Rethinking the Industrial Revolution

Historical Materialism Book Series

The Historical Materialism Book Series is a major publishing initiative of the radical left. The capitalist crisis of the twenty-first century has been met by a resurgence of interest in critical Marxist theory. At the same time, the publishing institutions committed to Marxism have contracted markedly since the high point of the 1970s. The Historical Materialism Book Series is dedicated to addressing this situation by making available important works of Marxist theory. The aim of the series is to publish important theoretical contributions as the basis for vigorous intellectual debate and exchange on the left.

The peer-reviewed series publishes original monographs, translated texts, and reprints of classics across the bounds of academic disciplinary agendas and across the divisions of the left. The series is particularly concerned to encourage the internationalization of Marxist debate and aims to translate significant studies from beyond the English-speaking world.

For a full list of titles in the Historical Materialism Book Series available in paperback from Haymarket Books, visit:
www.haymarketbooks.org/category/hm-series

Rethinking the Industrial Revolution

Five Centuries of Transition from Agrarian to Industrial Capitalism in England

Michael Andrew Žmolek

Haymarket Books
Chicago, IL

First published in 2013 by Brill Academic Publishers, The Netherlands

Published in paperback in 2014 by
Haymarket Books
P.O. Box 180165
Chicago, IL 60618
773-583-7884
www.haymarketbooks.org

ISBN: 978-1-60846-375-6

Trade distribution:
In the US, Consortium Book Sales, www.cbsd.com
In Canada, Publishers Group Canada, www.pgcbooks.ca
In the UK, Turnaround Publisher Services, www.turnaround-psl.com
In Australia, Palgrave Macmillan, www.palgravemacmillan.com.au
In all other countries, Publishers Group Worldwide, www.pgw.com

Cover design by Ragina Johnson.

This book was published with the generous support of
Lannan Foundation and the Wallace Global Fund.

10 9 8 7 6 5 4 3 2 1

Library of Congress Cataloging-in-Publication data is available.

For Mary Louise
who I knew as Mom

Contents

List of Tables and Diagrams xiii
Acknowledgments xv
Foreword xvii

Introduction

Why the Industrial Revolution began in England 3
The transition debate 8
Marx on property relations: Brenner's point of departure 17
The specificity of capitalism and agrarian capitalism 23
Market dependency 28
The elusive origins of capitalism and industrialisation 32
Conclusion 40

Part One: England Transformed

Manufacturing and Agrarian Capitalism, 1348–1783

1. The Pre-History of Industry 47
   Wage labour and the guilds 49
   The evolution of the guild system in England 57
   Queen Betty's law 66
   The economic context in Tudor and Stuart Times 70
   Nef's 'early industrial revolution' 74
   'Capitalism' in medieval and early modern mining 81
   Mining and agrarian capitalism: the instructive case of Whickham 86
   The so-called phase of proto-industrialisation 91
   Conclusion 101

2. Parliament and Revolution 105
   The crisis of the early seventeenth century 107

Parliament's civil war 116
Restoration to Glorious Revolution 136
The post-revolution settlement 146
The glorious financial revolution 148
'Free trade' 156
Conclusion 162

3. Agrarian Capitalism: The Key to Britain's Rise to Power 165
Views on the relationship between agriculture and manufacturing 166
War, debt and the land tax 171
The storm before the calm 174
Stability and 'old corruption' 182
The so-called agrarian depression: 1730–50 192
The return to war and the '45 206
Conclusion 212

4. An Empire in Crisis 215
Pitt and empire 218
The emergence of popular politics: Wilkes and George III 223
Rebellion at home and abroad 235
The survival of empire 244
Conclusion 248

5. Harvesting the Agrarian Revolution 253
The end of the demographic pause 256
Internal and external expansion 259
Parliamentary enclosures and the consequences of increasing agrarian productivity 265
The great enclosure debate 270
Conclusion 279

Part Two: 'Such Machines . . . As Cannot Err'

Capital and Technology in the Making of Industrial England, 1700–1800

6. Technology and History 283
The ahistoricism of technological determinism 288
The technology of Antiquity 301
Medieval to early modern technology 307

The technology of the Industrial Revolution 322
Conclusion 338

7. The Social Origins of the Factory 343
'Plen-ty of time': The multifarious conditions of labour, 1700–60 ... 348
Wages and the emerging labour market 355
Concentration and regional specialisation 359
Solutions for poverty 368
The first factory 379
'A gymcrak of some consequence' 384
The turning point 393
Conclusion 396

8. Factories and Machinery 401
Wedgwood 403
The specific role of machinery 415
Manufacture versus machinofacture 420
'King Cotton' and the cotton king: from factory to factory system 428
Technological versus organisational innovation 444
Discipline and control 451
The arrival of the power-loom 455
Conclusion 457

9. Capital and Industry 461
Woollens and worsted 462
Linen: the second-class textile 467
Iron and steam 469
Mining 479
Beer, paper and chemicals 483
The capitalist 490
Origins and definitions of capital 495
Conclusion 500

Part Three: Custom's Last Stand

The Rise and Fall of Artisan-Led Resistance to Capitalism in England, 1783–1848

10. Custom and Law 509
The paradox of custom 511

'A Whig state of mind': political economy, the bloody code and the decline of paternalism 521
'Is there any principle in these things?': the return of radicalism ... 532
'You offer no motives': outdoor relief and the problem of the poor .. 548
Conclusion 555

11. Rebellion and Reaction 557
'A tribute to Welsh pluck': invasion, rebellion and mutiny 558
'The Radicals are drinking Pitt's health': the Combination Acts in context 562
The tension within radicalism 572
'So simple is the plan, so faithful are the men' 577
The second generation of industrialists in charge 583
War, commerce and British Capitalism 585
Luddism and the repeal of Queen Betty's law 592
Conclusion 603

12. Class and the State 609
The postwar crisis 614
The 'Malthusian moment' 618
'Bread or blood' 624
The makings of a working class 633
'A land of Roast Beef and Plum-Pudding' 643
'A ramshackle and cumbersome machinery of government' 646
'A prey to be plundered': the reversal of the combination laws 656
Conclusion 673

13. Reform and the Oligarchy 677
High politics 678
Swing 689
'No kings, No lords, No inequalities' 697
Free labour 709
Grand Union 716
The New Poor Law 727
Capital formation and the railway boom 738
Conclusion 744

14. Chartists and Liberals 749
The People's Charter and the National Petition 750
The age of petitioning 761

The strike of 1842 765
Reform and disorder under Peel 768
Repeal of the Corn Laws and the Irish Potato Famine 773
'All men are brethren' 778
'A paddock and a pigsty' 785
Conclusion 790

Conclusion 793
The crisis of feudalism and the origin of agrarian capitalism 796
The sixteenth century 800
The seventeenth century 803
The eighteenth century 806
Technology and the labour process 812
Capital, custom and the law 817
The early nineteenth century 822
Summary 837

Epilogue 841

References 845
Index 869

List of Tables and Diagrams

List of Tables

Table 0.1: Rates of growth, Britain 1700–1831 32
Table 3.1: Rising wages in Lancashire 1700–90 193
Table 5.1: Corn output in England and Wales 257
Table 5.2: Growth of British imports and exports: 1720–90 258
Table 5.3: Enclosure bills in Parliament, 1740–1829 266
Table 7.1: Legislation against combination and property damage: 1718–26 350
Table 7.2: Regional specialisation in manufactures 1600–1750 362
Table 7.3: English patents sealed: 1660–1759 394
Table 8.1: Arkwright Factories built 1769–84 436
Table 9.1: Brewers in England and Wales in the eighteenth century 485
Table 13.1: The decline of hand-loom weaving: 1788–1860 738

List of Diagrams

Diagram 5.1: The pattern of causal relations in the economic context of the Industrial Revolution 254

Acknowledgments

The central thread of this work was inspired during valuable exchanges with Professors Ellen Meiksins Wood and George Comninel, whose own work has informed much of the present material. I am grateful for the exceptional care which both of these scholars took in reviewing drafts of my doctoral dissertation, completed in 2008, from which this book originates. I also wish to thank the third member of my dissertation committee, David McNally, for being ever-ready to answer questions and offer assistance as needed. Other professors at York University I wish to thank and acknowledge are: Robert Albritton, for providing me with the opportunity to test some of my ideas in debate, and John Saul, for his inspirational teaching during my graduate course-work. Florence Booth at the University of Iowa and Robert Reid at the University of Dubuque provided valuable assistance in helping me revise the outline. Appreciation is due to the staffs at the libraries of York University, the University of Toronto, the University of Iowa, the University of Dubuque, the University of Maryland and at the Bodleian Library in Oxford. A very special thanks goes to Dave Kelly at the Library of Congress for his invaluable assistance.

During the long writing and preparation of this work, I have been blessed by the support and encouragement of friends and colleagues in Toronto, Washington DC, Iowa City, Dubuque and elsewhere. Rather than list dozens of names, I simply wish to say thank you all for being there during what has at times been a difficult journey.

Finally, I wish to thank my family: to my sister Pauli for support and patience during the years we shared a house in Takoma Park, Maryland, where during many long hours of study I enjoyed the companionship of her late dog Zoe; to my brother Tom and his family: his wife Mary and my nieces Kate and Laura, whose spiritual journeys have encouraged me to 'rethink' more than just the Industrial Revolution; and to my brother Stuart, whose playful sense of humour always gives me hope. And there are simply not enough words to thank my father, Lee Zmolek, for his unfailing support. This book is dedicated to memory of my mother. Without the love and support of my parents, this work would never have been completed.

December 18, 2013

Foreword

Words of warning

There is something of a tradition where books on the Industrial Revolution are concerned. It seems almost obligatory to begin with some words of caution about the scope of the subject – what it is, and what it is not. Writing in 1917, the Hammonds caution us that:

> there is a sense in which it is impossible to explain anything without explaining everything. It is true, again, that there is an element of risk in any general statement about the Industrial Revolution.[1]

Eleven years later, Paul Mantoux cautioned that not only did the causes of the Industrial Revolution remain a mystery, but also that:

> in spite of the apparent rapidity of its development, the industrial revolution sprang from far-distant causes, and was destined to produce consequences whose process of development, after more than a century, is still incomplete. The distinctive characteristics of the factory system did not reveal themselves all at once.[2]

Twenty years later still, T.S. Ashton published his 1948 classic *The Industrial Revolution 1760–1830*, a concise account which remains among the most widely read texts on the subject. Ashton begins by cautioning us about using the term 'capitalism', but asks us to accede to the common understanding and usage of the term 'Industrial Revolution':

> The system of human relationships that is sometimes called capitalism had its origins long before 1760, and attained its full development long after 1830: there is a danger of overlooking the essential fact of continuity. But the phrase 'Industrial Revolution' has been used by a long line of historians and has become so firmly embedded in common speech that it would be pedantic to offer a substitute.[3]

1. Hammond and Hammond 1995, p. 3.
2. Mantoux 1961, p. 25.
3. Ashton 1969a, p. 4.

Writing eighteen years after this, Michael Flinn, also justifies this usage:

> Disaggregated, the individual elements in the industrial revolution look gradual and undramatic enough; viewed as a whole, the process amounts to a sufficiently drastic upheaval to justify, in spite of the historians of the interwar years, the expression 'Industrial Revolution'.[4]

Yet Flinn qualifies this by stating that:

> The process of growth is complex, and any attempt to explain an industrial revolution in terms of a single prime mover is bound to be misleading. Inevitably a wide range of factors is involved, and each of these factors has its own chronology. Thus, the chronology of an industrial revolution is the sum of a large number of contributory chronologies.[5]

The present study will challenge such a view by suggesting that while we must understand that there were multiple processes at work, it may be possible to place those processes in a larger framework to gain a more coherent understanding.

Three years after Flinn wrote this, Peter Mathias's *The First Industrial Nation*[6] was published. Mathias and many other authors of the succeeding period would appear to have heeded Flinn's advice, for his was one of a great many books that undertook a sector-by-sector analysis of the Industrial Revolution, one chapter per sector. Peter Mathias begins his 1969 work with his own words of caution:

> The term industrial revolution . . . should not be used just to denote industrial or mechanical innovation, an advance in a technique of production or the mechanization of a process in a single industry, or even the conversion of a single industry into a mass-production basis with large plants driven by more than human power. If the concept is to mean only this, then the search for its origin would be lost in the remote past.[7]

Here, we have a repetition of the theme that the Industrial Revolution involved multiple, complex and interwoven complexes. But in what way could we employ the term with precision?

Let us attempt to answer that question by breaking the term into its component parts. There is little ambiguity about the fact that this event was characterised by rapid change within, and rapid growth of, industry. The problem would seem to lie with the word 'revolution'. Writing a decade after Mathias, the master of the *longue durée* himself, Fernand Braudel, concludes his magnum opus

4. Flinn 1966, p. 103.
5. Flinn 1966, p. 93.
6. Mathias 1983.
7. Mathias 1983, p. 1.

Civilization and Capitalism[8] with a chapter on the Industrial Revolution. There, not surprisingly, he, too, offers words of caution, but here specifically about the term 'revolution':

> Historians are often criticized for misusing the word *revolution* which, it is argued, ought to be used in the original sense, to refer only to violent and rapid change. But when one is talking about social phenomena, rapid and slow change are inseparable. For no society exists which is not constantly torn between the forces working to preserve it and the subversive forces – whether perceived as such or not – working to undermine it. Revolutionary explosions are but the sudden and short-lived volcanic eruptions of this latent and long-term conflict. In any attempt to analyse the revolutionary process, the most difficult part is their relationship and the links between them. The industrial revolution in England at the end of the eighteenth century is no exception. It consisted both of a rapid sequence of events and of what was clearly a very long-term process: two different rhythms were beating simultaneously.[9]

This passage is not entirely helpful. On the one hand, Braudel appears to recognise the importance of identifying the complex linkages between different historical events in order for any complex overall patterns (or their absence) to be revealed. Yet Braudel gives us little clue as to the nature of the long-term process tied to the Industrial Revolution. Even if we are able to hold it in our heads that this event simultaneously involved both short-term and long-term processes, we are still faced once more with the problem of the term as a referent attached to no specific object or event. So what *was* or *is* the industrial revolution?

Eric Hobsbawm tells us that the term 'revolution' was borrowed from the experience of the French Revolution of 1789 and applied to the English experience sometime thereafter, gaining popular usage only by around the 1820s.[10] The Industrial Revolution is, for Hobsbawm, part of a 'dual revolution' – industrial in England, political in France. Certainly, such upheavals as Luddism, Peterloo, the Swing Riots and other social dislocations generated by the economic transformations associated with the Industrial Revolution compelled contemporaries, after 1789, to compare these events with the more purely political dislocations

8. Braudel 1981 and 1988.

9. Braudel 1988, pp. 537–8 goes on to cite Phyllis Deane for her reminder that the discontinuities in the English economy of the late eighteenth century were contained within a historical continuum in which '"breaks and discontinuities lose their identities as unique or decisive events"' (quoting Deane 1987). Additionally, Braudel warns that David Landes's description of the Industrial Revolution 'as the formation of a critical mass which eventually produced a revolutionary explosion' is appropriate, but 'the mass can only have been formed by the slow accumulation of all manner of necessary elements. Argue as we may, the long-term will always claim its due'.

10. Hobsbawm 1994, p. 43.

associated with the French Revolution. As such, the term picked up the word 'revolution' through an analogy. Is this inaccurate? Turning to the dictionary is not helpful. On the one hand, a revolution is 'an overthrow or repudiation and the thorough replacement of an established government or political system by the people governed', a definition clearly based on the American and French revolutions of the late eighteenth century (and others which followed, such as the Russian Revolution of 1917). On the other hand, revolution is 'a radical and pervasive change in society and the social structure, esp. one made suddenly and often accompanied by violence', and it also 'a sudden, complete or marked change in something: *the present revolution in church architecture*',[11] a definition which suggests something more along the lines of the English experience, in other words a revolution in the mode of social relations of production. It would appear that these two dictionary definitions simply mirror the two very different experiences of political and Industrial Revolution, the latter still borrowing the term from the former.

While the *consequences* of the industrial revolution were clearly profound, even if these results emerged somewhat gradually by comparison with the sweeping ramifications of the great political revolutions, it appears to be generally accepted that problem with applying the term 'revolution' to this historical event or period is that it is widely viewed as something which traces its origins and antecedents well into the past. Thus, taken as a subject, the Industrial Revolution presents any author with an immediate problem: its origins, causes and antecedents lay outside and prior to the historical period to which it belongs. Therefore, any effort to explain *why* the Industrial Revolution happened must account for the period in which these dramatic and revolutionary events took place, but also a long period of events stretching back into the distant past. The demands which this places on the author are immense.

It is a fair question to ask, however: to what precise 'historical continuum' does the Industrial Revolution in Britain belong? It will be a central contention of this work that the causes of the Industrial Revolution do indeed belong to a long historical evolution; but contrary to the predominant view of Braudel and others, who take this historical continuum to be common to Western Europe in general, this evolution can be traced to transformations in the agrarian social and class relations of early modern England.

---

11. There is, of course, the third sense of the term, which means quite the opposite of something 'radically new'; this is the sense of a revolution as something revolving, 'a procedure or course, as if in a circuit, back to a starting point', as in an orbit, 'a cycle of events in time or a recurring period of time' (Merriam-Webster 1993). The understanding of the term 'revolution' has always been controversial within Marxist theory; see Kiernan 1983, pp. 425–8.

Introduction

> Who would not be bewildered by the hundredth debate on this topic?
>
> Fernand Braudel[1]

The significance of the Industrial Revolution as a critical period of transition in human history can hardly be overstated. Yet there remains little scholarly agreement on even the most basic issues. Should we speak of only one industrial revolution, or several? Was the Industrial Revolution the dawning of the capitalist era, or merely its high noon? What were the basic causal factors leading to industrialisation? Why was England (Britain after 1707) the first nation to undergo an industrial revolution? These questions have found disparate answers from a wide variety of approaches.

The dynamic expansion of industry and technology from the latter half of the eighteenth century is generally understood across theoretical fences as the logical fulfilment of prior developments in trade and economic growth. Many scholars view industrialisation as something forever prefigured in the prior development of markets and manufacturing. Indeed, industrialisation is treated as a more or less direct response to new opportunities afforded by the dramatic expansion of commerce and the rise in population across Western Europe during the early modern period. It has become virtually axiomatic to assume that these opportunities were always already present in pre-capitalist forms of trade and manufacture. Industrialisation thus

1. Braudel 1988, Vol. 3, p. 556.

comes about simply through the application of scientific advancements to pre-capitalist methods of manufacturing, combined with the growth of trade and population. Theories which operate based upon such assumptions provide us with only a partial and distorted view of history. Such economistic approaches to the Industrial Revolution have generally ignored the role of class and social property relations in shaping and conditioning the process of industrialisation. As a result, they are unable to explain why industrialisation occurred when it did, and not in some previous period of commercial and demographic expansion, such as in ancient Rome or China. They are also unable to provide a satisfactory explanation of the relationship between capitalism and industrialisation.

The definition of 'capitalism' remains subject to widespread ambiguity and sharp divergences of opinion. Yet the prevailing view continues to be that capitalism developed across Europe in general, whilst industrialisation – oddly – began in only one country: England. This has led to the general tendency to treat industrialisation in relative isolation from considerations of capitalism. In turn, industrialisation is often understood as a process driven more by technological advance than by economic considerations, while capitalism itself plays a subordinate role by promoting 'economic rationality', thereby facilitating industrialisation. This downplays the historical specificity of capitalism as an economic system operating in real societies in favour of a view of capitalism as an eternal and natural system in continuous development bound up with the advance of science and technology.

The pioneering work of Robert Brenner, Ellen Meiksins Wood and George Comninel has offered a new approach to questions arising out of the debate on the transition from feudalism to capitalism. In considering the divergences between the French and English paths out of feudalism, this approach argues that while absolutism was developing in France, the transformation of agrarian social relations in England gave rise to a unique form of social relations, an 'agrarian capitalism', understood as a period of transition to industrial capitalism. There is now a significant corpus of work elaborating the theory of English agrarian capitalism. What nevertheless remains to be explained is how agrarian capitalism generated a set of conditions that allowed for incipient industrialisation in England. Ellen Meiksins Wood has argued that we cannot take for granted that the development of agrarian capitalism made the industrial revolution necessary. This is in keeping with her insistence that it is necessary to explicate historical developments, rather than take their causality for granted.

> Whether agrarian capitalism made industrial capitalism not only possible but necessary or inevitable is another question . . . the conclusion we can draw from the history of agrarian capitalism is that a capitalist dynamic rooted in a new form of social property relations preceded industrialization, both chrono-

> logically and causally. In fact, a kind of 'market society' – in which producers were dependent on the market for access to the means of life, labor, and self-reproduction, and subject to market imperatives – was not the *result* of industrialization but its primary cause.[2]

To date, there has been no work focused on demonstrating direct causal linkages between agrarian capitalism and the First Industrial Revolution. This is the lacuna which the present study is meant to address. By advancing an account of the Industrial Revolution and its origins which pays close attention to the importance on the role of class relations, class struggle and the development of the state in shaping economic outcomes, this study seeks to follow through on radical implications of the challenge to the predominant theories accounting for the origins of capitalism and industrialisation posed by Brenner, Wood and Comninel. In so doing, the stage is set for future work which could provide a new, alternative account of the Industrial Revolution and how it began.

Why the Industrial Revolution began in England

The capitalist system in England was brought into being through a transformation in social property relations in which the appropriation of peasant surplus by feudal lords was gradually superseded by a new system of surplus-appropriation involving a nexus of powerful landlords renting land to tenant-farmers, who in turn hired agrarian wage labourers from a growing pool of cottagers and rural poor. Where peasants had once enjoyed direct possession of the land, a growing number of these direct producers were losing their direct access to the means of subsistence and therefore becoming dependent upon markets for their access to subsistence goods. Simultaneously, their employers also became dependent on markets in land, labour and money for access to the necessary components of the production process, over which they enjoyed unprecedented control as owners of the means of production. This control gave them exclusive rights to the surplus accruing from that ownership – rooted in a novel and specifically capitalist system of property relations – in the form of profits. In pursuing the extension of this new system of surplus-appropriation to its logical ends, landlords and tenant-farmers were facilitating the expansion of the scope of market regulation of social relations and production decisions. A key aspect of this market regulation was the increasing pressure of market-based competition, which increasingly made the transformation of production an imperative. The expansion of agrarian capitalism was a long and protracted process, however, and landlords

2. Wood 2002a, p. 143.

and their tenant-farmers faced widespread resistance against the loss of access to the means of subsistence, including the wastes and commons. In order for agrarian capitalism to continue to develop, this resistance had to be suppressed.

Struggles to resist the imposition of such a system were led principally by direct producers. These struggles were not highly organised, as a rule. They were generally sporadic and episodic. They rarely rose to the level of a compact set of ideas forming a coherent ideological position. They were borne directly out of the economic and social pressures – often intense but equally as often protracted – to which direct producers threatened with loss of access to the means of subsistence were subject. Where resistance was organised, it often involved violence against property and occasionally involved violence against persons. Yet such struggles were generally localised. Capitalism was not born in a vacuum any more than it arose out of a democratic form of society. It was the successor to an exploitative manorial system under which freedom was the preserve of the lords and also of freeholders, while the majority of persons remained both the political and economic subjects of their local lords. From the sixteenth century onward, as agrarian capitalism developed, tenants rose in protest against enclosures. In the seventeenth century, aspirations for greater freedom and equality were voiced by the Levellers, who promoted the idea of universal manhood suffrage, and the Diggers, a smaller and more radical group who called themselves the 'true Levellers', as they advocated the abolition of private property and anticipated theories of communism.[3] During the eighteenth century, freedom of the press expanded enormously, but Britain was still a society in which relations of mastery and servitude remained widespread. It is, therefore, impossible to know for certain how broad the level of popular support was for machine-breakers and other protestors. By the third and fourth decades of the nineteenth century, just as trade unions were growing in strength and number, we witness the expression of mass opposition in the form of the Chartists' presentation of millions of signatures on petitions to Parliament, requesting

3. Thus a Digger manifesto reads: '. . . so long as we or any other doth own the earth to be the peculiar interest of the lords and landlords, and not common to others as well as them, we own the curse, and holds the creation under bondage; and so long as we or any other doth own landlords and tenants, for one to call the land his or another to hire it of him, or for one to give hire and for another to work for hire; this is to dishonour the work of creation; as if the righteous creator should have respect to persons, and therefore made the earth for some and not for all . . . And that this civil property is the curse is manifest thus: those that buy and sell land, and are landlords, have got it either by oppression or murder or theft; and all landlords lives in the breach of the seventh and eighth commandments, *Thou shalt not steal nor kill*' (Everard *et al.* 1973, pp. 84–5). Note, here, both the rudiments of an economic analysis of agrarian capitalism, as well as the careful reference to both lords (of manorial estates with open fields) and landlords (leasing out to tenant-farmers on enclosed lands).

universal manhood suffrage. Chartism reflected a new mentality, one which sought to expand the *political* rights of labourers where the struggles over *economic* rights had been lost. The defeat of Chartism was followed by widespread, but by no means complete, accommodation to capitalism among British workers.

Thus the Industrial Revolution owes its pedigree to a series of processes that brought about a transformation of social property relations resulting in widespread market dependence and market regulation of the economy. While this entire process involved class struggle in the form of resistance on the part of direct producers seeking to avoid loss of access to means of subsistence or loss of control of the labour process, and thus required active suppression of such resistance on the part of surplus appropriators, this emphasis on 'active' or 'conscious' suppression of resistance should not be taken to mean that landlords, tenant-farmers or state policy-makers were aware throughout the process that the long-term consequences of their actions would result in a capitalist society and an industrial revolution. It would be absurd to suggest that when English lords set about enclosing their fields between the fifteenth and seventeenth centuries – creating land markets and (proto-) capitalist farms in the process – they had anything approaching contemporary industrial and technological society in mind. It would also make little sense to suggest that landlords actually chose to impose market imperatives on themselves and their tenants. While it is true that certain thinkers have been able to articulate an awareness of the broader, long-term implications of class struggle, such as the way the participants in the debate at Putney in 1647 demonstrated an awareness of the centrality of property rights to what was essentially an argument between representatives of both the propertied and propertyless classes,[4] class-based actions taken at specific moments in history must be understood in terms of the social and economic pressures that provided the immediate motivation behind them. As the new forms of tenure and social property relations evolved in such a way that even the appropriating classes themselves became market-dependent in unforeseen ways, their own choices were shaped according to how they chose to respond to market imperatives which increasingly made economic survival in a competitive market environment contingent upon the ability to transform production. Market dependency, market imperatives and the social property form of capital, three terms which will be defined more clearly over the course of this study, emerged as the unintended consequences of a long-term process of economic agents pursuing short-term economic ends.

---

4. See Chapter Two, pp. 126–7.

While concurring with the prevailing view that the emergence of capitalism pre-dates the first Industrial Revolution, the present study takes the view that the reason the First Industrial Revolution took place in Britain is because capitalism first originated in only one country: England. Thus the Industrial Revolution in Britain was a thoroughly capitalist affair and its history cannot be considered independently of the development of capitalism.

If this perspective is correct, why has it not become conventional wisdom? While the 'Brenner Debate' is now well-established as a widely recognised contribution to historical social theory, the positions of Brenner, Wood, Comninel and others remain a minority position even within Marxist circles. According to Guy Bois, Brenner's alleged 'privileging' of political factors over economic factors amounts to the heresy of a 'political Marxism'.[5] For Ellen Wood, this misses the point of Brenner's method entirely, which is to explore 'the consequences of the *fusion* of the "economic" and the "political", the unity of "surplus-extracting" and "ruling" classes, which was, precisely, a constitutive feature of the feudal mode of production'.[6] How else would Marxist scholarship overcome the error of economism? More broadly, however, we would suggest that there is another reason why this perspective has not been more widely adopted.

By the eighteenth century, as the Industrial Revolution began to take shape and the pace of change quickened, it was becoming increasingly clear to some contemporary observers in Britain that the change around them was leading toward a new social order. If British commentators were generally more focused upon the clearing away of older economic forms than the specific nature of the new, this is likely attributable to the fact that agrarian capitalism had already been developing in England for centuries. Adam Smith's treatise on *The Wealth of Nations*[7] is an inquiry into a society that is only very marginally an industrial-capitalist society. Smith's work is in point of fact *the* inquiry *par excellence* into the economics of the first and only *agrarian capitalist* society. What is meant by agrarian capitalism will become clear in the chapters that follow. In spite of his brilliance, as the founding father of political economy, Smith bequeathed to future generations one major epistemological error that remains embedded like a cornerstone in the foundations of political economy's successor: modern economics. Smith *naturalised* economics. Smith did this in a peculiar way, however.

> In his view nothing indicates the presence of an economic sphere in society that might become the source of moral law and political obligation. Self-interest

5. See Bois 1978, pp. 60–9.
6. Wood 2002a, p. 56.
7. Smith 1957.

> merely prompts us to do what, intrinsically, will also benefit others, as the butcher's self-interest will ultimately supply us with dinner. A broad optimism pervades Smith's thinking since the laws governing the economic part of the universe are consonant with man's destiny as are those that govern the rest... Natural is that which is in accordance with the principles embodied in the mind of man; and the natural order is that which is in accordance with those principles. Nature in the physical sense was consciously excluded by Smith from the problem of wealth... Political Economy should be a human science; it should deal with that which was natural to man, not to Nature.[8]

The distinction between a Smithian economics based on the laws of human nature and the laws of economics being *among* the laws of nature was lost on later thinkers like Burke and Bentham, for whom the 'laws of commerce were the laws of nature and consequently the laws of God'. For them, it was just as well, too: 'Let the market be given charge of the poor, and things will look after themselves'.[9] To an extent, Bentham and Malthus stand in relation to Smith the way the social Darwinists stand in relation to Darwin. Smith's analysis was never so crude and he never lacked sympathy for the poor and working classes. In his first treatise, *The Theory of Moral Sentiments*,[10] Smith wrestled with issues of the corrupting influence of commerce. In short, his solution was to suggest that enlightened men of superior moral virtue, namely the community of country gentlemen leasing their land to capitalist tenant-farmers, were in the best position to govern society wisely and uphold laws that would keep the otherwise unbridled greed and self-interest of merchants and manufacturers in check. In *The Wealth of Nations*, Smith carries these themes forward as he advocates an expansion of self-sustaining growth in the context of an *agrarian* capitalism.[11]

It is only because Smith's contemporaries were already familiar with the logic of an economic system driven by competitive markets that *The Wealth of Nations*, written at the cusp of the Industrial Revolution, was properly understood as a description of the agrarian capitalist economy in which they lived, and not (as the text is often misread today) as a blueprint for an industrial-capitalist society. To Smith's British readers, the concept that the economic laws propelling the British economy forward were eternal and natural would not have seemed the least bit peculiar. It would take a pair of immigrants from Germany to recognise the peculiarities of British capitalism. For Marx and Engels, the rapid

---

8. Polanyi 1957, p. 112.
9. Ibid. After Bentham came Malthus, who popularised this notion in the early nineteenth century.
10. Smith 1979. For an in-depth discussion of Smith's project in writing *The Wealth of Nations*, see McNally 1988, p. 180.
11. For more discussion of Smith's project, see Chapter Ten, pp. 523–6.

transformation of social relations and what was happening to British *workers* in particular seemed quite *un*natural in contrast with the German principalities, which were only just beginning their conversion to capitalism. They saw in capitalism a form of class warfare whose laws were distinctively social. This, in turn, led them to the project of writing a critique of political economy.

Not only were Smith's followers taken by the notion that economic laws were natural laws, but this understanding promoted a tendency to universalise capitalism. Because they had never known any other system of economics, theorists of British political economy were not compelled to inquire into the origins of an economic system (capitalism) that was older than they were. Thus it was that in their critique of political economy, Marx and Engels criticised the tendency of the political economists to project the capitalist mode of production backward in time, and to imagine capitalist social relations where they had not existed. In Marx's early attempts at developing a theory of modes of production, he somewhat uncritically adopted Smith's episodic view of the history of economic systems as one which proceeds as a series of 'stages' (rather than as a series of complex overlapping processes). As Marx gained a deeper understanding of the specificities of the capitalist system, however, he increasingly emphasised the centrality of production and painstakingly sought to demystify the naturalisation of economics by exposing the relations of production as socially and artificially constructed, and therefore subject to change through conscious effort. Despite this increasing emphasis upon social property relations, Marx never took up the project of a systematic *historical* inquiry into the origins of capitalism. Meanwhile, for the followers of Smith, there was simply no inquiry to conduct, for if the laws of capitalism were eternal, then capitalism had no temporal origin. Industrialisation and the Industrial Revolution, however, *did* require an explanation. To date, no single approach to providing such an explanation has achieved general acceptance, and a plethora of authors offer words of warning,[12] stating that it is folly to embark upon the task of definitively answering what is arguably the most central historical question in all of the social sciences, namely: how did industrial society emerge? It was left to the followers of Marx and Engels's scholarship to initiate a 'transition debate' inquiring into the historical origins of the specifically capitalist system of social relations of production and property.

The transition debate

The collection of essays titled *The Transition from Feudalism to Capitalism*[13] encompasses the key arguments in what has come to be known as the 'transition

12. See the Foreword above.
13. Sweezy *et al.* 1978.

debate.' Rodney Hilton's introduction begins by mentioning Karl Polanyi's incomplete criticisms of Maurice Dobb's 1946 work entitled *Studies in the Development of Capitalism*.[14] According to Polanyi, Dobb had adopted Marx's labour theory of value (which Polanyi considered Marx's weakest theory) and in his otherwise excellent attempt to theorise the transition from feudalism to capitalism, Dobb had ignored Marx's '"fundamental insight into the historically limited nature of market organisation"'.[15] But Polanyi did not pursue the problem, and it was essentially dropped for thirty years, until it was picked up by Robert Brenner. Dobb's work had touched off a debate with fellow Marxist Paul Sweezy in the journal *Science and Society* in the 1950s. We could identify the three primary points of contention in the 'transition-debate' as:

1. the definition of a 'mode of production';
2. the role of commodity exchange (does trade transform the relations of production?); and
3. how different developments in England, France, Germany, Italy, and Spain all resulted in capitalism.[16]

The third of these is crucial for anticipating the work of Brenner, who rejected the theory of a single process across Western Europe, in favour of the theory of agrarian capitalism and the argument that England alone gave rise to industrial capitalism.

The exchanges between Dobb and Sweezy are at the centre of the debate. Sweezy criticises Dobb for equating serfdom with feudalism, because this does not identify a system of production. He is also critical of Dobb's thesis of the 'exhaustion of the peasantry'. Dobb has summarised this thesis as follows:

> . . . such evidence as we possess strongly indicates that it was the inefficiency of Feudalism as a system of production, coupled with the growing needs of the ruling class for revenue, that was primarily responsible for its decline; since this need for additional revenue promoted an increase in the pressure on the producer to a point where this pressure became literally unendurable.[17]

---

14. Dobb 1947.
15. Polanyi, as quoted by Hilton 1978, p. 9.
16. Hilton (1978, 13) sets out the seven central issues of the debate: 'the definition of serfdom; the origin of towns; the role of handicrafts; merchants and the money economy; the unfettering of simple commodity production; the alternative paths for the emergence of capitalist production; the concept of the "prime mover".' All of these issues are crucial, but we have conflated them to what we see as the three primary ones.
17. Dobb 1947, p. 42.

This unendurable pressure purportedly led to: a) flight to the towns; and b) insufficient labour on the demesnes. Sweezy says Dobb is taking too much for granted, here, and that basically he does not sufficiently explain how feudalism, as he defines it, gives rise to the towns and the 'money-' economy:

> Dobb reasons that if the only factor at work in Western Europe had been the rise of trade, the result might as well have been an intensification as a disintegration of feudalism. And from this it follows that there must have been other factors at work to bring about the actually observed result. What were these factors? Dobb believes that they can be found inside the feudal economy itself.[18]

Sweezy disputes Dobb's thesis as follows. He lists four factors which Dobb uses to explain the intensification of lordly demands on the direct producers: the low regard which ruling classes held for the interests of the serfs, warfare and brigandage, the demographic expansion of the ruling class, and the increasing extravagance of lordly demands. The first two factors were present throughout the period, says Sweezy, and Dobb does not demonstrate how and whether these factors increased in intensity prior to feudalism's collapse. The growth in size of the exploiting class was real, admits Sweezy, but it was matched by a growth in the size of the peasantry; moreover, as war took a heavier toll on the upper orders, it is doubtful that the growth of the exploiting class, in relative terms, was decisive. The fourth factor in Dobb's thesis – the growing extravagance of their demands – is an acceptable premise for Sweezy, but he argues that this may be understood as an external, not an internal factor: '[O]nce we look outside the feudal system we find ample reason for the growing extravagance of the feudal ruling class: the rapid expansion of trade from the eleventh century onward brought an ever-increasing quantity and variety of goods within its reach'.[19] Finally, Sweezy argues that the hypothesis that serfs would desert the manors *en masse* is dubious since flight would mean choosing a life of vagrancy and poverty, and while vagrancy did increase, this was due to there being less room on the manors, not to choice.

Having thus rebutted Dobb's main points in explaining the decline of feudalism, Sweezy offers a peculiar alternative. The rise of towns offered liberty, employment, and social status to peasants, and Dobb's theory of internal causes could be rescued, says Sweezy, 'if it could be shown that the rise of the towns was a process internal to the feudal system'. But Dobb himself recognises that the growth of towns was 'in proportion to their importance as trading centres. Since trade can in no sense be regarded as a form of feudal economy, it follows

18. Sweezy 1978b, p. 37.
19. Sweezy 1978a, p. 39.

that Dobb could hardly argue that the rise of urban life was a consequence of internal feudal causes'.[20]

Sweezy takes off from here in proposing that the decline of feudalism can be attributed to external factors, namely the rise of trade. Trade, for Sweezy, made its impact on the static feudal economy felt in four ways: a) it revealed the inefficiency of manorial production by supplying goods that could be purchased at a lower cost than they could be made; b) it transformed the attitudes of peasant-producers, who could now accumulate monetary wealth instead of heaps of perishable goods; c) it developed the tastes of the feudal ruling classes (*à la* Dobb); and d) the rise of towns opened up the prospect of a freer and better life. Relying as he does on changes in prospects, attitudes, and tastes, Sweezy's argument is weak inasmuch as he fails to identify the specific process by which changes took place. What, for example, explains the lords' access to the means of trade, in other words their wealth, and why should this be considered limitless? What explains the timing of the breakdown of feudalism? Why did trade not bring about the expected change at an earlier or later period? And most importantly, why would lords allow the end of serfdom without an 'internal' class struggle?

Justin Rosenberg has since argued persuasively that the Italian city-states in the Middle Ages, being centres of trade and manufacturing which serviced the feudal North, were not transformative of agrarian production, being economically rooted in the circuits of international commerce, and cannot be seen to be the precursors to the later rise of national states after Westphalia in 1648.[21] Sweezy's conception of 'dynamic' capitalist towns amidst a sea of agrarian stagnation is also counter-intuitive when one considers the dynamism of the 'agrarian' feudalism of 1050–1300, which saw the populations of England and France more than double, supplying armies for the Crusades; the building of Gothic cathedrals; the clearing of forests and the draining of marshes; and the colonisation of Eastern Europe by Western European knights, who brought peasant settlers with them.

As Kohachiro Takahashi, a third participant in the transition debate, points out, external factors themselves must be explained as internal factors to some historical process:

> If we say that historical development takes place according to external forces, the question remains, however, how those external forces arose, and where they came from. In the last analysis these forces which manifest themselves externally must be explained internally to history. The dialectics of history cannot go forward without self-movements (the contradictions of inner structure).[22]

20. Sweezy 1978a, pp. 39–40.
21. Rosenberg 1994, pp. 73–5.
22. Takahashi 1978, p. 79.

Responding to this, Sweezy says he never intended to deny that trade as an external factor was not itself internal to some process. 'The expansion of trade, with the concomitant growth of towns and markets, was external to the feudal mode of production, but it was internal as far as the whole European-Mediterranean economy was concerned'.[23] This poses a serious problem regarding the definition of a mode of production. Sweezy appears to be employing it in a very narrow sense of the extractive relations between serfs and lords, or between producers and exploiters, in other words in a rather economistic sense. The notion that there was a feudal mode of production operating somehow independently of circuits of mercantile trade seems to relegate the role of the state and ideological and/or normative modes of regulating social relations to a separate realm of inquiry.

Sweezy sets out the conditions for demonstrating that the growth of towns in feudal Europe was internal to the feudal process:

> One would have to show that the feudal ruling class took the initiative in building the towns and successfully integrated them into the feudal system of property and labour relations. Undoubtedly this did happen in the case of some towns, but it seems as if Pirenne has conclusively shown that the decisive trading centres typically grew up in an entirely different way. But what particularly indicates the non-feudal character of the towns was the general absence of serfdom.[24]

Sweezy concludes that the driving force of feudalism is to be found outside the system.[25]

Dobb responds by saying that he would see the interaction of both internal and external factors as together bringing about historical change, rather than seeing the question as one of 'either/or'. Dobb places primary emphasis upon internal contradictions 'since they determine the particular form and direction of the effects which external influences exert'.[26] Trade, in Dobb's view, 'accentuated the internal conflicts within the old mode of production'.[27] But 'external factors' (and Dobb seems to accept the rise of the towns as at least in part an

23. Sweezy 1978a, p. 105.
24. Sweezy 1978a, p. 105, n. 3.
25. Sweezy appears to assume that there is something about markets in general that makes them antithetical to feudalism. But with the right amount of regulation, constraint and monopoly, markets functioned perfectly well under feudalism as an integral aspect of the whole mode of production.
26. Dobb 1978, p. 60. Note how similar Brenner's later comments are regarding the role of class relations in setting the boundaries to economic growth. For a discussion in defence of Brenner's position on the role of class relations in economic development, see Zmolek 2000, pp. 144–6.
27. Dobb 1978, p. 61.

'external' factor), cannot determine the specific effect that they will have upon the internal structure of class relations. Thus the effect of the flight to the towns – itself due perhaps both to the lure of urban life as well as 'the repulsive force of feudal extraction' – upon feudal relations, would be determined by the specific character of the relationship between serf and feudal lord. The magnitude of flight may have been small, but the threat of it may have been sufficient to bring about concessions from lords, thus accelerating the breakdown of feudalism.

Dobb points out that Sweezy's thesis of the rise of trade does not explain 'the transition from coercive extraction of surplus labour by estate-owners to the use of free hired labour', which 'must have depended upon the existence of cheap labour for hire (i.e. of proletarian or semi-proletarian elements)'. For Dobb, this raises the question of what followed feudalism in Europe. As the period of high feudalism ended in the fourteenth century, the next two centuries are apparently suspended between feudalism and capitalism, and have to be classified as 'homeless hybrids'. Finding this an inadequate classification, Dobb conjectures that if the ruling class of this period was not bourgeois and capitalist, then the concept of 'bourgeois revolution' would make little sense, since the bourgeoisie would itself already have been in power by either 1640 or 1789. Either the events of these years were court and crown attempts at counter-revolution, or we must dispense with the concept of bourgeois revolution altogether. Finding neither alternative agreeable, Dobb proposes that the ruling class remained feudal because it continued to depend upon the exploitation of producers following the petty mode of production, a 'feudal' mode of production. By this logic, having come to the conclusion that the ruling class of the intervening period between feudalism and capitalism remained feudal, Dobb then seeks the source of capitalism in the rising class of 'kulak' yeomen farmers, whom he sees as 'key to understanding the class alignments of the bourgeois revolution' of seventeenth-century England.[28] We will see shortly how Brenner found this part of Dobb's analysis problematic.

Neither Dobb nor Sweezy appears to recognise the specificity of feudalism, as distinguished from the manorialism that followed the collapse of the Roman Empire, or how the introduction of what was arguably the most highly regulated system of production in history on the *seigneuries* formed the basis for what, by the standards of the time, was an explosion of agrarian production, and subsequent population growth.[29]

---

28. Dobb 1978, pp. 63–4.

29. We look forward to forthcoming work exploring this very topic from Professor George Comninel. In applying his theory to his own time, Malthus failed to appreciate how the constant increase of productivity through revolutionising the means of production could allow production to generally keep pace with population growth. Malthus' theory of population, however, is applicable to the feudal period, for once the limits of

Takahashi's important, if problematic,[30] contributions to the debate, although theoretically amounting mostly to a restatement of some of Dobb's major points, point to some of the problems which would become central for Brenner's later work. Most notably, Takahashi points out divergences between England, France, and Eastern Europe. In particular, following Tawney, Takahashi points out the peculiarity of the English development of the '"tripartite division into landlord, capitalist farmer and landless agricultural labourer" which is characteristic of modern English agriculture' and which because it 'had its origin within the structure of already existing English feudal society . . . there is no reason to ascribe it to trade as such'.[31] Takahashi also notes the absence of these developments in France. He mentions the writings of Arthur Young, who in his *Travels in France* noted the miserable condition of the French peasantry prior to 1789. Takahashi comments that the dissolution of the small peasant producers in France 'did not establish a capitalist wage labour system but initiated usurious land-proprietorship'.[32] Takahashi still amalgamates the English and French experiences together under the rubric of Marx's 'Way I',[33] which is the transformation of the small producer into a capitalist by his gaining control over the productive process. Thus 'the class of small- and middle-scale industrial and commercial capitalists . . . threaded their way to independence in the interstices of the merchant capitalist "control" and became the merchant-manufacturers'. Takahashi adds that Dobb should have 'given a more precise development' to his theory of way I, or the 'truly revolutionary way', 'in light of the internal organisation peculiar to English agriculture'.[34] Rather than following this up by interrogating further the differences between the English and French experiences, however, Takahashi distinguishes the English/French (Western European) experience, from the Eastern European route to capitalism. The former are held to have followed 'Way I', while the latter followed 'Way II', or the merchant becoming a capitalist through the putting-out system, whereby the small producers were subordinated to market forces by merchants controlling their access to the market.

Both Dobb and Takahashi, *contra* Sweezy, look for the dynamic of the system not in the relations between producers and the market, but in the relations between producers themselves, and between producers and their exploiters.

---

arable land were reached, population growth did indeed outstrip the food-supply (see Malthus 1960).

30. For example, Takahashi anachronistically employs the term 'labour-power' to pre-capitalist settings, and also speaks of the 'self-disintegration' of the peasantry, which is simply counter-intuitive.

31. Takahashi 1978, p. 77.

32. Takahashi 1978, p. 78.

33. Marx 1967, pp. 334–5.

34. Takahashi 1978, p. 94.

Rejecting Sweezy's understanding of capitalism as distinguished from feudalism in terms of a system of production for exchange versus a system of production organised primarily for use-values – the rise of capitalism as simply the growth and eventual predominance of production for exchange value – Dobb attempts to locate the agents of change in their social production relations, but in a very limited manner. Way I and Way II are taken as *general* paths to capitalism operating across feudal Europe (or post-feudal Europe, depending on how it is defined). The processes may vary widely in content, but as a rule each begins with a fairly generic feudalism and ends in the same result: a process of accumulation of capital through the subordination and control of landless, free wage labour. Aside from recognising England's precocious industrial development, the peculiarity of the English experience is not dealt with. Moreover, the subordination and commodification of labour is assumed as a fairly natural result of the growth of a capitalist class, which can impose capitalist conditions upon the entire country once it has broken the 'fetters' of feudalism, by overthrowing the feudal aristocracy in bourgeois revolution. However, the notion that bourgeois revolution represents the final and ultimate blow to the old structure of class relations, ushering in the new, capitalist system in one breathtaking moment, appears to simply reproduce Sweezy's explanation of the triumph of a system of exchange values over one of use-values. For although Dobb managed to pose the problem of the process by which the economic is separated from the political in capitalism by emphasising the 'extra-economic' character of feudal relations, this process is assumed, not explained, in the triumph of the bourgeois/proletarian (capitalist) class system over the lord/peasant (feudal) class system. The bourgeoisie becomes, in effect, the social agent which can institute a system of production for exchange and quash the former system of production for use-values.

Brenner credits Dobb for being perhaps the first 'to begin to understand feudalism in terms of its own internal contradictions and conflicts, not excluding but incorporating the growth of trade'. But providing a theory of feudal economic development and crisis is not to provide a full account of the transition to capitalism. Dobb accounts for the transition in terms of the 'unfettering' of petty commodity production. Here, however, the attempt to formulate a theory of transition to capitalism for Western Europe as a whole runs into trouble. For Dobb 'understates the pivotal role played by English landlords in short-circuiting and undercutting small peasant production, so as to provide the conditions for capitalist development by their commercial tenants'.[35] Dobb is hard-pressed to explain how 'feudalism' was overthrown in 1640, how the 'fetters' of feudalism

35. Brenner 1978, pp. 122–3.

had impeded capitalist development up to that point, and moreover to demonstrate that there existed, in England in 1640, any 'feudal' ruling class at all.

In rejecting trade as the external source of dynamism within feudalism, Dobb proceeded to an analysis of the feudal laws of motion. Dobb recognised that feudal class relations 'generated their own long-term development tendencies toward retrogression'. The crisis of the fourteenth century was the realisation of these tendencies, the result being a drastic reduction in population and subsequently a crisis in seigneurial revenues. The newly available untenanted land and the scarcity of labour opened the way for the peasantry to throw off lordly controls. Dobb is clear on all of this, says Brenner, but he does not draw the logical conclusion. At first he seems to suggest that the crisis of the fourteenth century itself determined the fall of serfdom, rather than resulting from a process of class struggle. Later he examines the seigneurial reaction, post-collapse, and asks why in some regions feudal rent was maintained whilst elsewhere (specifically England), lords were 'unable to prevent the supercession of serfdom by the rise of contractual relations between lord and peasant, or even the rise of peasant property'.[36] Strangely, Dobb comes to the following conclusion: 'All the indications suggest that in deciding the outcome economic factors must have exercised the outstanding influence'.[37] Here, Brenner objects: '[W]as not the essence of feudalism, as Dobb defines it, the encasement of economic-productive activities within a determined structure of extra-economic relations of surplus-extraction directly by force?'[38] The implication of Dobb's 'economic' argument, says Brenner, appears to be that the lords could dictate whatever outcome was suitable to their needs. Dobb failed to carry through his inquiry into the sources of class solidarity and class power among the peasantry, and among the lords. Instead, Dobb continued to rely on the assumption that once serfdom was abolished, peasant production will evolve:

> more or less automatically in the direction of capitalism. Under the impact of the market, larger petty producers will accumulate surpluses; their size will give them technical advantages over smaller plots; they will ultimately outcompete the smaller units on the market. The outcome is a bit-by-bit takeover by the larger producers from the smaller ones, the elevation of the larger producers into the ranks of rural capitalists and the depression of the smaller ones into the rank of the wage labourers... Nevertheless, to assume such a progression is to beg the central question. For it is to assume that there already exist social-productive relations in which the petty producers are deprived of

36. Brenner 1978, pp. 126–8.
37. Dobb 1947, pp. 50–4.
38. Brenner 1978, p. 128.

> the means of subsistence, so that they must sell on the market and thus productively compete in order to survive.[39]

Brenner contrasts the ability on the part of much of the French peasantry to hold onto the land, and the apparent absence of any dispossession of peasants by market forces, with *villein* peasants in England, who were unable to establish widespread proprietorship and were vulnerable to supersession by larger producers who held leases from landlords. In England, the impact of the market did, indeed, condition a significant pattern of differentiation. It is this, argues Brenner, which must be explained and which cannot be assumed: the separation of the direct producers from the means of production and their vulnerability to productive competition according to market principles.[40]

Marx on property relations: Brenner's point of departure

Adam Smith captured the essence of economic growth, and discovered its key mechanism, namely 'the presence in the economy of a systematic and continuous tendency or drive to transform production in the direction of greater efficiency'.[41] This drive entails specialised production for exchange on a competitive basis, which presupposes market dependence and a system of consistently seeking ways of reducing the price/cost ratio of output, which in turn requires further specialisation, accumulation of surpluses, and innovation, or the adoption of the best available production techniques. For Smith, this whole system is premised upon the natural human tendency for individuals to pursue their rational self-interest through exchange. What Smith fails to specify are the social conditions under which the commodification of all factors of production is both possible and rational in the eyes of the economic agents themselves. Smith assumes the existence of free economic actors who are not subject to extra-economic constraints, and also assumes that rational self-interest precludes any attempts to maintain non-capitalist systems of production.

Sweezy, according to Brenner, adopts the same problematic assumptions. Like Smith, Sweezy locates the source of the transformation in psychological factors, specifically the pursuit of rational self-interest. Thus lords adopted an 'exchange consciousness', and merchants and members of the feudal system alike adopted

39. Brenner 1978, p. 136.

40. Brenner 1978, p. 136 n. †, notes that Dobb did not neglect Marx's discussion of so-called primitive accumulation, and neither did he neglect the role of landlords; he merely fails to link these insights into his discussions of the transition and bourgeois revolution.

41. Brenner 1986, p. 24.

a 'businesslike attitude'.[42] In effect, capitalism always exists for Sweezy; it is merely inhibited by the feudal integument. Sweezy posits that the relationship of direct producers to the market determines their operation, their development, and their relation to each other, and not vice-versa. So like Smith, he locates the potential for development in the capacities of the system's component and isolated units, not in the system as a whole. Like Smith, Sweezy contrasts production for exchange versus production for use, but he does not ask: *under what conditions is exchange value able to predominate*?

For Marx, the domination of exchange value itself, and production which generates exchange value:

> presupposes alien labour capacity itself as an exchange value – i.e. the separation of living labour capacity from its objective conditions; a relation to them – or to its own objectivity – as alien property; a relation to them, in a word, as capital. Only in the period of the decline and fall of the feudal system, but where it still struggles internally – as in England in the fourteenth and first half of the fifteenth centuries – is there a golden age for labour in the process of becoming emancipated.[43]

It is this emancipation, or freeing of labour from its objective conditions of existence, which for Marx enables money-wealth to become capital. For it accumulates both the means of production on the one hand, and on the other hand purchases labour-power on a regular and ever-expanding basis, thereby subsuming production to its control and its own prerequisites of specialisation, maximisation and innovation in order to compete on the market place. Marx identifies the starting-point of the wage labourer and the capitalist as 'the servitude of the labourer', which in the transition to capitalism undergoes a change in form, a transformation from feudal exploitation to capitalist exploitation. Marx writes: 'Although we come across the first beginnings of capitalist production as early as the fourteenth or fifteenth centuries, sporadically, in certain towns of the Mediterranean, the capitalistic era dates from the sixteenth century'.[44] Note the use of the term 'capitalistic' in latter half of this sentence, contrasting with 'capitalist production' in the earlier part. This suggests ambiguity on Marx's part regarding the nature of capitalism prior to the Industrial Revolution (and its precursor in England, the expropriation of the agricultural producers). Since Marx writes of 'merchant capital' in the early modern period, he is obliged, at

42. Brenner 1977, p. 45.

43. Marx 1973, p. 510. Brenner 1977, p. 50 cites the same passage, but leaves the last sentence out. Below, we will discuss what Marx had in mind when he wrote of the 'golden age for labour in the process of becoming emancipated'.

44. Marx 1906, p. 787.

least, to speak of forms that are 'capitalistic' in this period. But by identifying 'capitalist production' in Italian manufactures in the sixteenth century, Marx appears to contradict himself, if he means to imply that *capital* as a social relation – the precise object which his study sets out to define – can be identified in sixteenth-century Italy. For in the very next paragraph, he identifies the revolutionary moments of primitive accumulation as 'above all, those moments when great masses of men are suddenly and forcibly torn from their means of subsistence, and hurled as free and "unattached" proletarians on the labour market'. Continuing, he writes:

> The expropriation of the agricultural producer, of the peasant, from the soil, is the basis of the whole process. The history of this expropriation, in different countries, assumes different aspects, and runs through its various phases in orders of succession, and at different periods. In England alone, which we take as our example, has it the classic form.[45]

Continuing further in a footnote, Marx notes that the emancipation of serfs first happened in Italy, and 'at once transformed him [the serf] into a free proletarian, who moreover, found his master ready waiting for him in the towns . . .' The use of the term 'master', here, is telling, for Marx's 'proletarian' is not heading for work in a factory, but in a manufacturing workshop regulated by custom, and as such the use of the term 'free proletarian' appears misleading.[46]

Despite being a prominent critic of Smith, Marx initially adopted the essentials of Smith's theory of the division of labour as the source of capitalist development. However Marx went on to develop a theory of modes of production, which provided him with a powerful point of departure from which to begin the critique of Smith's synchronic and ahistorical model. In theorising feudalism and capitalism as modes of production, Marx sought to explain how capitalism developed out of the action of feudal society itself. In particular, Marx hoped to explain how extra-economic surplus-appropriation – through rent and other forms of tribute – was dissolved, and how the separation of the direct producers from the means of production was brought about.[47]

Brenner argues that Marx's original formulation of the transition to capitalism, which relied heavily on the concept of bourgeois revolution, was explicitly techno-functionalist. While the later Marx focused on class and property

---

45. Marx 1906, p. 787.
46. In the next chapter, we will discuss how, in a different context, Epstein also equates waged labour with capitalist production. Interestingly, Marx goes on to explain that when Northern Italy's commercial supremacy was annihilated by around 1500, deurbanisation ensued. The reader could conjecture that this explains why no industrial revolution followed in Italy.
47. Brenner 1989, p. 273.

relations – and the connection between these relations to the process of development – class structure in Marx's early formulations depended on the occupational position of individuals in 'technically-constituted roles in the labour process'. Class and property relations were taken as mere appendages of the division of labour. Marx had only elaborated, not broken with Smith's theory. In his later writings, Marx defined property relations as both the relations between direct producers and the means of production, and the relations between the direct producers themselves. Both sets of relations structure the actions of direct producers in a way that allows them to reproduce themselves as agents within a rule-bound system at the same time as they reproduced the whole structure of social production-relations, including the property relations which govern the system. Marx now recognised that the structure of property relations, which was reproduced on a constant basis by the community:

> constituted a fundamental constraint under which economic actors chose their economic goals and, in turn, decided just how they would respond to the emerging opportunities for exchange that had played such a determining role in the first, Smithian version of Marx's historical materialism.[48]

This new approach turned Marx's earlier approach upside down. Instead of the forces of production determining the structure of production relations through the division of labour within the workplace, the structure of property relations – bound up as it is with the entire structure of social relations and the specific form of the state in a class society – governed the overall direction of economic change.

Brenner takes this conception of the role of property relations in social change – a conception held by the 'mature' Marx – as the basis for his understanding of feudalism. Central to his understanding was the fact that peasant producers and their overlords in pre-capitalist societies had direct access to the means of production. In the process of choosing their fundamental economic goals, the primary interest of the peasant would be to maintain access to the plot of land which he possessed, since this was the basis of – the *means* of – his and his family's subsistence.[49] To do this the peasant would have to maintain his standing in the village community, since this community mediated his relationship to the land. In short, it was in the peasant's interest to reproduce himself as a peasant. Moreover, given the uncertainty of harvests, and the subsequent uncertainty in food supplied through the market, it would *not* be in the peasant's 'rational

48. Brenner 1989, pp. 284–7.
49. This is assuming the average peasant head of household to be male, and thus the use of 'he', 'him', and such like. A minority of peasant households were, of course, headed by widows, unmarried women, and so on.

self-interest' to pursue production for the market. Specialisation in a given crop could spell disaster in the event of crop failure or a sharp decline in price due to a general glut of that product on the market. It was, therefore, sensible for peasants to avoid dependence on access to subsistence goods through the market, or on the sale of commercial crops at the market, as means of generating subsistence revenue. Subsistence could best be guaranteed through diversifying production so a maximum number of needs could be provided for through non-market means. Going to market with nonessential surpluses, if possible and if necessary, could be done to fill in when this strategy resulted in a shortfall in the fulfilment of specific needs, or to obtain petty luxury-goods if subsistence needs were met.[50]

Lords too, in pre-capitalist class societies, enjoyed direct access to their means of reproduction: ownership of land worked by peasants, as well as ownership of the means of coercion in the form of military equipment and manpower – what Brenner refers to as 'politico-military apparatuses'.[51] Lords were thus freed 'from the necessity of increasing their income for the purpose of increasing their productive capacity'.[52] To increase their incomes, lords had to coerce peasants into yielding a greater share of their surplus. For lords to pursue a strategy of improving the productivity of agriculture, they would have been required to employ overseers engaged in the direct supervision of the labour process, which would prove costly. They could not expropriate peasants from the land because peasant access to land was regulated by customary law, which bound lords and peasants in a web of mutual obligations. Moreover there was no class of free producers devoid of the means of reproduction to whom they could lease out their land or hire on a wage labour basis. The most rational and efficient avenue for lords to increase their consumption was to accumulate surpluses which they could invest in the means of coercion for use in guaranteeing and maximising their share of peasant surpluses, as well as for going to war and expanding their estates by colonising new lands. For these reasons neither lords nor peasants in pre-capitalist societies depended on the market for their subsistence, and neither would find it rational to become market-dependent. The pressures to engage in systematic specialisation, maximisation of price/cost ratios, and innovation in the productive process were simply not present. A fundamental barrier to the drive to systematically improve the efficiency of production was posed by the access which the direct producers had to the means of production in land. The factors of production: peasants' labour, land, and (insofar as peasants produced

50. Brenner 1989a, p. 287. See also Brenner 1972, pp. 26–32 and Brenner 1985b, p. 236.
51. Brenner 1972, p. 31.
52. Brenner 1989a, p. 290.

their own) implements, remained effectively outside of the circuit of commodity exchange.

To the extent that merchants played a role in pre-capitalist economic systems, it was one of maintaining, not transforming the system. Merchants profited through pursuing trade, not investing in ever more productive spheres of production. Building on Polanyi's observation that the character of trade before the advent of what he calls 'market society' was fundamentally non-competitive, Wood points out that buying cheap and selling dear was the operative principle, not market-driven competition. To the extent that competition within the marketplace existed, it was not driven by 'producing more cost-effectively', but had more to do with achieving dominance over trade routes or arbitrage between markets. 'This kind of trade, largely in luxury goods for a fairly limited market, did not in itself carry an impulse to improve productivity... The main vocation of the large merchant was circulation rather than production'.[53] Communal regulation of production both in the peasant villages and urban guilds predominated, not individual discretion. Only a radical restructuring of property and class relations could change this. The role of merchants was to secure the trade of urban handicraft production in luxury and military goods (for lordly consumption), in exchange for peasant-produced food and raw materials (needed in the towns for the artisans' subsistence). In order to ensure that they could buy cheap and sell dear, merchants sought and obtained the ability to control access to their markets. Gaining monopoly control over markets required political assistance, and thus the cultivation of alliances with the monarch or the lordly class was a major preoccupation of the merchant. 'Far from transforming the old system economically or subverting it politically, the merchant class thus tended to live off the old socio-economic order and to constitute one of its main bulwarks'.[54] Marx taught that commerce has a generally corrosive effect upon production,[55] because under the influence of commerce, production increasingly becomes production for exchange value, and products increasingly take on the character of commodities. But it is centrally important to note that Marx is unequivocal about the fact that merchant capital cannot by itself explain the transition to capitalism,[56] and that commercial change (economic growth or decline), does not determine the outcome of the process of social change. Marx wrote: 'to what extent [commerce] brings about a dissolution of the old mode of production depends on [the old mode's] solidity and internal structure. And whither the process will lead... what new mode of production will replace the old, does

53. Wood 2002a, pp. 77–9.
54. Brenner 1972, p. 291.
55. Marx 1967, pp. 331–2.
56. Marx 1967, pp. 327.

not depend on commerce, but on the character of the old mode of production itself'.[57]

Thus a mode of production involved a particular 'solidity and internal structure' of the system of property relations which governs the social relations of production, which gives it its distinctive character. In this way, Marx distinguished various pre-capitalist modes of production by their distinctive forms of property relations. Marx's theory of modes of production posed the problem of the transition in a new way, that being how pre-capitalist property relations were transformed into capitalist property relations.

Brenner takes Marx's theory and elaborates a causal sequence for changes in economic development. He argues that the form of property relations sets the rules for reproduction of the individual economic actors, and the carrying out of these rules will result, in aggregate, in the long-term pattern of economic development (or non-development). Given societies with diverging structures of property relations, then, the same demographic and commercial changes may develop along entirely different paths. Brenner locates the divergence that led to the transition to capitalism in English agrarian property relations.

The specificity of capitalism and agrarian capitalism

Both Ellen Meiksins Wood and George Comninel have credited Karl Polanyi for recognising the strikingly disruptive character of the self-regulating market under capitalism. No one, writes Comninel, 'has yet spelled out more clearly than he how truly peculiar it is for a society to have its fundamental processes of social reproduction organised in the manner of capitalism'. He adds: 'What Polanyi particularly denies is that there ever was a society, prior to capitalism, in which the market played a role comparable to its absolutely central role in capitalist society'.[58] Wood recognises that Polanyi has indeed broken with the standard accounts of economic development inasmuch as they stress the continuity of commercial activity from ancient times to the present. Polanyi's understanding of the development of capitalism however, writes Wood, is based on a belief that technological progress lay at the heart of it. In effect, Polanyi remains an economic (and a technological) determinist. 'Polanyi never actually treats the market itself as a social relation – as distinct from an impersonal mechanism which imposes itself on social relations'. In contrast to Polanyi's technological determinism,[59] Wood offers an alternative, by proposing, as we read in an

57. Marx 1967, pp. 326–7 as quoted in Brenner 1972, p. 292.
58. Comninel 2000, p. 6.
59. See Wood 2002a, p. 25 for her critique of Polanyi's technological determinism.

earlier quote from Wood, that that a 'market society' in which both direct producers and exploiters had become (or were in the process of becoming) dependent upon the market for access to the means of subsistence and of self-reproduction not only preceded industrialisation but served as its primary cause:

> Only a transformation in social property relations which compelled people to produce competitively (and not just to buy cheap and sell dear), a transformation which made access to the means of production dependent on the market, can explain the dramatic revolutionizing of productive forces uniquely characteristic of modern capitalism.[60]

Here, we see why the theory of agrarian capitalism represents such a sharp departure from long-standing, taken-for-granted assumptions about the development of capitalism. The overwhelming tendency has been to equate trade and/or waged labour – in whatever form – with capitalism, and thus to equate the growth of trade and/or waged labour with the growth of capitalism itself.[61]

The transition debate brought out the peculiarity of feudal and pre-industrial English developments, the backwardness of French agriculture relative to agrarian capitalism in England, and the importance of peasant/lord relations in the decline of feudalism and the rise of capitalism. We have just seen that in his later work, Marx revised his earlier Smithian formulations and recognised the historical specificity of different modes of production – capitalism among them – by virtue of their distinct systems of property relations. Furthermore, Marx recognised the importance of the expropriation of the agricultural population from the land, and the 'bloody legislation' against them, the 'classic form' of which took place in England. Yet Marx, Dobb and Sweezy all left unexplained what most needed to be explained, which is the actual historical *process* by which the direct producers became divorced from the means of production, thereby creating a proletariat and the conditions for industrialisation. Through this process all the agents of production became market-dependent, where before they had access to the means of subsistence outside of, or prior to, their relationship to the market. Through this process the production for the market ceased to be merely an option or opportunity. It became instead a system with 'specific laws of motion that uniquely compel people to enter the market, to reinvest surpluses and to produce "efficiently" by improving labor productivity – the laws of competition,

60. Wood 1994, p. 25.

61. As previously noted, although Marx broke with this conception, he tended to equate the expansion of waged labour with capitalism, without analysing the specific structures of property relations involved. Without the analytical tool of market dependency, one cannot show how producers enter a capitalist dynamic when they are subject to market compulsions and are subject to a *process*, the result of which is the commodification of labour-power.

maximisation, and capital accumulation.'[62] It should be clear then that the task at hand is to locate the logic of this process. To this end, the theory of agrarian capitalism has provided a beginning. The theory attempts to locate a rupture in the feudal system of property relations, which opened up a unique historical opportunity for the development of a *capitalist* system of property relations.

A necessary precondition for the development of agrarian capitalism in England was the decline of serfdom and feudal relations of direct domination by around 1450. The decline of feudalism was not caused by English agrarian capitalism – as this decline occurred broadly across Western Europe – nor did the decline of serfdom mean the simultaneous rise of capitalism, or capitalist forms of production. In Western Europe, new forms of surplus-extraction were developed through the centralisation of the state and the transformation of state offices into a new form of property: the tax-state office – a development that Wood, following Perry Anderson, has aptly described as the 'centralisation upwards' of feudal estate property.[63] Eastern Europe experienced a second serfdom, lasting into the nineteenth century. The Italian city-states lapsed into lordly somnambulism and forever lost the vibrancy they had previously enjoyed as republican communes serving as the hub of access to international commerce for the feudal North. Meanwhile, English property relations were undergoing a different kind of transformation. The different paths out of feudalism shared many features in common, such as the expansion of commercial activity or the centralisation of military force by the state. But contrary to deep-seated assumptions about human nature and economic evolution, there was no capitalism just waiting to be set free from the 'fetters' of feudalism.

The process by which capitalism came into being begins in England. The English body politic had since the Norman Conquest been more cohesive and more unified than most countries in Europe.[64] By the fourteenth century, landownership in England was peculiarly concentrated in the hands of larger lords. And, in general, the reserves that were the direct property of the lords in England were larger in comparison with the holdings of their counterparts on the continent. Ellen Wood suggests that there was a kind of trade-off where lords accepted the centralisation of state power in exchange for control over the land, becoming *land*lords in the process.[65] In the context of a loss of over half the population after the plagues, lords engrossed vacant lands and lands held by formerly *villein* tenants, in many cases converting the latter to leaseholds. To do this, lords turned the common law – unique to England – to their advantage

62. Wood 2002a, p. 15.
63. Wood, 1991, p. 23.
64. Comninel 2000, p. 22.
65. Wood 2002a, p. 99.

in asserting their rights to land as a form of personal *property* rather than as something they held legal jurisdiction over by virtue of their enfiefment as barons.[66] Between 1370 and 1470, lords began to lease out their manorial demesnes to tenants, rather than allowing peasant-proprietors to cultivate them directly. For many lords, the income from leased lands soon eclipsed that from those still regulated by customary rights and in this way, by adapting the king's law to promote their interests, they gradually began to transform themselves from manorial lords into landlords.[67]

The different classes of tenant – freeholders, copyholders, and tenants-at-will – were still present. But this system 'was in many ways being bypassed' as freeholders and copyholders, for example, let out lands to sub-tenants 'whose existence was not in the cognisance of the manorial system.'[68] Relying increasingly on economic rents enforced by contracts under common law rather than extra-economic power, England's landed aristocracy was the earliest in Europe to demilitarise.

By itself, this increasing reliance on economic rents did not constitute the beginnings of an agrarian capitalism, because production was still organised according to non-market, extra-economic rules, or customary modes of production.[69] Only when significant tracts of land were removed from the purview of customary law through enclosure did the capital relation make its first appearance. In the late fifteenth century, the elevated arable lands of Eastern Yorkshire were widely enclosed for the purpose of creating sheep runs. While pastures had been created elsewhere, this was the beginning of a new pattern of converting land from arable to pasture when the price of wool and mutton was high. In the Yorkshire Wolds region, both high and low lands were heavily manorialised with strong open field systems, but only the high Wolds, where the quality of the land was poor, were enclosed early for pasture, provoking a tremendous outcry from local tenants. The lowlands were among the *last* arable lands in England to be enclosed by parliamentary enclosure.[70] When grain prices recovered, there was a significant return to mixed farming after the original enclosure for pasture. Thus 'improved' agriculture, involving mixed or 'sheep-and-corn' farming, was introduced. What this example suggests is that the conversion of arable to

66. Comninel 2002, pp. 28–31.
67. Hilton 1985, p. 129; Brenner 1985a, pp. 46–9; Brenner 1985b, pp. 251–317.
68. Coleman 1977, p. 42.
69. The term 'customary modes of production' is used here cautiously, not in order to collapse distinctions between various non-capitalist economies with entirely different histories and laws of operation, but as a way of drawing a very broad distinction between economies still very much 'embedded' in social and political relations and capitalism, in which the economy (in theory and to a considerable degree in practice) has become 'dis-embedded' from extra-economic forms of regulation.
70. Yelling 1977, pp. 58–63, especially p. 63.

pasture through enclosure on the high Wolds was being made not in accordance with local manorial custom, but in direct response to market prices. While other regions saw enclosure of arable for conversion to pasture, the transformation was less dramatic, owing to the weakness of the field-systems relative to East Yorkshire.

In the context of an arrangement of social production relations where the right to property was absolute and production decisions could be made in accordance with the market, leasehold tenure took on a new character. For now individual lease-holders were in competition with other tenants not only in the search for paying customers to buy their produce, but most importantly for security of tenure in the form of leases. Failure to pay the rent on a lease spelled dispossession. In this increasingly competitive environment, production for the market became less and less about realising the opportunity afforded by the market to dispose of a surplus in order to earn additional income, and more and more about coping with the imperative to compete by increasing overall output on a tenancy – an imperative imposed on tenant-farmers by a competitive market in leases. Ultimately this would mean specialising in cash-bearing crops and innovating in production methods and technologies.

What began to emerge was a sphere of social relations increasingly governed by market regulation, as opposed to direct domination or 'extra-economic' coercion. It only 'began' to emerge, here, because this 'strictly economic' sphere of social relations first developed in the context of social relations which retained many of the basic characteristics of feudalism, including both lordly and royal hierarchies. Social relations in general were still subject to normative regulation through custom and convention. We are only at the beginning of a process by which that sphere of the economy governed by market regulation through competitive pressures expanded at the expense of normative, customary systems of socio-economic regulation.[71] This would entail many conflicts in the process of transformation. Typically, the process by which 'feudal' systems of property relations are dismantled is understood as the 'unfettering' of 'obstacles' to capitalist development, as though capitalism were ever-present in human nature in the form of rationality, technological development and/or commerce.[72] But here, we are tracing the point of rupture of the old system and the *beginnings* of

---

71. That evolutionary process is not complete even today. Polanyi argued that a truly free-market society would annihilate itself, and that for this reason the state had to play a role to 'buffer' the effects of the free market. Thus a fully-fledged or fully-developed capitalism, one in which *all* social relations came to be regulated by the market, could never come into existence. Despite this, followers of the Japanese Marxist theorist Kozo Uno's work, such as Robert Albritton, have adopted the approach that the best way to understand capitalism is to engage in 'pure theory', that is, to theorise in the abstract a purely capitalist society in which all social relations are regulated by the market (see Uno 1980). For a critique of pure theory, see Zmolek 2004, pp. 290–7.

72. For a discussion, see Wood 2002a, pp. 4–5.

something completely different: capitalism. And the amazing thing about capitalism, an economic system which promotes the regulation of production according to the dictate of the market ahead of all other forms of regulation, is that it developed out of feudalism, an economic system in which production was intensively regulated according to extra-economic rules and norms. Since capitalism did not develop in Asia or ancient Europe, it would appear that capitalism needed something to push against, that the repudiation of normative economic regulation was more likely to take place under conditions of intense normative control.[73]

Market dependency

What was unprecedented about agrarian capitalism is that as the system developed, the economic agents involved become increasingly *dependent* on the market in order to obtain the necessities of life. The development of market dependency is much more clearly evident in the wake of the enclosure movement. High prices for animal products in the late fifteenth and early sixteenth centuries prompted a wave of enclosures in regions more suitable for husbandry. But with the rise of grain prices by the late sixteenth and early seventeenth centuries, enclosures were increasingly undertaken on arable lands. With their income increasingly derived from economic rents, enclosure offered landlords a method by which they could extinguish customary rights and rid themselves of copyholding tenants whose status was protected under the customary law of the manor. The act of erecting fences or planting hedges around a field both symbolically and literally removed the land in question from the jurisdiction of customary law, cancelling customary obligations attached to the land, and making that land a piece of property or 'real estate' protected exclusively by common law.[74]

Brenner has argued that the development of an 'agrarian capitalism' in England set in train the long-term logic of self-sustaining growth which Adam Smith

---

73. This concept of capitalism as owing its origins, at least in part, to a rejection of the intense normative regulation under feudalism arises out of personal discussions with Professor George Comninel and are based upon his research into the question of whether feudalism could be considered a mode of production. Therefore, these comments anticipate his as-yet unpublished work. Additionally, the use of the term 'normative' here and throughout this work is not intended to stress morality or ethics, as is sometimes the case in political theory, but is rather intended in its more anthropological usage, and as used by Polanyi, to refer to 'economic' relations directly governed by social conventions, mores and customs, typically of a local origin. This will become more explicit as the work progresses, especially in Chapter Ten.

74. Prior to this, lordly property was protected under common law, but only in accordance with the dictates of customary law.

identified as a progressive element in capitalism. This development involved the conversion of the direct producers from peasants into landless poor, or semi-proletarians increasingly dependent upon the sale of their labour-power for their subsistence. As agrarian capitalism developed, both producers *and* their exploiters became subject to a situation of *market dependence*, for the exploiting class also became subject to market pressures that compelled them to maximise their productive output by innovating in productive techniques, or by specialising in a narrow range of commodities. In order to reproduce themselves as they were, they now had to rely on market exchange. This new logic (or set of rules) of the *market as imperative*, contrasted sharply, as Ellen Meiksins Wood has pointed out, with the pre-capitalist/feudal logic of the *market as opportunity*.[75]

Peasant production on the manorial estate was primarily geared towards consumption for subsistence. After the fall of the Roman Empire, the manorialism that prevailed across most of Europe involved little marketing of agrarian surpluses. But the advent of feudalism after 900 CE introduced a new and complex medieval field system, and an enormous increase in the number of fines, fees, rents and other monetary obligations upon the peasantry. This system promoted rapid growth of the population, the growth of both local and long-distance trade and compelled the sudden return to the minting of coins. Yet even as producers were increasingly compelled to market their surplus in order to keep up with the mounting burden of rent, tithes and other feudal fines and fees, production was itself ever more closely regulated by the custom of the manor and of the guild. On the open fields, production intensified not through the introduction of new and better methods, but through ever greater numbers of peasants being tied to the land, with ever greater amounts of tribute being exacted from them. Under such a system, there was minimal incentive for peasants to innovate in production. Moreover, peasants found it in their interest to engage in a subsistence strategy of diversifying their production rather than specialising, in order to protect themselves against the dangers of market failure. This they could do precisely because they continued to enjoy direct access to the means of production, which served as their means of subsistence. The law of the manor also placed restrictions on lords as well as peasants. All were bound by the custom of the manor.

Feudal lords, being dependent upon appropriation of peasant surplus for their livelihood, were also shielded from market dependence. Expanding their level of consumption and their extra-economic powers to extract surplus were the ends-in-view of the lords as economic agents. With the aid of an ideological system that enshrined hierarchy, they and their hangers-on oversaw and maintained the

75. Wood 1994, pp. 14–40.

social order which kept the peasantry subordinate in their role as direct producers. The lords achieved their ends either by squeezing peasants and appropriating greater surplus, or through territorial expansion. Any attempts by the lords to encourage specialisation or new methods yielding greater productivity were met with resistance on the part of peasants, precisely because such attempts required the elimination of customary rights, legal institutions which were themselves in part the product of peasant resistance to absolute servitude and slavery.

If production under feudalism was inherently antithetical to market regulation, how did market resistance become market dependency? Dobb posed the question: what, in the action of feudal society itself, brought about a rupture in the logic of the feudal system, leading to a new logic? In addressing this, Brenner locates the dynamic of this transition in the class relations between producers and exploiters in England, where through the enclosures and the extinguishing of customary law, the direct producers were divorced from the means of production and gradually rendered market-dependent. In choosing to make class-relations central to his analysis, Brenner asserts that he is offering an alternative to class analysis which treats class as arising more or less directly out of the requirements of surplus generation and the growth of production in response to the opportunities and pressures of trade. According to Brenner, economic development cannot be determined solely by the laws of supply and demand. Rather, the course of economic development is ultimately determined by structures of class relations which are the product of class struggle. Most debates that have dealt with the role of English agriculture in relation to the development of capitalism have focused almost exclusively on quantitative levels of output. Brenner has argued that economic models which understand economic development in terms of the response of given sectors of an economy to economic or demographic growth and the laws of supply and demand are doomed from the start by their implicit or explicit denial of the determining influence of class structure upon economic development. '[M]ost crudely stated', writes Brenner, 'it is the structure of class relations, of class power, which will determine the manner and degree to which particular demographic and commercial changes will affect long-term trends in the distribution of income and economic growth – and not vice-versa'.[76]

In dealing with the challenges thrown up by his critics, Brenner argues that their arguments tend to follow one of two well-tried models: the demographic model and the commercialisation model.[77] Brenner sets up a kind of proof

76. Brenner 1985a, pp. 10–11.
77. Wood identifies the 'Pirenne thesis' as one example of the commercialisation model. According to Pirenne, the revival of commerce in Europe in the twelfth century

whereby he shows that while all of Europe experienced a tremendous growth of population and a growth of trade in the early modern period, the effects of these phenomena were different in different regions of Europe.[78] Only in England did a system of agrarian capitalism develop whereby the peasantry was rapidly being displaced by tenant-farmers renting out enclosed fields in an incipient market involving competition for leaseholds. For Brenner, these differing results had to do with differences in class structure.[79]

Brenner's insistence upon the centrality of class issues in understanding historical change and economic development led him to a critique of what he calls 'neo-Smithian' Marxism.[80] Brenner criticises those Marxist authors who continue to rely on the classical-liberal understanding that what gives rise to self-sustaining growth or (capitalist) economic development is the on-going extension of the division of labour, leading to continual gains in productivity and an ever-expanding scope of trade. In the classical and neo-classical Smithian paradigm, the division of labour gives rise to innovation and improvement in material production; it improves dexterity, saves time, and facilitates and abridges labour upon the introduction of machinery. Smith wrote: 'It is the great multiplication of the productions of all the different arts, in consequence of the division of labour, which occasions, in a well-governed society, that universal opulence which extends itself to the lowest ranks of the people'.[81]

As the Industrial Revolution involved enormous productivity gains which were achieved in conjunction with the widespread introduction of new labour-saving devices, economic progress has commonly been associated with the advance of machine technology. In the (neo-) Smithian framework the logical site for the growth and elaboration of more and more refined production-processes is urban manufacturing – 'handicraft' production, as the perennial site of relatively more advanced technologies and division of labour. More or less uncritically, the Industrial Revolution has been viewed within this framework as the realisation of latent possibilities for productive activities prefigured in earlier developments, brought about by the continuation of the logical unfolding of the division of labour. This has served to obscure the importance of agrarian capitalism and

---

led to the emergence of new, more commercially-oriented cities and the 'revival' of a burgher or 'capitalist' class, making the expansion of markets inevitable. Wood notes that while this thesis 'has been controversial and generally superseded', its critics 'have seldom questioned the tacit assumptions on which it rested' (Wood 1995, pp. 152–3, citing Pirenne 1969).

78. See above, pp. 16–17.
79. Wood 1995, pp. 13 and 25.
80. Brenner 1977, pp. 25–92.
81. Smith 1957, p. 11.

the development of capitalist, market-dependent social relations in England, in laying the foundation for industrial capitalism.

The elusive origins of capitalism and industrialisation

The most difficult question regarding the Industrial Revolution in most accounts has been its timing. Some historians have completely opted out of the problem of how to explain the timing of the Industrial Revolution by denying that any such event ever took place. The view 'of the industrial revolution as a unique or important watershed in economic or social life' fell out of favour in the 1920s and '30s after J.H. Clapham's *Economic History of Modern Britain* was published, ushering in a period of orthodoxy for a gradualist interpretation[82] This interpretation was based on macro-economic views of the British economy and sector-based studies which showed that non-mechanised labour and small firms continued to predominate in industry into the second half of the nineteenth century.

Table 0.1: Rates of growth, Britain 1700–1831 (% per year)[83]

	Old estimates			New estimates		
	GDP	Industry	Culture	GDP	Industry	Culture
1700–60	0.7	1.0	0.2	0.7	0.7	0.6
1760–80	0.6	0.5	0.5	0.6	1.3	0.1
1780–1801	2.1	3.4	0.6	1.4	2.0	0.8
1801–31	3.1	4.4	1.6	1.9	2.8	1.2

While the gradualist interpretation no longer enjoys a position of orthodoxy,[84] what has survived is an understanding that aggregate rates of economic growth in Britain during the early Industrial Revolution were low (rarely exceeding 2 percent per annum) by comparison with later periods of economic boom. Despite this 'low' rate of growth, however, the gradualist approach no longer holds up when we look at more recent data. We can see from Table 0.1 that England experienced a steady and remarkable growth in output throughout the period, even if not achieving the kind of spectacular growth rates associated with Rostowian 'take-off'. Peter Mathias finds the metaphor of 'revolution' overdramatic. Nevertheless, he does support the notion of a historical watershed:

82. See Clapham 1926.
83. Source: Crafts 1994, p. 47.
84. The gradualist school did maintain its adherents. Thus, as late as 1982, professor Cameron wrote of the Industrial Revolution that 'The very concept is a positive hindrance to historical understanding' (Cameron 1982, p. 379).

> [J]udged against the long perspectives of recorded history, the late eighteenth century did see pivotal changes of this nature and the development of new trends which may be claimed in retrospect to have changed the entire nature of the economy and to have established the watershed between an essentially medieval and an essentially modernized context in the economic sense. There is a simple way of demonstrating the truth of this assertion. If the long-term trends in the rate of growth of the economy in the two centuries after 1780 are projected backwards before 1780, the economy would have virtually ceased to exist.[85]

Anyone who travels through towns like Bolton, Rochdale or Wigan in Lancashire will see hillside after hillside covered with honeycombed tracts of worker houses, thrown up in rapid fashion during the accelerated growth of the towns in this region during the early part of the Industrial Revolution, when the cotton mills were going up all around. In 1773, Manchester had barely 30,000 inhabitants; in 1790 it had 50,000; in 1801, 95,000. By 1927, the figure had reached nearly one million.[86] The towns of this region all experienced this enormous growth of population in a short time. This was due to the steady and ever-increasing influx of workers arriving to work in the cotton mills, and later, around Leeds, in the newly mechanised woollen mills.

In the late eighteenth century, wage labour was nothing new, either on the farm or in the manufacturing sector. It was the *scale* of the new factory operations which was decisively novel, not because the mills could employ hundreds of workers at a time,[87] but because of the steady and continuous increase in the numbers of people employed in the ever-increasing numbers of factories, and the quantity of the product produced. The effects of this transformation were of course profound. In his introduction to *The Condition of the Working Classes in England*, Engels cites the proletariat as the chief product of the Industrial Revolution: 'Population becomes centralized just as capital does; and, very naturally, since the human being, the worker, is regarded in manufacture simply as a piece of capital for the use of which the manufacturer pays interest under the name of wages. A manufacturing establishment requires many workers employed

85. Mathias 1983, pp. 3–4 reprints the figures from Crafts, given here in Table 0.1, but is apparently looking at an earlier edition of Floud and McCloskey's book. Thus the 'new' figures for Mathias appear slightly different from the 'new' figures in Table 0.1. This does not affect the argument here, however.

86. Mantoux 1961, pp. 27 and 358.

87. There were large concentrations of workers in manufacturing enterprises prior to the eighteenth century. John Winchcombe is said to have employed hundreds in his wool manufactory in the early sixteenth century (Mantoux 1961, pp. 33–4). We will take up the question of why such large operations did not herald the onset of the Industrial Revolution in the next chapter.

together in a single building, living near each other and forming a village of themselves in the case of a good-sized factory...'[88]

Engels, 24 at the time, was not focused upon statistical rates of growth, but rather on the effects of industrialisation upon the people of England.[89] For Engels, there was little question that the Industrial Revolution amounted to an enormous transformation in both economy and way of life.

In the 1950s and '60s, a number of 'heroic' accounts were written. These writings did not dispute the timing of the Industrial Revolution, but rather emphasised the importance of the innovative entrepreneur. Authors such as Aldcroft, Crouzet, and McClelland stressed the humility, austerity and formative childhood years of the great entrepreneurs. Such an emphasis seems to suggest that if such men were relocated to an earlier historical period or another geographical location, or that if they were reared in a similar fashion in other times or places, the Industrial Revolution might have happened earlier, or might have originated somewhere other than England. But the intellect or psychological constitution of the pioneers of industry is not the issue. These economic agents were operating within a specific historical, social and geographical context of an emerging social logic of market competition as an imperative, an imperative that was absent in other contexts.

There is no debate that the Industrial Revolution in England involved a tremendous growth in the application of new mechanical innovations in nascent industrial production. This fact has led to a tendency to give pride of place to machine technology in conceptions of the Industrial Revolution. In *Unbound Prometheus*, D.S. Landes proclaims:

> In the eighteenth century, a series of inventions transformed the manufacture of cotton in England and gave rise to a new mode of production – the factory system. During these years, other branches of industry effected comparable advances, and all these together mutually reinforcing one another, made

---

88. Engels 1993, p. 33.

89. Engels 1993, p. 33 even took note of the dysecological and health effects of urbanisation: 'The centralization of population in great cities exercises of itself an unfavourable influence; the atmosphere of London can never be so pure, so rich in oxygen, as the air of the country; two and a half million pairs of lungs, two hundred and fifty thousand fires, crowded upon an area three to four miles square, consume an enormous amount of oxygen, which is replaced with difficulty, because the method of building cities in itself impeded ventilation. The carbonic acid gas, engendered by respiration and fire, remains in the streets by reason of its specific gravity, and the chief air current passes over the roofs of the city. The lungs of the inhabitants fail to receive the due supply of oxygen, and the consequence is mental and physical lassitude and low vitality. For this reason, the dwellers in cities are far less exposed to acute, and especially to inflammatory, affections than rural populations, who live in a free, normal atmosphere; but they suffer the more from chronic affections'.

> possible further gains on an ever widening front . . . they may be subsumed under three principles: the substitution of machines – rapid, regular, precise, tireless – for human skill and effort; the substitution of inanimate for animate sources of power . . . thereby opening to man a new and almost unlimited supply of energy; the use of new and far more abundant raw materials, in particular, the substitution of mineral for vegetable or animal substances.[90]

Here, it is as if technological development is the 'motor' of industrial development. Landes's view is close to popular conceptions, still prevalent today (as evidenced in most contemporary science fiction), in which historical progress is seen as intimately bound up with the advance of machine technology, and may even depend upon it. Some contemporary Marxists have elaborated theories of technological determinism according to which the development of the productive forces acts as the 'prime mover' of historical change.[91] Technological determinism obscures the necessity of understanding the social and historical context underpinning what was a new imperative to seek out and integrate cost-cutting measures into an emerging system of capitalist industry.

Critics of the 'prime-mover' approach have emphasised productivity increases in many branches of early manufactures where no new machineries were applied. Hobsbawm and others have emphasised how relatively modest the technological advances were in, for example, the early cotton mills. Landes's claim that inventions transformed the manufacture of cotton seems to have put the cart before the horse. One clear advantage of Brenner's approach is that it encourages us to theorise technological development within nascent industries as change which reflects the imperatives of new forms of class relations, not simply as the application of scientific advancements to opportunities afforded by higher levels of trade. This logically leads us toward exploring the social and historical context of the Industrial Revolution in search of causes and factors that provided the impetus for a dynamic expansion of industry and technology. Thus in place of Landes's formula, a more plausible hypothesis would be as follows: new forms of the social organisation of manufacturing cotton, necessitated by competitive market pressures, transformed the method of integrating machine technology, into the labour process. The reorganisation of production along factory lines provided the basis for the productivity gains achieved. Thus the social organisation of labour is an integral part of the advance of technology. The integration of

---

90. Landes 1962, p. 42 as quoted in Hudson 1992, p. 23. Below, we will explain why Landes is *not*, strictly speaking, a technological determinist while G.A. Cohen, arguably, is. See Chapter Six, pp. 28–301.

91. See Cohen 1978, Chapter Six, 'The Primacy of the Productive Forces.' See previous footnote.

labour-saving devices within this framework further enhanced such productivity gains, and helped to 'tip the scales' decisively in favour of capital.

If there is anything about which there appears to be a general consensus within the literature, it is that there was no specific moment when the epochal event known as the Industrial Revolution occurred. Another approach to defining the Industrial Revolution is to see it as a distended process which divides two historical periods or epochs. For Carlo M. Cipolla, no revolution in history has been 'as dramatically revolutionary as the Industrial Revolution – except, perhaps, the Neolithic Revolution'.[92] The continuity which characterised the pre-industrial world, a continuity rooted in methods of production as well as in knowledge and methods of understanding, was, according to Cipolla, 'broken between 1750 and 1850'.[93] Having set these temporal parameters, and having made the strong case for the significance of the Industrial Revolution and its sweeping, transformative character, we might expect Cipolla to zero in on the period in question and offer an explanation of precisely what happened between 1750 and 1850 that so totally transformed the character of human society. Instead, however, Cipolla asks us to look deep into the preceding centuries in order to understand the origins of the Industrial Revolution. Cipolla suggests that the city-states of Northern Italy, and later, the Southern Low Countries and Northern France were sites of urban revolt against:

> the predominant agrarian-feudal order. It was the beginning of the end of a society in which power and economic resources were based exclusively on landed property and were monopolized by social groups whose ideals were chiefly fighting, hunting, or praying. In its place there began to grow a society based on commerce, manufacturing and the professions, inspired by the ideals of expediency, profit and, to some extent, reason. The warlord and the monk were replaced by the merchant and the professional. The civilization based on these two characters developed quickly and within a few centuries had conquered Western Europe. A *cumulative process* reinforced and refined its structures, both institutional and human.[94]

Cipolla appears to make four assumptions in this statement: 1) that modern, industrial society came about through the extension of urban trade and manufactures, while its precursor, feudalism, was intrinsically rural-based; 2) that this growth was driven forward by the rationality of profit-maximisation; 3) that this was a cumulative process; and 4) that such a historical process was experienced

92. Cipolla 1973, p. 7.
93. Cipolla 1973, pp. 7–9.
94. Cipolla 1973, pp. 9–10. Emphasis added.

in common across Western Europe. Each of these assumptions will be challenged in the course of this work.

Coming to Cipolla's explanation of the Industrial Revolution after 1750, we are told that there is an 'obvious continuity' between the sketches of Honnecourt, the machines of Da Vinci and the discoveries of Newton. By the end of the seventeenth century, this movement of an emerging mechanical conception of the universe reached its peak, recognisable in Baconian philosophy. At this critical juncture, Holland might have seemed the likely place for an explosion in productive improvements. By harnessing windpower on an unprecedented scale (as exemplified in the production of the *fluyt*, a smaller, slower, but more cost-efficient cargo ship), the Dutch attempted to maximise their profits not according to the age-old tradition of insisting upon the high quality of goods, and therefore maximising profit per unit of production, but by demonstrating a willingness to sacrifice quality in order to expand the quantity of goods sold. For Cipolla, this represented 'a decisive move toward mass production'.[95] Why then was Holland not the first country to experience an industrial revolution? Cipolla explains that 'she was imperceptibly ossifying into conservatism and she was losing leadership in a progressively greater number of fields. Moreover England possessed coal and Holland did not'.[96] Let us take note that Cipolla implies here that an industrial revolution in Holland was possible – even likely – had coal, and more progressive politicians been available. Historical accident apparently blocked this imminent potential.

Brenner's interpretation is that the Netherlands did in fact develop capitalist agriculture early on, but that its capitalist development was 'stymied' because, unlike England, this growth had not been accompanied by the development of the domestic market. Wood challenges Brenner's interpretation using Brenner's approach to the problem in analysing capitalist markets as a form of social property relation. For Wood, the Netherlands may have seen the growth of market dependence in agriculture, but she questions whether this was actually capitalist, involving the compulsion to revolutionise production, or merely the kind of market dependence that follows from large-scale growth of markets as opportunity. Charles Post adds that the absence of market compulsions inducing Dutch peasants to revolutionise their agrarian techniques would have posed a domestic limit to further growth, in addition to Brenner's external limit (the feudal-commercial relations of the European economy).[97]

Cipolla points to four factors which helped precipitate an industrial revolution in England: 1) privateering; 2) the aggressive pursuit of foreign trade; 3) the

95. Cipolla 1993, p. 259.
96. Cipolla 1973, pp. 10–11.
97. See Brenner 2001, pp. 169–241; Wood 2002b, pp. 50–87 and Post 2002, pp. 88–95.

protectionist policies of the British government; and 4) the role of immigrants as craftsmen, inventors, and especially merchants who facilitated the growth of foreign trade. Cipolla does not offer any clear causal explanation of the Industrial Revolution as it first emerged in England. Instead, Cipolla not only seeks to extend its origins back in time to the twelfth and thirteenth centuries in Northern Italy, but he also wants to expand the definition of the term forward in time towards the as-yet unfinished business of industrialising the non-industrialised portions of the globe. His earlier assertion that the Industrial Revolution ushers in a 'completely new' world now seems awkward, unless we are to understand it less as a description of a historical event, and more as a general organising principle for dichotomising the world into two halves: the 'advanced' industrial nations, and the 'backward' non-industrialised nations. What was the social basis for this imminent potential for industrial progress? By what social process did the mechanistic view of nature manage to effect such an ominous transformation as the Industrial Revolution? We will see in Chapter Six that though Da Vinci conceptualised many of the mechanical devices involved in the textile revolution of the eighteenth century, it still remains to be answered why the application of these designs took four centuries to be realised. These lingering questions leave Cipolla's analysis incomplete, at best.

Fernand Braudel and Immanuel Wallerstein are two authors who argue that the origins of the capitalist 'world-system' are traceable to the fourteenth century or earlier. Wallerstein dates the origins of 'a European world economy based upon the capitalist mode of production' from the sixteenth century. But capitalists did not 'flaunt their colors before the world' in this century, according to Wallerstein, nor was the ideology of free trade emergent any time before the eighteenth or nineteenth centuries.[98] Braudel goes further back in time, citing India's seizure (or penetration) of the East Indies, and Rome's hold on the greater Mediterranean as the beginnings of a 'biography' of capital in some form. Criticising those 'cautious' historians who would not speak of capitalism being present in the sixteenth or even eighteenth century, Braudel argues that the Industrial Revolution did represent a 'major break with the past,' but maintains that: 'throughout even this formidable transformation, capitalism remained essentially true to itself. Is it not in the nature of capitalism, a sort of rule of the game [Braudel asks], that it thrives on change, drawing strength from it, being ready at any moment to expand or contract itself to the dimensions of the all-enveloping context which, as we have seen, limits in every period the possibilities of the human economy everywhere in the world?'[99]

98. Wallerstein 1974, p. 67.
99. Braudel 1988, Vol. 3, p. 621.

If capitalism can, indeed, be compared to the rules of a game, several questions immediately arise: Who are the players, and who plays the role of referee and enforcer or interpreter of the rules? Where are the boundaries? What is it about the rules that gives them the internal consistency of a 'game', defining winners, losers, draws, foul play, a beginning and an end? And most crucially, where and when were the rules established, and by whom? In this passage, capitalism is again conceived as a general organising principle, a heading under which disparate processes of production and social life are grouped apparently by the fact that all involve some degree of profit-motive. Both Braudel and Wallerstein avoid offering any precise definition of capitalism, allowing the term to take on a meta-historical quality. By effectively universalising capitalism, they lose sight of its specificity and save themselves the trouble of inquiring into the specific geographical and historical origins of capitalist property relations.

What Braudel and Wallerstein stress is the commonality of developments across Western Europe from at least the fifteenth century. The rise of trade, the establishment of new and extensive international trading networks, the conquering of overseas territories, the settlement of colonies, the competition amongst empires for foreign territory and sources of minerals – all of these developments were common to Western Europe in the early modern period. While each state was quite distinct and had its own mode of operation, the emergence of an international system of European states and empires is, in fact, distinguishable as a transformative era in European history, with implications for world history. Furthermore, there can be no argument with the thesis that among the central factors behind industrialisation there were developments, such as the emergence of this international system of national states, which were common to Western Europe in the early modern period. The competitive expansion of empires is itself traceable to a certain logic and social dynamic which these states undoubtedly shared. But it bears asking: if capitalism and industrial revolution were prefigured in such early developments as the rise of the Northern Italian city-states, then why did it take five hundred years for this dynamic to be realised? The thesis that capitalism was common to Western Europe with deep roots into the feudal era, and that industrial revolution was foretold in the works of early modern scientists such as Da Vinci, amounts to a teleological thesis in which the Industrial Revolution stands as the culmination of many economic developments occurring in disparate geographical and historical settings. Whether capitalism is seen (as with Cipolla, Wallerstein or Braudel) in the rise of trade from the thirteenth century, or is to be understood (*à la* Weber) as existing wherever historians find markets present, the view that capitalism had long dominated European history prior to the Industrial Revolution shifts the causes of the Industrial Revolution away from questions linking it to the development of capitalism, towards issues specific to industrialisation *per se*, specifically the advance of technology. This de-linking of the issues of the origins of capitalism and the Industrial Revolution leads the prefigurative thesis to founder on three fundamental questions, best expressed by Eric Hobsbawm:

1) 'Why it was Britain which became the first "workshop of the world"'.
2) 'Why this breakthrough occurred towards the end of the eighteenth century and not before or after'; and
3) 'How it was ignited; and we may add, what stopped the first explosion from fizzling out after an impressive initial bang?'[100]

Abbreviated, these may be understood as the where, the when and the how of the Industrial Revolution. The *when* is critical. If Cipolla, for example, admits that the Industrial Revolution represented a radical break with the past, then why stress the *continuity* of capitalism? Putting forth the redundant argument that the Industrial Revolution was precipitated by applying scientific methods of engineering to manufacturing does not take us one step further in finding answers to Hobsbawm's 'where, when and how'. It is here that the theory of English agrarian capitalism looms so large.

Conclusion

By examining social change and social conflict during the period leading up to and including the early British Industrial Revolution, this work seeks to demonstrate how the direct producing classes – first in agriculture and then in manufacturing – sought to shield themselves from exposure to market forces, and how their defeat and subsequent exposure was integral to the development of capitalist industry. The transition to capitalism in England came about as a result of a protracted process involving class struggle between direct producers and surplus appropriators both acting as economic agents seeking to reproduce themselves as they were, but culminating in the unintended consequence of general market dependence and new economic imperatives. English peasants lost their direct access to land as the means of subsistence, whilst lords became landed proprietors appropriating rents from tenant-farmers, to whom they provided access to land, the means of production, by way of economic leases. Unlike peasants, agrarian-capitalist tenant-farmers became subject to new market pressures, in the form of competition for leases as well as price competition,

100. Hobsbawm 1986, pp. 36 and 40.

which made the transformation of production in the direction of greater efficiency an imperative. For the capitalist tenant-farmer, economic survival came to depend upon finding ways to maximise output by either increasing the scale of production or by improving productivity through specialisation and innovation. Economic leasehold gave the tenant command over all decisions affecting the production-process, thus allowing for the possibility of treating land and labour as abstract inputs and thus making possible the appearance of a new type of social property relation: capital. As all the agents of agrarian production: direct producers, tenant-farmers and landlords, came into a situation of market dependence; market imperatives and the capitalist system of production were reinforced by the growth of output, of population, of demand, by the steady improvement of agrarian productivity and by the steady decline in the cost of living. Central to this process was the abolition of customary law and the conversion of all land to freehold tenure under common law, thereby redefining the role of the state away from upholding social relations rooted in custom toward becoming the enforcer of property rights and economic contracts between buyers and sellers in the marketplace. Thus could the coercive powers of the state be invoked to suppress resistance to enclosures and the advance of agrarian capitalism.

During the centuries prior to the Industrial Revolution, English manufacturing underwent a considerable degree of transformation, much but not all of which can be attributed to the development of agrarian capitalism. In general, the production process continued to be regulated by customary or extra-economic forms of social regulation right down to the Industrial Revolution. In fact, the numbers of workers engaged in manufacturing grew tremendously as direct producers in agriculture were extruded from agrarian production and looked to domestic handicraft production as an alternative means to a livelihood. With the advance of agrarian capitalism and market dependency, the pressure of the market imperative continued to grow. The growing power of capital was first felt by domestic craft workers through the loss of direct access to markets. For example, merchant-employers engaging in 'putting-out' arrangements exerted control over not only the craft workers' access to markets but also their means of production. However, the strength of workers' organisations and state-level support for customary modes of regulating labour in manufacturing posed a significant barrier to the ability of capitalist employers to enjoy an unlimited capacity to transform production in response to market imperatives. This set the stage for an epochal class struggle between an artisan-led resistance seeking to defend custom, and employers seeking to abolish apprenticeship rules and all customary forms of labour regulation, and, ultimately, to assume full command over production decisions in manufacturing by taking direct control of the labour process away from the workers. The artisan-led resistance to these efforts was only successfully suppressed through the application of the powers of the state, both legislative and coercive, and only after many generations of class struggle involving successive waves of often violent conflict, climaxing in the first half of the nineteenth century.

Throughout this period, the landed oligarchy, whose wealth continued to be drawn primarily from agrarian-capitalist rents, managed to retain control over state power. Based on their experience with the success of 'improved' agriculture, the oligarchs would have shared an ideological bias in favour of the capitalist employers' efforts to 'improve' production in manufacturing. But the specific factors that drew the state into taking sides in the class struggle between capital and labour in manufacturing had more to do with politics than economics. Since the leadership and the core of support for the radical movement for popular democracy were largely drawn from the community of skilled artisans, artisanal organisations, particularly trade unions or 'combinations' of workers, it came to be perceived as a serious political threat to the Hanoverian state, one which had to be suppressed. The state's response to the revival of radicalism in Britain during and after the French and Napoleonic Wars thus hastened the advance of capital in manufacturing.

Contrary to those who would view the state as a passive agent in Britain's Industrial Revolution, the historical fact that the artisan-led resistance to the conversion to capitalism in British manufacturing was only overcome through the direct application of state power demonstrates that the state played a very active and central role in the Industrial Revolution. Moreover, the fact that this application of state power was directed not by a rising class of industrialists but by the ruling landed oligarchy testifies to the fact that the Industrial Revolution in Britain grew out of, and continued to be shaped by, the social property relations of agrarian capitalism. While the emergence of capital as a social property relation and its associated market imperatives arose from the unintended consequences of class struggle, being realised first in the form of agrarian capitalism, the fact that the development of both agrarian and industrial capitalism involved class struggle and the application of state force means that it is untenable to view capitalism as an economic system that resulted from the 'natural' evolution of European society and economy out of feudalism, fulfilling the latent potentialities of pre-capitalist commerce and industry. On the contrary, in order to be realised, the modern capitalist economy and social order had to be imposed upon those who sought to resist it. In order to fully explicate this thesis, it will be necessary to explore both the economic and the political history of Britain throughout this long period of struggle, paying particular attention to the role of the state in shaping events and outcomes.

The plan of this book is both thematic and chronological. Part One concentrates on the history of manufacturing in England in the context of the emergence of an agrarian capitalism which transformed the English economy from the fourteenth century onward. We explore the impact on manufacturing of the overall transformation of the economy through the extinguishing of customary law in agriculture, the expansion of the domestic system and putting-out operations, the growth of a domestic market fuelled by the increasing market dependence of workers, employers and landlords, the increasing productivity of English agriculture and the falling price of grain and, therefore, labour. We trace an evolutionary process of stratification within the old craft guilds, many of which were overtaken by the merchant or 'livery' element whilst small masters and journeymen struggled to either preserve or re-create their craft companies or formed friendly societies for mutual economic protection and support. In addressing the upheavals of the seventeenth century, we explore how the increasing wealth and power of landowners renting to capitalist tenant-farmers translated into their victory over the Crown and a transformation of the state whereby Parliament, as the expression of the power of the landed oligarchy, entered into a kind of ruling partnership with the monarchy. As we enter the eighteenth century, we examine how agrarian capitalism actually served to bolster ruling class solidarity whilst also providing the economic muscle necessary for Britain to prevail in successive wars with France, suffering defeat in only one of these wars: the American War of Independence. Despite the loss of America and other rebellions within the Empire as well as in England, agrarian capitalism and an emerging industrialisation at home helped secure Britain's young Empire, an Empire which was itself not specifically capitalist. Part One closes with an examination of the era of high parliamentary enclosures in the later eighteenth century. As the Industrial Revolution had been set in motion, the processes of agrarian capitalism were approaching their logical conclusion: the commodification of all land in Britain through enclosures and the extinguishing of customary law, bringing about a full conversion to market dependency.

Part Two deals with the question of the role of capital and technology in the Industrial Revolution. By briefly reviewing the development of technology throughout history, we seek to show that it was only under conditions of capitalist social relations in Britain that technology was first applied *systematically* to production in the interests of maximising productivity in the pursuit of profits. We then seek to understand how, in the early eighteenth century, the factory emerged alongside the workhouse as a means of putting idle hands and pauper children to work. We also examine the economic pressures that conditioned the systematic application of machinery to production. We argue that what was absolutely necessary for capitalist industry, even prior to the advent of machinery, was for the owner of the means of production to assume control over the labour process, a control that had heretofore always belonged to the labourers themselves. This sets the stage for the long-term struggle over control of the labour process between owner-employers and workers that becomes central to Part Three. Part Two concludes with a discussion of the different understandings of capital and its role in the Industrial Revolution. We seek to show how the capitalist transformation of manufacturing required not only the dismantling of customary control of the labour process but also the *positive* action of constructing new institutions that would lay the foundations for the Industrial Revolution and a capitalist social order.

In Part Three we turn our attention to the artisan-led resistance to industrial capitalism and the arrival of the factory, paying particular attention to the role of the state. Between the end of the American War and the early years of the French Wars, struggles over custom in both agriculture and industry came to the fore. We look at how the coercive and legislative powers of the state were brought to bear in defeating a popular resistance that sought to defend customary rights, specifically the Tudor statutes which had recognised and legitimised the customary regulations of the guilds. As these statutes were increasingly disregarded and ultimately would be repealed, Parliament introduced a long list of draconian laws designed to secure the absolute property rights of landowners. We examine how this 'bloody code' related to the growth and influence of political economy as an ideological defence of property and of capitalism. We then seek to understand the period between the end of the French wars and the defeat of the last Chartist petition in 1848 as one in which the power of the landed oligarchy reached its apex even as the growing wealth of capitalist manufacturers began to pose a challenge. Despite this apparent schism between two factions of the ruling class, the increasingly self-organised 'working class' was nonetheless confronted with a unity of class interests between landowners and industrialists through the state, and continued to resist the on-going imposition of the social relation of capital, some putting forward visions of an alternative society, while others sought to advance the interests of workers within the framework of capitalist social relations by pressing for a role in setting state policy through the expansion of the franchise. As these struggles played out, the general framework of industrial-capitalist class relations and corresponding state institutions took shape.

Part One

England Transformed

Manufacturing and Agrarian Capitalism, 1348–1783

Chapter One
The Pre-History of Industry

> An initial question: how can one talk about 'industry' in a society often called 'pre-industrialised' or even 'pre-industrial'? Is this not an obvious absurdity?
>
> D.C. Coleman[1]

As the title of this chapter suggests, we are interested, here, in exploring the status of manufacturing prior to the Industrial Revolution. The term 'pre-history' is used to convey the need to understand the continuity between pre-industrial manufacturing and industrial manufacturing, without losing the distinction. As Coleman writes:

> The concept of an industrialised society, brought into being by a process of industrialization or, more dramatically, by what has come to be called an industrial revolution, must carry with it the corollary of a non-industrialized or pre-industrialized society. The definitions and the distinctions are not precise; they do not have universal applicability; they are chronologically blunt. As useful labels... however, they convey meanings which other sorts of labels... fail to convey.[2]

Coleman has been perhaps the principal critic of the use of the term 'proto-industrialisation', and has thus held up the greater part of one side in what could be called

1. Coleman 1975, p. 11.
2. Ibid.

the 'proto-industrialisation debate'. In this chapter, we shall explore the evolution of manufacturing in England to the middle of the seventeenth century. In the process, critiques of both the theory of proto-industrialisation and J.U. Nef's concept of an 'early Industrial Revolution' will be offered. Before we begin that exploration, however, it is necessary to say more about the concerns to be addressed in this chapter, including how they differ from Coleman's concerns.

The theory of agrarian capitalism, as articulated by Robert Brenner, Ellen Meiksins Wood, George Comninel and others, contends that changes in English agrarian class relations were key to the development of capitalism in England, as the foundation was laid for a revolution in manufacturing that essentially played out principles already well-established in English agriculture. These principles include: the divorcing of the direct producers from the means of production, rendering them market-dependent; the control over production and therefore over the labour process by capital; and the subjection of production to market-pressures that compel the owner to make efforts to systematically improve productivity. In Chapter Four, we will examine the operations of agrarian capitalism in greater detail. Here, we shall explore the historical dynamic of the 'crafts', particularly in the sixteenth and seventeenth centuries. According to the theory of agrarian capitalism, the critical development of market imperatives and the growing market dependence of the agents of production were first realised in English agrarian relations. Given this, it remains to ask what role changes in pre-industrial manufacturing played in the transition. What changes can be understood as capitalist in nature? Were such changes merely necessary or were they sufficient? At a broad level, the argument, here, will be that such changes were necessary but not sufficient in and of themselves, without the critical transformation of agrarian class relations in England. This is not to deny the importance of changes in English manufacturing prior to the Industrial Revolution. Nor is the argument simply one of substituting the agricultural 'sector' for the manufacturing sector as the locus of the true dynamic of the genesis of capitalism. Ultimately, the transformation of class and production relations involves all sectors of the economy. But changes in agricultural relations are central to the process, due to the simple fact that the majority of the English population was employed in agriculture, and thus the weight of the entire class structure rested on agricultural labour. We will be attentive here to the ways manufacturing was transformed by the same process of growing market dependency in agriculture, and why this transformation took the form it did, without revolutionising manufactures until well into the eighteenth century.

Wage labour and the guilds

Wage labour in manufacturing has a history stretching back through the Middle Ages. In Europe, associations of craft artisans date from at least the first century BCE, as they played a role in the political upheavals of that turbulent century.[3] These 'Roman guilds' or *collegiae* were 'voluntary associations of traders or employers devoted to a specific line of commerce or commodity production'. Like the medieval guilds, Roman colleges had divine patrons and met in halls where social and religious activities were conducted. Solidarity and prosperity among the members was promoted. Those colleges in a position to negotiate with the state could earn some immunities and concessions, which increased their attractiveness to members. Unlike medieval guilds, slaves could be members and where present, were normally left with the heavier work. Moreover, the Roman *collegiae* 'did not regulate competition among their members or establish any work-rules or production-standards'.[4] The de-urbanisation that followed the collapse of the Western Empire was accompanied by a decline in the colleges. During the ensuing period of manorial agriculture, the demand for urban handicrafts fell as the manors proved to be largely self-sufficient, relying on the labour of free peasants as well as slaves. Records of the existence of medieval guilds date from the twelfth century, but whether any medieval guilds can trace their origins back to Roman times remains uncertain, and perhaps unlikely.[5]

With the spread of feudalism after 900 CE, the newfound power of the ban – 'the power to tax, to decree, to command and to punish' – held by lords, enabled them to command from their subjects such obedience and obligations previously incumbent only on slaves or other dependent persons.[6] Lords tied peasants to the land by forbidding their movement or flight and used access to land, the means of subsistence, as a means of control. While peasant villagers fell into the position of being a universally exploited class, those who dwelled in the towns, not being tied to the land, were increasingly free of obligations. The feudal system of agriculture promoted rapid population growth through a vast expansion of the land put under arable cultivation and, among other things, creating conditions under which children were both valuable for their labour contribution and important as heirs where title to land was hereditary. With

3. Epstein 1991, p. 13.
4. Epstein 1991, p. 18.
5. Weber 1961, pp. 118–19. Weber thought that the guilds in Italy (but nowhere else) were a survival from late Roman times.
6. Comninel 2000, p. 17.

lords looking to peasants as their primary source of surplus-extraction, towns enjoyed a remarkable degree of autonomy. Thus while rising population and commerce facilitated the growth of medieval towns, the independence of the towns was also a direct result of the way the legal-property relations of feudalism extruded non-agrarian workers whilst simultaneously generating the demand for a market in consumables arising as a corollary to the customary and non-market-based economy of the *seigneurie*. Although production decisions were based not on market considerations but on the extra-economic power of the lords to shape production according to their own consumption patterns, the resultant growth precipitated an increase in overall effective demand in the economy, manifested in the resurgence of trade with the East from the tenth and eleventh centuries. The growth of the Italian city-states was the most outstanding manifestation of this.[7] In such an economic environment, handicrafts were bound to flourish.

According to Epstein, it was at this juncture that waged labour became the standard form of productive employment in manufacturing. When slavery, serfdom and dependent employment in monasteries or in the service of the state remained alternatives, the fact that urban employers in manufacturing seized upon wage labour as the principal option is, for Epstein, remarkable. He even goes so far as to suggest that this development represents the 'true beginnings' of modern wage labour. Epstein writes:

> The recent controversy between Robert Brenner and his many critics about agrarian class structure, coercion, and the development of capitalism in late medieval Europe has generally been conducted without reference to the cities. The participants in the 'Brenner Debate' have chosen to omit wage labour, and only Brenner himself recognizes its significance, though he has pushed its effects into the later Middle Ages, past the urban origins witnessed here. The first wages may actually have been paid in the countryside, but regular wage labor by contract, regulated first by the guilds and then by the commune or the state, is an urban innovation. The consequences of this development, so fundamental to the evolution of capitalism in Europe, should encourage historians of labor in later periods to acknowledge the true beginnings of their subject.[8]

The predominance that wage labour came to have within handicrafts was, for Epstein, bound up with the spread of the idea of contract within feudal society. One of feudalism's 'enduring legacies', he writes, was: 'the idea of contract and

---

7. See Comninel 2000, pp. 9–22 for a more in-depth discussion. Some of the ideas presented, here, arise from personal discussions with Professor Comninel, some of which dealt with material he has yet to publish. See the Introduction, p. 28, n. 73 above.

8. Epstein 1991, p. 258.

that the voluntary tie of mutual dependence between fighters would eventually dispose the entire society to value and respect contracts. In this view, those who did not fit into the feudal hierarchy, the townspeople and traders, simply wanted the same personal rights enjoyed by the lords: in this case, the right to make a contract'.[9]

Epstein appears to be suggesting that the contract between lord and vassal may have conditioned the *form* of contract as executed between master and his waged labourers. While this matter is worthy of further study, another explanation for the relative freedom of artisans and towns and the stimulus for their growth is the development of feudal property relations and the evolving symbiosis between the rise of medieval towns on the one hand, and the extension and intensification of agrarian production under feudal agriculture on the other, together providing the basis for the Gothic golden age of cathedral building and crusades.

While slavery had been tolerated by Christianity, and while the Church itself owned slaves who worked on its land holdings, the Church sought to ameliorate the harshness of slavery and was instrumental in the decline of slavery by the medieval period. The declaration of the 'Peace of God' in 989 CE was intended to curb the lawless warfare of the feudal barons and to offer protection to 'women, children, travellers, strangers and holy clerks'.[10] During this period, the manumission of male slaves, *servi*, was common, but the manumission of female slaves, *ancillae*, was less common. Thus even while the institution of slavery declined from the tenth century onward, evidence suggests that where it persisted the majority of the remaining slaves were women, most labouring in agriculture, but others working in textile-workshops and great houses.[11] This casts doubt on the thesis, advanced by Epstein, that the decline of slavery occurred simultaneously with the expansion of the use of free, wage labour engaged in domestic manufactures in the towns.[12]

---

9. Epstein 1991, p. 73, citing Bloch 1961, pp. 450–1.
10. Flick 1909, pp. 357–9.
11. The matter is complicated by the decline of the usage of the term *servus* as meaning slave in the tenth century, and its coming back into usage two centuries later: and no longer connoting a slave, but merely servitude, or serfdom. The term *ancilla*, however, apparently persisted, and retained the connotation of women who passed on their condition as chattel to their children. See Stuard 1995, pp. 7 and 27.
12. See Renard 1968, p. 100. Renard refers to the 'spontaneous and independent' appearance of the guilds, as though the institutions themselves could not have appeared much earlier than the earliest surviving records testifying to their existence. Renard, however, sees this as but one of two opposing theories. The alternate theory suggests that guilds may have had deeper origins, whether in the Roman *collegiae*, or the *scholae*; in the Germanic associations resembling artificial families; in the feudal *ministerialies*: organisations of male servants in feudal households; or as modelled after the monastic orders and religious brotherhoods of the church.

We know from surviving records that medieval guilds had emerged across Western Europe by at least the latter half of the thirteenth century. On the continent, the revival of Roman law in the early modern period provided a potential legal framework for the regulation of urban artisans and their associations, but it had nothing to say about apprenticeship. Instead, hereditary status was emphasised. Guilds on the continent may have also found themselves 'in the unenviable position of late Roman colleges', which, under Roman law, subordinated them to the broader interests of state 'if any secular ruler or arm of government was capable of enforcing its rights in Roman law'.[13] In England, both towns and guilds received charters of incorporation from the Crown. As we shall see below, in the case of merchants, the relationship between the Crown and merchant companies became one of mutual interdependence, with important ramifications. Guilds served their members by providing legitimacy and protection whilst mediating between different sources of local authority, often with overlapping jurisdiction. In general, guilds strove towards monopoly control of markets and often succeeded in attaining the authority to police their craft, in such cases maintaining what Weber calls an 'industrial court'.[14] They also strove towards compulsory membership and the establishment of a guild district, though in England this was generally not achieved. Local monopolies could provide guild members with protection from the vagaries of market fluctuations, which no doubt increased in importance as the revival of long-distance trade advanced.

Mickwitz describes guild regulation of markets through the securing of local monopolies or the seeking of a 'just price' fixed by custom as arising from a pervasive fear of competition.[15] Epstein contends with Mickwitz's linking of custom with monopoly and the general attempt to limit competition by suggesting that 'The love of custom could just as easily go hand in hand with a zest for competition'.[16] While it is true that a competition between guild masters in the same line of craft production did take place, this was to see who could outdo the others in terms of turning out a high quality product. It was thus a competition to fetch the highest price, not to sell the greatest *quantity* and then lowering production costs by underselling competitors. 'A monopoly granted either to an individual or to a trading company', wrote Adam Smith, 'has the same effect as a secret in trade or manufactures. The monopolists, by keeping the market constantly under-stocked, by never fully supplying the effectual demand, sell

13. Epstein 1991 pp. 73 and 80.
14. Weber 1961, p. 114.
15. Mickwitz 1936 p. 250 as cited in Epstein 1991, p. 125. Epstein comments that: 'In the end, this continuity of monopolistic practices convinced Mickwitz that some continuity must exist from the ancient to the medieval guild'.
16. Mickwitz 1936, p. 100.

their commodities much above the natural price, and raise their emoluments, whether they consist in wages or profit, greatly above their natural rate'.[17]

Competition to fetch the *highest* price based upon or leading to monopoly and competition to sell the greatest *quantity* by lowering price are two diametrically opposed senses of competition. Yet Epstein seems to conflate the two in tracing the origin of modern, capitalist competition back to the medieval crafts. Epstein's suggestion that early forms of capitalist labour markets, market contracts and market competition were present in the medieval period is in keeping with the tendency within historiography to project capitalist social property-relations into the pre-capitalist era. By presupposing the existence of capitalist forms at the *onset* of high feudalism, Epstein's views would generally accord well with those of Weber and his followers. Thus, Immanuel Wallerstein proclaims that: 'It was in the sixteenth century that there came to be a European world economy based upon the capitalist mode of production . . . the stage was set in Europe but not elsewhere for the creation of a capitalist world-economy'.[18]

Fernand Braudel states his agreement with Marx (who later revised his view),[19] that capitalist production began in thirteenth-century Italy.[20] For Braudel, 'Capitalism and towns were basically the same thing in the west'.[21] Setting the clock back even further, Max Weber saw capitalism active in ancient Rome and China. As we shall see below, however, Weber did see something unique and distinct about what he called 'modern rational capitalism' or 'market capitalism'.[22]

It is precisely this tendency to treat capitalism as a universal economic form of 'profit maximising', present in all societies, thus rendering the term too non-specific for historical inquiry, that the present work seeks to challenge. The problem with presuming the *a priori* existence of the forms of modern capitalism is, as Robert Brenner has argued, that the very thing most in need of explanation is

---

17. See Smith 1957, p. 67 (Book I, Chapter 7). Smith openly advocated abrogating guild statutes: 'The pretence that corporations are necessary for the better government of the trade is without any foundation. The real and effectual discipline which is exercised over the workman is not that of his corporation, but that of his customers. It is the fear of losing their employment which restrains his frauds and corrects his negligence. An exclusive corporation necessarily weakens the force of this discipline. A particular set of workmen must then be employed, let them behave well or ill. It is upon this account, that in many large incorporated towns no tolerable workmen are to be found, even in some of the most necessary trades. If you would have your work tolerably executed, it must be done in the suburbs, where the workmen, having no exclusive privilege, have nothing but their character to depend upon, and you must then smuggle it into the town as well as you can' (Smith 1957, Book I, Chapter 10, p. 129).

18. Wallerstein 1974 vol. 1, pp. 67 and 63.

19. See the Introduction, pp. 18–19.

20. Braudel 1988, Vol. 3, p. 57.

21. Braudel 1988, Vol. 3, p. 514. Braudel cites Lewis Mumford who 'humorously claimed that capitalism was the cuckoo's egg laid in the confined nests of the medieval towns'.

22. See below, p. 83.

itself assumed away *without* explanation.[23] One reason this tendency may be so pervasive is that scholars writing in the capitalist age will tend to take for granted the laws of capitalist society and assume them as universal laws of history. The notion that pre-capitalist and non-capitalist societies may have been governed by different laws altogether poses a challenge to the imagination of those of us who have known nothing but capitalism. Prior to the development of capitalism, societies as a rule were regulated by normative, non-market principles. Human economies were, in Polany's terms, 'embedded' in the larger matrix of social relations. Polanyi writes:

> man's economy, as a rule, is submerged in his social relationships. He does not act so as to safeguard his individual interest in the possession of material goods; he acts so as to safeguard his social standing, his social claims, his social assets. He values material goods only in so far as they serve this end. Neither the process of production nor that of distribution is linked to specific economic interests attached to the possession of goods; but every single step in that process is geared to a number of social interests which eventually ensure that the required step be taken.[24]

The guild system was no exception to this rule, as Polanyi explains: 'Under the guild system, as under every other economic system in previous history, the motives and circumstances of productive activities were embedded in the general organisation of society. The relations of master, journeyman, and apprentice; the terms of the craft; the number of apprentices; the wages of the workers were all regulated by the custom and the rule of the gild and the town'.[25]

The expansion of wage labour, legal contract and markets in the medieval period provided important ingredients in the later emergence of capitalism. But it is erroneous to instil the concept that medieval labour was increasingly unregulated and left to the play of market forces. Labour in medieval society was very much a part of the 'moral economy' under which social life in general was regulated according to custom.

Epstein points out that guild masters 'were just as concerned about competing among themselves as they were interested in protecting themselves from foreign goods'.[26] But this seems to equate wage labour under a relatively autonomous system of guilds in towns, where urban residents were effectively free of the feudal burdens of agriculture, with a labour market of free wage labourers. The confusion is understandable. Epstein has argued that it was coincident with the

23. Brenner 1986, p. 24.
24. Polanyi 1957, p. 46.
25. Polanyi 1957, p. 70.
26. Epstein 1991, p. 100.

disappearance of slavery from manufactures that the guilds first appeared in the historical record. And this happened in the context of an emerging feudal system characterised by the parcellisation of sovereignty. Thus, unlike the Roman *collegiae*, which under the laws of Justinian were subordinated to the larger interests of the state,[27] the craft guilds were confronted not with a powerful and unified state, but a fractured and contested lordly sovereignty with its power base in the rural manors. This left the towns a relatively independent but contested terrain of power. Thus, according to Epstein, 'artisans and merchants everywhere found themselves in a social setting of competing forces', calling forth the guild as an institution to negotiate on behalf of artisans.[28] The guilds' statutes, however, would not spell the end of all competition or rivalry between independent masters. Far from it. In the case of cloth, leather or armaments, the article under production 'had to pass through the hands of more than one craft guild'. The increasing complexity of production often forced a single craft guild to split into two or more. 'It followed that the dividing line between guild and guild was often very doubtful, and this situation was continually giving rise to differences, quarrels, and lawsuits, some of which lasted for centuries'. To take but one example, the tailors sold new clothes but there were vendors who sold old clothes. Thus 'the courts laboured for years and years to fix the exact moment at which a new suit became an old one!' Such unending litigation was 'inherent in the guild system and could only disappear with the system itself'.[29] No institution could manage the conflict between guilds entirely. But guilds were precisely organisations which sought to regulate competition not only in the interests of individual masters, but in the interests of their members as a whole. Second only to the goal of pursuing the defence of the trade in the interest of its members, was the goal of 'fair play'. The guild sought 'to prevent the great from crushing the small, the rich from ruining the poor, and, in order to succeed, it tried to make advantages and charges equal for all. Its motto so far was: Solidarity'.[30] Therefore, while the focus of the guilds' statutes may have been to minimise the dangers of external competition, an exclusively self-interested pursuit of wealth by any individual master would soon enough appear as an 'external' threat in its own right.

In keeping with the above quotes from Polanyi, there would have been competition between masters, but its aims would not have been limited to the goal of acquiring material goods and wealth. The aims of masters also included status, prestige, reputation, and 'social assets' such as business connections with suppliers and buyers, access to higher circles of authority, and the perquisites that flow

---

27. Epstein 1991, p. 80.
28. Epstein 1991, p. 98.
29. Renard 1968, pp. 38–9.
30. Renard 1968, p. 40.

from being a well-connected and reputable individual in a town. Additionally, markets in general – whether involving international trade between different climatic zones, or the exchange of goods between town and country – were more complementary than competitive. For Polanyi, the late development of competitive internal markets was the result of state intervention, and as we shall see below, 'state regulation continued to prevail over competitive principles'.[31]

The freedom enjoyed by medieval artisans may well be a prerequisite to the later development of a market in free labour. But this relative freedom from feudal obligations did not mean that the contract between master and apprentice was a market contract. Rather, the regulation of labour through the guild typified the medieval mode of labour organisation, as it upheld the customary principles of protecting both producer and consumer by helping to ensure the quality of the product. The labour process was regulated by custom.[32] As such, artisans were shielded from full exposure to the market.

> A market economy can exist only in a market society . . . A market economy must comprise all elements of industry, including labor, land, and money. But labor and land are no other than the human beings themselves of which every society consists and the natural surroundings in which it exists. To include them in the market mechanism means to subordinate the substance of society itself to the laws of the market.[33]

Merchants and craftsmen sought charters of incorporation, and peasants sought to maintain their access to the means of subsistence through manorial law. Both rural and industrial producers and traders thus sought protection from exposure to the vagaries of the market through custom. Subordinating the substance of society itself to the laws of the market would have been unthinkable.

The question of custom will be treated in greater detail in Chapter Ten. Suffice it to say in summary, here, that Mickwitz may overstate the case when he claims that 'a pervasive fear of competition' accounted for the emergence of guilds, but if we substitute instead a 'pervasive concern with exposure to the market', we should have it about right. What may be perplexing from the perspective of those of us who live in an advanced capitalist society is that such a pervasive concern with exposure to the market could have existed. But let us try and step through the looking glass for a moment, and see it from the medieval point of view. To the members of medieval guilds, it would have seemed

31. Wood 2002a, p. 23.

32. Leeson 1979, p. 26. Leeson describes the minute detail of the rules governing the activities of guild members, down to the level of fines against members for using foul language or for missing attendance at a meeting.

33. Polanyi 1957, p. 71.

an equally bizarre notion to suggest that master employers begin treating their apprentices as mere factors of production in the interest of maximising the efficiency of their overall operation, lowering the price of the product, and sacrificing quality to profit. This is so because it would mean not only subordinating a host of non-material aims of the operation – the transmittal of the craft, the aims of honour and prestige embodied in the 'masterpiece', the solidarity of the collective – but also treating the labourer's labour as a commodity. This could only happen if the material exchanges of the economy were abstracted out from the structure of social relations as a whole, if land and labour became *abstract* land and *abstract* labour.

While custom served to protect corporate entities such as guilds from the dangers posed by commodification, it was not a thing, or a tactic, to be used by workers as a hedge against some inherent urge to commodify labour. Guilds emerged in an ethos of customary social regulation, and were one of many institutions operating according to customary norms of social behaviour and institutional protocol, others among which include even the state. Let us apply the distinction between *use value* and *exchange value* as first popularised by Adam Smith. In pre-capitalist societies production remained focused on producing socially necessary goods in their particular form. Production is not subordinated to capital in such a way that it is used by capital to reproduce itself on a larger scale. The aim of production remained focused on meeting the social need for *use values.* In this context, the emphasis of the guilds on producing articles of high quality served as a kind of guarantee to the consumer that each purchase would fulfil a *use value* need. In a market-society, by contrast, the paramount interest of employers can be the maximisation of *exchange value*, at the exclusion of use values or other social goods. This situation can only come about through the triumph of exchange values over use values, which by necessity involves the commodification of all elements of production, including labour.

The evolution of the guild system in England

Known variously as the 'crafts', 'companies', 'fraternities', 'misteries' or 'brotherhoods', the guilds were initially a way for the town crafts to deal with outsiders. But as they grew and adopted elaborate sets of rules, the guilds evolved into a kind of social safety net for their members, providing mutual aid for members' families when they were sick, widowed, and so on. The shortage of labour in the wake of the plague and the general crisis of the fourteenth century prompted the English state to act, in an attempt to control the cost of labour. The Statute of Labourers of 1349–51, the Royal Decree of 1360, the London Proclamation of 1383 – all these appear to have been designed to control the crafts in the name of protecting the consumer, but were likely more sharply motivated by panicked employers and landlords seeking to retain labour on their estates, which were depopulated by the plague.

The Statute of Labourers set up a régime of wage control, with hundreds of enforcers employed 'to tour the country and punish labourers refusing the statutory wage'.[34] Rulings in 1364 and 1373 confirmed that the Statute of Labourers applied to both agricultural as well as craft labourers. The enforcers were frequently met with discontent and protesting. Thus in the great Peasant Revolt of 1381, craftsmen had good cause to throw in their lot with the peasants. Just two years after the revolt was crushed and many of the rebels slaughtered, the London Proclamation of 1383 banned unauthorised 'assemblies, alliances, confederacies or conspiracies, or obligations to bind men together'. In 1388, the 'settlement law' laid the foundation for the next five hundred years, in which the state would 'harry the poor without alleviating their poverty'.[35] In the same year, all guilds were ordered to register with the Crown. The crafts thus lost their independence from local and national law, and their coming under state regulation changed the nature of the guilds themselves. This development was a reflection of the exceptional centralisation and strength of the English state in the fourteenth century as compared with states on the Continent.[36]

As English trade began to expand beyond local markets, a growing separation between masters involved in trade, and those directly overseeing production began to transform the guilds.[37] The presence of the merchant-employer within the guilds is reflected in many regulations in existence by the early fifteenth century. New legislation seeking to limit or suppress wages bolstered the standing of those masters who engaged in trade, and made it difficult for the poorer masters to compete. This process of stratification within the guilds was accompanied by an increase in entrance fees and other costs associated with attaining the status

---

34. Leeson 1979, pp. 38–9.

35. Leeson 1979, pp. 40–1.

36. See Wood 2000, pp. 22–7 and Wood 1991, p. 27. The unity of the English state had to do with the way in which England had never experienced the parcellisation of sovereignty, the devolution of the power of the ban to feudal lords or fragmented jurisdictions.

37. Unwin 1963, p. 46. Unwin describes this transformation as a separation of the guilds into 'two distinct classes representing the mercantile and the industrial interests'. Clearly a kind of stratification was taking place, which would ultimately place the merchants in a favourable position. But these are not 'classes' in the Marxian sense. They are upper strata vying for position in a system for dividing up the return from sale on a hierarchical basis, according to custom. By employing the term 'class', Unwin seems to imply that the merchant could exploit the small master in the modern, capitalist sense, and the master his workmen. We must seek to understand exploitation within the guild system on its own terms, and avoid the tendency to view relationships within the guild in terms of relationships within the modern capitalist firm.

of master. The bar was thus raised for those who sought to pass from journeyman to master. This was a trend across Western Europe, and thus, according to Unwin, after the onset of the plague there was in every craft an increasing number of workmen who 'had no prospect before them but that of remaining journeymen all their lives', and who were increasingly aware of their collective interest as apart from the interest of their employers.[38] Within the guilds, the question of loyalty shifted from one of protecting the independence of the crafts to one of loyalty of the workmen against the master. Fraternities of 'yeomen' suddenly appeared in the larger crafts,[39] such as the cutlers, blacksmiths, carpenters, and drapers. Leeson contends that the yeomen's associations were neither the earliest form of modern trade unions, nor ephemeral combinations to be immediately crushed by authority. In London, yeomen organisations were pervasive; in other cities they were less prominent or less stable:

> The yeomanry was not separate but an integral yet self-contained subordinate section of the craft company. The subordination is sometimes not so obvious and the masters and journeymen appear as equal partners, sometimes with the mayor as arbitrator, in disputes over the payment for altar lights, prices and other 'necessary and good matters', or more often arguments over the poor fund which was kept in a 'great chest lokkid with three lokkes' (a custom in craft organisation which was to last into the nineteenth century).
>
> The yeomanry, in fact, was a compromise, one giving the masters control over the men and the men a form or organisation which they could and did

38. Unwin 1963, p. 48. Unwin actually writes that they were 'bound together by an increasing consciousness of a class interest which separated them from their employers'. The use of the term 'class' in conjunction with the term 'consciousness' is problematic in this context as it conjures up the Marxist term 'class consciousness'. The term is clearly applicable to workers' movements in the nineteenth century and perhaps even in the late eighteenth century. But to speak of 'classes' within manufacturing in fourteenth-century England is anachronistic. This issue of what defines a 'class' will be addressed below.

39. The term 'yeoman' has a wide range of usages, making it a term lacking in precision. Its precise etymology is obscured by multiple suggested origins. One suggestion is that it is derived from *yew-man*, an older name for an archer, his bow being made of yew wood, thus representing military rank just below knights and squires and above foot-soldiers. Thus by the seventeenth century the term applied to a naval petty officer handling supplies. Another suggestion is that it is a contraction of Old English *iunge* (young) and *man*; thus 'young man'. Leeson's use of this definition suggests that this may have been how the term was understood within the crafts. Another possible derivation is from Old English *gae* (district, village) and thus *gaeman* (villager). This would accord with its widespread usage to describe middle-level tenants, from freeholders to well-to-do copyholders, and later tenant-farmers. The term also was used to describe a retainer or dependent in a royal or noble household, and came to be associated with loyal service ('a yeoman's job'). Tennyson made the first known usage of 'yeowoman' in 'The Foresters' in 1852: 'Then I am yeo-woman O the clumsy word!' Tennyson 1892, p. 90.

> use on occasion, [as well as] access to funds to relieve poverty, and the backing of the company to preserve their livelihood.[40]

By agreeing to such a compromise, the efforts of the journeymen to act independently of the guild 'were being in part sanctioned and in part counteracted by the policy of the masters in providing for them a subordinated form of organization in which any attempt at combined action was subject to oversight and control'.[41] In many guilds, the yeomanry was put to the task of overseeing the entrance of newcomers. The Blacksmith's Company of London, for example, granted the right of the journeymen to form a separate organisation, 'subject to an appeal to the master of the company'.[42] A representative of the journeymen was allowed to be present at the making of all covenants between employers and newcomers. A separate box was kept by the yeomen, into which half of all fines on newcomers was put, the other half going to the box of the masters.

Unwin sees the emergence of the yeomanry as the development of a new 'class' which, as he puts it, 'came to form a new rank below the *livery*'.[43] It would seem that he is right to describe the yeomanry as a 'rank' within a hierarchical organisation, but the term 'class' seems inappropriate.[44] To be sure, combinations of journeymen would have been seeking a higher standard of living, but this involved more than just a greater wage. Board and lodging were typically provided to journeymen, further allowing masters to keep them in a position of subordination. Journeymen began seeking the right to marry, to set up their own household and take work home, working on the basis of piecework. Once journeymen began contracting their own work, many were able to achieve near parity with their masters. This near parity is reflected in the fact that, alongside regulation barring unqualified journeymen from becoming masters, ordinances prohibiting masters from acting as journeymen began appearing in the fifteenth century.

Masters specialising in trade were sufficiently wealthy to lend money to the Crown and were also a significant source of tax revenues. In 1411, Henry IV had banned retainers from dressing in uniform or 'livery', but this ban did not apply to the crafts. Over time, the privilege of wearing livery became restricted to the wealthier masters. Hence from the mid-fifteenth century there were brothers 'in' and brothers 'out' of clothing, the latter paying lesser dues to the fraternity. Edward IV furthered the transformation of some companies into 'livery companies' by granting charters of incorporation separately to trading and craft guilds.

---

40. Leeson 1979, p. 45.
41. Unwin 1963, p. 51.
42. Unwin 1963, p. 51.
43. Ibid.
44. See above, n. 37.

The expansion of finished and unfinished wool exports in the thirteenth and fourteenth centuries, leading to greater exports of finished woollen products, facilitated this development, and by 1500 most guilds were divided into separate livery and yeomanry sections, with this development being most pronounced in London. At the same time as English manufactures moved in the direction of 'putting-out' weaving and spinning to the countryside under a domestic system whilst the trading interest came to dominate the urban guilds, guilds on the continent were embroiled in bitter conflicts to retain their monopoly status.[45]

Why then did the trading interest come to dominate the guilds so early on in England? This precocious development would appear to owe a great deal to the early centralisation and unity of the English state. Since the conquest in 1066 at least, England had been the most unified national state in Europe. This unprecedented degree of political centralisation was reflected in England's 'impressive network of roads and water transport that unified the nation to a degree unusual for the period'.[46] This unity was most clearly expressed in the common law, 'a unified legal system ... administered by a corps of judges who sat in the central courts in London and took the law into the provinces when they went on circuit to hold the local assizes'.[47] English common law, a legal system protecting 'economic' social property relations that had arisen in the course of the feudal era, complemented the legal system protecting 'economic' social property-relations that had been integral to feudalism. By the sixteenth century, 'political' property was eroding under the impact of enclosures, which involved the abolition of the customary law of the manor. As customary law was steadily and gradually extinguished, what remained was the legal framework of common law, which enshrined the abstract right to absolute private property. As they came to rely increasingly upon 'economic' property for their livelihood, the demilitarisation of the English ruling class was greatly facilitated with the cessation of hostilities at the conclusion of the fifteenth-century English civil wars (the so-called 'Wars of the Roses'). Furthermore, the cheapening of grain brought on by productivity gains in agriculture allowed wages to fall and/or labourers to buy more with the wages they received. This not only facilitated the growth of the domestic market, but it also allowed a greater share of sale to go to the traders, made home-based

45. Weber 1961, pp. 121–5. Consistent with his view of a transhistorical capitalism, Weber sees this development as 'the first conflict between industrial and trading capital'. As for the divergence between England and the continent, Weber points out that in Germany, towns incorporated in the principalities retained their independent guild-policies. In England, incorporated towns had representation in Parliament 'and in the fourteenth and sixteenth centuries – in contrast with later times – the overwhelming majority of the representatives came from urban circles'. This would lead to the centralisation of authority over guild policy and the Statute of Apprentices.

46. Wood 2002a, p. 99.

47. Upton 2001, p. 92.

domestic production more feasible and may also have enabled a standard of living sufficient enough for craftsmen that they were less prone to revolt than their counterparts on the continent, where these factors were not present or were less developed.

A 'town economy' in which craft specialisation arose in each town to supply local needs and wants had developed prior to the fourteenth century. In Thomas Smith's dialogue, *A Discourse of the Commonweal of this Realm of England*, written in 1549, an imaginary character laments the loss of the local market:

> ... as I knewe the time when men weare contented with cappes, hattes, girdelles, and poyntes and all manner of [garments] made in the townes next adjoyninge; whereby the townes then weare well occupied and set aworke; and yet the money paid for the same stuffe remained in the countrie. Nowe the porest yonge man in a countrey can not be contented either with a ... lether girdle or lether pointes, gloves, knives or daggers made nighe home. And specially no gentleman can be content to have eyther ... cappe, coate, doublet, hose, or shirt made in his countrey, but they must haue theire geare from London; and yet manye thinges thereof are not theare made, but beyonde the sea; whearby the artificers of oure townes are Idle, and the occupations in London, and specially the townes beyonde the sea, are well set aworke even vpon our costes.[48]

From the latter half of the fourteenth century, a national market in cloths had begun to emerge.[49] The peace and security that followed in the wake of the founding of the Tudor dynasty in 1485 further facilitated the rapid extension of the national market, bringing competition to the towns. In the new context, consumers exposed to new products became more discerning and more demanding. Local crafts struggled under the pressure of both domestic and foreign competition. Smaller operations creating the same articles in the towns now had to compete with goods produced outside the town on an economy of scale. This contributed to regional specialisation. Town-based craft guilds were weakened as a result, and this created the opportunity for the middleman trader to rise. As it grew to a disproportionate size, London served as the hub of England's emerging domestic economy, playing home to the largest and greatest variety of guilds.

As their wealth and rank set them apart from the 'commonalty', the livery masters in many companies claimed the right to elect the chief master and assistants. Incorporation allowed livery companies to own property, including land, from which the livery could derive an additional source of income. Between 1514

48. Smith 1893, pp. 125–6.
49. Thirsk 1984, p. 220.

and 1516, the twelve 'Great Companies' of London reached an agreement on 'The Order of Precedence'. The 'Great Twelve' were mainly trading companies, led by the Mercers, the wealthiest company of all. A trend that had started among the Taylors,[50] allowing in the guildmen who had never learned to sew, now caught on in other crafts. Alongside apprenticeship and inheritance, a third avenue to guild membership emerged – 'redemption', which meant buying in. The livery masters were now made up of masters turned traders and traders who bought their way into the guild. By the mid-sixteenth century, the appearance in some guilds of a 'Court of Assistants' – a committee of the livery meeting in private – completed the process of stratification, as lesser masters were excluded and their status declined. Members of the livery could take on two or three apprentices, the chief master up to four. But masters who had not attained livery status were restricted to one apprentice. Stratification also took on external forms, as wealthier companies absorbed smaller crafts and reduced their members to the status of employees. Thus the leather sellers took over the glovers; the cloth-workers absorbed the shearmen's and fullers' guilds, and so on.[51] Where one craft was overtaken by another in this way, the one doing the overtaking was typically the craft that was closer to the point of sale. So the Mercers, for example, were in the perfect position to secure the market to their advantage. And the saddlers were in a position to take control of the leather dressers.[52] As the smaller craft fraternities were absorbed into the larger companies, with journeymen and small masters who were awaiting entry into the livery forming yeomen's associations, outbreaks of 'variance and discord' were seen, such as that among the Founders over the Poor Box in 1508. In 1514, a petition sent to Parliament complained of the influx of foreigners and how their numbers would ruin the lives of English craftsmen. In 1517, the 'Evil May Day' uprising by a crowd of a thousand apprentices against 'aliens' anticipated the government's heavy-handed response to later 'riots' as it prompted the stationing of five thousand troops in London. Thirteen of the apprentices were hanged for treason.[53]

By the sixteenth century, rural handicraft-production, predominantly in spinning and weaving, had become widespread. Viewing the export of half-manufactured goods as a loss of potential for urban manufactures, efforts were made to restrict the country manufacturer from selling directly to foreign

50. Leeson 1979, p. 48. The Taylors gained royal permission to rename their guild the 'Merchant Taylors' in 1502. This reflected who among them was now at the head of the guild.

51. Leeson 1979, p. 48.

52. Weber 1961, p. 121.

53. Mackie 1952, p. 298. The attack itself had proved harmless. In all 400 persons were arrested, and all were released except the instigator, a broker by the name of John Lincoln, and thirteen others 'executed on the absurd grounds that an attack upon foreigners when the king was at peace with all princes is tantamount to treason'.

markets, so as to divert the trade through the towns. Predictably, a rivalry ensued between urban and rural producers of the same half-finished goods. The Weavers' Act of 1555 forbade country clothiers to possess more than one loom, or to hire out looms to others. It thus sought to keep weaving under the control of town employers by inhibiting the growth of their rural counterparts.[54]

The English Reformation facilitated the process of stratification within the craft trades. The dissolution of the monasteries meant also the end of many religious charities run by the guilds, as in 1547 the Crown asked the companies to hand over and then buy back the charities. The charities run by the monasteries themselves were not elaborate, but when the monasteries were dissolved, tens of thousands of dependents were turned out and became beggars or vagabonds, to face the extraordinarily harsh and punitive vagrancy laws. It was not only the end of the charities that helped to create a human surplus. Monastic lands being sold off by the Crown had not been subject to the law of the manor. Thus the addition of these lands to the emerging market for lands to enclose undoubtedly provided a great stimulus to the enclosure movement. From the 1520s and 30s, the primary type of fields to be enclosed shifted from pasture to arable. This period also saw the beginnings of the dissemination of 'improved' farming methods that appear to have originated on the grange farms of the Cistercian monasteries. While other orders held peasant tenancies, the Cistercian brothers worked the fields themselves, as their Trappist successors do even today. Having no tenants, their farms were not subject to the regulations of customary law. They practiced a model of grange farming that became the basis for the 'improved' agriculture practiced by tenant-farmers working on enclosed farms. Half the fields were kept in grass and the other in grain for a number of years before they were converted between these 'up' and 'down' usages. About 28 of the 101 monasteries dissolved under Henry VIII belonged to the Cistercian order.

Marx wrote that the forcible expropriation of the people received 'a new and frightful impulse' from the dissolution of the monasteries, whose inmates were 'hurled' into the proletariat (one estimate[55] puts the number of beggars on the roads in Henry VIII's time at 72,000). 'The estates of the church', wrote Marx, 'were to a large extent given away to rapacious royal favourites, or sold at a nominal price to speculating farmers and citizens, who drove out, *en masse*, the hereditary sub-tenants and threw their holdings into one'.[56] As Nicholls writes:

> Lay landowners set about outbidding one another for the privilege of acquiring a share of these immense spoils... Formerly quite restricted, the English land market became more dynamic, as wealthy men without acres, profes-

54. Unwin 1963, pp. 92–3.
55. Leeson 1979, p. 53.
56. Marx 1967, pp. 792–3.

> sionals and younger sons of peers competed with established noblemen and courtiers for monastic estates. Most of the land ended up in the hands of local families.[57]

The *extent* to which the dissolution of the monasteries facilitated both the spread of enclosures and the spread of improved farming methods is a subject for further research. But this second wave of enclosures may have been the first instance when we begin to see an emerging market in land, driven by economic imperatives that are distinctly capitalist in character. By 1551, the Crown had sold off most of the lands it had confiscated, squandering a precious resource and benefiting mainly private landowners.[58]

Sir Thomas More had described the new breed of landlord as 'eager for the profits of the expanding corn and wool trade, eager for land even more than labour'.[59] The landlords no longer pursued labourers to try and force them back on the land; they urged them onto the roads. Among those on the roads were craftsmen without work. Masters began demanding certificates granted by previous employers for skilled craftsmen, and out of this evolved a network for 'travelling brothers' that would last well into the nineteenth century.[60] Journeymen reacted to the stream of unemployed appearing at the gates of their towns. Their calls for restrictions on the employment of 'foreyns' in their trades met with some support from the livery. Another major grievance was directed at certain masters themselves when they were found to be circumventing restrictions on the number of apprentices they could take on.

> In the 1550s, seventeen craft companies seeking a way out of internal dispute asked the Common Council to fix by law the number of apprentices each master might take. But this did not put an end to the problem. For the richer masters had developed a double standard. They enforced regulations which held back the journeymen and small masters from competing while ignoring the restrictions on themselves.[61]

Already by the time of Henry VIII, some clothiers employed hundreds of spinners and weavers. The legendary John Winchcombe of Newbury was said to have employed as many as two hundred weavers, all assembled in one great room. They were assisted by apprentices. Other employees of Winchcombe were said to have included: a hundred women employed in carding; two hundred girls plying the distaff and the spinning wheel; one hundred and fifty boys and girls

57. Nicholls 1999, pp. 56–7.
58. Mooers 1991, p. 156.
59. As quoted in Leeson 1979, p. 53.
60. See Leeson 1979, chapters 6–8.
61. Leeson 1979, pp. 51–2.

sorting; fifty men as clippers; eighty men as dressers; twenty men at the fulling mill and forty men in the dye works. The numbers may be exaggerated, but the size and scope of Winchcombe's operation was extraordinary for his time, meaning that such experiments of assembling dozens or hundreds of workers under one roof were the exception which proved the rule.[62] Other clothiers employing hundreds of spinners and weavers, employed them in their own cottages, sending them wool and taking away their cloth.

The Tudor government was somewhat alarmed at these developments. Henry VIII, when encountering a string of carts laden with cloth said to belong to Winchcombe, is reported to have said: 'This Jack of Newbury is richer than I'.[63] Yet the government also wanted to foster the rapidly accumulating wealth of the merchants. It only sought to limit the effects of this phenomenon. State and municipal laws backed the powers of the livery. An example of this is the law of 1548–9 (Edward IV 2–3, c. xv), which banned craft 'confederacies' employing secret oaths that attempted to set the price and rate for labour. This law replaced the Statute of Labourers of 1351, and was itself not repealed until 1826. The new law would only frustrate the yeomen of the companies, and certainly did nothing to settle their grievances.

Queen Betty's Law

By the time Elizabeth assumed the throne in 1558, craftsmen were restive, common-law courts, which had always been limited to freeholders, now began to hear cases from copyholders. Yet at the same time, arguments in defence of ancient rights of commoners as defined by custom were increasingly treated as anomalous, effectively eclipsed by common-law definitions of property ownership. Custom still applied where manorial courts remained and exercised purview over the organisation and sharing of open fields. But in common-law courts, appeals to custom could only defeat the 'legal principle' of ownership when the custom in question could be proven to have peaceably enjoyed local consent continuously since antiquity.[64]

62. Mantoux 1961, pp. 33–4.
63. Mantoux 1961, pp. 34.
64. Patriquin 2004, pp. 205–6. See also Nef 1964, p. 38, who contrasts the way in which the royal courts in sixteenth-century France were successfully able to extend their jurisdiction, in general and specifically over industrial regulation, with the way in which similar efforts by the royal courts in England were met with opposition from common-law judges who 'claimed that their decisions could overrule those given in the royal courts. They even went so far as to maintain that common-law was superior to statute law. So jealous of their rights were the common law judges, and so influential were they in the house of commons, that the whole system of royal jurisdiction, which the Tudors had carefully cultivated, was swept away by act of parliament in 1641, on the eve of the civil

During the Elizabethan era, the governing bodies of the companies increasingly dominated by the trading interest were nonetheless bound by charters and ordinances which protected the handicraft tradition. The organised yeomen also served to preserve the craft tradition through grievances which, if the company Court of Assistants was not forthcoming, could be appealed to the Crown. By bringing the companies under the Crown's law in the fifteenth century, the custom of the guild was enshrined in statute law. It is possible then to view the statutes of the guilds and fraternal associations as the urban-manufacturing equivalent to rural-agrarian customary law. They come under full assault with the final assault on custom in the late eighteenth century, though as we shall explore, there was a long history of weakening first the guilds and then the position of the worker vis-à-vis the merchant. However, as enclosures extinguished customary law one parish at a time, it was difficult to carry out a similar assault on custom in the crafts. The principal barrier to this would be the Statute of Apprentices, which so long as it remained in place, gave self-organised workers' combinations a solid legal basis to continue to defend their customary practices.[65]

Having passed an Act of Settlement (1559) in an attempt to resolve the question of religion, Elizabeth's government now turned its attention to address another area of conflict. Though perhaps no more than eight percent of the English population was involved in manufacturing, their importance to the state was of a far greater magnitude. It should not surprise, therefore, that the Statute of Apprentices (1563) was passed only five years into Elizabeth's reign. As in the previous century, the pressures on the small masters and lesser companies were growing. Increasingly dependent upon the merchants for both supply and sale, small masters saw their share of the return from the product shrink as the merchant's share increased. Meanwhile, lesser companies continued to be absorbed by larger ones: the girdlers amalgamated with the pinners in 1568, the blacksmiths absorbed the

war'. This is a reference to the Habeus Corpus Act of 1641, which abolished the Star Chamber. Nef 1964, p. 52, seems to qualify the ramifications of this statement when he writes that the proclamations, letters patent and orders of council of the early Stuarts were met with increasing opposition when these 'interfered with the profits of powerful merchants and landed gentlemen interested in the progress of large-scale industry. It became almost impossible for the privy council to enforce any industrial regulations, *not embodied in statutes*, if they conflicted with the private interests of such merchants and gentlemen' (emphasis added). As we shall see, the struggle between arguments in defence of profits under common law and those in defence of customary regulation under the Statute of Apprentices would rage on for more than a century and a half after 1641.

65. Further research is necessary to explore the similarities and differences in the relationship between the common law and workers' associations on the one hand, and the customary law of the manor on the other. Note that 5 Elizabeth c. 4 is commonly referred to both as the 'Statute of Apprentices' and the 'Statute of Artificers', and sometimes as the 'Statute of Artificers and Apprentices'. For our purposes, we shall use the name 'Statute of Apprentices', except where one of these names appears differently in a quotation, as this seems to be the most common usage.

spurriers in 1571 and also attempted to absorb the clockmakers, and so on. We know from the example of the clothworkers that the absorption of one craft by another was not *always* a hostile takeover. Unwin speculates that in the case of the clothworkers, who in 1566 volunteered to turn over all their members engaged in cloth finishing to the Merchant Taylors, one of their main motives in making the offer may have been that releasing the workers would have freed them of the responsibility of poor relief for the craftsmen and their families.

By passing the Statute of Apprentices, Elizabeth's government sought to check the growing social rift within the trades by balancing the interests of apprentices, yeomen and livery masters. In 61 'remembered' trades, the rule of seven years' apprenticeship was to be enforced. Uncontrolled entry into the crafts, it was thought, could mean that 'men like ravenous fishes would feed on one another'.[66] Enforcement of this rule would keep down the wages of agricultural labour and would protect journeymen from any flood of newcomers or from cheaper, untrained rivals. The master craftsman would be protected from a rush of apprentices seeking to replace him. The public and traders would benefit from the protection of the quality of the product. And masters were protected by the rule that journeymen must serve until the age of 24. A third rule was that before any extra apprentice was taken on, there should be work for three journeymen. This enshrined the earlier custom of many trades allowing one apprentice for a master, two for a liveryman and three for the company master. Workshops employing the correct proportion became known as 'legal' or 'fair' shops. But in the rapidly expanding textile trades, employing ever-increasing numbers of workers in rural areas outside the scope of guild regulations, the law could not have been popular with the greater masters, who anyway tended to disregard it. The Statute also enshrined the requirement that new workers provide a certificate from their previous master. And it restated the terms of the 1549 Act prohibiting working people from setting their own pay, leaving the Justices of the Peace the power to limit wages.

The goals of 'Queen Betty's Law,' as it became known among the crafts, were to stabilise the various strata in the manufactures, to ensure greater regularity of employment and 'to bring wages into a steadier and more equitable relation to prices'.[67] By seeking uniformity of wages throughout individual crafts, the Statute had the effect of benefiting the least paid workers. But as wages were more

---

66. Leeson 1979, p. 61 attributes this quote to the character of Sir Thomas More in the play *Sir Thomas More*. Primary authorship of the play in question has since been attributed not to Shakespeare, but to Anthony Munday. Shakespeare is thought to have contributed but three pages.

67. Unwin 1963, p. 119.

often levelled downward than upward,[68] most journeymen stood to lose and masters stood to gain. In general, the new legislation strengthened the position of the masters over journeymen: 'The journeymen had lost all effective share in the yeomanry organization, and the only modes of common action open to them were either to appeal over the heads of the masters to the Court of Assistants, or to form an illegal combination and to strike. The second of these methods was ineffectually resorted to as early as 1565 . . .'.[69]

For the next century, journeymen's associations would decline into relative obscurity. The decline of the power of the town guilds, however, did not mean that urban manufacturing was faltering. Nor did the expansion of rural manufacturing come at the expense of urbanisation, as was the trend on the continent.[70] The typical Elizabethan company had achieved a compromise between the potentially conflicting interests of masters and traders. The craft masters had agreed to refrain from interfering with the trading operations of the merchants in the company, whilst traders would 'sanction the regulations designed to preserve the status of the craftsman', including rights of search and seizure.[71] But with the ever-expanding pool of journeymen held in check by the new framework of legislation securing the position of the masters, the industrial and commercial interests were now free to contend with one another, giving the companies a new tension and dynamic that was destined to transform the nature of the craft-organisation once again in the coming century.

68. Hay and Rogers, pp. 89–90. The practice of limiting wages under the Statute of Labourers of 1349–51 had fallen into disuse by the time of Henry VIII, who exempted employers from compliance. But inflation in the 1540s once again required the government to revive the practice. Under Elizabeth, the Statute of Apprentices was passed with a host of legislation in 1563, 'more such legislation than had ever been enacted in any session, including anti-enclosure legislation, reform of poor relief, licensing of middlemen in foodstuffs'. The Statute regulated contracts, wages, compulsory recruitment of labour, and guild-apprenticeship of seven years. The offences it outlined were: paying and receiving excessive wages, and refusing to work. In the late seventeenth and early eighteenth centuries, the legislation may have been employed more often to control high wages. But order was also an imperative, and so a 'customary minimum wage in times of decaying trade' or dearth was sometimes recognised and enforced.

69. Unwin 1963, p. 120.

70. Hudson 1996, p. 53.

71. Unwin 1963, p. 12. Unwin refers to the non-interference in trading operations by small masters as 'freedom of trade'. The merchant companies that arose out of this period, however, enjoyed royally sanctioned monopolies over markets, and thus we should be careful not to confuse internal non-interference with 'free trade'. In the course of the seventeenth century, the great merchant-companies would come under attack by merchant-interlopers, who favoured 'free trade', meaning markets open to (virtually) all comers. The use of the term 'free trade' in the seventeenth century is not to be confused with its later use as the 'doctrine of free trade', which advocated the lowering of tariffs and other forms of regulation in international trade to stimulate overall trade and investment.

For Unwin, the Statute of Apprentices 'presents two very different aspects to the historical student'. On the one hand, it was a monument to the progress of national unity in England, reflecting also the growing centralisation of the English state.[72] Where earlier legislation had dealt only with specific regions or sectors of the economy, the Act of 1563 attempted to regulate virtually all localities and working populations. On the other hand, the 'Act represented a vain endeavour to give fixity and permanence to a condition of things which already, in great part, belonged to the past'.[73] As Leeson puts it, the Statute of Apprentices 'was a hostage to the future'.[74] Although the Act broadly covered all forms of employment, the title 'Statute of Apprentices' implied a focus on employment in the crafts. This is significant, because it was precisely by seeking to preserve the hierarchical and normative system of the guilds that the Act most effectively sustained an area of the economy governed by customary forms of regulation. The Act should perhaps be seen not so much as a conscious attempt to preserve the old order as an effort to set a modern and thus national framework for an economy in transition.

The economic context in Tudor and Stuart times

During the Tudor period, multiple and varying forces and factors were at work in transforming the basic contours of the English economy. These included: a rapidly growing population; a revolution in prices; a deepening national market reflecting regional specialisation and evolving national unity; and a shortage of employment. From the late fifteenth century, the population of England and Wales began to rise again following the extreme population decline after the plague, which had struck Marseilles by the end of 1347 and spread northward, leaving only tiny pockets of Europe untouched. It reached London by the end of 1348. The recovery of the population in Europe only began in the sixteenth century. In England, population growth began to increase from the 1520s to the 1540s, and only slowed again after 1640 or 1650, after which the population remained stable or rose only slightly for about a century.[75] Unlike the Continent, however, England did not experience any serious population decline after 1650.[76]

72. Unwin 1963, p. 137. For Unwin, the Statute of Apprentices, being the first such legislation to cover the whole country, reflected England's national unity, in contrast to France. He notes that the fiscal motive underlying the French edicts was 'conspicuously absent' in the English case.

73. Unwin 1963, p. 139.

74. Leeson 1979, p. 62.

75. Coleman 1977, p. 12.

76. Hudson 1996, p. 52.

We can point to several factors conditioning this period of population increase. First, as noted previously, the end of the Wars of the Roses and the founding of the Tudor dynasty brought about stability and the chance for England's economy to grow and diversify. England was thus able to take full advantage of the rise of trade in Europe generally. Secondly, accompanying, and partly in response to this rise of trade, was a pan-European growth of population. This included the rapid growth of cities. London was exceptional in this regard. With a population of around 33,000 in 1500, London had grown to become the largest city in Europe by 1650, with a population of perhaps 400,000, surpassing Paris.[77] With the growth of population and rampant monetary inflation came a major expansion of grain production across Europe, with high prices attracting new investment. Thirdly and crucially, the uniquely English development of tenant-farming on enclosed fields also contributed to the growth of population. Improved farming methods began to be adopted widely on enclosed farms in the first half of the sixteenth century, thus coinciding with the onset of population growth. Improved farming meant higher yields per acre, and thus greater productivity. France produced an overall greater yield than England, for it had a much larger population. However, while customary law still prevailed in French agriculture, England was outstripping France in output per acre.[78] In absolutist France, the *taille*, a tax assessed on the village community collectively, increased by 300 percent from 1620 to 1640, sparking a series of peasant revolts. In Eastern Europe, high grain prices compelled lords not to adopt improved methods but to re-introduce serfdom in the face of a labour shortage. The Dutch played a lead role in transporting and re-selling grain from Eastern Europe. However, when the second agrarian depression struck, lasting to 1720, the Dutch were hit hard and England alone continued to advance in agriculture.[79]

It would be impossible to sort out the contributions each of these different factors made to population growth during the period in question. However, the

77. Coleman 1977, p. 20. Without the increased use of coal, the growth of London would have been limited. Coal supplied warmth for houses and fuelled industries for producing necessities for urban subsistence – soap and salt, for example – as well as those luxuries that made urban life tolerable, even preferable – glass, sugar, beer. London's growth set in motion a self-reinforcing mechanism of growth in the economy. Its expansion demanded more coal as well as bigger breweries and soap-boilers. Increasing demand for coal necessitated deeper mines, larger ships and improved transport-routes. During the seventeenth century, the number of collier ships jumped from 400 to 1400; the average cargo load from 60–70 tons to 250–300 tons (Wilson 1984, pp. 45 and 84). We must bear in mind, however, that coal was a secondary precondition to the growth of London, the first being food, and the increasing productivity of farming that enabled local farms to keep production at pace with London's ever-expanding demand for grain. See Hudson 1996, p. 52.

78. Wood 1996, p. 215.

79. Upton 2001, pp. 8–10.

enclosure movement and the corresponding extinguishing of customary law and common rights were undoubtedly principal factors in displacing significant numbers of people from the rural areas. This, in turn, may help to explain the exceptional growth of London. It was also an underlying cause of England's vagrancy problem, which in turn helped to prompt the implementation of the Elizabethan poor laws.[80] The poor laws could be seen as a kind of early welfare system used to buffer English society from the dislocating effects of an emerging capitalist economy with built-in structural unemployment.[81] Polanyi comments that the poor laws together with the Statute of Apprentices made up a 'Code of Labour', though the poor laws, while also a national policy, were administered locally at the parish level.[82]

Simultaneous with the growth of population was a period of rising prices. In the two centuries from 1450 to 1650, prices of basic household goods rose steadily. Grain prices increased more sharply between 1550 and 1650. The apparent trend, based upon limited evidence, suggests that wages rose about three-fold between 1500 and 1650, while cereals rose by seven-fold.[83] For agricultural and industrial labourers, then, it was likely a time of decreasing real purchasing power and thus decreasing standard of living. Coleman notes three main forces at work behind this price rise.[84] The first is short-term debasements of the coinage by the Crown, which can only account for temporary increases. A second factor of inflation was the inflow of bullion from Spanish America. The inflationary effects of this influx were felt across Europe. With population growth as the third factor, England was caught up in a pan-European economic crisis. The impact of Spanish bullion could only have been felt after the 1560s, when a new technique of extracting silver from its ore made mining operations in Bolivia and Mexico practical. As Spain made its payments increasingly in bullion, Spanish bullion began circulating rapidly throughout Europe. Much of it was used to mint new coins. This dramatic increase in the volume of money fuelled the spiral of increasing prices.[85] It also fuelled a new attitude on the part of increasingly wealthy merchants towards moneymaking: that money begets money. This, in turn, reflected in a new attitude towards craftsmen. 'To the merchants who made the fortunes and dominated the trading life of the nation, it must have seemed an outrage that their doings should in any way be governed by meetings of craftsmen and small shop-holders because they were all nominally members of the same company,

---

80. Hudson 1996, p. 52.
81. See Patriquin 2005, pp. 18–30. Slack 1999, p. 164 writes that: '... eighteenth-century England was already, in attitude and practice, a welfare state'.
82. Polanyi 1957, p. 87.
83. Coleman 1977, pp. 21–3.
84. Coleman 1977, pp. 24–6.
85. Ralph *et al.* 1997, pp. 712–13. See Leeson 1979, p. 60.

and that men whom they could buy and sell ten times over should lay down how many men should be employed, how many boys apprenticed and thus how the market should be divided'.[86]

High prices meant hard times for working men and women, and extraordinary opportunities for those who handled money. Despite the important role played by the influx of Spanish bullion, however, only the recovery of population since the devastation of the plague could explain the length of the price increase, and the disparity between food prices and industrial prices.[87]

At the village-level, population pressure meant several things at once: increasing population *density*, expansion of the area under cultivation and/or subdivision of tenancies, a surplus of (increasingly younger) agricultural labourers, and migration of labour out of the village. The landless unemployed grew so much that in 1573 the House of Commons complained of the increase of 'rogues, vagabonds and thieves'.[88] The demand for commercial agricultural produce increased dramatically, as an increasing number of people no longer produced their own subsistence goods. Whatever gains were made in agricultural productivity, they were insufficient to keep up with the pace of demand, and hence the high inflationary trend in agricultural products. 'Conversely', writes Coleman, 'the supply of manufactured goods was markedly more elastic'. Continuing, he writes:

> In a few industries there were technical advances which helped to restrain real costs as output increased. Far more important, however, was the highly labour-intensive nature of much industrial production, often susceptible to real reductions in real costs by organizational changes, notably an extension of 'putting-out' techniques. A substantial increase in population thus came as a great economic blessing to producers, especially of such goods as textiles. Their price consequently did not rise nearly so much as did the price of the land-intensive agricultural products.[89]

East Anglia developed an extensive putting-out system in the sixteenth century. It would not fully develop in Lancashire until the seventeenth century. Both the growth of London and the rural handicraft manufacturing that grew up alongside it were fuelled by a surplus population in search of employment. London's expansion meant ever-greater demand to stimulate agricultural and industrial production (some of it centralised and/or large in scale, as we shall discuss below). Overseas economic expansion in the form of colonialism and

86. Leeson 1979, pp. 60–1.
87. Coleman 1977, p. 25.
88. Coleman 1977, p. 359, citing Tawney and Power (eds.) 1924.
89. Coleman 1977, p. 26.

trading by the overseas merchant companies facilitated this expansion and gave further encouragement to regional specialisation. The domestic market continued to deepen.

As patterns of demand changed, combined with an overall expansion of trade, a gradual decline set in on the guilds. The guilds were unable to assert their authority over rural production or over new lines of production where they appeared. The decline of guild authority and the changes accompanying it 'was not a rapid or country-wide movement, proceeding at an even pace. In many provincial towns changes came only later in the sixteenth century...'.[90] The decline of the guilds from the sixteenth century on did not mean, however, that urban manufacturing faltered. 'Neither was there such a clear division of labour in England (as there may have been in other parts of Europe) between towns (providing mercantile, financial and finishing services) and the countryside (providing cheap family labour for mass production processes). The rapid growth of urban villages, unincorporated towns and suburbs in London and other large towns in the eighteenth century was associated specifically with expansion of employment in the low-wage, unregulated domestic and small workshop trades'.[91]

Although the English guilds, particularly those outside of London,[92] had begun to decline, struggles over the regulation of the craft-trades would continue.

Nef's 'early industrial revolution'

Arnold Toynbee's lectures of the 1880s conduced to cement the use of the term 'Industrial Revolution' to describe the emergence of industrialisation in England from about 1760. Toynbee's object was to lay out the comparatively backward state of the English economy in 1760, in light of what was to come. Thus in 1760, writes Toynbee: 'the old industrial system obtained in England; none of the

90. Coleman 1977, p. 74. Ogilvie 1996, pp. 30–3, points out that the decline of the guilds in England and the Low Countries in the sixteenth century occurred far in advance of the decline of guilds in other parts of Europe. The gradual disappearance of guilds in France did not begin until the early part of the eighteenth century. 'Almost everywhere else in Europe, proto-industries [rural handicrafts] were regulated by corporate groups of "capitalists", and often also of "workers", well into the eighteenth century'. Rural handicraft-workers also formed their own guilds. It would be instructive to examine any attempts by rural handicraft workers in England who may have attempted to form rural handicraft guilds from the sixteenth to the eighteenth centuries, as it might tell us more about the social relations and economic forces which militated against their emergence generally. Hudson 1996, p. 53 notes that the expansion of rural manufacturing in England 'did not appear to occur at the expense of urbanization' as it did on the continent.

91. Coleman 1977, p. 74.

92. Kellett argues that the guilds of London actually survived until the mid-nineteenth century. See Chapter Seven, pp. 348–9.

great mechanical inventions had been introduced; the agrarian changes were still in the future'.[93] Wool remained the primary export, and cotton production was minimal. 'England in 1760 was still to a great extent under the mediaeval system of minute and manifold industrial regulations. That system was indeed decaying, but it had not yet been superseded by the modern principle of industrial freedom'.[94] For Toynbee, 'The essence of the Industrial Revolution is the substitution of *competition* for the mediaeval regulations which had previously controlled the production and distribution of wealth'.[95] Half a century later, John Nef challenged this line of thinking, arguing that: 'the concept of an "Industrial Revolution" would seem to be especially inappropriate as an explanation of the triumph of industrial civilization in Great Britain. It gives the impression that the process was especially sudden, when it was in all probability more continuous than in any other country'.[96]

Nef cites an 'enormous economic expansion, beginning about the middle of the sixteenth century' in 'large-scale enterprise'.[97] In a later article, Nef states his position more forcefully when he declares that 'we have been mistaken about the time when the industrial revolution began'.[98] In making this claim, Nef certainly deserves recognition as a pioneer anticipating by half a century the outpouring of scholarship that rejects the classic Toynbeean view of the British Industrial Revolution.

From the 1540s onward, England saw the development of enterprises on a scale it had not hitherto seen. The new or expanding old lines of production included: coal, salt, glass, ships, alum, soap, cannons and gunpowder, mined metals, metal wares, paper, copperas, sugar, saltpetre, calamine, iron rods, metal wire,[99] as well as lime, starch, and brewed beverages.[100] The production of sugar and brass was new to England, as was papermaking. In the 1540s Britain was importing all or virtually all of its paper; in the 1550s paperworks began to appear, and 'foreign workmen were obviously the main source of the necessary skills'.[101] By the 1720s

93. Toynbee 1956, p. 7.
94. Toynbee 1956, p. 72.
95. Toynbee 1956, p. 58. Emphasis not found in the original.
96. Nef 1934, p. 24.
97. Ibid.
98. Nef 1943, p. 4.
99. Nef 1934, p. 13.
100. Coleman 1977, p. 86.
101. Coleman 1958, pp. 36–48, 76. The first paper mill recorded was at Fen Ditton, near Cambridge, built in 1557. In 1588, a German immigrant named John Spilman (or Spielman) set up paper mill at Dartford, Kent. He employed German workmen. The following year Spilman was granted a monopoly over the making of all white writing paper in Britain, but he apparently had trouble enforcing the patent in the face of other mills attracting away his labourers. Even if they were proving difficult to enforce, the granting of monopoly rights in paper manufacturing serves to underscore the point (to be made

about two-thirds of domestic consumption was being supplied by domestic manufactures. Other products, like saltpetre and gunpowder, had been produced in England previously, but in insignificant amounts.[102] The older lines of manufacturing undergoing extensive changes drew in larger numbers of workers. In copper smelting, steel-making, mining and metallurgy, brick-making, and glass-making, immigrant craftsmen from the continent brought many of the requisite skills and know-how to enable technical advance and expansion of scale.

Nef cites three major technical developments that facilitated the growth of large-scale manufacturing units in the century before 1640: the introduction of new 'capitalistic' industries; the application of old technical processes to new industries; and 'the discovery and application of new technical methods'.[103] For most of these newly expanding industries, the key development, according to Nef, was the increasing use of coal as a power source. The use of coal could lower the cost of production, thus aiding in market expansion. Moreover, the introduction of coal as a power source made possible the introduction of essential technical advances. New techniques in such lines of production as glass, bricks or malt yielded a product 'more suitable for commercial purposes than that obtained from fires of charcoal, wood, and straw'.[104] The substitution of coal for wood also eased regional shortages of wood, freeing up timber for ship-building and other wood-based production. According to Fernand Braudel, the 'decisive feature of this revolution' was the increasing dependence on coal use, precipitating a vast expansion in coal mining: 35,000 tons in 1560 rising to 200,000 tons by 1600.[105] Under the reign of Elizabeth I, mines grew in terms of output, the numbers of workers employed and the scale of investment:

> By a legal decision rendered in 1566, before the great expansion of the coal industry, all minerals except those containing gold or silver were excluded from the *regale*. During the next century and a half the development of coal-mining led to the digging of pits and addits and the making of paths, cartways, and wagonways in hundreds of manors in many counties.[106]

The use of coal spurred technical advance by facilitating the development of new techniques or posing technical problems that required a solution. Charles Wilson notes that by the end of the seventeenth century, 'substantial progress

---

below in our discussion of mining) that sixteenth- and seventeenth-century manufacturing continued to be regulated in 'extra-economic' ways. In other words, a system of industry regulated by the free play of market forces (industrial capitalism) had not yet come into existence.

102. Nef 1934, p. 6.
103. Nef 1934, p. 5.
104. Nef 1966a, p. 325.
105. Braudel 1988, p. 553.
106. Braudel 1988, p. 329.

had been made towards a solution of the technical problems created by the use of coal instead of wood' in 'every industry save one – iron'.[107] Nevertheless, iron-works grew in scale, employing blast-furnaces and water-powered bellows.

Braudel has expressed puzzlement as to why this so-called 'first industrial revolution' should have taken England from being an industrial laggard[108] to being a leading industrial nation in Europe by the eve of the Civil War: 'But why did this happen in England, when all the major innovations of the period – I am thinking for example of blast-furnaces, the various apparatus used for underground mining: tunnels, ventilation systems, pumps and winding gear – were all borrowings, demonstrated to the English by German miners hired for the purpose? Why England, when it was the craftsmen and workers of more technically advanced countries – Germany, the Netherlands, but also Italy (for glass) and France (wool and silk textiles) – who contributed the necessary techniques and skills for the establishment of a series of industries quite new to Britain – paper mills, powder-mills, glass, mirrors, cannon-founding, alum and copperas (green vitriol), sugar refining, saltpetre, and so on?'

> The remarkable thing is that when these industries did arrive, England should have developed them on a scale hitherto unknown: the growing size of firms, the dimensions of the buildings, the rising numbers of workers, soon running into tens or even hundreds, the comparatively high level of investment which was reaching thousands of pounds, whereas the *annual* wage of a worker was only about £5 – all these were completely new and indicate how extraordinary was the expansion of English industry in this period.[109]

Braudel is apparently as impressed as Nef is over these developments. But it should be noted that while seventeenth-century England did see this remarkable growth of industries that for England were unprecedented in size, similar examples from the Continental powers can be cited. Moreover, it was not until the latter half of the eighteenth century that England took a decisive lead.

Nef's thesis rests on the presupposition that there is something inherently 'capitalistic' about large-scale manufacturing in the sixteenth and seventeenth centuries. Likewise, Braudel sees that the adaptation to coal as a power source

107. Wilson 1984, p. 198.

108. Nef 1966a, p. 322. As it suits his thesis, Nef expresses less surprise and comments on this change simply as a matter of fact: 'What marks off the economic history of Great Britain in this period from that of her continental neighbours', he writes, 'is both the extent of general economic development, and the difference in the kind of industry which developed most strikingly. A country which had remained throughout the Middle Ages economically in a backwater rose to a place in the front rank'.

109. Braudel 1988, p. 553.

led to 'a concentration of the workforce and *inevitability of capital*.'[110] But were these larger firms specifically 'capitalist'? And if so, why?

According to D.C. Coleman, centralised production is necessitated by any of four conditions: the immobility of fixed capital equipment, the immobility of a power source (as in wind or falling water), the immobility of the raw material in an extraction process, or by an assembly process requiring multiple parts to be fashioned into a larger objects (such as a ship). 'These conditions', writes Coleman 'are technical, not economic... They tell us nothing whatever about the optimum economic size or scale of any plant'.[111] For Coleman, the larger operations employing hundreds of workers were the exception that proved the rule. He finds in Nef's thesis 'a great deal of nonsense'[112] and a tendency to exaggerate. Of the bewildering variety of types of mills to emerge:

> only a very few gave rise to large enterprises or had more than half-a-dozen or so workers dependent on them. Many a mill was owned by the landlord; sometimes, in the early period, it was still the manorial mill to which the tenants brought their corn for grinding; but as such practices declined the mill was often rented out for more overtly industrial purposes.[113]

Moreover, many of these operations failed when they reached a size that presented insuperable technical and managerial difficulties. By the 1620s, the larger textile operations run by the Winchcombe and Dunham families in Newbury had been abandoned 'due to changes in the commercial and regulatory climate'.[114] The Mines Royal and the Mineral and Battery Works, both set up in 1658 and later 'let to farm', serve as examples. 'Among the causes of failure', writes Sidney Pollard, 'must be reckoned technical difficulties and the inability to efficiently transplant Continental methods, overestimate of the yield of copper mines and inability to deal effectively with ore which was different in composition from German ores' in addition to: high costs, poor supervision, waste in the form of bribery, inability to raise capital, fraud, and sheer 'mismanagement'.[115] Some of the largest operations that did survive, such as the ship-building industry in the naval dockyards, were not based on private enterprise but were dependent upon state patronage.[116] State demand for ships, iron for cannons and other metals played a major role in facilitating the growth of large, centralised operations in manufacturing from the mid-sixteenth century.

110. Nef 1966a, p. 322. Emphasis not found in the original.
111. Coleman 1975, pp. 35–6.
112. Ibid.
113. Coleman 1975, p. 38.
114. Jackson (ed.) 2004, p. xxviii.
115. Pollard 1965, pp. 14–5, 23.
116. Coleman 1975, p. 40, citing an earlier publication of his from 1953.

What can also account for the ability of new lines and techniques to thrive in England where they were less successful on the continent is the unprecedented expansion of England's domestic market. The growth of a highly productive agriculture produced on land farmed under economic leases or by capitalist tenant-farmers responding to market imperatives supported a growing domestic economy and regional specialisation. New lines of manufacturing and new techniques in this context would have a high probability of success in an economy where disposable incomes were on average increasing, and where the consumer-market was beginning to expand and diversify below the level of elite consumption of luxury goods. Soap, glass, and salt are all goods that the common folk of England were consuming in greater numbers.

The importance of Nef's thesis is that his emphasis on the emergence of 'new' industries helps to frame the question: what economic forces were at work in facilitating the development of such new industries in England? Nef highlights a significant development of large-scale enterprise long before the Industrial Revolution and draws what seems an obvious conclusion: that the evolution of industrial capitalism had a much longer and extended history than is generally imagined. Capitalism's origins long pre-date 1760. But Nef is focused on the form and not the process. Moreover, Nef is making a case for a pan-European 'early Industrial Revolution', which we dispute. In spite of this, however, he repeatedly finds examples of ways in which England was unique. Furthermore, Nef's work focuses more or less exclusively on the growth of large-scale manufacturing. He does note the 'growth of an elaborate network of middlemen, who supplied the materials upon which thousands of domestic workpeople laboured at their spinning-wheels and looms', which he views as 'so remarkable in the late sixteenth and early seventeenth centuries that the changes in the face of industrial Lancashire were scarcely less important than between 1760 and 1832'.[117] Yet Nef himself had little to say about the development of rural cottage manufacturing. This was a subject to be picked up later by others in what became the literature on 'proto-industrialisation', another theoretical approach (to which we shall turn momentarily) that seeks to trace the origins of the Industrial Revolution through pre-industrial manufacturing.

If the implication of Nef's thesis is that it should be possible to trace a continuous development of 'factories' and industrial capitalism from this period, the thesis is untenable. Large-scale production could be found in Roman times, but these did not give rise to an industrial revolution. Nef's work does not bring us closer to explaining the *timing* of the Industrial Revolution in the eighteenth century. He emphasises the 'importance' of these developments; so it bears

117. Nef 1934, p. 4.

asking: in what way were these developments particularly important? What did the expansion of the scale of some industrial operations in the sixteenth and seventeenth centuries contribute to the rapid growth of English industrial output in the late eighteenth and early nineteenth centuries? The contention here is that the emergence of large-scale, mostly state-run enterprises in sixteenth-century England did not by itself generate the momentum – the social dynamic – capable of yielding the dramatic burst of English industrial output in the late eighteenth century. And while developments like the spread of the blast-furnace were necessary conditions for that 'revolution' in manufacturing, they were far from sufficient. The emergence of large-scale manufacturing enterprises by the mid-seventeenth century reflected the increasing strength and coherence of the English state, its strength in part premised upon the increasing scope and depth of the domestic market. Since the numbers of those employed in manufactures remained relatively low when compared to the rapid growth of factories in the later eighteenth century, it does not appear to be the case that these 'early factories' were absorbing large numbers of peasants turned wage labourers displaced by the process of enclosures and expanding agrarian capitalism, even if they stood to benefit from the resulting cheapness and wider availability of wage-labour. Indeed, there were large-scale industrial enterprises in France, Sweden and other nations where agrarian capitalism was not developing. Moreover, English exports continued to be dominated by textiles. By 1701, woollens still accounted for over two-thirds of British exports.[118] It is thus difficult to see how the expansion of mining and other industries that Nef cites as part of his 'early Industrial Revolution' might have brought about an overall transformation of the economy sufficient to merit the 'revolution' label.

As Coleman states, the commonality such industries share is the nature of the technical process itself, which does not allow dispersal of workers and requires concentration. However, the robustness of these industries in seventeenth-century England can be explained at least in part by the development of new market imperatives that necessitated a transformation of agrarian production, resulting in an agrarian capitalism and regional specialisation in a growing domestic market. By calling for a protracted view of the Industrial Revolution as a long-term process, Nef's work (perhaps unintentionally) places an emphasis on the historical *process* that led to the Industrial Revolution. This suggests that the whole confusion about whether the Industrial Revolution was a slow or sudden development confuses causal process with the *outcomes* of the change itself.

Nef tells us that the centralisation of production in these large manufacturing operations made capitalism inevitable because large sums were needed for

118. Deane and Cole 1969, p. 30.

investment in fixed capital, including new techniques and some machinery. Yet Nef tells us virtually nothing about the social relations involved in production. Are we to imagine the presence of a class of capitalist employers emerging from this period?[119] To address this question, let us consider the positions of several authors who, when specifically examining medieval and early modern mining operations, have answered this question in the affirmative.

'Capitalism' in medieval and early modern mining

Max Weber has argued that the increasing concentration in mines from the thirteenth to the seventeenth centuries meant increasing capital requirements, necessitating capitalists employing wage labourers. According to Weber, in the thirteenth century the strength of German miners induced landed proprietors to grant 'free mountains', whilst in England mining rights were at this time reserved to the Crown.[120] The implication seems to be that German mining became capitalist from a very early period, and well before England.[121] Lewis Mumford has similarly suggested that the Fuggers of Germany, an exceptionally wealthy mercantile family of the fourteenth century with extensive mining interests, were among the first true capitalists.[122] The Fuggers were a German merchant family who traded in silk, spices and fine arts. By 1502, Jacob Fugger was 'the foremost fiscal agent of Rome' and collected Papal revenues across Europe.[123] He had entered into a partnership with the German mining engineer Johan Thurzo in 1494 and the Fugger-Thurzo trading company came to operate an extensive network of copper and silver mines leased in Germany, Tyrolia and Hungary, employing hundreds of workers in mines and smelting works in what was, prior to the opening of mines in South America, 'probably the largest-scale business which had developed to that time'.[124] Enjoying extensive patronage and little competition, Fugger nearly achieved a global monopoly on the copper trade

119. Some questions for further research remain: What did these industries contribute in terms of experience with financing large-scale enterprise or labour management? To the extent that valuable experience in large-scale industry was gained, by whom was it gained exactly?

120. Weber 1961, p. 143. As noted above, Nef cites a legal decision of 1566, under Elizabeth I, as opening up ores other than precious metals to private mining. According to Weber, the change came later, under Charles I.

121. See Weber 1961, pp. 134–44.

122. Mumford 1934, pp. 76–7 (plate IV) writes: 'Jacob Fugger II... is the very model of the pure capitalist. His dominance symbolizes the perversion of life-economy into money-economy'.

123. Flynn 1941, pp. 38–9.

124. Ibid.; Strieder 1966, p. 106.

in the first quarter of the sixteenth century.[125] Did such an amassing of merchant capital translate into 'capitalist' relations of production in the workplace? According to John Flynn: 'the mines, of course, under the feudal system, were the property of the Duke, the owners holding them as feudal grants. The Duke, therefore, was entitled to a share of all the copper and silver taken out of them by the operators'.[126] The fact that the leasing arrangement retained a feudal character suggests that the mode of labour organisation also continued to follow longstanding customary practices. In other words, there is little evidence to suggest that fifteenth- and sixteenth-century mine owners wrested control over the labour process away from their labourers in the same manner as English textile-mill owners did in late eighteenth-century England. In fact, in English mining the struggle over control of the labour process persisted well into the latter half of the nineteenth century.

It is not surprising, however, that Weber would identify such operations as capitalist, since Weber finds capitalism wherever he finds trade. Weber defines a 'capitalist economic action' as one which 'rests on the expectation of profit from the utilization of opportunities for [peaceful] exchange'.[127] In effect then, capitalism is equated with the accumulation of wealth and with trade; wherever you find a flourishing trade, as in ancient Rome or China – or even Babylon[128] – you find capitalism. As Weber explains:

> Merchants have existed in all parts of the world, wholesale and retail, local and foreign; there have been money-lenders of all kind, and banks with a variety of functions... Wherever public bodies have had monetary finances, the money-lender has appeared, whether in Babylon, Greece, India, China or Rome: he has financed, above all, wars and piracy, contracts and building of all kinds... This kind of entrepreneurial figure, the capitalistic adventurer, has existed all over the world. With the exception of trade, and credit and banking activities, the basic opportunities sought by such men have been either in purely irrational speculation or in acquisition by violence, and above all in

125. Strieder 1966, pp. 126–8.

126. Flynn 1941, p. 42. The Fuggers were active traders out of Antwerp, a key hub of new activity during the period when the centre of trade was shifting from the Mediterranean to the North-West of Europe. Ehrenberg comments: 'we begin to hear of fairly large financial transactions on the Fugger's part in Antwerp. Hitherto the factory there (which had a house to itself in 1508) had really only been used for dealing in commodities, a business where pepper figured alongside of copper and silver', adding in a footnote: 'Factory is used in the eighteenth century sense of a depot' (Ehrenberg 1985, p. 71, n. 3). This again suggests that the Fugger operation was largely governed by the logic of mercantile operations. It also reminds us that terms like 'factory' can have a wide variety of meanings.

127. Weber 1974, p. 17.

128. Collins 1980, p. 4.

> acquisition of booty, either in an actual war or by the fiscal plunder of subject-peoples over a long period.[129]

If the unifying definition of capitalism is reduced simply to 'acquisitive activity', rendering it ahistorical and universal, the term is emptied of its specificity. In the case of ancient Rome, Weber was at least more specific: *ager publicus* was, for Weber, the pristine form of communal agrarian property that the Romans inherited when they began, but the key development of the Romans was *ager privatus*, private property in land that came to involve a business-like form of organisation (based on the pursuit of profits) so uninhibited that he even recognised it as an 'agrarian capitalism'. In the present work, we are discussing an entirely distinct conception of 'agrarian capitalism' set in early modern England. So as not to invite confusion, let us make it clear that Weber's conception of an ancient agrarian capitalism is not of a system of agriculture driven by market forces and market imperatives, but is rather of one that still involves the application of 'extra-economic' or coercive, political force.

How do we know this? Because Weber drew a distinction between modern and earlier forms of capitalism. Notwithstanding Weber's sweeping definition of capitalism, Weber did see something unique and distinct about what he called 'modern rational capitalism' or 'market capitalism'. 'The West' writes Weber, 'has given capitalism a degree of significance such as it has never had elsewhere',[130] for in the modern West, 'there exists a completely different form of capitalism, which has developed nowhere else in the world: the rational capitalist organisation of (formally) *free labour*'.[131] It bears asking, here: of what utility is it to work with two contradictory definitions of capitalism? In reviewing Weber's *Agrarian Sociology of Ancient Civilizations*,[132] John Love takes note of this dual definition. Initially, Weber offers the following definition: 'Where we find that property is an object of trade and is utilised by individuals for profit-making in a market economy, there we have capitalism'.[133] But later in the same work, Weber distinguished 'political capitalism' as a mode of profit-making involving the application of force from 'market capitalism' or 'bourgeois capitalism' involving acquisition by peaceful methods. Love finds this distinction useful because

---

129. Max Weber 1978, pp. 335–6. According to Mueller 1986, pp. 1–20: 'Capitalism meant something very specific to Weber: the organization of formally free labour in methodical, rational and disciplined work'. While the more sweeping definitions we have quoted above seem to indicate that Weber was not so consistent about adhering to this labour-based definition of capitalism, as with the broader definition, this more specific definition is still a kind of 'ideal type' that could be applied to many different societies in different time periods.

130. Weber 1978, pp. 335–6.

131. Weber 1961, p. 208.

132. Weber 1976.

133. Weber 1976 as cited by Love 1986, p. 162.

'it assists in explaining those acquisitive activities that possess capitalistic features without identifying the ancient forms with modern capitalism'.'[134] But this is only to re-state the problem. Even if Love wishes to shy away from Weber's claim that capitalism existed in the ancient world, he still suggests that 'capitalistic features' were present. What made certain features of ancient society 'capitalistic'? Either Love is measuring ancient society against the measure of 'modern capitalism' to anachronistically label features of ancient society as 'capitalistic', or like Weber, he defines what is 'capitalistic' so broadly that it could be applied to virtually any society.

For our purposes, we recognise profit-making and the acquisition of large-scale wealth in ancient society as a form of private property based upon 'extra-economic' methods of surplus-extraction. Weber appears to recognise this distinction when he writes that ancient capitalism 'was rooted in *politics*: that is, it depended on the private exploitation of relationships of political domination in an expanding city-state'.[135] Here lies the rub, for it is precisely the 'extra-economic' character of ancient property that distinguishes pre-capitalist forms of property and it is precisely the 'strictly economic' character of property governed by market imperatives that distinguishes the form of private property found under conditions of (modern) capitalism.[136] As such, Ancient society was a form of European class society involving large-scale private property, but it was not in any meaningful sense capitalist. As Ellen Wood explains, the Romans developed 'a conception of property more individualistic and exclusive than ever before', but:

> Rome was not a capitalist society, nor a 'liberal democracy'. It is certainly true that, unlike any other ancient civilization, the Romans created a régime with two distinct poles of power, in which a well-developed central state coexisted with strong private property; and it is no doubt also true that, as the imperial state grew, there were tensions between propertied classes and an increasingly burdensome state. But there never existed in Rome a system of appropriation, like capitalism, which depended on extensive growth, rooted in profitably competitive production, rather than on the extensive growth of property in a massive grab for land. Territorial expansion in the empire was an extension of land concentration at home; and public power of the state, its coercive force, played a more immediate role in the acquisition of private wealth.[137]

---

134. Love 1986, p. 172.
135. Weber 1978, p. 312.
136. For a discussion of the concept of market imperatives see Wood, 1994, p. 25.
137. Wood 2006, p. 125.

By clarifying the distinction between an economic system based on well-defined rights of property but still rooted in various forms of extra-economic surplus-extraction and an economic system in which the economic sphere is 'insulated' from extra-economic 'interference' so that market regulation becomes paramount, Wood avoids reduplicating Weber's confusing dual definition of capitalism without failing to acknowledge the contribution which the development of strong private property in the ancient world made to the subsequent development of feudalism, absolutism and capitalism.

Neil Evans makes an argument similar to Weber's with regard to mining in claiming that the mining region around Newcastle in the North-East of England was 'capitalist' from early on. Evans gives two reasons to justify his claim. First, he notes that Newcastle enjoyed international trading links from as early as 1500 or before. 'Danzig and the Netherlands were important trading partners'.[138] Here, Evans resonates with Weber in equating capitalism with trade and with the commercialisation model or any theory ascribing the rise of capitalism to the rise of trade in the early modern period.[139] Second, however, Evans notes that from the early 1600s, relations between landlords and tenants had already become contractual.[140] Mining, claims Evans, attracted labourers who were effectively proletarian from early on:

> The coal industry from an early stage developed a detailed division of labour and a proletariat recruited from the wandering poor, criminals and civil war prisoners. Many came from Scotland and the whole workforce was given none of the status accorded to people who worked the land or to craftsmen. No guild organisation ever emerged in coal mining. The product was seen as being offensive and the people carried its taint.[141]

As menial jobs with low wages, these would have been the jobs that men in the 'honourable trades' eschewed. It does appear, therefore, that English mining operations involved the employment of proletarian or semi-proletarian labourers. By attracting those displaced souls who had little else available to them as a means of making a living, mining operations played the role of absorbing a portion of the displaced population without access to the means of subsistence

---

138. Evans 1989, p. 206 writes: 'The region illustrates the dominance of what Thompson calls an agrarian bourgeoisie', citing Thompson 1978, p. 40. Evans notes that 'the phrase is implied rather than used directly', however a checking of both hardback and paperback versions of Thompson's book reveals nothing remotely connected to this suggestion.

139. For a discussion and critique of the commercialisation model, see Brenner 1985a, pp. 10–11 and Wood 1995, pp. 152–3.

140. Evans 1989, p. 206.

141. Evans 1989, pp. 204–5.

whose numbers had been increasing in England since at least the sixteenth century.

It may well be that many European miners from the thirteenth to the seventeenth centuries became dependent upon the market for both earning wages and spending those wages to acquire the necessities of life. But there is nothing inherently capitalist about the practice of wage labour as such, as wage labour has existed in many pre-capitalist settings. If these early mining operations were indeed capitalist, we would expect to find evidence that they operated according to a logic of price competition in a marketplace generally free of extra-economic forms of market regulation between employers who are themselves not only dependent upon market exchange for access to labour and the realisation of profits, but also subject to a market imperative to transform production by making it more efficient and cost-effective in order to ensure their economic survival. Nevertheless, what the available evidence suggests about these early mining operations is that rather than being driven by market imperatives, the relations of production continued to be regulated by extra-economic forms. While the workers mostly retained direct customary control over the labour-process and therefore over the means of production, the employers were effectively merchants enjoying monopoly rights over their mines which freed them from competitive pressures that might otherwise have led to their seizing direct control over the labour process in order to transform production.

Mining and agrarian capitalism: the instructive case of Whickham

If one accepts the seemingly counter-intuitive suggestion that it was a transformation in *agrarian* class relations that formed the crucial rupture that enabled the development of a distinctly 'economic' sphere of social relations in which production could be regulated directly by the market and thereby became subject to the pressures of market competition, making the transformation of production an imperative, what then of manufacturing in England during the period of so-called agrarian capitalism? To address this key question, we continue our discussion of proletarianisation and capitalism in mining by way of considering Levine and Wrightson's case study of the growth of mining in the manor of Whickham.[142]

Whickham was a manor in the Tyneside with large coal deposits, making it destined to become one of the principal coal-mining sites around Newcastle. 'From the later sixteenth century it had witnessed the emergence of industrial undertakings of striking scale and complex organisation, of 'specialized and

142. Levine and Wrightson 1991.

distinctively industrial settlements', and a hitherto unknown concentration of industrial workers'.[143] Coal mining also attracted other industries to the area: 'salt, glass and lime, ship-building, copper, and iron'.[144] It was here in 1691 that Sir Ambrose Crowley would establish his mighty Winlaton ironworks that would soon become one of the largest manufacturing complexes of the early eighteenth century.

In the late sixteenth century, a Grand Lease had been awarded to the local landlords allowing for mining on the open fields. The award led directly to a dispute between two factions. On the one side were the 'ins' or the 'Grand Lessees', most of whom belonged to the Company of Hostmen, admission to which was generally restricted to those owning or leasing coal mines. On the other side were the 'outs', who called themselves the 'Non Grand Lessees' and were comprised mainly of 'smaller coal owners whose interests were ignored by the ruling faction'.[145] The interloping 'outs' soon complained that the Lessees had used their monopoly position in order to raise the price of coal from 4*s*. to 9*s*. per caldron, taking their complaint to the Bishop of Durham and to London. At stake was not so much the question of monopoly as such, but control over the municipal government itself, by which control over mining operations could be assured through the exercise of patronage and extra-economic power. The matter was settled in favour of the Grand Lessees in the form of a new charter for Newcastle, granted in 1600, which guaranteed the control of the municipal government to the 'ins' and provided for the incorporation of the Company of Hostmen. What did Queen Elizabeth get in return? First, a steady supply of coal for the rapidly expanding City of London was guaranteed. And second, an increase on the tax on coal was agreed upon, raising it from 4*d*. to 1*s*. per chaldron.[146] It was a historic bargain, and one which allowed for the further growth of centralised mining operations.

Whickham was still unenclosed in 1600 and pastoral agriculture was predominant. While the mining activities that took place in the late sixteenth century did little to disrupt the way of life of local producers, this was in part due to the fact that copyholders were vigorous about protecting their rights. By 1610, a suit by the copyholders of Whickham and a counter-suit by the Grand Lessees both

---

143. Levine and Wrightson 1991, p. 78.

144. Levine and Wrightson 1991, p. 79.

145. Sweezy 1938, pp. 5–6 writes: 'The circumstances surrounding the origin of the Grand Lease are somewhat mysterious, but it seems clear that in the year 1582 a certain Thomas Sutton, acting on behalf of the Crown, obtained from the Bishop of Durham a lease running for ninety-nine years, on all his coal lands in the manors of Whickham and Gateshead'. Sutton subsequently sold the lease to two of the wealthiest merchants in Newcastle on the promise that they turn over the lease to the mayor and burgesses of Newcastle. But instead they opened it up to private interests.

146. Sweezy 1938, pp. 6–8.

found their way to court. 'The documents that were generated as they proceeded show the lines of conflict very clearly drawn. The copyholders complained bitterly of their recent usage at the hands of the Grand Lessees, expressing themselves roundly in submissions and testimony crackling with resentment and indignation'.[147] Anticipating the struggles of English textile workers in the late eighteenth century, the peasants emphasised that the rights to the land that they enjoyed were rooted in custom. They complained that their fields were being entered upon and mined without their consent. And they 'challenged the coal owners' right to proceed "at their pleasures", for they explicitly accused them of arrogating to themselves an extra-legal *absolute power*'.[148] Absolute it may have been, but it was not extra-legal. The Grand Lease was no doubt a royal concession, and as such had the status of common law.[149]

The imposition of mining rights on lands still held in common under the law of the manor inevitably created a situation characterised by a state of friction between the two parties. The court case did lead to an attempt at a settlement in 1621. To meet the grievances of the copyholders, they were to be consulted on roadways and recompensed for damages. 'They were also to receive fire coal for their homes at a price of 1*d.* per bowl'.[150] Wasted pits were to be filled, and so on. But the copyholders were ordered not to hinder the mining and carriage of coal by the Grand Lessees. 'They were forbidden to enter into any "agreement or combination amongst themselves not to leade but at such and such Rates as themselves shall agree", and if they and the Lessees could not agree, the commission was to set wage rates'.[151] Thus, the copyholders did not come away empty-handed, but 'on all essentials, they had lost'.[152] As mining on the open

147. Levine and Wrightson 1991, p. 121.

148. Levine and Wrightson 1991, pp. 121–2.

149. Levine and Wrightson 1991, p. 123 cite a lecture by E.P. Thompson, given in 1986, in which Thompson advised that it is 'unwise to posit too sharp a distinction between law and custom'. In other writings, Thompson pointed out that custom often enjoyed the status of law. Thus while the Grand Lease was not extra-legal, neither were the efforts of the peasants to defend their rights by appealing to custom. We have two legal systems in conflict, here.

150. Levine and Wrightson 1991, p. 130.

151. Ibid. Note here the early ban on combinations.

152. Levine and Wrightson 1991, pp. 131–3 write: 'In effect, the decision of 1621 meant that the fate of the copyholders of Whickham was sealed'. An instructive exception was the case of Robert Harding, a freeholder, who claimed that his land was not affected by the decision of 1621 because it was a freehold of the neighbouring Hollinside manor, and not part of Whickham. After four years in court, Harding was awarded damages of £720 for the coal that had been removed and £500 for the resultant decline in the value of his property. As a freeholder, Harding would have been able to make his case at common law, and we can only speculate that this was the true reason for his success, that is, his ability to assert absolute legal title to his land in the king's court. Were he a copyholder, his case would have involved a boundary issue between two adjoining manors, in either of which his tenure would have remained insecure at best.

fields proceeded apace, Whickham was not depopulated, but *grew* in population, thanks in large part to the fact that the mining operations were now attracting outsiders looking for employment in mining as well as in a local agriculture that was responding to rising prices driven by the increasing demand for agricultural produce to feed the growing number of people employed in mining and other industries. This demand for greater agricultural output was a major factor in the later decision to enclose the parish in 1678. Enclosure in Whickham had social consequences that are more familiar to us through the examples of late eighteenth-century parliamentary enclosure: accelerated social polarisation, mounting poor law rates to deal with the growing numbers of the poor, and by 1750, the establishment of a workhouse at Swalwell.[153]

The case of Whickham is instructive because it serves as an example of the conversion of tenancies to economic leaseholds and the subsequent enclosure of the parish being undertaken for purposes other than agrarian ones. Here we have a case of peasants appealing to customary manorial law in their legal struggle to preserve their customary rights against the claim of the holders of an economic lease not for purposes of tenant-farming or putting up a sheep-run, but for 'industrial' mining operations. In his study of *The Rise of the British Coal Industry*, John Nef recognises how such conversions to economic leaseholds and subsequent enclosures of land for purposes of coal mining contributed to the distinctly English path of economic development. Nef writes that:

> only a curtailment of the mineral rights claimed by manorial tenants could have made the private ownership of royalties tolerable. Wherever collieries were started, we find a movement to prevent the peasants from working coal, or hindering the lord of the manor or his concessionaire from working it, in both their own lands and the manorial waste. Portions of the wastes which contained coal were often enclosed in order to facilitate mining. It is not unlikely that some lords ejected tenants because of their claims or potential claims to share in the revenue arising from the working of coal. The growth in rural districts of other industries, encouraged by the expansion of coal mining, also interfered with the rights of small tenants. Coal was therefore a factor of some importance in the decline of peasant-proprietorship and the increase of the large estate. Together with sheep-farming and the confiscation of property of the religious foundations, coal mining helps to account for the differences between the agrarian history of England and that of the Continent.[154]

This is a remarkable observation coming from the same scholar who proposed an 'early industrial revolution' marked by the rise of large, centralised manufac-

153. Levine and Wrightson 1991, pp. 148–51, 378.
154. Nef 1966a, pp. 329–30.

turing operations in sixteenth- and seventeenth-century England. We are not aware of Nef having drawn any causal connections between 'the agrarian history of England' and the emergence of these larger manufacturing units. What we do know is that in his view, coal mining profoundly shaped the course of English history. 'The rise of the coal industry during the Stuart period', he writes, 'helped to establish parliamentary government... it is not too much to say that the general economic and social development of the period from 1550 to 1700 cannot be understood unless account is taken of the part played in it by the coal industry'.[155] While attributing major political developments to the conversion to a new source of power smacks of economism in the extreme, this is not to say that the unprecedented expansion of coal use played anything less than a critical role in the development of capitalism in England; it did.

England became the first nation to convert from reliance upon 'current local sunlight'[156] as an energy source to what we now commonly refer to as 'fossil fuels.'[157] This marks a pivotal moment in human history. In addition to the advantages of allowing for new techniques of production to be devised or freeing up English timber for other uses, coal offered clear advantages over water and wood. Wood, 'with its greater bulk for calorific value and less readily controllable heat, was a poor basis for many industrial processes'.[158] Coal was readily transportable and more controllable; it could be mined and burned year-round, whereas water wheels were subject to ice flows, floods and decreases in water flow. Ultimately the conversion to coal and away from wood and muscle as sources of power allowed for the release from dependence on fixed power sources such as water and wind in the form of the steam engine and later, with the discovery of the potential of oil as a fuel source, the internal combustion engine, with such long-term ramifications as global warming resulting from the release of greenhouse gases and mercury poisoning in the fish supply due to the exhaust from coal-fired power-plants.

As far-reaching as the implications of this shift away from 'ancient direct sunlight' may have been in terms of making possible new ways of applying energy to production, however, this development was ancillary to the transformation of class and property relations involved in the emergence of agrarian capitalism, understood as a transitional stage leading to the transformation of agrarian and subsequently industrial production in ways that would necessitate innovations

155. Ibid.

156. Hartmann 2004, p. 83 contrasts the use of 'current direct sunlight' with the use of 'ancient sunlight,' in other words so-called fossil-fuels. See next footnote.

157. There is apparently some disagreement with the prevailing view that so-called fossil fuels are actually derived from ancient plant and animal life ('ancient sunlight', see previous footnote), or whether oil is in fact a 'primordial' geologic material (for a discussion, see Engdahl 2004).

158. Black 2001, p. 47.

in energy production and usage. Additionally, by increasing agrarian productivity and thereby lowering the prices of agricultural goods, agrarian capitalism could act as the primary stimulus to the unique and unprecedented expansion of the domestic market in England, a development in which the growth of London played a central role. The growth of the domestic market and population translated into increasing demand for manufactures. In turn, the expanding demand for fuel in both manufacturing and for domestic use in expanding urban centres put increasing pressures on supplies of timber, encouraging the conversion to coal use. Thus it could be argued that it was the economic compulsions of a developing agrarian capitalism which led to the drive to expand coal production, while the expansion of coal use, in turn, expanded the limits of what was possible in terms of both 'improving' or innovating in production and the growth of urban populations.

What the case of Whickham demonstrates is that the imposition of common-law property rights in land in favour of operations employing both waged and casual labourers, where the profits accrued to the owner or lease-holder, not only took place outside of the agriculture 'sector' but during the same time period as the development of agrarian capitalism. It also demonstrates that whether for agrarian or 'industrial' purposes, the curtailment of the rights of customary tenants in favour of the rights of the holders of economic leases or the wholesale extinguishing of the customary law upon the enclosure of the manor had similar consequences, namely: the divorcing of direct peasant producers from the means of production and contributing to the growth of a proletarian labour force.

If mining is taken as an industrial as opposed to agrarian form of production, does it still make sense then to think of this period in terms of the development of *agrarian* capitalism in early modern England? As a productive activity vastly in the minority next to agriculture and husbandry, coal mining may have transformed the regional landscape and the regional economy of such sub-regions as that of the Tyneside, but it is difficult to see how coal mining did more than *contribute* to the development of agrarian capitalism, being but one (highly significant) line of manufacture in a society still dominated by agrarian production.

The so-called phase of proto-industrialisation

Although the term 'proto-industrialisation' had been used before, Franklin Mendels, writing in 1972, was the first to use the term systematically.[159] Peter Kriedte and Hans Medick later offered a neo-Marxist approach to the theory.

---

159. Mendels 1972, p. 241. Gullickson 1983, p. 241, comments: 'In 1972 Franklin Mendels introduced the term proto-industrialisation into the vocabulary of economic and social historians. The term had been used before, most notably by E.J.T. Collins, E.L. Jones and J. Woolf in analysing advances in European agriculture, but it had no systematic usage'.

They saw proto-industrialisation as the second in a three-phase process, the first being the growth of domestic manufacturing not tied to international markets, the third being factory mechanisation.[160] As one commentator has noted, the greatest contribution of the term 'proto-industrialisation' may be that it has generated such a range of studies on the same generalised phenomenon in a wide variety of contexts.[161] At the same time, however, criticism of the theory in both its original (Mendels) and neo-Marxist (Kriedte and Medick) variants, by authors both sympathetic (Ogilvie)[162] and hostile (Coleman; Houston and Snell)[163] has exposed the theory's lack of a solid foundation. In the previous section, we discussed the development of centralised industrial production in England from the Tudor era onwards, yet proto-industrialisation theory tends to ignore these developments. Coleman comments that: 'If the purpose of the theory is to shed light on the way in which industrialisation came about it is surely necessary to look at other sorts of industrial activities and at urban manufacturing as well as rural in order to see if they conduced to or, equally important, failed to conduce to, industrialisation proper'.[164]

What Nef's argument and proto-industrialisation theory have in common is that both suggest a 'stage' of development within a larger process of historical evolution. As such, the same problem or question applies to both theories: what is the *process* at work behind the rise of larger, centralised firms in the sixteenth and seventeenth centuries or the expansion of rural manufacturing throughout the early modern period?

The most striking inconsistency to be found in proto-industrialisation as a stage-theory is that in some regions proto-industry is seen to have led to industrial revolution while in other regions it led to 'de-industrialisation'. This robs the theory of the potential for having any intellectual rigor, 'especially since the factors which decided whether a proto-industrial region would industrialise or de-industrialise [remain] largely unclear'.[165] What we can say for certain is that various forms of rural domestic manufacturing expanded significantly from the sixteenth and seventeenth centuries in regions scattered across Europe. Some of those regions later underwent full-scale industrialisation; others saw rural manufactures decline and a return to agricultural predominance. But the move from phase two to phase three – to full industrialisation – did not take place all at once. Significantly, Mendels sees proto-industrialisation on the conti-

160. Kriedte, Medick and Schlumbohm 1981.
161. Ogilvie 1996, p. 37.
162. Ogilvie 1996, pp. 7–11.
163. Coleman 1983; Houston and Snell 1984, pp. 473–92.
164. Coleman 1983, p. 444.
165. Ogilvie and Cerman 1996, pp. 1–11.

nent as delayed, and as primarily a response to English proto-industrialisation.[166] Likewise, Kriedte writes that industrialisation on the continent 'was primarily a response to the English challenge'.[167] But if proto-industrialisation was an intermediate phase between the post-feudal domestic system and fully-fledged industrialisation, why should its development and the subsequent process of full industrialisation on the continent be delayed? And why should these processes be dependent upon English developments?

In England, rural domestic and putting-out manufacturing linked to overseas markets grew up alongside the guild system, experiencing periods of expansion and contraction 'over six successive centuries'.[168] Periods of economic expansion saw peasants taking advantage of market opportunities by producing goods for the market in their cottages, especially during the winter months. As we noted above, by the sixteenth century the development of rural handicraft production in England was concentrated in spinning and weaving. By constructing 'putting-out' arrangements in the countryside, urban merchants could circumvent company restrictions limiting the number of employees they could put to work, thus contributing to the exceptional expansion of rural manufacturing in the English countryside. Hudson finds it surprising that the bulk of the theory on proto-industrialisation has focused on continental Europe, given the fact that England led the way in the transition to an industrial society:

> If any environment were to provide a test case for various hypotheses derived from the work of Mendels and others it was likely to be England. Not only did several proto-industrial regions later become the heartlands of a more fully-fledged urban industrial society but they did so without competition from earlier mechanized and transformed industries in other parts of Europe. In addition, the social structure, the expansion of markets and the framework of law and taxation in England were such as to provide every encouragement to the unfettered expansion of commercial manufacturing, proletarianization and wealth accumulation, compared with social and institutional environments in many areas of continental Europe.[169]

While the English case may seem like the ideal case for exploring so-called 'proto-industrialisation', it actually poses enormous problems for proto-industrialisation theory, for when looking at rural manufacturing in England, one quickly finds that there is no single pattern of transition from rural manufacturing to industrialisation proper. Criticising the argument put forward by Kriedte *et al.*

166. Mendels 1972, p. 245.
167. Kriedte, Medick and Schlumbohm 1981, p. 139.
168. Coleman 1983, p. 440.
169. Hudson 1996, pp. 49–66.

that the putting-out system [*Verlagssystem*] involved greater concentration and control of capital-accumulation than the domestic system [*Kaufsystem*], Randall writes:

> The theory of proto-industrialization assumes that *Verlagsystems* were more adaptable to transition to the factory than were the more "backward" *Kaufsystems*. The English woollen industry does not bear this out. In fact, the opposite is correct. Just as the Domestic System had proved itself adaptable to rapid growth in the eighteenth century, with the onset of mechanisation it was able to absorb much of the new technology within the existing structure and advance still faster.[170]

According to Hudson, English proto-industrialisation involved a variety of household structures with no simple linear development.[171] The location of 'proto-industries' in England has been associated with such variables as the type of soil, pastoralism, seasonality of agriculture, fragmentation of holdings, weak manorialism, and access to common rights.[172] Coleman identifies ten areas of England where the theory identifies proto-industrialisation and finds that only four of these industrialised, the others leading to de-industrialisation. 'The obvious difference which separates the four' he claims, was their proximity to coal fields.[173] Moreover, notes Coleman, North-East and South Wales had little or no rural manufacturing, and yet these regions took part in the early Industrial Revolution. Clearly the development of rural manufacturing was not a necessary phase for a region to undergo in order to arrive at industrialisation. At the same time, proximity to coal did not ensure a successful transition for 'proto-' or full industrialisation, as Hudson points out, writing: 'the eclipse of the Kentish Weald, East Anglia, the West Country and several other proto-industrial regions occurred before coal became a vital locational influence'.[174] There is little doubt that more proximate causal factors such as geography and institutional arrangements at the village-level were important factors in determining where rural manufacturing appeared, the types of trades that were adopted and in what form. But Coleman finds such heterogeneity in the various locations where rural manufacturing were found that he questions whether it is even possible to define the regions in England where 'proto-industrialisation' developed. He proceeds to question whether enclosures were perhaps more significant than poor soils and

---

170. Randall 1991, p. 26.
171. Hudson 1996, p. 57.
172. Hudson 1996, pp. 55–6.
173. Coleman 1983, p. 443.
174. Hudson 1996, p. 58.

weak agricultural incomes in prompting rural dwellers to seek additional income in industrial by-employments, a suggestion relevant to our discussion.[175]

Kriedte *et al.* specify that what they refer to as 'the general framework of capitalist industrialisation' was a necessary condition for proto-industrialisation to lead to full industrialisation. Note that this 'general framework of capitalist industrialisation' is not explained in the theory, but is simply taken for granted. Such an assumption, writes Coleman: 'puts proto-industrialisation itself in a wholly indeterminate position, leaving us unable to tell how much was caused by it and how much by all the other things comprehended within that "general framework". We are back with that familiar collection of possible causes stigmatized by new economic historians as the "shopping-list"'.[176]

As is perhaps to be expected of any concept around which a theory develops, the theorists of proto-industrialisation go in search of the causes of the phenomenon of so-called proto-industrialisation, but can only resort to caveats when the core concept of the theory itself is challenged or beset by problems. The 'shopping list' of proximate causes in proto-industrial theory also includes enclosures. Below, we will argue that the full significance of enclosures can only be understood as part of a long-term historical process, specifically one involving the transformation of property rights. In fact, any discussion of a general framework of social relations would be incomplete without a discussion of class and property relations. Therefore, since the general structure of capitalist social relations is a necessary condition for the successful transition from cottage manufacturing to factory industrialisation, explaining how cottage and putting-out ('proto-industrial') manufacturing contributed to the Industrial Revolution would require a theory to explain the origin of capitalist property-relations, a topic about which proto-industrialisation theory has very little to say. The theory is caught in a tautology: what is used to explain how domestic manufacturing forms (in some instances) a causal link between earlier forms of manufacturing and capitalist industry is nothing other than the 'general structure' of capitalist industry itself. Kriedte writes: 'Proto-industrialisation stands between two worlds: the narrow world of the village and the world of trade that crosses all boundaries, between the agrarian economy and merchant capitalism'.[177] Thus for Kriedte, trade is the dynamic capitalist element, acting upon the stagnant, feudal agrarian sector. Here we see the neo-Smithian conceptualisation of the

175. Coleman 1983, pp. 440–1.
176. Coleman 1983, p. 445.
177. Kriedte, Medick and Schlumbohm 1981, p. 37. It is worth noting that the three authors of that volume are not in agreement on the nature of proto-industrialisation. Kriedte and Medick see proto-industrialisation as a separate economic system, while Schlumbohm views it as part of the feudal system. See Ogilvie and Cerman 1996, p. 3.

problem at work.[178] Trade, which is assumed to be inherently capitalist, liberates 'proto-industry' from its backward and presumably feudal 'fetters', allowing it to naturally develop into full-scale factory industrialisation. A discussion of the origin of capitalist class relations is at best a subject for further inquiry, and at worst is left out of the inquiry altogether.

The theory is perhaps most vague about precisely when the so-called phase of proto-industrialisation begins. Indeed, the writing in Kriedte, Medick and Schlumbohm's *Industrialization Before Industrialization* is so abstracted from specific historical events, that it seems to reify a timeless 'proto-industrial household' at the expense of bearing in mind the transitional character of this form, or of doing justice to the heterogeneity of rural handicraft arrangements.[179] With no clearly defined historical period for the onset of the proto-industrial phase and with the outcome of the phase being either industrialisation or de-industrialisation of the region in question (a truism), it becomes very hard to see how the various appearances and disappearances of rural manufacturing cohere into a distinct 'phase' at all.

In theory then, proto-industrialisation also stands 'between two worlds' in a larger historical and temporal sense – that is, between feudalism and capitalism. Mendels argued that as it developed, proto-industrialisation broke down the general institutional framework of feudal agrarian society and developed a new framework of markets. Kriedte, Medick and Schlumbohm make a similar claim when they write that:

> Viewed from the long-range perspective, [proto-industrialization] belongs to the great process of transformation which seized the feudal European agrarian societies and led them toward industrial capitalism. On closer inspection, however, it becomes clear that proto-industrialization could establish itself only where the ties of the feudal system had either loosened or were in the process of full disintegration.[180]

This thesis is empirically false. By contrast to Western Europe, Eastern Europe experienced a 'second serfdom', and yet cottage manufacturing still developed in the context of 'strong' feudal institutions. In Bohemia, lords urged and sometimes compelled their peasants to engage in by-employments in manufacturing, and could keep costs low 'through "forced wage labour", exploitation of labour services for "proto-industrial" auxiliary tasks, and restricting peasants' alternative options'.[181] In England, the Low Countries, Switzerland and the Rhine, on the

178. Brenner 1977, pp. 25–92.
179. Ogilvie and Cerman 1996, p. 8.
180. Kriedte, Medick and Schlumbohm 1981, p. 6.
181. The extent, if any, of 'putting-out' arrangements in Bohemia is uncertain. Underlying the exploitation of Bohemian peasants by forcing them into a situation of waged labour was a doubling of the population in the century before 1750, creating a surplus

other hand, village communities and the traditional institutions regulating access to land were already weakened prior to the development of significant 'proto-industrialisation'[182] Ogilvie suggests that 'what mattered for proto-industry was not so much the "strengthening" or "weakening" of feudalism, but the specific effect of feudal institutions on industrial costs'.[183] In general, there is significant disagreement about to which areas of Europe the theory of proto-industrialisation actually does or does not apply. Houston and Snell find 'that the heuristic value of the theory seems to be limited to north-western Europe'.[184] At the same time, however, they find, with Coleman, that the demographic predictions of the theory do not bear out for England. Some German scholars have insisted that Germany followed a 'special path' to industrialisation and that the theory is not applicable to German conditions.[185] In considering the case of the *pays de Caux* in France, Gullickson finds the thesis that 'proto-industrialisation' developed only in areas not suitable for surplus cereal production is not tenable.[186] As Houston and Snell write, 'the problems abound.'[187]

It is enough trouble that one of the central premises of proto-industrialisation theory – that proto-industrialisation is corrosive to feudal social relations – can be disproved by the evidence. But the larger issue is that the theory seeks to encompass far more than it can bear. It is not only that the primary attention given to rural manufacturing – at the expense of urban handicrafts and more centralised manufacturing operations – is unwarranted for a theory seeking to explain the transition to industrial revolution. It is also that the theory in its original formulations sought to explain *both* the decline of feudal institutions *and* the onset of industrialisation in one go. What is at issue is the underlying assumption that these two processes are one and the same. What is behind this assumption? Kriedte writes:

---

of labour, more than could be put to work on the land. Thus labour-costs were low, but they were artificially pushed lower by heavy feudal burdens. By Klíma's account, industrial by-employments do not appear to have played a 'corrosive' role on feudal relations. Klíma 1987, pp. 198–212.

182. Klíma 1987, 24.

183. Ogilvie 1996, p. 29. Ogilvie's use of the term 'proto-industry' is understood by the author to equate with 'cottage industry' in general.

184. Houston and Snell 1984, p. 478.

185. See Ogilvie and Cerman 1996, p. 9.

186. Gullickson 1983, pp. 848–9, writes: 'The proto-industrialisation of the *pays de Caux* poses problems for the usual models of proto-industrialisation in acute form . . . The expansion of the cottage textile industry in the fertile and well-farmed Caux demonstrates that large-scale cottage industry could and did spread in regions of commercial cereal agriculture, as well as in regions of subsistence agriculture, and suggests that seasonal unemployment and landlessness – not subsistence agriculture – were the distinguishing features of proto-industrial regions'.

187. Houston and Snell 1984, p. 492.

> Then, as the social division of labour deepened and became the agent of the economic process, it ceased to be purely the division of labour between town and countryside. In fact, the division of labour between town and countryside, where it was upheld, increasingly turned into an obstacle to further development of the forces of production. Economic growth could throw off its fetters only if the self-sufficient peasant production unit could be cracked open.[188]

Once the 'fetters' to (capitalist) economic development are removed, so the assumption goes, economic growth is no longer inhibited. So it already exists in embryo, waiting to be liberated. But what if feudal social relations in Western Europe declined without immediately producing capitalism? What if capitalism did not simply exist 'in embryo' within the womb of feudalism, but had yet to be realised as a new form of social relations?[189] The problem is that capitalism's emergence into history is not explained; capitalism is simply assumed to already exist. The 'phase' or 'stage' of proto-industrialisation is the transitional link between two ideal types of society or two vastly generalised modes of production. But whether we fill in the gap with rural domestic manufacturing or urban centralised manufacturing, or by theorising an 'articulation' of modes of production, there remains the work of explaining the logic of the *process* of change itself. It is not difficult to see why rural cottage manufacturing could be construed as the 'link' between an agrarian feudalism and urbanised industrial society, since it combines so many elements of both: manufacturing in an agrarian setting, urban merchants setting to work rural dwellers and all this happening in many locations that would later witness industrialisation. Kriedte claims that proto-industrialisation 'did indeed provide certain conditions for a capitalistic industrialisation' yet admits that these conditions 'were not however sufficient to actually introduce the process of industrialisation'.[190] If this is the case, why then should rural cottage manufacturing stand in as the 'proto-type' of later industrialisation?[191]

The concept of proto-industrialisation has also come to be applied not only broadly across the map of Europe, but outside of Europe.[192] Various studies

188. Kriedte, Medick and Schlumbohm 1981, pp. 12–13.

189. Wood 2002a, pp. 40–2, credits Paul Sweezy with first posing the problem of whether the dissolution of feudalism was the same process as the growth of capitalism.

190. Kriedte, Medick and Schlumbohm 1981, pp. 145–6.

191. Checking his dictionary, Coleman 1983, p. 447 writes: 'According to the *O.E.D.* the prefix "proto", derived from the Greeks, means first in time, earliest, original, primitive or, less commonly, first in rank or importance, chief or principal. Proto-industrialisation, as defined in the theory, has no claim to conform to either of these definitions, especially to the more common meaning of being the earliest or original form of something'.

192. See Patnaik 1972 (Anatolia); Quataert 1986 (Brazil); Libby 1991 (Japan); Howell 1992 (Japan); Dublin 1991 (North America) and Sokoloff and Dollar 1997 (North America), to name only a few examples.

suggest the presence of 'proto-industrialisation' in India. In justifying his application of the term to Minas Gerais, a Brazilian "slave society",' Douglas Cole Libby explains that because the model of proto-industrialisation has been challenged to account for examples that resulted not in industrialisation but de-industrialisation: '[Proto-industrialisation] is no longer exclusively viewed as a preparatory phase in the industrialisation process ... The practical result of the critical revision of the proto-industrial model has been a broadening of the concept which tends to allow for the inclusion of a much wider range of observable historical phenomena within what might be labelled as proto-industrial phases or tendencies'.[193]

Libby defines proto-industrialisation as: 'wide-scale rural production of industrial goods destined for distant markets and based on low-cost peasant labour'.[194] Given such a definition, the question arises: if such peasant production is no longer a preparatory phase anticipating industrialisation, why is it necessary to utilise the 'proto-' prefix at all? Even if the term is to be stripped of whatever geographic or historical specificity it may have once carried, the etymological implication of something that is indeed a preparatory ('proto-') phase anticipating industrialisation remains. How then can the application of the term to any type of situation involving rural or peasant manufactures, whether or not it preceded industrialisation, be justified? And how is that better than simply calling it something like 'peasant-based manufacturing' or 'commercialised, rural manufactures'?

In spite of the persistent rejection of the usage of the term by many social scientists, there are those who still call for a continuation or revival of the term's usage. Describing proto-industrialisation as more of a 'research strategy' than a 'historical period', Julie Marfany argues that those who believe that the theory is disproved by the failure of proto-industrial regions to industrialise are viewing a theory that was simply intended as 'a point of departure' in 'excessively rigid terms'.[195] It is 'undeniable', writes Marfany, 'that many areas of Europe between the sixteenth and eighteenth centuries witnessed the rise of a new form of industrial production for non-local markets, production that usually remained rural and domestic in nature, and was practised alongside agriculture. The distinctive nature of proto-industry demands recognition as a particular area for research'.[196]

193. Libby 1991, pp. 1–2.
194. Libby 1991, p. 2.
195. Marfany 2010, p. 943.
196. Ibid.

Yet the extant research that proceeded upon the assumptions of the founders of the theory, and found them to be false, has thereby called into question the 'distinctive nature' of so-called 'proto-industry'. There is nothing controversial about calling for comparative studies of rural, commercially-oriented manufacturing across different parts of Europe or even around the globe, but it is hard to see how insisting upon the usage of a term laden with the baggage of disproven theses will serve to do more than perpetuate the confusion.[197]

This review of some of the fundamental points of criticism should show why the theory of proto-industrialisation is strained to breaking point. The growth of the literature on proto-industrialisation over the last forty years has generated a new wealth of (often interdisciplinary) research into phenomena that clearly need to be addressed within the larger context of the transition to industrialisation. For John Davis, 'the important common feature is the emphasis these studies place on the ways in which economic growth has been influenced by social, institutional and other non-economic factors'.[198] He suggests that it may make 'better sense to think of "proto-industry" as a frame of references rather than a theory'.[199] Likewise, Jean Quataert, following Medick, argues that proto-industrialisation theory: 'should not be seen as an effort to conceptualize the whole transition from feudalism to industrial capitalism in one new, overarching category. Its contribution is more modest, and the need is to formulate generalisations from local and regional studies instead of conducting empirical research on the basis of preconceived theories'.[200]

Ogilvie calls for deeper investigation of various frameworks of social institutions and their effects to explain the profound differences and divergences among European societies all having in common the development of rural manufacturing in the early modern period.[201] And Houston and Snell call for 'a less schematic and limiting approach which takes more account for the diversity of European social and economic development in the passage to industrialisation'.[202]

---

197. Marfany's study of the village of Igualada in Catalan is significant for a reason having nothing to do with the theory of proto-industrialisation. Robert Brenner, who pioneered the theory of English agrarian capitalism, views Catalonia as one of only two regions outside of England where agrarian capitalism (as he understands it) may have developed, the other being Holland (See Brenner 1985a, p. 49 n. 81). Marfany 2010, p. 944, acknowledges that 'Catalonia is [a] "success" story in that proto-industry was followed by factory industry…' The question arises: to what extent did agrarian capitalism, or some process very much like agrarian capitalism, contribute to the successful industrialisation of Catalonia? Moreover, was the situation in Catalonia before industrialisation comparable to the case of the Netherlands (see the Introduction, p. 37), which Wood views as involving the development of market dependence in the absence of capitalism?

198. Davis 1990, p. 63.

199. Ibid.

200. Quataert 1988, pp. 3–22, citing Medick 1983, p. 269.

201. Ogilvie 1996, p. 37.

202. Houston and Snell 1984, p. 492.

These suggestions may point us in the right direction, but is the game worth the candle? It is the use of the prefix '*proto-*' which binds the various writings together around the theoretical assumption – whether implicit or explicit – that the development of cottage manufacturing and putting-out systems is a logical and necessary step in the direction of full industrialisation. We submit that this assumption is a fallacy.

Conclusion

In seeking to explain the origins of the Industrial Revolution, it is to be expected that theorists would attempt to trace a direct line of development endogenous to the manufacturing sector from the era of the guilds to modern, capitalist industry. But since the guilds were organised on a basis so completely antithetical to capitalist industry, it becomes necessary to identify an intermediary 'stage' or 'phase' linking the one to the other. Thus Nef points to the growth of large-scale (mostly state-run) manufacturing enterprises in the sixteenth century, while proto-industrialisation theory looks to the growth of cottage manufacturing for explanations. As we have seen, both theories are fraught with logical contradictions. Both theories suffer from the methodological flaw of attempting to read too many elements of Britain's Industrial Revolution of the eighteenth and nineteenth centuries back into the sixteenth and seventeenth centuries. Both theories share this tendency toward anachronism as well as a high degree of economism with political economy in general. The way out of this trap is to re-introduce social and political factors into the analysis and also to situate early modern manufacturing in the proper context of being a 'sector' within an economy still very much dwarfed by agrarian production.

In early modern England, the centralisation of state power facilitated the class solidarity of an emerging landed oligarchy asserting its power through Parliament. The expansion of economic leaseholds on land treated as exclusive private property recognised under common law was an expression of this ever-rising class power of the oligarchy. The transformation of social property relations associated with agrarian capitalism involved the growing market dependence of both the direct producers and the appropriators of surplus, who were increasingly operating under the compulsion of market imperatives. The dispossession of customary tenants of their access to land and the growing market dependence of the population fostered the rise of cottage manufacturing and the growth of the national market involving regional specialisation to meet rising levels of market demand. Improved yields and falling grain prices further promoted the development of the domestic market, including an expansion of both urban and rural manufactures, and facilitated the internal stratification as well as the early decline of guilds in England relative to Europe. Craft masters and merchant-employers expanded their operations by concentrating production and putting-out work to domestic workers in the countryside. In the face of an emerging price competition, the guild logic of monopoly control of markets to maintain quality and price at a high level was put under increasing strain.

Responding to the apparent crisis within the crafts, the Tudor state under Elizabeth sought to regulate the crafts by elevating the customary practices set out in company by-laws, the apprenticeship rule in particular, to the level of national policy. This would have the peculiar effect of giving such forms of customary control over the labour process the backing of state authority that would ultimately provide domestic workers with a powerful bulwark against the imposition of capitalism. This, in part, helps to explain how it was possible for capitalism to advance sooner in agriculture than in manufactures. Yet even without the state's effective sanction of customary labour practices in the crafts, it is likely that resistance to capitalism would anyhow have been fiercer in manufactures than in agriculture. The process at the heart of agrarian capitalism was the conversion of land to capital, which implies not just the commodification of land but its transformation to a specific form of property whereby the owners and direct producers working the land are operating under conditions of market dependence and according to market imperatives. As we have seen in the case of mining, where land served centrally as the primary of production just as it did in agriculture, the land was subject to a form of enclosure whereby the owner gained strict property rights under common law and local, customary claims on the land were extinguished. It is one thing to divorce direct producers from the means of production, rendering them market-dependent in the formal sense. It is quite another thing to render workers completely market-dependent by extinguishing the customary regulations that provide them protection from full exposure to the market. At the heart of the Industrial Revolution was the conversion of labour to capital, which implies not only the commodification of labour, but the subsumption of all manufacturing to the same logic governing agrarian capitalism, whereby under conditions of market dependence for both employers and workers and in response to price competition in the marketplace, economic survival for employers comes to depend upon making improvements in the efficiency of production, including of course the efficiency of labour, ultimately through taking direct control of the labour process. Employers are therefore compelled to abandon the age-old and customary conceptions of labour in favour of conceptualising the capacity of workers to labour, their 'labour-power', as *abstract labour*, as but one additional cost factor in the production process. However unlike land, labour-power is inseparable from the human beings whose capacity to labour is being 'owned' as a form of capital during the labour process, human beings who also have the capacity to resist their subsumption to capital.

In the centuries prior to the Industrial Revolution, however, the subsumption of manufacturing or craft labour to capital was more formal than real, and was achieved mainly through capital assuming control over marketing arrangements and the means of production.

The exceptional rise of cottage manufacturing in Britain is in large part a story of the conversion of peasants into part-time agricultural labourers and part-time domestic labourers. As enclosures encroached upon open field tenancies, domestic by-employment offered a means of compensating for the loss of access to the means of subsistence, as well as a substitute for production strategies designed to protect peasant families from the vagaries of market fluctuations. But urban domestic workers and full-time rural artisans themselves had no such alternatives. Here is another reason why it is not surprising that their resistance was more concerted and fiercer than the resistance that peasants and agrarian labourers put up against enclosures.

By the seventeenth century, English society was subject to previously unknown strains and contradictions. England's unique developments – the expansion of agrarian-capitalist tenant-farming on enclosed estates, the growth of regional specialisation within a domestic market and the centralisation of the state – would all come to bear upon the outcome of a showdown between the patrimonial powers of the Crown and the growing wealth and power of the landed classes, the outcome of which would stun elite society in Europe. The growing contradictions and disparities within the manufacturing and mercantile communities would shape the way in which merchants and craftsmen came to play key roles in this conflict, including the emergence of radical voices from the ranks of artisans calling for democracy and even a levelling of classes or what would later be understood as socialism.

Chapter Two
Parliament and Revolution

> All the main thing that I speak for,
> is because I would have an eye to property.
>
> General Henry Ireton, the Putney Debates[1]

During the seventeenth century, the Tudor framework for regulating craft manufacturing would begin to fully unravel. As we have seen above, the legislation of the Tudor era – the Statute of Apprentices in particular – sought to give fixity to Tudor-era social relations, which broadly remained based on custom, hierarchy and privilege. At the same time it sought to give a 'modern' cast to these by bringing their regulation under the purview of the central state. Unwin claims that the 'industrial world had outgrown its medieval framework'.[2] There were certainly pressures that were straining that framework to breaking point – the subordination of most companies to the trading interest, the expansion of rural and suburban manufacturing escaping regulation, the concentration of production in some lines of manufacturing and the problems this posed for customary modes of labour regulation. Yet to assert that manufacturing had *already* outgrown this framework is surely premature. In 1600, the struggles that would ultimately transform the nature of regulation within manufacturing still lay in the future. In London, the growth of suburban London and 'illegal' craft-production in these areas outside the old City

1. Thompson 1991, p. 25.
2. Unwin 1963, p. 136.

contributed to the increasing inability of the companies (still known as 'guilds' in London), to restrict entry into their trades to those who had served their apprenticeships and to restrict competition for 'foreigners' outside of London.[3] However, a series of mostly provincial common-law decisions in London between 1599 and 1614 served to challenge:

1. the authority of guild company by-laws;
2. the enforcement of the seven year apprenticeship rule;
3. the right to bar non-apprenticed or suburban craftsmen from joining the guild;
4. the right to prohibit merchants from contracting out to 'foreign' artisans (Tailors); and
5. rights of search and seizure (Dyers).

Throughout the seventeenth century, these cherished rights of the craft-guilds remained suspended in a kind of legal limbo, having lost precedent at common law, but still enforceable under company by-laws. Early in the century, the City's Common Council sought regulation of the trades, but liberal arguments would later begin to sway Council decisions away from enforcement.[4] Outside of London, craft guilds presumably faced an even greater struggle. Instead of serving as the bedrock of the trades, 'Queen Betty's Law':

> became a battle cry in the class struggle ... relations among the crafts were destined to be the major social battleground of the future and the two groups whose mutual welfare was supposed to be assured by the Statue were destined to be the main antagonists. Almost every point of the Statute was to become an area of conflict and the main principles were the first to be disregarded.[5]

It may be that within ten years of its passage, the Statute was widely regarded as a dead letter due to the lack of any effective mechanism for enforcement. Yet when it suited their purpose, employers and journeymen would appeal to authority to enforce language in the statute favourable to their interests. Compulsory registration for all masters, journeymen and apprentices was proposed. Alternately, the idea of allowing offenders to become legal by paying a fee to the Crown was proposed repeatedly, even as late as 1638, but was probably never put into effect.[6] On occasion, when it suited the interests of the Crown, the early Stuarts supported the interests of craftsmen over traders. The Crown

3. Kellett 1958, p. 382. Attempts to ban construction in the suburbs or to force suburban craftsmen to join the city guilds were largely unsuccessful.
4. Kellett 1958, pp. 381–4.
5. Leeson 1979, pp. 59 and 63.
6. Unwin 1963, p. 141.

saw wisdom in arguing for protectionism as a reason why the King should be allowed control of taxation. The cash-strapped Stuarts soon saw the granting of monopolies as an important source of extra-parliamentary revenues for the Crown. By this means, the Crown supported the growing wealth and power of merchants, but the Crown also sought to regulate the effects of this growth. The new opportunities for merchants came from both exports and re-exports.

> There was wealth from the trade plunder voyages to the West and East Indies, wealth from the great export of cloth which the Crown channeled through London to the distress of other cities, wealth which flowed into larger-scale farming and larger-scale manufacture, with London's clothing trade employing thousands (even the glovers numbered 400 shop-holders and 3,000 workpeople). This wealth the Crown sought to tap by tax, excise, and charter fee, or by joining in the business ventures which seemed to make money out of nothing. If there was advantage (the seventeenth century name for profit) in trading spices, cloth or the lives of Black Africans, there was even more in trading in money. Worthy Puritan merchants were ready to make 50 percent on loans to brothers of the faith colonising the bleak New England shore, though the Bible said usury was a sin and even Parliament said 8 percent was enough.[7]

The unprecedented expansion of English commerce had many ramifications for the conflicts that would dominate most of the seventeenth century. Hence merchants were near the centre of the disruption.

The crisis of the early seventeenth century

Upon the death of Elizabeth and the accession of James I in 1603, the bringing together of England and Scotland under the same king meant that England no longer needed to defend the Scottish frontier. As an island nation, England was also spared the need for a standing army or the ravages that war had frequently brought to France, and would soon devastate the German provinces and much of Central Europe in the Thirty Years' War. In 1604, England made peace at last with Spain. But James had inherited a significant war debt from Elizabeth.[8]

---

7. Leeson 1979, p. 60.

8. England was no exception in this regard; the only European governments not financially overextended in 1600 were Denmark and Bavaria. In particular, the Spanish budget was sorely overextended, a combined effect of the inflationary effect of Spanish bullion on European prices, exacerbated by raids on Spain's transport vessels by English and other privateers; epidemics that claimed about ten percent of Spain's population in the 1590s; its limited financial manoeuvrability in relation to the church and its trading partners; and of course the exorbitant and fruitless Spanish Armadas sent to conquer England which had depleted the state's coffers more than once. It was in this financial condition that Spain entered the Thirty Years' War in 1618, and with the aid of hindsight

He also inherited an antiquated and nearly broken-down system of public finance and raising Crown revenues.[9] James's plans for a union with Scotland dominated the Parliamentary session from 1604–7. This, his first major project, failed, and it would take a full century before union could be achieved. James next turned to the matter of the Crown's debt – then totalling £280,000. He asked Parliament to pay off the debt, as well as to supply the Crown with a regular income. The total request came to £600,000, including the budget for the Royal Navy. Parliament grieved, asking that all forms of taxation should have parliamentary approval, castigating monopolies and seeking to curtail the powers of the Crown. James responded by dismissing Parliament.

Periods of arbitrary rule throughout the early Stuarts' reign resulted from an inability of Crown and Parliament to reach a compromise between the Crown's desire to increase its tax base and Parliament's desire to restrict the Crown's capacity to raise taxes without parliamentary authority. The conceptual framework of the time held that the monarchy was to 'live of its own', with Parliament only providing for its 'extraordinary' expenses. Unwilling to submit to Parliament's demands in return for a subsidy or an increase in its regular sources of extra-parliamentary income, the Crown turned to other non-parliamentary sources.[10] These included customs, the use of the prerogative powers of the Crown for monetary purposes, and the combination of social and fiscal policies. James turned to syndicates of businessmen – 'men of substance' – to collect customs duties in exchange for paying an annual rent to the Crown. By arrangement, the Crown simply drew upon these customs 'farmers' by means of 'tallies'. In effect, they became government bankers advancing loans to the Crown on the security of current and future customs revenues. The Crown also levied additional extra-parliamentary revenues by invoking its extraordinary powers through the prerogative courts, 'that residuum of the ancient duty of the king to act in the national interest'.[11] Employing a wide variety of methods, the Crown could, for example, levy an impost on any merchandise involved in foreign commerce, as foreign trade could fall under the category of conduct of relations with foreign states. 'Ship Money' could be so invoked when the King determined that the whole kingdom was in danger. Finally, the Crown also held what was equally a prerogative power – the power to grant concessions, in the form of charters, monopolies or patents. By tradition, authority over matters of economic and social regulation belonged to the Crown. Where Elizabeth had shied away from monopoly contro-

---

we can see how much at risk of losing its empire Spain was at the outset. 'This was a society', writes Upton, 'that repeatedly demonstrated that it was incapable of adaptation' (Upton 2001, pp. 73–90).

9. Wilson 1984, p. 89.
10. Brenner 1993, p. 666.
11. Wilson 1984, pp. 98–9.

versies, the early Stuarts set about incorporating a record number of new royal companies. Many, if not most, of the new companies were justified primarily on the basis of the ability of the petitioners to pay for their privileges.[12]

The relationship between the Crown and the merchant political elite of London, notably the directors of the East India Company, was one of constant collaboration. Many of the greater merchants were in charge of the tax farms set up a century before, and while their companies needed the Crown's support for the maintenance of their privileges against interlopers, the Crown also needed them as its principal lenders.

James faced an acute fiscal crisis for a number of reasons. The first was perhaps the exorbitant spending of the court, which was justified as a means of shoring up support among his retainers. More directly, the Crown's subsidy had fallen from £138,000 to £55,000 in the century before the 1620s.[13] In spite of expanding the extra-parliamentary income of the state through selling offices, Crown lands, charters and through increasing customs, the profligate spending of the Stuarts kept them in fiscal insolvency, and exacerbated the emerging crisis and conflict with Parliament. Taxing trade presented the best option for the Crown to make up the shortfall. For the King, this posed the danger of alienating at least a significant part of the merchant elite. But this was the last group the Crown had to worry about:

> If London's company merchant community and the royal government were thus natural allies, Parliament and the City's overseas traders tended to be natural opponents. This was because, from one point of view, Parliament was an amalgam of grower, manufacturing and outport interests, and because each of these interests had an understandable desire for freer trade and thus the weakening of the London merchants' companies and privileges.[14]

Quite unlike the company merchants, the landed classes who dominated Parliament 'no longer required immediate and direct access to political power in order to maintain themselves economically'.[15] Unlike lords in Eastern Europe who relied on extra-economic coercion to extract rent and feudal dues from the tenants, unlike the French aristocrats who increasingly relied on state taxation to support them in offices of state, and unlike England's merchant elite who were dependent upon the privileges they held at the behest of the Crown, England's landed classes:

---

12. Wilson 1984, p. 101.
13. Brenner 1993, pp. 199–201.
14. Brenner 1993, p. 203.
15. Brenner 1993, p. 204.

> were able to subsist very well off broad commercialized landed estates, from which they collected rising economic rents deriving from what were roughly free markets in land and labor. As a result, they were free to oppose arbitrary government in general and unparliamentary taxation in particular as straightforward threats to their absolute property. . . .[16]

The makings of a conflict were well in place by the beginning of James I's reign. And in 1604, the Commons shot the opening salvoes of this conflict when it passed a bill for free trade. James intervened to ensure the bill did not become law. In 1606, Parliament passed a bill to establish free trade with France, Portugal and Spain, and again the Crown intervened to put a halt to it.

In 1612, Robert Cecil, Earl of Salisbury and Lord Treasurer since 1608, died. Taking Robert together with his father William (Lord Burghley), the Cecils had provided the English crown with more than half a century of exceptionally pragmatic counsel. The younger Cecil had managed to reduce the Crown's debt from £1,000,000 to £300,000 in his first two years as Lord Treasurer. Under his successor, Robert Carr, a Scottish favourite, the debt rose in a year to £680,000, with expenditure outrunning revenue at £200,000 per year.[17] Cecil's pragmatism would be sorely missed, but the fiscal crisis of the Crown was not due solely to laxity in bookkeeping or profligate spending. England was entering a period of profound economic crisis. In 1614, the year Parliament reconvened, cloth exports from London reached their highest level at 127,000 pieces, up from 100,000 in 1600. The economic prosperity, combined with peace with Spain, and the 1609 truce in the Netherlands, suggested to contemporaries a return to economic normalcy and even increasing prosperity. Yet all sides knew that the peace was fragile, and had only deferred dealing with the issues that had led to war in the first place.[18] By 1622, however, cloth exports in the 'old draperies' had fallen to little more than half of their 1614 levels. It was the beginning of a long period of stagnation and intermittent depression, leading into the Civil War.

When Parliament reconvened in April 1614, impositions were now bringing in £70,000 per year to the Crown. Parliament would only agree to a grant if impositions were abolished; a conundrum. In June, James dissolved the 'Addled Parliament', which had failed to pass a single bill. The Crown's reputation was sinking, a result of the combination of the growing mistrust between Crown and Parliament; the exorbitant spending on royal (especially Scottish) favourites; the proliferation in sale of noble offices (seen to cheapen the status of peerage), Crown estates and royal charters; and the increasingly heavy burden of customs

16. Ibid.
17. Wilson 1984, pp. 92–5.
18. Upton 2001, p. 42.

and excise. Then, in 1614, the Crown struck a devastating blow to the Merchant Adventurers by giving sanction to a plan to reorganise England's export of cloths, a plan which would result in disaster. Unfortunately for the Merchant Adventurers, they had no recourse to Parliament, where the Commons was 'simply unalterably opposed, both by interest and principle, to the chartered commercial companies'.[19]

The plan in question ran as follows. Sir William Cokayne, a rich merchant, alderman and creditor to the Crown, along with his partners, had managed to convince James to grant a royal charter for a new company, the 'King's Merchant Adventurers'. The new company would achieve a dual objective: to break the virtual monopoly held by the (other) Merchant Adventurers, and to recapture England's position of predominance as cloth exporter to the Baltic region. The export of unfinished cloth, mostly to the Netherlands where it was dyed and finished, was seen as a net loss for England. The scheme required all cloths to be dyed and finished prior to export. But the highly-skilled crafts of dyeing and finishing were not sufficiently developed in England in order for England to compete with Holland. Worse, the Dutch took reprisals once the plan took effect, banning the import of English cloth. The new company quickly admitted defeat, and sought to obtain permission to export unfinished cloth. The old Merchant Adventurers were soon able to bribe their way back to having their old charter.[20] In the resultant crisis of overproduction, five hundred bankruptcies were reported. Unemployment soared and weavers protested in Gloucestershire and Wiltshire.

The Cokayne project was widely blamed for the economic slump that followed, and that continued through the 1620s. It was certainly a terrible blow to royal prestige, and exposed the dangers of leaving economic regulation to the 'well-meaning mercies of the royal amateur and his self-interested associates'.[21] The real causes of the long-term slump, however, were basically external, having to do with currency manipulations by local princes in Germany, Poland and the Baltic, resulting in higher prices for English goods in the Baltic region, and thus an export-slump for England.[22] The trade depression was significantly ameliorated by the expansion of exports in a line of 'new draperies' – bays, says, camlets, fustians – the only branch of cloth manufacturing to significantly prosper

19. Brenner 1993, p. 210.

20. Brenner comments: 'Naturally there was a price. According to one well-informed source, the Crown originally extracted an annuity of £20,000 a yard for granting the charter in 1617, but Cranfield persuaded Buckingham to accept in its place a lump-sum payment of £80,000. This was in addition to gifts and bribes to courtiers'. (Brenner 1993, p. 211).

21. Hill 1961, pp. 27–8.

22. Wilson 1984, pp. 54–5.

during this period.[23] Yet the 'new draperies', which had taken root in East Anglia upon the arrival of Flemish immigrants in the 1560s, would not reach their true peak until the 1660s. Meanwhile, Dutch competition and the disruption of markets due to the onset of the Thirty Years' War meant that markets continued to sag, though England was probably spared the worst by maintaining neutrality throughout the war.

The Cokayne project was an exceptional venture, but it was nevertheless part of a general trend to entrust monopolies to speculative investors.[24] The 'peculiarly English' compromise that had held the amalgamated companies of the Elizabethan period together – whereby merchants would observe the regulations that preserved the status of the craftsmen, while craftsmen would not interfere with the purely trading functions of the merchant – was now being upset. Seeking to preserve their status as honourable craftsmen in control over their own trade, small masters sought separate incorporation, and in some cases were successful. The Stuarts were willing – for the right price – to grant monopolies to individual masters, who paid a lump sum and an annual rent for the patent. Thus in 1604 the feltmakers gained a charter from the King, securing their independence from the haberdashers. In 1612, the leatherworkers began agitating for separate incorporation, which they gained in 1638. The problem faced by

23. Coleman 1977, pp. 62–4.

24. Unwin 1963, pp. 141–7 and 183. Unwin calls these speculative investors 'capitalists'. The contradiction in the following passage by Unwin is instructive: 'During the preceding century England had experienced the beginnings of that development which was to make her predominantly an industrial and commercial country. Labour and capital were acquiring a new mobility; and the population was leaving its settled abodes and customary forms of employment in order to meet the requirements of a wider economy of production. Henceforward the manufacturing interests of the country were to show a steady relative increase, and the agricultural interests a steady relative decline. In the end this process involved a corresponding gain of the town population at the expense of the country; but the immediate effect was not of this character; indeed, in many cases it was exactly the opposite. England's greatest manufacture was leaving its older seats in the privileged cities and boroughs for the freedom and the cheapness of the countryside; and the great urban industrial centres of the future were to be looked for in a number of prosperous villages and unincorporated market towns' (Unwin 1963, p. 139). What is problematic about this passage is the rather teleological statement that 'Henceforward the manufacturing interests... [would] increase, and the agricultural interests... decline' when at the same time Unwin tells us that the 'immediate effect' was an exodus of wealth and labour from the cities to towns in rural regions. Despite this trend, Unwin sees a clear linear progression from the guild to the factory, and any growth or accumulation in that sector is seen to demonstrate this. While assessing the impact of agrarian change is surely outside the scope of Unwin's study, the idea that agricultural interests underwent a steady relative decline *vis-à-vis* manufacturing in the *countryside* obscures the dynamic growth of agriculture in England, as well as the linkages between an evolving agrarian capitalism displacing peasants, many of whom find new employment in expanding rural manufacturing made possible by the cheapening of grain that was also a result of improved agriculture under conditions of agrarian capitalism.

small masters in these situations was one of raising sufficient investment to fully exploit the opportunities afforded by a chartered monopoly. In the case of the playing-card makers, they had to resort in 1637 to asking the Crown to save their enterprise. Charles obliged by making a weekly purchase of cards, in return for a fine on all cards made and sold in England, accruing to the royal purse. The Beavermakers' Company, manufacturing beaver hats very much in vogue at this time, attained independence from the feltmakers under a charter from Charles I. But the haberdashers and feltmakers ignored the monopoly. In 1639, Charles declared felt-making and beaver-making as separate callings. But in a problem peculiar to the method of craft organisation of that time, this proved the ruin of the beavermakers because they were prohibited from making mixed (felt and beaver) hats, the selling of which had been their primary source of income.[25] Ultimately, the movement by small masters seeking independence from companies dominated by traders ended in disappointment, as the new monopolies came under the control of larger investors. The expansion of markets undermined the ability of individual crafts to assert monopolistic control over the line of production. Lacking sufficient investment to carry on the enterprise and meet growing demand, incorporation afforded small masters the possibility of setting up a common fund, a 'joint-stock'. But in general, such schemes were unsuccessful and it was not until the mid-eighteenth century that conditions were ripe for applying the joint-stock principle to manufacturing at large.

In the 1620s, the slump in the wool trade meant not only that masters were ignoring apprenticeship clauses, but weavers complained that their wages were being abated as well. Many took to the roads in search of work. The ranks of the 'yeomen' within the companies swelled with embittered small masters and journeymen alike. Hill remarks that the discontent of the populace before 1640 has not been adequately brought out. The years 1620–50 rank among the lowest points for the economy in England's history. The collapse of export markets in the Baltics was exacerbated by periodic bouts of poor harvests and the plague. Revolts by unemployed workers in Gloucestershire in 1622 were cause for alarm. In 1625, an outbreak of the plague paralysed London's economy, bringing exports to a virtual standstill.[26] The so-called 'Western Rising' of 1628–31 involved plebeian protest against the Crown's plans to sell off parts of the royal forests in Dorset, Wiltshire and Gloucestershire to courtiers and speculators. At issue was the loss of common rights on the forests and adjacent lands scheduled for enclosure.[27] These protests took place in the context of poor harvests in the years 1627–9,

25. Unwin 1963, pp. 124–47.
26. Wilson 1984, p. 53.
27. Outhwaite 1991, p. 48; Wood 1999, p. 250. The forests in question were the forests at Braydon, the Forest of Dean and Chippenham Forest.

which continued through 1631. Participants in grain riots in the southern grain-producing counties in 1630–1 were protesting primarily against the siphoning off of grain surpluses from rural areas to meet the growing demand of the City during a time of grain shortage. While it was widely understood that poor harvests resulted from poor weather, and that resulting grain shortages were exacerbated by 'villainous' middlemen as well as the siphoning off of grain for urban consumption, there was also 'a long and widely held tradition which believed enclosure to be the real cause of dearth. Enclosure was held to withdraw land from tillage, raise the price of grain and increase (if not create) the risk of scarcity'.[28] Charles I's response to the crises of 1627–31 was to issue the *Book of Orders*, which instructed commissioners to seek out and halt the activities of middlemen seeking extra profits at a high time of grain prices through the practice of forestalling and engrossing of grain. At markets, or when buying directly from farmers, the poor were to be given pre-emptive rights to buy at charitable prices. Such orders put a heavy burden on local Justices of the Peace. The last such issuing of the *Book of Orders* came in 1631. The reason for the discontinuation of this practice may have had to do with the reaction to Charles's wide expansion of such royal prerogatives during the period of personal rule in the 1630s. Other forms of government-intervention during periods of dearth included restrictions on grain exports and restrictions on usages of grain. All these forms of intervention declined after the 1630s, and lacking central organisation, government intervention in the grain trade became piecemeal and less effective.[29]

The swelling of discontent and opposition to the arbitrary rule of Church and Crown in the 1630s and 1640s was in part driven by the sense of outrage by small masters and journeymen at their weakening ability to have a say in company affairs. The top grievance within the crafts was the violation of apprenticeship rules. It is worth considering to what extent the later demands for democracy on the part of radicals in the army during the Civil War were conditioned by the struggle to hold onto what democracy remained within the crafts. Disenfranchised within their own companies, craftsmen may have transferred their thoughts of gaining enfranchisement to doing so in that greatest of companies, the state. While John Lilburne was a Leveller and Gerard Winstanley a Digger, both had experience among the rank-and-file of London's trading companies. Charters granted the power of selecting officers to the 'commonalty', which to the small masters and journeymen quite certainly meant the 'freemen' of the company. But to lawyer Edward Coke and the livery of the clothworkers, it

28. Walter and Wrightson 1984, pp. 112–13 and 116. The belief that enclosure caused or exacerbated grain scarcity was central to the Midland Rising of 1607.

29. Outhwaite 1991, pp. 35–43.

meant the master and wardens only. The yeomen Founders protested this move in their own company by refusing to pay their quarterage.[30]

The high grain prices of this period were an encouragement to enclosures of arable land. Where high prices for wool had encouraged enclosure of pasture in the sixteenth century, the trend now reversed. The Tudor and (less emphatically) the early Stuart régimes had imposed fines for enclosures. The first bill facilitating enclosure was 1621. But the monarchy under Charles I, during the period of personal rule, resumed the practice of fining enclosers, fining 600 persons between 1633 and 1638. Archbishop Laud's unpopularity with the gentry stemmed in part from his stern opposition to enclosures. But the Crown itself enclosed fields, and granted approval of enclosures to its friends, in particular to those who loaned it money.[31] The struggle over enclosures not only took place on open fields, but also over commons, marshlands ('fens') and forests.[32] Dorset and Wiltshire saw particularly strong opposition to enclosure. Led by the fictitious 'Lady Skimmington', a male figure dressed in women's clothes, a band in the Forest of Braydon revolted in defence of the loss of access to the commons

30. Leeson 1979, pp. 60–70.

31. Professor Wilson (Wilson 1984, pp. 103–5) writes: 'No aspect of early Stuart policy . . . illustrated the desperate ambiguities of the royal situation better than the manipulation of Crown Lands'. Under James, estates were granted away or sold off in large numbers. The 1607 survey of Crown lands was motivated by a search for unimproved lands to be drained or otherwise improved. Wealthy landowners and tenants lent their support, but commoners resisted. A drainage scheme at Hatfield, promising handsome profits, found the local commoners of the Isle of Axholme rising in protest to destroy the works as an invasion of their common rights. 'A monarchy committed to a high view of its social responsibilities towards the poor was thus tempted to betray its own professed ideals. It was the royal advisers who invented an ingenious method of extinguishing common rights to make way for improvement. The Commissioners of Sewers would lay an impossible tax on land (usually common) judged to be 'hurtfully surrounded' by water. If the tax remained unpaid, the community would be adjudged in arrears with its rates and the commons could be sold to an 'undertaker' to drain. His reward was a proportion of the land drained. In the earlier stages of the drainage craze – as late as the early 1630s – the largest beneficiaries seem to have been the large local landowners – men like the Earl of Lindsey, Sir Anthony Thomas, Sir John Monson and others. As the King's finances declined, he began to exact a larger share of the profit and demand more say in the management. After seven years of wrangling, Charles took a full third of the acreage drained in 1637–8. The King had effectively to assume the role of entrepreneur himself in order to make sure that he secured a large enough bite out of the improved acreage dispute between King, local landowners, drainage contractors and peasantry. The monarchy thus became a party to local feuds, sharing the hatred that was vented on the local improvers'.

32. The use of 'forage crops (clovers, sainfoin, ryegrass and to a lesser extent turnips) and floated water-meadows (that is irrigated pasture), spread very widely, though far from uniformly, from the middle years of the seventeenth century': Jones (ed.) 1974, p. 129. More fodder meant more animals and more animals meant more manure, more manure meant higher grain yields and the ability to expand arable onto lands formerly suitable only for pasture.

through enclosure. It was not to be the last time that a rebellion against capitalist intrusion upon customary right would be led by a fictitious male personage dressed in women's clothing. As an act of protest against enclosure, the tearing down of wooden fences had a dual advantage: the barriers themselves could be rendered ineffective, and the wood could be carted off to be used as firewood.[33]

Enclosures of arable lands, of course, resulted in the displacement of peasants. They joined the swelling numbers of the dispossessed who had no rights to speak of. There were insufficient employment opportunities to absorb dispossessed peasants, decommissioned soldiers and those otherwise disenfranchised after a long period of population increase that was now slowing. As wages fell in relation to prices, the poor faced extreme hardship. This explains the 'general background of potential unrest' during the early seventeenth century. Vagrancy was punishable by whipping. Entry into the cloth-manufacturing trade was limited to forty-shilling freeholders under Queen Betty's Law. Justices of the Peace set wages for working women between the ages of 18 and 30, 'as though no woman over thirty was likely to be capable of working in the fields'.[34] But as the lower orders were generally less able to supply for their own subsistence-needs, their growing market dependence was a stimulus to the expansion of a domestic market in consumer goods – food, clothing, household-wares and coal for the hearth.

Parliament's civil war

The economic crisis of the early seventeenth century exposed the incapacity of the patrimonial system of royal charters to cope with the changing demands of the economy. There was a built-in contradiction in the state's financial system, exacerbated by the Crown's ever-increasing need for more revenues, and its reliance on customs as a means of meeting that need. For like other institutions within the economy, the Crown was steadily becoming more and more dependent upon an *expansion* of trade. The function of royal companies, however, was to maintain the quality and restrict the supply of goods in order to maintain high prices:

> . . . as the market widened, in Europe and beyond, so the rival possibility appeared of selling large quantities of lower-quality goods – as the Dutch had begun to do. In a competitive world the future lay with the lighter and cheaper New Draperies, produced in relatively free conditions, and so more adaptable to changing market demand.[35]

33. Bushaway 1982b, pp. 76–7.
34. Hill 1961, pp. 18–19.
35. Hill 1961, p. 29.

The companies were still needed for convoys and ambassadors, but neither they nor the Crown were committed to any concerted policies of actively expanding or protecting English commerce. The proliferation of new occupations, the unusual degree of social mobility, the unfolding of a *mass* consumer market in London; in short, the exigencies of an unfolding domestic market of unprecedented depth and scope produced needs that demanded a progressive economic policy not forthcoming from Crown and companies.

At root, however, a deeper conflict was at work. 'At every point, English "manufactures" were intimately connected with the land', writes Wilson, 'Crops like flax, hemp, saffron, woad were grown specifically for manufacturing . . . England's trade – in wool, leather, grain, hops, minerals – grew directly out of her land and farms . . .'[36]. So the unprecedented expansion of England's domestic market was largely if not primarily a function of the transformation of English agrarian social relations. What role then did merchants and commerce play in this transformation? The theory of agrarian capitalism as first articulated by Robert Brenner and others was discussed in the Introduction. We now turn to a discussion of Brenner's novel interpretation of the English Civil War in order to arrive at an understanding of the ways in which the events of 1640–8 did and did not prepare the way for further transformations in manufacturing prior to the Industrial Revolution. The following passages are drawn primarily from Brenner's extensive treatment of the subject in *Merchants and Revolution*.[37]

We have yet to explore the role of Parliament as the representative body of the landed classes in English affairs of state. This, of course, will become crucial to our understanding of the civil wars of the seventeenth century. The nature and function of Parliament had changed and was continuing to change by the early seventeenth century. With the decline of feudal systems of extra-economic coercion, Parliament was increasingly the voice of an ever-more unified landed interest. The basis of this transformtaion was the squires' increasing reliance on economic rents from their estates. In the process, lords were disbanding their military retainters, thus giving up their capacity to coerce the peasantry, and instead yielding this capacity to 'a new form of unified state with an unprecedented level of jurisdictional and legal unity and a novel monopoly on the legitimate use of force'.[38] Economic rents provided lords with income sufficient enough for them to dispense with royal patronage in the form of office and perquisites.

The 'central fact about English social history between 1540 and 1640', writes Stone,

36. Wilson 1984, pp. 36 and 69.
37. Brenner 1993.
38. Brenner 1993, p. 651.

> was the growth in numbers and wealth of the landed classes and the professions. The number of peers rose from 60 to 160; baronets and knights from 500 to 1400; esquires from 800 to 3,000; and armigerous gentry from perhaps 5,000 to 15,000. The landed classes thus trebled in numbers at a time when the population scarcely doubled.[39]

Another title that grew vastly in number during this period is the number of Justices of the Peace. Stone gives the example of Hertfordshire, where there were 23 JPs in 1558 and 58 in 1662. Stone attributes the enormous growth in the gentry to the sale – often at artificially low prices – of Crown and Church lands. Stone observes that land was flowing into the hands of the gentry from two directions. On the one hand, rising rents and inflated prices were putting increasing pressures on copyholders and leaseholders. On the other hand, the aristocracy resold to members of the rising gentry much of the Church lands they had acquired after the dissolution of the monasteries. The changing fortunes of the gentry were so dramatic, writes Stone, that in some areas their standard of living grew fourfold in a century. This was further compounded by the transformation of the gentry, who with rising fortunes and growing confidence were coming to see themselves less and less as faithful retainers of local magnates or loyal subjects of the crown, and more as 'men of substance', who were 'full citizens of the commonwealth'. This growing economic strength and self-confidence of the gentry helps explain the shift of power toward the House of Commons in Parliament. Add to this the increasing power of the merchant community in both London and provincial port towns, and we see that between 1540 and 1640 there was 'an overall shift of wealth away from Church and crown, and away from both the very rich and the very poor towards the upper middle and middle classes'.[40]

Quite unlike the situation in France, Germany or Poland, the relationship between Crown and gentry in England was one whereby the King relied upon the landed classes to voluntarily staff the administration of local government and relied on Parliament to supply the Exchequer with revenues, significantly in the form of the land tax, which fell upon the landed classes themselves. English landlords 'ceased to require forms of state, of political community, either local or national, that had as one of their central functions the economic support of the members of the dominant class by means of the maintenance of *politically-constituted forms of private property*', whether in the form of levies on peasants (feudal lordship) or by constituting property in the form of central or local offices supported by peasant taxation.[41] Politically constituted property was not extinct

39. Stone 1972, p. 72.
40. Stone 1972, p. 75.
41. Brenner 1993, p. 651. Emphasis not found in the original.

however, for the monarch, being a great patrimonial lord in his own right, could mobilise the resources to sustain his own following – the 'patrimonial group' – that was dependent upon politically-constituted property.

England's landholders had long relied on the common law to protect their rights to private property in land. Strict enforcement of common-law rights of property would protect their rent-yielding lands from encroachment, would uphold their claim to absolute private property in land against the claims of peasants seeking to maintain or recover what they perceived to be their customary rights to land use, and would ultimately reserve to them the right to evict landless squatters. The Crown's administrative and financial dependence upon the landed classes allowed them to obligate the Crown to collaborate with them. Thus Parliament served not only as a forum to ensure their interests and their property, but also as the vehicle for collaborative governance with the Crown. The landed classes were involved continuously in making commercial policy and regulating manufactures for the growing domestic market.

But this arrangement was beset with tensions. With limited patrimonial followings of their own, lords had limited ability to check the Crown's tendency to exact greater levels of taxation for the purpose of expanding its patrimonial group in a move towards arbitrary rule. So, on the one hand, lords required a powerful state with a monopoly on the legitimate use of coercive force capable of enforcing their claims to private property and reducing the threat of local neo-feudal magnates. But on the other hand, they needed to limit the power of that state to defend themselves against over-taxation and the threat of arbitrary rule. The conflicting goals of having a powerful, centralised administration versus having a smaller, cheaper state tended to create disagreements between and among the landed classes themselves. The issues that tended to exacerbate the tensions between Parliament and the Crown involved taxation, use of administrative resources and especially those resources attached to the church hierarchy. These were often touched off by disagreements over foreign policy. The threat of papacy at home and abroad remained a high priority in the minds of the Protestant majority, and so they saw a Calvinist-Protestant state as essential to defending their interests. To this end they were willing to allow the expansion of taxation and state bureaucracy, even under the early Stuarts. Yet at the same time they sought royal acknowledgment of Parliament's perceived liberties and rights. The different outlooks on the role and nature of the state began to take on a permanent ideological character, anticipating the later development of political parties.

The Crown had good reason to resist an anti-papist, Protestant foreign policy. For one thing, alliance with the Dutch republicans was not in itself an inviting prospect for the monarchy. Elizabeth's chances of finding a suitable spouse had been brighter during periods when she could maintain an alliance with France or Spain. The fiscal weakness of the Crown could also be aided by an alliance with France or Spain. Elizabeth had recruited Catholics and over-zealous Calvinists to her administration, balancing them off one another to retain her authority. Charles I leaned more heavily on the Church, cracking down on dissent. But the less trustful wing of Parliament was already forging alliances with Puritans and Dissenters. This provoked controversy just as the Crown's expansion of extra-parliamentary forms of taxation did.[42] Initially, company merchants were content to acquiesce to the extension of customs duties under the early Stuarts, in exchange for the maintenance of their charter privileges. But as we shall see, this had its limits.

The Bohemian Revolution of 1618, which sparked the Thirty Years' War, brought the differences between Parliament and Crown to the fore.[43] In 1621, the Protestant cause in Europe appeared bleak. Parliament took up debate on foreign policy and took a militantly anti-Spanish position, favouring 'war by diversion' (supporting the Dutch so as to divert Spanish resources from Bohemia) and a 'blue-water' policy of attacking the Spanish fleet in the Americas. In 1624, Parliament won a minimal commitment from James to pursue an anti-Spanish foreign policy. But as Charles veered from the course and Parliament's support fell off in 1625–6, Charles responded to growing opposition by dismissing Parliament. Each side now sought political alliances, with religious differences coming to the fore. Charles consolidated his support from the Arminian clergy, granting high church appointments. Parliament in turn sought alliances in the counties, and among the militant Calvinist clerics and in London. In London, resistance to the Crown could be found not only among Dissenters, but also among small masters embittered by company merchants' control of trade, journeymen unable to advance, and an ever-expanding pool of paupers unable to find sufficient employment.

---

42. For the foregoing, see Brenner 1993, pp. 651–5.

43. When Ferdinand I, the Catholic Hapsburg ruler of Bohemia made a decision to curtail religious toleration for Protestants and Hussites, Bohemian nobles in Prague registered their protest by throwing two of the king's advisors out of a castle window, whereupon they landed in a pile of manure and survived. A year later Ferdinand was deposed, and Protestants and Hussites in Prague sought to replace him with the Elector Frederick, son-in-law to James I. If successful, this would have given Protestants a majority of the seven votes necessary to elect future Holy Roman emperors. The Catholic Hapsburgs ruthlessly counterattacked. James sought to secure an alliance with Spain and a Spanish marriage in hopes of a handsome dowry that would alleviate his financial troubles. Parliament sought an alliance with the Protestants in Europe and war with Spain. A ferocious campaign of propaganda was launched, and James responded to the 'stinging petition' on religion in 1624 with repression. He promoted the Arminian clergy, who held fewer grievances against Catholicism than other Protestants, and broke with his policy of a balance of power among religious tendencies. The result 'was a period of not insignificant political polarization, foreshadowing in important ways . . . the polarization of the later 1620s and indeed that of 1639–1641' (Brenner 1993, pp. 674–5).

Yet by 1626, Charles's attacks on the company merchants made them ready for resistance, too.[44] A forced loan and impounding of supplies provoked a reaction by merchants to refuse to ship any goods. Significantly, the East India Company shied away from the revolt, the Merchant Adventurers did not.[45]

Even if such taxes affected them minimally, the parliamentary landed classes offered 'consistent, militant and principled opposition to unparliamentary taxes on trade'.[46] Arbitrary taxation threatened the parliamentary liberties that were now central to the property rights supporting their existence. Thus on 24 June 1628 Parliament deemed extra-parliamentary taxation 'a breach of the fundamental liberties of this kingdom' and encouraged resistance.[47] But the company merchants held a contradictory position in relation to the Crown. They feared arbitrary rule, but were dependent on the Crown for their privileges. In light of the revolt by many company merchants against the Crown, it was clear by 1629 that Charles had to reconsolidate their support. As the Crown reined in the chartered company merchants, Parliament set about making alliances with merchants who stood in opposition to the monopolies granted to the old company merchants.

These were the colonial interlopers, the 'new merchants'. By this time, the American trade had posed too much risk for the old company merchants. So the trade was left to a new merchant leadership that, after some time, and due to some spectacular commercial and productive innovation, enjoyed success in tobacco and later in sugar planting. These merchants did not depend on the crown for politically-constituted forms of property, but rather favoured 'free competition' in trade. In 1629, key members of the new merchant community sought to undermine the East India Company's monopoly over Indian trade.[48]

---

44. 1624 was a high point in the Commons' attack on company merchant privileges, as Charles I and Buckingham gave their blessing to an assault on the Merchant Adventurers and refused to renew the Virginia Company's charter, enabling the Levant East India Company combined to gain ascendancy. In 1626, Charles removed control of the customs farms from the merchants. Thereafter Charles allowed England to drift into a war with France, an act which was 'simply incomprehensible' to city merchants trading with that country (Brenner 1993, pp. 237–8).

45. In 1626 Charles imposed a forced loan, imprisoning many resisting MPs. In reaction to a seizure of a shipment of currants, merchants revolted against unparliamentary impositions of tonnage and poundage. This galvanised merchant opposition in the City in 1629, climaxing in a complete halt of merchant trade and thus curtailing a major source of Crown revenues (Brenner 1993, pp. 197–239).

46. Brenner 1993, p. 670.

47. Brenner 1993, pp. 672–3.

48. Brenner 1993, p. 115 and pp. 170–81. Where in the 1620s new merchants Samuel Warner and Gregory Clement faced penalties for transgressing on the privileges of the East India Company, by the 1630s the new merchants had gained sufficient strength to make a serious challenge to the older City monopolies. By 1641, William Courteen, son of the Anglo-Dutch merchant and lender to the Crown of the same name, could demand

Initially the interlopers invaded the trading territory in West Africa held by the English Guinea Company, which was weakened as a result and was thus compelled to pick up the slack by becoming a major supplier of slaves. This was the starting-point of large-scale slave trade to the Americas and the so-called triangular trade between Europe, Africa and the Americas.[49]

The stage was now set for conflict within London itself, which was dominated by 'profoundly oligarchic political and ecclesiastical institutions'.[50] The control of city government by the Arminian clergy and the old company merchants was deeply resented and was matched by a profound radicalism among large sections of the London populace. This radicalism was driven by support for Parliament's calls for religious and political reform. Through a complex series of events in 1641–2, the City's Common Council was elevated to power over the aldermanic court, and the radicals came to power in a City revolution, with the relatively small, and narrowly-based, colonial-interloping new merchants playing a pivotal role. 'The new merchants' social origins and their continuing participation in domestic commercial activities gave them strong and extensive ties to that broad layer of City shopkeepers, mariners and artisans who largely made up the City radical movement'.[51] For Parliament, the radicalisation of the City was only a necessary evil, and this evil was a major source of the split in Parliament that led to the Civil War. The principal need of Parliament for the resources of London was for an army, as the landed classes no longer had their own private military followings. London was both the most strategic politico-military base in England, and also held the necessary men and material for the construction of a formidable army. Yet the urban masses of London posed the greatest threat to social order. The city's growth was astonishing, and this created serious problems of law and order. Crime was rampant. So for a large section of the landed classes, the sanctioning of a mass movement and the subsequent necessity of pursuing further religious reform were going too far.

It was foreign policy that touched off the dispute that led to Civil War. Charles had stopped short of an alliance with Spain, but when revolt broke out in Scotland, he faced pressure to seek Catholic support within the Isles and moved toward a real alliance with Spain.[52] This provoked a reaction from Parliament in the form of a legislative revolution. Parliament sought to ban taxation without its consent, and to eliminate the prerogative courts (Star Chamber and High

---

and receive compensation from the Crown when instructed with other interlopers to cease violating company privileges. By 1645, the new merchants were in a position to essentially dictate the terms of a merger to the Company.

49. Brenner 1972, p. 382.
50. Brenner 1993, p. 319.
51. Brenner 1993, p. 395.
52. See Brenner 1993, p. 690.

Commission). It attacked monopolists, it moved towards the adoption of a militant campaign against Spain in the Atlantic and West Indies, it attacked the religious programme of Bishop Laud and impeached both Laud and the Earl of Strafford (who was subsequently executed) and it sought to establish Parliament as a permanent and indissoluble institution. This bold programme of the Long Parliament was facilitated by Parliament's alliance with the London radicals.

Parliament's radical initiatives in revising the London constitution, attacking company merchants and pursuing Puritan revolution from below all led to a strengthening of support for the Crown amongst conservative landed classes and company merchants from the latter half of 1641. The King drew upon support from overseas merchants to counter Parliament's base in London. He also warned of the threat of popular and religious radicalism, and a rising of the common people who would 'destroy all rights and properties, all distinctions of families and merit; and by this means this splendid and excellently distinguished form of government end in a dark equal chaos of confusion . . .'.[53] Charles also drew support from the Company of Hostmen in Newcastle. An army of Scottish covenanters blocked the port of Newcastle in 1640, choking the supply of coal to London for three years, and finally forcing Charles into a truce whereby the supply would be released in return for payments to maintain the Scottish army in Northern England. Both King and Parliament vied for the support of the hostmen, and they came down on the side of the King. But the victory of Parliament would lead to the decline of the Royalist faction and the introduction of 'new blood . . . into the coal industry through the sale, doubtless at bargain prices, of "parts" in collieries belonging to delinquents. Furthermore, the area of coal mining was expanding'.[54] This division and expansion of mining in the Tyne would open up the field to interlopers.

Large-scale anti-enclosure protests over large parts of England as the nation descended into Civil War in 1640–3 were put down by the Crown, but with full support of Parliament. During the Civil War, much of the land that had earlier been drained by the Crown 'was seized back by the peasantry, some of it permanently'.[55] In effect, Professor Hill tells us, this background of unrest caused both sides in the civil-war dispute to assume that the threat of an uprising would induce the other to agree to their terms. The acute depression in trade also factored into the crisis. In 1640, export of unfinished cloths, still England's prime

53. From 'His Majesties Answer to the Nineteen Propositions of Both Houses of Parliament', in Wootton (ed.) 2003, p. 174.

54. By the time Ambrose Crowley leased his first mine in 1691, the hostmen would be in full decline. They were coming 'to recognize that their interests were really the same as those of the unfree mine owners, and to constitute themselves as a distinct group in the coal trade' (Sweezy 1938, pp. 17–21).

55. Wilson 1984, p. 105.

export commodity, had fallen to just 45,000 pieces.[56] Charles was successful in converting significant sections of the parliamentary classes to accepting the ecclesiastical hierarchy as indispensable to the protection of tradition, privilege, order and property. Rising gentry who had succeeded in securing offices at Court or in insinuating themselves into lucrative fen drainage projects were naturally more likely to support the Crown; those who felt their power weakened by exclusion were more likely to support Parliament.[57]

The event that brought matters to a head was the rising of the Irish. '[A]t last liberated from Strafford's iron hand' the Irish revolted in October of 1641 and 'hundreds, probably thousands, of Englishmen were killed'. If the revolt was to be crushed, an army had to be raised. But who should control the army? By the narrow margin of 11 votes, Parliament adopted the Grand Remonstrance, 'a comprehensive indictment of royal policy'.[58] By now, parties had formed. The King responded with defiance. He refused a plan by Pym and Bedford to settle and subsequently sent an armed contingent to the House to arrest Pym, Hampden and three other opposition leaders, who took refuge in the City, drawing mass support. The King had lost control of London, and announced he would go to Scotland. Parliament's only means of warding off an absolutist coup was to sanction the revolution in London. For a near-majority of the landed classes, however, even if most abhorred the Laudian program, entrusting reform to the King was preferable to opening the door to the 'root-and-branch' challenge to hierarchy and social order. The result was civil war.

Emboldened by Parliament's support, the radicals went on the offensive. First of all, the new merchants had not waited for Parliament to put a coherent anti-Spanish policy into effect. From 1638–41, they engaged in a highly successful series of raids against Spanish possessions in the Caribbean. And in response to the Irish uprising, they organised the Additional Sea Venture to Ireland largely on their own resources. This act of Puritan imperialism involved 1,000 foot soldiers, 500 seamen and 15 vessels who set off at the end of June 1642 for 'six months of private war and plunder in Ireland'.[59] This was accomplished despite Parliament's exaction of £100,000 from London for its efforts against the king. The striking ability of the new merchant leadership to organise on an autonomous and voluntary basis can be explained in part by their preference for an independent religious view. Meeting in new independent churches provided a source of exceptional solidarity.

---

56. Compare this with the level of exports in the sixteenth century. Between 1559 and 1600 they 'did not fall below 93,681 or rise above 103,132 ... These levels were sustained, or exceeded, until after 1614' (Brenner 1993, p. 8).
57. See Wilson 1984, pp. 113–14.
58. Hill 1961, p. 94.
59. Brenner 1993, p. 404.

As the war had brought initial successes for the royalists, the London radicals in control of the militia committee organising the parliamentary army pursued their own demands. They called for putting the squeeze on royalists to sequester funds for an independent army of godly citizens and replacement of the unsteady aristocratic military leadership with more resolute commanders. This initiative suited Parliament's need for fundraising, but the funds were insufficient. Parliament set up its own commission for customs, specifically to support the navy. With the old company merchants backing the Crown, Parliament turned to the new merchants, who provided over sixty ships. When the customs-commission collapsed, Parliament started to tax the royalists in September of 1643. In the summer of 1643, as the tide was turned from the near collapse of parliamentary forces through to victory in 1645, the radicals lost their influence among the London citizenry to a more moderate group of Presbyterians and Independents.[60] The moderates sought to complete the Puritan revolution, but to suppress radicalism.

Parliament allowed the new moderate leaders of the city to construct their own citizens' force, but this was no match for the New Model Army. And although the radical element within the army continued to haunt Parliament by its cries for popular sovereignty, dismantling the army was not an option, since the danger of a return of the monarchy remained. Hence in 1647 and again in 1648 the army was able to march into London unopposed and place the city government under its control. Each time, this brought the Independents to power, and the colonial-interloping merchants rose to the pinnacle of their influence. They had remained quiet during the ascendancies of the political Presbyterians, but were now thrown back into the arms of the democratic radicals. The Army's invasion in effect completed the failed radical city revolution of 1642–3. A city militia was organised. A new army committee assembled with old radicals on board. Top municipal officers were purged.

Control of London gave Parliament control of the bulk of customs revenues as well as a vast reservoir of manpower.

---

60. The fall of Bishop Laud was followed by the emergence of a bewildering variety of Puritan sects, which alarmed orthodox Presbyterians and led to a series of controversies which were quite central to the Parliamentary debates of the 1640s. Among these sects were the Independents, who rejected the orthodox Presbyterian idea of regional Presbyters and sought full independence for each congregation. Orthodox Presbyterians accused the Independents of threatening the existence of the Church of England and of advocating tolerance for all Dissenters, claims which the Independents rejected (see Zakai 1989). Debates over religion during the tumultuous years of mid-seventeenth century England were central to the course of events, as George Yule (Yule 1970, p. 133) reminds us: 'religious radicalism was regarded as radicalism just as much as was political radicalism'.

> As long as London was under parliamentary control, the king could not win the war, but until 1645 he had enough resources to field armies in each campaigning season, adequate to keep the conflict going on fairly level terms militarily . . . It seems clear that [Charles I] was willing to risk any extremities to himself personally rather than yield any of the basic sovereign powers of the monarchy. This obduracy left the victorious parliamentarians at a loss.[61]

When Parliament's victories in 1645 turned the war permanently in its favour, what remained were mostly mopping-up operations. Attention now turned to the challenges arising from the first attempt in English history to sustain a standing army over an extended period of time. Desperation arising from the fact that regular pay of soldiers was gravely in arrears led to a wave of mutinies and threats of disbandment sweeping across more than thirty English counties and much of Wales in the spring of 1646. By 1647, régiments in 36 of the 40 English counties were variously involved in such actions as refusals to obey orders, threats of disbandment, systematic plunder or the seizure of officers or other officials.[62] The crisis was compounded by a disastrous harvest in the autumn of 1647, which came at the conclusion of hostilities. It was at this point in time that the influence of the Levellers peaked, with the circulation of the Agreement of the People and the debates at Putney between the radical leaders led by Colonel Rainsborough and the Independent-minded generals, notably Cromwell and Ireton.[63]

The radicals put forth an argument for universal adult male suffrage, demanding to know, if that were denied, what else they had fought for. The radical position had been outlined by many pamphleteers, most notably John Lilburne. Lilburne and other like-minded spokesmen were labelled 'Levellers' for their support for levelling hedges in opposition to the concentration of wealth brought on by enclosures, and their presumed intent to level property distribution in general. But as the Putney debate shows, the Levellers actually stopped short of calling for a redistribution of property, most probably because they were small property holders themselves.[64] When pressed, however, Rainsborough, speaking for the army radicals, did give higher position to the rights of persons over

61. Upton 2001, pp. 101–3.

62. Morrill 1984, pp. 186–211.

63. Brenner 1993, pp. 427–515; Mendle (ed.) 2001. The Putney debates, of which we have a full transcript, provide an astonishing, detailed account of the rationale of both the so-called Levellers and the generals of Parliament's New Model Army. Not all of the radicals for whom Rainsborough spoke were as radical as Rainsborough himself. Many would likely have been content with something less than absolute male suffrage.

64. It was left to another radical sect to call for abolishing private property and levelling of classes, namely the 'Diggers', whose most prominent spokesperson was Gerrard Winstanley. The Diggers saw themselves as the 'True Levellers,' and even attempted to set up what might be understood as early communes. Though couched in religious language, Winstanley's writings anticipate later communist and socialist ideas.

the rights of property. To this, General Ireton responded that only those with a fixed or permanent interest in society have a real stake in the state. The rest are little different from foreigners, and so if they are unhappy with the shape of government, they are free to leave. The radicals were unimpressed with this argument, and it is clear that by the end of the debate, neither side had convinced the other.

> The Levellers keep insisting on their native rights and ask what the soldiers have fought for in the war, if they are now to be denied those rights . . . Ireton's reply is straightforward: what the army fought for was the right to be governed by a representative body and a known law rather than by the arbitrary rule of one man. And they fought for the freedom to do business and acquire property. Their true birthright is the English constitution itself, principles of property and government that have stood the test of time, and the security they derive from this constitutional order. To put it another way, the Levellers demanded something like democracy, literally 'rule by the (common) people'. Ireton offered them constitutional or limited government instead.[65]

For the brief period in which they were a party to be reckoned with (roughly 1647 to 1649), the Levellers were perceived by the ruling elite as posing a significant threat that needed to be eliminated. Was the defeat of the radicals a setback for democracy, costing centuries of lost progress? The radicals in the New Model Army believed themselves to be fighting for democracy as a means to preventing the worsening of the condition of the poor. Had they prevailed, democracy in their time would likely have made a tremendous difference in terms of improving the conditions of the working poor, at least in the short-term. Such a democratic programme might also have threatened the further development of capitalism. Universal male suffrage would take another three centuries and more to be achieved, by which time all of the substantive issues such as property rights and customary protections of the labourers' rights to regulate production had been decided against them. The increasing power of the rising class of landed property owners in seventeenth-century England, however, posed a formidable force united against democracy.

With neither the moderate Presbyterians nor the radicals enjoying sufficient support to win the day, the fate of the country lay in the hands of the middle-group of Independents who were now in the commanding position at the head of the New Model Army. Unable on the one hand to settle with the King, and facing the pressure of a rising radical movement within the army rank-and-file on the other, the army leaders were faced with the prospect of a revolutionary take over of state power. But in order to accomplish this, the army leaders would

65. Wood 1997, p. 87.

need to neutralise the influence of the Presbyterians, the Levellers, the Royalists and other factions in Parliament. Consequently, the political Independents in the city were in a position to exert extraordinary influence: 'They could firmly consolidate their new position of power in the City and nationally by virtue of the pivotally important political base they could offer a new Commonwealth government that was profoundly isolated from almost all elements within the old governing class and desperately in need of allies'.[66]

In the wake of the King's trial and execution in 1649, a year of acute depression, the social gulf between the artisan-based Levellers and the 'silken independents' became manifest. Many 'freemen' who had thrown their weight behind Parliament returned to find their shops occupied by 'intruders'. The grievances of small masters and journeymen were as hot as ever. The Levellers and the democratic movement were perceived by the Independents as a threat to social order and were destroyed. The principal power at this juncture, the New Model Army, sought regular sessions of Parliament, redistribution of seats, legal reform, and religious tolerance.

During the Commonwealth, a number of companies underwent a short-lived democratic revival. Leeson suggests that the contradictions within the position of the Levellers can be better understood by keeping in mind that within the company rank-and-file, both small masters and journeymen had ambitions that could threaten this 'class' solidarity. Journeymen tried to set up on their own. Small masters sought to expand their operations. It was by its very nature an unstable alliance between different ranks within a crumbling hierarchy.

Overall, the Commonwealth 'took on a rather distinctive political character – and projected a definite if limited radicalism – that distinguished it from all English governments that preceded and followed it'.[67] The Independents did have a vision: 'They wished to transform England, Scotland and Ireland into a godly Commonwealth, fit to be the leading actor in promoting God's plans for the world'.[68] For the Levellers, of course, this radicalism was pale indeed. But the Rump Parliament was nonetheless very radical by the standards of the times, too radical in fact for most pre-1648 and post-1660 MPs.

The Independents had no refined theory of politics, yet they were not merely reacting to events. The Commonwealth meant the achievement of their goal of parliamentary sovereignty, based in theory upon popular sovereignty, an idea that had been circulating as early as 1643.[69] But this was a popular sovereignty

66. Brenner 1993, p. 707.
67. Brenner 1993, p. 559.
68. Upton 2001, p. 105.
69. Brenner 1993, p. 564.

reduced to little more than parliamentary supremacy itself.[70] The programme included attacking privilege and opening careers to talent. They sought cheap and efficient government, a revamped salary and expenditure structure and particularly a reduction in the enormous budgets for entertainment attached to the offices of sheriff and lord mayor. Legal reforms were studied, but not seriously acted upon. The most striking successes of the Commonwealth were achieved in the area of commercial policy and diplomacy. A militant, expansionist foreign policy to secure the hegemony of English merchants over the Dutch was pursued. To this end, the Navigation Acts of 1650 and 1651 attempted to restrict the carrying trade to and from England to English ships, initiating what became known as the 'old colonial system' that was to last for more than a century.[71] Maximum investment, expansion and innovation in trade were encouraged.[72] The East India Company and the English Guinea Company were granted charters, but were subject to the new merchants' demands for reform and allowing the new merchants to become partners in the new joint-stock.[73] In short, the Commonwealth realised perfectly the aspirations of the new merchants. But this was its great weakness: the narrowness of interests it represented. When the Commonwealth's opponents in the army moved to dismantle it in 1653, it went with a whimper.[74]

---

70. Brenner 1993, pp. 707–8.

71. Hill 1961, pp. 97 and 134. Wilson 1984, p. 63 comments: 'With the navigation Act we have arrived at a fully fashioned conception of economic policy in an essentially national form. Its dynamic was no longer the achievement of social justice through Christian ethics working against private greed or exploitation. It was – supposedly – the welfare of the Leviathan'. Representing such a narrow range of political interests politically, perhaps the Commonwealth was pressured to pursue more vigorously policies that stood to benefit all in the interest of securing broader support. At the same time, however, it is worthwhile to consider the degree to which the imperatives of the emerging domestic market conditioned the need for a new maritime policy. There can be little doubt that it played a significant role.

72. Brenner 1993, pp. 707–8.

73. The founding of the Dutch East India Company in 1602 marks the first appearance of a joint-stock company. This is often cited as a key development in the growth of capitalism, allowing investors to purchase stock and achieve a higher rate of interest than they would otherwise have earned by depositing their money in a bank, whilst not themselves becoming actual *owners* of the means of production. Yet joint-stock as a form of business did not actually begin to become prevalent until the mid-nineteenth century, when capitalism was coming into its own. Moreover, the great joint-stock companies that traded in East India later became the anachronisms of their day, icons of the old monopoly school of doing business and targets of the 'free trade' touting New Merchants. The fact that this form of joint-stock thrived under conditions of industrial capitalism, and that some of the great joint-stock merchant companies survived as well suggests that joint-stock as a form could succeed under both capitalist and 'mercantilist' or rather pre-capitalist commercial economic conditions.

74. Brenner 1993, p. 709.

The generals of the army were divided between conservatives willing to come to terms with the 'natural rulers of the country' and those who would use military-dictatorship to push through radical reforms of law and church. The Barebones Parliament passed some of the radical bills which the Rump had prepared, but this deeply threatened men of property. Worse still was the affront of having the Leveller leader, John Lilburne, return to London from having been exiled on pain of death by the Rump. He argued that with the dissolution of the Rump his sentence was invalid. No jury could be found to convict him and he was exonerated, to the great joy of the London crowds. But those in Parliament sympathetic to the radicals failed to rally around Lilburne. 'The Barebones Parliament was dissolved without incident'.[75]

The war itself had caused great disruption, swelling the roads, once again, with vagabonds.

> Most of the vagrants were discharged soldiers and freed prisoners, those lucky enough not to have been 'barbadozzed'... But neither Cromwell's Protectorate nor Charles II's Restoration government 'suffered them to wander' to the extent that soldiers of previous wars had done. In 1654, Cromwell issued an order that discharged soldiers were to be free to follow any trade 'without let or molestation'.[76]

This gave a new meaning to the term the 'King's Freemen'.[77] It could only further dilute the expanding pool of craft labour, and thereby undermine the struggle by journeymen and small masters to preserve their status. Richer masters were in a position to take advantage.

Despite the inability of Parliament and the army to come to terms, morale had been raised by the generally successful war against the Dutch from 1652 to 1654. The army pushed forward with plans to reorganise the franchise under a new constitution, the Instrument of Government. Army and Parliament were unable to come to terms over ultimate control of the executive. Parliament was dissolved once more in 1655. The army set about reconstructing the administrative apparatus of the state. Local gentry were generally unwilling to serve, so men of lesser rank were in both local and central authority. Policies tended thereby to

75. Hill 1961, p. 114.
76. Leeson 1979, p. 71.
77. The original meaning, of course, goes back to William the Conqueror and the Norman conquest of 1066. William ensured that in each of the territories to be governed by his lordly knights, there would be 'freemen' loyal to the king and not the local lord. William died a year after the Domesday survey in 1087 and was succeeded by William II (King Rufus), an unpopular king who died in mysterious circumstances in 1100. The throne went to the Conqueror's youngest son, Henry I, who consolidated Norman rule and whose jurists were responsible for the common law, to whose courts only freemen and nobles had access.

favour the poor. Poor-relief funds that had been appropriated by local oligarchs were restored. Enclosures in some areas were checked. Town corporations were purged. 'The rule of the Major-Generals was honest and efficient', writes Hill.[78] But having crushed the radicals within its ranks and without, the army could no longer fall back upon the radicals as a base of support. Nor could the army turn to the landed classes. The army's refusal to submit to parliamentary authority confirmed the worst fears of the landed classes just as Charles I's dismissal of Parliament had done in 1629. It appeared that they had fought a civil war only to be subjected to an even more powerful Leviathan. Both the decimation tax upon royal estates and outright sequestering were failing to generate anticipated revenues. Still the burden of taxation upon the landed classes mounted. It was used to pay for a government vastly more expensive than the one that had been deposed, mainly due to the vast expense of maintaining the New Model Army. They were appalled by the army's repression, by the rising of lesser men into positions of governmental authority, and fearful that their own estates would soon become the object of decimation taxes to sustain the 'many headed monster'. 'Slowly the logic of events was driving the men of property to reunite'.[79]

When Parliament reconvened in 1656, most of its members were from areas where Royalists had been disenfranchised. It nevertheless put forward the same demand that Parliament had sought since its first confrontations with James I: limited monarchy, and offered Cromwell the crown. Recognising the need to compromise, the army accepted control of an upper house with the power of veto over a restored Parliament. For his part – and contrary to his romantic portrayal in film as a man too principled to even consider it – the historical Cromwell, as *Lord Protector* Cromwell, pondered the crown for a month before refusing. He surely recognised that his true power base was the army, and that upon taking the throne he would have to disband the army, at which point a Cromwell dynasty could not possibly survive. Cromwell must also have realised that his religious goals were equally unattainable. He sought to create 'a broadly-based national church, with toleration of radical Protestant groups outside it who were prepared to keep the peace' by which 'he hoped to permit the individual Protestant conscience protection from its enemies, whom he identified as Catholics and Episcopalians'.[80] Faced with the return of old enemies in the restored Parliament of January 1658, and in the midst of pursuing an unpopular and expensive war with Spain, Cromwell dissolved Parliament again in February. He died unexpectedly in September, having nominated his son Richard as successor to the title of Lord Protector.

78. Hill 1961, p. 115.
79. Hill 1961, p. 116.
80. Hutton 1993, p. 6.

Richard inherited a government that was bankrupt, and heading into a depression fuelled by war that would hit bottom in 1659. Unable to secure loans at home or abroad, he had little choice but to call upon Parliament for aid. New elections in December–January of 1658–9 produced a huge Parliament of 549 members, many or most of them obscure and lacking experience. Little was required of them to bring down the Protectorate. 'A paralysed and chaotic body would ruin the Protectorate just as effectively as a hostile one'.[81] Parliament's hostility to the military had already surfaced when it got its report on the nation's finances in April: 'It was certainly clear and concise. The government was now nearly £2.5 million in debt, its regular revenue was falling short by nearly £333,000 per annum, and it owed the army nearly £890,000 of arrears'.[82]

Parliament immediately sought to assert its control over the army. Richard went further, and declared the Army Council dissolved. In the midst of the political explosion, Richard summoned his soldiers and found that he had but two hundred men to match the thousands gathering at St. James's Palace in support of the army. The army forced Richard to dissolve Parliament once more. On 5 May the army restored a remnant of the Rump to Parliament 'and Richard retired into oblivion'.[83] Violence was now the only effective means by which the army could collect taxes. London's city government refused to co-operate. In the midst of this chaos, General Monck in Scotland was authorised by some of the recalcitrants to act on their behalf. Rich with funds recently supplied by the Scots, Monck was able to win over a sufficient number of sorely underpaid rank-and-file deserters from the army sent to confront him under Lambert that Lambert's army simply melted away. Monck then marched on and took control of London. A pragmatist, Monck cleared the way for new elections, the return of a Presbyterian-Royalist majority in Parliament, and the acceptance of Charles II's Declaration of Breda, which set the conditions for his return. On 25 May 1660, Charles II returned and the republic was ended with the Restoration of the Stuart monarchy.[84]

In tracing this complicated path through the civil wars and the Interregnum, a striking feature of the conclusion by way of Restoration is how quickly the landed classes were able to reunite after having split into opposing camps to fight a Civil War.[85] The Restoration amounted to a repudiation of the parliamentary revolu-

81. Hutton 1993, p. 29.

82. Hutton 1993, p. 35.

83. Hill 1961, p. 99.

84. Hill 1961, p. 100. Charles's conditions included 'an indemnity, settlement of disputes about land sales, payment of arrears to the Army, and liberty of conscience'.

85. Hill 1961, p. 121, cautions that we should not be deceived by the popular rejoicing at the Restoration. While 'Men of property were pleased to feel that law, order and social stability, liberty and property, were being restored with the King, discipline with the Bishops', those who were not so pleased did not dare to seem opposed to the current. But

tion of 1641. The Crown could once more pursue an open agenda of expanding its patrimonial group, and a subversive agenda of promoting Catholicism.[86] But for the time being, this posed the lesser of evils in terms of the varied threats to the landed classes and their interests in private property. The threat of papacy had by now largely abated, with Spain's defeat by the conclusion of the Thirty Years' War in 1648, with the Treaties of Westphalia and Münster.[87] With victory over Holland in the First Dutch War, England's primary commercial rival had

---

if the city radicals had suffered utter defeat by the end, those among the landed classes who had supported Parliament could reflect upon the significant accomplishments of the period, and the fact that they had escaped the threat of radicalism that they had unleashed, including the more real threat posed by the army and its cul-de-sac political trajectory.

86. While not religious himself, Charles II had been impressed by the Catholic monarchies during his exile and, more importantly, was well aware that Catholics in Britain had been the most steadfast royalists. Aware of this, the Earl of Shaftesbury launched what may have been 'first attempt by an aristocratic court faction to mobilize public opinion in order to secure control of the House of Commons and force a change of government on the king' (Upton 2001, pp. 145–6) by renewing public fears of a papal plot to bring absolutism and Catholic rule in Britain.

87. The Treaty of Westphalia of 1648 had three major outcomes: 1) the tacit granting of religious pluralism within the Empire; 2) the granting of sovereignty to the principalities of the Empire; and 3) the formal definition of borders to the emergent nation-states. Being an island nation with pre-defined geographic borders, Britain was thus little affected by Westphalia. More significant to Britain was the Treaty of Münster, which concluded the long war between Spain and the United Provinces. A long-time enemy and major rival in trade had been reduced in half a century from Europe's leading imperial power to a second-rate monarchy. 'The Spanish monarchy', writes Upton, 'disposing of the most powerful military machine in the world, had waged some 80 years of warfare to subdue the rebel United Provinces and had failed completely' (Upton 2001, pp. 57–61). Astonishingly, the now sovereign United Provinces, some 1.5 million souls strong, had managed to emerge from those eighty years of warfare as the most prosperous society in Europe, with an economy based upon serving as Europe's foremost entrepôt for re-export in grain and cloth (Upton 2001, p. 109). Holland also became a centre of banking and financial innovation. The war effort had been 'entirely financed by borrowing on public credit. That was why the public debt of the Union rose from 5 million guilders in 1607 to 80 million in 1715. In any other political context this would have spread ruin' (Upton 2001, p. 111). The implications of Dutch success for Britain were that Britain's long-time Protestant ally was now its major economic rival. But as the three Dutch Wars would demonstrate, Holland's fleet was no match for Britain's. Another implication was that Dutch financial experience would be brought to England when William of Orange 'conquered' Britain, as many Dutch prefer to view the events of 1688–9 to the present day. With the threat of Spain and of Holland out of the way, Britain's future eighteenth-century rival was obvious. France had not been sitting idle. By 1670 Colbert's reforms had effectively balanced the state budget, expanded France's manufacturing sector using government regulation, subsidies and tariffs, initiated the canals that made navigation from the Bay of Biscay to the Mediterranean possible and, most significantly, France began building a state-commissioned army that grew from 50,000 in the 1660s to 250,000 in 1672, peaking at around 400,000 in 1697, at the end of the War of the Spanish Succession, the first in a century of intermittent wars against Britain and its allies (Upton 2001, pp. 121–2).

been humbled. England's future rival for the next century would be France. The radicals had been soundly defeated and suppressed. The many-headed monster that was the New Model Army – the child of Parliament's unstable marriage (and subsequent divorce) with London's radical movement – had been eliminated. Paradoxically, the threat of royal absolutism was once more the primary threat to the programme of sustaining and elaborating a system of surplus-appropriation based upon an evolving agrarian capitalism. Equally as paradoxical, the frightening experience of the Interregnum provided the basis for a more coherent unity with which the landed classes would confront the restored Stuart monarchy.

The basis for this rediscovered unity was an even more deeply rooted interest in private property in land. The old hierarchical order of 'peers, knights, esquires, yeomen, retainers and customary tenants' that was already in deep decay before the war was now irretrievably shattered. 'The war itself destroyed many of the great castles ... With them went the great armouries and the stables of great horses for armed men'. The civil wars were 'the last echo of military feudalism.'[88] The first order of business in the House of Commons after hearing the Declaration of Breda was to confirm Acts of Parliament in 1646 and 1656 abolishing the Court of Wards, the authority that enforced feudal dues. In return, the Crown would henceforth receive a fixed annual subsidy of £100,000. This legal action is something the lords had sought since medieval times.[89] All sorts of legal ambiguities surrounding lordly rights of land ownership that had existed since at least the Statute of Merton of 1235 were now suddenly cleared up. Lords now had unlimited rights in their estates, 'an absolute power to do what they would with their own, including the right to settle the inheritance of all their lands by will'.[90] All land was effectively converted into freehold. Further, landholders were now free of all military and monetary services to the Crown, 'and of the burdensome

88. Wilson 1984, p. 4.

89. The idea of abolishing wardship (whereby during a minority in the family the land reverts to the King until the end of the minority, with possible fines attached) and purveyance (the King's right to levy supplies at below market costs when the royal household moved around the country, something no longer practiced) was first proposed in the 'Great Contract' submitted to James I in 1610. James had asked for £200,000 and the price proved too high. Hill remarks that the £100,000 Charles II received was a bad bargain for him, as it barely covered the loss of purveyance alone. For the landlords, however, it was a true bargain, relieving them of a form of taxation and shifting the burden to the poor in the form of the excise-tax (Hill 1961, p. 185). The total revenue per annum for the Crown voted by Parliament was £1,200,000. When receipts fell £250,000 short of what had been voted, a Hearth Tax of two shillings on every hearth (exempting the poor), was added in 1662 (Hill 1961, p. 186). In the last instance, the consumer or common householder could be called upon to cover revenue shortfalls. Such taxes were sorely unpopular, however, and often short-lived.

90. Hill 1961, pp. 126–7.

relics of feudal theory, by which, at the death of a tenant, land reverted to the lord'.[91] Since the law no longer obligated tenants to perform military service, landowners felt entitled to more from their tenants. As the land market became more fluid, with urban and mercantile wealth buying its way into the estate business, older families were under pressure to maintain their standard of living. The market in land was becoming a market in *rents*, and thus the competitive pressures of the market *compelled* landowners to seek the full value of rents.

The conversion only applied to those who held land under common law. The movement to win the same rights in land for copyholders was defeated. 'In no sphere was the defeat of the radical movement more decisive', writes Hill. Landlords were now free to evict copyholders in order to enclose or consolidate 'their' lands. The Prerogative courts that under the Tudors and early Stuarts had (rather tepidly) sought to check enclosures had been abolished during the Interregnum and were not restored. Protests during the Civil War had checked the enclosure of forests, commons and wastes. But 'Henceforth, encouragement of agricultural improvements was a major object of government policy; attempts to prevent enclosure were abandoned'.[92] Hill dramatises these developments in buttressing his case for treating England's seventeenth-century revolution as a bourgeois revolution.[93] Focusing on the historical moment when laws which England's lords had long sought to change were overturned can mean losing site of the long-term process at work. It is true that by means of revolution England's landed classes positioned themselves to be able to move their class agenda forward as never before, furthering what was a capitalist project even if they themselves were not 'capitalists' as such. But to equate a legal landmark with the economic transformations that it facilitates precisely misses the bigger picture. Perhaps seventy-five percent of farms were still unenclosed in 1660. The manorial structure and medieval custom did not simply disappear. A century and a half of struggle over enclosures lay ahead. And as we shall explore further below, the effort to expel custom from manufacturing would prove an even longer struggle. Yet one major outcome of the civil wars was the legal and political defeat of popular (and mostly urban-based) radicalism, which would not resurface for a century to come.[94] Since popular radicalism was a political force that the revolution itself uncorked, the character of politics after the Restoration was

91. Wilson 1984, p. 8.
92. Hill 1961, pp. 127–8.
93. Hill's embrace of the concept of 'bourgeois revolution' belongs to the more hesitant expressions of the concept than the unbridled expression of it in the 1940s, which Hill certainly abjured.
94. Unwin 1964, p. 210, writes: 'The democratic movement within the companies was the rally of a dying cause. As far as its immediate object was concerned, the practical results were very slight. After the Restoration they entirely disappeared, and the older influences resumed complete possession of the disputed ground.'

deeply similar to that before the revolution began. Seeing a bourgeois revolution in 1660 is thus very difficult. But we have yet to deal with the Glorious Revolution of 1688–9.

Restoration to Glorious Revolution

After the Restoration, landed property remained the basis of politics, but 'generally the social and economic purposes and consequences of landholding were changing, and with them its political significance'.[95] The market in leases for enclosed farms grew, but whole estates were also increasingly up for sale as land in general was losing its extra-economic character, and gaining the character of a commodity to be bought and sold freely. Lawyers who profited from the increasing litigation that a vigorous land market involves, along with wealthy merchants and financiers:

> all bought large estates, acquired knighthoods, baronetcies and even peerages, married their daughters into the gentry and aristocracy, and sometimes founded dynasties. Conversely, the younger sons of old gentry families commonly took to trade to make their fortunes . . . younger sons came to London, made a fortune in trade or finance and later reverted once again to their traditional status as country gentlemen.[96]

There was no strict legal definition for either 'gentleman' or 'yeoman'. Whether or not men of business who invested in land proved to be more efficient and frugal estate managers, the increasing social mobility gave the 'upper and middle classes a common stake in economic efficiency and a common interest in economic progress'.[97]

The Restoration marked the beginning of a century of relative stability and plenty. Food-prices were kept high by corn exports and a prohibition on corn-imports. Despite relative prosperity for the well-off, the expanding and increasingly market-dependent labouring class suffered hardship as wages rose steadily and real prices of most commodities other than grain fell. Government policy was gradually shifting from one of protecting the consumer to stimulating production and protecting the employer. Regrating and engrossing,[98] long-time taboos under guild regulation, were permitted in an act of 1663 designed to encourage

95. Wilson 1984, p. 8.
96. Wilson 1984, p. 10.
97. Wilson 1984, p. 15.
98. In this context, to 'engross' meant to purchase large quantities of a commodity in hopes of selling it later at a higher price, while to 'regrate' typically meant buying provisions that one would sell again in or near the same market where it was purchased.

the cultivation of wastes. Tea, known in Holland since mid-century, is said to have been introduced to England by Catherine of Braganza, who married Charles II in 1662. The first coffeehouse in England had opened at Oxford in 1650,[99] though as early as 1637 a Greek man was sighted drinking coffee in Oxford.[100] As the market widened and more people had larger disposable incomes, the consumption of luxury commodities such as tea, coffee, chocolate, tobacco, sugar, glass, watches and so on was gradually expanding among the middle and lower classes. It was the beginning of the mass market.

By the 1660s, the status of the small masters was generally in decline. They were being displaced 'by a body of larger employers on the one hand, and by a mass of journeymen on the other'.[101] The defeat of the radical politics and of the politics of the army they had had a role in creating meant a strengthened position of the employing classes as a whole. Many workshops employing, say, half a dozen labourers increased to a dozen or two. In each craft the struggle was increasingly one between yeomanry and livery, between the 'handytrade' and 'non-manual' elements. In some crafts, such as the yeomen carpenters, they came to accept their lot as waged labourers with little room for advancement. In most, the yeomanry continued to fight for their right to a say in company affairs, but it was increasingly a losing battle.

As noted, the disbanding of the New Model Army added to the surplus of men in search of work. The Act of Settlement in 1662 was meant, in part, to address vagrancy by empowering local Justices of the Peace to turn away from the towns any vagrants who might become a 'charge' on the poor rate. A new thinking about labour and poverty was emerging, one that saw cheap labour as 'the source of true riches'.[102] Landlords supported the export of corn because keeping the price of corn high meant both higher rents and labourers who were motivated to work for dear life. If it also meant higher wages, what was that to the landlord? It might put a tenant-farmer out of business, but there were plenty of others who could pay the rent.

> The assumption behind the [Act of Settlement] was that a pauper was idle, vicious, and rightless. The impotent poor received relief in their parish of settlement, at minimum rates. Workhouses were deliberately made unpleasant in order to discourage applicants for relief; so they helped to keep down wages outside. This harsh code was more effective in villages than in towns. Hence

---

99. By 1694, there would be two thousand coffeehouses in England, where clients would meet their patrons to make contracts, where lectures were given and promissory notes exchanged. London Science Museum, visit by Author, October 1997.

100. Bramah Tea and Coffee Museum, London, visit by author, October 1997.

101. Unwin 2001, pp. 198–9.

102. Hill 2001, p. 177, quoting the historian of the Royal Society.

> the drift to the greater freedom and economic opportunity of the cities, where a mass of casual labour prevented wages rising too rapidly and began to form that new phenomenon, the mob.[103]

Wilson does not doubt that the act led to 'grievous hardship', but he cautions against assuming it was motivated by the desire to ruthlessly exploit. The act served to protect the conscientious parish-based provisioning for their own poor from being inundated by paupers.[104] Leeson argues that the principal effect of the Act was to create a rootless workforce, more at the mercy of the new employers. Unemployed persons without papers from a local vicar or leading citizen willing to support them increasingly faced the whip if caught in a state of vagrancy. While the woollen trade continued to expand, absorbing surplus-population in suburban and rural spinning and weaving, an increasing number of labourers were without access to any means of self-subsistence, and without any serious opportunities for advancement in their trades. But where the structures of protection and regulation of trade were crumbling, custom survived and carried older traditions into the new era. Craft solidarity meant that brothers in the craft who were 'tramping' continued to be entitled to 'live off the box' if they could not find work.[105]

'Free Trade' in the later seventeenth century meant primarily the freedom to enter a trade without a royal charter. Everywhere, the principle of royal protection was under assault. Appeals to Queen Betty's Law were increasingly in vain.[106] In the rebuilding after the Great Fire of London (2–5 September 1666), the traditional half-timbered houses were replaced with new structures of stone and brick. Charles II 'had powers of conscription over the builder [but] chose instead to stimulate the reconstruction of the City by letting loose the forces of free trade', by ignoring the company controls enshrined in the Masons' charter. 'Forrens' were employed in the building trade. The Rebuilding Act of February 1667 'offered the freedom of the City for seven years (which could be extended for life) to all those who worked on the rebuilding'.[107] The London building crafts petitioned in vain, but continued to practice 'searches' inspecting credentials and levying contributions. But the trade would ultimately never recover from the blow.[108] The sawyers tried to form a craft union in 1670, but master craftsmen said it would bring the trade to a standstill.[109]

---

103. Hill 2001, pp. 177–8.
104. Wilson 1984, p. 137.
105. See Leeson 1979, pp. 68–73.
106. Leeson 1979, p. 75. On occasion it was strengthened, as in 1662 when a special act was passed affecting the Norwich worsted trade, limiting the number of apprentices taken in to one per journeyman.
107. Inwood 1998, p. 248.
108. Leeson 1979, p. 74.
109. Hill 1961, p. 178.

The fire itself dealt a blow to many trades in other ways. Shops and markets were destroyed. Stocks were lost, the Stationers' Company losing £200,000. The poor remained where the fire had driven them, typically outside the city walls. Devastating as the fire was financially, it presented the opportunity to reshape London:

> for its role as the centre of a large metropolis, to solve the problems of traffic congestion, overcrowding, inconvenient food markets, inadequate riverside facilities and fire danger which had grown worse as the population grew. At first, it was felt that the best way to achieve this would be to adopt one of the grandiose plans put forward within days of the Great Fire by Christopher Wren, John Evelyn, Robert Hooke and others for a completely redesigned city of wide boulevards and grand piazzas, a city fit for a great European monarch. By mid-September, though, the King, Parliament and the City had agreed that the practical and financial difficulties involved in adopting a plan which ignored all existing property rights, however attractive it might seem on paper, were insuperable.[110]

Tenants bore the greatest burden for reconstruction, and although a fund was set up to provide compensation, disputes over leases were widespread. Speculators and landlords seized the opportunity and the suburbs rapidly expanded westward. There, tradesmen relocated and set up shop and manufacturing grew up beyond the reach of guild controls. In order to entice 'unfree' craftsmen and shopkeepers to re-inhabit the vacant houses and shops in the old city, the city offered legal recognition for a low fee, dropped the prosecution of 'forrens' in 1672 and granted freedom to anyone offering to take up permanent residence in the newly built shops and houses.[111] Thus guilds faced loss of control on three fronts: in the suburbs, in emerging manufacturing towns like Manchester and Birmingham where there were no guilds, and in rising manufacturing trades in textile, metal-working and mining dispersed throughout the countryside. 'By the 1670s there were "illegal men" in all occupations'.[112] An influx of French craftsmen further weakened the ability of the guilds to control their trades. Machine, breaking by ribbon-loom weavers in London in 1675, protests against the Dutch Loom in Cockney in the same year, and protests by weavers in Colchester in 1676 and in Trowbridge in 1677 attest to the increasing frustration by journeymen-workers.[113]

These incidents had only a local and incidental impact on the textile trade. Norwich's new draperies were coming into fashion in the 1660s. And in the 1670s,

110. Inwood 1998, pp. 244–6.
111. Kellett 1958, pp. 382–3.
112. Wilson 1984, p. 177.
113. Hill 1961, p. 178; Wilson 1984, p. 194.

Devon's serges 'swept the board'.[114] Merchants and larger masters understood free trade as meaning as large and as cheap a workforce as they could employ. They attacked the principles of the Statute of Apprentices as 'common errors'. They became more and more reluctant to sanction 'the search'. Dramatic episodes within the company minute books tell of bachelors' companies being dismissed from the hall, or from the company altogether. Protests by the yeomanry in the form of withholding quarterage payments were met with wage deductions, or reductions in collections for the box. The Elizabethan companies were strained to the breaking point. The democratic impulse within the companies that informed the radicals during the Civil War and the Interregnum, was now channelled into attempts by journeymen to form themselves into new corporations to defend their collective interests. The trading classes viewed the incorporation of journeymen or small masters as a Pandora's box, and fervently opposed it on the grounds that it would be an 'evil example' for employees to have a separate organisation. But most journeymen were anyway unable to incorporate (as in the case of the tailors, or attempts by the nailers) and were driven to combine in secret.

Thus began the emergence of the 'friendly societies', which Unwin identifies as the direct ancestors of the modern trades unions. This new form emerged not only out of the old companies, but in the countryside as well. There, the wool trades had never had the same controls as the crafts, yet:

> a militant spirit showed itself. Where the law was unable or unwilling to protect their earnings from the attacks of the clothiers, the wool workers took to the streets. In Colchester and Trowbridge they marched to the sound of horn and fiddle and in Colchester the militia were called out. But in seeking independence from the clothiers, the woolcombers of a number of centres sought formal incorporation of the traditional kind. The Devon combers found Royal Charter too costly for them. In Coggeshall, the combers withdrew from the clothiers' company and formed a "Woolcombers 'Purse'."[115]

This purse inaugurated a 'corporation without a charter'. And such 'box' clubs began to become common. The purse could be used to look after the welfare of the members (as the masters were never less inclined to do so), as well as to raise funds to take 'intruders' to court. With the small masters now generally reduced to the same status of journeymen, the source of conflict between these two strata gradually began to fade.

The failure of incorporation by first the small masters and then the journeymen, and the passing of control of the companies into the hands of the trading

114. Wilson 1984, p. 291.
115. Leeson 1979, p. 77.

interest did not mean the journeymen were at this juncture completely reduced to the status of proletarians, as Unwin might suggest. We must consider what traditions, customs or privileges the emergent 'friendly societies' were seeking to preserve. Their trades would remain 'honourable trades' in their eyes for another century, and this had to do with how labourers in manufacturing continued to possess the means of production and to be in control of the labour process, as rooted in custom and enshrined in Queen Betty's Law.

The Second Dutch War began in the year of the Great Plague of 1665, lasting through 1666 – the year of the Great Fire in London – and ended when England was forced to make peace after the sailing of the Dutch fleet up the Thames to destroy English ships. These events were all a shock to the English economy. A brief alliance with Sweden and the Netherlands against France was reversed in 1673 when Charles entered upon the Third Dutch War in alliance with France. Secretly, he had signed a treaty with Louis XIV which gave him a subsidy in return for declaring himself a Catholic when the political weather in England permitted. Charles's sympathy for Catholicism (he declared himself a papist on his deathbed), led him to seek alliance with Catholics and also with Dissenters. He issued a Declaration of Indulgence, and Parliament responded with the Test Act, requiring that all government officials in the military service and the new and expanding civil service[116] declare for the Church of England and against Catholicism. Charles's brother James – Duke of York and heir to the throne – responded by resigning his commission as Lord High Admiral. In 1678, an alleged Catholic plot to assassinate the King led to a panic. Those suspected of being involved in the conspiracy were purged and executed. In the same year, Parliament moved to exclude James, an avowed Catholic, from the succession. Three parliaments were convened and rapidly dismissed by Charles between 1679 and 1681, and Parliament was not to meet again until after his death. Political parties that would later be known as Whigs and Tories emerged in this period. As tensions mounted, the lessons of 1640–60 were not lost on the landed classes. The Whigs in opposition to the King were not ready to risk anything like a civil war, and their opponents, the Tories, were thus successful during the period of personal rule that lasted until Charles's death in 1685. James II thus succeeded peacefully to the throne. He was even granted an annual subsidy of £200,000,

116. One of the major changes between the early and late Stuarts was the survival of a professional administrative apparatus from the Interregnum, during which time parliamentary control of government through committees had set new standards of efficiency. The exercise of royal patronage now involved primarily appointment to state offices, a responsibility which was itself passing 'slowly into the hands of ministers'. Returning royalists were forced to work with former Cromwellians. '[T]he naval code of discipline published in 1661 and the military code of 1666 were substantially those of the commonwealth' (Hill 1961, pp. 192–3).

about twice what Charles had received in 1661. In 1685, James successfully put down the risings of Argyll in Scotland and the rebellion led by Lord Monmouth, Charles's illegitimate son whom the Whigs had earlier promoted to succeed his father. The reprisals taken against the plotters in the Monmouth rebellion were particularly brutal. In the same year, James clashed with Parliament over the repeal of the Test and Corporation Acts, and dismissed Parliament. It would not meet again under his reign.

In 1685, the courts ruled that 'apprenticeship was necessary only for servants hired by the year, thus exempting most wage labourers from it'.[117] This was a major blow to the crafts. Yet it was only an early milestone in the long and steady decline of apprenticeships.

James sought to appoint Catholics to high positions. He made two declarations of indulgence in 1687 and 1688. Bishops who protested were sent to the tower, but found not guilty. But it was only when a son was born to him, and the threat of the indefinite continuation of a papist Stuart dynasty presented itself, that the landed classes could tolerate no more. Rumours were circulated that the child was a bastard. William of Orange, James's nephew and husband to his daughter Mary, was invited to invade England and depose James. James attempted to make concessions, but the plan went forward. The Glorious Revolution of 1688 brought William and Mary to the throne, and the hapless James fled to France and into exile.

The overriding theme in the conflicts between Parliament and Crown under the later Stuarts had to do with religious disputes. Yet 1688 also marked the completion of a transformation with an unmistakable class character. Parliament was no longer simply a vehicle through which the propertied landed classes could collaborate in governance with the Crown. Parliament was to meet annually, and would have authority over virtually all financial decisions. In this way, Parliament held the powers of the Crown firmly in check. The threat posed by the absolutist tendencies of the Stuarts appeared to have been permanently removed. Parliament could be prorogued no more.

The revolution was 'glorious' precisely because Parliament had not divided, and had not resorted to rally the support of the lower orders in order to attain its objective. Though the gentry continued to fear the threat of revolution from below and arbitrary rule from above, financial control of the state meant that this class possessed extraordinary powers to deal with threats to its power, authority and hegemony. As the Whigs and Tories patched up their differences over the legitimacy of William and Mary's succession, the solidarity of a ruling class of agrarian-capitalist landlords was clearly evident. 'The country was, for the time

117. Hill 1961, p. 176.

being, politically unanimous as it had not been since the days of the Spanish menace'.[118] This 'unanimity' was of course based upon the triumph of the ruling gentry and the defeat of the radicals half a century earlier. While they may not have felt safe to state their positions in public, in all likelihood wage labourers and small craftsmen privately acknowledged that the weakening of the Crown lessened their prospects for incorporation or other forms of royal protection. For them, this change signalled an even more rapid decline in protection and regulation of manufacturing.

As noted above, the number of peers and of the landed classes in general had grown disproportionately in relation to the growth of the general population since 1540. Colin Mooers rightly corrects those who would interpret the triumph of the landed classes and the expansion of the peerage in particular as the triumph of an *ancien régime*. The survival of the monarchy and the strength of the landed classes in England to this day is a paradox of British history. Mooers points to the growth of the landed classes *as a whole*, and interprets it as the result of a transformation in the *entire* social structure:

> That the gentry had greatly strengthened its social power against the Crown is clear. That they had also gained the upper hand against the peerage is less clear. Much debate has surrounded the question as to whether or not the peerage, which constituted the basis of the traditional aristocracy of the 'court', was a declining feudal aristocracy being out-stripped by the rising capitalist gentry of the 'country' in the sixteenth and early seventeenth centuries. The growth of agrarian capitalism had not just altered social relations in the countryside, it was also beginning to shape the character of trade and commerce as well, from which much of the peerage drew their incomes.[119]

Both peerage and gentry were undergoing a transformation into 'a new type of ruling class'.[120] According to Zagorin, this class 'constituted a single economic class, for what they had in common was the possession of capital for the end of profit and capital accumulation'.[121] Mooers emphasises that even the peerage was engaged in accumulation, based upon land ownership. It is true that peers and gentry alike were amassing new fortunes from the economic rents on their estates. Accumulation by itself, however, is neither revolutionary nor capitalist by definition. What made the character of the English economy specifically 'capitalist' in this period were the competitive pressures of the emerging market in economic leases on land, which compelled tenant-farmers to maximise,

118. Wilson 1984, p. 216.
119. Mooers 1991, p. 157.
120. Ibid.
121. Zagorin 1965, p. 51 as quoted in Mooers 1991, p. 157.

specialise and innovate on their farms. Landlords had every incentive to invest in improvements on their land, and they did so. They thus held the combined roles of owners of *and* investors in the means of production. But it should be made clear that they were not themselves directly subject to the competitive pressures of the market in the way that their tenants were. They were holders of a specific kind of 'capital': commodified land, in the Polanyian sense. This did not make them 'capitalists' in the sense that we understand the term today. Yet they played an absolutely pivotal role in bringing about the emergence of capitalism, and capital in the abstract – capital as a social relation. Mooers makes it sound as if the defeat of the Crown in the revolutionary upheavals of 1640–88 *by itself* brought about a transformation resulting in capitalist property-relations. He then cites Thompson to back up his point:

> A victory of royal absolutism would have had a profound effect on the fortunes of the bourgeois opposition. It would have meant that those who owned property were not free to dispose of their wealth as they saw fit. The Crown had persistently attempted to intervene in relations between landowners and their tenants and to exert the prerogatives of the Crown over those of private property. What was at issue, from one aspect, was exactly a capitalist redefinition of 'the basic property statute', from 'ancient right' to 'natural law' and purchase; of the mode and rationale of production from quasi-self-sufficiency to the marketing of commodities for profit; and of productive relations, from the organic compulsions of the manor and gild to the atomized compulsions of a free labor market.[122]

This accords well with Mooers's point that the defeat of the crown enabled a redefinition of property rights and freed the landed classes from the threat of an absolutist check on their ability to dispose of their private property as they would. But the quote from Thompson continues: 'And, from another aspect, the real movement was enormously complex and protracted, commencing . . . with the great monastic wool farmers of Domesday, and passing through the enfeeblement of the barons in the wars, the growth of "free labour", the enclosure of the sheep-walks, the seizure and redistribution of Church lands, the pillaging of the New World, the drainage of the fens, and thence through revolution, to the eventual acceleration of enclosure and the reclamation of wastes'.[123]

Mooers does not follow up on Thompson's point here about the whole process being 'enormously complex and protracted'.[124] Mooers seems to want to gloss

122. Thompson 1965, p. 316 as quoted in Mooers 1991, pp. 158–9.
123. Ibid.
124. Mooers continues by discussing the critical importance of the popular struggles, which pushed Parliament farther than it would ever have gone and proved decisive in

over the protracted nature of the transformation, and create the impression that it was in these years that the 'real' transformation of the economy and social relations took place. Yet, again, the process of extinguishing customary law through enclosures was ongoing; the greatest struggles over enclosure lay ahead. Checking the absolutist tendencies of the Stuarts did not mean the executive would no longer wield enormous power or that it would no longer come to loggerheads with Parliament, as we shall read in the next chapter. Mooers is correct to suggest that a new type of ruling class and a new type of state were emerging from the revolutionary period. But the completion of the revolutionary project was the political end of a much larger, more protracted process which was centuries in the making, as Thompson so sagely points out in qualifying his own assertions. The revolution may have succeeded in establishing the political framework for the full elaboration of a capitalist economy based upon private enterprise. But this was, on the one hand, only the completion of a longer process of separating 'state' and 'civil society', bringing an end, in Brenner's words, to 'the age-old "fusion" of the "economic" and the "political".'[125] And on the other hand, as we shall discover below, the process still had a long road ahead before realising the more 'fully-developed' form of capitalism in industrial capitalism.[126]

The chief difficulty with interpreting England's seventeenth-century revolution as a *bourgeois* revolution is of course that it was not led by any bourgeoisie.[127] To the extent that wealthy urbanites were involved, these were the merchants,

---

the defeat of the Crown. This point is agreeable and important in its own right, but serves to gloss over the key issue at stake (see below).

125. Brenner 1985b, p. 299.

126. Mooers's object is to counter the Nairn-Anderson thesis, which argues that seventeenth-century England experienced a precocious yet incomplete capitalist revolution. Anderson, for example, finds that England's lack of a 'second revolution' after a takeover of power by the bourgeoisie, and the lack of a centralised, 'modern' bureaucracy are signs of England's 'backwardness'. Against this view, Mooers (Mooers 1991, p. 171) counters that England in fact serves as the 'classic' example of bourgeois and capitalist revolution. He bases his argument on the claim that the English state after 1688 was 'uniquely suited to the requirements of capitalism'. This claim is uncontroversial. Yet Mooers's thesis rests on the premise that there is a necessary connection between 'bourgeois' revolution and capitalism. Elsewhere, Mooers's attempt to fit the revolutions in England (1640–88), France (1789) and Prussia (1871) into the same mould of 'bourgeois revolution' has been criticised on the grounds that the English Revolution was led by a rural, landowning gentry, not by a professional urban bourgeoisie (Zmolek 2000, pp. 147–51). Like the term 'proto-industrialisation', the term 'bourgeois revolution' is simply too broad to be of much value to the task of historical analysis, and its application to the English experience is especially misleading. These points of critique take nothing away from Mooers's excellent summary of the reorganisation of the English state after 1688, which we shall draw upon in the next section.

127. For more extensive elaborations of the critique of the bourgeois paradigm, see Comninel 1987, p. 53 (Chapter Three); Brenner 1989, pp. 271–304; and Wood 1991, p. 1 (Chapter One).

who, as we have seen, were sorely divided at the outset of the hostilities. If the temptation to force an interpretation of the English Revolution as a bourgeois revolution can be laid to rest, we must still acknowledge the significance of the changes that were brought about in facilitating the further development of agrarian capitalism.

The post-revolution settlement

William of Orange's motivations for accepting the invitation to invade England involved the prospect of reinforcing the Dutch struggle against Louis XIV's expansionism. Commercial rivalry gave way to an Anglo-Dutch alliance against France, England's new commercial rival. Thus the War of the Grand Alliance (1688–97), fought mainly in Flanders, dominated England's foreign policy under William.[128] While England had not fought a war in Europe since the time of Henry VIII, it was now governed by a King with an intimate knowledge of continental politics, in sharp contrast to his Stuart predecessors.

The legislative revolution that followed the Glorious Revolution laid the groundwork for a more stable, more tolerant British state and society. Freedom of the press, the rapid growth of newspapers, and the new position of Catholics as the target of religious animosity would all have enormous implications, especially in the latter half of the eighteenth century. Stability, however, did not arrive immediately. Britain's political elite was still deeply divided, and there were still conflicts that would have to be played out. The resolution of these political conflicts did not mean that economic rifts were also healing. On the contrary, for even as all this was being accomplished, economic forces were pushing the scales further and further against the small producer in favour of the landlords, merchants and large masters in manufacturing.

The acts passed by Parliament in the post-revolutionary period were exceptional in number and laid out a new framework for government. Providing guarantees against the abuses of power and prerogative that had been committed by James II and his Stuart forebears, the Bill of Rights, passed in 1689, reaffirmed Parliament's claim of control over taxation and legislation. It also banned royal interference in elections and royal impingement on freedom of speech. When combined with the decision to allow the Licensing Act to lapse in 1695, these

128. The Grand Alliance consisted of a broad coalition of Catholic and Protestant states (including Britain, Holland, Denmark, Austria, and the many German States), all fighting against France. Before England joined, the alliance against France was known as the League of Augsburg. Hence the name, the 'War of the League of Augsburg', among other names (King William's War; The Nine Years' War; The War for the English Succession).

actions gave an enormous boost to freedom of the press. A 'newspaper revolution' ensued,[129] and the now common practice of meeting at coffeehouses for political discussion and debate became even more widespread. Individual rights were also enhanced in the courts, as the King was forbidden to establish his own courts or to sit in the capacity of a judge. Excessive bail or fines were lowered, and cruel and unusual punishments banned. The Bill of Rights did not reduce the King to a figurehead. Certain royal prerogatives were preserved, such as the appointment and dismissal of ministers, and the ability to veto legislation or declare war. The authority to summon and dissolve Parliament still belonged to the crown. Yet the Bill put the crown on notice that 'Parliaments ought to be held frequently'. The Triennial Act passed in 1694 was a resurrection of the first Triennial Act, assented to by Charles I in 1641.[130] It required a new Parliament to be assembled every three years. Longer sessions of parliament and more frequent elections quickened the development of political parties. The King was also forbidden to maintain a standing army in time of peace without Parliament's consent. Parliamentary control of finances was strengthened, deliberately rendering William and Mary dependent on Parliament. 'When princes have not needed money they have not needed us', was the reasoning of one Member of Parliament. 1694 was the same year the Board of Trade was established along with the Bank of England as a mechanism for lending money to the crown. Yet as the national debt depended on parliamentary guarantees, the Bank of England did not loosen the Crown's dependence on Parliament. In 1689 the Toleration Act was passed as a kind of reward to Nonconformists for their refusal to side with James II. While the bill restricted both Nonconformists and Catholics from service in government, freedom of worship was granted to Nonconformists, but not Catholics. This act of state reflected a major shift in popular sentiments. Around the 1670s, Catholics came to be seen as a greater threat to political stability than Nonconformists, and anti-Catholicism, which was 'in essence . . .

---

129. The growth of newspapers and advertising was bound up with the growth of land transport and stage coaches. Improved transport facilitated the improvement of inter-regional communications and also came to rely on it. Even before the Licensing Act of 1697, the newspaper industry had been growing. The phenomenon was not restricted to London. The *Reading Mercury* for example, dates from 1697. The first daily, the *Daily Courant*, began in 1702, followed four years later by the first evening paper, the *Evening Post*. As the newspaper spread to provincial towns, aided by the falling costs of paper, the first wave of commercial advertising further spurred on the growth of regional economies (Coleman 1977, p. 146).

130. This was a resurrection of the first Triennial Act, assented to by Charles I in 1641, in response to pressure from the Long Parliament. The act ensured that Parliament was in session for a minimum of 50 days every three years. Within a year, the first Civil War broke out, and so the Triennial Act was not used until the Restoration in 1660. Charles II managed to have the act repealed in 1664.

political, patriotic, and anti-clerical rather than religious',[131] was widespread, cutting across class lines. The Test Act of 1673 had established that anyone who wished to hold public office must regularly attend church, and an Anglican church at that. In 1702 and 1704 the Occasional Conformity Acts were intended to rein in Dissenters who were in the habit of getting around the Test Act by only attending church occasionally. Daniel Defoe was arrested under this act in 1704 for a pamphlet he wrote on dissenting. Yet while being pilloried, the crowd threw flowers instead of rotten eggs. Defoe, often credited as the 'father of journalism' and for writing the first true novel in English, *Robinson Crusoe*, was let off easy, his victory seen as another step forward for freedom from censorship.[132]

The glorious financial revolution

The financial reforms initiated under William III were undertaken in response to a severe fiscal crisis beginning in the early 1690s and the subsequent outbreak of eight years of war with France. Many historians have equated these reforms with a 'financial revolution'. William required huge sums for his war, and tax revenues alone were clearly insufficient to the task.[133] The new political unanimity and the new relationships between Parliament, Crown and the people proved favourable to a reorganisation of the state's funding devices and indeed the whole apparatus of government. The burden of taxation now fell heaviest on the landed classes through the land tax and on the poor through the excise (perhaps half of which fell on the national beverage: beer). It follows, of course, that if Parliament was tapping the members of its own class of landholders for the single largest source of taxation, this also gave Parliament unprecedented control over the finances of the state, and specifically over the army and navy.

Ever since Charles I's seizure of bullion in the tower in 1640, goldsmiths and scriveners had begun accepting deposits, discounting bills and issuing notes. The professional banker had begun to emerge. As practice taught that a larger volume of notes could be issued than the volume of cash deposited, the banking

---

131. Gregg 1980, pp. 15–6, citing Roberts (ed.) 1975, p. 66.

132. Defoe was a man of many talents. He was associated with 26 journals. A soldier in William's army in 1688, he served as a secret agent under Queen Anne, and played an important role in bringing about the Act of Union with Scotland. The Licensing Act had lapsed in 1695, ending censorship of the press. 'Grub Street flourished, and in the ensuing years Swift, Defoe, Pope, Addison and Steele were to be the greatest of the notable authors of Queen Anne's reign' (Gregg 1980, pp. 131–2).

133. From the outset of the hostilities in 1689, it was clear that 'governments and parliaments were faced with the need to produce funds on a hitherto unimagined scale' (Upton 2001, pp. 151–2). Across Europe, governments could not ignore the increasing wealth of merchants and bankers, who were soon to become indispensable as the lenders who kept the state afloat.

practice began to add liquidity to the financial community as a whole. 'From 1650 onwards, writers on economic problems focused their attention increasingly on this aspect of banking: as a means of enlarging trade and releasing the nation from that nightmare of "a scarcity of money" by which it was always haunted'.[134]

Charles II and his brother after him began to systematically anticipate revenues by borrowing from these wealthy specialists *in specie*. Their borrowing was based upon anticipated revenues from any taxes recently approved by Parliament. Hill calls this 'a decisive factor in the evolution of banking'.[135] The abandonment of tax farming in 1671 opened up a new and rapidly expanding branch of civil service.[136] In that year alone 763 customs officers were added to the state-bureaucracy.[137] A stop in the Exchequer in 1672 and the resultant bankruptcies of five large bankers shocked the banking establishment. This led to a hike in the rate of interest paid by the government. Public confidence in the Crown was at a low ebb. Parliament protested against loans to the Crown that often resulted in bribes offered to members in the form of fat pensions. Sir George Downing was scandalised. He had sought in 1671 to tax lenders on amounts accruing more than the standard rate of 6 percent interest, in a vain attempt to encourage lenders to make deposits directly with the Exchequer. The crisis of public finance under the later Stuarts was eventually patched up by annual government disbursements to lenders.[138] 'England had stumbled, as it transpired, into the device of a funded debt'.[139] But it was only after the Glorious Revolution that public confidence would be sufficiently restored to enable the realisation of Downing's dream of 'statutory guarantees of appropriation and interest, and assignability under Treasury control'.[140] By erasing public suspicions of the threat of Stuart absolutism as well as the Crown's suspicions of the threat posed by a national bank, the Glorious Revolution provided the confidence and unanimity among the ruling classes

---

134. Wilson 1984, p. 209.

135. Hill 1961, p. 188.

136. Tax farming had ended in 1643, but was resumed again in 1662, largely as a way for Charles II to compensate ex-cavaliers, resulting in considerable corruption. Only customs farming ended in 1671. Tax farming for the excise lasted until 1683. The Hearth Tax, introduced in 1662, was farmed from 1667 to 1684, and abolished in 1688. (See Hill 1961, p. 187 and Wilson 1984, p. 212).

137. This development brought the state 'into closer connection with business life, at the same time that individual gentlemen and their families profited' (Hill 1961, p. 187).

138. The Stuarts were aided by a recovery of trade in the 1670s, bringing greater revenues from customs and excise and thus greater relative freedom from parliamentary control of finance (Hill 1961, p. 187).

139. Wilson 1984, p. 215.

140. Wilson 1984, p. 216 adds: 'Under Downing, the country had taken a major step forward to a modern system of public finance'. Downing died in 1684, and thus did not live to see the later realisation of his project. Symbolic of the restored confidence, William was to repay £1,300,000 to Charles's bankers, so devastated by the stop of 1672 (Hill 1961, p. 189).

which, combined with the strength of the market under conditions of agrarian capitalism, would allow both an extension of taxation and the underwriting of the national debt.

The demands of war and the declining value of sterling, upon which Britain's colonial trade depended, led to an acute fiscal crisis. By 1693, England's trade balance with the American colonies – the trade which England counted on to underwrite her healthy trade balance with Europe, based upon re-exports of staple commodities such as sugar, tobacco and cod – had fallen by 50 percent.[141] Various solutions were tried, such as public lotteries, the sale of annuities and coin clipping. But these provided only temporary relief.[142] The next measure, the establishment of a national debt, was effectively formalised in an act of 1693. Subscriptions totalling £1 million were taken. The subscribers could choose between a lifetime annuity at 14 percent, tax free, or gamble and take 10 percent until 1700, with uncertain terms thereafter.

> Two principles [combined for the first time] were thus firmly established. The annuitant was not to see his capital again. And the creditor lent not upon the security of the King's word but on the security of an Act of a sovereign Parliament which included provision for severe penalties against any servant of the Crown who disobeyed the terms of the Act. What had happened by accident in 1672 was now established as an accepted principle of public finance... From this device of allocating specific duties for the payment of perpetual but theoretically redeemable annuities, repeated over and over again, came the National Debt. In return for a statutory promise to pay interest on a long-term basis, the Government secured a large volume of spending power to tide it over its immediate emergency.[143]

141. See Jones 1988, p. 226, Table 7.4. The East India trade, though lucrative, meant a constant outflow of silver since India preferred silver bullion to English commodities. A temporary suspension of the East India trade could bring temporary relief to the depreciation crisis, but the loss of profits would soon disrupt the economy as a whole. So this was not a solution.

142. The face value of silver coin was left unchanged, and a new industry of clipping provided employment and a fillip to the home economy. The bullion provided from coin clipping was used to pay off the government's debts. 'The total recorded export of molten silver between 1689 and 1695, including what the East India Company exported in this form (though not as foreign coin) since clipping was the likelier source of this, amounts to 8,402,087 ozs. Compared with this, the total silver known to have been lost from silver coin between these dates amounts to some 9,174,200 ozs. So the amount exported is large enough to account for the bulk of the loss through clipping from the silver coin' (Jones 1988, p. 226).

143. Jones 1988, p. 218.

Inspired by the apparent success of this scheme, a jumble of additional schemes for raising state revenues based upon the concept of a National Debt now came forward.

The most significant of these arose out of the ongoing rivalry between the East India Company, which itself had been suffering a cash shortage since the 1680s, and interlopers attacking its monopoly. Competition between the Old Company and its rivals would set the stage for a process of private companies outbidding one another to give loans to the state. Through spies, bribes and by withholding a tax instalment due to the cash-strapped King William, the Old Company initially prevailed and managed to win a new charter with capital of £1.5 million. But many of the interlopers refused to subscribe. Instead, the 'late solicitors against the East India Company' outbid the Old Company by offering a more generous loan to the crown. This resulted directly in the founding of the Bank of England in May 1694.[144] It was effectively a hybrid between a commercial banking scheme backed by reliable men of wealth in London, and a scheme to lend money to the government. Advancing the whole of its credit to the government in the same year, the Bank of England quickly became indispensable as the primary bank of the country. The English stock market, which had first developed around the purchase and sale of the securities of the great merchant companies such as the East India Company, now 'grew enormously, thanks to vastly increased government needs (brokers, jobbers and price-lists all quickly emerging to expedite the rapidly growing business)'.[145] While initially a success, the Bank itself was caught up in the ongoing fiscal crisis of the next two years.[146]

---

144. Jones 1988, p. 218. The loan itself was not actually cash. Wine-merchant Gilbert Heathcote, a 'man of outstanding shrewdness and tenacity', whose London syndicate was 'by far the biggest investor in government securities of all kinds', teamed up with his colleagues to offer, in exchange for £1.2 million in government debt, banknotes worth the same amount. The £720,000 taken in for subscriptions was reserved for banking practices. The bank combined standard banking practices, a perpetual loan and the issuing of stock. In this ingenious arrangement, everyone came out ahead. The government traded debt for paper currency which it could use, the bank received 8 percent (£100,000) annually on its capital of £1.2 million, and the shareholders got a secure investment. See Carswell 1993, p. 23.

145. Jones 1988, p. 13. Part of the troubles experienced by the Old Company in the 1680s was attributable to stock-jobbing practices.

146. By late 1694, clipping coin had run its course, and silver coin no longer passed at face-value. Parliament attempted to ban bullion exports, but this proved 'worse than useless' (Jones 1988, p. 23). Merchants were suffering heavy losses. A scramble ensued for Old Company stock, as it was perceived to be the most stable. But while many were trying to get 'in' on the East, many of the Company's own agents were seeking a way 'out' of a company in crisis and back into the centre of things in the London financial market. The growth of specialisation in either import or export trade made it a still more attractive place to be. During the first week of May 1695, only 'two days after the last date for clipped money to be paid in at face value as tax, there was a serious run on the bank.

When William landed in Holland and took command of the allied force on 7 May 1696, the treasuries of both France and England were bare. His aim now was merely to subsist, and to do this he needed cash. But who would provide it? Before his departure the king had appointed a commission, led by Robert Harley and Thomas Foley, to collect subscriptions from the landed gentry for a National Land Bank. The scheme had a certain obvious validity, and serves as a testament of the degree to which land was becoming commodified.

A major advance of trade since the 1670s was generating unprecedented concentrations of landed wealth. Where medieval policy had been based upon the notion of provision (a concern with distribution), the direction of state policy since the Restoration had shifted to a concern for the encouragement and protection of home production. The Corn Laws of 1663, 1670 and 1689 were intended to encourage the producer of corn. Whether or not these laws can be credited for the change, English agriculture was embarking upon a long period of vast improvement.[147] The extensive building of new and elegant mansions in the last decades of the seventeenth century, and the smaller, more comfortable houses that sprang up all over the country, testified to the rising standards of living everywhere: glazed windows and plentiful supplies of coal freed the houses of many commoners from the hazards of winter. Just as a new market in financial and manufacturing interests was opening up for investors, competition for land had driven prices upward over the course of the seventeenth century. Larger merchants and financiers (usually those who were getting on in years) were increasingly seeking to purchase estates and see their sons take their place among the gentry. Probationary periods before full acceptance into the local world of county families, however, could be frustratingly long. Estates became available for purchase when hereditary owners went bankrupt or were unsuccessful at making improvements. Wilson finds it unlikely that the influx of men of new wealth from the town into the estates had any serious impact on the efficiency of estate management. Those 'aspirants to social status would not always want to remind their neighbours of their commercial origins by attending too officiously to the business of their estates', and it was among the larger squires 'that most evidence is to be found of enterprise and innovation in estate management'.[148] The expense of making improvements added to the general expense of owning land, raising the bar for entry, and making the situation for smaller farmers increasingly untenable. Though expensive, enclosure was such a profitable undertaking that landlords were compelled to embark on a wave of

---

As a result, the Bank's operations were almost crippled for the rest of the year . . .' (Jones 1988, p. 23). See also: Macaulay 1886a, Chapter XXII.

147. Wilson 1984, pp. 236–7.

148. Wilson 1984, pp. 158–9 and 153.

enclosures on an unprecedented scale. The first private act, inaugurating the era of parliamentary enclosure, would not be presented to Parliament until 1710.[149] The government that had once fined private landowners for enclosing their land now became the tool for effecting enclosure and enforcing the increasing dispossession of small landholders. The wave of extravagant and ostentatious spending by the landed classes contributed to a subsequent crisis of liquidity when a series of poor harvests ensued in the early 1690s. 'Diaries, letters and lawsuits of the time all tell the same tale of estates "encumbered" with debt'.[150] Many cavaliers who had managed to recover 'delinquent' lands taken from them during the Interregnum had done so only through heavy borrowing. Now they were faced with having to borrow more to sustain existing levels of consumption. Many landlords, or land stewards or bailiffs operating on their behalf, were compelled to negotiate for higher rents and new leases with their tenants. The crisis deepened the resentment towards financiers and the King's 'placemen' on the part of the landed classes who received no return on their 'investment' in the form of the land tax. To them, 'it seemed all the profits were being drained off to the money power'.[151] 'From 1688 to 1695 we have a paradox: almost a decade of bad summers, unknown since the 1620s, accompanied by an outburst of company promotion and financial speculation likewise unknown since the 1620s, and not paralleled until the boom of the South Sea Bubble'.[152] Driven by the need for greater spending power, schemes came forward from the landed classes to create a 'land bank', lending to landowners as well as the government at low rates of interest.

The act presented to Parliament combined several schemes in one.[153] The Land Bank, it was hoped, would help underwrite the war with France. For this entire proposal, £564,700 was advanced. The scheme was an instant failure. The proceedings of Parliament tell a sad tale. The plan passed the Lords on 27 April 1696.[154] The expected sum to be raised was £2.6 million. Very attractive terms were offered.[155] Apparently initial subscriptions were poor, as subsequent efforts were made to allow for clipped and unclipped money, Guineas, Bank of England Bills and Notes and Plate all were allowed to be used as forms of payment for

149. Mooers 1991, p. 171.
150. Wilson 1984, pp. 155–6.
151. Upton 2001, pp. 151–2.
152. Wilson 1984, p. 183.
153. The title of the Bill read as follows: 'An Act for continuing to His Majesty certain Duties upon Salt, Glass Wares, Stone and Earthen Bottles; and for granting several Duties upon Tobacco Pipes, and other Earthen Wares, for carrying on the War against France; and for establishing a National Land Bank; and for taking off the Duties upon Tonnage of Ships and upon Coals'.
154. *British History Online* 2006a, pp. 745–7.
155. *British History Online* 2006b, pp. 593–8.

subscription. Generous discounts, starting at 15 percent in June and lowering to 5 percent by December, were offered. The King himself subscribed £5,000. But by 19 June only £500 more had been subscribed for the Land Bank specifically, and by 3 July no more had been added. A request for £300,000 to save the programme was denied.[156] By 1 August, £2,100 had been subscribed. In the midst of a crisis, country gentlemen had shown they were anxious to borrow, but not anxious to lend. By December, those who had advanced the initial sum of £564,700 would be petitioning Parliament to be 'restored to their former Securities', without which they would be 'ruined'.[157]

With the delusion of the Land Bank exposed by August, William sent word that without a new source of private credit, he faced mutiny or desertion.[158] The Directors of the Bank of England (who had been dismayed by the whole Land Bank adventure) were approached once more, and now were more amenable. A loan of £200,000 was raised 'in return for a promise of compensation for the losses suffered by the depreciation of the exchange'.[159] As the Bank's position became entrenched, its influence was felt internationally. Rather than provisioning the troops through supply lines, England found it more expedient to buy locally. And it was through the Bank's correspondents in the financial centres on the Continent that pay and provisions for the army were subsequently arranged.[160] Through 1695, 'inflationary hyperactivity' kept the economy going, but the monetary crisis peaked in 1696–7, when the cloth markets lost nearly 20 percent of their trade. To resolve the problem of devaluation, the government finally recalled all silver coin for recoinage in May of 1696. The scheme 'could never have succeeded but for the great underlying strength of the economy'.[161] At last, the value of silver began to recover.

A professional administration of commissioners, overseen by committees appointed by Parliament, was now in charge of new funding devices, supported after 1696 by a 'revivified administrative system' and a reformed coinage. The government was now 'able to take immediate control of economic and financial resources that far exceeded its income from taxation'.[162] Where others faltered,

156. *British History Online* 2006b, pp. 593–8.
157. *British History Online* 2006b, pp. 619–20.
158. 'The failure of English payments coincided with news of the defection of Savoy, and of the consequent neutralization of Italy . . . defeat was a very real prospect' (Jones 1988, pp. 24–5).
159. Ibid.
160. Carswell 1993, p. 25.
161. Carswell 1993, p. 15. The result of recoinage, writes Carswell, 'was to make sterling the hardest currency in Europe. In 1696, before the recoinage began, sterling at Amsterdam varied between 31 and 27. From 1698 to 1703 it never fell below 34, and sometimes touched 37'. The recovery of the relative value of silver must be factored in to this. But here again is another reference to the superior strength of England's economy.
162. Wilson 1984, p. 216.

the Bank survived the recoinage of 1697 that 'pricked the bubble of inflation that had grown since early in 1695', causing prices to fall rapidly. The Bank's notes approached half those in circulation. Its stock soared.[163] The creation of a stable system of financing state activities, combined with the expansion of credit in the economy, generally provided the framework for a buoyant economy and freed up funds for a boom of investing. The boom was driven by a burst of speculative investments in manufacturing, which the government now actively encouraged through acts of Parliament. A statute in 1689 had thrown investment in copper mining open to all comers. Two further acts encouraged landowners to dig for minerals on their estates. It was in this period that a large number of joint-stock operations were established, only to run into serious problems. Only 19 joint-stock companies were given charters in England between 1610 and 1660. In the next 60 years, 54 charters were granted, most of these in the 1690s. Of the 54 charters, 23 of these were for mining or manufacturing operations, 11 for overseas trade, and the remaining charters were distributed between 'banking and finance, water supply, insurance, and fishing'. There were also unincorporated joint-stock operations. In 1695, estimates placed the total number of joint-stock companies in England and Scotland at 140. Listings of quotations on stocks in newspapers evidenced an embryonic stock exchange. Land had ceased to be virtually the only investment for men with surplus income, as higher rates of return on securities (at much greater risk) attracted increasing numbers of investors. Marine insurance had developed in the 1680s. Life insurance was now made possible by the new science of statistics emerging in the wake of a mathematical renaissance.[164] Coleman finds that unlike in shipping and insurance, there was in fact little need in manufacturing for joint-stock organisation at this time, since the personal networks of large masters provided sufficient security, and at the same time, borrowing was not difficult as there was an abundance of capital.[165] 'A vigorous and highly speculative market in stocks and shares flowered in the City; thunders of disapproval rumbled against the "pernicious art of stock-jobbing"'.[166] Stock-jobbers were speculating on the value of holdings in the emerging securities market. When the boom went bust in 1697, they took much of the blame for the losses resulting from the deflation that followed. An 'Act to

163. Wilson 1984, pp. 220–1. Upton 1991, p. 152 comments that the Bank was established to serve 'as a hedge against any reversal of 1688, which would throw the legitimacy of the national debt into question'.

164. See Hill 1961, p. 233. 'The greatest scientific minds of the day like Boyle, Hooke and Newton did not disdain the practical conundrums of invention and technology. Isaac Newton was from 1699 a diligent and successful Master of the Mint who raised it to new standards of accuracy and precision' (Wilson 1984, pp. 221–7).

165. Coleman 1977, pp. 169–71.

166. Coleman 1977, 170.

restrain the number and ill-practice of Brokers and Stock-jobbers' was passed. It limited their number to 100, required them to keep books, wear a badge and obtain a license. This fiscal crisis did not last long: a rapid recovery followed, based mainly upon the strength of the new fiscal institutions. 'Shipping revived, and foreign trade expanded to a total of £13.5 million by 1700–1, an increase of about 90 percent over the 1696–7 figure'.[167]

The establishment of a national debt, managed by the semi-private Bank of England, marked a major milestone in the financial revolution that would profoundly alter the traditional relationship between the English government and private businessmen. Unlike the Stuart kings, who had 'gained little in power from the buoyancy of the economy over which they presided', William was now mobilising finances for war on a scale previously unthinkable.[168] The fiscal reforms of the revolution settlement managed to harness a portion of that burst of financial activity that had been pent-up for years.[169] A euphoria for paper-wealth erupted. Shares and bonds were coming to be viewed as a more convenient means of securing a future than land. The public's confidence in paper and in the national debt, however, remained untested.

'Free trade'

Before the eighteenth century, European trade had expanded rapidly in the early feudal period (1050–1250) and in the sixteenth century, when population rebounded from the effects of the crisis of the fourteenth century. The contraction in volume of trade within a crisis-ridden Europe in the seventeenth century served to reinforce attitudes and policies associated with the 'mercantilist' view of competition in trade as 'a continuous fight over a cake of limited size, a prize more or less fixed in quantity and value'.[170] The great hope was that new markets in lands newly discovered by Europe would aid the growth of domestic manufacturing. When buyers in the East showed a preference for silver over European manufactures and America proved too shallow and too poor a market, these hopes proved to be premature.

From the Interregnum onward, England's foreign trade had experienced steady and unprecedented growth. This growth can be attributed in large part

167. Wilson 1984, p. 183.

168. Where the attempts of the 'absolutist' Charles I to collect relatively modest taxes without parliamentary consent had triggered the civil wars, the parliamentary monarchy of William III deployed 'a veritable army of tax collectors to bring in vastly greater sums without causing serious political disturbance' (Harling 2001, p. 22).

169. A hundred joint-stock enterprises were in existence by 1695, most of them tied to the exploitation of patents. Carswell 1993, p. 13.

170. Coleman 1977, p. 131.

to the reforms passed under Cromwell, who sought to build up the fleet and raise England's status as a maritime power. From 1600 to 1660, Holland had gained pre-eminence in trade by building a large and efficient fleet.[171] The Navigation Acts cut off Dutch access to English colonial markets. This 'age of trade wars and trade treaties' was fought 'by tariffs and prohibitions as much as by armies and navies'.[172] But what secured England's rise to supremacy in trade was victory in the three wars with Holland between 1651 and 1674, all of them centring on a struggle for predominance in trade. Subsequently, England began to imitate Holland's role as *entrepôt* inasmuch as its trade was increasingly driven by a surge of imports for re-export. At the same time, the English continued to expand their colonial trade and to improve manufacturing techniques so that finished cloths could be exported directly from England.

In general, however, the economy was still characterised by parochialism, where a decline of trade for one article could impact upon the region specialising in its production, leaving other areas unaffected. Enclosures and the gradual conversion of smallholders into market-dependent labourers or unemployed poor was also a regional affair, as was, by consequence, unemployment. The numbers of the poor in search of work rose steadily, too. Many were prompted to propose solutions to the widely recognised 'problem of the poor'. Combined public and private charities for the most poor scarcely came to £1 per head per year, enough only to stave off the worst of immediate hunger and cold. Some were aided by the expansion of employments in textile manufacturing in the London suburbs and the Midlands, but charity and poor relief remained the only prospect for survival for a great many. The problems of underemployment were made acute by the economic fluctuations of the 1690s. Emigration, transportation, kidnapping of labour for the plantations, service in the military – all these factors had contributed to a lessening of population pressures. So much so, perhaps, that there were complaints by employers of a shortage of hands. 'In 1696 the Commissioners for Trade and Plantations deplored "the dearness of labour". It should be bought as cheaply as possible if English exports were to capture foreign markets against the competition of French and Dutch industry protected by tariffs'.[173]

---

171. Emerging from its own wars of independence as a significant economic power for a small country, Holland specialised in re-exports, promoting *entrepôt* trade across the globe. Command of trade brought command of raw materials. From England, the Dutch imported white cloth for dyeing and re-selling. From Germany, the Dutch imported unfinished linens. Once finished, such goods were-sold in Holland and around the globe for high profits (Carswell 1977, pp. 65–6).

172. Carswell 1977, p. 132.

173. Hill 1961, p. 229.

The 1662 Act of Settlement was now criticised for restricting the mobility of labour, thus putting a break on the advance of manufactures. It was relaxed in 1697.[174]

> By 1700 all sections of the population were to some extent cash consumers for goods produced outside their areas, and to meet this there was a highly developed regional specialization. 'There are shopkeepers in every village', Defoe observed, 'or at least in every considerable market town'. . . . The home market was variously estimated at from 6 to 32 times the foreign market.[175]

The market was responding to an overall increase in effective demand for luxury and semi-luxury items among not only landlords but also successful farmers as well as to the increasing dependence of 'middling' and working-class consumers on the market for basic subsistence and domestic items. Yet before 1688 investment in manufacturing production had been retarded. The early 1690s saw a boom in manufacturing projects. Of 236 patents for invention issued between 1660 and 1700, 64 were issued in 1691–3. Foreign trade was depressed in the early years of King William's war, and capital had to seek its outlet at home.[176] The increased investment in domestic manufacturing combined with decreasing prices for necessities – particularly food, drink and clothing, releasing consumers' spending power for other, often novel, items – contributed to the 'feverish interest in industrial invention' of the 1690s, particularly the later 1690s.[177] Inventions were not as yet generally made in the laboratory: 'In industry as a whole, technology was largely then, as occasionally now, a matter of knack, of local knowledge, often inherited and often secret, rather than of scientific reasoning and inquiry. Such were the skills of the brewer, forge master, tanner, dyer, mason and many others'.[178]

Technology remained overwhelmingly embodied in the knowledge of skilled labourers.[179] Despite important advances in technique and management, there was overall little radical reorganisation of the production process outside a few lines of manufacturing.[180] Nevertheless, the customary arrangements of

174. Ibid.
175. Hill 1961, p. 264.
176. Hill 1961, p. 227.
177. Wilson 1984, p. 187.
178. Ibid.
179. The immigration of Huguenot refugees after the revocation of the Edict of Nantes in 1685 brought an influx of hundreds of different kinds of skills into Britain, leading to many modifications in methods of manufacture, trade and finance. Many of the patents of this period bear their names. To take another example that we shall read more about in a later chapter, Richard Arkwright's workingmen were offered bribes to come and build cotton mills in Scotland.
180. Glass-making and brewing did show signs of radical reorganisation of production. Abraham Darby was apprenticed in the malt trade, where presumably he gained

the domestic system were increasingly threatened. As noted, the size of enterprises was expanding and management was increasingly separated from ownership in firms run on a partnership or joint-stock basis. Workers here found more demanding and less humane working conditions. At Crowley Iron Works, 'the old autocrat, Crowley, found it necessary to design an entire civil and penal code, running to more than 100,000 words, to govern and regulate his refractory labour-force'.[181] By 1700, 'Small masters in most City companies had lost all influence in running their affairs; everywhere oligarchy ruled'.[182] In 1690 the Leeds clothworkers tried and failed to halt cloths leaving Leeds until they had been dyed and dressed. By 1720, the Leeds Company was a dead letter. Justices of the Peace overseeing Quarter Sessions were increasingly ignoring apprenticeship-regulations.

Given all these changes, labourers were not simply idle. For example, in 1698 the journeymen feltmakers formed a combination to collect funds, to strike for higher wages and to take action against 'blacklegs'. Weavers' unions were to be found in Devon, Wiltshire, Somerset and Gloucestershire in the early eighteenth century.[183] It is hardly surprising that there was this expansion of activity among trades-'unions' after 1688. Their appearance signals the beginnings of the self-organisation of a proletarian class. Journeymen's associations in many trades created a 'Purse' to form 'friendly societies': 'As well as looking to their members' social welfare they raised money to take intruders to court – "from such as would our rights invade, or would intrude into our trade, or break the law Queen Betty made", as the popular rhyme put it'.[184] Customary contact with other workers was maintained through members travelling in search of work. The 'Purse' was a sign of things to come. Yet as we shall see, there was significant continuity of practice held over from the forms of labour organisation that preceded them.

Under William, the state devoted its resources towards the promotion of trade and colonial interests – a revival of the policies of the Commonwealth. Throughout the seventeenth century England's trade had grown in volume and diversity of exports. Overseas trade was 'the major advance of the period'.[185] Tobacco imports grew from 50,000 pounds in 1615 to 38 million pounds in 1700, most of it re-exported but a large share now consumed at home by the middle

insights that later enabled him to resolve the problem of coal's application to iron working. For 'In every industry save one – iron – substantial progress had been made towards a solution of the technical problems created by the use of coal instead of wood' (Wilson 1984, pp. 198–9).

181. See Thompson 1993, pp. 383–5. See pp. 411–13 for a discussion of Crowley's operations.

182. Hill 1961, p. 178.

183. Hill 1961, pp. 229–39.

184. Leeson 1979, p. 78.

185. Wilson 1984, p. 268.

classes and even labourers. Sugar imports rose from 160,000 cwt after 1660 to over 370,000 cwt by 1700, with about two-thirds being consumed at home. Sugar boiling, refining and marketing industries expanded in the Western ports. The Levant and East India Companies brought home spices, silks and fine fabrics in increasing numbers. Cod from New England poured in. Exports and re-exports to West Africa were exchanged for human cargo while slaves were shipped or re-exported to the West Indies. An increasing volume of manufactured goods was exported to the protected markets of the colonies, as well as to Europe – 'brass, copper, and iron wares, silk and linen, tallow, glass, earthenware, paper, cordage, leather and, of course woollens'.[186] Coal and grain exports were not exports of high value, but demanded shipping tonnage. Shipping tonnage may have doubled between the Restoration and the Glorious Revolution. By 1700, shipping was one of the largest employers of labour, employing perhaps 10 to 20 percent of the labour force outside of agriculture.[187] Between 1687 and 1703, the number of naval yard workers jumped by 475 percent. The navy was at this time arguably the largest manufacturer in the country.[188] London lost its place of absolute predominance as the ports of Bristol and Liverpool expanded thanks to the Navigation Acts. Cheap raw materials from the colonies lowered the costs of manufacturing. Where exports to Europe increased by 18 percent between 1660 and 1700, exports to the colonies increased by over two hundred percent. Although colonial exports stood at just eight percent of the total, the protection of such exports under the Navigation Acts allowed British manufacturing to expand to the point of being able to compete in European markets. The indirect subsidy to shipping, however, and the lucrative re-export trade, had the effect of diverting investment away from heavy industry.[189]

England's primary export remained cloths, though the share of cloths in proportion to the total of exports decreased. Between 1660 and 1700, the value of cloth exports may have nearly doubled.[190] A statute in 1689 threw the export of cloth open to all traders, ending the monopoly of the Merchant Adventurers, whose full privileges had been restored in 1683. The woollen and weaving manufacturing trades were opened to all in 1694. In 1673 the Eastland Company's trade in the Baltic had been thrown open to all on payment of two pounds after the company refused to lower its administrative fee. By 1688, it had virtually ceased to exist. By 1728 it was reduced to a dining club. The Hudson's Bay Company lost its exclusive privileges in 1697. The Royal Africa Company lost its charter in

186. Wilson 1984, p. 170.
187. Wilson 1984, pp. 169–71.
188. Hill 1961, p. 228.
189. Hill 1961, pp. 131–83.
190. Wilson 1984, p. 185.

1698, and trade to Africa was thrown open on condition that the forts of the now decommissioned Company would be maintained. The Russia Company lost its control of the Muscovy tobacco re-export in 1699. As the navy's ability to deal with the threats of piracy and rivalry improved, the usefulness of monopolies declined.[191]

> As the responsibility for diplomatic negotiations passed increasingly to the appropriate departments of states and their envoys accredited to foreign Powers, it was no longer necessary for merchants in strange lands to live under corporate rule as the Italian 'nations' had once lived in Bruges, the Merchant Adventurers in Dordrecht or the Eastland merchants at Elbing. The custom of appointing state envoys had been growing since the end of the fifteenth century amongst the European States. But it was some time before satisfactory and unanimous agreement could be obtained on protocol, even on the fundamental question of legal diplomacy.[192]

Thus 1688 essentially spelled the end for the old style of commercial monopolies in overseas trade. But this did not mean the end of all the great companies themselves. The Levant Company's by-law restricting the trade to apprenticed merchants was condemned in the Commons in 1694, but the company would survive until the 1750s. Trade to the East having expanded enormously, the East India Company flourished, despite its charter being cancelled in 1693 and then renewed with obligations to export commodities to the value of £100,000 per year. In 1698 a New East India Company was formed to rival the 'Old' Company. A fierce parliamentary battle ensued, but for a trade of such a long-distance, the advantages of a monopoly to protect traders were still deemed useful, and the two companies united in 1709.

In short, international commerce was by and large thrown open to 'free trade'.[193] The proponents of this new policy were once again the new merchants.[194] By achieving the revocation or compromising of the old companies' charters, the proponents of 'free trade' had reversed the basic principles of restricting output and maintaining quality and prices that had supported those companies since medieval times. With a domestic population increasingly dependent upon

191. Hill 1961, p. 183; Ashton 1964, p. 130.
192. Wilson 1984, p. 270.
193. 'Free trade' applied to British exports only; Irish cloth manufacturing was ruined by the competition from cheap English cloths in 1699. In 1700, Parliament banned imports of calicoes from the Orient; re-exports were permitted (Hill 1961, pp. 224–5). The ban was widely ignored in England, but Indian textile manufacturing suffered, though it would continue to prosper until after 1757, when the British set out forcibly to destroy hand-looms in India.
194. See above, pp. 121–5.

a diversifying home market for subsistence goods – food, clothing, household-wares – the manufacturers and the traders who sold their wares were increasingly faced with the prospect of being able to continuously expand their sales. Prospects, when open to all, become competitive pressures to see who could best fulfil demand with supply at the best price. The clamour to open up foreign trade to 'freer trade' – in its restricted, seventeenth-century meaning[195] – would have been strongly motivated by the realisation among merchants that the unlimited expansion of foreign trade could mean better prices for their produce if they had a larger number of buyers, and continual lowering of the costs of production in an economy of scale, and thus more profits and greater advantage in the competitive struggle to secure the largest share of markets. Thus free trade had everything to do with the development of England's domestic market (and as we shall discuss in the next chapters, of agrarian capitalism). England was already by this time the largest area in Europe without internal customs barriers hindering trade. When the Act of Union would be passed in 1707, joining Scotland with England, sending 'the price of Scottish cattle soaring'[196] as the Scots gained direct access to English markets, the largest free-trade area in Europe would become even larger.

Conclusion

The revolutionary upheaval from 1640 to 1688 constitutes a period of English history that needs to be understood in its own terms. The French bourgeoisie may have played a leading role in the revolution that came to France a century later, but attempts to conceptualise the Glorious Revolution as a 'bourgeois' revolution, even if an 'incomplete' one,[197] do serious injustice to the complexities of seventeenth-century English history. While urban-dwelling merchants and craftsmen played important roles in these struggles, the merchant community was divided between monopolists and free trade supporting interlopers, while the radical movement among the artisans was suppressed. What precipitated the English civil wars was not a conflict between an aristocracy and a bourgeoisie, but rather a conflict between a king and his parliament. By expanding extra-parliamentary sources of Crown revenue and resorting to arbitrary rule in their efforts to bypass Parliament's control of the purse, the Stuart monarchs stoked the fires of violent opposition from large segments of the landed class.

195. Wilson 1984, p. 271.
196. Hill 1961, p. 228.
197. As in, for example, the thesis of a 'mediated' bourgeois revolution put forward by Tom Nairn and Perry Anderson. See Anderson 1964, pp. 27–53; Anderson 1987, pp. 20–77 and Nairn 1988. For a critique, see Wood 1991, pp. 11–17.

The Stuarts' attempt to expand the patrimonial state in the direction of French absolutism was rooted in the logic of pre-capitalist economics based upon extra-economic forms of property. In a very real sense, this ran into conflict with the rising force of agrarian capitalism. For the growing power and independence of the landed classes was rooted in their increasing reliance upon strictly economic rents from farming undertaken by tenant-farmers on enclosed estates. As the rift between Crown and Parliament widened, both the merchant community and the landed classes themselves were divided. From the ranks of the labourers came a groundswell of dissent and calls for democracy ranging from merely extending the male franchise to the abolition of private property and the levelling of classes. Since the latter posed a potential threat to *both* capitalist and patrimonial or extra-economic forms of property, the suppression of radicalism, even the limited radicalism of the Independents who ruled under Cromwell during the Interregnum, became an imperative. In this sense, the whole period of upheaval from 1640 to 1688 might be said to amount to a counter-revolution as much as a revolution.

It is a general misnomer to see political revolutions as events which result in the immediate overhaul of whole economic systems. But this is not to say that revolution does not facilitate such change. As noted, the Restoration largely restored the political state of affairs that had existed before all the trouble began. This meant that the threat of Stuart absolutism had remained, and so the Glorious Revolution removed this threat by way of a revolution without radicalism. As the ascendant party in politics, the landed classes acting through Parliament in a new environment of political unanimity were now in a position to advance policies that would promote the social relations of agrarian capitalism, and the assault on customary or extra-economic forms of regulating manufactures, as well as commerce, now began in earnest.

Chapter Three
Agrarian Capitalism: The Key to Britain's Rise to Power

I can calculate the movement of the stars, but not the madness of men.

Sir Isaac Newton, after losing £20,000 in the South Sea Bubble[1]

During the first half of the eighteenth century, the British economy managed to weather two periods of agrarian depression, to underwrite the cost of putting its own army in the field of war and still provide unprecedented subsidies to allies in wartime, and to undergo regional transformations that created conditions favourable to industrialisation in the North and West of England. The basis for this dynamism was the continued growth of the domestic market and regional specialisation being driven by increasing rates of agricultural productivity and falling prices attributable to the continued expansion of agrarian capitalism.

Between 1688 and 1815, Britain fought six major wars with France, a nation with three times its population, and would suffer only one defeat: the American War, which unlike the wars fought on the Continent, was primarily a rebellion of colonists against the Empire. England enjoyed several advantages: the protection of the Channel, a superior navy and multiple allies in coalitions against France within which Britain was the major player. Moreover, England's colonial trade was more extensive than any of her rivals. This trade,

1. Carswell 1993, p. 108. This ubiquitous quote varies in the last word between 'men', '[the] people' and '[the] crowds'.

however, was in part a function of the expanding domestic market, which made the expansion of trade necessary and far more lucrative. Manufacturing in the early eighteenth century witnessed numerous portentous developments that signalled the approach, if not the arrival, of the Industrial Revolution: Darby's discovery of coke firing for the blast-furnace in 1709, Newcomen's steam engine of 1717 and the construction of the Old Silk Mill, to name but a few examples. Yet agrarian capitalism was already steering the economy in the direction of a broader capitalism by the time these key developments in manufacturing arrived. With output per head and overall agricultural productivity rising, exports of grain rising, food consumption and standards of living rising, Britain was out stripping all her rivals in the field of agriculture. To be sure, Britain had geological advantages over Europe. While trade in Europe was confronted with a more difficult terrain, a lower population density, rivers that were less readily navigable and wider distances between river basins, England enjoyed an exceptional range of geologically varying environments.[2] 'Nature had not been so kind as to Britain'.[3] But the key to Britain's rise as a world power was its economy, which was on a new footing, involving a unique market-based or capitalist system of agriculture.[4]

Views on the relationship between agriculture and manufacturing

There remains widespread scepticism over the significance of the role played by agriculture in helping to precipitate the Industrial Revolution. Before Brenner, most historians and historiographers saw the unique developments in English agriculture as playing an important but minor role as a causal factor in the Industrial Revolution. Agriculture forms one 'sector' among a dozen others in countless studies seeking the primary causal sector, while many reject the idea that such a 'smoking gun' exists. As we saw in both the Foreword and the Introduction, many resolve that the process of pristine industrialisation is too complex to be reduced to a single sector.

Fernand Braudel writes that agriculture 'rightly' tops the list of sectors in most studies of the causes of the Industrial Revolution. 'Was agriculture an integral part of this mighty achievement?', he asks. 'To ask this question is to be exposed to a thousand contradictory replies'.[5] Flinn and Habakkuk say no. Bairoch and Jones say yes. For his part, Braudel can only pose some tantalising questions. He notes that the English countryside had been integrated into the domestic economy; that English farms had managed to feed the urban populations into the

2. Jones 1977, p. 499.
3. Landes 1991, pp. 126–8, as quoted in Jones 1977, p. 499.
4. John 1961, p. 18 and Coleman 1956a, p. 288.
5. Braudel 1988, p. 558.

nineteenth century; and that by 1780 English agriculture was providing enough demand for about two to three hundred thousand tons of iron per year for the production of farm implements. Meanwhile, England imported large quantities of iron from Sweden and Russia. Braudel asks: '[W]as this not because the English domestic iron industry had insufficient capacity to meet the increasing demand largely accounted for by agriculture? And does that not suggest that agriculture was on the move before the development of industry?'[6] For Braudel, even in 'the apparently absurdly backward seventeenth century', everything 'was really on the move'.[7] Braudel finds that the Industrial Revolution is linked to the development of inland trade within Britain. But in asking: 'why did it develop so early in England?' he can only pose the question.[8]

Clarkson argues that by 1700 the skeleton of the manorial structure may have survived, but it was beginning to take on new flesh, that of enterprise and profit. He finds that the 'causes of this metamorphosis are obscure . . .'[9] Yet regarding its consequences, he states unequivocally that:

> the very considerable developments in agricultural techniques and organization in pre-industrial England, and the resulting increase in agricultural output did not transform the economy before 1750. Instead, it prepared the way for the industrial revolution of the late eighteenth century by permitting the gradual release of factors of production into industry and commerce, by contributing to a modest rise in effective demand among wage-earners and receivers of incomes from non-agricultural sources, and by fostering the growth of a market economy. By 1750 the agrarian yoke on the economy had been eased: it was not removed until the nineteenth century.[10]

This seems something of a contradictory formula. For although he qualifies the allegedly non-transformative, but multifold changes brought on by new agricultural techniques as 'modest' and 'gradual', the claim that agriculture 'paved the way' for the Industrial Revolution seems a fairly strong statement in favour of causal linkage. Flinn also prefers to see the contribution of agriculture as 'modest'. Despite the coincidence of agrarian enclosures with industrial changes, for Flinn: '[I]t must remain extremely doubtful whether the agricultural developments themselves would be sufficient to have played more than a modest part in stimulating an industrial revolution'.[11] For Berg, however, this kind of 'anti-agrarian prejudice' has contributed to 'an enormously mistaken view based on a rather

6. Braudel 1988, pp. 563–4.
7. Braudel 1988, p. 587.
8. Braudel 1988, p. 581.
9. Clarkson 1974, p. 68.
10. Clarkson 1974, p. 74.
11. Flinn 1966, p. 96.

insignificant place for agriculture in British Industrialisation'.[12] Berg claims that the evidence is now clear that the innovations that brought about most of the key technical changes in agriculture – irrigation, drainage, crop rotations and the use of root crops – were developed in the seventeenth and early eighteenth centuries, contributing to a dramatic increase in England's agrarian surplus. This surplus sustained population growth and the expansion of cities, which in turn helped to expand domestic and international markets. Joan Thirsk seeks to shift the emphasis away from demography, and argues that the type of farming community and the form of social organisation conditioned the pattern of growth in by-employments, especially in pastoral or dairying regions.[13] Both Berg and Thirsk tend to see the growth of cottage manufacturing as a development arising out of agrarian conditions and contributing to the development of industry, but do not necessarily embrace the view that cottage manufacturing consists of a stage of 'proto-industrialisation'.

Where English agriculture is concerned, theorists of proto-industrialisation have not entirely overlooked England's uniqueness in constructing a theory that makes a claim for a pan-European path to industrialisation. This is crucial because it demonstrates that even though the thrust of proto-industrialisation theory has been to try and support the concept of a pan-European development of cottage manufacturing as a precursor and progenitor of capitalist industrialisation at the expense of considering other causal factors, these theorists were nonetheless compelled by the facts to consider England's uniqueness. Peter Kriedte in particular writes several passages that would mesh well with the theory of agrarian capitalism, for example:

> England was most deeply affected by the development of the rural relations of production. The appropriation of social surplus labour in the form of feudal rent was discarded and the adoption of short-term modern leases changed the feudal rent into capitalist ground rent. Since the sixteenth century, English agriculture became commercialised, and relations of production were increasingly determined by the laws of the market.

Everything in the passage above concurs with what we discussed in the previous chapter. Where the theory of proto-industrialisation departs from the theory of agrarian capitalism is in its understanding of how all of this came about: 'Population growth, a deepening social division of labour, and the growing demand for wool generated by an expanding textile industry converged and destroyed the traditional agrarian structures'.

12. Berg 1985, p. 93.
13. Thirsk 1961, pp. 22–3, as cited in Berg 1985, p. 103.

Here it seems we have the demographic model, the commercialisation model and proto-industrial theory all rolled into one. The text continues: 'The collectivism which had hitherto determined the village economy was replaced by "agrarian individualism" (Marc Bloch). This opened up the possibility to introduce modern agrarian methods like convertible husbandry'.[14]

This is yet another striking example of assuming what needs to be explained. Demography, the extension of the division of labour and foreign trade spurred on by proto-industry are said to have 'destroyed' feudal relations, and then – *voila!* – commercial agriculture spontaneously came into being. This assumption is clearly apparent when Kriedte writes: 'The steadily progressing disintegration of the peasant economy opened the path for an agrarian production that was entirely market oriented'.[15]

Kriedte's main concern is with the rise of rural manufacturing, and how 'cottagers who lost their main source of income when the common land was partitioned and distributed among private owners were practically forced into rural industry'. But which is cause and which is effect? Does English 'proto-industry' stimulate trade which then breaks down traditional agrarian structures? Or does the division of the land through privatisation and enclosures (which left a 'deep mark on the rural social system', a definite understatement), force dispossessed rural dwellers into cottage manufacturing?

Kriedte is clear that England is the exceptional case when he writes: 'No-where did the development of industrial commodity production in the countryside run so directly parallel to the re-organisation of the rural relations of production according to the laws of the market as it did in England'. But what explains England's peculiarity? Kriedte has no answer other than to appeal to the idea that 'England was ahead of her continental rivals'.[16] And to the rule that says proto-industrialisation develops under conditions of subsistence-agriculture, Kriedte can only add the caveat that it could also develop in regions with commercial agriculture.[17] Yet at the same time Kriedte recognises that what allowed England to avoid the income reductions in agriculture that befell the continent was the increasing productivity of English agriculture. Increasing productivity meant a steadily growing domestic market for goods produced in 'cottage industry'.

14. Kriedte, Medick and Schlumbohm 1981, p. 21.
15. Kriedte, Medick and Schlumbohm 1981, p. 30.
16. The context of this quote should be made clear. Kriedte is discussing how England was able to overcome problems in the shortfall of supply for cottage manufacturing by replacing wood with coal. The full quote is: 'Here as in so many other cases, England was ahead of her continental rivals' (Kriedte, Medick and Schlumbohm 1981, p. 30). The 'other cases' for Kriedte include: the conversion to convertible husbandry, the 'steadily progressing disintegration of the peasant economy' and advances in productivity, which will be discussed below.
17. Kriedte, Medick and Schlumbohm 1981, p. 26.

That market was stabilised by the intensification of agrarian production through increasing inputs of labour and capital, which improved the soil and reduced dependence on the vagaries of nature. England was able to weather the seventeenth-century crisis in agricultural prices because with median incomes rising (as a result of the productivity of agriculture), the fall in prices did not mean an overall loss of purchasing power in the agrarian sector. Thus the prerequisites for rural manufactures were more favourable in England than on the Continent. Kriedte sees the divergence as located in the 'relations of production'.[18] But what does Kriedte mean by 'relations of production'? His analysis is sensitive to the pressures of trade, population and productivity on different economic agents in English agriculture. But he says little about changes in the structure of property-relations, or the class character of social relations of production. It is unclear if Kriedte means that further research into these areas not covered in his own study holds the key to explaining England's distinctiveness.

Ogilvie is clear about this when she calls for 'deeper investigation' of social institutions, since this 'may hold out the best perspectives for explaining differences in economic development, certainly in early modern Europe, and perhaps in pre-industrial societies more generally'.[19] Ogilvie is also clear when she states that 'there is no evidence that it was proto-industrialisation which led to the development of commercial agriculture, rather than agricultural surpluses which led to the growth of both proto-industries and – crucially – towns and cities'.[20] While Mendels originated the claim that 'proto-industrialisation' breaks down the traditional framework of agrarian relations (something that was 'theoretically assumed, rather than empirically demonstrated, and subsequent work on proto-industrialisation has not confirmed it'),[21] he nonetheless recognised that the creation of a domestic market in agriculture in England was crucial to supporting 'the growing section of the population that was no longer entirely self-sufficient in food'.[22] Proto-industrialisation theorists recognise the uniqueness of the English agrarian economy, but as they are wedded to the concept of cottage industry as 'proto-industry' and the stage prior to industrialisation in a sequence of developments, they entirely miss the importance of enclosures, market dependence and the effects of falling prices due to increased agrarian productivity under conditions of agrarian capitalism. Both Mendels and Kriedte recognise that English agricultural development was distinctly 'advanced' and

18. Kriedte, Medick and Schlumbohm 1981, pp. 31–2.

19. Ogilvie 1996, p. 37. Hudson (Hudson 1995, p. 59) finds that social and institutional factors are paramount in determining which regions of cottage manufacturing industrialised and which 'de-industrialised'.

20. Ogilvie and Cerman (eds.) 1996, p. 11.

21. Ogilvie 1996, p. 24.

22. Mendels 1972, p. 245.

that agricultural productivity was the key to supporting a growing non-agricultural population. Yet they see 'proto-industry' as either *the* cause of (Mendels) or a key factor in (Kriedte) the 'destruction' of traditional agrarian social relations. Not only is this understanding not confirmed by the evidence, writes Ogilvie, but in England, the Low Countries, Switzerland and the Rhine, landholding patterns were already 'weak' long before the development of cottage manufacturing tied to international markets (namely, 'proto-industry').[23] Only if we abandon entirely the notion that the expansion of rural manufacturing was responsible for the breakdown of feudal agrarian structures can we resolve this contradiction. This notion is itself based not upon the idea that there had to be a causal agent that released capitalism from the 'fetters' of the feudal structure. It is not based on a concern for how feudal social property relations were *transformed* into capitalist property relations, which would precisely require us to examine social relations of production and social institutions to understand both the dissolution of feudalism and the rise of capitalism. That is one of the goals of the present study.

War, debt and the land tax

England entered the eighteenth century between two wars with France. The most phenomenal aspect of the way in which war impacted upon the English state was its cost. In peacetime, a state expenditure of two million pounds per annum was considered excessive. Combined, the War of the Grand Alliance (1688–97) and the War of Spanish Succession (1702–13) cost British taxpayers £150 million. Of this sum, approximately one-third was raised through government borrowing, one-third from the land tax, with the final third coming mainly from customs and excise. There was considerable opposition to the growth of the excise. Unlike under the early Stuarts, this opposition had to do not with any renewed threat of absolutist or pro-Catholic tendencies on the part of the monarch, but rather with the concern that they would mean higher wages and lower profit margins. 'In other words, opposition to excise duties was motivated by a set of concerns which were distinctly *capitalist* in character'.[24]

The ultimate guarantee that the system would be maintained was the land tax. Being in possession of control of taxation, Parliament jealously guarded the land tax, as well as the appointment of the commissioners who supervised the local assessments, voting for it one year at a time. The land tax was assessed on the tenant, who then deducted the same amount from the rent paid to the landlord. Thus in stark contrast to absolutist France, where taxation fell heaviest upon the

23. Ogilvie 1996, p. 24.
24. Mooers 1991, pp. 162–4.

peasantry, England's landowners were taxing themselves through Parliament. Since it was a tax on the ground rents paid increasingly by a growing number of capitalist tenant-farmers exploiting rural wage labour, the actual proceeds were in fact rooted in this form of capitalist exploitation; specifically, the tripartite structure of agrarian capitalism. In both France and England, indirect taxes grew significantly during the early eighteenth century. In France, the expansion of indirect taxation was to fuel the seemingly limitless extension of noble offices in the absolutist state. In England, by contrast, these taxes were tolerated inasmuch as they went to pay for wars that forwarded English commercial expansion. A likely reason for the failure of Harley's Land Bank scheme is the simple fact that country gentlemen were already paying for the war through the land tax, which typically rose during wartime. Lending more money to the Crown might only encourage looser spending and result in an even higher land tax.

Government borrowing for wartime expenditure was nothing new. What was new was the political infrastructure. 'The credit-worthiness of the new régime, based as it was on a parliamentary title, was negligible without the clear understanding that the propertied classes would ultimately be prepared to foot the bill'.[25] As war dragged on and the debt mounted, the pretence that the debt could be repaid grew ever thinner. Anxieties mounted as well. Contemporaries believed that trade suffered disastrously due to war. The demands of the navy drew ships and men from the shipping trade. Sailors and soldiers died, meaning the loss of 'intangible human qualities'.[26] Domestic works such as the building-trade faced a lack of supplies. To 'those who had a shrewd perception', however, the advantages of political stability generated by this 'machinery for channeling private wealth into public expenditure' were becoming clear.[27] The ability of the English state to tap these vast new financial resources, based as it was on the still emerging structure of agrarian-capitalist relations in the economy, underpinned England's successes in the wars with France. Whereas England under the later Stuarts had earned the reputation on the Continent as 'little more than a pensioner of France', Britain emerged from its victories at Blenheim, Ramillies, Gibraltar and Minorca as 'a major force in Continental politics, a substantial power in the Mediterranean, and a worthy competitor for France overseas'.[28] War no doubt drew resources away from the economy, though contributing to it in other ways, such as ship-building, state demand for iron to make cannons, wool to make uniforms, and so on. The wars were also wasteful, and directed with a significant level of incompetence. But it was through war that England beat out its rivals

25. Langford 1986, p. 357.
26. Wilson 1984, p. 276.
27. Langford 1986, p. 357.
28. Langford 1986, p. 356.

in becoming the predominant transatlantic carrier in trade, holding a monopoly of trade and transport over a vast area. 'The rise of the British economy', writes Wilson, was based 'on the conscious and successful application of strength; just as the decline of the Dutch economy was based on the inability of a small and politically weak state to maintain its position against stronger states'.[29] This is a potentially misleading statement. It is true that Britain could not have expanded its empire without the use of force; other powers would have claimed these territories instead. And for any empire, expansion widened the sphere of trade. But what distinguished Britain was its ability to sustain levels of production to meet demand. By 1700, as much as forty percent of England's economy had moved out of agrarian employment. Within agrarian Europe, only the commercially-oriented economy of the Dutch Republic had seen a similar development. In non-capitalist countries the economy was limited by the low level of agricultural productivity. As non-agrarian employment expanded, demand for food rose, driving up food prices, wages and thus the price of manufactured goods. As prices rose, buying power was undermined, thus forcing the domestic economy to contract. But in England, constant improvement in agricultural productivity allowed the steady expansion of the manufacturing sector and the sustained expansion of the domestic market, allowing England to meet the challenge of expanding its international markets by steadily expanding production at home.[30]

Furthermore, England was uniquely able to provide extraordinary subsidies in the hundreds of thousands of pounds to its allies during the War of the Grand Alliance,[31] a trend that was to continue. The ability of the landed class in control

---

29. Wilson 1984, pp. 286–7. Wilson continues: 'Without the wars, the entire course of world history might have been different. The Bourbons might have triumphed and survived, neither learning nor forgetting. New France might have gone on, authoritarian, bureaucratic, orthodox, neo-feudal. The United States might never have emerged, and Britain herself might have declined into the economic lethargy of Sweden or Holland'. We can always speculate about how things might have been. But let us note that Wilson is surely not accounting for England's economic advantage, its agrarian capitalism.

30. Brenner 1985a, pp. 51–4.

31. To get the full scope of England's military commitments over the years 1688–97, it must first be considered that a force of some forty-eight thousand six hundred soldiers was committed to suppressing the Irish rebellion in support of James II in the wake of the Glorious Revolution, lasting until 1691. At the very same time (1689–91), England paid for between five thousand and twelve thousand troops serving in the Low Countries, and repaid a loan of £600,000 that the Dutch Estates General had made to William for his expedition to England in 1688. During these years, England began paying annual subsidies of £20,000 for Prussian troops in Flanders, £95,000 to aid Savoy's campaign in Italy, and more still to aid Hapsburg and Bavarian troops fending off a French assault. Subsidies picked up once the Irish campaign ended. By 1692–3, England supported an army of nearly forty-one thousand in Flanders, of whom over twelve thousand were foreign mercenaries. Annual subsidies of £25,000 and £35,000 respectively to Saxony and Hesse Cassel supported more troops in Flanders, and the numbers increased. From 1694 until 1697, England supported an army of forty-eight thousand English subjects, twenty

of Parliament to pay the tax even when it rose to new heights during wartime attests not only to the success of the financial revolution in England, but also to the strength of the domestic economy and the growing domestic wealth, based as it was upon agrarian-capitalist methods of production that could be mobilised for war. As the rivalry with France played out over the course of the eighteenth century, agrarian capitalism would generate the economic might necessary for Britain to outdo France in the game of imperialism, even as it was laying the foundations for the first industrialisation ever undertaken by any country.

The storm before the calm

As England entered the eighteenth century, the political convulsions of the seventeenth century left a volatile legacy. The apparent unanimity of the landed classes after 1688 appeared threatened by the rift between liberal Whiggism and country Toryism. The schism turned on the legitimacy of the régime, and Tory sympathies for the Stuarts. But beneath this was an increasing anxiety among country gentlemen, some of whom were hard-pressed to keep up with the pace of economic change, over William's financial revolution and the increasing number of 'placemen' in charge of the nation's finances, making handsome fortunes during a period of agrarian hardship. The schism was also characterised by differences over the conduct of war, with the Tories favouring peace and the Whigs holding out to press England's advantage. The real possibility of another restoration of the Stuart line gave this schism its profundity.

By 1697, France was ready to sue for peace, and having managed to stave off financial collapse, England was able to gain an honourable draw with the Treaty of Ryswick. The English economy had not been seriously impaired by war expenditure, and the fiscal crisis of 1693–6 by no means signalled an overall crisis in the economy, only a 'defective state of that instrument by which her material wealth was distributed'.[32] By 1700, England had broken its dependence on Europe and had reversed the terms of trade such that Europe now depended upon England as an *entropôt*. Between 1622 and 1700, imports of tobacco and sugar, taken together, had risen from two percent to 15 percent, while textiles had fallen from 41 percent to 26 percent of total imports. Between the 1660s and 1700, exports of foodstuffs rose from 3 percent to 11 percent while textiles fell from 74 percent to 69 percent of total exports.[33] Trade with the Baltic began to undergo a dramatic shift away from exporting woollens in exchange for grain

thousand five hundred foreign soldiers, added to which were Prussian, Saxon and Hessian troops living from English subsidies (Jones 1988, pp. 7–8).

32. Macaulay 1886, p. 578.
33. Coleman 1977, pp. 121–2 and 139–141.

toward a trade of re-exports, raw materials and other exports for imports of timber, iron, hemp and flax. While exports to Europe continued to grow, the overall percentage fell due to a rapid increase in colonial trade.[34] Thus it was not only the volume of trade, but its shape that was changing.

However, a severe slump in England's textile exports followed the peace at Ryswick. Cloth was at this time still very much England's primary export, and wool led the way. One cause for the slump was the decline of Holland's *entrepôt*-trade, whereby former customers were bypassing the Dutch middlemen and dealing directly with producers. Another cause was the rising competition from Irish Linens. In response, a prohibition was placed on all woollen manufacture in Ireland, and all Irish exports of wool had to pass through England, placing the entire Irish wool clip at the disposal of English manufacturers. This prohibition was consistent with the Navigation Acts; primary materials within the Empire were to be reserved for the benefit of domestic manufacturing in England.

At the same time as England was ruining the Irish woollen trade, a policy devised to reverse the terms of trade with India began with a ban on all imports of silks and printed calicoes. By 1700, 14 percent of English imports were made up of textiles and spices from India. Indian cottons produced 'a near-revolution in textile fashions'. British consumers seemingly could not get enough of calicoes and muslins from India, 'and sundry other exotically-named cotton fabrics which started to flood into England' in the late seventeenth century. In Lancashire, where cotton had made its way into textile manufacturing in the form of fustians and other mixed cotton and linen products, the competition of Indian cotton posed a serious threat to domestic cloths.[35] The cotton cloth manufacturers lobbied for protective tariffs and got them. The first in a series of bans passed in 1701.[36] These bans had the effect of stimulating the re-export trade. Experiments in imitating Indian cottons were also given stimulus, though with

34. Specifically, the advance of the period was led by a surge of imports from New England (whale oil, lumber, furs and provisions), the Carolinas (tobacco, rice, silk, indigo) the Caribbean (sugar, molasses and wood) and Asia (spices, cotton goods). From Africa, gold dust, ivory and the lucrative slave trade further enhanced Britain's colonial commerce (Ashton 1964, p. 154).

35. Coleman 1977, p. 162.

36. In 1698, the interlopers had finally managed to gain a Charter for a 'New' East India Company, creating a situation of two rival East India Companies that lasted until 1702 and lingered until their eventual merger in 1708. Its directorate included nineteen merchants actively engaged in the East India Trade, as compared with only four actively trading among the directors of the 'Old' Company (Jones 1988, p. 288). The 1701 ban signified a victory for woollen-manufacturers over the East India Company, in an ongoing trial of strength, coming as it did during the 'great schism' between the two rival East India Companies. The ban was less than successful, as consumers continued to prefer the Indian prints. This led in 1721 to a ban on the wearing of imported printed fabrics (Coleman 1977, pp. 162–3). The course of the legislation ran as follows:

limited success. Most importantly, by sheltering and providing stimuli to the domestic cotton industry, 'a new body of experience in cotton textile technology' was created.[37]

It was also under the protection of tariffs that silk manufacturing would give rise to the first factory. In some instances, protective tariffs actually gave rise to whole new industries in Britain, or they made giants out of infants. The British paper industry initially produced only brown paper. After improving its technique, it managed to become the primary source of fine white paper and of printing paper for journals, which began proliferating rapidly after 1710.[38] Bans and restrictions on imports, however, were not the only means of protecting domestic production. They were also placed on exports, with the goal of reserving primary materials for the benefit of the home industry. Wool was the primary instance of this. Not only was the export of raw wool banned, but so were textile machinery and the emigration of artisans. Such protective policies were not in any way driven by the imperatives of capitalist industry, for English manufactures could not yet be seen as integrally capitalist, and capitalist production outside of England was still unknown. The goal was to create 'a protected home market, to restrict imports, and to encourage a positive balance of trade in manufactured products'.[39] Since the 1670s, the system of government bounties on grain exports had been in place and these enabled grain exporters to sell grain at below cost price abroad, leading to an expansion of English grain exports, sparking complaints from the Dutch and others over the flood of cheap English grain. The War of the Spanish Succession (1701–14) also disrupted production on the Continent, creating market space for English textile exports. Thus England experienced an export boom during the 1700s, based upon huge increases in grain and woollen-textile exports to Holland, Germany, Russia, and Poland.[40] This boom created an overall favourable balance of trade and underwrote England's ability to expand

- 1699: Irish exports of wool and woollen textiles to foreign and colonial markets banned
- 1700: imports of silks and printed calicoes banned or restricted
- 1701: import, save for re-export , of printed calicoes and other cottons prohibited
- 1721: wearing (or consumption) of all imported pure cotton prints prohibited
- 1736: printed fustians exempted from the 1721 act

37. Coleman 1977, p. 163. This technology 'was to have its bigger and more famous consequences in the second half of the eighteenth century'.

38. Wilson 1984, p. 306.

39. Black 2001, p. 69.

40. While England's competitors were crippled by war, they remained unable to compete or to uphold tariffs to keep English goods out of markets they previously controlled. For example: '[W]hen Spanish Flanders was won over into allied control in 1706, the English and Dutch set about dismantling the prohibitive tariffs created under French influence against their goods in 1701 and replacing it with a new tariff which gave an even more favourable position than that enjoyed under the earlier 1680 tariff' (Jones 1988, p. 195).

her military operations and subsidies to foreign powers on a scale outstripping that of the previous war.

In 1697, Louis XIV had recognised William's legitimacy as part of the Treaty of Ryswick. But when James died in 1701, Louis XIV now recognised his son, James Francis Edward Stuart (the 'Old Pretender') as the rightful heir to the English throne. The following year William died, passing the crown to Anne, second daughter of James II. Anne had been the first heir apparent to attract opposition politicians to her apartment at Whitehall, a pattern that would be followed throughout the century.[41] Under the Act of Settlement (1701), should Anne die without an heir, the crown would pass to Sophia, Electress of Hanover. Out of seventeen pregnancies, only one of Anne's children survived past the age of two. But when the young William Duke of Gloucester died only a few days past his eleventh birthday in 1700, Sophia became the heir apparent. The weakness of Sophia's claim could only strengthen that of the Old Pretender. Next to him, her genealogy was remote. Anne herself was 'an undoubted (and undoubting) daughter of the Church of England'. In 1704, her thirty-ninth birthday was marked by the introduction of a bill in the Commons, later known as 'Queen Anne's Bounty',[42] for the Crown to surrender from £16,000 to £17,000 of its traditional income to the Church for the purpose of aiding the woefully inadequate stipends of local clerics. The Tories drew their strength from the 'twin pillars of loyalty to the house of Stuart and the Church of England'.[43] For her part, the Queen took the Tory cry of the 'Church in Danger'[44] as a personal insult. But she nonetheless favoured the Tories during her reign, despite committing herself to the Elizabethan principle of national unity, serving as the disinterested arbiter between opportunistic parties.

41. 'Prior to the reign of James II, Stuart monarchs co-operated closely with their heirs apparent; from the Revolution, however, the heir to the throne was usually the nominal head of the opposition. The success of the Revolution had legitimized opposition to the personal wishes of the monarch, but not to the crown; as the distinction between monarch and crown remained uncertain, politicians who were not in royal favour sought the aid of the heir apparent to cloak their activities with some degree of respectability' (Gregg 1980, p. 74).

42. The Bounty was immediately popular, and did much to counteract High Tory propaganda. As the Queen pointed out in her message to Parliament, she sought 'the advantage of the Church of England as by law established, for which nobody can have a more true and real concern than myself' (Gregg 1980, p. 179).

43. Gregg 1980, p. 133.

44. This was the Tories' strength in a country that was ninety percent Anglican. However: 'The old Tory battle-cry of "Peace and the Church in Danger" could not rival in popular appeal the Whig slogan of "Trade and the Protestant Succession", to which Hanoverian Tories no less than Whigs could be expected to rally. Rent by internal dissent, the Tory ministry staggered on, while Bolingbroke indulged in fantasy by planning a wholly Jacobite Administration and trying to gain control of the army and of strategic points in the kingdom' (Owen 1975, p. 3).

By recognising the Old Pretender's claim, Louis XIV had solidified English public opposition to his designs and by resurrecting the Jacobite cause and the threat of a French-backed invasion of England he had secured the Anglo-Dutch alliance to prevent Louis XIV from inheriting the Spanish throne.[45] The War of the Spanish Succession that followed would not end during Anne's reign. The scope of the land war was bewildering; with simultaneous battles being fought in Spain, Italy and the Spanish Netherlands. Initially, success in 1705 and 1706 led Parliament to allot unprecedented sums of money to the war effort, 'in the hope of final victory in 1707',[46] though 1707 brought a reversal of fortunes. In the same session, plans for union with Scotland proceeded, arising out of security-concerns for both countries. For England, concern lay in the very real threat that Scotland might reject the Hanoverian succession, and thereby also the Revolution Settlement, and recognise, instead, the Old Stuart Pretender as heir to the Scottish crown. For Scotland, union might allow it to avoid being turned into a bloody battleground as a pawn in European politics. Scotland had economic reasons to support the union, however. Scotland's chief export was linen and England was by far the largest market. Union would mean access to a free market and the end of paying duties on exports to England.[47] Though bitterly opposed by the Tories, the Act of Union with Scotland was ratified on 1 May 1707.[48] The two parliaments were merged, as were the two fiscal systems, creating the largest

45. The drift back to war had already begun by this point. While Louis XIV had reluctantly agreed to lay his claim to the Spanish throne aside in favour of his grandson, Philip, Duc d'Anjou, who became Philip V of Spain, the rest of Europe waited to see whether Philip would be his own man, or a puppet of his grandfather. When Louis sent his troops to rebuild fortifications in the Spanish Netherlands in February 1701, the English and the Dutch began their preparations for a return to the battlefield to check French expansionism once again, and to prevent a Franco-Spanish behemoth from emerging. Louis had also cut off England and the Netherlands from trade with Spain. The fate of both the Spanish Netherlands as a trading partner and Spain's American possessions as a potential export market were of the utmost concern to Britain, as later events would bear out (Hoppit 2000, p. 109).

46. Gregg 1980, p. 239.

47. While England could easily obtain linen from other sources, Scottish linen-makers depended upon the English market. 'How much this influenced the final decision is impossible to assess; the merchants of Edinburgh certainly asserted in 1710 that "the great inducement made use of to engage Scotland in this Union was the prospect of improving and vending our linen . . . by a direct exportation"' (Durie 1979, p. 233).

48. The Tories saw a threat to the Church of England in the recognition of Presbyterianism as the established church of Scotland. The Tories also represented a long tradition of English snobbery (or worse) directed at the Scots. When James VI of Scotland became James I of England in 1603, he made attempts to unify the two nations. However, in his proposal to unify the laws of the two nations, but not their parliaments, Parliament smelled a rat. Debates at Westminster revealed a disdain for the Scots bordering on the hysterical: "'Zoological metaphor', remarks S.G.E. Lythe, 'was strained to the limit to describe the ravening hordes of Scotsmen waiting the chance to flood southwards'." (Smout 1969, p. 177, quoting Lythe 1958, pp. 219–28).

free-trade area in Europe. The loss of national independence generated strong anti-union sentiments and Scotland became ripe for a Jacobite attempt. So the Old Pretender, twenty-year-old James Francis Edward Stuart, prepared a plan to invade in March 1707. Although he never set foot on British soil, the threat was enough to cause a panic on London's financial markets, and to precipitate calls for new elections to Parliament. In the elections, the Whigs won a crushing victory. The winter of 1708–9 was one of the worst in memory. Famine conditions in France led Louis XIV to sue for peace, but with the Whigs back in power insisting on a policy of 'no peace without Spain', the war would carry on for another four years.

The costs of the war were extraordinary. By 1710–11, Britain was 'paying for fully 171,000 officers and men (58,000 subject and 113,750 foreign) to fight abroad in Europe.'[49] Britain was able not only to field an army composed mainly of hired foreign mercenaries,[50] but also once again to provide subsidies to its allies. At the same time, transporting supplies not being an option, local purchase for provisioning the troops was necessary.[51] Thus most of the spending on foreign supplies would not provide any backflow to aid the trade balance. Critics who felt that England should concentrate on her naval superiority were dubious at the costs of a 'double forward commitment'.[52] As noted, the total bill of the two wars of succession came to £150 million. In peacetime, military expenditure of £2 million per annum was thought excessive. How was England once again able to sustain such enormous outlays for war? The new financial institutions that had

49. Jones 1988, pp. 10–11.

50. Although 'Marlborough was the leading military figure in the alliance, the war was very much a collective enterprise and one where Britain's direct military contribution was relatively small. In 1702 the Empire was meant to put 82,000 men into the field, the Dutch 100,000 and the British 40,000. However, Britain only sent just over 13,000 to the continent, buying in foreign troops to make up the deficit. Even at its peak, in 1709, only 28,000 Britons were serving under Marlborough. Subsidies – mainly to Savoy and Portugal – [reached] an absolute peak of £875,000 in 1710' (Hoppit 2000, p. 115).

51. England's forces under the Duke of Marlborough were not innocent of atrocities. From October 1702 to May 1703, during a streak of stunning victories in a campaign to secure the Eastern frontier of the Austrian Empire, Marlborough's army 'destroyed everything in its path in a vain attempt to force the Elector, Max Emmanuel, to change sides – Marlborough oversaw the futile and awful destruction of some 500 villages' (Hoppit 2000, pp. 114–20). But the fact that England laid out huge sums to pay for local supply suggests that England committed fewer atrocities in relative terms when we consider that the *Kontribution*, a holdover from the Thirty Years' War, was still in use by other armies. 'In Poland, down to the defeat of the Saxons at Fraustadt early in 1706, Russian, Swedish, Polish and Saxon armies repeatedly moved to and fro levying ruinous *Kontribution* as they went . . . In classic fashion, plague breaking out between 1706 and 1713 compounded the miseries of war . . .' (Jones 1988, pp. 183–204).

52. The 'double forward commitment' refers to a policy whereby the army was deployed forward on a permanent basis and the navy most of the time (Jones 1988, pp. 41–3).

sustained the first war once more proved indispensable. But in order to borrow, there had to be private wealth that could be lent, and this is where England held an advantage which stemmed from England's superiority in agricultural output:

> Over the century or so preceding the wars there had been significant economic developments, the most fundamental being the introduction of various forms of convertible husbandry (almost unique in Europe), with a resulting increase in agricultural output. This not only transformed England's subsistence position, but also made more wool available for her textile industries. On this basis, England was in a superior position to command the resources to meet the demands of a Double Forward Commitment.[53]

The double forward commitment testified to the dynamic growth of wealth in England's unique domestic economy, which was being transformed by the forces of agrarian capitalism.

Unprecedented violence marred the elections of 1710. The Tories were able to successfully take advantage of the discontent with the Whigs over the Sacheverell affair to divide the public and guarantee an electoral victory. Once in power, the Tories took full advantage of the public mood against nonconformists, passing new legislation against them. The Tories also moved swiftly into negotiations for peace.

When the Queen fell ill in December 1713, her imminent demise set off a crisis in the Tory party leadership. An out-and-out struggle for power ensued between the more moderate Oxford, and the Jacobite-leaning St. John, newly titled Viscount Bolingbroke, who had unforgivably allowed himself to be seen publicly with the Pretender during the peace negotiations. In April, Parliament passed legislation confirming the Hanoverian succession. It offered a reward for the Pretender 'dead or alive' should he set foot on British soil. This was merely an attempt to cover up political divisions so deep that they provoked Charles d'Iverville, the French Envoy to England, to comment: '"Affairs are moving in such a manner that civil war is becoming inevitable in England"'.[54] In May, Electress Sophia died, leaving her son Elector George Lewis as heir to the British crown. George 'was a convinced supporter of the claims of the Habsburg Charles VI to the throne of Spain; he was also a soldier with a warm admiration for the duke of Marlborough'. Put 'so much out of patience by Hanoverian intrigues with the Whigs', Oxford himself made final appeals to the Pretender to declare himself a Protestant in the early months of 1714. The Pretender adamantly refused.[55]

53. Jones 1988, p. 43.
54. As quoted in Gregg 1980, p. 380.
55. Holmes (ed.) 1969, p. 227. Both men had made such appeals to the Pretender since 1710. Their early winter negotiations of 1714 were kept secret from each other and from the Queen. Where Bolingbroke's appeals to the Pretender were aimed merely at

The timing of the Queen's death in July 1714 seemed to pre-empt the imminent crisis that had been brewing. The accession of George I came off initially without incident. The arrival of the House of Hanover, which would last until the death of Victoria in 1901, heralded an extraordinary era of political stability and economic prosperity. The initial quietude, however, was broken when protests erupted in over thirty towns on the day of George I's coronation. Violence also marred the elections of that year, in which the Whigs came to power, despite the Tories having held a huge majority of some 240 seats. A Whig majority was necessary for the Hanoverian succession to succeed. And it may have reflected a new elite consensus, but it was far from reflecting overall popular sentiment. The outpouring of popular discontent with the rule of George and the Whigs was sufficient for the Whigs to pass the Riot Act, suspending *habeas corpus* and inciting further anger and frustration. Thinking there may be no place for them in the new régime, the Tories began to look to the Pretender.[56] Taking both the government and the unprepared Tories by surprise, the embittered Earl of Mar was the first to raise his standard in Scotland on 6 September 1715, proclaiming James III true king of Great Britain. The campaign had very little chance of success. By 22 October, the Scottish and English risings combined forces, but still only totalled a tiny force of one thousand four hundred men on foot and six hundred men on horseback. Seeking support, they marched toward Lancashire and the force trebled before confronting government troops and surrendering unconditionally on 13 November. Retributions followed. With the rising defeated, the Tories discredited and leaderless, the Whigs now set about strengthening their formidable position. Any Tory was now tainted with the suspicion of having harboured support (if not having given it outright) for the rising. Those who lost the most out of the 'Fifteen' were the Tories, who went from having a huge majority in Parliament to losing major party status, all in the span of a few years.[57] For Holmes, the Tories had virtually self-destructed: 'By spurning the limited yet important favours which George I was prepared to bestow on them; by bungling their election campaign in the winter of 1714–15 and so failing to capitalize on a natural majority in the constituencies, by withholding their support but not

---

expediency, Oxford was seeking a sincere and immediate conversion. Gregg (Gregg 1980, p. 377) comments of James Francis Edward Stuart that his 'private refusal to dissimulate his religion was the fatal decision which determined the course of his future career. In this, he displayed his full share of Stuart arrogance and lack of remorse . . .'

56. Speck 1977, pp. 176–8.

57. '[How] a party which commanded a natural majority of the political nation, which had enjoyed since 1710 a position of unprecedented strength in the House of Commons, and whose members had engrossed by 1714 almost every important civil office in the kingdom, thereupon disappear[ed] from the political map, as a potent force, for three-quarters of a century . . . [is] one of the strangest riddles in British political history' (Holmes 1969, p. 216).

their sympathy from the rebels of the '15, they virtually offered themselves up as a sacrifice to their enemies'.[58]

The extent of Tory support for the Jacobite cause is impossible to verify. Feiling writes of the 'disgrace of their leaders and the pillorying of them all for the sins of a few', adding that 'the Tories did penance for their years of tampering with lost causes', the Anglican bishops turning against them out of the '"abhorrence" of rebellion'.[59]

Given the astonishing speed with which the Tories collapsed, how justified were fears of civil war? With the deaths in the years 1712–16 of Anne, Sophia, Marlborough and others 'who had served their political apprenticeships in the Restoration era',[60] came the passing of a generation that had carried those fears forward.[61] The outlook of a new generation weary of war was not haunted by memories of the civil wars. Anne's reign, writes Gregg, 'proved to be the great watershed between the violence of the seventeenth century and the stability and prosperity of the eighteenth century'.[62] In retrospect, the real threat of Jacobitism lay in the threat of a French invasion. With France's recognition of the Hanoverian Succession at Utrecht and the subsequent failure of the 'Fifteen', Britain's landed elites had much to lose and little to gain by allowing a dispute amongst them to carry on any longer.

Stability and 'old corruption'

After the 'Fifteen' and the Bubble of 1720, Britain's landed class enjoyed a period of peace, a decreased land tax, and a stable political system characterised by the extensive use of patronage ('old corruption') under the guidance of Robert Walpole. In effect, this amounted to the full consolidation of the political régime of agrarian capitalism. The economy as a whole continued to flourish as paper money and country banks vastly expanded the supply of local credit. Continued growth and regional diversification within Britain's domestic market, combined with the continued expansion of trade, particularly colonial trade, created the conditions for the rise of domestic consumerism and the pre-emergence of a middle class. The rise of consumerism, combined with the increased tolerance

58. Holmes 1969, p. 234. Above all, Holmes blames the destructive power struggle between Oxford and Bolingbroke for this failure, since it paralysed the party.

59. Feiling 1938, p. 16.

60. The new generation 'knew James II and arbitrary authority only by repute and . . . had come to the fore in an age of toleration towards Dissenters, frequent elections, annual parliaments, terrible wars, heavy taxation, enormous national debts, and a burgeoning press' (Hoppit 2000, p. 312).

61. Ibid.

62. Gregg 1980, p. 400.

and freedom of the press, facilitated the growth of literacy, political consciousness and ultimately popular politics. Despite their growing numbers, urban professionals did not yet approach the status of 'a class with its own institutions and objectives, self-confident enough to challenge the managers of "old corruption" ... As surveyors, attorneys, tutors, stewards, tradesmen, etc., they were contained within the limits of dependency ...'[63] Despite growing resentments at this state of dependency, and the strong desire for independence, this pre-middle class required allies in order to check the rampant parasitism of the elite. These they found in the disaffected Tory squires, the press, the elevation of the courts increasingly to play the role of neutral arbiter of disputes and the 'ever-present resistance of the crowd; a crowd which stretched at times from small gentry and professional men to the poor ...'[64] There was, however, much room for ambiguity. For even as these forces challenged the control that elites exercised over their lives through various forms of paternalism now entering a period of decline, they were also faced with increasingly unregulated *market* forces that were being developed amidst the decline of such paternalistic forms of control.

The opening of some sixty years of Whig hegemony[65] was not, however, without its fireworks. Doubt was cast on Whig integrity when they passed the Septennial Bill in April 1716, fixing Parliamentary elections to occur every seven years instead of three. Protests erupted when the Duke of Somerset introduced the Peerage Bill in 1719, seeking to consolidate the number and thus the power and privilege of the peerage at the expense of royal power. It was prudently withdrawn. These events were overshadowed by a diplomatic revolution when Britain entered into an alliance with its long-time rival France. Meanwhile, a 'Swedish plot' to supply a force of ten thousand men for another Jacobite rising was exposed.[66] In June 1718 the Royal Navy defeated the Spanish fleet that had

63. Thompson 1993, p. 32.
64. Thompson 1993, pp. 33–5.
65. Colley challenges the notion that the stability of Georgian England rested on the proscription and ultimate dissolution of the old Tory Party. Specifically, she challenges Habakkuk's postulation, adopted by Plumb, namely that the engrossment of estates between 1714 and 1750 came at the expense of Tory estates and thus explained the party's decline: 'It was so convenient to assume that this decline in small landowners was the economic counterpart to the political decline of the Tory party; that the increasing rigidity of the eighteenth-century land market which Habakkuk had postulated was the necessary libretto to the operatic extravaganza which was Whig oligarchy and Walpolian success ... It was this combination of supposed economic obsolescence and supposed political impotence which has made the proscribed Tory party so unattractive to historians ...' (Colley 1982, pp. 6–7). Writing half a century earlier, Feiling also finds that between 1714 and 1747 'all this time the fragment called Tories were not extinct' (Feiling 1938, p. 55).
66. George I was generally preoccupied with his native Hanover, where he felt far more welcome than in Britain. Peace with France meant that he could concentrate on

invaded Sicily in a short, one-sided affair between two nations who were not yet at war. In July Britain entered into a Quadruple alliance with Austria, France and Holland against Spain and its bid to reclaim Italian possessions given up at Utrecht.[67] Threatened with more losses, Spain quickly made peace in January 1720. That same year the adventurous Charles XII of Sweden died in an apparent accident and the Great Northern War (1700–20) quickly came to a close. For the first time in generations, Europe was faced with the extraordinary prospect of lasting peace. It was at that precise moment that Britain, France and their trading partners were engulfed in the frenzy of speculative financial bubbles.

In 1708 a City bank known as the Sword Blade Company had become involved in a legal dispute with the Bank of England. Its aim was to challenge the Bank's hegemony, but when its own mortgage scheme went sour, it blamed the Bank.[68] One of the causes of the Tory victory in 1710 was the growing fear about the national debt. In 1711, the Tories announced a public lottery designed to help pay it off. The Sword Blade Company outmanoeuvred the Bank in fulfilling subscriptions for a public lottery scheme by selling all tickets in four days, whereupon Robert Harley, whose Land Bank scheme of the 1690s had failed miserably, announced to Parliament on 7 March that the Government's total unsecured debt now came to £9 million. The next day, 8 March, he was stabbed, and John Blunt, Secretary of the Sword Blade Company, took charge of the Treasury. Blunt immediately announced a second lottery. Harley returned to Parliament in April. On 2 May, he announced his scheme to convert the entire £9 million into shares of capital for the South Sea Company. In return, the Government agreed to pay interest and granted trading privileges in the Spanish Main, privileges later secured when Britain gained trading rights in Spanish America under the *Asiento*. The announcement was greeted with euphoria. Harley was made Earl of Oxford.

But the slave trade with Spanish America that was supposed to be the real business of the Company was not turning a profit. And when war with Spain broke out in 1718, the Company's property, valued (perhaps overvalued) at £300,000, was seized, leaving the Company exposed as a naked finance corporation. Meanwhile in France, a Scotsman by the name of John Law was entrusted with France's entire national debt, valued at £130 million, which he converted into shares of his

---

Hanover's interests in the Baltic, where he had drawn Britain's navy into action in the Baltic on the side of an alliance against Sweden, to which Hanover was a party in the Great Northern War (1700–20) (Hoppit 2000, pp. 399–400).

67. In turn, Spain took up support for the Jacobite cause, sending an invasion force in early 1719 which, reminiscent of the Armadas, was turned back by inclement weather. A second and smaller force of three hundred Spanish soldiers reached Scotland, and joined with one thousand clansmen before being quickly defeated.

68. Carswell 1993, p. 32.

Company of the Indies. The masters of the South Sea Company were challenged to match Law's success; they even sought to amalgamate the Bank and the East India Company into their South Sea enterprise. Their objective, however: 'took no account of the contrast between English and French economies. The French economy was stagnant and needed a stimulus which the already overheated British economy did not require, and they never seem to have foreseen that a mountain of credit unsupported by yield would inevitably collapse'.[69]

By 1720, the total unsecured national debt stood at £31 million and the South Sea Company outbid the Bank for the next round of conversion with an offer of £7.5 million. South Sea stock soared.[70] Like the lotteries, subscriptions sold as soon as they were on the market, enabling the directors to realise their profits even before the debt had been converted. In May, rampant inflation burst the bubble of Law's scheme in France, the currency collapsed and a drastic restructuring of French state finances was ordered.[71] This only bolstered the value of South Sea stock, allowing it to dominate European markets. The Company was now offering sweet deals for cash. For example, the Company would announce that it would advance £300 worth of shares for every £100 in currency deposited. Unlike the French cash bubble, the South Sea bubble was a credit bubble. Short of cash, Blunt would prepare each new subscription to mop up existing cash with more credit-based shares. Between February and July, the value of South Sea stock rose from £175 to £1,000. In September, the bubble burst. By the end of that month, it had fallen back to £180. The Company had no alternative but to turn to its arch-rival, the Bank, for assistance. The damage was widespread. Urban workmen in London, such as builders, suffered mightily at the loss of trade, being forced to halt work on half-finished ships and houses. The 'experts' had lost credibility. A wave of public scrutiny and moral judgment ensued with pamphleteers and journalists demanding answers and reprisals. 'Let us pursue

69. Note that here we have yet another author reflecting upon the exceptional dynamism of Britain's (agrarian-capitalist) economy. 'In modern values', writes Carswell, the £130 million in converted French debt would be about £20 billion, so that the Company of the Indies, even today, is still one of the largest capitalist enterprises that has ever existed' (Carswell 1993, pp. 65–77).

70. Within an hour of the books opening on 14 April, a million shares had already sold, including a purchase worth £100,000 by the King himself. By now, fortunes were being made and lost. The greatest fortune was made by Thomas Guy, whose total reward for stock sold was £234,000. The hospital built from these funds was 'the best memorial the Bubble left behind it'. Sir Isaac Newton withdrew his £7000 of South Sea stock on 20 April, having made a hundred percent profit on his investment (Carswell 1993, pp. 41–5 and 113).

71. On 21 May, Law's 'extraordinary decree' reduced the value of all fixed notes and shares by 25 percent. 'Paris, reported Stair, was like a town taken by storm, and he put the loss to British subjects alone at £3 million. Troops appeared in the streets...' (Carswell 1993, p. 121).

to disgrace, destruction, and even death', cried one journal, 'those who have brought this ruin upon us . . .'[72]

Robert Walpole, who had withdrawn his shares from the bubble early, and who had resigned as Paymaster-General in 1717, now became Chancellor of the Exchequer and took charge of the recovery plan, under which the Bank and the East India Company absorbed nearly half of the South Sea Company's £38 million in paper capital. Money subscribers lost, on average, fifty percent of their investment; holders of annuities lost between one and two-thirds.[73] Despite all this, most were grateful for the settlement because without it subscribers stood to lose the full amount of their subscriptions and annuitants all but a fraction of their incomes. At the same time, however, Walpole's task involved 'screening' those in high places from charges of corruption, whilst satiating those crying for revenge. For this he became known popularly as the 'skreenmaster general'. It was only the beginning of a system of patronage which would keep Walpole in power for over two decades.[74] Walpole's system of justice had a decided class bias.[75] He was duly rewarded with the office of First Lord of the Treasury in April 1721. His subsequent leadership (or control through patronage) of the Commons would later earn him recognition as Britain's first Prime Minister.

While the bubble resulted in many losses, the economy as a whole continued to flourish. The introduction of paper money in the countryside gave a boost to the agricultural revolution and brought a permanent improvement in the accessibility of rural credit. The first country bank had been set by James Wood of

72. Trenchard and Gordon 1995, pp. 145–6 as cited in Hoppit 2000, p. 406.

73. Dale 2004, p. 146.

74. Wilson 1984, pp. 259–60. Robert Walpole was one of the few (and one of the last) statesmen to make a fortune as a politician. In the 1720s and 1730s Houghton Hall was transformed from a modest country house into a small palace. When he died in 1745, he left debts of £50,000 on a mortgaged estate. His assets outweighed his debts, however, and in this respect his case may have been a typical one.

75. To give some examples: Despite damning evidence against him, Charles Stanhope escaped censure in large part thanks to Walpole's efforts to manipulate the vote in his favour. In March 1720, Stanhope was credited 'with £50,000 of fictitious South Sea Stock at the then market price of £250, which he "sold" three months later at a price of £750. He thereby netted an extraordinary profit of £250,000 which was paid to him via a nominee account at the Sword Blade Bank'. A clumsy cover-up ensued in which his name in the SSC's cash book was altered to read as 'Stangape'. Apparently, no effort was made to pursue the matter any further. Even John Aislabie, who served as the scapegoat for the whole affair, being expelled from the House and sent to the Tower with all his assets frozen, would later be reprieved and allowed to spend the rest of his life practicing landscape gardening on his Studeley Manor in Yorkshire, having retained £165,000 out of £210,000 in assets, again thanks largely to the intervention of Walpole, whose sympathies and standards of justice were decidedly on the side of those with money and influence (Dale 2004, pp. 150–2).

Gloucester in 1716,[76] the first in a wave of country banks that would peak in number around 1800 and nearly vanish by 1900. By the mid-1720s, the revolution in public finance was effectively complete, and it had an enduring effect on the finance of business that was sustained right through the period of the Industrial Revolution. By 1750, the buying and selling of government stock had been reduced to a routine. London, while rivalled in trade by the rise of the Western ports, remained steadfastly the financial centre of the country, and increasingly, of Europe.[77]

With the recent experience of the bubble and panic at the outbreak of plague in Southern France, few would have foreseen the stability that lay ahead. The Tories returned only 170 members to Parliament in 1722. The Whigs prepared for another seven years of hegemony, further secured by the exposure of the 'Atterbury plot' later that year.[78] While the buoyancy of economic life in London after

---

76. Ashton 1969, p. 71. According to Mathias (Mathias 1983, p. 151), the first country bank was set up in 1716 in Bristol.

77. See Wilson 1984, pp. 324–7. Berg (Berg 1994, p. 183) rejects the notion that the financial revolution and the Industrial Revolution had very little to do with one another, noting that an increasing number of connections between financial innovations and industrial development are/were being uncovered at the level of the firm. 'It is too early to assign specific authorship to a story that is still being written and revised, but it is certainly high time to devise an analytical framework within which the various threads of the tale can be examined and pieced together'. Neal 1994, p. 180, is far less cautious about the matter: 'It is very interesting that the regression coefficients on the Consol yields are so similar for the two time periods, whose economic and financial characteristics are so different, as indicated by marked changes in the coefficients on lagged bankruptcies and lagged exports'. This suggests that the revolution in public finance, completed in England by 1725, had an enduring effect on the finance of business that was sustained right through the period of the Industrial Revolution (whenever it began!). The web of credit among merchants, manufacturers and bankers, however, had grown in terms of its radius, density and strength. By the end of our period, marked by the Banking Act of 1844, it extended into all the trading regions of the world as well as into every niche of the domestic economy. From 1723, when the pre-eminence of the Bank of England as the premier financial institution in England was assured and the state had developed the perpetual annuity as its primary form of long-term debt, this web of credit was anchored securely in the City of London. Without this anchor, it is very doubtful whether the British economy could have made the structural changes in techniques, products and markets that characterised its transformation from 1760 to 1850.

78. Atterbury, High Bishop of Rochester and a well-known Tory, was banished for allegedly conspiring to organise a Jacobite rising. The Pretender's presence in Spain, about to set sail in October 1722, did cause a minor panic. The ' "Atterbury Plot" demonstrated with near complete finality the impotency of the Jacobite cause. On 18 June 1723 Atterbury sailed away and with him went many of the last hopes of the High Church and the Tories. Walpole assiduously cultivated the public perception that both were virtually synonymous with Jacobitism'. It did not help matters for the Tories that Bolingbroke (having obtained a royal pardon by way of a bribe) returned to England in the same month – his presence a reminder of the Tories' agonising relationship with the Pretender (Hoppit 2000, pp. 411–12). As the Prime Minister himself referred to it, the 'firm of Townshend and Walpole' was now solidly established (Speck 1977, p. 209).

1688 was shattered by the bubble, what came after was an 'age of cautious conservatism, hardening social distinctions, ever more clearly formalised patronage, and hostility to change'.[79] Population growth, political life, and, to a large extent, even the life of the country squire would remain stagnant for a generation. The Bubble Act, which supporters of the South Sea Company had passed to restrict the joint-stock ventures of their competitors, remained in effect and had a dampening influence on the stock market. In Parliament, the opposition viewed Walpole's system as a 'gigantic machinery of corruption which threatened to undermine the constitution and to destroy the very fabric of society'.[80] This perception seemed to be justified in light of numerous parliamentary investigations which turned up extensive corruption in high places.[81] While the Tories were a spent force politically, Tory wits such as Pope, Gay and Swift with his *Gulliver's Travels*, published in 1726, were celebrated for their commentary on the moral poverty of the contemporary world.[82] Their literary attacks on the régime helped to spur debate and coffeehouse gossip outside the voting oligarchy, among artisans, shopkeepers, merchants and scornful dissenters. If 'old corruption' was secure for now, a new political consciousness sceptical of oligarchy was coming into being. Meanwhile, the exposure of massive public corruption was matched

79. Carswell 1993, p. 242.

80. Speck 1977, p. 223.

81. 'The lord chancellor was found guilty in 1725 of embezzlement and corruption [for organizing the sale of judicial offices], and fined £30,000. In 1727 a government supporter was expelled from the Commons after having been detected in a fraud concerning estates forfeited from former South Sea Company directors [sold to the trustees of the Derwentwater estates at artificially low prices]. In 1732 the Charitable Response Corporation, which was supposed to use its capital to lend small sums of money to the poor, was discovered to have employed it for the financial benefit of its projectors. Next year another scandal was exposed involving the York Building Company. Yet although supporters of Walpole were involved in all these cases, he emerged relatively unscathed. A generation which could stomach the South Sea Bubble could swallow the lesser scandals with little effect. Walpole himself was quite cynical about the allegations of corruption made by the opposition. As he put it "I am no saint, no Spartan, no reformer"' (Speck 1977, p. 228). See also Langford 1986, p. 366.

82. Thompson (Thompson 1993, pp. 30–1) opposes his critique to that of those 'historians who have become habituated to seeing this age in terms of the apologetics of its principal actors', with the disclaimer that 'the alternate view which I offered should come with no sense of surprise. It is, after all, the criticism of high politics offered' by Swift, Pope, Johnson, Mandeville and others. Satire was a weapon that literary critics could wield in a time when no effective class or political force was in a position to challenge the Whigs and their system of old corruption.

by the growth of private corruption in the form of 'a flourishing economy of crime,'[83] and the corresponding elaboration of the 'bloody code.'[84]

The bloody code was part and partial of the consolidation of power by the new Hanoverian régime. Its development has been described as 'an organic process of adaptation by a society concerned to protect new forms of property and to restrict the benefits of a huge increase in wealth.'[85] Several major pieces of legislation were foundational to its development. The Riot Act of 1715 was specifically directed at violent crowds of Jacobites and their detractors burning effigies of the Pretender or attacking Scotch and Irish Catholics. But by fixing the labels of 'mob' onto the crowd and 'riot' onto a protest, popular forms of direct action now became tainted with the suspicion or the general assumption that the intent of the participants was criminal rather than communal. This blow did not immediately undermine the legitimacy of forms of popular protest, however. Such legitimacy declined only slowly over the course of the century. Before 1718, the most common punishments for felonies were whipping and branding, but the Transportation Act gave magistrates the option of transporting felons to America, thereby reducing the numbers of those to be hanged, and reducing even further those who had, for want of an alternative, to be freed back into the community. Transportation became by far the most common punishment meted out by the end of the century.[86] Most important was an act which itself stemmed from a localised conflict between wealthy enclosing landowners consolidating their property estates and commoners reacting to the loss of access to rights of commons. Responding to these disturbances at Enfield Chase, Walpole himself assumed the rangership and swiftly curtailed the customary rights of the commoners.[87] Then, in an extreme act of legislative overkill, Parliament enacted a piece of legislation that gave local officials unprecedented legal power

83. Langford 1986, p. 367. The success of the master thief Jonathon Wild – whose racket consisted mainly of restoring goods stolen by his minions to their original owners (for a profit of course) – depended largely upon the collaboration of corrupt JPs and their officers in the city. The prisons were equally open to corruption.

84. We will consider the 'bloody code' in relation to political economy, law and custom in Chapter Ten, pp. 521–7.

85. McLynn 1989, pp. xi–xii.

86. McLynn 1989, p. 286. Hence prison populations were low in early eighteenth-century Britain. Rule 1992a, p. 241 citing Beattie 1986, pp. 620–4.

87. Thompson 1990, pp. 181–2. The Act was specifically directed at 'blacking' or deer-poaching in the forests in the South of England. The 'blacks', so-named because they blackened their faces for purposes of anonymity, were led by the mythical 'King John' and enjoyed considerable local sympathy and support. They opposed the granting of licenses for hunting all game aside from deer in the forest and for the felling of timber, for this, they held, violated their customary rights to cut timber on their own farms, to graze their animals and to haul clay, gravel and chalk and cut furzes. They retaliated by poaching deer, which were seen as a symbol of the authority of local officials and their new-fangled deer parks. The conflict was heightened by the acute shortage of timber.

to punish offenders against property in the name of the maintenance of order.[88] Passed in 1723, the same year as the Workhouse Test Act,[89] the Waltham Black Act 'provided an overarching capital statute covering almost every conceivable criminal activity'.[90] The Black Act was 'neither necessary, nor especially effective, in dealing with the particular "emergency" which served as its excuse'.[91] This was so in part because the legislation, while empowering local gentry and loyal citizens of the hundreds to enforce the act, did not provide the necessary funding they would have required to do so. But what the Act did was provide the régime with 'a versatile armoury of death apt to the repression of many forms of social disturbance' as well as 'a model for subsequent terrorist legislation against disaffected Highlanders, Irish agrarian rebels and English smugglers'.[92] It became a capital offence under the Black Act to steal a deer, even a fawn;[93] to fire a gun inside a dwelling place even if no one was hurt; or to commit arson.[94] Other legislation confirmed and supported the bloody code, such as the Vagrancy Act of 1744, which allowed for the whipping or imprisonment of 'beggars, gamblers, strolling actors, gypsies, and "all those who refused to work for the usual and common wages"'.[95] The Black Act thus served as a precedent for the expansion of capital punishments in the eighteenth century.[96] The Act outlasted Walpole, being renewed five times after its passing and then being made perpetual in 1758.[97]

To many, Walpole was the embodiment of the corruption of his time. But aside from dispensing patronage, he did have other skills. Walpole's meticulous attention to the proceedings of the Commons, on the one hand, and his pursuit of pragmatic policies that would be attractive to a broad spectrum of the political nation on the other, were key to his success. Another key was his ability to marshal a phalanx of placemen in the Commons. The creation of a court party in the Commons dated from the reign of Charles II, and corruption was widespread

---

With the enclosing of the forests, blacking accelerated and the authorities were anxious to proscribe customary access to timber.

88. Thompson 1990, pp. 64, 98, 134, 145, 159, 188 and 191.

89. See Chapter Seven, p. 376.

90. McLynn 1989, p. xvi.

91. Thompson 1990, p. 192.

92. Thompson 1990, pp. 192 and 197.

93. 'Edward Elliott, aged only seventeen, went to the gallows because he had strayed from his fellows (during the raid on Alice Holt) trying to catch alive a young fawn as a present for his girl-friend' (Thompson 1990, p. 161).

94. McLynn 1989, pp. 38 and 84.

95. McNally 1993, p. 39.

96. 'Blacking', or dressing in disguise by poachers illegally hunting deer in the forests of Hampshire and Berkshire, caused an enormous affront to respectable society. Thompson 1990, pp. 49, 63 and 197.

97. Thompson 1990, p. 206.

under the reign of Anne, adding to the grievances behind the instability of her reign. When George II succeeded George I in 1727, like his father he chose to proscribe the Tories. This paradoxically brought greater stability to the government. 'Court Tories were more determinedly courtiers than they were Tories, and the prospect of permanent exclusion from place and profit was more than many could bear'.[98]

In 1727 some minor skirmishes with Spain, now allied with Austria against Britain, France and Prussia, provoked fears of a return to war. But only the threat of war loomed. When George II took the throne that year, he would have preferred to promote a member from the opposition, but he quickly realised that there was none other than Walpole that he could look to for stable, continuous government under a Parliament now very much operating in a routinised manner. In 1730 Walpole negotiated the Treaty of Seville behind the back of Townshend, his partner who until now had handled foreign affairs. The infuriated Townshend resigned, and was succeeded by the Duke of Newcastle. When the War of Polish Succession (1733–5) broke out, Walpole sent no aid to help Austria defend itself against the attacks of France and Spain. He later boasted that '50,000 men had been "slain this year in Europe, and not one Englishman" '.[99] He judged correctly that the landed classes were more interested in lower taxes than war.

Now in control of both domestic and foreign policy, Walpole took a survey of the entire system of taxation. Walpole's watchwords were 'peace, low taxes, unrestrained exports, and unlimited toleration for Dissenters'.[100] He constantly sought cheaper government and better rates on the national debt. He sought to reduce the monopoly of the East India Company and failed, but not before obtaining a payment of £200,000 and a lower rate of interest on the debt held by the Company. He loosened restrictions on colonial trade. And faced with the collusion between customs officers and smugglers, he sought to shift the burden of taxation from the point of entry to the point of sale.[101] By doing so, he could reduce both customs and the land tax at the same time. By 1730, he was able to reduce the land tax to two shillings on the pound, down from four during the War of the Spanish Succession. His goal was to eliminate it altogether.

The policy of reducing the land tax was naturally popular with Tory squires and the great Whig landowners alike. It comes as no surprise, then, that this master manipulator should pursue peace in foreign policy, since it allowed him to appease his would be opponents by lowering the land tax. The Whigs were

98. Langford 1986, p. 371.
99. Speck 1977, p. 234.
100. Hoppit 2000, p. 410.
101. In 1732 Walpole reported the findings of a committee to inspect frauds and abuses in the customs houses. It found that six customs officers had been murdered and 250 assaulted in the previous nine years. Speck 1977, p. 213; Leadam 1969, p. 343.

liberals of the grandiose sort, believing their leadership in conjunction with the crown was the best way to secure liberty, a liberty which they defined in Lockean terms as being rooted in private property. But those who held out as Tories, being relatively less wealthy, nonetheless embraced a fairly principled liberalism of their own, rooted in their opposition to arbitrary government and their preoccupation with corruption. Thus, many Tories found little difficulty in switching to the new Whig principles in exchange for renewed access to the court. The Whiggery of Walpole was not demanding. In the countryside, loyal Tory families did remain resilient, and could make life difficult for their comrades who defected to the Whigs. Stability may have been more apparent than real.[102] But between the two parties, there was no real quarrel over the nature of the state, and both supported the expansion of private property in land through enclosures.

The so-called agrarian depression: 1730–50

With a slump in both agriculture and trade, the British economy during the first half of the eighteenth century scarcely seemed poised for an industrial revolution. Low grain prices between 1670 and 1750 led to heavy rent arrears. The *York Courant* reported on 20 February 1739: 'Last Monday [12 February] . . . the best shipping wheat for £6 [a load] which is so low, that it is impossible farmers can live and pay their rents at such prices; and as wool likewise bears so low a price, unless some care be speedily taken, and the people eased of the present heavy taxes, most of the lands of the kingdom will be flung up into the landlords hands'.[103]

Yet what stands out as the most remarkable fact of the early eighteenth century was that the output and productivity of agriculture were *rising* during a period marked by long bouts of agricultural depression. Despite falling prices, rents rose, 'remarkable as it may seem'.[104] If rents were rising, why was this period widely viewed as a period of agrarian hardship?

After 1660, the long period of rising prices for agricultural goods that had lasted since the 1520s came to a close. A long period of economic expansion from the 1620s to the 1750s facilitated a vast improvement in agriculture. The concept of 'improvement' had been in the air since at least the mid-sixteenth century. It now became the mantra of a movement that was transforming British agriculture in entirely new ways. The period was characterised by a demographic pause and expanding supplies, with an overall trend of falling prices, interrupted by

102. '. . . [F]or example, when one of their aristocratic leaders, Earl Gower, joined Henry Pelham, the result at the general election of 1747 was rioting of almost unparalleled ferocity in Gower's home county of Staffordshire' (Langford 1986, p. 371).
103. As quoted in Black 2001, p. 31.
104. Wilson 1984, p. 248.

Table 3.1: Rising wages in Lancashire 1700–90[105]

	1700	1750	late 1780s
Lancashire	8*d.*/day	12*d.*/day	20*d.*/day
Oxford	14*d.*/day	14*d.*/day	16*d.*/day
London	20*d.*/day	24*d.*/day	24*d.*/day

periods of poor harvests prompting price spikes.[106] As labourers enjoyed cheaper bread, real incomes rose. The data suggests that nominal incomes rose as well (see Table 3.1).[107] The slow rate of population growth would have suppressed the growth in the number of able-bodied workers during a time of expanding employment of waged labour on farms and in manufactures.

Overall, low prices and expanding real incomes created a favourable environment for what we would refer to today as 'import substitution'. The depth of domestic demand was increasing rapidly and expectations were rising. 'The periodic fair was already declining in importance by 1700. Its place, as a method of distribution, was increasingly taken by the weekly market and the shop'.[108] British consumers began to find an increasing variety of foreign articles available in local markets, from coffee, tea, sugar, tobacco and molasses, to Indian prints and porcelains from East Asia. As meat and dairy prices held stable and incomes rose, Britons ate more meat. They bought better quality furniture, including better clocks. The metal trades were expanding in the Midlands and South Yorkshire as Britons were buying more and cheaper harnesses, 'brass locks, buttons, candlesticks and nails'. While exports 'certainly made some contribution to this activity', the main stimulus was domestic demand.[109] Indeed, the increasing output of glasswares, pig iron, textiles and so on is often taken as a function of foreign demand, but for A.H. John, what is of 'vital significance' is the 'demand released by increased agricultural productivity'.[110]

The only plausible explanation for how it was possible to have falling grain prices and rising rents at the same time is that the continued expansion of improved agriculture meant that the rate of productivity in agriculture continued to climb during a period of low prices, and even as the resultant overproduction had a further depressing effect on prices, increasing yields per acre

105. Source: Ashton 1964, p. 232.
106. Wilson 1984, pp. 237–8.
107. Table 3.1 indicates that wages in Lancashire grew by fifty percent between 1700 and 1750, and by another seventy-five percent between 1750 and the late 1780s. These percentages reflect nominal wages only. When we take into consideration falling bread prices, real incomes for labouring people in Lancashire grew by much more.
108. John 1961, pp. 185–6.
109. John 1961, p. 183.
110. John 1965, p. 24.

meant more value was being realised out of the same amount of land, thus allowing rents to rise *and* the food supply to increase. This was a historically novel response to agrarian depression. Under conditions of peasant-based farming, low prices bring about a decrease in production. But in early eighteenth-century England, the ability of capitalist tenant-farmers to respond to market prices by intensifying rather than withdrawing production marked the approach to a nearly complete conversion to capitalist principles governing agriculture.[111] As improved agriculture spread, more and more land was subjected to the competitive pressures of the market. These pressures compelled farmers to innovate, resulting in further productivity gains. Rising rates of productivity led to falling prices on the one hand, and still afforded the possibility for rents to rise. Falling prices meant higher real wages, which in turn meant greater overall consumer demand. Higher domestic demand stimulated imports as falling prices stimulated exports. Britain became a net exporter of grain.[112] Grain exports peaked around 1745, and remained strong for at least a decade, followed thereafter by a gradual decline and eventually, a reversal, beginning in the 1760s. Falling prices also facilitated engrossment of agricultural holdings, wherein improved methods generated better yields, contributing to the increasing level of agrarian productivity and so falling agrarian prices, creating a feedback loop and making the whole process self-reinforcing. To the extent that land was being converted to capital, the evidence would seem to point to a process in which capital becomes self-expanding.

A second feedback loop involves husbandry, one that has been referred to as a 'virtuous circle'.[113] From the middle of the seventeenth century, forage crops

111. Ashton (Ashton 1964, p. 30) provides a succinct summary of the conditions of agriculture during this period: 'Agriculture had its peculiar features. Its techniques differed from place to place. Of its varied products a large part was consumed on the spot. The esteem that attached to ownership of the soil affected its progress. But generally, like other callings, it was ruled by the forces of the market'. Indeed, in examining Gregory King's economic tables of 1688, Deane and Cole (1969, p. 3) find that only 'cottagers and paupers' could be treated as subsistence producers, and they account for only 5 ½% of the population of England at the time, even though 'interpretation on his categories suggests that between 70 and 80 percent of the occupied population was primarily engaged in agriculture.' Writing a century later, Colquhoun distinguished 'no cottager class as such.' Deane and Cole (Deane and Cole 1969, p. 93) reach a similar conclusion to that of Ashton: 'For centuries English agriculture had had extensive ties of varying strength with the market, and by the eighteenth century it was largely organised on a capitalist basis: the typical farmer was not a peasant toiling for his own subsistence, but an employer of wage labour holding his land at an economic rent from men who not infrequently ploughed their profits back into agriculture, or into transport, industry and trade'.

112. John 1965, pp. 19–26.

113. Jones 1968, pp. 58–71. Although Braudel (1988, p. 560) references p. 62 of Jones's *Past and Present* article, one does not find any reference there to a 'virtuous circle'. It is, therefore, unclear whether the specific term 'virtuous circle' originates with Braudel or Jones.

for husbandry and irrigation began to spread widely, though not uniformly. More fodder from forage crops allowed for the retention of more animals, and more animals meant more manure. More manure meant better fertilisation, which in turn spelled greater yields of corn. Of course this also meant greater yields of fodder. Thus a positive feedback loop emerged whereby new methods meant more animals and thus better manuring, which in turn meant more fodder, which could sustain even more animals, and so on.[114] More manure also afforded new opportunities for improvements in the cultivability of less fertile soils, allowing for their continuous cultivation. This was especially the case for the lighter, sandy soils of Southern England, which had hitherto been mainly employed for pasturage. As a result of this virtuous circle: 'English grain output increased automatically, effortlessly so to speak, to the point of exceeding home demand. Hence the fall in the price of cereals which were increasingly exported until 1760'.[115] It is important to note that none of these processes were to be found operating in France. The agronomist Arthur Young, during his tours of the French countryside between 1787 and 1789, noted that three-field rotations on open fields were scrupulously observed and found that while France enjoyed a climate more favourable to agriculture than that in England, this disadvantage was more than offset in England by improvements wholly lacking in France.[116]

Another feedback loop that we can identify, one involving brewing and distilling, might be seen as a way of short-circuiting the previous process. These industries produced huge amounts of spent grain left over from the infusion of barley and malt, as well as 'wash' left over after the spirits had been distilled out from the vat, leaving vast quantities of waste material which provided an excellent source of feed for cattle and pigs. While brewers typically sold their 'offals' off premises, distillers could feed hogs completely on their unmalted grains without supplementing beans or peas. As a result, the primary distillers brought hogs into their own operation and set up fattening operations of their own. The result was pork of lower quality, but also of lower price. In 1745, when prices were still near their lowest point, a complaint by farmers in the form of a petition led to an investigation by Parliament, which concluded that the fall in hog prices could not be blamed on the distillers. By 1750, the primary distillers were fattening around one hundred thousand hogs for market and provisioning another twenty thousand or more for the Victualling Office.[117] Thus urbanisation contributed to an expansion of brewing and distilling, which in their own way supported

114. Jones 1974, p. 129.
115. Braudel 1988, p. 560. Italics found in the original.
116. Comninel 1987, p. 191; and Wright 2003, pp. 518–19.
117. Mathias 1979, pp. 252–60.

the expansion of husbandry, which in turn helped to sustain the population of growing cities.

A fourth feedback loop involved the relationship between agriculture and non-agrarian labour. In the period 1700–50, we begin to see new forces emerge that draw labour away from the countryside. New developments in transportation provided demand for labour and had an upward effect on wages. There developed new seasonal migrations to coastal towns, such as Newcastle-upon-Tyne, where additional labour for loading coal was needed. Cheap and unskilled labour was sought, and this often meant a preference for women and children. A permanent migration to the larger towns also developed to meet the demand of an expansion of urban manufacturing. 'London, of course, exercised the greatest pull; but other industrial centres like Birmingham, Sheffield, and Manchester also attracted their quota'.[118] Agrarian conditions were harsh and entry into apprenticed trades difficult for rural agriculturists, and they were thereby compelled to seek by-employments locally, through seasonal migration, or to migrate to the cities in search of full-time employment.[119] The growth of cities and towns, in turn, placed greater demand on the domestic market for food and manufactured goods, promoting further improvements in agriculture and expansion of manufactures. This tendency was more pronounced on the heavier clay soils of the Midlands where arable lands were being converted to pasture, resulting in the release of labour from the land, and possibly cancelling the effect of the South's more intensive cultivation and greater demand for labour.[120] Smaller farmers in the Midlands now faced falling prices and competition from the extension of farming in the South. They tried and failed to pass legislation '"to suppress the Improvements in the Southern Parts"'.[121] Others sought to suppress the sowing of clover in the Midlands.

118. John 1965, pp. 29–30.

119. In a similar vein, Braudel (1988, p. 561) outlines the process by which, in his view, the crisis of the seventeenth century promoted the Industrial Revolution. First, it encouraged high-yield agriculture capable of meeting demand resulting from the sudden demographic explosion after 1750. Second, it promoted the rise of cottage manufacturing, which in turn provided a malleable and trained workforce, a reserve labour force on which the Industrial Revolution would draw. Braudel comments that the Industrial Revolution would draw on a workforce trained by cottage manufacturing 'rather than on the strictly agricultural workforce which maintained its previous levels, contrary to assumptions made by commentators from Marx to the present day'. Braudel would apparently credit improved agricultural productivity with creating the conditions for the growth of cottage manufacturing, but apparently wants to downplay or ignore the impact of agriculture on divorcing the direct producers from the means of production, whether or not they go on to acquire industrial skills.

120. John 1961, p. 180.

121. Worlidge 1669, p. 26, as cited in John 1965, p. 130.

A fifth feedback loop could be identified in the self-sustaining relationship between the expanding domestic market and improvements in transportation infrastructure, including roads, river- and coastal navigation. England's roads had a reputation as being among the worst in Europe. Whereas the Roman roads were built by state-employed soldiers, road-repair had been a local affair since medieval times in England. The Statute for Mending of Highways of 1555 placed responsibility on parish surveyors. Starting in 1696, turnpikes were established by private trusts, responding to the strength of the local economy, the volume of transport and profitability.[122] Accordingly, the movement slowed during the period of low agricultural prices, but picked up again in the 1750s. Efforts to improve the navigability of rivers also began in the sixteenth century. Slowed by the wars with France, the pace picked up again between 1719 and 1721. Improved navigation provided a cheaper means of transporting bulky goods, especially coal. At the same time, improvement in coastal shipping involved the development of ports, docks and harbours, the use of buoys, improvements in lighting, dredging, and the building of piers. Coal shipments from the Tyne travelling along the East coast (seventy percent of it going to London) rose from over four hundred thousand tons in the 1660s to over six hundred thousand tons by 1730–1 and nearly eight hundred thousand tons in 1750.[123] These improvements in navigation and the development of a national turnpike system set Britain apart from its neighbours

---

122. Since funds for investment were crucial to the success of the trust, the widespread (though not complete) success of the various trusts reflected widespread confidence of investors in the health of local economies and in the profitability of more active links. Black (Black 2001, p. 61) writes that: 'The desire of local merchants and manufacturers for growth was important, but turnpikes were not just commercial ventures: trusts were dominated by noblemen and the squirearchy, and the turnpikes were seen as a form of improvement'. He seems to be suggesting that the gentry approached the trusts with a lack of self-interest, and even that a selfless commitment to the spirit of improvement was more important than the profit-motive in driving the effort to improve the roadways. This seems to contradict his earlier statement: 'Rather than following some master plan, the road system came in large part to reflect the degree of dynamism of individual trusts, and the ability of particular routes to produce revenue'. Many estate-owners were anxious to enhance transport systems in general (although for those with coal and other minerals on their estates, improvements in water navigation which greatly lowered costs of transporting bulk products were a greater priority). Landlords renting to farmers had a clear motive to support cost-cutting improvements in transport, and agricultural goods were better placed to benefit from roadway improvements than coal and other minerals.

123. Black 2001, pp. 67–8. Compared with what Black calls the 'scant improvement in the condition of marine transport', the growth of the merchant marine had far larger implications. Wilson (Wilson 1984, p. 247) comments: 'Put in terms of the balance of payments, the growth of the mercantile marine meant that what had often been an invisible import item was turning perceptibly into a profitable item of invisible export. While inland transport might remain poor, the British economy was being provided with an increasingly efficient system of external transport, exploiting an ingeniously protected market'.

because these improvements came into being not through government initiative and finance, but through private enterprise at the regional level responding to commercial imperatives. While consumers resented the tolls, farmers, landlords, mine owners and master manufacturers all benefited from the steady fall in transport costs and times, stimulating further economic growth and more demand for cheaper, faster transportation.

Eighteenth-century Britain was a prominent contributor to the field of agrarian literature. Between 1692 and 1750, a significant number of books and periodicals on improved methods of farming appeared.[124] The early eighteenth century also saw a remarkable spread of technical innovation in agriculture in terms of mechanical devices, the floating of water-meadows and the spread of new planting techniques. Tull's introduction of the seed drill in 1701 marked a major development, and Tull soon followed up by introducing the horse hoe. In the 1730s, the 'Rotherham plough' was introduced. New planting techniques included the widening use of artificial grasses (clover, as well as sainfoin and lucerne) and the growing of turnips as a fodder crop within the rotation. Viscount Charles 'Turnip' Townshend popularised turnip planting in the 1730s. With more fodder, better grasses and more land available for pasture, the food supply for animals was improved. As 'new possibilities of crop rotation' were realised, 'better use could be made of the land by the extension of convertible husbandry and by further specialization according to types of soil'.[125] Combined with Tull's straight rows, turnips yielded better economies of cost and greater yields. The result was better profits for farmers and higher rents for landlords.[126] Ashton finds that 'nearly all the improvements of agricultural technique of which there is record were made on land already enclosed or in process of enclosure'.[127] On the other hand,

---

124. Contemporary titles included: John Houghton (ed.), *A Collection for the Improvement of Husbandry and Trade* (periodical, 1692–1703); Timothy Nourse, *Campania Foelix, or a Discourse of the Benefits and Improvements of Husbandry* (New York: Garland, 1982 [first published 1700]); Thomas, 6th Earl of Haddington, *The Short Treatise on Forest Trees, Aquatics, Evergreens, Fences and Grass Seeds* (1735), (as cited in Black 2001, p. 39). In 1700, probably one of every two adult males was still engaged in agriculture, 'a proportion that probably had not differed much for a long period of time' (Hay and Rogers 1997, p. 4).

125. Coleman 1977, p. 116.

126. Wilson 1984, p. 247. Turnips aside, the expanded cultivation of specific crops may not signify the spread of new techniques, but is indicative of growing demand and new markets for such crops, and of a growing commercialisation of agriculture. Thus potatoes became a field crop in this period. Apple- and pear-orchards arose in the West Country, while apple and cherry orchards appeared in mid-Kent. Vegetable gardening expanded in the vicinity of London. The hop excise in 1711 encouraged its growth; output rose from 9 million lbs between 1712 and 1721 to 19 million in the period 1745–56. Likewise, the cultivation of flax, hemp, madder, woad, saffron, wheat and barley also expanded in this period, with exports of wheat and barley on the increase.

127. Ashton 1964, p. 34.

enclosure did not automatically equate with improvement, or greater efficiency; improved drainage, adapting to new methods and introducing new machinery required outlays that not every farmer or landlord could afford.

If the source of agricultural innovation was profitability alone then we should not expect to see innovation in this period of agrarian hardship and low profits. But in an emerging agrarian-capitalist system, agrarian distress heightened the competitive pressures of market-based agriculture. Thus in such a time of distress, investing in the means to improve agricultural efficiency could save the landowner and his tenants from bankruptcy. The smallholder 'was at the mercy of the weather, but he was much more at its mercy than his more progressive and larger neighbours. As they increased their output, and as the increase was reflected in a larger national output, it was their prices that ruled the market'.[128] His distress was compounded by falling prices resulting from productivity gains on mostly larger farms; gains which he lacked sufficient capital to effect. For most landowners, manorial rents were no longer of great economic consequence. Their income came mainly from tenant-farmers whose advantage lay in seeking to continually lower the cost of production.[129] As the 'third class' that defines agrarian capitalism,[130] landlords were directly affected *by* the competitive pressures of the emerging land and grain markets, but were not themselves directly subject *to* those pressures. As we shall discuss shortly, the competitive pressures they faced were real, they simply were driven by a different logic: the competition for status, not by the logic of the capitalist market as such. Landlords could afford to relax spending on investments in their estates and buy more luxury items. The tenant-farmer could not.

In the earlier period of agrarian depression (1690–1715), it was high agrarian prices driven by recurring bad harvests that brought hardship. The distress was compounded by high wartime taxation and a slump in trade. Agrarian and industrial labourers were also adversely affected by high grain prices. But in the so-called agrarian depression of the 1730s and 1740s, we have falling prices and

---

128. Wilson 1984, pp. 249–50. Wilson might better have stated that while the little man was at the mercy of the weather, he was much *more* at the mercy of his larger neighbours. He continues: 'Quite apart from the short-term fluctuations caused by the weather, the price structure of an increasingly commercial, capitalistic market for agricultural produce was shaping against the small peasant farmer'.

129. Coleman (1977, p. 123) observes that: 'The market for grain approached that of a perfect economic market: no individual producer could control prices or rents'.

130. Marx 1967, Part VII, Chapter XLVIII struggled to come to terms with the 'three classes' when he wrote about the 'trinity formula'. It does not appear that Marx ever fully appreciated the role that landlords played in facilitating the transition to capitalism through an agrarian capitalism that was unique to England, despite seeing England's route as the 'classic' one.

good harvests.[131] Real incomes for labourers were rising. However, rents piled up and many farms fell into disuse. Landlords 'were forced to write off such arrears, to make concessions, to provide capital for farm buildings or improvements, in order to retain good tenants – on whom they so much depended'.[132] It is 'the sudden appearance of heavy arrears of rent', writes Mingay, 'which justifies the view that the failure of rents to rise at this time is a sign of depression'.[133] Writing in 1785, *The Economist* postulated that agrarian stagnation and the decrease of purchasing power for landlords and farmers offset gains in other areas of the economy. Similarly, Habakkuk argued that low agricultural prices 'had a depressing effect on agricultural investment and indirectly on the demand for industrial goods'.[134] But A.H. John argues that this thesis does not hold up to scrutiny. He argues that buoyancy in the economy was sustained throughout the period, and that on the whole, this was not a period of economic stagnation: farmers were increasing their stock; evidence of labour migration suggests economic growth in multiple sectors; and the overall increase in the volume and range of consumer goods as well as the growth of the linen industry suggests a period of considerable growth. Two additional trends bring the stagnation thesis into question. First, luxury consumption increased, and this increased diversion of capital from productive uses may mask the overall increase in agrarian incomes. Landlords began to spend more – 'they had armies of servants . . .'[135] Some landlords were lucky enough to find minerals or coal, or simply converted their properties into fortunes when they sold out to urbanisation. Secondly, landlords were investing more capital in improvements, and hence sinking more of their wealth into productive investment.[136] In general, landlords could consolidate farms on old enclosed areas, and their investment allowed them to reshape and re-let farms at higher rents.[137] We must conclude, therefore, that the complaints of distress

131. Both Coleman (Coleman 1977, p. 124) and Mingay (Mingay 1956, p. 336) cite Wimpey 1775, pp. 492–3 as one contemporary to whom the results of improvement were clear: '. . . All history cannot furnish twenty such years of fertility and abundance as from 1730 to 1750 when the average prices were the lowest ever known. Another reason we assign to the fall of price, is the great improvements made in agriculture in the last fifty or sixty years'.

132. Coleman 1977, p. 124.

133. Mingay 1956, p. 325.

134. Habakkuk 1956, pp. 437–8, as cited in Deane and Cole 1969, p. 90.

135. Rule 1992a, pp. 22–3.

136. John 1965, pp. 20–2, 32.

137. 'Thereafter, the farmers tended to take on a large share of the burden of investment in agricultural improvement' (Rule 1992a, p. 22). Indeed, as Mingay writes, during the 'depression' years of 1730–50, 'The landlord's expenses for repairs and new construction of farm buildings, fences, gates, embankments and cottages were generally heavy . . .' But such outlays declined in the decade between 1750 and 1760: 'The burden of making repairs and the expenses of any improvements were now largely thrust upon the tenant' (Mingay 1956, p. 330).

were coming from the lesser gentry who had less resources to invest in improvement and keep up with those who were engrossing and consolidating enormous estates. In other words, this was not so much a period of depression or stagnation as one of *differentiation* in the countryside.

This applied to the tenants as well. Landlords naturally preferred wealthier tenants and those with experience at making successful improvements and turning out more abundant harvests. Falling grain prices facilitated differentiation between agrarian producers with low outputs and relatively high costs and those with high outputs, causing the share of investment to shrink relative to the total cost of the operation.[138]

> Farms were growing larger. The old idea that a holding should be of a size sufficient to maintain a family and no more was beginning to give way to a belief in bigger units of production. These could introduce division of labour, utilise larger capital, and supply markets more efficiently.[139]

The new idea was that a farmer should produce thrice what he consumed, with the other thirds allocated to rent and expenses related to production (including hired labour). There was very little about the emerging logic of agrarian capitalism that favoured smaller farmers.[140] All producers were increasingly drawn into a real agrarian-capitalist market.

While the older peasant way of life was fading, local circumstances could aid its preservation.[141] The open field system was not entirely without its advantages: rents were generally lower and ready access to the means of subsistence combined with rights of grazing, gathering firewood and fishing on the commons afforded

---

138. Not everyone, therefore, rejoiced at harvest-time. But the capitalist tenant-farmer did. Wilson describes him as: 'the human pivot on whom the new rural arrangements turned. He was the symbol of a new society that no longer relied on customary relationships based on the ownership or part-ownership of land, but on legal and contractual relationships designed for a world of commerce. He survived so long as he could honour his contract and pay his rent' (Wilson 1984, pp. 253–4).

139. Ashton 1964, p. 37.

140. The tenant-farmer as a category for a real socio-economic agent was defined by social relationships built on new, non-customary foundations. Since his entire production operation was geared toward the market, any use of productive output for immediate consumption for the self-subsistence of himself and his family, were secondary concerns. The rising incomes of a growing number of farmers was laying the foundation for the emergence of a middle class, able to afford and provide effective demand to stimulate the domestic market in household consumer goods (soap, cotton garments, tea and sugar). And 'it was the large proportionate size of the middle-income groups which distinguished English society' (Rule 1992a, p. 23).

141. 'There were still many owner-occupiers of small holdings of ten acres or less who could still borrow, free of charge, the 'town plough'. It was said that in Cumberland, juries could always be relied upon to find for the tenant in any landlord/tenant dispute (Wilson 1984, pp. 250–1).

a degree of protection from the market.[142] Nor was the old system completely inflexible.[143] By adapting to improved methods, by specialising in husbandry, dairying peasants or small farmers working on common fields still unenclosed could remain viable, giving landlords less incentive to enclose. Nevertheless, the overall trend was for the gradual disappearance of the small producer, primarily copyholders, especially in regions where dairying or conversion to permanent pasture could not be substituted for traditional agriculture. A minority of copyholders managed to transform their share in the reapportioned fields upon enclosure of the village into a productive, capitalist operation. But whether or not their land was enclosed, most could not afford to invest in improving the drainage systems, much less to put up hedges or build stone fences. They remained uncompetitive. Their best option was often to seek the highest price for their land, upon the sale of which they joined the ranks of the growing numbers of cottagers, wage labourers or landless poor. The freeholder held a clear advantage over the copyholder. By transmuting the value of his land into stock, seed and manure for fertiliser, he obtained the necessary funds to invest in improvements.[144] Freeholders were often the first to enclose their properties by agreement and/or by unity of possession. And so we see yet another self-reinforcing process at work, for the failure of small producers in the face of competition from large farms with improving techniques reinforced the tendency for concentration as these lands were absorbed into larger farms. Larger farms operating on an economy of scale could afford greater investments in improvements, further tipping the scales against the small producer.

A great deal of ink has been spilt disputing the assertions of Marx and others to the effect that the peasantry was forcibly expropriated.[145] Kussmaul claims

142. Black 2001, p. 37. In later chapters, we will see more clearly how custom and parochialism factored into efforts to resist market pressures.

143. 'It has been said that the necessity of conforming to the communal time-table for sowing and harvesting, of following the agreed rotation, and observing the customs of the village or manor, ensured that cultivation did not fall below certain standards. Open-field farmers could agree to exchange strips so as to get larger contiguous holdings, and sometimes they added a crop to the customary cycle or made arrangements to hold meadows in severalty: there is no need to think of the arrangement as inflexible. But it was unfriendly to the individual who wanted to move ahead of his fellows' (Ashton 1964, p. 33).

144. Wilson 1984, p. 252, citing Trow-Smith 1951. In 1688, Gregory King reckoned that farmers and freeholders made up 5.5 per cent of the population, with 'better freeholders' making up less than 1 percent (Hill 1961, p. 13).

145. Marx's description of the process is quite dramatic. For example, Marx 1906, p. 805 writes: '. . . the fraudulent alienation of the State domains, the robbery of the common lands, the usurpation of feudal and clan property, and this transformation into private property under circumstances of reckless terrorism, were just so many idyllic methods of primitive accumulation. They conquered the field for capitalistic agriculture, made the soil part and parcel of capital, and created for the town industries the necessary supply of

that opinion is now widespread that 'that the commons were purchased rather than stolen from the commoners', [146] and there is limited evidence to support the idea of a 'deliberate and calculated expropriation'.[147] Many if not most villages were enclosed by legal arrangement. In such cases, however, peasants did not always give up their rights without a legal battle. What is indisputable, however, is that the loss of access to the commons and the subsequent full expropriation of the peasantry brought hardship and uncertainty to the poor.[148] This raises the question of how it had been decided that common-law property right should trump tradition and community interest. How enclosure was accomplished, and what its immediate effects were, is in some sense trivial beside the fact that millions of cultivators of the soil lost access to the commons and then (even if they were bought out) lost possession of land to till and were 'hurled' into the ranks of men, women and children seeking to sell their labour for a wage, even as the rich continued to consolidate their estates.

As the Hanoverian era opened, the late seventeenth-century trend of expending enormous sums on country houses and their accompanying landscaped parks rose to new levels of extravagance, astonishing observers. Nature was brought to serve a Promethean arrogance. Hillocks were levelled, streams dammed and diverted, lakes manufactured, and trees planted by the thousands. Great houses were built from incomes derived from vast landholdings or offices of state. The construction of two-hundred-room houses on parks stretching for thousands of acres testifies to a degree of wealth unknown since the days of Caesar and Crassus. Sir Edward Coke amassed enough land throughout his lifetime to provide land for all his children, a true exception in the era of strict primogeniture.[149]

---

a "free" and outlawed proletariat'. It is noteworthy, however, that in quoting contemporary accounts of the tearing down of villages, he notes that 'The complaints of these old chroniclers are always exaggerated . . .' (p. 790). Marx's sweeping narrative on the topic deals less in the specifics of enclosure than in the overall process of transforming land into capital and peasants into proletarians.

146. Kussmaul 1994, p. 4.

147. Wilson 1984, p. 250.

148. In part, this is indisputable when one considers that contemporaries were quite aware of the hardships enclosure could bring about: 'When in 1759, Reverend John Loder, the lord of the manor of Hinton Waldrist in Oxfordshire, informed his tenants that he wanted to enclose the land, they replied that it would create much hardship for those who only had short tenure, that it would be expensive to grow and maintain hedges, and would be divisive: " 'tis likely to create uneasiness amongst us as long as we live and one will be ever thinking another's land better than his". Despite this, an Enclosure Act was passed the following year' (Black 2001, p. 37). Likewise, when in 1712 the Marquis of Powys enclosed Benefield in Northhamptonshire, 'even the local gentry thought [this] imposed great injustices on the poor' (Wilson 1984, p. 250).

149. Most younger sons moved to the city in search of a career in trade, in the bureaucracy or the military. Coke accomplished this feat in spite of losing £79,000 (the equivalent of approximately £7 million today) in the scandal of the South Sea Bubble (Wilson 1984, pp. 259–60).

It took Thomas Coke thirty years (1734–64) and £90,000 to build Holkham Hall near the Northern Sea coast of Norfolk. The project continued, however, and by 1800 the surrounding park covered three thousand acres.[150] Even this was no match for Lord Lonsdale's four-thousand acre Lowther Park, or (not to be outdone) the Duke of Norfolk's five-thousand acre estate in Cumberland.[151] At these lofty heights of the elite, there could be little social mobility. A healthy rent-roll squeezed from the tenants thanks to improved farming methods might only encourage higher aspirations of elegance and grandiosity.[152] As the costs of running an ever more luxurious establishment accumulated, it became necessary to carry a running debt in order to maintain sufficient liquidity. For many, this would lead to eventual bankruptcy. The seething animosity between the two parties in the first fifteen years of the eighteenth century becomes more understandable if we consider that in order to keep up with the sumptuous lifestyle he had known, many an old Tory Squire found himself borrowing from Peter to pay Paul. Chronically in debt, it is no wonder that he turned his wrath upon the 'placemen' profiting from schemes of lending to private interests and the state alike.[153] As the eighteenth century progressed, however, there were fewer bankruptcies, even though the debts carried were larger. What had changed was that the revolution in the financial system had vastly improved the supply of credit. And as land was considered good security, bankers were eager to lend to landholders.

There were no urban fortunes to rival those of the countryside. But this is not to say that there were no urban fortunes being made. Moreover, urban professionals often sought to buy their way into the gentry by purchasing estates and

150. The estate today, still active and still privately owned, employing some 160 persons, covers twenty-five thousand acres (Holkham Hall and Estate 2008).

151. Rule 1992a, p. 37. See also p. 186, n. 74 above.

152. Not all landlords saw the importance of investing in improved agriculture. Whether or not they did would influence the long-term prospects of their estate. For many, it was certainly possible to spend productively and conspicuously at the same time.

153. See Coleman 1977, p. 126: 'Some changes followed, directly or indirectly, from the effects of Civil War and Interregnum. During the Interregnum there was confiscation and sale of some "delinquent" Royalist lands, as well as those of Church and Crown; other Royalists sold or borrowed to pay fines in order to "compound" for their support of the wrong side. But at the Restoration the sales of confiscated lands – though not other sales – were invalidated; and most Royalists regained their lands. It seems unlikely that, as a direct consequence of these forced transactions, there occurred any substantial transfer of land to lawyers, merchants, soldiers, rich citizens, and the like who were then responsible for putting into operation the improved methods of farming and estate management. Nevertheless, many former Royalists and other landowners whose lands bore heavy debt charges, whether incurred because of or before "the troubles", found themselves in a very disadvantageous situation as rents and prices fell in the post-Restoration years. Legal developments since the earlier seventeenth century had facilitated the growth of a mortgage market; and some money-lending scriveners did very well out of this flourishing business...'

with landlords increasingly taking up residence in the town. In these ways, the rural-urban distinction was at least beginning to become blurred.[154] Wealthy merchants, lawyers, bankers and contractors professed a longing to go into the country, to establish a family nest in an ostentatious display 'to prove to one's self and others that one was as grand as one's neighbour by being palpably more grand'.[155] Joining their quest there were:

> ironmasters and coal owners; shippers, shipbuilders and sugar planters; East India magnates; and a miscellany of professional men and place-men. Like their Tudor predecessors they acquired landed estates, built splendid new houses, married their children into the peerage or into older families, and started new landed families. Many, especially the parvenu amongst them, got themselves buried under some of the biggest pieces of memorial sculpture to be seen in English churches, almost all dating between 1650 and 1750.[156]

Many of the estates they purchased were indeed from old families no longer able to keep up the pace. Rule concurs with the Stones' notion that England did not have an 'open elite',[157] at least among the families of the aristocracy. 'The eighteenth-century titled aristocracy was one of the most closed in Europe, despite the fact that there was no legal definition of noble blood'.[158] The peaks, writes Rule, could not be scaled, but he asks 'what of the foothills?' Contrary to the Stones, Rule finds that the way was not barred for men of new money to be able to climb into the ranks of the gentry, and suggests the issue was not access but attitude; the newcomers were not inclined to adopt the substance of the old ways. In fact, most of these wealthy townsmen who purchased rural estates maintained their urban residences. During the periods of agrarian depression, they might speculate on urban construction schemes as an alternative to investing in the countryside. Absentee landlordship grew, and as a result owners needed to hire stewards to manage their estates.[159] Their position served to

---

154. 'A foreign visitor in 1727 considered the elite of London's merchants to be wealthier than "the sovereign princes of Germany and Italy"' (Rule 1992a, p. 53).

155. Wilson 1984, p. 257.

156. Coleman 1977, p. 127.

157. See Stone and Fawtier Stone 1984, p. 403. This book looks at the market for country houses to inquire whether the apparent myth of an 'open elite' into and out of which flowed merchants, financiers and industrialists could move freely. The idea that the landed gentry was regularly replenished by successive waves of fresh, newly bourgeois outsiders, write the Stones, 'is clearly not more than a hoary myth, which should now be laid reverently to rest'. 'During the whole 340-year period covered by this study there were only 137 men of business who bought their way into the elite in our three counties'.

158. Rule 1992a, p. 50.

159. The steward assumed broad responsibilities. Cottagers and tenants alike typically negotiated their leases with the steward, not the landlord. Stewards often took charge of dispensing charity to locals. On very large estates, the position required men skilled in

maintain or increase the social distance between the very rich and the very poor. On the larger estates, the sheer scale and increasing complexity of the enterprise made the steward indispensable. 'He was in a unique position to speed the rate of rural change and agrarian progress'.[160]

The distress of the lesser gentry came in a period of low prices, but we find little cause to describe the decades between 1730 and 1750 as a period of agrarian depression. Rather, it was a dynamic period involving agrarian *differentiation* or stratification. While some may recall a particular period as one of distress, others meanwhile prospered mightily. Barring an analysis of how surplus is appropriated and property is expropriated, the tendency will be to view economic failure as individual failure to take advantage of the opportunities others managed to exploit and by which they gained.

The return to war and the '45

Walpole's efforts to shift the burden of taxation onto the consumer were welcomed by merchants as well as landlords, for they corresponded neatly with a growing sentiment among wealthy merchants and landowners that labouring people were too well-off and should be taxed. Evidence of this could be seen in the increasing ability of working people to have the means to buy luxury items – evidence of 'a dangerous spirit of luxury and debauchery which ought to be checked'.[161] In 1723, Walpole had extended an experimental system, first applied in 1709 to imports of pepper, of holding imports in bonded customs houses without exacting customs. The advantage of the system was to stimulate the colonial re-export trade by removing mark-up for customs. Goods that travelled inland were subject to an excise payment equivalent to the otherwise foresworn customs duty. The 1723 extension included tea, coffee and cotton, and increased revenues by approximately £120,000 per annum. Now Walpole prepared to add wine and tobacco to the system. To sell his scheme, he presented a report in 1732 on the rampant corruption of the customs system, which could

---

assessing and negotiating rents and leases, good knowledge of farming methods, and the ability to oversee the employment of dozens of men. Their salaries were high. 'It took the Duke of Bridgewater six years in the 1720s to persuade a yeoman farmer to act as his steward, eventually getting him for £100, a house and a horse at the duke's cost' (Rule 1992a, p. 70). Even owners of modest properties required stewards in their absence. Here, far less skill was required. But a strong knowledge of and ability at effecting agrarian improvement would have been highly-sought qualities in a steward. For the absentee-owner expecting to maximise his rents, a manager who could maximise efficiency and productivity was crucial. But even an excellent steward could not prevent a crisis if the lord of the house overspent.

160. Wilson 1984, p. 260.

161. Jubb 1984, pp. 136–7.

be ameliorated by the drastic reduction in customs duties put forth in his proposal. The uproar that followed demonstrated how Walpole's own reputation for corruption could be used against him.[162] Walpole admitted defeat, which was welcomed with delirium. The bells of London rang for two days; 'bonfires blazed in the streets'[163] The outpouring of popular resistance to the mere idea of a general excise was testimony to the growing power of consumers with rising incomes. The government's attempts to license the sale of spirits between 1729 and the Gin Act of 1736 likewise proved ineffective.[164] Dwelling-houses became dram shops, 'a carnival of drunkenness ensued,' which combined with economic distress, contributed to widespread protesting during the year of 1736.[165]

With his excise scheme having failed, Walpole was determined to crack down on smuggling. In May of 1736 a bill was introduced to make smuggling punishable by transportation for life. The bill passed, despite strong objections from the two heads of the judicature on the grounds that it included language criminalising not merely the act of smuggling, but the *intent* to do so. This only encouraged

162. The opposition, having rehearsed their arguments in the previous year when the excise on salt was reintroduced after a two-year lapse, set out to inflame public opinion against the scheme, claiming that Walpole sought to unleash an army of officers upon the public to enforce a general excise. 'A phrase of Pulteney's, "that monster, the Excise; that plan of arbitrary power", caught the public ear. Caricatures and pasquinades representing excise as a devouring dragon, a universal tax upon all commodities, especially bread and meat, flooded the country, among them a political ballad, "Britannia Excisa",' by Pulteney. The Craftsman week by week invented hideous pictures of its effects. The essays, some of them from Pulteney's pen, bearing in a collected form the title Arguments against Excises, fed the flames of popular fury. "No slavery – no excise – no wooden shoes", the last symbol to arbitrary monarchy like that of France, became the universal cry. In vain the ministry dispersed pamphlets unmaking the imposture' (Leadam 1969, pp. 344–5). Excise duties were 'first levied by Pym in 1643, but they had always been unpopular in the country, partly because they affected many of the necessities of life, and partly because the activities of the excise officers made evasion of payment very difficult' (Owen 1975, p. 30).

163. '. . . the effigies of Walpole with a blue paper ribbon of the garter and of a fat woman representing the queen, fed the flames. Cockades were worn inscribed "Liberty, Property, and no Excise" '. Leadam interpreted the whole affair as 'the triumph of passion and prejudice, excited by the interest of the numerous traders who profited by smuggling, against a scientific adjustment of taxation' (Leadam 1969, p. 345). However, examining the voting on the bill, Speck concludes that Walpole's loss of the support of the Commons was due not to the pressure of the London crowd, but to doubts among placemen about the King's backing for Walpole during a moment of crisis (Speck 1977, p. 215).

164. Owen 1975, p. 38.

165. This included the Porteous riot in Edinburgh, which involved smuggling and drunkenness. In April, the execution of one Andrew Wilson, a smuggler, led to stones being thrown from the crowd and under the command of one Captain John Porteous, shots being fired into the crowd, killing six and wounding eleven. Porteous was found guilty of murder. Upon obtaining a reprieve from the Queen, Porteous was subsequently hanged by an angry crowd that stormed the gaol. The crowd was dispersed. The opposition, led by Carteret, sought to embarrass the ministry over its handling of the Scottish administration (Leadam 1969, pp. 350–2).

the smugglers to engage in more violence. The new law failed to address the causes of smuggling, which was rampant. The real problem was that smuggling was made profitable due to the high rate of duties. The fact that the authorities charged with suppressing illicit trade were themselves corrupted did not help matters. Contemporaries complained that smuggling had corrupted the entire nation. Certainly the practice enjoyed widespread legitimacy, given that a large volume of goods could be obtained at a better price from smugglers, if they could be legitimately obtained at all. Indeed, Walpole himself, 'despite the savagery of the measures he proposed to suppress smuggling, personally carried his fine French wines past the Custom House'.[166] Not until the 1740s would the smuggling crisis come to a head.[167]

When Parliament met in January 1738, the opposition's new weapon against the ministry was a long list of grievances against Spain for harsh treatment and frequent searches of British traders. If smugglers were to receive no mercy from Walpole's ministry, those engaging in illicit trade in the Spanish colonies would receive none either. Since 1713, a thriving illicit traffic had arisen, provoking a clampdown by the Spanish coastguards. Between 1713 and 1731, 180 British ships had been appropriated by Spain. After a lull, the clampdown was renewed in 1737, and the cry for reprisals against Spain became an uproar when, in March 1738, Captain Jenkins brought his ear to Parliament – pickled in a bottle – which he claimed had been cut off by the Spanish in 1731. Walpole could hardly come out in favour of illicit trading, but he did commence negotiations with Spain. The Convention of Pardo in 1739 compensated innocent British traders hurt by Spain's activities, in return for enforcing the payment of Spain's outstanding claim of £68,000 from the South Sea Company. The opposition was indignant. A frenzy of public denunciations and lampoons of the ministry ensued. Petitions denouncing the Convention poured in. Carteret and Chesterfield led the attack, followed by the Duke of Argyll and the Prince of Wales. Still, the ministry carried on. When the South Sea Company refused payment, Spain in turn suspended the *Asiento*. The uproar now became a torrent. At last Walpole's guiding principle of appeasing the landed classes with peace and a lower land tax proved incapable of staving off the march to war, a war now known to posterity as the 'War of Jenkins' Ear'.[168] The King refused Walpole's resignation. In July 1739, as fighting commenced in

166. Winslow 1975, pp. 147–9.

167. In Sussex, the growing level of violence approached the level of an insurrection. 'Pitched battles with customs officers, aided by soldiers, continued of frequent occurrence. In one such, near Pevensey in 1744, a hundred mounted smugglers were victorious' (Leadam 1969, p. 353). In 1748, the capture, torture and murder of a revenue officer and an informer, William Galley and Daniel Chater, 'finally fixed the attention of the entire nation' on the smugglers in Sussex and led to an 'extraordinary campaign' to suppress the practice, led by the Duke of Richmond (Winslow 1975, p. 136).

168. Speck 1977, p. 234; Leadam 1969, pp. 357–9.

the West Indies, Walpole came under fire for allowing the ships of the fleet to fall into disrepair. In October, the death of Charles VI of Austria and Prussia's subsequent invasion of Silesia signalled the beginning of the War of Austrian Succession. With Prussia and Austria at war, 'The entire continental system constructed by England as a barrier against French aggressions had fallen to pieces in a few weeks'.[169] While England, as a signatory to the Pragmatic Sanction, was obliged to come to the aid of Maria Theresa of Austria, King George removed to Hanover and quickly settled a treaty to keep the electorate neutral. News of the agreement proved a decisive blow against Walpole's reputation. After Parliament reconvened in December 1741, the ministry quickly lost its majority on the second vote. By February, Walpole resigned all his offices and was immediately promoted to the House of Lords, accepting the title of Earl of Orford.[170]

In finding a successor to Walpole, the King had to choose between two factions of ambitious and self-promoting members of the opposition, and naturally chose against the faction led by Prince Frederick. William Pulteney succeeded as Prime Minister, and John Carteret was chosen to handle foreign affairs because he would indulge the King in supporting a pro-Hanoverian policy. As in the past, the policy was deeply unpopular and generated a constant stream of complaints. Britain quickly became a major player in the war, doling out huge subsidies to its allies. As the centre of the conflict shifted to Italy, Carteret promised Sardinia's Charles Emmanuel an annual subsidy of £200,000. In the Netherlands, Hanoverian

169. Leadam 1969, p. 366. Although Austria and Great Britain briefly found themselves belonging to opposing alliances in the 1720s, the two powers had since the 1690s generally been in an alliance that sought to counterbalance French territorial ambitions in Europe. The assumption 'that Austria and Britain were natural allies against French ambitions was deeply rooted in the minds of British statesmen' (Anderson 1995, p. 11). Frederick's invasion of Silesia demonstrated that it was not France alone that had territorial ambitions in Europe, that it was not France alone that might be willing to renege on agreeing to the Pragmatic Sanction and that it was not France alone that would happily see the Habsburg Empire dismantled.

170. Walpole's ministry had long used the committee of privileges and elections to increase its majority by tossing out the petitions of aggrieved opposition candidates whilst supporting the grievances of candidates backed by the ministry. Now this committee had for the first time in recent memory fallen into the hands of the opposition. The unscrupulous methods of this committee were turned against Walpole's government, and anticipating the outcome, Walpole resigned on 1 February, one day before the ministry was defeated in a vote of 241 to 225 to refuse the petition of defeated Court candidates at Chippenham in favour of opposition country candidates (Speck 1977, pp. 237–8). The new Earl of Orford was the subject of an investigation after his downfall as Prime Minister. A motion by Lord Limerick 'into the conduct of Robert Earl of Orford during the last ten years' passed 252 to 245, and a secret committee was struck with Limerick acting as chairman. The committee's results were, according to Leadam, 'so lame and impotent' that they 'provoked a reaction of opinion in favour of Orford'. Even an eloquent speech by Pitt, in favour of a motion to revive the inquiry, failed to move the House, which voted 253 to 186 against in December 1742 (Leadam 1969, pp. 369–70).

troops were put on the payroll in order to secure Dutch participation. And of course Austria, whose existence now depended upon British support, received subsidies as well. In 1743, George II led British forces to victory in the battle at Dettingen. It would be the last time a British sovereign would lead his troops in battle.[171] After Dettingen, George II hesitated, and lost the advantage. Newcastle complained that had the advantage been pressed, France could have been forced to submit '"to reasonable and proper terms of peace"'.[172] The perception was that British interests were being sacrificed to Hanoverian interests.[173] The King announced to Parliament in February 1744 that the Young Pretender, Charles Edward Stuart, was planning an invasion from France. Reminiscent of the first Spanish Armada, the invading fleet was turned away by gale-force winds. The invaders lost twelve ships. France and England exchanged declarations of war in March. The pressures against a pro-Hanoverian policy were now strained to breaking point, and Carteret resigned under pressure. Allied with his brother the Duke of Newcastle (Thomas Pelham Holles), Henry Pelham assumed leadership over a new and shaky ministry that became known as the 'Broad Bottom Administration', being composed of a wide spectrum of politicians. George finally gave up on Hanoverian neutrality and declared Hanover as a principal in the war. He chose his son William, Duke of Cumberland, to lead the campaign. A series of defeats ensued,[174] leading to a truce, negotiated by the British, whereby Austria agreed to cede Silesia to Prussia, effectively relinquishing its status as a great power.

In July 1745, 'Bonnie Prince Charlie' landed in the Hebrides of Western Scotland 'with about a dozen companions and hardly any resources'.[175] By 17 September, Charles seized Edinburgh and was proclaimed King James VIII of Scotland. On 21 September, the rebels routed a British force of some two thousand three hundred under the command of Cope, the resident commander-in-chief in

171. 'In England the news of Dettingen aroused an excitement out of proportion to the merits of a victory due rather to the folly of the opposing general' than to the skill of the allied army. 'The King's courage and that of the young Duke of Cumberland were the theme of universal praise' (Leadam 1969, p. 377).

172. Speck 1977, p. 243.

173. William Pitt, never timid about insulting the King, charged that England had been 'reduced to the status of "a province to a despicable electorate"' (Speck 1977, pp. 242–3).

174. Only in North America were the British triumphant that year, taking Louisbourg, the French garrison at the mouth of the Saint Lawrence (Leadam 1969, pp. 383–90).

175. Within weeks he had an army of one thousand five hundred men, and in August raised his white, blue and red standard at Glenfinnan. While Scots as a whole remained divided throughout the affair, supporters of the Young Pretender joined for a variety of reasons. Catholics and Episcopalians sought religious reform. Many Scottish nationalists had long opposed what they saw as the subjugation of Scotland by England in the Act of Union. Others simply resented customs and excises imposed on Scottish products. 'And doubtless there were those who went along for sheer adventure and hopes of booty' (Speck 1977, pp. 248–9).

Scotland, near Prestonpans. By early December, the Jacobites, aided in no small way by the atrocious state of the roads in the West Midlands, took Derby; they were less than one hundred and thirty miles from London. In London, astonishment turned to panic when the news arrived on 6 December, 'Black Friday'. Shops closed and the Bank of England only averted disaster by paying out in sixpences to clients making a run on the bank. But the Jacobites were already in retreat. With less than five thousand men, the Jacobite army would be no match for an army of ten thousand under Cumberland, and two more armies of the same strength. In April, Cumberland smashed the rebel army of less than eight thousand at Culloden. Vicious reprisals followed.[176]

One of the consequences of the trials was the determination that the hereditary feudal and jurisdictional rights of the highland clans of Scotland should be abolished under the Disarming Act of 1747. Financial compensation was offered, and the forfeited estates were applied to the encouragement of agriculture, fisheries, and the establishment of industry, including instruction in linen and stocking-weaving. Speck notes that 'These acts eradicated, as far as legislation could, a complete culture and way of life'.[177] Thereafter, agrarian capitalism would make rapid progress in Scotland.

The Jacobite rebellion touched off yet another crisis in the government. William Pitt managed to sufficiently ingratiate himself with the King to succeed to the post of paymaster of the forces. Pitt now found himself advocating the very subsidies he had thunderously denounced in the past. 'Subsidies of £400,000 for 50,000 Austrians, £300,000 for the King of Sardinia, and £310,000 for 18,000 Hanoverians were carried in one day by 255 to 122 votes'.[178] The national debt, which had stood at nearly £47 million in 1739, would soar to over £76 million by 1748. By 1746, peace negotiations were underway at Breda. Far away in India, British victories over French ships in the fall of 1747 would ultimately contribute to British supremacy in India. France's victory over the allies at Lauffield signalled a coming French invasion of Holland. But when the Whigs returned 338 seats against 97 opposition Whigs and 117 Tories[179] in 1747, a triumphant Henry Pelham moved quickly to extract Britain from the war. At Aix-la-Chapelle,

---

176. Transported to England for trial, rank-and-file rebels were forced to draw lots, 'one in twenty to be hanged, the rest to be transported' (Leadam 1969, p. 408). In all seventy-seven were hanged, drawn and quartered or beheaded. Most declared their allegiance to the Jacobite cause to the end; a few bought their freedom in exchange for betrayal. Three peers were beheaded as traitors. At first celebrated as the saviour of the nation, as news of the reprisals filtered back, Cumberland was soon being referred to as 'Billy the Butcher'.

177. Speck 1977, p. 251.

178. Leadam 1969, p. 412.

179. In this election the Tories 'held a majority of the English shires, where representation was most real . . .' (Feiling 1938, p. 55).

negotiations led to an offsetting of territorial gains. Britain did not gain territory, but obliged France to expel the Pretender and once again recognise the Hanoverian succession. Spain renewed its grant of the *Asiento* to Britain until 1750. A bloody, destructive and expensive war, the 'futile and unintelligible' War of Austrian Succession (1740–8) ended with very little having changed or having been gained by any side.[180] Peace negotiations were followed by Pelham's subsequent efforts to reduce the burden of the nation's debt. In two short years, he reduced Britain's armed forces from 50,000 to fewer than 19,000 in the army and from 51,000 to 10,000 in the navy. Horace Walpole commented: 'You will hear little news from England, but of robberies; the numbers of disbanded soldiers and sailors have all taken to the road or rather to the street; people are almost afraid of stirring after it is dark'.[181]

Pelham reduced the interest rate, consolidated the national debt and lowered government expenditure from £12 million to £7 million pounds per annum. The land tax was reduced from four shillings on the pound to two. These efforts freed up capital for heavier investment in agriculture, just in time for the era of high parliamentary enclosures.

Conclusion

At the outset of the eighteenth century in England, the re-found unity of the ruling landed elite appeared to be in jeopardy once more as the Tories enjoyed a revival of power during Anne's reign, and inter-party disputes sharpened over issues of popular sovereignty, the divine right of kings and the threat of a Jacobite rising possibly accompanied by a French invasion in support of a Stuart restoration. Yet in spite of fighting two wars with France over the span of 26 years (1688–1714) interrupted by only four years of peace (1697–1701) and an agrarian depression lasting throughout most of this period, exports surged ahead and England managed to position itself as Europe's primary *entrepôt* state as well as the leading exporter of cheap grain. The favourable balance of trade was essential to enabling England to maintain a permanent deployment of the army and a near-permanent deployment of the navy (the 'double forward commitment') as well as providing unprecedented military subsidies to its allies.

While a positive trade balance with Europe, an upswing in colonial trade and the financial reforms of William III were all necessary factors in explaining how England was able to hold its own in the battlefield against France, a country three times its size, the expansion of trade and empire were themselves largely

180. Owen 1975, p. 69. Walpole's comment came on 31 January 1750.
181. As quoted in Leadam 1969, p. 420.

made possible by the growth of agrarian productivity and the expansion of the domestic market. The effective annexation of Scotland in 1707 broadened this domestic market and made Great Britain the largest free-trade area in the world. Many lines of production enjoyed protective legislation to foster their continued expansion. The building of stately country houses also gained momentum as larger landowners increasingly consolidated their holdings, with smaller landlords finding it increasingly difficult to keep up with the game even as merchants and other urban ('bourgeois') men of wealth sought to buy their way into the gentry by purchasing estates.

Between the Whig electoral victory in the violent elections of 1714, the passing of Queen Anne and the defeat of the Old Pretender in the following year, the Whiggish forces of limited popular sovereignty effectively buried their Tory opponents who had long sought to uphold the divine right of the Stuart kings to reclaim the throne they had lost in 1688–9. As in those years, ruling-class unity and hegemony was once again restored. In the decades to come, Whig hegemony would mean stability with corruption, continued expansion of foreign trade, a deepening of empire and the rise of great landed houses to new heights of opulence as enclosures, improved farming, land consolidation and agrarian-capitalist tenant-farming continued to spread. Parliament, acting as the body representing the landed classes once again secure in their refound unity and hegemony, set about a process of 'enclosing' agrarian property rights in a battery of harsh, new and punitive laws in what became known as the bloody code. Under the leadership of Robert Walpole, Britain's first Prime Minister, the landed elite would also now begin to wean the state off of the land tax and shift the burden of taxation away from the landlord class and onto the working poor.

The relative ease with which the economy recovered from the bubble of 1720 testifies to the underlying buoyancy of the expanding agrarian-capitalist economy. Most remarkably, during the so-called agrarian depression of 1730–50, rents rose even as prices fell. After reaching their lowest point in 1743, when prices stood at 92 percent of their 1700 equivalent, grain prices began rising again, and the British economy partook in the burst of post-war growth in trade that took place across Western Europe from 1748–52. Since this recovery was not unique to Britain, we can list this as, in part, an exogenous factor coming to the economy's rescue. Population growth likely compounded the effect of the recovery of foreign trade in stimulating prices. It was precisely in 1751, the same year that the heir to the throne died suddenly of pleurisy,[182] when the first in a series of bad

182. At the time of his death on 20 March 1751, Prince Frederick was in the midst of laying plans for his succession, which he intended to usher in a new era free of corruption. Frederick's son George, 12, suddenly became the subject of intrigues in a struggle over who should act as regent upon the death of George II.

harvests hit, further stimulating prices but putting the squeeze on real wages. Large exports of grain continued until 1755, after which they steadily declined. The trend of low prices for primary products and grain exports went into reverse. Rising prices caused domestic consumption to falter, and it appears that this meant more goods were available to fuel the export boom. 1756–7 brought the worst harvest of those years, and the series of bad harvests that had begun in 1751 lasted until 1758 and ensured that agrarian prices stayed high. With the cost of bread and the demand for labour rising simultaneously, wages rose in turn.[183] According to A.H. John, it was only when the cost of labour increased that machinery such as the fly shuttle; the gig mill and the warping mill were adopted more widely. 'It was when costs and prices altered in a drastic way during the late fifties and sixties that the way was open for more radical changes'.[184] For John:

> the unique importance of the years 1680–1750 lies in the emergence, for the first time, of a situation in which the terms of trade between manufactures and primary products turned in favour of the former for reasons other than a fall in population. Until then the major variable had been the size of population, and relative changes in these two categories of production followed as a consequence.[185]

John cites numerous factors to explain how this change in the terms of trade came about, including: a redeployment of resources with capital chasing cheaper labour in the North and West, the process of achieving national financial unification, and the addition of skilled labour to the economy through the expansion of industry into new regions. However, John concludes that 'a large measure of the credit' for the fact that by 1750 Great Britain was the largest free-trade zone in the world 'must go to agricultural improvement, which coincided with a long period of slowly growing population'.[186] If it was possible for agriculture to respond to falling prices with intensified production and improved productivity, what then could be achieved in manufacturing?

---

183. John 1965, pp. 26–8 and 33.
184. John 1965, p. 31.
185. John 1961, p. 187.
186. John 1961, p. 190. John was perhaps the first to systematically examine the linkages between the dramatic developments in agriculture and the growth of manufacturing in the decades anticipating the onset of the Industrial Revolution. By placing a heavy emphasis on prices and demographics, however, John's economic approach leaves the impression of a merely incidental relationship between productivity, falling prices and changing terms of trade for manufacturing and stops short of identifying the specifically *capitalist* dynamic driving agrarian change.

Chapter Four
An Empire in Crisis

> England should bee endeavoured to bee made the shop of Europe, and it with other countries the markets. To doe this all trades and workmen should bee encouraged and all manner of compendious ways invented wherby they may come to undersell the manufactures and commodities of all other countrys. This would bee better then to strengthen their monopolizing corporations in ignorance and idleness.
>
> William Petty[1]

> It was no weak state that provided the force to put together one of the greatest commercial empires in history.
>
> John Rule[2]

To argue that agrarian capitalism was the key to the establishment of British preeminence among European empires does not mean to imply that the empire itself operated on capitalist principles. British imperial expansion was driven by the same strategic considerations as its rivals, with perhaps the key consideration being geopolitical rivalry, which was itself 'extra-economic' in character. Like absolutist Spain and France, Britain applied military force directly and often ruthlessly for the purpose of expanding commerce and access to key raw materials needed for expanding manufactures. The British imported slaves to work their sugar and tobacco plantations in the Caribbean

1. Wood 2003, p. 85.
2. Rule 1992a, p. 27.

and America, as did the Portuguese and the Dutch. In the widely used and very loose definition of capitalism, wherein capitalism is generally equated with markets, European imperialism in general is understood as a wholly capitalist affair. But in this study, we are seeking to understand the specific process that led to the development of industrial capitalism in Britain, wherefrom it has spread throughout the world. Within this perspective, capitalism is identified with a very specific form of property, the social relationship of *capital*, which involves the fictitious commodification of land and labour. And the development of this specific form of property was most pronounced in, if not unique to, Britain in the eighteenth century.[3] Rather than 'capitalist', the term we prefer to apply to eighteenth-century Europe is 'European class society', for this was a highly *commercial*, militarist society in which class divisions were stark. Moreover, agrarian capitalism, absolutism, Italian commercialism and neo-feudalism in Eastern Europe are all different forms of class society existing and interacting simultaneously. In general, the British Empire operated in accord with the same commercial and military framework as rival empires.

However, the one major exception to this was England's first colonial project: Ireland. Here, as Ellen Meiksins Wood has shown, Irish landholders were forcibly displaced by Cromwell's soldiers and replaced by colonial settlers in an attempt to transplant the social relations of agrarian capitalism from England to Ireland. The rationale was supplied in the quote above from William Petty, Cromwell's surveyor in Ireland. Rather than maintain a system of monopolies specialising in luxury items, Britain could gain the advantage through competitive production, as opposed to mere commercial exchange. Petty's understanding of the advantages of competitive production was based upon the experience of English tenant-farmers who were subject to the compulsion of a land market based on competitive land leases. Irish agriculture was not subject to the same economic compulsions. Irish land was less productive because it was not 'improved'; and was therefore less valuable when value is measured in terms of the productivity

---

3. While Brenner pioneered the theory of agrarian capitalism, he has written of regions outside Britain where agrarian capitalism developed, namely in Catalonia (see Brenner 1985a, p. 49 n. 81), and in Holland (see above, Introduction, p. 37 for a discussion that includes the dissenting views of Wood and Post). And as also noted above, Weber and Mumford both seem to believe that German mining became capitalist from a very early period (see above Chapter One, p. 81). Entering a debate over whether capitalism actually developed in any of these places is outside the scope of the present work, so we allow for only a brief comment. Proletarianisation, the separation of the direct producers from the means of production, advanced quite early in mining operations. And while industrial capitalism has involved the development of a proletariat, this does not mean that where we find proletarianisation we find capitalism. As we shall discuss more fully in Chapter Ten, the organisation of production continued to be organised along mostly customary lines in British mining throughout the nineteenth century, despite the high degree of proletarianisation.

of labour. By applying English agrarian-capitalist methods to Irish land, the Irish themselves would stand to benefit because the level of production across Ireland would increase. But Ireland was unique in that it was the only English settler-colony where the English were able to transplant the distinctive social property relations of agrarian capitalism.[4] Even here, the effort to recreate the landlord, tenant-farmer and wage labourer triad of agrarian social relations in Ireland was moderately successful in the North, but was resisted in highly agrarian southern Ireland by such groups as the Whiteboy movement, resulting in the reversion of customary forms of organising agrarian production.[5] In America, the development of a competitive market in leases in support of a class of rentier landlords proved unfeasible, as farmers could too easily own their own land.

What we can observe is that within the non-capitalist framework of European imperialism, British imperialism was conditioned by agrarian capitalism in a number of ways. No other imperial power could afford to relocate such large numbers of settlers to the colonies, and this was due to the increasing numbers of British who were being 'freed' from the land, creating a surplus population. The British were latecomers to the slave trade, seizing a significant share only after 1670 and quickly becoming the pre-eminent slave traders. Slavery, observes Coleman, 'was in no way peculiar to capitalism'.[6] But the use of large numbers of slaves was essential to running Caribbean plantations to meet the exceptional demand of Britain's domestic market for sugar and tobacco, imports of which inclined sharply in the 1740s.[7] Export levels tell us something about production and productivity, but import levels are also telling. Imports began to incline

4. Wood 2003, p. 87.

5. The effort was only moderately successful because Irish landholders largely came into possession of their estates as spoils of war rather than through purchase or inheritance, and were thus not subject to competitive market pressures to the same degree as English agriculture. They thus tended to resort to 'squeezing' absolute labour increases out of their tenants as opposed to investing in raising the level of productivity, which explains the yawning gulf between very wealthy landlords and extremely poor tenants observed by Arthur Young during his travels in Ireland in the late 1780s. See Wright 2003, pp. 484–5.

6. Coleman 1977, pp. 143–4. Wright 2003, p. 342, finds no differences between the way the English, French, Dutch and Spanish organised slave labour on their plantations. Yet he finds it 'reasonable to suggest that the capitalist emphasis on the pursuit of profit, as the primary social objective, could be expected to exert increasing levels of influence on the conduct and practices of at least some of the members of parliament, for these individuals were very heavily drawn from the same landed class who actively engaged in transforming English agrarian relations into the capitalist format'. It is an interesting suggestion, but the emphasis on the profit-motive seems off the mark. Below, however, in Chapter Thirteen, pp. 710–11, we will consider an early nineteenth-century example in which Wright's observation might be more salient, and which speaks to the obverse suggestion: that the English may have applied to their construction of a capitalist labour market things they had learned from their experience as slavemasters.

7. Wood 2003, p. 106.

sharply in the 1740s. Cole and Deane write: 'Clearly the years 1745–60 constitute a landmark in the history of this branch of trade'.[8]

By the eighteenth century, with the unprecedented expansion of the domestic market in Britain, driven by falling prices and increasing productivity in agriculture, Britain's economy was outpacing its rivals in terms of the rate of growth and the ability to expand trade. This superiority was reflected in the decisive military victories over France in the eighteenth century, the Seven Years' War in particular, which resulted in an enormous geographic extension of the Empire. From Spain, Britain sought the *Asiento*, not colonial territory to control, but the rights to trade within Spain's American colonies, effectively the right to *compete* with Spanish producers in what were otherwise monopoly markets for Spain. In the third quarter of the eighteenth century, as Britain sought to consolidate the new territories it had annexed as a result of the Seven Years' War, it was confronted with different forms of resistance arising from a variety of causes. Meanwhile, increasing social dislocation through enclosures as well as population growth contributed to growing unrest at home in the form of an emerging popular politics. At home and abroad, the view that the King and his government were tyrants was becoming more widespread. The unrest culminated in simultaneous convulsions at home and in the colonies and a costly defeat for Britain at the hands of the Americans and their allies, most notably the French. Despite the loss of America, Britain was able to adjust and maintain its empire, and even to expand it further. It is doubtful whether any other imperial power could have fared as well. The British economy soon recovered and surged forward once more, riding the strength of the most productive economy in the world, now approaching the full expression of its agrarian-capitalist logic. Moreover, Britain was about to enter upon the first industrial revolution, driven by a recently emerging industrial capitalism, which after 1782 would begin to demonstrate its potential.

Pitt and empire

The eight years of peace that followed the War of Austrian Succession allowed space for matters of social reform to take priority. Britain was on the Julian calendar, which had been ten days behind the Gregorian in the seventeenth century and was eleven days behind in the eighteenth. In March of 1751 an act was passed to convert Britain from the Julian to the Georgian calendar by suppressing the eleven days between 2 and 14 September 1752. 'The resultant outcry "give us back our eleven days" is often dismissed as the blind reaction of an ignorant mob; but

8. Ibid.

in fact the change gave reasonable grounds for concern at all levels of society, necessitating nice calculations about rents, leases, debts and wages, as well as superstitions about saint's days and holy days which were exploited by almanac makers . . .'[9]. The losses were surely small compared to what they might be if a similar change took place today, but would any other country have witnessed such an outcry over the effect of such a change on rents and wages?

Another attempt at reform was the effort to crack down on the perceived problem of increasing public drunkenness, thanks to the cheapness of and easy access to gin. Penal laws were made more severe, to little effect. Novelist Henry Fielding, who was also a police magistrate, published *An Inquiry into the Causes of the Late Increase of Robbers, etc.* in January 1751, denouncing intemperance as a source of the increase in criminal activity. The attempts at licensing under the Gin Act had failed to check the spread of drinking. The 'tippling act' reformed the licensing laws and established a more centralised, restrictive and effective liquor law that remained in effect until 1828. A second offence at unlicensed retailing of spirits was made punishable by whipping; third offences resulted in transportation. In June of 1753 the Marriage Act was passed. It obliged would-be newlyweds to obtain the explicit consent of guardians (in the case of minors) and proof of residence.[10] Earlier, in May, the Jewish Naturalization Act received royal assent. Immediately, 'The great clamour of 1753' ensued, in which the opposition press wildly exaggerated its scope. As Walpole had learned with his excise scheme, so Pelham learned with the Naturalization Act that it is unwise to provoke popular resistance to a measure on the eve of an election, Pelham bowed to public pressure and repealed the measure within a year of its passage.

But Henry Pelham did not survive in time for re-election and was succeeded as First Lord of the Treasury and Prime Minister by his timid and compulsive brother Thomas Pelham Holles, Duke of Newcastle. In his long tenure as a leading Whig administrator, Newcastle epitomised Whig stability and commitment to the Protestant succession. While Newcastle was the master of electoral patronage, he was also a hard-working administrator 'prepared to do the essential donkey work'.[11] By now it had been established by Walpole's example that it was necessary to have the King's minister present in the Commons in order to manage it. A peer himself, Newcastle had two choices: Henry Fox, Secretary at War, and the thunderous Paymaster William Pitt, neither of whom he found

9. Speck 1977, p. 255.

10. It also established that marriage records should be kept. This put an end to clandestine marriages before fraudulent clergymen. See Owen 1975, p. 74.

11. Speck 1977, p. 258. The full comment reads: 'The very fact that he left behind him the largest collection of papers for any politician of his age in itself documents the astonishing degree to which he was prepared to do the essential donkey work of a system which depended upon patronage. There was scarcely a sphere of activity left untouched by this noble drudge'.

acceptable. When Pitt attacked Newcastle for having sought to bribe German princes against allying with France, Pitt was dismissed and Fox was given the job. Spurned, the man capable of 'spellbinding the Commons with scathing denunciations'[12] now unleashed his fury at Newcastle's foreign policy of allying with Prussia to protect Hanover, which provoked an alliance between Austria and France.[13] Subsequently, when Newcastle resigned in the wake of the French seizure of Minorca in May 1756, the Duke of Devonshire was made First Lord of the Treasury, but the indomitable Pitt became the *de facto* Prime Minister.

Pitt's first act was to recall troops to England to protect against a French invasion. His militia bill passed the Lords only after the total projected force was reduced by half to 32,000 men. When it went into effect in the fall, it was greeted in six counties with protests against entrapment of troops. As the Old Corps remained loyal to Newcastle and Pitt himself sought his support in the country gentlemen, the ministry was set on a weak foundation. Pitt sought to impress upon the King that his principal objective was to see Britain fight from her strength, at sea, and not another stagnant land war on the continent. The King was unmoved, and the country gentlemen were shocked and dismayed at the thought that the 'country' policy they had hoped for would not materialise. In March 1757 Captain Byng was hanged over the loss of Minorca, a hanging Pitt opposed, but one which nonetheless cost him his popularity. He was dismissed by the King and for nearly three months there was no government. The solution to establishing a new government was at once an absurd and an obvious prospect – Newcastle and Pitt should form a ministry together. Both Pitt and Newcastle were 'Whigs' after all, despite Pitt's close association with and acting as a spokesman for the country gentlemen, about half of whom were Tories. Numerically, the Tories were by now reduced to the status of being but one of five distinct factions among the opposition.[14] With the general support of

12. Speck 1977, pp. 261–2.

13. Britain's traditional allies had been Austria and the Netherlands. When, in 1755, Newcastle looked to renew the Anglo-Austrian treaty against the French, Austria sought language providing for a defence against Prussia, her primary concern. Mainly concerned with protecting Hanover, the Duke turned first to Russia and signed the Convention of St Petersburg, by which subsidies would be paid to Russia. This so alarmed Prussia, whose central concern was Russia, that the King of Prussia sought to neutralise its effect by coming to terms with Britain. Prussia and Britain signed the Convention of Westminster in January 1756. The diplomatic revolution was completed when in response to this convention, France and Austria agreed to a new alliance. 'Newcastle's alliance with Prussia to protect Hanover was grist to Pitt's mill that British interests were being sacrificed for the defence of the Electorate. Pitt argued that he was prepared to allow Hanover to be overrun while Britain concentrated on obtaining French territory outside Europe. Then when war ended extra-European gains could be traded for the recovery of the Electorate' (Speck 1977, p. 263).

14. These five factions under Newcastle were: 'the Cumberland corps led by Bedford and Fox, the Cobham group (though the old lord had died) of Pitt, Lyttleton, and the

both Court and Country, the new administration was virtually unopposed. On 29 June, Newcastle became the nominal Prime Minister once again. Pitt would serve as secretary, but was in actuality the premier and heir to Walpole's station in the Commons. This remarkable marriage of convenience was only to last three years until the death of George II in 1760. But as a moment of extraordinary ruling-class unity and hegemony, it does stand out as a moment of closure on the political schism between court and country that pre-dates the Revolution. Ever since the defeat and effective silencing of radical dissent in the form of Levellers and more moderate Independents – partly during the civil wars, completely after the Restoration – the politics of state had been thoroughly elitist in character and the struggles in politics were intra-elite struggles. The intra-elite schism between court and country had undergone a series of transmogrifications – Royalists versus Roundheads giving way to Whigs and (Jacobite and pro-Hanoverian) Tories, giving way to the 'Old Corps' and the country gentlemen (Whig and Tory). But throughout, the power of the landed classes as expressed in Parliament continued to grow.

During the interim between governments, an annual subsidy of £670,000 for Prussia's King Frederick had been voted by the British parliament. Subsequently, on 1 May 1757, France joined Austria and Russia in signing the Second Treaty of Versailles, agreeing jointly to invade and carve up Prussia. Russian troops began marching westward. Now, just five days from the founding of the new ministry, news arrived from Germany that in response to Prussia's invasion of Saxony, the Austrians had defeated and inflicted heavy losses on Frederick's army at Kolin in Bohemia. Coinciding with this, news arrived from India of the fall of Calcutta the previous June (1756) to Suraj-ud-Daulah, the Nawáb of Bengal. The public gloom was magnified when news spread of the horror of the 'Black Hole of Calcutta.'[15] Needing to score a quick victory for Britain that could calm the public's nerves, Pitt sought to attack Rochefort in September, only to see the expedition abandoned.[16] By October, the Russians had taken Berlin while the

Grenvilles, the Court of Leicester House, and the Tories. But the dividing lines were made soft and spongy by the common Whigdom of four groups . . .' (Feiling 1938, p. 59). Thus it becomes comprehensible that a man could be recommended to Newcastle as '"a Dissenter and a good Whig . . . a leading man among the Tories"' (Feiling 1938, p. 72, quoting Robert Nugent).

15. This was an incident involving the mass-murder of over 125 persons belonging to the vanquished British camp by Suraj-ud-Daulah, who took Calcutta with an army of 50,000 men against a settlement defended by 264 soldiers and 250 residents. Leadam 1969, p. 452.

16. Pitt dispatched General Sir John Mordaunt to attack Rochefort in September 1757, but Mordaunt doubted the practicability of the expedition, and returned to Portsmouth on 3 October. 'The exasperation in England at these failures was intense. A court-martial on Mordaunt condemned the project of the expedition, and by Mordaunt's acquittal Pitt sustained a mortifying rebuff' (Leadam 1969, p. 454).

French were in control of Ostend. For Britain, it was the lowest point in the war thus far. In November and December, Frederick handed defeat to a combined Franco-Austrian force at Rossbach and Leuthen. A series of costly and unimpressive victories for Britain ensued, deflecting French attention from Prussia.

But Pitt's thoughts were turned to the West. His main objective at this stage was to launch a major offensive in America. Determined to contain the westward expansion of British settlers, the French had by 1756 constructed a chain of forts from Quebec to New Orleans, and formed alliances with a majority of the native tribes.[17] British defeats at Fort Henry, Lake George and Ticonderoga in 1757–8 were followed by the seizure of Fort Duquesne (renamed Fort Pitt) in November 1758. Further victories secured Pitt's position and gave him free reign to carry out his plans. The Tory country gentlemen and Whig landowners rallied to Pitt's support. £10 million was voted for the war effort.

Pitt pre-empted a French plan to invade England and Scotland with 62,000 men by attacking French ports. A French fleet was defeated near Lagos, Portugal. In November and December, Frederick II scored impressive victories, and Pitt sent 10,000 men to Germany, in response to pressure to aid Prussia's successes. This brooked no controversy. 'By 1759 no fewer than ninety-one thousand British soldiers (excluding the militia) and sixty thousand men were serving in the various theatres of war, and nearly £13,000,000 was voted for the coming year without a word of protest'.[18] Despite the dispatch of soldiers and the huge annual subsidy to Prussia, 1759 brought more defeat for Britain's allies on the continent. But in North America, Wolfe took Quebec in September. This was followed by the victory at Quiberon Bay. Britain was now in command of the seas. 1759 was declared 'the great year' in Britain. Pitt was at the height of his career. He was in command of Britain and saw no reason to stop now. He rebuffed calls from neutral Spain for a peace settlement. He sought to expand the armed forces from 91,000 to 175,000 men, and increased the supplies granted from £12,761,000 in 1759 to £15,500,000 in 1760. 'This budget, which no other minister could have carried, was voted with unanimity'.[19] It was Newcastle, of course, who had the charge of raising these prodigious sums.

---

17. Hence the Seven Years' War became known by British settlers in America as the 'French and Indian Wars'.

18. Owen 1975, p. 90.

19. Leadam 1969, p. 470. In these budgets was the £670,000 annual subsidy for Prussia, which Pitt now supported, contradicting his earlier opposition to Newcastle's subsidy system. In 1761 Pitt claimed 'paradoxically . . . that he had conquered Canada in Germany'. Speck writes: '[T]here were so many contradictions in [Pitt's] approach to strategy that it is hard to see how he reconciled them even in his own mind'. He finds Pitt's war planning 'paradoxical', offering the example of Pitt contradicting himself on his earlier critique of subsidies (Speck 1977, p. 271). But this does not seem a very strong example, for when one takes into account popular outcries of support when Prussia

While news of events in the Americas could reach England within a matter of months, news from India took more than a year to arrive. Thus while the expulsion of the French from India actually followed swiftly upon the expulsion of the French from Canada; celebrations would have to be delayed. In February 1757, the British defeated the Nawáb, installed a puppet successor and were effectively governing Bengal. Two years later, France was driven out of Madras. Later in 1759, a plot to check British dominance in Bengal with Dutch aid was blocked when seven Dutch ships bearing 1,400 troops were seized. On 22 January 1760, the British seized the fortress of Wandiwash, and with their coastal headquarters surrounded, the French surrendered Pondicherry on 15 January 1761. All that remained were French possessions on the West coast, which soon fell, ending the presence of French military power in India.

When King George II died on 25 October 1760, news had reached Britain only a month prior to the decisive battle of Wandiwash, and only nine days prior to the conquest of Canada. Policies such as his preoccupation with the security of Hanover and his treatment of Pitt were widely forgiven in the moment of victory. All the same, Britons were not indifferent to the costs of the war, and many were now calling for peace.

The emergence of popular politics: Wilkes and George III

Upon the death of George II in October of 1760 'the fires of party controversy were burning lower than at almost any time in the eighteenth century',[20] but this was about to change. On the surface of things, there appear to be few direct causal links between the new developments in converting manufacturing to capitalist industry and the mayhem in politics. Much of the controversy can be attributed to party, faction, distrust of the King and personalities. With the revolution settlement now three-quarters of a century behind it, the unprecedented volume of legislation Parliament had to consider meant that its work had become routine, and annual sessions a necessity. There was plenty of economic legislation to deal with, including matters of taxation, loans and subsidies for war and a rapidly increasing number of acts of enclosure. But there was little controversy in Parliament over these matters, and a high degree of consensus concerning

---

scored major victories, Pitt's change of course seems little different from any other politician willing to change his mind when the new course of action is sure to be popular with the public at large. When in opposition, Pitt needed to consolidate his base in the country gentlemen, including the Tory squires who clung to the old notion of a 'blue water' policy. Once in power, and having achieved success in war to make him popular to all, Pitt could clearly afford to make decisions that would displease his base of support, but which would go over well with the public and especially the King.

20. Christie 1982, p. 55.

economic affairs, where formal politics is concerned. Given the sustained unanimity of the ruling class concerning most economic matters, political ruptures took on a more specifically *political* character.

This is not to say that we cannot discern *any* causal links flowing from the economic to the political sphere in this period. Indeed, it is in this period that large-scale, mostly urban, popular protest begins to take on a life of its own, fuelled in part by the expansion of popular print media. And just as the radicals in the English Revolution were drawn in large part from the ranks of journeymen and small masters in manufacturing, so in the late eighteenth century the ranks of protesting crowds were drawn from the ranks of working men and women. While some of these may have belonged to the embryonic industrial proletariat working machines in cotton factories or simply facing dislocation and unemployment, the greater portion were more apt to be those in the 'honourable trades' who still owned their own spinning wheels, looms or cropping shears and who could see in the factory system the sign spelling the eventual end to their independence and way of life. These labouring men no longer had recourse to guild regulations and were increasingly losing the government's support in enforcing apprenticeship rules, or any of the regulations of the trades set out in the Statute of Apprentices. Their primary concern was to maintain their independence by retaining control of the labour process. Thus while, on the one hand, the radical discourse of extending the franchise that had ended with the suppression of the radicals under Cromwell was revived, an inherently conservative current also ran among independent craftsmen who favoured 'reform' but who found their interests running against the oncoming wave of industrial 'progress'. They could find allies among the opposition in Parliament who likewise supported reform, albeit in the form of tepid support for extremely limited and piecemeal measures, but those same allies would not hesitate to pass an enclosure bill or grant patent rights for factory machinery. Shorn of customary law in the village or guild regulation of manufacturing and proscribed from political life, working people often resorted to popular protest. As parliamentary enclosures resulted in unprecedented numbers of people being divorced from their means of subsistence, domestic manufactures and factory industry expanded. This, combined with the resurgence of population growth, contributed to the growth in numbers of those employed in both large and small manufacturing enterprises.

The accession of George III, son of Prince Frederick and grandson to George II, spelled the end of the proscription of Tories from holding public office. The re-engagement of the old Tory squires back into politics meant, in turn, that the ghost of the now hopeless and twice defeated Jacobite cause could finally be laid to rest. Under George II, the Tory party's members had become 'scattered all through the political spectrum of the House'.[21] At the same time however, the 'Old Corps' of the Whigs, led by Newcastle, also gave way upon his resignation in 1762. The political divisions that had lasted since the exclusion crisis of the 1680s were no longer resonant. In due course, new allegiances and voting patterns and disputes would emerge among the elite.

At the age of 22, George III came to power at a moment of extraordinary optimism for the British and their empire. The recent military victories over France meant that Britain was emerging as the world's pre-eminent military, economic and imperial power. Great Britain was ready to emerge from the Seven Years' War as 'the most powerful state in Europe, or indeed in the world'.[22] George added his voice to those calling for peace. Overseas trade had doubled in thirty years; trade with North America had tripled. The old economy with its open field system was being swept away by an unprecedented wave of parliamentary enclosures. Any ruler would have found it difficult to avoid getting carried away with optimism, but how revealing of his character it was when, three days after his succession, George III issued a proclamation '"for the encouragement of piety and virtue, and for the prevention of vice, profaneness and immorality". A naïve young man of twenty-three was about to clean out the Augean stables'.[23] No other English sovereign began his or her reign with so much promise in the air only to encounter so much adversity and personal tragedy.

Things started well enough for George. Where Charles I had gone to war with Parliament over Crown revenues, George 'surrendered his hereditary revenue in

---

21. Christie 1982, p. 29.

22. Upton 2001, pp. 343–4. In the continuing passage, Upton struggles to provide reasons for Britain's new pre-eminence: 'This was because it was structured differently from the great continental monarchies'. Like all early modern societies, Upton adds, the British state was highly devolved and most government was local. But the real difference from the continental monarchies 'showed at the level of central government'. Powersharing was the rule: '[P]olitical hegemony of the landlords replicated at lower levels by the control of the localities by gentlemen JPs, disguised the existence of the money power . . . Uniquely in Europe, the British governments did not have to worry about a possible state bankruptcy, and they could maintain the world's biggest navy and hire soldiers with a freedom denied to their rivals. But perhaps the best evidence of the power of money was the consistency with which the Whig landlord oligarchs made the protection and furtherance of commerce the basis of their public policies'. Upton goes on to suggest that a second factor was 'an unusually high degree of politicized public opinion' and cites the massive expansion of newspapers. Further on he points out that the growth of national identity in Britain rested on two basic emotions: anti-popery and patriotic imperialism. What is strikingly absent is any mention of the uniqueness of the British economy and/or how this uniqueness has shaped the structure of government or has provided the economic strength necessary to sustain the government's new financial system based upon publicly-funded debt.

23. Owen 1975, p. 169.

return for a fixed annual Civil List of £800,000, and a supply of nearly £20,000,000 was voted for the coming year without too much difficulty'.[24] However, George's youthful inexperience and moralistic attitude would lead to trouble soon enough. He viewed politicians in general with contempt. The 'broad bottom' coalition of Pitt and Newcastle was doubly offensive to George, for in the Elder Pitt he saw 'a renegade, "the blackest of hearts" and "a snake in the grass"', while he held Newcastle responsible for the corruption he found reprehensible.[25] George was thus anxious to remove these noxious ministers, but he faced an enormous challenge in finding a harmonious combination of men who both met his approval and also had the necessary experience of managing Parliament.

In the aftermath of Britain's stunning successes against France in the West Indies and North America in the *annus mirabilis* of 1759, Pitt rose to the status of a national hero. But despite enjoying popular support outside Parliament, especially through his connections to the City electorate, this could not change the political reality that he lacked the backing of a sound political constituency inside Parliament. After suffering the loss of Belleisle in Newfoundland, Dominica in the West Indies and Pondicherry in India, France indicated its willingness to discuss terms of settlement. But during the negotiations, Minister Choiseul threatened that Spain might enter the war if French and Spanish grievances were not settled. Over the objections of Newcastle, Pitt broke off negotiations, demanding action against Spain: a declaration of war, seizure of Spain's treasure fleet and attacks on Spanish colonies. When these demands failed to win the support of the cabinet, Pitt resigned. Victory had seen his popularity soar, but he failed to understand how popular peace had become in the face of the war's enormous cost and when the enemy appeared ready for peace. Pitt's stance on the matter was vindicated when war against Spain was declared after all in January 1762. This left Newcastle increasingly isolated. The King's favourite, the Earl of Bute, was put in charge of the military and his brother, James Stuart Mackenzie, was in charge of negotiations with France. The war continued to spell victory for Britain. But in stark contrast with Pitt, Bute's reaction to victory was to panic at the prospect of an expanding war. As Frederick called for more subsidies, and in the face of a new threat from Catherine II of Russia, Bute moved to cut subsidies

24. Owen 1975, p. 170.

25. Christie 1982, p. 56; Turner 1999, p. 12. In 1755, Pitt had allied with George's favourite, the Earl of Bute, 'as a stepping stone to office, only to find after a brief and bitter experience that he could not at the same time serve both the king and the heir'. From the first 'it was obvious that the policies of the prime minister and the attitude of the new monarch were fundamentally at variance. It was an ironic fate for Pitt, who had risen to prominence as a patriot who had attacked the Hanoverian connection on most occasions, to be committed to a major war in defence of Hanover at the accession of a patriot king who boasted that he gloried in the name of Briton, and despised "that horrid Electorate"' (Speck 1977, pp. 273–4).

to Prussia. Infuriated at the betrayal of an ally, Newcastle resigned, to be succeeded by Bute. The fall of the Pitt-Newcastle coalition precipitated a period of political instability and a rapid succession of chief ministers over the remainder of the decade.

Bute's abilities did suffice to keep him in power for nine months.[26] But, unnerved at the widespread resentment and suspicion that greeted him, Bute resigned on 8 April, suggesting George Grenville, Pitt's brother-in-law, as a replacement. This choice only deepened the King's gloom as he complained of having to listen to 'a crashing bore, with a mind like a cash-register',[27] It was in the midst of this grim moment for the King that the comedy of legal errors known as the Wilkes affair began to unfold, adding insult to the King's injury.

While in office, Bute's press hirelings had levelled attacks against William Pitt for his decision to accept a pension and a peerage for his wife, which alongside Newcastle's decision to decline a pension upon his retirement cast Pitt in an awkward light. Pitt's City supporters responded in kind, 'led by the witty journalistic frondeur John Wilkes'.[28] Wilkes was a wicked polemicist. Publishing under the patronage of Earl Temple – who was a brother to both Bute and Grenville, his political alignment with Pitt and the Grenvilles no doubt gave him a sense of security. His attacks took aim at Scots in general and their undue influence over the Crown in particular. In No. 45 of the *North Briton*[29] he published a scathing denunciation of the King's speech in praise of the peace settlement, echoing Pitt's denunciations. A warrant was issued for his arrest on charges of

26. In negotiating the peace, signed on 10 February 1763, he managed to steer clear of both extremes in avoiding heavy concessions for Britain whilst not imposing heavy terms that would drive France to desperation, terms such as those favoured by William Pitt, who came out of retirement to deliver scathing condemnations of the peace treaty and still demanding that France be excluded from the Newfoundland fisheries and stripped of her colonial possessions. See Christie 1982, p. 62.

27. Owen 1975, p. 175. The quote is from Owen the author, not from George III. The King's quip about Grenville runs as follows: '"When he has wearied me for two hours, he looks at his watch to see if he may not tire me an hour more"' (as quoted in Christie 1982, p. 67).

28. Christie 1982, p. 59. Born in Clerkenwell, a suburb of London, John Wilkes was the son of a wealthy London distiller. He married an older woman, the heiress of Aylesbury, located just east of Oxford. She bore him one child before a mutually consented-to separation, arising from Wilkes's loose life and companions. The full flavour of Wilkes's scurrilous behaviour and sense of humour is revealed in an incident involving the secret 'Society of Sir Francis Dashwood', to which Wilkes belonged. Summer meetings in the ruins of St. Mary's Abbey at Medmenham were rumoured to have involved obscene orgies and parodies of Roman Catholic ritual. While the reality may not have lived up to rumour, the society was dissolved after Wilkes pulled a practical joke on Lord Orford. Orford was leading a mock prayer to Satan when Wilkes released a baboon disguised as a devil from a box, whereupon Orford nearly went mad at the thought that his supplication had been answered. (Encyclopedia Britannica 1910–11, Vol. 23, p. 608).

29. Wilkes 1776.

seditious libel. His arrest and imprisonment in the tower evoked popular sympathies. Seen as the victim of tyranny, Wilkes became known as the 'friend of liberty', with 'No. 45' and 'for Wilkes and liberty' becoming popular slogans of the time. At issue was the immunity parliamentarians were supposed to enjoy from the use of warrants except in the case of treason. Not lacking in means, Wilkes was able with the help of friends to secure a hearing, making his case on a writ of *habeas corpus*. Chief Justice Pratt, who was a friend to Pitt, dismissed his case on account of a breach in parliamentary privilege. Rejoicing crowds greeted him upon his release. 'With splendid effrontery Wilkes pressed home his advantage by re-publishing his libels, suing Halifax and his undersecretary, Robert Wood, and recovering £1,000 damages'. Wilkes went unchallenged through the summer, until Parliament, upon reconvening in the fall, voted 237 to 111 to declare No. 45 'to be a "false, scandalous and seditious libel", likely to excite "traitorous insurrections against his majesty's government".'[30] Further, Lord Sandwich, a former associate of Wilkes, obtained a private printing of his pornographic tract *The Essay on Woman*, and 'read out the text to a half-scandalised, half-convulsed chamber of peers'.[31] The text was deemed blasphemous for its attributing notes in the obscene text to the Bishop of Gloucester. Wilkes was now condemned by both houses, with warrants out for his arrest on charges of seditious libel as well as blasphemy. Then, in what many suspected was a government plot to murder him, Samuel Martin, an open supporter of the King who had spent the summer at target practice, challenged Wilkes to a duel, which took place on 16 December. Taking a shot in the stomach, Wilkes was seriously but not mortally wounded. A week later, Parliament voted to take away parliamentary immunity in the case of publishing seditious libels. Having removed to his daughter's residence in Paris, Wilkes failed to appear in court to face his charges and was expelled from the Commons in January 1764.

Wilkes was, for now, out of the picture. But the fallout continued to plague the ministry. Wilkes' counter-suits resulted in a long and technical process issuing in a series of judgments that came down against the use of warrants to arrest those under suspicion of seditious libel. Since the Licensing Acts passed under the Stuarts had been allowed to lapse in 1696, the use of warrants to suppress sedition was considered of dubious legality. They had been used with little controversy against suspected Jacobites during the previous half century, but here they were being used in high-handed fashion, against a single, vociferous Whig. Judge Camden ruled that the precedents no longer existed. The opposition in Parliament seized upon this issue and moved to declare the warrants illegal. The motion was narrowly defeated. The legal controversy over the use of warrants

30. Owen 1975, p. 176–7.
31. Christie 1982, p. 65.

was merely part of a far greater issue which was to become the focus of City radicals and Opposition members alike, that of the 'liberties of the subject' threatened by an alleged royal conspiracy.[32] By attacking the King and his ministry head on, Wilkes had become the symbol of resistance to improper authority.

Grenville's heavy-handed response to the Wilkite rebellion would have long-term implications, but even more full of portent was the outrage stirred up by his policy in the American colonies. After more than half a century of perceived neglect, North American colonists felt themselves ready and deserving of self-government. Where the colonists had declined to expend the necessary funds for their own defence until Pitt promised reimbursement, in Britain the gentry, whose land tax was contributing to the defence of the colonies, felt it was time to reassert the mother country's authority. To this end, Parliament passed a series of restrictive acts between 1763 and 1765, which unwittingly ignited the first sparks of colonial rebellion.[33] Pitt attacked Grenville's American policy, claiming that Parliament had the authority to legislate for the colonies, but not to tax. He called for a Declatory Act reasserting Parliament's power of legislation, and for the repeal of the Stamp Act. When the Americans responded with popular protests against the Stamp Act and a trade boycott, Pitt's advice was

32. As stated above, George III saw it as his God-given duty to restore royal prerogatives. Like Queen Anne, he believed the Crown's role was to play the umpire, rising above party faction. For if not the sovereign, who else had the authority to act as neutral arbiter betwixt factions? 'The public neither had the information nor had it the electoral machinery at its disposal to enable it to make choice of governments. Unless the King were conceded some rights he would become a non-entity manipulated by aristocratic factions whose claims to power lacked any real legitimacy' (Christie 1982, p. 22). But to orthodox Whigs, George III broke with constitutional practice in his attempts to increase the powers of the crown. This view, which first arose when it appeared that Bute exercised improper influence, later became known as the 'Rockingham legend', after Rockingham and his followers, who perpetuated the notion. This animosity toward the Crown and its ministry, largely based on exaggeration, would serve as a focus and rallying cry for the opposition for decades to come (Turner 1999, pp. 13, 18–19; Christie 1982, pp. 22–3).

33. Intended to ease tensions between the colonists and native Indians, who under Ottawa chief Pontiac had captured Fort Detroit in May, The Royal Proclamation of 7 October 1763 restricted settlement beyond the sources of Atlantic rivers, beyond which the colonies were temporarily restricted. The new policy sought control of western lands for Britain and wealthy English speculators against control by provincial governments and invading squatters (Petulla 1988, p. 48). The Plantation Act of 1764 was meant to subsidise the colonial army and to maintain the status of the colonies as a captive market for British manufactures and as a supply of raw materials for British arms and industry. Grenville's Currency Act of 1764 banned the circulation of colonial bills of credit, provoking widespread resentment in the colonies. The Quartering Act required the colonies to provide barracks and supplies for British troops. The Stamp Act of 1765 imposed duties on newspapers, legal and business documents, dice and playing cards. It was the first internal tax on Americans. An additional policy of Grenville's that would hold portent for the future was his reduction of the British army from 120,000 down to 30,000 and financial neglect of the navy 'to the point of danger' (Owen 1975, pp. 178–9).

followed by the new ministry under the nominal leadership of the Marquis de Rockingham. What most likely circumvented a spiralling cycle of repression and rebellion that could have led to an early revolution in the colonies was the agitation by merchants in Britain who, already hit by the post-war depression, were now doubly hit with a trade boycott by the Americans. They began forming local associations and petitioning the Commons. 'All stressed the disastrous effect of the crisis upon trade and the widespread unemployment in manufacturing and commercial districts'.[34] Fears of social unrest and national bankruptcy led to the passage of reforms proposed by the merchants: free-trade ports in the West Indies through which the Americans could smuggle sugar and export raw cotton bound for Manchester and through which the West Indians could smuggle Spanish bullion. Under Rockingham, an act restraining the import of foreign silks, was welcomed by the silk-weavers in the London suburb of Spitalfields. In cases of alleged libel, warrants and seizure of papers were made illegal. A new commercial agreement was signed with Russia.[35] While some saw the Rockingham ministry as guided by Enlightenment ideals, the guiding principle was more likely one of a panicked ministry seeking to stay in power by granting concessions wherever they were demanded. When the Rockinghams, acknowledging the weakness of their support, sought an alliance with their adversaries the Bedfords and Grenvilles, George could take no more. In July 1766, he approached 'the blackest of hearts', and five days later Pitt agreed to form a new government.

Pitt's return heralded a return to relative stability. However, the mutual contempt that had developed between Pitt and the Rockinghams over issues of being excluded from patronage meant that an alliance between them was impracticable. Pitt further weakened his position by accepting a peerage as Lord Chatham and moving to the House of Lords. In 1768, only 49 self-described 'Tories' would be re-elected. Within the Whig party, a new party had emerged as champions of the 'true Whig' cause, focusing their efforts on a reduction in the land tax from four to three shillings. Chatham's removal to the upper house, combined with a mysterious illness beginning in March, meant that Townshend became the chief orator for the Ministry in the Commons. Negotiations with the colonists took place in a climate of hostility. Townshend resolved that if the colonists would only submit to 'external' taxation, he would give them what they wanted in

34. Owen 1975, p. 183.

35. Russia was a natural trading partner as a source of naval stores and market for British manufactures. After the peace of 1763, Russia was on a collision course with Sweden, Poland and Turkey, all French client states. Although a shared enmity toward France would have made Russia a natural ally for Britain, no agreement was reached. Regardless, any conflict in the Balkans would certainly find Russia working towards the same ends as Britain; a formal alliance may have been a moot point. See Christie 1982, pp. 48–50.

spades. Passed as the Revenue Act of 1767, the 'Townshend duties' imposed a tax on tea, glass, lead, paint and paper. The duties antagonised the colonists further.

If the Chatham ministry had a poor grasp of the situation in America, it had an even poorer grasp of the situation unfolding in India, where the East India Company was racked by political divisions stemming from the factions in Parliament. Chatham sought to assert the Crown's authority over, and rights to, revenues flowing from newly-acquired Bengal, Bihar and Orissa. This was 'a feasible proposition for a trading company, but scarcely for the British Crown'.[36] Chatham's position was ignored and, reduced to a virtual non-entity, his actions in pursuit of the goal of ending party factions had only served to harden them. It was at this point, in December 1767, that John Wilkes returned to publish his next searing attack, not on the King, but on Chatham, the very man on whose defence he had launched his career as the champion of liberty.

With elections pending, Wilkes saw his only means of avoiding debtors' prison in standing for election and recovering his seat in the Commons. The Government did not wish to re-enact the events of 1764 by arresting him, so he moved about the City with impunity. Failing to secure election for the City of London in May of 1768, Wilkes managed to win support from the majority of voters in the elections for Middlesex a few days later, during which 'crowds of weavers blocked the roads to Brentford and barred access to all who did not show his colours'.[37] Post-war depression and unemployment, a severe winter and bad harvests, and renewed rumours of Bute's secret influence over the King all aided his cause.[38] As soon as he secured his victory and re-gained parliamentary

---

36. Chatham's approach 'was based on a misconception of the Company's power in India, where it had no territorial possessions as such, but merely held the revenues in quasi-feudal fashion in return for administering the provinces as Diwan of the Mogul Emperor' (Owen 1975, p. 190). Shelburne led the negotiations and guided four acts through Parliament which amounted to a temporary measure of reform that confirmed the Company's territorial rights for two years in return for an annual payment of £400,000 to the crown.

37. Christie 1982, p. 75.

38. Writes Feiling: 'Trade had never recovered from post-war depression, American troubles were beginning to produce unemployment, bad harvests accelerated a rise of prices. The capital city was a den of misery. Irish immigrants, drunken and criminal, filled the cheap boarding-houses of Bloomsbury and St. Giles; Jews, Germans, and Dutch swarmed in Houndsditch and Chelsea. The Spitalfields weaving industry was full of fluctuation, blind-alley employment, starved apprentices. Gin at 1d. a quart from the grocer's shop had brutalized a whole generation. Infantile mortality ranged round 75 percent, and Parliament had just roused itself to deal with the misery of parish children. The two Fieldings had begun police reform, but gangs of criminals still murdered and robbed in broad daylight, highwaymen and their women holding open festival at the Dog and Duck and other sinks of iniquity round St. George's Fields' (Feiling 1938, p. 105). It must be pointed out that the miseries of overcrowding and underemployment were more pronounced in London than anywhere else in Britain. This would help explain why Wilkite radicalism was so specifically based in London.

immunity, he then gave himself up to justice, to the tumult of the excited crowds of shopkeepers and craftsmen who followed him. As Wilkes awaited sentencing before the King's Bench, troops fired on a crowd of protesters in the adjacent St George's Fields, killing six and wounding fifteen. Chaos reigned in London for three weeks. Found guilty for past offences, and sentenced to pay a fine of £1,000 and serve 22 months in prison, Wilkes prepared a petition of his grievances from prison, and violently denounced the 'massacre of St. George's Fields' as a ministerial conspiracy against the people. Wilkes continued to win elections, first as a ward alderman, and then, after his second expulsion from the House of Commons on 3 February 1769, an uncontested by-election for Middlesex. The House expelled him again, and declaring him incapable of election to Parliament, 'an unwise step, for . . . eligibility for election arguably was a matter determined by the common and statute law and not by the law and custom of Parliament'.[39] Wilkes won a second by-election, and Parliament again expelled him. In April, a climate of intimidation hung over the third by-election and in a low voter-turnout Wilkes polled 1,143 votes, as against 296 for his opponent Henry Luttrell. Yet the House declared Luttrell the winner on grounds of Wilkes's ineligibility. While tolerable precedents for exclusion of a candidate could be cited, 'Middlesex electors could not be treated as if they were a handful of voters in a rotten borough'.[40] The decision to exclude Wilkes and appoint the loser posed a threat to the right to vote itself, taken as a form of property; if taken as a precedent, the Commons could use it to remove all opposition candidates. This touched off a storm of protest and criticism, as the very idea of representative government was seen to be under threat. Moreover, it lent credibility to the rumours that the Earl of Bute and the King's mother were pulling the strings from behind the scenes. Popular protests and strikes gripped the City and '45' was scrawled on doorways 'for Wilkes and Liberty'.

A group of lawyers formed the Society of Supporters of the Bill of Rights in late 1769 to support Wilkes and pay off his debts. They did not stop there. Soon they were putting forward calls for extensive reforms, and the Wilkite political movement began to emerge as something of a party. They condemned general warrants and sought to end the immunity of authorities to the full scope of the law. They sought to reform criminal law and ensure that juries, not judges, decided what passed for seditious libel and what did not. They sought shorter parliaments and secret ballots. They called for a Place Act to exclude office holders from the Commons, and a requirement for the taking of an oath against bribery upon election to office. They called into question the continued existence of

39. Christie 1982, p. 76.
40. Langford 1986, pp. 352–418.

rotten and pocket boroughs[41] and demanded a greater number of MPs be elected by the growing metropolis. With Wilkes in prison, leadership of this growing movement of radical metropolitan agitators was assumed by William Beckford, London's Lord Mayor and a close associate of Chatham. The Supporters of the Bill of Rights sought to organise petitions in the countryside in favour of shorter Parliaments, place and pension bills, and reform of the franchise. Their success was limited. Owen comments:

> The electorate as a whole had no wish to become dupes of metropolitan radicals . . . Country gentlemen were basically conservative in their politics, and the freeholders were mostly ignorant or apathetic. The country was not yet ripe for reform.[42]

The radical movement was principally an urban phenomenon. Between 1768 and 1770, the government was facing its most profound crisis since the days of Queen Anne, with no minister able to form a stable majority in Parliament, the embarrassments of the Wilkes affair, America moving to open revolt with Bostonians adopting a non-importation agreement in reaction to the Townshend duties and a loss of prestige when France prepared for the annexation of Corsica and the Chatham government made no attempts at diplomacy or naval coercion to prevent this. Chatham resigned in October 1768 only to come out of retirement the following summer to blast the Grafton ministry for its handling of agitations at home and abroad. Responding to the new wave of discontent in the colonies, the Cabinet met on 1 May 1769 and repealed the Townshend duties, with the portentous exception of the duty on tea. Chatham stood alone with Camden in calling for the repeal of the Declatory Act that he had insisted upon four years earlier. The repeals of the Stamp Act and the Townshend duties testified to the lack of consistency in the ministry. Edmund Burke wrote of the need for solidity of politics and party loyalty, marking a point of origin for party politics of the modern kind. Tired of presiding over a disunited ministry enjoying what appeared to be only a slim majority in the House during a period of increasing

41. A 'rotten borough' was a constituency that had declined in population to the point of near absurdity when put next to the growth of urban centres, including Manchester, a city which had over 24,000 residents in 1773, but which had no representatives in Parliament (see Wadsworth and Mann 1965, pp. 509–11). Old Sarum, in Wiltshire, was perhaps the most notorious of the rotten boroughs. Originally a Roman fort, the town had but three houses totalling fifteen inhabitants in 1831, the year before the reform bill was finally passed. A 'pocket borough' was a constituency controlled by a patron who could simply nominate the representative, often by virtue of owning the majority of houses in the town. Newcastle was said to have seven boroughs 'in his pocket'.

42. Owen 1975, p. 195.

political instability, Grafton at last resigned on 25 January 1770. There was little sign that a decade of instability was about to come to an end.[43]

Lord North shared some traits in common with John Wilkes, namely that he was described as awkward and ugly, but had a keen wit and skill in debating. That skill would serve him well in the Commons, which for the first time since Grenville now had a Prime Minister who could manage the House in person. After suffering some narrow votes in the Commons, North was able to consolidate his position. With Chatham and the Rockinghams continually at odds, the opposition was divided, and North was to enjoy seven years without significant threat from the opposition in Parliament. But this is to say nothing of extra-parliamentary opposition. Wilkes returned to the centre of politics again in February 1770 when a bootleg printing of a parliamentary debate irritated one Colonel George Onslow, who was described in the printing as 'little cocking George'. The House summoned the printers to answer charges against them, since technically, printing of parliamentary debates was a breach of privilege. When the King issued a proclamation for their apprehension, two of the three printers were brought before City aldermen, one of these being John Wilkes. They were dismissed on the grounds that no charges had been brought against them. According to plan, the third printer was to give himself up to arrest, whereupon the messenger from the Commons was himself apprehended first, brought before the Lord Mayor and the aldermen, and charged with a breach of the peace. A furious House summoned Wilkes and his collaborators to face further charges of breach of privilege. Wilkes declined to attend in any other capacity than MP for Middlesex. The Ministry 'was so chary of tangling with him again that it even adjourned Parliament for ten days so that the order for his appearance might lapse'.[44] Nonetheless, the Lord Mayor Crosby and Alderman Oliver were brought to the House on 25 March and duly sent to the tower, provoking a walk-out by many of those in opposition disgusted at the authoritarian handling of the affair. Protests followed, and the affair culminated when Crosby and Oliver were greeted with wild celebration in the City upon their release at the end of the parliamentary session. The Wilkite radicals had won another major victory, this time for freedom of the press. Combined with the earlier victory ending the

43. Customs officials in Boston had suffered occasional harassment, and when four régiments were sent to Boston to restore order, the City council would not allow the Governor to deploy them. The idle soldiers became a focus of resentments and on 5 March 1770 a squad of redcoats fired on a protesting crowd, killing five and injuring more in what quickly became known as the 'Boston Massacre'. What more proof was needed to prove that the colonists were living under a 'military tyranny'? 'Few could have guessed that the political instability of the previous decade would be ended within eighteen months of North's accession to power; fewer still that he would preside over the only major war that Britain has ever lost' (Owen 1975, p. 197).

44. Owen 1975, pp. 203–5.

use of general warrants, this extra-parliamentary party that had emerged around the issues of reform and liberty was widening the scope of civil rights and demonstrating the power of popular mobilisation as a means of influencing politics.[45] Beyond small businessmen and urban craftsmen, 'Wilkes and Liberty' was gaining support outside the world of the urban petit-bourgeoisie. 'Seamen and petty artisans identified with [Wilkes's] campaign against naval impressment. Striking seamen, silk-weavers, hatters and coal-heavers found Wilkes a useful signifier for their own struggles'. For a time, the popularity of 'Wilkes Holidays' eclipsed those of the official calendar. In his 1772 publication *Thoughts upon Liberty*, John Wesley openly deplored Wilkes's popularity, speculating that Wilkes's name and face were 'more celebrated than that of any private man ... in England for these thousand years'.[46]

Rebellion at home and abroad

As far as North was concerned, if the centre of gravity for opposition to the Ministry had moved outside Parliament itself, so much the better. Embarrassing as it may have been to receive a black eye from the radicals, their support outside the City remained limited, and if anything, the reaction of elite opinion was likely to play in North's favour. For who among respectable society – with the possible exception of the iconoclastic Chatham – would wish to risk being seen as sympathetic to the likes of Wilkes and his followers? With the political winds blowing generally in his favour, North set about the task of tidying up the nation's finances. His success in this endeavour further secured his position. After 1771, the land tax was kept at three shillings on the pound. A new tax on luxuries was introduced as a means of tackling the national debt, as well as a revenue lottery. In general, North's domestic policies were a success. It was in managing the Empire that he ran into trouble. The sheer scale of Britain's global enterprise was daunting. With Captain James Cook returning from his discovery of Australia in 1771, the British Empire was busy annexing previously uncharted continents.[47] In India, the financial reforms, steep tax increases and outright

45. Christie 1982, p. 79.
46. Hay and Rogers 1997, pp. 172–3. Wesley detested the London radicals and the '"Bedlam" of mob activity'. For Wesley, the cry for liberty had become 'an "Epidemic Madness" that needed to be curbed'. In this, Wesley was out of touch with popular thinking, and shared more in common with reactionary forces.
47. Cook would go on to discover the Northwest Passage. Cook's sightings on the British Columbia coast and brief stop on Vancouver Island supported a British claim of discovery which almost led to a subsequent war with Spain, a war which was later avoided by an agreement of joint rights. Eventually, Britain successfully expanded the claim to all of Western Canada. See James 1994, pp. 139–45.

looting of the state treasury of Bengal by the East India Company brought on what was surely the greatest man-made famine in history to date. An estimated ten million human beings died in the Great Bengal famine of 1769–79. What was a holocaust for Indians translated into a financial meltdown for the Company. Faced with a shortage of Indian tax revenues in a period of rising expenditures, combined in 1772 with a general financial crisis in the form of a shortage of credit in Europe, the Company was brought to its knees. North moved an act in Parliament for internal reform, and a loan of £1,400,000 was forced upon the Company, with provisions. Finally, the Company's tea sales were in a serious slump. Fully half of the fourteen million pounds of tea consumed by Brits annually was reportedly smuggled. The solution put forward was the Tea Act, which set out a scheme to dump surplus tea on America.[48] When twelve hundred chests of tea arrived in the American colonies, bearing the hopes for a solution to that Company's financial woes, the colonists responded by either turning away the shipments, or putting them unsold into storage. In Boston, 340 of the chests were ceremoniously dumped into the harbour on 16 December 1773.[49]

As America edged closer to open rebellion, events in Ireland seemed to follow a parallel course. If anything, the Irish were more oppressed than the Americans. A small caste of Episcopalian landowners enjoyed control over the land and a transplanted agrarian-capitalist system while they simultaneously enjoyed explicit control over government, at the exclusion of both the Catholic majority – comprising some three-quarters of the population, and the Irish Presbyterians – debarred from holding office in municipal government under the Test Act and Corporation Act.[50] Hopes were dashed when upon his accession George III made clear his steadfast opposition to any form of Catholic relief. Despite the increasing prosperity of Irish commerce in the face of restrictive trade policies designed to limit Irish competition, poverty was rife amongst the Irish peasants who

48. Under this act the government offered its own agents (on commission) to directly arrange for sale of the surplus. They were to dump the tea in North America, granting full drawbacks. When the government refused to additionally abolish Townshend's 3*d.* per pound duty, however, the scheme amounted to naught for the Company (Christie 1982, pp. 85–6).

49. Just prior to the arrival of the tea, radical passions had been ignited when the printer Benjamin Franklin published the private letters of Governor Hutchison of Massachusetts and his Lieutenant-Governor, which stated that in order to prevent the break-up of the empire '"there must be a diminution of what are called English liberties" in Massachusetts' (Miller 1959, p. 331). The resentment that this type of attitude provoked among colonists burst into active resistance. In Britain, the 'Boston Tea Party' was condemned by the Ministry and opposition alike.

50. 'Since the settlement of 1690 Ireland had been under a Protestant landlord ascendancy. The original Catholic proprietors were almost eliminated, the leadership of the Catholic peasantry fell to the priests, and their resentments flared up only in occasional outbreaks of rural banditry against the landlords and their agents' (Upton 2001, p. 352).

constituted a majority of the population. 'Absentee landlords, sub-letting, rack-renting, and the rapacity of land-agents, seem to have been mainly responsible for this state of affairs, which caused many rural areas to be in a state of chronic insurrection'.[51] For now, however, both the Irish opposition and the American colonists conceived their struggle in terms of winning concessions from, and remaining a part of, the British Empire. Upon a visit to Ireland in 1771, Benjamin Franklin saw that the grounds were ripe for making common cause with Irish grievances. He stated his hope that '"by joining our interest to theirs [there] might be obtained for them as well as for us, a more equitable treatment from [England]".'[52] Charles Townshend had offered the Irish reforms in exchange for an agreement to pay for an increase in the number of soldiers stationed in Ireland from 12,000 to 15,000, but these offers were basically rescinded upon Townshend's premature death in 1767, only a few months after they had been made. In America, the British government had granted trade concessions in response to American boycotts, but had given no ground on the constitutional right of Britain to tax and legislate for its colonies. It was toward challenging these prerogatives that the discourse now moved. From where North sat, it appeared that a few conspirators in Boston had gone outside the law and would need to be brought to heel in order to restore law and order lest they spread ruin throughout the Empire. This attitude was shared by most Britons, and because of this, North's ministry could only restore order by taking firm action. North passed the 'Coercive' or 'Intolerable' Acts, shutting down Boston's port, demanding that damages be paid to the East India Company, curtailing the unruly 'democratic' element by reducing the independent power of the Massachusetts Council and requiring the Americans to provide quartering for British troops. The response was an outpouring of material support for Boston, and the calling of a Continental Congress to organise the resistance.

A flurry of publications and public denunciations of the government's policies towards its colonies erupted in the colonies in the summer of 1774. Thomas Jefferson's *Summary View of the Rights of British America*[53] envisioned a separate empire for America, whose sole connection to Britain would lie in a joint sovereign. In September, the First Continental Congress met in Philadelphia and adopted the Suffolk Resolves, which demanded that colonists defy the Coercive Acts and withhold taxes until such time as all rights had been restored to Massachusetts. The Continental Association was formed to block trade to or

51. Christie 1982, p. 97 continues: 'But the peasants' welfare was not an issue which the landowners dominating the Dublin parliament interested themselves, nor at this time did it present itself as a problem to the British government'.
52. As quoted in Christie 1982, p. 99.
53. Jefferson 1774.

from Britain, and enforce non-consumption of British products. While Chatham and Burke were ready to concede to Congress's demands for the vision Jefferson had put forward, to most ministers in Britain it was beginning to become quite clear that only force could determine whether the colonies would remain a part of the British Empire. North proposed that if the colonists would agree to tax themselves to Parliament's satisfaction, 'Parliament would merely forbear to exercise its rights'.[54] It was the first major concession, but it came too late. On 18 April 1775, British soldiers and colonial minutemen exchanged fire at Lexington. In June, the Battle of Bunker Hill demonstrated that the colonists 'were not the despicable rabble that Englishmen had envisaged . . . pride demanded total victory. The time for debate was over'.[55] The King rebuffed the Olive Branch Petition sent by Congress.

For men like Thomas Paine, this reinforced the Rockingham legend, according to which the King was a tyrant. In *Common Sense*,[56] Paine pushed the Rockingham legend further, attacking the institution of kingship itself, and arguing for an independent, republican America. Over the course of 1777, the Rockinghams began to argue that only the repeal of all acts since 1763 could stave off independence, though if this failed, independence should be recognised. In October, Burgoyne's force of 5,000 men surrendered at Saratoga. When the news reached Britain, crisis set in at Parliament, not to abate for another six years. North's initial reaction was to open secret negotiations with American diplomats led by Franklin in Paris, only to discover that the Americans would now settle for nothing short of independence, and moreover that France and Spain were ready to agree to an alliance whereby they would enter the war if independence were not granted. France signed an alliance with the Americans on 6 February 1778. A rebellion within the Empire was now poised to become an international war with global ramifications. North, meanwhile, was faced with weakening support and a debate in the cabinet on how to conduct the war. The debate was between those who favoured a strictly seaborne campaign and those who did not. Recognising the gravity of the situation only too late, the King dispatched the Carlisle Commission to America with instructions to concede to all of the Americans' demands short of independence. But having tasted victory at battle, and with the might of France at their side, the colonists would settle for nothing less than independence or an immediate withdrawal of British forces. In mid-June of 1779, Spain followed France in declaring war on Britain. Britain added another coun-

54. Owen 1975, pp. 215–16.
55. Owen 1975, p. 217.
56. Paine 1986.

try to the list of its enemies when it declared war on Holland for supplying the Americans with munitions.[57]

Events in Ireland and Scotland contributed to the Ministry's erosion of support and control. When news that the Carlisle Peace Commission had offered the Americans dominion status, the Irish raised the bar, feeling that they deserved a similar offer of their own. In March 1779 a non-importation agreement modelled on the Americans was adopted at a public meeting in Galway. In response to the threat of a French invasion and Britain's unpreparedness to defend Ireland, the overwhelmingly Protestant 'Volunteers' were organised and reached perhaps over 40,000 men by autumn. Encouraged by the opposition's renewed attacks on the Ministry, the Irish were moving in the direction of open rebellion. Seeking to nip the Irish rebellion in the bud, Parliament quickly granted free trade with all British colonies to Ireland.[58] Like the Americans before them, the Irish responded not with gratitude but with an effort to press their advantage, pushing ahead with demands of constitutional reform. Grattan's motions in the Irish Parliament, which amounted to a declaration of independence, were defeated, but they left a clear signal that Ireland was ripe for rebellion. Meanwhile in Scotland, North's proposal to extend the 1778 Act, granting mild relief for Catholics, provoked such violent 'No Popery' protests in the lowlands in 1779 that it had to be withdrawn. These anti-Catholic protests foreshadowed coming events in London.

In the midst of the growing crisis, those with social or economic grievances were able to gain a broader audience, aided by the growth not only of newspapers but of stamped and unstamped materials, including handbills and cartoons. 'The idea spread that a free press would ensure responsible government'.[59] Caricatures became important means of swaying the opinions of the uneducated. The Rockinghams had begun to develop a coherent ideology as the party whose mission was to protect British liberties, their target audience remained 'respectable opinion'. But when the Rockinghams latched on to the cause of reform, it was not long before popular forces followed suit and took their own initiative. Under the leadership of the conservative Yorkshire parson Christopher Wyvill, a new petitioning movement promoting reform spread not in the City but in the counties. Between February and April 1780, Wyvill and his followers delivered no

57. Holland had been clandestinely shipping the majority of munitions and supplies destined for the American rebel forces, using the island of St. Eustatius as a transfer depot. In 1778 and 1779, St. Eustatius became the 'world's busiest port' (Hough 2005).

58. Membership in the Levant Company was also granted to Catholics, a significant move, signalling that Catholic emancipation in Ireland was not far off, though it may have contributed to perceptions in Scotland and England that the Ministry was under the influence of 'popery' (Christie 1982, pp. 131–3).

59. Turner 1999, pp. 15–17.

less than forty-one petitions to Parliament calling for lower taxes, fiscal accountability, the removal of placemen from Parliament and the redistribution of seats in Parliament. Rotten boroughs were to be eliminated and seats re-distributed. The petitions were rejected,[60] but like the Wilkites before them, Wyvill and his associates had raised the level of political awareness 'in a more ordered and focused way than Wilkes had attempted'.[61]

Not two months after the rejection of the petitions, London exploded in 'an outburst without equal'.[62] At home, there did not appear to be any cause for open riot or rebellion. The London radicals may have had sympathies for the American colonists, but they had grown quiet of late, with their hero Wilkes having taken up the position of Lord Mayor of London in 1774. The apparent motivation for the protests in Edinburgh and Glasgow in 1779 and London in 1780 was a reaction to the Catholic Relief Act of 1778 which lifted many restrictions on Catholics,[63] but clearly far more elements were involved. First, the 'Gordon Riots' were named after Lord Gordon, a Scotsman with shoulder-length, flowing red hair. The Scots were still grieving at their harsh treatment in the aftermath of the '45': the proscription of Scottish culture, the subjugation of the Scottish church and state to England, and the wholesale introduction of agrarian capitalism in the form of enclosures for sheep.[64] Second, the relatively progressive Quebec Act

60. See Owen 1975, pp. 225–9.

61. 'The petitioning movement of the 1780s provided the model for later single-issue campaigns for change . . .' (Upton 2001, p. 355).

62. Nicholson 1985, preface. The so-called 'Gordon Riots' constituted the largest rebellion since the Duke of Monmouth had raised his standard in 1685. Bread- or food-protests were common, and occurred in nearly every town and every county until the 1840s, but local protests were small in scale, were not driven by religious sectarianism and did not compare with the scale of 1780.

63. The Catholic Relief Act (Papists Act 1778, 18 Geo. III, c. 60) removed restrictions on the treatment of Catholic priests as felons, the prohibition of purchase of land and the confiscation of property from Catholics who sought an overseas education (Olsen 1999, p. 285). Between the accession of Elizabeth I in 1558 and the Jacobite uprising of 1745, Catholics had few if any successes in their long-standing rivalry with Protestantism in Britain. While no longer seen as politically suspect after the '45', Catholics were still widely viewed as 'superstitious, treasonous, and idle (owing to the large number of religious holidays in the Catholic Calendar)' (Ashton 1964, p. 19, citing Parrott 1752, p. 83). Out of some 69,000 Catholics in England in 1780, only 11,000 actually lived in London. More than twice that number lived in Lancashire, and the rest were mainly country gentlemen whose frequent succumbing to the temptation to convert was probably largely responsible for the declining numbers of Catholics.

64. 'Any notions of equality or federalism that might have tinged the Act of Union had died at Culloden . . . Within a decade of the defeat the highlanders would see sheep coming to replace them. The "management" of the Scottish estate would be more profitable with animals than with human brutes' (Nicholson 1985, pp. 8–9). Marx comments that 'what "clearing of estates" really and properly signifies, we learn only in the promised land of modern romance, the Highlands of Scotland. There the process is distinguished by its systematic character, by the magnitude of the scale on which it is carried out at

of 1774 generated hostile reactions from American and British Protestants arising more from a sense of betrayal than from direct hostility toward Catholics, since the Ministry's objective in allowing the French in Quebec to retain Catholicism as the official religion was to be able to recruit Catholics there to fight against the rebellious American Protestants.[65] Third, the outburst took place in London, home to the radical movement rooted in working-class artisans. In the country cities of Manchester, Nottingham, etc. the growth of factories was only nascent and barely beginning, but in London the ranks of the poor and working class were swelling, increasing the pressure to lift restrictions on entry into London's craft trades and at the same time adding to the increasingly miserable conditions for the City's poor.[66] Finally, the systematic assault on the City's prisons was likely a response to the expansion of the prisons to accommodate those being charged under a host of new crimes against property.

Some fifty thousand or more marchers gathered on Friday, 2 June 1780 at St. George's Fields[67] in Southwark – the site for most of the City's prisons – as Parliament was set to vote on another Catholic Relief Act. They marched through the City in orderly fashion, bearing a petition with nearly 120,000 signatures calling for the repeal of the Relief Act. Upon arriving at Parliament they roughed up some of the MPs. Inside, Gordon moved for a vote on the petition. The result was 192 against, six in favour. After skirmishes with soldiers brandishing swords, the crowd dispersed. This prompted the calling of troops into the City and a declaration of martial law. John Wilkes, now the Lord Mayor of London, recruited a force from his own ward and reported his group for military duty, and likely took part himself in the armed suppression of the rebellion. It should not be forgotten that Wilkes launched his career by penning attacks on the Scottish. The rebels now declared their intent to destroy 'the Bank, Gray's Inn, Temple, Lincoln's Inn, the

---

one blow . . . [and] finally by the peculiar form of property, under which the embezzled lands were held' (Marx 1906 vol. 1, p. 800). How enclosures were affected overnight in Scotland, with dramatic results both in terms of productivity and misery is worth a study in its own right.

65. Since efforts were already underway to recruit British Catholics to fight in America, the Act of 1778 was surely viewed in the same light. Nicholson points out three ironies: 1) Catholic Scots 'being asked to fight for the German king whose uncle had butchered them [in 1745]' against French Catholics fighting in support of Protestant America; 2) a war 'to impose a tyranny on the descendants of those who had fought such evils' using Catholic troops to defeat Protestants; 3) 'For the Scots these paradoxes went even further . . . Here was an English king recruiting Catholics in Scotland to fight Protestants in America because he claimed they were being helped by Catholic France! The more likely fear was of another Catholic attempt on Scotland' (Nicholson 1985, pp. 11–12).

66. It seems likely that these increasing pressures contributed to the sudden outburst of rebellion in London, but the matter is a subject for further study.

67. St. George's Field was, not coincidentally, the very site where some twelve years prior six protestors, demanding Wilkes's release, were killed when troops opened fire on the crowd, leading to three weeks of unrest. See p. 232 above.

Grand Arsenal at Woolwich, and Royal Palaces'.[68] To the poor, the Bank stood for finance and a swindle against the people by those who manipulated numbers on paper.[69] Even as the rich multiplied the number of offences against property, they invented new methods to *legally* manipulate wealth into their own pockets. Ropes and barricades turned back the first assault. Twenty rebels fell to gunfire. At Blackfriars Bridge, the toll booths, symbols of oppression and the new system of corruption, were set on fire, casting a light on the rebels who were trapped once the troops arrived. Their corpses 'fell like rats into the river beneath', writes Hibbert, with the condescension of posterity.[70] By Thursday morning, only after the arrival of the troops, corpses could be found strewn everywhere. Soldiers now took open reprisals. Captured rebels were court-martialled and executed, their bodies hung from the lamp posts. In horror of what it had set loose, and in the face of vociferous condemnation by Burke and others in the opposition, the Ministry disclaimed martial law.[71]

Arrested, Gordon accepted no responsibility and was set free. He would later die in a debtor's prison after having been found guilty of libel against the entire legal system by publishing his opposition to using transportation to Botany Bay.[72] Not only did the use of transportation as a form of punishment continue, but the rebellion prompted a movement of reformers who would specify that new prisons be built to limit prisoners' contact to the outside world and keep them in confinement. Gordon had been the man in Parliament giving voice to the combined Scottish nationalist, American, Protestant and London City-radical opposition to perceived tyranny, whether it be the tyranny of Parliament, the Crown or Popery (at home or abroad). The 'Rockingham myth' of royal tyranny and the 'Bute legend' may have started with the opposition, but it took on a life of its own amidst the public. It took but one voice in Parliament to rally them. By the

68. Holcroft 1944, p. 27.

69. The troops guarding Langdale Brewery had been called away to protect the Bank. When it was attacked it produced an enormous fire, compounded when the fire hoses were connected to the brewery cellars and more gin was poured on the blaze. The stills burst and the undistilled spirit gushing onto the street caught fire. The blaze and fumes left many dead. But the decision had paid off. Instead of a run on the Bank as ordinary, transactions ran at £80,000 less than usual, 'a proof that the arrival of the troops had quieted their fears' (Holcroft 1944, p. 28).

70. Hibbert 1958, p. 145.

71. Nicholson 1985, pp. 72–3. 'The final score looks like rioters nil. Authorities over a thousand', writes Nicholson. This figure is usually put at little over three hundred, including later executions of 18 of 68 rebels, the other 50 presumably being consigned to floating ships awaiting transportation. Nicholson seeks to account for those whose bodies were never found.

72. Transportation to America was no longer an option; hence the shift to recently discovered Australia. One of the many grievances of the colonists in America had been the dumping of criminals on their society as a means of easing pressures on the British prison system.

standards of the age, King George was less a tyrant than others, but his inability to acknowledge the grievances of the Americans and his slowness to respond to growing demands for reforms and freedoms at home amidst a widening of the sphere of popular politics helped to perpetuate the legend.

One of the effects of the rebellion was that it dismayed the Opposition in Parliament. 'Nothing could have been more calculated to alienate both the Rockinghamites and the independent landed gentry'.[73] The rebellion drove such a wedge between City and the opposition in Parliament that North was even compelled to approach Rockingham in July to discuss a coalition. But Rockingham wavered in his support for full American independence and economic reform, and no coalition could be arranged. News of success in the Carolinas, and especially of loyalists in America taking an active role in the war, gave such an additional fillip to North's revival that he dissolved Parliament one year early, throwing the Opposition once again into turmoil. When Parliament reassembled in December, North would enjoy comfortable majorities through the summer.[74] Once again, North's administration was the beneficiary of division in the opposition. But it would be the last time.

Through the summer and autumn of 1781, North's ministry enjoyed a period of relative calm and stability. It was during this time that attention turned once again to the East India Company's troubles. The India Act was passed, renewing the Company's charter for another ten years. The act once again avoided the question of the Crown's rights to territorial revenues, and left the administration of conquered Indian provinces in the Company's hands. Yet with a swelling bureaucracy of over 1,000 officials and a growing army in India of over 40,000 men, it was only a matter of time before the government would have to step in and take charge of governance in India.[75]

News of Cornwallis' surrender at Yorktown reached England on 25 November 1781, just two days before Parliament was set to reconvene. It was immediately apparent both that the war was lost and that North's ministry would not survive. For George, the end of the American War seemed to spell the end of Britain's great power status; the loss appeared too great to accept. He talked of abdication. Who could foresee at that moment that in the next thirty to forty years Britain's economy would propel her to become the 'workshop of the world', that Britain

73. Christie 1982, p. 138.

74. Owen 1975, pp. 231–3.

75. The Regulating Act of 1773 had been extended beyond its six-year term through 1779 and 1780, owing to the war in America and an emerging rebellion in Ireland. As the devastation of the rural population of Bengal continued, so did the complicated conquest of India by a merchant company. A complex situation arose in the Carnatic whereby the presidency called for aid from Bengal. In the late 1770s, the Opposition had extended the Rockingham myth to include the notion that the Nawab of the Carnatic wielded some secret influence over the ministry (Christie 1982, p. 124).

would triumph in spades over an imperial France or that Britain would go on to expand its own empire to undreamt-of proportions? On 27 February 1782, a disunited Parliament voted to end offensive operations in North America.[76]

The survival of empire

In the wake of North's resignation, the largest faction in Parliament, with 100 votes, was Rockingham's. In George's eyes, Rockingham and his party were 'the archetypal example of an aristocratic faction out to dictate to the crown. Its nonsensical theories about hidden cabals and secret influence appeared to him to be directed against his exercise of his few remaining legitimate constitutional functions'.[77]

But only Rockingham could hope to command the support of independents, and George had no option but to agree to his terms. Rockingham took over the Treasury; Fox became Foreign Secretary and Shelburne Home Secretary.[78] The first order of business for this short-lived ministry was to carry three major pieces of legislation attacking the vast sums given by the Crown to members of Parliament in the form of patronage. But these acts had little impact, and served to sow doubt about the veracity of the Rockingham legend. Wyvill, who had high hopes for the Rockinghams when they took power, soon became a fierce critic of the Ministry.[79]

More lasting effects of the brief Rockingham Ministry were felt in Ireland. In March and April the Irish Commons passed and reaffirmed Gratton's motions calling for Irish independence.[80] In April, shortly after the Duke of Portland arrived to take up his post as the new Lord Lieutenant, the Irish Commons reaffirmed the motions. Coming as this did at a highly precarious moment in the war, and given the Ministry's open sympathies for Irish reformers, the Ministry reluctantly granted huge concessions. The Irish gained full and equal constitutional, legislative and judicial rights. In return, Ireland voted to put up £100,000 for the navy, and would commit 5,000 soldiers to the Foreign Service. Ireland had

---

76. Owen 1975, pp. 233–4. North went on to resign in March, and serious instability would plague the Government for the next two years.

77. Christie 1982, p. 139.

78. Turner 1999, p. 20.

79. Crewe's Act disenfranchised all revenue officers. Clerke's Act excluded government contractors from the Commons. Burke's Civil Establishment Act abolished several government and court appointments. Crewe's Act affected few boroughs and made little difference. Clerke's Act also made little impact, since the number of contractors in the Commons had shrunk from 37 to 17 since the first year of George III's reign. The 'good stout blow to the influence of the Crown' predicted by Fox missed its mark (Christie 1982, p. 140; Owen 1975, pp. 237–8).

80. Christie 1982, p. 141.

gained, in short, the very type of arrangement that Britain had denied America and fought a war to prevent. Moreover, the Catholic Relief Act of 1782 put an end to restrictions on land tenure for Catholics and legalised the Catholic clergy in Ireland.

Rockingham and his faction sought to extract Britain from the war in America. But Britain had by now lost its naval dominance over the Baltic, the Atlantic and most importantly the Caribbean, to which the centre of the war had shifted. In April, a decisive victory over France in the enormously destructive Battle of the Saintes stemmed further British losses in the West Indies, protected the sugar islands and, once the Bahamas were recaptured from Spain and British outposts along the Central American coast regained, re-established British naval supremacy in the West Indies.[81] Historians credit North's naval reinforcements for this victory, along with the carronade, a short cannon manufactured by the Carron ironworks at Falkirk. 'The new technology of the Industrial Revolution had rescued the empire', cheers James.[82] Britain lost Minorca to Spain but recovered Gibraltar in the autumn and managed to evade a French plot to invade Jamaica. As news of the negotiations took its time to reach India, Admiral Hughes fought running battles in the Indian Ocean with French Admiral Suffren through until June 1783. Pondicherry, Cuddalore and Trincomalee on Dutch Ceylon had fallen to Britain but were recaptured. French losses were enormous, and the expenditures on the war set France on the path to bankruptcy and revolution.[83] Exhausted, and believing they had achieved their primary objective of reducing the might of the British Empire through securing American independence, France and Spain were ready to negotiate peace.

When Rockingham died suddenly, just three months after taking office, George offered the Treasury to Shelburne, whereupon his rival Fox, who one day before Rockingham's death had moved a failed resolution to grant full recognition to the United States of America, resigned.[84] Shelburne inherited the burden of negotiations. Upon assuming office, Prime Minister Shelburne promoted a sweeping programme of reform: 'The national debt and the annual charge upon it were to be reduced by conversion of existing loans to lower rates of interest and by the

81. Hough 2005 comments: 'One wonders if the British took the approach of sinking or capturing all Allied shipping they could so that after the war, the only commercial ships available for commerce would be British. Actually, the British probably were in a better trading position after the war than before as they were able to take over much of the Dutch commerce'.

82. James 1994, p. 81.

83. The French military historian Capt. Joachim Merlant summarised French losses during five years of war to have been 45,289 men, 63 ships, 3668 and $50,000,000 in 1918 dollars (Hough 2005, citing two works by Merlant 1920 and 1918.) These enormous costs would factor into the looming bankruptcy of the French state in the 1780s.

84. Turner 1999, p. 24.

re-establishment of an effective sinking fund; the revival of commerce was to be encouraged by the adoption of some of the free-trade measures advocated by Adam Smith . . .'.[85] Shelburne's proposal 'of an Anglo-American partnership in commerce, foreign policy and defence'[86] was too liberal for the majority of Britons, who felt the Americans deserved no part in the empire they had forsaken, and this would be his undoing. Under the agreement signed on 30 November 1782, all lands between the St. Lawrence and the Ohio were ceded to the Americans, while the Mississippi would remain open to all traders. In return for agreeing to honour debts to Englishmen held prior to 1775, the United States gained favourable terms for trade in British ports, access to the Newfoundland fisheries and an agreement of reciprocal trade with Canada.

Shelburne's ministry did not survive long enough to conclude negotiations with the European powers. For five weeks, George III held out in vain against what he described as a 'monstrous plot' to form a Fox-North ministry, with the Duke of Portland as its nominal head. The coalition came to power over a vote to censure the peace deal Shelburne had negotiated. Denied the right to make appointments, the King believed himself reduced to a figurehead. He pleaded in vain with Pitt to form a ministry and once again talked of abdication. The result of the negotiations, led by Fox, was effectively a return to the *status quo ante*. Despite the loss of the Americas, 'the important gains made at the expense of France in the Seven Years' War did remain substantially intact – Canada, the Maritimes, the Newfoundland fisheries', not to mention Ireland.[87] Britain also paid careful attention to securing trading agreements out of its negotiations, with an eye, as always, to underselling its rivals. As a result, Britain recovered from the war more quickly than France or Spain. Here was an island kingdom that had fought five wars at once, and still came out as the foremost military and commercial power in the world, reclaiming a control of the seas that it was to retain until the Second World War.[88]

The economic chill between Britain and America did not last long. Britain's economy needed American timber and raw materials and American and Irish consumers demanded British manufactures. By 1784, Britain's colonial trade was exceeding pre-war levels. Ten years later, the Jay treaty of 1794 would allow the small vessels from America to trade in the West Indies, and also opened up East India to American trade. In return, the Americans would agree to relax restrictions on British shipping. Trade between the two nations would double

85. Owen 1975, p. 241.
86. Owen (ibid.) finds this idea 'eminently sensible'.
87. Christie 1982, p. 146.
88. Hough 2005.

over the next seven years.[89] Even trade with France resumed to a brisk pace in the 1780s.

The American War had diverted attention away from the as-yet unresolved crisis of the East India Company. Several years of research by two parliamentary committees – dominated by Edmund Burke and Lord Dundas – had by 1783 produced a vast amount of information on the Company's affairs, and it was now apparent to all that further reform involving greater government control over the company was urgently required. Being a Rockinghamite who did not trust the King, Burke proposed to hand over responsibility for all territory held by the Company in India to a parliamentary commission made up of seven members. 'Fox's India bill' as authored by Burke was seen as an attack on the liberties of the subject that had been enshrined in the Company charter, and furthermore an attack on private property. Burke was, to his credit, a vehement critic of the injustices suffered by native Indians living under the Company's rule. But his motives were hardly antagonistic to private property as such, only to private property in the form of tribute. In Burke's view, the East India Company was a dinosaur engaged in a costly, non-capitalist form of commerce based on non-competitive exchange of products that was not bringing sufficient revenues to the state, partly due to corruption within the Company. By now, British manufacturing was led by capitalist manufacturers eager to break in to the Indian market. Despite public hysteria that it would create a 'Carlo Khan' by giving Charles James Fox more power than the King,[90] the bill passed by 208 to 102 votes on 8 December, when many independents had left for the Christmas holidays. Their absence should have given Fox pause, for with public opinion on his side, George was now able to carry out a political coup and place the ministry into the hands of the younger Pitt. A message from the King was read to the Lords declaring that anyone voting for the bill would be considered his enemy.[91] The Lords rejected the Bill on 17 December. Parliament was dismissed on 18 and 19 December, after Fox and North had been called to return their seals of office. The younger Pitt assumed command of the Treasury. The Rockingham weapon of swaying public opinion to check the influence of the Crown had been turned against them, and now emerged as a major component not to be underestimated in parliamentary elections.

Nevertheless, Burke's prescription for India would eventually be implemented in the form of a new bill that set out a board of control to supervise the East

89. Christie 1982, pp. 166–7.
90. Owen 1975, pp. 245–6; Christie 1982, pp. 153–4.
91. Turner 1999, p. 30. During the debate, Pitt had cleverly moved his own India Bill, which took a co-operative rather than confrontational approach to the Company. This would later pay dividends after he took power. See Derry 2001, p. 37.

India Company's affairs. British cottons soon flooded India's markets, spelling ruin for native manufacturing in India which could not compete with British goods now being produced on a capitalist basis. The wholesale destruction of India's domestic spinning industry reversed the situation of 1700. The depressive effects this had on India's economy only attracted deeper British involvement. As Wood explains, 'while the British state became more and more involved in India as a means of rescuing the empire from the non-capitalist logic imposed on it by the East India Company, it was constantly pulled back to the non-capitalist logic of the Company and the military state'.[92] Thus Britain's engagement with India was constantly caught between the capitalist imperatives driving the need for imperial expansion and the necessity of operating the empire 'based on direct military coercion and surplus-appropriation by extra-economic means'.[93] The East India Company had 'governed' India through tax-sharing agreements with native magnates. In taking over this racket, the British state's governance in India would become entrenched in such extra-economic forms of surplus-appropriation by application of military force.

Conclusion

An important question worth further exploration that arises out of the events covered in this chapter has to do with the relationship between private property under conditions of (agrarian) capitalism and the emergence of popular demands for an expansion of civil liberties. If the emergence and evolution of capitalism involves the establishment of an economic sphere insulated from the political sphere through the process of defining rights of property in ever more stringent terms, then capitalism's emergence involves the setting of new limits upon state power or upon state interference in individual affairs. It follows that this opens up a new space (meaning a greater objective potentiality) for the successful pursuit of individual rights beyond the ownership of private property. Since the pursuit of accumulation of property was an avenue closed to the majority of working people, what other avenue might one expect the majority to pursue upon the opening up of this new space than the pursuit of greater civil liberties *vis-à-vis* the state?

Following decades of relative Walpolean stability, old corruption and peace abroad, Great Britain emerged from the Seven Years' War as the foremost imperial power in the world. Yet the new Empire was confronted with rebellion not only in the colonies, but at home as well. If the Pitt-Newcastle administration

92. Wood 2003, p. 114.
93. Wood 2003, pp. 114–15.

of 1757 testified once again, as in 1688 and 1714, to the overall unity of England's ruling landed oligarchy and its ability to set aside intra-elite disputes, the Wilkite rebellion which followed seems to testify to the way in which, amidst the gradual dissolution of long-standing paternalistic and customary relations between patricians and plebs, there was at the same time an emerging and growing horizontal unity among working people, who began to demand an expansion of *their* rights through placing further curtailments upon the ability of the state to suppress or limit their freedoms. The fact that this current of protest from the 1760s was initially led by John Wilkes, a parliamentarian and renegade member of the lesser gentry, would seem to underscore the fact that the masses of working people were still constrained politically by their dependence upon a nominal member of the ruling class to give expression to their grievances. Throughout this period, the Rockingham myth of undue influence in the court of George III was sustained perhaps less as an article of faith than as a useful means of putting the rulers of state on the defensive as would-be reformers inside of government and popular protesters outside pursued an expansion of civil liberties, notably in the area of freedom of the press. To the extent that this (re-)emergence of an artisan-based popular radicalism posed a challenge to oligarchic rule, it actually served to strengthen the unity of the ruling elite, a unity once again consolidated under Lord North. In the 'Great Liberty Riot' of 1780 in London, Wilkes sided against popular rebellion, taking direct part in the repression of the protesters attacking the Bank of England. The so-called 'Gordon Riots' were so-named after Lord Gordon, a Scottish nobleman who had led the presentation of a petition to Parliament that preceded the rioting. But Gordon would later deny playing any role in inspiring or organising the rioting which followed upon Parliament's dismissal of the petition. Thus the rioting proceeded without the leadership of a member of the ruling landed elite and in this context, no constraint in the use of state violence and coercion to suppress the popular rebellion was observed for several days, during which an untold number of protesters were shot or hanged. Here, we might suggest, were the beginnings of a sharpening class divide between a ruling elite with an interest in protecting and expanding the development of agrarian-capitalist tenant-farming on enclosed estates and the mass of direct producers increasingly drawn into a situation of market dependence and the real (in the countryside) or more formal (in manufacturing) subsumption of their labour to the control of capital. As noted, the protesters generally operated within the scope of accepted customary forms of protest, but the authorities did not. The events of 1780 in London thus mark a highly significant milestone in the breakdown of the customary and paternalistic bonds between patricians and plebs.

We are, here, merely raising the question of the relationship between the expansion of agrarian-capitalist social relations and the emergence of popular protest in demand of civil liberties. None of this is meant to deny the importance of a long and proud discourse of the 'liberties of the subject' in English history stretching back through the early modern period, or to suggest that we can simply read political events as 'determined' by economic developments. The question has to do with the relationship between the two. And it is at least provocative to interrogate whether, in addition to being informed by the Rockingham myth and a shared commitment to the cause of 'liberty', the demand for greater civil liberties behind the rebellions in each region during this period was at least conditioned by the social property relations of agrarian capitalism in the manner we have suggested. For each of these regions was, in a different way, affected by the development of capitalism, with Scotland undergoing a wholesale conversion to agrarian capitalism after Culloden, with an experiment in agrarian capitalism by Protestant settlers in Ireland and, in America, with an economy informed by English agrarian social property relations, specifically by methods of improved farming for commercial purposes. Only in America, where there was no landed oligarchy as such, were Britain's landed elites unable to consolidate their hegemonic rule. In Britain and Ireland, remarkably, they would stay in power for another century.

Britain was able to emerge from defeat in the American War as the preeminent world power because its capitalist economy was the only economy in the world that could generate the level of demand for colonial products and export sufficient numbers of settlers from its surplus population to farm the colonies, whilst simultaneously reaping handsome profits by supplying competitively-priced manufactures to its colonies and to a newly independent America. Britain's expanding domestic economy enjoyed a relationship with the colonies whereby surplus production in the domestic market could be exported to the colonies in return for raw materials that would prove vital to industry. Britain would establish unchallenged control of the Pacific, about which the British knew more than any other power, once French interests there declined after the revolution of 1789. Although the Pacific did not give Britain a huge boost in commerce, its effective annexation was a vast expansion of what now became an indisputably global empire.

Despite the fact that the domestic economy of Britain was capitalist, with an agrarian capitalism now operating alongside an emerging industrial capitalism, the Empire as a whole, while being conditioned by the imperatives of domestic capitalism, was never specifically capitalist. The project of Empire required the construction of an imperial state based on the application of extra-economic force. The disjuncture between, on the one hand, the economic imperatives arising from capitalist market competition compelling a drive toward ever greater efficiency in production, resulting in a vast expansion of surplus production necessitating (and by constantly lowering prices, facilitating) the expansion of markets, and the extra-economic imperatives of the imperial state project of violence and plunder on the other, defined the contradictory nature of the British imperial project down to its dissolution in the twentieth century.

Chapter Five
Harvesting the Agrarian Revolution

> In truth the agrarian revolution is but a current in the wake of mightier movements.
>
> R.H. Tawney[1]

> I do not believe that it would be going too far to say, that nine-tenths of the farmhouses of England have been destroyed since the day that the 'good old King' came to the throne... Nothing that man could devise would be more injurious to the country than this.
>
> William Cobbett[2]

While the period 1760 to 1820 is generally identified with the first wave of the Industrial Revolution, possibly the most impressive area of economic performance during this period was to be found in the rate of increase in agrarian output. This period coincides with the era of parliamentary enclosures, which extinguished the open fields and the customary courts that governed them on the remaining half of the land that remained subject to open field farming after the middle of the century. Since most arable land became subject to economic leases after enclosure, this meant a steady addition of new land to the growing competitive market in land leases. This, in turn, helped to accelerate the growth of the domestic market, the spread of innovations in agriculture, including: mechanical devices, continued improvement in agrarian productivity and a resumption of rapid population growth adding to

1. Tawney 1912, p. 408.
2. Cobbett 1824, p. 147.

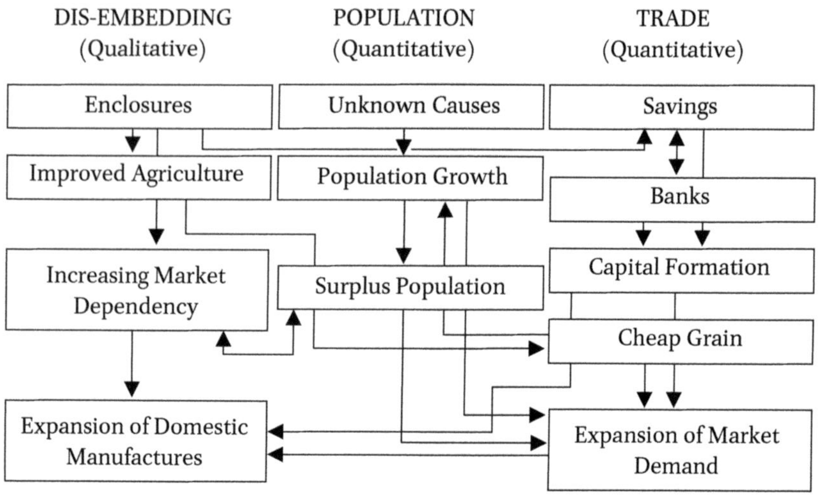

Diagram 5.1: The pattern of casual relations in the economic context of the Industrial Revolution.

the expanding pool of landless labourers and poor in both city and country. While the growth of population and the expansion of cottage manufacturing were common developments across Europe at this time, no other country witnessed the expansion of cottage manufacturing on the same scale as Britain. The economic processes set in motion by agrarian capitalism were now culminating in an extraordinary economic transformation that was unfolding before and, once it began, alongside the Industrial Revolution. In this chapter we will explore this transformation in order to better understand the nature of the economic context within which the Industrial Revolution started and unfolded.

Of the key factors that made up the economic context in which the Industrial Revolution emerged and was sustained, most can be linked to the previous and ongoing development of agrarian capitalism. These include: a price recovery; renewed population growth contributing to an expanding surplus population no longer tied to the land, with increasing numbers already engaged in domestic manufacturing; an expanding supply of grain based on improved agriculture capable, with imports, of meeting the bulk of the demand for food amongst the growing population; sufficient domestic demand to sustain a rapid increase in manufacturing; accumulated savings for capital formation along with a growing system of country banks and a rapidly improving system of transportation on turnpiked roads and canals. The expansion of colonial markets is an additional factor that can be associated with success in war and empire-building and with the growth of domestic production, the former expanding demand for manufactures whilst supplying the raw materials to be worked, the latter generating the supply to meet overseas demand. This impressive but incomplete list presents a challenge in terms of sorting out what is surely a complex pattern of causal relations. A tendentious sketch is offered in Diagram 5.1. The factors are grouped under three general headings: dis-embedding, population and trade. In the three sections that follow, we will discuss these three areas: population, trade and dis-embedding, in that order.

As previously discussed in Chapter Three, during the so-called period of agrarian depression, increased investment in improved methods and agrarian technology was itself an attempt to compensate for losses due to falling prices by intensifying cultivation and boosting overall productivity. Left to its own devices, the process of generating ever greater productivity gains in response to low prices would only have served to drive agrarian prices down even further. By the mid-1740s, prices reached a low, and the number of enclosure bills faltered. By the 1760s, the low agricultural prices, stagnant population growth and sluggish trade that had characterised the economy in the first half of the eighteenth century had undergone a reversal. Grain exports, having peaked in 1745, continued until 1780 when, as a result of recurring poor harvests, Britain was compelled to import considerable quantities of grain (238,000 quarters) for the first time.[3] Rising prices would have made British grain less attractive than previously to buyers in foreign markets, but this could not be the primary reason why grain exports reversed. Nor could it be due to increasing agrarian productivity, since this had continued to increase during the period of low prices, and continued to grow further as prices recovered. The primary reason why grain exports dried up had to be that a growing population (with steadily rising average incomes) would have served to soak up the agrarian surplus. The recovery in prices also appears to generally follow the resurgence of population growth. Thus, upon first examination, population growth appears to be the primary causal factor behind the unsteady recovery. At the same time, we cannot overlook the important contribution made by the expansion of overseas trade in allowing for further expansion of the domestic market. This presents the opportunity of reconsidering both the demographic model and the commercialisation model at the same time, and contrasting these with the significance of agrarian capitalism, treated as a long-term transformation in social property relations.

---

3. Berg 1985, p. 94.

The end of the demographic pause

While the population of Britain grew by 57 percent over the course of the eighteenth century, most of that growth came after 1750, when the demographic pause ended and rapid population growth resumed. During the 1720s and 1730s, the population of England and Wales may have actually declined slightly, falling just under six million inhabitants. Growth began again at a pace of around four percent in the 1740s, approaching seven percent in the 1760s and 1770s and exceeding 11 percent in the 1790s.[4] Contemporaries were slow to notice.[5] Remarking on the simultaneity of the upswing in population growth and agricultural output, Deane and Cole write: '[I]t is impossible not to be struck by the close connection between the pattern of growth at home and the course of population change, and it is natural to inquire how far the two were causally related'.[6] There can be little doubt that population growth as a factor exerted tremendous force on the economy, or that economic growth and population growth were intertwined. But population growth was a double-edged sword. During economic recessions (as during the American and French wars), population growth could lead to depressed wages and increased misery. During periods of heavy investment and growth (as during the interwar periods of 1763–76, 1783–92 and after 1815) population growth could contribute to speedy recoveries by cooling the pace of wage increases.[7] Commenting on a later period, the early nineteenth century, when demand for labour was high, Schofield asks: 'Was this acceleration in both the population and in the demand for labour coincidental? Did the population grow in response to the demands of an expanding economy; or was the economy stimulated by the demands of an increasing population?'[8] Here, we have the demographic model in the form of questions, if not as assertions. To address the question, we must first consider the causes of population growth.

---

4. Deane and Cole 1969, p. 6, Table Two.
5. Even by 1780, 'some writers were speculating that the population was actually declining, but by that time parish clergymen, who kept a close watch on the local social scene, were finding clear indications that this was far from the case' (Christie 1982, p. 3).
6. Deane and Cole 1969, p. 89.
7. This way of putting it might lead to confusion by implying that war simply depressed the economy. Several times in this study we have seen how war both stimulated production and diverted capital from investment, with the two trends somewhat offsetting one another. However, in the specific period we are considering, the economy grew throughout, so it would be quite misleading to imagine that during the American and French wars economic growth slowed tremendously or came to some sort of standstill. The point is simply that growth tended to be more robust during the inter- and post-war periods.
8. Schofield 1994, p. 60.

Table 5.1: Corn-output in England and Wales[9] (thousands)

Year	Population	Domestic consumption (quarters)	+Net exports -Net imports (quarters)	Net output (quarters)
1700	5,826	13,109	184	13,293
1750	6,140	13,815	1,006	14,821
1800	9,024	20,305	−1,313	13,991
1820	12,088	27,198	−2,112	25,086

The upswing in population growth was preceded by a long period of low agricultural prices alongside increasing productivity gains in agriculture. But where the decision to have children is concerned, human behaviour must be taken into account. Cheap food and plentiful employment are economic factors that can contribute to cultural change by creating the conditions whereby couples may find it more feasible to marry and start a family at a younger age.

But we cannot simply deduce the specific causes of population growth from economic variables. The specific causes may be many and complex. Contrary to the predominant view that decreasing mortality rates were the primary cause of population growth, Schofield suggests that for the nineteenth century, the actual cause may have been increasing fertility rates. He suggests further that higher rates of fertility may have been caused by young persons marrying at an earlier age.[10] Another suggestion is Philpot's 'enclosure hypothesis', by which enclosures are thought to have 'freed the common wastes of disease-ridden cattle and sheep which had infected the human population with brucellosis, tuberculosis and anthrax and so caused high mortalities in the years up to about 1750'.[11] Other cultural factors may have played an important role as well, such as the loss of access to herbs with contraceptive properties by urban women.[12]

9. Source: Deane and Cole 1969, p. 65.

10. Schofield 1994, p. 73 adds the comment that: 'in the sixteenth and seventeenth centuries, changes in celibacy emerge as very much more important than changes in the age at marriage in causing changing GRRs' [GRRs = Gross Reproduction Rates]. In concurrence, Youings 1984, p. 137 asks why the rate of population growth was slow during a time of plentiful resources, and suggests that the answer lies in the delay in the onset of marriage. See Zmolek 2001, p. 136.

11. Philpot 1975, pp. 19–46 as cited in Hodgson 1979, p. 83.

12. 'Some women, who were unmarried or simply unwilling to risk the very real dangers of childbirth, resorted to chemicals and plant extracts, like wormwood, saffron, hyssop, ergot, pennyroyal, and savin, in hopes of aborting a fetus. Some believed that drinking heavily or being bled in the feet would do the trick' (Olsen 1999, p. 51). It has been suggested that as cities grew and populations lost access to forage in the forests, knowledge of certain herbs that may have been known by midwives and some physicians since time out of mind to have properties that suppressed pregnancies or stimulated stillbirths would have been lost. Where before women may have quietly and secretively used such

Yet while economic factors may not be treated as the sole, direct causes for demographic fluctuations, the food supply does both enable and set an upper limit on the growth of the population. And here, the early eighteenth-century productivity gains made in agriculture affected not only birth and mortality rates, contributing to the resurgence of population growth. Continual improvement in productivity through the end of the century and beyond enabled Britain to break the Malthusian cycle and support a constantly expanding population.

Of course, not all Britons had equal access to the food supply. What impact did the simultaneous expansion of the food supply and population growth have on diets? As we might expect, there is no clear evidence to suggest that the average consumption of cereals per head changed very much in the eighteenth century. As a greater range of commodities became available through foreign trade and new seeds, many found a greater variety of food on their table. Meat consumption, however, does not seem to have risen, and in areas where wages fell, meat consumption probably declined for the poor.[13] The quality and size of livestock may have improved, and the rate of meat production probably increased, but the supply of beef could not keep pace with population growth.[14] As a result, Scotland and Ireland expanded their sales of beef and dairy produce to England.[15] If the poor were in some regions tightening their belts, the tables of the gentry and prosperous tenant-farmers had no need to go without. British exports were sufficiently robust to allow for the importation of whatever foods were necessary to cover domestic shortages.

Where food is concerned, population growth and increasing grain yields may have tended to offset one another when considered in terms of consumption

Table 5.2: Growth of British imports and exports: 1720–90[16]

	Imports	Exports
1720	£6.1m	£6.9m
1750	£7.8m	£12.7m
1770	£12.2m	£14.3m
1790	£17.4m	£18.9m

herbs as a kind of 'morning-after pill', their access and knowledge to these options may have been lost or cut off with the move to the cities, thus removing an option that in the past may have served to limit the fertility-rate to whatever degree (John King, King's Cross College, University of Oxford, personal discussion, October 1997). If this is a valid hypothesis, it serves as an example to demonstrate how challenging research into the cultural factors behind population growth (or decline) can be.

13. Deane and Cole 1969, p. 64.
14. Deane and Cole 1969, pp. 68–71.
15. Deane and Cole 1969, p. 74.
16. Source: Black 2001, p. 69.

per head. But in general, population growth added to the total demand in the economy, stimulating expansion. Since we have also seen that growth in the food supply provided the enabling factor for population growth, the answer to Schofield's question is that population and (agrarian) economic growth are mutually stimulating. But given that Britain's economy continued to expand during the long demographic pause, even during a mild population decline, the demographic model cannot hold. While population growth may have provided a powerful stimulus to growth, it remains one variable among others.

Internal and external expansion

In the second half of the eighteenth century, British trade roughly doubled (see Table 5.2). The most striking feature of British trade was the spectacular growth in colonial trade, rising from ten to 57 percent of England's domestic exports over the course of the eighteenth century. The growth in exports to North America was most impressive, rising from £0.27 million in the years 1701–4 to over £2 million in 1786–90.[17] Deane and Cole conclude that 'the increase in British exports in the course of the century was almost entirely due to the expansion of trade with the new, colonial markets in Ireland, America, Africa and the Far East'.[18]

Restrictions on exports and imports remained in effect throughout the century. This included bans on exports of raw materials, including wool and sheep, exports of textile machinery, and the emigration of artisans. Manufacture of steel, iron and iron wares in the American colonies was banned in 1750. Attempts to ban imports of manufactured cloth persisted, including a ban on the import of all manufactured silks and velvets in 1766. From 1775 to 1783, the Irish silk trade collapsed, just as the ban on imports of Irish cattle from 1699–1759 had hit depressed Irish cattle exports. 'The Irish and colonial economies were regulated and restricted in order to make them assist, not rival, that of Britain'.[19]

Britain emerged from the wars with France the pre-eminent power in Europe, effectively in command of the seas. Yet might the Industrial Revolution have happened sooner in the absence of these wars? Ashton has answered in the affirmative, pointing to the loss of ships and persons, the 'deflection of energies' away from human needs. Ashton writes: 'If there had been no wars the English people would have been better fed, better clad, certainly better housed, than they were'.[20] Nef, on the other hand, finds that on balance, war provided a positive

17. Ibid.
18. Deane and Cole 1969, pp. 83–8 and 34.
19. Black 2001, pp. 70–1.
20. Ashton 1959, p. 177, as cited in Wilson 1984, pp. 276–7.

economic stimulus.[21] Wilson finds that aside from the major depression in the economy during the years 1761–2, which may have been brought on by the diversion of capital out of the domestic economy for the war effort, war cannot be held directly responsible for other periods of economic slump. Clearly war had both positive and negative effects on economic development.

On one side of the balance sheet, we can list the depressive effects that war had on the domestic economy. War demanded raw materials, and where civilians found an inadequate supply of goods that were in demand for the military, the impact of war would have been directly felt. The diversion of capital toward the war effort meant higher interest rates. This would tighten up credit and slow down the rate of investment. Heavier taxation meant higher wages. Both high interest and high wages cut into profits. Higher taxes also took money out of the pockets of consumers, reducing purchasing power and thus serving as a source of drag on the whole economy. More broadly, war was an added source of instability and uncertainty in the economy, alongside the vagaries of nature, such as the threat of a bad harvest or a harsh winter. Economic growth may thus have been delayed by war. On the other side of the balance sheet, we can list the ways in which war provided a positive stimulus to economic growth. First of all, the 'diversion' of capital out of the private sphere of the domestic economy toward state expenditure on war was largely no diversion at all. The army and navy demanded guns, cannons and shot, stimulating the iron, brass and copper industries. Ship-building prospered under navy contracts, and stimulated demand for 'coal, metals, tar, ropes, as well as for the skilled and semi-skilled labour of carpenters, sailmakers, anchor makers and the like'.[22]

The impact of the textile industry is more complex, since clearly war interrupted exports to overseas markets. At the same time, imports declined, easing up competition and freeing up space for domestic produce on the domestic market. Simultaneously, the demand for uniforms allowed much of the industry, especially woollens, to offset the loss of overseas markets by acquiring government contracts. Yet even if on balance manufacturers were forced to cut back on production during wartime, they had reason for long-term optimism, provided that Britain prevailed in war, for the acquisition of new territory by wars meant new markets.

---

21. 'The French Revolution and the Napoleonic Wars helped Great Britain to gain a tremendous lead over Continental countries in industrial development, just as the Religious Wars and the Thirty Years' War had helped England to become the foremost country of Europe in the development of heavy industry during the late sixteenth and early seventeenth centuries' (Nef 1943, pp. 24–5). While in the case of the Napoleonic Wars, Nef certainly means to include victory as an important part of the stimulus to industrial development. Throughout his writings Nef makes references to state demand for production (such as ship-building) being generated by war.

22. Wilson 1984, p. 280.

The acquisition of the world's largest colonial empire was achieved by war and served as the basis for Britain's supremacy as a trading power. The interruption of colonial trade during the American War would have been had a more severe impact and the recovery would have been slower had Britain not acquired such a vast colonial empire. This raises the question as to whether foreign trade is more than a supplement to domestic growth.

McCloskey challenges the notion that foreign trade was as significant for growth as is widely believed, and specifically attacks the 'primitive' and old-school notion – championed by the likes of Rostow as well as Deane and Cole – that foreign trade acts as an 'engine of growth'. McCloskey invokes Harberger's law to draw the conclusion that: 'Only 13 percent of any change in income . . . can be explained by foreign trade'.[23] This, explains McCloskey, is insufficient to account for figures such as an overall growth in the economy of 100 percent between 1780 and 1860. Furthermore, McCloskey challenges the notion that growth in trade can explain economic growth, noting that: 'Exports are not the same thing as new income. They are new markets . . .'[24] At the same time, McCloskey argues against treating the British economy as if it developed in isolation, arguing that British prices were set by European trends. But what of trade barriers? McCloskey admits that trade barriers did have a huge impact on domestic prices. One can not simply dismiss tariffs as a caveat, as if free markets otherwise ruled the day in the eighteenth century. Where this study departs from the views of McCloskey is in emphasising the importance of productivity gains in agriculture. McCloskey does discuss productivity gains other than in terms of how to measure such gains using price indexes, but does not ask how it became an imperative for Britain to seek out and/or create overseas markets, or how Britain was able, for the first time in history, to break through the limits to growth and continue indefinitely to supply a steadily rising demand for its products.

The expansion of the domestic market and the completion of the commercial revolution, discussed in chapter three, allowed for real incomes to rise even as population growth rose, with both of these factors contributing to the expansion of market demand. And it was the expansion of the domestic market that demanded not only regional specialisation in new goods, but a whole new infrastructure for trade, as reflected in the 'turnpike mania' that commenced in

23. Named after the economist A.C. Harberger, Harberger's law states that 'if one calculates a gain amounting to some fraction from a sector that amounts to again a fraction of the national economy one is in effect multiplying a fraction by a fraction'. Showing that the average gross barter terms of trade varied by a ratio of as much as around 2 percent over the course of the eighteenth century (meaning that at most, roughly, terms of trade doubled), McCloskey then multiplies this rough estimate of a possible 100 percent increase in the terms of trade by the share of the UK's GNP taken up by foreign trade, which was 13 percent (McCloskey 1994, pp. 253–6).

24. Ibid.

1751–2, years in which 389 turnpike trusts were established.[25] Up to this point, the need for faster and better transport to and from London's expanding metropolis, which had fundamentally driven the turnpike system since the seventeenth century, had been fulfilled as turnpikes were set up on the main roads in and out of the capital, lowering travel times and possibly expense as well. Now, rising towns such as Liverpool, Manchester and Birmingham began to exert a demand for better feeder routes. During the 1750s and 1760s, turnpike acts were passed at an average of forty per year, as compared with an average of eight per year between 1700 and 1750.[26] In the early eighteenth century, regulations were passed to limit the load weight, the number of horses, the size of wheels and the width of axles as a policy 'of making the traffic conform to the roads', but the enormous increase in domestic trade and traffic necessitated a shift of emphasis. New policy stressed improving the roads to conform to the traffic, and this would require new feats of engineering.[27] The results of improved roads and improved coaches would prove to be dramatic. In 1754, it took four days to go from London to York; by 1785 one could reach Newcastle in three. Despite the dramatic improvements, the turnpike system could not by itself sustain the required level of expansion or growth necessary to meet the rising needs of a growing economy and population. The development of a parallel system of domestic transport would be required.

The improvements in coastal shipping in the first half of the eighteenth century were followed by the canal era in the second half. The canal era coincides more or less precisely with the era of parliamentary enclosures and the Industrial Revolution. Like the Industrial Revolution, two necessary factors for the canal boom were expanding market demand and investment capital. But the domestic market itself would in turn be reorganised by the provision of a faster and less expensive means of transporting goods.

---

25. Deane 1987, p. 74. This number was more than in either the preceding four decades or the following 6½ decades.

26. Deane and Cole 1969, p. 236.

27. Ashton 1969, p. 59. A blind engineer named John Metcalf devised a method of road-building similar to that the Romans had used, packing chipped stone to form a camber for drainage on top of a foundation of stone blocks, and digging roadside ditches to improve drainage. On soft subsoils he used heather to promote drainage by creating a convex surface. Later, during the construction-boom years of 1788–95, Thomas Telford and John Loudon Macadam developed further innovations. Telford stressed solid foundations and used multiple layers of different types of stones, covering the surface with gravel. Macadam's less expensive (and less durable) method was to form a foundation using packed stones, covering this with broken stone or flint which would settle to form a hard and arched surface. These methods were not significantly improved upon until the advent of the steamroller in the 1860s (Deane and Cole 1969, pp. 74–5; Ashton 1969, pp. 59–60; Mathias 1983, pp. 103–4).

The story of Foss Dyke sheds perspective on the timing of the canal-boom. First constructed by the Romans[28] as a waterway connecting the city of Lincoln to the River Trent, Foss Dyke was restored under Henry I in 1121. From 1620 to the 1740s, Foss Dyke changed hands several times, but was never made profitable. Richard Ellison re-opened the waterway in 1744, and by 1766 it was bringing in £595 per year, a figure that approached £3,000 per year when the canal passed from the hands of Richard Ellison II to (Colonel) Richard Ellison III.[29] So having been available for centuries, why did Foss Dyke only become profitable coincident with the canal era? 'If canals, say, are to explain part of the growth of income', writes McCloskey, 'it must be explained why a technology available since ancient times was suddenly so useful'.[30] The general answer is that the demands of the domestic market made canals profitable. The specific answer has everything to do with coal, for which canal barges posed an ideal means of transport.

Britain's first *bona fide* canal, or constructed waterway independent of any river, was built by the engineer James Brindley, in the employ of Francis Egerton, the Duke of Bridgewater, for the purpose of providing a better means of transporting coal from Bridgewater's Worsley mines to Manchester.[31] The Bridgewater Canal opened for business between 1761 and 1763. The extent to which its construction was driven by market considerations is striking. By halving the price of coal in Manchester, Bridgewater's canal signalled an entirely new market for investors, who would on average earn about an 8 percent annual return. From the outset the process was driven by competition between the builders. 'A contemporary calculated that 90 out of the 165 [Canal Acts] passed between 1758

28. Historians are not in agreement as to whether the Romans actually built the first canals in Britain. That the Romans did build the first navigable waterways in Britain is not in doubt. And the first of these, according to some historians, was Foss Dyke. While some argue that Foss Dyke and other Roman waterworks were merely built for drainage purposes, others contend that by connecting the River Witham at Lincoln (Lindum Colonia) with the River Trent, the Romans surely must have applied their expert sailing skills to take advantage of this man-made waterway. Regardless, Roman waterways fell into decay for centuries (Hardcastle 2005).

29. Hardcastle 2005 notes: 'Another waterway, very similar to Foss Dyke, named Car Dyke, was also built by the Romans. It headed south from Lincoln towards the River Cam near Cambridge'.

30. McCloskey 1994, p. 262.

31. Not only was Brindley's canal a stunning achievement in its own right (and an instant success), but Brindley also built an underground canal out of the mines to connect with the main canal and to help with mine drainage. He also built a 38-foot high aqueduct spanning the Irwell at Barton. These engineering achievements 'stirred the imagination of a public that believed passionately in man-made improvement' (Deane 1987, p. 79). More stirring, perhaps, was the effect the canal had on lowering the price of coal, and it was probably this more than anything which stimulated a wave of investment in canal-building in the 1760s and early 1770s.

and 1802 had coal as their main prospective traffic'.[32] The demand for coal was driven by the growth of towns and – following Darby's method of smelting with coked coal spread beyond Coalbrookdale in the 1750s – by the iron industry.

The strategic considerations that hastened and shaped the building of the canal system came from sellers, who were chiefly landlords, and buyers, with rising industrialists like the potter Josiah Wedgwood among them. Wedgwood became the treasurer of the Mersey to Trent Canal, 'which was to pass though the Potteries and thus enable Cornish clay to be brought there at a cheap rate'.[33] Carriers and innkeepers opposed the scheme, afraid of losing traffic on their roads. Some landowners also refused to sell. When Brindley presented the plans before Parliament in London, Wedgwood joined him to point out its utility, arguing that not only the Potteries would benefit, but also that 'the iron industries of Warwickshire needed water communications, and were condemned to stagnation as long as means of transport were lacking'.[34] The Trent and Mersey Canal opened in 1777, and included over 708 locks and five tunnels, one as long as two miles.[35] But the T and M was just a part of Brindley's grand plan for a national network of canals he called the 'Grand Cross'. The American War of Independence interrupted this first wave of canal-building. As the war drew on, canal investors were drawn away toward investing their funds in the government's war to retain the American colonies. But investing picked up even stronger after the war. The canal mania of the 1790s was driven by the building of extensions, linking middle-sized cities like Lancaster, Leicester, Sheffield, Basingstoke and Andover to the network. The T and M was the first part of the main line that would stretch from the Mersey in the northwest to the Thames at London in

32. Mathias 1983, p. 102.

33. Wedgwood, the potter, together with his friend and associate Thomas Bentley, busied themselves with 'indefatigable zeal' over the Mersey to Trent Canal (Mantoux 1961, p. 387).

34. '...When at last, on July 26, 1766, the work was begun, Wedgwood had the honour of turning the first sod. Almost immediately, on the line of the canal, he bought the land on which his great Etruria factory was built shortly thereafter' (Mantoux 1961, pp. 128–9). Combined with improvements made to the local roads, the whole district was transformed by population growth, conurbation and the reputation that comes with growing wealth. In a later speech given 'to a new generation of inhabitants, [Wedgwood] could justly say: "I would request you to ask your parents for a description of the country we inhabit when they first knew it; and they will tell you that the inhabitants bore all the makers of poverty to a much greater degree than they do now..."' (Mantoux 1961, p. 387; citing Wedgwood's *An Address to the Young Inhabitants of the Pottery* [Wedgwood 1783, pp. 21–2]). Other industrial capitalists who shared Wedgwood's vision of how canals would expedite the flow of commodities within the domestic market were Matthew Boulton and Samuel Garbett, both of Birmingham.

35. Brindley was initially ridiculed for his project of building the tunnel, but now people 'came from miles around to see it, proclaiming it one of the wonders of the world' (Hardcastle 2005).

the Southwest, upon the eventual completion of a 'Grand Union' line running between London and the T and M. The 'cross' across this main trunk would be canals connecting the Severn in the Southwest and the Trent in the Northeast, by way of the Bridgewater Canal connecting with the Leeds and Liverpool Canal, which would cross the Pennines. The Grand Union Canal was by far the largest project. It was approved by Parliament in 1793, opened in 1805, and only fully completed in 1813.

By the late eighteenth and early nineteenth centuries, Britain had developed the most advanced transport and communications infrastructure in the world. The cost may have been as much as £20,000,000, which 'was far exceeded by the reduction in transport costs'.[36] More remarkable still is that whereas the risk, expense and time requirements are typically too great to attract anyone but governments to the building of such public works, in Britain 'it was almost entirely native enterprise that found both the initiative and the capital to lay down the system of communications which was essential to the British Industrial Revolution'.[37] Acts of Parliament, however, were essential. They allowed land to be acquired and prodigious sums of capital to be raised without the investors bearing the liability. 'Canal shares became freely negotiable and were quoted on the Stock Exchange like government securities at the end of the eighteenth century'.[38] Canal-building, then, was every bit as much a form of private enterprise as enclosing or factory-building. Although industrial demand provided a part of the stimulus and industrial capitalists partook in the strategic planning, canal-building was mainly responding to the demand for coal and of the expanding domestic market more broadly. The steadily expanding output of grain would also travel on the canals.

These examples of extraordinary cost and effort being expended on improving and developing the transportation facilities, what we call the infrastructure of trade, remind us that markets do not automatically appear once the producer has produced and the consumer is ready to consume. Marketing as an activity itself requires the expenditure of labour-power.

Parliamentary enclosures and the consequences of increasing agrarian productivity

Second and key is that the proportion of the population no longer dependent upon the land but increasingly dependent upon the market for their

36. Owen 1975, p. 314.
37. Deane 1987, p. 73.
38. Mathias 1983, p. 106.

Table 5.3: Enclosure bills in Parliament, 1740–1829[39]

Years	No. of bills
1740–9	36
1750–9	137
1760–9	385
1770–9	660
1780–9	246
1790–9	469
1800–9	847
1810–19	853
1820–9	220

subsistence was continuing to rise. The number of enclosure bills presented before Parliament between 1720 and 1754 never went over 50 per decade, after which the numbers rose rapidly.[40] By 1760, most of East Anglia and South-East England had been enclosed without acts of Parliament. Over fifty percent of the acts of parliamentary enclosure passed after 1760 were for enclosing fields in the core counties of Cambridgeshire, Huntingdonshire, Northamptonshire and Oxfordshire. Starting in the 1770s, the last assault on rural common rights commenced with a new wave of enclosures. In all, some 2.95 million acres of open fields and their associated commons in fourteen counties were enclosed by acts of Parliament between 1760 and 1820, representing over 69 percent of the total open fields and associated commons in England.[41] The effects of enclosure were profound. The demand of an increasing herd of animals on the land for pasture meant forests were felled and trees pushed to the margins of the Britain's unique quilt-patchwork geography of fields divided by fences or hedges. In the England of 1760, poor land use 'and the ravages of animals had almost stripped the country of trees', and the peasants in their wake.[42] Of the two types of parliamentary enclosure, the conversion of arable land was more controversial than the conversion of wastes and commons because it directly removed the tenant's access to the means of subsistence. Obtaining an act of enclosure brought in not only the strong arm of the state to force the issue, but the arguments of influential critics of those who defended common-right. Since resistance to enclosure was almost entirely a local affair, the 'liberal' critics were able, from the 1760s on, to

39. Source: Deane and Cole 1969, p. 95, n. 1.

40. 'Between 1760 and 1815 over 7,000,000 acres were enclosed by act alone – an average of more than 125,000 acres per year compared to the mere 7,300 from 1715 to 1760' (Christie 1982, p. 159).

41. Mingay 1997, p. 16; Christie 1982, pp. 4–5; Rule 1992a, p. 132 following Blaug 1964, p. 243.

42. Christie 1982, p. 5.

frame the debate in terms of the interests of the nation against the conservative and parochial interests of the countryside.[43] Not coincidentally, it was in the period of parliamentary enclosures that the professional lobbyist appears. 'After 1770 customary tenancies and medium-sized farms began to disappear under the impact of agricultural improvement, accentuating the gulf between the larger tenant-farmers and the mass of the rural poor'.[44] Cottagers were increasingly consigned to having simply a cottage and a garden, although in many areas they still retained access to wastes and commons. And labourers likely rented even their own dwelling. The number of enclosure acts slowed after 1777 (no doubt in large part due to the American War), 'and for a time, at least, arrears of rent testify to comparatively depressed conditions for the farming community'.[45] Yet once the pace of enclosure acts recovered, the pace doubled, and continued to accelerate until 1820.

As the rate of population growth accelerated after the 1750s, it reinforced the expansion of the domestic market. It also reinforced – or after 1760 may have been the primary source of – the growth of the non-agrarian sector of the population.[46] But the key point, here, is that it would be all too easy to overlook the window between the recovery of prices and the onset of accelerated population growth and simply attribute the recovery in prices to population growth, without weighing the considerable impact that the increasing market dependency of the population would have on prices. Since the growth of the domestic market is part and parcel of the expansion of the growth of the non-self-subsistent or market-dependent portion of the population, the commercialisation model is describing the same process as the theory of agrarian capitalism, but where it fails is in seeing only a quantitative change in the growth of markets while missing the critical qualitative change to market dependency. By itself, the British population's increasing dependence upon the market for the necessities of life would have increased the overall level of demand, having an upwards effect upon prices. The demographic model is one step further removed from the matter than is the commercial model, since it confuses what is essentially an effect of rising productivity and falling prices, namely population growth, for the cause.

Whatever the relative contribution of these three factors to the recovery of prices, what is of critical importance is the dispossession of the tenantry from the land as a qualitative change, where the other factors are essentially quantitative. Only the qualitative change can explain the break with patterns of the

43. Neeson 1996, p. 46.
44. Hay and Rogers 1997, p. 198.
45. Deane and Cole 1969, p. 95.
46. According to Berg 1985, p. 101: 'It is now widely argued that agricultural improvement was labour-using rather than labour-saving, so that most of the industrial labour force must have arisen out of population growth'.

past, for it was the ability of the agrarian capitalist economy to break through the limits on the expansion of the non-agrarian sector of the population on the basis of increasingly productive agriculture that set Britain apart from any other economy. In discussing the release of labour from the agricultural to the industrial sectors, Nick Crafts recognises the critical importance of increasing agricultural productivity. Given a situation of rapidly rising agricultural demand *and* rising population growth, how on earth, asks Crafts, could the economy afford to release labour *from* the agricultural *to* the industrial sector, allowing the Industrial Revolution to take place at all?

> Suppose agriculture is characterised by diminishing returns to labour and suppose also that food demand grows at the same rate as population. If the relative share of labour [in agriculture] is to fall, it is necessary that the growth rate of the labour force in agriculture is less than the growth rate of population and the labour force overall. This appears to pose problems, for whilst the demand for food grows with the population the food supply grows less rapidly, even if all the extra labour were to be used in agriculture (which would, of course, amount to deindustrialization). Clearly, to feed all the extra population and also industrialise it is necessary to secure rising output per agricultural worker, which itself requires either innovation or investment in agriculture to permit the release of labour… It is clear that between 1700 and 1760 the condition for the release of labour was easily met by British agriculture.[47]

In fact, writes Crafts, '…the sector could also cope with the additional demand for food associated with higher incomes per person'. What allows this condition to be met, for Crafts, is the rising productivity of agriculture.

Note, however, that Crafts speaks only of productivity growth, a quantitative factor, and does not acknowledge the transformation of class and property relations in the development of agrarian capitalism that facilitated increasing agrarian productivity, or the extension of that qualitative transformation in the expansion of the share of the population becoming market-dependent. It should not surprise us then, that Crafts falls back on that third of the three quantitative models of change, the technological model, to explain the Industrial Revolution, by stating that there is 'a good case for regarding the timing of the famous inventions in cottons and textiles as a random exogenous shock', with the implication that 'the rapid structural changes characteristic of the Industrial Revolution were not readily predictable in the mid-eighteenth century. In other words, technological change provoked a serious switch in direction from the course which was

47. Crafts 1994, p. 57.

inherent in the type of growth experienced up to that time and the outcome can be regarded as truly revolutionary'.[48]

Regardless of how 'large' a contribution is attributed to the agrarian sector in making the Industrial Revolution, the fundamental causes of the Industrial Revolution are typically imagined as either exogenous to agriculture, or as too complex to be intelligible. It is here that the contribution of the gradualists only served to further confound the debate by seeking to diminish the suddenness of the 'shift' to industrialisation, without providing any new causal hypothesis to explain the protracted nature of its onset.

Rather than seeing the continuity between an agrarian economy generating greater and greater (and eventually unrivalled) productivity gains, and the application of machinery to industry as driven by the same economic logic behind a drive for improving the productivity of *labour*, Crafts maintains a hermetic seal between the two sectors of the economy. His immediate concern is merely to explain how a release of labour away from agriculture was possible under conditions that would on the surface seem to militate against it. Then, out of the blue, along comes the application of new technologies to industry and the entire economy is 'shifted' in a new direction. Without underestimating the severity of technology's impact on productivity, one might fairly ask whether the Industrial Revolution 'shifted' the economy in a new direction, or actually 'completed' the unfolding logic of a new, capitalist economy based on market principles by bringing these principles more fully to bear upon industry. We will explore this problem more fully in the coming chapters.

The era of high parliamentary enclosures came more than a century after the civil wars and the redefinition of Parliament as the instrument of state power expressing the unanimity of the ruling landed class, specifically in economic matters. Parliamentary enclosures followed upon the last Jacobite rising in 1745, and began to accelerate during the Pitt-Newcastle Ministry, which had brought a symbolic closure to the lingering Whig-and-court versus Tory-and-country schism. The prospects of a vast expansion of empire and the establishment of commercial linkages between rural manufactures and far-flung overseas markets combined to render parochialism increasingly obsolete. What was traditional, customary and local stood against improvement, progress and economic growth. Thus the proponents of enclosure argued that the poor would ultimately benefit. The debate may have still raged in the 1760s, but any attempts by the state to put a stay to enclosing were beyond historical memory. The necessity of legislating enclosure, then, did not really arise out of a need to apply the power of the state to tip the scales of class struggle towards the elite and from the poor. The

48. Crafts 1994, p. 59.

process was much too far along to require that. The most obvious precipitating factor is the recovery in prices, which increased the overall profitability of enclosing. Population growth, the expansion of the market and the correlative expansion of market dependency all added to the market pressures compelling farmers and landlords to enclose. Each trend reinforced the other, creating an overall economy of self-sustaining growth within which the arable, pastoral and rural-to-urban feedback-loops explored in the previous chapter continued to function.

The great enclosure debate

The impact of enclosures upon the inhabitants of the village has been a topic at the centre of a running series of debates over the course of the last century. To call this controversy a series of debates is accurate because a very wide range of specific topics are involved. This complexity has to do with the complexity of the enclosure movement itself. At the same time, however, it could be argued that all of the controversy amounts to a 'Great Debate' between scholars representing the Marxist and liberal approaches to economics. On one side are the 'pessimists', who place class struggle at the centre of the analysis and have tended to view enclosures as leading to immiseration through the loss of access to land and commons for the peasant, cottager or smallholder. On the other side are the 'optimists' who put contracts between 'free' buyers and sellers in the marketplace at the centre of their analysis and tend to see enclosure by agreement as a kind of democratic exercise that afforded even smallholders the opportunity to benefit from enclosure by taking advantage of new market opportunities. In this sense, perhaps it is more accurate to say that the 'Great Debate' has incorporated a discussion of enclosures, rather than to say that there has been a 'Great Debate' over enclosures.

Three distinct features of enclosure are: the demarcation of a piece of land by erecting a fence or a hedge, the abolition of mixed properties and holdings on the same field of arable land and their combination into units farmed by one cultivator rather than many, and the extinguishing of customary tenancies on arable land and rights to use of the commons. According to Butlin, these three processes:

> were not inevitably concomitant or simultaneous: 'the simple world in which all land was either common or enclosed turns out to be imaginary. Reality was far more complex'. Open field land could, in theory and practice, be in severalty, that is free from common rights. Equally, enclosures – fenced parcels – occurred in common fields. The basic distinctions to be made, therefore, are

> between open or enclosed land (a physical criterion) and land which was either in common or in severalty (a legal and operational criterion).[49]

We have already noted in Chapter Three that improvement could be undertaken on open fields, and thus did not require enclosure.[50] Nor did enclosure automatically translate into improvement. Funds needed to be invested in order for the land to be 'drained, limed or marled'.[51] Landlords naturally preferred farmers with the means to invest in improvements, but might let out smaller or marginal holdings to those of lesser means who were unlikely to make improvements. There were many other motives for enclosing besides improvement.[52] Suffice it to say that in terms of the technical details as well as motivations, the enclosure movement was an extraordinarily complex process subject to a wide range of regional and local variation in terrain as well as custom and culture.

Writing in 1911, the Hammonds described how parliamentary enclosures 'broke the back of the peasant community'. Enclosures, they wrote:

> created a new organization of classes. The peasant with rights and a status, with a share in the fortunes and government of his village, standing in rags, but standing on his feet, makes way for the labourer with no corporate rights to defend, no corporate power to invoke, no property to cherish, no ambition to pursue, bent beneath the fear of his masters, and the weight of a future without hope. No class in the world has so beaten and crouching a history...[53]

The pro-poor class bias of the Hammonds as well as the moralistic tone that pervades much of their work have drawn the criticism that their work lacks objectivity. The critics' main focus has been the way in which the Hammonds presented enclosure as a catastrophe for the peasantry. The class-based approach of R.H. Tawney, a Marxist scholar, came under heavy criticism for tending to treat agrarian producers in early modern England as proletarians. 'Revisionists'

49. Butlin 1979, p. 65 quoting Kerridge 1968, p. 16.

50. Neeson 1996, p. 105 argues that while common-field farmers were less likely to innovate than demesne farmers, 'where significant piecemeal enclosure did occur, the result may have been an invigorated common-field agriculture co-existing with a proto-enclosed one. And where this happened the two agricultures may have fed one another'.

51. Wade Martins 2004, p. 18.

52. For example, in the case of parliamentary enclosures, Mingay explains that 'The object of the enclosure Act was sometimes merely to get rid of the last rump of the open fields and commons, or to confirm an enclosure carried out previously by agreement among the owners, or to complete the exploitation of the waste and tidy up an inconvenient and confused accumulation of small closes' (Mingay 1968, p. 19). The use of the term 'merely' here betrays Mingay's dismissiveness of the importance that the 'last rump' of commons may have had to the local producers who relied upon it for firewood, for grazing their animals or for collecting fertiliser for their fields.

53. Hammond and Hammond 1974a, p. 81.

like G.E. Mingay and Eric Kerridge have argued that enclosure was not such a zero-sum game and that enclosure by agreement was common, involving smallholders being compensated for their losses or even surviving enclosure. Mingay succinctly summarised the revisionist position when he wrote: 'Modern opinion does not support the view of the Hammonds that the process by which an Act of Enclosure was obtained and executed was deliberately rigged against the small owner'.[54] The course of the debate followed the trajectory of revisionism, which sought to correct errors and exaggerations of pessimists like the Hammonds, followed by a counter-revisionist critique which at least partially restored the pessimists' case.

Turner cites research by the Soviet historian Lavrovsky, who found that the percentage of land held by landowners not belonging to the nobility, gentry or church was higher the later the enclosure. For Turner, the implication of this is that in regions like the South of England, where early enclosures took place, the peasantry was virtually extinguished, but elsewhere the peasantry's resilience became a factor in delaying enclosure. Subsequently, high agrarian profits during the French Wars induced these recalcitrant 'peasants' to enclose.[55] Turner then makes a salient observation, noting that studies like Lavrovsky's showed the dynamism of agrarian change and that enclosure was not necessarily the dominant aspect. 'It followed that the real issue was not necessarily the social upheaval at enclosure but more broadly the social upheaval caused by all elements of agrarian capitalism'.[56] It is doubtful that Turner has in mind the same definition of 'agrarian capitalism' as used in this study, but at face-value this statement is in complete accord with the thrust of the present study. Turner also follows Lavrovsky's work through to the conclusion that the 'peasantry' as a whole was weakened by enclosure as wealth was concentrated in the hands of larger landowners.

The work of Davies and Chambers corroborated Lavrovsky's findings that the period 1780–1830 saw an *increase* in the number of owner-occupiers in parishes where enclosure came late, at least in the East Midlands. The problem with Davies's work, however, was that he based the idea that the number of owner-occupiers holding 20 acres or less, not on any extant records of landholding but by translating records of land-tax payments into holdings. While Chambers

54. Mingay 1956, p. 23.

55. Turner 1968, p. 67 adds: 'Some of these "peasants", in fact, were behaving like capitalists, and we must recognize that a strong, commercially minded small landownership structure is not incompatible with a Marxist interpretation of the eighteenth century.' Certainly, Marx recognised that many peasants turned to what he called petty commodity production to supplement their incomes, but Marx surely recognised that a peasant turned petty producer turned capitalist was no longer a peasant.

56. Turner 1968, p. 66 citing Lavrovsky 1932–1934.

found that there were larger numbers of owner-occupiers in parishes after enclosure, this may have been a factor of the practice of recognising the legal rights of squatters and cottagers who held no land in arable at enclosure.

Mingay reaches the general conclusion that small farmers did decline but did not disappear. For Mingay, the agricultural revolution is a 'slow and protracted affair', a 'long-drawn-out process' in which the effects of 'parliamentary enclosures were by no means so sweeping as was once supposed'.[57] Mingay also finds that the major period of decline for smallholders came in the seventeenth and early eighteenth centuries.[58] Echoing this, Kerridge has put forth the claim that by 1700 only a quarter of the land left to be enclosed remained in open fields, such that '"the hoary fable of the supreme importance of parliamentary enclosures should be relegated to limbo"'.[59] This leaves Turner to the tentative conclusion that the 'best that we can say' is that enclosures before 1700 appear more important than previously thought, but involved less enclosure by agreement, while parliamentary enclosure would only become important after 1700.[60] Another tentative conclusion offered by Turner is that even if the numbers of smaller owner-occupiers did not decline after enclosures, many of them nonetheless sold their holdings shortly after enclosure, thus providing a landless labour force.[61] This leads to the next area of controversy: did enclosures, by releasing labour from the land, directly provide the landless, proletarian workforce for the Industrial Revolution?

Chambers did not question the Marxist notion that proletarianisation was an institutional rather than a natural development, but he challenged the notion that enclosure was the responsible institution. He argued, instead, that it was the 'unabsorbed surplus of rural population and not the main body which became the industrial workforce',[62] a surplus resulting from population growth, not enclosure. Crafts challenged Chambers's work by looking at counties other than Nottinghamshire (the sole focus of Chambers's study), where he found no evidence of population growth after enclosure alongside evidence of out-migration. Even if absolute numbers of workers engaged in agriculture rose, Crafts noted, relative to population growth this still meant that a declining share of the population was engaged in agriculture and an overall release of labour out of the agrarian sector. Turner adds to this discussion the proposition that relative price factors between land, labour and industry may have played a role, in that as land prices rose, the increasing use of labour after enclosure may have reflected the

57. Mingay 1968, pp. 16–17.
58. As cited in Turner 1968, p. 72.
59. Kerridge 1968, p. 24 as cited in Butlin 1979, p. 75.
60. Turner 1968, p. 35.
61. Turner 1968, p. 82.
62. Turner 1968, p. 77.

decreasing relative value of labour to the newly improved (and therefore more valuable) land. Turner then suggests that if enclosure so 'anchored' labour on the land by improving efficiency, then 'if relative rural depopulation occurred, the institutional creation of a labour force was not enclosure nor agrarian capitalism, but industry itself', which, Turner muses, 'could lead to an ultimate turnabout in the Marxist view of this history; enclosure anchoring the labour force on the land and industry trying to pry it off'.[63] In this way, Turner combines Chambers's thesis that enclosure was not responsible for rural depopulation with Crafts's argument that a release of labour nevertheless did occur.

The revisionists' reliance on land tax records and aggregated data leaves us with information only about the *size* of holdings, and not the legal status of tenures. To speak only of small occupiers disguises the more important transition from open fields being cultivated by 'peasants' to enclosed farms being cultivated by small tenant-farmers.[64] Moreover, and as noted, 'smallholders' typically sold their holdings soon after enclosure, being unable to compete with larger farmers with greater means and now producing on an economy of scale. Second, there appears to be a tendency to look only for proximate linkages between enclosure, population and the labour supply; long-delayed causation does not seem to be factored in. But it has been our thesis, here, that the main effect of the development of agrarian capitalism upon the economy was to lower prices by improving productivity and thereby to lift the ceiling on population growth previously set by the level of the food supply. So when Chambers argues that population growth, rather than enclosure, created a surplus population in the countryside, he is discounting the contribution which previous enclosures may have had in lifting the ceiling on the food supply and thereby allowing for demographic growth. We concur with Mingay that it was a long and drawn-out process, and with Turner's suggestion that the social upheaval brought about by agrarian capitalism in general, rather than specific enclosures, is the real issue. But we are still left with the problem of what role the enclosure movement *did* play in bringing about a transformation from customary to market-based tenures.

Mingay argued that the 'common-field system was wasteful, expensive, and difficult to work so long as dispersed holdings, common grazing rights, and sharing of the commons remained its basis'. Enclosing offered 'a means of rapid transformation to lower costs per acre, higher yields, and greater profits on a larger cultivated area'.[65] Neeson has countered this view of the open field system as inefficient by arguing that:

63. Turner 1968, pp. 76–9.
64. Saville 1969, p. 71.
65. Mingay 1968, p. 19.

> Living off the produce of commons encouraged frugality, economy, thrift. Productive commons had always been the insurance, the reserves, the hidden wealth of commoners – they were the oldest part of an ancient economy. They gave commoners the fuel, food and materials that kept them out of the market for labour and out of the market for consumption too. And the more productive the common the more independent the commoners.
>
> The habit of living off commons made the habit of regular employment less necessary. For commoners it was customary to make a living first out of the materials on hand; after all, the common came first, wage labour was a relatively recent arrival. This is not to deny the existence of wage labour; earning wages was necessary, but until they became the lion's share of income they were supplementary not central to a communing economy. Looking for regular, constant employment was unnecessary where commons were rich reserves.[66]

Nor did 'commoners' (a term Neeson uses to describe direct producers still living on either open fields or in part from access to the commons)[67] necessarily *want* full-time employment, for the independence which access to the commons afforded them meant that time was freed up for family, for sporting or just enjoying nature. As we have noted, such independence was increasingly viewed by landlords and farmers as laziness and idleness, which was but another way of expressing regret at the lost opportunity to exploit their labour-power. Another problem with the revisionist approach is thus its tendency to uncritically adopt the attitudes of the proponents of enclosure and their harsh criticisms of common-field systems, commoners and squatters. Neeson objects that common-right cottagers were valued members of the community, paying rents and placing no additional burden on the poor rates. She cites the case of the village of Welton in 1754, where some landlords argued against enclosing because the loss of access to the commons would remove the source of their tenants' livelihood. Thus not only commoners but also landlords in the mid-eighteenth century continued to see access to the commons as a right. The transition to seeing this as a privilege would be a long and difficult process.[68] Furthermore, Neeson argues that the attitude of deploring the management of the commons was not so much a constant as one which tended to develop specifically in the context of enclosure.

---

66. Neeson 1996, p. 177.
67. Neeson 1996, p. 297 explains that she 'reluctantly but necessarily' uses the term 'peasants' interchangeably with 'commoners' because it distinguishes these people from agrarian wage labourers and because 'it emphasizes a continuity with the past, a continuity based on the occupancy of land and rights in the common-field system'.
68. Neeson 1996, pp. 85 and 163.

Not only was it the case that impending enclosure tended to draw out arguments rooted in self-interest, but where only portions of a parish were enclosed, the balance of resources was upset and the once viable lifestyle of the commoners now put under strain.

> Enclosure transformed relationships in common field villages – changed the terms of the argument – as soon as it looked certain. But it is important to note that *enclosure* was the reason for this change in behaviour, not the common-field system.
>
> And it was in the context of enclosure that improving opinion in general began to deplore commons' management: 'that Ruskins' – the overstocker, the trespasser, the agister, the unscrupulous champion who 'robbeth by night / and prowleth and filcheth by day' – staulks the pages of enclosers' account of the common fields from Tusser on. For this reason, as critics of common fields, they missed the point. They failed to look at the system in its own terms. If we do this, we see at once how imperative was the *need* for common pasture to work efficiently, and therefore how vital was effective regulation. We remember the centuries of agricultural production generated by the common fields. Simply put: common pastures had to serve the common stock adequately, and grain had to be grown. In the end, common fields gave way to enclosed farms. But this does not mean the 'good' agriculture triumphed over 'bad', like some conquering hero in a gothic romance.[69]

To argue that the common-field system was 'inefficient' is in some ways to treat it as a capitalist operation, or perhaps more to the point, to see customary rights as nothing more than a 'break' upon the development of capitalist rationality. This follows from the Smithian tendency to universalise capitalist economics, which we discussed in the Introduction. Neeson's work has helped us to understand the custom-based social relations of the open field system on their own terms. Although as we noted it was not always the case, enclosure typically meant the extinguishing of customary law and associated customary rights and the conversion of enclosed fields to the status of freehold tenure as property over which the individual owner held absolute rights of ownership as recognised in common law. Both the higher rents enjoyed by enclosing landlords and the imperative arising from market-competition compelling landowners and tenant-farmers to assume control over the production process in order to more efficiently respond to the dictates of the market contributed to the drive towards converting land to capital.

For landlords, on the other hand, enclosure was unquestionably a good deal. The higher rents usually translated into a return on their investment of 15 percent

69. Neeson 1996, p. 156.

or more. Mingay argues that 'it must have been correspondingly profitable to the farmers whose greater productivity allowed them to pay much increased rents', by which he means 'farmers commanding capital'. Both landowners and 'farmers commanding capital' must have favoured enclosures out of their 'desire ... to take advantage of the market more readily and more completely than could be done under the limitations of the common fields'.[70]

For the small landowner, 'enclosure was of dubious value'.[71] Those who had been freeholders before enclosure were now as vulnerable as the copyholder who had received some land as compensation for the loss of the right to cultivate strips in the open fields. Exposure to the market meant higher rents, higher poor rates and in general, competitive market pressures that they had not been exposed to prior to enclosure. Being responsible for improvements, they might try to mortgage their holding in order to borrow the funds for investment, but this left them in the precarious situation of having to generate a sufficient profit to repay the loan, and in being in such a vulnerable position during a bad year could easily result in foreclosure. For the cottager, enclosure brought the 'double blow' of loss of access to land *and* rights of common. 'No argument about the rise and fall of classes can do justice to this effect of enclosure', writes Neeson. 'Whether the English peasantry disappeared or not, the effect of enclosure on the last generation of open field peasants was profound'.[72] The loss of access to land and commons meant the loss of access to the means of subsistence, which is but the correlate to their being rendered exposed to the market and ultimately dependent upon the market for wages with which to buy food and other means of subsistence.

Neeson credits E.P. Thompson for being the first to challenge the revisionist view that enclosures were accepted by commoners with relative passivity, arguing that 'commoners were more active in their own defence than historians – including the Hammonds – have allowed'.[73] Commoners resorted to petitions, negotiations, moral suasion, tearing down fences or hedges and burning ricks. The record of their resistance has been underestimated in large part because they kept few records.[74] Once an enclosure bill became an act, opposition generally became unlawful. While Thompson acknowledged that recent scholarship (in the time he was writing) had shown that the 'rules of the game' were played more fairly than the Hammonds had portrayed it, stressing that in spite of this there lay a danger in losing sight of 'the larger fact that what was at issue was

70. Mingay 1956, pp. 19–20.
71. Neeson 1996, pp. 254–5.
72. Neeson 1996, pp. 243 and 236–9.
73. Neeson 1996, p. 262.
74. Neeson 1996, pp. 272–7. 'It cannot be emphasized too strongly that the absence of records of illegal opposition makes any attempt to establish its dimensions impossible'.

a redefinition of the nature of agrarian property itself',[75] Neeson has challenged the revisionists' claim of fairness. She points out that Parliament would in many case waive or bend the rules, such as ignoring orders that the bills be publicly displayed in the parish before being introduced, ignoring the informal rule that four-fifths of the land to be enclosed should be held by supporters of the bill.[76] This could only add to the 'visceral hostility' felt by the poor who lost out at enclosure.

The first peak in parliamentary enclosures came in the 1770s, and was interrupted by war in America. This wave of enclosures was focused mainly upon enclosing the remaining open fields. The second peak came during the wars with France and focused upon enclosing the wastes and commons as well as light lands.[77] According to Mingay, 'between 1793 and 1815 a million acres of waste and commons were enclosed by Acts, in addition to that enclosed by agreement'.[78] Much of the debate covered, here, is based upon on research on enclosures in three counties which saw over fifty percent of their land enclosed between 1750 and 1818: Oxfordshire, Cambridgeshire and Northamptonshire. Mingay has argued that during the French Wars, long leases at low rents were offered to attract 'farmers of capital'.[79] Turner points out that while 'marginal' owners may have even taken part in promoting enclosures during the wars, it was during the deflation in the aftermath of the wars, with the decommissioning of soldiers flooding local labour markets and a fall in grain prices that farmers were caught holding large loans and faced with insufficient profits to pay off their debts. Meanwhile, those holding 100 acres or more tended to prosper and engross their farms.[80] Thus, while building their case on evidence from the period in which the evidence is most supportive, the revisionists ignore the counter-evidence from the period that follows. This undermines their argument.

George Comninel takes Eric Kerridge to task for making two unwarranted assumptions about enclosures. First, Kerridge appears to assume that, in the case of enclosure by agreement, tenants had no room for grievance when their interests had been respected under the law, even if the law said that they had no 'legitimate' claim to the land – as if laws cannot be bent for unfair or illegitimate purpose. Second, the doctrine of estates was natural and inevitable, rather than being a specific feature of English common law. What Kerridge and fellow revi-

75. Thompson 1991, pp. 237–8.
76. Neeson 1996, p. 273.
77. Wade Martins 2004, p. 33.
78. Mingay 1956, p. 21.
79. Mingay 1956, p.
80. Turner 1968, p. 69. More than one author has commented on the paucity of research on the farmer or local farmer associations, despite the absolutely pivotal role which farmers played in the transition we are here describing. See Wade Martins 2004, p. 1; and Fox 1979, p. 44.

sionists take for granted is that not only England, but every society prior to the advent of capitalism, was based upon agrarian labour regulated by customary norms that dictated how production was carried out. What the revisionists fail to explore is the normative social relationships of the field system, which they tend to treat as simply an obstruction blocking the development of an already existing capitalism that had to be removed in order for capitalism to grow. Enclosures generally involved the extinguishing of not only customary rights and tenures but also the manorial courts which enforced these rights. Enclosure was thus necessary for the development of agrarian capitalism because it enabled the owner to escape entirely the jurisdiction of customary law, something which could only be effected through the complete enclosure of the manor, thereby extinguishing the local court. But it was more than a matter of clearing away the old to allow the new to develop. Enclosure was something that required positive action and which could create social upheaval at the local level. That positive action was the establishment of absolute rights of property ('real estate') under the common-law doctrine of estates. Where Kerridge imagines estates as the 'natural and inevitable development of social progress', Comninel challenges the notion that 'the creation of farms held and operated exclusively in severalty, without community control', an arrangement that runs against the normative structure of social production in not only England but virtually every agrarian society that had ever existed, should be taken for granted as natural and inevitable.[81] To customary tenants losing their tenancies in the name of 'improvement', enclosure and the assertion of individual legal rights to enclosed land under the common law must have seemed very strange indeed, and very unnatural.

Conclusion

We saw in Chapter Three that the establishment of agrarian-capitalist relations of production enabled British agriculture to respond to a fall in prices not by withdrawing land from production, but for the first time in history by intensifying production. It was during the unsteady recovery from the so-called agrarian depression of 1753–50 that Britain became a grain exporter and British population growth began to rise rapidly, alongside the turnpike- and canal-manias, and a rapid acceleration of trade and production during the period when the Industrial Revolution began in earnest. The recovery of agrarian prices attracted more investment in enclosure, the pace of which doubled after the American war and accelerated even further during the French Wars. In the process, enclosures were ensuring that an ever greater percentage of the growing population

81. Comninel 2000, pp. 38–42.

would lack access to the means of subsistence, thereby adding tremendously to aggregate domestic demand, and thereby accelerating the cycle of self-sustaining growth. In the latter half of the eighteenth century, agrarian capitalism bore its fruit: bitter fruit for agrarian labourers and smallholders, extravagant fruit for landowners and larger farmers.

As Neeson has argued, enclosed farms were not necessarily more efficient than farming on open fields. At issue, then, is not the efficiency of farms, but efficiency for whom? Although tenants on open fields did sometimes introduce improvements, the problem which open fields posed for the improving landlord was two-fold. First, communal control of production decisions did not allow for a tenant-farmer to control production and make production decisions in accordance with the market. Second, the by-laws of the manorial court continued to hold jurisdiction not only over open fields but to every holding in a parish that had not been experienced wholesale enclosure and/or the abolition of the manorial court. Enclosure became an imperative in the context of an increasingly competitive market in grain and in land leases. It enabled the tenant-farmer to escape the jurisdiction of customary law so as to assert absolute individual rights of property over the land, thereby allowing him to respond directly to market compulsions by undertaking improvements, as well as maximising production and specialising in single crops. To this end, parliamentary enclosures proved both useful and effective.

Part Two

‘Such Machines . . . As Cannot Err’

Capital and Technology in the Making of Industrial England, 1700–1800

Chapter Six
Technology and History

> If the nation's strength was built on 'practical tinkerers', to use Professor Landes' words, what so inspired them here to break through their ancient restraints, to seek something other than simply another design, another set of colours, or to try to copy some finish already in use elsewhere? What, to be more specific, in a national industry that had to rely on one parson to invent the stocking-frame, on another one two centuries later to invent the power-loom, and on a barber to develop a spinning machine invented by a carpenter, what was it that moved inquiring men towards drastic mechanical change and away from mutations and imitations? It is a question which still remains to be answered.
>
> D.C. Coleman[1]

In considering the origins of the highly technological societies of the twenty-first century we rightly look to the Industrial Revolution for answers. Fundamental changes took place that set European and ultimately all human societies on a new trajectory involving the unprecedented growth and application of technology. While technological development up to that point in history was significant, the Industrial Revolution, which started at a relatively modest pace, involved the first application of machinery to production on a systematic basis, initiating the constant and ongoing process of revolutionising the means of production.

1. Coleman 1973, p. 13.

Eventually, this process of constant improvement in production gave rise to the internal combustion engine, telephones, spacecraft and the microchip. On its own terms, technological development is by nature progressive; it is subject to constant improvement. While technical knowledge can be lost upon the death of a scientist or inventor, or when whole civilisations die out, the character of technology is such that new devices are premised upon the discovery of many previous technological principles and innovations. Each discovery, each new device, has the potential to make possible an unlimited amount of further new innovations. Granting this, it is tempting to see the Industrial Revolution as being, in the main, the result of so many prior technological developments reaching a 'critical mass', whereby the clustering of a number of key discoveries at approximately the same time produced a burst of new innovation that was quite sudden by comparison with all that had come before, and which set in motion a kind of chain reaction of technological innovation that ultimately led to the development of the highly industrialised world in which we now live. This is another way of saying that it was bound to happen, or that the Industrial Revolution was a technological inevitability. But was it?

In his treatment of the British Industrial Revolution, author David Landes repeatedly finds that British economy and society were exceptionally responsive to market opportunities and incentives. Yet he has no theory to offer that would explain why this is so. For Landes, Britain's leap forward from relative technological backwardness to technological superiority is mysterious. Contemporary testimony, he explains, was mixed. Some saw the British as creative innovators, and there was definitely a display of talent. But 'England was not the only country with such artisans, and [yet] nowhere else do we find this harvest of inventions'.[2] Landes is stumped. He knows there is something peculiar about Britain. But to the extent that he seeks to explain why the Industrial Revolution happened in Britain by examining the development of technology and machinery, he can provide no general explanation for that peculiarity.

By studying the particularities of Britain's 'harvest of inventions', we are bound to learn a great deal about why the Industrial Revolution began in Britain and nowhere else. But theoretical attempts to explain the Industrial Revolution by making technology the 'prime mover' generally fall apart when confronted with some of the most basic historical problems. For example, if the progress of technology determines the course of history, then the Industrial Revolution either should have developed simultaneously across Europe,[3] or, if it had to start in one country, should have begun in seventeenth-century France. Here, under the

2. Landes 1991, p. 61.
3. There is no space, here, to entertain the question of whether Europe in general enjoyed technological superiority in the period just prior to the Industrial Revolution.

reign of Louis XIV, a system of state-run factories was established by Minister Colbert. They were giant operations which produced mainly luxury items for royal consumption and for the public. Colbert believed that large-scale manufacturing required state sponsorship to survive.

> If the hand which built and upheld this structure was withdrawn, everything broke down and ruin was imminent. These undertakings only lived on protection and privilege. Left to themselves many would have disappeared at once, and so when, under Louis XV, the government paid them less attention, they began to decline.[4]

Mantoux is explicit in rejecting the notion that this development bore any relationship with the privately-led Industrial Revolution in Britain a century later:

> The creation of royal manufactures in the seventeenth century must not therefore be confused with the spontaneous growth of the factory system in the following century. It is indeed a fact of very limited significance, though no doubt it contributed to the prosperity which Colbert sought to give France. It produced no general consequences and no relationship can be traced between it and the economic system of our times.[5]

Whatever the level of technology involved in these *Manufactures Royales*, the marked difference with England is that instead of setting in motion a constant process of revolutionising technology, they declined. The structure of the labour process was not the forerunner of our modern capitalist system, because despite generous state subsidies, work was organised in guild-like fashion where the workshop predominated with journeymen enjoying a share of the profit from the lace, glass, mirrors, silk, tapestries and other specialty goods that were produced.

So if France represented the highest level of technological development in the seventeenth century, and if it is primarily technological development that determines the course of history, why was it in Britain and not in France that the Industrial Revolution 'took off' a century later? And at the same time as Britain was building factories, why were the lords of Eastern Europe still building castles on their estates?

---

4. Mantoux 1961, pp. 29–32. Rather than directly promoting greater efficiency of labour in production, Colbert's policy of promoting manufacturing relied on tariffs as well as the recruitment of foreign specialists. 'N'oublions pas, au nombre des moyens mis en œuvre par Colbert pour développer l'industrie française, le recruitement à l'étranger, par les ambassadeurs et consuls, des ouvriers les plus habiles en tout genre. C'est ainsi que la France lui dut l'industrie des draps fins, des dentelles, points et glaces de Venise, des belles tapisseries de Flandre, du goudron, du fer-blanc...' (Clement 1874, p. 306).

5. Mantoux 1961, pp. 29–32.

A solution to these historical problems has already been suggested in the Introduction.[6] There, we reviewed Brenner's critique of what he calls the commercialisation model and the demographic model, and his conclusion that both models come up short in terms of being able to explain the development of capitalism. We saw that such models are unable to provide satisfactory answers to Hobsbawm's three questions: Why Britain? Why the late eighteenth century? And how did the spark that ignited this revolution get lit? These questions are equally salient in the context of the present discussion because what we could call the *technological model* is equally incapable of providing answers to these three questions. In the same manner that Brenner applied his three-region 'proof' in critiquing attempts to explain the first emergence of industrial capitalism by employing the demographic or commercialisation models, we can employ this proof to critique explanations of the origins of industrial capital society according to a technological model.

The rise of trade and population growth were experienced across Europe. The scientific revolution was also a pan-European phenomenon. Pre-eighteenth century technological development in Europe was not particularly concentrated in any one country. And as we have seen, technological advancement was more prominent in seventeenth-century France than it was in England. In fact, England had long been among the most backward regions of Europe, as Louis Mumford explains:

> The fact is that England, throughout the Middle Ages, was one of the backward countries of Europe: it was on the outskirts of the great continental civilisation and it shared in only a limited way in the great industrial and civic development that took place in the South from the tenth century onward. As a wool-raising center, in the time of Henry VIII, England was a source of raw materials, rather than a well-rounded agricultural and manufacturing country... It was not until the sixteenth century that various traders and enterprisers began to develop mines and mills and glassworks on any considerable scale.[7]

Moreover, Mumford is at pains to point out that England *borrowed* many of the innovations that were key to the Industrial Revolution: '...the observations of the new industrial methods, after Adam Smith – who was too early to appraise

---

6. See above, Introduction, pp. 31–2.

7. Mumford 1934, p. 152. The excerpted text reads: 'and with the destruction of the monasteries by the same monarch, England's backwardness was only accentuated'. Whatever Mumford has in mind in terms of the negative impact the dissolution of the monasteries may have had on England's economy, he clearly has no conception that this act of property confiscation by Henry VIII may have actually *stimulated* economic growth by adding more land to the growing acreage of land in England that was subject to economic leases. For a discussion of how the monasteries may have informed improved agriculture, see Chapter One, pp. 64–5.

the transformation – were made by economists who were ignorant of the technical history of Western Europe, or who were inclined to belittle its significance. The historians failed to appreciate the debt of England's navy under Henry VIII to Italian shipbuilders, of her mining industry to imported German miners, of her waterworks and land-clearance schemes to Dutch engineers, and her silk-spinning mills to the Italian models which were copied by Thomas Lombe'.[8]

Beyond that, Mumford insists not only that we acknowledge the inventors of the machinery that was borrowed, but that we also trace the origins of the specific invention back to the first thinkers who struggled with or posed the technical problem which the invention solved. Credit must be given to all those who worked on the problems and contributed advances that ultimately led to the solution. The 'modern machine age', writes Mumford, 'cannot be understood except in terms of a very long and diverse preparation. The notion that a handful of British inventors suddenly made the wheels hum in the eighteenth century is too crude even to dish up as a fairy tale to children'.[9] Indeed, an invention does not emerge out of thin air. It arrives upon the solution to a technical problem, usually one that has been long-standing and tried at by many minds. Thus we may concede the point that the technical and scientific contributions to the mechanical innovations involved in the initial phase of Britain's Industrial Revolution came largely, if not primarily, from beyond Britain's shores. But what does this tell us about the role of technology in the British Industrial Revolution? If anything, it helps to demonstrate further that Brenner's three-region critique applies to technological as well as commercial and demographic models. A technological model could neither predict nor explain England's shift in position from economic backwater to economic and technological powerhouse. If technological advancement determines economic advancement, then how *could* Britain have achieved economic and technological superiority on the basis of borrowing continental technologies or realising the solutions to long-standing technological problems that were known throughout Europe? Here again, the question looms, what was so special about Britain?

Brenner's answer to this question, as we have seen, has to do with the differing arrangement of class relations in three different regions. Let us briefly consider the course of technological development in each region. The state-sponsored factories of seventeenth-century France were a logical expression of technological development in the context of absolutism, a society dominated by the regulatory functions of the state bureaucracy. Eastern Europe saw the return of feudalism in the fifteenth and sixteenth centuries, and where machinery was later introduced, it was typically worked by landless poor or peasants on feudal

8. Mumford 1934, p. 152.
9. Mumford 1934, p. 109.

estates seeking a source of supplementary income.[10] In Britain, the peculiar way in which the society was so commercially oriented and responsive to the market was not simply a function of the character of the people, as Landes seems to suggest, but with the social relations of agrarian capitalism that were transforming British society, and which continued to do so even after the Industrial Revolution got underway.

This chapter sets out to challenge theories that give primacy to the role of technology in historical development by demonstrating that such arguments cannot explain the where, when and how of the Industrial Revolution. The systematic and progressive application of machine technology to production upon the Industrial Revolution, and the subsequent acceleration of technological progress, did not happen because this was inevitable, or because science and engineering had reached a critical mass. It happened in a specific place: England. And it happened during a specific time period: the eighteenth century. And it happened at the same time as English agriculture was undergoing a rapid and nearly final conversion to market regulation. Over the course of the seventeenth and eighteenth centuries, agrarian capitalism continued to evolve, and as it did so it gradually exerted ever stronger economic pressures upon manufacturing, including the same market-driven compulsion to seek ways to constantly improve productivity as were already being experienced in agriculture. While the growth of population, the rise of international trade and the development of technology were all necessary and integral developments, none of these phenomena explain the transformation of class relations and the corresponding growth of an unprecedented, integrated and specialised domestic market that *preceded* the Industrial Revolution in England and Britain. In the absence of other major factors to point to, it is difficult to draw any other conclusion than that this explains why Britain was home to the first Industrial Revolution.

The ahistoricism of technological determinism

To the extent that Mumford has suggested the British Industrial Revolution can be explained by borrowing, adapting or realising exogenous technologies, he is

10. In discussing eighteenth century Bohemia, Klíma writes that in contrast to wealthier peasants there were 'the vast majority of smaller peasants whose holdings yielded barely enough to supply the essential needs of their families – and also the overwhelming majority of the landless who, to supplement their earnings from the agricultural sector (usually not sufficient to support their families), sought seasonal work in such domestic manufacturing trades as spinning and weaving, glass-making and the like. For a large section of the rural population, domestic manufacturing trades such as these continued to provide supplementary part-time employment well into the capitalist period' (Klíma 1987, pp. 208–9).

engaging in a form of technological determinism. But this is an easy charge to make, and only a handful of authors actually identify themselves as technological determinists. Most susceptible to the charge are authors of works on the history and origins of technology and technological change, and perhaps the most prominent of these is David Landes. The very title of Landes' masterful work: *The Unbound Prometheus*, suggests a technology simply waiting to be liberated of its fetters.[11] Thus Landes flirts with ideas that sound like technological determinism.[12] But Landes is no determinist; he carefully avoids single-issue explanations. The problem is that when dealing with the history of technology, it is difficult to avoid generalisations that ultimately support notions of technological determinism.[13] Any theorisation about technology, or any other 'sphere' of social interaction, is bound to involve some degree of reification, leading to the assumption that a given 'sphere' is structurally autonomous from other social spheres. When technology is treated as a structurally autonomous sphere of social relations that in and of itself 'determines' social outcomes, the charge of technological determinism can and should apply.

Much of the contemporary literature on technological determinism is preoccupied with twentieth and twenty-first century technology. The debate

11. This of course reflects the tendency to assume that which itself is most in need of explanation, just as in the case of the origin of capitalism. The text of *The Unbound Prometheus* itself largely reflects the author's exuberance for, and confidence in, technological development as progress, although Landes does manage at various junctures to recognise the social injustices that accompanied the Industrial Revolution, such as when he writes: 'For many – though by no means for all – the introduction of machinery implied for the first time a complete separation from the means of production; the worker became a "hand"... The factory was a new kind of prison; the clock a new kind of jailer' (Landes 1991, p. 43). It is important to note that despite his exuberance for technology, Landes recognises the oppression that accompanied the Industrial Revolution, even if writers such as Marx and Mumford are far more apt to emphasise the 'achievements' of the Industrial Revolution that were hardly worth celebrating.

12. Landes writes: '... it took a marriage to make the Industrial Revolution ... it required machines which not only replaced hand labour but compelled the concentration of production in factories – in other words, machines whose appetite for energy was too large for domestic sources of power and whose mechanical superiority was sufficient to break down the resistance of older forms of hand production' (Landes 1991, p. 81). Kristine Bruland reduces this quote to: 'the new factory system was "compelled" by developments in machinery', and argues that Landes' work is 'essentially determinist', as is the work of Toynbee, for whom (according to Bruland) 'British economic growth and change since 1760 was solely caused by four key innovations in textiles, and by the innovation of a new power technology, Watt's steam engine: "we find," remarked Toynbee, "the all-prominent fact to be the substitution of the factory for the domestic system, *the consequence of the mechanical discoveries of the time*"' (Bruland 1990, p. 155 citing Toynbee 1956 [Bruland's emphasis]). While we do see elements of technological determinism in the thinking of both authors, the work of both Landes and Toynbee is so much oriented toward simply providing a survey that to pin either down as a technological determinist is not possible, and Bruland's claims are overstated.

13. Chandler 2000.

thus deals with problems that arose long *after* the first systematic application of machinery to production. It is one thing to interrogate the role of technology in the emergence of the Industrial Revolution. It is another thing entirely to interrogate the role of technology within a highly technological society. However, it would seem that the debate has reached a general consensus that, at best, only a 'soft' rather than a 'hard' technological determinism makes for a viable argument. According to Fernand Braudel, the view of technology as 'pump-primer' had lost ground by the 1970s. He reminds us that despite the introduction of the power-loom after 1800, hand-loom weaving remained predominant in woollens and worsteds until the 1840s, due to the steady decline in wages earned by weavers. Only when the power-loom became more cost-effective than the handloom did weaving finally succumb to the factory. This example, writes Braudel, demonstrates how the uptake in the use of any newly introduced technology was dependent upon the state of the market.[14] The seed drill, the gig mill and the flying shuttle provide earlier examples, although in these cases custom may have played a greater part than relative market cost-effectiveness in delaying their application. Nevertheless, such examples clearly demonstrate that once a superior technology is discovered, its application will not necessarily follow immediately as a matter of course. This throws up a challenge to the concept of technological autonomy.

The ever more preponderant role that technology plays in our contemporary lives probably serves to reinforce, rather than discourage, the tendency to view technology as an autonomous force. As Heilbroner puts it, the abundance of technology creates the appearance that it is autonomous, and this is why the question of technological determinism is so important, adding that this is particularly a problem of high capitalism.[15] It is important, therefore, to proceed with caution, and to heed Usher's warning that 'technology makes sense only when

14. Braudel 1988 vol. 3, p. 567. Braudel adds that according to Chaudhuri, it was competition with Indian cottons that stimulated the development of textile machinery in Britain. So in this case, it is competition in international trade that is thought to induce technological change, another example of how technology is dependent upon the state of the market.

15. Heilbroner 1967, p. 345. In the context of capitalism or the context of a socialism based on maximising production or minimising costs, writes Heilbroner, 'the continuous appearance of technical advance and its diffusion throughout the society assume the attributes of autonomous processes... This is why, I think, the problem of technological determinism – of how machines make history – comes to us with such insistence despite the ease with which we can disprove its more extreme contentions'. '*Technological determinism is thus peculiarly a problem of a certain historic epoch* – specifically that of high capitalism and low socialism – *in which the forces of technical change have been unleashed* [*sic*], but when the agencies for the control or guidance of technology are still rudimentary' (emphasis found in the original). Heilbroner does not spell out the means by which under a truly socialist society the control or guidance of technology would move beyond the rudimentary form, but one would expect that his intent, here, is to

read forward'.[16] For it would be easy to let twentieth-century views colour our discussion of the role of technology in eighteenth-century Britain. The debate on the issue of technological determinism in the twentieth century was preoccupied with issues of human freedom, with fatalists like George Orwell, Kurt Vonnegut and Jacques Ellul viewing technological autonomy and the 'technological imperative' as a threat, whilst optimists like Alvin Toffler arguing that technology expanded the realm of human freedom. This debate has little bearing on the causal origins of the Industrial Revolution. At the same time, however, by borrowing some of the terminology of the discourse, we shall seek to refine the terms of this discussion of technological determinism.

Let us begin with the three approaches to technological determinism as identified by Bimber.[17] One of these approaches involves addressing the role of technology in terms of unintended consequences. So for example, the makers of the automobile could not foresee its detrimental effects in terms of pollution, urban congestion, suburban sprawl and so on. Bimber finds no overarching patterns, here, and concludes that the unintended consequences of technological development are merely facts of social action. If the economic and social effects of technology are unpredictable, this is a case of *in*determinacy, not determinism. It is thus worth coining the term *technological indeterminism* to describe the unintended social consequences of technological development. Another of Bimber's three approaches to technological determinism is what he calls the logical-sequence approach. This refers to the concept that technological processes require society to commit to their outcomes regardless of their desirability. Bimber cites Miller, who believes that technological developments follow a kind of naturally given logic, and are therefore not socially determined.[18] Heilbroner, in a clear-cut case of hard determinism, goes further and asserts that history itself is determined by scientific laws. The steam mill follows the hand mill, writes Heilbroner, because the steam mill represents the next 'stage' in 'a technical conquest of nature that allows one and only one grand avenue of advance'.[19] To make his case, Heilbroner points to incidences of simultaneous discovery (examples include the sewing machine) and the possibility of technological prediction (a contemporary example of which can be found in Moore's law, which successfully predicted that 'the number of transistors that could

---

suggest a reassertion of normative or communal regulation over economic processes, limiting the free play of market-forces.

16. Molella 2005, p. 786 citing Usher 1982, pp. 5 and 60 (see p. 46 in the 1954 revised edition).

17. Bimber 1990, p. 334.

18. Bimber 1990, p. 338 citing Miller 1985, p. 174 ff.

19. Heilbroner 1967, p. 336. Were Heilbroner to make this claim in terms not of technological advances *per se*, but in terms of the sequence of the discovery of scientific and technological principles, he might have a stronger case.

be placed on an integrated circuit would continue to double at short, regular intervals...').[20] Bimber concludes that the logical-sequence approach is the only one that is actually useful or applicable to technological determinism.

Bimber's third approach, the norm-based approach, refers to an absence of wilful control over technical practice. The implications of this definition are immediately familiar. Once the machine is put into a factory, the worker becomes an appendage of the machine. The repetitive action of the machine itself shapes or 'determines' how the factory is organised and operated. What is peculiarly missing from the twentieth-century debate is any discussion of the role of custom, or normative regulation over production. This is no surprise, since, as we shall explore in greater depth in the next chapters, at the very heart of the Industrial Revolution was a process of extinguishing custom in manufacturing, such that by the twentieth century customary regulation of production was no longer prevalent. Bimber concludes that the norm-based approach is not useful, which is precisely what we should expect a twentieth-century commentator to conclude. But consideration of how normative economic regulation affects the introduction of technology is highly applicable to our exploration of the Industrial Revolution in the eighteenth century. In considering the role of norms upon technological development, we may identify issues that continue to have salience in the twentieth and twenty-first centuries. For example, under industrial capitalism, efficiency of production becomes the prevailing normative standard by which the success of technological outcomes is judged,[21] at the exclusion of other norms, such as whether or not the technology is or is not harmful to the environment, or whether or not the technology serves the many or only the few. The extinguishing of customary control over production did not mean that norms disappeared; it only meant that the norms and values of capitalism became prevalent within production. But this is what is precisely taken for granted in the twentieth-century literature on technological determinism, where capitalism is effectively assumed to be a universal condition. To ask whether technology drives history begs the question of what was going on *before* the Industrial Revolution and before capitalism. And as we seek to demonstrate, it was not technology so much as capitalism that was key to the Industrial Revolution. This work seeks to argue that a pre-industrial agrarian capitalism preceded and established the capitalist economic framework that enabled the Industrial Revolution to happen at all, and that the conversion of production in

20. Ceruzzi 2005, pp. 584–93. Moore's law has held true, according to Ceruzzi, ever since it was introduced in 1965, 'although the interval soon stretched from twelve to eighteen months'. Ceruzzi concludes by asking us to 'step back from a social constructionist view of technology and consider that, in at least one instance, raw technological determinism is at work'.

21. Bimber 1990, p. 339, citing Staudenmeier 1985, p. 136 ff.

manufacturing to capitalist principles created the proper environment and may even have required the systematic application of technology to production.

In order to show why it is so problematic, let us consider some examples of technological determinism. We begin briefly by mentioning Arnold Toynbee, who wrote 'the first systematic work on British industrialisation', in which he argued 'for example that British economic growth and change since 1760 was solely caused by four key innovations in textiles, and by the innovation of a new power technology'.[22] Toynbee finds the substitution of the factory for the domestic system to be ' "the consequence of the mechanical discoveries of the time" '.[23] It is significant that Toynbee viewed machinery as having *caused* the rise of the factory, given how influential his work has been.

Turning to other examples, anthropologist Leslie A. White, in describing what he calls 'cultural systems', presents a kind of layer-cake model for the functioning of societies. He describes 'three horizontal strata' which are:

> the technological layer on the bottom, the philosophical on the top, the sociological stratum in between... The technological system is basic and primary. Social systems are functions of technologies; and philosophies express technological forces and reflect social systems. The technological factor is therefore the determinant of a cultural system as a whole. It determines the form of social systems, and technology and society together determine the content and orientation of philosophy.

Let us repeat one sentence from this quote: 'Social systems are functions of technologies'. That is about as straightforward and as 'hard' as technological determinism can get. Yet White then proceeds to qualify this passage:

> This is not to say, of course, that social systems do not condition the operation of technologies, or that social and technological systems are not affected by philosophies. They do and are. But to condition is one thing; to determine, quite another.

We are confronted here with the ambiguity of language. For in all this discussion of what determines what and what conditions what, we are of course dealing with theory at the broadest level of abstraction. To say that social systems are functions of technologies certainly sounds like a complete subordination of the social to the technological, leaving little room for other factors to do their 'conditioning'. It is thus worth mentioning at this juncture that the literature on technological determinism and that advancing a technologically deterministic

22. Bruland 1990, p. 155, again citing Toynbee 1956.
23. Ibid.

argument in particular is largely devoid of historical reference. Continuing further, White even takes us to the level of the cosmic:

> We are now in possession of a key to an understanding of the growth and development of culture: technology. A human being is a material body; the species, a material system. The planet earth is a material body; the cosmos, a material system. Technology is the mechanical means of articulation of these two material systems, man and cosmos.[24]

The reductionism and determinism of this passage is evident not only in the way in which 'primacy' is assigned to the 'technological system', but also in the way that 'technology' is reduced to 'mechanical means', as if knowledge played either a secondary role or no role at all in this system.

White's three-level ontological system bears a strong resemblance to theoretical elaborations of Marx's base-superstructure metaphor taken to its (il)logical extreme. In the hands of Stalinist determinism and Althusserian structuralism, the metaphor of the economic 'base' as what 'determines' the social superstructure became the basis for an economic determinism so rigid that Wood is left to conclude that it 'has always been more trouble than it is worth'.[25] It was, after all, intended as a metaphor, a short-hand way of expressing a highly sophisticated conjuncture of social relations. Another overstated quote from Marx is his famous aphorism: 'The hand-mill gives you society with the feudal lord; the steam-mill society with the industrial capitalist'. This well-worn phrase has been taken as proof that Marx was a technological determinist. In reviewing the debate on this topic, Bimber concludes that Marx believed that technology was ultimately at the service of humanity and that in general technology is more of an enabling factor than a cause.[26] At the heart of the controversy is how Marx understood the relation between what he termed the productive forces and the relations of production. On the one side, G.A. Cohen, Robert Heilbroner and William Shaw defend the view that Marx's intent was to proffer a theory of the primacy of the productive forces. Against this view, Robert Brenner and Joshua Cohen have argued that the forces of production have no primacy over aggregate human factors.[27]

---

24. White 1969, pp. 366–7. Interestingly, Chandler leaves out the latter half of this quote, beginning with 'This is not to say...' In other words, he leaves out the qualification. While White's qualification does not save him from the charge of technological determinism, it nonetheless appears as an attempt to avoid the charge. Note White's use of the word 'articulation,' which suggests the influence of the 'articulation of modes of production' school of Althusserian Marxism. For a discussion, see Comninel 1987, pp. 95–103.

25. Wood 1995, p. 49. We shall hear more from Wood on this point below.

26. Bimber 1990, p. 34.

27. Ibid.

In his impressive, sweeping and quite ahistorical opus *Karl Marx's Theory of History: A Defense*, G.A. Cohen advances what he describes as a '"technological" interpretation of historical materialism'. Cohen's argument runs as follows. Productive forces – which incorporate not only the technology embodied in the means of production but also the labour-power and the raw materials processed by labour and machinery combined – do not constitute a subset of production relations, and are not a part of the economic structure. Instead, argues Cohen, Marx intended the term 'productive forces' to refer to 'objects' bearing the property of productive power, as opposed to 'relations'. While the legal and political superstructure arises out of the economic structure constituted by production-relations, Cohen represents productive forces as something developing *autonomously* of production relations and thus as a 'material' force distinct from the 'social' milieu of economic relations. Cohen argues that Marx assigned primacy to the productive forces, such that the level of development of the productive forces explains the nature of the production relations of a given society.[28] According to Cohen's reading of Marx, production relations constitute the economic structure, 'the "real foundation" upon which a superstructure arises'. And the economic structure is 'the sum total of production relations ... provisionally construed as sets of rights of persons over productive forces'.[29] Cohen substitutes the concept of rights over productive forces for the concept of property in order to expunge the superstructural element of law from the equation.[30] This last step is the real *coup de grâce* against 'social' or 'political' readings of Marx and Engels' historical materialism. History proceeds according to the level of development of the productive forces, which explains the nature of social production relations, which in turn support the nature of the legal system and the state (the superstructure). The development of class relations, legal-property relations, cultural relations and so on can be explained according to the level of the productive forces, which can be qualitative (as in technological development) or quantitative (as in pyramid building). Yet capitalism is the only mode of production that systematically develops the forces of production. Cohen notes that in the *Grundrisse*, Marx pointed out that 'Between the full development of [the] foundation of industrial society and the patriarchal condition, many intermediate stages, endless nuances [occur]'.[31] Nevertheless, claims Cohen: '[even while the] "end-

28. Cohen 2000, pp. 134–5 and 142–50 backs this up with his own favourable (and highly questionable) interpretation of a long list of quotations taken from Marx's writings. He qualifies this statement by adding that 'it is sometimes the sheer quantity of power, sometimes its qualitative embodiment, and sometimes both, in which explanation resides'.
29. Cohen 2000, pp. 142–50.
30. Cohen 2000, pp. 216–9.
31. Marx 1973, p. 193.

less nuances" in pre-capitalist class history resist theorisation as sets of production relations whose succession reflects a series of rises in the level of productive power... the resulting damage to historical materialism, on our strongly technological construal of it, is smaller than at first might appear'.[32]

To explore Cohen's attempt at damage control on this point, we must introduce another of Marx's well-known formulas.

In his earlier writings, Marx asserted that at a given stage in history, the development of the productive forces reaches a level at which the social relations of production constitute a 'fetter' on their further development, necessitating social revolution to remove the fetters and allow the further development of the productive forces. The key word here is 'stage', since in this formulation, Marx and Engels more or less uncritically adopted the four-stages approach to history from the liberal historians of their day, an approach premised upon the idea of a natural progression of technology based upon the unfolding of the division of labour.[33] In brushing aside the above-mentioned discomfiting observation, Cohen offers his own version of this four-stage theory. Since capitalism represents the third stage, and socialism the fourth, only two moments of transition in previous history require explanation according to the fetters paradigm: the transition from pre-capitalist class society to capitalist society, and, prior to that, the transition from pre-class society to pre-capitalist class society after the Neolithic revolution at the end of the last Ice Age.[34] In this way, Cohen avoids having to deal with such 'lesser' transitions (now reduced to the status of 'nuances') as the collapse of the Roman Empire, or the emergence of feudalism, in terms of the fetters paradigm. In his attempt at damage control, Cohen argues that it is possible to explain the 'endless nuances' between patriarchal society and capitalism by pointing out that different types of productive forces present different sets of economic needs, and as a result different sets of production relations arise.[35] In short, Cohen essentially dodges the problem.

Here, we have an interpretation of the theory of historical materialism resting on the claim that historical development is primarily determined by the level of the productive forces, in which the development of technology is a central feature. And yet the author simply brushes aside the discomfiting observation that little historical evidence exists to support the idea that pre-capitalist history was characterised by the progressive development of the productive forces and technology (!). This serves as a dramatic example of how far the structuralist reading

32. Cohen 2000, p. 200.

33. This incorporation of liberal thought by Marx and Engels into their theory has been revealed and subjected to critique by Comninel 1987, pp. 140–63.

34. Cohen 2001, pp. 198–201.

35. Cohen 2000, p. 201.

of historical materialism has been preoccupied with theory at the expense of history. Cohen inspires even less confidence in his theory when in his conclusion he expresses his own doubts about its validity, writing: 'I have come to wonder whether the theory which [this] book defends is true...I do not now believe that historical materialism is false, but I am not sure how to tell whether or not it is true'.[36] Might history serve as a guide? If the historical record does not provide a sufficient measure for checking the validity of one's theory of socio-economic development, what else would?

Furthermore, as we saw in the Introduction, Marx eventually broke with the liberal and techno-functionalist conception of property relations (and therein, the productive forces) as mere appendages to the division of labour, in favour of a theory which saw the structure of property relations, not the forces of production, as governing the overall direction of economic change.[37] It is not difficult to understand why Cohen finds it an attractive proposition to imagine it were possible to explain historical and social development in terms of the growth of technology and the productive forces 'determining' the outcomes of class struggles and social development in general. If the theory were true, it would lighten the burden on historical explanation by an enormous factor, since all we would need to do is study the development of the productive forces, while the study of social relations could be relegated to the function of mopping up the details. As Wood explains, Cohen's technological determinism: 'means that the "natural" impulses which propel the material sphere – the development of the technical forces – prevail over, and in one way or another causally determine, the historical development of social forms. The premise is that there is a natural and perennial impulse, independent of social and historical conditions, grounded in human nature and rationality, toward the improvement of technological forces'.[38]

By giving primacy to the 'natural' (as opposed to social) development of the productive forces, Cohen reproduces precisely the tendency of the political economists to naturalise and universalise economic relations, and capitalist social relations in particular, that Marx and Engels were at pains to argue against. The political economists tended to simply assume that history was guided by 'natural' and perennial forces, involving the extension of the division of labour, which in turn facilitated its further extension and the improvement of technology. Marx and Engels demanded, instead, that social and economic changes be understood in their historical specificity, and in terms of the outcomes of class struggles resulting in new structures of property relations rooted in

36. Cohen 2000, p. 341.
37. See above, Introduction, p. 20.
38. Wood 1981, p. 70.

class structures involving domination and exploitation.[39] They sought to demonstrate precisely that the division of labour and class relations were not 'natural', but were in fact social constructions. Societies based upon stratification had developed out of societies that once knew social egalitarianism. The exploitation of one class by another was not an eternal law, but was a social relationship that had been constructed by human beings and could therefore be dismantled by human beings as well. To the extent that most non-Marxist scholarship has not dealt with questions of the origins of class exploitation and capitalism on these terms, the tendency to treat technological development as something happening independently of specific social and historical conditions and independently of class relations and class struggles is widespread, even within theories that are not explicitly based upon a technological determinism. It is thus one of the great ironies in the of history of scholarship that historical materialism was developed into a rigidly deterministic theory, beginning in the Second International and culminating in the official Marxism of the Soviet Union under Stalin, and that subsequently Marx's theory of historical materialism came to be dismissed on the grounds that it was determinist.

While brushing aside the charge of technological determinism, Cohen does not directly refute it.[40] Presumably Cohen would embrace the term 'productive force determinism', a term which Shaw coins to emphasise that 'productive

39. Notwithstanding writings by Marx and Engels which reproduce liberal technological determinism. It 'must be admitted that support for such determinism can genuinely be found in a number of brief statements of [Marx and Engels'] work...' (Comninel 1987, p. 154).

40. Wood claims that 'Cohen's object is to establish that historical materialism is a technological determinism' (Wood 1981, p. 70). Cohen argues that critics of the primacy thesis argue that it is demeaning to humanity and so cannot be attributed to Marx. 'Those who take this line stigmatize the thesis as "technological determinism", and complain that it presents machinery and allied subhuman powers as the agencies of history. On the technological view – so it is felt – the inhuman prevails against men'. (Note the centrality of machinery in the formulation of productive forces as 'machinery and allied subhuman powers'.) Setting up the problem thus, Cohen then dismisses the criticism, responding with the argument that 'the development of the productive forces is centrally an enrichment of human labour-power' and therefore 'the emphasis on technology loses its dehumanizing appearance'. This is a peculiar defence, since it hinges on a moral judgment of technology, not the question of whether or not the theory is staking a claim that technological development determines social change. It needs little reminding that the question of whether or not a theory is based upon a technological determinism bears no inherent relationship to the question of whether or not technology can be dehumanising. Yet having cast the matter in these terms, Cohen then skirts the question entirely, writing in a footnote: 'Technological determinism is, presumably, two things: it is technological, and it is determinist. One may envisage a non-technological determinism, and, as it were a technological non-determinism. Our version of historical materialism may be called technological, but the issue of determinism will not be discussed in this book' (Cohen 2000, p. 147).

forces' includes more than machinery and technology.[41] The deterministic reading of historical materialism by G.A. Cohen and others is, in the last instance, deeply rooted in a technological determinism that requires expunging not only such superstructural elements as the legal system and the state from the hallowed sphere of 'pure theory', but historical specificity as well.

Lewis Mumford, while not a Marxist, puts forward a theory based upon three historical 'phases' in the history of technics. Mumford's use of the term 'technics' closely resembles the meaning of the term 'productive forces', though it puts a greater emphasis on collective knowledge and science. The eotechnic phase dates from the tenth century. This phase is associated with wood and water, and its machines include the water mill, the windmill, the printing press and the wooden lathe. The paleotechnic phase, dating from the eighteenth century (and so naturally corresponding with the early Industrial Revolution) is associated with iron and coal, and its machines include of course the steam engine, the power-loom and other power-machinery built from iron. The neotechnic phase is associated with 'instantaneous personal communication over long-distances' and the application of science to 'every phase of human experience and every manifestation of life'.[42] This includes the application of liquid fuels and mechanical stokers, which emancipated 'a race of galley slaves, the stoker, those miserable driven men' whose work was cruel.[43] This is not a rigid stage theory; all three phases can and do persist even today. Mumford showers scorn on what he sees as the dehumanising aspects of the paleotechnic phase, in contrast with the liberating aspects of the neotechnic.[44] While clearly not an example of hard

41. Shaw 1979, p. 158. Shaw only uses the term 'productive force determinism' to put a fine point on his explicit embrace of technological determinism, as he attributes it to Marx.

42. Mumford 1934, pp. 241 and 217.

43. Mumford 1934, p. 235.

44. This scorn anticipates the flourishing of critiques of modernism under the banner of post-modernism in the late twentieth century. Critics of modernity writing under the banner of post-modernism would embrace Mumford's scorn for paleotechnic notions of progress when Mumford (Mumford 1934, pp. 182–3) writes, with a strong dose of sarcasm: 'In the nature of progress, the world would go on forever and forever in the same direction, becoming more humane, more comfortable, more peaceful, more smooth to travel in, and above all, much more rich... With the rapid development of machines, the vague eighteenth century doctrine received new confirmation in the nineteenth century. The laws of progress became self-evident: were not new machines being invented every year? Were they not transformed by successive modifications? Did not chimneys draw better, were not houses warmer, had not railroads been invented?... Here was a convenient measuring stick for historical comparison. Assuming that progress was a reality, if the cities of the nineteenth century were dirty, the cities of the thirteenth century must have been six centuries dirtier: for had not the world become constantly cleaner?' Writing five decades later, Mumford (Mumford 1970, p. 199) describes the doctrine of progress thus: 'those who favored progress simple-mindedly believed that evils were the property of the past and that only by moving away from the past as rapidly as possible could a

technological determinism, Mumford's writing is deeply imbued with notions that could be characterised as soft technological determinism.

Karl Polanyi, despite his insights on the implications of turning land, labour and money into commodities, appears to follow a technological model in his description of how the conversion to market society came about. For Polanyi, this transformation was 'so complete that it resembles more the metamorphosis of the caterpillar than any alteration that can be expressed in terms of continuous growth and development'.[45] Polanyi points to large-scale machinery, which requires an economy of scale and a high volume of goods sold in order to be profitable. This in turn requires that all transactions be 'turned into money transactions, and these in turn require that a medium of exchange be introduced into every articulation of industrial life'.[46] Elsewhere, he clarifies that: 'It was not the coming of the machine as such but the invention of elaborate and therefore specific machinery and plant which completely changed the relationship of the merchant to production',[47] a decisive shift in which manufacturing ceased to be an accessory to commerce, and grew to relatively greater importance. Once industry grew in complexity, inputs of land, labour and money had to be safeguarded for its use, and this necessitated that these elements of production be commodified, even if the commodification of whole parts of human societies is ultimately fictitious.

From these examples, we see that the notion of technology as the 'prime mover' of the industrial revolution can be found in many differing epistemologies. The tendency of political economists and liberal historians to naturalise history and universalise capitalism, based upon a stages theory of history, which was initially and uncritically incorporated into historical materialism, resurfaces in various subsequent theories of history based upon or including some form of technological determinism. While Cohen's work may represent one of the most *explicit* examples one can find of an attempt to put forward a theory of history based upon technological determinism, imputing this theory to Marx, the Smithian tendency to naturalise the economy and assume a teleological development for technology remains widely unchallenged and is therefore *im*plicit in much or perhaps even most non-Marxist scholarship.[48]

The point of this discussion is not to simply condemn all forms of technological determinism. As noted, any discussion of technological change or the

better future be assured' (as cited in Chandler 2000). While these statements anticipate or dovetail with postmodernism, Mumford's relative optimism for the neotechnic phase would both resonate with and clash with the later work of modernity's critics.

45. Polanyi 1957, p. 42.
46. Polanyi 1957, p. 41.
47. Polanyi 1957, pp. 74–5.
48. Molella 2005, p. 785.

history of technology can scarcely avoid explaining technological development on its own terms. The point has been to problematise the tendency and to briefly explore the development of the concept, and its historical origins in scholarship. In explicating the historical progression of scientific discovery and technological innovation, there is a seductive tendency to get caught up in the perception that human history in general is one long series of innovations with new technologies being the end results of the historical process that mark its stages of development. This tendency does not merely promote such a myopic view of history focused upon technological change. It also supplants cause and effect within the sphere of science and technology for cause and effect in the relationship between science and technology, on the one hand, and social and historical development, on the other. In other words, the insularity and circularity involved in the tendency to engage in technological determinism reproduces theories that are either devoid of historical specificity, or that produce history devoid of any serious examination of the way social relationships are structured and the process of their evolution in real human societies.

The technology of antiquity

Mechanical devices capable of being applied to production and of improving the productivity of manufacturing have been in existence since ancient times, but by themselves these technologies did not bring about an industrial revolution. Why? If the prime mover behind socio-economic change in history is technology, or technics or the 'material' productive forces, why did the Industrial Revolution not begin in ancient China, in the Roman Empire, in fourteenth-century Venice or in seventeenth-century Holland? Shaw argues that capitalism failed to take root in ancient Rome because the level of the productive forces was insufficient.[49] But without a measure of what would constitute a sufficient level of the productive forces to precipitate the development of capitalism, this is little more than a tautological argument. Pre-capitalist societies were certainly capable of producing goods matching the quality of those produced under capitalist conditions. 'Such ancient handicraft products as linen and porcelain . . . were clearly as good as, if not better than, modern manufactured goods. Mechanisation allows production in volume and reduction in cost, but neither guarantees superior products'.[50]

Productive volume and the ability to cheapen the product were mainly what pre-capitalist modes of production lacked, not the ability to produce quality

49. Shaw 1979, p. 163.
50. Molella 2004, pp. 786–7, following Usher.

goods. But did ancient or medieval societies possess the technical knowledge or the component parts they would have needed had they been compelled to industrialise? Let us have a brief look at the historical record.

Fire is arguably the oldest and most fundamental technology of human society, its use dating back approximately 600,000 years. The myth of Prometheus stealing fire from the gods and giving it to man is just one variant of a universal myth found in all cultures.[51] The use of fire precedes the advent of clothing, shelter, the spear and the spear-thrower or *atlatl*, the axe, painting, the bow and arrow, ceramics and pottery, the needle, the paintbrush, the harpoon, the net, boats, rope, basket-weaving and the hammer, all of which date to 10000 BCE or earlier. We now know that trepanation (brain surgery) was practiced from the late Stone Age.[52] Not long after the end of the last Ice Age, with the beginnings of permanent settlement and agriculture (with granaries and alcoholic beverages following soon after), several key innovations preceded the formation of the earliest states in Egypt, Mesopotamia, the Indus Valley and the Andes. Between 7000 and 5000 BCE the spindle (or distaff), metal-working, bricks, the grindstone and irrigation were all discovered. These early civilisations were thus able to produce clothing; metalwares; houses, temples, ziggurats and pyramids; flour and grow crops during dry seasons. On the eve of the formation of the earliest states, between 5000 and 3000 BCE writing; ink and papyrus; sailing vessels; canals; nails; cement; plywood; the wheel and the cart; the yoke; glass; silk and barbed fishhooks all made their appearance. Around 3500 BCE bronze was discovered, allowing two crucial innovations essential to the formation of states: the bronze sword and the bronze plough.

Improved weaponry meant it was now possible to organise coercive violence in the form of militias as never before, enabling rulers to rule and conquerors to subjugate foreign peoples possessing inferior arms. This statement would appear to be an example of technological determinism. Indeed, the notion that states arose out of the technologies developed in the wake of the Neolithic Revolution

51. Campbell 1988, pp. 127–8 views the Greek myth of the theft of fire from the gods by Prometheus as a universal theme in all cultures, a foundational act in the evolution of human civilisation. 'Often, it's a trickster animal or bird that steals the fire and then passes it along to a relay team of birds or animals who run with it. Sometimes the animals are burned by the flames as they pass the fire along, and this is said to account for their different colorings... The fire theft sets man apart from the animals. When you're in the woods at night, you light a fire, and that keeps the animals away. You can see their eyes shining, but they're outside the fire range... [The fire theft myth is meant] to evaluate the fire, its importance to us, and to say something about what has set man apart from the beasts' (Campbell 1988, pp. 197–228).

52. The practice was apparently widespread: 'Trepanned skulls have now been discovered at burial sites of most of the great civilizations of the past, from the megalithic builders of ancient Europe to the Incas of Peru' (James and Thorpe 1994, p. 24). For a fuller discussion, see Rudgeley 1999, p. 9.

would seem to concur with G.A. Cohen's suggestion that the only revolution made necessary by the growth in the level of the productive forces outstripping the capacity of the social relations of production and necessitating social revolution prior to the advent of capitalism came with the transition from pre-class to class society. Yet we must pose a chicken-and-the-egg problem, here. For what gave rise to the need for weaponry? Was it external aggression? Or did large and aggressive societies first arise through the process of social stratification? Stratified societies are those in which two persons of the same sex and age group do not enjoy equal access to society's productive surplus. Morton Fried argues that the preservation of stratification required the organisation of coercive violence in order to prevent the return to a form of society based on egalitarian principles, which for Fried is the same as saying that it required the formation of the state.[53] If Fried's suggestion is correct then a transformation in the social relations governing production and distribution of the social surplus may have been the cause of state formation and may have called forth the demand for superior weaponry in the form of bronze. Of course, it is possible that this need was conditioned by both indigenous and exogenous factors. Yet even in the case of the exogenous threat of war, the need to form and equip a militia may precede the discovery of the weaponry that that militia will deploy. The discovery of a new technology opens up new possibilities, but the search for a solution that leads to that discovery may in almost every case arise out of perceived social needs conditioned by changes in social relations. So is the technology cause or effect?

Gandhi's famous quip in response to being asked what he thought of Western civilisation – that he thought it would be a good idea – is more than a light-hearted joke. States have been with us for 5,000 years now, and show little signs of going away. 'Civilisation' in general (not just in the West) is generally associated with the formation of states, because with that development, societies grew larger, more complex and the pace of technological development quickened. Stratified societies have bequeathed both the abundant fruits of advanced civilisation in terms of technology and the arts, alongside the ever-expanding capacity of state societies to commit acts of destruction, violence and even annihilation of whole populations. States have, therefore, left behind a very mixed legacy. It is, after all, the improvements in the quality of life brought about by advances in technology which have always been cited in order to justify the continuation of states. A large measure of these technological advances arose out of improvements in the means of warfare. Early states developed such civilising innovations as soap, rulers, currency, standardised weights and the toilet in Mesopotamia; the alphabet and glass vessels in Phoenicia; the balance, the

53. Fried 1967.

swape (well sweep),[54] the shower, candles, copper surgical instruments,[55] the water clock and the sundial in Egypt; the tidal dock, buttons, the artificial sewage system and dentistry in the Indus Valley; bells, coins and silk looms in China. At the same time, we enter the age of the chariot (Mesopotamia) and body armour (Greece) – the age of organised warfare.[56] The Scandinavians gave us the sledge, or sled, in the first millennium. The Mayans and Aztecs made shoes, cloth and balls for sport out of rubber as early as 1600 BCE.

Between the onset of the Iron Age around 1100 BCE and the development of classical antiquity around 500 BCE, ships and wagons underwent considerable improvement, and the range of carpenters' tools was widely extended to include: lathes, saws, pegs, shears, scythes, axes, picks and shovels.[57] While most of the inventions mentioned thus far have endured until modern times, we find little evidence in pre-classical antiquity of mechanical devices involving the transmission of power by way of a transmitting mechanism to the tool or device working some object or raw material.[58] The exception is the swape, which demonstrated the principle of the lever. By the time we get to classical antiquity, the principle of the lever is manifested in what Hero of Alexandria described as the five simple machines ' "by which a given weight may be moved by a given force" ': the wheel, the axle, the pulley, the wedge and the screw. These provided the building blocks of mechanics. Treating the lever itself as the sixth of these, only the seventh of the fundamental devices was lacking:

> no form of crank motion appears in any of the evidence. Nearly all the elementary pairs appear. We find the five other kinematic 'chains': the *screw* chain, the *wheel* chain, the *cam* chain, the *ratchet* chain, and the *pulley* chain. The *crank* chain only is missing. The treadle attachment to produce rotary motion is the earliest form of this type of mechanism; it does not appear until later. We may thus say that this period is concerned with fundamental statements of elementary principles and with the study of motion. The development

54. The swape involved one of the earliest examples of the lever. 'The lever appears in the well sweep (swape) which is to be found in Egypt as early as 1550 BCE under the name of "shaduf," and in India as the picotab' (Usher 1982, p. 122).

55. James and Thorpe 1994, p. 12.

56. Platt 1994.

57. Mokyr 1990, p. 19, n. 1.

58. Usher writes: 'The term "machine" presents an almost hopeless problem. Popular usage is extremely lax . . . The general position is concisely stated by Marx: "All fully-developed machinery consists of three essentially differentiated parts, the motor mechanism, the transmitting mechanism, and finally the tool or working machine". This definition ignores the distinction that can advisedly be made between mechanical elements and an extensive train of mechanism. The history of invention is more readily understood as a cumulative process if it is actually analyzed as a progressive development of larger and more elegant trains of mechanism, which are synthesized and composed by the arrangement of individual parts to achieve specific objectives' (Usher 1982, pp. 116–17).

> and applications of power involved changes in scale rather than changes in principle.[59]

Thus the mechanical achievements of pre-Christian antiquity were concerned mainly with facility in the production of motion, and were limited to 'the lowest-power units, with only the smallest extensions beyond the field of human muscular effort'.[60] But while classical antiquity may not have excelled in mechanics, excellence was achieved in other technologies: in science, mathematics and geometry, in medicine, architecture and coinage. The mechanical devices that existed did not necessarily come into widespread use, and were not systematically applied to production. Economic growth derived instead 'from those aspects for which the Greeks and Romans are famous: organization, trade, order, the use of money, and law'.[61] In stark contrast to the way in which the Industrial Revolution was led by private enterprise, it was in public works that the Romans excelled.

> The history of the Roman Empire, especially, reveals the importance of men such as Agrippa and Apollodorus, who helped their respective masters (Augustus and Trajan) carry out vast public works. The Rome of 100 A.D. had better paved streets, sewage disposal, water supply, and fire protection than the capitals of civilised Europe in 1800. Most agriculture, manufacturing, and services were carried out by the private sector, however, and achievements there were few and slow.[62]

Roman architecture was mainly borrowed from the Greeks and the Etruscans. The Romans excelled in the use of the arch, building aqueducts and bridges, and in the use of cement, out of which the dome of the Pantheon was built, one of Rome's greatest architectural achievements. The Greeks and Romans also excelled in hydraulics, applying the water pump to a range of activities from mine drainage to firefighting.[63]

In military technology, the major advances came less in technological advances than in the form of military organisation, as was reflected in the *scutum*, the large, curved shields that allowed the legionnaires to form a wall and march forward against their foe, driving them back, anticipating modern crowd-control

59. Usher 1982, p. 160.
60. Ibid.
61. Mokyr (ed.) 1990, pp. 19 and 29.
62. Mokyr (ed.) 1990, p. 20.
63. The Romans regularly flooded the floor of the Colosseum for water games on ships. As of 1997, research was ongoing in order to discover how the Colosseum could be flooded and then drained in time to hold gladiator competitions on the same day (author's interview with researchers during personal visit to the Colosseum, Rome, Italy, September 1997).

tactics. The Greeks introduced the catapult around 400 BCE and it remained the largest instrument of war down to the age of cannons. The Romans improved upon Greek weaponry mainly by making them larger.[64]

Two inventions of the classical era are of particular interest with respect to the Industrial Revolution. The first of these is the waterwheel, invented in Greece around 85 BCE. Its predecessors were the chain of pots and the *noria*, both first noted by Philo of Byzantium in the third century BCE.[65] The *noria* was a wheel turned by a stream capable of lifting water to somewhat less than half its height. The step from *noria* to waterwheel involved gearing or a 'train of mechanism' to transmit the power from the motion of the turning of the wheel to drive a device, which in the case of the Greek invention involved the turning of a millstone. This appears to be the only use to which waterwheels were applied down to the fifth century CE. While the *noria* resembled the modern upright waterwheel, the early Greek waterwheels lay horizontal in the stream. The earliest upright waterwheels were undershot wheels, and could be as large as 40 feet in diameter. The more efficient overshot wheel, which harnessed the power of gravity rather than the motion of the stream, was not known until the third century CE. How widespread the use of the waterwheel was in Roman times is still a matter of speculation, though it is certain that its use stretched all the way to Britain.[66] However, just as the steam engine later offered the advantage of mobility, the Romans often favoured the donkey mill because it could be located anywhere. The other invention that draws our attention is the *aeolipile*, sometimes referred to as the steam engine. It was invented by Hero of Alexandria of the late first century CE.[67] This device was applied to open temple doors, not really for productive purposes, but with the same function in mind as the coin-operated vending machine (also invented by Hero): to awe the faithful. Hero is also credited with measuring instruments such as the *dioptra* for surveying and the *theodolite* for measuring angles. Alexandria produced another great inventor in the third century BCE: Ctesibius, who is credited with the invention of the force pump, the hydraulic organ, the water clock and metal springs. Since many devices made of wood and leather have not endured the centuries, and given

64. Mokyr (ed.) 1990, pp. 21–5; Platt 1994. The Chinese had invented the trebuchet by around 500 BCE.

65. Usher 1982, p. 131.

66. The Romans used the waterwheel in the goldmines of West Wales and for grinding corn. Two examples of wheels for grinding corn can be found at Hadrian's wall. 5,600 wheels were recorded in the *Domesday* (Museum of Science and Industry, Manchester, visit by author, November 1997). Usher 1982, pp. 80 and 181, comments: 'Domesday is probably the most extensive enumeration of mills in this early period. A complete list of all the mills and their rentals is given by Bennett and Elton. The striking feature is the wide range in yearly rental values'. See also Mokyr (ed.) 1990, p. 27.

67. Mokyr (ed.) 1990, p. 22.

the destruction of Rome by its invaders, it is possible that the level of classical age technology was more advanced than we know. Indeed, recent archaeology suggests that the Romans were capable of applying gears and turntables akin to modern ball and rolling bearings. The discovery of the Antikythera, a highly sophisticated astrolabe built in the first century CE capable of reproducing the motions of the Sun, the Moon and the planets, has prompted one scientist (who reconstructed the device) to suggest that '"Men who built this could have built almost any mechanical device they wanted to."'[68] But Mokyr is more cautious, arguing that the Antikythera only demonstrates that classical civilisation had 'mastered the use of gears and applied geometry beyond what was previously believed possible... [and]...had the intellectual potential to create complicated technical devices. The question remains why so little of this potential was realized and translated into economic progress'.[69] A full answer would require an exploration of classical economics, a subject which lies well outside the scope of the present work.

Let us note, however, that the Romans had the ability to harness the power of water and steam and the ability to construct highly sophisticated mechanisms with complex gearing, technologies which later made essential contributions to the Industrial Revolution. Moreover, Rome had established the greatest commercial empire in Europe before modern times, and this enabled the Romans to absorb technologies from the peoples they conquered or traded with – stone arches, paved streets, false teeth and sewers from the Etruscans; transparent glass and shipping techniques from the Phoenicians; wooden barrels, spoked wheels, the hub-box, soap and enamelling from the Celts; to say nothing of what technologies the Romans borrowed from the Greeks, the Egyptians and the Chinese. The Roman Empire also experienced enormous population growth. Thus all three models: the technological, commercial and demographic, are faced with the enormous challenge of explaining why Roman civilisation with its high levels of technology, trade and population growth, did not undergo an industrial revolution, and why, over a millennium later, Britain did.

Medieval to early modern technology

In considering the origins of the technology that was known in Europe at the time of the Industrial Revolution, the degree to which Europe lapsed into the state of virtually being a technological backwater is often left unmentioned. It is

68. Price 1975, p. 48 as cited in Mokyr (ed.) 1990, p. 22.

69. Mokyr (ed.) 1990, pp. 22–3. The Antikythera mechanism 'could predict the Sun and Moon trajectories over decades and calculate a lunar anomaly that gave headaches to Isaac Newton himself' (Anitei 2006).

important for its own sake to acknowledge that the Europeans had no monopoly on invention, and during the so-called 'Dark Ages' of Europe, other civilisations discovered or made use of technologies that were still unknown to Europe. While the pre-Columbian civilisations of the Americas had no contact with, and thus could not have contributed to the science and technology of, Europe, we have only recently begun to gain an adequate appreciation of their accomplishments. Consider, for example, that while in the early eighteenth century the Archbishop Usher of Armagh in Ireland calculated that the Earth was created at 9:00 a.m. on 26 October 4004 BCE, a thousand years prior to the making of that calculation the Mayans had calculated the age of the cosmos to be 90 million years old. This is considerably closer to current scientific views that the earth is at least 4.4 billion years old and the universe about 13.7 billion years old.[70] Builders of pyramids and astronomical observatories, Mayan calendars predicted astrological events with great accuracy. The earliest known use of a symbol for the number zero as a place-holder in a numerical system is found in the Mayan Long Count calendar, which dates to 36 BCE.[71] While Ptolemy was using a symbol for zero as a place-holder by 130 CE, the actual symbol for our modern zero originates in Cambodia and Indonesia in the late seventh century and was brought to Europe by the Arab mathematician Mohammed ibn Al-khwarizmi in the eighth century.[72] The use of zero in the Hindu-Arabic system as a decimal digit arrived in Europe in the eleventh century. While Mayan civilisation fell into decline from the tenth century on, we now know that Andean civilisation had a virtually unbroken history from 2500 BCE to the arrival of the Conquistadors. In Meso-America, the Spaniards were astonished at the sise of Aztec capital city Tenochtitlan, which had between 200,000 and 700,000 inhabitants at the time the Europeans arrived. In North America, the city at the site of Cahokia (near St. Louis) had between 5,000 and 40,000 inhabitants at its height, which was between 1000 and 1300 CE. The population of London at this time was 1,500.[73]

India gave us sugar, the waterwheel, the water mill and wootz steel between 500 and 350 BCE. The surgeon Sushruta recorded the first known use of

70. Despite the destruction of the Mayan libraries by the Spanish in 1562 CE, the deciphering of Mayan hieroglyphs since the 1950s has begun the process of gaining a greater appreciation for the achievements of this civilisation. Even today, we are only entering the golden age of Mayan archaeology.

71. It is possible that the concept of zero was not invented by the Mayans, but was actually inherited from their predecessors, the Olmecs.

72. Platt 1994, p. 17.

73. The city was abandoned after 1300 for reasons still unknown. Scientists have discovered that the diamond-shaped plaza of the city, a mile long on each side, was expertly levelled. It remains the largest man-made plaza in the world today (Cahokia Mounds Museum at the Cahokia Mounds State Historic Site, visit by author, 1998).

plastic surgery sometime after 200 BCE.[74] The first stirrups (for the big toe only) appeared in India around 100 BCE. In the sixth century CE innoculation against smallpox was devised, but whether in India or China is still in dispute. In the tenth century, Indian sailors devised fore-and-aft rigging and the lateen sail. The first spinning wheel was developed by textile workers in India between the sixth and early eleventh centuries.

The Chinese had discovered magnetism and the primitive compass[75] by the fourth century BCE and the crossbow by the third century BCE. They had excelled in horse riding for a millennium before the introduction of the saddle sometime in the first century CE, along with the stern-mounted rudder, followed by paper[76] in 105 CE. Chinese inventor Zhang Heng invented the water-powered armillary, the first seismometer and the odometer in the second century CE. The wheelbarrow appeared in China in the third century, and paired stirrups by the fourth. Buddhist monk Yi Xing developed the first escapement mechanism in the eighth century to control the inner workings of an armillary. In the ninth century, the Chinese developed the *camera obscura* and bookprinting, followed by gunpowder, the solid rocket, the banknote, and the canal lock in the tenth, and movable type printing (Bi Sheng) in the eleventh, and the cannon and bead abacus in the thirteenth. Nearly all of these inventions would eventually find their way to Europe and would have a transformative impact. The Chinese were meanwhile improving their silk-reeling machines, which developed into a spinning wheel that twisted the threads together before reeling them onto a bobbin. The spinning wheel only reached Europe in the early fourteenth century, and is a machine so basic in its importance to textile manufacturing in Britain and Europe that we sometimes take it for granted. Sandpaper appeared in China in the fourteenth century, the toothbrush in the sixteenth.[77]

---

74. James and Thorpe 1994, p. 21.

75. The *sinan* was composed of a ladle made with magnetic iron ore set on a polished surface as a crude compass. It was actually employed by Jade miners who used it to keep the bearings on long journeys. The use of a magnetic needle as a compass was possibly discovered much earlier, in Meso-America, by the Olmecs (James and Thorpe 1994, pp. 93–7).

76. 'The Chinese guarded the secret of papermaking jealously; it did not reach Europe for more than a thousand years'. Subsequent Chinese inventions involving paper were the stencil (500 CE), paper money (618 CE), and movable type (c. 1040 CE), and the Chinese also adapted wood-block printing from the Japanese (740 CE), (Platt, 1994) Europeans were still replacing papyrus with parchments in the 800s. Paper reached Europe in twelfth century, but paper did not begin to realise its full potential in Europe until Gutenberg invented the printing press in the 1450s.

77. Toothpaste had appeared in Egypt in the fourth century CE. Apparently it was used more as a mouth rinse prior to the appearance of the toothbrush, that is, for eleven centuries.

The collapse of the Western Empire and the survival of a continuous and highly urbanised civilisation in the Eastern Empire, much of which would be conquered by the Muslims from the eighth century onward, shifted the centre of culture and learning to the East. In Asia Minor and the Eastern Mediterranean, under the surviving Eastern Roman Empire (Byzantium) and the Islamic Empire, the technologies of the high Roman era were extended and improved upon. New technologies from Asia would be adopted here first, and only later transmitted to Western Europe.

Western Europe experienced de-urbanisation and attention focused on agriculture. The innovations of this era centred on the horse. Around 600 CE, the mouldboard plough was invented and spread amongst the Germanic peoples. Around 900 CE, the horseshoe made its first appearance in Europe and was widespread by the eleventh century.[78] The moist soils of Northern Europe made the horseshoe an imperative, since horses' hooves are sensitive to moisture. This improved the horse as a military asset, but another step was necessary if horses were to replace oxen in pulling the plough. The ancient yoke harness worked well for oxen, but when applied to the horse 'the neck-strap pressed on its jugular vein and windpipe, tending to suffocate it and to cut off the flow of blood to its head'. This was replaced by the modern harness with a padded collar. As horses could plough faster and for longer hours than the ox, the contribution of the horse to medieval agriculture was to be profound.[79] At the very least, one can suggest that these innovations that allowed the horse to work the fields, when combined with the intensive system of regulating agrarian production under the

78. White 1965, pp. 57–9. '[T]here is no literary evidence that the Greeks, Romans or Franks had the horseshoe: the closest they came were hipposandals and *solae* attached with thongs or wires either for ornamentation or to help the healing of a broken hoof... The earliest unambiguous excavated evidence of horseshoes comes from nomadic rider-graves of the Yenisei region in Siberia in the ninth to tenth centuries. Simultaneously, nailed horseshoes are mentioned in the Byzantine *Tactica* of Emperor Leo VI, who reigned from 886 to 911. And in the West we probably hear the first sound of shod hooves in the last decade of the ninth century...' Whether horseshoes travelled from Siberia to Byzantium to Europe is unclear, but from this it does appear that Europe inherited rather than invented the horseshoe.

79. White 1965, pp. 61–2. 'Although it cannot yet be proved, it is probable that from the eighth century onward the increasing weight of armour created a knightly demand for more powerful horses, and that these were bred systematically before any such selective breeding was developed for cattle... As compared with horses, it is safe to assume that cattle were relatively weaker in the Middle Ages than they are today. We must conclude that any modern advantage which can be shown for the use of the horse in farming should be augmented as applied to the Middle Ages. Modern experiments show that while horse and ox exert roughly the same pull, the horse moves so much more rapidly that he produces 50 per cent. More foot-pounds per second. Moreover, a horse has more endurance than an ox, and can work one or two hours longer each day'.

feudal system, the subsequent doubling of Europe's population by around 1250 CE becomes more explicable.[80]

The fourth invention related to the horse is the stirrup, appearing in the eighth century, and which Leslie White, in a stark display of technological determinism, claims led directly to the development of feudalism in Europe. White's argument runs as follows. By giving 'lateral support in addition to the front and back support offered by pommel and cantle, [the stirrup] effectively welded horse and rider into a single fighting unit capable of violence without precedent.'[81] Combined with the demand for breeding heavier horses, the stirrup established the superiority of mounted soldiers, creating the need for maintaining large numbers of mounted and armoured knights. 'Because both horses and iron were scarce, the entire economic system had to be geared toward paying for these armies.'[82] Even if one accepts the general premise of White's widely criticised thesis, feudal warfare arose in the context of the political parcellisation of sovereignty, which such developments in the techniques of war may have helped to extend, but which was ultimately a legacy of the collapse and fragmentation of the Roman Empire, or in other words, a historical and political phenomenon. Other innovations of Europe during this period are related to overcoming the harsh northern winters: chimneys, the use of coal for heating, plaster for better insulation, window glass, the crank-driven grindstone, better soaps and stronger alcoholic beverages.

While Northern Europeans were finding better ways of toughing out the harsh winters, Islam served as the bearer of the knowledge and technology of classical civilisation. 'It was a society literate beyond Europe's wildest dreams . . . Between 700 and 1200 the Moslems know more about the different parts of the world than any other civilization'.[83] Paper came to the Islamic world after 800 and by 1000 CE 'the entire Islamic world was enjoying bound books, wrapping paper, and paper napkins'.[84] The texts of the Greeks were translated into Arabic and were thus preserved for rediscovery by the Europeans after the Renaissance. Like the Mayans of the same period, the Muslims were highly advanced in mathematics and astronomy. They were also advanced in chemistry, making improvements on glass and ceramics and inventing *naptha*. In medicine the Muslims were

80. At issue is the timing. England lagged behind, with only some regions using the horse rather than the ox by the late twelfth century. But 'Normandy was in advance of Britain: two thirteenth century documents indicate that in the Duchy peasants were doing all of their ploughing with horses' (White 1965, p. 65). Presumably this had been the case in Normandy for some time.

81. White 1965, p. 2.

82. From Mokyr's summary of White's argument, see Mokyr (ed.) 1990, p. 36, n. 4.

83. Mokyr (ed.) 1990, pp. 39–40.

84. To say nothing of toilet paper, another Chinese gift to world civilisation (Mokyr [ed.] 1990, p. 41).

cataloguing a large number of medicinal cures and were learning how to quarantine those with contagious diseases, whilst Europeans still believed that leprosy and the plague were transmittable by sight alone. Iraqi surgeon Ammar ibn Ali al-Mawsili used a glass syringe to remove cataracts in the ninth century. The Moor scholar Abbas Ibn Firnas made the first attempt at a parachute jump in 852, and the first attempt at flying a hang glider in 875, six centuries before da Vinci and a full millennium ahead of the Wright Brothers. Tajik scholar Abu-Mahmud al-Khujandi invented the first sextant in Persia in 994 CE. The pendulum originated in Egypt in the tenth century, and is credited to the mathematician Ibn Yunus. Other Arab technology included resolving the limitations of the lateen sail so that it could be used on larger ships, allowing ships to sail up to 65 degrees off wind. In the late twelfth century, Arabs invented the rudder, which greatly improved steering. Since the earliest known appearance of the compass in Europe precedes its earliest known appearance in the Muslim world, it remains an open question whether the European compass was an independent invention or was transmitted from China via the Arab world. Street lamps and window panes both originated in the Arab Empire. Under the Muslims, textile qualities improved greatly. Cotton production and cotton clothing were introduced. Damasks (Damascus linens), cotton muslins, and cotton-linen fustians are names of fabrics that would later be among Europe's textile exports. The Muslims also produced superior water clocks, including some which could represent the movements of the Sun and Moon and the stars in the zodiac. The Muslims were at this time the leaders in hydraulic technology. They made widespread use of the water mill, applying it not only to grinding but to sugar processing and sawing. Around 1000 CE near Basra, the first tidal mill was invented to harness the energy of the tides. The eighth-century physician and alchemist Jābir ibn Hayyān is thought to have discovered many of the basic chemicals and is widely considered the 'father of chemistry',[85] although the Persian physician Ali-Rhazi or Rhazes, born 850 CE, is also credited by some for laying the foundations for 'the preparation of pure hydrochloric, nitric, and sulfuric acids by Europeans in the thirteenth century'.[86] Finally, the windmill was invented in Persia in the seventh century and 'is mentioned in Islamic sources from the ninth century on'.[87] However, it did not gain widespread use in the Muslim world.

What the history of inventions between 500 and 1200 CE suggests is that whilst other civilisations enjoyed a golden age as literacy, the arts and

---

85. Jābir ibn Hayyān, who studied in Baghdad, was given the pseudonym 'Geber' in the fourteenth century, and chemical historians refer to the author of works attributed to him as 'pseudo-Geber' (Greenburg 2007, pp. 64–5).

86. Brock 1993, pp. 19–24, as quoted in Greenburg 2007, p. 136.

87. Mokyr 1990, p. 41.

technological innovation flourished, Europe had become a technological back water. But around the thirteenth century, fortunes begin to reverse. For reasons that remain a mystery, technological innovation in both China and the Islamic Empire had already begun to slow by the time the Mongols destroyed Baghdad in 1258 and conquered China in the 1260s. In the twelfth and thirteenth centuries, meanwhile, the population of Europe was growing on the basis of the intensive farming under the feudal system of agriculture, enough that armies in excess of 100,000 could be raised and sent off to fight the Crusades. After 1200, European innovation grew whilst other places lapsed into relative technological stagnation. Given that Europe *regressed* whilst others moved ahead, and then rebounded while others lapsed, can arguments based on technological determinism help to explain this pattern? Shaw writes:

> broadly speaking, a society can be characterised as managing the productive forces at hand either successfully or unsuccessfully. When the economic structure fails to exploit society's capacity adequately, when there is a dislocation of the forces and relations of production, then systemic difficulties in the socio-economic organisation of society become apparent and dissatisfaction with the old way of doing things grows. The existing social equilibrium is disrupted, and impetus given to the reorganizing of material production.[88]

This formula implies an inherent drive toward greater productivity in pre-capitalist societies. Yet Roman and Mayan civilisations fragmented, China and Islam stagnated. Where was the impetus to reorganise material production? Shaw continues: 'Equilibrium can be restored only by bringing the relations of production and productive forces into correspondence. Since men do not wish to sacrifice their productive gains, they alter their relations of production to accommodate their productive forces – even when this transforms the basic character of production'.[89]

Here Shaw quotes Marx: 'as the main thing is not to be deprived of the fruits of civilization, of the acquired productive forces, the traditional forms in which they were produced must be smashed'.[90] The only thing that can stabilise the society again, writes Shaw, is 'a new economic order'. This model of social change would appear to be quite applicable to the development of capitalism, which is a system governed by market regulation, but it does not appear to fit the pattern of pre-capitalist societies, which in general were governed by normative or customary forms of social regulation. In the broadest sense, the pattern of technological progress appears to be more one of ebb and flow or even a kind

88. Shaw 1979, p. 161.
89. Ibid.
90. Marx and Engels 1975, Vol. 6, p. 175, as quoted in Shaw 1979, p. 161.

of 'leap frog' rather than one of continuous development, with Europe rebounding by innovating in agricultural techniques appropriate to its soil and climate, and subsequently adopting (or independently discovering) the innovations of the East and taking them further. Indeed, all of the history discussed so far in this chapter comes before the invention of the pendulum clock in thirteenth-century Europe, and only with its diffusion across Europe by the fifteenth century, did the concept of measuring productivity according to time take hold.

> [The clock] permitted a more accurate measurement of productivity. After all, implicit in our notion of efficiency is the need to measure time: productivity is a flow concept. Clocks brought home differences in efficiency: more productive workers and better implements and tools could be seen to produce more output per hour. Productivity comparisons became easier, and with them the choice between the faster and the slower.[91]

For Mumford:

> The clock, not the steam engine, is the key-machine of the modern industrial age . . . here was a new kind of machine, in which the source of power and the transmission were of such a nature as to ensure the even flow of energy throughout the works and to make possible regular production and a standardized product. In its relationship to determinable quantities of energy, to standardization, to automatic action, and finally to its own special product, accurate timing, the clock has been the foremost machine in modern technics: and at each period it has remained in the lead: it marks a perfection toward which other machines aspire . . . The clock, moreover, is a piece of power-machinery whose 'product' is seconds and minutes: by its essential nature it dissociated time from human events and helped create the belief in an independent world of mathematically measurable sequences: the special world of science.[92]

Music also felt the profound impact of the clock. If we accept that the invention of the clock was even half as fundamentally important to the development of science and the regulation of production as Mumford suggests, we can choose to view its impact in terms of an incidental discovery that happened to have a transformative impact, particularly with regards to the regulation of production, or we can ask: how did the need for such an instrument arise? Out of what configuration of social relations? Mumford suggests that the clock was 'an almost inevitable product' of monastic life and was created as 'an instrument for striking the hours at intervals or for reminding the bell-ringer that it was time to strike

91. Mokyr (ed.) 1990, pp. 50–1.
92. Mumford 1934, pp. 14–15.

the bells'.[93] Whether or not Mumford is correct, we must still ask why the clock was so quickly adopted for so many uses outside the monastery and whether these uses can be related to the development of intensive regulation of agrarian production under the feudal system.

Asking these questions takes us outside the realm of possibility proscribed by technological determinism. To suggest that the course of historical development is shaped by socio-political organisation as much or more than it is shaped by technology is not to deny that the evolution of technology has a certain 'inner' logic, governed by the limitations that prevail at a given time, and the new possibilities opened up with each new discovery. It is only to suggest that the impact of technological development on society and on production is mediated by the configuration of social relations that prevail. We find few examples of the systematic application technology to production. The assumption that state (or 'civilised') societies in general are characterised by an inherent drive toward greater productivity is a reading backwards of capitalist laws of motion onto earlier societies. This was and remains a common assumption among liberal historians and political economists, and was initially adopted in its essentials by Marx, who as we saw in the Introduction reformulated his thinking on the matter later in life. Thus, this assumption is at the root of the tendency toward determinism to be found in both Marxist and non-Marxist historical theory. Let us bear in mind, however, that peasant labour under the feudal system, with its unique emphasis on regulating production, was the predominant form of labour in Europe between the feudal period and the Industrial Revolution, the same period in which Europe went from backwater to leader in technology.

It bears more than a footnote's comment to add that a great deal of national and racial pride lies at stake in the discourse on the origins of innovations, and this, of course, means that all evaluations are inevitably tainted with some degree of subjectivity. A sense of racial superiority among Europeans was at least buttressed by, if not actually founded upon, the scientific and technological advances of post-Renaissance Europe. Consider how in the following dismissive passage concerning the technology of antiquity in Europe, McCloskey, by omission, appears even more dismissive of non-European advances:

> 'Give me a lever and a place to stand on', said boasting Archimedes, 'and I shall move the world'. What is odd about his world of the classical Mediterranean is that for all its genius it did not apply the lever, or anything much else, to practical uses... The 'Dark Ages' contributed more to our physical wellbeing than did the glittering ages of Pericles or Augustus. From classical times we got toy steam engines and erroneous principles of motion. From the ninth

93. Mumford 1934, p. 13.

> and tenth centuries alone we got the horse collar, the stirrup, and the mouldboard plough.[94]

Why these three inventions should out-rank the long and still incomplete list of both ancient and non-European advances we have listed above is less than self-evident. But McCloskey continues with a list of 33 innovations that 'we got' from 'an explosion of ingenuity down to 1500'.[95] Of these, 19 appear to be of uniquely European origin, and they include: the blast-furnace, cast-iron pot, chimney, coal-fuelled fire, cog boat, cross-staff, eyeglass, hops in beer, marine chart, nailed horseshoe, printing press, ribbed ship, shingle, ski, spring watch, water-driven bellows, weight-driven clock, whisky, and the obscure 'whippletree'. As noted above, Europe may or may not have invented the compass independently of China. As we have also seen, the cam, crank, pump, treadle and waterwheel were all known in ancient Europe, the suction pump, treadle loom and overshot wheel being later improvements. All of the remaining eight inventions mentioned by McCloskey are either improvements upon or direct borrowings from inventions outside of Europe. They include: the cake of soap (Mesopotamia), the canal lock (China), carrack ship (Phoenicia), flywheel (Andalusia), grindstone (pre-historic), spinning wheel (India), wheelbarrow (China), and the windmill (Persia). While this omission of Europe's debt to the rest of the world is striking, McCloskey nonetheless may be pointing in the right direction when repeating the observation (omitted from the quote above) that *applied* technology 'was a northern European accomplishment'.[96] All the great civilisations appear to have exhibited ample amounts of genius, and many inventions outside Europe played important roles in production, but in Europe after 1200, the tendency to gear technological innovation toward enhancing production became more pronounced.

A good example of this is the unprecedented expansion of the utilisation of inanimate power in the form of watermills and windmills. The first drawing of a mill since Roman times appears in 1169, and shows the use of crown and pinion gearing, allowing for higher speeds of operation. The overshot wheel also made its first definite appearance in feudal Europe. By the thirteenth century, gearing was in common use in various types of mills. The first recorded windmills in Europe appear in the late twelfth century, notably in Yorkshire. Europeans were the first to build windmills with a horizontal fan, as opposed to the vertical fan from Persia. This modification, however, required mounting part of the mill or the entire mill on a pivot to allow it to turn with the wind, making for

94. McCloskey 1994, p. 267.
95. Ibid.
96. McCloskey 1994, p. 267, cites Jones 1981. Mokyr (ed.) 1990 was the first to make this observation.

a more efficient means of capturing the wind.[97] While grinding grain remained the predominant function of mills, they were put to other uses. Fulling mills, for example, employed waterwheels to power the engine which drove the hammers (fulling stocks), which scoured and milled the cloth. Dating from the eleventh century, they spread in England in the thirteenth century. West Yorkshire had eleven mills by 1327. In 1377 Parliament banned the export of cloth not properly fulled.[98] Such mills were set up as public utilities to be used collectively by clothiers.

The Romans experimented with sawmills, but they fall out of the record 'until we come to the "Album" of Villard de Honnecourt, [a French] ecclesiastical architect of the thirteenth century. Here we find two sketches of saws, one of which, at least, is supposed to be driven by water power'.[99] Honnecourt's album also contained the first reference to a primitive escapement, the essential mechanism for the self-operating, weight-driven, mechanical clock to be able to mark precisely equal periods of time. Between the thirteenth and eighteenth centuries, wind and water remained the sources of inanimate power (donkey and horse mills were still common) applied to mills prior to the application of Watt's steam engine. But larger, more durable and more sophisticated mills were constructed, and the understanding of gearing developed in mills as well as clocks.

In the thirteenth century, Northern Italy was the centre of European commerce and therefore the point where new technologies, such as gunpowder, were introduced. It was also the source of several significant technological developments, with an emphasis on reading and sight. The first manufacture of paper began in Italy around 1270. Eyeglasses were invented in Venice in 1286. And whether or not he was aided in his discovery by the use of eyeglasses, Giotto demonstrated the first use of perspective in his paintings a few years later. The functional button for clothing was another invention to emerge in thirteenth-century Europe. The spinning wheel arrived from India in this century, and was applied to various threads, including silk, which the Italians had long been producing.[100] In England the magnifying glass had been invented in 1200, nearly three centuries before the discovery of the telescope and the microscope. Another British

---

97. As noted, it remains uncertain whether windmills in Europe were borrowed from Islam or were an independent development. 'In so far as there was borrowing, it was creative borrowing', writes Usher 1982, p. 173.

98. Jenkins 1973, p. 255.

99. Usher 1982, p. 185.

100. Silk production was a secret retained by the East until the Emperor Justinian in 500 CE persuaded two Persian monks to risk their lives by smuggling silkworms in the hollow of their bamboo canes from Cathay to Byzantium (Sykes and Sykes 1920, p. 214). This enabled Italy and later France to undertake silk production until the silkworm plague of the nineteenth century.

contribution in the thirteenth century was the longbow, invented in Wales. It was also during the thirteenth century that the horizontal bench lathe appeared.

The fourteenth century saw the first working escapement clocks, the first alarm clock, and the introduction of knitting. The hand cannon, precursor to the pistol and rifle, were known by mid-century. For reasons that would seem obvious, we see little record of new inventions between 1347, when the plague first arrived in Europe, and the fifteenth century. Key inventions of the fifteenth century were concave lenses, oil painting, the trigger and the astrolabe. In metal-working, German and Bohemian engineers were constructing larger furnaces using water-powered bellows, allowing the iron to absorb carbon, thereby lowering its melting point and allowing it to be cast into moulds.[101] The blast-furnace pouring pig iron fully emerges in the sixteenth century, but its evolution took place mainly in the fifteenth. The availability of better, cheaper iron was an important contribution to another major invention of the fifteenth century: the printing press. Usher expounds on the significance of the invention of the printing press, and the many innovations that had to take place in order for this machine to be realised:

> Printing is one of the first instances of the substitution of mechanical devices for direct hand work in the interests of accuracy and refinement in execution as well as reduced cost. By capitalistic methods and mass production, a new and superior product was evolved. All the economic consequences of these inventions were thus characteristic of the new order; and even at the outset, the printing office disclosed the features of a factory enterprise rather than those of the craft shop.[102]

Two comments are in order, here. First, as in mining, it may have been the case that printing grew up as a form of production in which ownership of the means of production was concentrated and the workers were highly or relatively proletarianised at an early stage, but it is unthinkable that production decisions were being made strictly in accordance with market indicators, as they might be later under conditions of a well-developed capitalism. Second, printing employed far fewer workers even than mining, and so the effect of printing on advancing proletarianisation throughout the economy would have been minimal.[103]

---

101. Mokyr (ed.) 1990, p. 48. Mokyr notes another advance in metallurgy that took place in the fifteenth century: 'a process to separate silver form copper ores by means of lead, developed around 1450'.

102. Usher 1982, pp. 238–9. He continues: 'The history of paper is in some ways a separate subject, but it must be evident that the generalization of printing could not have proceeded significantly with any other medium'.

103. The case of proletarianisation in metallurgy and mining is discussed above in Chapter One, pp. 81–91, Chapter Seven, pp. 363–6 and Chapter Ten, pp. 496–75.

Usher continues: 'The entire achievement embodied in the printed book with illustrations presents a striking example of the multiplicity of individual acts of invention that are requisite to bring about a new result. In its entirety, this accomplishment involves: the invention of paper and of inks made with an oil base; the development of engraving on wood and on metals; the development of type founding and metal reproductions of wood blocks; the development of the press and the special technique of press work involved in printing'.[104]

In effect, the emergence of the printing press was really the completion of a series of inventions in engraving, casting and most critically, and late in the process: typefounding. While Usher is thus unclear about what it was, exactly, that Gutenberg invented, Mokyr is more certain. For Mokyr:

> The printing press is justly famous, because it is the first medieval invention for which the name of the inventor and the time of the invention are reasonably well-established, and for which we know that the inventor single-handedly solved the entire problem to the point that within a short period the new gadget was in use all over Europe... Like the windmill, the printing press spread with dazzling speed. By 1480, there were over 380 working presses in Europe, and in the 50 years following the invention more books were produced than in the preceding thousand years.[105]

While the printing press thus served as a model for modern machinery because it produced a superior product, more efficiently and in far less time than did hand manufacture of books, this does not mean that there was anything inherently 'capitalistic' about the printing press.

One other important contribution of the early printing press was that it enabled the posthumous distribution and popularisation of the manuscripts of Leonardo Da Vinci. Da Vinci 'laid the foundations of the new experimental sciences; he broke away from mere empiricism to the concepts of an applied science of mechanics capable of general application throughout the whole industrial field'. The sketches in his notebooks included novel features that 'were too far in advance of the technique of the period to admit of practical application. But much of the inventive effort was worked into practice by Leonardo himself and those around him, so that even apart from his manuscripts these devices exerted a powerful influence upon his time'.[106] Da Vinci's sketches testify that he had already conceptualised nearly every invention necessary for mechanising woollen manufacturing. He conceived of a u-shaped spinning

---

104. Usher 1982, pp. 238–9. He continues: 'The history of paper is in some ways a separate subject, but it must be evident that the generalization of printing could not have proceeded significantly with any other medium'.
105. Mokyr (ed.) 1990, p. 49.
106. Usher 1982, p. 215.

machine, a faster shuttle and a power-loom, a gig mill, and a shearing engine. Although 'there are numerous schemes for the shearing engine, the essential principle was naïve and incapable of development'.[107] Da Vinci also diagrammed a winding apparatus for silk, though it is unclear if he had contact with Zonca, the sixteenth-century inventor whose design was similar and more complete. Usher provides an exhaustive list of Da Vinci's accomplishments in the field of applied mechanics, noting that perhaps most of his conceptions were wrongly credited to later inventors, some of them key figures in the later 'scientific revolution'. These accomplishments ranged from hydraulics to military engineering to general mechanics, including spiral gears and various other studies in gearing, swinging and rotary motion, anti-friction rollers, link chains, a screw cutter, die and collar for coining, and a coining machine. Da Vinci's sketch of a file-cutting machine is but one example of his efforts to apply the principle of the self-automated mechanism from clockwork to machinery in manufacturing. Assessing the amazing breadth of Da Vinci's work in terms of the contributions made to the advance of technology requires venturing into the realm of speculation. According to Usher: 'It is only with Leonardo that the process of invention is lifted decisively into the field of the imagination; it becomes a pursuit of the remote ends that are suggested by the discoveries of physical science and the consciously felt principles of mechanics'.[108] How then do we account for the role of the imagination in advancing hypotheses about technological advancement? Da Vinci conceptualised most of the machinery that revolutionised textile production five centuries before its application. If societies in general are characterised by an inherent drive towards adopting new technologies and raising the level of productivity, why were Da Vinci's conceptions not put into practice sooner? Some of the answers should already be apparent. Quite contrary to the notion that 'men do not wish to sacrifice their productive gains' (Shaw), the guilds of the medieval and early modern period, and the craft workers who succeeded them were hostile to the introduction of machinery, which they rightly saw as a threat to their livelihood, and this contributed to the delay in its full invention and its application to production. What of the alternative hypothesis that we have suggested above? That is, as the structure of the social relations of production changes, needs for solutions to technical problems are created or made more urgent than previously, increasing the probability that these problems will be solved sooner. This formula also seems to fall short of being able to account for the role of Da Vinci as a visionary. This is not to say that Da Vinci was anything other than a product of his time, building on previous advances and

107. Usher 1982, pp. 219–20. Usher notes that 'Da Vinci's 'sketches for the loom and flying shuttle are incomplete…'

108. Usher 1982, pp. 236–7.

finding solutions to problems left by others. But in 'lifting' invention to the level of the imagination, Da Vinci surely also began to work on problems that only he had imagined. The majority of Da Vinci's conceptual inventions were eventually put to practical use, but they were mostly worked out in theory, and much of his work would have been as unthinkable to contemporaries as the imaginary devices we read of in 'science fiction' today. So while we discount the notion of a 'technological imperative' where technology advances autonomously, shaping society in its wake, we must leave room for the role of the human imagination to envision desired outcomes, thereby shaping the course of technological change as it develops in the context of evolving socio-economic structures, responding to needs and pressures as they arise.

In the sixteenth century, Hero's treatise on the 'five simple machines', which had been preserved in Arabic translations, came to the attention of European scholars studying mechanics. Although 'mechanics' for Hero applied strictly to the lifting of heavy weights and the machines were in fact the basic components of lifting apparatuses only, the doctrine that these five mechanisms were the basis of all machines actually survived into the nineteenth century.[109] It is in the sixteenth century that the scientific revolution got underway. Logarithms, the microscope, the telescope, the thermometer and the Mercator projection are among the scientific achievements of this century. In warfare, the grenade was first used in France in 1528, and the wheel-lock and match-lock rifles were introduced. In machinery, perhaps the major advances of this period were made in the area of machine tools. Leonardo's sketches suggested improvements to the lathe and French engineer Jacques Besson also made significant improvements, such as adding guides to allow the cutting of irregular shapes and introducing a screw-cutting lathe. The mandrel lathe, which allowed the work to be attached to a spindle, expanded the range of possibility further.[110] One invention that would go on to play a key role in the British Industrial Revolution was the stocking-frame, the first knitting machine, which was invented in 1589 by William Lee, a clergyman from Calverton, Nottinghamshire. Soon thereafter, around 1604, the 'Dutch Loom' or ribbon loom appeared in Holland, the invention of one Willem Dircxz van Sonnevelt, which enabled one weaver to weave 12 ribbons at once, and 24 ribbons at once by 1621.

In the early seventeenth century, the flintlock rifle was introduced, but did not come into wide use until the 1640s, leaving the parties to the Thirty Years War to fight with the more expensive and troublesome wheel and match-lock rifles and pistols, alongside pikes and swords. James I had commissioned the first submarine from Dutch inventor Cornelius Drebbel, although it was far from ready for

109. Usher 1982, p. 120.
110. Usher 1982, pp. 361–3.

application in warfare.[111] Another troubled experiment by a Dutchman was that of Christian Huygens attempting to apply the pendulum clock he had invented in 1673 for use on sailing ships: 'the operation of the instrument was hopelessly inaccurate in rough weather and in 1674 Huygens recognized that the variation of gravity at different latitudes would be an insuperable obstacle to the use of the pendulum at sea'.[112] Huygens subsequently turned his attention to smaller projects, patenting the pocket watch in 1675.[113] Huygens and his English counterpart in clockmaking Robert Hooke, inventor of a machine for cutting clock wheels (1671), were both members of the Royal Society. Founded in 1660, the Royal Society gave institutional form to the scientific curiosity of the age. Many other scientific inventions of this century also reflect the emphasis on science, while the level of machinery remained relatively undeveloped:[114] the sliderule, the calculator, the precision microscope, the vacuum pump and the universal joint.

On the eve of the eighteenth century, European science was making unprecedented strides, and the pace of invention was brisk. But there were as yet few attempts to systematically apply machine technology to production in the effort to attain constantly increasing productivity and therefore profits. We could hypothesise that this was due to the monopolistic regulations of the guilds, but in England the guilds had been in a state of steady decay since the sixteenth century. We could subsequently point to the role of custom in regulating markets and restricting their potential. But this would be to assume that there exists some inherent drive toward productivity that custom was blocking. It might also be to assume that there was an already existing industrial capitalism waiting to have its 'fetters' removed so that it could it naturally 'unfold'. Perhaps neither one of these assumptions is correct. Perhaps the historical record speaks plainly when it shows that pre-industrial European class society was highly inventive, but did not revolutionise production or even show any clear signs that it was about to do so. Moreover, perhaps the revolutionising of production did not even require the application of machinery in the first place.

The technology of the Industrial Revolution

If the controversy over whether the 'Industrial Revolution' is itself an appropriate term had focused strictly on technology, the gradualist school might have

111. Platt 1994, p. 25. 'Although the submarine leaked badly, the 12 oarsmen succeeded in rowing it along London's Thames River at a depth of about 13 ft (4 m)'.

112. Usher 1982, p. 325.

113. Huygens invented the pocket watch by improving on existing (larger) portable clocks and adding a spring to the balance wheel.

114. Owen 1975, pp. xi and 313.

won the day, at least if the discussion were restricted to the eighteenth century. Throughout the eighteenth century, key innovations appeared that would have far-reaching consequences, and certainly the momentum picks up as the century wears on. But looking back from 1800, it is hard to see these developments as a *technological* revolution.

The agrarian innovations of the early eighteenth century such as floating water-meadows, the use of turnips as fodder, artificial grasses and the seed drill, have already been discussed.[115] It bears reminding that agriculture as much as manufacturing was subject to 'improvement' in the form of innovation in the early eighteenth century. British inventiveness continued in the latter half of the eighteenth century, the most notable example being the invention of the threshing-machine by the Scotsman Andrew Meikle in the mid-1780s. The 'thresher' or 'thrasher' was powered by hand, by horse, by water and eventually by steam.[116] Within industry, the major British innovations of the eighteenth century occurred within two broad areas: the various branches of the textile trades on the one hand, and the nexus of iron, coal and power production on the other. We begin this overview with the latter.

Sixteen hundred years after Hero of Alexandria developed his *aeolipile*, the first known development of a steam engine, the British Parliament granted a 99-year monopoly to the Marquis of Worcester and his heirs for a 'water-commanding' engine. Worcester had visions of enormous profits from his proposal to develop a waterworks supply for the City of London. We know little of his contraption, however, including whether or not the subsequent patent taken out by Thomas Savery of Devon in 1698 for a steam-driven engine was for an entirely novel invention, or one based upon Worcester's earlier effort.[117] Savery was hoping to sell his device to mineowners seeking to cut costs. As the mines in England and Wales were growing ever deeper, drainage costs were becoming exorbitant. Savery proposed to use his device for drawing water out of mines. The drawbacks of Savery's invention were largely overcome with the subsequent development of the single-cylinder 'atmospheric' or 'beam' engine of Thomas Newcomen, also of Devon, around 1710.[118] By 1712, the first Newcomen engine

115. See above Chapter Three, pp. 198.
116. Beckett 1990, p. 25.
117. Usher 1982, pp. 344–6.
118. Usher (Usher 1982, p. 347) showers extraordinarily high praise upon Newcomen's achievement: 'The invention of the atmospheric engine in this form [Newcomen's] was the greatest single act of synthesis in the history of the steam engine and must be regarded as one of the primary or strategic inventions. The important work of Watt and his contemporaries was crucial rather than synthetic, and though new devices had to be invented they are, after all, improvements of the Newcomen machine, which can scarcely be rated as greater inventive achievements'. It should be noted that Newcomen was inspired by the work of French inventor Denis Papin, who had worked with Boyle,

was in operation near Wolverhampton. By the 1720s and 1730s, Newcomen's steam engines were at work in coalmines, especially the deeper ones as in Northern England, as well as in tin mines and mines extracting other non-ferrous ores, which saw an upsurge in the late 1740s.[119] Newcomen's engine helped to solve not only drainage problems, but problems of water shortages slowing or halting waterwheel driven furnaces and forges in the iron industry. Steam now took its place alongside wind and water as a source of inanimate power to be harnessed for productive purposes. By 1767, fully fifty-seven Newcomen engines were employed in the mining industry.

One of the most critical inventions of the early eighteenth century initiated a major step forward in British iron production by applying a modified form of coal to the iron-smelting process. The Quaker Abraham Darby, son of a locksmith, began applying coke to smelting in 1702. Experiments in smelting with coal had been attempted since at least 1612, most famously by Dud Dudley, Darby's great uncle.[120] By 1790, Darby had successfully managed to smelt iron with

---

Huygens and Leibniz and who invented the steam-digester, and even developed a model piston engine, which inspired Newcomen's work (Usher 1982, p. 344). Thus we see again that a single invention can be traced to the work of many previous scientists and inventors. And we have another example of the British borrowing from the work of Continental inventors (Papin was a Huguenot and did spend much of his life in London). Where Newcomen secured his reputation is in successfully *applying* his invention to good productive use, for had he failed in that, the fame likely would not have followed.

119. Deane and Cole, 1969, pp. 54–5.

120. Coke had been discovered in the Middle Ages, and by the seventeenth century was used as a fuel in processes where it could be kept from making direct contact with the raw material, such as in glass-making and dyeing. But because iron-smelting involves direct contact between fuel and ore, the impurities found in coked coal prohibited its application, and most furnaces therefore relied on the cleaner, but inefficient charcoal before 1750. Trinder notes that Darby used coke from the first, and his success was probably due to the fact that 'Shropshire clod coal from which the coke was made was largely free of sulphur' (Trinder 1974, p. 19). It was the same Shropshire coal used by his great uncle Dud Dudley, whose success in making iron using pit coal, however limited, undoubtedly benefited from the quality of the coal he was using. Dudley was one of eleven illegitimate children born to Edward Sutton, the fifth Baron Dudley, and his mistress Elizabeth Tomlinson, making him a distant cousin of the famous Robert Dudley, Queen Elizabeth's favourite, and Robert's younger brother Guilford Dudley, the doomed spouse of Lady Jane Grey. With such connections within the nobility, Dud was able to show samples of his work to King James, and later had a patent that was renewed under Charles I. 'He endured the usual disappointments of inventors', writes Mantoux. His blast-furnaces at Stourbridge were destroyed by floods. Removing to Sedgely, Staffordshire, his works were again sacked by the workmen of jealous ironmasters. He was unable to renew his patent, even after the Restoration, despite having fought as a colonel in Prince Rupert's cavalry. According to Mantoux, when he died 'unnoticed' in 1684, 'his secret, if he had one, died with him'. Or did it? It is curious that Mantoux did not notice the family connection between Dudley and Darby, for Abraham Darby's grandmother Jane was Dud Dudley's sister. Could Darby have been taking advantage of a family secret? (See Mantoux 1961, pp. 285–91.)

coke,[121] although the process of perfecting his discovery to the point of being able to use coke to make wrought iron of comparable strength and malleability as that made by using charcoal continued for a generation after his untimely death in 1717.[122] A second coke-fired blast-furnace was not established until 1749.[123] After 1750, prices of coke and charcoal reversed and coke smelting began to spread beyond Coalbrookdale,[124] but even some eighty years after Darby's discovery there were some large furnaces in Shropshire still smelting with charcoal.[125]

In 1718 James Puckle took out a patent on the first machine gun, but this early weapon of mass destruction only brought financial ruin to its maker. Around this time George Sorocold was building the first silk-spinning factory for Thomas Lombe at Derby. The factory employed large, circular spinning frames approximately fifteen feet in diameter, powered by water. The designs for these frames are thought to have been stolen from Italy by Thomas' brother John Lombe, power-driven silk-spinning having been known (secretly) in Italy since the early seventeenth century, if not before,[126] being based upon the designs of Zonca and/or da Vinci. The machines Lombe installed in his factory 'were basically a large version of a hand technique'.[127] But if the technology was not new, and the machine itself no major technological advance, what was novel was the design and layout of the factory itself, which set the standard, being of unprecedented scale. The huge waterwheel turned 'no fewer than 25,000 small wheels that simultaneously threw and reeled silk on a vast scale'.[128] The advent of the factory in Britain, and the mode of labour organisation it implied, introduced a new technology of labour organising. Anticipating later developments in cotton

---

121. Darby had leased a 'small and derelict ironworks at Coalbrookdale' in 1708, bringing his workers with him from Bristol, and within a few months 'was able to achieve an innovation which would ultimately revolutionize the iron industry' (Trinder 1974, p. 14). This account might leave the impression that Darby started from scratch, which is unlikely (see previous footnote). 'The Darbys took out no patents, the second Darby refusing to "deprive the public of Such an Acquisition" ' (Letter of Mrs. Abiah Darby, cited by Ashton 1963, p. 250 and by Hammond and Hammond 1974b, p. 137). Only the Darbys produced cast-iron products on such a scale that they could make coking pay. The Darbys also kept secret another patent of Abraham Darby, who had discovered in 1707 a superior way of making thin-walled castings poured straight from the foundry furnace, for which pig iron was more applicable than wrought iron (Deane 1987, p. 108).

122. Landes 1991, p. 90. There were many factors involved in the quality of the charcoal or coke, which had to be sufficiently porous, sufficiently strong and with the right amount of oil in order to produce steady heat and flames.

123. Braudel 1988, p. 553. The greater cost initially involved in making pig iron from coke compared with pig from charcoal contributed to the delay. Meanwhile, England lagged behind Russia, Sweden and France in metallurgy.

124. Braudel 1988, p. 569.

125. Wilson 1984, p. 301.

126. Reynolds 2002.

127. Berg 1985, pp. 244–5.

128. Mokyr (ed.) 1990, p. 68.

and woollens, silk-spinning was mechanised whilst silk-weaving continued in the traditional, artisan mode of organising production.

The earliest railways were used in the coal-mining industry. In 1726, the first railway bridge in the world was built in Durham. The first railways were built on wooden rails, but iron bindings were soon being tried, and cast-iron wheels were put to general use by the 1780s.[129]

By comparison with the relatively quiet 1720s, the 1730s saw a virtual flurry of inventions. The pace of innovation was brisk, but not yet brilliant. In 1730, the making of pots was transformed by the introduction of moulds and the use of the plaster of Paris for making common pots and decorations. Now only finer wares required a thrower, and new classes of pottery workers came to predominate: carvers, designers and pressers. Double firing, introduced by Enoch Booth, reduced the risk of the ceramics being damaged in the ovens, but the lead-based glaze he also introduced brought a scourge on the pottery workers: lead poisoning.[130] John Kay introduced his flying shuttle to weaving in 1733, but it would take decades before it would come into widespread use. In the same year, William Kent invented the baby carriage. Wyatt and Paul patented their roller-spinning machine in 1738. Caissons to allow underwater foundations to be constructed were also developed in England that year. In the 1740s, Benjamin Huntsman discovered the process of making steel with a coke-fired crucible. In 1741, Physician William Brownrigg invented water carbonation. Two years later Thomas Boulsover invented silver plate and thus Sheffield silver. Benjamin Franklin introduced the Franklin stove in 1742 and ten years later performed his famous experiment with a kite, discovering electricity and inventing the lightning rod.[131]

---

129. Black 2001, p. 47. The first railway bridge, 'Causeway Arch, was built for the movement of Durham coal across the Causey Burn towards the Tyne. It had the largest span of any bridge built in Britain since Roman times, and the architect had to work from Roman models'.

130. According to the Hammonds 1974b, pp. 167–8: 'These several changes of method had made the complete reorganization of the industry on a capitalist basis inevitable'. To justify this claim, they argue that 'an industry which imports and exports cannot be conducted on the scale of a peasant industry which uses local materials and supplies a local market. The needs of the old industry had been served by master potters, each of whom had a single oven with six men and four boys, fired once a week, and drew a weekly profit of ten shillings, together with six shillings for his own labour. Before the middle of the century the more enterprising masters began to add oven to oven. Thus the factory arrived'. How adding ovens or expanding the size of the operation translates into factory production is far from clear. This claim is reminiscent of Nef's thesis, and also the commercialisation model.

131. Franklin went on to invent bifocals in his later years (1784) (Platt 1994, p. 32). Egyptian temples from the third century BCE were built with copper-covered masts, while records suggest that the Minoans built temples in the mountains with spear-shaped metal masts to attract lightning. Were these early examples of lightning rods? (James and Thorpe 1994, p. 151).

In 1748, Lewis Paul and Daniel Bourn were awarded separate patents for their respective designs of a carding engine.[132]

Every invention discussed thus far was invented or adapted either in Britain or in America, which was still a British colony. Outside the English-speaking world, the scientific revolution carried on, and the preoccupation was with measurement. The mercury thermometer was invented by German physicist Daniel Gabriel Fahrenheit in 1714, and in 1742 Swedish astronomer Anders Celsius invented the Celsius scale. But the British made major contributions to measurements in this period as well, specifically in the area that made them masters of the seas: marine navigation. English mathematician John Hadley and American inventor Thomas Godfrey independently invented the octant or 'mariner's quadrant' in the years 1730–1, finally improving upon Hipparchus' astrolabe of ancient times. In 1757, Englishman John Campbell improved upon the octant to invent the sextant. Two years later Englishman John Harrison invented the first successful marine chronometer, allowing accurate timekeeping at sea. Outside of Britain, the preoccupation with measurement continued, with the invention of the hygrometer (to measure humidity) by Swiss physicist Horace de Saussure in 1775. And could we fail to mention that most enduring legacy of the French Revolution, the metric system?[133]

Nef remarks that 1760 'is too early a date for marking the beginning of the industrial revolution, but it is much too late a date for marking the beginning of the intellectual development which made a revolution possible'.[134] Thus Nef recognises the Industrial Revolution as something separate from his 'early industrial revolution'. And at the same, time, he lends some credence to Toynbee's now famous line: 'Previously to 1760 the old industrial system obtained in England; none of the great mechanical inventions had been introduced...'[135] No doubt the great mechanical inventions to which Toynbee is referring include the following inventions that would soon revolutionise the textile industry:

---

132. Bourn took out his Patent No. 628 in January 1748. Paul took out Patent No. 636 on 30 August 1748. Wadsworth concludes that 'It was probably the grant of this patent [to Bourn] which decided Paul to apply for one for his own carding machine...' (Wadsworth and Mann 1965, p. 441, ns. 7 and 8).

133. Devised by 12 scientists appointed by France's revolutionary government, the goal was to standardise France's notoriously chaotic systems of measurement. In 1824, the British Government introduced its own standardisation: imperial measures, based on the 'imperial units' known as the yard and the pound (Platt 1994, p. 32).

134. Mechanical inventions, writes Nef (Nef 1943, p. 25), 'were a product of a movement in natural science and technology which was in progress long before the middle of the eighteenth century'. See Nef's long digression here.

135. Toynbee 1956, p. 7, continues: '... the agrarian changes were still in the future', an assertion we would contest, although most certainly a reference to the fact that parliamentary enclosures were only just beginning.

- the spinning jenny, introduced in 1765, and normally credited to James Hargreaves, a weaver and carpenter from Stanhill, Lancashire, although Thomas Highs may have been its original inventor;[136]
- the ribbing stocking-frame, for which Jedediah Strutt took out his patent in 1766; and
- the water frame, almost certainly devised by Thomas Highs but introduced for application by Richard Arkwright between 1767 and 1768, and operating in a factory by 1771.[137]

The spinning jenny was basically an adaptation of its precursor the spinning wheel, for it made it possible to work eight, and later as many as a hundred spindles by a single wheel, whereas the old spinning wheel worked one spindle and one alone'.[138] The appearance of the spinning jenny and the water frame at the same time helped to solve the immediate problem of a shortage of yarn, which was attributable in good measure to the success of John Kay's 'flying shuttle' loom. After a delay that can be attributed in part to resistance from weavers who saw it as a threat to their livelihood, use of the 'flying shuttle' loom, which could weave cloth out of cotton or woollen thread, began to spread in the 1750s and 1760s. Its use led to a surge in output of woven cloths and a crisis on the spinning side of the industry by way of a shortage of yarn. Finding a solution to the

---

136. To Hargreaves's great misfortune, the courts refused his application for a patent on the grounds that his invention had already been employed in industry prior to his application. He did not die a poor man, but the £4,000 left for his family upon his death was a paltry sum next to the fortune made by his rival, Richard Arkwright. The jenny did lead to the development of factory production, but was mostly located in cottages, replacing the earlier spinning-wheel. According to Guest (Guest 1823), Thomas Highs, a comb-maker and inventor from the village of Leigh in Lancashire, was the true inventor of the jenny, just as he was the true inventor of the water frame. According to another account, having completed a machine suitable only for making the weft, he set out to make a machine that could produce thread suitable for the warp, namely the water frame. The jenny's output 'was too soft to be used for warp, which still had to be manufactured from linen, made from the stem of the flax plant. There is some suggestion that, at this stage, Highs handed the jenny over to James Hargreaves – the two families certainly knew each other, at least later in life – and returned to tackle the problem of drafting rollers' (*Cotton Times* 2006).

137. According to Arkwright, he invented the water frame in 1768, with the aid of a Warrington clockmaker by the name of John Kay (no relation to the inventor of the shuttle-loom). He obtained a patent the following year. The machine itself apparently bore a strong resemblance to that introduced by John Wyatt and improved upon by Lewis Paul, differing 'only in its details'. 'A wheel sets in motion four pairs of increasing rapidity of rotation. The top cylinder of each pair is covered with leather, whilst the lower one is ribbed or grooved lengthwise. After it has gone through the rollers, whose progressive acceleration stretches it more and more, the thread is twisted and wound on vertical spindles' (Mantoux 1961, p. 223).

138. Hammond and Hammond 1974b, p. 181.

problem of domestic spinning being unable to keep up with the new, faster pace of the weavers became an imperative. In 1761, the Society for the Encouragement of the Arts and Manufactures had offered up a prize for the inventor who could find a solution.[139] How greatly this prize was coveted by inventors is not of issue here, but it does suggest a conscious preoccupation in Britain with the need to resolve economic pressures by way of invention.

New and key innovations in the textile industry continued to appear in Britain from the 1770s onwards. Various inventors made successive improvements on the carding engine, likely building upon the models of Paul and of Bourn. One of these inventors was John Lees, who in 1772 improved upon the carding engine by adding the feeder mechanism. In the same year, James Hargreaves added the crank and comb. Thomas Highs also made his contributions. In 1774 a Mr. Wood succeeded in obtaining perpetual or endless carding.[140] And in 1777, American Oliver Evans presented a design for a machine to make the teeth for the carding engine.[141] In 1779, Samuel Crompton introduced his 'mule', so-named because it borrowed features from both the spinning jenny and the water frame, having both rollers and spindles.[142] It was invented in secrecy and Crompton at first used it only for his own spinning. But the quality of thread it produced attracted curiosity mixed with greed. 'Ladders were used to peep in at his windows and holes were bored into his walls'.[143] As the mule was an adaptation of the water

139. This competition is surely one that Deane and Cole 1969, p. 97 had in mind when they commented that it was not 'entirely by chance that these discoveries came when they did, for by the 1760's competitions were being held for the best inventions.' Mantoux 1961, p. 215 comments that Wyatt and Paul, who had tried and failed to manage a small factory based on their spinning machine, 'were too early.' Mantoux was apparently unaware of Richard Guest's account wherein Guest asserts that Arkwright actually procured a model of the water frame from John Kay in 1767, Kay having worked with Highs on both the jenny and the water frame (see Guest 1823, p. 21).

140. Guest 1823, p. 18.

141. This was his first invention. He would go on to be the first to patent the designs for a grist mill in its entirety and to make improvements on the steam engine. His designs for a steam carriage, a steam-powered dredge and a refrigerator run on vapour were not realised until later inventors took them up.

142. Hammond and Hammond 1974b, p. 182. Born into a Lancashire family of cottagers who combined domestic spinning with agriculture, Crompton had known Arkwright personally when he was still a barber at Bolton.

143. Mantoux 1961, p. 236. The initial subscription was £67 6*s*. 6*d*, though not all made good on their promise. A subsequent subscription of £500 was raised in 1802, and Parliament made a grant of ten times this amount in 1812. Crompton also invented a carding machine, but apparently destroyed it to prevent anyone from stealing his innovation. Where the jenny's thread was fine but weak and the water frame's thread was strong but course, 'The mule gave both strength and extreme fineness', whereby the mule 'enabled British manufacturers to outdo the renowned skill of the Indian workers and to manufacture muslins of incomparable delicacy' (Mantoux 1961, pp. 235 and 238).

frame, Crompton stood little chance of gaining a patent. He thus decided to make a gift of it to the public, and the manufacturers raised a small subscription.

Several Scotsmen made important contributions to the textile industry. In 1783, Thomas Bell replaced hand-printing with a copper roller, thus introducing the revolving press, and allowing one workman to print as many calicoes as a hundred hand-printers in the same time.[144] The shearing frame, perhaps the most contentious piece of machinery in the later Luddite disturbances, was invented in 1787 by Sheffield clergyman John Harmer.[145] In 1790, a Scot named William Kelly adapted the mule to water power. 'From that time forward the mule became the spinning machine *par excellence*, and took the place, in current use, of Hargreave's jenny'.[146]

As spinning surged forward, the weavers could not keep up with the demand. It was Edmund Cartwright who proved the sceptics wrong by devising the first working model of a power-loom by 1785.[147] Cartwright set up a 400-loom steam-powered factory in Manchester in 1791, only to see it burned to the ground by angry weavers a month later. Eli Whitney invented the cotton gin in 1792, a critical contribution because it enabled cotton production to keep pace with the demand of a rapidly expanding cotton-cloth production industry in Britain. In 1797, Neil Snodgrass of Lancashire invented a scotching or blowing machine to clean the straw out of raw cotton.[148] By 1800, the demand on the part of manufacturers, the government and probably a good share of the public for a power loom began to outdo the resistance to it posed by weavers and their supporters. So severe was the shortage of yarn felt, that a campaign was undertaken to ban its export. Power-weaving was revived, and after 1800 the power-loom was triumphant as over the next four decades the wages of the weavers would fall from bringing them near middle-class prosperity to a level of grinding poverty.[149] New innovations in the hosiery trade continued to emerge, such as John Heathcote's bobbin-net machine for making bobbin lace of 1808.[150]

Just as in textiles, the 1760s was a kind of turning point for developments in Britain's iron industry. After decades of experimentation, Darby's process of smelting iron with coke had improved to the point where it could be profitably disseminated in the 1750s and 1760s. New coke-fired furnaces began to be built not just at Coalbrookdale, but also at Carron, Scotland and Dowlais, South

144. Mantoux 1961, pp. 244–5.
145. Randall 1991, p. 122.
146. Randall 1991, p. 237.
147. For more about Cartwright, see below Chapter Eight, pp. 455–6.
148. Fitton 1989, p. 168.
149. Regarding the arrival of the power-loom, see Chapter Eight, p. 455.
150. Pollard 1965, p. 96.

Wales and the Wrexham district of North Wales.[151] Coke blasting required larger furnaces, and so as this process spread, the size of the furnaces increased. This in turn required larger draughts. Leather bellows could not keep up with the larger furnaces, and although better, neither could Isaac Wilkinson's cast-iron blowing cylinder, which was first introduced in 1760 at Carron ironworks in Scotland.[152] Further improvement in this area would have to await the arrival and first application of the steam engine in 1776. In 1766, the Brothers Cranage took out a patent on the refining of pig iron using a reverbatory furnace in a coke-fired forge, anticipating Cort's later discovery. In 1767, the first iron rails had been cast at Coalbrookdale by Richard Reynolds, who managed the Darby operation during the years when the third generation of Darbys had not yet come of age. The iron rails replaced the wooden rails that connected Coalbrookdale's blast-furnaces with the nearby mines.[153] The implications of these developments were far-reaching.

Probably the most far-reaching development of the 1760s was James Watt's separate condenser engine, which he had devised by 1765 and for which he took out his first patent in 1769. Many improvements had been proposed to improve upon Newcomen's engine, which was recognised as inefficient in terms of its consumption of fuel and loss of energy, but Watt was the first to resolve 'the practical difficulty of dealing with steam pressures'.[154] Among those who had struggled with steam pressures was Frenchman Nicolas-Joseph Cugnot, who applied the steam engine (without a separate condenser) to a large horse cart or *fardier*, and (barely) achieved successful self-propelled automobile motion in 1769. Succumbing to problems of weight distribution, his invention never achieved practical success. Another Frenchman, Claude-François-Dorothée, the Marquis de Jouffroy d'Abbans, was responsible for the first successful steam-powered ship, which operated in 1776. Fascinated with new forms of transport, the French would later develop the hot-air balloon[155] (the Montgolfier brothers)

151. Christie 1982, p. 11.

152. Mantoux 1961, pp. 306–7, n. 4, citing Ashton 1963, p. 22, credits Isaac Wilkinson for this advance. In 1757, Wilkinson 'had taken out a patent for a system by which "a furnace, forge, or any other works may be blown from any waterfall... to several miles distant... by means of a pipe". [Patent No. 713, 12 March 1757]'.

153. Mantoux 1961, pp. 299–300.

154. Usher 1982, p. 356.

155. The first actual recorded manned flight of a balloon came in 1709, when the Brazilian Father Bartolomeu de Gusmão gave a demonstration to the Portuguese court in Lisbon. There is speculation that the ancient Nazcas of Peru, who were fascinated with flying, had actually pioneered balloon flight, and that this rather than alien visitations might explain the impressive gigantic animal figures and straight lines carved into the Nazca Plain (James and Thorpe 1994, pp. 109–10).

and the first parachute (Louis Lenormand), both inventions appearing in 1783.[156] In 1775, iron master John Wilkinson took out a patent on a new type of boring machine that produced metal cylinders with greater accuracy.[157] These he supplied to Watt, who without them would not have been able to complete his first successful separate condenser steam engine in 1776. In 1782, Watt introduced the double-acting steam engine, which doubled the power of the steam engine and would later prove suitable to the locomotive.

The 1780s saw a sudden leap in iron output in Britain that would last until the 1810s and 1820s. The spread of coke-fired furnaces was surely a part of the reason, but we must also consider the broader context of falling prices, falling wages, a growing and accelerating domestic market with constantly emerging new developments and demand for new goods. Iron-production facilities and the firms that ran them grew along with the size of the productive equipment and gave the owner an advantage over his rivals. The same held true in the brewing industry. In brewing, the means by which the technology could be improved to expand the scale of production was simple and did not require the arrival of steam or the railroad: the size of the vat and the utensils could be increased. By itself, this change 'gave economies of scale in costs of construction and materials'.[158] As the scale of production increased, an extraordinary degree of capitalisation was required in both the iron- and brewing industries. As vats and bellows expanded, so did the uses of iron. In 1775, American David Bushnell invented an iron submarine known as the turtle, the first ever to be used in combat. John Smeaton, the first self-described civil engineer began using the first cast-iron axle in 1778.[159] Samuel Harrison invented the first steel-nib pen in 1780, replacing the long-used quill pen. In 1779, Thomas Pritchard, John Wilkinson and

156. While he had studied physics and chemistry under Lavoisier and Berthollet, Lenormand's work may not have required much financing (his initial parachute-jump from a tree used simply two modified umbrellas). The Brothers Montgolfier, on the other hand, were underwritten by a committee of the Académie des Sciences de Paris, and: 'Given the scope of the project, the ministry of finance was quick to assume control of the financing for the venture' (Fortier 2004, p. 6). In general, inventors in France enjoyed greater state patronage while inventors in Britain tended to be self-financed amateurs (see Mathias 1972, pp. 79–81).

157. This patent was surely inspired by that taken out in 1758 by Wilkinson's father Isaac [Patent No. 732] for 'a new method of invention for casting Guns or Cannon, Fire Engines, Cylinders, Pipes and Sugar Rolls and other such like instruments… [to be cast] in an expeditious manner' (Soldon 1998, p. 35).

158. Mathias notes that one brewer, Richard Meux, gave '200 people a dinner to celebrate the opening of his huge vat – inside the vessel…' (Mathias 1979, pp. 214–6 and 247).

159. Museum of Science and Industry, Manchester, visit by author, November 1997. According to the Museum, Smeaton began using wrought-iron brackets on his wheels in 1780. The first use of iron *rims* on wheels, however, dates to the Celts, who used them on their chariots. Otherwise, wheels before Smeaton were made entirely out of wood.

Abraham Darby III completed the construction of the world's first iron bridge, with a hundred-foot span at a height of forty-five feet. As a visible demonstration of the versatility of wrought iron, it attracted world-wide attention. Larger iron bridges soon followed at Sunderland across the Wear in 1796 and another along the Severn in 1797. In 1784 Henry Shrapnel of Wiltshire, a lieutenant in the Royal Artillery, produced the hollow, exploding cannon-ball or 'shrapnel shell'.[160] In 1787, Wilkinson defied his critics by successfully launching the first iron barge on the Severn. Before his death in 1805 he envisioned iron ships.[161] In 1788, Matthew Boulton developed a coin-making machine powered by Watt's rotative engine. In 1797, he prevailed upon Parliament to pursue counterfeiters and standardise the coinage.[162] Also in 1797, New Jersey blacksmith Charles Newbold received a patent for the first cast-iron plough. Preceded by many experiments, the first 'practical' steam boat was realised through the application of William Symington's patent steam engine to a paddlewheel boat designed by Patrick Miller of Dumfries, Scotland. In 1802, the vessel successfully towed two barges along the Forth and Clyde Canal, commencing the era of the steam-powered towboat.

As coke smelting began to spread, it quickly became apparent that its application was limited to producing pig iron,[163] which was suitable for casting but too brittle for much else. In order to produce an iron with greater 'malleability, tensile strength, ductility, and other virtues' – namely, wrought iron – the metal was reheated in a forge and pounded with tilt hammers to reduce the carbon content

---

160. Shrapnel's name was erroneously applied to fragmentation from artillery shells, the current usage of 'shrapnel' today, for Shrapnel's cannonball was soon replaced by high explosive rounds.

161. In 1788, Wilkinson astonished his contemporaries when he supplied the city of Paris with cast-iron pipes totalling forty miles in length for the expansion of its waterworks. 'Towards the end of his life [Wilkinson] liked to repeat that iron was destined to take the place of most of the materials then in use, and the day would come when everywhere would be seen iron houses, iron roads, and iron ships. When he died in 1805 he was buried, in accordance with his wishes, in an iron coffin'. (Mantoux 1961, pp. 307–9; Christie 1982, p. 162.

162. Boulton wrote that a boy of 12 could operate his machine. Up until this time, coin-making was very labour-intensive. An additional advance was the retaining collar. In 1805 the Royal Mint left the Tower of London for Little Tower Hill. Contracts were made to buy machinery from Boulton, and by 1812 were furnished. In 1817 local coinage was forbidden in France, and Boulton supplied the machinery to standardise the coinage in France and several other countries (Soho House Museum, Birmingham, visit by author, 29 October 1997).

163. Pig iron was named after the process involved in its making. At the foundry, iron-ore mixed with lime was superheated for up to two weeks until it became liquid. It was then poured into sand furrows on the ground, the main furrow being the 'sow' and twenty-some furrows shooting off the saw known as 'pigs'. 'When sufficiently cool, but still plastic, the iron in the several pigs was broken off from the iron in the sow. The iron in the sow was then broken up into a number of pieces of the length of the pigs. The pig-iron was now ready' (Hammond and Hammond 1974b, p. 132).

and remove other impurities.[164] By 1750 and well after, this process relied mainly on charcoal and was both cumbersome and expensive. The search was on for a better method of making wrought iron. A partial solution was discovered in the use of reverbatory fire, known since medieval times but only applied to smelting in the late seventeenth century, which kept the flames from direct contact with the metal. In 1728, William Wood devised a method of enclosing the iron in crucibles to prevent sulphur contamination.[165] This method, known as 'potting and stamping', spread to all stages of refining around the year 1780, and according to Braudel was responsible for the subsequent seventy percent jump in iron output. But British iron was still of inferior quality. Henry Cort's trials with reverbatory fire, which led to patents in 1783 and 1784, delivered the crucial advance that allowed the British iron industry to excel in quality as well.[166] Known as 'puddling', Cort's technique involved removing the carbon by heating and cooling the metal until the higher quality metal could be separated out as a consequence of its higher melting point. Cort also invented 'rolling', which replaced hammering by squeezing out the dross. As opposed to hammering, rolling 'worked perhaps fifteen times as fast; and by grooving or otherwise performing the rolls, one could now turn out an almost unlimited range of those standardized crude shapes – beams, bars, rails and the like – that have come to constitute the framework of industry, construction, and transport'.[167] Potting, puddling and rolling revolutionised the British steel industry. Only the making of steel could not yet be made with coke. By now, Watt's steam engine was applied to the draught, enabling the larger furnaces to operate at greater capacity.[168] For Britain, this development had enormous ramifications. The switch to coked coal meant that the assault on the diminishing forests could be somewhat abated. And meanwhile, Britain's dependence on foreign bar iron was checked.[169]

---

164. The forge was called a 'finery' (hence the process was known as one of 'fining' the iron) or a 'chafery'. 'The pig-iron was reduced to the proper consistency in the finery, and then placed under a big hammer worked by a waterwheel, and beaten into a thick square or 'half bloom'. The heating and hammering were repeated a second time, and the product was then known as a 'bloom', a square bar with knobs at either end. These knobs had to undergo more heating and hammering before they were turned into bars' (of wrought or bar iron) (Hammond and Hammond 1974b, p. 132).

165. Henrycort.com 2007.

166. In what is apparently another case of simultaneous invention, puddling was also discovered and patented by Peter Onions, an obscure foreman at one of the iron works in Merthyr Tydfil in Wales (Patent No. 1398, 7 May 1783) (Mantoux 1961, p. 293, n. 6).

167. Landes 1991, p. 91.

168. Though it was not until 1829 – with Neilson's discovery that preheating the air could raise the limitations imposed by the capacity of the bellows – that another significant improvement in the draught was made (Landes 1991, pp. 90–1).

169. Deane and Cole 1969, p. 221.

The earliest accurate metal-working lathes, including iron mandrel lathes, date to around 1700. The achievements of Sweden's Christopher Polhem (1661–1751) in advancing machine tools were exceptional. He applied water power to the manufacture of various metal objects: 'Plowshares, harrow teeth, and hammer heads were among the coarser articles made; gun locks, door locks, clock wheels, tinned plates and [other] vessels were among the lighter and more elaborate shapes'.[170] Polhem's use of power shears and the rolling mill would be emulated outside of Sweden. Polhem's water-powered factory for producing clocks was built in 1699 in Stjärnsund, Sweden, pre-dating the Lombe factory by around two decades.[171] Around 1750, the mechanical slide rest appeared in Britain, and around the same time the tool-holder carriage was attached to the lathe as well. In 1778, French gunsmith Honoré Blanc called a group of politicians, scholars and military men together to demonstrate his discovery of interchangeable parts. Having disassembled a thousand muskets, he reassembled them from parts drawn at random. While the French government rejected his invention, Thomas Jefferson visited his workshop and wrote back to America about it. In 1783, Frenchman Samuel Rehe invented the grinder for sharpening tools. Around 1790, Massachusetts inventor Jacob Perkins devised the nail-making machine. Between 1795 and 1798, American inventor Eli Whitney took up Blanc's idea and made a similar demonstration of interchangeable parts before Congress, which quickly took up the idea. These were key contributions from France and America. However, in the late eighteenth and early nineteenth centuries, Britain yielded an exceptional number of foundational innovations in machine tools. In 1770, Jesse Ramsden invented the screw-cutting lathe, and in 1797 Henry Maudslay would build one entirely out of metal, which could cut screws with higher precision and enabled the standardisation of screw-thread sizes. In 1793, Samuel Bentham developed machines to more efficiently produce the wooden pulley blocks used in the rigging on sailing ships. In the early nineteenth century, Maudslay and engineer Marc Brunel would work with Bentham to improve upon his invention, which bored, mortised and finished the blocks.[172] Birmingham engineer Ralph Heaton invented the button-shank machine in 1794. 'Heaton's button shank machine is one of the earliest examples of a fully self-acting device capable of performing a whole series of consecutive operations without re-setting'.[173] Other notable inventions by Maudslay were the compound slide rest (1794) and the first bench micrometre (1805), pushing the detail of measurement to one

170. Usher 1982, p. 376.

171. The factory met with resistance from workers who feared they would be replaced by machines, an early example of a kind of 'Luddism' outside of Britain. The factory was mostly destroyed in a fire in 1734, but it continued to produce clocks.

172. Usher 1982, p. 378.

173. Workshop of the World 2007.

ten-thousandth of an inch. Maudslay's father-in-law was the reputable inventor and locksmith Joseph Bramah, who is credited with inventing the flushing toilet (1778), impenetrable locks, the hydraulic press (1795) and the hydraulic jack (1812). The contributions to the world of machine tools underwent a period of intensive refinement down to 1850.

If Britain was excelling in machinery, what were inventors outside Britain doing in the era of Napoleon? Bavaria gave us lithography, developed by Aloys Senefelder in 1796. Italy gave us the modern battery,[174] developed by Alessandro Volta in 1800. The Austrian Empire gave us the gas stove, developed by Moravian chemical manufacturer Zachäus Winzler in 1802. But the most prolific inventing nation next to Britain in this era was surely Britain's rival across the Channel. The French gave us a much improved oil lamp, the Argand Lamp (Ami Argand, 1784), which became the standard for home lighting down to the appearance of the kerosene lamp in 1850.[175] Carl Wilhelm Scheele of Sweden, born in Germany, is credited with being the first to isolate oxygen in 1771 and with discovering chlorine in 1774.[176] The French aristocrat Anton Lavoisier, the 'father of modern chemistry', named both oxygen in 1778 and hydrogen in 1783, disproved phlogistan-theory and developed the first table of elements. Comte Claude-Louis Berthollet was a chemist who became an inspector of a dyeworks in 1784, whereupon he was able to develop the use of chlorine as a bleaching agent.[177] Nicolas LeBlanc was awarded a prize by the French government in 1791 for discovering a process (the 'LeBlanc Process') for making sodium carbonate, much desired for use in French glass manufacturing, from common sodium chloride. Also in 1791, dentist Nicholas Dubois de Chemant took out a British patent on the manufacture of false teeth. This was an improvement upon the work of his partner, who in 1770 had introduced porcelain false teeth. In 1792, Napoleon's chief physician, Dominique Larrey, developed the *ambulance volantes* to carry wounded soldiers to designated hospitals. Equally useful for the French army was the optical telegraph, the first means devised for relaying detailed information over long distances, developed by Claude Chappe in 1793. The first successful

174. The concept of the battery may have been known in ancient Mesopotamia. In Baghdad, the discovery in 1936 of a small clay jar containing a copper cylinder sealed with bitumen has left scientists with no plausible explanations other than that it may have served as a battery sometime between 250 BCE and 250 CE (James and Thorpe 1994, pp. 149–50).

175. The Argand lamp was patented in London (12 March 1784) and was manufactured by Matthew Boulton. Like many inventors, Argand suffered chronic debt problems and while 'Boulton treated Argand very badly' he did comply with a request to forgive a debt of £475 (Delieb 1971, pp. 107–9).

176. Ede 2006, p. 123.

177. Daintith 1994, p. 78. In 1785, James Watt introduced bleach to England (Mantoux 1961, p. 245).

papermaking machine was patented in 1799 by Nicholas-Louis Robert, who sold the patent to the paper mill owner Leger Didot, who did nothing with it in France, but who in 1801 went to England, 'the one country in the world, which at that time possessed the capital, the enterprise, and the skill necessary to develop industrial mechanization'.[178] He approached Henry and Sealy Fourdrinier of the firm Bloxam and Fourdrinier, the leading wholesale stationers in London, and by 1806 the 'Fourdrinier' was working in several factories, and would soon revolutionise the entire papermaking industry. At the manufacturing exhibition in Paris in 1801, Joseph-Marie Jacquard of Lyons exhibited his 'Jacquard head' that allows punchcards to control the operations of a dobby loom in order to make specified patterns. His invention had a significant impact on textile manufacturing, but it was also an advance presaging the use of punchcards in computers. Silk-weavers in Lyons took to destroying his machines, but after a decade its use spread in France, and after 1820, in Britain. In 1826, French inventor Nicéphore Niépce produced the first permanent photograph on a polished pewter plate covered with bitumen. Thereafter, Niépce worked with Louis Daguerre in experimenting with silver and chalk compounds, and Daguerre introduced several improvements of his own after Niépce's death in 1833, laying the foundations for modern photography. In 1826, Benoit Fourneyron turned the waterwheel on its side to develop the first outward-flow water turbine, a far more efficient mechanism than the reactive turbine or 'Segner-wheel' (developed by Hungarian Ján Andrej Segner around 1750) and the inward-flow water turbine (Jean-Victor Poncelet, 1820). Finally, the classic case of simultaneous invention is the sewing machine, patented by Frenchman Barthélemy Thinomnier in 1830. Four years later, American inventor Walter Hunt, apparently without knowledge of Thinomnier's invention, developed a better model using a lock-stitch.

While the French were making scientific contributions to chemistry, dentistry, weaving, sewing and power generation, Britain continued to be the most prolific nation for inventors. In 1798 physician Edward Jenner devised the vaccination method. After 1807, gas lighting appeared in Europe's major cities, thanks to the Natural Light and Heat Company. In 1815, Humphrey Davy invented the miner's safety lamp and three years later Marc Brunel (a Frenchman who had lived in America and Britain) developed the tunnelling machine. By 1820 John McAdam had introduced Macadamised roads, improving the strength and drainage properties of road-building. In 1821, Michael Faraday introduced the electric motor. The reaping machine, forerunner of modern combine harvesters, was developed by Scotsman Patrick Bell in 1826. In yet another case of apparent simultaneous

178. Coleman 1958, pp. 179–82. The background to the development of papermaking machinery in France had to do with rising labour costs and strikes in the industry by the powerful *compagnages*, the forerunners to the early French trade unions.

invention, American Cyrus McCormick independently developed a rather different type of reaping machine five years later. Two additional American inventions of our period are: the revolver, patented by Elisha Collier and Artemis Wheeler in the same year (1818), and the pin-making machine, patented by Lemuel Wright in 1824.

We end this review with the advent of the locomotive, which for many signified the advent of the 'second' industrial revolution. In 1802, Cornish engineer Richard Trevithick introduced the next major step in the development of steam engines when he unveiled the first prototype for his high-pressure engine.[179] The following year he introduced the first successful locomotive. This was followed by Matthew Murray's 'Salamanca' engine in 1812, Christopher Blackett's 'Puffing Billy' in 1813, William Hedley's engine for the Wylam Colliery Railway, and George Stephenson's 'Locomotion' in 1825, which was the first public transport by steam locomotion. Stephenson went onto become the Arkwright of the railway, his company becoming the pre-eminent builder of railways in Britain, America and Europe.

Conclusion

It becomes quite apparent from this brief synopsis of the history of technology that human societies of all continents and races have been consistently inventive. The pace of invention appears to have received a significant boost from the formation of states, which could patronise science, education and the arts, and could organise production in new ways. Early masters of invention such as Hero or Zhang Heng undoubtedly enjoyed healthy stipends from the state, freeing them to focus on their labours. State societies appear to undergo periods of exceptional inventiveness. The scientific tradition that the Greeks handed down to the Romans and the Romans to Europe has left a powerful legacy. Arguably, the inventions devised in China between the Han and Ming dynasties had an even greater impact. Between the fall of Rome and the rise of the early modern states, Europe made few contributions outside the sphere of agriculture, and the Arab empire carried forward Greco-Roman knowledge and contributed substantial advances. The pace of European invention gathered momentum between the Renaissance and the Industrial Revolution. And this fact has facilitated the view of a continuous pan-European progress moving in teleological fashion in the 'technical conquest of nature that allows one and only one grand avenue of

179. Watt's patent had expired in 1800 'and the field of steam-power was thrown wide open'. Trevithick's 'high-pressure engines were soon applied successfully in transportation and mining, whereas low-pressure engines like Watt's remained the prime form of steam-power in manufacturing' (Mokyr 1994, p. 24).

advance',[180] with Britain 'precociously' being the first nation to realise what is sometimes assumed to be an inevitable outcome of historical and technological development for all nations: the Industrial Revolution.

After all, to the extent that we can measure progress or 'development' writ large, technological advance offers an easy empirical method of setting the benchmarks. This is the seductiveness of technological determinism, which as we have seen, shades the thinking of even those who consider themselves quite opposed to the concept. Max Weber wrote that machines did not call the factory into being, but adds that there is a correlation between the two. His claim that: 'The specialisation of work and Labour discipline within the workshop, however, formed a predisposing condition, even an impetus toward the increased application and improvement of machines' is followed by the stunning and possibly absurd claim that: 'Economically, the significance of the machines lay in the introduction of systematic calculation'.[181] Here, Weber seems to be conflating the systematic nature of bookkeeping and economic calculation with the systematic and repetitive motion of all machinery, treating the advance of the machine in the factory as the logical outgrowth of 'rational commerce'.[182] We could add a fourth model to our list: the rationality model. Enlightenment rationality, for Weber, was the *deus ex machina* that explains the Industrial Revolution. This points to something particular about European class society, and perhaps suggests an examination of social relations, but Weber gives us little by way of class analysis. What all the models we have discussed have in common is a degree of reductionism. Whether in the form of economism, 'demographism' or technological determinism, the tendency to assume that different societies will change along the same lines when the same phenomena affect them is widespread. This is not to say that studies that generally follow such an approach invariably lead to inaccurate conclusions. As has been shown, few if any authors actually embrace the idea that they are 'determinists'. The problem is rather one of incompleteness. And what is typically left out or ignored is an interrogation into how differing structures or the configurations of class relations between different societies affected by the same economic, demographic or technological events or phenomena generate completely different outcomes.

It is no doubt tempting to leap to the conclusion, as Heilbroner does, that the fact of independent invention (such as the parachute, the glider or the compass) and more dramatically *simultaneous* independent invention (the octant,

180. Heilbroner 1967, p. 336. Were Heilbroner to make this claim in terms not of technological advances *per se*, but in terms of the sequence of the discovery of scientific and technological principles, he might have a stronger case.

181. Weber 1961, p. 136.

182. 'Rational commerce is the field in which quantitative reckoning first appeared, to become dominant finally over the whole extent of economic life'. Weber 1961, p. 170.

the typewriter and the reaping machine) demonstrates that all societies are moving along the same 'grand avenue of advance' when it comes to technology. Yet, following Usher, we have argued that every invention is but the culmination of the work of many previous inventors working out solutions to problems. Each advance in machine engineering (gearing, interchangeable parts, electric automation) presents new possibilities for solving a particular problem or meeting a specific human need through mechanisation. The same principle of advancement applies not only to machines but to all applied sciences, such as medicine or chemistry. So as innovations appear and spread from one society to another, the possibility and likelihood of solving other problems or meeting other social needs may be enhanced. So long as societies are exchanging technologies, the general progression appears to follow a logical sequence. We know that the scientific revolution involved considerable sharing of results across national borders, so that scholars in many countries could be confronted with the same scientific problems at the same time, and for long periods of time. (Tracing the incremental advances is something that has to be done singly for each field.) Are these factors not sufficient to explain the occurrence of simultaneous invention without jumping to the conclusion that because the progression of innovation moves only in a forward direction, all societies are governed by a single, overarching logic of technological progress? Even if we concurred that this was so, we would still be at pains to explain why the Industrial Revolution started in Britain and Britain only.

One of the clues to some major differences in social relations can be ascertained from our review of inventions, especially when we examine the different emphases and the sponsors of the various inventors. What we observe is that the discoveries outside of Britain, particularly in France, are far more focused upon scientific principles, while Britain took the lead in machinery and components arising out of productive facilities. Mathias notes that in France there was: 'much greater state patronage through the *Académie des Sciences*, by military sponsorship, and direct industrial sponsorship, as with the research department attached to Sevres porcelain factory working on glazes, enamels and paints. Provincial academies also flourished in the main regional cities'.[183]

By contrast, in Britain there was a strong interest in 'amateur science' with an emphasis on relating science to industry, 'and in this, England is certainly unique in Europe'.[184] In England, local science societies 'flourished with very tiny material resources... being amateur and self-financing'.[185] In Europe, state patronage in the eighteenth century favoured the theoretical sciences. Calls for

183. Mathias 1972, p. 80.
184. Usher 1982, p. 78.
185. Usher 1982, p. 81.

greater empiricism in the mechanical arts were not heeded in a timely manner.[186] The key difference between Britain and the Continent is that manufacturing in Britain was coming to be regulated by market considerations and pressures; innovation was largely, but not entirely, a private affair. Scientific and industrial advancement in the rest of eighteenth-century Europe was still state-led. Thus the discovery of similar processes by which the refining of foundry iron in significant quantities could be carried out was discovered in Britain by the elder Darby, an iron founder whose aim was to be able to mass produce hollow iron ware, and in France by Réamur, a scientist whose primary aim was to understand the metallurgical properties of different grades of iron.[187] Explaining this disparity requires an examination of the historical development of social relations of production in different countries. And what such an examination reveals is that capitalism had been germinating in Britain for centuries, developing to the point where it could transform manufacturing even as it completed its transformation of agriculture. This provided a new social context in which practical innovation responded to the market-driven compulsion to revolutionise production in order to cut costs and raise profits. As new machines appeared, they contributed to and reinforced the transformation of manufacturing. But it was the competitive market logic of capitalism, not technology or machinery that led this transformation. In the process, the logic of capitalism demanded new technologies to further the transformation of manufacturing. To bring this point home, in chapter eight we will consider an example of how manufacturing could be revolutionised with little or no application of mechanical technology at all.

186. Wolfhard Weber credits Christian Wolff and G.W. von Leibniz for calling for a complete accounting of 'the mechanical possibilities of the territory [Germany] in order to establish . . . a much more perfect state as machine'. Wolff in particular stressed the need for 'cooperation between the mathematical-physical and empirical methods'. But 'With the professorships of cameral sciences institutionalized and with officials being more interested in jurisprudence than in technical and mathematical aspects the Wolffian concept of technical officials was delayed for decades' and only after the Seven Years' War was Wolff's cry taken up with any seriousness in Germany (Weber 1979, p. 74). Here is another example demonstrating the absence of capitalist social property relations and market imperatives on the continent.

187. Usher 1982, p. 374.

Chapter Seven

The Social Origins of the Factory

> In the schemes for elaborately organized workhouses and spinning schools, which filled the minds of reformers after the Restoration, the outlines of a factory system were already shaping.
>
> A.P. Wadsworth[1]

> The private factory emerges imperceptibly from antecedents that include the workhouse – the first experiment in organizing labour in concentrated groups.
>
> Charles Wilson[2]

Marx's well-known formula of the formal versus the real subsumption of labour implies a certain logical progression from earlier modes of production, through a kind of intermediate phase of formal subsumption to the real or fully-capitalist mode of production.[3] For shorthand, he referred to the intermediate phase as the period of manufacture, which lay between the

1. Wadsworth and Mann 1965, p. 91.
2. Wilson 1984, pp. 350–1.
3. In his 'Economic Manuscripts of 1861–63' (Marx 1989), Karl Marx defined the real and absolute subsumption of labour to capital as follows: 'I call the form which rests on absolute surplus-value the formal subsumption of labour under capital. It is distinguished only formally from other modes of production, in which the actual producers provide a surplus produce, a surplus-value. i.e. work more than the necessary labour-time, but for others rather than for themselves…With the real subsumption of labour under capital, all the changes we have discussed take place in the technological process, the labour process, and at the same time there are changes in the relation of the worker to his own production and to capital – and finally, the development of the productive power of labour takes place, in that the productive forces of social labour are developed, and only at that point does the application of natural forces on a large-scale, of science and of machinery, to direct production become possible'.

periods of guild predominance and machinofacture. This formula surely informed the conceptions behind the theory of proto-industrialisation. Yet the formula does not require that the causal forces that brought about the formal and real subsumption of labour in manufactures were restricted to manufactures alone, or that labour in agriculture did not follow a similar evolution. Indeed, broadly speaking it was agricultural labourers who were the first to experience the real subsumption of their labour through the extinguishing of their customary land rights at enclosure, whilst laws upholding customary regulation in manufactures tended to shield craft workers from full exposure to the market – and real subsumption to capital – for a longer period. We have already seen how by the seventeenth century, the trend across the entire English economy was toward a reduction in the independent status of labourers, or toward the formal subsumption of labour. But tracing the actual history of this movement is difficult because of the complexity and the number of variables.

As with any period of transition, the economy of early eighteenth-century Britain was full of contradictions. Each line of production followed its own course of development. Some lines of manufacturing, like silk and cotton were relatively exempt from the same strict customary regulation as found in woollens. And while as late as the early nineteenth century, weavers and shearmen in the woollen trade were still struggling to stave off the real subsumption to capital, as early as the 1720s and 1730s a small number of silk and cotton spinners were already working in mechanised factories. In agriculture meanwhile, open fields were still worked by 'peasants',[4] whilst at the same time enclosed fields were worked by a growing corps of tenant-farmers and wage labourers. And while it was predominantly in agriculture that the direct producers were being rendered market-dependent, exposing them to the prospect of becoming wage labourers subject to the full subsumption to capital, both parliamentary enclosures and the zenith of cottage manufacturing still lay ahead, paradoxically coinciding with the onset of the Industrial Revolution of the late eighteenth century.

In Chapter One, we traced the process by which the medieval guild hierarchy of master craftsman, journeyman and apprentice steadily eroded under pressure from merchants seeking control over company functions and seeking in general to expand production. By interposing themselves between the producer and the market, merchants were able to steadily increase their control over company functions. In the Elizabethan companies, they compromised for a bargain allowing them control over trade functions, but under which they were obligated to adhere to the regulations protecting the status of the craftsmen. In the Stuart

4. The term 'peasants' is placed in scare quotes because the social property relations that once defined the role of the peasant were now severely eroded. Rather than using the term peasants, Neeson adopts the term 'commoners'. See Chapter Five, p. 275, n. 67.

era, they gained more or less full control over most companies, provoking strong reactions from the craftsmen, including attempts at separate incorporation for craft lines and for journeymen. In rural manufacturing, merchants found an outlet for investment in enterprises that could circumvent the rules protecting the status of the craftsmen, and which would allow them to expand the scope of production. Here also, the putting-out system enabled merchants to control the direct producers' access to the market. Thus in both urban and rural contexts, large merchants were playing an increasingly dominant role in the context of an expanding marketplace.

For Nef, Unwin and so many others, the combination of waged labour, accumulation of profits and an expanding circuit of trade and investment is sufficient to label merchant-employers and small masters who have risen to become large masters as 'capitalist employers'. Kriedte writes that 'Merchant capital, by drawing an essentially pre-capitalist social formation – namely peasant society – into its sphere, promoted the process of accumulation and became the pacemaker of the general acceptance of the market principle'.[5] Yet as we have seen, we do not have a clear theory from these authors that delineates what is specifically 'capitalist' about mercantile trade and wage labour. Moreover, Kriedte's identification of the agrarian sector as 'an essentially pre-capitalist social formation' highlights the uncritical assumption that urban trade and manufacturing equate with capitalism and progress, while associating agriculture with tradition and stagnation. Clearly the dissolution of customary craft regulation and the subsequent development of an expanding workforce of wage labourers without the formally recognised protection of guild or company contributed to the rise of a proletarian labour force that could be moved into factories. But this 'internal' causal factor was not a sufficient condition for the Industrial Revolution any more than were demographic and commercial trends across Europe. We cannot assume that by tracing the dissolution of customary regulation of labour, we have explained how the Industrial Revolution in the eighteenth century was made possible. As we shall see, there were other factors conditioning both the formal and later the real subsumption of labour in manufactures.

Throughout the eighteenth century and well into the nineteenth, journeymen and other direct producers in the 'honourable trades' continued to resist the reduction of their status to mere wage labourers. How was this possible? We can, of course, point to the friendly societies. But in the putting-out system and certain other lines of manufacturing, there were workers with no such organisation to protect them. Why then were they not fully expropriated in the seventeenth century? There are at least two reasons. First, we must remember that

5. Kriedte, Medick and Schlumbohm 1981, p. 37.

merchant-employers were still merchants, focused on maximisation of profit by *trade*. Where increased demand meant the need to increase production, the typical solution for the merchant was to increase the scale of production by employing more workers. In seeking to circumvent restrictions on the number of apprentices, merchants turned to the countryside, where they found a plentiful supply of domestic labourers who lacked the protections enjoyed by urban workers and their organisations, which meant that the merchants could disregard state law and company rules. In particular, by ignoring apprenticeship rules, merchant-employers could expand their absolute surplus by employing more labourers at the loom or the wheel. Whereas we find few examples of employers making a conscious effort to effect increases in *productivity* prior to the latter half of the eighteenth century, it is useful to characterise this situation as one of formal but not real subsumption. Secondly, to the extent that the merchant-employer was a capitalist, he was a merchant capitalist, employing merchant capital. The materials he may have put out and the looms and wheels he may have let out to the producer were part of his capital-as-stock, but the labour of the semi-dependent worker was technically not a part of his capital, not yet a 'fictitious' commodity in Polanyi's terms. In order to achieve increases in productivity, employers would need to be in a position to dictate the terms of employment by seizing control over the labour process. In agriculture, the tenant-farmer employing a hired hand was technically in such a position. And some degree of mechanisation took place in eighteenth-century agriculture, but it was not yet systematic. The majority of hiring was probably casual, being either part-time throughout the year or seasonal at planting and harvest-times. The principal importance of agrarian labourers being deprived of their customary access to the land is that their conversion to market dependence facilitated the expansion of both: 1) domestic markets generally, as ever greater numbers of people shifted from self-sufficiency to accessing their means of subsistence and other consumer goods from the market; and 2) a growing national labour market. In short, the extinguishing of customary rights through enclosure left agrarian producers exposed to the vagaries of the market in a way that their urban counterparts were not.

Control over the labour process is the last thing that organised, honourable craftsmen in the towns were willing to yield. As independent craftsmen, journeymen and masters who owned their own tools (individually or collectively), they therefore owned a critical component of the means of production. Even in putting-out arrangements, or when craftsmen were paid by the piece, the tools or machines (looms, knitting frames, and so on) were also in the possession of the producer, not the merchant-employer or his factory. The seventeenth-century craftsman was separated from direct access to the *market*, but not the means of production. According to Unwin, manufacturing in this period was characterised by various

> intermediate forms of industrial organization which have been grouped together under the term 'domestic system'. The decay of those forms and their ultimate displacement by the factory system was due to the growth of industrial capital. As long as the small master owned most of the industrial capital required for the exercise of his calling, he was not a mere wage-earner, however much he might be dependent on the capital of the trader. With the appearance of the industrial capitalist, who organized manufacture on a large scale and supplied not only the circulating but sometimes also the fixed capital, the small master was reduced either to the position of a journeyman, or to that of a wage-earning master scarcely distinguishable from a journeyman.[6]

Unwin apparently sees a 'proto-capitalist' in the small master. But how many small masters or their successors ever went on to succeed as industrial capitalists? In the midst of a growing domestic market, probably most small masters derived considerable benefit from the expanding labour market. But to the extent that customary modes of regulating the workplace were followed, their 'capital' was not a social relation of capital. We understand the 'growth of industrial-capital' in this passage to mean merchant capital or stock, but not necessarily capital as a social relation, as understood by Marx. Prior to the appearance of the first factories in the eighteenth century, we find much evidence of employers and putter-outers seeking to expand their operation to achieve economies of scale or to intensify production by demanding greater output from workers, but little evidence of the conscious arrangement of the labour process by a capitalist employer whose 'capital' is not merely investments in buildings, machinery and other forms of wealth, but who in effect 'owns' the very process of production as a wealth-generating form of private and exclusive property. This includes the ownership of the worker's labour-power as a form of capital. In the absence of the critical elements of *ownership* of the means of production and control over the labour process by the capitalist employer, pre-industrial manufacturing in general lacked fully-capitalist principles of operation.[7] Once factory production made its appearance, labourers in the 'honourable trades', organised in unions and friendly societies consciously (and sometimes violently) resisted any attempts that threatened their autonomy as independent craftsmen or their control over the labour process. Industrial capitalism did not arrive unopposed. Yet like the first enclosures, the first factories encountered less resistance than those that came

6. Unwin 1963, p. 225.

7. Kriedte notes that even under conditions of 'proto-industrialisation', workers have 'considerable control over the workforce' (Kriedte, Medick and Schlumbohm 1981, p. 53).

later, mainly because they employed mainly women, children and transient male workers, and thus beyond the future they portended, posed little direct threat to the independent craftsmen who, like the copyholder, had a legal basis upon which to appeal to custom in defence of their independent status.

This chapter attempts to chart a course through the murky waters of labour relations in manufacturing in the early eighteenth century by first discussing the overall economic environment, and secondly by exploring the ties between the increasing numbers of dislocated workers (in the midst of a demographic pause, which tells us that population growth could not have been the only cause of their increasing numbers), and the earliest factories.

'Plen-ty of time': The multifarious conditions of labour, 1700–60

By the early eighteenth century, the remaining guilds that had once functioned as fraternal orders to protect the rights and privileges of labouring men increasingly faced being overtaken or pushed out of their companies by merchants and larger masters. As craftsmen and craftswomen (prior to the 1760s the term 'journeymen' often encompassed both sexes),[8] they still required some type of association through which to assert their collective power, and these associations often attempted to assert the same rights once enjoyed by the guilds. In many crafts, the journeymen broke away from the bigger masters and founded their own 'friendly societies', in part as a means of using collective solidarity to try and enforce and preserve the regulations under 'Queen Betty's Law'. Typically operating without a charter, such companies could hold sway over local politics, especially those in which small masters could vote. Among the first to break away were the hatters, who had organised themselves in 1700, followed by the journeymen curriers in 1708. The boundaries between guilds, friendly societies and combinations or unions was never definite in the eighteenth century, and only a comprehensive study of the evolution of all the trades would clarify precisely how each trade developed and where the distinctions fell.

In London, one reason why craft companies became less prominent is that by the early eighteenth century they had begun to engage in a more strategic approach to prosecuting interlopers, that of persuading individuals to inform the authorities on their behalf. Since this was costly to the individual, some encouragement was needed. And so in response to petitions calling for clarification of

8. Berg provides examples of the smallware weavers in Manchester in the 1740s and 'an informal union of female wool spinners called the sisterhood' which in 1788 'stirred the men to riot over pauper labour and machinery'. Starting with the Spitalfields silk-weavers in 1769, however, 'women were increasingly excluded from the organizations if not from the trades' (Berg 1985, p. 160).

the rules which the Common Council had not addressed in over a century, the Corporation passed an act in 1712 reaffirming the status of company by-laws as well as its intent to punish interlopers. This revitalised, for a time, the practice of making rounds for the purposes of search and seizure. But this practice was now highly unpopular, the fees that were raised rarely covered the expense of the procedure and the liverymen who were members of the court of assistants had little incentive to invest their time in it. The act also suffered from other problems, such as the inability of some employers to find freemen to work in their trades. Another issue was that employers were increasingly less concerned about outside competition than they were about inside combination amongst their journeymen. By 1720 the Council was receiving petitions for repeal. A compromise was later worked out in 1750 when the Common Council began to sell licenses for employing non-freemen.[9]

Against the view popularised by the Hammonds that trade unions date from the end of the eighteenth century, Dobson cites literary evidence of the formation of a union of weavers, wool-combers and labourers striking for higher wages in 1677: 'Goeing forth he saw a great company of men ffollowing a ffidler . . . he heard Aaron Atkins say he was the man who made the Proclamacon and that the intention thereof was to engage as many as he could for the raising of their wages sixpence per weeke'.[10]

In 1717, troops were dispatched to Devon to break up a crowd of 900 weavers 'marching from town to town, cutting looms and breaking the masters' jars of oil'.[11] In London, tailors and curriers formed unions and tested 'the indictment for conspiracy as a legal weapon against strikes'.[12] In 1721, more than 7,000 journeymen tailors are said to have entered into combination to raise wages and leave work an hour sooner. A famous judgment of that year in Cambridge concluded: ' "[I]t is not the denial to work except for more wages than is allowed by statute, but it is for a conspiracy to raise their wages, for which these defendants are indicted" '.[13] The strike resulted in an act to punish tailors who enter into combinations to seek higher wages with two months' imprisonment. The act also fixed the tailors' hours and wages. Combining to effect a raise in wages was treated as an act of conspiracy under common law, but this required employers to wait

9. Kellett 1958, pp. 381–94 argues that while some authorities, such as Unwin, have argued that the licensing scheme equalled the official abandonment of the old guild-system of regulation, it was in his view an attempt to overhaul the system and make it more effective. Not until 1856 were the guild laws fully abolished in London.
10. Dobson 1980, pp. 19–20 citing Howard 1932, pp. 259–60.
11. Dobson 1980, pp. 19–20.
12. Dobson 1980, p. 21.
13. Ibid., citing 'a famous judgment against some striking tailors of Cambridge in 1721' as quoted in Cole and Filson 1965, pp. 88–9.

Table 7.1. Legislation against combination and property damage: 1718–26[14]

1718	Royal proclamation against journeyman's clubs
1719	Act to punish frame breaking
1720	Act making combinations illegal among London crafts
1721	Act to discipline journeymen tailors
1726	Acts against unlawful clubs and societies

until the next quarterly session to prosecute. This, the first anti-combination act, was designed to speed up the process by allowing summary judgment at trial before two justices of the peace.[15] Dobson listed 23 industrial disputes occurring before 1730, and 383 overall between 1717 and 1800.[16] In 1717 and again in 1725 the Wool-combers led militant strikes, destroying looms and serges, and 'the Mayor of Bradninch, attempting to put down a riot, narrowly escaped being killed'.[17] An act punishing the formation of combinations among woolcombers with three months' imprisonment was passed in 1726. Passed within three years of the Black Act, it also made loom breaking a capital offence. Balancing this out, the act also barred employers from paying workers in truck.[18] The so-called 'gin riots' in 1736 are normally attributed to the Government's attempts to restrict sales of gin and spirits. But these protests:

> also involved the resentment of building workers and weavers at being displaced from employment by the cheaper Irish. At one point the grievance brought out an East End mob 4,000 strong which destroyed some Irish public houses. Among nine taken into custody were a weaver, sawyer, carpenter, brewer, blacksmith and several servants. The combers of Norwich went on strike for better wages and to protest blacklegs being brought in to replace them, one comber asking: "We are social creatures and cannot live without each other, and why should you destroy community?"[19]

---

14. Leeson 1979, p. 86 and Owen 1975, p. 36. Note that these dates follow the defeat of the Jacobite rising of 1715, after which harsher penalties in general were meted out for all crimes under a régime that felt itself more secure, with fewer enemies to pursue than in the past.

15. The Act (7 Geo. I, st. 1, c. 13) required the judgment be made within three months of the offence. It was improved upon during another bout of unrest among the Tailors during the Wilkes disturbances in 1768 (8 Geo. III, c. 17). Orth 1987, pp. 181–4.

16. Dobson 1980, pp. 22–5.

17. Wilson 1984, p. 291.

18. This act (12 Geo. I, c. 34, §2) was renewed in 1756 (30 Geo. II, c. 12, §1) with new language empowering the justices of the peace to fix wages for weavers. Orth 1987, p. 186.

19. Wilson 1984, p. 291.

The evidence would appear to be clear: 'organisations recognizable as trade unions were in existence by the first two decades of the eighteenth century'.[20] By the 1750s, the organisational rules that were followed by some of these organisations 'show already meticulous attention to procedure and to institutional etiquette'.[21]

Faced with tremendous new opportunities based on the expansion of trade, the state was now setting broad economic policy and Parliament was eager to help employers fighting the battle under the banner of free trade, as the term was understood at that time. This sympathy for employers would eventually be cultivated by an employers' lobby. Long before the Combination Acts of 1799–1801, large employers managed to secure the passage of combination-busting legislation specific to their trade (see Table 7.1). In 1758, weavers in the Manchester area launched a major strike seeking a return to 1730s prices and recognition of their Manchester Smallware Weavers' Society. They were defeated by prosecution for illegal combination. In 1760, Worsted weavers in Manchester were similarly defeated by prosecution. On balance, the eighteenth century was one 'of active industrial legislation, but of a distinct class character'.[22] We note the elitist attitude of the merchants and larger employers in this period: 'In 1716 the master masons decided that the "whifflers" or stewards at the Lord Mayor's procession should not dine with them but have three shillings and sixpence to eat elsewhere. In 1724 a surgeon was called to attend to a master coachmaker following a "riot" at the annual celebration and several journeymen were prosecuted'.[23]

The Government had many reasons, however, not to favour a free and unregulated labour market. For example, when duties were imposed on indentureships after 1701, the state had at that time a financial incentive to preserve them. In 1725, the making of broadcloth in the West Riding was restricted by an Act of Parliament to persons who had served their seven-year apprenticeships. The act was repealed in 1733, however. In 1751 a report by a committee of the Commons argued strongly against compulsory apprenticeship.

The Statute of Apprentices (1564–1814) was still widely observed in 1700, though henceforth a prolonged battle to break 'legal' or customarily 'fair' limits on the number of apprentices ensued. The bigger masters cried that the old craft rules denied them labour, or in other words cheap labour, as they argued against wage rates set by custom. The seven-year apprenticeship rule as well as the limit on the ratio of boys to men was another obstacle that stood in the way of them expanding their workshops. But to the smaller masters, apprenticeship brought

20. Rule 1992a, pp. 206–7.
21. Thompson 1991, p. 457.
22. Leeson 1979, p. 87.
23. Leeson, 1979, p. 90.

fees paid upon indenture, and was for that reason not undesirable. The primary group interested in preserving the system of apprentices was the journeymen, who were prepared to wage a fierce battle to defend the apprenticeship rules and keep 'boys' and 'forrens' out of their trade. Their wages were kept high by limiting the numbers of journeymen in the trade:

> This element of control over entry to the trade was crucial to the prospects of artisan unions. A frontier of skill had to be defended against dilution by the unskilled, including large numbers of women. 'Unfair' workers, 'knobsticks' as the calico printers called them, were not to be worked with, and in this defence, fundamental to all other purposes such as maintaining or improving wages or hours, the artisans were able to claim a legitimacy not only from the 'customs of the trade' but from the statue of artificers passed in 1564 and popularly known as '5 Elizabeth'. This statutory requirement for an apprenticeship to be served before trade could be taken up was not repealed until 1814 in the face of organised trade union opposition. Although throughout the preceding century case law decisions had narrowed its scope and denied its extension to any trade not in being at the time of its passage, it had remained nevertheless of great importance as a legitimating symbol of skilled labour's 'rights'.[24]

In general the cleavage within the various craft trades deepened between journeymen, their allies and small masters on the one hand, and merchants and larger manufacturing masters on the other.[25] Wherever possible, the larger masters attacked the apprenticeship rules.

In the newer towns such as Birmingham, Manchester, Leeds or Wolverhampton, it was often unnecessary to have served an apprenticeship in order to enter a specific trade. Men of 'native wit, though of little education' found in these places 'a climate favourable to their enterprise'.[26] 'Neither Birmingham nor Wolverhampton was hampered by the remnants of medieval gild control that lingered at Coventry or Lichfield'.[27] Josiah Wedgwood (a figure we shall examine in greater depth in Chapter Eight as the leading industrialist in the potting trade of the later eighteenth century), was just 15 years old in 1745, the year in which

---

24. Rule 1992a, pp. 208–9.

25. Leeson 1979, pp. 83–4. Standing in the way of the larger masters was the seven-year apprenticeship rule as well as the limit on the ratio of boys to men, both of which employers were lobbying the government to suspend and were anyway violating despite this being ancient practice. Employers also increasingly expected journeymen to train orphans and children recruited from the workhouses, accepting a premium from the parish-funds in the process. 'Finally, when the apprentice was trained, they would have pupil replace teacher at the loom or bench. This process was still able to provoke the skilled worker to fury in the 1890s'.

26. Ashton 1964, p. 16.

27. Wilson 1984, p. 300.

he signed a formal Indenture of Apprenticeship binding him to five years of service in return for which his master would '"learn his Apprentice the said Art of Throwing and Handleing"'.[28] But Wedgwood's case may have been exceptional, since apprenticeships of this sort had declined since the late seventeenth century. Between 1710 and 1760 only 29 apprentices had registered in the Potteries, among whom nine (including Josiah Wedgwood) became master-potters. 'The difficult art of throwing on the wheel was the most highly rated of all the potter's skills and only those who were expected to become master craftsmen served such an apprenticeship'.[29]

And yet at the same time, the economic climate of the early eighteenth century was favourable to the small producer of manufactures. Falling agricultural prices may have brought considerable hardship to the countryside, but in the towns it meant a more comfortable living could be had on the cheap. And so long as the small producer 'owned his tools and stock-in-trade and sold his product on the market, he was clearly the owner of a business concern ...'[30] The key difference, here, is whether the product could be sold on the open market, or as with most of the many stages of textile production, the product only served as raw material for the next stage in the process. 'A small man might make and market a piece of kersey: he could hardly do the same for a piece of worsted or a variety of smallwares'.[31] Another benefit to the small producer was the increasing availability of credit. Credit was not a one-way street; it ran in all directions. So merchants lent to manufacturers, but manufacturers also supplied goods to merchants on credit. Poor labourers were generally forced to provide what amounts to credit by foregoing wages. For example, farm servants were typically paid at the end of the year. Between payments, they generally received only board and lodgings. In manufacture: 'The employer was accustomed to make up his accounts with his workers, not weekly, but at the end of a period that might run to two or three months: when the worker was able and content to wait from one settlement to the next he was, in effect, giving credit to his employer'.[32]

Since few workingmen could afford to wait the full period, interim measures were required, and borrowing from outside the workplace was the non-confrontational alternative to seeking higher wages. In times of crisis, friendly

28. Reilly 1992, pp. 3–4.
29. Ibid.
30. Ashton 1964, 97. It is unclear which part of the eighteenth century Ashton is referring to in this passage, but the independence of the skilled workman faced far greater threats in the second half of the century than the first.
31. Ashton 1964, pp. 97–8.
32. Ashton 1964, p. 207.

societies could offer a kind of insurance against sickness, periods of unemployment or, what was more common, underemployment.[33]

In textiles and mining as well, full-time employment was rare. And, of course, few wage labourers on the farm worked the whole year round. Workers could be called away from their farms when there was work to be done improving a local road. In agricultural regions, employment probably reached its highest point from July to October, when looms fell idle as the chores associated with bringing in the harvest – 'making hay, reaping corn, picking hops and fruit' – took precedent. There is, of course, no neat way of distinguishing between wage labourers on the farm and those in manufactures. 'In Cornwall men divided their time between mining and fishing for pilchards; in Yorkshire the fulling mills often worked only between October and Whitsuntide, when water was plentiful...'[34] Yet being under-employed was still far from being a matter in which labourers had no choice. Ashton writes:

> It would be wrong to imagine that what the ordinary man sought above all was continuity of work. Casual methods of hiring naturally engendered casual habits. It is true that the workers resented the imposition of unemployment... But leisure, at times of their own choice, stood high on their scale of preferences. If it is true that they observed fewer holy days than their fellows of Papist France, it would be idle to deny that a large part of their energies went into channels largely outside the economic system. In most parts of the country there were annual fairs or wakes during which little or no work was done.[35]

These many and seemingly random and endless sources of work stoppages might be expected to have caused great concern for employers, yet far more serious was the tendency for workers to extend their weekend by taking a holiday on 'Saint Monday'. The pace of work in manufactures generally was irregular, and that applied to the working week as much as the working year: 'The work pattern was one of alternate bouts of intense labour and of idleness, wherever men were in control of their own working lives... On Monday or Tuesday, according

33. Wilson 1984, p. 336.

34. Ashton 1964, pp. 202–3. In addition to the seasonal ebb and flow of agrarian activities, other 'use-value obstacles' could result in idle hands: heavy storms could make roads impassable, temporarily cutting off access to markets with the same effect as a sharp fall in demand for a particular product; a local epidemic could have a similar effect, and a drought could render harvesting activities pointless. To these problems we must add war, as well as occasional riots and other social disturbances. (On the use of the term 'use-value obstacles' see the following two articles that initiated a debate in the *The Journal of Peasant Studies*: Albritton 1993, pp. 427–8; and Zmolek 2000, pp. 155–6.

35. Ashton 1964, pp. 203–4. In this passage, Ashton quotes Smith 1969, p. 390.

to tradition, the hand-loom went to the slow chant of *Plen-ty of Time, Plen-ty of Time*: on Thursday and Friday, *A day t'lat, A day t'lat*'.[36]

Saint Monday was a source of great lament for moralists and masters, though not all found fault with the cycle of labour as it was in this form.[37] We must bear in mind that work was still largely unsupervised. In the textile trades, it was carried out in the home, and the merchant-employer engaged in putting-out raw materials would have been in the first instance concerned that the work be done by the arranged time for pick-up. Small masters were often sanguine about the practice, and used Monday for personal business or such tasks as banking.

Wages and the emerging labour market

Conclusive data concerning wages for our period is lacking, but what does exist suggests that the early eighteenth century was a period characterised by falling prices and steady wages, which in turn suggests that real incomes rose moderately in all regions. Thus, surprisingly, incomes moved inversely to the movement of prices. Meanwhile, greater liquidity in the form of a new abundance of credit also helped to ease pressures on the economy to prevent monetary deflation.[38] Rising incomes could be attributed to the price of food falling faster than the price of manufactured goods, and the slow rate of population growth, which contributed to scarcity in the emerging labour market. The *rate* at which wages rose, however, varied greatly from region to region: 'After a period of uncertainty in the first two decades real wages rose in all four districts in the twenties and thirties by amounts ranging from 10 per cent in the case of labourers in the southern rural districts to 45 per cent or more for both labourers and craftsmen in the North. In the forties and fifties, however, the trend was generally downward, until by 1760 the gain registered in the earlier decades by workers in the rural South (but not in London and the North) had apparently been wiped out'.[39]

36. Thompson 1993, p. 373.

37. Smith 1957, Vol. 1, as cited in Ashton 1964, p. 205 was among those who felt that 'Great labour . . . is in most men naturally followed by a great desire for relaxation'.

38. Coleman 1977, pp. 99–100.

39. Deane and Cole 1969, p. 21. Deane and Cole appear to contradict themselves when they write on p. 18 that the regional variation in wage rates narrowed over the course of the eighteenth century and then write on p. 21 that regional trends in wages diverged more widely after 1750. The contradiction may be more apparent than real if we consider that the rapidly industrialising North-West and Midlands saw wages rise from the lowest to nearly the highest in this period, while the growth of wages in other areas not experiencing the same rapid growth in manufacturing was far slower (if not stagnant or declining in some regions). Thus it was possible that while the factors controlling wage rates produced extremely different results in the late eighteenth century, the expansion and increasing interconnectedness of the domestic market was gradually bringing common factors to bear on the wage rates of all regions. Furthermore, it would appear that

But there was more to this regional variation than the previously discussed differentiation between the expanding manufacturing districts of the North and the agrarian-capitalist South. While there was an emerging labour market in which ever larger numbers of market-dependent labourers sought employment, non-market factors still governed wages. In many towns, wage rates for unskilled labour in specific lines of work appear to have been set by custom alone:

> According to Dr. Gilboy, at Westminster and Southwark the wages of the mason's labourer stood at 2*s.* a day for more than fifty years after 1731, and at Oxford the pay of the builder's labourer stood at approximately 1*s.* 3*d.* a day from 1700 to 1770. Generally the wages of skilled workers were less rigid. But over the period 1700–1790 the daily rate of bricklayers, masons, and plumbers at Westminster and Southwark never fell below 2*s.* 6*d.* or rose above 3*s.* For seventy-eight years the plumber's wage stood at 3*s.*, and for fifty-six years the plasterer's wage never varied from the same figure. Nor was this rigidity peculiar to building. At Griff colliery in Warwickshire in 1729, the normal daily wage of 1*s.* 6*d.* was the same as had existed in 1701.[40]

Despite these examples of rigidity of wages in specific areas, wages for the same occupation could vary widely between one region and the next. Smith regarded higher rates of pay in some areas 'as compensation "for those anxious and desponding moments which the thought of so precarious a situation must sometimes occasion" '.[41] Ashton comments that were it simply a matter of equity, 'large numbers of women, and scores of thousands of labourers in London . . . might have established as convincing a claim to high wages as that of the building workers or coal-heavers'.[42] Higher wages were intended to retain labourers who otherwise would have sought employment elsewhere, or in other words, wages were in large part determined by *local* supply and demand. However, for unskilled labour, where supply was effectively unlimited, customary notions about what constituted a just wage, or where such wages had stood 'time out of mind' could be a major determining factor. Broad changes across trades and skill sets operated on a longer time scale. Lancashire began the century relatively under-populated; the labour supply was low and demand high. As investment in manufactures gathered momentum, wages in Lancashire grew more than in any

---

for agrarian wage labourers in the South, low prices and moderately rising wages in the 'depressed' 1740s meant that times were good for them, while after the unsteady recovery that followed their relative incomes shrank, which would demonstrate again that the so-called agrarian depression was only a depression for some.

40. Ashton 1964, pp. 219–20.
41. Smith 1957, Vol. 1, Chapter Eight, as cited in Ashton 1964, pp. 221–2.
42. Ashton 1964, pp. 219–20.

other region, starting below average and rivalling the high wages of London by the end of the century.

Some apprentices and journeymen were paid out of the wages of those who directed them. Collective payment was common. Working in pairs, sawyers received a joint daily wage. Payment could come in the form of cash, or a portion of the product. Some worked in their homes, others such as coalminers were provided with a cottage for little or no rent.[43] The unit of time for pay could be the hour, the day, the week, or in some cases even the year. Weavers, stockingers and spinners, among others, were paid by the amount of product they produced, even though piecework was not officially allowed before 1755.

More than just regions and varieties of working conditions add to the complexity of understanding wage rates in this period. 'Differences of race, age, and sex operated through demand or supply, to produce marked differences in rates of wages'.[44] Spinning was generally done by women and children in their own homes. Few women found employment in coal mining or iron works, but Irishmen, noted for their strength, were employed at low rates as coal-heavers, dock-workers and the like. Few Christian employers would take on Jews as apprentices. As most were refugees, and since they could not work on the Sabbath, their position in the labour market was weak. Immigrants as a whole, however, made an enormous contribution to the development of British manufacturing. The new industries growing up in this period – silk, paper and glass – 'owed much to immigrants from Europe; and the list of names of merchants who presented their congratulations to George III on his accession is eloquent of the part played by men of continental origin in the commerce of London'.[45] As with the paucity of data on wages, so too there are no reliable statistics on either immigration or emigration in this period, particularly because the bureaucracy lacked the capacity to monitor the ever-increasing flow of goods and people as the growth of the ports increased.

As the century progressed, by-employment in agriculture became less common and more households were gaining income strictly from manufacturing work. Waged work in agriculture, however, continued to be characterised by endemic underemployment.[46] Additionally, work was increasingly paid in wages, while the portion paid in kind steadily declined. 'A survey of the measures passed [between 1703 and 1777] to suppress embezzlement and delay in returning

43. Ashton 1964, pp. 217–18.
44. Ashton 1964, pp. 222–4.
45. Ashton 1964, p. 10.
46. Kussmaul 1994, p. 3.

materials shows a progressive increase of penalties'.[47] Inspectors appointed by local JPs formed a kind of industrial police. As the wage relationship became more predominant, and 'as other forms of social control and influence, such as that of the lower clergy, diminished, the people were given a space in which to make their own culture. This freedom did not necessarily find expression in forms which were in conflict with the ruling patrician elite'.[48] In fact the gentry patronised popular leisure, with a willingness to tolerate it and be functionally involved. For example, the popularity of horse racing expanded in the eighteenth century, involving the 'ultimate level of participation as a mass spectator sport reaching down to the betting proletariat'.[49]

The gradual spread of the practice of paying monetary wages was a key aspect to the process by which labour was being dis-embedded from customary forms of regulation. Cash payments to the poor in the form of poor relief further facilitated the growth of the money-wage economy. Money wages made credit easier to obtain, and more directly linked workers to the emerging markets in consumer goods, exposing new wage-earners to a compulsion they had not previously experienced so directly: the compulsion to consume. The falling prices of the period facilitated the beginnings of a consumer market as the pace of consumption in new and old household wares increased: window panes, cast-iron pots, brass door handles and other metalwares, coal, silk, cotton cloths, molasses, sugar, tobacco, coffee and tea. The increasing pace of consumption 'is at first too slow and too slight to show through the crude arithmetical apparatus we use to measure these things, but the churning vitality of industry was widely visible'.[50] Providing a typology of the multitude of various arrangements and forms of labour in this period would require a full study in its own right. But the broad outline presented here is one of a labour market in the process of being dis-embedded from the age-old economy dominated by custom. In the process, both the play of market forces and the force of normative rules based in mostly local custom act upon prices, wage rates and the production process,

---

47. Ashton 1964, pp. 210–11, citing Macpherson 1804, pp. 44 and 72. In Chapter Ten, we will explore the question of 'takings' in more depth.

48. Rule 1992a, pp. 162–3.

49. Rule 1992a, p. 46. The preference for leisure activities on the part of workers not restricted to non-market activities, as testified in the 1730s and 1740s by the soaring amount of gin and other spirits produced and consumed by the lower orders. Employers increasingly complained of excessive drinking by their employees, and not without reason. 'Consumption of gin increased six-fold between 1700 and 1743'. Leisure and luxury were not entirely the realm of the rich, working people did invest their money and their 'emotional capital' in leisure pastimes.

50. Wilson 1984, p. 288 and Coleman 1977, pp. 164–72.

giving rise to endless variations, contradictions and, for labour, a situation aptly summarised by the phrase 'formal subsumption to capital'.

Concentration and regional specialisation

Writing on the period 1650–1750, Coleman writes that the historian of industry 'is often faced with seemingly contradictory evidence, of enterprise and complacency, of growth and stagnation'.[51] But the long-term trend is clear, adds Coleman: this was an age of investment and enterprise in English industry, not manifest in the kind of spectacular changes seen in the succeeding century, but vitally important in providing the stronger and more flexible bases from which that later revolution could be launched. Despite the 'churning vitality of industry', manufacturing remained rooted in particular localities. As the expanding domestic market grew more integrated, it afforded greater concentration of particular types of production in particular regions. Geography typically shaped such trends. The early furnaces were erected near forests needed to supply charcoal, later ironworks arose near coalfields; the Potteries grew up in an area abundant in both coal and clay. Tanners and papermakers required large volumes of water for their trade, and so those in London settled south of the Thames:

> The textile trades abhorred hard water. And so, though they existed in almost all parts of England, they congregated in East Anglia and about Dartmoor, the Cotswolds, and the Pennines, where the streams were pure and free from lime. Many industries made use of water for power. Flowing water was employed to work the pumps of the miners, the machines of the papermakers, the fulling mills of the woollen manufacturers, the bellows, hammers, and slitting mills of the iron masters, and the grindstones of the Sheffield cutlers and Black Country tool-makers.[52]

As one line of manufacturing became rooted in a particular region, 'subsidiary trades grew up to minister to the principal occupation: the making of spindles, reeds, combs, and cards in the textile areas, of grindstones and crucibles at Sheffield, of shoemakers' knives and awls in leather-working centres such as Kendal . . .'[53] Concentrating on one line of production in one locality led to comparative advantage, as regions gained a national reputation for the quality of

51. Coleman 1977, p. 151.
52. Ashton 1964, pp. 93–4.
53. Ashton 1964, pp. 96–7.

their wares. If 'a razor or knife was made at Sheffield, or a file at Warrington, [this] gave it an advantage over one made elsewhere.'[54]

Overall, in the form of organisation and the type of enterprise the constant was variation; there existed no single model of labour organisation running through all trades. Industries, writes Berg, 'did not fit into any "logic of managerial enterprise" which associated scale, scope and market power'.[55] Yet despite this, it is possible to identify some significant trends. The competitive pressures that drove the tendency to 'truck, barter and borrow', and to innovate, specialise and maximise, also compelled masters in manufacturing to consolidate larger operations, just as landlords and larger farmers were compelled to consolidate their landholdings. But this did not mean that large, centralised operations were common; rather, they were the exception. Among large-scale operations, a large number of smaller units was the rule. According to Ashton, a sailmaker at Warrington claimed to employ 5,000 workers; while a silk manufacturer reported that prior to 1762 he employed 1,500 persons in London, Gloucestershire, Dorset and Cheshire.[56] These were vast operations for the time period, but not all the operations of the firm were occurring under one roof. The boundaries of the firm were often ill-defined, for there was an increasing integration between cottage manufacturing and more centralised operations. For those working for employers with thousands of employees, they might never meet their employer directly. Domestic producers who bought and sold their materials to the same merchant or factor did not think of themselves as employees, servants or even outworkers, but as independent craftsmen and women who did their own transporting of materials between the cottage and the local merchant's headquarters or warehouse. While production processes changed little, the linkages formed by putting-out and other means by which cottage producers marketed their wares grew in number and complexity as the eighteenth century wore on. 'The Norwich draper, the Leeds clothier, the Manchester warehouseman, and the Nottingham hosier, each, like a spider at the center of a vast web, gave out material and drew in finished or semi-finished goods from hundreds, or even thousands, of spinners and weavers'.[57] Putting-out operations were typically subsidiary to some type of more concentrated operation, such as spinning, and as such tended to be concentrated in suburbs like those around London and in unincorporated towns like Birmingham. By comparison with the growth in the size of centralised operations, expanding networks of putting-out operations involved the

54. Ashton 1964, pp. 96–7.
55. Berg 1994, p. 127.
56. Ashton 1964, p. 100. For more examples of larger concerns of this period, see Pollard 1965, pp. 31–3.
57. Berg 1994, p. 128.

merchant-manufacturers' investments being tied up in goods in circulation, not in fixed equipment. In some cases these investments 'must have run into scores of thousand pounds'.[58] With the loosening of apprenticeship rules, domestic workshops were able to expand beyond what had long been the customary size. In the early 1720s, for example, Nottingham saw workshops employing forty or more parish apprentices under the same roof, whilst their masters were simultaneously engaged in putting out materials.[59]

Wilson notes that despite the sense of independence enjoyed by the domestic producer, and the greater incentives and field for enterprise for the northern worker, 'everywhere the "domestic" organization of employment pressed hard on the worker, affording him an uncertain employment in squalid surroundings that tended to destroy health and decency. We need waste no tears on its later disappearance'.[60] Ashton comments that 'the notion that the coming of factories meant a "depersonalization" of relations in industry is the reverse of the truth'.[61] The conditions could be abysmal. The requirement to leave a window open even in Winter increased the threat of frostbite. Few workers lived past the age of fifty. Nor were industrial dangers restricted to workers alone: 'Dressing and tanning leather polluted water supplies and was therefore kept outside cities: in London on the banks of the River Wandle south of the Thames. The kilns of brick and tile works produced smoke and fumes'.[62] Laws restricting the pollution of water, land and air were limited and 'there was no systematic scrutiny or drive for improvement'.[63] Yet once the factory system arrived, the rates of pollution were only set to further intensify. And factory labour conditions a century later were in some cases worse. So is it fair then to blame the domestic system itself for the immiseration with which it is often associated, or should we instead look to the larger economic forces that had dispossessed the peasantry of the means of production, that were centralising large-scale property into fewer and fewer hands, or that maintained the position of the domestic worker at a bare subsistence level? Worse than being employed in the home was having no employment at all. As we shall see, the remedy reformers devised for dealing with poverty could be worse than the disease.

58. Ashton 1964, pp. 99–102.
59. Berg 1985, p. 212.
60. Wilson 1984, p. 299.
61. Ashton 1964, p. 103.
62. Black 2001, p. 18.
63. Ibid.

Table 7.2. Regional specialisation in manufactures 1600–1750[64]

	Region	Industry
1500s on	Staffordshire	Pottery
1540–1813	The Weald (Sussex and Kent)	Iron-smelting
1600s on	Sheffield, South Yorkshire	Cutlery
1600–1700	East Devon	'Honiton' lace production
1600–1700	Midlands (West of Birmingham)	Nailing
1650 on	Nottinghamshire, Derbyshire and Leicestershire	Framework knitting, Hosiery
1650–1712	Buckinghamshire, Kent	Papermaking
1680–1720	Buckinghamshire & Northamptonshire	Lace
1680–1720	Bedfordshire (from Hertfordshire)	Straw plaiting, especially for hats
1686 on	Cheshire, Derbyshire, Dorset, Warwickshire, (London: Spitalfields)	Silk-weaving
1700 on	Buckinghamshire	Needle-making

More centralised operations still tended to be state-run operations or else privately owned operations serving as major suppliers to the state. Around 1700, the naval shipyards at Portsmouth and Chatham dwarfed nearly all private enterprises of the time, each employing well over a thousand men building ships of five hundred tons and more for the Navy. And they were continuing to expand. Large ships were also built in London to supply the East India Company. The more rapid growth in ship building of this period, however, was in lighter ships of 150–200 tons built in smaller coastal ports for transporting timber and coal. Not only the ship building and shipping trades grew around the larger ports such as London and Bristol, but others: sugar refining, tobacco processing, brewing and distilling, paper milling and tanning – all heavily dependent upon sea transport.

Between 1650 and 1750, English paper manufacturing grew sevenfold, causing paper imports to decline in an early example of import-substitution, first in brown paper, then in finer white paper. By 1712 there were over 200 paper mills in England, mostly concentrated in the Home Counties of Buckinghamshire and Kent to serve the London market. A handful of mills also rose up around Edinburgh and Glasgow in Scotland. Paper mills typically used water to power the Hollander engines. They were small operations, similar in size and nature to corn-grinding and fulling mills, and could be converted from or to these types of mills. Three workmen – the 'vatman' the 'coucher' and the 'layer' – performed the essential tasks.[65] Demand came from the expansion of business generally, and more specifically from the advent of provincial newspapers, the first being the *Norwich Post*, which made its first appearance in 1710. Despite the natural assets

64. Jones 1974, pp. 58–71; John 1961, p. 184.
65. Coleman 1958, pp. 29, 49–59 and 81.

of plenty of wood, fuel and water, the success of the paper industry depended on government protection. Paper was 'a classic case of an infant industry brought to maturity under the shelter of a protective tariff'.[66] Exports of paper, along with glass, tallow and candles all expanded rapidly in the 1740s,[67] driven by the decline of prices down to 1745, after which prices began to rebound and these exports slowed.

Iron continued to be produced in the same regions that had supplied it since time out of mind: 'the Weald, Forest of Dean, the Birmingham Plateau, North Staffordshire, Nottingham and south Yorkshire'.'[68] What these regions offered was not only an abundance of ore, but of timber to fire the forge as well. In the Midlands and around Birmingham, where metalwares in copper, tin, brass and lead were all being produced for export, demand for iron and coal grew. With a seemingly limitless expansion of demand for coal and a chronic shortage of iron, especially quality iron, there existed strong incentives to find innovations in production or transport that could lower costs or speed up delivery times. While the growth of both mining and transport spurred innovation, coal obviously had a greater impact on efforts to improve transportation systems as it was produced in the millions rather than tens of thousands of tons.

> In 1725–26 the first railway bridge in the world, Causeway Arch, was built for the movement of Durham coal across the Causey Burn towards the Tyne. It had the largest span of any bridge built in Britain since Roman times, and the architect had to work from Roman models. The system of wagonways developed greatly during the period as techniques improved. The wagons ran on wooden wheels, which were later flanged. By the 1730s iron bindings were being tried, and by the 1780s cast-iron wheels were in general use. After the formation of the Grand Alliance of leading coal-mining families in North-East England in 1726, a process of sharing and rationalizing existing wagonways and of improving the system led to an increase in the length of wagonways and thus in their efficiency. New links included the New Western Way opened in 1739, and the extension of the Wear system to Pelton Fell by 1746. Wagonways

66. Wilson 1984, pp. 305–306 citing Coleman 1958, p. 145. A monopoly over the making of 'all types of writing- and printing-paper' was granted to the Governor and Company of White Paper Makers in England in 1686 and extended in 1690. Coleman notes that paper makers were expressing their anti-French sentiments at this time. The Company was surely a leading voice in the cry for protection, but it was not alone: 'It seems highly likely that before the expiry of the patent in 1704 effective competition had developed' (Coleman 1958, pp. 66–74).

67. Deane and Cole 1969, p. 58.

68. Black 2001, p. 50.

> developed to link other coalfields to riverside wharves and to ironworks, for example from the East Shropshire field to wharves on the Severn.[69]

With the coming of improved systems of transport, coal could serve as the basis for the creation of buoyant mixed-industrial regions with large pools of labour and demand, and specialist services. For rapid growth, the essentials were capital, transport, markets and coal. While the number of blast-furnaces in England and Wales fell from 86 to 49 between the 1650s and the 1740s, iron output grew from over 23,000 to nearly 33,000 tons, thanks to bigger and better furnaces and a dramatic decline in the use of low-grade ores. Rolling mills were applied to the making of tin-plate in the first half of the eighteenth century, and England enjoyed a competitive advantage. Despite the growth in output, supply could not keep up with the demand of an expanding trade in wrought iron, and nearly as much iron was imported as was produced domestically, most of it from Sweden. High-grade iron from Sweden was brought in because what was produced at home was still more expensive due to high labour and transport costs.

In 1682, Ambrose Crowley, having served his apprenticeship, founded a nail 'factory' at Sunderland. In 1691 he set up a more extensive iron works at Winlaton, near Newcastle. His business expanded markedly after he secured contracts to supply the Navy in 1693. He subsequently established additional iron works at Winlaton Mill in the late 1690s and Swalwell in 1707. The Crowley warehouse was located in London, where he would serve as Alderman of London, Common Councillor and, apparently briefly, Director General of the South Sea Corporation. Crowley was an early pioneer in industrial management and drafted an extensive *Law Book* as an attempt to set out a rigid code of organisational discipline. The *Law Book* established committees to govern the operation of the works, including an oversight Council with an 'inner committee' which operated much like the Prime Minister's Cabinet. There were actual courts to enforce the laws and resolve disputes. An idiosyncratic but innovative element was the setting out of a ten-week cycle of time reckoning (a century before the French Revolution brought about the metric system). Great emphasis was placed on encouraging informers, but the *Law Book* did not just dispense negative discipline. 'More than one official was instructed "to give the workmen a ready and cheerful dispatch" '.[70] The *Law Book* continued to be revised down until the last Crowley died in 1782 and the firm was sold to the Millington family, but most of it was written by Sir Ambrose before his death in 1713. Upon his death, his son John Crowley took over the works, and when his wife Theodosia was widowed in 1728, she ran the works for another forty years and more.

---

69. Black 2001, p. 47.
70. Flinn 1957, p. xxvi.

By the 1720s, the industrial landscape around Newcastle amazed observers 'Defoe was impressed by a story of a wonderous underground explosion in which almost sixty people died. On the road to Newcastle he had "a view of the inexhausted store of coals, from whence not London only, but all the south part of England is continually supplied...we [in London] are apt to wonder whence they come and that they do not bring the whole country away"'.[71]

Crowley Ironworks was 'a massive manufacturing complex with forge, mills, furnaces, warehouses and workshops', rivalled in size only by the naval shipyards, according to the historian of the firm.[72] Large as it was,[73] the workmen in Crowley's operation still worked in separate shops led by small masters, each workshop producing a different item: '"nails, locks, chisels and all sorts of ironmongery..."' They 'got tools and material from the works "ironkeeper", employed their own hammermen and prentices, and were credited with the selling price of their goods less cost of material; in which, it must be assumed, would be included some overhead charges and profit for Crowley, now Sir Ambrose, "ironmonger"'.[74]

This type of subcontracting had a long history in both British and Continental mining operations. According to Pollard: 'Far from antedating the rise of modern capitalistic industry to some period before 1700, it should rather be stressed how much of the older system was left in the interstices of the new factory organization, making adjustment easier and postponing, to that extent, the development of modern management techniques. The survival of subcontract, which at once reduces the problem of management to that of the workshop size, is perhaps the most important'.[75]

As subcontracting remained a common form of organisation, especially in the metal and mining trades well into the nineteenth century, and as it remains a common practice in such industries as the construction trade today, it is difficult to specifically identify it as either a 'feudal' or a 'capitalist' mode of labour-organisation. The putting-out system was itself a kind of subcontracting. Pollard argues that as these systems were effectively a way of overcoming the sophisticated problems that arise from establishing what he calls 'unitary firms', as opposed to 'several scattered mine properties or of many outworkers operating

71. Evans 1989, p. 205, citing Defoe 1971, pp. 534–5.
72. Levine and Wrightson 1991, p. 79. See also Jones 1988, p. 309.
73. In 1707, Sir Ambrose Crowley extended his iron works, started in 1691, by buying out his rival Edward Harrison of Swalwell. By 1728 the manufactory and slitting mill at Swalwell was employing hundreds of men, and was potentially the largest industrial unit in the country outside the naval dockyards. It was 'a massive manufacturing complex by the standards of the day, comprising forges, mills, furnaces, warehouses, and numerous workshops'. Levine and Wrightson 1991, p. 79.
74. Clapham 1926, p. 176 as cited in Berg 1994, p. 137.
75. Pollard 1965, p. 8.

with their own tools or within their own four walls, and only loosely controlled', they: 'could provide precedents only for certain aspects of the tasks which faced the entrepreneurs of the new factory industry. The task, in its totality, with its complex interrelationship of many different objectives in a flexible environment, had to be pioneered from the beginning within the framework of the British Industrial Revolution'.[76]

These large operations were, after all, exceptional. Crowley's works depended upon securing large contracts from the Navy. He thus enjoyed a quasi-monopoly. The challenge was to achieve a successful subsumption of labour in the *absence* of an open or 'free' labour market and its self-regulating and disciplining functions. It was common practice in such large mining and metal-working operations therefore to seek extra-economic means of disciplining labour 'either by legal compulsion or discipline, or by dominating the workers' whole lives inside their townships within the framework of long-term "bindings", a method which goes back to some large Renaissance firms, particularly on the Continent'.[77] Other common forms of control included payment by piece or in truck.

Perhaps more than anything, it was the scale of such operations that set them apart as pioneers into a new type of organisation involving vertical integration, one that was easily distinguishable from the traditional workshop headed by the small master with his several journeymen and apprentices. In these operations: 'the manufacturer owned the premises, the power source and some of the machinery, but did not become deeply involved in the details of the manufacturing process. Instead employees carried on the traditions of workspace and use of gas and power'.[78]

Arguing for the 'capitalistic' character of these operations, Nef points out that some of the top officials were converted to salaried employees. Yet the tools used remained traditional tools and there was little application of new machinery beyond the application of water and steam to power hammers and forges. The power source, the train of mechanism and the tool aspect of the mechanism were all larger, but the work still involved basic manual labour. Unlike the water frame, the mule and the power-loom, such machinery may have dwarfed the worker, but it did not make him a mere appendage to the machine. Moreover, it is undeniable that where subcontracting preserved the basic organisational model of the traditional workshop – where small masters and their journeymen carried on as they would have in small workshops, but benefiting from a steady demand for their product – customary modes of labour organisation within larger operations continued.

---

76. Pollard 1965, pp. 59–60.
77. Ibid. See our discussion of capitalism in early mining above, Chapter One, p. 81.
78. Berg 1994, p. 137.

The story of the subsumption of labour to capital in the mining and metal-working trades, with the irregular rhythms of work that were involved, appears to be one of an extremely long and drawn-out struggle where relations remain somewhere between the formal and the real subsumption of labour. The continuing role of custom can be seen in the demands made during strikes, the reactions of the owners and in the application of extra-economic force. When iron workers and miners in Shropshire demonstrated over a shortage of bread and flour in 1756, Abraham Darby II's wife Hannah urged her husband to distribute food and drink '"to keep them quiet"'.[79] Nonetheless, a posse of farmers, farm labourers and tradesmen 1,500 strong put down the demonstration, taking ten prisoners and executing two of the leaders. Crowley's pitmen organised strikes in 1731 and 1765. In the 1765 strike, 'blacklegs' and armed force were called in, and while the result was a stand-off, the pitmen achieved what was probably their primary goal: to get their employers to repudiate the rumour that the pitmen would not be allowed to make a bond of brotherhood.[80] The pitmen may have been highly proletarian, but they were still able to organise according to the norms of the 'honourable trades'. These observations indicate that to a very large extent, the labour process remained in the control of the labourers, that customary modes of labour organisation still governed the workshop, and from that we must conclude that the subsumption of labour was still more formal than real.

By 1700, the shortage of wood in England was severe, and coal production was soaring. Over half a million tons were being shipped from Newcastle-on-Tyne, up from a figure of just over 30,000 tons in 1599.[81] Nef makes the dramatic claim that the 'entire production of the rest of the world did not perhaps amount to much more than a sixth of that of Great Britain'.[82] Between 1710 and 1726, the Grand Alliance of leading coal-mining families in northeast England was formed 'for joint-stock mining and for restricting output and raising prices',[83] and lasted until the third quarter of the century. As one of the few instances of monopoly power based upon industrial concentration from this period, the Alliance sought to regulate the output and price of coal, which it did with considerable success between 1733 and 1751, after which a period of intense 'cutthroat competition' set in.[84]

---

79. Soldon 1998, pp. 159–60.
80. Levine and Wrightson 1991, pp. 388–417.
81. Nef 1966a, Appendix D, table (i).
82. Nef 1966a, p. 325.
83. Berg 1994, p. 127.
84. When an industry is undergoing rapid expansion, writes Sweezy, 'there is nothing to be feared from cutthroat competition. There is no need for regulating quantities produced, and the incentive to add a little something to profits by pushing prices even higher than they are may be weak and easily overbalanced by the trouble involved. Such a period began for the Newcastle coal trade in the autumn of 1751, and, as we shall see

Solutions for poverty

Since at least Elizabethan times, the growth in the ranks of England's poor had occupied a central place in elite discourse. Although the poor laws may have served to stave off a greater crisis, the ranks of the poor continued to grow, as did the controversy surrounding the question of how they should be dealt with. With the landed classes enjoying unprecedented wealth, the widening gulf separating rich and poor was reflected in social attitudes. Inadequate housing, an insufficient supply of fuel to keep warm throughout the winter, malnutrition leading to stunted growth, greater susceptibility to disease and – what is a sad curse for the manual labourer – a general lack of energy, were the real consequences of poverty. In general, such maladies were assumed to be self-inflicted. What is more, given the extreme variety in working conditions within both manufacturing and agriculture, and the fact that so many workers lived on the brink of poverty, there was a tendency to identify working people 'with that sub-stratum of the population which was rarely, if ever, regularly employed'.[85] By the early eighteenth century, some attitudes had already hardened into a view held by many pamphleteers – anticipating the teachings of Reverend Malthus by nearly a century – blaming the insecurity experienced by labouring people on defects of character. England's elites were increasingly alarmed at the thought that working people often laboured only four days of the week, and preached that the poor needed guidance from the more educated and well-to-do, who should hold them to industry and guard their morals. In 1697, John Locke had proposed to the Board of Trade that if the poor refused to work they should be whipped or even mutilated.[86] The only way to make workers more temperate and industrious, wrote William Temple in 1739, was '"to lay them under the necessity of labouring all the time they can spare from rest and sleep, in order to procure the common necessaries of life"'.[87] As the century wore on and it became increasingly clear to some that while the material condition of both the elite and the middling sort had been improving steadily for some time, there was little evidence to suggest that the lower orders had seen much benefit themselves. Wilson comments: 'The proportion of total heads and hands of the nation – perhaps as much as a

---

in the next chapter, there is good reason to believe that it lasted, substantially without interruption, right down to 1771' (Sweezy 1938, p. 31).

85. Ashton 1964, p. 200.

86. Black 2001, p. 105; citing Locke 1876.

87. Ashton 1964, p. 202, quoting Temple's *Reflections*, from Smith 1969, p. 30. Forty odd years later Arthur Young would put it more bluntly: '"everyone but an idiot knows that the lower classes must be kept poor or they will never be industrious"'. Ashton adds: 'Enclosure was desirable if only because rights of common led to irregularity of work' (Ashton 1964, p. 202, quoting Gilboy 1936, p. 144). From this, it would appear that enclosers were quite aware of the effect enclosing had upon the conditions of labour.

third or more – left stranded by progress in 1750 disposes of any lingering fallacy that unemployment is a creation of the Industrial Revolution'.[88] Yet if not the Industrial Revolution, what then of capitalism?

By the early eighteenth century, this process of extinguishing customary rights in agriculture through enclosure was by no means complete, but it was already generating enormous change. An emerging labour market, characterised by the spread of wage labour and the increasing monetisation of an economy now characterised by its capacity for self-sustaining growth was developing in the context of an unprecedented expansion of the domestic market. At the same time, there was an ever larger underclass of unemployed and under-employed persons.

Poor relief was the primary social and legislative mechanism by which the English government buffered this effect of agrarian capitalism. When the system was performing its intended role, it specifically helped to prevent chronic malnutrition. Aside from those who were wholly dependent on aid – the elderly, orphans and the infirm – poor relief was only available as a means of supplementing wages when existing wages were insufficient to allow any given household to meet its dietary requirements. Any 'able-bodied' person was expected to work as much as they could before receiving relief. Since the price of bread fluctuated wildly, the numbers of those receiving relief also fluctuated, falling as low as five percent of the population in good years and rising as high as forty percent in bad years, typically averaging around ten percent.[89] In times of high prices or low employment, it was single women who tended to face the harshest economic situations, and, therefore, depended more upon relief; an example of how the system anticipated contemporary forms of welfare.

If the fact of being deprived of access to commons and land for subsistence-farming meant that the poor faced periods of exceptional suffering during economic downturns, poor relief at least helped to ameliorate that suffering. According to Rule, historians are largely agreed that 'eighteenth-century... relief in general was neither ungenerous nor ineffective'.[90] One of the inherent limitations built into the system of poor relief when it was first enacted under Elizabeth, however, was that because it was built upon the parish system, it thus required funds to be raised from among the parishioners themselves. The harder the times, the heavier the burden upon the rate-payers, who already faced shrinking budgets as well as higher taxes *before* paying poor rates. Moreover, economic crises could have a greater impact in some regions than in others. Most of the farmland in the agrarian South and East was enclosed before 1760, so the overall proportion of the working population that was fully market-dependent

88. Wilson 1984, p. 347.
89. Hay 1982, pp. 131–3.
90. Rule 1992a, p. 118.

would have been higher here than in other regions. In good times, more intensive farming meant heavier employment of wage labour on farms, but in bad times, unemployment soared whilst at the same time there were fewer options for by-employment than there were in many industrial regions. These built-in contradictions made the system of poor relief inherently unstable. Moreover, as agrarian capitalism continued to develop, moving British society in the direction of ever greater market dependence, the problems resulting from increased social dislocation only continued to increase.

The growth of London in the fifteenth and sixteenth centuries prompted City authorities to establish four 'hospitals' (understood less as medical facilities than as institutions providing hospitality to the unfortunate) for dealing with orphans or foundling children, invalids, elderly or incurable persons and the mentally ill. They were among a host of new public 'corporations' that had to be established 'to fill the vacuum left by the dissolution of religious orders and fraternities'.[91] What remained was to deal with idle persons: prostitutes, vagabonds, 'vicious rogues' or 'sturdy beggars'. In 1552, Edward VI transferred the abandoned palace of Bridewell, once the residence of his grandfather Henry VII, to the City for purposes of initiating the first experiment in *creating* work for the idle poor. Previous efforts 'had commonly focused on supplying an *existing* demand for labour'.[92] The methods of enforcing a rigorous labour discipline could be quite harsh, including putting the residents to harsh labour and enforcing this with whipping as needed. Corporal punishment was a holdover from previous methods of dealing with the idle poor, what was new about Bridewell was an effort not only to punish 'sin' but to reform the poor by putting them to work, forcing religious observance and exercise. The emphasis on saving souls and reforming individuals meant that Bridewell focused on the most problematic individuals rather than those who were merely suffering from material want and lack of employment. In the midst of an ever-expanding metropolis, however, the capacity of Bridewell to handle up to five hundred committed vagrants at a time was quickly overwhelmed. 'Particularly as it became clear that Bridewell offered no final solution to the sturdy beggar problem, it became possible to argue that its ambitious régime was in practice too harsh, that the petty delinquencies of the poor were not best corrected by such rigours'.[93]

Moreover, 'Bridewell's promoters appear to have been overoptimistic in proposing to blur the boundaries between relief and punishment', and were 'quickly branded as a rogues' hospital'.[94] The dual function of London's bridewell was

91. Slack 1999, p. 26.
92. Innes 1987, pp. 42, 52–3.
93. Innes 1987, p. 60.
94. Innes 1987, pp. 55–6.

reflected in the establishment of a separate school in the 1560s for teaching boys manufacturing skills. But perhaps the main function of a bridewell was to be used simply as a threat or a deterrent in coercing the poor into some form of employment or out of licentious behaviours. The bridewell would have offered an attractive option to JPs faced with punishing offences such as leaving work unfinished under the Statute of Apprentices of 1563. An Act of 1572, making compulsory the collection of rates for local poor relief, made a distinction between those unemployed through no fault of their own and 'professional' beggars, who were to be bored through the ear on the first offence and, if found to be persistent offenders, hanged. In 1576, Parliament passed an act which first ordered the establishment of bridewells in every county, placing an emphasis on putting the poor to work in manufactures. The typical bridewell had two rooms, one for men and one for women. Some had a separate room to be used as a workroom and would be stocked with implements for crushing flax or for combing wool or twisting thread, but the work performed in bridewells was neither well-regulated nor profitable, despite the fact that some of the 'masters' or 'keepers' were themselves manufacturers.[95]

In spite of the criticism, lack of profitability and charges of mismanagement and even corruption, local prison-hospitals on the bridewell model were built in more than a dozen towns and at least a quarter of English counties by 1600. By 1630, 'a network of bridewells covered the whole of England'.[96] Similar institutions in France, Germany and Holland did not develop on any scale until after 1750, with apparently only 19 ever having been established in Holland and 44 in Germany by the late 1700s, by which time England had over 170. Joanna Innes states that it is 'not obvious that English social and economic arrangements were so different from those prevailing *everywhere* on the Continent as to account for so distinctive a governmental response'.[97] She seeks an explanation in the role

95. Innes 1987, pp. 76–7. The work of a 'keeper' was usually not full-time work. Bear in mind that a 'master' overseer in the sixteenth century would not have been a factory owner, but perhaps a successful master overseeing a traditional guild workshop.

96. Innes 1987, pp. 61–76 and Patriquin 2005, pp. 18–19. In 1598, Essex had plans to build 23 bridewells in the county. In 1600, Wiltshire had plans to build one in every hundred.

97. Innes 1987, pp. 63–8. Innes (Innes 1987, pp. 44–5) is sceptical of scholars who view the emergence of bridewells as specifically associated with the emergence of capitalism, although she recognises that they emerged in the more advanced cities of Europe. Key to her argument is the claim (Innes 1987, p. 47) that 'bridewells clearly played no part in *inaugurating* [the early modern system of labour relations]: they arrived too late in the day. A substantial free wage labour sector existed in England from the later middle ages'. Reminiscent of Epstein's claims (see Chapter One, p. 50), Innes appears to associate capitalism with the emergence of wage labour across Western Europe from the early modern period. Where she is sceptical of the relationship between bridewells and capitalism, to us the early appearance of bridewells in greater numbers in England would appear as a fairly logical response by the English state to the greater numbers of tenants

of the local JPs in imposing central government policies at the local level, with the poor laws forming an important context. Without stating it, Innes is here emphasising the exceptional degree of centralisation of the English state. Innes makes no mention, however, of agrarian capitalism or how the loss of access to the means of production by rural direct producers may have contributed to the growing ranks of the poor.

Alongside the Elizabethan poor laws, charities had been dispensing various forms of material aid to the poor for centuries. Whether motivated by self-interest or genuine concern, hundreds of trusts – a thousand in London alone – were in operation by 1700, in what has been referred to as the 'Age of Benevolence'.[98] Likewise, thousands of charity schools were set up to provide elementary education to children who would otherwise go without. Founded in 1698, the Society for the promotion of Christian Knowledge (SPCK) coordinated the movement. Initially more passive in character, over time the charity schools expanded their services in the direction of providing pauper children with education or apprenticeship in a trade. In the stream of pamphlet literature that was produced during the reigns of William III and Anne I, 'economic principal and philanthropic argument were closely intertwined', adding 'to a notable enlargement of the concept of social welfare' that was 'something more than the mundane necessity of keeping the poor from starvation'.[99] While charity schools had their critics, the debate surrounding them 'was negligible compared with the passions that raged round the proposal for workhouses'.[100]

Workhouses date from at least the early seventeenth century. Paul Slack situates the emergence of the workhouse as part of a campaign of:

> ambitious local experiments in social welfare which were erected on the statutory foundation of the poor law. They occurred chiefly in corporate towns, and – in the period from 1570 to the 1630s – in municipalities ruled by Puritans. In Norwich and other East Anglican towns in the 1570s, in Salisbury, Dorchester and other western towns in the 1620s, alliances of godly magistrates and ministers sought to remodel their little commonwealths, and they used the management of the poor as a tool for that purpose. If idleness were rooted out, drunkards, bastard-bearers, hedge-breakers and other rogues would disappear. Poverty itself might be conquered along with ungodliness, if only there were sufficient investment in social engineering. Accordingly, there were censuses and listings of the poor, workhouses and schooling for poor children,

---

being displaced from their tenancies by the conversion of land to private property and agrarian-capitalist tenant-farming.

98. Wilson 1984, p. 348, citing Jones 1938, p. 3.
99. Holmes 1969, pp. 12–13.
100. Ibid.

> storehouses and hospitals, municipal enterprises such as the breweries of Dorchester and Salisbury . . .[101]

Workhouses were thus part of a broader social-welfare campaign in early modern England that was both religiously inspired and at the same time inspired by the concept of the 'common weal', which had long lost its meaning of simply the realm and had come to refer to the general well-being of the people. One of, if not *the*, earliest was the workhouse at Newbury, established in response to the economic downturn of the 1590s, which opened in 1628. The Newbury workhouse was informed by, if not inspired by, the large and centralised textile operations that had previously existed in Newbury:

> By the mid-1620s, the large-scale factory system of manufacture developed by the Winchcombe and Dunham families in Newbury in the early sixteenth century had long been abandoned, due to changes in the commercial and regulatory climate. However, the benefits of centralized production were never totally abandoned, and some of the town's more successful and prosperous clothiers continued to operate centralized integrated workshops, concentrating those stages of manufacture that required close supervision on their own premises, and utilizing outworkers for processes such as spinning, which employed large numbers of part-time workers, and fulling, which demanded large-scale production to provide a direct return on the substantial fixed-capital investment needed. It was to this form of organization that the corporation turned when setting up the workhouse.[102]

Other early experiments with workhouses dating from the 1630s were 'isolated and short-lived'.[103] Larry Patriquin points to the difficulty of distinguishing between early bridewells and early workhouses, noting that the Webbs suggested the first workhouse was set up in the London suburb at St. Giles-in-the-Fields in the 1640s.[104] As workhouses emerged, they were operated in close association with bridewells, being directed at addressing the needs of the unemployed rather than 'sturdy rogues'.

In 1649, the London Corporation for the Poor opened. Ambitious in and of itself, its promoters had a much grander programme in mind: 'free medical assistance

101. Slack 1990, p. 24. We note in passing the mention of hedge-breakers and the notion on the part of reformers that the refusal to accede to enclosure was equivalent to sin. The movement may have been understood by enclosers as one to promote the 'common weal', but others saw enclosers alongside engrossers as 'enemies of the commonwealth' in both senses of being enemies of the state and of the general welfare (Slack 1990, p. 7).
102. Jackson 2004, pp. xxxviii–xxix.
103. Brundage 2002, p. 11.
104. Brundage 2002, p. 32.

and education; encouragement to cultivate wastes and grow flax to employ the nation's poor; a London Corporation to cover the whole metropolis...'[105] They had to settle for a programme of workhouses in the old city teaching or setting to work eighty children at a time and putting a thousand adults to work, most in their own homes. The expense proved more than the body politic was willing to support and the scheme failed at the Restoration, but it served as a model for later experiments, such as the Clerkenwell workhouse established in 1662, a workhouse at Exeter in 1672, a flax-spinning project by the London Quakers in 1677 and a workhouse in Bristol in 1696.[106] Within a decade many other cities had followed this lead, by 1711 some 15 cities had established Corporations of the Poor.[107] Worcester established a workhouse in 1703 'in which "Beggars and idle people" could be compelled to work'.[108] A bill to establish workhouses across all of Britain failed in 1704, but in the following year numerous workhouses were erected nevertheless.

Workhouses were intended to improve the lot of the poor by inculcating Christian values of piety and industry. Idleness and sloth were widely assumed by the upper classes to be the root of poverty; if the poor could be made more industrious, poverty could be overcome. As private institutions, however, the Corporations 'were expected to make an absolute profit from the labour of the poor'.[109] 'Profit for the rich, (which will be life to the rest)', was first among three expected positive outcomes of employing the poor, according to the Quaker economist John Bellers writing in 1695, the second and third outcomes being a 'plentiful living for the poor' and 'a good education for youth'.[110] Far from turning a profit, however, the early workhouses were a financial disaster from the start. Like the bridewell movement of a century earlier, the workhouse movement also blurred boundaries, but not so much between relief and punishment as between relief and profit.

They employed low-skilled labour in producing goods for which demand was limited and maintenance costs were high. Finding those with the necessary experience and expertise to be effective supervisors and organisers of the labour undertaken inside the poor house proved intractably difficult. While the workers included children and able-bodied adults, they also included criminals and the mentally ill. The output of the workhouses could not compete with private enterprises producing the same hand-made goods. The workhouse at Bristol had lost £1,980 during its first seven years of operation. A workhouse belonging to the

105. Slack 1999, p. 86.
106. Slack 1999, pp. 89–90; and Slack 1990, p. 25.
107. Hitchcock 1992, pp. 145 and 148.
108. Black 2001, p. 107.
109. Hitchcock 1992, p. 149.
110. Hitchcock 1992, p. 148, quoting Bellers 1980, p. 12.

London Corporation of the Poor was £3,300 in debt by 1711. These two facilities were soon converted into a hospital and a house of corrections respectively. 'Tiring of the failure of their good works, the guardians slipped back to the simpler palliative of outdoor relief'.[111] It had not taken long to recognise that maintaining the unemployed in workhouses was more expensive than simply providing them with small payments in cash.

The Corporations for the Poor founded in the seventeenth century had been promoted by sectarian and dissenting bodies. Founded as an Anglican response, the SPCK took charge of the workhouse movement at the outset of the eighteenth century and thereby reduced the level of controversy surrounding workhouses.[112] In the context of the still heated controversy over the Hanoverian succession, however, critics charged that the charity schools promoted by the SPCK would become breeding grounds for Jacobitism. Moreover, Bernard Mandeville and others levelled a straightforward argument rooted in strict class prejudice when they charged that the students in charity schools would be educated beyond the 'blissful ignorance' of their station in life. The SPCK found the workhouse movement useful for dealing with such criticism and in 1712 proposed to train children of the respectable poor in simple tasks suitable to their lot, alternating working days with education days. By 1714, the Society had managed to facilitate the establishment of some 55 charity schools providing elementary education and teaching Christian knowledge to over 2,000 children in London, and another thousand charity schools in the countryside. But lack of funding and experience caused the working schools to fail and the charity school movement lost its momentum. Nearly a century later, the movement had 'lost both momentum and idealism, turning in some cases into mere juvenile workhouses',[113] and their decline left a void in Britain's educational system. By contrast, despite the fact that the workhouse as a model for employing the poor was clearly a financial failure, the construction of workhouses was about to take off, but not because a way was found to make them profitable.

Local JPs typically favoured any scheme which promised to reduce the burden of the poor rates on their parishes, and workhouses were not the only proposed scheme. In 1721, a government official named Elias Barnes proposed a scheme to establish charity schools throughout the kingdom to teach women and children how to spin fine yarn at low cost. In making this proposal, he appealed to the interests of the rate-payers. '"Surely if we do not find a way to employ

111. Wilson 1984, pp. 350–1.
112. Hitchcock 1992, p. 149.
113. Wilson 1984, p. 394.

our taxable poor they must be maintained out of the produce of our Lands" ',[114] Barnes argued. This was an appeal to the kind of thinking that went into the passage of the Workhouse Test Act in 1723. In response to the outcry from rate-payers at rising poor rates, the Act made work a prerequisite for the able-bodied to receive relief. The Act itself may have had little direct impact. It was passed at the behest of a religiously inspired reform movement organised through the SPCK. Just as scientific and industrial developments in Britain came from private initiative,[115] so Parliament played only a minimal role in facilitating the development of workhouses.[116] The Workhouse Test Act transferred authority over poor relief to local magistrates, giving local parishes the right to deny poor relief to anyone who refused to labour in a workhouse.[117] What this reflected was the abandonment of any effort to make the workhouse a profit-making endeavour in favour of continuing to build workhouses for the simple reason that they had proven themselves to be a useful deterrent in keeping a significant proportion of able-bodied paupers off the poor rates.[118] The expense of the workhouse could now be justified by the savings it brought to local rate-payers. Finding a way of making employing the poor profitable would require the discovery of an entirely separate institution: the factory.

A flurry of workhouse construction ensued. By 1725, 124 workhouses had been founded. By 1730, every parish in Nottingham had one. Lancaster built a workhouse in 1730. Birmingham built another in 1733.[119] At Manchester, only one of four buildings to be set around a quadrangle was ever completed, but its ambitious design approached the scale of a factory: four stories with rooms for Dutch looms and accommodation for between 120 and 140 persons.[120] Cork opened a workhouse in 1735. In 1740 the vestry of Nazeing in Essex opened a workhouse. Edinburgh opened a workhouse in 1743 and by 1757 it had 701 inmates. Parishes combined for the purposes of erecting common workhouses.[121] 'There can have been few regions to which the idea of the concentration of workers under a single roof was wholly unknown'.[122] A 1777 survey found 1,196 workhouses across England housing an estimated 90,000 paupers and deterring a far greater

---

114. Barnes's proposal was never acted upon, and he afterwards removed to the Continent, where he appealed to the German, French and Dutch governments to try his scheme, with minimal success (Wadsworth and Mann 1965, pp. 121–4 and 414).
115. See Chapter Six, pp. 340–1 and Chapter Eight, pp. 414–5.
116. Hitchcock 1992, p. 146.
117. Owen 1975, p. 38.
118. Patriquin 2005, p. 32.
119. Black 2001, p. 107.
120. Wadsworth and Mann 1965, p. 406. The project was initiated around 1730.
121. Patriquin 2005, pp. 32–3.
122. Ashton 1964, p. 114.

number.[123] Most had been built before 1750 and in the countryside, where the earliest workhouses had been built mostly in the towns. None of them were financially self-sufficient, but they continued to be built. By 1803, there would be around 3,765, roughly one in every market-size town. By 1815, 'the workhouses seem to have become mainly asylums for the helpless poor and rarely employed the able-bodied; aged people and children predominated in them'.[124] Another century and more would pass before the workhouse would outlive its usefulness in keeping the poor rates down.

Private employers in manufacturing cried foul about workhouses as a source of unfair competition, yet their cries were tempered by the fact that they also benefited from the way in which workhouses and the poor laws together tended to drive down the price of labour. Moreover, by providing a social safety net for much of the working poor, the poor rates absorbed surplus labour during periods of low employment, preventing or easing crises and in effect stabilising the transition to – and the expansion of – a national labour market. This was particularly true in agriculture, where a majority of labourers, dispossessed of the means for self-subsistence, required assistance in surviving through seasonal downturns in work. It was also true in domestic manufacturing, where the putting-out merchant faced with shortages of demand or supply could respond by simply decreasing the number of orders he put out.[125] An emerging system of 'tramping' also eased labour surpluses whereby friendly societies issued 'blanks' to unemployed members, giving them entitlement to travel to another town in search of work, whilst meanwhile being supported by their society. A wool-comber could by this method claim support from any wool-combers' society in England.[126] Hence employers had cause to welcome, or at least not to oppose, both the poor laws and the tramping system, as together these served to keep wages low and to ease oversupplies of labour. Rate-payers may have grumbled at the personal expense of the poor laws, but from 'the perspective of the landed classes', writes Patriquin, 'poor relief was the price to be paid for an "improved" method of exploitation'.[127]

Despite their failure to be an effective means of resolving problems of poverty, workhouses survived throughout the nineteenth century, eventually becoming the habitation of last resort for the destitute. 'Workhouses were always more successful at looking after individuals who were on permanent relief. Indeed, over time they had become virtual asylums, caring for orphaned children, the

---

123. Hitchcock 1992, p. 145.
124. Crowther 1981, pp. 24 and 28. Not until 1871 was there a move to soften the 'grim reputation' that the workhouse had gained (Crowther 1981, p. 54).
125. Rule 1992a, p. 119.
126. Ashton 1964, p. 230.
127. Patriquin 2005, p. 38.

chronically ill, the mentally disabled, the aged, and unwed mothers'.[128] They became a place where the most vulnerable of the population were sent to toil, to suffer and to die, quietly and out of public view. 'When Jonas Hanway, a Russia merchant who helped to promote the Foundling Hospital and other charitable institutions, inquired into fourteen parishes in London, he estimated that the infant death rate in the workhouses set up since 1720 was 88 per cent. Some parishes admitted that "no infant had lived to be apprenticed from their workhouses" '.[129]

Workhouses were far from the only places where the horrors of poverty were played out. In a society where disease and violence were common, the cruelties of the workhouse did not necessarily stand out in sharp relief.

As philanthropists abandoned the workhouse as a solution for poverty, private employers were effectively in a position to take over the project. 'The private factory', writes Wilson, 'emerges imperceptibly from antecedents that include the workhouse – the first experiment in organising labour in concentrated groups'.[130] Let us reflect for a moment on this statement by Wilson, for it suggests one direct line of development between agrarian capitalism and the Industrial Revolution. Centuries of enclosures, accelerating in the eighteenth century, had dislocated the English peasantry and given rise to a class of paupers, vagabonds and small cottagers facing unemployment or chronic underemployment, stimulating an elite discourse on what to do about the 'problem of the poor' and a debate on how to put idle hands to work. The work of agrarian labourers employed by tenant-farmers renting farms on enclosed fields was probably not as intensified or as exploitative as factory work, but it is doubtful that agrarian labourers observed 'Saint Monday' as artisan craft workers still did, since too much idleness would surely have met with being docked pay or a termination of employment. By the late seventeenth century, liberal thinkers were seeking ways to lessen the burden of poor relief by putting more hands to work, thereby increasing the wealth of the nation. Eventually they hit upon an idea for how to accomplish this through a legal form common to this period – the corporation. Thus the initial attempt at combining labourers under one roof, subject to supervision, and the coordination and assigning of tasks emerged as a new scheme to deal with the twin problems of poverty and underemployment, both resulting largely from the dislocation of agrarian producers associated with agrarian capitalism.

What is conspicuously absent from the early eighteenth-century calls for founding workhouses is any concept of using the profit-motive to induce managers to respond effectively to market competition by seeking ways to increase

128. Patriquin 2005, pp. 33–4.
129. Wilson 1984, p. 352, citing Hutchins 1940, pp. 47–75.
130. Wilson 1984, pp. 350–1.

worker productivity through intensifying the labour process. But the profit-motive, trade skills and the potential for competitiveness were not lacking in the private factory. Once conditions of labour in England had reached the point where workhouses – in which any control over the labour process by combinations of craftsmen was a dead letter – had become widespread, it was but a small step for the private employer to argue that he could offer the same or better terms of employment in the form of an operation with greater long-term viability, he could thus make the case that by setting up a factory he was providing a vital service to the community. As Wilson notes, 'These new factories often with their schools and dormitories for child workers closely resembled the earlier workhouses. Unlike them, they were equipped with machinery...'[131] It appears as less than sheer coincidence that the first 'factory' in the sense of the word as we now know it, with large numbers of workers under one roof operating power-driven machinery, became fully operational in 1724, just one year after the passage of the Workhouse Test Act.

The first factory

According to the *Oxford English Dictionary*, the usage of the word 'factory' to refer to a manufacturing site dates back to 1618. A 'factory' could be a colonial warehouse, a processing station or it could simply refer to the activities of mercantile agents. One definition offered by Webster's is: 'a station where resident factors trade'. Hence the term is derived from 'factor', which refers to the merchant's middle-man and is directly traceable to the Latin *factor* meaning 'doer'. This explains how contemporaries referred to a variety of large-scale production operations overseen by factors (agents representing merchant-employers), as 'factories' well before the Industrial Revolution. Today, we generally associate the word with the multi-storey textile mills housing hundreds of workers operating power-driven machinery and subject to a strict labour discipline. By this definition, the first factory in England was not a cotton mill, and it was not built in Manchester.[132] It was a silk mill in Derby, built on the banks of the River Derwent in 1717. Today, the 'Old Silk Mill' serves as a museum dedicated

131. Wilson 1984, p. 351.

132. Weber 1961, p. 135 writes that we have 'almost no record' of new factories down to 1700, but that 'it is impossible that they were entirely absent' since government no longer barred such industry. What Weber means by 'factory' may simply be synonymous with 'mill', for he writes of the Huguenots forming 'small' factories in Amsterdam, Haarlem and Utrecht to make mirrors, silk and velvet. Suffice it to say that prior to the Derby silk mill, few if any other large-scale operations involving large numbers of machines driven by an external power source had previously existed. Polhem's clock mill may be one of these few (see Chapter Six, p. 335).

to industry in general.[133] It was partially destroyed by fire in 1826, and again in 1910, and nothing of the building's original interior remains. Yet standing outside the structure, taking in its red-brick facade, belfry tower and smokestacks, one can imagine the familiar scene of silk workers arriving early and waiting for their employers to open the large wrought-iron gates, and one can ponder how it could have been built fully half a century before the boom of cotton factory construction following Richard Arkwright's introduction of the water frame.

That the first factory was a silk factory should not surprise. In the late seventeenth and early eighteenth centuries, the demand for silk stockings, particularly for men, was very high; hence the high demand for silk thread. Silk was a luxury item relative to other textiles and the higher prices to be earned from silk thread no doubt helped to sustain the profitability of the operation. At the same time, however, silk could never be cheapened to the point of enabling a vast expansion of demand, as later happened in the case of cotton. Although silk production in England dates as far back as the fourteenth century, it received a tremendous boost after 1685, when Louis XIV revoked the Edict of Nantes. Huguenot refugees from Tours and Lyons fled to England bringing with them the advanced silk-weaving skills that had long served France to the envy of other nations. They settled outside of London in the district of Spitalfields, where by the early eighteenth century there were some 15,000 to 18,000 silk looms. However, attempts by the London companies to enforce their restrictions and control silk production in the interests of a small group of masters provoked many of these immigrant craftsmen to relocate to the East Midlands counties of Nottinghamshire, Leicestershire and Derbyshire, where stockings had been produced for over a century using Lee's stocking-frame (invented in 1589). A Royal Lustring Company was founded in 1692 and, citing a decline in the number of looms operating in England, managed to persuade Parliament to prohibit the import of imported silks from France in 1698 and from India and China in 1701. Heavy duties on imported silks continued until 1765, when all imports of manufactured silks were prohibited, a policy that lasted until 1824. The English silk industry thus enjoyed near or full protectionism throughout the eighteenth and well into the nineteenth centuries.[134]

A solicitor named Thomas Cotchett, born in the Derby area, set up as a 'reeler' (a supplier) of textile equipment in the London area, where he would have been familiar with the high demand for silk thread in the cottage manufacturing at

---

133. Derby Industrial Museum, visit by author, November 1997; this museum is housed in the building that once was the Old Silk Mill.

134. Hertz 1909, pp. 710–11. A tariff system that went into effect continued to provide protection for English silk manufacture and was gradually reduced until it was abolished in 1860, under a new commercial treaty with France, whereupon the English silk industry went into an immediate and irreversible decline.

Spitalfields. Thus in 1702 he chose to set up a small water-driven mill on the Derwent in Derby to power silk-reeling machines and Dutch 'engine-' looms.[135] Built by the well-respected engineer and inventor George Sorocold, who specialised in waterworks, the 'Old Shop' housed Dutch machines for 'doubling' or strengthening silk thread, and could accommodate 48 doublers.[136]

One of those doublers was John Lombe. Having seen the frustration at the poor quality of thread produced by the Dutch machines, Lombe is said to have gone off to Italy to study the design of the Italian machines that produced the finest *organzine* silk thread,[137] whereupon he brought the designs back to England in an act of industrial espionage for which it was believed he later paid with his life. (Legend suggests he may have been poisoned by a suspicious Italian woman who appeared briefly in Derby just prior to his death). John Lombe had returned from Italy around 1717 and in 1718 his half-brother (or by some accounts, his cousin), Thomas Lombe, a London silk merchant, obtained a patent on 'three sorts of engines never before made or used within this our Kingdom of Great Britain, one to wind finest raw silk, another to spin and the other to twist the finest Italian raw silk into organzine in great perfection which was never before done in this our Kingdom, by which means many thousand families of our subjects may be constantly employed in Great Britain, be furnished with silks of all sorts of the manufacture of our subjects, and great quantities exported into foreign parts by being made as good and cheap as any foreign silk can be'.[138]

Patent in hand, Lombe called upon Sorocold to undertake the construction of a new mill. Built beside the 'Old Shop', on a far more impressive scale, the 'Italian Works' mill was completed in 1721. It was 110 feet long, five stories and 55 feet high, 39 feet wide, and had 468 windows. It could accommodate about three hundred workers operating relatively complex machinery for spinning silk thread. One large undershot wheel, 23 feet in diameter, drove all the machinery.[139] A smaller doubling shop was also built, adjacent to the main Italian Works. Thomas Lombe made a fortune from this operation. Although he played down his profits, perhaps to discourage his competitors, he left his wife the sum of £120,000 upon his death in 1738.[140]

---

135. Chapman 1987, p. 14.
136. Butterton 1996, pp. 5–11.
137. 'Details of the mechanism, which had long made Italian engines for winding, spinning and twisting raw silk into organzine the envy of the world and the source of an absolute monopoly of that material, had been published in England in 1607 and 1621, but had never been adopted in practice' (Hertz 1909, p. 719).
138. Butterton 1996, pp. 5–11 quoting the original patent.
139. Derby Industrial Museum.
140. Apparently when the patent expired in 1732, Lombe petitioned for a renewal, writing to Parliament: 'That the works had taken so long a time in perfecting, that there had been none to acquire emolument from the patent'. Hutton comments that 'he had

A surviving letter-book from the firm that purchased the factory after Thomas Lombe's death gives us some clues as to the kinds of problems that the mill's owners faced. There are complaints about the poor conditions of the roads, and the problem of obtaining a steady supply of high quality raw silk.[141] The elements took a heavy toll on the machines, waterwheel and support beams of the factory, all of which were made from wood. Rains would cause the beams to rot; ice in the river would shut down or damage the waterwheel, requiring the machines to be powered by hand. Not only were workers dismissed when technical or supply problems slowed production, but production was also slowed when workers were 'drunk and disorderly' (indicating a lack of worker discipline) or when they observed traditional holidays.[142] Wages were 'generally low', a weaver in 1715 making about 5*d.* per week and eighty years later 4*s.* 6*d.* for single-hand work or eight to 12 shillings if working at a loom.[143] Children served as unpaid apprentices and were employed to tie the threads, which often broke. Pollard writes that the silk mills 'employed, proportionately, far more children, and far younger children, than other mills'.'[144] William Hutton speaks of 'that wonderful machine' (referring to the whole mill), inside of which he laboured as a child:

> Some have earnestly wished to see this singular piece of mechanism; but I have sincerely wished I never had seen it. I have lamented, that while almost every man in the world was born *out* of Derby, it should be my unhappy lot to be born *in*. To this curious, wretched place, I was bound apprentice for seven years, which I always considered the most unhappy of my life . . . the severity was intolerable, the marks of which I yet carry and shall carry to the grave. The inadvertencies of an infant, committed without design, can never merit the extreme of harsh treatment.[145]

In Hutton, the factory children of the nineteenth century had an early prophet.

A rare glimpse of the culture of the workforce is given by a visitor writing in 1778:

---

forgotten to inform them that he had already accumulated more than £120,000; thus veracity flies before profit' (Hutton 1817, p. 167).

141. Contributing, at least, to the shortage in supply was the prohibition, on pain of death, of exports of raw silk from Piedmont by the King of Sardinia in 1724 (Hertz 1909, p. 719). John Lombe's 'theft' of the Italian machinery designs was not easily forgiven in Italy.

142. Another problem for management was theft. In 1757, the compting house was robbed and a reward was offered to information about the culprit, suspected to be a worker (Butterton 1996, p. 31).

143. Hertz 1909, p. 725.

144. Pollard 1965, p. 96.

145. Hutton 1817, pp. 158–9. Note that apprenticeship rules were followed, even within a factory system.

> These mills employ about 200 persons of both sexes, and of all ages, to the great relief and advantage of the poor. The money given by strangers is put into a box, which is opened the day after Michaelmas-day, and a feast is made; an ox is killed, liquor prepared, the windows are illuminated, and the men, women and children, employed in the work, dressed in their best array, enjoy in dancing and decent mirth a holiday, the expectation of which lightens the labour of the rest of the year. It is customary for the inhabitants of the town, and any strangers who may be there, to go to see the entertainment; and the pleasure marked in the happy countenances of these people, is communicated to the spectators, and contributes to the provision for the ensuing year.[146]

From this we can observe that by this time the mill had become a part of the traditional life of the community. We are left asking whether the observance of such a communal holiday meant that the workers in the factory had their own organisation, and if so: what was its nature? To what extent did the management feel obliged to concede to workers' appeals to customary observances, rights and norms? When we consider that the processes of winding and doubling were done on hand-powered machines which could be set up at home by cottage workers, with only the thread-twisting processes being done on large machines demanding an external power source, we can imagine the difficulties faced by management in training and disciplining a workforce in the context of other workers in the trade being accustomed to setting their own hours, setting up friendly associations and in short, overseeing their own labour process. Nonetheless, working hours would have been regulated by the ringing of the bell at set intervals. Each floor would have had its own overseer. A rudimentary engineering department would have been necessary to maintain the transmission of power from the waterwheel to the machines. The architecture itself seems to attest to the fact that it was a distinctively capitalist operation.

The superior advantages of cheap water for power, cheaper labour and superior machinery to be found in the Midlands meant that silk-throwing at Spitalfields in London would eventually go into decline.

Parliament declined Thomas Lombe's request for an extension of his patent and the designs were made available to the public upon his death in 1739. This opened the way for the construction of mills modelled after Lombe's, beginning with several mills in Stockport and Cheshire in the 1730s, Chesterfield and Macclesfield in the 1750s and additional mills in Derby, Congleton, Leek and Knutsford in the 1760s. By 1770, Stockport had at least six silk mills supplying mainly the hand weavers at Spitalfields and Macclesfield had seven large mills and a dozen smaller mills employing nearly 4,000 labourers. Thereafter,

146. Bray 1783, p. 32.

the construction of silk mills on the Lombe model expanded into the Southern counties in the late eighteenth century.[147] The industry continued to struggle, however, due to restricted supply of high quality silk owing to high import duties on raw silk from China and shortages of raw silk coming from Italy. Since the only substitute was a lesser quality supply from Persia, most of the new silk factories concentrated on producing an inferior quality of silk thread known as 'tram'.

Thus it 'was the production of "tram" silk that led to the first wave of factory production in Britain'.[148] This history has been overshadowed by the far more spectacular success of Richard Arkwright's factory system based upon the cotton-spinning water frame, as has a small but significant development of machine-driven cotton-spinning mills, beginning prior to Toynbee's red-letter date of 1760, that anticipated Arkwright's later success.

'A gymcrak of some consequence'

In the early eighteenth century, England's textile industries were undergoing a shift in direction, characterised by local crises. The growth in the triangular trade between England, Africa and the West Indies meant an expanding market for English textiles, especially in coarse goods such as linens, the textile of preference for clothing slaves. But the previously overwhelming share of exports held by textiles and led by wool was declining, and this can be attributed to the growth of the domestic market and the emergence of many new industries. Manufacture of Britain's leading export cloths, woollen and worsted, had historically been centred on three regions: East Anglia in and around the city of Norwich, the West of England between Dorset and Gloucestershire, and the West Riding of Yorkshire. Lancashire also had a strong tradition of woollen production that survived into the nineteenth century. The only area of concentrated woollen production in Scotland was Aberdeen, but 'any incipient Scottish woollen cloth industry had long been suppressed as a result of English competition after the Union'.[149] With the Peace of Utrecht in 1713, certain English cloth exports to Holland were hit hard by the drop in re-exports from Holland as former customers of the Dutch *entrepôt* trade were finding that in the new environment of peace it was easier and to their advantage to trade directly with the manufacturers, circumventing the Dutch middlemen. Exeter had another problem: high-quality Irish linens were claiming a large share of the traditional market in serges. The serge trade was simply falling prey to 'one of those striking changes of fashion which from

147. Jones 1987, pp. 76–7.
148. Butterton 1996, pp. 33 and 49.
149. Christie 1982, p. 13.

time to time stretch the ingenuity of the manufacturer and consign the unenterprising to perdition'.[150] Where the serges had seized the cloth markets in the 1670s, they now fell prey to the latest trend out of Norwich: Norwich 'stuffes'. Another reason for this shift, aside from fashion, may have been lower wage rates in Norwich. The depression in local exports from Exeter embittered labour relations, and heated protests took place in 1717 and 1724.[151] Following the 1724 protest, workmen's clubs were banned locally in 1725. Attempts by clothiers to import ready-spun and combed worsted from Ireland and to introduce new fabrics that might appeal to the changing tastes of the market were frustrated by these labour disturbances. Devon clothing manufacturing continued to decline steadily, worsening in the 1720s with a spate of local bankruptcies, and would reach full stagnation in the 1740s. Despite the success of the new 'stuffes' out of Norwich,[152] increasing imports from India in the form of new cottons and muslins brought unwanted competition. While British weavers enjoyed the same quality of implements as their counterparts in India, their fingers lacked the same dexterity and skill. The Norwich drapers petitioned the Commons for relief between 1695 and 1721. The first bill seeking a ban on Indian cloths came in 1696, but failed in the House of Lords, where the East India Company had a strong influence. In 1701, a bill had passed forbidding English citizens to wear calicoes and other cottons from India, or silks from either India or China. It proved an extraordinarily difficult law to enforce, as smuggling was rampant.

At the same time, however, the domestic printing industry in England was flourishing. The new printworks were based in London, where demand was concentrated. Norwich drapers continued to petition for relief and managed to persuade Parliament to place an excise duty on printed linens and calicoes in

---

150. Wilson 1984, p. 290.

151. 'When Celia Fiennes visited Exeter in 1698 she wrote admiringly in her journal that the industry "turns the most money in a week of anything in England:... She had caught the atmosphere of a boomtown. Surviving figures show that Exeter's own export trade, mainly to Holland, had also expanded rapidly so that around the turn of the century it was probably responsible for nearly fifty per cent of the country's exports of this type of fabric, which in turn accounted for about twenty per cent by value of all woolen exports. But the competition of Norwich, where wages were lower, and Yorkshire, already switching from its decaying kersey trade to the new worsted stuffs, soon began to leave its marks of distress. By the 1740s a correspondent could write of the "lamentable condition of the woollen trade especially in these parts [between Taunton and Exeter], a thing so universally known that I think it almost needless to crowd a letter with any of my observations upon it"' (Coleman 1977, p. 161, citing Fiennes 1935, p. 76).

152. 'At its height the Norfolk industry commanded some 12,000 looms. They worked to the orders of some thirty very large clothier-dyers, and kept 72,000 workers – six to a loom – busy in and around Norwich. The annual output of a loom was valued at about £100' (Wilson 1984, p. 294). In this period, this was one of the largest operations in the clothing trade, all done with hand looms, without power, and in scattered workshops, not the factory.

1712, doubling these duties again in 1714. With both the silk- and woollen trades in a slump upon the renewal of war with Spain in 1719, renewed pressure for action from Parliament came about in the form of petitioning and protesting. Woollen manufacturers viewed the popularity of printed goods as the 'source of all their ills'.[153] In 1721, when resistance from the Company was weakened in the aftermath of the Bubble, Parliament responded with an act banning all foreign cloth, mixed or cotton, printed or painted, excepting muslins, neckcloths, blue-dyed calicoes and fustians. The exceptions were partly a concession to the East India Company and were partly meant to allow British printers to continue to print cloths that could not be confused with Indian cloths. Nevertheless, dozens of calico printers were forced out of business. With their competition reduced, Norwich clothiers would enjoy general prosperity from the 1720s to the 1760s. Still, the clothiers were hypersensitive to competition. Their focus was increasingly upon domestic, not foreign, competition, in the form of coarse worsteds and cheap cottons from Yorkshire. Filling the gap in the market created by the ban on imports, British printers had found a way to make faux calico prints with engraved plates. Consumers did not seem to mind the loss of quality. This aroused domestic opposition.

Coleman's data shows that despite these various types of shifts, where the woollen manufacturing in one region pursuing one line of cloth production faltered or failed while another region advanced, the overall trend for woollen exports from the 1650s to the 1750s was a steady advance.[154] Initially, the ban on Indian cloths led to their being replaced by fustians and linens, mainly from Germany but also from Scotland and Ireland. Over time, fustians from Lancashire improved in quality and claimed the largest share of materials used in printing, so much so that by 1735 the Norwich drapers again complained to Parliament. This resulted in an act of 1736 which reaffirmed that fustians were a cloth made of linen yarn and cotton wool, and as such, were exempted from the ban. During this time, Switzerland, Holland and Germany all had no such prohibitions on Indian imports. As a result, any attempts at domestic cotton production in these countries could not compete with the low prices of Indian wares. France did not permit domestic printing until 1759. Thus the growth of both cotton- and silk manufactures in England were supported by protective legislation, and likely would not have developed as significantly as they did without it.

For cotton, a protected market formed an ideal environment for innovation, and the two key innovations that would eventually enable the first successful spinning and carding factories were worked in this period. An early patent on a machine for spinning linen was granted in 1678 to Richard Dereham of London

153. Wadsworth and Mann 1965, pp. 130–4.
154. See Coleman 1977, p. 16, Table 18.

and Richard Haines of Sullington, Sussex. The machine involved six to a hundred spindles attached to a single crank turned by human labour. Patronised by Prince Rupert, the inventor, Haines, claimed his machine could 'cheapen the cost of giving work to the poor, because spinning could be done upon it in one-third of the time usually occupied', thereby affording employment to 'pauper children and criminals' and enriching the nation.[155] In 1723, London weaver Thomas Thwaites and Yarmouth merchant Francis Clifton patented a machine to '"Spin and Mix in the first Thread Wool, Flax, Cotton, Silk, etc., into a fine even and better Thread..."'[156] No designs or specifications of this invention remain.

The small wares 'engine' loom or 'Dutch' loom had been brought to London in the early seventeenth century by immigrants, and was seen as a threat to English weavers. These machines increased productivity in weaving ribbons and tapes. By the 1660s the loom was known in Manchester. In 1725, some masters were apparently profiting from the use of it sufficiently to incite the comment that 'it had made manufacturers who could "vie with some of the best gentlemen" of the locality'.[157] Later, in 1745, the inventor John Kay of Bury (of whom we will learn more below), took out a patent on a mechanism for transmitting water power to drive the loom. Kay was thus involved in ongoing experiments using water to supply power to machinery that was gaining momentum in Lancashire during this period. By 1750, as many as 1,500 Dutch looms of different types were in use in Manchester alone. Thus here is another example of operations gathering significant numbers of machines under one roof that were becoming increasingly common in the decades prior to Arkwright's success. Lombe's mill, and subsequent silk mills that followed, provided a model to be emulated. But the first power-machine-driven *cotton* factories in England were actually built not using Richard Arkwright's water frame, but using a spinning machine invented by Lewis Paul and John Wyatt.

The story of these mills reveals important details about the emergence of factories in England. Lewis Paul, who claimed to be the descendant of French Huguenots, had by 1732 invented a 'pinking machine for making the edges of shrouds'.[158] He apparently used this to run a successful trade in London. John Wyatt, a ship's carpenter from Lichfield, Staffordshire, is credited with several

155. Coleman 1977, p. 414. According to Fitton 1989, p. 11: 'eight more attempts were made' after Dereham and Haines, before Lewis Paul began his experiments with roller spinning. Fitton does not detail these attempts.

156. Wadsworth and Mann 1965, pp. 414–5 and Coleman 1977, pp. 155–6.

157. This comment was met with the mocking response: '"I wonder what any country gentleman can be supposed to envy them for! Is it their houses? Which country gentleman has reason to envy the possession of a house of four, five or six rooms of a floor with warehouses under and warping rooms over?"' (Rule 1992a, p. 83, citing Bowden 1965, pp. 150–1).

158. Wadsworth and Mann 1965, p. 420.

inventions: a harpoon to be shot from a gun, improved weighing machines, a road-levelling machine, a boring machine and a file-cutting machine. When in 1732 the rights to Wyatt's boring machine were turned over to Paul, the two men began an unsteady business relationship that lasted for ten years.[159] According to Wyatt's son Charles, in 1733 near Sutton Coldfield just northeast of Birmingham, his father invented a two foot square machine that 'spun the first thread of cotton ever spun without the intervention of human fingers'.[160] Wyatt was reportedly excited with suspense to the point of trembling, and wrote to his brother: '"I think I have a gymcrak of some consequence"'.[161] While Wyatt was clearly the engineer who assembled the device, Paul is typically credited with the path-breaking principle that would form the basis for the subsequent revolution in textile machinery, which is the use of rollers to spin the thread to a finer quality and produce a twist, though the machine may have been insufficiently effective in the latter. A second principle applied was the use of spindles which turned independently, stretching and possibly twisting the thread. Of course, the invention was not without precedent. The circular plan of the machine echoed the twin-cylinder mechanism that was 'the heart of Lombe's adaptation' on the Italian model.[162]

A telling part of this story was Paul's concern for the plight of those whom the machine might put out of work, which he expressed in his patent application of 1736. Wadsworth explains:

> All the inventors after Haines echoed his hopes of employing the poor, but what troubled Paul, at any rate, was the opposite argument that his machine would take the bread out of their mouths. The Attorney-General, in issuing the patent, took the rather unusual course of stating his reasons at some

---

159. Mantoux 1961, pp. 45–8. Wyatt's various designs can be found in the Birmingham Central Free Library.

160. Mantoux 1961, p. 210.

161. Mantoux 1961, pp. 209–11, citing an undated letter from Wyatt written in or prior to 1733 (Wyatt 1885, p. 9). Also, regarding the contending claims of original invention, cf. specifically p. 209, n. 1. It is significant that Wyatt appears to have been well-aware of the potential of the invention. He pondered whether such machines would increase the profit of the manufacturer at the expense of the public and the workman. He concluded against this supposition, writing that the resulting increase in industry would provide more employment and more wealth: '"an additional gain to the clothier's trade naturally excites his industry as well as enables him to extend his trade in proportion to his gain by these machines..."' Of the 33 per cent left unemployed, the employer will surely take some in to expand his operation, and more, since he will need more weavers, shearmen, etc. '"Every such improvement in trade must certainly be a gain to the country, especially a country which so much raises its trade as ours..."' (Mantoux 1961, p. 213, citing Wyatt 1885, p. 34). This was written more than forty years before Smith published his *Wealth of Nations.*

162. Butterton 1996, p. 33.

> length.... the balance was turned in favour of Paul by the argument that the better quality and lower price of the yarn to be spun on the machine would restore to England that superiority in the woollen trade which was endangered in Continental markets by French competition. Even the prospect of unemployment... was balanced by the fact that the machine would afford work for the very young, the old and the blind.[163]

For his part, Wyatt issued an elaborate statement rationalising the introduction of the machine in which he envisaged the establishment of works based on this machine '"dispersed all over the kingdom"' and employing women, children and the infirm at a saving to the employer, the parish and the kingdom as a whole. His argument may have persuaded the Attorney General to grant the patent, put in Paul's name, in 1738.[164] But what Paul's concerns appear to demonstrate is how customary conventions pertaining to the rights of artisans remained prevalent in the culture as a whole.[165]

In all, one workshop and four factories were set up using the Wyatt-Paul spinning machine. The original machine was set up in the workshop of James Johnson, a checkmaker of Spitalfields in 1740, and it was quickly discovered that a mechanical solution to carding was needed to keep pace with it. The machine drew considerable interest, and several investors were putting up money for spindles. One of these investors, Dr. Richard James, could clearly see the machine's economic potential, when he wrote: '"I am certain that if Paul could begin with £10,000 he must, or at least might, get more money in twenty years than the City of London is worth"'.[166] The first mill using multiple machines, tended by ten female workers and powered by 'two asses walking round an axis'[167] was set up in Birmingham in the summer of 1741, but was hampered mainly by the fact that its engineer, Wyatt, found himself in debtors' prison at the Fleet from 1742–3. Wyatt apparently attempted to restore the derelict mill upon his release from

163. Wadsworth and Mann 1965, pp. 416–17.

164. For a copy of the original diagram filed with the Patent Office, see Delieb 1971, pp. 114–15.

165. Wadsworth comments: 'It is some measure of the remarkable change in economic opinion wrought in the thirty years between Paul's patent and Arkwright's that the promoters of the former should have been seriously troubled enough about the social objections to their invention, while Arkwright, so far as we have any evidence, does not appear to have been troubled at all' (Wadsworth and Mann 1965, pp. 415–8). It is worth asking whether Paul's comment was motivated out of fear of the wrath of the craftsmen who might be dispossessed. We note that in the Attorney General's grant the machine was intended for spinning wool. What prompted the shift from spinning wool to spinning cotton was most likely the fact that cotton fibres proved more adaptable to roller spinning, but Paul's personal acquaintance with cotton checks and stripes through his London pinking business may also have been a factor.

166. Wadsworth and Mann 1965, p. 430.

167. Fitton 1989, p. 12.

prison, but little more is known of the fate of this first mill, which had showed some promise. The fact that prices were at an all-time low in 1743 may have been a factor in its demise. Birmingham may seem a most unlikely place for the first cotton mill, but it had long had its own cloth-making industry supplying the local market. As early as 1730 'we hear of machines being invented to twist a number of threads simultaneously'.[168] These 'twist mills' were large machines, driven by horse capstans, and surely informed the first attempts by Paul and later by Arkwright, in setting up factories.

The second Wyatt-Paul mill was erected in London, possibly at Holborn, by the wealthy Edward Cave, founder of the *Gentleman's Magazine*, who was meanwhile seeking a better location for the operation where he could apply water power. In London, he was apparently overwhelmed by the difficulty of training a workforce to observe regular hours. ' "I have not half my people come to work today", he wrote to Paul, "and I have no great fascination in the prospect I have to put myself in the power of such people" '.[169] When Lewis Paul's Birmingham mill failed, he sold it to Cave, who in 1742 moved it to Northampton, where he faced similar problems. The mill had five machines powered by a waterwheel and each having fifty spindles, and a carding machine invented by Paul. It employed fifty 'girls' in carding and spinning, and keeping them to their task was an issue. But the larger issue at Northampton had to do with defects in the machinery, which required constant and expensive repair, as well as the inability to resolve the fundamental problem of achieving constant carding. In 1744, the mill was the site of one of the earliest known accidents involving child labour in a factory when a boy had three fingers torn off by one of the wheels (apparently in the driving mechanism) and broke his arm.[170] The Northampton mill 'barely maintained its existence' until 1764. Later, it was sold to none other than Richard Arkwright himself.[171] The fourth Wyatt-Paul mill was set up at Leominster by Lancashire native Daniel Bourn, who apparently achieved a measure of success

168. Stanley D. Chapman 1967, pp. 43–4.
169. Wadsworth and Mann 1965, p. 433.
170. Wadsworth and Mann 1965, p. 445.
171. Mantoux 1961, p. 214. Wadsworth writes that '...one cannot conclude with M. Mantoux that Paul's machine came into Arkwright's hands at the beginning of his experiments' (Wadsworth and Mann 1965, p. 483), and his reasoning seems to be that shortly after the mill was actually broken up, possibly as late as 1764 the machinery 'disappeared' (Wadsworth and Mann 1965, p. 446, n. 6). Since neither author indicates what year Arkwright may have come into possession of the Northampton mill, we can only guess how much time elapsed, but we must assume it was only after Arkwright had achieved success with his own early mills. The connection is nonetheless intriguing, and Wadsworth speculates that Arkwright's water frame may have had strong similarities to the machine described in Paul's first patent, which involved a series of rollers. Another question is the extent to which Thomas Highs, now widely viewed as the true inventor of the water frame (see Chapter Six, p. 328, n. 136) borrowed from Wyatt and Paul.

with an improved carding engine that he patented in 1748. Paul, who had been experimenting with a carding engine at the Northampton mill, took out his own carding patent later that same year. Both machines likely contributed to later, more successful carding mechanisms. The Leominster mill burned down in 1754, and the *Manchester Mercury* commented afterwards that the cotton works 'had been viewed with great pleasure and admiration by travellers and all who had seen them', and that their destruction by fire presented 'an immense loss of the ingenious artist and to the poor who were employ'd therein from the town and adjacent country'.[172] These observations, combined with the fact that investors in the Northampton mill in the 1750s apparently viewed spindles as '"a valid security"' suggests that the Paul-Wyatt mills may have enjoyed considerable success in their day, even if mechanical defects, poor management and an inability to achieve a consistent carding mechanism all contributed to their ultimate failure.

There were other inventors working on machinery for spinning in this era. John Kay of Bury, the inventor of the flying shuttle, took out his first patent in 1730 for a spinning machine, but did not make immediate use of it. Lawrence Earshaw of Mottram invented a machine 'to spin and reel cotton at one operation'[173] but being concerned as Paul was about its effects on the poor, destroyed it without patenting it. James Taylor, a clockmaker from Ashton-under-Lyme, invented a machine resembling the later jenny. The deficiency of surviving documentation may make the task of sorting out the complex interrelations between all of these contributions impossible, but the fact that so many different inventors were simultaneously pursuing a practical solution to the same problem attests to the way in which the market imperative to transform production was gaining hold of this line manufacturing in English textiles.

The career of John Kay of Bury is instructive in a number of ways, particularly in how it suggests differences between the economies of early eighteenth-century Britain and France. Kay was most famous for inventing the 'wheel shuttle' or 'flying shuttle', which he patented in 1733.[174] The mechanism involved a small cart on rollers moving on a track to insert the weft through the warp threads in the loom, effectively automating what had forever been a manual process of pulling or tossing the shuttle from side to side. The reaction to Kay's shuttle was immediate. Weavers in Colchester petitioned the King in September of 1733,

172. *Manchester Mercury*, 5 November 1754, as quoted in Wadsworth and Mann 1965, p. 444.

173. Wadsworth and Mann 1965, p. 472.

174. 'The modern title of "fly shuttle" or "flying shuttle" seems to be a translation of its French name, *navette volante*, and was not used in England until towards the end of the eighteenth century' (Wadsworth and Mann 1965, p. 450; see also Wilson 1984, p. 297; and Coleman 1977, p. 156).

saying that if the shuttle were adopted it would ruin them, since it would enable one weaver to do the work of four. By Kay's own account, he was confronted at some point with a crowd of angry weavers who threatened to kill him, and who destroyed a number of the shuttles, but exactly when or where this took place is unclear. Worse still for Kay, he not only had difficulty collecting from those who signed agreements to rent the use of his patent, but other weavers were found to be violating his patent by installing their own wheel shuttles and tracks. He pursued the interlopers in numerous trips to Chancery Court. On one occasion, an accused weaver claimed that a board for shuttles to run upon had been known for fifteen years or more, and that Kay's most significant improvement, putting a hole in the shuttle so that a single and larger bobbin could more evenly release the thread, was not included in his patent, but only came afterwards in 1735.

Having failed in Chancery Court, Kay took his case to Parliament, to no avail. He subsequently removed to France in 1747 in hopes of better success with the application of his shuttle-loom and to continue pursuing work on numerous other inventions. After jointly applying for a patent with the firm of Scalogne, woollen manufacturers in Abbeville, Kay was again complaining of interlopers, whereupon the French government promptly sent officials to suppress them.[175]

What is most instructive about Kay's story, aside from the travails to be faced by eighteenth-century inventors, is what the different courses of progress made by the fly shuttle in England and in France can tell us about differences in the two countries. By 1790 its use had almost completely died out in France. But in England it had made slow and steady progress, if only in Lancashire. It seems doubtful that the flying shuttle had a dramatic impact on increasing the output of weaving in England before the arrival of a working power-loom in 1803, but even then it had another forty years to spread among manual weavers. What is more, it provided the working principle of an automated shuttle that would serve as the basis for the power-loom's design. The fact that the flying shuttle took root in England, where there was both strong opposition to and simultaneous interest in the new machine, while it did not take root in France, attests to the different structures of social relations of production prevailing in the two countries. Mann describes the contrast as one 'between a country in which industry was subordinated to a highly organised and, on the whole, a very efficient body of officials, and taught to look to the Government for the encouragement of new processes, and one where the tradition of Government control and assistance was almost dead'.[176] The fact that governmental control was 'almost dead' in England points to the dynamism of an economy increasingly regulated by market considerations in an environment of increasingly sharp competition between private interests.

175. See Wadsworth and Mann 1965, pp. 449–72.
176. Wadsworth and Mann 1965, p. 206.

The turning point

According to Deane and Cole, the 1740s 'constitute a landmark' for several branches of manufacturing. Increasing demand from the West Midlands for the use of metals in production also stimulated the growth of mining in copper, tin, brass and lead.[177] By the 1740s, Newcomen's engine was applied to Cornish mines in non-ferrous metals. From the 1740s, the output of tin (previously used mainly for pewter but now driven by the production of tin-plate) and copper, grew rapidly. For copper mining: 'the year 1748 marks the beginning of a great wave of expansion which lasted for nearly forty years', after which decline set in. The output of tallow candles and glass rose rapidly from the 1740s onward.[178] Between the 1730s and the 1740s improvements on the 'Hollander' engine – which derived (as its name suggests) from continental origins, though improved upon in England – made its appearance in the paper industry and was used for pulping linen rags, after which English paper production may have increased threefold by 1800.[179]

In 1740, textiles still composed a third of all manufacturing output in Britain.[180] When agricultural prices reached their lowest point in 1743, there was regional depression.[181] The cloth trade out of Devon was wiped out: Tiverton declined absolutely, while Exeter was just able to maintain a steady population as 'small masters drifted into shopkeeping and a variety of other occupations'.[182] Only two years later, woollens, cottons, linens and silk all began not only to recover, but to start on a long-term trend of unprecedented growth. The shift of textile-manufactures from the South to the North began to accelerate, but this did not become widely apparent until the 1760s, when it became clear that the high quality woollens from East Anglia were quickly losing their share of the domestic market to Yorkshire products of inferior quality: worsteds and cheap woollens. Wool production as a whole grew by around eight percent per decade from 1700 to 1740, and exceeded 14 percent in the decades thereafter.[183] In West Yorkshire, a class of small clothiers grew as the woollen trade was open to any weaver who could come up with £100 to £150 for a loom. The opposite trend

177. Coleman 1977, pp. 153 and 167.
178. Deane and Cole 1969, p. 56.
179. Deane and Cole 1969, pp. 57–8, citing Coleman 1956b, pp. 1–22.
180. Wilson 1984, p. 289, citing Hoffmann 1955, pp. 18–9.
181. Wilson 1984, p. 292. For Devon, it was 'a particularly bad year, when the gloom of the cloth trade, prevalent unemployment, bankruptcies and crowded workhouses of the towns and villages were equaled in the countryside. Record numbers of estates were up for sale. Record numbers of farms to be let. Yet observers noticed that the cloth industry elsewhere did not share these burdens'.
182. Wilson 1984, p. 292. Dobson 1980, pp. 32–3 notes that following violent protests in Tiverton in May of 1738, loom-cutters became clandestine in their activities.
183. Deane and Cole 1969, p. 53.

Table 7.3. English patents sealed: 1660–1759[184]

Years	Patents
1660–9	31
1670–9	50
1680–9	53
1690–9	102
1700–9	22
1710–19	38
1720–9	89
1730–9	56
1740–9	82

held true in worsted manufacturing, which was dominated by big clothiers like Sam Hill. Hill had set up as a worsted clothier in Halifax by 1737, declaring he was ' "studying to outdo all England" ' with his shaloons and Long Ells. Whether or not Hill lived to fulfil his claim, Yorkshire's worsted industry itself would see it come to fruition. What was even less apparent to contemporary observers in the early eighteenth century was that the other and much greater rival to Southern textiles coming out of Lancashire and Scotland (in and around Glasgow),[185] would be cotton. Much of it imitating Indian prints, the range of cotton prints had grown enormously by mid-century, even if by 1750 the consumption of raw cotton was only double what it had been in 1710.

Significant as this growth was, it was but 'a pale anticipation of what was to come'.[186] This is partly because, as we have seen, the application of machinery to textile production was still quite limited. Counting the numbers of patents granted is only a crude measure of the rate of innovation, but what can be seen from Table 7.3 is that after a burst of applications in the aftermath of the Glorious Revolution, followed by a lull, the general trend was toward more patents each year. The second half of the eighteenth century would bring a sharp upward trend, with 647 patents in the 1790s alone. But the figures for 1700–50 'are not pointers to a stagnant economy'[187] Why was innovation on the rise in this half

184. Coleman 1977, p. 155.

185. 'It may be significant', writes Wilson (1984, p. 296), 'that these were the two areas where linen manufacture flourished before the age of cotton'. Before 1700, Scottish linen manufacturing had been insignificant. But 'its rise to national prominence was one of the striking features of Scotland's economic history in the earlier part of the eighteenth century' (Deane and Cole 1969, p. 52).

186. Deane and Cole 1969, p. 52.

187. Coleman 1977, p. 155. Some were of 'dubious originality and limited economic value (like "Back-frames for the Bed-Ridden" and a monopoly for importing lobsters)', writes Wilson, 'but the majority could claim to have a *prima facie* connexion with

century? Ashton points to the 'decline of strict apprenticeship and corporate regulation of industry [that] released native talents' as well as the lower costs 'of experimentation and the construction of new appliances', attributed to the 'greater abundance of capital and lower interest rates', but he commits to 'no sure answer'.[188] Why did innovation in the first half of the eighteenth century not compare to the outburst of the second half? Black points to the size of workshops and the role of custom. The limited size of most operations, he writes:

> helped ensure that there was very little specialization, either in machinery or labour... Artisan mentality included a sense of the importance of traditional values and communal stability. There was a general disinclination to innovate, understandably so in a culture where training was largely acquired on the job and where tradition determined most industrial practices.[189]

In both of these explanations, it is the customary mode of organising the labour-process that is understood to be the force holding back the otherwise already existing drive to innovate. We have seen examples that would justify such a view, such as the hostility of Lancashire weavers to Kay's shuttle, and we shall meet more examples like this. Yet we also saw in the case of Kay that weavers were perhaps more eager to adopt the new technology when they were inclined to see it as an advantage. Meanwhile in France, the shuttle and other inventions failed to catch on, and while French inventors were patronised by the state, French manufacturing seriously lagged behind British manufacturing when it came to applying new technology to productive purposes. Could more be at work in this contrast than simply the presence of extensive regulation of manufacturing in France versus the absence of regulation in Britain? And what, at any rate, explains the difference? Let us here suggest that the difference was quite simply that capitalism had taken root in Britain, but not in France.

We begin with agrarian capitalism, which through the extinction of customary rights in agriculture by enclosure was creating an ever larger percentage of the producing population that no longer had direct access to the means of subsistence. By the early eighteenth century, this process was by no means complete, but it had generated two phenomena. First, there was an emerging labour-market, which we would characterise by the spread of wage labour and the increasing payment of wages in money rather than in kind. This labour market grew up in the context of the unprecedented expansion of the domestic market in an economy now characterised by its capacity for self-sustaining growth. Second,

---

economic processes of genuine importance – smelting ores, dyeing textiles, making explosives, swords, boats, ploughs, mills, locks, soap, glass, oil, pumping engines, etc'. (Wilson 1984, p. 102).

188. Ashton 1964, p. 105.

189. Black 2001, p. 55.

there was an increasingly large underclass of unemployed and underemployed persons. As the numbers of the underclass grew, various reformers called for ways to deal with the 'problem' of what to do with would be workers who had no land to work and no jobs to fill. Both the poor laws and the workhouse were favoured as solutions, and both tended to help keep the cost of labour down. During this period of falling prices, real wages held steady or rose moderately, and this encouraged employers to expand their operations, whether in the form of extending their networks of putting-out operations or expanding the size of an already centralised operation. Customary modes of labour organisation were increasingly disregarded. The workhouse precedes the factory, and serves as a kind of prototype for gathering workers under one roof and putting them to work on machinery. But even in what appear to be explicitly capitalist operations, the earliest factories, we see that the communal and customary norms that workers bring to the workplace continue to frustrate their capitalist managers.

Ashton and Black, by focusing on the way custom appears to impede the 'progress' of innovation, circumvent the key question, which is: what is it that custom is up against? What is custom impeding? It is as if the answer is so obvious that it need not be stated. Yet without clarifying what capitalism *is*, we can have no explanation for how it came into existence. The explanation offered by Ashton and Black, like so many accounts, seems to treat industrial capitalism as both already in existence before 1750 and also as an inevitability that renders the struggles of craftsmen to hold on to their customary modes of labour organisation moot. But as Hutton's childhood experience at the Old Silk Mill suggests, much was at stake, starting with how a society treats its children, how it rears them, and how, or if, it provides them with skills and an education.

Conclusion

Capitalism is more than a system of government *laissez-faire*. It involves a peculiar social relationship, the social relation of capital, a form of property which is wholly market-dependent. The development of agrarian capitalism involved the increasing market dependence of not only direct producers but also surplus-appropriators, who were increasingly compelled by market imperatives to transform production in the direction of greater efficiency. This growing necessity to transform production necessitated their taking direct command of the production process, which in the case of agrarian capitalism was achieved in part through enclosures and declaring absolute individual property rights over land under the common law.[190] In a highly developed capitalist economy, capital is

---

190. Comninel, 'Capital as a Social Relation,' draft essay (York University, n.d.).

a social relationship that comprises all factors of production – including land, labour and money – and virtually all aspects of production (even social reproduction) are subordinated to the exigencies and compulsions of market-based competition, although there has never been and never will be a perfectly capitalist economy because the physical environment, human labour and money, which exist in their own right independently of the market, can only be understood to take the form of capital in a fictitious sense. In examining this period just prior to the onset of the Industrial Revolution, we have seen that it is a period characterised by a wide variety of labour arrangements and types of manufacturing firm. If we can agree that Lombe's factory was at least a recognisably 'capitalist', how are we to describe the wide variety of manufacturing operations of different size and type of arrangement of this period? There is a certain parallel between the factory and the enclosed farm. Both enclosure and the factory developed in response to competitive pressures acting upon the tenant-farmer or manufacturing employer, making the transformation of production necessary in order to ensure their economic survival. Both institutions virtually extinguished any role for custom to play in regulating production.[191] Both the capitalist tenant-farmer and manufacturing employer came to enjoy complete command over the means of production so that production decisions could be made in accordance with the dictates of the market, with the profits of production accruing solely to the owner. This does not mean that capitalism as an economic system had already achieved dominance in manufacturing; in general it could still be characterised as in transition, operating within the social framework associated with the social relations of agrarian capitalism – a ruling landed class, capitalist tenant-farmers, and a growing pool of agrarian producers 'freed' of the means of subsistence. To fully convert manufacturing to the control of capital and full subjection to the market imperative would require an industrial revolution. And the factory would provide one of the vital institutions for making that happen.

In Chapter One, it was proposed that the proper way to understand the changes within craft guilds was in terms of stratification, not of class. In the early eighteenth century, the effective dismissal of craftsmen from the companies and their scramble to reassert their collective power in the form of friendly societies and charterless companies has all the appearance of one class consolidating its power to face another. This consolidation took place in one trade at

191. We say 'virtually' because, as we have seen, customary notions of how production was to be organised still intruded into the operations of the early factory, and to whatever minute degree they have into the operations of every factory since. This is because custom is not only rooted in legal arrangements and by-laws governing the operations of units of production. As we shall see, custom is rooted in culture, in social understandings of 'how things are done', transmitted from generation to generation. Chapters Ten and Eleven will provide a fuller discussion of the role of custom.

a time, however, not collectively. While agrarian waged labourers who had lost access to both the means of subsistence and the means of production (which in agriculture are effectively the same) were by definition proletarian, the direct producers in domestic manufacturing were at least semi-proletarian in character inasmuch as they did not possess any means of subsistence and had to work for wages. Most craft workers, however, possessed (if they did not own) their own means of production – the tools and equipment necessary to proceed with their craft. Prior to losing direct access to markets, as in the era of the guilds, they were also traders inasmuch as they had to realise a value for their product in order to obtain money or other goods to exchange for the necessities of life. The loss of access to markets by increasing numbers of domestic workers brought them under the sway of the capitalist market imperatives that were driving merchants and large employers to intensify production.

The 1750s saw an intensification of conflict between large employers and craft-workers seeking to defend custom. The increased frequency of harvests after 1750 meant that both food protests and industrial disputes grew more common. In Lancashire, which had already become dependent on imports of grain to feed its growing manufacturing population, the impact of rising prices and bad harvests was particularly acute in the 1750s. Sharp price rises in 1753 prompted protests in Manchester and a request by the justices that workers return to work. In 1756, a bad harvest brought about widespread protesting among the ' "half-starved manufacturing people" '.[192] A worse harvest in 1757 brought unrest in all parts of the country. Manchester was put under armed guard. Liverpool armed its citizens with muskets and bayonets against incursion from the countryside in search of grain. In the context of such distress in the 1750s, combinations were induced to 'come out of from the secrecy of the club-room into the light of publicity, and into open conflict with the employers'.[193] Their demands asserted or re-asserted rights long-held in custom. In 1756, Gloucestershire weavers successfully persuaded the magistrates to fix their wages. In Manchester, worsted smallware weavers were pressing for higher piece-rates. They and the check weavers published 'apologies' for their trade societies. The check weavers would soon launch a 'great strike'. 'In March of 1758, the silk-weavers of Manchester announced their intention to limit apprentices'.[194] Do these demands suggest that 'the artisan-craft tradition by which the British trade-union movement more than any other was deeply marked' was 'a pre-industrial and pre-capitalist tradition?'[195] This usage of the term 'pre-capitalist', can be misleading, writes John Rule:

192. Wadsworth and Mann 1965, p. 359, quoting Touzeau 1910, p. 508.
193. Wadsworth and Mann 1965, p. 361.
194. Wadsworth and Mann 1965, pp. 361–2.
195. Fox 1984, pp. 124 and 141 as cited in Rule 1992a, p. 202.

> The rise of a class of capitalist employers predicated the emergence of defensive labour organizations, but this separation of interests long pre-dated the arrival of the factory and the 'industrial revolution' as normally envisaged. Unions of journeymen commonly sought to retain the restrictive and regulative customs of the 'trade' over such institutions as apprenticeship and expected of the state that it continue to guarantee 'rights' against, in particular, the 'infringements' of innovating masters. They even inherited much of the ceremony and ritual.[196]

These labour organisations were very much caught up in the transitional process that had taken hold of manufacturing in this period. They had a dual character inasmuch as they did anticipate the trade unions of the nineteenth and twentieth centuries, while at the same time forcefully seeking to preserve customs of the past. We see the emergence of large operations involving large 'capitals', but with few exceptions, the production process itself remains directly regulated by non-market conventions rooted in custom. At the same time, however, the role of custom in regulation manufacturing was being undermined as the declining cost of food alongside rising levels of demand increased the competitive pressures on traders and employers to improve productive efficiency by intensifying production. This they did by assuming control of the marketing of manufactured goods, thereby controlling the direct producers' access to the market. The result of this 'formal' subsumption to capital was an increasing level of exploitation, even if workers generally continued to maintain direct control over the labour process. This was still a society governed by a landed oligarchy and the advantages of improved, market-driven agriculture were well-known, informing the increasing tendency for justices to rule against combinations in the courts on the grounds that trade ought to be free and unregulated. State-level support for the customary mode of labour regulation was rapidly eroding.

From all of this, it follows that the factory owes its origins not specifically to the amassing of wealth, the concentration of units of production or the introduction of machinery, but to the economic forces generated by agrarian capitalism – the divorcing of the direct producers from the means of subsistence, creating an expanding pool of increasingly market dependent employed, semi-employed and non-employed workers, the subsequent market dependence of surplus appropriators faced with the necessity of transforming production in accordance with market dictates for their economic survival, and the expansion of the domestic market, including the beginnings of a national labour market. All of these factors combined formed the vital economic conditions for the emergence of the factory as a complete expression of the social relation of capital in manufacturing. At the

---

196. Rule 1992a, p. 202.

same time, the factory owes its origins to more than just economic factors. The factory came about in part as a remedy to the perceived social 'problem' or 'ill' of poverty, to which the workhouse was proposed early on as a remedy. Proposals for erecting a factory were pitched on the grounds that they would provide much needed employment for the poor: if agrarian capitalism brought about widespread poverty, industrial capitalism, it was argued, would cure it.

Chapter Eight
Factories and Machinery

> [T]he agglomeration of workers into factories was a natural outgrowth of the putting-out system (a result, if you will, of its internal contradictions) whose success had little or nothing to do with the technological superiority of large-scale machinery. The key to the success of the factory, as well as its inspiration, was the substitution of capitalists' for workers' control of the production process; discipline and supervision could and did reduce costs *without* being technologically superior.
>
> Stephen Marglin[1]

> Machines and new techniques alone are not the Industrial Revolution, they meant gains in productivity, a shift in the relative importance of the factors of production from labour to capital. But by revolution we mean a transformation of the organization as well as the means of production. In particular, we mean the assemblage of large bodies of workers in one place, where to accomplish their tasks under supervision and discipline; we mean, in short, what has come to be known as the factory system.
>
> David Landes[2]

The winding down of operations in America and the resignation of Lord North were followed by a period of political instability prior to the ascension of the Younger Pitt to office. It was also a period of recovery

1. Marglin 1974, p. 84.
2. Landes 1991, p. 114.

as economic resources that had been diverted toward the war were now turned once again to domestic purposes. Parliamentary enclosures were renewed. And starting in 1782, 'almost every statistical series of production shows a sharp upward turn'.[3] 1782 also coincides with the beginnings of a rapid expansion of the factory system and the use of new machinery, the jenny in particular, in domestic production of textiles. A spinner in 1812 is said to have been able to produce as much yarn as two hundred spinners prior to the invention of the jenny.[4] Clearly machinery played an important role in the Industrial Revolution by making dramatic increases in productivity possible, but in the emergence of industrial capitalism, was machinery more cause or more effect?

Mokyr, like Toynbee, puts the turning point at 1760: 'before 1760', he writes, 'stability was the rule and inventions the exception; afterwards, it was the other way around'.[5] Yet as we have seen, there was plenty of innovation to go around before 1760. Furthermore, even if Mokyr's sweeping statement were in some sense accurate, placing the emphasis on innovation begs the question of *why* the pace of innovation increased in the latter half of the eighteenth century. In textiles, some machines such as the fulling mill and gig mill had been in use for centuries, whilst the designs necessary for mechanising other stages of the textile-production process had been worked out as early as the sixteenth century. Landes's metaphor of a 'harvest of inventions'[6] is therefore somewhat misleading. One might suggest that the Industrial Revolution was not so much a harvest of inventions but rather a harvest in the ways in which both old and new technologies were applied to production. The question then becomes not one of explaining any sudden burst of *technology*, but how to explain this virtual explosion of *productive output* and *productivity* in specific branches of industry toward the end of the eighteenth century, particularly after 1782. Since on the one hand there was a broad upswing in output across most industries in Britain, while on the other hand the spread of machine-driven production and of factories was limited to certain industries in the last decades of the eighteenth century, it is clear that there were other factors besides machinery and technology which contributed to this increase.

A relatively small number of factories appeared in the period between the Glorious Revolution of 1688 and the 1780s, when the factory system began to spread. Nevertheless, during this century a kind of fever for mechanical invention caught hold. There were many examples of failed inventors that we know of, but there were surely many more innovations of which no record survives. Wadsworth notes that:

---

3. Ashton 1964, p. 125.
4. Deane and Cole 1969, p. 183, citing Ellison 1886.
5. Mokyr 1994, p. 13.
6. Landes 1991, p. 61.

> The idea of mechanical production had seized the [cotton] industry. Scores of men were making machines, and equipping small factories; scores of inventive minds were at work, contributing a modification here, an adaptation there, which had passed into the common stock. There was no machine without its history of trial and error, and the men whose names have become household words were surrounded by a whole society of inventors to whom the progress of cotton machinery owes hardly less than it does to them.[7]

Thus the economic and social context in which the factory system emerged was one characterised by an already existing obsession with machinery, based on experience that was replete with technical problems needing to be worked out. It would seem obvious that this fever for invention was motivated by the same competitive market pressures that were driving the subsumption of labour to capital. As we have noted, these pressures were strengthened by the spread of market dependency, an increasingly unregulated domestic market and the growth of a national force of wage labourers. What role did machinery play? Was mechanical technology itself a driving force or merely a tool in this process?

We have argued that the development of capitalism involved more than simply removing the 'fetters' of the feudal integument, with all its complex customs for normatively regulating economic life. This suggests that the question that needs to be posed is: how was industrial capitalism *made*? In Chapter Seven, we argued that while Britain in the early eighteenth century saw growing 'capitals' or growing concentrations of wealth in manufactures engaged in putting-out operations or running centralised operations employing large numbers of workers, the character of this emerging industrial capitalism could in general be characterised by a formal as opposed to a real subjection of labour to capital. The problem we shall address in this chapter is: what was required in order for the industrialist to establish a fully capitalist operation in which he enjoyed the capacity to transform the production process in order to achieve more efficient production in response to market imperatives? In other words, how was the 'real' subsumption of labour to capital achieved? These questions will guide us into the heart of the early Industrial Revolution.

Wedgwood

Among the key regions of the Industrial Revolution in Britain, the West Midlands hosted more *types* of manufacturing going into the Industrial Revolution than any other. County Staffordshire was not only home to coal and iron production, but it was also the 'home of English pottery'. And pottery was as profoundly transformed by the Industrial Revolution as any other line of production. 'The

7. Wadsworth and Mann 1965, p. 503.

Potteries' comprised five towns within an area of twelve square miles: Stoke-on-Trent, Burslem, Tunstall, Hanley and Longton. In this area, 'lying on the sloping base of a long chain of hills', clay was to be found which had the fine 'qualities of the clay of Samos and Etruria'.[8] In the seventeenth century, pottery was basically manufactured by peasants. It was a source of by-employment for some, not very different from weaving or spinning or other lines of cottage manufacturing. The potters here were ignorant of the use, then current all over England, of copper oxide for adding colour. Toward the end of the sixteenth century, Gilbert Wedgwood, great-great-grandfather to Josiah Wedgwood, settled at Burslem, where he established a small pottery which supplemented the family income from farming. By legend, one-third of Burslem's inhabitants would come to bear the Wedgwood name by 1700.[9]

Numerous developments in the early eighteenth century provided excellent conditions for an unprecedented expansion of pottery manufacturing in Britain. First, the growth of tea drinking and the spread of coffeehouses locally brought about new demand for quality ceramics. Second, according to a story that bears some resemblance to the story of John Lombe's trip to Italy to steal the secrets of silk-spinning machinery, two local potters by the names of Astbury and Twyford managed to steal the secret for using salt-glazing to make red and black teapots that was held as a family secret by the Eelers, two Dutchmen who according to legend had come over from Holland with William of Orange in 1688.[10] The Eelers had set up their wares in London and Bradwell, and Astbury and Twyford managed to find employment with them long enough to steal the trade secret.[11] They subsequently set up works with Thomas Wedgwood, grandfather to Josiah Wedgwood, and the region began to gain a reputation for its fine glazewares. Astbury went on to introduce the use of powdered flint as a whitener in 1720. This practice became a blight on potters, however, as the inhalation of

8. Hammond and Hammond, 1974b, p. 163. The region provided the necessary resources for pottery manufacturing: 'Burslem had a population of enfranchised copyholders, men of initiative and independence, who could dig for clay and even for coal on the adjacent waste, while six miles away they could obtain the lead ore that they needed for glazing'.

9. Lord 1966, p. 45.

10. The method actually posed an environmental hazard. 'The burning salt sent up dense clouds of black smoke, and by the middle of the century on Saturday afternoons, when the firing was going on, people had to grope their way about the streets of Burslem' (Hammond and Hammond 1974b, pp. 165–6).

11. Idiots 'were employed at the thrower's wheel in preference to normal workmen'. Astbury, pretending to be an idiot, worked for the Eelers for two years and got all their secrets. Twyford did likewise and each set up potworks. The Eelers departed for London, 'and remained the best potters in England till Josiah Wedgwood displaced them' (Lord 1966, p. 45).

powdered flint caused a fatal type of lung disease that became known as 'potter's rot'. Despite Thomas Benson's discovery of a method to grind the flint in a water mill and avoid exposure during its production, the use of powdered flint as a whitener continued until the end of the century, and many lives were destroyed. Third, and perhaps most portentous, was the revelation of another trade secret, one that had been kept from Europeans for a millennium. The secret of making Chinese porcelain became known to Europeans after 1708. The first English porcelain manufactories were established in the mid-1740s.[12] By the middle of the century Europe was in the grip of a porcelain mania.[13] Meanwhile, European methods of pottery manufacture and design had undergone such an improvement that they were able to compete with porcelain as a cheaper alternative. While the demand for porcelain was almost universal, it was too expensive for most. 'It was the dream of every ambitious potter to develop a fine, white earthenware that could imitate the appearance of porcelain without incurring destructive losses in production'.[14] Fourth, key among the new innovations was the introduction in 1730 of moulds and the use of the plaster of Paris for making common pots and decorations. Now only finer wares required a thrower, and new classes of pottery workers came to predominate: carvers, designers and pressers. The use of moulds 'required specialised block cutters, flat and hollow ware pressers, and casters'.[15] Double firing, introduced by Enoch Booth, reduced the risk of the ceramics being damaged in the ovens. But like Astbury, Booth introduced yet another scourge on the pottery workers: lead poisoning, for the new and cheaper glaze he introduced was lead-based.

According to the Hammonds: 'These several changes of method had made the complete reorganisation of the industry on a capitalist basis inevitable'.[16] To justify this claim, they argue that:

> an industry which imports and exports cannot be conducted on the scale of a peasant industry which uses local materials and supplies a local market. The needs of the old industry had been served by master potters, each of whom had a single oven with six men and four boys, fired once a week, and drew a weekly profit of ten shillings, together with six shillings for his own labour. Before the middle of the century the more enterprising masters began to add oven to oven. Thus the factory arrived.[17]

12. Young 1999, pp. 257–8.
13. Reilly 1992, pp. 9 and 14.
14. Reilly 1992, p. 16.
15. McKendrick 1961, p. 31.
16. Hammond and Hammond 1974b, pp. 167–8.
17. Hammond and Hammond 1974b, p. 168.

The Hammonds appear to equate adding ovens, or rather expanding the size of the operation in response to increasing demand in trade, with a transition to factory production. But much more was involved. It was Josiah Wedgwood who pioneered the factory system in pottery. An examination of his methods reveals much about the essence of factory production.

The potting trade was not mentioned in the Statute of Apprentices of 1562, for it had always been a craft undertaken by potters dispersed throughout the countryside; not being a town-based craft it had no guild. 'Nevertheless, the trade seems to have imitated the organisation of the rest of industry as a matter of convenience, for it was considered the normal thing to serve an apprenticeship of seven years as in other trades'.[18] In the early eighteenth century, employers increasingly sought to circumvent the apprenticeship system. Customarily apprentices were not paid, and in 1744 London passed a law confirming this. But by the later eighteenth century the practice of paying nominal wages to apprentices 'had become so widespread that provision was being made for the entry of wages on the standard printed indenture forms'.[19] So even apprenticeships were being marketised. Josiah Wedgwood himself served a five-year apprenticeship before he went into partnership with Thomas Whieldon in 1754, provoking Josiah Spode, one of Wielden's apprentices, to leave him. Spode would go on to become Wedgwood's foremost competitor.

Whieldon was the first potter to rent accommodations for his workers and in 1759 was among the first to subscribe to the first turnpike road reaching the vicinity of the Potteries.[20] By 1765, Wedgwood was master of his own works and in that year introduced his own creamware, the production of which he had brought to such a high standard that it superseded salt-glazed ware 'and, in due course, ruined the trade in tin-glazed wares, not only in Britain but throughout Europe'.[21] Over the next three decades, Wedgwood established the most successful pottery enterprise in Great Britain, if not in the world, by meticulously organising the production process, by experimenting in and introducing new glazes and other technical advances, by aggressively marketing his pottery in London showrooms and even abroad and by securing the development of turnpikes and canals through the region, guaranteeing good access to distant markets for his work and that of the other potters.

---

18. Lord 1966, p. 47.
19. Whiter 1970, pp. 4–5.
20. The roads in and around the Potteries were exceptionally bad thanks in large part to a local custom whereby any freeholder had the right to dig at any time for any quantity of clay or coal on any unenclosed land. While the custom ceased to be observed after 1720, many of the resulting holes in the roads could be more than a century old. The sorry state of the roads is considered to have been a factor in enabling Bonnie Prince Charlie to reach Derby without opposition in 1745 (Reilly 1992, pp. 21–2).
21. Reilly 1992, p. 29.

Wedgwood's success as an industrialist and entrepreneur depended upon other factors besides the expansion of markets for British pottery. He was the beneficiary of trade skills and pottery works handed down from generation to generation. He built upon the introduction of new techniques and benefited from the uncovering of long-held trade secrets. As in most trades, customary regulations such as apprenticeship rules were increasingly being disregarded as masters sought to expand the scale of their works beyond previous limits set by custom. Wedgwood not only imitated these larger masters, but by radically restructuring the organisation of production, he rendered toothless the customary norms that had prohibited certain market behaviours as unacceptable and which had once constrained the size of the operation by restricting the number of apprentices. Wedgwood's initial success in developing a new method of producing a line of pottery (creamware) that was superior in quality, competitive in price and matched a recent surge in demand for such wares, provided him with a distinct advantage over other master potters. Throughout his career, he would manage to maintain this lead through further innovation and specialisation. But what enabled him do so, and further, what enabled him to maintain the quality of his product, to expand his operation so as to simultaneously maintain multiple areas of specialisation and to maximise production to meet periods of unprecedented expansion in demand for his wares, were his innovations in labour management methods. These methods anticipated practices that did not become widespread across various industries for many decades, and even anticipated twentieth-century Taylorism and Fordism.

Before discussing Wedgwood's radical reforms of the traditional workshop-methods of pottery production, it is necessary to clarify or reiterate a few points. We have identified that the expansion of the market for pottery was an important factor behind Wedgwood's success, and have also noted that it was one of several factors. Second, while it is true that the observance of customary restrictions on the trade had weakened, it is important to bear in mind that this weakening was itself the product of a long struggle within the crafts and one that involved conscious agency on the part of merchants and masters, albeit at the collective level. Third, one must be clear in saying that Wedgwood's decisions (as an individual master) were shaped by the competitive pressures of the market is not the same as saying that the capitalist logic of production was already implicit in the existence of increasingly unregulated and increasingly (but not yet fully) competitive markets in his trade. What competition did was to compel such entrepreneurs as Wedgwood to seek out new techniques and new methods of production in order to gain an advantage over other competitors in the marketplace. Wedgwood stands out as exceptional because the way in which he reorganised production was surely the most radical break from the customary way the labour process was regulated in the potteries. Some have labelled works like

Wedgwood's the 'immature factory'.[22] And yet, while the scale and complexity of Wedgwood's operation may pale in comparison to the conveyor belts of the twentieth century, in terms of the revolution in the reorganisation of the labour process, Wedgwood's operation was perhaps the most advanced of his time.

Aside from his innovations in production, another way in which Wedgwood serves as an example to demonstrate that the establishment of industrial capitalism required the conscious *building* of new institutions and new social relationships is in the field of marketing. From his letters, Wedgwood appears as a man far more preoccupied with figuring out the most effective ways of marketing his wares than with innovation in methods of production. Dividing his time between his pottery works in Staffordshire and his showroom in London, Wedgwood was constantly in search of new markets, constantly monitoring trends of style and taste in the market so that he could quickly innovate to match the changing cycle of demand. Wedgwood was a merchant for his own wares. This made him one of those merchants who, as Smail writes, 'did as much to shape the pace and character of economic growth in the eighteenth century as did producers or consumers, for merchants created the constantly evolving markets where the efforts of producers met the needs of consumers'.[23] To a large extent the history of how merchants and merchant-manufacturers like Wedgwood created new markets remains to be written, and Smail's is a pioneering work in this regard. It is important to recognise that markets did not simply arise out of the dissolution of the medieval integument; new markets had to be created, discovered, adapted to and closely followed. Our attention is drawn to Wedgwood as both an innovator in the capitalist mode of production and the capitalist mode of marketing.[24]

Bruland identifies three key elements to Wedgwood's system.[25] The first of these was a subdivision of the labour process into a series of discrete tasks. Increasing the division of labour in this way 'implied the substitution of homogeneous for heterogeneous work; work consisting of repetition of similar tasks, rather than tasks proceeding vertically'.[26] Wedgwood's designs 'aimed at a conveyor belt progress through the works: the kiln room succeeded the painting room, the account room the kiln room, and the ware room the account room, so that there was a smooth progression from the ware being painted, to being

---

22. Pollard 1965, p. 12, quoting H.D. Fong.
23. Smail 1999, p. 1.
24. Smail (Ibid.), suggests the term 'mode of marketing', which together with the mode of production and the mode of consumption shaped the overall pattern of economic growth in the eighteenth century, and presumably thereafter.
25. Bruland 1990, p. 161.
26. Bruland 1990, p. 162.

fired, to being entered into the books, to being stored... He organized his men on the same basis...'[27]

Each labouring man or woman was trained in a specific skill associated with a single, discrete task in a process of producing pottery that had been broken down into dozens of tasks. Where once there had been a world of journeymen potters moving from '"one kind of labour to another, just as impulse or convenience prompted"',[28] now there were specialists exclusively trained to master but one of the many distinct phases of the new production process. In jasperware,[29] for example, 'there were ornamenters, turners, slip-makers, grinders, scourers, and mould-makers', and the jasperware workshop was kept separate from the coloured ware and black ware workshops, which had their own set of specialists.

Pottery was not the first industry to see the introduction of a significant division of labour. 'Early in the eighteenth century the [pin-making] industry had... achieved that high degree of division of labor by Adam Smith's description'.[30] The watchmaking trade had achieved an 'intense' division of labour by 1747: 'there were wheel-forgers, wheel-cutters, pinion makers, spring makers, cap and stud makers, jewelers, engravers, chasers, and enamellers, besides the finishers who assembled the various parts and the key makers and chain makers who provided the accessories'.[31] Coalminers in 1700 were mostly either getters or drawers. By 1800, 'a growth in the size of the pits, and the use of capital appliances, had created specialised occupations including those of holers, hammermen, ramblers, punchers, loaders, trammers, hangers-on, and blanksmen'.[32] While Wedgwood's conception of an advanced division of labour was surely informed

27. McKendrick 1961, p. 32.

28. Arthur Young, writing in 1768 as quoted by the Hammond and Hammond 1974b, p. 172.

29. Wedgwood introduced jasperware well after his creamware. It involved pressing white ornamentation such as Greco-Roman figures onto a soft blue background. This reflected the trend of innovation in pottery in the latter decades of the eighteenth century where new surfaces and glazes were introduced, along with enamelling. Wedgwood's rival, Josiah Spode the elder, had introduced 'blue-printed' ware after 1780, once a satisfactory method of printing pre-designed illustrations onto the vessels. 'Blue-printed' quickly became the standard in 'useful ware', and it soon found its way into nearly every middle-class home. Spode's son, Josiah Spode the younger, discovered a method of making cheap china by introducing bone paste into the mix. While the Wedgwoods set the standard for high-end ceramics, both the Spodes and the Wedgwoods made their fortunes by mass producing low-end 'useful ware'. Wedgwood also set the standard for the new mode of mass production, leading the dramatic transformation of the whole trade (Hammond and Hammond 1974, pp. 170–1; Wedgwood Museum, Barlaston, Stoke-on-Trent, Staffordshire, visit by author, November 1997).

30. Usher 1982, p. 375.

31. Ashton 1964, p. 103, citing George 1965, pp. 173–5.

32. Ashton 1964.

by developments in other trades, he was likely also informed by the extensive division of labour that was used in the production of porcelain in China, where:

> In the manufacture of porcelain, the division of labor is carried very far. The best is made at the village of Kiangsee, which contains a million of inhabitants. Seventy hands are sometimes employed on a single cup.[33]

The possibility that Wedgwood may have been influenced by principles of production in China, a country in which the economy was highly regulated by the government, lends further weight to the point that the introduction of the capitalist factory system required more than simply removing the fetters of customary and normative forms of regulation in the economy. It required the introduction of new methods of production and new institutions. The fact that porcelain production in China involved an advanced division of labour does not mean that the economy in eighteenth-century China was capitalist. Rather, it suggests that there is nothing specifically capitalist about specialisation or the division of labour. The results of adapting an extensive division of labour to a capitalist mode of production in British pottery yielded dramatic results, and served to inform other lines of industry in Britain. Such was not the case in China.

The second key element was the recruitment and training of a labour force. While the family craftsman in pottery had long since given way to the master potter with an increasing number of apprentices and journeymen, Wedgwood encountered the problem of having to constantly train his workers in their discrete roles, and resistance in the form of grumbling and reticence to learn new techniques. In a letter to his nephew dated 19 May 1770, Wedgwood wrote:

> You observe very justly that few hands can be got to paint flowers in the style we want them. I may add, nor in any other work we do – We must make them. There is no other way. We have stepped forward. Beyond the other Manufactures & we must be content to train up hands to suit our purpose. Where amongst our Potters could I get a complete Vase maker? Nay I could not get a hand through the whole Pottery to make a Table plate without training them up for that purpose, & you must be content to train up such Painters as offer to you & not turn them adrift because they cannot immediately form their hands

33. Meanwhile, 'Silk and cloth are cultivated and manufactured in families, each man spinning, weaving and dyeing his own web' (Clarke 1871, p. 43). Wedgwood familiarised himself with porcelain production in China by reading contemporary French travellers and porcelain experts Jean-Baptiste du Halde and Francois Xavier d'Entrecolles. 'The industrial assembly line was the result, and the Etruria factory was the first pottery in Europe to be designed specifically for mass production on these principles' (Reilly 1992, p. 134).

> to our new stile, which if we consider what they have been doing all this while we ought not to expect from them.[34]

Naturally Wedgwood found over time that his best workers were those he had trained from youth. The 'central feature of pre-industrial production', writes Bruland, 'was that technological knowledge took the form of craft skills and those who possessed these skills controlled the production process'.[35] McKendrick argues that the division of labour under Wedgwood 'did not destroy skill: it limited its field of expression to a particular task, but within those limits increased it'.[36] While the question of whether this amounted to 'de-skilling' is, for Bruland, open for debate, what is not in doubt is that 'Wedgwood controlled the production of skill, and he required workers who were willing to train on his terms'.[37] This is precisely where his break with past practice is so radical. The ramifications of this seemingly simple step can hardly be overstated. Wedgwood's taking control of the technical knowledge, the skill and the organisation of the labour process, enabled by and combined with his conversion to a complete wage system in which being the owner of the means of production he accrued all profits, mark Wedgwood's operation as distinctively capitalist.

While Wedgwood retained portions of the apprenticeship system in his operation, he adapted it to his purposes. Old hands might undergo a second apprenticeship, but were less likely to succeed in producing at the level of perfection desired by 'Owd Woodenleg'.[38] In the 1770s Wedgwood introduced women and girls into the works in large numbers. 'He paid the men more to persuade them to accept female apprentices' and 'countered their objections with indignant rage'.[39] While the introduction of females was difficult at first, it proved a lucrative investment due to the lower price of their labour. In 1790, fully twenty-five percent of Wedgwood's 278 employees were apprentices.[40]

The third key element of Wedgwood's system was imposing a rigorous discipline on the workforce. Like Lombe, Wedgwood faced the challenge of breaking the customary habits of the workers. 'The stoppages for a wake or a fair or a three-day drinking spree were an accepted part of the potter's life – and they proved most difficult to uproot'.[41] The extensive system of discipline which Wedgwood

34. Wedgwood 1903, pp. 346–7. Abbreviations as found in the original.
35. Wedgwood 1903, p. 159.
36. McKendrick 1961, p. 32.
37. Bruland 1990, p. 162.
38. Wedgwood, who walked with a wooden leg after his amputation, followed a custom whereby he would stomp through his workshops and smash anything that was substandard. '"...my name has been made such a scarecrow to them, that the poor fellows are frightened out of their wits"' (as quoted in Reilly 1992, p. 138).
39. McKendrick 1961, p. 38.
40. Reilly 1992, p. 135; McKendrick 1961, p. 35.
41. McKendrick 1961, p. 38.

introduced involved strict hours of work regulated by bells and clocks, forfeits for violations and detailed written instructions on how to perform one's specified task. He was apparently the first to introduce the institution of 'clocking-in'. Initially, attempts at introducing a single overseer to manage the entire operation while he was away at his shop in London proved disastrous, as 'the incorrigible potters returned to many of their old ways'.[42] Wedgwood's solution for this was to place one overseer in each workshop, in effect reproducing or imitating the organisational structure of the traditional workshop with the master working alongside his journeymen and apprentices. Yet the new arrangement was in actuality a radical break with the traditional workshop. Wedgwood's apprentices could no longer look forward to a career of rising from journeyman or even dream of eventually being their own master. So long as they remained employed they served only one overall master throughout their life. Where those employed in the traditional workshop were vulnerable to a general downturn in the market for the general line of pottery their workshop produced, specialists were vulnerable to fluctuations in demand for the specific style of ware they were locked into producing. 'When the fashionable world turned against gilding for instance, Wedgwood wrote, "Gold, the most precious of all metals is absolutely kicked out-of-doors, & our poor Gilders I believe must follow it"'.[43] 'Such violent changes in taste', adds McKendrick, 'were fortunately rare and, in a world of expanding markets, the potter in general gained from specialisation. Certainly the quality of the pottery improved, and that was Wedgwood's major consideration'.[44] McKendrick is also keen to point out that Wedgwood's high standards for discipline and hygiene were partly motivated out of consideration for the workers, such as standards designed to protect them against lead poisoning. Wedgwood 'provided very adequate compensation' for his workers' 'loss of freedom',[45] presumably referring to their freedom to observe St. Monday or other holidays, spontaneous or otherwise, or to engage in lax working habits. But McKendrick makes no mention of the workers' loss of control over the labour process which again, above all else, marked Wedgwood's operation as capitalist and demarcated a new faultline in power relations within the industry.

While Wedgwood was able to reinvest a large percentage of his profits in order to expand his operation whilst simultaneously building up a personal fortune, his workers generally spent all that they earned as soon as they were paid and had little if any margin for savings. Discontent erupted in 1772, when the painters struck and Wedgwood sacked the strike leader as well as all his house servants

42. Thompson 1993, p. 386.
43. McKendrick 1961, p. 33.
44. Ibid.
45. McKendrick 1961, p. 54.

along with the head former on his estate for 'robbing us of everything they could carry off',[46] and during a depression in 1783 when Wedgwood was compelled to summon in the armed forces to disperse an insurrection at his Etruria works.[47] The fact that Wedgwood was able successfully to appeal for the state to intervene in a labour dispute by applying coercive force is itself testament to both the exceptional position of power that Wedgwood the capitalist enjoyed, and the role of the state in demarcating power relations within the new capitalist order by decisively defending large-scale private property.

We have chosen to begin this chapter with a discussion of Wedgwood for two reasons. First of all, Wedgwood serves as a classic example to demonstrate the rule that what distinguished the great capitalist entrepreneurs of the Industrial Revolution was how their complete reorganisation of the labour process brought about the total or 'real' subsumption of the labourer to a capitalist logic governing the workplace. Secondly, however, if that rule implied the application of machine technology to production, Wedgwood serves as the perfect counterexample. Wedgwood carried off the whole reorganisation of the labour process without the aid of machines. The closest example we can find, in terms of Wedgwood's contributions to machine technology, is the trundle cart that was used to carry the pots and vases from workshop to workshop as they passed through the various stages of production. The potteries continued to rely on the throwing wheel, a technology known to the ancient Egyptians, as the basic instrument of production. When the steam engine arrived at the potteries in 1792, it was merely applied to grinding flint. This is not to say that there were no technological advances at all to be found in Wedgwood's operation. We know that Wedgwood was a genius at mastering the chemical properties of his glazes, and that he invented many new types. This surely gave his operation a much needed edge over his rivals, which in turn may have ensured the success of his operation. So it would, therefore, be untrue to hold Wedgwood up as an example of an early capitalist master whose success did not derive from any technological advances whatsoever. Yet the chemical properties of his glazes cannot be said to be governing factors in how Wedgwood organised his workers. What did govern how Wedgwood organised his workers were his innovative labour management techniques, and these were surely much more fundamental to his success. And inasmuch as technology is defined as the practical application of knowledge, these techniques were themselves a form of technology. But at the same time

46. Reilly 1992, p. 138.

47. McKendrick 1961, p. 52. 'He may have believed in liberty, but it was not the liberty to riot, and when in 1783 a riot broke out at Etruria he summoned the military and dispersed the mob by force. Two men were arrested, both of them convicted, and one of them subsequently hanged'.

they were more than merely a type of technology, as the ramifications of such a reordering of the relations of production in the workplace involved a broader reorganisation of the social relations of production in the economy as a whole.

In Chapter Six, we alluded several times to the way in which during the Industrial Revolution technology came to play a different role than it had in all of previous history, by pointing out that it was specifically applied to production for the purposes of maximising output. To the extent that the capitalist reorganisation of the workplace was a kind of technology, then it was a technology specifically involving the control of the labour process by the owner of the means of production, which governed the application of other technologies during the Industrial Revolution and under capitalism ever since. In the remainder of this chapter, as we review the progress of other early industrial capitalists, we will seek to explicate the specific and important role played by machine technology in the Industrial Revolution, bearing in mind that the example of Wedgwood demonstrates how it was possible to transform an entire branch of industry without the aid of any significant advances in mechanical technology.

It can hardly be said that Wedgwood lacked access to the science or technical know-how that might have afforded the opportunity to apply machine technology to his operation, for he was a member of the Lunar Society, probably the best-known amateur science association of his day. Here he had access to some of the greatest industrial, scientific and inventive minds of the era, including inventors such as Boulton and Watt, instrument maker John Whitehurst, gun manufacturer Samuel Galton Jr. and fellow chemists James Keir and Jonathan Stokes.[48] While 'the Royal Society was in its doldrums during this period',[49] provincial societies of amateur scientists and gentlemen-manufacturers were appearing across England. 'Relatively obscure towns like Spalding, Northampton, Peterborough, and Maidstone for example, boasted such gatherings. Almost thirty are known to have existed'.[50] As previously noted, this contrasted sharply with France, where state rather than local and private patronage paved the way for French advances as grants were provided 'through the *Académie des Sciences*, by military sponsorship, and direct industrial sponsorship, as with the research

48. A listing of 14 of the major members can be found in Schofield 1972, pp. 139–40. A separate listing can be found in Gale 1952, p. 19. Less active members and correspondents included such notables as Richard Arkwright, Benjamin Franklin and Thomas Jefferson.

49. Schofield 1972, p. 137.

50. Mathias 1972, p. 77. To demonstrate the importance of these amateur science societies, Mathias points to 'a growing list of examples of innovations which sprang, or appeared to spring, from this fertile soil of scientific discourse and social nexus between men of science and industry. Steam-power above all; but also the adolescent chemical industry with chlorine-bleaching, sulphuric acid production, soda making, coal distillation. James Watt, Roebuck, Josiah Wedgwood, Lord Dundonald, George and Charles Macintosh were all well-known individuals who personify these connexions.'

department attached to the Sèvres porcelain factory working on glazes, enamels and paints'.[51] Even in chemistry, 'where the linkage between scientific knowledge and industrial innovation was probably most intimate',[52] state patronage was dominant in France. For example, when Nicholas Leblanc patented a process for making alkali (sodium carbonate), he was responding directly to Louis XVI's offer of a cash prize for the solution. Mathias notes that the extent of interest in 'amateur science' and the efforts to apply science to industry set England apart within Europe. We have already seen that state-led industrialisation in seventeenth-century France did not result in an industrial revolution while privately-led industrialisation in Britain did. In Britain, private enterprise and proletarianisation were far more advanced than in France by the late eighteenth century. As customary regulation of manufacturing gave way to market regulation, leading manufacturers like Wedgwood were faced with the challenge of responding to changing and growing markets by finding new ways to innovate, specialise and maximise. It was only logical that they should seek out the advice of scientists, share views with others like themselves and that scientists and inventors should seek them out. There was profit in it as never before. The results are part of the story of the Industrial Revolution itself.

The specific role of machinery

If it was possible for one of the leading entrepreneurs of the Industrial Revolution to transform his trade – pottery – into a capitalist, industrial operation without the aid of machinery, then it remains for us to examine the critical role that we know machinery did play in the Industrial Revolution. We also know from our review in Chapter Six that even if Britain was not necessarily exceptional in terms of producing technology, it was exceptional in terms of applying technology to the production process and with greater frequency as the eighteenth century wore on. Before seeking an explanation for why this should have been the case, let us first examine what some prominent scholars have suggested about the role of machine technology in the Industrial Revolution.

Adam Smith saw machinery as arising out of the division of labour, which he saw as the result of the expansion of the market. For all of the attention that has been given to Smith's discussion of the technical division of labour in his example of the pin factory, Smith's praise for the division of labour rests more heavily on the advantages of the social division of labour that compels producers to specialise in any given line of production, thus providing a productive service

51. Mathias 1972, pp. 79–80.
52. Ibid.

from which all others may benefit through market exchange. Smith credits common labourers for developing most of the improvements that the great inventors would go on to take credit for. The workmen, he writes, 'who, being each of them employed in some very simple operation, naturally turned their thoughts towards finding out easier and readier methods of performing it'.[53] For Smith, the primary significance of machinery was its capacity to save labour. But he also suggested that a saving of labour to the employer would likely mean an increase in his trade and hence more employment to be provided for the workforce.[54]

Karl Marx reiterated and also challenged these points using his own terminology. Marx's dictum that under capitalism the labourer became an appendage to the machine, and thus subordinated to the condition of wage slavery, is well-known. In his critique of the argument of Smith and other political economists – that the machinery which displaces labourers also frees up capital that will then be used to employ an even greater number of labourers, Marx emphasises the countervailing tendency for machinery to reduce the amount of labour necessary to produce an even greater quantity of commodities which sell at a lesser price, thus throwing the labourers out of work.[55] Additionally, when the same commodities are being produced both by machinery and by hand, the machine-owning capitalist is able to derive exceptional surplus-value and thus exceptional profits based on the comparatively greater efficiency of the labour-power he pays for, since he is able to 'replace the value of a day's labour-power by a smaller portion of the value of the day's product'.[56]

Echoing Smith, Max Weber wrote that what formed 'a predisposing condition, even an impetus toward the increased application and improvement of machines' was the 'specialization of work and labor discipline within the workshop'.[57] For Weber, specialisation and division of labour within the workshop and therefore also the introduction and spread of machinery were all part and parcel of the

53. Smith 1957, p. 9. Applying Smith's discussion of machinery to the present discussion presents the danger of anachronism. Writing on the cusp of the Industrial Revolution, Smith does not appear to have anticipated the vast increases in industrial output that were about to take place (see Smith 1957, p. 272). Smith should be read as a theorist not of industrial capitalism, which had scarcely begun by the time he was writing *The Wealth of Nations*, but as a theorist of agrarian capitalism.

54. Smith 1957, p. 272.

55. His argument continues as follows: the labourers, being trained in a given skill, now rendered useless, will be hard-pressed to find new work, even if the advance of their industry calls forth supporting industries that put others to work. Yet for the others, the same process will repeat itself: 'The number of the men condemned to work in coal and metal mines increased enormously owing to the progress of the factory system; but during the last few decades this increase of number has been less rapid, owing to the use of new machinery in mining' (Marx 1967, p. 484).

56. Marx 1906, pp. 443–4.

57. Weber 1961, p. 136.

spread of rationality, which he equates with capitalism.[58] Weber believed that capitalism had been around since Antiquity, but gained its fullest expression in the factory. We saw in Chapter Six that Karl Polanyi attributed to large-scale machinery and the factory the role of requiring the elements of production to be commodified.[59] For Polanyi, the factory and large-scale machinery were responsible for a sudden transformation to capitalism, or market society. Wood points out that Polanyi's account lacks 'an appreciation of the ways in which a radical transformation of social relations *preceded* industrialisation'.[60] What Polanyi and Weber have in common is a tendency to define capitalism as well as the technology of capitalism in strictly economic terms.

Fernand Braudel sees the inventions of the late eighteenth century as part of a 'first wind' in the Industrial Revolution, but belonging to a 'second generation' of inventions. England: 'entered these rough waters just as the "second generation" of inventions was coming into being: the spinning jenny (1768); the water-powered frame (1769); the powered drill (1775); the rotary steam-engine (1776–1881); iron puddling (1784); the first usable threshing-machine (1786); the perfected form of the lathe (1794) – cumulatively a huge technical investment paving the way for recovery'.[61]

The next upturn in the Kondratieff cycle after 1791 came in 1850, a 'second wind' when continuous growth had at last appeared. Ironically, Braudel adds that: 'The cotton revolution was accomplished without any major technical innovations',[62] by which he means that cotton was revolutionised prior to the application of steam-power. This downgrading of the new spinning machinery to the status of minor inventions is peculiar, and beyond measurable force, it is unclear what Braudel's criteria for rating different types of technology are. But what interests us about Braudel's approach to the technology of the Industrial Revolution is the way innovations come in waves, responding to broader

58. Ibid. Weber equates capitalism, its emergence and its spread, with 'rational commerce'. 'Rational commerce', writes Weber (1961 p. 170), 'is the field in which quantitative reckoning first appeared to become dominant finally over the whole extent of economic life'. It is clear that Weber follows a kind of commercialisation model in his thinking.

59. See Chapter Six, p. 300.

60. Wood 2002a, p. 26. Wood is concerned on pp. 21–6 to rescue the rational kernel from Polanyi's tendency toward economism along Weberian lines. See also Wood 1995, pp. 168–73, to read her critique of Weber's economism, which includes a discussion of Polanyi's tendency to follow Weber's lead.

61. Braudel 1988, pp. 571–2. We may fairly ask: was not the combination of machinery with labour in a factory setting itself a major technical innovation? Of course, power-driven factory production of textiles began in silk, but cotton soon eclipsed silk, which was already in decline by the end of the eighteenth century.

62. Braudel 1988, p. 572.

economic trends and pressures. Here, it is not innovation in machinery driving the economy; but economic change driving innovation.

Each of these authorities tells us something about what machinery did in the workplace, but so far we have no historical account of *how* or *why* machines came to play such a central role in production. In her brief but key essay, Kate Bruland has offered a concise account of the how and the why. Bruland argues that a 'purely managerial and organizational' transformation of the workplace, such as that effected in pottery by Josiah Wedgwood, 'could produce growth in output and productivity, falling costs of production, and changes in industry structure'.[63] However, she finds that Wedgwood is an atypical example, as he effected a far more rapid and clearly thought-out transformation than most. 'Nevertheless', she writes:

> the overall process of change which it implies was very widespread; it occurred in many industries, over a longer time-scale, with less clarity in terms of objectives and less clarity in terms of objectives and greater confusion in terms of methods . . . It is certainly possible to suggest . . . that the basic economic development in eighteenth and early nineteenth century Europe was change in the organization, and control of work at the level of the enterprise.
>
> This large-scale historical change had two significant consequences. On the one hand it led directly to economic growth. On the other, it established a production system in which technological change could occur. For entrepreneurs, it was a relatively short step from changing the technical division of labour and the control of work to seeking to change the instruments of work: seeking, that is, to make innovations in equipment. Changing the nature of work in the enterprise was the single most important pre-condition for this.[64]

This account goes a long way to answering *how* machines were adopted in the production process, and it provides a logical explanation for *why* the application of machinery to production and further innovations associated with that development were an effect of the reorganisation of the labour process, not the cause. But what brought about the reorganisation of the labour process? Bruland notes by way of what she calls 'some tentative answers':

---

63. Bruland 1990, p. 164.

64. Ibid. Bruland suggests that Wedgwood-style organisational transformations were 'a key element in so-called "proto-industrialisation" processes'. The extent to which cottage-manufacturing-based organisation, such as in putting-out systems, contributed to the organisational methods later applied in factories, is an area in need of further research.

> ... the changing character of work was central to the overall process. It was the long historical process through which entrepreneurs gradually removed control of the production process from the individual craftsman or artisan which opened up the possibility of technical innovation and mechanical methods. This is because, from a technical point of view, it gave entrepreneurs a control of the overall production process which made it possible to envisage and install mechanical innovations; and from an economic point of view, the fact that entrepreneurs could appropriate the economic benefits – in the form of increased profits – gave them a powerful incentive to seek innovations.[65]

Bruland has identified the key to understanding both how capitalist industry was made possible, and how machinery came to play a central role in capitalist industrialisation, which is the direct control of the production process by the capitalist, motivated by a desire for increased profits. But if the profit-motive were by itself the primary motive for this action by employers, why did this process take place only over the course of the early modern period and not before? Another problem with Bruland's account is that she appears to consider 'organizational innovation of a very radical kind' as something that was not specific to Britain but took place across Europe. Curiously however, she also notes that these changes diffused outward from Britain, the 'originating economy: British workers, in most parts of Europe, played a significant role in spreading the new work systems, in training local workers, and in the adaptation of the workforce to the new rhythms of work'.[66] Why British entrepreneurs and labourers were brought to France and other countries to introduce new techniques of management and production requires an explanation.

What the theory of agrarian capitalism suggests is that the 'incentives' that encouraged the entrepreneur to innovate were actually market *imperatives* arising from market competition between different entrepreneurs in an increasingly unregulated marketplace, specifically the English domestic market, which as we have argued was expanding as part of the development of English agrarian capitalism, which led the way not only in terms of extinguishing customary control of production, placing control over production decisions in the hands of the employer and creating a proletarian wage labour force, but also by lowering the costs of necessities, beginning with food, which in turn lowered the cost of labour and thereby sorely undermined the ability of customary craft organisations to resist the growing power of capitalist merchants and employers.

65. Bruland 1990, p. 165.
66. Ibid.

Manufacture versus machinofacture

Explanations resting upon technological determinism or a technological model give technology a primary causal role in the development of industrial capitalism. As we argued in Chapter Six, this is to mistake cause for effect. The application of machinery to production was secondary to the reorganisation of production in a capitalist direction, that is, in order that production decisions could be made to respond to market indicators in an environment of market competition. Smith and Weber appear to have recognised this inasmuch as they trace the 'predisposition' to introduce and innovate in machinery within production to the division of labour. But they do not take the analysis any further than this. Since both tend to equate markets with capitalism, in effect universalising the capitalist economy, the expansion of the division of labour is seen as merely a function of the growth of the market. Braudel recognises that the application of machinery comes in response to *specific* trends in economic history, but his account also universalises capitalist relations of production. Where normatively regulated, pre-capitalist forms of production enter such liberal accounts, they are typically treated as impediments to the growth of an already existing capitalist marketplace. This is where Marx took issue with liberal accounts, for as we have seen, in his view the machine was a weapon in the hands of the capitalist, a tool in the class struggle. To the liberal economist who universalises capitalist economics, the conflict between employer and employee is reduced to disagreements over a market contract, and when customary labourers break machines or attempt to impose extra-economic or customary modes of regulation of markets or the labour process, or in any way oppose the extension of the market to the point of reorganising production, they are engaging in a form of resistance that is both irrational and futile. This reduces generations of labourers who resisted the introduction of capitalism to ignoramuses at best and criminals at worst.

Capitalism was resisted. The introduction and development of agrarian capitalism was a long and gradual process. It is highly unlikely that capitalist landlords and their tenants had any sort of grand vision whereby they could correctly imagine the long-term implications of their actions. Intentionality was surely limited to short-term goals in the larger framework of history. However, over the course of the eighteenth century, the principle that markets and later the economy in general should be 'free' and unregulated grew in popularity, culminating in Adam Smith's *Wealth of Nations*. The generally localised and sporadic resistance of populations affected by the introduction of capitalism, which took place before the Industrial Revolution and long after it began, shows that they were aware of the adverse impacts of capitalism that they were facing. The gig mill was banned under Edward VI because it was seen as posing a threat to trade.[67] By the eighteenth century, this logic was increasingly seen as outmoded. Agriculture now served as a remarkable example of how investing considerable sums for purposes of improvement could greatly enhance profitability. The same was true of transport, as investors turned from turnpikes to the mania of canal-building, starting in the 1750s.

As the advantages offered by machines grew steadily more apparent, the legitimacy that customary opposition to machinery enjoyed steadily eroded. We shall explore below the ways in which the right to halt the introduction of (or to destroy) machinery that threatened a trade had a legitimacy rooted in custom, even if that legitimacy waned between the seventeenth and nineteenth centuries. Here, we will consider some of the key innovations normally associated with the Industrial Revolution, their advantages, to whom they were advantageous and to whom they were disadvantageous.

While the advantages of machinery were multifaceted, the advantage of reducing the necessary labour-time required to produce a given item that they offered was not unknown outside the factory. When placed in the workshop of a small master, the benefits could possibly be enjoyed by not only the small master but also his journeyman (if any) or his family. This was possible with a simple, manually powered mechanism like the spinning jenny. According to legend, once the jenny was introduced, protests broke out between the years of 1768 and 1770, forcing the jenny's reputed inventor, James Hargreaves, to remove to Nottingham, where he and his partner Thomas James set up a small factory employing jennies. But this story is mired in 'inextricable confusion'; while it does appear that there were attacks on the jenny, it remains unclear whether it is actually true that Hargreaves was attacked and forced to leave.[68] Once in Nottingham, Hargreaves took out a patent in 1770 and set up Hockley Mill, a workshop employing 100 workers at 50 jennies driven by power from a horse capstan. Hargreaves was unable to maintain the secrecy of his workshop just as he was unable to successfully defend his patent. For by now, jennies of

---

67. Oldland (2007, p. 102) suggests that West Country's employment of gig mills as a means of mechanising and thus accelerating the process of wet-napping the cloth 'is testament to a fully integrated cloth industry producing finished cloth... in the fifteenth century'. An earlier ban on using wire cards in gig mills was imposed in 1463–4. The 1551 ban was probably motivated by the perception that gig mills challenged the dominance of the towns (and their guilds) in the cloth-finishing trade.

68. Part of the confusion arises from the fact that in 1768 there were violent demonstrations over an election in Preston: 'for three months the town [was] held up by bands of hired factions who had done much damage to life and limb and property'. A day after the election ended, two men were arrested for 'signing a paper "declaring that 10,000 men would come and destroy Blackburn"' (Wadsworth and Mann 1961, pp. 479–80). Whether the violence that subsequently took place at Blackburn had to do with this threat or the jenny is unclear.

various (often pirated) designs were in use across much of Lancashire.[69] It is also possible (though not certain) that Hargreaves had trouble defending his patent because the original inventor was actually Thomas Highs.[70]

What is certain is that when the attempt to introduce the jenny into the West of England was made some years later, it met with resistance. In 1776 at Shepton Mallet, Somerset, the local gentleman clothiers engaged in the experiment of employing the jenny at the local workhouse, but the machines were destroyed around two o'clock in the morning on 11 July. In September and October, gentlemen clothiers from Somerset, Wiltshire and Gloucestershire met in Bristol and Bath, after which they publicly called for the introduction of the jenny on a trial-basis, lest the West of England fall behind the progress that was being made with the machine in Yorkshire. Randall provides the following excerpt of one of their statements: 'And whereas reports have been industriously propagated that the poor by the introduction of spinning machines will be deprived of a considerable part of their labour and consequently become burdensome to their parishes, they [the clothiers] do, upon the most mature consideration, declare that no mischievous consequences are likely to ensue... [However] they will be ready to discontinue the use of the machines if after a proper trial they shall be found in any degree prejudicial to the poor'.[71]

The polite tenor of this statement says a great deal about the state of relations in manufacturing at the outset of the Industrial Revolution. Feeling the pressures of competition coming from the North-West, the clothiers are nonetheless confronted with the prospect of violence against their property coming from the local wool workers. The wool workers themselves responded to the clothiers' persuasions by petitioning Parliament to abolish the jenny. Upon rejection, the workers conciliated and agreed to allow only the workhouse to operate with jennies, under their inspection. Another incident of jenny-breaking took place in nearby Frome in 1781, the last major incident against the jenny. Owing to the inability of the jenny to cope with the finer yarns used in the specialised woollen production of the West of England, the jenny was not reintroduced until the trade boom between approximately 1787 and 1793 when it gained wide acceptance (amidst lingering resentments).[72]

The woollen trade in the West was organised around the gentleman clothier, who oversaw a complex putting-out operation inclusive of each stage of the production-process. In West Yorkshire, by contrast, the master clothier (or small

69. Wadsworth and Mann 1961, p. 481.

70. The alleged inventor of not only the jenny, but also of the water frame. See Chapter Six, p. 328, n. 136.

71. Randall 1991, p. 74 citing the *Gloucester Journal*, 14 October 1776.

72. Randall 1991, pp. 70–5.

master) often undertook scribbling, spinning and weaving in his workshop or home, selling his product in an unfinished state at the cloth hall to the gentleman merchant, who put out for the finishing.[73] Thus in Yorkshire, the master-clothier who introduced the jenny into his workshop gained an advantage over his fellows, and at least after some early resistance of an unclear nature in the late 1760s, the jenny began to spread quickly. Some of the larger masters would go on to add more machines, to the point of setting up small factories. But in the West of England, spinning was still a domestic affair and spinners saw that while the jenny would benefit the gentleman clothier, it offered them no immediate advantage, which may explain why the first experiment with it took place in a public workhouse. The woollen trade in the West of England knew a greater concentration of capital, greater specialisation and skill development and a greater degree of proletarianisation than it did in West Riding. Yet in West Riding machinery spread rapidly, while 'craft consciousness and solidarity proved to be one of the major stumbling blocks to the mechanisation of the industry of the West Country'.[74] Randall points out that this is precisely the opposite of what 'proto-industrialisation' theory would predict.[75]

Spinning, which paid the lowest wages in the textile trades, had long been conducted by women: wives, girls and unmarried 'spinsters'. It should not be surprising then (though it may challenge the stereotype of the docile English woman), that women played a prominent role in the anti-jenny demonstrations in the West of England between 1776 and 1781.[76] Some women were able to increase their productivity and wages using the jenny at home, while others moved into 'jenny factories' where they 'lost control of their own labour as well as early windfall gains to a male manufacturer'.[77] But for most women who spun, the jenny would quickly displace them from that occupation,[78] particularly spinners in agrarian districts. Their labour would be increasingly absorbed in other occupations, not only by the growing number of silk and cotton factories but

73. Randall 1989, pp. 180–1. See below, Chapter Nine, pp. 462–7, for a discussion of the woollen and worsted-producing regions of West Yorkshire.

74. Randall 1991, p. 26.

75. According to 'proto-industrialisation' theory, says Randall, the *Kaufsystem* 'characterized by artisan domestic production in by-employment with agricultural activities' approximates to the situation prevailing in West Riding, and is supposed to develop in the direction of the *Verlagsystem* 'in which capitalist control has been extended into a putting-out system where workers, divorced from agriculture, depend entirely on wages from industrial production'. Yet while production relations in the West of England approximated the *Verlagsystem*, and industrialisation was stalled, West Riding moved straight from *Kaufsystem* to industrial revolution (see Randall 1991, pp. 23–6). Problems with proto-industrialisation theory continue to abound.

76. Randall 1991, p. 102.

77. Berg 1987, p. 79.

78. Randall 1991, pp. 71–2.

also in 'new rural industries' that industrialisation promoted: 'in lace, straw plait manufacture, glovemaking and shirt button-making, boot and shoemaking, nail-making and in the new urban sweated trades, especially in tailoring which flourished in the 1830s'.[79] The jenny itself survived alongside the (shuttle-) loom and the stocking-frame as the quintessential machinery of cottage manufacturing, operated mostly by 'small masters' whose trade survived so long as a supplement to factory spinning was still called for.

While Kay's flying shuttle had met initial resistance in West Riding in the 1770s, it was in general use by the 1780s. Its introduction in the West of England, however, was met with extraordinary resistance, starting with protests at Trowbridge in 1785 and 1792. A non-violent protest persuaded the clothier Nathaniel Watts to take down his loom in Rodborough, Gloucestershire in 1793. He complied, and it was not reintroduced until 1798 when weavers were in high demand. In other textile-towns of the West, the shuttle did not arrive until as late as 1803.[80]

Based on the stocking-frame, invented by William Lee in the sixteenth century, the manufacturing of silk, woollen or cotton hosiery was well-established in Nottingham before the civil wars. The stocking trade expanded continuously after the Restoration, first around Nottingham and then in Leicester and Derby. In 1730, a Nottingham workman produced the first pair of cotton hose ever made by mechanical means.[81] By 1750, the stocking trade had virtually disappeared from London, although the City remained its primary market. [82] In 1758, the Royal Society of Arts awarded a prize to Samuel Unwin for his improvement on the stocking-frame, which he patented. In the same year, Samuel Need and Jedediah Strutt took out a patent on an innovation that enabled the frame to make ribbed stockings. Strutt's innovation ushered in 'an era of experimenting in the production of new meshes on the frame'.[83] As 'merchant-manufacturers', Strutt and Unwin profited handsomely from their inventions. They sat atop the hierarchy of hosiery manufacture, with the wholesalers below them and the 'bag-' hosiers or middlemen organising production in the villages at the base. Overall, hosiery remained a domestic line of manufacturing, with most stocking-frames located

79. Berg 1987, p. 77.
80. Randall 1991, pp. 98–9.
81. Fitton 1989, p. 22.
82. 'As evidence of the industry's growth, the number of stocking-frames employed in the provinces is said to have increased from about 150 in 1664 to 15,000 in 1812. After a famous test-case in 1728, in which Nottingham magistrates refused to recognize the validity of the restricting ordinances of the London Company of Framework Knitters, the migration of the hosiery trade from London accelerated, and a new class of provincial merchant hosiers began to emerge' (Chapman 1967, p. 18). Thus the hosiery trade settled in Nottinghamshire.
83. Chapman 1967, p. 38.

in the knitters' homes.[84] However, larger merchant-manufacturers like Strutt opened manufactories where their new inventions were worked by a workforce that included women and children.[85] Chapman argues that a primary motivation for the hosiery masters to establish manufactories may have been the need to retain control over the secrets of their innovations,[86] an observation which underscores how markets were becoming increasingly competitive. After 1784, greater diversification and expansion set in with the introduction of techniques for making lace and point-net. Lace was considerably more lucrative than other lines of hosiery. According to Chapman it probably diverted capital and skill away from the cotton industry in the late eighteenth century.[87]

In the garret or spare room of the domestic producer, the jenny, the stocking-frame or the shuttle-loom could be employed to increase personal income through a saving of labour. Alternatively, as the machine could produce the same amount in less time, it could mean more time for leisure. But as the general adoption of a given mechanism would lower necessary production time across the trade, these options would in the long run face diminishing prospects in the face of falling prices. The size of the machine that could be operated in the domestic workshop was limited by the domestic worker's reliance on muscle as a source of power. Larger machinery required non-human power sources (*equidae*, water or steam). The first factories of Wyatt and Paul were powered by donkeys, Arkwright's first mill by horses. These were no small steps. They were early trials in switching the source of the machine's power to a non-human source, and that

84. Chapman 1967, pp. 36–7 provides two examples of how the domestic workshop was expanded to accommodate extra frames. In Nottingham, where the failure to enclose was driving up the price of land, this involved building three-storey dwellings for the workers. In Leicester 'later work-shops containing a dozen or more frames, were built as an annexe to workers' houses and cottages, though this development was only just beginning at the end of the eighteenth century'.

85. Since the early 1700s, Samuel Fellows had managed a large workshop in Nottingham employing boys aged ten to twelve, whom he provided with boarding, having purchased their apprenticeship at £5 each from the parishes. Girls and boys were made to work until eleven at night. Parish officials complained that the masters would take on the apprentices solely for making a profit before turning them loose, after which they were seen as a burden on the local parishes (Chapman 1967, p. 40). However, it was probably more expensive for these masters to provide boarding for their child apprentices, as opposed to apprenticing children in the countryside. A cheaper solution called 'colting' was later introduced which dispensed with formal apprenticeship, drawing condemnation from the framework knitters' unions.

86. For example, having purchased the secret to a method for producing imitation 'Spanish' eyelet-hole mitts, contrived by Samuel Betts and Ferdinando Shaw, Samuel Fellows built a large factory in Nottingham. This, according to Chapman, was the first attempt to build a factory as a 'safe box' for a trade secret, while others with new or stolen innovations then followed suit in Nottingham and elsewhere (Chapman 1967, p. 38).

87. Chapman 1967, p. 27.

switch actually facilitated two further steps: the concentration of machinery into larger workshops or factories and the taking control of the labour process itself out of the hands of the workers.

For Marx, machinery played a critical role in the conversion of manufactures to *capitalist* industry because it played a role in separating the direct producers from the means of subsistence. Marx argued that to say 'machinery cuts off the workmen from their means of subsistence is ... in economical parlance tantamount to this, that machinery liberates means of subsistence for the workman, or converts those means into capital for his employment'.[88] Following Poncelet, Ure and Babbage, Marx identified three components of the machine: 'All fully-developed machinery consists of three essentially differentiated parts, the motor mechanism, the transmitting mechanism, and finally the tool or working machine'.[89] Usher, being more concerned with the history of engineering than the role of the machine in the social and industrial revolution, found that this definition 'ignores the distinction that can advisedly be made between mechanical elements and an extensive train of mechanism'.[90] He cites the medieval clock makers as the forerunners of the modern engineer who made the large-scale gearing of the factory possible. This puts all the focus on the skilled work of the engineers. Gearing, waterwheels and steam engines made large-scale machinofacture possible, but these did not supplant the work of masses of domestic workers. As Marx explained, it was specifically that part of the machine that worked upon the product, the tool aspect, powered by water or steam transmitted through gearing that did. 'The machine proper is therefore a mechanism that, after being set in motion, performs with its tools the same operations that were formerly done by the workman with similar tools ... It is this last part of the handicraftsman's implement that is first seized upon by the industrial revolution, leaving to the workman, in addition to his new labour of watching the machine with his eyes and correcting its mistakes with his hands, the merely mechanical part of being the motive power'.[91]

In effect, the machine obviated the need for a detailed division of labour. Manual work is *literally* taken from the hands of the workers by the substitution of the machine for the tools and hands of the worker who, now alienated from the

88. Marx 1967, p. 480. Applying Marx's extensive chapter on machinery in *Capital* to the present discussion presents the danger of anachronism, for in that chapter Marx is mainly concerned with the state of machinery as used in factories in the mid-nineteenth century, a period we will come to discuss only when we reach Part III.

89. Marx 1906, p. 407.

90. 'The history of invention is more readily understood as a cumulative process if it is actually analyzed as a progressive development of larger and more elegant trains of mechanism, which are synthesized and composed by the arrangement of individual parts to achieve specific objectives' (Usher 1982, pp. 116–17).

91. Marx 1906, pp. 412–13.

craft aspect of work, is left to attend to all the remaining chores subsequent to the actual productive activity itself. One activity, the repairing of threads, makes for an exception. The children who were charged with this task must have understood how vital this activity was, since they were interacting with the material in the midst of the process of production, and this may have provided them with a greater sense of their own importance to the operations of the factory as a whole. Rules and oversight were necessary, but mainly in the service of attending to the *machine* to ensure its uninterrupted operation. During the early years when Arkwright's factories ran through the night, the machines were idle for only one hour to allow for dusting and cleaning, yet when profits were high even that hour was not spared.[92] By contrast, the means of production in Wedgwood's potteries were the potter's wheel, the clay, the stencils and other hand tools. In order to effect a truly *capitalist* operation, in order to make 'such machines of the Men as cannot err',[93] Wedgwood would have to devise an extraordinary code of factory discipline in order to reduce the actions of the worker to simple, discrete operations, very much as would be expected of a machine.

What then of innovations *not* specifically designed to supplant the manual labour of workers? Can it be said in general that machines were built and exist because the one thing they all have in common is that they are labour-saving devices? Ashton would say no: '[I]t is by no means true', writes Ashton, that the sole object of industrial discoveries 'was to economise labour'.[94] Telford's innovative 'method of dressing the roads with small angular fragments of stone, so as to make the surface impervious to water', for example, 'was prodigal of labour'.[95] While some of the early innovations of the Industrial Revolution tended to replace unskilled labour – donkeys, rails and carts replaced human coal-heavers; spinning machinery replaced the domestic spinning of women and children; Kay's flying shuttle allowed one weaver to produce a broadcloth, thus replacing his assistants – machines could also produce savings in terms of natural resources, capital, or direct savings resulting in the creation of new wealth. The overshot wheel which, when it replaced the undershot wheel, produced a tremendous saving of natural energy. Newcomen's engine when applied to pumping water out of mines obviated the need for keeping large numbers of horses for that purpose, yielding a saving of capital. '[A]lmost all technological change',

92. Fitton 1989, p. 152.

93. McKendrick (McKendrick 1961, p. 34), quoting a letter from Josiah Wedgwood to Thomas Bentley dated 9 October 1769 from the manuscripts of the Wedgwood Museum. The full letter can be found in Wedgwood 1903. Wedgwood (Wedgwood 1965, p. 82) dates the letter 7 October 1769; it is thus unclear whether there were multiple drafts of this letter or whether Wedgwood used the phrase more than once.

94. Ashton 1964, p. 112.

95. Ashton 1964, p. 113.

writes Mokyr, 'saves *all* factors of production relative to output, although it may save some more than others'.[96] The general emphasis was on *time*-saving, for the longer that goods remained in production or storage, the greater the cost. In no respect, writes Ashton, did the men of the eighteenth century differ more from their predecessors than in their attitude towards time: '[N]o one can read through the correspondence of the period without noticing the stress laid on punctuality and the exasperation caused by any unnecessary delay'.[97] Nevertheless, time-saving and labour-saving largely amounted to the same thing where production was concerned. As Mokyr observes: 'The speeding up of production and distribution by the new machines and new means of transport made it possible to transmute circulating into fixed capital. The process is at the center of what is called the Industrial Revolution'.[98]

The application of machinery accomplishes precisely this result: the transmutation of circulating into fixed capital through a reduction in necessary labour-time. In the hands of the capitalist, any saving in the time it takes to produce something amounts to a saving of capital.

'King Cotton' and the cotton king: from factory to factory system

While rising labour costs favoured the adoption of machinery in general, one trade in particular was the first to introduce a factory 'system' based on machine production. As we have seen, cotton enjoyed the advantages of protection and of being an unregulated trade.[99] Additionally, the cotton industry was not subject to domestic price pressures on imports of raw cotton from the Levant or the West Indies.[100] Prior to the 1770s cotton remained one of the

96. Mokyr 1994, p. 15.

97. Mokyr 1994, pp. 111–12. A Bristol merchant observed in 1695 that the halving of prices on many goods in the preceding decades '"proceeds from the ingenuity of the manufacturer, and the improvements he makes in his ways of working: thus the refiner of sugars goes through that operation in a month, which our forefathers required four months to effect; thus the distillers draw more spirits, in less time ... than those formerly did who taught them the art ... Books are printed instead of written ... Lead is smelted by wind furnaces instead of blowing with bellows; all of which save the labour of many hands, so the wages of those employed need not be lessened"' (Coleman 1977, p. 157, quoting Cary 1972, pp. 322–3).

98. Mokyr 1994, pp. 111–12.

99. As Mantoux (1961, p. 204) summarises, cotton had 'instead of privileges, all the advantages of freedom. The fact that it was not fettered by tradition and stood outside the regulations which stopped, or at any rate hampered technical development, made it, so to speak, a field for inventions and for every kind of alternative. Thus a favourable ground was prepared for the building up of machinery'. And yet for all these advantages, cotton remained a lesser trade until the introduction of machinery, to which it was uniquely receptive.

100. Shapiro 1967, pp. 204–5.

lesser trades, and 'little more than a subsidiary occupation for a few thousand agriculturalists'.[101] Based upon the volume of raw imports, the growth of cotton production can be approximated. In 1700, imports ran at little more than a million pounds a year. By the 1740s, this figure had doubled, and by around 1770 it had doubled again, perhaps spurred on by the now more widespread adoption of Kay's flying shuttle in Lancashire in the 1760s (and other counties over the course of the next forty years), which boosted the output of weavers and so made improvements in spinning the thread imperative. Up to this point, cotton cloth was made with a linen warp and a cotton weft, but the water frame enabled the spinning of thread strong enough to serve as warp and the production of 100 percent cotton goods was undertaken. That this development should again double the demand for cotton imports would not be surprising, but well beyond doubling, imports of raw cotton rose from between five and six million pounds to over fifty million pounds by 1800. 'Here then', write Deane and Cole, 'is a pattern of growth which, in both its magnitude and timing, accords very well with the view that the Industrial Revolution became effective in the last twenty years of the century'.[102] The introduction of machinery, with its capacity to accelerate the productivity of labour by degrees, into factories, clearly made this burst of output possible. Let us consider *how* 'machinofacture' developed in cotton production.

Since time out of mind, cotton, like silk, was a specialty of the Orient, with India being the world's greatest exporter of hand-woven cotton cloths. While cotton had first found its way to Europe in the fourteenth century, settling in the Dutch city of Antwerp, the cotton industry in England was not established until 1641 when cotton production was first undertaken in the unincorporated town of Manchester, which by the late seventeenth century had become the hub of a local network of cotton cloth production. Cotton thus started its career in England 'free from the impediments that were to be found in smaller towns that possessed a charter'.[103] While Mantoux has argued that the damp and cool weather of South Lancashire provided the ideal geographic setting for the growth of the cotton industry by making it 'possible to spin exceptionally fine counts' of thread,[104] Mann finds this claim 'more than doubtful', and cites Ogden who 'attaches more importance to the abundant supplies of soft lime-free water'.[105] Besides these apparent natural advantages, Lancashire enjoyed an abundant supply of coal.[106] It was not only cotton which enjoyed these

101. Deane and Cole 1961, pp. 182–3.
102. Deane and Cole 1961, pp. 51–2.
103. Hammond and Hammond 1974b, p. 180.
104. Mantoux 1961, p. 202.
105. Wadsworth and Mann 1965, p. 172, citing Ogden 1927, pp. 8–30.
106. Hammond and Hammond 1974b, p. 181.

advantages. Linen production developed in South Lancashire prior to the cotton boom, and continued alongside it; the same held true in Scotland around Glasgow.[107] West Lancashire remained in pure linens. Sailcloth manufacture and a putting-out system for watch-making and file-making were also important Lancashire trades. Pure woollens were the staple product of central Lancashire around Rochdale, and remained strong there until well into the nineteenth century. Even Manchester had a strong putting-out system for woollens in 1824.[108]

It seems doubtful that, as is often suggested, the use of Kay's flying shuttle had become so widespread in and around Lancashire that a shortage of cotton thread was creating a crisis by the 1750s and early 1760s. It is more plausible that a shortage was being created because more cottagers were becoming weavers (most not yet employing the shuttle), thereby increasing the demand for thread, while meanwhile rising prices and labour costs were compelling merchants and employers to seek lower production costs and to better regulate supply through mechanisation. These are the pressures that induced the Society for the Encouragement of the Arts and Manufactures to offer up the previously mentioned prize in 1761 for the inventor who could find a solution.[109] While both the spinning jenny (1765) and the water frame (1767) had been invented within six years, Mann finds 'no reason to suppose that the awards had any direct influence' on the development of these machines, for 'by the time of their invention, the Society had abandoned the idea of encouraging attempts to spin on anything more complicated than the ordinary wheel'.[110]

---

107. Wadsworth and Mann 1965, p. 171.

108. Walton (1989, pp. 43–8) struggles with the issue of whether to define eighteenth-century manufacturing in Lancashire as 'proto-industrial'. While he finds some evidence of putting-out systems in West Lancashire around Kirkham, the overall proto-industrial model does not seem to fit even here, and so he (p. 51) suggests: 'At most, one might invite the wrath of Professor Coleman by calling west Lancashire "sub-proto-industrial" in the third quarter of the eighteenth century'. Jumping ahead to the early eighteenth century, Walton (1989, pp. 67–8) finds that rather than a transition from domestic to factory industry, the two could be found alongside one another, 'enabling mixed domestic economies to emerge. All this took place in a setting which was neither proto-industrial nor yet fully industrial'. So then, he asks, what shall we call it? 'With tongue slightly in cheek, but with a genuine belief that the label may have its uses, I suggest that it is "post-proto-industrial"'. This half-serious straining to make sense of the theory of proto-industrialisation by adding a 'post-' to a 'proto-' further testifies to the way in which this attempt to theorise an intermediate 'stage' of manufacturing before industrialisation, as opposed to explicating a process, is fatally flawed. As Walton (Walton 1989, p. 64) writes, in order to explain 'the chain of events which began in the 1770s and gathered such overwhelming momentum in the nineteenth century, we need to go beyond the proto-industrial mode of analysis'. Amen.

109. See Chapter Seven, pp. 328–9. Mantoux (Mantoux 1961, p. 215) comments that Wyatt and Paul, who had tried and failed to manage a small factory based on their spinning machine, 'were too early'. If sufficient records survive, a full study of the Wyatt and Paul story would be a welcome contribution to the literature.

110. Wadsworth and Mann 1965, p. 476.

The man who introduced the water frame into large-scale cotton spinning was Richard Arkwright. While his life is sometimes portrayed as a rags-to-riches story, it is notable that in 1761 he married into wealth.[111] Having developed the water frame by 1767, probably on the original model of Thomas Highs,[112] Arkwright obtained a patent in 1769. In his early career as a barber, he had travelled extensively collecting hair for wigs, and would have been familiar with the rising hosiery trade in Nottingham, where the shortage of yarn was most acutely felt. Perhaps also in response to the violent demonstrations in his hometown of Preston in 1768, Arkwright followed Hargreaves and took 'the golden road to Nottingham',[113] where he succeeded in gaining the support of two of the city's leading merchant-manufacturers – Samuel Need 'the wealthiest hosier in Nottingham', and Jedediah Strutt, 'the leader of the Derby trade'.[114] With their support, Arkwright set up his first workshop in Nottingham. Housing only a handful of water frames powered by horses, it was initially reminiscent of the Wyatt and Paul workshop set up in Nottingham thirty years earlier.[115] Both were probably informed by twist mills, which by the 1760s were being used to twist warp threads for cotton looms in Lancashire.[116] By 1772, Arkwright's Nottingham mill had four storeys and would employ 300 workers, declining to around 200 by 1777, the majority being children.[117] Need and Strutt began using Arkwright's finer

111. Arkwright stood apart from the other innovators in the cotton trade – Wyatt and Paul, Kay, Highs and Hargreaves – primarily on the basis of his business acumen, but there is nothing like financial support to build confidence. Arkwright was born in Preston, and his first occupation was as a barber in Bolton, Lancashire. He was known for his ambition, his drive for self-improvement and his vanity. After losing his first wife to illness, Arkwright married Margaret Biggins 'a propertied woman from Pennington' (Rupp and Townsend 1999, p. 4). By this marriage 'he acquired sufficient capital to became an itinerant dealer in hair for wigs' (Chapman 1967, p. 62), operating out of Wirksworth. He soon '. . . came into possession of a valuable, secret chemical for dyeing hair' (Rupp and Townsend 1999, p. 4). This is consistent with his later apparent appropriation of the inventions of others.

112. See Chapter Six, p. 328, n. 136.

113. Chapman (1967, p. 32) writes: 'The pages of the trade historians are filled with the stories of artisans who took the golden road to Nottingham. They came not only from the framework-knitting districts, but also, in a few cases, from regions beyond; indeed, by the early 1820s Nottingham was even attracting German clockmakers'.

114. Chapman 1967, p. 62.

115. One might suggest that Arkwright's establishment of the factory system was to the early cotton factories of Wyatt and Paul what the explosion of parish workhouse construction after the passage of the Workhouse Test Act in 1723 was to the earlier Corporations for the Poor.

116. 'Before Arkwright began his career in cotton, twist mills with forty or fifty spindles were common and 200 spindles were not unheard of' (Chapman 1967, p. 43). It is unclear whether any of these operations were later converted to using the jenny or water frame, but it is far from unlikely.

117. According to the guide at the Arkwright Museum in Cromford (personal visit by author, October 1997), the Nottingham mill was primarily used by Arkwright as a showcase to attract capital for future projects. Chapman, however, suggests that the Cromford

thread to produce stockings of a superior quality and 'as warp to produce calico, a plain, white, serviceable cotton cloth. For the first time in England, a cloth made solely of cotton was manufactured'.[118] Unsatisfied with the results of using animal power, Arkwright sought out a location in the West Midlands where he could take advantage of the fast-flowing streams and where he could withdraw from the possibility of resistance from competitors and workers opposed to mechanisation. Arkwright may also have hoped to take advantage of the cheap labour arising from the failing lead-mining trade in that region. With assistance from his partners, Arkwright began building the first of two large mills as part of a factory in Cromford, Derbyshire in 1771. Not far from Derby, the new factory building and adjacent workshops were built using the Old Silk Mill as a model.[119] Within a year Arkwright was employing more than three times as many workers as Hargreaves and James employed at their Hockley mill.

When Arkwright obtained his next patent on a carding machine in 1775, Hargreaves and James were ruined.[120] The carding patents of Bourn and Paul had expired in 1762, and Arkwright combined these and subsequent carding improvements into one working cylinder engine, with the novel addition of the crank and comb, though even this – considered by some his only true contribution[121] – is alleged to have been first developed by Hargreaves and perfected by Wood.[122] Where Arkwright was clearly a master was in the practical application of new inventions and in securing patent rights in order to monopolise their use. It should be pointed out that patents survive today as a holdover from the guild-era practice of granting monopoly charters.[123] What is different

mill was actually less successful, owing to its remote location, citing 'very real handicaps which transport costs and isolation from the centre of the cotton textile industry imposed' (Chapman 1967, p. 67).

118. Rupp and Townsend 1999, p. 6.

119. Lombe's mill was an influence not only in design, but also in working conditions. Commenting in 1816 on working conditions at his Belpor and Milford mills, Strutt declared that the working hours were six before and six after dinner, each period including time for breakfast and tea. '"This has been the invariable practice at the original silk mill in Derby [and] in this neighbourhood for more than a hundred years"'. '...what is significant is that the second generation at Belper should attempt to justify their practice by allusion to the Derby silk mill. The impression given from the Strutts' remarks is that not only the design of the buildings, but also the details of administration and organization at the Derby mill had been absorbed by the local business community and accepted as precedents' (Chapman 1987, p. 41).

120. Chapman 1967, p. 50. James left Hargreaves to set up a mill with water frames, paying for the use of Arkwright's patent. Hargreaves passed away only a few years later.

121. Wadsworth and Mann 1965, p. 478.

122. According to Guest (1823, p. 18), Hargreaves invented the crank and comb in 1772, and this allowed Wood to achieve perpetual or ceaseless carding by 1774.

123. The first 'letters patent' was granted by Henry VI in 1449 to a Flemish man, giving him a twenty-year monopoly on the manufacture of stained glass. This was in keeping with the typical English practice of offering inducements for the importation of new

about the patent as opposed to the company charter, however, is that a patent grants *individual property rights* to the holder, and does not presume the existence of a semi-egalitarian community of merchants or craftsmen.[124] As the holder of patents over the two prime pieces of technology for cotton spinning, the water frame and the first truly effective machine for continuous carding, Arkwright now held the keys to developing his own economic empire. While his patents lasted, Arkwright made a considerable fortune from the construction and licensing of water frames alone.[125] Others who wished to set up factories based on the water frame had to seek Arkwright's authorisation and pay him a royalty.[126] One of those was the industrialist Robert Peel Senior.[127] Like Kay and Paul, Arkwright faced the pirating of his patent, but he surpassed their skill in the practical business application of the machines. Moreover, because the water frame required external power and could not be adapted to manual work, the pirating he faced was only from larger, more easily identifiable masters. Continuous power-spinning on rollers required less attention for repairs and less time to produce more yarn than the jenny, which was subject to the intermittent motions of manual work. The result was cheaper yarn of superior quality. While the jenny had raised the quality of thread from 16 to 20 hanks for hand spinning into the low twenties, thread produced on the water frame could surpass 60 hanks.[128] All these benefits of machinery accrued to Arkwright.

---

techniques. For example, in 1238, Henry III offered the Mayor of Bordeaux a fifteen-year monopoly to practise the use of a secret dye in England (Kahrl 2001, pp. 2–10).

124. As a grant of individual property rights, patent rights by definition fall under common law. Further study into the origin of patent rights in Britain in relation to the development of individual private property under common law should prove a fruitful area of inquiry.

125. This would require the training of workmen in the building of the machines, which were built on-site. There was no manufactory for building water frames or carding engines as such (Arkwright Museum, Cromford, visit by author, October 1997).

126. There were those who managed to get patents on improvements to the water frame. Samuel Unwin, one of Arkwright's business partners, 'experimented to improve the early roller-spinning machinery and, early in 1772, his own patent (No. 1,009) was registered. The ideas were to minimise breakages in the yarn by eliminating the use of cog-wheels in winding and doubling... Another patent was taken out in 1772 by Coniah Wood, a turner who at one time worked for Arkwright at Nottingham. Wood's patent suggests an attempt to combine the principles of the jenny and roller-spinning' and thus would seem to anticipate Crompton's mule. However: 'The jenny and Arkwright's patent were the only successful techniques of mechanized spinning that emerged before the mule' (Chapman 1967, pp. 73–5).

127. Robert Peel, First Baronet, was the son of Robert 'Parsley' Peel and father of the nineteenth-century Prime Minister Robert Peel, Second Baronet (of whom we shall hear much more below). He had prior experience in the industry, as earlier he had offered assistance to John Kay in the development of his shuttle-loom.

128. Chapman 1987, p. 21.

In 1776, Arkwright employed over two hundred workmen at Cromford in erecting a second mill seven storeys high and 120 feet long. Completed in 1777, it would soon double Cromford's output,[129] but he faced a setback when multiple attempts to resolve the insufficient water flow led to the inadvertent flooding of local lead mines. The lead miners retaliated by sabotaging his floodgates, bringing his operations to a standstill. Worse for Arkwright, this led to a five-year legal battle, which he lost.[130] Meanwhile, Arkwright returned to his home county of Lancashire a wealthy and famous man to erect a factory south of Preston at Birkacre near Chorley, with plans to carry on the 'whole process of Picking, Carding, Roving, Spinning and Peeling of Cotton' under one roof.[131] This statement exemplifies Arkwright's conscious design to establish a system of what Stanley Chapman refers to as 'flow production', which for him is what set Arkwright's factories apart from their earlier predecessors, which for the most part were engaged in 'batch production' and which explained Arkwright's 'spectacular financial success'.[132] At a cost of over £4,000, Birkacre was already partially operational by the Autumn of 1779, and his foray into the heart of manual cotton-spinning country appeared on the verge of success. But on 4 October 1779, two days after an initial assault, a crowd of some four to five thousand bearing arms broke in, destroyed all the machinery and burned the factory to the ground. Arkwright called for military support, but only horsemen and dragoons could be spared. Angered that one member of their company had been shot dead and many others wounded, the protesters continued the violence into mid-October. A dozen or more mills were destroyed, Birkacre being the largest by far. Travelling through Lancashire at the time, none other than Josiah Wedgwood encountered a crowd of some of them, who he described as '"eight thousand, and marched by the beat of drum and with colours they rounded the mill"', and reported that the machine-breakers intended to make their way to Manchester, Stockport and even Cromford '"to destroy all the engines, not only in these places, but throughout all England"'.[133] The crowd never got within fifty miles of Cromford. Had they reached the town, they would have been greeted by a force of 1,500 men whom Arkwright had organised, bearing arms and spears on long poles to defend the town and Arkwright's mills.

---

129. The second mill was powered by two overshot wheels in a pit twenty feet deep, sitting along a half-mile long culvert, or underground drainage channel called a sump. This provided an advantage over the rivers at Nottingham or London which froze over in winter, because by channelling the water underground Arkwright could guarantee a continuous supply of water to drive the wheels. The first mill still stands, but the second mill has been destroyed, and recent excavations have uncovered the pit where the wheels of the second mill turned (Arkwright Museum, Cromford, visit by author, October 1997).

130. See Chapman 1967, pp. 63–4.

131. Fitton 1989, p. 51.

132. Chapman 1974, p. 470.

133. Fitton 1989, pp. 51–3, quoting Wedgwood.

The background to this and other disturbances of these years[134] was the American War, which had brought depression to the trade, causing many small workshops to fall idle, even while the factories continued to work. One rebel explained how the plight of the spinners led to the revolt: '... being no longer able to endure the remediless cries of our husbands, wives and children, and not having it in our power to put food into the mouths of those to whom, under God, we gave existence; in an unhappy hour of depression, prompted by want and poverty, we pulled down and demolished several of these Machines, the causes of our calamitous situation'.[135]

Observers like Wedgwood were quick to point to economic depression arising from the war as the underlying cause of the revolt. The machine-breaker quoted above noted both causes, and while it would be difficult to gauge the extent to which power-machine spinning was already affecting prices and turning spinners out of work by this point, he was at least prescient enough to recognise that this was the trend set for the future. While the machine-breakers directed their attacks against Arkwright frames and carding engines and also against jennies and twisting machines, remarkably all jennies under 24 spindles were spared. The smaller jenny was welcomed by master spinners for the simple reason that it did not threaten to alter the customary modes of labour organisation.[136] The use of the jenny in small workshops and 'jenny factories' survived in economically and geographically peripheral regions such as the Peak District, continuing to satisfy a demand for coarser yarns.[137]

In the same year of 1779, when water frames were attacked and smaller jennies spared, Samuel Crompton introduced his spinning mule.[138] He tried to set up a small spinning mill in Oldham, then in Bolton, but like other inventors he lacked a talent for business and died poor. Where the jenny's threads were fine but weak and the water frame's thread was strong but coarse, the combined fineness and strength of threads produced by the mule 'enabled British manufacturers to outdo the renowned skill of the Indian workers and to manufacture muslins of incomparable delicacy'.[139] Where England had once moved to ban the

---

134. Months later, in early 1780, there were anti-machine revolts in Leeds, and anti-Catholic revolts took place in Scotland and London in both years.

135. As quoted in Wadsworth and Mann 1965, p. 499.

136. 'Far from favouring the progress of capitalism, the jenny seemed to have provided the small master with a new weapon with which to safeguard his independence. This was the secret of its success in a country which was, above all others, the home of small-scale industry' (Mantoux 1961, p. 264). As we shall see, the master clothiers of the West of England only came to realise the usefulness of the jenny too late, for by the time they did, machinery was already moving in to take over the trade in West Riding, producing cloth of quality too fine and too cheap for the West of England to compete.

137. Chapman 1967, pp. 50–1.

138. See Chapter Six, pp. 329–30.

139. Mantoux 1961, pp. 235 and 238.

import of superior Indian cottons, Britain was now poised to out-compete the Indian handloom-woven cotton industry.

The first blow to Arkwright's virtual monopoly came in 1781 when he lost a legal challenge against nine other spinners who had constructed machines only slightly differing from the water frame. Sued by Arkwright, they succeeded in overturning Arkwright's patent by pointing to the language of the patent itself, which was obscure and even appeared to have been written in such a manner as to obfuscate the actual design. The water frame patent, which was anyway set to expire in July of 1783, was revoked. Arkwright's defeat, proclaimed the *Manchester Mercury* '"relieves the Public from a Monopoly, which they have too long submitted to, under plausible and mistaken Apprehension"'.[140] Parliament found that he had already '"realised such a Fortune as every unprejudiced Person must be allowed to be ample compensation for the most happy Efforts of Genius"'.[141] Fitton attributes his loss to 'his foolish insistence on prohibitive premiums, and his claims to inventions that were not his own', which 'brought the wrath of the whole trade upon him'.[142] Arkwright now turned his efforts against those he alleged were infringing his 1775 carding patent, forcing some to comply but losing most in an atmosphere of intense feelings.[143]

Table 8.1: Arkwright Factories built 1769–84[144]

	Town	County
1767	Nottingham	Nottinghamshire
1771	Cromford (upper mill)	Derbyshire
1777	Cromford (lower mill)	Derbyshire
1779	Cressbrook near Tideswell	Derbyshire
1779	Birkacre near Chorley	Lancashire
1780	Keighley	West Riding
1782	Bakewell	Derbyshire
1783	Wirksworth	Derbyshire
1783	Manchester	Lancashire
1783	Matlock (Paper Mill)	Derbyshire
1784	Matlock (Masson Mill)	Derbyshire
1784	New Lanark	Lanarkshire

140. Fitton 1989, p. 98.
141. Ibid.
142. Fitton 1989, p. 76.
143. It is important, write Wadsworth and Mann 1965, p. 495, 'to remember how intense was the Lancashire feeling against protective patents'.
144. Source: Chapman 1967, pp. 67–8.

The loss did not deter Arkwright. In 1782, his annual profits exceeded £40,000. Less than two years after his Birkacre factory was destroyed, he returned to Lancashire to build a factory with the tallest chimney in Manchester.[145] Elsewhere, he pressed forward with the building of many more factories, including his giant Masson Mill, a red-brick structure seven stories high. He built it along the Derwent, just upstream from the Cromford mills, alongside his recently built paper mill. By this time (1784) Arkwright had established at least a dozen mills (see Table 8.1).

Arkwright appealed and won back his patent, with damages, in early 1785. In the process, he had also managed in the previous year to convince Parliament to lift the 1721 ban on printed cottons and pure cotton goods, which could now be made in Britain thanks to the water frame providing thread of a suitable quality for the warp. The court decision to restore Arkwright's patent was challenged before the King's Bench, and this time the vagueness of both his patents were used as evidence to support the claim that the poor Lancashire inventor named Thomas Highs was 'beyond any reasonable doubt'[146] the true inventor of the water frame.[147] Both patents were cancelled. Arkwright 'told fellow manufacturer Josiah Wedgwood... that he intended to take revenge on an ungrateful Britain'.[148] The field was now open to all competitors and soon there would be hundreds of operations setting up shop all over the country using the water frame. By 1788, there were at least 208 cotton mills in Britain, most having been

---

145. The factory was five stories high. 'The mill's chimney, the highest in Manchester, occupied a base of forty square yards, dominating the landscape to the awe of the crowds...' (Fitton 1989, p. 63). After his partners pulled out, Arkwright sold the Manchester mill to Richard Arkwright Jr. in 1784. In 1786, a second mill, also five stories high, was built.

146. Wadsworth and Mann 1965, p. 482.

147. Highs's testimony was supported by the same John Kay who had worked with Arkwright on his original model, and who testified that he had revealed Highs's designs to Arkwright. Kay's wife and the widow of James Hargreaves also testified. The fact that Hargreaves's widow supported Highs's claim that not only was he the inventor of the water frame, but also of the jenny would suggest that both were true. Arkwright had no background as an inventor before 1768. Highs had been experimenting with machines in an effort to improve the model of Lewis and Paul since his marriage in 1747, and had in fact attempted to set up a business using his inventions, but lacked the business skills to succeed. Highs apparently went on to invent the throstle, which applied the principles of Crompton's mule to the twisting of wool. He was thus apparently an inventor of great skill and possibly the single most important inventor of the early Industrial Revolution, as far as textiles are concerned. See Mantoux 1961, pp. 227–32 and Guest 1823, pp. 22–7. 'There never was a greater practical attempt made to mystify a subject since the creation of the world', writes Guest, 'than this specification of Mr. Arkwright's'. The bias in favour of Highs and against Arkwright in Guest's work leaves his entire work open to question.

148. Arkwright vowed to share his designs with other countries. Six years later, the United States granted a patent on the water frame to William Pollard of Philadelphia, '"ass[ignée] of Richard Arkwright", for a machine for "Spinning and Roving Cotton"' (Wallace and Jeremy 1977, pp. 404–5, citing Fitton and Wadsworth 1958, p. 88).

built since Arkwright's patent was first successfully challenged in 1781.[149] Capital began to be diverted from the contracting pottery manufacture outside the Potteries in Staffordshire, and from the contracting iron and lead industries in Derbyshire into the building of cotton mills.[150]

The 'geographical distribution of Arkwright's mills largely determined the location pattern of the Midlands cotton-spinning industry'.[151] He was but one of the many key figures in the development of the textile industry who relocated to the West Midlands from elsewhere.[152] But his decision to place the capital of his empire at Cromford cut him off from centres of innovation, such as Nottingham, ensuring that his dominance of the trade would not last. He had enjoyed sixteen years of near-monopoly over factory spinning, which ended in 1785. And where he needed credit to start out, by 1784 he could purchase the massive Masson mill with cash. The factory empire he would bequeath to his son upon his death in 1792 was valued at over half a million pounds.

Unfortunately, little by way of any record of how labour was organised in Arkwright's factories remains,[153] and there is in general a want of data about labour conditions in the early factories.[154] As in the early silk mills, the labour force in the cotton mills was made up predominately of women and children, not because they were cheap but because 'otherwise the mills would have been without sufficient labour, or at least without sufficient child labour in relation to the number of adults'.[155] Men supplied the skilled labour to construct the mill and its machinery. Parents 'were only too eager for their children to be accepted into the mills'.[156] At Cromford in 1789, only 150 of the 1,150 workers were men.[157] Arkwright, who employed *mainly* pauper children, had no trouble finding children at Nottingham or later in Manchester, but at Cromford any hopes he may have had of recruiting from the local lead-mining force were soon dashed, and he initially had to recruit from nearby towns. In general, the factory masters' demand for child labour was greater than local supply even in a time of

149. Chapman 1987, p. 27. This number corrects Colquhoun's pioneering census of Arkwright-type mills in 1788, which noted only '143 mills dispersed over 27 counties in England, Scotland and Wales…'

150. Chapman 1967, pp. 93–4.

151. Chapman 1967, p. 68.

152. The hosier Samuel Fellows was from London. The Lombe brothers of London were originally from Norwich. Lewis Paul was a descendant of Huguenot refugees from France. Hargreaves, Arkwright and the Peels all came from Lancashire (Chapman 1967, p. 46).

153. 'We have no records of the work processes' (guide at the Arkwright Museum, Cromford, visit by author, October 1997).

154. Chapman 1967, p. 174.

155. Pollard 1965, p. 165.

156. Ibid.

157. Chapman 1967, pp. 164–5.

rapid population growth, and pauper children were imported by the score from Middlesex and the large towns to serve as indentured labour in the rising factories of the Midlands.[158] Most were eight to ten years of age. Mortality rates were high. Chapman suggests that since the factory owners in general attended well to the health of the children, the high mortality rate was probably due to the fact 'that they were collected from the unhealthy dregs of society'.[159] No doubt many pauper children may have arrived at the factories in a state of malnourishment, but the fact that even more ran away tells us conditions were generally miserable. Chapman also plays apologist for the cruel punishments used in the factory, including the 'progressive' use of a log weighing up to six pounds fixed around the child's neck, or the suspension of children above the machinery in a basket.[160] Commenting, John Rule reminds readers that 'the objective position is presumed to be that of juryman, not counsel for the defence'.[161] Factory workers were typically not allowed to sit during their long shifts, and breaks were infrequent. The gruelling, repetitive work alongside noisy, dusty machines could only have been an overall detriment to a child's health. In the early days, the machines were kept running through the night,[162] with the children taking alternating shifts. As discussed in Chapter Five, Chambers suggested that the population that moved into the factories came not so much from those dislocated by enclosures as from the rapidly increasing population of Britain in the late eighteenth century. Here

---

158. Writing some sixty years later, Engels commented that: 'The memory of the shameless and brutal treatment of women and children at that time, which was quite relentless while there was still a single muscle, sinew or drop of blood to be exploited, is still very much alive among the older generation of workers in England. Some of these workers still carry this memory with them in the form of a crooked back or crippled limb, and all are haunted by it on account of their irrevocably damaged health' (Engels 1975b, p. 97).

159. Chapman 1967, p. 171. Chapman's treatment of the question of cruelty toward children is somewhat confounding. He presents the case of Ellis Needham as the exception to the rule. Needham was a factory master of the Litton mill, located near Tideswell in Derbyshire, a copycat of the Arkwright system. In the *Memoir of Robert Blincoe*, an interview of a child labourer sent to work in Litton Mill in 1802, Needham is accused of gross sadism, including suspending children above the machines by their arms. Chapman finds the author of the *Memoir* to be a 'gullible sensationalist', casting doubt on the charges, but then proceeds to suggest that some of the cruelties practiced by Needham, such as suspending a four-to-six-pound log around a child's neck or caging or suspending children, 'were, in fact, advocated by progressive educationalists' of the period, and that Needham was merely copying them (Chapman 1967, pp. 199–209). The power dynamics in the early factory alone are such that it is virtually impossible *not* to believe that abuses were common, that most went unreported and were in some cases extreme.

160. Chapman 1967, pp. 203–4.

161. Rule 1986, p. 149.

162. 'The Arkwright mills, it was said in 1784, "are worked night and day or at least 23 of the 24 hours, one hour is allowed for examining, oiling and cleaning"' (Fitton 1989, p. 152).

we have a demonstration of how this might have worked, with the masters effectively skimming off a share of each new generation of the children of the poor.

As a rule, larger masters were better able to provide for their workforce. Arkwright's 'initiative in building an inn (in 1779) and a market (in 1790) at Cromford was almost unique',[163] but as the largest and most successful capitalist of his day, he would have had the means. Arkwright and Strutt also threw a feast for five hundred workers at Cromford in 1776 and annual balls until 1781.[164] When in 1802, in response to a report telling of the poor health and stunted growth of factory workers, Peel's Health and Morals of Apprentices Act was passed by Parliament, subsequent factory inspections revealed sound conditions amongst the wealthier operations, but poor ventilation and hygiene in smaller operations.[165] When we set out to measure the cruel treatment of women and children versus the abysmal conditions of the domestic system or abject poverty, or when we note that industrial protest lessened during periods of higher employment, we are already, at this early date, on the terrain of the standard of living debate.[166] Here, it is sufficient to point out that to put the focus on the morality of individual factory masters is to lose sight of the larger process at work.

Inasmuch as machines themselves greatly facilitated a capitalist structure of ownership and division of labour, this made the reduplication of the factory driven by machines far more expedient than a factory relying solely on a minute division of labour and extensive training of the workforce. So here is another advantage of the machine: facilitating the easy reproduction of factories, thus enabling the elaboration of a factory 'system'. If we are to give Arkwright credit as an innovator, then it is in the introduction of a factory 'system' that his true genius resided. Power-spinning 'set in motion a sequence of technical and organisational changes in connected branches of the industry'.[167] Earlier stages now required improvement: cleaning, batting, carding, drawing, roving would now be 'accomplished simultaneously'.[168] The result 'was the perfection of a system of continuous (or flow) production in which the cotton was mechanically handled from the moment the bales were hoisted from the drays to the top floor of the mill to that at which it was dispatched, in carefully graded yarns, from the

---

163. Chapman 1967, p. 162. By 1790, Arkwright was providing 'a public house, a weekly market and garden allotments to retain his workforce…' Other leading capitalists like Strutt or Dale offered similar incentives in what appears to be a competition for labour (Chapman 1987, p. 47).

164. Pollard 1965, p. 183.

165. Fitton 1989, p. 154.

166. For a brief discussion of this debate, see the summary pages of the Conclusion below, pp. 836–7.

167. Chapman 1987, p. 22.

168. Rupp and Townsend 1999, pp. 3–7.

ground-floor warehouse'.[169] Flow production 'required workers at each stage of the process to work at the same pace to prevent bottlenecks'.[170] We can easily make a comparison, here, with the feedback loops discussed in Chapter Three. For here again, the falling price of the industrial (as opposed to agricultural) product sets in motion a self-reinforcing process of change. Factory production intensifies production, increasing productivity, thereby creating a surplus of supply in one component of the production process, necessitating the application of automation or factory discipline to the production of other components. As a result, new factories arise and the factory system expands. Feedback loop number one. As factory production expands, it gradually extinguishes domestic manufacturing, or subordinates it to its needs, thus requiring the disciplining of the new work force, thereby expanding the supply of trained factory labour. Feedback loop number two. In good times, new capitals enter and set up new factories. Competition is intensified and drives the compulsion to innovate further. Feedback loop number three. As production lurches forward, especially with the aid of machinery, supply outstrips demand and prices fall in a crisis of overproduction. As a result, many firms (mostly smaller firms) are culled by bankruptcy. Idle buildings and machinery can be purchased for a song, thus attracting capital and encouraging concentration. A new wave of investment ensues. As demand catches up with supply, production recovers and factory-building resumes with smaller capitals getting back in the game. And so on.

Such cycles of boom and bust were already to be witnessed in the cotton trade of late eighteenth-century Britain. In 1788, a depression hit the trade and those regions using the jenny were hardest hit, with widespread shut-downs and the dismissal of many hands in Lancashire and Cheshire. The price of no. 100 cotton yard had fallen from 38 to 35 shillings a pound. Supply was outstripping demand, and falling prices only encouraged spinners to increase production further, leading to a crisis of overproduction. The recovery was swift, and building soon started up again. In 1791, John Kennedy and his partner James McConnel set up a mule-spinning shop in Oldham with a capital of '"not more than £600 or £700"'.[171] A year later, John Byng would write from Oldham that '"every vale swarms with cotton mills, some not bigger than cottages"'.[172] But in 1793, the price of no. 100 had fallen to just 15 shillings a pound, and again depression set in. This time the depression was actually part of a larger financial crisis due to the shortage of credit that was only partially attributable to the unprecedented 'boom' of 'King Cotton'. Other industries such as iron were simultaneously taking

169. Chapman 1987, p. 22.
170. Geraghty 2006, p. 25.
171. Fitton 1989, p. 150.
172. Fitton 1989, p. 147.

part in a booming trade, and as the financial system could not keep pace, a 'bust' followed. Pitt helped to restore confidence by issuing new treasury bonds, and the cotton boom was soon back on track.[173]

The extraordinary versatility and elasticity of cotton in comparison with linen or wool made it the ideal fabric for Britain to market in the midst of an international trade boom and expanding markets in the colonies.[174] The production of raw cotton in the Americas was rising fast, facilitated by the invention of Whitney's gin. In 1789, the influx of American cotton broke the age-old monopoly of Asia on cotton growing. 'Moreover, whilst India and China only exported their surplus crop, practically the whole of the American crop was sent to European ports. In this way a double stream of imports converged on Liverpool'.[175] It is little wonder that among the first canals of the canal boom was one connecting Liverpool and Manchester, and that the first railroad line traced the same route. By the 1790s, capital was diverting away from the construction of factories on the Arkwright system and into mule-spinning. In 1790, a Scot named William Kelly adapted Crompton's mule to water power.[176] In 1795, M'Connel & Kennedy of Manchester succeeded in applying a Boulton & Watt steam engine to the two "heavy" motions of the four-movement cycle of the mule, [and] many of the pioneers of the Arkwright system, like the Peels and Douglases, began to direct their investment into the new and rapidly developing technique'.[177] While the water frame had attained thread of over sixty hanks, the mule soon produced thread in excess of eighty hanks, reaching over three hundred hanks by the end of the century.[178] The 'slubbing billy', a jenny-like machine for preparing the cotton for spinning, and the 'throstle' also came into use in the 1790s.[179]

According to Professor Chapman, the textile-printing industry in England dates from around 1676, when printworks making calicoes in imitation of those that had for a long time been imported from the Orient, chiefly India, began settling along the Southern tributaries of the Thames in the vicinity of East London, where bleaching and dyeing operations had long been established. Since

---

173. See Mantoux 1961, pp. 251–5.
174. Walton 1989, p. 64.
175. Mantoux 1961, p. 201.
176. 'From that time forward the mule became the spinning machine *par excellence*, and took the place, in current use, of Hargreave's jenny' (Mantoux 1961, p. 237). By this time, Samuel Oldknow of Nottingham was already the leading maker of fine muslins using the mule. His first workshop may have been supplied by yarn spun by Crompton himself in the early 1780s (Unwin 1968, pp. 4 and 69).
177. 'The leviathan of the [mule-spinning] industry, Livesey, Hargreaves & Co. of Blackburn, employed about 900 workers shortly before their bankruptcy in 1788' (Chapman 1987, pp. 21–3).
178. Chapman 1987, p. 21.
179. See above, p. 437, n. 147.

waterwheels on the Lea, the Wandle and the Cray rivers provided the motive power for bleaching, dyeing, grinding, polishing (the copper plates) and printing, 'most of the large calico works could easily have qualified as factories if we adopt the elementary criterion of identifying factories as manufacturing plants where power was employed'.[180] By 1763, there were at least eighteen larger works in existence and dozens of smaller works to be found in London, but also in Lancashire, Scotland and in Dublin, Ireland.

The Peels were exceptional in that most entrepreneurs who entered the cotton trade in the Midlands were either already established in the hosiery trade, shifting their investments out of declining trades such as lead mining, iron-smelting or other textiles, or were simply speculators.[181] But the Peels started out in cotton in Lancashire and expanded into the Midlands. Combining the latest technology and turning out high volume, Robert 'Parsley' Peel and his son Robert Peel set quality standards and prices for printed cloths as well as thread based on mule-spinning, just as Arkwright had done when the water frame was the cutting-edge technology. Also like Arkwright, the Peels experimented in vertical integration, combining spinning, weaving and printing within one large operation.

In 1789, Arkwright had some eight hundred souls employed at his Cromford mills, while Jedediah Strutt had six hundred working at his Arkwright-system mill at nearby Belper. By 1800, the factory system run by Arkwright Junior was still the largest in Britain, but from the mid-1780s its decline had been foretold in the 'failure of Arkwright and son to keep abreast of technical developments'.[182] By 1802, Cromford was in decline but the Strutts had survived several depressions and continued to expand, employing over twelve hundred workers at Belper.[183] The Strutts continued to adapt to technological developments, even introducing the first fire-proof factory with iron framing and a heating system. Robert Peel II had only a small clothing shop in the 1770s, but by 1803 he had over twenty mills between Lancashire and the Midlands and a total workforce of some 15,000, a considerable number of these working in textile-printing works.[184] Cotton's new kingdoms had arrived.

---

180. Chapman 1987, p. 459. For more background on the Peel family, see Chapter Thirteen below, pp. 686–7.
181. Chapman 1987, p. 99.
182. Chapman 1987, p. 70.
183. Fitton and Wadsworth 1958, pp. 224–5.
184. Chapman 1967, p. 87.

Technological versus organisational innovation

Thomas Geraghty suggests that the Peels enjoyed a 'dual competitive advantage... in both quality and high volume', which depended upon 'both mechanization and organizational innovation'.[185] The centralising of weavers into manufacturing warehouses did not appear to have provided any great advantage, however, and the Peels were willing to settle for offering inducements to weavers to move closer to their works. Despite viewing these types of centralised operations that combined machinery with manual work like hand weaving as rudimentary factories – due to the application of water (and later steam) power – Chapman prefers to consider these works not as factories proper, but as 'proto-factories', or Type II factories, engaged in 'batch production', where Type I is simply the single-process workshop that has been centralised and expanded beyond the scale typical of the early modern period, and Type III is the 'factory proper', engaged, as Arkwright was, in 'flow production'. Chapman's 'proto-factory' involved centralisation of the various processes in one location, combining mechanical and manual production, but lacking what can only be found in Type III factories: the 'synchronisation of a sequence of highly specialised machines' that could allow round-the-clock, twenty-four hour operations.[186] This insistence that the application of machinery is required in order for a factory to be a 'true' factory suggests that, in seeking an explanation for the origin of the factory, Professor Chapman may subscribe to a technological model. Yet his emphasis on the machine has everything to do with the role that machinery plays in the way that production within the factory is organised.

Longstanding debates over the way in which the capitalist factory came into being have tended to turn on the apparently opposing poles of technological versus organisational innovation within the factory. Geraghty has suggested a way out of the conundrum by way of a synthesis. On the one hand, writes Geraghty, we have what he calls the economies of scale hypothesis, which is based upon a technological model: technological innovation required greater investment in fixed capital, necessitating centralisation. On the other hand is the transaction cost hypothesis, which proposes that organisational innovation allowed manufacturers to reduce transaction costs in the form of reducing the amount of time workers were idle or limiting workers' embezzlement' of raw materials. The transaction cost hypothesis is supported by the existence of non-mechanised factories, such as Wedgwood's pottery works. Because the growth of factories was faster in cotton and worsted production, which were the first lines of textile production to mechanise, than in flax or wool, Geraghty cannot

185. Geraghty 2007, pp. 14–15.
186. Geraghty 2007, pp. 470–2.

accept the implication of the transaction costs hypothesis that organisational innovation was more important than machinery in the development of the factory.[187] In place of either hypothesis, Geraghty offers his own *complementarity* hypothesis, in which he suggests that factory production expanded as a result of *both* organisational innovation and the adoption of machinery, thus bypassing the question of which of the two factors was primary. What may appear as a two-sided debate between proponents of a technological model and proponents of an organisational model is in reality a terrain for much debate which, we would argue, is even more complex than it may already appear.

Stephen Marglin's 1974 essay, entitled 'What Do Bosses Do?' touched off significant debate on this terrain.[188] In a number of ways, Marglin's essay resonates with (and may have indirectly informed) the general thesis of the present work. For example, readers of Marglin's essay will recognise this when they read that: 'The minute specialization that was the hallmark of the putting-out system only wiped out one of two aspects of workers' control of production: control over the product. Control of the work process, when and how much the worker would exert himself, remained with the worker – until the coming of the factory'.[189]

This insight is as central to Marglin's thesis as it is to our own. Additionally, where Marglin's argument dovetails with our own is in refusing to accept capitalism as a natural or inevitable system and pointing to the resistance of artisanal labourers to the coming of the factory system as evidence to that effect. Where Marglin's thesis diverges from that of the present work is in the suggestion that the drive for technological superiority did *not* inform the development of capitalist industrial organisation. In the first of four specific propositions, Marglin argues that: 'The Capitalist division of labor . . . was the result of a search not for a technologically superior organization of work, but for an organization which guaranteed to the entrepreneur an essential role in the production process, as an integrator of the separate efforts of his workers into a marketable product'.[190]

Posing a rhetorical question, Marglin asks why the division of labour under the putting-out system entailed not only the separation of tasks but also specialisation, to which he answers: 'In my view the reason lies in the fact that without specialization, the capitalist had no essential role to play in the production process'.[191] Using a divide-and-conquer strategy, Marglin argues, the capitalist putter-outer insinuated himself in the production process and thereby ensured

187. Despite the fact that silk was the first line of textiles to industrialise, Geraghty leaves silk out of this discussion because of the relatively low numbers of workers employed in silk production (Geraghty 2007, p. 47).
188. Marglin 1974, pp. 60–112.
189. Marglin 1974, p. 81.
190. Marglin 1974, p. 62.
191. Marglin 1974, p. 70.

'that he would remain essential to the production process as integrator of these separate operations'.[192] This important step, which facilitated the formal subsumption of labour to (merchant) capital, was clearly a major and important step along the road to the real subsumption of labour, when the labourers lose their control over the labour process upon the capitalist master taking direct command of production. But Marglin is confusing the how with the why, implying that the capitalist employer wanted control of production for control's sake. There is no acknowledgment of the possibility that, under pain of losing market share to his competitors and facing the possibility of bankruptcy, the employer in a putting-out arrangement would have been confronted thereby with the economic compulsion to introduce task specialisation, a detailed division of labour, product specialisation, product maximisation and, eventually, to innovate further in productive methods including taking direct command of the labour process. Contrary to Marglin, it is our contention that the emergence of the factory arose *directly* out of the search by employers to find a more efficient form of production.

Part of the difficulty with Marglin's argument is that while it does rely on a host of historical references, it is aimed at critiquing specific assumptions arising out of the abstract economic modelling of neoclassical or neoliberal economics. Marglin's approach begins by taking aim at one of the core suppositions of classical political economy, namely Adam Smith's contention that what explains how the capitalist division of labour came into being is its technological superiority. Under the economist's model of perfect competition, argues Marglin, the terms technological superiority and technological efficiency lose all their specificity and are reduced to meaning the same thing as *economic* superiority and *economic* efficiency: 'Under text-book assumptions of perfect and universal competition, the technologically efficient method of production is the one that costs least, and cost reduction is an index of technological superiority'.[193] According to economic theory, Marglin argues, the hierarchical or pyramidal structure of capitalist industry actually plays no essential role: 'neoclassical theory says only that hierarchy must be technologically efficient to persist, but denies the superiority of capitalist hierarchy (workers can just as well hire capital, remember!). This is to say very little...'[194] Here, Marglin is taking economics to task by showing how

192. Marglin 1974, p. 80.
193. Marglin 1974, p. 65.
194. Marglin 1974, p. 66. In what follows, Marglin develops his argument by criticising Smith's use of the example of the pin factory to buttress his argument about the superiority of the division of labour, but does not return to his critique of neoclassical economic assumptions about perfect competition and technological superiority by way of providing a summary. This leaves the argument somewhat unfinished and thus open to criticism.

the problem of justifying the hierarchical organisation of production is evaded by a slight of hand. At the same time, however, Marglin effectively adopts this point to argue that the role of the capitalist and of hierarchy in production is unrelated to improving technological efficiency in production. 'The social function of hierarchical work organization', he writes, 'is not technical efficiency, but accumulation'.[195] Here Marglin seems to divorce the drive for efficiency from the drive to accumulate. Are the two not intimately related?

The most controversial assertion from Marglin comes when he writes that it was 'technologically possible' for a 'workman, with his wife and children' to realise 'the advantages of dividing the overall production process into separate tasks' *without* specialisation. This proposition prompted a condescending rebuttal from none other than that fan of Prometheus, Professor Landes.[196] Landes proceeds to break down the complicated problem of efficiency and defend the reputation of the capitalist by way of a long digression on the commercial and organisational requirements that make the capitalist indispensible. Landes argues, persuasively, that the capitalist employer *does* contribute to overall technological efficiency, with much of this contribution taking place outside the sphere of production and more in the mode of marketing. The hypothetical question arising from Marglin's suggestion is: in the absence of the introduction of machinery, should it not have been possible for independent, artisanal labourers to produce the same amount of goods by applying the same amount of labour-time as under (non-mechanised) putting-out arrangements of factory conditions by adopting the same standards of labour discipline and the detailed division of labour? All things being equal, perhaps. But the likelihood of independently organised labourers adopting a labour process involving an intensification of labour that in some respects surpasses that of slavery is improbable in the extreme because independent labourers were not subject to the same pressures as capitalist employers, who were drawn into market competition with one another, such that they were compelled to transform and reorganise production to make it directly responsive to market imperatives.

---

195. Marglin 1974, p. 60.

196. Landes 1986, pp. 594–601. Notwithstanding the almost tongue-in-cheek tone of Landes's entire essay, his condescension shows itself in full at the conclusion, when he writes (p. 623): 'In the last analysis, then, I see Marglin's essays as exercises in optative economics, useful for the historical questions they raise, but directed primarily to true believers as a vision of what might have been and ought to be. His aim, implicit if not explicit, objective if not subjective, is to delegitimize the capitalist today . . .' And Landes's aim, no doubt, is to defend the capitalist today. By questioning the legitimacy of the capitalist and not the nature of capital as a social relation, Marglin was bound to provoke this kind of reaction. Nonetheless, Landes's parting shot by way of a charge of pure utopianism: 'But as every good economist knows, there is no such thing as a free utopia' is unjustified and undeserved.

There is no question that the adoption of machinery accelerated the further development of factories, for by accelerating the speed of physical production well beyond what human muscle power can achieve through the transmission of water, steam and later electrical power to the assembly line, machines have the capacity to increase productivity at a rate that simply cannot be achieved through organisational innovation alone. But within the capitalist employer's toolbox of cost-cutting, labour-saving measures, machinery formed only one (very important) component. The transformation of production along capitalist lines generally preceded the introduction of machinery and therefore was not a precondition necessary to making such a transformation possible.

If machinery was not absolutely required in order to revolutionise production along capitalist lines, an interesting question arises: could the factory system have continued to evolve without machinery? Despite his strenuous arguments against Marglin emphasising the indispensability of the capitalist's contributions to the transformation or production at the level of re-organising production and co-ordinating marketing, Landes delivers an emphatic: 'No, what made the factory successful in Britain was not the wish but the muscle: the machines and the engines. We do not have factories until these were available, because nothing less would have overcome the cost advantages of dispersed manufacture'.[197] Notably, however, Landes does not follow up this claim with any evidence to support it. A comment from the Committee on the Woollen Manufacture of England, writing in the early nineteenth century, similarly suggests that the factory system would have stagnated without rapid advances in machinery: 'the major part of the economic advantage of the factory springs from the use of machinery capable of performing very quickly, and the use of power which can make the machinery go at high speed. Until these elements of speed become possible, the factory system did not possess any very great advantage over the cottage industry'.[198]

Despite these assertions, there seems little question that Wedgwood's eighteenth-century works, which continue to this day to produce pottery using the same manual techniques and careful division of labour and oversight, produced pottery superior to that produced under the domestic system. So we see no reason why organisational innovation could not have continued to generate greater efficiency in production in the absence of machinery, since short of some sort of competitive pressure it would have continued to compel the transformation. The 'technological imperative' to introduce and to constantly revolutionise machinery only becomes an imperative once a particular type of machine, such as the spinning mule or the power-loom, is introduced into a particular line of production. Once that happens, other factories in the same line of production are

---

197. Landes 1986, pp. 606–7.
198. As quoted in Pollard 1965, p. 11.

hard-pressed to survive without adopting that machinery or, what is even more important, without keeping up with the latest innovations in machinery. It is competition which creates the imperative to constantly innovate in production in order to stay afloat financially. Once this logic of competition-driven innovation took hold of the factory, an imperative towards expansion was created, and this posed new challenges. As Pollard states: 'technology made it imperative, if progress was to continue, that business should grow beyond the size which a single proprietor or a small group of partners could directly overlook. Firms had to cope, and they learnt to do so'.[199] Certainly investment in machinery could contribute to the imperative to grow, but we must be clear that this formed only a part of the imperative to innovate.

Landes summarises what he sees as Marglin's 'main point . . . that the key to an understanding of technological choice is power, that is political power . . . Technology, he says, is not autonomous . . . and inexorable. Man makes technique and then chooses; or dictates what techniques to look for.'[200]

Landes agrees with this conclusion:

> up to a point. That point is, the choices are not accidental . . . there is an inherent logic to technological change, which is governed by the law (condition) of minimisation of inputs; or conversely, of maximisation of output. The aim is to get the most for the least.[201]

In this striking statement, which gives all the appearance of an argument rooted in technological determinism,[202] we see Landes treating the 'laws' of capitalism as eternal and inexorable, taking capitalist social relations for granted and therefore having nothing to say about how they came into existence. This is no less true in the case of Oliver Williamson, whose contribution to the discussion amounts to a firm defence of the transaction-cost hypothesis. Williamson argues that since it can be shown that the hierarchical organisation of production does serve to economise transaction costs (and thereby contribute to technological efficiency), 'an alternative explanation for the historical events to which Marglin . . . [refers] warrants serious consideration'.[203] Hierarchy, concludes Williamson, 'is ubiquitous within all organisations of any size . . . inveighing against hierarchy is rhetoric; both the logic of efficiency and the historical evidence disclose that non-hierarchical modes are mainly of ephemeral duration'.[204] Here, as in the case of Landes's sturdy defence of the substantive contributions of the capitalist,

199. Pollard 1965, p. 24.
200. Landes 1986, p. 620.
201. Ibid.
202. See Chapter Six, pp. 288–9.
203. Williamson 1980, p. 11.
204. Williamson 1980, p. 35.

Williamson's rather brutal defence of hierarchy and his straightforward conclusion that 'the organization of work is, predominantly, a transaction cost issue',[205] are somewhat inescapable, *so long as* we admit that while these assertions may be true of capitalism, they do not necessarily apply to non-capitalist modes of production.

To his credit, Landes is careful to acknowledge that Marglin bases his argument upon an understanding of efficiency measured not in cost savings, but in labour-time.[206] Noting this, we can draw out of Marglin's essay the implied argument that the partial/formal or direct/real control of the production process enjoyed by the capitalist employer could bring about cost savings while at the same time decreasing the efficiency of labour so far as the labourer is concerned. It is not only possible, but it is in fact central to Marx's critique of political economy, that the labourer may work longer hours in return for the same or less money as before, or may experience an intensification of his labour for a wage that is the same as it was before, or less. In other words, the capitalist factory may contribute nothing or may even reduce the efficiency of labour, if measured in terms of the remuneration for the duration and intensity of the work performed. In keeping with his engagement with neoclassical economics and its propensity to conceptualise economies in the aggregate, Marglin's second essay explores the question of savings and, building on the argument of the first essay – that accumulation, not efficiency, justifies capitalist hierarchy – elaborates that the function of hierarchy under capitalism is to perpetuate a high rate of capital formation among the rich and a correspondingly low rate of saving among the working class.[207] In short, underpinning Marglin's two essays is the question: efficiency for whom?

Returning to Marglin's problematic assertion that the role of the capitalist employer was superfluous, in a footnote Marglin further weakens his case on this point through the following concession: 'This is not to say that the putter-outer or "master manufacturer" never contributed anything of technological importance to the production process. But where the capitalist did contribute a useful technological innovation, he could effectively appropriate to himself the gains (of what in economic terms is a "public good") . . .'[208]

205. Ibid.
206. Landes 1986, p. 594.
207. Marglin 1975, pp. 20–37.
208. Marglin 1974, p. 71, n. 11. The quote continues: '. . . he could effectively appropriate to himself the gains (of what in economic terms is a "public good") by preventing others, particularly his workers, from learning and imitating his trade secrets. What better way to achieve secrecy than to insist that each worker know only a part of the whole?' This last observation touches on a key point in our investigation, however much it inverts the equation. For it was by keeping secret the 'mysteries of the trade' that guilds and their successor organisations maintained control over the labour process and excluded

This would seem to lay bare Marglin's true agenda, which is not actually to make the seemingly wrong-headed claim that the very individuals who organised production along capitalist lines contributed nothing to increasing the efficiency of the productive unit as a whole, but rather to argue that the efficiency gains that were and are achieved were and are effectively appropriated by the capitalist class, resulting in an *aggregate* functioning of the whole social system that could be characterised as massive *inefficiency*.[209]

Discipline and control

If we are satisfied that the re-organisation of production-relations was essential to the capitalist transformation of industry and that machinery was more effect than cause in this transformation, let us now ask the obverse to our rhetorical question of whether the factory system could have continued to evolve in the absence of machinery, which is to say: could the factory system have been driven by machinery without organisational innovation to facilitate it? By way of answering this question, we will point to the lengths to which all of the early factory masters had to go in their efforts to discipline the labour force, with or without machinery. Geraghty offers numerous examples of early industrialists who struggled to find ways to impose a régime of order and discipline in the factory and to instil new work habits in their workers. Like Wedgwood, the Peels invested a great deal of effort in recruiting and training new workers. They developed 'a "system of punctuality and regularity which approached the discipline of military drill". A portion of supervisors' pay depended on both quality and output, and a sort of internal labor market was established in which promotion within the business was emphasized, with especially talented managers offered partnerships'.[210]

The Midlands cotton factories adopted many of the labour-discipline techniques that had been employed in Lombe's original spinning mill: bells to ring at set intervals; set hours (and long hours) of work with few breaks; overseers who meted out punishments, including corporal punishment; rules; fines and forfeits and gated communities. At his Stockport mill, where Samuel Oldknow employed mule-spinners producing fine yarn for muslins, the emphasis was on the productivity of each spinner. Spinning records, warping books, cutting frames, books

---

unwanted 'forryns'. Seizing direct control of the labour process also meant seizing control over knowledge *of* the labour process, or in other words the ability to transmit the skill from one generation to the next.

209. As measured, for example, in terms of the balance of savings between the wealthy few and the masses.

210. Geraghty 2006, p. 13; quoting Chapman and Chassagne 1981, pp. 36–9.

for trimmers and a 'disgrace account' recorded workers' behaviour. At his larger Mellor mill using the water frame to produce coarser yarns, the emphasis was on team output and personal discipline. Oldknow set up an elaborate system of paper notes for paying his workers in truck. 'By his shop notes of 1792–3 he almost eliminated the use of money in his wages.'[211] Jedediah Strutt started out employing framework knitters producing hosiery on a decentralised basis. He established an employers' association to prosecute knitters who embezzled raw materials or damaged machinery. After breaking his partnership with Arkwright he retained two Arkwright-model mills at Belper and Milford. The list of forfeits under Strutt's system of discipline runs for several pages. Robert Owen, the famous factory owner at New Lanark, Scotland sought to apply communal pressure on the factory floor through snap checks and a colour-coded 'silent monitor' at each workstation; slacking, absenteeism, embezzlement and drunkenness were not tolerated. John Marshall of Leeds pioneered flax spinning in the late eighteenth century, introducing a hackling machine that fed directly into a spinning machine, making him the Arkwright of flax spinning. In his factories he recorded the productivity of each worker on cards placed on each machine. Punishments for absenteeism, tardiness, shirking or even talking included fines or dismissal. George and Samuel Cortauld operated a factory for throwing crape-silks at Braintree in Essex. Before adopting machinery they relied on outsourcing, and had a system of fines they imposed on outworkers who fell below their quotas, an example of discipline imposed prior to the adoption of factory methods.

The firm of McConnel and Kennedy was possibly the first to adopt mule-spinning. The mule required semi-skilled labour, and as it could be manually powered (normally requiring a man's strength), it could be housed in workshops, but was typically found in concentrated operations. The spinners were paid through piecework, and their wages were higher than other spinners, but were also far more vulnerable to price fluctuations.[212] McConnel and Kennedy had a 100 percent annual turnover rate among workers,[213] which underscores that this was not skilled labour as such. As the mule began to supersede the jenny and the water frame in spinning factories from the 1790s, a unique arrangement of subcontracting arose, whereby the employer and owner of the mule left the mule operators in charge of hiring, paying and overseeing the 'piecers', usually children, who assisted them.

> The activities of the overlookers were typically limited to recording output and waste, or helping the mule operators to adjust the machines when a different yarn count was to be produced. Mule-spinners were able to establish this craft

211. Fitton and Wadsworth 1958, p. 240.
212. Collier 1965, p. 4.
213. Bruland 1990, pp. 166–7.

> control over the production process due to the skill requirements of the job, and their ability to conceal their true effort levels by manipulating machine settings and speed of operation... The subcontracting system thus originated as a method of getting around this asymmetric information problem by making the supervisory function part of the mule-spinner's job.[214]

Not surprisingly, this arrangement was unsatisfactory for the owners, and in the 1810s McConnel and Kennedy tried to replace the spinners with female and child labour, but they were overcome by the strength of their former adult male spinners' local combination, gaining from them but one concession: that the spinners would set aside time each day for cleaning and maintaining the machine. In 1835, Richard Roberts invented the self-acting mule, 'the world's first complex automatic machine', which would render factory masters '"independent of the working spinners, whose combinations and stoppages of work have often been extremely annoying to the masters"'.[215] Bruland cites this an example of using machinery to 'innovate around' labour conflicts. In all of these examples, we note the persistence of the factory masters' efforts to find a way to gain full control of the labour process. Clearly factory discipline was not only an imperative, but was also very difficult to achieve. It was one thing to wrest control of the product from the workers; quite another to seize control of the labour process by abolishing the labourers' collective control, rooted in custom.[216] All of the examples above point to an ongoing struggle inside the workplace which took place on a trade-by-trade basis. Many of these struggles lasted well beyond the mid-nineteenth century.

Several other forms of disciplining workers were practiced. The employer could prosecute employees who ran away or took extended leave.[217] It is difficult to draw firm conclusions about corporal punishment, but it became the main complaint against factory owners.

> 'We beat only the lesser, up to thirteen or fourteen... we use a strap', stated Samuel Miller, manager of Wilson's mill in Nottingham, one of the few to admit to this to the Factory Commission. 'I prefer fining to beating, if it answers... [but] fining does not answer. It does not keep the boys at their work'.[218]

---

214. Geraghty 2006, pp. 18–19.
215. Bruland 1990, p. 167 citing Baines 1966, p. 208.
216. If the labour market was to operate, capitalism needed a mobile and wage-responsive workforce, 'and this meant an interim period in which old forms of control were eroded before newer and more appropriate forms of social and industrial control had fully emerged to take their place' (Rule 1992a, p. 159). It is extremely difficult to generalise about the beginning and end dates of this interim period, except perhaps on a trade-by-trade basis.
217. Fitton and Wadsworth 1958, p. 233.
218. Pollard 1965, p. 186.

Maintenance of low wages was another mechanism of discipline. Daniel Defoe, anticipating Keynes, supported high wages in the interests of greater consumption. But William Temple, the seventeenth-century statesman, believed that the only way to make the poor '"sober industrious and obedient"', was to remove the means of '"idleness and intemperance, such as high wages". The best goods were made when subsistence expensive and workers were "oblished to work more and debauch less"'. A century later, Arthur Young said 'great earnings' cause workers to work just four to five days of the week.[219] It was over the course of the eighteenth century that attitudes towards the working class hardened, and the intolerance for idleness grew ever stronger. Yet the practice of taking off a day of work on 'Saint Monday' persisted long into the nineteenth century wherever workers maintained customary control of the labour process. To the artisan, it was a time-honoured privilege. Moreover, while looms and spindles may have sat idle for an extra day, the spinner or weaver may have busied him or herself with personal matters or marketing activities.[220] Significantly, the field labourer had no Saint Monday, a reflection of the fact that he had already been proletarianised.[221]

The purpose of factory discipline, with all its rules, forfeits, fines, bells and various punishments was not merely to put a stop to longstanding, customary habits of work and behaviour. It was also intended to inculcate *new* habits and to impose what Thompson calls 'a new time-discipline ... In mature capitalist society all time must be consumed, marketed, put to use; it is offensive for the labour force merely to "pass the time"'.[222] Richard Whipp finds Thompson's sharp distinction between the 'task-orientation' perception of time in customary societies and the emphasis on 'time-measurement' under capitalism problematic, arguing that perceptions of time are more subjective than this formula allows and that 'time in relation to work has been continually shaped, defined and contested by workers and employees in the context of changing structural pressures contained within the spheres of production and social reproduction'.[223] Surely, Thompson would be the first to grant the working class its own subjective concepts of time, and it is clear that Thompson acknowledges the subjective nature of time when he writes: 'There is no way in which we can quantify the time-sense of one, or of a million, workers'.[224] For our purposes, what is useful

219. Rule 1992a, p. 18.

220. Thompson 1993, pp. 375–6. In Sheffield as late as 1874, 'it had become "a settled habit and custom" which the steel-mills themselves honoured'. Up until the eighteenth century, at least, it was not uncommon to take a Saint Tuesday as well.

221. Thompson 1993, p. 378.

222. Thompson 1993, pp. 394–5.

223. Whipp 1987, pp. 210–11.

224. Thompson 1993, p. 396.

is the contrast, the way in which one thing is being *substituted* for another: time-measurement for task-orientation. This speaks to an active process in which a new mode of producing things and a new labour process is supplanting the 'way things had been done' before.

The arrival of the power-loom

With the introduction of the mule, cotton spinning surged ahead. The situation of the previous generation, where there were too many weavers and not enough thread, was now reversed: high-quality thread was readily available and it was the weavers, still working on manually powered looms, who were in high demand. A 'fever of production' caught hold in the decade before 1785. Thousands of jennies were in operation and the weavers could not keep up the pace. '"The old loom-shops being insufficient, every lumber-room, even old barns, cart-houses and outbuildings of any description, were repaired, windows broke through the old blank walls, and all fitted up for loom-shops"'.[225] With the demand for weaving high, weavers' wages rose accordingly: 'So they gave themselves great airs, and could be seen parading about the streets, swinging their canes and with £5 notes stuck in their hatbands. They dressed like the middle class and would not admit workmen of other trades to the public houses they patronized'.[226]

The weaving trade naturally began to attract thousands of newcomers, and thus the greater part of the decline in weavers' wages that set in during the late 1790s can be attributed primarily to the increase in their number. It was around this time that the power-loom arrived, but its application to weaving on any significant scale was only about to begin.

Edmund Cartwright of Nottingham may be the most unlikely inventor amongst all those who contributed to the Industrial Revolution. He was the son of a Nottingham gentleman who prior to becoming an inventor had excelled in literature at Oxford. He had no background in mechanics. Whilst on holiday in the early 1780s at Matlock, near Arkwright's Cromford mills, Cartwright became engaged in an argument. He proposed that Arkwright should invent a weaving mill to end the bottleneck in weaving and maintain his leading edge, but his opponents said '"that the thing was impracticable"'.[227] Cartwright set out to prove them wrong. His first model was working by 1785, but it worked only poorly. His first factory, run on animal power, was set up in 1787 at Doncaster, South Yorkshire with 20 looms. His brother and radical reformer Major John

225. Mantoux 1961, p. 246, quoting Radcliffe 1974, p. 65.
226. Mantoux 1961, pp. 238–9.
227. Mantoux 1961, p. 241, quoting Cartwright.

Cartwright established the Revolution Mill at East Retford, Nottinghamshire in 1788. It was intended for weaving, but used for spinning worsted. Both mills failed. In 1791, with the backing of the Brothers Grimshaw, a 400-loom factory powered by steam was set up in Manchester. 'But the first machine had hardly been fitted when the weavers' violent hostility broke loose. The owners received threatening letters, and a month later the whole place was burnt to the ground'.[228] This was twenty years before the Luddites. Cartwright found himself in a situation similar to many previous inventors, 'struggling with merciless creditors and dishonest debtors', forced to sell his patents, and waging legal battles to maintain control over his next invention, a wool-combing machine.

By 1800, the demand for power-weaving had grown and resistance to it had weakened. The first revival of the power-loom took place in Glasgow, where one James Lewis Robinson set up two looms powered by none other than a newfoundland dog. Mr. Monteith of Pollockshows, financed again by the Brothers Grimshaw, set up a factory of 200 looms powered by steam. And an all-metal power-loom was introduced by Horrocks of Stockport in 1803. The power-loom now began to spread quickly. As the nineteenth century began, several million spindles were spinning cotton thread, while only a few hundred power-looms were in operation. Although the decline of domestic weaving was foretold in the form of the power-loom, falling wages increased the attractiveness of the domestic option for owners and suppliers against the cost of machinery, and thus paradoxically prolonged the survival of domestic weaving.[229] Over the next four decades, the wages of the weavers would fall from bringing them near middle-class prosperity to a level of grinding poverty. We shall see in the remaining chapters how the tragic plight of the weavers was a central tale within the larger narrative of the Industrial Revolution.[230]

The plight of the weavers was part of the paradox that Marx saw 'at the heart of industrial capitalism – the manufacture of the machines of large-scale factory industry was conducted by small-scale artisans; the source of the automatic power of the machine was lodged ultimately in the skill and craft of individual

228. Mantoux 1961, p. 242.

229. Mantoux (1961, p. 244) comments: 'More recently a repetition of the same phenomena has been witnessed in certain industries which have not been completely transformed by the industrial revolution. There lies the explanation of the survival of a belated technique in small domestic workshops, the last home of the sweating system. But the obstacles which machinery raised against its own progress could never be anything more than temporary'. However, so long as the prices of products produced in domestic or 'sweat' workshops can compete with the price of goods produced in factories, it can survive.

230. Mantoux 1961, pp. 242–3. For his part, Cartwright got a £10,000 grant from Parliament for his contribution to industry, and unlike Crompton, died in relative prosperity.

human effort'.[231] Only after 1850, Marx noted, did machines begin replacing manual labour in producing bobbins, shuttles and spindles.[232] It is no accident that societies of skilled labourers like the engineers and the masons are among the few which can trace a continuous history back to the Industrial Revolution or before. Their skills in building factories and assembling machines, whilst still manual labour, were and generally remain essential to the functions of industry.

Conclusion

In both the pottery works of Wedgwood and the factories of Arkwright, the labour process was no longer controlled by the workers themselves but was strictly dictated by the capitalist owner responding to market compulsions. Where Wedgwood and Arkwright might be seen as operating at different ends of a spectrum, in point of fact their operations were quite similar. Both were engaged in distinctively capitalist operations. Arkwright's machinery was used in effect to supplant the skilled aspect of his labourers and his factories thus requiring little training. Wedgwood achieved a similar result by recruiting and training his workforce to submit themselves to the intense discipline of a labour process characterised by the minute division of labour. Both applied discipline in the interest of imposing control over the labour process. Without the aid of machinery, Wedgwood had to go to greater lengths, but the objective of taking control of the labour process was largely achieved – largely, because as we have seen, even factory labourers continued to assert customary rights and practices, and to resist ceding full control of the labour process. Given that the majority of manufacturing was done not in factories but by independent domestic workers still very much operating under customary modes of labour regulation, it is not surprising that the ethos of customary labour practices would be carried over into the factory.

---

231. Berg 1994, p. 136. 'The distinction between these tools and the body proper of the machine, exists from their very birth; for they continue for the most part to be produced by handicraft, or by manufacture, and are afterwards fitted into the body of the machine, which is the product of machinery' (Marx 1906, p. 408). Here, Marx specifically identifies the tool aspect of the machine as that which continued to be made by hand, while the 'body of the machine' is assembled from elements produced with the aid of other machines. Presumably he means wooden beams and gears made on lathes and other machine tools, cast-iron parts made in a foundry, both of which are nonetheless labour-intensive and could pass as forms of manufacture or non-factory labour. Nonetheless, there is a sense of poetic irony in this identification of a process by which manual labourers continue to make with their hands the same specific tool parts that when 'fitted into the body of the machine' replace manual labour.

232. Marx 1906, p. 408, n. 1.

It would seem, then, that machinery was neither responsible for giving rise to capitalist industry nor absolutely necessary to a capitalist transformation of manufacturing. We have identified a number of clear advantages that machinery offered to the capitalist, such as reducing the value of labour-power, enhancing the production of surplus-value and of profits, offering (temporary) comparative advantage and perhaps most importantly, being easy to reproduce and thereby making possible the rapid construction of new machine-driven factories. Machines also did much of the work that in Wedgwood's operation had to be instilled through direct training and oversight, namely habituating the worker to performing simple, discrete operations or task-work. But machines also helped competitors to level the playing field.

There was much cruelty in the harsh exploitation of child labour and the deskilling of workers in general, robbing them of the chance to learn skills that would fetch better-paying jobs and it would be easy to see the capitalist as the embodiment of such cruelty. And while it is particularly true of these early masters that they themselves were the pioneers who actively promoted the realisation of a capitalist system of industry, it is important not to lose sight of the context in which the early capitalists were operating. First, as the guarantor of private property in general and specifically in land, the British state in general did little to inhibit the establishment of factories. As we saw in the previous chapter, since agrarian capitalism was generating a gulf between rich and poor – even wider perhaps than what had prevailed under feudalism – private entrepreneurs and statesmen saw workhouses and factories as fine solutions to the problem of 'what to do' with the ever-increasing numbers of paupers. Moreover, in the coming chapters, we will trace the steady erosion of the laws that respected the customs that had long regulated the labour process under worker control, had ensured the transmission of skill from one generation of workmen to the next and had provided protection from full exposure to the market. Secondly, we must not lose sight of the fact that Arkwright and Wedgwood had competitors. Even the early capitalists were compelled to organise the production process in such a manner that they could respond to market competition with greater efficiency. On this point it should be noted that while machinery may have enhanced the capitalist's ability to respond to changes in the market, a capitalist like Wedgwood also enjoyed the inverse advantage: in the absence of any machinery having yet been developed for his line of industry, his competitors also lacked such machines that could enhance their efficiency. The fact that Wedgwood's pottery works are still going strong while Arkwright's empire crumbled under the weight of enormous competition soon after his death would seem to attest to the significance of this point.

As stated in the Introduction, it is extremely common for capitalism to be treated as a form of society that merely had to be 'liberated' of its 'fetters' in order to develop and expand. Such a view creates the impression that where customary modes of regulating labour and the economy are concerned, their primary function is to stand in the way of capitalist progress and that, once removed, the natural unfolding of capitalist principles will occur. We have tried to stress throughout this work that, on the contrary, popular resistance to the elimination of customary tenures and customary control over the labour process in manufactures had to be suppressed in order for capitalism to advance. Even in terms of the origin of capitalism, the social relation of capital that emerged in English agriculture during the early modern period was a new type of social property-relation. In no other society prior to the Industrial Revolution do we find farmers engaging in systematic efforts to improve output in response to market imperatives as we do in agrarian-capitalist England. The continuing development of agrarian capitalism would require the invention or application of new methods, techniques and devices in agriculture. The same process would later play out in manufacturing. In this chapter, we have seen a number of examples of how, in the process of building an industrial-capitalist economy, one form had to be *replaced* with another: the worker's tools with the tool element of the machine, task-orientation with attentiveness to time-measurement, Saint Monday with clocking-in. What is critical is not so much what is the old that is being replaced but what is the new that is replacing the old, for *that* is what will shape the future.

Yet as we look back through time from the perspective of living in a capitalist society whose laws of motion are as familiar and as invisible to us as the air we breathe, it is that which is *strange* to us, the traditional, strange customs, the seemingly irrational actions of the Luddites seeking to check the progress of machinery, the notion on the part of workers that they have a *right* to take home (to 'embezzle') a share of the 'takings' of the production process, that attracts our attention. It is likely that this is why the notion that capitalism came into being simply by removing the customary 'fetters' that inhibited its otherwise inevitable development has survived. It may also be the reason that machine-breakers such as the Luddites get such a bad rap.

Machine-breakers may or may not have understood the broader implications of losing control over the labour process, of being 'de-skilled', but they clearly understood that those whose trades had already been converted had lost something that they too stood to lose. Not only were the bonds of solidarity among craft workers dissolved, but their bargaining position *vis-à-vis* the employer was thereby weakened as the experience of being a worker was atomised according to the individual contract between employer and worker. As we shall see, this also opened up new possibilities for workers. For as the bonds of solidarity within any given trade were weakened, the potential for solidarity *across* trades increased. In fact, this potential was already being anticipated early on in the tramping system and other forms of co-operation.

Bruland's idea that employers use machinery to 'innovate around' conflicts with labour captures only one side of the equation by suggesting that machinery helped rid the employer of the 'annoying' fact that mule-spinners exercised considerable control over the labour process. What this metaphor does not capture is the clear objective of the factory owner to *replace* the skill-based knowledge of the mule-spinner with his own complete control over the labour process. Likewise Geraghty, in drawing the conclusion that the factory system came into being through 'complementary' processes of both technological and organisational innovation, loses sight of the deeper question of why industrialists were driven to innovate in the first place until the end of his essay, when he asks several pertinent questions that take us to a deeper level of analysis:

> [W]hat was it about the Industrial Revolution that made manufacturers less willing to accept this cost [of corner-cutting and embezzlement by the worker]? Did improved machinery 'raise the bar' in terms of potential quality, so that corners cut were more costly? Did the doctoring of raw materials in the course of embezzlement impair machine performance? Did more intensive competition increase the importance of establishing a reputation for quality?[233]

Geraghty has effectively answered the first question with those that follow. The manufacturers of the Industrial Revolution were increasingly subject to the pressures of market competition which created an imperative to innovate in production, under pain of bankruptcy. It is not just that idleness and embezzlement stood in the way of industrial progress; far more significant is the fact that the old mode of producing was *insufficient* to keep the owner of the means of production in the competitive game. *This* is why it had to be not merely done away with, but replaced with something that could. We often speak of 'the market' or 'markets' as a universal constant, but with the development of land and labour markets in England under agrarian capitalism, the very nature of markets is transformed. Where previously markets were sites where the produce of land and labour are exchanged, now land and labour themselves are subsumed into the sphere of exchange as commodities. In effect, human society and the natural environment become mere factors in the 'rational' calculations of the capitalist. Polanyi recognised the ultimate fiction behind capital's claim to 'own' labour and the environment. But it is not pure fiction. And that is the significance of the factory owner taking full control over the labour process. It may come only at the end of a long process of gradual subsumption of the workforce to standards of discipline subversive to customary practices, but that final step, as it is reduplicated across all the various trades, is the threshold over which we cross into a new social order.

233. Geraghty 2007, p. 48.

Chapter Nine
Capital and Industry

> I sell here, sir, what all the world desires to have – power.
>
> Matthew Boulton[1]

There is much that could be read into this quote from Boulton. The steam engine provided a much improved source of motive power that would revolutionise industry and break the factory's dependence on the waterwheel. But it does not seem as if Boulton were talking only of power in the form of energy. Ownership of a steam engine also implies a good measure of social power. Does that power come from the machine or from the fact of property ownership? The answer we offer, as might be expected by now, is that since the purchase of a steam engine required capital and since the application of the steam engine took place within factories where we could define the relation between the owner and employee as a social relation of capital, then it follows that the power of capital precedes, and is a necessary precondition, to the application of the power of the steam engine.

In this chapter, we turn to the inquiry of the social property relationship that is capital. In the conclusion to Chapter Seven,[2] we argued that capitalism as an economic system involves more than policies promoting government *laissez-faire*; that what makes capitalism is the social relation of capital, which could be

1. Ubiquitous quote prominently on display at the London Science Museum, visit by Author, October 1997.

2. See Chapter Seven, p. 396.

said to exist when all the factors of production are in possession of the owner/employer who in response to competitive market pressures making the transformation of production an imperative is able to treat the factors of production as abstract inputs into the production process in pursuit of a profit that accrues solely to the owner of the means of production. In order to set the stage for the remaining chapters where we trace the long struggle between workers resisting the imposition of capital in manufactures, and capitalist employers seeking to impose it and turning to the state for assistance, this chapter will consider the emergence of the capitalist entrepreneur, the sources of investment capital and different understandings of the definition of capital. First, however, we shall continue our review of the different sectors of the British economy as they were transformed by the Industrial Revolution by turning to those lines of industry that were in general less well-developed along capitalist lines, starting with textiles other than cotton.

Woollens and worsted

Several factors explain why the woollen trades, long the staple of British exports, took a back seat to cotton at the end of the eighteenth century. The key difference between the cotton industry and the woollen and worsted industries was of course that the latter were regulated, while the former was not. While the guilds had long disappeared, workmen's combinations in the woollen trade: combers, carders, weavers, fullers and shearmen (or 'croppers' as they were known in West Riding) were well-organised in the late eighteenth century and could mount serious resistance to any perceived threats to their occupation. Solving the technical difficulties of adapting machinery to processing wool also proved difficult in certain lines of production, and this contributed to the delay in industrialising woollens. Woollen production involved no less than 34 steps between the sorting of the wool and the folding of the finished cloth.[3] The spinning jenny was adapted to spinning the shorter fibres of woollen cloth not long after its introduction. Being a machine that basically expanded the number of threads the spinner could spin at once; it was well-suited to the domestic pattern of work in Yorkshire and was quickly and easily adapted to household production. 'Far from favouring the progress of capitalism', writes Mantoux, 'the jenny seemed to have provided the small master with a new weapon with which to safeguard his independence. This was the secret of its success in a country which was, above all others, the home of small-scale industry'.[4] But the jenny was found unsuitable for spinning the long-fibred wool required for making worsted.[5]

---

3. See Baines 1859, p. 4.
4. Mantoux 1961, p. 264.
5. The making of wool cloth came in two primary forms: woollen and worsted. Woollen cloth is made from loosely spun short-fibred wool, which gives the final product

Each of the regions of woollen and worsted manufacture had developed a different form of organisation. Worsted, which takes its name from the town of Worstead, Norfolk, where it was produced as early as the thirteenth century, made steady progress from the late seventeenth century. In Norwich, the trade was less centralised and centred on the weaver. In the West of England production was centralised around the gentleman clothier. The same was true of the worsted trade in West Yorkshire, but in the woollen-producing region of West Yorkshire, as we have seen, the small clothier and the gentleman merchant were predominant. In Wales and Scotland it was the spinners who did the putting-out of any work they could not do themselves.

By the eighteenth century, rapid changes were taking place in the woollen and worsted trades. Norfolk had been complaining about competition from Yorkshire since the 1740s. After 1750, Yorkshire began to differentiate from the other regions.[6] Woollens and worsted from Yorkshire accounted for about a fifth of total exports in 1700, about half in 1770 and about 60 percent by 1800. This rise to pre-eminence is remarkable given that Yorkshire 'had few natural advantages. In transport, raw material supplies and the price of labour there were none'.[7] Roads were poor, wool was in short supply and after 1750 Yorkshire had no advantage in terms of labour costs. What Yorkshire did have were fast-flowing streams well-suited for turning water mills. Much of West Riding was still unenclosed in 1750 and this meant that workers in the widespread woollen and worsted trades also enjoyed access to land as a supplementary means of subsistence. This gave a strong underpinning to the artisanal structure of employment, where domestic manufacturing was predominant in the woollen trade. Production itself was mainly carried out by small master manufacturers who did the weaving and whose family carried out the spinning and the scribbling, though these could also be put out. Fullers cleaned and prepared the cloth before the small master took them to the cloth hall, where gentlemen merchants bought the unfinished cloth, put it out to finishers and then sent it to market. The system here was thus centred on the gentleman merchant, who by virtue of being unencumbered by the production process, did not have to share his profits with a 'factor' or middleman. This:

its high nap and bulkiness. The fuzzy, bulky woollen blanket provides a good example. Named after Englishman Thomas Blanquett, who apparently 'invented' it in the early fourteenth century, the woollen blanket became a staple product of the woollen industry of West Riding. Worsted cloth is instead made from long-fibred wool spun into yarn that is smooth and compacted, making for a napless, tightly woven cloth such as that used in suits. Arkwright had engaged in experiments to adapt the water frame to wool spinning, without success. See Chapman 1967, p. 102.

6. Jenkins and Ponting 1982, p. 2, and pp. 8–10.
7. Wilson 1973, pp. 235 and 248.

> benefited the entire industry for it ensured that the merchants could always pay on the nail for the cloths they bought in the cloth halls. Thus, the master clothier saw a quick return on his investment in wool and labour and was able to continue production requiring much lower levels of credit than a minor producer in the West of England would have needed. This rapid circulation of capital was without doubt a major reason for the vitality of the West Riding Wool industry.[8]

The advantages of better organisation and more rapid circulation of trade have been cited as perhaps the key factor to explain West Yorkshire's exceptional growth.[9] There is much more to the story than this, however. Broadly speaking, cloth production here was separated into two regions, both characterized by 'the ubiquity of freehold as opposed to copyhold tenure'.[10]

A worsted-producing region west of and including Bradford and Halifax was characterised by poor soils, prevalence of husbandry, early enclosures and proletarianisation, partible inheritance and, as noted, the dominance of the merchant-clothier engaged in putting-out operations. Here, enclosures of waste for sheep farming in the sixteenth and seventeenth centuries had weakened manorial custom and increased social polarisation between large freeholders and leaseholders on the one hand, and small cottagers and landless persons on the other. The increased market dependency of the majority of the population encouraged the spread of putting-out operations.

The woollen-producing region within and around Leeds, Huddersfield and Wakefield retained its 'mixed' character and was characterised by better soils, mixed farming, late enclosures, and the prevalence of the independent small clothier or an 'artisan' structure of work organisation.[11] The independent clothier of this region typically had 'a reasonable-sized farming plot and a fairly viable dual occupational structure which cushioned him against years of bad trade and supported the accumulation of capital'.[12] The Industrial Revolution played out quite differently in these two zones of production. What seems to have contributed to the exceptional pre-factory growth in output in both regions is a combination of high population growth combined with the exceptional prevalence of freehold-tenure, in turn facilitating the growth of towns under civic control which established their own national and international trading networks. In imitation of the

8. Randall 1991, p. 22.

9. What appears to account for Yorkshire's 'growing supremacy' is the active role played by merchants in towns such as Leeds and Wakefield versus the more passive or absentee role of London merchants monopolising and placing restrictions upon the Norwich trade (Wilson 1973, pp. 236–41).

10. Hudson 1981, pp. 34–53.

11. Hudson 1981, pp. 43–4; Hudson 1983, p. 125, see map.

12. Hudson 1986, p. 137.

growth of London, the towns of West Yorkshire increasingly operated as centres of credit and finance, and as wholesale markets for food from East Yorkshire, while the local population was increasingly dependent upon manufacturing as a source of income.[13] The greater reliance on foreign markets made the Yorkshire trade more vulnerable to serious fluctuations in demand.

While the woollen industry experienced developments in the direction of industrialisation before 1790, with nearly two-thirds of all woollen mills built in Yorkshire after a recession in the years 1778–81, the volume of trade tripled between 1783 and 1792.[14] Since the thirteenth century, fulling mills had provided a service to paying clothiers, who paid monopoly prices to the landlord.[15] The advent of the Industrial Revolution brought about a bottleneck in fulling, leading to the establishment of new fulling mills. There were 104 in Yorkshire in 1780 and 197 by 1800, by which time most fulling mills housed scribbling and carding machinery.[16] The slubbing billy and the scribbling engine, machines that prepared the fibres for carding, had come into general use in the 1780s. Slubbing was a step added by the introduction of mechanised scribbling and carding, and thus met little resistance as it did not displace an existing workforce. In the woollen-producing district of West Riding, the scribbling engine provided the main stimulus for the conversion of cornmills, the addition of such engines to fulling mills or the building of new mills. The number of new mills increased from 36 to 243 during the 1790s. Typically, new mills using scribbling engines were located alongside streams so that they could be run by water power. One such mill located alongside the river Aire was built by Joseph and John Wainwright at Armley Mill near Leeds.[17] As a result of this expansion, thousands of domestic scribblers were put out of work, their outsourcing trade being displaced. At the same time, the establishment of 'company mills' operating on a co-operative basis was seen. 'The company mill performed the fulling, scribbling, carding and slubbing processes; some included dyeing and some of the later ones also did rag grinding and spinning on commission'.[18] Quite unlike the initial effects of the Arkwright system on cotton spinning, the co-operative 'company mill' did little to disturb the structure of production in the central woollen region of West

13. Hudson 1989, p. 78.
14. Jenkins and Ponting 1982, p. 60.
15. Hudson 1986, p. 136.
16. Jenkins and Ponting 1982, pp. 26–7.
17. Jenkins 1973, pp. 253–6. There was a fulling mill on this site as early as 1590 known as Casson Mills, named after the owner Peter Casson. The mill would later be added to Benjamin Gott's industrial empire after 1805, and with Gott's new buildings would become the largest woollen mill in the world, conveniently located alongside the Leeds and Liverpool Canal. Armley Mills Museum, outside Leeds, visit by author, October 1997.
18. Hudson 1983, pp. 135–6.

Yorkshire.[19] Weaving and spinning continued to be conducted in domestic workshops and garrets, except where domestic workers were brought into mills where the employer could oversee the quantity and quality of their labour.

There were some larger mills that appeared in the region before 1800. Benjamin Gott and his partners would establish his mill at Bean Ing in 1792, which 'by the late 1790s had 38 scribbling and carding machines ... but the average number of machines per mill was probably nearer six to eight'.[20] Gott, who started out as a merchant, became Mayor of Leeds in 1799 and died a millionaire, was the exception to prove the rule. In the woollen districts of West Yorkshire, it was generally the small clothier who provided the basis for the slow but steady growth of the factory system by accumulating enough capital to purchase machinery to start a private spinning or weaving mill whilst being able to pay into the operations of a company mill for his 'outwork' and remain competitive.

In the worsted districts, the first worsted mill was started in 1787 at Addingham, and a small number of water-powered mills, some combining cotton-spinning, appeared in the early 1790s. As spinning mills, these were typically much larger than the woollen mills. Unlike the jenny, the water frame was found unsuitable for spinning the short-fibred wool required for woollens.[21] Once Arkwright's patents were invalidated, the field was open to other inventors to find a way to adapt the water frame. After a period of inactivity, John Coltman, a hosier from Leicester, motivated by a desire to overcome the bottleneck in worsted yarn for the new and expanding worsted hosiery trade, found a way to adapt the water frame to worsted spinning. As had taken place in cotton, the shortage of yarn was overcome and now there was a plentiful supply. Both the hosiery trade and hand-loom weaving were able to expand, except in Leicester.[22] 'By 1800, there were eighteen power-driven worsted spinning mills, four powered by steam, the rest by water power. Only after 1800, however, did investment in these factories pick up once the quality of the yarn improved to the point where these factories could compete with domestic production'.[23] The number of worsted mills increased from 22 to 54 between 1800 and 1815. As these operations were far from any source of coal and had a plentiful supply of water, the

19. Pollard 1965, p. 36.
20. Jenkins and Ponting 1982, p. 28.
21. See above, p. 462, n. 5.
22. Coltman's attempt to introduce his adapted frame to the works of master comber Joseph Whetstone met with demonstrations in Leicester, and 'the Corporation forbade them to operate the machine within fifty miles of the town'. Coltman relocated to Bromsgrove, Worcestershire to start another partnership that spun high quality worsted-yarn. Another successful attempt to spin high quality worsted was made by the partners Robert Davidson and John Hawksley who built Arnot Mill at Arnold, outside Notthingham (Jenkins and Ponting 1982, pp. 102–15).
23. Jenkins 1973, pp. 263–4.

steam engine would only make slow progress in the northwestern worsted districts of West Riding. Remoteness from the coal fields also delayed the advent of steam in Scotland, and it was 'almost unknown in Wales and the border counties of Northern England'.[24]

The West of England was slower still to take up the steam-driven factory. Coal here ran at four times the price it did in Yorkshire. Only one Boulton and Watt engine was in use by 1805 in Gloucestershire and Wiltshire. While the scribbling engine was accepted with a minimum of resistance in Gloucestershire, in parts of the West of England, the scribbling engine encountered prolonged resistance. There were violent protests against it in the Wiltshire towns of Trowbridge and Bradford-on-Avon in 1791 and 1792, and at Shepton Mallet, Somerset in 1794.[25]

Linen: the second-class textile

Undoubtedly 'the least known of the major English textile industries'[26] is linen. The reason for this is straightforward. English demand for linen was high, and this meant that a high volume of linen imports flowed into England, comprising about fifteen percent of total imports during the first half of the eighteenth century. 'Linen was, in fact, the most important manufactured import into pre-industrial England. Until the end of the eighteenth century imports of "linens" ranked second only to imported "groceries" in total value'.[27] Meanwhile, English production before the early eighteenth century was mostly local and not for export. Thus we have good records of the volume of linen imports and poor records of English production. The reason linen was in such high demand was that it served so many uses, from household wares such as napkins and bedding to industrial uses such as sacks, canvas and sailcloth. Linen production took place in all four corners of England: in eight counties of the South-West; on the Lancashire plain in the North-West; in Yorkshire, County Durham and Northumberland in the North-East; and in East Anglia. In Lancashire and Scotland, linen production served as the basis for the growth of the cotton industry, providing the warp to be combined with cotton weft for the making of fustian

24. Jenkins and Ponting 1982, pp. 52–6.
25. Randall 1991, pp. 80–2 and 94. In May 1791, a crowd of some five hundred workers stoned the house of a prominent clothier in Bradford-on-Avon. The clothier, Joseph Phelps, fired on the crowd, killing five protestors, including a boy, whereupon, 'his nerve broken, [he] handed over the [scribbling engine] to be ceremoniously burned on the bridge'. At Trowbridge, a crowd of the same size protested in September, and again in August 1792 when they joined with local miners and attacked both scribbling engines and shuttle-looms.
26. Harte 1973, p. 74.
27. Harte 1973, p. 75.

(jean, velvet, velveteen, corduroy, and so on), prior to the water frame and the making of cotton thread suitable for warp. By 1700, however, English linen was produced mainly for local consumption 'and was still, for the most part, bumpkin ware'.[28]

The story of the rise and fall of linen in the eighteenth century hinges on the imposition of duties on imports and later bounties to encourage exports. The goal of the British government was to reduce dependence upon foreign supplies of linen, and this included the encouragement of linen production in Scotland and Ireland to fill the gap. For both Scotland and Ireland, linen was the prime export product, and was second only to agriculture in numbers of workers employed. While Parliament had banned Irish woollen exports in 1699, Irish linen had been allowed to enter English markets duty-free since 1696, and shipping to the colonies was allowed after 1705. For Scotland, the Act of Union in 1707 brought an end to the payment of duties on linen exports to England. Scottish linen was of poor quality, and in 1727 an Act was passed ' "for the Better Regulation of Linen and Hempen Manufactures in Scotland", and henceforth linen that reached the required standards of quality, length and breadth was stamped'.[29] From 1743, a bounty was established to stimulate English exports. It was periodically allowed to lapse and then renewed, lasting until 1830. The bounty was also applied to Scottish linens. The impact of such subsidies was profound. It stimulated the rapid growth of linen production in England. Its effect on Scottish linen production can be demonstrated by the fact that when it was withdrawn, depression immediately set in.[30] By around 1780, English, Scottish and Irish exports of linen had all risen dramatically, but different regions suffered different fates.

In Ireland, the peak years of linen exports were 1780 to 1825. However, the expansion of Irish linen production contributed to rural impoverishment and the development of a disarticulated economy. High population growth meant an almost unlimited supply of cheap labour. The availability of marginal lands that could be put under flax also kept prices low. These factors meant that rural, mostly female spinners who increasingly depended upon flax spinning for their subsistence were stuck at a level of producing for bare subsistence, even as the linen industry in Ireland expanded rapidly.[31] In East Anglia, the last decades of the eighteenth century brought about a dramatic reversal of fortunes. The once wealthy region became one of the poorest regions in England as a result of

28. Wilson 1984, p. 197.

29. Evans 1985, p. 121.

30. Scottish output of coarse *Osnaburg* linen, an imitation of German Osnabrück linen, soared 'from just over 0.5 million yards in 1747 to 1.1 million in 1753 and 2.2 million yards in 1758, and became within a decade a major Scottish product and export commodity', but 'when the bounty was briefly withdrawn in the mid-1750's, production of Osnaburg fell by half' (Durie 1979, pp. 27 and 65).

31. Gray 2005, pp. 39–41 and pp. 149–50.

rising population and the decline of rural manufactures exacerbated by wartime-inflation. As rural poverty set in, the poor rates in East Anglia soared. The decline of linen manufacture here was part of an overall decline in rural manufactures in the face of these pressures and competition from the emerging factories in the North.[32] In Lancashire the cotton industry developed in large part as an outgrowth of the linen industry. '"The linen manufacture in Lancashire hath declined within these last few years", a leading London draper stated in 1786, "from the great increase of the cotton manufacture in that country"'.[33] Linen itself did undergo mechanisation, however. Edmund Cartwright attempted to apply the power-loom to weaving coarse linens in 1787. Flax spinning was first achieved by John Kendrew and John Porthouse in 1787. A year later, John Marshall of Leeds established the first of his two mills in the vicinity of Leeds for spinning flax. His became a major concern, involving intense factory discipline, and Leeds became the new centre of linen production in England. 'By 1790 the English linen industry was following its offspring cotton into a period in which the main factor in its development was to be technological change rather than protection'.[34] Other flax and linen mills followed Marshall's example, but the progress was not comparable to that of 'King Cotton'. As in Lancashire, the linen industry in Scotland provided the basis for the growth of the cotton industry. In the 1770s, linen manufacture was still the foremost industry in Scotland, but by the 1790s it had been overtaken.[35]

Iron and steam

We have already seen how within the mining and metal-working trades there existed a tension between, on the one hand, the high degree of proletarianisation of labour and the assertion of absolute property rights in land in the form of mines, and on the other hand, the continued use of such practices as subcontracting within mines and the putting-out of materials to domestic workshops, leaving the control of the production process in the hands of the workmen, thereby preserving certain customary forms of labour organisation. While skilled labourers in the textile trades, such as engineers, continued to assert a high degree of control over the labour process well into the nineteenth century, where unskilled labour was concerned the development of the factory system drew a fairly sharp contrast between a customary or traditional

32. Evans 1985, pp. 127–8 and p. 151.
33. Harte 1973, p. 112.
34. Ibid.
35. Durie 1979, p. 95 (see the chart on p. 23). This did not mean that linen production in Scotland declined. It continued to expand, but suffered serious setbacks followed by recoveries early on in the nineteenth century.

mode of production, in which the knowledge and control of the production process still belonged to the worker, and a capitalist mode of production in which they belonged to the owner of the means of production. With exceptions, there was no corresponding development within the mining and metal-working trades. This is largely due to the fact that, and as previously discussed, while the size of forges, furnaces, hammers and vats increased, the work remained predominately manual in nature. This is particularly true in mining, where the coal seam or rock continued to be worked with pick-axe and shovel. The key innovations here were process innovations, not product innovations. A deeper inquiry into the stages of capitalist development in this sphere would require detailed analysis of both larger and smaller firms, the various forms of labour practices that were applied and a study of how these evolved over time. As Ashton comments: 'These issues are under-studied'.[36]

Coal and iron were two metal/chemical industries that were closely interlinked by necessity, and the great metal-working industries grew up in districts where coal was abundant. The principal region of coal mining in England, as we know, was in the Northeast around Newcastle, where the Grand Lessees, Grand Allies and the Crowleys had enjoyed dominance. South Wales was also of great importance as a source of coal, and ironworking rose and fell beside it. A third region was the Scottish lowlands. And great metal-working industries grew up in and around Birmingham in the West Midlands. Iron production plays a peculiar role in the story of the Industrial Revolution. Without the expansion of iron production, the gears, wheels, levers, coils, shafts, pistons and rails that made up the machinery of the Industrial Revolution could not have been built. Yet iron production itself was not initially affected by the rapid development of new machinery that we commonly identify with the Industrial Revolution. In the eighteenth century the West Midlands became the heart of Britain's iron industry. Through this region flowed the River Severn and its tributaries, providing both water power and transport. Here, iron ore, coal and wood were abundant. Wherever iron, coal and streams could be found together, new metal-working industries were bound to appear, and along the Severn, scattered iron works were 'constantly exchang[ing] iron at different stages of production' along 'one of the busiest commercial waterways in Europe'.[37] Open fields persisted here, subject to piecemeal enclosure, and in some areas a division of labour arose between those who intensified their crop rotations, or specialised in raising carriage horses, and those who specialised in metalworking and began to keep fewer animals. In

36. Ashton 1963, p. 196.

37. 'Various subsidiary industries, earthenware potteries, glasshouses, tobacco pipe manufactories, tar distilleries, and salt works had grown up in the area' (Trinder 1974, p. 14).

both agriculture and manufacturing, economic exchanges had long been based on cash.

As we have seen,[38] it was also here in the West Midlands that the elder Darby made his discovery that would ultimately revolutionise British iron production; Abraham Darby II took over his father's works in 1730 and continued to perfect the method.[39] He introduced vertical integration into the works, signing the rights to lease coal mines in the surrounding region, and opening several new blast-furnaces.[40] Additionally, only the Darbys specialised in making cast-iron products on such a scale that they could make coking pay.[41] The Darbys' Coalbrookdale Works grew from a single blast-furnace started in 1702 to what one observer in 1768 described as '"that variety of horrors art has spread at the bottom"' of the otherwise romantic and beautiful valley that is Coalbrookdale, '"the noise of the forges, mills, etc., with all their vast machinery, the flames bursting from the furnaces with the burning of the coal and the smoak of the lime kilns, are altogether sublime..."'[42] The spread of coke-fired blast-furnaces in the West Midlands would revolutionise not only the local economy 'but also its settlement pattern and landscape'.[43] By the 1760s, 'there was already a large skilled workforce dependent on industry for a living, and a wide diffusion of manufacture, marketing and management'. Large landowners 'became much more active in developing the mineral assets of their estates', though they generally 'took no direct part in manufacturing industry',[44] but rather focused their efforts on facilitating their access to minerals by enclosing, and on canal building for the transportation of their minerals to more distant markets.

---

38. See Chapter Six, pp. 324 and 330.

39. Mantoux 1961, p. 291. Darby not only improved methods of smelting with coke, he made stronger, water-powered bellows and pioneered the use of reagents such as ore limestone.

40. 'In all nine blast furnaces were built within four miles of Coalbrookdale in the four years between 1755 and 1758' (Trinder 1974, p. 31).

41. Deane (1964, p. 13) found it odd that Darby would have brought his workmen with him from Bristol at a time when employers were seeking ways to circumvent the irritating craft restrictions that still held sway in older towns, but part of this story is that one of his workmen and fellow Quaker, John Thomas, had succeeded in casting bellied iron pots, for which Darby took out a patent in 1707. 'Thomas signed an agreement that he would only work for Darby in the casting of pots, and that he would not teach his secrets to anyone else for a period of three years' (Trinder 1974, p. 14). The Darbys also kept secret another patent of Abraham Darby, who had discovered in 1707 a superior way of making thin-walled castings poured straight from the foundry furnace, for which pig iron was more applicable than wrought iron.

42. Young 1785, p. 168, as cited in Hammond and Hammond 1974b, p. 137. Iron Bridge Gorge Museums and Blists Hill Open Air Museum, visit by author, November 1997.

43. Rowlands 1989, p. 124.

44. Rowlands 1989, pp. 121–3.

While John Wilkinson's father Isaac had been among those who set up a coke furnace modelled after the Darbys, his success was not that of an inventor but of the next generation of 'men quick to note new inventions, to realize their practical value and to use them for their own profit'.[45] He had his own warehouse in London, his own coalfields, foundries in South Wales and Indret, France, near Nantes and interests in Cornish tin mining, Wilkinson followed in the footsteps of the Crowleys and Darbys in pioneering vertical integration. He developed what Mantoux describes as a kind of 'industrial state, which [he] governed with a strong and autocratic hand. This State, more important and much richer than many Italian or German principalities, enjoyed a credit which they might well envy…'[46] His works made the first iron chairs, iron and lead pipes, and huge vats for the expanding breweries, and we have already mentioned his involvement in making iron bridges and barges.[47] Wilkinson relied heavily upon subcontracting to 'charter masters', or 'butties' who worked on monthly contracts and hired their own holers and pikemen, skilled labourers paid by the day, and bandsmen, casual workmen who were paid twice per week. Payment in credit notes redeemable only in a tommy shop was common, and the truck system was apparently so advanced under Wilkinson that like a German prince he coined his own money with his own image upon it. Workers were generally provided with on-site housing, coal to heat their homes and when the work was particularly strenuous, free ale at the brewhouse.[48] Apprenticeships were served, and according to Soldon 'the structure of the industry, involving as it did apprenticeships, resembled something of the form or spirit of the old guilds of ironmongers and founders'. But according to Pollard, under the butty system, the 'butty was a capitalist employer, whose profits depended on reducing the men's wages below the bargain price he made with the coal-owner'.[49] Here again, we must ask to what extent such ostensibly capitalist practices were balanced by the continuity of custom.

In the Scottish Lowlands, John Roebuck borrowed £12,000 to set up the first major Scottish ironworks along the Carron River in 1760, where Darby's method was introduced with dramatic success.[50] English workmen from the West Midlands

45. Mantoux 1961, p. 301. 'His major ironworks were centred in four main areas: around Wrexham (Bersham and Brymbo), near Broseley (Old Willey and New Willey), near Birmingham and Wolverhampton (Bradley and Bilston) and near Wellington (Hadley)' (Soldon 1998, p. 47).
46. Mantoux 1961, p. 301.
47. See Chapter Six, pp. 332–3.
48. Soldon 1998, p. 157.
49. Pollard 1965, p. 41.
50. Christie 1982, p. 11.

counties were brought North at considerable expense to take the skilled positions.[51] The firm was initially poorly managed, Roebuck, the principal, went bankrupt in 1773, having overextended himself in coal, salt and chemical operations. New management under Charles Gascoigne brought 'draconian rule' and a restoration of profitability, the profits accruing mainly to Gascoigne.[52] The Carron Company expanded rapidly in response to government contracts for the American War.

In 1750, the economic position of Wales in relation to England was similar to that of the colonies, being a supplier of raw wool, unfattened cattle and coal. Between 1700 and 1750, Wales produced just less than three per cent of Great Britain's coal output. Between 1750 and 1800, however, this figure leapt to over eleven percent. During the same period, North Wales saw the growth of copper mining, which failed soon thereafter. And over a longer period, iron mining and iron-making in South Wales saw a tremendous expansion, followed much later by contraction. Ultimately coal would endure as the primary industry of South Wales.

Initially, poor roads hindered the development of what was otherwise an obvious site for setting up ironworks. But in 1765, an iron ore merchant named Anthony Bacon and his partner William Brownrigg obtained a 99-year lease granting a concession on all mines within forty miles of Merthyr Tydfil, paying an annual rent of just £100. In 1771, the road to Myrthyr Tydfil was turnpiked, providing better access to Bacon's four ironworks: Cyfarthfa, Dowlais, Penydarren and Plymouth works. Richard Crawshay, the son of a Yorkshire farmer, could be said to have had incredible good fortune. He received a large dowry upon his marriage to Mary Bourne in 1763 and bought out Brownrigg's share in the works for £1504 in 1777. Then, in 1779–80 he won a state lottery and bought his way into Bacon's partnership. By his retirement in 1782, Bacon had grown rich from supplying government orders for artillery to be used in the American War.[53]

The inventor Henry Cort also set up iron works, in the hopes of supplying the Admiralty. As a former agent of the Royal Navy, he had grown concerned about the deficit in the quality of English iron against that of Sweden or Russia. Leaving his post in 1775, he set up an iron works at Fontley, Hampshire, and in 1783 received his first patent on the puddling process.[54] Following the all too familiar

---

51. Hammond and Hammond 1974b, p. 148. Roebuck may be better remembered for underwriting the research of a still unknown engineer and inventor by the name of James Watt during the period of his experiments leading to a patent (see p. 473 below).

52. Pollard 1965, p. 20.

53. Addis 1957, pp. 1–7.

54. Patent No. 1420, 13 February 1784 (Mantoux 1961, p. 294, n. 1). We have already reviewed the steps leading to the development of potting, puddling and rolling. See Chapter Six, pp. 333–4.

pattern of other inventors, Cort was unable to bring his invention to commercial success, being ruined by the calling in of his debt upon the death of his financier. But Richard Crawshay and Samuel Homfray, who had taken over Bacon's Penydarren works 'were the first ironmasters to use the puddling process, and they grew rich while Cort was ruined'.[55] In 1787, the Cyfarthfa works was only producing ten tons of bar iron per week. Soon after, a meeting with Richard Cort led Crawshay to adopt the puddling and rolling method and output leapt to two hundred tons per week. The puddling process removed the barriers to integration in the iron industry, allowing for forges and furnaces to be integrated into a single works, and facilitating a rapid growth in output and the building of new ironworks.[56] Cort's primary goal, improving the quality of English iron, was also achieved. 'Iron, produced by Cort's process, took the place of wood in shafts, gears, wheels, and machines, and this, also, powerfully aided the growth of scale of the factory or works'.[57] In 1794, Crawshay bought the entire rights to the Cyfarthfa Ironworks. Like Wilkinson, Crawshay 'founded a dynasty of ironmasters', earning him the moniker 'the Iron King'.

With the advent of puddling and rolling, a new division of labour appeared at the foundries and forges. Charcoal burners, keepers, bridge servers and fillers tended the furnace, typically numbering seven men in all, with women and children employed to sort and prepare the ore. Making bar iron at the forges required skilled finers and a master hammerman, who served in the role of foreman and was among the 'aristocracy of labour'.[58] To become a 'Master of the Bloom' required a three to seven years' apprenticeship. Therefore, as we ought to expect, where we find skilled labour we again find the customary mode of labour organisation: masters and apprentices, no doubt with the accompanying notion of this being an 'honourable trade'. Since making pig iron at the foundries involved mostly unskilled labour, the condition of the workers was probably proletarian in character.[59] But given the higher degree of necessary skill and the risk involved, metal-workers tended to make wages considerably higher than farm-workers or miners.

---

55. Mantoux 1961, p. 302.
56. Owen 1975, p. 309.
57. Ashton 1964, p. 117.
58. Ashton 1963, p. 191.
59. A third site of production, aside from foundries and forges, was a slitting mill, where bar iron was cut up for the making of nails. 'The slitting wheel, which was worked by water, broke or cut up the cold bar into short lengths; these lengths were then heated and when hot put under the rollers, also worked by water, and roller flat. Finally they were put through cutters of different sizes… When it left the slitting and rolling mills the iron was ready for the smith… In the slitting and rolling mills a different set of workers [than at the forge] were employed, but not much is known of their circumstances' (Hammond and Hammond 1974b, pp. 133–4).

As with the Potteries in Staffordshire, the small metals and 'toys' trades in Birmingham were seeing the development of an increasingly detailed division of labour: 'each branch was carried on by a small master with possibly half-a-dozen workmen on piecework and without the aid of any except muscular power. The work was done to the order of the merchants who secured and distributed the orders [and] organized the selling and export of the products'.[60]

For well over a century, Birmingham had been a centre for making hardware and 'toys' including '[b]uttons, buckles, watch-chains, chatelaines, snuff boxes, corkscrews, sugar nippers' and sword hilts.[61] Birmingham offered several attractions to manufacturers. There were plenty of forests nearby. Like Manchester, it was an unincorporated and therefore unregulated town. And after the Restoration, Birmingham, which had solidly backed Parliament in the Civil War, attracted many Dissenters who brought with them new energies, talents and technical knowledge.[62] By the latter half of the eighteenth century, a number of Birmingham industrialists, including Henry Clay, John Taylor, Sampson Lloyd, Samuel Garbett, John Gimblett and Matthew Boulton, employed large numbers of workers. Clay reportedly employed three hundred workers. Taylor's workforce apparently rose from five hundred in 1755 to between six hundred and seven hundred in 1762. It is likely that these numbers include a large proportion of outworkers. It appears that Taylor's works, while never making the full transition from workshop to factory,[63] took the division of labour within the workshop to its logical extreme. Button-making, for example, involved seventy separate processes. 'Lady Shelburne called him the "principal" manufacturer in Birmingham in 1766 . . . When he died in 1775 his estate was valued at £200,000'.[64]

When John Boulton died in 1759, he left to his son Matthew a small workshop at Snow Hill that had been engaged in making buttons and small metal wares. Three years earlier Matthew Boulton married his distant cousin Mary Robinson, an heiress to a large fortune. Both Mary Robinson's father and John Taylor bore the title of 'esquire'. 'The word "esquire" in the middle of the eighteenth century still had some significance. It was only given to men who were members of the lesser gentry or who came of well-established middle-class families'.[65] Having married into the gentry, Boulton 'could easily have settled down as a country gentleman', writes Mantoux but 'he loved industry'.[66] One assumes the same holds for John Taylor. The question is: what was the attraction? One suggestion is that they

60. Dickinson 1937, p. 41.
61. Gale 1952, p. 35.
62. Goodison 1974, p. 36.
63. Pollard 1965, p. 82.
64. Goodison 1971, p. 5.
65. Mantoux 1961, p. 325, n. 6.
66. Mantoux 1961, pp. 325–6.

found the increasingly competitive nature of the Birmingham small metal wares trades alluring, particularly when both men enjoyed a distinctive advantage in the form of private wealth drawn from estates. We can only imagine how smaller masters in Birmingham viewed Boulton's arrogance when he declared that it was his task to cleanse 'Birmingham's bad reputation' by insisting upon only 'the best materials and the most skilled workmen'.[67] Boulton conceived of using his wife's wealth to build a large manufactory in which he could bring all the operations of the trade together under one roof and supervise the works, thereby ensuring a high standard of quality, reducing his overheads, conducting his own warehousing and merchandising and enjoying the profits of both merchant and manufacturer. He located a suitable plot of land at Handsworth Heath along the road to Wolverhampton, where he tore down a water-powered metal-rolling mill and at a cost of £10,000 erected the Soho Manufactory between 1759 and 1766. The work was sub-divided into separate rooms, with foremen or subcontractors supervising a workforce comprising mostly women and children working 'primitive' and largely hand-driven machinery supplemented by power transmitted by belts and pulleys from a waterwheel, including lathes, stamps, presses, dies or polishers replacing 'simplified tasks'.[68] As the scale of the operation and the range of items increased – the workforce approached a thousand by 1770 – the division of labour was extended and co-operation between departments allowed for innovation and the creation of novel items of manufacture. Boulton's works is called a manufactory and not a factory because unlike a factory, it was not engaged in mass-producing standard products, but rather in individually crafting pieces of high-quality artisanship in the same manner as his close colleague Josiah Wedgwood produced pottery.[69]

In many ways, Boulton's career parallels that of Wedgwood. Out of the small-metals trade, Boulton and his partner John Fothergill ventured into the high-end market of metal wares, such as gold-plated bronze, also known as 'ormolu'. They soon earned 'a name for quality which was second to none' and were thus 'widely patronized by the aristocracies of both England and Europe'.'[70] Just as Wedgwood needed to sell his 'useful ware',[71] Boulton and Fothergill relied on the small metal wares trade to sustain the scale of the operation, their highly sought ormolu and other ornaments being insufficient for this purpose. Fothergill's role as merchant was to keep the works informed of changing tastes and styles in foreign and domestic markets. Like Wedgwood, Boulton hired skilled artists and

---

67. Ibid.
68. Pollard 1965, p. 81.
69. Berg 1985, p. 302.
70. Goodison 1974, p. 1.
71. See above, Chapter Eight, p. 409, n. 29.

decorators that were beyond the reach of most of his competitors. Competition for skilled craftsmen amongst the large employers was intense, especially between Taylor and Boulton. Poaching was not uncommon.[72]

In the midst of a trade that would continue to be dominated by workshops for another century and more, the Soho Manufactory was an oddity. Boulton's pioneering efforts in vertical integration and organisational innovation were undoubtedly informed by the methods of Crowley and Wedgwood. In its early days, 'Soho alone... "combined, in a factory, all classes of workmen engaged in the manufacture of its various products; and in the owner of this factory was vested the technical as well as the entire economic control over his employees" '.[73] Yet this control had limits, and the almost direct transference of independent workmen into such a factory-style setting is surely the cause for some of the management problems which were faced. 'Never had the two systems of "manufacture" and factory so nearly approximated', writes Mantoux, 'and never had the distinction between the two [been] harder to make without becoming involved in subtleties and arbitrary distinctions'.[74] The manufactory employed over six hundred workers by 1762 and possibly over a thousand by 1772, with a turnover that rose from £7,000 in 1763 to £30,000 by 1767.[75] In a works of this scale, subcontracting and contractors profiteering by squeezing wages was likely to be common. Boulton rejected piecework, however, paying his unskilled workers between two and twenty shillings per week and his department heads the unheard of sum of £9 per week.[76] An Insurance Society was established for the workers, offering sickness and funeral benefits. Rule III of the rulebook reads: 'Each member shall pay to the treasure box agreeable to the table following, which is divided into eight parts, viz. the member who is set down at two shillings and sixpence per week, shall pay one halfpenny per week; five shillings, one penny...' etc.[77] Here, we see that the safe box of the friendly society was also directly adapted. Like Arkwright and Strutt, Boulton hosted communal events for his workers, such as a ball attended by seven hundred people upon his son's coming of age.[78] With benefits and high wages, Boulton was able to fulfil his

72. 'Set as he was against the use of London goldsmiths', Boulton 'nevertheless had to lure silversmiths, chasers, braziers, coppersmiths – all manner of craftsmen – away from their original master' (Delieb 1971, p. 37).
73. Roll 2013, p. 5.
74. Mantoux 1961, p. 327.
75. Goodison 1971, p. 14.
76. Gale 1952, p. 25; Delieb 1971, p. 39.
77. As quoted in Delieb 1971, p. 38.
78. 'Communal feasts, as part of the old pattern of leisure activities, were to be throttled together with other relics of an older morality' (Pollard 1965, p. 183). Lombe, Wedgwood, Arkwright and Boulton all struggled with and to some extent accommodated lingering expectations of custom and paternal benevolence.

quest of attracting the best talent, and with its high standards of quality and workmanship, Soho became a kind of private academy for skilled engineers and craftsmen.[79] But relatively high wages also cut into profits and invited abuse. Like Wedgwood, when Boulton was away on business, this invited indiscipline, misunderstandings and delays.[80] Boulton demonstrated an idealism that, unlike most manufacturers of his time, could only have come from someone whose personal financial security was guaranteed.[81] Boulton's fame and fortune as an industrialist were assured, however, by his partnership with James Watt.

Born in Greencock, Scotland, Watt attended the University of Glasgow where he became interested in steam engines. In 1765, he conceived of the separate condenser engine, and it was on his way to the patent office in 1768 that he met Matthew Boulton. The meeting was followed up by a letter from Boulton in which he wrote: 'I was excited by two motives to offer your assistance, which were the love of you and love of a money-getting ingenious project. Engine would require money, very accurate workmanship...'[82] Since Watt's backer, John Roebuck, was in financial straits,[83] Boulton was able to acquire Roebuck's share in Watt's project in return for the cancellation of a debt Roebuck owed to Boulton. A patent was granted in 1769 and extended in 1775. After initial difficulties in perfecting a marketable product, the first engine began operating at a colliery in Tipton, a few miles from Soho, in 1776. John Wilkinson ordered the second engine to power a bellows for one of his furnaces at his Willey ironworks. Two engines were installed at the Darbys' Ketley works in 1778 and 1780. In 1781 the old Newcomen engine at Coalbrookdale was replaced and the new Boulton and Watt engine was named 'Resolution'.[84] Richard Arkwright was the

---

79. Among the skilled craftsmen whom Boulton attracted to work at Soho was John Wyatt, the same who had partnered with Lewis Paul in patenting the first cotton-spinning machine (see Chapter Seven, p. 387–91). At Soho, Wyatt and his son Charles introduced the wood screw, 'a double-acting lathe with lever-motion, and tools for cutting pearl buttons and button-moulds' (Delieb 1971, p. 116). The son of John Gimblett (one of Boulton's competitors who had sought to undercut Boulton's prices) later found himself working at Soho as an associate partner (Delieb 1971, p. 36).

80. James Kier, Lunar Society member of Edinburgh, was asked in 1778 to manage the manufactory, and declined, but he did send 'two critical letters, which revealed some of the malpractices of the workmen, and the mismanagement which took place when Boulton was away on his travels... much silver is at the mercy of the workmen' (Delieb 1971, p. 112). Fothergill was a poor manager, and when John Scale was hired to oversee in Boulton's absence, he found himself overwhelmed. This led to the consideration of paying in piecework, common among other manufacturers (Goodison 1974, p. 17).

81. Boulton was beset with a constant shortage of capital, and this may have had something to do with his policy of allowing his customers six months to pay, whilst paying his own suppliers inside of six weeks (Goodison 1974, pp. 17–18).

82. Letter from Boulton to Watt, 7 February 1769 (from display at Soho House, Birmingham, visit by author, 29 October 1997).

83. See below, p. 487, n. 122.

84. Trinder 1974, p. 39.

first cotton spinner to inquire about the expense of a steam-engine, visiting Soho in 1777, but the first factory master to purchase one was Peter Drinkwater of Manchester in 1789. Arkwright bought his a year later for his Nottingham mill.[85] Under their patent, Boulton and Watt required payment of a third of the savings in fuel that the installation of a separate condenser engine produced. This demonstrates how conscious they were of the incentive for large manufacturers to reduce costs of production.[86] Marx credited Watt's genius in recognising that his invention, unlike most others, was built not for a specific purpose, but had universal applicability.[87]

The story of the spread of steam-power is well-known. Boulton's interest in buckles, buttons and ormolu soon flagged in the face of the profit potential of steam. Parts of his manufactory were converted to the making of components for 'Boulton and Watt' engines: 'As the end of the patent period approached, however, the firm decided to become a large-scale producer of complete steam engines, and erected in 1795 the "Soho Foundry" for this purpose ... Among its outstanding innovations were careful and most elaborate costing, planning of the flow of production and of products, standardization of components and processes, and subdivision of labour among the many skills, some of which the firm itself had introduced and developed'.[88]

It was here that 'the technical as well as the entire economic control [of the owner] over his employees' was achieved, for at the foundry there were no centuries-old craft traditions to negotiate with. Like Wedgwood, Boulton could recruit '"plain country lades", waifs, and orphans'[89] and train them up from scratch. Thus a more perfect commodification of labour could be achieved at the foundry. At the same time, however, by training skilled engineers, Boulton and Watt contributed to the emergence of a new stratum of skilled craftsmen.

Mining

The eighteenth century saw the growth of mining and metallurgical operations of considerable scale in Britain and Ireland. A 'promotion mania' in the 1690s had brought forth a number of large concerns, some of which succeeded, some of which failed almost immediately.[90] The Mine Adventurers of England, having taken control of some silver mines and smelting works in Cardiganshire in 1698,

85. Fitton 1989, p. 63.
86. Gale 1952, pp. 13–15.
87. Marx 1906, p. 412.
88. Pollard 1965, p. 79.
89. Delieb 1971, p. 39, quoting Boulton in a letter to James Adams.
90. Pollard 1965, pp. 17–21.

was a fraud that offered lottery tickets for shares. The English Copper Company was founded in 1691 and amalgamated with other concerns in 1720. A successful operation, it survived into the nineteenth century. Notable copper mines were located in Cornwall, Cumberland, at Anglesey where a deposit of rich copper ore was discovered at Parys Mountain in 1768 and at Ecton Hill in Staffordshire, which by 1790 was the largest single source of copper in Britain, but soon ran dry. Copper smelting and brass works gave rise to large operations, such as the Warmley Company of Gloucestershire, employing 2,000 workers in 1746. 'It was in the copper smelting industry and the related brassworks that some of the largest firms and some of the most interesting managerial experiences were developed'.[91] By 1746, the Warmley Company of William Champion, Thomas Goldney and Sampson Lloyd employed two thousand workers at Bristol in brass works. By 1765, it was bankrupt and in 1767, with a capital of two hundred thousand pounds, it was sold to the British Brass Company. The 'copper king' Thomas Williams, a lawyer who leveraged his way into the position of being a managing partner of the Parys Mine Company, went onto acquire copper works in Cornwall and Lancashire, and enjoyed a partnership with John Wilkinson.

Brass had been introduced in Britain around the time of the Restoration, and 'greatly extended the scope of the Birmingham metal-working trades'.[92] It was another home industry that enjoyed protection. Bristol and Swansea were centres for copper and zinc working and brass works, but the late eighteenth century saw several large operations rise up in Birmingham: the Birmingham Brass Company (1780), the Birmingham Mining and Manufacturing Company (1790) and the Rose Copper Company (1793).

In lead mining, the London (Quaker) Lead Company, amalgamated in 1704 from three companies that had appeared in the promotion mania of the 1690s, 'the company was mining and smelting lead, over its long history, in Wales, Derbyshire, Ireland, Scotland, the Isle of Man, and the North of England, and survived until 1905'.[93] Despite a slow-down in activity after the death or retirement of the first generation of owners around 1730, the company revived after 1792 thanks in part at least to 'its carefully-thought-out training and promotion programme, and its social welfare schemes for workers coupled with an unusually tight discipline over them'.[94] Lead mining in Derbyshire around Wirksworth dates to the Roman era. In the eighteenth century most mines in Derbyshire were small, but in the third quarter of the century the largest, the Gregory mine,

91. Pollard 1965, pp. 17–24 and 61–84 is used as the source in the foregoing section on mining and metallurgy, except where noted.
92. Goodison 1974, p. 3.
93. Pollard 1965, p. 17.
94. Pollard 1965, p. 18.

averaged 1,500 tons per annum. By the fourth quarter, lead mining here was in full decline just as the textile factories were arriving.

Tin mining in Cornwall has a long history, and larger works appeared early. In the tin and copper mines, many works adopted the 'cost-book' system under which the partners met quarterly to divide up the profits, leaving little capital for re-investment. Depression in the trade and drainage problems at the turn of the seventeenth century had called out for a solution as 'one pit after another was being drowned out and the future of the industry seemed very precarious'.[95] John Costar 'successfully used a single large waterwheel to drain some of the deeper mines' in 1710. William Lemon achieved his success at Wheal Fortune Mine after applying a Newcomen engine to the works in 1720.[96]

At least two other minerals in England were mined on a scale involving considerable numbers of workers. Slate quarries were worked in Wales and Cumbria, with works of up to a thousand men seen as early as 1782. Salt had been mined in Cheshire in Roman times and was rediscovered in 1657. By 1675, 26,927 tons of salt were manufactured in Cheshire annually. A second centre of salt manufacture was in Durham at Shields.[97] Salt-works employed far fewer men than in other mining operations. In Scotland, sea salt was collected along the northeast and northwest coasts.

From 1765 on, writes Pollard, 'the northern coal-mines could be said to have become large industrial units of recognizably modern type'.[98] After some two decades of virtually unregulated coal trading, the cartel, sometimes known as 'The Limitation of the Vend', sought to control coal prices by limiting the output of its members. This practice would continue on and off until 1845.[99] These larger owners also sought to control the trade by purchasing most of the mines less than 60 fathoms deep. Beginning in 1778, interlopers were sinking shafts of one hundred fathoms and more, weakening the control of the 'Grand Alliance', and by the 1820s and 1830s the trade was 'profitable, progressive and booming'.[100] The Alliance probably never controlled more than sixty per cent of the mines, and the control of the larger owners progressively weakened over time.[101] Alongside the continuation of this ongoing attempt at monopoly was the continuation of the venerable practice of requiring colliers to agree to annual 'bindings', annually-negotiated contracts under which the collier and his family were

95. Pollard 1965, p. 34.
96. Lord 1966, p. 38.
97. Lord 1966, p. 49.
98. Pollard 1965, pp. 63–4.
99. Sweezy 1938, pp. 36–7. The 'Grand Alliance' was also still referred to in the late eighteenth century.
100. Pollard 1965, pp. 62–3.
101. Robinson 1941, pp. 103–4.

obligated to work the mines for the duration of the bond, in return for housing, steady employment and the guarantee that sons would be brought up in the trade. This security of employment encouraged high birth rates and a steady supply of labour for the owners. It was also the basis for a unique culture that was hostile to outsiders and laid a strong foundation for trade union activity in the nineteenth century.[102]

The coal owners in Cumberland enjoyed a 'monopolistically controlled market in Ireland'[103] and the mines were quite advanced by the early eighteenth century, turning out thirty-eight thousand tons by 1709. By 1813 there were twenty miles of underground railroads, six hundred employees and a thousand horses at work. Subcontracting was most prevalent in the Midlands and South Wales in the form of the 'butty' system, which came in the form of the 'little butty' in which the subcontractor worked alongside his employees and the 'big butty' in which he merely negotiated prices, provided tools and equipment and pocketed about a quarter of their earnings. The most extraordinary growth in coal mining was in South Wales, which contributed little to British output in 1760, but represented 42 percent of British output by 1830. In that year, fifteen firms exceeded 10,000 tons in annual output, and twelve of these were in South Wales. In Yorkshire, Nottinghamshire, Derbyshire and Staffordshire the coal mines were small by comparison. In the Forest of Dean, Gloucestershire, miners enjoyed common rights to cut wood and graze their beasts at least until 1777, when the Mine Law Court was abolished, sparking six decades of strife during which miners fought to defend their customary rights. Here then we find another direct parallel between agrarian enclosures and what we have suggested could be called 'coal enclosures'.[104] The West Lancashire collieries were worked by few hands, being subject to extreme fluctuations in output and in wages. Colliers worked in family groups and the high percentage of women and girls employed astonished observers. After 1730, output grew rapidly, as did population growth among colliers. The Worsley colliery had 331 colliers working underground in 1783, and it was of course here that miles of underground canals were dug. The

102. Langton 2000, p. 38. The foregoing short section on coal is drawn from Langton 2000, pp. 36–44, except as noted.

103. Pollard 1965, p. 64. Cumbria was a poor agricultural region with similarities to South Wales. It had been a mining region since at least the sixteenth century. Iron, copper, lead and slate were all mined here. As the manorial courts declined in the eighteenth century, a variety of manufacturing and other by-employments arose, including dairying, gunpowder manufacture, paper making, and from the late eighteenth century, bobbin manufacturing. Despite considerable growth of iron mining and smelting in Cumbria through the eighteenth century, along with the growth of these other lines of manufacturing and an emerging middle class, the iron industry was ultimately destined to contract along with the rest of the economy as external competition undercut the region's economy (Marshall 1989, pp. 133–5, 149).

104. See Chapter One, p. 86.

structure of mining resembled the domestic system in textiles and probably discouraged innovation.

The most striking continuation of what was not only a customary but an effectively *feudal* mode of labour organisation was in the coal mines of Scotland. Here colliery serfdom was the rule. The collier and his family were bound to the mine owned by the lord. 'Whole families were valued, along with horses and equipment, in inventories and deeds of sale'.[105] Prevalent in Lothian and Fife, colliery serfdom lasted until 1799, being phased out by successive pieces of legislation.

In general, the insularity of coal mining, with kinship systems controlling recruitment and its high rates of endogamy gave rise to distinctive cultures that varied extremely from one region to another. As a production process with limited options for close supervision, and no prospects of replacing manual labour with large-scale mechanisation, the direct control of the labour process remained in the hands of the colliers. Owners thus employed ongoing 'extra-economic' measures meant to guarantee labour supplies, whilst also engaging in contracting, subcontracting and negotiation which anticipated fully free labour markets. Under the practice of binding in the Northeast, for example, there were two weeks out of the year where such contracts were renegotiated and rates of relocation in and out of mines by workers was high. Overall, this meant relatively high wages for colliers, led by skilled labourers who directly worked the seams (such as the 'pikemen' in the West Midlands). Their sons and grandsons would lead the great strikes to come a half century later.

Beer, paper and chemicals

The iron and brewing industries saw parallel developments, the most obvious of which was that the increase in the size of the productive equipment facilitated the expansion of the firm and gave the owner an advantage over his rivals. Both therefore involved an extraordinary degree of capitalisation. For both, there were chemical processes involved, which were subject to experimentation and improvement. The biggest difference was that one trade was urban- and the other rural-based. Where the brewer could situate his operation right in the midst of his market, the ironmonger profited by placing his furnace and forge in close proximity to a supply of coal, iron and water power, having to endure transport costs as a penalty.

As the brewing industry underwent a complete revolution over the course of the eighteenth century, it stands out as an exceptional case. Since Tudor times there had been common brewers in the City, some of them larger breweries located

105. Langton 2000, p. 37.

near the Tower which provided victualing for ships in addition to exporting their brew. After 1672, the Common Brewers had an incentive toward centralisation in the form of an allowance of three duty-free barrels out of every thirty-six for 'wastage'. The larger breweries were under the constant supervision of excise officers checking for fraud.[106] Similar supervision over the tens of thousands of small victuallers scattered throughout the country would have been impossible. In the larger cities, meanwhile, victuallers were gradually reduced to serving as publicans ('pubs'), while larger breweries focused on production, leaving sales up to the merchants. Thus increasingly the interest of brewers became aligned with the banking and mercantile interests of the City, and the great brewing families began to marry into families represented in the Commons. Throughout the eighteenth century, no less than six Members of Parliament were brewers, and Southwark and even London became known as 'brewers' boroughs'.[107] As an industry, brewing had a unique advantage: demand for its product was virtually universal. To the extent that brewing settled in any 'region', it centred on London as the largest urban market and was thus perfectly suited to an intensive expansion in the scale of production. The increasing concentration of operations also meant the decline in the number of common brewers in London (see Table 9.1). As concentration ensued, brewing was subject to innovation in several ways. First, brewing became more scientific. There were no highly revolutionary inventions, but there was considerable progress in adapting known scientific instruments to the measurement and control of the brewing process. The discovery of porter revolutionised the industry by allowing the brewers themselves to mature it in vat and cask, thereby affording them control of both production and distribution. By cutting out the middlemen, porter further aided the concentration of the industry.[108] Secondly, as in smelting, the means by which the technology could be improved to expand the scale of production was simple: the size of the vat and the utensils could be increased. By itself, this change 'gave economies of scale in costs of construction and materials'.[109] This also economised labour further in an industry which was already among the least labour intensive.[110]

---

106. 'Excise officers were evidently supervising the bigger breweries continually on a six-hour shift as early as 1724' (Mathias 1979, pp. 216–17).

107. Mathias 1979, pp. 227 and 247. In no industry, writes Mathias (Mathias 1979, p. 210) was the 'familial structure more marked or tenacious than in brewing'.

108. Michael Combrune first applied the thermometer. James Baverstock and John Richardson introduced the hydrometer to measure the relative density (specific gravity) of the brew. In 1722, an 'obscure London brewer, Ralph Harwood, is said to have first brewed porter', a heavy, darker and slightly bitter beer. For his part, Harwood made no great fortune, but his innovation would add to the growing fortunes of the large brewers (Mathias 1979, pp. 235–7).

109. Mathias 1979, pp. 214–16.

110. The actual brewing process, prior to racking, storing and distributing barrels, required relatively few labourers. 'Only one man was needed at the valve-cock to transfer

Table 9.1: Brewers in England and Wales in the eighteenth century[111]

	Brewing Victuallers		Common Brewers	
	England & Wales	London	England & Wales	London
1700	39,469	–	746	174
1750	48,421	–	996	165
1799	23,690	–	1,328	127

Third, by the 1790s breweries and their vats were reaching massive proportions. The total outlay on raw materials for a single brewing house might be one hundred thousand pounds per annum. As soon as the steam engine was available to them, the large brewers took advantage of it. By 1805, virtually the entire process up to the point of racking the barrels had been mechanised.[112] By 1830, 'the London brewing industry resembled precociously the business situation of later times, with integration, imperfect competition and pricing agreements'.[113]

The Statute of Apprentices does not mention the paper trade because in 1563 it scarcely existed.[114] But as the trade developed, combinations of workers formed along familiar lines. There 'were neither sensational technical advances . . . nor sweeping extensions in markets' in the paper industry during the eighteenth century, but it did undergo a 'slow but worthy' expansion.[115] The number of mills grew and their distribution spread away from the concentration of Kent and Buckinghamshire to the West Midlands in particular, but by 1800 there were mills in virtually every county, driven by the need for paper in all of the expanding industries, a typical mill costing between four and five thousand pounds.[116] While paper mills remained small and rural, stationers were concentrated in the rising towns doing a brisk trade. The two most significant developments were the application of the Hollander engine after 1730 and the application of chlorine, after its discovery in 1774, to bleaching. In 1788 a combination of 'journeyman papermakers was noted in or near Manchester and in

the contents of the largest vat to the utensil below'. As the scale of production increased, the structure of the labour process changed little and therefore the share of labour costs out of overall operational costs shrank as a result (Mathias 1979, p. 216).

111. Source: Mathias 1979, p. 232.

112. Mathias 1979, pp. 226–7.

113. In 1830 Charles Barclay of Barclay Perkins Brewery told a committee of Parliament that 1.2 million out of the 1.4 million barrels of beer produced by tax-paying houses in London were produced by the twelve largest breweries. ' "We are the power-loom brewers, if I may so speak" ', was his remark (Mathias 1979, pp. 210 and 227).

114. See Chapter One, p. 75.

115. Coleman 1958, p. 90.

116. Pollard (Pollard 1965, p. 100) finds it unlikely that more than one or two firms had more than two hundred employees.

1790 some workers in the industry in Hertfordshire were indicted for conspiring to compel their employer to increase their wages'.[117] The 1790s brought a crisis to the paper industry in the form of inflation. Rags, labour costs and taxation were all rising sharply, and there were calls for mechanisation. When the paper-making machine was introduced from France in the first decade of the nineteenth century,[118] it 'represented a straightforward mechanisation of what was formerly done by hand' and brought about the retarded but 'entirely analogous' revolution in paper making that was seen decades earlier in the textile trades.[119] Machine-based paper factories did not begin to spread widely until 1830, after which they spread most quickly in Lancashire, Yorkshire, Durham and Scotland, a development which 'almost certainly owed much to the ready availability of coal in these regions' whilst the industry 'declined in the remoter areas distant from assessable supplies'.[120]

Landes writes that chemical production, 'the most miscellaneous of industries' and the one in which scientific research played a larger part than in any other industry, has been neglected by historians of the Industrial Revolution due to the advanced knowledge necessary to grasp the complexities of chemistry, its secondary importance next to other industries and its 'unrevolutionary character' as an industry that saw little by way of productivity advances or any re-organisation of the labour process. Yet advances in chemistry were absolutely necessary in order for the Industrial Revolution to happen: 'There was not enough cheap meadowland or sour milk in all the British Isles to whiten the cloth of Lancashire once the water frame and mule replaced the spinning wheel; and it would have taken undreamed-of quantities of human urine to cut the grease of the raw wool consumed by the mills of the West Riding'.[121]

Prior to 1750, work in chemicals was mostly subsumed under the operation in question: dyes and bleaches for textiles, grease for machinery and special glazes for pottery. Linen was bleached by alternately boiling it with ashes and lactic acid (sour milk), applying sun exposure between boilings. Sulphuric acid, known as 'vitriol' to medieval chemists, was used in place of sour milk, but was prohibitively expensive. In 1736, the London pharmacist Joshua Ward and his partner John White, applying the method of the seventeenth-century German-Dutch chemist Johann Glauber, used glass vessels to increase the scale of sulphuric acid production a thousandfold, thereby dramatically reducing the cost. John Roebuck of Sheffield was able to improve upon this method by replacing the

117. Coleman 1958, p. 262.
118. See Chapter Six, pp. 336–7.
119. Coleman 1958, p. 191.
120. Coleman 1958, p. 195.
121. Landes 1991, p. 108.

glass vessels with lead containers, thus allowing industrial-scale production. In 1748 Roebuck, with his partner Samuel Garbett, transferred his acid manufactory and fifty workmen to Prestonpans, Scotland, in hope of expanding his sales to manufacturers in the growing linen industry there, but also in hope of maintaining the secrecy of his process. The process was patented in 1771, but when the partners set out to enforce it, the matter went before the courts and the patent was overturned the following year.[122] As textile manufacturers discovered that sulphuric acid was not only cheaper but faster than lactic acid, vitriol works spread rapidly.[123]

Subsequent developments in the industrial use of chemicals in Britain depended upon the discoveries of the French chemists.[124] In fact, during the Napoleonic Wars, France leapt ahead of Britain in producing sodium carbonate (soda) based on the LeBlanc and later the Solvay Process. Britain had to rely upon potassium carbonate (potash) for use in glass-making, scouring, fulling, leather softening, bleaching, cleaning, gunpowder-making and alum-making until soda works were widely established from the 1820s.[125] Berthollet's isolation of chlorine in 1784, by contrast, led to major advances in Britain. Combined with salt, sulphuric acid yielded hydrochloric acid as a by-product, and from this chlorine could be produced. The industrial use of chlorine was slowed by its highly corrosive properties, and while after 1790 chlorine came into use as a bleaching agent, it was noxious and difficult to produce on-site. In 1796, the French developed Javel water (potassium hypochlorite) 'which has remained a household cleaning agent ever since',[126] but which was not applicable to the growing textile industry. Charles Tennant of Glasgow patented a method of passing the chlorine through a combination of lime and water,[127] and this reduced costs but had drawbacks. Tennant's partner Charles Macintosh 'solved the problem completely with his process for absorbing chlorine in dry lime – the first gas-solid

122. As with Arkwright's water frame, the process was deemed not to be original. Roebuck quickly ran into financial difficulties and sold out to Garbett, who set up a second vitriol works in his native Birmingham, where demand was increasing in the up-and-coming brass 'toys' trades, but soon disinvested himself of the whole enterprise (Clow and Clow 1972, pp. 148–51; Pollard 1965, p. 97).

123. Where lactic acid bleaching took up to eight months, sulphuric acid reduced the necessary time to about four months (Chapman 1987, p. 23).

124. See Chapter Six, p. 336. Landes writes that 'the really important research in theoretical and applied chemistry was being done abroad, where the education of chemists was already more systematic and thorough than in Britain'. But he recognises the difference in Britain's advance in that Britain enjoyed an economy of scale, which made it the leader into the late nineteenth century (Landes 1991, p. 114).

125. Landes 1991, pp. 110–11.

126. Landes 1991, p. 110.

127. Patent No. 2209, 1798 (Hardie 1972, p. 182).

reaction to be technically exploited'.[128] This key innovation, the discovery of bleaching powder (chloride of lime), 'opened the flood-gates of textile manufacture' by removing any significant limitation that would otherwise have been posed by the limited options available for bleaching.[129] By 1814, Tennant would go on to buy out his partners in the St. Rollox works near Glasgow, which on the strength of bleaching powder sales would become easily the largest chemical works in the world by the 1830s.[130] Macintosh went on to make several additional discoveries including naptha rubber for making 'life-preservers', namely rain jackets, new processes that would lead to advances in steel-making and a process of using coal tar, a waste product which up to that point had simply been dumped into rivers, as a furnace fuel. 'Coal tar', writes Hardie, 'was the subject of one of those peculiar reversals of technological importance, by which the by-product of a process becomes more important than the product for which it was originally carried on'.[131] Such a recycling of a waste product provided 'a powerful stimulus to innovation', writes Landes, as there was 'the positive lure of profit'.[132]

Two other chemical entrepreneurs merit discussion. In 1738 William Champion of Bristol patented a process for distilling zinc from zinc oxide, and set up a manufactory. The making of quality brass had depended upon zinc imports from India, and in response to Champion's initial success, East-Indian traders drastically lowered their zinc prices, forcing Champion to revert to using calamine in his brass works at Warmley.[133] When his patent was extended in 1750, it was opposed by metal-workers. Champion went bankrupt in 1769,[134] and his story serves as not only another example of an inventor who failed as a businessman, but as the typical British entrepreneur interested in innovation for profit rather than state prizes. His contribution spurred on the brass metal-working trades of Birmingham. James Keir, a member of the Lunar Society, had set up

---

128. Patent No. 2312, 1799. The patent was taken out in Tennant's name and Tennant is widely credited for the invention, but Hardie (Hardie 1972, p. 182) clarifies that Macintosh was the inventor.

129. Hardie 1972, p. 183. 'In the history of the first seventy-five years of the chemical industry', writes Hardie, 'it is almost impossible to overemphasize the significance of chloride of lime'. There is an obvious parallel, here, with the steam engine, in that without this innovation the growth of industry would have been limited until some other alternative for expanding the ease and scale of bleaching was found.

130. Landes 1991, p. 112.

131. Hardie 1972, p. 190. This was no doubt a trade-off in the form of polluting the air instead of polluting the water, but the savings ran into the millions of pounds.

132. 'The story of chemicals in the first two-thirds of the nineteenth century is in large part this effort to use up all the materials…' (Landes 1991, p. 113). In addition to the profits to be earned from a new enterprise, there were the additional savings to the manufacturer in the form of having less lawsuits to contend with.

133. See above, pp. 479–80.

134. Pollard and Heron 1996, p. 208.

a glass works at Stourbridge near Birmingham in 1772 where he experimented in alkalis. His partners were the Birmingham industrialist John Taylor and the vitriol manufacturer Samuel Skey. He abandoned the glass works in 1778 to set up a soap and alkali factory at Tipton, where he pioneered in organisational innovations in the chemical industry.[135]

After 1799, many industries began manufacturing their own chemicals on-site, but chemical works also spread. Aside from the Glasgow area, the two other centres of the chemical industry in Britain were the Tyneside, where access to water transport and coal was abundant, and Merseyside, with easy access to coal and Cheshire salt, concentrating on soda ash for making soap and sodium sulphate for glass-making.[136] Chemistry was another capital-intensive industry where the concentration of labour was small – only 9,172 adult workers in the whole industry by 1851, over a thousand of which worked at St. Rollox alone.[137] But its importance 'was clearly out of proportion to its numbers, or even its capital investment'.'[138]

There are a host of other industries that are of interest, such as sugar refining, soap-boiling, glass-making, and coach-making, to name a few. These industries remained small in scale and saw few major technical developments in the eighteenth century. One industry which emerged purely out of an accidental discovery was the gasworks. In 1604 one Reverend John Clapton of Wigan noticed flames on the water that he later determined to be gas released from a nearby coalmine. Nearly two centuries later, the gas lamp was invented, perhaps simultaneously, by William Murdoch, an engineer at the Soho foundry (the first building to be lit with gas lighting) and Philippe LeBon of Paris, who used it to light his house and gardens. Soon cities like London and Paris would erect gas lamps along the parks and walkways, powered with gas piped in from the new gas works.

---

135. Pollard 1965, p. 113. Keir's connection to the Lunar Society is important, as both Wedgwood and Boulton were members. This strongly suggests that the Lunar Society's members discussed far more than just science.

136. Landes 1991, p. 112.

137. Pollard 1965, p. 97. George Macintosh, father of Charles and maker of boots and shoes, had joined in a partnership with George and Cuthbert Gordon in erecting and operating a dye manufactory in Dunchatton. The factory was circled by a high wall, within which with five hundred Scottish Highlanders worked. Like the factory of Roebuck and Garbett at Prestonpans, the wall, and in this case the employment of Gaelic-speaking workers who rarely left the compound, were apparently efforts to protect secrets of the process. It 'must have been one of the strangest factories in the records of industry' (Hardie 1972, pp. 175–6). By its size, it was probably the largest of its time. In a word, it was exceptional.

138. Landes 1991, p. 113.

The capitalist

Where did the entrepreneurs – the capitalists – of the Industrial Revolution themselves come from? In agriculture, as we have seen, landlords themselves were actively involved in supplying capital for improving the farms they leased. The Duke of Bridgewater set the canal revolution in motion by investing exorbitant amounts of capital, both his own and that he borrowed. Thus landowners were themselves major investors. Merchants and manufacturers also invested in the turnpike roads, canals and later the railroads. Urban improvement schemes were invested in as well, and opened up opportunities for the middling classes, who could be a 'part of a pluralistic, propertied endeavour for improvement'.[139] In general, awareness of both the risks and the potential for very lucrative gains to be made by getting in on any number of emerging investment opportunities was widespread in eighteenth-century British society. By 1750, there is already 'unmistakeable evidence of a rising rate of capital accumulation in roads, canals, buildings and agricultural enclosures'.[140] The landed gentry often supplied the capital needed for larger industrial projects, while the entrepreneurs themselves would often be the younger sons of landed families who had the contacts, the resources and access to education and training to develop their talents as industrialists.[141] Among the early entrepreneurs, few started out as labourers. Many if not most had access to savings in their own family or the family into which they had married. Their position demanded organisational skills. These included: marketing, maintaining a careful oversight of management, ensuring the supply of raw materials was steady and of good quality, and sufficient understanding of the technology they employed to be able apply it to the production process. Only rarely did they themselves demonstrate a great talent for invention. This talent

139. Hay and Rogers 1997, p. 193.

140. Deane and Cole 1969, p. 261. They add: 'If parliamentary enclosures can be taken as evidence of increased investment in the reproducible capital of agriculture (fences, buildings, equipment, livestock, etc.), the fact that the acreage statutorily enclosed in the period 1761–92 was seven times that of the preceding three decades is significant enough'. The conversion of land to capital may in fact have been the fundamental development in the creation of a capitalist economy.

141. An example in the seventeenth century was the wealthy Flemish merchant William Courteen, a lender to the crown who had organised an interloping expedition to East India in 1635 (see Chapter Two, p. 141, n. 48). Courteen purchased the manor of Laxton in Nottinghamshire, 'obviously with the intention of making his estates pay'. The Governor of the East India Company, Sir John Banks, married his daughter to the Earl of Aylesford and earned a fortune off of his rent-roll (Wilson 1984, p. 158). In the eighteenth century, Richard Arkwright and Sir Robert Peel both 'acquired titles, bought estates, built country houses and founded landed families' (Stone and Stone 1984, pp. 411–12). According to the Stones, however, these were exceptional cases, and in general the landed elite enjoyed a kind of cultural isolation which gave them a general monopoly on power and status, prizes which for now eluded the industrialists.

more often rose from the ranks of working men. Those who came up with new methods of production and the inventions that flowed from them were probably for the most part wage labourers or journeymen, and were rarely credited for their contributions. '[M]any of the first engineers and machine builders – Joseph Clements, Bramah, Henry Maudslay – were sons of peasants or humble weavers, and they began life as carpenters and blacksmiths'.[142] The Duke of Bridgewater's engineer, James Brindley, was from a successful family of craftsmen and farmers in the Peak District, but had no formal education as a child.[143]

The transition from a manufacturing base characterised by independent domestic workers owning their own looms or spinning wheels, or renting them from the merchant who 'put out' the raw materials they worked, to a manufacturing base characterised by factories or operations considerably larger in scale than the typical workshop in 1700 with perhaps a dozen or less persons employed, came about through a process involving a multitude of 'shifts' in the economy. Mathias provides two key examples. First, many of the early entrepreneurs originated in closely-related branches of industry, shifting operations from the merchandising to the production of their goods. Second, many merchants who relied on the domestic system and who were aggravated by the inconsistency of supply were compelled to assume control over part of the production process.

> Many grain merchants or maltsters became brewers or set up a son as a brewer; the characteristic industrialist in the woollen industry had set up a factory from being a 'putter-outer' or a woollen merchant. An instance of this sequence was Benjamin Gott of Leeds, who went into woollen production to fulfil the demands of regularity of supplies and consistency of quality which he needed as a merchant. In the metal industries most of the iron masters had been in the secondary metal trades – making final products from refined metal – and they then moved back to making iron.[144]

Taking direct control of a production operations allowed merchants to ensure the quality and supply of commodities. It also allowed them to control and to upgrade production techniques in order to provide goods of uniform quality and sufficient supply to the buyer. Making this 'shift' also allowed them 'to bypass public markets and the independent merchants who owned and distributed raw materials to small manufacturers, buying themselves from the importers and laying down their own specifications'.[145] In the face of competition within rapidly expanding markets, these factors became imperatives if one wanted to stay in

142. Mathias 1983, p. 140.
143. Malet 1990, p. 14.
144. Malet 1990, p. 141 citing Wilson 1957, p. 115.
145. Mathias 1983, p. 137.

the game. 'The market', writes Mathias, 'decided the nature of production', quoting Charles Wilson, who wrote that the role of entrepreneur required '"a sense of opportunity combined with the capacity to exploit it"'.[146]

New economic roles emerged as new economic habits and practices came into being. A 'class' of industrial capitalists did not suddenly appear on the scene, either as the effect of an industrial revolution or as its cause. For Mathias, they formed a *type* but not a *class*, given that they 'arrived from every social class and from all parts of the country'. This *type*, however, fulfilled particular needs driven by economic imperatives in an extraordinary economic context – one of rapidly expanding markets in an expanding empire, markets driven by competition in a way as never before. 'If the momentum of expansion was to be maintained', writes Mathias, 'unscrupulous' industrialists were compelled to adopt 'instruments which increased the exploitation of labour'.[147] These instruments included 'long pay' or – in the place of cash wages – issuing tokens or credit slips as titles to purchase in the tommy shops. Ashton has argued that the government's inability to provide a steady supply of currency is partly to blame for the problems these shortcuts were meant to stem. But these problems are specific to the imperative to expand faced by the early industrial capitalists; where they existed in the past, they were never so acute. Aside from short-changing workers, another means to increase the rate of expansion was credit.

Currency supply was a money problem. Credit, in this context, is a problem of the movement of capital. In the age of the guilds, when the goal was to establish a monopoly over markets in the name of ensuring the high quality of the product, markets were conceptualised as more or less static. Credit played a role in lubricating the commercial transactions of merchants, but there was no imperative to progressively expand units of production, and thus a limited need for credit. Once a company gained monopoly control of a given market by charter, competition was eliminated and so any competitive imperative to expand, innovate or maximise production was reduced or even minimised. Under conditions of agrarian and then emerging industrial capitalism, however, the market imperative to expand production generates an urgent and permanent demand for credit as what one might call an artificial means of accelerating the movement of capital through the circuit of production, exchange and reinvestment.

Mathias notes that: 'In the pre-factory, domestic system . . . almost all capital lay in stocks of materials, with a very small fraction indeed in fixed assets such as buildings or machinery. Even in the early factories, in textiles, breweries and the like, amongst the most heavily capitalized less than one-seventh or one-eighth of total assets typically were in buildings and plant; six-sevenths to seven eighths

146. Mathias 1983, p. 138.
147. Mathias 1983, p. 140.

and more still being absorbed by "movables" or "circulating capital" – raw materials, goods in the pipeline, goods being sold but not yet paid for'.[148]

As the Industrial Revolution progressed, these ratios would shift toward heavier and heavier outlays in fixed capital, but in the early days of the factory system investments lay preponderantly in circulating capital. We may note, however, that Professor Mathias fails to include the wages of labour among the elements of circulating capital. The importance of this omission will become apparent below. Given such a low ratio of fixed to circulating capital, it meant that the early factory masters were mainly in need of sources of short-term credit. As we have seen, the rise of the country banks in the late eighteenth century came to their aid. Before the arrival of the country bank, however, the entrepreneur had to rely heavily on either personal resources or personal acquaintances: family members, friends and business associates to cover not only short-term capital needs, but also to accumulate enough capital to start a business or to invest in buildings and equipment. Early on, it was possible to set up a new business with one's own resources, if they were sufficient. Owen, Watt, Arkwright, Marshall, the Darbys and Wilkinsons all used personal resources or borrowed from friends and family to get started. Once established, it was essential to reinvest profits into the enterprise, which, at least when they were starting out, often meant abstinence or strict discipline involving limiting spending for the entrepreneur and his family. When profits were insufficient, loans were required. Since success depended so heavily on the organisational, managerial and marketing abilities of the entrepreneur, 'respectability' was important. Those with whom one did business with regularly were less reticent to lend, particularly those working in a related branch of the same industry. Hence 'spinning mill owners were the main source of capital for the provision of power-looms in Lancashire in the 1820's and 1830's'.[149] Eventually, an elaborate system of credit arose that would be able to meet the demands for large-scale loans to finance large-scale projects of the nineteenth century, specifically the railroads. By that time, the scale of such enterprises had outgrown the sole proprietor model and corporate enterprise was a prerequisite. By the late eighteenth century, the ratio of fixed to circulating capital required to start and sustain a firm was becoming significant. For the entrepreneur considering his investment choices, this raised the stakes. 'In an effort to reduce his own share of the risks of a cyclical fall in demand he shifted as much of it as he could on to his labour-force. Hence the long drawn-out agony of the handloom weavers who bore most of the losses of the early nineteenth century cotton trade slumps'.[150]

148. Mathias 1983, pp. 133–4.
149. Deane 1987, p. 179.
150. Deane 1987, p. 171.

Credit provided the mechanism by which savings could be mobilised for investment. Eighteenth-century England was a country comparatively wealthy in savings.[151] The difficulty lay in finding a way to leverage credit for the use of borrowers. As we have seen, this void was filled by the various mechanisms of credit that developed. But what was the source of the savings that was translated into the capital that fuelled the Industrial Revolution? Mathias points to land:

> An important direct flow of savings from the land, being created from farming profits and agricultural rents, fertilized agricultural improvement, mining, transport improvements in turnpike trusts and canals. Once country banks were established in most market towns in the second half of the eighteenth century another conduit for transfers of rural savings came into action. At the same time other flows of capital came back to the land with new recruits to the landed classes, from commerce, industry, and the professions. It is impossible to say if the net flow was towards or away from the land.[152]

One area of the economy where a great deal of wealth was transferred from the land was canal-building in the form of locally raised funds,[153] starting (as we have seen) with the Duke of Bridgewater.[154] The canal boom made it clear that there was, indeed, an abundance of capital in England in the late eighteenth century. Deane points out that during the canal-building era England was not short of capital *per se*, only of *productive* capital. 'There was a good deal of capital invested in the Funds, in land, and in game preserves and country-houses . . . yielding a very low return indeed, in either money or in goods and services, compared with what it could be made to yield in canals and turnpike trusts'.[155] David Ricardo would complain in 1817 that the unproductive nature of many of their investments put the interest of the landed class generally at odds with the greater progress of capitalism.[156] By contrast, investment in transport had a multiplier effect on the economy by reducing costs, opening access to new markets and new business relationships, increasing confidence and security and reducing turnover times and so speeding up the rate of profit. 'The fact is that an efficient market, whether it be in goods or capital or men or ideas, depends largely on a rapid and free flow of information as well as of things'.[157] By 1815,

151. One might venture to guess that it outstripped all its rivals in this category, and that we could credit this to agrarian capitalism.

152. Mathias 1983, pp. 52–3.

153. 'In most cases the new navigations were the product of corporate enterprise initiated by local businessmen and landowners and supported by shareholders and bankers and city corporations and even sometimes by universities' (Deane 1987, pp. 80–1).

154. See Chapter Five, p. 263.

155. Deane 1987, pp. 84–5.

156. Ricardo 1987, pp. 224–6.

157. Deane 1987, p. 85.

perhaps as much as twenty million pounds had been invested in canals,[158] an enormous sum for the times. Yet this money was being invested at a time when virtually all sectors of the economy were seeing increasing investment. Rentier investment was only one source. We must also consider the profits being made in capitalist tenant-farming and the emerging capitalist industries. In both cases, the increasing rate of the exploitation of labour may provide a key. To elaborate, it is necessary to discuss briefly how different authors appear to have different understandings of capital.

Origins and definitions of capital

The term 'capital' is used fast and loose throughout the literature, but it seems clear that not all are in agreement as to its definition. The work of economic historians like Deane, Mathias and others is vital to establishing an accurate understanding of the complexity and the gradual nature of the process that is the Industrial Revolution. As we have just seen, from their work we gain the understanding that the 'capitalist' did not simply emerge one day as a category of economic agency, but that the role emerged gradually, and out of various economic shifts and different social backgrounds. Yet it appears that 'capital' for these authors is strictly an economic term, an umbrella category that encompasses the investor's cash, the industrialist's stores (stock) of raw materials, and forms of credit. In other words, the term is inclusive of all the forms that capital takes as it moves through the cycle of production, circulation and reinvestment in production. All the forms save one, for there is little discussion of capital taking the form of commodified labour. Nor is there much consideration of the social implications of land, or access to land, coming to be treated as a commodity. Let us call this the economic or static definition of capital. It is in short a definition that restricts capital to the pantheon of economic terminology, thereby avoiding a careful examination of capital *itself* as a manifestation of a unique set of social relationships, as a web of social relations. 'Capital' is treated as a universal concept, potentially present in all societies where there is trade: ancient Mesopotamia, ancient China, or perhaps even in ancient Caral in the Andes. Despite the recognition that an unprecedented *growth* of capital is taking place simultaneous with the Industrial Revolution, restricted to its economic aspect, capital can grow in quantity but its universal quality remains unchanged.

A second definition, what we might call a social or dynamic definition (and the one pursued in this study), would see capital not simply as the financial and material resources of owner-employers, but as a social relationship and a form of property that is market-dependent. The social relation of capital arises out

158. Owen 1975, p. 314.

of a situation in which the transformation of production in response to market indicators becomes not a choice but an imperative necessary for the economic survival of the market-dependent owner of the means of production to whom all the profits of production accrue. The owner is thereby compelled to assert rights of legal ownership over all the inputs of the production process, including not only raw materials but also land, labour and money. The spread of the capital relation and the growing market dependence of both direct producers and surplus appropriators both stimulated, and are reinforced by, the growth of the national domestic market. Where during the transitional period that saw the rise of agrarian capitalism in England the transformation of production by way of converting *land* to capital was central, it was the conversion of *labour* to capital that was more central to the Industrial Revolution.[159]

In Chapter Three we considered two major sources of the capital that fuelled the Industrial Revolution: investment and credit, which are but two sides of the same coin. Those authors using the static definition of capital tend to think of an increase in the nation's capital as roughly equivalent to an increasing rate of investment. Thus Deane points out that capital grew faster between 1750 and 1800 than between 1700 and 1750; while in that same first half-century England and Wales saw a fifty percent growth in the population, a doubling of the national income and a tripling in the volume of overseas trade. Given these enormous rates of growth, Deane concludes that for the century between 1750 to 1850: 'the level of investment would have had to increase by something like 50 percent just to keep the capital stock growing at the same rate as the labour force', yet there is no 'convincing support'[160] for the hypothesis that there was an increase in savings large enough to double the rate of investment. Deane and Cole cite Lewis, who claims that while underdeveloped countries save just six percent of their national income, developed countries save twelve percent or more. They also cite Rostow, who argues that for a country to be able to reproduce Britain's industrial 'take-off', a five to ten percent increase in savings is required.[161] Yet if the growth of savings did not meet these standards in the planet's first industrial revolution, then where *did* the capital come from to enable a fifty per cent increase in the level of investment between 1750 and 1800?

159. Comninel n.d.

160. Deane 1987, p. 167.

161. Deane and Cole 1969, pp. 260–1, citing Rostow 1960, p. 7; Lewis 1955, p. 208. Lewis actually defines the term industrial revolution according to the investment rate: 'All countries which are now relatively developed have at some time in the past gone through a period of rapid acceleration in the course of which their rate of annual net investment has moved from 5 per cent or less to 12 per cent or more. This is what we mean by an Industrial Revolution'. It would be hard to find a more brazenly economistic definition of the term 'Industrial Revolution'. If social science could be reduced to such tidy equations, there would be little work left to do.

By way of addressing the problem, Deane pursues the question of when the upward shift in capital formation took place. She casts doubt upon Rostow's claim that a doubling of capital formation took place between 1783 and 1802 for three reasons:

1. there is evidence of prior capital formation
2. the developments of those two decades were not massive enough for this kind of impact
3. the railway age (still to come) had a totally unprecedented impact, and would serve as a more likely period.

Thus for Deane, the evidence suggests that the sharp upturn more likely took place after 1830, during the railroad boom and the peak period of mechanisation in the cotton industry, followed by the mechanisation of the woollen industry after 1850.[162] The evidence assembled by Deane and Cole do point to 1830 or 1832 as a real break point in the trends.[163] Yet the problem remains: how did capital formation *before* 1832, and indeed before 1800, keep pace with an unprecedented growth of population, trade and income?

Throughout the literature it is pointed out that savings were not in short supply in eighteenth-century Britain, only the means of *leveraging* savings into investment. Are we to conclude then, that the growth of the banks in London and the country was sufficient to leverage enough extant savings to account for a fifty percent growth in the level of investment between 1750 and 1800? No doubt their unprecedented growth during this period did mean a greatly expanded funnel through which otherwise idle savings could be converted into investment. But this can hardly account for the difference. Also widely pointed out in the literature is the fact that early industry required minimal investment in fixed capital, but the proportion of fixed to circulating capital grew as time wore on. Thus investment outlays in early industry would have started out at low levels, but would have grown steadily. Still, the growth of banks and a low investment threshold for industry cannot explain a doubling of the national income and a tripling in the volume of overseas trade. Not just investment, but *capital* had to grow, and grow exponentially.

Let us suggest that a static definition of capital is incapable of explaining this growth because it takes a warehousing approach to the problem, sticking to quantitative accounting and sidestepping issues of qualitative transformation. How many pounds were shifted from savings to investment? How much income

162. Deane 1987, pp. 168–9; Deane and Cole 1969, pp. 262–3.
163. See Chapter Thirteen, p. 740, for a discussion of the importance of landed capital's share of total national capital formation in the nineteenth century.

from foreign trade was put back into production? How much of the national income did the landed classes consume? These questions of accounting are essential to good analysis, but we learn very little about the social dimensions of capital from such trade-offs. Following Gregory King, the closest to a concise definition of capital given by Deane and Cole is the '"productive and reproducible national capital"'.[164] They are at pains to point out that the whole effort to quantify the rate of capital formation, especially for the eighteenth century for which no records exist, is 'highly conjectural'.

How is capital formed? All that we can learn from accounts that employ a static definition of capital is that capital grows when the technical instruments, the buildings and the commodities involved in production increase. How do they increase? More money is invested, or more profits are reinvested, in production. Capital is effectively treated as just stock. It moves from one part of the national warehouse to the other, or it gets exported and money or other goods return to take its place. Deane and Cole have remarkably little to say about the role that capital played in the *social* transformation that accompanied the Industrial Revolution. To address this requires an understanding of capital as a form of property. Unlike the factory master's *stock*, the term *property* immediately invokes the existence of social institutions such as the courts, the legislature and ultimately the state.

Another related problem with attempting to measure the national capital of Britain before, during and after the Industrial Revolution is one of defining relative values. Suppose that arable land is to be including in our accounting of the nation's capital. What is the value of land? We can derive a number for average rent per acre and multiply that by the total arable farmland. But what of unenclosed lands that are not subject to market rents and market principles? Our calculation will be skewed. And in 1700, only half the land in England was enclosed.[165] It is no wonder that Deane and Cole's attempt at measuring the growth of Britain's national capital in the eighteenth and nineteenth centuries is

164. Deane and Cole 1969, p. 260 citing Gregory King.

165. In developing or underdeveloped countries today, the problem is similar. Indian environmental activist Vandana Shiva, commenting on the Green Revolution that revolutionised agriculture in India and other developing countries from around the 1970s, writes: 'Biological products, which were not sold on the market but used as inputs for maintaining soil fertility, were totally ignored by the cost-benefit equations of the Green Revolution miracle. They did not appear in the list of inputs because they were not purchased, nor in the list of outputs because they were not sold. Yet what was seen as "unproductive" or "waste" in the commercial context of the Green Revolution is now emerging as productive in the ecological context and as the only route to sustainable agriculture': Shiva (ed.) 1994, pp. 131–2. Elsewhere, Shiva has pointed out in her work that in one year in the late 1980s or early 1990s, the Indian government created the *appearance* of a sharp burst in economic growth where there was none, simply by including for the first time statistics for non-market agricultural production under traditional methods.

'highly conjectural'. It is an economy where land in both its commodified form and land in its non-commodified form exist side-by-side, with a process at work converting the one into the other. The same can be said for labour. In such an economy, there exist dual methods for calculating values, even if one method is ascendant. The problem is that these dual methods involve more than quantitative problems; they are the respective products of different sets of social relations, different cultures and even different meanings.

The political economists had a hard time of it as well, as McCloskey points out:

> Economics was for long a British, even disproportionately a Scottish, subject. What is odd is that the British economists did not recognise the factor of twelve as it was happening. The economists' theories took useful account of little changes – a 5 percent rise of income when cotton textiles grew or a 10 percent fall when Napoleon ruled the Continent. But they did not notice that the change to be explained, 1780 to 1850, was not 10 percent but 100 percent, on its way to 1,100 percent. Only recently has the enquiry into the nature and causes of the wealth of nations begun to recognise this astonishing oversight.[166]

The 'factor of twelve' mentioned here by McCloskey is referring to 'the factor by which real income per head nowadays [circa 1980] exceeds that around 1780, in Britain and in other countries that have experienced modern economic growth'.[167] McCloskey reviews all the possible factors to explain the factor of twelve, and comes up with nothing but 'nots'. When one factors in population-growth between 1780 and 1980, the factor of twelve translates into a much more astronomical sum in terms of overall economic growth. McCloskey credits the historian Thomas Babington Macaulay for standing almost alone amongst his contemporaries in being able to consider the implications of contemporary trends of economic growth. In 1830 (that watershed-moment for Deane and Cole) Macaulay wrote: 'If we were to prophesy that in the year 1930 a population of fifty million, better fed, clad, and lodged than the English of our time, will cover these islands, that Sussex and Huntingdonshire will be wealthier than the wealthiest parts of the West Riding of Yorkshire now are … that machines constructed on principles yet undiscovered will be in every house … many people would think us insane'.[168]

Why should it take a historian to grasp what the economists could not? And why are economists still searching for a convincing hypothesis to explain the

166. McCloskey 1994, p. 243.
167. McCloskey 1994, p. 242.
168. McCloskey 1994, p. 243, citing Macaulay 1858.

phenomenal growth of the Industrial Revolution?[169] One might at least consider looking to the exploitation of labour as holding some of the answers to this dilemma. If Deane and Cole exclude labour (power) from their accounting of the national capital, they exclude the possibility of accounting for the phenomenal growth of capital by considering how methods of squeezing more surplus labour out of the labourer were used to progressively increase the capitalist's profit, and in the process to allow capital to 'self-expand'. It may not be sufficient to account for how much capital is moved from one part of the warehouse to another, or in and out of the warehouse . . . Perhaps the stock is growing where it sits.[170]

Conclusion

Innovation is a creative process, one requiring conscious effort. The Industrial Revolution did not simply spring forth from the 'interstices' of post-feudal, early modern British society. New institutions such as the factory had to be imagined, built, organised, financed and regulated. While we have tried to lay out how conditions for the emergence of factories and the general upturn in industrial output across Britain were propitious, this does not mean that it was inevitable that Wedgwood would revolutionise the pottery trade, that cotton factories based on the water frame and the mule would number in the hundreds by 1800, or that Watt would discover the separate condenser engine. What science and technical innovation have in common is that they proceed by moving from one problem to the next, each new problem posing a challenge to find a solution. With hindsight, we can trace the evolution of discovery and change. But hindsight quickly lapses into tunnel vision when the path of discovery and evolution begins to appear like a single path directed toward the *telos* of the present. Staring into the future, the scientists and inventors of the Industrial Revolution could no more accurately predict what discoveries lay ahead than their contemporary counterparts can foresee the discoveries of the future. At the same time, however, forecasting is not complete guesswork: we can identify what problems are being worked on, what solutions are being sought and suggest probable outcomes. The

169. Of course, for authors of the gradualist school, beginning with Clapham as discussed at the outset of this work (see Introduction, p. 32), this growth was not as 'phenomenal' as others may think.

170. What is meant by this is that the industrialist's store of commodities in the warehouse represents only one phase in a circuit of the reproduction of capital in which value is constantly being added in the production process itself. We are not referring to any appreciation of value in the conventional sense of increasing demand or shrinking supply pushing up prices, but rather to the value that is invested in the product in the process of production.

confusion comes when, in looking at the past, we lose sight of the fact that multiple outcomes were possible, and presume that there was only one.

It is crucial to bear this in mind as we consider the broader forces at work in bringing about economic and social change, or in the case of the present study, the Industrial Revolution. So while we have seen how the introduction of the factory required the wilful act of inculcating habits of time-thrift in the place of task-orientation, or substituting a machine for the manual skill of the craft-worker, these actions did not take place in a social and economic vacuum. Any analysis that shows how the course of economic change threw up general problems that were solved in specific instances with specific solution runs the risk of being dismissed as 'economistic', 'determinist' or 'teleological'.[171] These charges should not deter us from seeking to identify the broader forces at work in social and economic change, for the alternative is to simply lapse into analysis that only considers what is contingent and specific. The goal should be to produce analysis that can situate specific developments within the broader course of historical change, whilst ascribing inevitability to neither. This means that broader-scale change, while more immutable, is also open to other possibilities. This can be identified in terms of limitations set by technological factors. For example, had the separate condenser engine not been discovered, the spread of textile factories would have continued to rely on water power, which would soon have reached an upper limit beyond which the system could not expand. It can also be identified at the political level. For example, had Spain managed to land at least one of its armadas, conquer England and overthrow Elizabeth, it is possible that the Spanish crown could have sought to establish an economy on the same foundations as Spanish absolutism, thereby possibly extinguishing agrarian capitalism and even terminating the development of capitalism itself.

So bearing in mind, with due diligence, that there were other possible outcomes, let us consider some of the broader forces at work in making up the historical context in which the crucial innovations of the Industrial Revolution occurred. Let us start specifically with competition. We know that in agrarian capitalism the competition that compelled tenant-farmers to introduce new techniques on their farms was a factor of the emerging market in land leases, wherein the farmer who failed to innovate risked being unable to pay the rent and so lose the farm. How did competition in manufactures come about? The short answer is that markets themselves were transformed. Throughout the eighteenth century, an increasingly unregulated labour force emerged. At the same time we see the emergence of increasingly large-scale manufacturing operations of varying type. The growth of the domestic market and of population both

171. Thus Robert Albritton (2002, pp. 125–34) has argued that the perspective taken here is teleological, reductionist and so on.

contribute to these developments. And in the first instance, we can trace both of those developments to the prior emergence of agrarian capitalism, which does several things. First, it lifts the ceiling on population growth by expanding the food supply. Second, it divorces direct producers from the means of subsistence, creating an expanding supply of labour for manufactures. Third, agriculture itself becomes subject to market imperatives, creating self-sustaining growth, which we explored in Chapter Three. Key to this change is the way in which the tenant-farmers themselves are rendered market-dependent, and enclosing landlords themselves become dependent upon markets in land and labour to guarantee their rental income. What is the parallel transition in manufactures?

In making this analogy, let us first recognise that manufactures had no lordly class as such. Craft workers were subjects of a state dominated by the power of a class whose economic base was rooted in the ownership of land, but unlike peasants they did not pay feudal dues or rents. The paradox of domestic manufacturers is that while custom continued to regulate their mode of production longer than it did in agriculture, they had always been by definition market-dependent in a double sense, since they were both divorced from the means of subsistence and also relied upon the sale of their products in the marketplace. But royal charters and customary norms of organising relations in the workshop meant that manufactures, while commercially-oriented, were not capitalist. Asking how the capitalist entrepreneur became market-dependent is tautological. We must first ask how the merchant, the small master or anybody else became a capitalist, as in a factory master. So long as the division of labour between merchants who handled trade and craftsmen who controlled both the means of production and the labour process survived, the revolution in industry would not be complete. In the previous chapter we saw how through the imposition of a detailed division of labour in pottery and factory machinery in cotton spinning, capitalists such as Wedgwood and Arkwright pioneered the real subordination of labour to capital. In the woollen and worsted industries, a far more diverse set of developments arose. The large factory owner like Benjamin Gott was the exception, and even Gott's operation was not only heavily dependent upon domestic outworkers but, this was a dependence which, as we shall see, could still bring his entire operation to a halt.[172] The more characteristic development of the factory in the woollen district of West Riding is the emergence of small operations combining fulling mills, slubbing billies and scribbling engines in converted cornmills in a manner that generally did not disturb domestic weaving and spinning. Some of these 'company' mills apparently operated on a co-operative basis, with workers exercising a degree of collective control over production in a the setting of a

172. See Chapter Eleven, p. 580.

small factory,[173] while others were run by small owners with varying degrees of adherence to customary norms of organising labour. Meanwhile, independent producers and small masters had long made significant headway using the jenny and the shuttle-loom. While Gott, the merchant turned manufacturer, serves as a classic example of Marx's 'way II', the general development of the woollen industry in West Riding conforms perhaps more closely than any other example to Marx's 'truly revolutionary' way, or 'way I', in which the small producer gains control over the production process and becomes a capitalist. While delayed by difficulties in developing machinery and disadvantages of geography, the worsted districts of West Riding appear to have followed a more straightforward path toward the large spinning and weaving factory. With the adaptation of spinning to flax by Kendrew and Porthouse in 1787, linen also appears to have moved quickly toward the factory, with Marshall as the counterpart to Gott or Arkwright.

The case of the West of England reminds us that *regional* competition played an important role in shaping outcomes. Here, early enclosures appear to have had the paradoxical effect of more firmly entrenching customary norms and expectations in woollen spinning and weaving, allowing for stronger resistance to the introduction of machinery, including the jenny and the shuttle-loom, with the long-term result that the West of England was unable to withstand the price competition from the relatively more rapid advance of machinery even among domestic producers in West Riding. One must also remember that by serving as a competing region of woollen production, the West of England played a role in the development of capitalist and mechanical woollen production in West Riding.

Before the arrival of the papermaking machine after 1830, the paper mill resembled the company mill in woollens, being a small manufacturing operation with a simple division of labour. What the expansion in the *number* of paper mills throughout England attests to, however, is the extraordinary expansion of the domestic market and domestic demand. Brewing provides a striking case of an industry rapidly converted to a capitalist structure of labour organisation. This was made easy by the fact that brewing requires minimal labour, and minimal machinery, since the ability to expand the size of the vat and utensils to mammoth size was and probably remains the surest way to meet price competition by producing on an economy of scale. Metallurgy, much like clockmaking, generally remained the preserve of the domestic craftsman or craftswoman. Boulton's manufactory was exceptional in this regard, although as in mining the structure of the independent workshop was largely preserved inside

173. See Hudson 1986, pp. 259–60. More will be said of this development below in Chapter Eleven, p. 741.

the manufactory. Moreover, the sheer range of products being produced probably made it difficult to establish the same degree of labour discipline. Such deficiencies in the ability to effect necessary changes in the production process as required by market competition were overcome when Boulton and Watt, starting from an entirely new blueprint that ensured they would enjoy complete control over the production process, established the Soho Foundry for producing separate condenser engines. A parallel would be seen at Coalbrookdale when the Darbys found that the production of steam engines made up for the decline of profitability in the small cast-ironwares trade.

The striking thing about iron and coal production is that, despite the absence of major revolutions in the means of production, these were able to expand after 1782 at a rate sufficient to keep the textile revolution going, and later the railroad boom. There were generally two ways that the scale of production could be increased without revolutionising the production process. Fist, as in brewing, foundries and forges were able to expand the scale of output without revolutionising the means of production in any way other than increasing the size of the forge, furnace, bellows and hammers. The second way was to expand the size of the workforce. To a great extent this is what happened in mining, where new mines were opened up, and metal-working, where the size of the tools was enlarged.

The butty system is a good example of the formal subsumption of labour to capital and the way in which such operations were becoming capitalist in their overall orientation, whilst retaining useful aspects of earlier, customary forms of labour organisation. The butty, or team leader, was himself subject to market-pressures to reduce costs by exploiting his workmen, a break from customary norms of labour organisation, and one very much driven by the increasingly cheap supply of labour. Under this system, we do not see the development of highly subdivided tasks, as the workmen still maintained direct control of the labour process. But employment for the colliers was increasingly insecure as large employers were increasingly able to access an emerging national labour market in which labour was increasingly commodified. As the supply of labour increased, even in those industries where the factory system was not developing, there was a growing tendency towards viewing labour as simply one input among others in the production process, or in other words as *abstract labour* or as *capital*. In the coming chapters we will visit examples of how in these industries the movement from a formal to a real subsumption of labour continued, but was a long and protracted process.

To the extent that the commodification of labour presupposes a social property relationship between a class of owner-employers paying wages in exchange for the labour-power of a class of free workers, we might expect to see clear evidence of these classes by the late eighteenth century. In the case of employers, we have seen that in nearly every industry there were industrialists accumulating large amounts of wealth and stock and employing hundreds, and in some cases thousands, of labourers at their operations – Wilkinson and Crawshay in iron, Williams in copper, Arkwright, Strutt and Peel in cotton, Gott and partners in wool, Marshall in linen, Taylor, Boulton and Champion in metallurgy, Barclay in Brewing, and so on. Certainly, they were amassing capital in the static sense, and we have been at pains to suggest that while the social relation of capital was first established in agriculture, the rate at which the conversion from traditional manufactures regulated by custom and monopoly to the formal subsumption of labour to capital, to the real subsumption of labour to capital varied in different lines of manufacturing. We have seen how many of the early industrialists were enthusiasts for science and made connections through amateur science clubs like the Lunar Society. There were only the beginnings of an indication that they saw themselves as a new class. Arkwright's life-long ambition was to join the ranks of the gentry. Wilkinson was an improving landlord. The Darbys incorporated farming into their increasingly vast operation to supply horses for railways and wagon-teams, and sold clover, wheat, barley, bark, horses and sheep.[174] The success of the Darbys had depended upon innovation; one generation building upon the advances and insights of the previous one. By the end of the century, the Darby works would produce in excess of thirteen thousand tons of iron per annum, an increase of twenty-five-fold since the time of the first Darby.[175] The pioneering capitalists of the Industrial Revolution displayed a remarkable capacity for self-reproduction in terms of passing on their works to sons bearing the same name. Thus the second generation of industrialists included Richard Arkwright II, Josiah Wedgwood II, Josiah Spode II, James Watt II and Matthew Boulton II. The Soho foundry was taken over by the sons of Boulton and Watt, as intended, with Murdoch's aid. In the case of the Darbys, Abraham Darby III and Samuel Darby, who died in 1789 and 1796 respectively, passed Coalbrookdale onto the fourth generation: Francis Darby, Edmund Darby and Abraham Darby IV.[176] These second, third and fourth generations of the early masters would go on to articulate the interests of industrialists in a more certain expression of a class. But their fathers did combine in order to attempt to influence policy according to a perceived common interest.

It was Samuel Garbett who spearheaded the General Chamber of Manufacturers, an early lobby group which was perhaps the first attempt by the

174. Trinder 1974, p. 40.
175. Mantoux 1961, p. 300.
176. Trinder 1974, pp. 51–8.

manufacturer to seek to influence policy separate from the mercantile interest. Acting on a 'general conviction that the Ministry was hopelessly ignorant of the problems of industry and foreign trade', Garbett sought to organise manufacturers to press for a commercial treaty with the newly independent United States in 1782. Only a loose federation was ever achieved, put under the presidency of Josiah Wedgwood. Garbett and Wedgwood soon split over the decision of whether to make concessions and work with Pitt's ministry, which Garbett favoured, or side with the opposition, as Wedgwood preferred. This schism persisted in discussions over the signing of a commercial treaty with France in 1786, with the opposing faction arguing that the only industries to benefit would be those that enjoyed the advantages of technological superiority, speculation and credit, such as Manchester's cotton masters, whilst the older industries 'firmly established on the solid foundations of the English agricultural economy',[177] such as Bristol's brass trade, would lose their protective tariffs and be exposed to ruin from foreign competition. Such a schism attests to the fact that, by and large, capitalist entrepreneurs were still a *type* and not a class. The Chamber soon fell apart. But regional associations continued, and this first attempt was only the beginnings of an increasingly 'class-conscious' group of industrialists whose power rested in the control of capital.

As we shall see below, it would take several decades before the first efforts to establish organisations representing a working class in general, in the form of the early cross-trade combinations or *trades* unions (not to be confused with single-industry *trade* unions). Every economy is but the ensemble of that society's social reproduction, which is realised in specific social forms and foundations that are *never* universal or simply natural. The development of a capitalist economy may be implied by the dominance of a certain set of interests with a powerful intrinsic logic, such as the drive to transform production in accordance with market competition, but the social relationships of capitalism still must be realised in society. And in society, there were and are powerful interests capable of mounting significant resistance to the introduction or imposition of the social property relation of capital.

---

177. Norris 1958, pp. 450–60.

Part Three

Custom's Last Stand

The Rise and Fall of Artisan-Led Resistance to Capitalism in England, 1783–1848

Chapter Ten
Custom and Law

> Her memory still is dear to journeymen,
> For sheltered by her laws, now they resist
> Infringements, which would else persist:
> Tyrannic masters, innovating fools
> Are check'd, and bounded by her glorious rules.
> Of workmen's rights she's still a guarantee.[1]

In the late eighteenth century, the Saddlers, who had just emerged from a dispute in which they presumably prevailed, composed this 'Ode to the Memory of Queen Elizabeth'. The ring of nostalgia and the need to eulogise the Statute of Apprentices to which it refers are undoubtedly the result of at least a century of case law decisions that had resulted in the scope of 5 Elizabeth c. 4 being considerably narrowed in comparison to how it had been applied in the past.[2] In the 1790s, cottage manufacturing – which afforded a relatively comfortable existence for the vast numbers of British people who were displaced from subsistence farming, their numbers rising along with the unprecedented rise in population – was reaching its zenith. Yet signs of its coming demise were everywhere. The customary laws that had shielded many peasants and craftsmen from full exposure to the market were coming under full attack in the name of progress. Parliamentary enclosures were reaching their peak, bringing

1. Rule 1987, p. 105.
2. Rule 1992a, p. 209. Note that 5 Elizabeth c. 4 is commonly referred to both as the 'Statute of Apprentices' and the 'Statute of Artificers', and sometimes as the 'Statute of Artificers and Apprentices'. For our purposes, we shall use the name 'Statute of Apprentices', as this seems to be the most common usage.

about the final extinguishing of the customary law of the manor, specifically by dismantling, parish by parish, the last of the customary courts that regulated the production relations of the village. Under the banner of 'free trade', commerce was increasingly opening up to allow all comers who had the means to take part to enter. Now it was manufacturing's turn. Factories and workhouses were being built apace. Britain's cities and towns were filling up with factory workers, outworkers and a 'reserve army of labour' of the poor and unemployed. Crime and policing were set to grow alongside one another. Harsh new laws against theft and vagrancy were directed primarily at the poor, while laws such as 5 Elizabeth and the customary social arrangements it enshrined were running up against the new liberal ideology embodied in the recent and increasingly popular writings of the political economists. In this chapter, we will examine the period between the accession of the younger Pitt to the office of Prime Minister in 1783 and Parliament's adoption of the Speenhamland system in 1795, with an eye to solving the riddle of why during this period appeals to custom and customary forms of protest became *more*, not less prominent a social phenomenon in British social life and politics.

We have already seen how the customary regulation of manufactures as enshrined in the Statute of Apprentices was increasingly disregarded by employers throughout the eighteenth century. With the full repeal of the statute in 1814, it might be expected that this closed the final chapter on customary regulation of production in Britain. But this was not the case. The peculiarity of custom is that while it was reflected or enshrined in laws and statutes, custom goes beyond law. Custom defies simple definition. Custom is rooted in communities, in local culture; it is *lex loci*. The cultural norms and practices that regulated economic life before capitalism could not simply be legislated out of existence. As the legal framework upon which customary modes of social and economic regulation were founded was dismantled, resistance to the imposition of capitalism and in defence of custom persisted and took on new forms.

Custom was not merely a 'fetter' or a 'brake' on the inevitable development of an already existing market society. Markets had existed before, but market society had not. Custom regulated both markets and production in pre-capitalist society. The fact that custom comes to the fore just as the legal foundations of customary, normative economic regulation are being dismantled underscores the fact that what is being created in capitalism is something entirely new, and that the resistance put up by local communities of labourers and craftsmen was based in the cultural understandings that they shared, having no other precedent upon which to base their response. Those who engaged in forms of resistance to capitalism and industrialisation that appealed to custom were not backward, self-interested and myopic as they have often been portrayed. They were not engaging in a resistance against a form of society that already existed; rather, they were resisting efforts to *construct* a new form of society that had never previously existed. What was strange and unusual was not the way in which labourers 'fell back' on appeals to custom in defence of their traditions and their control of the labour process in manufactures. What was strange, new and unusual was capitalism, and the efforts to impose capitalist economic regulation of production by market forces. Since this was a protracted process which started in agricultural relations and advanced in some lines of manufacturing before others, as the process wore on working people were able to get an ever clearer picture of what type of society was being brought into existence, and the disadvantages and losses they would suffer if their resistance failed. Thus, they were seeking to preserve and protect their communities, their way of life as they knew it, and their independence from being destroyed and from being replaced by something entirely new, which being new and therefore full of unforeseeable consequences, appeared to pose enormous risks. Rather than take a leap in the dark, craftsmen and their allies sought to preserve the mode of production that they had known and relied on since time out of mind.

The paradox of custom

How could custom, which had always been associated with tradition and conservatism, become associated with rebellion? The great paradox of the eighteenth century, writes E.P. Thompson, is that 'we have a *rebellious* traditional culture'.[3] This was, as already suggested, a reflection of the profound transformation in social relations taking place in British society. Prior to the eighteenth century, custom was in general associated with order, obedience and conservatism: 'It was the religious duty of everyone, whatever their position in the hierarchy, to render unquestioning obedience to their divinely ordained superiors and to impose it on those entrusted to their charge. Without this control, the innate wickedness of fallen man would result in general anarchy and insecurity'.[4]

In this way, the Church was the institution most responsible for promoting and maintaining a highly conservative social order in which the economy was embedded in and inseparable from the culture, and was normatively regulated by prescriptions and rules based on an understanding of what constituted 'custom'. Over 'a broad spectrum of public affairs, there was no necessity to analyse and discuss what needed to be done; to every problem there were answers based on

3. Thompson 1993, p. 9.
4. Upton 2001, p. 16.

what had always been done before'.[5] Society was comprised of a wide variety of self-financing, self-governing collectives, each with its own rules, and upon which government depended. In order to serve as the arbiter in the endless disputes that arose between these groups, the state wielded the stick of requiring deference and obedience to a pre-ordained hierarchy and offered the carrot of patronage.[6]

In eighteenth-century Britain, the forces of agrarian capitalism and the beginnings of an industrial capitalism were uprooting the institutional foundations of custom and inducing a radical transformation subversive of the traditional social order. The traditional bonds of mutual dependence between plebeian workers and peasants and patrician gentry and peerage were being eroded, and in the process the gap between the cultures of the rich and the poor was widening. In the context of the onslaught against customary rights and customary forms of property, the public ceremonies of popular culture became more visible. They were codified with greater exactitude. This was no longer *just* a 'traditional culture' writes Thompson, 'powerful self-motivating forces of social and moral regulation were at work' and the customary norms being defended were 'not identical with those proclaimed by Church or authority', they were coming to be 'defined within the plebeian culture itself'.[7] A crucial point to derive from Thompson's work for the purposes of this study is that poor and working people were neither passive agents simply swept away by the newly 'unleashed' forces of the market, nor mindless contrarians pitting themselves against the inevitability of progress and the factory system. They were dynamically engaged with the process of change that confronted them, and so in the process of the broad transformation of social relations, the idea of custom itself changed as plebeians sought to assert their rights in both old and new forms. In investigating the gamut of rituals of eighteenth- and early nineteenth-century plebeian culture in Britain – well dressings, rush-bearings, harvest homes, skimmington ridings, shivarees, the stag-hunt, 'groaning', rough musick and wife sales – Thompson finds that 'far from having the steady permanence suggested by the word "tradition", custom was a field of change and of contest, an arena in which opposing interests made conflicting claims'.[8] This meant that custom in the eighteenth century was 'in continual flux', having increasingly become 'the rhetoric of legitimation for almost any usage, practice, or demanded right'.[9] In eighteenth-century Britain, as the elite launched an all-out assault on customary rights in the name

5. Ibid.
6. Upton 2001, pp. 21–5.
7. Thompson 1993, p. 8.
8. Thompson 1993, p. 6.
9. Ibid.

of private property and free trade and as customary law was extinguished, the status of customary labourers was gradually eroded whilst women, children and paupers were pressed into factories and workhouses.

In the midst of this assault on custom, the plebs employed the discourse of customary right *creatively*, not only in defending those long-held rights and privileges that were under assault, but also in asserting new rights in the form of *new* customs. While at the level of skimmington ridings and the like, the paradoxical invention of new customs may be seen as a useful tactic in the class struggle, at the level of tenancy rights it was most controversial. 'Squatters and other migrants', write King and Tomkins, were:

> agents in the fabrication of their own economy of makeshifts: inventing traditions where there were none, claiming rights by virtue only of residence, manipulating custom in their own interest. Settlement at the margins of a forest economy was not, therefore, a survival *strategy* legitimately played out in a context of widely recognized ethical rules, but a survival *tactic* which ingeniously exploited the "unstopped cracks in the wainscoting of power" . . . All of which brings us to the vexed question of who actually was *entitled* to common-right. In the early seventeenth century, at a time when there were perhaps 170 households in the parish, Brigstock possessed fifty-three suit-houses, two half, and nine quarter suit-houses, whose tenants were allowed housebot (the right to take timber for house repairs) by order of the forest courts . . . the tenants of the ancient commonable cottages resented the poor migrants who claimed customary right simply on the basis of residence . . . For the poor migrant to the forest, therefore, custom came to be regarded not as *cohesive* but rather as a *restrictive* ideology, one of the structural constraints within, and around, which survival tactics were perforce developed'.[10]

This adds a layer of complexity to our discussion of custom that must not be overlooked. The observance of custom was conservative as a rule, but it was subject to bending by those, like the forest squatters here, who sought to claim rights that had not hitherto been recognised in local customary law. That this should have offended the 'legitimate' customary tenants should remind us that early-modern England was a deeply stratified society; those who had tenancy rights, however minimal, were still in a better position than those who had none.

From this it follows that in seeking to understand the role of custom during the period of the Industrial Revolution and the reasons why it became so 'robust', especially in the late eighteenth century, we need to examine far more than the strict institutional foundations of the customary law of the manor. At the same time, we can point to the long-term process of the extinguishing

10. King and Tomkins (eds.) 2003, pp. 46–50 and 53.

of customary law through enclosure as having already initiated the first major assault on customary rights in the interests of promoting agrarian capitalism. Manorial customary law varied widely from region to region in its details, but its scope generally extended well beyond the delineation of field boundaries and the inheritance rights of copyholds and freeholds. It also governed the rights of commons, including right of pasture, 'defining which animals, how many, and where, could take "bite of mouth" on the open fields after harvest';[11] right of estover, or the right to take wood from the commons, wastes or forests for various purposes; right of turbary,[12] or the right to cut peat or turf (furze) for fuel or to make ashes for fertiliser; right of piscary, or the right to fish in parish-streams and ponds; as well as hunting rights or rights to collect acorns, berries, mast for pigs, sand or gravel (among other items) from the commons. All these customs were governed by the manorial court, which 'settled disputes, made bylaws about the maintenance of the fields and common pastures, protecting them from overstocking, fined transgressors, and supervised a small bureaucracy of pinters, fieldsmen, even mole-catchers'.[13] These customary rights were also sanctioned by the Church, which was directly involved in their maintenance. Gleaning, the right to gather left-over grain after the reaping, was sanctioned by the Bible – 'neither shalt thou gather any gleaning of thy harvest: thou shalt leave them unto the poor, and to the stranger' (from 23: 22, King James version) – and the parish bells were often rung upon the opening of the fields after harvest.[14] All of these rights were threatened, if not eliminated, upon enclosure.

More recent historiography has revealed that resistance to Parliamentary enclosure was more extensive than previous scholarship had allowed. Actions ranged from petitions to tearing down fences to public protests. Hay and Rogers give several examples: a crowd of football players in Northamptonshire abruptly turning on and burning two thousand pounds worth of fences, anti-enclosure protesters being subdued in Wilbartson and forced to unload waggons of fencing under the watch of armed cavalry, a crowd of sixty women in Burton-on-Trent pulling down fences in 1771, subsequently arrested, gaoled and rescued by a crowd of three hundred. This last vignette testifies to the impact of enclosures

11. Hay and Rogers 1997, p. 86. Right of pasture included 'levancy and couchancy', defined as '"a stint of common in contradistinction to common sans nombre, and signifies only so many as the messuage or fawn will by its produce maintain"': Hurlstone and Coltman (eds.) 1866, p. 28 citing the case of *Rogers v. Benstead*. The reader will note that with the extinction of agrarian customary law and the associated normative social relations, an entire vocabulary of terms entirely fell out of usage from the English language.
12. Gonner 1966, pp. 14–15.
13. Hay and Rogers 1997, p. 87.
14. Ibid.

on women, who made the most use of the commons, and who underwent significant proletarianisation as a result of enclosures.[15]

With the earlier, piecemeal enclosures, the loss of common rights could be gradual. But the parliamentary enclosures of the late eighteenth century were typically wholesale, enclosing the arable fields, wastes and commons. The remaining tenants were typically cottagers. Some limited access to commons in the form of gleaning and other customary rights may have persisted, but these were proscribed over time and even grazing rights would become subject to market contracts.[16] Between 1793 and 1813, some two thousand acts of enclosure were passed by Parliament, twice the figure for 1760–80.[17] So it is against this background, as the remaining quarter or third of open fields was being enclosed and the remaining 'commoners' rendered market-dependent,[18] that the domestic upheavals of the era of the French Wars took place. Britain's population was truly becoming the first people in the world to depend primarily upon markets for access to the means of subsistence.

To the complexities of war and the high tide of enclosures we must add a series of poor harvests. Between 1793 and 1818 only three abundant harvests were brought in, while fourteen were deficient. The years 1795–6 and 1800–1 were described in some parts as 'famines'. Unprecedented numbers of agrarian labourers took part in food protests as they could scarcely supply their families with bread.[19] Another low point came in 1813.[20] The increasing pressure on food supplies and grain markets which the displacement of self-subsistent agriculturalists, now 'hurled' into a situation of market dependence, added to the pressures of population growth could only have exacerbated hardships. It cannot be coincidence that grain imports doubled in this period, while grain exports virtually ceased. In the 1950s, Professor Chambers's work, which seemed to confirm the optimism of political economy with regard to enclosure, enjoyed a brief orthodoxy. Based on evidence from Nottinghamshire, Chambers argued that the effect of enclosures was to increase overall demand for agrarian labour. But this orthodoxy was short-lived, as subsequent studies suggested the contrary,

---

15. Hay and Rogers 1997, pp. 100–1.
16. Thompson writes that: 'even in hardheaded terms there are sound reasons for affording latitude in minor common rights. It is better that a labour force should remain resident and available for the heavy calls of hay and harvest and incidental calls for labour including the extensive women's service in hall, farmhouse and dairy' (Thompson 1993, pp. 150–1). This passage is in reference to unenclosed parishes around 1750, but such considerations would have applied after enclosure as well.
17. Owen 1975, p. 301; Christie 1982, p. 159.
18. For an explanation of Neeson's use of the term 'Commoners' see Chapter Five, p. 275, n. 67.
19. Hay and Rogers 1997, p. 198.
20. Rule 1992a, p. 131.

and that post-enclosure parishes experienced out-migration, less regularity of employment and increases in the poor rates. Another major factor was the loss of rights of turbary. What had been a closely regulated right of commons now became a crime. The customary right of taking firebote or 'snapping wood' from the commons was probably the longest to survive and the most coveted. Wood was used for many purposes, and being in short supply, it was in high demand. The large numbers of prosecutions for 'stealing' wood in the late eighteenth century mainly arose from attempts by commoners to assert their customary rights after these rights had been effectively criminalised.[21]

To all of these pressures we must add the impact which the spread of the factory had on forms of by-employment such as spinning. Cottage manufacturing had provided a kind of safety net for countless peasant households who had now become cottagers. By 1788, there were sixty thousand hands employed in factory spinning and over ten thousand in hand weaving. By 1806 there would be ninety thousand factory spinners and one hundred and eighty-four thousand hand-weavers.[22] The swelling in numbers of those engaged in rural domestic manufacturing during the late eighteenth century meant that many more were becoming domestic producers of handicrafts at the very same time as the customary regulations that had long governed such trades were coming under increasing strain and attack. In effect, the rural population was caught in the cross-currents of the successive waves of agrarian and industrial capitalism. It is only logical to expect that direct producers who found themselves proscribed from exercising their customary rights of ancient origin would become, upon shifting to reliance upon the sale of yarn, cloth or other goods produced in their domestic workshops and garrets, particularly attentive to the customary rights of their trades.

As we have seen, Elizabethan law had been based upon the regulations of the now defunct guilds, and were directed at the urban-based guilds of the sixteenth century. With the expansion of *rural* manufactures in the eighteenth century, the *principles* of customary craft regulation that had been enshrined in Elizabethan law were now being asserted in both new and old trades at a time when employers were already seeking to circumvent what they saw as restrictions upon freedom of trade. In this context, rights that were asserted in the name of custom were in reality 'claims, encroachments, negotiating positions, between employers and workers, masters and servants, or members of different trades'.[23]

As in the case of such customary rights as gleaning in agriculture, the remnants of production in manufacturing also became an object of deep contention.

---

21. Bushaway 1982b, pp. 71–2; Rule 1992a, p. 133.
22. Berg 1985, p. 259.
23. Hay and Rogers 1997 p. 91.

The existence of extensive opportunities for resale in manufacturing areas meant that it was easy to realise the value of appropriated raw materials, and often hard to prosecute. Legislation seeking to curb the unauthorised absconding of raw materials by employees stretches from 1512 to 1792. It was a particular problem in putting-out operations, where direct supervision was lacking. Since employers or putter-outers sometimes suffered serious losses, the problem of embezzlement was surely a significant impetus toward the centralisation of production. Pollard notes that putting a check on embezzlements by employees was one of the main achievements of the imposition of rigorous discipline in the factory or workshop.[24] For the labourer, the sale of embezzled materials (or products made with them) could amount to an increase in income of twenty per cent or more. Just as smuggling was widely condoned by labouring people, so too was embezzlement, or claiming the 'takings'. In part, the ambiguity arose from the fact that at certain times in certain industries, such rights were recognised as customary. 'Braziers took "filings", textile workers took "fents and thrums" [the fringes and ends left over from cloth production], shipwrights took "chips" . . .'[25] There was an ebb and flow at work in this process. During periods in which the money-supply was short, employers were happy to negotiate a partial payment of wages in kind, reinforcing the notion of the workers' right to take home some of the raw materials. In good times, the extent of such perquisites might be extended. But in hard times, they might tighten their enforcement of fines and deductions. All of this added to a general legal ambiguity regarding the status of materials which passed through the hands of relatively independent workers. The expansion of the domestic market in the eighteenth century made it possible in large-scale operations for whole subsidiary trades of considerable lucrativeness to arise out of the marketing of such post-production materials. Where workers had once been allowed to take home otherwise valueless waste materials for domestic use, such takings were now seen as a loss of value. Eighteenth-century legislation codified previous practices, extended the length of sentences for embezzlement and shifted the burden of proof from the accuser to the accused. By the end of the century, the number of convictions grew enormously as a government subsidy supported a private policing system designed to curb the practice in the Yorkshire wool and worsted industries.[26]

Not only production, but also trade had been regulated by custom since at least Anglo-Saxon times. The pattern follows a very similar trajectory to the role of custom in crafts. The entitlements and expectations of both craft trades and markets were codified in Tudor legislation and inscribed in local practice and

24. Pollard 1965, p. 210.
25. Hay and Rogers 1997 pp. 91–2.
26. Ibid. See Styles 1983, pp. 173–205.

ritual. It was under 5 and 6 Edward VI, c. 14 that the normative regulation of markets was enshrined in common law and the primary offences of forestalling, regrating and engrossing were defined. These prohibitions were concerned almost exclusively with the marketing of food provisions. Forestalling was the act of pre-empting the otherwise natural operation of the market by intercepting the product before it reached the point of sale with the intent to artificially induce a higher price. This was considered an infringement on the rights of customers to the lowest possible price on household necessities. Regrating and engrossing were each considered variations of forestalling. Regrating meant 'the buying of corn or other dead victual in any market and selling it again in the same market, or within four miles of the place'.[27] The primary concern about regrating was that it would lead to forestalling, or specifically that it would drive up the price, and so in some towns, such as Oxford, the resale of goods through middlemen was effectively regulated by a system of fines, which were not disincentives so much as 'a roundabout way of licensing the practice'.[28] Engrossing meant 'the buying up of a large quantity of corn or other dead victual, with a view to sell it again, by which means an individual of sufficient wealth might engross the whole of any necessary of life within a certain district, and raise the price of it at his pleasure'.[29] Other offences at the market included spreading false rumours or forming combinations (monopolies) with intent to inflate prices, employing false weights and measures, or selling adulterated food. In the early decades of the seventeenth century, the government codified laws against these offences in the *Book of Orders* and 'an administrative structure to survey markets and detect market criminals' was established.[30]

The Tudor laws had expressed the government's fear that 'social disasters might coincide with external threats to stability of régime'[31] and so particularly in times of dearth it was essential that profiteering middlemen be checked from sweeping markets clean, inflating prices to their own advantage and depriving the poor of their access to the 'necessaries of life'. But such laws had no teeth without the participation of the affected population. Informers were often paid for tipping off authorities about engrossers and regraters. But more important was the participation of the local population in public demonstrations or 'food riots' against such corruptions of the market. The aims of the 'mob' were typically to seize food that was scheduled to be exported, to expose and punish forestalling, regrating and engrossing and most of all, to demand that food be

27. Chitty 1824, p. 260.
28. Patterson and Alsford 2007.
29. Chitty 1824, pp. 260–1.
30. Hay and Rogers 1997, p. 93.
31. Hay and Rogers 1997, p. 92.

sold locally at a 'just price'.[32] Such demonstrations were known in virtually every town in seventeenth- and eighteenth-century Britain. They were recognised as something of an orderly ritual in which the local population asserted rights and expectations that had been codified in law. The acquiescence of the local JPs in order to placate the 'mob' was anticipated. 'Indeed', write Hay and Rogers, 'the established meaning of "police" until late in the eighteenth century was the effective governance of towns, and especially the policies that ensured food supplies and good order'.[33] When it came to disputes, the JPs had long presented themselves as referees in a society comprised of self-governing collectives with conflicting interests. The local JP had a strong interest in preserving his reputation as a fair and neutral arbiter. Moreover, local officials had their own interests in established custom: inheritances, various and sundry petty fees which they collected, membership in the local vestry were all seen as property rights rooted in ancient custom. In fact, it was a long established custom for the Crown to grant exclusive rights to hold markets. Here then is an entirely separate source of opposition to forestallers, regraters and engrossers, quite distinct from the government's need to keep the price of grain low in the public interest: the interests of *licensed* monopolists to exclude would be interlopers, as well as the government's interest in collecting licensing fees.[34] As the practice of licensing monopolies over holding local markets fell out of use, so this source of opposition to the practices of middlemen lost its force.

By the middle of the eighteenth century, the strict enforcement of these laws had long fallen into desuetude, although local magistrates continued to pursue them. But they did enjoy something of a partial revival; the *Book of Orders* was privately reprinted and its usage urged upon government officials in 1758. Under 31 George II the ban on forestalling was reaffirmed where cattle being brought to London was concerned. Such legislation, by promoting the idea that engrossers and regraters rather than poor harvests were responsible for local shortages of grain, may have actually encouraged attacks upon these middlemen.[35] At the urging of Edmund Burke, the Edwardian ban on forestalling was reduced to a misdemeanour in 1772 under 12 George III, c. 71 on the grounds that the prohibitions had 'in themselves a tendency to prevent free trade, and enhance the price of provisions, especially to the labouring and manufacturing poor'.[36] This was the language of political economy. It is notable that the justification for repeal could be grounded in the same concerns as those that gave rise to the prohibitions in

32. Hay and Rogers 1997, pp. 137–8.
33. Hay and Rogers 1997, p. 94.
34. See Letwin 1954, p. 370.
35. Outhwaite 1991, pp. 40, 52–3.
36. Chitty 1824, p. 260.

the first place. The courts however, responding to public outcries against these practices, continued to hand out convictions over the next several decades.[37]

For most of its centuries-long history, agrarian capitalism had rendered only a part of the population dependent upon the market for access to food and other means of subsistence. While more than half of the cultivable land in England had been enclosed by 1750, rights of common were still widespread. The extinguishing of customary rights to the remaining open fields, wastes and commons by Parliamentary enclosure during the latter half of the eighteenth century brought the greatest hardship to the cottager and the smallholder. The Tudor laws, particularly the Settlement Act of 1662, were written at a time when vagrants and vagabonds were seen as a threat to social order. The solution was for all hands to be put to work, and this could be accomplished if all recognised their natural superiors in a hierarchical order. The displacement of large sections of the agrarian population from access to the means of subsistence had created the *necessity* of offsetting their new vulnerability as market-dependent producers to the price of food in the form of the poor laws and the close regulation of markets by the state in the interest of protecting the poor from starvation. But what happens when, in the context of an unprecedented growth in population, virtually the entire population is in the process of becoming dependent upon markets for food?

Now you had a new situation. A large and growing displaced population meant rising poor rates. If local protests over food had once served as a kind of local barometer, indicating the need for state intervention in order to restore the local equilibrium between the interests of sellers and the necessity of local food supply, the transformation of social relations brought on by agrarian capitalism was now prompting a new and entirely different response from authorities. Increasingly, the legitimacy that the 'food riot' had once enjoyed was waning; authorities were coming around to the view that it was neither a reasonable way for the local population to invoke state intervention to protect local food markets, nor even

---

37. In *Rex v. Rusby*, 1799, the defendant Rusby had been indicted for regrating thirty quarters of oats, and probably appealed to the 1772 repeal. Lord Kenyon nevertheless found him guilty, penning in his finding: '"though in an evil hour all the statutes which had been existing above a century were at one blow repealed, yet, thank God, the provisions of the common law were not destroyed"... The vigour of Kenyon's address... so inflamed the public that a mob... tried to lynch Rusby, and ended by pulling down his house. The public was apparently not so convinced by Burke, Smith, and Parliament that forestalling was economically beneficial, or, at least, that laws prohibiting it were more harmful than the thing itself' (Letwin 1954, p. 372). The last conviction was in 1800, when two men were sentenced to three months in prison for forestalling cattle. In 1812, a case against engrossers of whale oil was dismissed. In 1844, the final repeal of all statutes against these offences was repealed in 8 Victoria, c. 24. This act repealed all legislation banning forestalling, regrating and engrossing stretching back to the first ban on forestalling registered in the statute books in 1266 (see Herbruck 1929, pp. 365–88).

a legitimate way of releasing pent-up social anxiety. Instead, by being lumped in with all forms of 'riot', the 'food riot' began to be seen as a *threat* to social stability. In the crisis years of 1795 and 1801, farm labourers were among the main participants in such disturbances.[38] Amongst farm labourers as well as domestic workers, factory workers, colliers and the poor, the growing prosperity of tenant-farmers was increasingly evident and resentment was not in short supply. Local Justices of the Peace were caught between the need to uphold the image of impartiality versus the pressure to enforce the new and harsh laws which criminalised protests and other threats to private property. In legal disputes between labourers and their employers, JPs tended to side with labourers for the simple reason that a lowering of wages resulted in a greater burden on the poor rates. In order for such tendencies to be broken, what was needed was a doctrine which would convince them of the rectitude of the law and to which they could refer in leaning towards the law and against custom.

'A Whig state of mind': political economy, the bloody code and the decline of paternalism

There is nothing more political than the making of laws. It is profoundly curious how political economy as a body of scholarship gave rise to modern neoclassical economics, which eschews politics and dwells almost strictly in the imagining of the 'purely' economic. Political economy was after all *political*; its principal aim was to direct state policy-makers in shaping and managing the economy. And it was under Pitt's administration in the 1790s that its doctrines first came to be implemented in any systematic fashion. The Hammonds describe the influence of political economy upon the thinking of Britain's elite as 'economic fatalism'.[39] This required, first of all, the re-casting of trade in a new light. Rather than being a zero-sum contest between nations, a conception Adam Smith associated with mercantilist thought, it was, instead, government interference with trade which, by interfering with Smith's 'obvious and simple system of natural liberty', restricted the actions of merchants and capitalists and held back the growth of economic prosperity. Additionally, rather than being opposed to the interest of the workman (or work-child), the self-interest of the employer was actually in accord with it because, as Burke wrote, the greater the profit-motive, the greater the desire of the employer would be in attending to 'the good condition of those [upon] whose labour his gains must principally depend'.'[40] We must be careful not to

38. Outhwaite 1991, p. 198.
39. Hammond and Hammond 1995, p. 196.
40. Burke 1829, p. 383 as cited in Hammond and Hammond 1995, pp. 196–200.

invite confusion. Burke's employer was a farmer, not a manufacturer. The latter notion no doubt resonated with manufacturers, but Adam Smith's principal appeal was to the gentry and yeoman farmers of the countryside. What is important to recognise about the meteoric rise to popularity of Smith's work is that it depended not upon any grounding in history or fact but in providing a systematic *theoretical* rationale that informed capitalist landlords, tenant-farmers and manufacturers of the self-evident moral justice that lay behind the principles of liberal thought and the emerging capitalist system. It was later compared to a system of metaphysics.[41]

One of Smith's purposes in writing *The Wealth of Nations*[42] was to provide 'a model of the workings of the economy',[43] not any specific economy, but *the* economy in general. By universalising the principles of the capitalist economy, Smith's work laid the foundation for the subsequent tendency to imagine that the capitalist system had long or always been in existence, waiting in the interstices of feudalism, and that its further growth and unfolding required only the removal of the hindrances or 'fetters' upon its growth and development. Secondly, Smith's work was intended as 'a policy recommendation of free trade and laissez-faire generally'.[44] 'What political economy forbade', writes Thompson, 'was any "violent interferences with the course of trade", including the prosecution of profiteers or hoarders, the fixing of maximum prices, and government intervention in grain or rice dealing'.[45] Markets, or rather *the* market, like *the* economy, were elevated to an abstract principle, as is strikingly evident in the following passage from Burke, who writes: ' "Market is the meeting and conference of the *consumer* and *producer*, when they mutually discover each other's wants ... The moment that government appears at market, all the principles of market will be subverted" '.[46] The 'principles of the market' are here conceptualised as universal truths, existing independently of history or any given set of social relations. Markets had thus always already existed and needed only the removal of the fetters of government regulation and custom in order to follow their 'natural' course.

This method of thinking was deeply informed by the methods of the natural sciences, such as physics, where it was necessary to conceptualise the interaction of moving or colliding bodies in the abstract, free from all other interferences. So here, we see Burke, under the influence of Smith, writing of 'market' in the same

41. By the author and clergyman Sydney Smith, according to Hammond and Hammond 1995, p. 205.
42. Smith 1957.
43. Raphael 1985, p. 46.
44. Ibid.
45. Thompson 1993, p. 282.
46. As cited in Thompson 1993, p. 273. Emphasis found in the original.

way one might write about 'gravity'.[47] The affinity of political economy with the natural sciences appeared to give it greater weight as a 'scientific' discourse and definitely added to its appeal. The *Wealth of Nations* impresses Thompson, however, 'less as an essay in empirical enquiry than as a superb, self-validating essay in logic'.[48]

At the time that Smith was writing *The Wealth of Nations*, the cause of *laissez-faire* was moving forward and appeals to custom were losing their sway, such as when legislation banning the practice of forestalling was repealed in 1772.[49] For eighteenth-century liberals, the greater abuses arose from 'the network of customary and legal restrictions which impeded the entrepreneur of relatively modest size who sought to exercise his abilities... "the grand enemy of the age" ' noted Tawney, ' "was monopoly" '.[50] The ideal society in the mind of British Enlightenment theorists ' "was a society where each man had free access to the economic opportunities which he could use and enjoy the wealth which by his efforts he had created" '.[51] Smith's work fits into this liberal tradition, but with some important departures.[52]

Smith was also very much a product of his time. If we can look beyond its ahistoricism and tendency to universalise capitalist economics, in some ways Adam Smith's *Wealth of Nations* reads like a snapshot of the state of agrarian capitalism at the barest advent of industrial capitalism and just prior to the advent of the factory system. Smith had spent time in France, was a personal friend of Quesnay and was influenced by the thinking of the Physiocrats. While he did not agree with their view that the source of all wealth was agriculture, their influence was evident in his view that agriculture was the best investment, as he writes: 'The capital... that is acquired to any country by commerce and manufactures, is all a very precarious and uncertain possession, till some part of it has been secured and realised in the cultivation and improvement of its lands'.[53] Only two of the book's 900 pages reference machinery, and then only to

---

47. Thompson points out that while the term 'market' can refer to *a* market or to *the* market as metaphor, 'too often discourse about "the market" conveys the sense of something definite – a space or institution of exchange (perhaps London's Corn Exchange at Mark Lane?) – when in fact, sometimes unknown to the term's user, it is being employed as a metaphor of economic process, or an idealization or abstraction from that process' (Thompson 1993, p. 273). At least Burke was careful enough to drop the definite article.
48. Thompson 1993, p. 203.
49. Thompson 1993, p. 201.
50. Fox 1985, pp. 46–7, quoting Tawney 1961, pp. 21–2.
51. Fox 1985, pp. 46–7. This remains a core doctrine of libertarian thought.
52. McNally provides a far more in-depth and nuanced discussion of Smith's thought than can be offered here, discussing the various influences on Smith's thought, including the Commonwealth tradition, the tradition of natural jurisprudence, the Whigs and the Physiocrats (McNally 1988, Chapters Four and Five).
53. Smith 1954, p. 395.

argue that the application of machinery, which for Smith arises out of the division of labour, is very advantageous because it tends to lower the cost of goods and is likely to increase rather than decrease employment.[54] The farmer and the landlord were, according to Smith, 'the least subject to the wretched spirit of monopoly... [and] are generally disposed rather to promote than obstruct the cultivation and improvement of their neighbours farms and estates'.[55] Unlike manufacturers, gentlemen and farmers openly share their discoveries in innovation of production, and being dispersed throughout the countryside, they cannot easily form combinations. Consistent with his hostility to monopolies, Smith was critical of employer combinations and attempts by merchants and manufacturers to reduce competition in the interest of depressing wages and increasing their profits. This, for Smith, would deprive working people of their rightful benefits in a growing and prosperous economy. While Joan Thirsk found Smith's harsh criticisms of rural domestic manufacturers too simplistic, even a 'grotesque caricature of the weaver farmer',[56] Maxine Berg clarifies that Smith's denunciations were not directed at the independent craft labourer, but at the merchant-employer operating on the putting-out system:

> The countryside and its workforce had been put at a disadvantage by a long history of economic policies designed to promote the interests of urban-incorporated industries at the expense of agriculture and other rural enterprises. Smith was, indeed, critical of these developments, but in his model of the natural progress of opulence what better, sustained analysis and prescription for the agricultural origins of industry? What greater praise for the significance of basic domestic commodities catering to a home market, and for the importance of the rural industries which gave rise to the fastest growing urban areas of the period? Smith was a theorist whose economic analysis was a social and moral tribute to the growth of agriculture and the development of the country region, with its own integrated towns, as opposed to the wealthy mercantile city. And he was a theorist who found in tenant farmers, country labourers and independent artisans a class whose individual interests and attributes were pre-eminently conducive to the growth of the wealth of the nation.[57]

54. Smith 1954, pp. 9 and 272.

55. Smith 1954, pp. 428–9. See McNally 1993, p. 60. One should observe that as agrarian capitalism was advanced by this time, while capitalism in industry was just starting to achieve real control over production, it makes perfect sense that Smith would find farmers and landlords to be less beholden to the spirit of monopoly. Fifty or a hundred years later, these relative outlooks would appear very different.

56. Thirsk 1978, pp. 150–1 as cited in Berg 1983, p. 44.

57. Berg 1983, p. 53.

Far from condemning the unregulated labours of rural artisans, Smith was their champion. In all of this, Smith stands as the classic spokesman for agrarian capitalism and as an expression, to a certain extent, of the older school of British conservatism in which it was seen as the obligation of the ruling landed elite to look after the interests of the poor.

This points to the deep tension within Smith's work and within agrarian capitalism itself. On the one hand, Smith declared his hostility to the 'traditional' policies of mercantilism and of customary order: chartered monopolies, employers' combinations, fixed wage rates, restrictions on labour mobility and indentured servitude all had to go. On the other hand, Smith tacitly approved of the poor laws and in what was a traditional view, looked to the 'natural aristocracy', the landed gentlemen, to 'exercise those civic virtues without which corruption and decay were inevitable'.[58] While idealising markets as offering all classes the means to increase their own share of the national wealth, the landed classes with their supposed virtues were to provide the moral check on the forces of coercion and exploitation that could be unleashed by the de-regulation of markets.

This tension went deeper than a conflict between agrarian capitalism and emerging industrial capitalism, or between custom and free markets. The growth of capitalism has always presented choices in the form of trade-offs. For the landed classes, the expansion of capitalist tenant-farming on enclosed farms came with the decline of the employment of servants-in-husbandry and the customary bonds of deference and dependence. For merchants and manufacturers, the expansion and deregulation of markets came with heightened competition and the decline of chartered monopolies. And for the growing numbers of wage-labourers who often asserted traditional rights based in custom, the liberal creed of free markets, freedom of contract and self-realisation had a definite allure. This is a crucial point. For while the radical movements of the late eighteenth and early twentieth centuries sought to retain rights and privileges rooted in custom, there would be no nostalgia for the decline of indentured servitude or the traditional hierarchy in which each was born to a station in life with little room for upward mobility. As Fox writes: 'However much wage-earners might look back to a supposedly golden age of guild or state protection when they contemplated their workplace predicament, there were many respects in which they looked forward to a condition of individual rights and liberation'.[59]

Inasmuch as Smith was true to his principles and consistently defended the interests of working populations within the new market order, he invited adherents amongst the working class. It is thus no surprise that self-described 'Smithian socialists' emerged among the radicals by the 1820s.[60] Yet inasmuch as this

58. McNally 1993, pp. 40–61.
59. Fox 1985, p. 48.
60. McNally 1993, p. 43.

concern was rooted in the conservatism that had its origins in the paternalistic ties of master and servant of the old economy, it was virtually inevitable that later apologists for capitalism would strip Smith's teachings of this moral component and retain the market rhetoric, which, 'joined to a moral crusade against the "indolence" of the poor', would 'serve as a powerful ideological weapon against the working class in the age of the industrial revolution'.[61] To this we must add the growing body of criminal law directed at poor and working people. Confronted with this combined arsenal, the pressure on the non-propertied classes to seek out new forms of emancipation was only intensified.

With the expansion of the domestic market and the conversion to a money economy and money wages over the course of the eighteenth century, the corresponding rapid expansion of wealth brought with it a heightened desire for security of property. Responding to this concern, Parliament passed one act after another, making crimes against property punishable by the death penalty. The cornerstone of this 'bloody code' was the Black Act of 1723, which set down a wide variety of new capital punishments for actions as trivial as stealing a fawn, giving the landed oligarchs a 'versatile armoury of death'[62] with which to confront any challenges to the security of their landed property.[63]

The new wealth of the patrician elite offered tempting rewards to the burglar, the footpad and the highwayman. And London's metropolis, where it was not possible to exercise the same level of paternalistic control as in the countryside, was unique in seeing the development of a criminal underground. To the pickpocket and the thief, the City offered the advantage of anonymity, narrow alleys and slum districts where police did not tread. Unlike rural thieves, who often stole food or were prosecuted under new laws against what had once been rights on the commons, London's thieves stole money and household goods such as plate silver. While the eighteenth century saw a number of master thieves, such as Jonathan Wild, Dick Turpin or Jack Sheppard,[64] most crimes involved petty thievery and were motivated primarily by urban poverty.[65] There was a perception that wickedness in general was on the rise. But we must consider that crime may not have grown in equal proportion to the expansion of wealth, and we must also bear in mind that the expansion of capital offences was out of all proportion to the growth of crime.

This expansion of capital offences can be partly explained by a kind of snowball effect: 'If you hanged for sheep-stealing, logically you had also to hang

61. McNally 1993, p. 59.
62. Thompson 1990, pp. 192 and 197.
63. McLynn 1989, p. xi.
64. See McLynn 1989, pp. 22–32.
65. Inwood 1998, pp. 372–3.

the man who stole a cow or a goat. There would literally be no end to the crazy cycle of "deterrence" '.[66] The crime of murder nearly always arises from entirely deep-seated personal motives, like passion or family disputes, and the severity of the punishment has never seemed to have much deterring effect. The homicide rate in Britain was well below that of Europe, but the expansion in the number of capital offences was out of proportion with the crime rate. Moreover, the new offences being added were nearly all in defence of property rather than of person. Burglary was the most common crime committed, and most typically what drove men and women to steal was poverty. But the absurdity of the vast expansion of capital offences is that it had virtually no deterring effect, since the new laws did nothing to address the poverty and distress underlying crimes against property.[67]

As customary and communal rights in the countryside and the chartered rights and privileged monopolies in crafts and trade were being dismantled, they were replaced with what were effectively new forms of absolute individual property rights. 'For Adam Smith', writes Thompson, 'property was either "perfect" and absolute or it was meaningless'.[68] The 'elevation of property above all other values', writes Thompson, was 'a Whig state of mind'.[69] 'Again and again', writes Hay, 'the voices of money and power declare the sacredness of property in terms hitherto reserved for human life. Banks were credited with souls, and the circulation of gold likened to that of blood'.[70] At the same time, the belief in a world imbued with magical powers was in decline.[71] The burning of witches and the tormenting of heretics were punishments belonging to the past, but summary justice was not. Secure on their estates where they were surrounded by servants and guards, the landed gentry and peerage had little reason to care about petty thievery or the occasional murder in London. As members of Parliament, they gave the true guardians of their class, the local Justices of the Peace, sweeping powers 'to convict offenders without the trouble of legalistic indictments or tender-minded juries. In cases involving grain, wood, trees, garden produce, fruit, turnips, dogs, cattle, horses, the hedges of parks and game, summary proceedings usually yielded a speedy and simple conviction'.[72] The focus of such legislation – including the Black Act – testifies to an obsession with *agrarian* property.

---

66. McLynn 1989, p. xiv.
67. McLynn 1989, p. 90.
68. Thompson 1993, p. 162.
69. Thompson 1993, p. 197.
70. Hay 1975, p. 19.
71. Except, perhaps, when it came to the ritual of public execution. While the King no longer condescended to offer the 'touch' to victims of scrofula, 'the "death sweat" of executed malefactors was still held to possess the power to cure this disease' (Linebaugh 1975, p. 110).
72. Hay 1975, p. 17.

Between 1688 and 1765, the number of capital offences rose from less than fifty to around one hundred and sixty, and by 1815 the total was around two hundred and twenty-five. This included only those offences explicitly carrying the death penalty; the number of offences *potentially* carrying the death penalty put the figure far higher. Yet the use of execution did not grow to match. Occasional public hangings in the face-to-face community of the towns served to set an example. 'The landed rulers of England did not *need* to hang all those indicted for felony; the assumption was of exemplary rather than retributive punishment'.[73] In unpacking this issue, Hay responds to contemporary critics who complained that the low number of prosecutions showed that the law was not an effective deterrent of crime by countering with the suggestion that ideology was as important as coercion in the efforts of the ruling class to utilise the law as an instrument of securing their rule and their hegemony. To this end, they deployed 'levers of fear and mercy' to invoke terror, yes, but also to sustain belief in the legitimacy of the law by frequently granting pardons or preserving the prerogative to deliver sentences well short of the harsh penalties prescribed by the law. The show of paternalistic benevolence in the courtroom was intended 'to move the court, to impress the onlookers by word and gesture, to fuse terror and argument into the amalgam of legitimate power in their minds'.[74] Such theatre was not only necessary, but, indeed, proved effective in maintaining a certain level of confidence in a legal system that was increasingly invoked to fill the breach created by the decline in traditional beliefs that could no longer be sustained through religion.[75] As the law increasingly focused on rights of property, this began to make itself felt outside of ruling circles.

Eighteenth-century Britain was a society rife with patronage and bribery. Positions from 'the City Recorder to the merest turnkey in the Fleet prison had to be bought, citizens who petitioned for justice had themselves to line the pockets of those who had bought these "places" '.[76] Educated men fallen from favour took to the highways and claimed a desolate stretch of road as, in effect, their property, politely (for the most part) extorting valuables from their unwary victims. This was consistent with the mid-eighteenth century concept of 'property' as encompassing both customary rights and perquisites, whether truly of ancient standing or recently invented. In this sense, the defence of custom by commoners was not strictly backward-looking, for increasingly those who claimed rights in custom adapted the language of their claims to that of the emerging market culture.

---

73. Rule 1992a, p. 237.
74. Hay 1975, p. 29.
75. McLynn 1989, pp. xvi–xvii.
76. McLynn 1989, pp. 20–1.

Smith's achievement in the *Wealth of Nations* was to collect the work of previous thinkers and package them in a systematic theoretical framework.[77] Thompson describes the potency of this new economic theory as 'no less far-reaching than the more widely-debated dissolution of restrictions upon usury'.[78] In elite discourse, custom came to be defined as 'usurpation, archaic ignorance, immorality, even criminality'.[79] Smith dismissed customary arguments against forestalling and engrossing 'as superstitious on a level with witchcraft'.[80] But it was precisely in relation to the economy of food where the theory was and remains the most controversial. Political economy promoted the notion that high prices were a necessary if painful remedy for food scarcity because the law of supply and demand dictates that supplies will be attracted to a region where prices are high. This logic leads, however, to what Thompson calls a 'most unhappy error'. It ignores the problem that arises when a portion of the population lacks the purchasing power to obtain grain at high prices or in some cases even when prices are low. 'Rationing by price', writes Thompson, 'does not allocate resources equally among those in need; it reserves the supply to those who can pay the price and excludes those who can't'.[81] For a society nearing the completion of a

77. Fox 1985, p. 47. For a review of some of the seminal thinkers in British political economy before Smith, see Berg 1983, 36–43. The author thanks Professor Sally Zerker at York University for clarifying this point.

78. Thompson 1989, p. 201.

79. Hay and Rogers 1997, pp. 97, 216 and 220.

80. Thompson 1989, p. 203. As a member of the jury of a 1779 case in which a man was convicted for regrating oats, Lord Kenyon wrote: ' "I wish Dr. Adam Smith had lived to hear the evidence of today, and then he would have seen whether such an offence exists and whether it is to be dreaded. If he had been told that cattle and corn were brought to market, and then bought by a man whose purse happened to be larger than his neighbours, so that the poor man who walks the street and earns his daily bread by his daily labour, could get none but through his hands, and at the price he chose to demand; that it had been raised 3d, 6d, 1s, 2s and more a quarter on the same day, would he have said that there was no danger from such an offence" ' (as quoted in Herbruck 1929, pp. 384–5). For his part, Smith opposed any policy that would raise prices above their 'natural' level as tending to 'diminish the public opulence'. At the same time, he criticised merchants and manufacturers for complaining of the expensiveness of labour but staying silent when their own profits rose to a level harmful to society. Thus Lord Kenyon's attack may seem misplaced when put against these sentiments of Smith, but at the same time, Smith's 'natural price' was precisely that which was governed by the law of supply and demand. As McNally 1988, pp. 219–20 comments, 'Smith's theory of value was riddled with inconsistencies'.

81. Thompson 1989, p. 285. Thompson borrows from the work of Amartya Sen on late twentieth-century food shortages. Sen's work is based on entitlements to food, which could range from self-subsistence agriculture to food supplied by the master in living-in arrangements to food purchased on the market. Once food entitlements are lost, poor people can find themselves outside the market, and a self-reinforcing cycle can lead to famine. Rather than preaching inaction along the lines of Smith, Sen says the only way to break the cycle is to rapidly import large amounts of grain into the affected region (See Sen 1981).

transition from self-subsistent peasant agriculture to one in which all economic actors come to be dependent upon the market for their subsistence, imposing a new dogma that preached government inaction was dangerous in the extreme, and in many regions Britain came nearer to famine in 1795–6 and 1800–1 than it had since the upheavals of the seventeenth century, despite the enormous expansion of wealth that had since occurred. The famines which later took place in India and Ireland were also to a considerable degree attributable to the implementation of policies by the British state designed to promote free trade at the expense of economic relations that had previously buffered direct producers from the effects of exposure to the market.

In 1750, as much as half the population of Britain still practiced self-subsistent farming on open fields. By 1815, this number had shrunk to a small minority after the passage of over 3,000 acts of enclosure. In the 1750s, wage fixing and apprenticeship regulations were still in force within the woollen trade. By 1815, these had been abolished. In 1749, the broadest expansion of anti-combination legislation prior to the Combination Acts of 1799 and 1780 was passed and the provisions of the weavers' combination act were extended to many other textile crafts.[82] In 1751, a committee of Parliament had recommended revocation of all apprenticeship laws.[83] When Lancashire cotton weavers were faced with an influx of cheap labour in the year 1756, they sought to extend the apprenticeship-rules of 5 Elizabeth to their trade but were refused.[84] In 1773, Parliament passed the exceptional Spitalfields Act, which limited the number of apprentices at two per weaver and sought to stabilise the wages of the Spitalfields silk workers by empowering Justices of the Peace to set wages and fine employers for paying any other rate. It was also a combination act, banning combinations – but not petitions – for higher wages.[85] This act was exceptional in the way it amounted to government interference in the free action of market wages. It was effectively coerced out of Parliament through violent demonstrations on the part of the Spitalfields weavers protesting against the introduction of the Dutch 'engine'

82. The trades covered under this act (22 Geo. II, c. 27, §12) included: 'Dyers and hot-pressers, felt makers and hatters, and all persons employed in the manufacture of silk, mohair, fur, hemp, flax, linen, cotton, fustian, iron and leather... as well all persons employed "in or about any of the woollen manufactures"' (Orth 1987, pp. 189–92). The ban against combinations among hatters was specifically extended by an act of 1777 which offered the 'modest concession' of requiring masters to hire one journeyman for every apprentice they employed.

83. Hay and Rogers 1997, p. 104.

84. Rule 1987, p. 106.

85. The Act (13 Geo. 3, c. 68, §1), was specific to the London area. It was extended in 1792 to include the production of cloth made of silk mixed with other fibres. Orth 1987, pp. 190–1.

loom into their trade, which led to armed clashes in the years 1768–9.[86] Its real intent, according to magistrate John Fielding, was to divert the matter back to the courts.[87] But the legislation held for another half century, during which Spitalfields enjoyed stable and tranquil labour relations. In most other trades, appeals to custom were losing their sway in the courts, such that by the 1790s probably the majority of judges in England had conformed to the outlook of the political economists. An example from a Lancashire weavers' society exemplifies how such organisations responded to the increasing hostility of the courts to the customary rights of the craft trades. Their standing orders were rewritten to set out a code of strict reverence and observance of etiquette. With this in place, they felt better able to meet any 'grand objection that may possibly be made to the whole, and that is, That it will be acting too much against Common Law', to which they might answer, '"That we have hitherto been acting more so, than we shall, when once Unity, Order and Decency is established among us"'.[88] They were ahead of their time.

The so-called Gordon Riots marked an important turning point in the decline of custom. The worst elite fears of a 'mob' running amok were played out. The response was brutal. Thompson viewed this as the point of climax:

> For a hundred years [the poor] were not altogether the losers. They maintained their traditional culture; they secured a partial arrest of the work-discipline of early industrialism; they perhaps enlarged the scope of the poor laws; they enforced charities which may have prevented years of dearth from escalating into crises of subsistence; and they enjoyed liberties of pushing about the streets and jostling, gaping and huzzaing, pulling down the houses of obnoxious bakers or Dissenters... [But the Gordon riots were] the apotheosis... of plebeian license; and inflicted a trauma upon the rulers which was registered in a growing disciplinary tone in the eighties...[89]

The violence of the response no doubt elicited even greater trauma among common people. There was widespread shock that so many of those sent to the gallows were teenagers. McLynn considers the Gordon Riots 'the greatest civil disorders in England since the 1685 Monmouth rebellion' and 'the nearest thing to the French Revolution in English History'.[90] The outrage conjured up new and venomous responses on the part of the elite, setting the stage for the repression

86. See McLynn 1989, pp. 229–30. Part of the dispute involved attempts by male silk-weavers to exclude women from higher paying work.
87. Leeson 1979, p. 88.
88. Wadsworth and Mann 1965, p. 346; unclear citation.
89. Thompson 1989, p. 95.
90. McLynn 1989, pp. 236–8.

of the 1790s. By 1785, long-standing resistance to the deployment of a professional police force yielded to the passage of the London and Westminster Police Bill.[91]

If it were possible to delineate a point at which the patriarchal system of old ended, leaving only what Thompson calls a 'patriarchal tinge' or its weaker alternative: 'paternalism', 1780 might be it. But the dissolution of the patriarchal bonds of the pre-capitalist estate or guild had been a long process which may have made this sort of convulsion inevitable. This is because as bonds of reciprocity were being replaced by wage contracts, as parading crowds attempting to drum up support with fiddles, cornets and drums could no longer count on the compassionate benevolence of the local JP to intervene in the name of the law and bring regulated order to the local market, being met instead with force, the once 'active and reciprocal relationship', or 'societal "field-of-force"'[92] that had long existed between the plebeian crowds and the patrician elite could clearly be seen to have broken down. In 1780 this breakdown, which had already been experienced in many local villages, was now experienced on a mass scale in the metropolis. While the focus of the disturbance was Catholic relief, and while the real political grievance likely had much more to do with the American War, underneath all that was the growth of a kind of semi-proletariat in the City. The Government's response in the use of force signalled the end to the old reciprocities, and while it remained unclear how rulers and subjects would interact in future, the factory posed a dismal sign of what the future portended for workers in manufacturing, whilst commoners in the countryside were everywhere seeing their access to means of subsistence eroded. It may be impossible to gauge the level of anxiety about the new economic realities and what role they played in 1780. But looking backward from Peterloo, 1780 could be seen to mark not so much the end of the old moral economy as much as it did the beginning of four decades of sharpening class conflict in which the role of custom in the economy was a central matter of contention.

'Is there any principle in these things?': the return of radicalism

Followers of Enlightenment thought had high hopes when George III entrusted the government to the Younger Pitt in 1783. Pitt recognised the need for reform, was a humanitarian, a close friend to William Wilberforce the abolitionist,

91. McLynn 1989, pp. 32–3 and 237. This bill was a triumph for the famous novelist Henry Fielding, the J. Edgar Hoover of his day, who served as Chief Magistrate in London until 1754. Fielding proposed establishing a light horse régiment in London to be at the ready upon reports of highway robberies. In 1749, he set up the Bow Street Runners, who were at first little more than 'glorified bounty-hunters', but who would go on to become a formidable precursor to Scotland Yard and the British police force.

92. See Thompson 1989, pp. 57 and 73; Hay and Rogers 1997, p. 140.

had met Adam Smith and had read his work.[93] The most pressing problem he faced upon assuming office was dealing with a national debt that had doubled since the outset of the American War, now standing at £243 million. While Pitt proved to be one of the most dedicated and capable statesmen in Britain's history, he inherited a system of administration and tax collection that was both cumbersome and ancient. Government accountants still employed wooden tally sticks, and the system was 'cluttered with ancient survivals of practices and of offices, the original purpose of which was almost forgotten'.[94] While Pitt's initial handling of reform leaves the impression of 'rather desperate and unsuccessful innovation',[95] he benefited from the recommendations of a commission that had been struck by Lord North in 1780 to examine public accounts. Although he was no doctrinaire follower of *laissez-faire*, Pitt was partly influenced by Smith in his pursuit of freer trade, including the reduction of duties on tea, wine and spirits and negotiating a commercial treaty with France under which tariffs were lowered on both sides. The specific object of the French treaty was to take the profit out of smuggling; and in this it was successful. The loss of revenue from customs and excise was made up for in the form of lotteries and a plethora of new taxes that targeted mainly luxury items such as servants, horses, hackney coaches, windows, bricks, ribbons, candles, shops, hats and even hair powder.[96] In general, Pitt's policies were successful: smuggling was reduced and by 1785 the debt had been cut by over £10 million. The new taxes, however, amounted to a general shift of taxation onto the consumer and away from the land tax. Dryden summed up popular sentiments about the new taxes in his *Alexander's Feast*: 'Monarchs first of taxes think; Taxes are a monarch's treasure; Sweet the pleasure; Rich the treasure; Monarchs love a guinea, clink'.[97]

The sharp reactions to the new fundraising policies meant that many of them were quickly withdrawn, including the proposed increased excise on textiles, a tax on coals, a tax on shops and an act to license bleachers, printers and dyers at £2 per annum. Later, in 1797, in what was 'perhaps the most unpopular' and 'certainly the most unsuccessful of all of Pitt's assessed taxes',[98] the tax on clocks

93. Plumb 1963, p. 139.
94. Christie 1982, p. 185.
95. Ibid.
96. Ibid. A tax on 'linen and cotton in 1784', writes Briggs (Briggs 1979, p. 119), 'was a serious economic mistake and, although Pitt had the sense to withdraw it later, the fact that he levied it at all showed that his understanding of the needs of the new industrial sector of the economy was strictly limited'.
97. As quoted in L'Estrange 1874, p. 154.
98. The 'average' working man, writes Thompson, became more methodical and 'subject to the productive tempo of "the clock" ' in the years between 1780 and 1830. Pitt and his friends at the Exchequer based the tax on the assumption that a watch was a 'luxury item'. But this 'small instrument which regulated the new rhythms of industrial life was at the same time one of the more urgent of the new needs which industrial capitalism

and watches proved impossible to collect, provoked a buyers' strike and plunged the domestic watch trade into a depression. Further financial reforms included the establishment of a commission for the audit in 1785; the gradual elimination of sinecures for customs officials by allowing them to lapse upon falling vacant; imposing greater fiscal discipline on the Navy and checking common abuses of such privileges as franking mail. In 1786, Pitt sought to put an end to the perennial raids on his sinking fund by setting up a board of commissioners charged with the task of reform.[99] Many of these acts were probably more geared toward restoring confidence in the system than actually reducing the debt. However, Pitt's quiet but steady reform of the administration did help to restore confidence. He phased out sinecures and replaced fees with salaries going much further in reducing 'influence' than the Rockinghams had done during their tenure.[100] Pitt's personal commitment to political reform was demonstrated when, in knowing defiance of the King's opposition, he introduced a bill in April 1785 to disenfranchise 36 rotten boroughs which would also have provided the patrons compensation for their loss.[101] The bill went down by a vote of 284 to 174. The House was not to seriously consider the matter of reform for another half century. As part of Pitt's reform package, he also introduced a bill in 1796 to address the distress arising from recent poor harvests by reforming the poor laws and creating 'schools of industry' for the employment of children in workhouses where they would produce leather and textiles. This bill also failed.[102] By demonstrating his commitment to administrative, financial, economic and electoral reform, Pitt took some of the bite out of the opposition's long-standing charge that George III's administration was rife with corruption (the Bute Legend), which had been revived with Fox's return to opposition.

The Whig Club, made up of followers of Fox and former followers of Rockingham, promoted the idea that Pitt had come to power unconstitutionally. When Pitt's Ministry challenged Fox's re-election in 1784, only to withdraw the challenge, this proved a source of embarrassment. Another embarrassment arose out

---

called forth to energise its advance'. A labourer coming into a small windfall might blow it on a watch and thus gain an item that was both useful and a symbol of prestige. 'Moreover, the time-piece was the poor man's bank' that could be hocked in a time of need. Requiring as it did a system of espionage for its enforcement, the tax proved utterly unenforceable. Thompson 1989, pp. 365–9 and 450.

99. Christie 1982, p. 184–8.

100. Christie 1982, p. 253.

101. Turner 1999, pp. 36–7.

102. Pollard 1965, pp. 163–4. The bill was extensive, and reflected both a paternalistic outlook and the influence of Smith. It included 'a gamut of proposals for the alleviation of the condition of the poor – family allowances, a rate in aid of wages, money to purchase a cow, schools of industry for poor children, reclamation of waste land, a relaxation of the Law of Settlement and measures to assist the provision of insurance against sickness and old age' (Stedman Jones 2004, p. 77).

of Pitt's failure to satisfactorily resolve the emergence of a tariff war between Ireland and Great Britain. The Radical movement led by the Volunteers was still very strong in Ireland as the excitement of the Revolution in America had not fully cooled. Two reform bills introduced by Sir Edward Newenham in 1782 and Irish MP Henry Flood in 1784 were roundly defeated, but they put demands on the table for the reform of the Irish Parliament, extension of the franchise and Catholic emancipation. Demonstrations in Dublin pressured the Irish Parliament to approach Britain and ask for concessions. Pitt proposed free trade in foreign and colonial goods, equalisation of duties and imports, a halt on new duties or subsidies and limited reform. In return, Ireland would have to contribute to the defence of the empire. But this was a non-starter for the Irish, as it echoed proposals Britain had made to the American colonies a decade earlier. Nor did the Irish wish to end their own highly successful policy of providing manufacturing subsidies for textiles, gloves and hats, glass or their emerging sugar-refining industry. At home in Britain, the General Chamber of Manufacturers had formed, being perhaps the earliest expression of class solidarity amongst the emerging industrial-capitalist entrepreneurs. Led by Josiah Wedgwood and ironmaster Samuel Garbett, the Chamber had successfully lobbied for the repeal of the cotton tax in 1784. Now the manufacturers flooded Parliament with petitions in opposition to Pitt's proposed treaty with Ireland. While they were not opposed in principle to a mutual lowering of tariffs in the interests of expanding trade, they saw the treaty as granting favouritism to Ireland – which had just been granted major concessions during the American conflict – and to Irish manufacturers. Noting Ireland's favourable conditions for manufacturing: lower taxes, government inducements and bounties and a plentiful supply of fast-flowing water, the manufacturer Robert Peel threatened (probably not seriously) to relocate his operation there, should the treaty pass. The manufacturers also complained that they were losing workmen who were being lured away by the newly-built Irish factories. The bill did offer much to landowners and little to manufacturers. Pitt and his ministers treated the manufacturers with condescension. The manufacturers therefore adopted a strategy of adding amendments that would ensure that it was no longer acceptable to the Irish Parliament. In this they succeeded.[103]

After this defeat, Pitt acted with greater caution. Proposals from the United States in 1785–6 for a new commercial treaty with Britain were similarly rejected, under the influence of ministers who sought adherence to the Navigation Acts, which they viewed as essential to Britain's prosperity.[104] A commercial treaty with France, however, was signed in late 1786 and was strongly supported by

103. Bowden 1924, pp. 655–74.
104. Christie 1982, p. 197.

the General Chamber of Manufacturers under Wedgwood's leadership. Critics among the manufacturers, however, charged that only the cotton, iron and pottery industries were the beneficiaries. Industrial interests favouring monopolistic policies, feeling they had not been well represented, soon took charge of the Chamber, which fell apart shortly thereafter.[105]

In Europe, a crisis erupted in Holland in the following year. Prussian troops invaded Holland in support of Frederick William II's sister, the Princess of Orange. Pitt subsequently forged a Triple Alliance between Britain, Prussia and Holland. This temporarily erased French influence in Holland and convinced the Bourbons that Britain was an implacable enemy bent on the destruction of France. The move came at a moment of French weakness, domestically and internationally. Isolated in Western Europe and with Prussia seeking to preserve the balance of power in the East by limiting any territorial gains to be made by Russia or Austria after the recent outbreak of war with Turkey, France had few allies to turn to. Domestically, having overextended its finances in the American War, France was mired in insoluble debt and heading for bankruptcy. Half the crown's revenues were being expended on interest payments alone. Britain, meanwhile, was able to achieve its principal aim of limiting French influence in the Low Countries, and this included stemming a rebellion against Austrian rule in Belgium by prevailing upon the Emperor to abandon an unpopular effort to rationalise and centralise the local administration in the Austrian Netherlands.[106] Whether by luck or by skill, Pitt had achieved early success in foreign affairs, the field where he had the least experience.

Domestically, Pitt was also shoring up his position against the Foxite opposition, whose promotion of the Bute legend was increasingly becoming irrelevant and whose alliance with the unpopular and flippant George Augustus, Prince of Wales, was increasingly becoming a liability. This liability was temporarily transformed into opportunity during George III's sudden outbreak of madness from porphyria in 1788. As Fox was holidaying with his mistress in Italy at the time, it fell on Sheridan to press for the Prince to take over at once as Regent, offering Lord Thurlow the opportunity to remain at his post as Lord Chancellor in the event of a change of ministry. Rather than opposing the idea, Pitt called for a survey to determine what precedents had been set in the past, and based on its recommendations sought to impose limitations on the Regent's power and to enable Parliament to exercise sovereign authority in the absence of an acting king. When Fox pressed for greater powers for the Regent, Pitt managed skilfully to divide the opposition over the issue of parliamentary authority. When

105. Bowden 1919, pp. 18–35.

106. Frederick William II had ascended the Prussian throne on the death of his father Frederick the Great in August 1786. Christie 1982, pp. 194–5; Owen 1975, p. 256.

George III subsequently recovered, the Foxites were divided and Pitt's authority was virtually unassailable.[107] By the time the Revolution of 1789 broke out in France, Britain was enjoying the success of having simultaneously achieved the long-sought goals of political stability at home, a foreign policy that successfully checked French influence on the Continent and an unprecedented growth of foreign trade.

Britons generally greeted the French Revolution with approval. The attitude of Pitt's ministry was one of 'condescension and complacency'. It was assumed that the recently signed Eden treaty could now be extended even further.[108] Fox openly celebrated the fall of the Bastille. The Society for Commemorating the Revolution (later known as the Revolution Society), which a group of dissenters had formed in order celebrate the centenary of the Glorious Revolution, greeted events in France as the serendipitous French equivalent.[109] One of these dissenters, the Reverend Dr. Richard Price, delivered an address to the Society in November of 1789 in which he not only lavished praise on the American and French revolutions as signs of the spread of enlightenment principles, but also spoke of how the Glorious Revolution was incomplete, making a strong case that Britain also stood in need of reform. This sermon provoked Edmund Burke to respond with his essay *Reflections on the Revolution in France*, which quickly gained a wide audience and the endorsement of the King. Around 19,000 copies sold in the first year of its publication and perhaps 30,000 in the five years to follow. Burke rejected the idea that the Glorious Revolution of 1688 had involved the same sharp break with past precedent as appeared to be the case at present in France. Price's sermon, he wrote, 'is in a strain which I believe has not been heard in this kingdom … since the year 1648'.[110] In Burke's view, Price wilfully misinterpreted the events of 1688 in order to advance the proposition that the people of England had acquired and exercised the right to choose their own governors and frame their own government, or to 'cashier them for misconduct'.[111] The Act of Succession may have been a deviation from principle, but Price and his followers, wrote Burke, 'take the deviation from the principle

107. Derry 2001, pp. 46–50.

108. Derry 2001, p. 53.

109. The Society sent a congratulatory address to France in 1789 and 'urged that "the two first kingdoms in the world" should together promote the common cause of freedom' (Briggs 1979, p. 131).

110. Burke 1973, p. 23.

111. 'No government could stand a moment, if it could be blown down with anything so loose and indefinite as an opinion of "*misconduct*" '. Against such a right, Burke counterposed the long-standing practice of impeachment. While Burke was a staunch Whig, his defence of 1688 as generally a revolution which conserved the basic political framework of the English constitution means his work is today treated as a charter-document of modern conservatism. Burke 1973, pp. 27 and 39–40.

for the principle' itself.[112] Burke saw the creation of the National Assembly out of the Third Estate as precisely such a repudiation of past principle, and a dangerous arrogation and centralisation of power by the revolutionaries. More than that, he uncannily predicted that the French Revolution would lead to tyranny, a rejection of Christianity in France and a cataclysmic war in Europe. Burke's essay attracted many published responses. His critics attacked his romantic portrayal of the French monarchy and his seemingly undue pessimism, in which he stood virtually alone.

In the summer of 1791, Burke met with Pitt and warned that Britain stood on the brink of a crisis threatening all that had been since the Glorious Revolution. Pitt was not moved by the warning. During the debates concerning negotiations with Spain over Nootka Sound and settlement rights on the Pacific coast of North America, pro-French sympathisers among the opposition interpreted the lack of French support for Bourbon Spain as evidence that the new government in Paris had abandoned dynastic ambitions. Pitt's Canada Act of 1791, by proposing special accommodations for Catholics and French Canadians, invited comparisons with revolutionary France. Sheridan and Gray went out of their way to provoke Burke, causing him to publicly distance himself from the Foxites during the subsequent debates in 1791, leaving the opposition in Parliament still weaker than before.[113]

The pace of events seemed everywhere to quicken in the 1790s. Parliament was passing act after act approving enclosures, new turnpike trusts and other projects of 'improvement'. Canal mania was in high gear, with huge sums being invested in multiple projects. Attention now turned to the task of completing Brindley's proposed 'grand cross', which would connect all parts of England and would incorporate London, the largest market of all, into the network. For the moment, traffic had to travel up the Thames to Oxford and north along the narrow Oxford Canal – a journey of two hundred and twenty-eight miles.[114] To provide a better alternative, the Grand Union Canal was proposed in 1791, and an act of Parliament would authorise the scheme two years later. 1792 was a boom year for trade. The Foxite Whigs formed the Society for the Friends of the People, ostensibly in the hopes of shoring up support for themselves and for the French Revolution, but specifically in an effort to claim leadership over the reformist movement and outwit the radical element. But given that the Society was 'unrepentantly aristocratic',[115] it was unlikely that this effort would succeed in

112. Burke 1973, p. 34.
113. Derry 2001, pp. 56–61.
114. Prior to the opening of the Coventry and Birmingham & Fazeley Canals, the route between London and Birmingham was fully two hundred and eighty miles.
115. Derry 2001, p. 63.

attracting working-class adherents. And indeed, the London Corresponding Society (LCS) was established soon after, itself comprising mainly artisans. While not denying that the LCS was rooted in the 'working class', Thompson suggests that the organisation may be better described as a 'popular-radical' society.[116] This appellation accurately places the descriptive emphasis on the political nature of the organisation, for the primary goal of the LCS was political reform, with universal male suffrage being its key demand.[117] This was, indeed, a demand that had scarcely been heard since 1648 in the wake of the debates at Putney, and Burke had accurately forecast its formation. Political radicalism and reformism were not the only expressions of disaffection with the government; religious groups from Wesleyan congregations that had broken with mainstream Methodism to the followers of Richard Brothers, the millenarian prophet 'who saw the French Revolutionaries striking down Babylon',[118] also expressed dissent.

The French Revolution now breathed new life into the radical cause. For what sense could it possibly make that not only the former colonists in America but now even the common people of France, long the symbol of papist despotism, enjoyed greater personal liberties than British subjects? Ever since the suppression of radicalism during the Civil War and the Interregnum, popular-radical resistance was caught in a narrow channel. On the one hand, the state did not tolerate challenges to the social hierarchy. After 1660 it abandoned any attempts to restrict enclosures and grew increasingly lax on enforcing labour laws which enshrined custom. On the other hand, customary law in both town and countryside still existed. The Elizabethan statutes were still official policy and artisans could appeal to them. Yet the ongoing commercialisation of social relations through enclosures and concentration of manufacturing operations meant a steady wearing away of the force of custom. Two factors made the context of the 1790s entirely different from the 1640s. First, while support for the Radicals in the 1640s was drawn primarily from the London artisan community, the spread of cottage manufacturing and the growth of towns such as Manchester and Birmingham meant that there were now far more artisans and they were far more widely dispersed. Second, artisans in the 1790s, unlike those in the 1640s, faced an ominous threat to their livelihood. Were they able to achieve their reformist goals and gain the right to vote, they undoubtedly would have sought to use their newfound political power in an effort to protect themselves against exposure to the market and the growing factory system.

116. Thompson 1991, p. 23.

117. Other demands of the LCS included 'the abolition of the property qualification for MPs, equal electoral districts, the payment of MPs, annual parliaments [and] the secret ballot' (Derry 2001, p. 63). These demands do not amount to a call for 'levelling' of classes and certainly do not merit the label 'socialist'.

118. Hay and Rogers 1997, p. 184.

Just one month following the publication of Burke's *Essay*, Mary Wollstonecraft's *Vindication of the Rights of Woman* was published in December of 1790. It was perhaps the most radical of all the published responses. Casting Burke as the 'champion of property,' passages of her wide-ranging essay echoed the Levellers of the Putney debates, if not Winstanley and the Diggers:

> Why cannot large estates be divided into small farms? These dwellings would indeed grace our land. Why are huge forests still allowed to stretch out with idle pomp and all the indolence of Eastern grandeur? Why does the brown waste meet the traveller's view, when men want work? But commons cannot be enclosed without *acts of parliament* to increase the property of the rich! Why might not the industrious peasant be allowed to steal a farm from the heath? This sight I have seen; – the cow that supported the children grazed near the hut, and the cheerful poultry were fed by the chubby babes, who breathed a bracing air, far from the diseases and vices of cities. Domination blasts all these prospects; virtue can only flourish amongst equals . . .[119]

Such an open attack on elite privilege and the sacredness of property was bound to cause excitement. But Wollstonecraft was attacked more on the basis of her being a woman with an unorthodox personal life than on the merit of her arguments. Thomas Paine's equally irreverent essay *The Rights of Man,* the first part of which appeared in February of 1791 followed by the second part a year later, garnered far greater excitement by virtue of its extraordinary popularity. After the publication of the second part, Pitt began writing to ministers about the possibility of suspending *habeas corpus* and issuing legislation to suppress dissent. Where Wollstonecraft had attacked Burke's defence of property, Paine sought to challenge Burke's interpretation of the Glorious Revolution, suggesting that Burke's argument amounted to granting the dead (meaning the revolutionaries of 1688) a right to fix a political settlement 'for all time' upon the living. Paine saw nothing 'glorious' about 1688 when set next to the revolutions in America and France. 'The very rights men and women now sought had not even been debated then . . .'[120] Paine attacked the absurdities of the British electoral system:

---

119. Wollstonecraft 1997, p. 94. Wollstonecraft's essay was shockingly irreverent for its time: 'It is impossible to read half a dozen pages of your book without admiring your ingenuity, or indignantly spurning your sophisms. Words are heaped on words, till the understanding is confused by endeavouring to disentangle the sense, and the memory by tracing contradictions' (Wollstonecraft 1997, pp. 85–6). In Wollstonecraft's work, there is a mixture of fatalism and revulsion in reaction to the excesses of wealth being built up in the midst of distress and poverty that was surely widely felt.

120. Claeys 1989, p. 87. Paine's essay was 'stridently egalitarian, anticlerical, and quite original in its advocacy of redistributive taxation to finance public education and welfare' (Hay and Rogers 1997, p. 181). Paine stopped short of advocating a redistribution of property, however.

'The town of old Sarum which contains not three houses, sends two members; and the town of Manchester, which contains upwards of sixty thousand souls, is not admitted to send any. Is there any principle in these things?'[121] By contrasting the evidently more equitable and rational representative systems of America and France with that of Britain, Paine advanced a powerful case for reform. At the same time, the secret to Paine's success – by 1793, radical societies had already sold between two and three hundred thousand copies of *The Rights of Man* – may be explained by the way he positioned himself alongside the advocates of Enlightenment progress whilst simultaneously writing with enough wit, sarcasm and humour to appeal to a growing audience of literate commoners. Moderate reformers such as Christopher Wyvill despaired at the popularity of these new voices of a resurgent radicalism, seeing in them the doom of any efforts for reform. In the short run, Wyvill was correct.

When war in Europe broke out in April 1792, virtually no other Briton but Burke thought it would last very long. Upon introducing the budget in February, Pitt had confidently remarked that there had never been a time when ' "we might more reasonably expect 15 years of peace than we may at the present moment" '.[122] On 20 April, France declared war against Austria over its leniency toward French *émigrés*. Also factoring into the declaration of war were the demands by German princes in French-controlled Alsace for a restoration of their feudal privileges and status, prompting Frederick William II to join the war in aid of Austria and the German princes. In Britain, the declaration of war led to a run on the banks and the shortage of cash in circulation was exposed. This forced several country banks to stop payment on their notes, sending a jolt through the financial system. The French invasion of the Austrian Netherlands was routed, with French soldiers defecting in large numbers. At this stage, had Austria and Prussia not been entangled with Russia in a dispute over the disposition of territories in Poland, the Revolution might have ended with a joint invasion by Austria and Prussia.[123] Instead, the revolutionaries in France had time to contemplate what the division of Poland meant by way of an example. Faced with the prospect of an occupied France being dismantled and shared out by rival powers, the young Republic 'discovered or invented total war: the total mobilization of a nation's resources through conscription, rationing and a rigidly controlled war economy, and virtual abolition, at home or abroad, of the distinction between soldiers and civilians'.[124] Europe was about to embark upon nearly a quarter-century of virtually uninterrupted war in which French armies would overrun the 'feudal'

121. Paine 1973, p. 312.
122. As cited in Christie 1982, p. 212.
123. Breunig 1977, pp. 30–1.
124. Hobsbawm 1994, p. 88.

régimes of the Continent. As it had done repeatedly since 1688, Britain would once more be called upon to dig deep into its agrarian-capitalist pockets and subsidise the war effort against France.

At home, the outbreak of hostilities on the Continent served to cast a light of suspicion upon reformists and supporters of the revolution in France. Alarmed at the popularity of Paine's *Rights of Man*, the government charged Paine with sedition. In August, Thomas Hardy and friends published an *Address to the People* promising ' "taxes diminished, the necessaries of life more within the reach of the poor, youth better educated, prisons less crowded, [and] old age better provided for" '.[125] The artisan outlook of this *Address* is unmistakeable. Briggs comments: 'They thus pointed the way forward to the development of working men's politics in the nineteenth century, particularly to Chartism . . .'[126] Paine appeared in court on 8 June 1792, only to have the trial postponed. Paine was granted French citizenship and was elected to four *départements* in the Convention. On 14 September, Paine departed for France. A fresh warrant for his arrest arrived at Dover only twenty minutes after Paine's ship set sail.[127] In a letter published after his departure he broke 'from his previous strategy as well as his moderate associates, and argued that a British convention should assemble to abolish the monarchy'.[128] Such a call for a popular-democratic insurrection helped to galvanise elites in Britain behind a campaign of reaction and repression. Further inflaming these tensions, France declared the Edict of Fraternity in November, reserving the right to come to the aid of 'subject peoples' struggling for liberty and against despotism. In December, with the King of France on trial for treason and (false) rumours circulating of an impending uprising in Britain, the lawyer John Reeves founded the Association for the Preservation of Liberty and Property against Republicans and Levellers, the most prominent in a wave of Loyalist associations that began to form across Britain. The Loyalists focused their efforts on detecting and prosecuting 'subversive' authors using tactics of threats and intimidation. Nominal membership in Loyalist organisations was high, but given the climate of intimidation and the levels of surveillance that were used to pressure citizens to join regardless of their true loyalties, the depth of genuine support is impossible to gauge. Tactics involved 'beatings, inquisitions, sackings and ostracism'.[129] There were many examples. To take one that speaks to the dynamics of agrarian-capitalist social relations: 'The Quaker John Payne of

125. Briggs 1979, p. 133.
126. Ibid.
127. Claeys 1989, p. 27. In July, Paine had considered going to Dublin, where he had been elected a member of the United Irishmen. Paine never returned to England. The Convention in France had recently replaced the National Assembly.
128. Claeys 1989, p. 28.
129. Emsley 1985, p. 802.

Newhill was warned by Earl Fitzwilliam in 1792 that his involvement with the [radical] Sheffield Society for Constitutional Information might cost him the tenancy of his farm'.[130] The Loyalist societies' attack on freedom of expression prompted the formation of the Friends of the Liberty of the Press a year later, which counted twenty opposition MPs among its members.[131] Britain was not yet at war with France, but the French Revolution had already set in motion the forces of counter-revolution within Britain.

This meant that resistance in the form of protests against enclosures or machine-breaking was also cast in the light of suspicion, more so the activities of 'combinations' among workers. Strikes were becoming increasingly common and 1792 was the year that the term 'scab' made its first appearance.[132] At Leeds in West Riding, the cloth merchants announced their intention to introduce machinery in a public manifesto and 'more than one Leeds mill was destroyed by croppers in the next ten years'.[133] A government official in Scotland observed that ' "The spirit of insubordination increases with the increase of manufacture" '.[134] In the West of England, where 'food riots' were particularly common, large crowds protested against the introduction of the scribbling engine and the shuttle-loom in the early 1790s. The outbreak of machine-breaking probably served to heighten tensions over the perceived threat of Jacobinism. But among artisans, the Government's campaign of repression also compounded hostility towards the introduction of machinery, the threat of factories and violations of the Tudor statutes.

The Government's attention turned to the friendly societies, which were appreciated for their work in providing a kind of welfare for the sick, the elderly and the unemployed, thereby freeing the rate-payer of an enormous burden.

---

130. Emsley 1985, pp. 802–4 goes on to provide further examples.

131. Among these MPs were Samuel Whitbread and Thomas Erskine. Outside Parliament such reformists as John Thelwall, Major John Cartwright and John Horne Tooke were active members (Broich 2007, p. 139). Reeves's Loyalist association was not the first. The Church and King Club formed in Manchester in 1790 was later superseded by the Association for Preserving Constitutional order in late 1792. Links were formed with local authorities and 'mob' violence against reformers was encouraged. Birmingham had seen "Church and King" disturbances in July of 1791 and similar disturbances took place in Manchester in June and December of 1792. See Turner 1999, pp. 97–8.

132. Leeson 1979, p. 88. The racially-charged label 'blackleg' appears to have already come into existence by this time. In hearings for the consideration of a bill against combinations in papermaking in 1796, employers reported that a refusal to raise wages by 5s. per week 'had provoked a strike amongst the men who were supported, it was said, from a general fund and who took action against "black-legs", amongst whom were men from the North of England and from Scotland' (Coleman 1954, p. 42). Within the Brief Institution, a union of cloth dressers, 'The threat of blacklegs was largely obviated by the highly-skilled nature of a cloth dresser's work . . . and, because the establishment of the Brief Institution extended union influence nationally' (Randall 1991, p. 139).

133. Thompson 1991, p. 573.

134. Thompson 1991, p. 97.

Numbering on average between one hundred and two hundred members, they had come to be less associated with particular trades and more closely identified with the local community. Their growth since they first began to emerge in the 1690s, and especially since mid-century was phenomenal, rising to some 7,200 by 1801, with 648,000 members. Only the churches enjoyed larger followings.[135] In the context of the threat of Jacobinism, their growing numbers aroused suspicion: 'Those advising the government, even the liberal-minded Sir Frederick Eden, felt that many of the friendly societies, with their passwords, loyalty oaths, and their drinking habits, were breeding grounds for rebellion, offering, in the words of the Board of Agriculture in 1793, "commodious opportunities to foment sedition" '.[136]

In an effort to bring regulation to this sphere of social activity, in 1793 an act was passed to encourage the friendly societies through regulation. But fearing persecution and a seizure of their funds, nearly a quarter of them refused to register.

Having found documents that proved conclusively that Louis XVI had conspired to encourage a foreign invasion of France, a majority at the Convention in Paris voted in favour of his execution, which took place on 21 January 1793. Pitt took this as a pretext to expel France's diplomatic representative, and in February the Convention responded with a declaration of war against Britain and Holland. Pitt was aware that war would mean abandoning most of his programme of reform. He thus held out for peace as long as possible. It would also mean a serious delay in securing the abolition of the slave trade, a cause Pitt supported.[137] It was thanks in large part to Pitt's financial and administrative reforms that Britain was in a far stronger position to engage in a war than it had been in 1783. Nevertheless, the Navy had only 16,000 sailors in uniform, down from 100,000 at the close of the American War. The Army had only 13,000 soldiers in uniform. Even with the addition of the usual Hanoverian and Hessian mercenaries operating under British pay, this was clearly no match for the army of half a million men that France was raising through the *levée en masse*. The only conceivable strategy for Britain, now unquestionably the wealthiest power in Europe, was to return to the policy of raising 'gold' to offer subsidies to its allies. By the Summer, Pitt 'had agreed to subsidize Austria, Prussia, Sardinia, Spain and Naples on condition that they abandoned the unrealistic aim of a Bourbon restoration'.[138] The

135. Rule 1986, pp. 165–6.
136. Rule 1986, p. 98.
137. Christie 1982, p. 255. In 1787, Granville Sharp had formed the Abolitionist Society. In 1788, under the influence of his eloquent friend William Wilberforce, Pitt introduced a motion to set up an enquiry into the slave trade.
138. Christie 1982, p. 262.

national debt had been lowered to £228 million, but soon Pitt would be faced with a war expenditure of £50 million *per annum*.[139]

By now, the French were quite accustomed to the British policy of waging war against France through subsidies and mercenaries. The Girondists, who had been forced by the Mountain to consent to the execution of the King, were no less radical when it came to speeches against their common English enemies. On 13 January 1793, the Girondist Armand de Kersaint explained how England could be defeated:

> The credit of England rests upon fictitious wealth; the real riches of that people are scattered everywhere... Bounded in territory, the public future of England is found almost wholly in its Bank, and this edifice is entirely supported by the wonderful activity of their naval commerce. Asia, Portugal, and Spain are the most advantageous markets for the productions of English industry; we should shut these markets to the English by opening to the world.[140]

The treaty of 1786, which had served the Southern wine growers well but which was despised by the Northern manufacturers faced with the competition of a flood of cheap British goods, was now seen by the revolutionaries in Paris as merely part of a conspiracy by Pitt to bankrupt the French. As we shall see, the mistaken conception held by many Frenchman that England's prosperity was based upon the 'fictitious wealth' of its colonial trade would ultimately bear bitter fruit for revolutionary France, and for its manufacturers in particular.

What Pitt did not have to face was a serious challenge to his authority to prosecute the war. Events in France were helping to solidify nationalist sentiments in British public opinion. War with France quickly became the national cause. Repression and Loyalist intimidation served to marginalise dissent. Parliament was in no mood for reform, as Grey found out when his reform bill was roundly defeated in May 1793.[141] Lord Braxfield felt secure enough to comment that '"the landed interest alone has a right to be represented... [and]... as for the rabble, who have nothing but personal property, what hold has the nation on them?"'[142] Scottish reformers were asking just this question when they convened the British Convention of the Delegates of the People in Edinburgh in October 1793. Fiery speeches were heard for a fortnight before authorities shut down the convention. Leaders were prosecuted, some convicted and transported. This provoked the English radical societies into outright defiance. In January a full meeting of the LCS was held, at which it was resolved that '"upon the first

139. Briggs 1979, pp. 118, 124, 139 and 170; Deane 1987, p. 74.
140. As quoted in Rose 1893, pp. 704–5.
141. Turner 1999, pp. 66–7.
142. As quoted in Briggs 1979, p. 99.

introduction of any Bill or Motion inimical to the liberties of the people...a general convention of the people should be summoned" '.[143] The Constitutional Information Society, led the veteran Wilkite Horne Tooke, went further, and began planning for a convention. The Pitt government had seen enough. Had not the King of France been executed by another convention just the previous year? On 12 May 1794, a Committee of Secrecy was appointed to draft a report and two of the most prominent rabble-rousers were arrested: Thomas Hardy, shoemaker and founder of the LCS, and Daniel Adams, secretary of the Society for Constitutional Information. Four days later the Committee issued its report recommending the suspension of the writ of *habeas corpus*, referring to the plan to summon a convention as ' "an open attempt to supersede the House of Commons in its representative capacity" '.[144] These arrests were later followed by the arrests of John Horne Tooke, the poet and peace advocate John Thelwall and ten other leading reformers. All were charged with treason. Their papers were seized and the Committee of Secrecy sought evidence to be used against them. An orchestrated propaganda campaign employing newspapers and ballad-singers on street corners promoted the idea that the arrested had been involved in a Jacobin plot to overthrow the Government. The LCS responded by establishing a secret executive committee, a September meeting of which was intruded upon by the Bow Street Runners,[145] who arrested the acting secretary. The member of the committee who most strongly protested against the arrest was one 'Citizen Groves'. Sensing a betrayer in their presence, Groves was accused of being a spy and was subjected to a formal trial before the full General Committee of the LCS. Satisfied with the evidence Groves presented of his devotion to the Society, he was 'triumphantly acquitted'; however, ' "Citizen Groves" *was*, in fact, a spy...After each meeting of the secret executive his full reports came in, for

143. As quoted in Christie 1982, p. 226.

144. 'Few were aware', writes Emsley (1985, pp. 807–8), 'of the legal niceties which left queries over who could issue writs of *habeas corpus*' or that individuals imprisoned by order of Parliament could not apply for the writ. 'Yet whatever the limits of the legislation, belief in its potency was strong'. *Habeas* had previously been suspended during the Jacobite emergencies and the American War.

145. The brainchild of novelist Henry Fielding, the Bow Street Runners initially numbered eight men when they were set up in 1749. As Chief Magistrate, Fielding employed them to apprehend criminals nation-wide. They operated out of his office at No. 4 Bow Street. John Fielding succeeded his brother as Chief Magistrate in 1754 and maintained the force. The increasing incidences of highway robbery prompted Fielding in 1757 to propose a light cavalry to pursue highwaymen. An act of 1792 established seven additional offices for the Runners. Shootings of Bow Street Runners became common, and those found guilty were hung in chains. Bow Street 'was the embryo of Scotland Yard. In 1798 crime on the Thames resulted in the establishment of the River Police, following the proselytizing work by Patrick Colquhoun' who acknowledged his debt to the Fieldings (McLynn 1989, pp. 32–5). The Bow Street Station closed in 1993, and the neighbouring Bow Street Court closed in 2006 (BBC News, 2006).

the perusal of Pitt or Dundas or the Treasury Solicitor. It is only thanks to his peculiar skill that we are able to describe the events of these months at all'.[146] In October, the trial of Hardy attracted national attention. A large crowd gathered outside the Old Bailey. A guilty verdict was sure to provoke a violent demonstration of protest. Hardy was acquitted, to the celebration of the crowds.[147] By December, Tooke, Thelwall and the other arrestees were acquitted as well, to the deep embarrassment of Pitt's government. But this would be 'the last great victory of English civil liberties for many years',[148] followed by decades of 'profound alienation between classes in Britain'.[149] In February, the suspension of *habeas corpus* was renewed for another six months. Then in July, as thousands of French citizens were being marched to the guillotine in the Terror, the Home Office would come to be occupied by the Duke of Portland, who being disgusted with the Foxites' tolerance for revolutionary activity at home and abroad, had finally decided to split with Fox and his followers and join Pitt. Pitt 'could not have found more zealous an advocate of a crack-down on radicalism'.[150] By June, as France was retaking Belgium at the Battle of Fleurus, its first major victory of the war, the Commons Secret Committee in Britain reported on a plot to overthrow the government. The Foxites derided the report, refusing to believe 'that "eighteen pike-heads, ten battle axes and twenty blades unfinished" amounted to a national conspiracy'.[151] But Portland believed that his spies had successfully infiltrated the 'military' wing of the LCS, and had foiled the plot.

In October of 1795, the LCS was able to gather a crowd of 150,000 for the opening day of Parliament. Whilst *en route* to Westminster, George III's coach was subsequently mobbed by an angry crowd. Their cries of 'bread!' suggested that their protest was motivated by hunger, but Portland suspected Jacobinism. The swift response was the Seditious Meetings Act of 1795, imposing restrictions on meetings of more than fifty people, and the Treasonable Practices Act, which expanded the definition of treason to incorporate plots to harm the King, plots to foster foreign invasion or the use of coercive language against Parliament.

---

146. Thompson 1991, pp. 144–7.

147. Thompson 1991, p. 148 notes that 'The public found in Hardy once again one of those images of independence in which the free-born Englishman delighted: a firm and dignified commoner, defying the power of the state'. The fact that Hardy was a commoner also meant he would never play the state the way that John Wilkes had.

148. Briggs 1979, p. 136; Turner 1999, p. 89.

149. Thompson 1991, p. 195. The full quote reads as follows: '. . . in the decades after 1795 there was a profound alienation between classes in Britain, and working people were thrust into a state of *apartheid* whose effects – in the niceties of social and educational discrimination – can be felt to this day . . . The "natural" alliance between an impatient radically-minded industrial bourgeoisie and a formative proletariat was broken as soon as it was formed'.

150. Mori 1997, p. 240.

151. Ibid.

Only the former was ever put into effect. Again the Foxites reacted with ridicule, charging the Government with intimidating its critics in the name of national security.[152]

The number of political prosecutions between 1793 and 1800 fell short of two hundred, most of these having been carried out by 1795. Scores more were held in prison without trial, provoking deep resentment. '[R]eformers directly affected by repression would not have agreed that there was no reign of terror, and there were enough people held in prison without trial, or whose health, reputation and livelihood were harmed by arrest and trial, for a reign of terror to become embedded in the developing radical consciousness'.[153]

Pitt's attack on English liberties earned him comparisons with Robespierre which, though ludicrous, were also within the compass of 'good, and traditional political propaganda'.[154] The arrests of Jacobites in 1715, 1722 and 1745 had been far more severe.[155] The logic of imposing repressive legislation against workers who had no say in the making of that legislation meant that those same workers would ultimately demand the right to vote in order that they might one day change it.[156] Radicalism, based on the recognition of the need for fundamental change, is by definition a form of resistance against not just coercive repression but also hegemony. Since Britain's radical movement in the late eighteenth and early nineteenth centuries was made up of working people, resisting hegemony also became an exercise in class self-definition, even if the 'class' in question was not well-developed and was led by artisans in possession of their own means of production, not feeling the full exposure to the market as wage labourers working on capitalist farms and in capitalist factories. Moreover, as the bonds of mutuality had once obligated both patricians and plebs to observe custom and paternalistic deference were in decline, including the protections and perquisites previously afforded by custom, artisans and labourers were compelled to strengthen horizontal bonds between them in the interest of protecting themselves against repression and, in the context of capitalism, against exposure to the market.

'You offer no motives': outdoor relief and the problem of the poor

As we have seen, by the late eighteenth century, Britain ceased to be an exporter and was now an importer of grain. The primary reason for this was the

152. Turner 1999, p. 69.
153. Turner 1999, pp. 72–3.
154. Emsley 1985, p. 802.
155. Emsley 1985, p. 822.
156. Leeson 1979, p. 102.

extraordinary growth of population from the middle of the century onwards, itself in part a result of the major advances in agrarian productivity. The emergence of the factory system and the application of new machinery such as the flying shuttle and the spinning jenny to domestic manufacturing enabled the textile industry to respond positively and swiftly to rising levels of demand.[157] The poor harvests of 1794 and 1795, however, made it apparent that Britain faced a chronic food-shortage problem. Britain's new reliance on food imports was seen as a dangerous policy in a time of war. Wartime inflation combined with shortages of grain drove the price of wheat to previously unseen heights: '108*s*. a quarter in London, 160*s*. in Leicester, while in many places it was unobtainable'.[158] In Berkshire, the Justices of the Peace met at an inn in Speenhamland in May of 1795 to discuss how to respond to the shortage of grain. They introduced a schedule for supplementing wages in accordance with the price of bread, effectively setting a minimum income for poor and working families in their county. Subsequently, their schedule was widely adopted, with variations, across England.

Historians are still debating the effects of this adoption of the 'Speenhamland system'. In *The Great Transformation*, Karl Polanyi makes Speenhamland a key component of his account of the origins of the free labour market. By this point in time, argues Polanyi, a free market in land and in money had largely been established, but not in labour. Polanyi interprets Speenhamland as an unconscious attempt by the landed classes in England to preserve paternalism and forestall the emergence of proletarianisation and a free labour market. The decision to supplement wage rates 'amounted to the abandonment of Tudor legislation not for the sake of less but of more paternalism'.[159] According to Polanyi, despite their best humanitarian intentions, the Justices of Berkshire had invented a system that, once unhindered by Speenhamland, would lead to an overall decline in labour productivity, a fall in wages to a level below that of subsistence (the difference being made up by relief) and a delay in the emergence of a free market in labour that would ultimately allow for overall wealth and incomes to rise. While the burden of rising rates fell on the yeoman tenant-farmer, this was partially offset by low wages and free labour organised through the roundsman system, which allowed employers to forego paying the rates if they employed labourers making the 'rounds' in search of employment. While Polanyi offers a contradiction to his thesis when he argues that had agricultural labourers been allowed to form legal combinations, the effect of the system might have been to *increase* wages, thereby at least suggesting that the true cause of rural immiseration was the Combination Acts, he nevertheless places the blame more or

157. Wells 1977, p. 8.
158. Thompson 1991, p. 156.
159. Polanyi 1957, p. 79.

less squarely on the 'ambiguous humanitarianism' of the Speenhamland system, the 'supreme abomination' of which he argues was to artificially reduce the worker to the status of a pauper.[160] According to Polanyi, Speenhamland was a reversal of the equally humanitarian intent of the relief behind the Poor Act of 1782 (Gilbert's Act), which had expanded the scale of relief to the able-bodied poor. This act had been undertaken for two reasons. The humanitarian element recognised that workhouses were best suited to attending to the needs of the orphans, invalids, the sick and the elderly. As many parishes struggled to build or maintain effective workhouses, these were now to be organised on a collective basis by grouping parishes together to build common workhouses. The pragmatic element of Gilbert's Act was a recognition that as workhouses could not be made to become self-sustaining, it would be cheaper to provide 'outdoor relief' to able-bodied poor in their own homes than to provide 'indoor relief' in workhouses. Samuel Whitbread Jr., son of the famous brewer, introduced a bill in the Winter of 1795 proposing that the Statute of Apprentices be expanded to include 'the fixing of minimum wages by yearly assessment'.[161] Setting a minimum wage, writes Polanyi, ran contrary to the intent behind the partial lifting of the provisions tying labourers to their native parish under the Act of Settlement of 1662, the intent being to allow wages to find their 'natural' level according to the market. Aid-in-wages did not run counter to this intent; it merely enabled the 'natural' price of labour to fall below subsistence levels due to their being supplemented out of the poor rates. In 1796, the option of setting a minimum wage was bypassed when Parliament adopted the Speenhamland system.

Two decades after the publication of *The Great Transformation*, Mark Blaug argued that the common interpretation of Speenhamland and the Old Poor Law as stifling the emergence of free labour and acting not to raise the living standards

---

160. Polanyi 1957, p. 99. Earlier, Polanyi (pp. 89–92) seems to suggest that this is someone else's argument, but not his own, when he writes: 'The inexplicable increase in the number of the poor was almost generally put down to the method of Poor Law administration, and not without some good cause'. Continuing, he suggests a deeper cause: 'Actually, beneath the surface, the growth of rural pauperism was directly linked with the trend of general economic history'. What general trend is he talking about? He points to 'an increase in what we would today call invisible unemployment' that resulted from fluctuations in trade. 'Much of the social damage done to England's countryside sprang at first from the dislocating effects of trade directly upon the countryside itself. The Revolution in Agriculture definitely antedated the Industrial Revolution' (on that, we all agree!).

161. Polanyi 1957, p. 289. The following year in the commons, Whitbread and Pitt debated the particulars of their respective bills designed to address the distress of the poor. Sir Frederick Eden opposed Whitbread's minimum wage but also felt that Pitt's measures went too far. In his essay 'on the state of the poor' in 1797, he spoke specifically of the 'labouring class' which should benefit from the reform of the poor law but might become less industrious with an increase in relief (Stedman Jones 2004, pp. 77–8; Eden 1996, pp. 419–20).

of the poor, but rather to trap the poor in a 'vicious spiral' of increasing poverty, resulted from the uncritical adoption of the views expressed in the *Poor Law Commissioners' Report of 1834*, which 'has seriously distorted the history of the Industrial Revolution in Britain', and was both ahistorical and based on evidence consisting of 'little more than picturesque anecdotes of maladministration'.[162] What one takes away from the work of Blaug and others critical of the *Report* and those like Polanyi who have repeated its arguments is first of all the degree of oversimplification behind the 'snowball effect' argument that aid-in-wages set in train a 'vicious spiral' of soaring poor rates and progressively increasing poverty. For one thing, the methods and goals applied to the administration of the poor law were subject to serious regional differences and differences across time. 'With a system so heterogeneous, any generalization is bound to be subject to serious qualification'.[163] This is the key weakness behind both the *Report* and Polanyi's account. It is a problem of economic theory in general, that of making arguments in the abstract without historicising them and with a limited range of variables. For Blaug, the resultant population growth from subsidies may contribute to a long-term decline in wages, but in the short-term the 'effect of a subsidy to workers is to lessen the supply', and 'if the supply curve of labour is positively sloped, the result is that wages will *rise*'.[164] Polanyi recognises this tendency, but sees the issue not as one of supply, but rather one of allowing workers to combine and struggle for higher wages; he otherwise appears to take at face value the notion that aid-in-wages will depress wages overall.

What Blaug adds to the discussion in his effort to expose the myth of the Old Poor Law is historical context. He points out, first of all, that by the time of the *Report* and the proscription of outdoor relief in 1834, the Speenhamland system had largely been abandoned. Plotting the available statistics for poor relief between 1802 and 1834, Blaug demonstrates that there was little difference in the overall levels of poor relief in counties where the Speenhamland system was widely used and those where it was not, and between agricultural versus non-agricultural counties. Neither differences in the administration of poor relief, nor the 'alleged deterioration of agriculture under the influence of allowances-in-aid-of-wages' provide any 'evidence whatever' to support the 'snowball effect' theory claiming that wage subsidies exacerbated the perennial agrarian distress from 1795 to 1834.[165] Blaug's statistics do confirm that rates were generally higher in

162. Blaug 1963, pp. 152 and 177.
163. Blaug 1963, pp. 156–7.
164. This, according to Blaug, is 'elementary economics' (Blaug 1963, p. 153).
165. Rule 1992a, p. 132. Rule notes that in many counties, when prices approached famine levels, the authorities would purchase large quantities of grain and re-sell them to the poor below market prices. This was another form of providing relief in the form of a subsidy, distinct from aid-in-wages. Might this help explain why Blaug found little

certain counties, mainly in the Southeast, where the Speenhamland system was also applied. His interpretation of the Speenhamland system is that it was a fairly rational solution to the problem of chronic unemployment in regions where wages were substandard. An example of this was the corresponding roundsman system, which was used to provide farm work during summers and winters when the demand for agrarian labour was low.[166] Blaug also makes the obvious argument that supplementing wages meant supplementing diets, which could allow for a higher calorie intake by workers and thus translate into greater productivity. Certainly, once established, a withdrawal of aid-in-wages could threaten the sheer physical output of those workers.

According to Larry Patriquin, contemporaries hardly saw Speenhamland as a landmark policy. The practice of topping up wages with poor rates had been increasing since the 1770s. The fame of Speenhamland 'lies in the fact that the Berkshire "bread scale" was published and became relatively well-known'.[167] To this we must add the international political context of a war with France, which reduced the landowners of England and Wales to 'quietly accepting' the addition of some 100,000 more able-bodied men to the total number of those receiving poor relief. By 1802, that total included more than one in every ten persons in England and Wales. This acceptance can only be understood in light of the perceived threat of domestic Jacobinism amidst flagging support for the war effort. The fact that the consensus on providing such relief fell apart at the conclusion of hostilities with France in 1815 would appear to confirm this link.[168] This vast expansion of outdoor relief and the soaring rates were eventually bound to bring about a response from those who took away the impression that the underlying problem was idleness. It seems, however, that the underlying problem was lack of employment. So what was the cause of such high rates of unemployment in agrarian regions? Snell's work demonstrates an 83 per cent correlation between enclosures and variations in poor relief.[169] 'Enclosure,' writes Rule, 'may not have been the only or even the most potent of the forces increasing and impoverishing the proletariat in the southern and Midland counties, but it was important in bringing many to a *total* wage-dependency'.[170] In the South and East, another likely factor was the decline of rural textile manufacturing. Other factors promoting proletarianisation cited by Rule are the spread of wheat

---

variation between Speenhamland and non-Speenhamland counties? This seems doubtful if the method was, as described, only a temporary emergency measure. Aid-in-wages under the Speenhamland system was also initiated as an emergency measure meant to be temporary, but it quickly became perennial, at least in certain counties.

166. Rule 1992a, pp. 170–1; Blaug 1964, p. 241.
167. Patriquin 1996, pp. 207–8.
168. Patriquin 1996, pp. 211–14.
169. Snell 1985, p. 315, as cited in Patriquin 1996, p. 216.
170. Rule 1992a, p. 133.

growing which demanded less year-round labour, and the decline in boarded farm servants, which Speenhamland facilitated by subsidising labour and thus making wage labour cheaper than the cost of maintaining boarders.[171] Patriquin argues that the modifications to the system of poor relief represented by Speenhamland amount to a response to 'a crisis of capitalist agriculture'.[172] He points out that under the manorial system lords had commandeered labour for work on their demesne lands during periods of the highest demand, such as harvest-time, while the rest of the year peasants were able to focus on farming their own holdings. With the breaking of the customary agricultural practices of the manor through enclosures, such extra-economic exploitation of labour was no longer possible. Thus the roundsman system and other methods of putting the unemployed to work not only had an historical antecedent, but like the poor laws, which Patriquin sees as an early system of welfare cushioning the effects of the introduction of agrarian capitalism, such modes of labour organisation provided an additional means of buffering the dislocation of labour being divorced from access to land and rights of commons by the final wave of parliamentary enclosures, with the added shocks of wartime inflation and poor harvests.

The crisis in question was fundamentally one of widespread and increasing poverty resulting from increasing market dependency combined with a want of employment. Rule may be correct in surmising that enclosures as such might not have been the 'most potent' causes of poverty, but enclosures were only one very important form of change in a broader process by which the land was commodified and the population was rendered market-dependent. The conversion from customary to market regulation of the economy, to capitalism, was the broader process that enabled some to rapidly accumulate wealth whilst others lapsed into poverty.

It should be made quite clear that if there was a crisis of agrarian capitalism it did not mean a crisis for farmers holding roughly one hundred acres or more. Wartime inflation meant high prices and high profits. The farmers' cry of distress in these years had not to do with lost profits but with soaring poor rates (and for those who were struck, with occasional crop failure). For the successful tenant-farmer, it was a time of excitement and opportunity as new lands, such as wastes and commons, were brought into cultivation and markets widened. In the interest of promoting new techniques in farming, the semi-official Board of Agriculture was established in 1793, with Arthur Young as its Secretary.[173] 'This curious body,' writes Plumb, 'had no bureaucratic function or authority'.[174]

---

171. Rule 1992a, pp. 133–4.
172. Patriquin 1986, p. 215.
173. Briggs 1979, pp. 39 and 163.
174. Plumb 1963, p. 152.

What stimulation was needed when Parliament was rubber stamping each enclosure act?

Poverty was one of the three great questions occupying the minds of the thinkers of the day, the other two being population and education. As Polanyi points out, contemporaries everywhere were befuddled to answer the question: where do the poor come from? Some earnestly suggested that the principal culprit was the consumption of tea.[175] In 1796, the same year as the Board of Health was established to deal with a rash of fever in the aftermath of two failed harvests and localised famine, the Society for the Bettering the Condition of the Poor was established for the purposes of turning charity into a science.[176] Reverend Malthus was still at this time preparing the manuscript of his famous essay on population, which would announce his discovery of the principle that poverty resulted from the geometric progression of population outstripping the arithmetic growth of the food supply. His puerile discovery would occupy the minds engaged in polite discourse on the 'problem of the poor' for a generation. For the wealthy, it was only too convenient to assume that poverty simply arises from a lack of initiative and not exploitation and unemployment. It was perhaps easier for the poor to grasp the true nature of the problem. ' "You offer no motives" ', a pauper is said to have exclaimed to Arthur Young, ' "you have nothing but a parish officer and a workhouse. Bring me another pot" '.[177] Another Reverend, Rev. Davies of Berkshire, wrote of poverty:

> 'Hope is cordial, of which the poor man has especially much need, to cheer his heart in the toilsome journey through life. And the fatal consequences of that policy, which deprives labouring people of the expectation of possessing any property in the soil, must be the extinction of every generous principle in their minds'. To Davies, the plight of the poor was not the consequence of defects of character, but defects of character the consequence of poverty. Most of his suggestions for alleviating that poverty, however, were relentlessly disposed of by Malthus, for whom official action was more likely to increase poverty than to make it more tolerable.[178]

---

175. Polanyi 1957, p. 90.
176. Briggs 1979, pp. 16 and 34.
177. Briggs 1979, p. 58. Malthus's essay would play an important role in prompting Parliament to pass the Census Act in 1800. The resultant census of 1801 would reveal that England and Wales had a combined population of 8.9 million, up from an estimated six million in 1700 and 6.5 million in 1750. Scotland was revealed to have 1.6 million people living there. No census was taken in Ireland. The numbers revealed that the population was in fact growing rapidly. The early censuses were not thorough, and only from the late 1830s do we have good statistical data on British demographics (London Science Museum, visit by author, 4–5 September 1997; Schofield 1994, pp. 61–6).
178. Schofield 1994, p. 60 citing Davies 1795. Malthus, for his part, did not believe that the poor rates contributed significantly to the increase of population, as many others did.

It would, of course, be a gross exaggeration to suggest (based on Blaug's argument) that aid-in-wages did not contribute in the slightest degree to the demoralisation of workers and to shoddy work. What Blaug convincingly refuted was the assumption upon which the Poor Law Commissioners of 1834 based their recommendations: that aid-in-wages *worsened* poverty. During the three decades leading up to that point, there must have been more Reverend Davieses at the local level than there were Reverend Malthuses.

Conclusion

The process we are describing, here, is in a very real sense one of local custom being supplanted by state law. Specifically, by asserting absolute property rights under the common law, British landlords and capitalists were uprooting the local foundations of customary law in the form of the village court leet and its jurisdiction over local tenures and common-right, and in the form of a wide variety of normative modes of organising labour, many that had existed since time out of mind. This process, as we have seen, had been developing over centuries, but parliamentary enclosures now represented the move to effect a wholesale conversion from a society of self-subsistent peasant agriculturalists and independent craftsmen to one based on the exploitation of market-dependent wage labourers. This conversion involved more than just the supplanting of custom by law. The spirit of custom could not be exorcised through legislation alone. Custom is rooted not only in local laws and by-laws but also in culture and ideology, and these forms would prove resilient even after the laws that enshrined normative beliefs and practices were abolished. A new order required a new ideological push, a coherent body of thought capable of de-legitimising and even criminalising such time-honoured customary forms as the 'food riot', 'takings' and restrictions on forestalling and regrating, whilst elevating absolute property-rights as the highest social value.

We have placed considerable stress on the Gordon Riots because, in many ways, the logic of how this upheaval in London played out mirrored the logic of a myriad of smaller conflicts at the village and town level where custom played a central role. When faced with a disappointing response from Parliament to their peaceful protest, the reaction of the London crowd was generally within the bounds of what had long been considered a customarily acceptable level of violence. But the overwhelming use of deadly force to put down the protests signalled that the old reciprocities had broken down, symbolically at least bringing closure to a process that had started sixty-five years earlier when the English crowd was criminalised as a 'mob' with the passage of the Riot Act.

Thus when the unanticipated revolution in France reverberated through British society, the Hanoverian régime was itself in the midst of a crisis of legitimacy, one whose origins were entirely different from that facing the Bourbons. If the initial burst of enthusiasm for Jacobinism in Britain spelled prospects for revolution at home, the onset of war quickly dampened them by obliging Britons to show their patriotism and rally to the national cause. The combined effects of dearth, the loss of overseas trade due to war and large-scale unemployment in the countryside meant that conditions were harsh and ripe for protest. But as repression set in and radical leaders were arrested, protesters in general were increasingly treated as though they were part and parcel of the political movement that was radicalism. Under the Speenhamland system's provision of outdoor relief, the poor rates soared, buffering untold numbers of rural dwellers from starvation. Despite cries of distress at the high rates from landowners and tenant farmers, high prices for grain products during the war meant relative prosperity for owners and employers. But for agrarian labourers, more than any other social group, it was the onset of a period of dire distress. As the vast majority of them were now rendered largely if not wholly market-dependent, attention turned to the laws that continued to shield domestic manufacturing workers from full exposure to the market.

Chapter Eleven
Rebellion and Reaction

> It is as if the English nation entered a crucible in the 1790s and emerged after the Wars in a different form.
>
> E.P. Thompson[1]

As the conflict ground on during the 1790s, it was slowly becoming clear that this would be no quick war. At home, Britons were engulfed in an economic and social crisis that ran deeper than the suppression of radicalism in the name of patriotism might suggest. Before the wars would end, huge political battles would result in decisive outcomes that would permanently affect the social relations of production in manufacturing.

In the aftermath of France's failed invasion of the Austrian Netherlands in 1793, France was confronted with multiple internal rebellions, invasions by Prussia, Austria and Spain as well as a naval blockade by Britain. But by 1797, the situation was almost completely reversed. The First Coalition had dissolved and France occupied both of the Low Countries, the Rhineland and much of Italy. The turning point began in 1794 when France repelled and invaded Spain, overran Belgium and seized the Rhineland. When France overran the Netherlands in 1795 and declared the Batavian Republic, Prussia and Spain sued for peace. Naval superiority enabled Britain to win naval victories off the coast of Brest and off of Corsica, and consistently to defeat France in the colonial theatre,

1. Thompson 1991, p. 209.

seizing most French holdings in the West Indies, Pondicherry in India and Dutch territories in Ceylon and the East Indies. These successes certainly 'served to boost waning morale, [but] they could scarcely counterbalance French domination in Europe'.[2] In 1796, Spain re-joined the war, now fighting alongside France. Advancing across Germany, the armies of Generals Jourdan and Moreau were initially repelled by Archduke Charles in 1796, but when Bonaparte's army took Sardinia and then the Tyrol in 1797, Jourdan and Moreau advanced once again. Facing the fall of Vienna, Austria signed the Peace of Loeben in April and the Treaty of Campo Formio in October, ceding the Rhineland and much of Italy to France. The War of the First Coalition was ended and Britain now faced France alone.

'A tribute to Welsh pluck': invasion, rebellion and mutiny

The threat of a Jacobin insurrection at home having effectively been checked or having yet to materialise, the Hanoverian régime now faced the much more real prospect of an invasion from France. In countries and territories they occupied, French forces claimed to 'liberate' local populations, introducing the Napoleonic Code and abolishing the ancient privileges of the landed elites associated with feudalism. Even after Waterloo, the Code generally remained in effect where it had been established and such privileges were not restored. The clearing away of these specific forms of politically-constituted property did help prepare these parts of continental Europe for the eventual adoption of capitalism, modelled after industrial capitalism in Britain, but it is important to note that the removal of such 'fetters' did not simply 'unleash' the forces of any previously existing capitalism. The status of agrarian tenures in France and the territories it had annexed was complex by 1815, but it by no means equated to the presence of an agrarian capitalism or the complete absence of politically-constituted forms of agrarian property. Further discussion of this issue lies beyond the scope of the present work. Had France defeated Britain, however, it would undoubtedly have abolished many of the forms of politically-constituted property that remained in Britain: peerages, sinecures, tax farms and, of course, that largest of all patrimonial estates: the monarchy itself. As for abolishing the 'feudal' privileges of lordly estates, however, this had already been accomplished by the development of agrarian capitalism. Recognising, therefore, that in actual practice Britain was far more advanced on this score than the Continent before the French Wars began, it is important to recognise the enormous influence of English liberalism not

2. Owen 1975, pp. 262–3.

only upon French Enlightenment philosophers such as Voltaire and Rousseau, but on the Physiocrats and on the revolutionaries themselves. This topic in itself deserves at least a book's worth of study. It would be important to explore the role which British political economy, with its radical theoretical assault upon monopoly and upon custom, played in shaping conceptions of 'liberty' and hostility to 'feudal' privilege in both the American and French revolutions. For our purposes, it is important to point out the awkward position Britain's landed elite found themselves in at this juncture. On the one hand, they ruled the most economically advanced (and the only capitalist) nation in the world with an expanding domestic economy based upon the establishment of a legal framework that defined property in strictly economic terms. Yet on the other hand, the 'citizens' of Britain, a term rarely encountered heretofore, could not claim to enjoy the same degree of rights and liberties as former British colonists in revolutionary America or (at least in theory) the French 'citizen' so celebrated in the new French constitution.

This seeming contradiction points to the unique legacy of the monarchical régime that survived 1797 (and still survives), a legacy that has unfolded along with the development of agrarian capitalism. The centuries-long unfolding of agrarian capitalism involved the transformation of the feudal estate, whose relations of production were rooted in customary law, into landed estates based upon economic rents, strictly defined as such under common law. The midwives of this long, slow birth of capitalism were the landed classes themselves, whose seizure of control of the state in the seventeenth century enabled them to carry out the project. The failure of republicanism at the Restoration meant the survival of the patrimonial monarchy and the titled aristocracy, its power expressed in the House of Lords. Both of these institutions survive to the present day, living inheritances of the uniquely British social relations of agrarian capitalism which shaped them. Is it not indeed ironic that the same state which eagerly sought to abolish the force of custom in regulating social relations of production should have retained such a deep attachment to ancient titles and rituals? This points to the class character behind the assault on custom. It was one thing to abolish the customary rights of commoners and artisans, and quite another for the peerage to contemplate offering commoners and artisans a voice in the affairs of state, to say nothing of establishing a republican form of government.

The French actually did attempt to invade England, though the attempt was somewhat less than serious. In 1796, the British government uncovered a conspiracy by the United Irishmen to collaborate with revolutionary France. One of the Society's founders, young Theobald Wolfe Tone, offered to go into voluntary exile in America and the Government accepted the offer. Naturally, Tone took the opportunity to travel to Paris. There he persuaded the French to send a liberation force to Ireland. In an almost farcical re-enactment of the fifth and final Spanish Armada, a force of 43 ships carrying 15,000 troops arrived at Bantry Bay and anchored off Bere Island, County Cork in December of 1796, but the effort was abandoned due to fierce gales and the failure of the United Irishmen (who were not aware of the plans) to arrive and join forces. Subsequently, on 22 February 1797, four French warships under the command of the Irish-American Colonel William Tate landed and were dispatched on a mission to destroy Bristol, Britain's second largest city. Turned back by a gale, they landed near Fishguard on the coast of Wales, but Tate, realising that his force of freed prisoners and prisoners of war and pressed émigrés was not up to the task, asked for negotiations. The Welsh locals, meanwhile, were taking matters into their own hands, including heroine Jemima Fawr, who rounded up twelve French soldiers with her pitchfork. An organised militia under the command of Lord Cawdor arrived in the area. Cawdor's written reply to Tate's call for negotiations asserted that his force greatly outnumbered the one thousand four hundred French, when in fact his Pembroke Yeomanry force was not even half as strong. But the bluff worked and Cawdor was able to secure Tate's unconditional surrender. In all, it was 'a tribute to Welsh pluck'.[3]

The effect of this dubious affair was, nonetheless, to cause 'a panic run on the country banks who in turn presented their Bank of England notes for repayment'.[4] The Bank had issued notes totalling more than ten times the value of the gold it held in store and could not pay. Order was temporarily restored by a loan of Exchequer notes from the Government to merchants, but this put government funds in short supply.[5] Large imports of grain necessitated by the dearths of 1794–6 and unprecedented expenditures on material and ships for the Army and the Navy (not to mention the usual loans and subsidies to the allies) had seriously compromised the Government's balance of payments. Parliament responded to the crisis by forbidding the Bank of England to make any payments in gold or silver other than to the armed forces and bypassing the Bank Restriction Act (the Currency Act) in May of 1797. Bank notes were now treated as legal tender for the first time. The predictable result was inflation, for which both the country banks and the Bank of England were blamed. However, 'by borrowing, and spending the proceeds, [thereby raising] the money income of the public

3. 'Most of the prisoners captured at Fishguard were returned in exchanges within two years. Among them was their American commander, William Tate, of whom little more was heard. He had, however, at least achieved something that Bonaparte himself had never managed – he had invaded Britain' (Latimer 2008).

4. Deane 1987, p. 193.

5. Ashton 1964, p. 103.

out of all proportion to the volume of goods available for civilian consumption',[6] the true fault for the inflation lay with the government.

Further adding to the crisis were the naval mutinies from April to June of 1797. The first mutiny, at Spithead, was resolved peaceably with an agreement for a pay raise and a royal pardon. The Government followed this up with the Seduction from Duties Act, which made the administering or taking of unlawful oaths (seducing servicemen from their duty) punishable by seven years' transportation. Almost immediately, the government would find its opportunity to set an example. In July, shoemaker Robert Fuller was found guilty of having offered seditious papers to the Guards. He was sentenced and hanged.[7] Another mutiny, at Nore along the Thames, involved demands concerning not only compensation and working conditions, but also the dissolution of Parliament and an immediate peace with France. When only a pardon was offered, the mutineers blockaded the Thames. But the mutiny quickly fell apart. Thirty of the mutineers were hanged, and others flogged, transported or imprisoned. Subsequent mutinies throughout the colonial fleet followed in the same year. These risings were mainly due to the appalling state of pay and working conditions throughout the Navy (the Army was little better), the use of press-gangs and the mixing of inexperienced commoners with hardened sea veterans. Discipline was brutal; 'the floggings and the brutality horrified even eighteenth-century Prussians'.[8] Morale was certainly given a boost later in the following year upon Admiral Nelson's August 1798 victory over the French fleet in the Battle of the Nile, stranding Bonaparte and his army in Egypt and effectively shattering his dreams of conquest in the Near East.[9]

France's attempt at fostering an insurrection in Ireland prompted harsh legislation giving magistrates extra-legal powers of search and seizure. The United Irishmen, now several hundred thousand strong, had formed in 1795, the same year in which the Government had organised the Orange Order. The Government had looked the other way when Orderists had looted and burned homes in Armagh. Now in early 1798, as General Lake set upon a brutal campaign of disarming the rebels, the Order came to prominence in Ulster. A 'full-blooded loyalist terror' ensued and Pitt was compelled to urge Camden to curb the savagery of the Loyalists.[10]

---

6. Ashton 1964, p. 103.
7. Like the other repressive legislation, the Seduction from Duties Act (37 Geo. III, c. 123) was intended as a temporary measure, but was prolonged until 1800 and then extended another seven years. Emsley 1985, pp. 814–15.
8. Plumb 1963, p. 200.
9. Owen 1975, p. 264.
10. Emsley 1985, p. 823.

In February, several United Irish leaders were arrested, along with LCS member John Binns,[11] who had come from Britain to show solidarity, and Edward Marcus Despard, the Irish-born British colonel turned revolutionary. Their arrests led to calls for a general rebellion. A date of 23 May was set and was to include the taking of Dublin. But the plan was exposed and the rebellion quickly fell apart. After their trial in May, Binns and Despard were held for several years in prison before being released. Only one of the arrested, the Reverend James O'Coigly, was found guilty of treason and executed. In August, the arrival of a thousand French troops in northwest Ireland would come too late for the rebellion. The rebellion convinced the Pitt ministry that the Protestant minority could no longer govern Ireland, and that Britain's best security lay in unifying the two parliaments. Pitt hoped to offer reconciliation to Catholics thereafter by removing most restrictions. While Catholics were generally agnostic about the prospect of union, Protestants were generally favourable. The act breezed through the British Parliament. But fearing a reduction in their rent-rolls due to agrarian disturbances, Protestant MPs in Ireland offered some initial resistance and the Act of Union failed upon its first reading in the Irish Parliament, whereupon Pitt offered compensation packages of £15,000 to Irish MPs who stood to lose their seats. The United Kingdom was to become a reality on 1 January 1801.[12]

'The Radicals are drinking Pitt's health': the Combination Acts in context

In England, 1798 brought not only a fresh suspension of *habeas corpus* but a fresh round of arrests and the Suppression of Seditious and Treasonable Societies Act, which specifically outlawed the LCS, the United Irishmen and the United Scotsmen. It also extended clauses of the Seditious Meetings Act and made publication of libel punishable by a year in prison. This had the immediate effect

11. Emsley 1985, pp. 813–17. A key reason for the acquittals was that the Government did not wish to reveal the identity of its spies who had infiltrated the United Irishmen. It seemed more prudent to use the suspension of *habeas* to detain radical leaders than to sentence them. Thus much evidence was kept secret, fuelling suspicions about Pitt's government. Fox, Sheridan and Grey also testified on O'Connor's behalf. Binns had been arrested in 1796 under the Seditious Meetings Act and acquitted. He had been arrested along with fellow LCS member John Gale Jones, (known by friends as John 'Gaol' Jones for the many prison sentences he served), who was found guilty but was not sentenced.

12. Powell 2002, pp. 424–8. 'The state of Ireland in 1798', writes Thompson, 'was enough to disorder the mind of any Irish patriot. And if we suppose (as we reasonably may) that Despard and his circle had access to former contacts of the L.C.S. as well as to the "United Irishmen" in Britain, and that there was some loose link between them and such organizations as the "Black Lamp" in Yorkshire, then the conspiracy was serious business' (Thompson 1991, p. 526). See pp. 574–7 below for more on Thompson's views of the LCS and Thomas Spence's influence.

of muting the Jacobin newspapers in Manchester and Sheffield.[13] Both the Suppression Act and the first Combination Act received royal assent on 12 July 1799. Given the context we have laid out here, it should hardly merit surprise that George III assented to both acts on the same day. But in fact the question of whether the Combination Acts actually formed an integral part of the 'Pittite Repression' has prompted serious scholarly debate. On one side of the debate we have the Webbs, the Hammonds, E.P. Thompson, Adrian Randall and others concluding that they did. On the other side we have M. Dorothy George, C.R. Dobson and A.E. Musson saying they did not. Let us briefly consider this debate, with an eye to whether the Combination Acts furthered the dismantling of the Tudor legislation which enshrined custom.

The Combination Act of 1799 arose out of an attempt by the abolitionist William Wilberforce to amend a bill to ban combinations among the millwrights. Since strikes by millwrights meant an interruption in the supply of bread to London, this was no trivial matter. Suggesting that combinations were a 'general disease' in society, Wilberforce proposed to amend the bill so that it would apply to all trades in the same way that an act of 1749 had prohibited combinations in most textile trades. His amendment was ruled out of order; whereupon the original bill passed the House and moved onto the Lords, at which point Prime Minister Pitt, no doubt acting at the behest of his good friend Wilberforce, interrupted the bill and proposed instead a bill that would apply to all workmen, modelled on the act of 1796 that banned combinations among the papermakers. Pitt was probably attracted to the Papermakers' Act because it allowed for summary judgments to be made within one month of the offence by a single justice of the peace, as opposed to two justices as prescribed in most of the earlier anti-combination acts, thus enabling the swiftest possible form of prosecution under law. But the Papermakers' Act also represented a diversion from previous acts in another important respect. Aside from setting working hours for vat men and dry workers, the act specified no other role for the government in terms of regulating the trade. Instead, it 'voided all contracts to raise wages, to reduce hours or work, to hinder employment of other workers, or "in any way whatever to affect" employers in conducting business'.[14] The day after Pitt had made his case in the Lords, his bill was moved in the Commons by Secretary to the Treasury George Rose and passed. In the House of Lords, Lord Holland, Fox's nephew, asked whether masters might be taking advantage of the temper of the times in order to ' "render their workmen more dependent than they had hitherto been" ', but the bill nevertheless also passed through the upper house and the first Combination Act quickly became law. Within the year, the vagueness of

13. Emsley 1985, pp. 817–18.
14. Orth 1987, p. 193.

the act was criticised and petitions from workmen all over England poured into Parliament. All of them protested the loss of trial by jury. One particular novelty of the bill was that it enabled a justice to grant employers licenses to hire non-apprenticed labour. This was seen as a serious blow to the Statute of Apprentices. Responding to the outcry of grievances, a committee was struck to draft a new bill which passed in July 1800. The new bill sought to balance the legislation somewhat by adding a new crime: combinations by employers. But rather than three months in gaol, the punishment for offending employers would be twenty pounds. The number of justices was increased from one to two, and the power of review was restored. While these were welcome changes for workers, the new bill also included a new provision outrageous to workers: the possibility of trial *in abstentia*.[15] Here, we see the Government seeking to preserve at least the minimal appearance of neutrality by making concessions to both parties in the territory of dispute, in keeping with typical eighteenth-century modes of justice, but also following the eighteenth-century trend toward greater summary justice.

According to M. Dorothy George, combination was just 'monopoly in the old sense' and the Combination Acts 'introduced no new principle and created no new offence'.[16] She points out that combination was treated as a conspiracy at common law, being a restraint of trade, alongside engrossing, regrating and forestalling. The primary purpose of the Acts, therefore, was to 'avoid the delays and expense'[17] of common-law trials by introducing a process of allowing summary justice. Quoting the Webbs, who claimed that these laws 'remain the most unqualified surrender of the State to the discretion of a class in the history of England',[18] George seeks to portray the acts as being, on the contrary, rather a damp squib, being passed 'casually' and 'almost "a dead letter"' as soon as they were made into law. 'Little more was heard of the Act until the agitation for repeal'.[19] Echoing George, Dobson rebuts E.P. Thompson's view that the Combination Acts sought not simply to ban conspiracy 'in the old sense', but the threat of *Jacobin* conspiracy among workers. Dobson argues that: 'the link, if any, between the lower-middle-class corresponding societies and the trade societies of wage-earners was by no means self-evident, and before 1800 there is little to show that the authorities seriously suspected any. The reports of the Committee of Secrecy said nothing of combination of wage-earners, and the English

15. Orth 1987, pp. 195–203.
16. George 1936, p. 172. By 'monopoly in the old sense' George surely means unauthorised monopolies, not legal monopolies in the form of chartered companies of merchants, and earlier, of guild craftsmen. For those organisations, monopoly was quite legal, but merchant monopolies began to give way to interlopers and 'free trade' in the seventeenth and eighteenth centuries.
17. George 1936, p. 173.
18. George 1936, p. 172, quoting Webb and Webb 1902, pp. 1–64.
19. George 1936, p. 173.

"Jacobins" were dealt with, not by the Combination Laws, but by the quite separate Corresponding Societies Act of 1799'.[20]

But is it possible, asks Randall, that Pitt himself had access to information overlooked by Dobson? According to Dobson, only after January of 1800 did 'plain clothes policemen' (government spies) began taking 'an active interest in trade-union affairs'.[21] Randall rebuts this argument by pointing out that from at least early August 1799, if not earlier, the Government had been spying on the trades. Among others, the government informant William Barlow had been spying on trade combinations in the Midlands and the North, reporting indirectly to the cabinet. Thus Pitt was taking a direct interest in trade societies in the immediate wake of the passage of the first act, if not before. Randall fails to mention that in November 1799 the Home Office sent another agent to check on Barlow's reports from Sheffield, and he could find no substantiation for Barlow's reports, finding Barlow to be '"a complete alarmist"', after which Barlow was dismissed.[22] The fact that spying was going on this early does indicate that the Government was concerned about the possibility of trade union activity becoming revolutionary. Upon reviewing petitions from the Lancashire weavers' association in August of 1799, the Duke of Portland wrote: '"...it is manifest that if nothing injurious to the safety of Government is actually in contemplation, associations so formed contain within themselves the means of being converted at any times into a most dangerous instrument to disturb the public tranquillity"'.[23] Such evident suspicion and alarm suggests to Randall that the acts did form a part of the general legislative repression as they were in fact meant to ban unions.[24] 'How deep the links between militant trade unionism and radicalism ran can only be surmised', writes Randall, 'but clearly the juxtaposition of industrial and political discontents constituted a dangerous mixture'.[25] In her argument, George suggested that a source of the confusion was the tendency to equate 'combinations' with 'unions', equating 'combinations' specifically with conspiracies to raise wages and 'unions' with 'associations of workmen'.[26] In the 1790s, however, the term 'combination' was generally applied to associations, whilst the term 'union' had not yet come into widespread usage. Nonetheless, the specific connotation of 'combination' in *legal* parlance did refer to attempts to manipulate wages or

20. Dobson 1980, p. 122. Dobson makes no mention of the fact that both acts received royal assent on the same day.
21. Dobson 1980, p. 144, n. 91.
22. Dinwiddy 1974, pp. 114–15.
23. Letter to Bancroft, 8 August, 1799, as quoted in Randall 1991, p. 270.
24. Randall 1982, p. 255. Agent Barlow makes an earlier appearance in Thompson's *Making of the English Working Class* (Thompson 1991, p. 546).
25. Randall 1991, p. 270.
26. George 1936, p. 177. She bases this argument on fact that the acts were little used, a point we shall come to shortly.

the product, whether it was employers or workers. Indeed, the anti-combination legislation of the earlier eighteenth century was mainly directed at *employers* who were paying too much in wages, and was usually passed at the insistence of other employers threatened by competition. It follows that the Combination Acts were not *specifically* intended as a measure of repression solely against associations of labourers, and thus Randall appears to overstate the case. At the same time, however, the acts were hardly unimportant. George argues that, in practice, the Combination Acts were 'a very negligible instrument of oppression'.[27] If this were true, how then to explain the way in which the Combination Acts came to enjoy such pride of place in the history of labour relations? George suggests simply that the act of 1800 has mistakenly been equated with *all* the anti-combination legislation repealed in 1824. This raises the question of the symbolic as well as psychological impact of the acts, both during the period they were in force and after their repeal.

Emsley points out that quite apart from previous anti-combination legislation, the distinctive aspect of the Combination Acts was that they were directed against actions made not by weavers, or hatters or bakers, but against workers as a discrete social *class*.[28] In this sense alone, the acts stand as a landmark piece of legislation. But more than symbolism was at work. As we have seen, the 1796 act against combinations in the paper trade specifically proscribed any interference in the business of employers and any violations of contract. Being based upon this act, the 1799 Combination Act dropped even the minimal amount of regulation (setting of hours) in the 1796 act. The 1800 act then introduced the power of review absented from the 1799 act. The effect of these changes, which may appear subtle, in fact represented a profound shift in government policy. Orth explains this shift in some detail:

> In 1799 and 1800 parliament outlawed collective action and voided collective agreements. The paradigmatic employment contract was between individuals: one employer contracting for the services of one workman. The Tudor-Stuart policy of wage regulation by the justices of the peace was ending. Within the new legislative scheme the role of the justices was to prevent group action and to enforce the individual contract. In place of their historic role as regulators, the justices received a limited role as arbitrators. In this last area the 1800 Act made a major contribution. Arbitration was not new in the industrial context, but before 1800 it was limited to specific industries. By the Combination Act of 1800 it was for the first time extended to 'all disputes' respecting [prices, injuries, delays in finishing the work, or poor quality of work]. This extension

27. George 1936, p. 177.
28. Emsley 1985, p. 820.

> of arbitration is comparable to the extension of the ban of the Combination Act to all trade unions. Just as parliament had come to think of 'workmen' in place of tailors, papermakers, and millwrights, so it had begun to think in terms of 'all disputes' rather than stoppages in particular trades.
>
> The parliamentary history of the arbitration sections reveals a conscious turn from the old policy of *regulation* toward the new policy of *arbitration*.[29]

Here, then, is a clear example of how it was not enough to simply remove the 'fetters' restraining trade, but to develop a new policy to replace the old. The paternalism of a state dominated by the landed class did not end at this point, as we shall see. But here, at least, is the beginning of a redefinition of the state's role as paternal overseer in the direction of a new role as neutral arbiter between contracting parties. Labour law in general was set on a new foundation, one based on conceptualising the relationship between employer and employee as a contract between two individuals trading commodities at the market, in this case wages for labour-power. While only a legislative step, such a reformulation of state policy was absolutely essential in order to accommodate the process of labour being commodified, or becoming abstract labour.

Both Rostow and E.P. Thompson have been criticised (for different reasons) for promoting the view that the 1780s or the 1790s were crucial decades of transition in the Industrial Revolution. As Malcolm Chase writes, the 'tendency now is to view British industrialisation as a much flatter, evolutionary process'.[30] Certainly the present work has sought to uncover the logic of the historical process at work, rather than treating sudden, episodic changes as being singularly causal. At the same time, much of the literature sees 1782 as a watershed for British trade, which grew exponentially thereafter. So in trade specifically there may be grounds for speaking of a 'take-off'. With regard to Thompson's work, which has generated so much controversy and has invited considerable misinterpretation of his argument, the question of how, whether and why the 1790s were a critical decade in the contemporary definition of concepts of *class* remains. If Thompson places too much emphasis on the links between radical Jacobinism and incipient trade unionism, we would like to offer an alternative explanation.

Let us start by asking where the impetus to shift labour policy from regulation to arbitration came from. Certainly political economy and liberalism inveighed against economic regulation in general (though as we shall see the banning of combinations was later itself seen as a form of interference with the free play of market forces). But the acts were the work of politicians, not economists. Thus we point to objective factors operating in the economy

29. Orth 1987, p. 204, citing 39 and 40 Geo. 3, c. 106, §18. Emphasis not found in the original.

30. Chase 2000, p. 70.

at the time, starting with the dislocations caused by enclosures. When Wilberforce proposed a policy to address 'a general disease' of conspiracies everywhere to raise wages, he was speaking to the fact that the 1790s had seen the greatest number of strikes and labour disturbances of the eighteenth century. While striking for higher wages was nothing new in factory or domestic manufacturing, what *was* new were strikes by agricultural labourers outside of harvest time. In November of 1790, a strike for higher wages by agricultural labourers in several villages of northern Norfolk prompted a swift response by local justices, who dispatched some of the ringleaders to the local bridewell. Previous strikes by agrarian labourers had either protested against the employment of Irish hands (1736, 1774) or took place at haymaking or harvest time (1749, 1761, 1763, 1766, and 1775).[31] Occurring in November, the Norfolk strike represented perhaps the first instance of agrarian labourers demanding higher wages during a season of low demand for labour. Throughout the 1790s, such strikes became more common, especially in East Anglia and the South East. In general, these strikes were severely dealt with. A trial of the leaders of an 1800 strike in Essex resulted in sentences of one-year imprisonment, and binding on recognisance for £100 each. '*The Times* reporter at the trial urged that the sentences be widely publicised to show agricultural labourers "what would be the consequences of combining to distress their employers"'.[32] The extent to which the panic that this new pattern of strikes among agricultural labourers sowed played into the passage of the Combination Acts as perhaps a key part of Wilberforce's 'general disease' is a question for further study. It is hard to see how it could not have been a factor, for Parliament was still a body dominated by the landed class, who would have been much more directly affected by agrarian strikes than by strikes in manufacturing. Yet with the resumption of parliamentary enclosures after the American War and in particular the increasing restriction or denial of access by commoners to rights of common, dependence upon wages, especially in the agrarian South, was steadily increasing as other options were foreclosed. The payment of relief in the form of aid-in-wages helped monetise agrarian employment relations. Above we followed Patriquin's suggestion that the roundsman system and other methods of mobilising agrarian labourers by means other than the market may in fact be the agrarian-capitalist answer to the loss of the feudal right of the lord to command peasants to work so many days out of the year farming his demesne lands. Likewise, upon the dissolution of customary law, the local justice of the peace effectively filled the void left by the lord as head of the manorial court, being now an official representing common law at the local level. As the

31. Dobson 1980, p. Appendix: 154–65.
32. Chase 2000, pp. 71–2, citing multiple sources.

process of enclosing nearly all the arable land in England over the course of four or more centuries drew to a close, rendering the agrarian population increasingly market-dependent and wage-dependent, the need for the local JP to regulate customary rights, to fix wages and hours or generally to fill the role left by their lordly predecessors of enforcing what remained of customary law waned. Meanwhile, the need for arbitration (or outright suppression of striking labourers) in wage disputes increased. In this context, the Speenhamland system could be read as offering a means by which the local JP could quiet agrarian labour disputes without asking for concessions from employers. Added to the dislocations of enclosures, the 1790s brought the national emergency of war, wartime inflation, the dearth years of 1794–6 and 1800–1 and the fiscal crisis of 1797. All of these added factors would have served to compound the hardships suffered by agrarian labourers faced with loss of access to means of subsistence and subsequent market dependency.

None of this is meant to declare the 1790s as *the* decade in which capital and labour made their appearance as distinct classes. What we are trying to point to is the empirical basis for the somewhat conscious recognition by the state of its shift from a policy of regulation to one of arbitration in labour disputes, and the concomitant recognition by the state of 'workmen' defined not by the particular function they played in terms of their unique contribution to the economy, but in their role as wage labourers. A change of such magnitude has to register some time. There may be other examples, but the Combination Acts serve well to demonstrate the point. Adding further caution, we must stress that the Combination Acts did not spell the sudden death of paternalism. Nor were they effective in curbing combinations in the least. Indeed, among papermakers, whose craft was the focus of the bill upon which the first Combination Act was modelled, combinations of both masters and their labourers were highly active in the immediate aftermath of the passage of the Combination Acts.[33] Part of the reason for their ineffectiveness was that there existed no effective method for policing combinations on a national scale. 'The Home Office during the 1790s was tiny, never more than two dozen persons including, at the top, the Secretary of State, and, at the bottom, the delightfully named "necessary woman"'.[34] The Bow Street Runners still maintained only a small office in London and were anyway charged with running after highwaymen and other common criminals.

Despite broad consensus among historians that the act was scarcely enforced, we cannot be certain that this was so since no definitive study of the life of the

33. Coleman 1954, p. 51.
34. Emsley 1985, p. 820.

Combination Acts has yet been written.[35] Thompson points out that since the crimes defined by the Combination Acts were not new; most prosecutions in this area took place under previous legislation, including the common law of conspiracy and the Statute of Apprentices.[36] However much they were actually enforced, the 'psychological and practical impact' of the Combination Acts on the development of trade unionism was enormous, as Chase explains:

> The typical penalty of two months' gaol and £5 costs was not negligible and it is small wonder the existing habits of secrecy and ritual became more deeply ingrained, shaping the cultural tone of craft trade unionism for more than a century to come. However well-managed a trade union might be, it was cast in the role of an enemy to the establishment until the repeal measure in 1824. The mere presence of such a measure on the statute book underlined the convergence of landed and manufacturing interests in opposition to those of labour, and even its perfunctory application constituted a powerful reminder of the power relations within contemporary society.[37]

It is highly unlikely that Pitt or Wilberforce actually intended to drive workmen into underground association. Pitt's main concern was to root out sedition. Leeson suggests that if Pitt's aim was to keep the radical Corresponding Societies from joining forces with the conservative artisans, its effect was the opposite: to drive them together in a search for mutual self-defence. 'From Lancashire with the passing of the Acts came the report, "The Radicals are drinking Pitt's health" '.[38] If the government was worried that the trades would learn organisational techniques of secrecy and enforcing loyalty, writes Leeson, they probably had it the wrong way around – if anything, the methods of enforcing secrecy and loyalty were transferred *to* political organisations *from* friendly societies and worker combinations.

At the same time, it seems likely that Pitt's adoption of the Papermakers' Act as a model for his Combination Act could have been made on the suggestion of anxious employers or more likely still, magistrates who recognised the advantage of preferring arbitration to regulation. Lord Kenyon, who presided over most combination trials at King's Bench in the 1790s and who consistently upheld Tudor legislation against forestalling, regrating and engrossing, suggested at one trial that it should be left to the workers to seek a better contract, the

35. Chase 2000, p. 84. To make her case, George offers but two examples of attempts at enforcement, both failing to result in prosecution. The reader is left feeling that this is both a selective sampling and something far short of representative.
36. Thompson 1991, p. 551.
37. Chase 2000, pp. 84–5.
38. Leeson 1979, p. 101.

courts being the improper forum for redressing such grievances.[39] And Spencer Perceval remarked in 1804 that prosecutions under the Act '"had better be in the hands of the Masters than of Government"'.[40] These comments reflect the fact that the Combination Acts were a form of enabling legislation that enabled criminal prosecution of combinations, but did not obligate the government to pursue the violators.

If it was left to employers to pursue prosecutions, why were there apparently so few? Leeson points to the intimacy of the small workshop, where a sense of mutuality persisted. Of course, in many cases it was simply easier for an employer to negotiate an end to a strike than to call upon the law for assistance. More broadly, employers could face serious consequences, including reprisals, by seeking to discipline workers under the act. Beyond that, there were advantages in allowing workers to organise. Where teamwork was an important component of the production process, it might be prudent for an employer to allow combination. Organised workers tended to discipline or expel slackers. Collections were taken and used to care for the sick or provide other social services. The term 'tramp' came into its own around 1800, by which time 'woolcombers, hatters, curriers, papermakers, cordwainers, calico-printers and others had begun their tramping contacts with "tickets" or "blanks" and "houses of call" where hospitality and news of work were to be found'.[41] By making it easier for the workman to relocate, tramping made prosecuting the combiner more difficult. The partial lifting of the Settlement Acts may also have facilitated tramping. The need for secrecy because of the Combination Acts probably made for better, or at least more strongly independent, organising. One reason for employers not to move against tramping was that it actually facilitated the mobility of skilled labour. Tramping also linked up different trades and helped disseminate political information and ideas.[42] In the decades following the Combination Acts, the number of permanent combinations of workers greatly increased. The policy of looking the other way by employers and officials certainly aided this, but we should keep in mind that the combined forces of population growth, the expansion of the domestic economy and especially of the manufacturing sector, the social dislocation brought on by enclosures and the decline of custom as enshrined in customary and common law were all factors contributing to the beginnings of an increasingly unregulated national labour force.

---

39. Dobson 1980, p. 131.
40. As quoted in Chase 2000, p. 87.
41. Leeson 1979, p. 112.
42. Leeson 1979, pp. 113–14; Chase 2000, pp. 88–90.

The tension within Radicalism

The years 1799–1800 saw poor harvests, the effect of which was to depress the textile trades in particular. Where the crisis of 1795 was hampered at the outset by an insufficient importation of grain, the initial government response to the dearth of 1799 generally tided stomachs over during the winter. But a second poor harvest in 1800 came at a point when reserves had been exhausted, producing an absolute scarcity in September. An abundant harvest in 1801 put an end to twenty-four months of extremely high grain prices. The effect of both periods of dearth seems to have been particularly acute in West Riding.[43] High prices, of course, meant dearth and distress for labourers but high profits and rents for farmers and landlords. Thus when prices remained low from 1801–4, profits fell and the economy slowed, even if hunger was averted. But prices climbed again from 1804 to 1814. The high prices of these years factor into the distress that lay behind the 'outrages' of violent protest and machine-breaking by artisans. We are now moving into that period of the long, slow decline in the plight of the weavers from a peak in their wages in the 1790s to their complete immiseration by the 1840s. The turning point in their real wages likely began with the dearth of 1794–5. High food prices clearly factored into falling real wages, but so did the growth of factories and other large-scale operations in textile production, which by providing a vast expansion of the demand for weaving, enabled the numbers of hand-loom weavers to expand even as use of the power-loom gradually began to increase alongside. While the power-loom was, as we have seen, met with immediate resistance upon its invention, its re-introduction in the early 1800s and its subsequent spread met with far less resistance for the simple fact that demand for hand-loom weaving remained steady, even if wages continued to decline. The shearing frame and the gig mill, however, posed an immediate threat to the finishing trade conducted by the cloth dressers, known as 'croppers' in West Riding and 'shearmen' in the West of England. The period in which they were resisted corresponds roughly to the years of high food prices as well as the war against Napoleon: 1797 to 1814.

By the time of Napoleon's return from Egypt, whereupon he assumed power on 18 Brumaire as First Consul of France in a *coup d'état*, Britain had organised the Second Coalition against France, which included Austria, Naples and Sicily, Portugal, Ottoman Turkey and of course French Royalists in exile. Russia also joined the coalition, scoring a victory against France in Italy but suffering defeat in Switzerland, and taking part with Britain in an unsuccessful attempt to drive France out of Holland, before Tsar Paul I withdrew his forces from the war out of disgust with Austria's strategic blunders and unwillingness to share

43. Wells 1977, pp. 1–7.

information. Britain's assertion of the right to seize ships in the Baltic for search subsequently led to Paul's decision to revive the League of Armed Neutrality, which included Russia, Prussia, Sweden and Denmark.[44] This would lead to armed conflict between Britain and Denmark in early 1801 at the Battle of Copenhagen, where Nelson, in defiance of orders, sank many a Danish ship before a truce was declared. While France appeared everywhere on the defensive in 1799, in 1800 Napoleon reclaimed northern Italy and General Moreau seized Bavaria. French troops were again threatening to march on Vienna and just as it had done in 1797, Austria sued for peace once more. The terms of the Treaty of Campo Formia were renewed in the Treaty of Lunéville. Once again Britain was the last major power confronting France. In Egypt, however, Turkish and British forces under Abercromby managed to expel France. Britain had also seized Malta in July 1801 and engaged the French off of Gibraltar in the costly Battle of Algeciras. These military successes brought a renewed sense of military confidence and eased fears of a French invasion. 'While the French navy had been reduced by more than a half between 1793 and 1801, the British navy had grown from 15,000 to 133,000 men and from 135 ships of the line and 133 frigates to 202 ships of the line and 277 frigates'.[45] However, Britain, with its mounting war debt, and Napoleon, anxious to consolidate his power within France and over newly conquered territories in Europe, were both war weary and ready to discuss peace. By this time, Pitt was no longer in power.

Pitt had fallen not over his efforts to raise funds for the war by re-organising the land tax and introducing the first income tax, as he had done in 1799, but rather over his efforts to lift restrictions on Catholics in the wake of the Act of Union, efforts which were staunchly opposed by the King. In January 1801, Pitt resigned, amidst negotiations with France and with the King suffering a renewed bout of madness. Henry Addington, a close associate of Pitt, assumed the office of the Treasury. Addington's negotiation of the Treaty of Amiens (March 1802) was greeted with bitter criticism at home both for making too many territorial concessions and even more so because it failed to include language that assured British merchants renewed access to European markets. The treaty was also conspicuously silent on the status of French-occupied territory in Holland, Italy and Germany. As in the years from 1697 to 1701, the treaty did not resolve all outstanding conflicts, although during this interlude of peace, Britain enjoyed an obvious naval superiority that put it in a position of being ready 'to renew hostilities against the French whenever it seemed desirable to do so'.[46]

44. Breunig 1977, p. 59.
45. Briggs 1979, p. 143.
46. Breunig 1977, p. 80.

That the ministry found itself in this position in 1801–2 did not mean the end of the repression. Nor did radicalism subside. Addington continued the repressive policies of Pitt. Mass meetings were called at the end of April 1801 to celebrate the restoration of *habeas* and the expiry of the Seditious Meetings Act and the Treasonable Practices Act. 'The government took these demonstrations as proof that danger still existed, renewed the acts and again suspended *habeas corpus*'.[47] This prompted radicals to return to organising in secret. The *Leeds Mercury* took note of the frequency of 'secret' midnight meetings. New members were urged to pledge their desire to see a total change in the system to the point of risking their lives, to promote the brotherhood of the 'friends of freedom' and to take every opportunity to obtain important political information.[48] Thompson points to the influence of Thomas Spence, who promoted radical decentralisation verging on agrarian socialism, as being widespread, particularly among LCS members.[49] Spence's pamphlet *The Real Rights of Man*, which appeared in Newcastle in 1775 but did not make its way to London until the early 1790s, advocated radical decentralisation of government, with authority to devolve to the parish level, each parish electing a representative to a national assembly. According to Thompson:

> Spence did not believe in a centralized, disciplined underground. His policy was that of the diffusion of agitation. [The intention of the Spenceans] seems to have been to make disaffection so amorphous that the authorities could find no centre and no organizing sinews. This was not the method of the 'Black Lamp' and of Luddism. But it provides a clue, in the very policy of diffusion. For the illegal tradition, from 1800 to 1820, never had a centre.[50]

There were more reasons for there being no 'centre' to radicalism besides a commitment to decentralisation. For one thing, the 'gagging acts' simply prevented the emergence of radical leaders who could express their views to the public. Censorship and intimidation had rendered its spokespersons effectively inarticulate until William Cobbett broke through much later.

Another reason was that the radical movement itself was heterodox and complex, full of a wide range of contending ideas and arguments. Methodism had a powerful influence upon the working class in instilling habits of self-discipline and regularity that were favourable to the spread of capitalist industry. But the 1790s also saw the rebirth of ideas associated with the antinomian heresy of the seventeenth century, upon which even the leading thinkers of the day drew.

---

47. Turner 1999, p. 90.
48. Thompson 1991, pp. 518–20.
49. Thompson 1991, pp. 176–7. 'Thomas Evans', writes Thompson, was a follower of Spence who 'was the first to give Spence's agrarian socialism a more general application'.
50. Thompson 1991, p. 543.

LCS members had to contend with crackpots as well as with radicals whose views were considered far too extreme. Spence was one of the latter. Francis Place would later write that Spence's views on politics ran virtually counter to that of the radical leaders of the day. In this sense, members of the LCS and other 'respectable' organisations did at least make efforts to assert a kind of hegemony within the underground radical movement, to the extent that this was possible under censorship, and to distance themselves from those radicals whose views seemed 'inarticulate, unrespectable, unenlightened, and hence illegitimate'.[51] Of course what one deems illegitimate is a matter of perspective. To the libertarian-minded followers of Paine, what was 'illegitimate' about Spence's radicalism was his disregard for what libertarians held and still hold most sacrosanct: property. To argue as Spence did for the abolition of property must have seemed nostalgic to middle-class liberals and libertarians who saw their property as the source of their growing prosperity. Radical statements are replete with the argument that a worker's labour was his only property. This could be seen as a reflection of the growing commodification of labour.

This points to the philosophical tension between popular-radicalism and the incipient trade union movement. While old-school trade unionists may have been inclined toward 'Leveller' philosophies such as that of Spence or Godwin, within the larger community such views were likely seen as utopian. For the conservatism of artisan workers was quite empirical and of the moment: they were mainly seeking to preserve a status quo under threat. If there was an issue upon which co-operation between the trade unionists and the popular-radicals could founder, it was the crafts' struggle to preserve what were effectively monopoly rights over a given trade as against the enthusiasm which Paine and his followers showed for free trade.[52] We have no doubt that trade unionists showed up for radical meetings. Radicals from outside the crafts showing up for strikes and direct action seems far less likely. This tension within radicalism is important to the present study on two levels. First, because while many trade unions were actively resisting the commodification of labour and the making of a capitalist system, there is a high degree to which other radicals were readily accommodating their thinking to conditions of market dependency and capitalism. Second, because while it was the elite artisans, the 'old' skilled labourers, who put up the fiercest struggle against the introduction of capitalism, by the middle of the nineteenth century, with the utter defeat of the artisans, the skilled labour of the factory system sought to protect its position of privilege by adapting to the logic of liberalism, and, indeed, even helping to shape the development of liberalism.

51. Makdisi 2003, pp. 20–4.
52. Chase 2000, p. 79.

The Despard affair suggests that at least a significant portion of radicals were ready and even preparing for an insurrection. But the depth of the plot and the support for it are impossible to know. Colonel Despard had a distinguished military record, having served in the West Indies and British Honduras. Nelson remembered him as a comrade-in-arms. He came from a family of Irish landowners, which is significant because in the 1790s he had moved within the circles of the LCS, the United Irishmen and the United Englishmen. In November 1802, he was arrested and accused of building an underground military organisation intent on overthrowing the Government. Evidence showed that he held many meetings at London taverns. Soldiers were apparently recruited and organised in divisions. Allegations suggested that the organisation was extensive with divisions within London and the countryside, and that it involved a plot to stage a coup in which the men would seize the Tower and the Bank and capture or assassinate the King, that being the signal for the London crowd to rise. At his trial, Despard himself offered little evidence either to confirm or deny these allegations, but Thompson interprets his statement as an admission of a conspiracy which Despard may only have been drawn into by others. Furthermore, Thompson suggests that if Despard had been in touch with secret organisations such as the 'Black Lamp' in West Riding, the conspiracy may have been quite widespread and quite serious, the 'Black Lamp' being noted as perhaps a code name for the organisation holding secret meetings on the byways outside Leeds under cover of night, as noted in a letter from Mayor Cookson to Fitzwilliam.[53] Dinwiddy points out that Thompson's evidence of an actual conspiracy in the North is completely hypothetical, being based on this one report from an agent who did not actually hear the content of the meeting, and on the distribution of handbills, which the authorities noted but found to contain no clear evidence of any revolutionary conspiracy.[54] While Thompson states his own caution of drawing clear links between popular-radicalism and trade unionism, he also points out

53. The letter describes what appears to be a spy seeking to infiltrate a secret meeting being held in a hollow six miles outside Leeds: '"... he found an irregular and moving line of scouts, who asked his business, and upon his continuing to proceed towards the 'Black Lamp' of men, a whistling was made, and he heard expressions and tones of voice that quite deterred him from his purpose"' (as quoted in Thompson 1991, pp. 520–7). See next footnote.

54. Dinwiddy (1974, pp. 119–20) writes that Thompson offers 'one substantial piece of evidence' connecting Despard to the secret meetings in Yorkshire: papers found on the men arrested along with Despard which re-stated a declaration about the '"objects for which we contend, and ... swear to be united" ... [But Thompson] does not mention that the leaflet of the "United Britons" in which this formula appeared had been cited over a year previously in the report of a house of commons committee of secrecy – a fact that seems to have been noted by Fitzwilliam, who observed in a letter to the Secretary of State in August 1802 that the oath and declaration which the disaffected were said to be using were "of several years' standing"'. Any connection, Dinwiddy concludes, remains speculative.

that the work of organising in either field would typically fall upon the few most active and competent individuals. The history of successful coups and revolutions would suggest that in each case the bold leadership of a relatively tiny group of leading conspirators is required. When the plot fails, the extent of the conspiracy can often only be gauged from fragmentary evidence. Our concern here is not whether Thompson is seeing a broader conspiracy than may have existed, but rather to suggest that the incongruity between artisan-based trade unionism, with its conservative attachment to custom, and Jacobin popular-radicalism, with its commitment to tearing down the old paternalist order and establishing a republican form of democracy, could explain – beyond attributing success to the policies of repression – why Britain did not, in fact, experience a revolution in imitation of the French and American models. In other words, while weavers, framework knitters and cloth dressers had serious grievances with the Government, their actions demonstrate a set of concerns grounded not in ideology but very concrete social property relations.

Malcolm Chase has warned that 'a fixation with the drama of Luddism can deafen us to the steady background noise of workplace complaint and grievances'.[55] Machine-breaking and property destruction were not tactics of first resort. The drama of machine-breaking came at a point in time when these artisans were faced with the elimination of their trades, or at least the reduction of their status as workers from being among the labour elite to living at the level of bare subsistence. More than that, the culture associated with the trades was itself under assault in the form of the dismantling of custom and its replacement with factories and policies promoting a 'free' labour market based on contracts between individual labourers and employers. Faced with the destruction of their trades, which for the artisans themselves posed an existential threat, and after polite options had failed, machine-breaking and property destruction posed an option that was in some cases successful. Ultimately, to prevent the intrusion of the social relationship of capital into their trades would have necessitated abolishing agrarian capitalism as well. The Spenceans may represent those who understood this to a degree. But the tactics used reveal a strategy with vastly more short-term ends-in-view. They do not suggest any inspiration by events in France, where the customary crafts had not been under the same long-term pressures.

'So simple is the plan, so faithful are the men'

The West of England had seen disturbances by the cloth dressers against the introduction of the gig mill as early as 1768, when shearmen pulled down a gig

55. Chase 2000, p. 95.

mill at Horningsham, Wiltshire and were punished with fines, whippings and imprisonment. Despite other, less violent tactics by the shearmen of Wiltshire and Somerset, the gig mill came into general use in the region for lower-quality cloths, but when it began to be applied to finer quality cloths in 1794, Gloucestershire shearmen alerted Parliament in a petition that their trade was threatened. They invoked 5 and 6 Edward VI, c. 22, 'An act for the putting down of gig mills', passed in 1552 and still in force. While the petition arrived too late for the parliamentary session, the gentlemen clothiers were nevertheless irate and called for a meeting at which they threatened the shearmen with wage reductions, dismissal and blacklisting. The position of the shearmen so weakened, there was no further resistance to the gig mill in Gloucestershire, and likewise the shearing frame was little resisted in Gloucestershire after its introduction in 1799. The use of gig mills began to spread in Wiltshire and Somerset between 1799 and 1802, prompting strikes and eventually direct action.

The peace of 1802 brought a slump to the woollen trade. And while this surely caused distress, Randall takes issue with the idea that episodes of violent machine-breaking such as the 'Wiltshire Outrages' of 1802 were the irrational actions of desperate men. There were, after all, little more than a dozen gig mills at work in Wiltshire and Somerset at the time. According to Randall:

> Violence was the pre-emptive, calculated choice of a powerful labour elite, not the desperate last gasp of a demoralized trade. Violence was controlled and specifically directed against men who in the cloth dressers' eyes were engaging in immoral and illegal practices. The Wiltshire shearmen were pragmatists, not pyromaniacs, and the outrages must be seen in terms of a mounting level of industrial intimidation against key innovators, seeking to force them back into compliance with the established customs of the trade. If to achieve this it was necessary to fire a few ricks and barns, this was justified by the innovators' own disregard for customary negotiation as legitimated by an Act of Parliament which the courts, on dubious grounds, refused to enforce.[56]

In all, three mills were destroyed during the 'Wiltshire Outrages' of 1802, one at Littleton, another at Clifford and a third at Trowbridge. The destruction of the Littleton mill succeeded in intimidating the gentlemen clothiers to agree to a wage increase. Randall provides an inventory of the other property destroyed: 'at least six ricks, one barn, two dwelling houses, one stable, several outhouses and one dog kennel were burnt down, trees were cut down, numerous windows broken…'[57] Many anonymous threats were issued, but no violence was committed against any person. Six years later, an attempt was made to murder one

56. Randall 1991, pp. 183–4.
57. Randall 1991, p. 179.

of the mill owners whose mill had been threatened in 1802. Three suspects were acquitted. The Wiltshire Outrages prompted the Government to dispatch militia to guard the mills. Government officials seeking information had difficulty comprehending the high level of support the perpetrators enjoyed from the local community. One shearman, Thomas Helliker, was tried and hanged, based solely on the evidence of a mill manager. Those who took part were armed with pistols, swords and other weapons and were in their late teens and early twenties: 'Dodging dragoons around damp fields in the night was not the place for men of riper years'.[58] To a considerable extent, both the non-violent and violent resistance against machinery in the West of England was successful in delaying its introduction. To the extent that this was the case, this also contributed to the West falling behind Yorkshire's lead. Randall goes so far as to suggest that worker resistance may have been the primary factor in the long-term slump in the West's woollen trade, and not vice-versa.[59]

In West Riding, the croppers had long managed to contain the use of gig mills to the environs of Huddersfield. So strong were the croppers' associations that they managed to quash efforts by masters to introduce the gig mill in 1791. In 1796, the Brief Institution, a union of croppers, was formed by John Tate. Only a few years before the passage of the Combination Acts, the Privy Council recognised the strength of this organisation:

> 'To contend with the men in their now united state would be very imprudent in every master. They know and feel their power and it gains such accession by every struggle that it becomes a matter of discretion now not to attempt resistance'. It was almost impossible to break their ranks, William Cookson, then mayor of Leeds, lamented in 1802, 'so simple is the plan, so faithful are the men to their oaths'.[60]

By 1802, the Brief Institution claimed membership among all of the cloth dressers in West Riding and the West of England. Use of the gig mill began to spread in peripheral parts of Yorkshire, but one merchant's attempt to set one up in Leeds

58. Randall 1991, p. 183.

59. 'Hostility to change therefore may have proved a major factor in delaying the mechanization of the West of England woollen industry and thereby have contributed to its slower growth rate than that in Yorkshire. Worker resistance may thus have been responsible for depressed trade and not the reverse as economic historians have often concluded' (Randall 1991, p. 105). Hobsbawm writes that the labour movements of this period 'were neither negligible nor wholly unsuccessful. Much of this success has been obscured by subsequent defeats: the strong organization of the West of England woollen industry lapsed completely, not to revive until the rise of general unions during the first world war...' (Hobsbawm 1952, p. 58).

60. Randall 1991, p. 131, quoting 'Observations respecting combinations', a Privy Council document, and a letter from Cookson to Fitzwilliam dated 16 August 1802.

in 1799 resulted in its immediate destruction. By 1801, the number of water- or steam-powered mills for scribbling wool in Yorkshire had grown from 26 in 1790 to 243, most having six to eight machines. Benjamin Gott's Bean Ing factory was the exception.[61] The number of fulling mills in West Yorkshire had grown from 104 to nearly two hundred in the previous two decades, and most of these mills now contained some scribbling machinery. In the worsted district, there were only 22 mills by 1800. The employment by Gott and other large employers of domestic spinners and weavers inside the factory offered the advantages of supervision and saved travel costs in dealing with outworkers. As the factory system grew in large towns like Leeds, the domestic system in peripheral villages declined.[62] When Gott attempted to introduce the gig mill at Bean Ing in 1801, he was forced to give it up. From September 1802 to January 1803, croppers working for Gott went on strike and were supported by funds from the Brief Institution's dues-paying members. Gott resorted to advertising and recruiting in the West of England, apparently to no avail. Other manufacturers refused to finish Gott's cloths by putting-out or employing their own croppers. Gott apparently did not contemplate invoking the Combination Acts. Mayor Cookson noted that an employer seeking prosecution would stand to lose business whilst awaiting a judgment and so would '"be exposed to incalculable injuries"'.[63]

Sporadically throughout the eighteenth century, merchant-clothiers in the West of England had set up loomshops, where weavers were concentrated under one roof. This effort became more concerted from the 1780s. It garnered the hostility of local weavers who laboured under the putting-out system, unlike the weavers in Yorkshire who set themselves up as small masters.[64] A major factor in the depression and unemployment that hit the trade following the Peace of Amiens was the loss of both government *and* continental demand for uniforms and blankets. Peace also meant stronger competition against British goods and high tariffs blocking access to continental markets, thanks to the incompetence of the Addington administration in handling peace negotiations with France. Because setting up as an independent weaver was a relatively easy affair, economic downturns had often seen those pushed out of work in other trades turn to weaving. Former scribblers and even some former shearmen now looked to weaving for employment. The decommissioning of soldiers, many of them woollen workers, meant an influx of labourers looking for work in an already overpopulated weaving trade just as production was nearing a standstill. The threat

61. See Chapter Ten, p. 466.
62. Jenkins and Ponting 1982, pp. 27–8.
63. Randall 1991, pp. 124–44 and 177, quoting a letter from Cookson to Fitzwilliam dated 8 September 1802 (p. 144).
64. Randall 1991, p. 187.

of machinery was now eclipsed by the threat of too many illegal workers (those who had not apprenticed or who had not been established in the trade for seven years). Gloucestershire weavers commenced a campaign to petition for government assistance in keeping interlopers out of the trade by enforcing not only the apprenticeship clauses of 5 Elizabeth, but also the statutes passed under Queen Mary that limited the number of looms that a weaver might possess. The Woollen Cloth Weavers' Society was formed for this purpose. It was modelled after the friendly societies, but was in fact a trade union, and was successful in chasing a hundred or more would-be weavers out of the trade. When the Society began threatening interlopers with prosecution, the innovating employers were compelled to petition Parliament for the repeal of the very statutes the Society was out to enforce. The employers also sought government help in suppressing the property destruction in Wiltshire and Somerset by force, and managed to secure several prosecutions of weavers under the Combination Act. When word of the struggle reached West Riding, small masters and journeymen united and formed the Clothiers' Community to oppose the repeal.[65] The gentlemen merchants and larger clothiers there joined the petition favouring repeal, insisting that the ruling should also apply to Yorkshire.

Among the members of the Commons Select Committee who would be responsible for the report in favour of suspension was Sir Robert Peel, the spinning and printing factory owner from Lancashire. Peel was, of course, a strong supporter of *laissez-faire*. Peel was also an Anglican Tory, which made him exceptional at a time when many factory owners were Dissenters, and thus brought to his factories an old-school conservatism and its belief that the poor were the charge of the rich. Peel was disturbed by the poor health and apparently stunted growth of the pauper apprentices working in his own mills.[66] Thus in 1802 he sponsored and succeeded in passing the Health and Morals of Apprentices Act. The name is informative, since it was conceived as an extension of the Statute of Apprentices to govern the employ of parish apprentices in cotton and woollen factories. But it became commonly known as the first factory act. Within the factory, the apprenticeship system was essentially nothing more than a means by which children were turned into indentured servants, since while severe punishments applied if they violated their apprenticeship 'contract', the 'skills' they were taught offered them little hope of advancing beyond a life as a permanent factory hand. Peel sought to set standards of cleanliness in the factories. The act banned the employment of children between 9 p.m and 6 a.m., and limited their work to 12 hours per day. It also mandated that the children be instructed

65. The Clothiers' Community lasted until 1806, when support in opposing repeal was garnered from the trustees of the cloth halls. Randall 1991, pp. 215–18.

66. Fitton 1989, p. 154.

in reading, writing and arithmetic as well as religious instruction.[67] Richard Arkwright II believed the bill's value lay in prompting factory owners to improve working conditions voluntarily, commenting that in some cases '"it would be rather an invidious task for magistrates to inspect the mills of their neighbours and friends"'.[68] Too few inspectors were appointed to make the act have much impact.

Shearmen and other artisans were equally subject to the pressures that came with peace and the slump in trade. And so they, too, took part in what became a long, very expensive and ultimately fruitless campaign from 1803 to 1806 against fully repealing the Statute of Apprentices as it applied to the woollen trade. The case put forward by the woollen workers appearing before the Select Committee involved social, economic and legal arguments all imbued with moral suasion. The moral argument was premised upon the characterisation of factories as institutions which fostered vice and immorality. Randle Jackson, counsel for the shearmen, argued that factories broke down the 'happy' relations of the domestic system and by destroying the 'moral and political instruction' of apprenticeship, knocked down barriers that had heretofore provided a check upon 'early licentiousness'. By contrast, he argues, the domestic system preserved the coherence of family values. Domestic work allowed fathers to prevent their children from succumbing to temptations, whereas the factory, by absenting the parent, served to encourage the vices of youth. The factory system encouraged social polarisation between rich monopolists and impoverished workers, and a society in which the new species of employer, the industrial capitalist, sought to destroy the independence and the customs of domestic workers. The appeal to tradition found sympathy among the true conservatives of the landed classes, and was also shared by smaller masters in the woollen trade who wished to see the growing power of the larger factory masters checked. Foremost among their economic arguments was the very demonstrable claim that the introduction of machinery led directly to unemployment among the artisans. When added to the claim that this in turn put a burden on the parish rates, this argument had extra pull with the landlords. They claimed that machines produced cloth of an inferior quality (which was likely true for a considerable time after a machine such as the power-loom was first introduced, but improvements would eventually turn the tables). They also asserted the view that their trades were their property just as

67. Collis and Greenwood 1977, p. 24. Notably, the employment of children during the night was to be allowed until June of 1804 for factories employing between 1,000 and 1,500 spindles. Clearly some manufacturers, perhaps Peel himself, needed time to withdraw from the habit of working children through the night. See a full version of the bill in Douglas *et al.* (eds.) 1996, p. 723.

68. Fitton 1989, pp. 154–5, quoting Richard Arkwright, who did not stop taking children under the age of 10 until 1806 either.

the clothier's factory and machinery were his capital. In this, and in their argument that unlike cotton manufacturing, where increased cultivation of cotton and Whitney's mechanisation of ginning had produced a virtually unlimited supply of cotton, woollen manufacturers suffered from a limited supply of wool (a weak claim brutally attacked by the clothiers), the cloth workers revealed their conception of a static economy with limited supplies of raw materials and a limited, rather than growing, output. Under such conditions, for the employers to enlarge their share of the pie at the expense of the workers' share was distinctly immoral. Most of all, they rested their case upon the legal argument that the Tudor prohibitions against non-apprenticed workers, interlopers and machinery should be enforced in accordance with existing practice and custom.[69]

The innovating masters and factory owners dismissed these arguments out of hand. They presented an alternative conception of an economy based upon continuous growth, a growth driven by innovation and machinery. Such an innovation would enable all trades to flourish and was the 'principal means by which we have excluded other nations from the foreign trade'.[70] Some unemployment was better than to allow a whole line of trade to fall behind regional or foreign competitors and collapse entirely. Here, we see the standard of living debate in embryo. In July 1803, both houses of Parliament would vote to suspend the statutes in question, and a bill for full repeal would be ordered.[71]

The second generation of industrialists in charge

By now, the sons of the first generation of factory masters had taken over production operations from their fathers. Arkwright junior had inherited his father's factory empire. Arkwright senior had located his primary factories at Cromford in the Derbyshire dales against the advice of his partners. 1797 had brought a series of bankruptcies for Midland spinners, commencing the decline of an industry that had been set on a weak foundation. Arkwright junior would reduce his father's empire to three mills spinning coarse yarn. Manchester was now the unrivalled centre for machine-building in the textile trades and the mule had become the standard spinning machine for cotton. The power-loom was just beginning to spread. Wartime inflation contributed to a shift in consumer demand away from wool and in favour of cotton. Cotton was king. Nottingham continued to serve as a centre of the hosiery trade, but the 'merchant hosiers and their class were generally content to be patrons of mechanical ingenuity in

69. Randall 1986, pp. 8–17.
70. Randall 1986, pp. 6–8.
71. Randall 1991, pp. 187–205; Gregory 1982, p. 123. The statutes in question are 5 Elizabeth c. 4, and 2 and 3 Philip and Mary c. 11.

others'.[72] The silk factories in the Midlands also saw a contraction, likely the result of an interruption in the supply of raw silk during the wars.[73] 'Lancaster triumphed with the mule', writes Chapman, 'and the West Riding with the throstle'.[74]

In the iron industry, the second generation was faring well. James Watt II and Matthew Boulton II had taken charge of the Soho Foundry, with the aid of their fathers' chief engineer, William Murdoch. It was here that Murdoch continued to pioneer new inventions, installing the first gas lighting at the Soho Foundry, which soon began filling orders for this new technology, and devising his model steam locomotive, which had been included in Watt's 1782 rotative engine patent. Before it could be developed further, this invention would await the arrival of engineer Richard Trevithick, who adapted the design to the world's first working locomotive,[75] which Trevithick first demonstrated to the public at the Penydarren ironworks near Merthyr Tydfil in February 1804.[76] A traveller and possible spectator of the event was struck by the concentration of capital at the massive ironworks.[77] Trevithick had invented his high-pressure experimental engine and ran the first steam-railway locomotive on the plateways at Coalbrookdale in 1802.

With Edmund Darby, the nephew of Abraham Darby III in charge at the Coalbrookdale, the works were filling a large number of orders for steam engines, and were still supplying orders for Newcomen engines as well. By filling orders for steam engines, the foundry became the profitable side of the business, while the manufactory was mired in the production of an infinite variety of cast-iron products for distant markets.[78] During the Napoleonic Wars the French

72. Chapman 1967, pp. 210–18.

73. Butterton 1996, p. 51. Only seven active silk mills were recorded in the area in 1817.

74. Chapman 1967, p. 212. The 'throstle' was apparently the project which Thomas Highs worked on after completing the water frame, being an adaptation of the same principle to the spinning of wool fibres. 'What is called the throstle-frame is only an improvement of the water-frame, both machines being the same in principle. In the throstle-frame all the rollers on either side are connected together, whereas in the other each head has a distinct act of gearing, and is driven by a separate motion : hence the throstle requires considerably less power to drive it' (*London Quarterly Review* 1860, p. 34). Thus based on Chapman's comment it seems that small, water-powered throstle factories emerged in West Riding and, before the coming of larger power-machinery, apparently went some way toward displacing the jenny.

75. Gale 1952, pp. 28–9. From discussions it is known that Murdoch also contemplated building steam engines and built a special engine for the purpose. The Foundry adopted Cort's process in 1808.

76. Aspin 1995, p. 11.

77. Evans 1989, p. 215.

78. Trinder 1974, pp. 53–6. L-shaped 'Jinney, Ginney or Jenny' plate rails developed by John Curr replaced the earlier edge rails; the new type of rail was cheaper to lay, but it

occupation of the Lowlands cut off Britain's access to the small-arms manufacturers of Liége, and thus 'the Carron Company became one of the great arsenals for Europe: about 1805–6 it was casting cannon at the rate of over 5,000 per year'.[79] The works' capital now exceeded £150,000, and as the enormous, short and broad guns it was turning out, known as 'carronades', proved effective in battle, its fame spread.[80] From Shropshire, first-generation industrialist John Wilkinson was supplying not only the British government with cannon, but the French government as well, even as the two nations were at war.[81] Most of the ironmasters were only too happy to provide the desired armaments. Being Quakers, the Darbys at Coalbrookdale were the exception, refusing to provide material in support of war.

War, commerce and British capitalism

The Peace of Amiens proved to be more of an armistice than a real peace. It reflected the stalemate that had been reached between British naval dominance of the seas and French army dominance of continental Europe. Many British tourists quickly resumed the practice of taking a holiday in France, Charles James Fox among them. The terms of Amiens included British recognition of the French Republic and an agreement that Britain would return Malta to the Knights of St. John, while the French would evacuate Piedmont and Naples. But Bonaparte refused to withdraw and continued his expansionist policies. He supported a coup in the Batavian Republic (Holland), he invaded Switzerland, where he declared himself mediator, and he reversed the Revolution in Saint-Domingue (Haiti) led by Toussaint L'Ouverture, re-imposing slavery in Haiti and throughout French territories. Britain ultimately refused to withdraw from Malta, fearing that France would seize it and thereby threaten to control the Mediterranean and re-occupy Egypt. Since France now controlled Holland, the Cape of Good Hope was effectively under French control. Allowing France to control Egypt and thus possess the ability to block British vessels from the East at both points was, therefore, unthinkable. When talks in Paris broke down in May 1803, Addington summoned up the nerve to declare war. A volunteer movement was organised, and 150,000 recruits enlisted in Britain.[82] When Napoleon had himself crowned

---

was a cul-de-sac and its being laid all over the region may have caused a lack of railway innovation thereafter.

79. Christie 1982, pp. 11 and 162.
80. Mantoux 1961, p. 303.
81. Hammond and Hammond 1974b, p. 147.
82. Addington's Army of Reserve Act of 1803 empowered the Government to recruit *en masse* and 'brought forward so large a force – ultimately 380,000 men in Britain and

Emperor in January 1804, the move alienated even the Jacobins. 'No True follower of Paine could stomach this',[83] writes Thompson. Napoleon began amassing a force at Bologna, in apparent preparation for an invasion of England.

Addington faced relentless criticism, primarily from the opportunistic Foxites and the re-emerging Grenville faction. When Pitt withdrew his support in the summer of 1804 in the aftermath of Parliament's ill-informed impeachment of Henry Dundas (now Lord Melville), Addington resigned. Pitt was the logical choice to once again unite the factions, though his second ministry would prove to be much weaker than the first. Pitt set about trying to unite the ministry in the name of patriotism. In Europe, he sought to build the Third Coalition against France, which included the usual suspects: Britain, Russia, Austria, Portugal, Naples and Sicily, now including Sweden.[84] Napoleon's strategy involved attempting to draw the British fleet away from the Channel by launching attacks in the West Indies. During the same period, Lord Mannington led an expensive but mostly successful campaign in Central and Western India against the Maratha armies receiving training from French privateers from 1803 to 1805.[85] In October 1805, the French fleet under Villanueva was defeated in the Battle of Trafalgar by Nelson, who paid for the victory with his life. Napoleon was forced to abandon his grand plan to invade England and concentrate once more on the Continent. In Europe, Austria's invasion of Bavaria resulted in its being routed at Elm, leading at last to the occupation of Vienna by French troops. This was followed by the defeat of a combined Austria and Russian force in Moravia. Austria effectively surrendered with the Treaty of Pressburg, under which the eight-and-a-half centuries of the Holy Roman Empire were brought to an end with the abdication of Francis II as Holy Roman Emperor. With Austria out of the war, the familiar stalemate ensued.[86]

Pitt's health had been failing, likely from cancer. The failure of his military strategy in the Third Coalition proved a severe blow. In January 1806, Pitt died at the age of 46, 'as much a victim of the war as the 47-year-old Nelson was its hero'.[87] In the wake of the loss of both Nelson and Pitt, there followed years of political chaos. Grenville succeeded Pitt at the Treasury and assembled the 'Ministry of all Talents', an attempt to unite the various opposition factions. Fox, however, was the dominant figure in the ministry, with George III having finally relented in allowing him to assume control of the Foreign Office. Sharing power

---

another 70,000 in Ireland – that it took months to provide many of the units with arms' (Christie 1982, p. 262).

83. Thompson 1991, pp. 494–5.
84. Derry 2001, pp. 87–103; Owen 1975, p. 267.
85. Christie 1982, pp. 266–76.
86. Turner 1999, p. 78; Christie 1982, p. 274; Briggs 1979, pp. 148–50.
87. Briggs 1979, p. 148.

and under pressure to find funds to supply the war effort, Fox and his party, having previously denounced increases in Pitt's income tax, now found themselves raising it by another 60 percent.[88] When the government then sought an excise tax on pig iron to fund the war, 'a nation-wide combination among iron masters arose to resist it'.[89] The Talents came to power seeking to pass acts to grant Catholic relief and to abolish the slave trade. Both issues underscored the Foxites' commitment to principle over expediency. The argument against abolition was that other nations would take up Britain's role and thereby gain an advantage. The case for abolition was led by William Wilberforce and the 'Saints', evangelicals who claimed divine inspiration and who seeing their chance under the Ministry of all Talents, launched a campaign of petitioning and public meetings, putting abolition at the top of the public agenda. The passage of the Abolition of the Slave Trade Act was the one genuine success of the Ministry.[90] Also among the Talents' objectives was the conclusion of a new peace with France. Fox soon realised that France was only interested in negotiating peace while it sought to break the alliance with Russia. Britain continued to inflict losses on the French fleet in the Mediterranean. Prussia's occupation of Hanover at France's urging was met with a British blockade of Prussian ports. There was now a British Blockade in effect from Brest to the Elbe. In September, Fox died and with him went any hopes for peace. Napoleon announced the Confederation of the Rhine. Prussia responded with a declaration of war against France. One month later, Prussia's armies were routed in the Battle of Jena.

From Prussia, Napoleon issued the Berlin Decree, which proclaimed a blockade against Britain, barred all English ships from French-occupied ports and the seizure of all English goods, letters and subjects in any French-occupied territory. A French policy of seizing British goods on carts and ships had been in effect since 1796.[91] In 1803, it was extended to Spain and now it was being extended to

88. Christie 1982, p. 277.

89. Addis 1957, pp. 18–19. Again reflecting the continued aspirations of master manufacturers for a life among the landed gentry, ironmaster Richard Crawshay, before his death in 1810, is reported to have told his son-in-law '"nothing but land can be considered as safe"'.

90. Turner 1999, pp. 79–82.

91. The Republic declared in 1796 that ships bearing British goods could be seized and detained. In 1797, the Council of Five Hundred broadened this to mean that any ship bearing any British goods could be taken as a prize and adding that neutral vessels known to trade in British ports were barred from French-controlled ports. 'It is needless to say that these decrees were inoperative' (Rose 1983, pp. 705–6). Such policies had previously been adopted during the Seven Years' War. Of overland trade Sloane writes: 'On December 4, 1798 . . . without warning, strong military detachments were placed at all the gates of Paris and every vehicle was carefully searched; domiciliary visits were commenced by the customs authorities and were continued until all English wares were removed from commerce; and French public opinion supported these proceedings, which the English stigmatised as "legal robbery"' (Sloane 1898, p. 215). Sloane notes that

all of Europe. The apparent basis of the Berlin Decree was a paper presented to Napoleon by an advisor on his secret cabinet, the Comte de Montgaillard, arguing that since the passage of the Navigation Acts in 1651 Britain had become a tyrant of the seas, ignoring any international law that did not serve the expansion of her commerce, an expansion necessitated by the extraordinary growth of her onerous national debt. Echoing Kersaint's 1793 speech in which England's wealth was viewed as 'fictitious', Montgaillard proposed that ' "To destroy British commerce is to strike England to the heart" '.[92] Cutting off British access to the East had in fact been the object of Napoleon's expedition to Egypt, as the Directory's orders to then General Bonaparte make clear.[93]

On 24 March, the Talents resigned. The next day, the Abolition of the Slave Trade Act became law.[94] The Talents had fallen not over the war, but like Pitt in 1802, over public and royal opposition to any relief measure for Catholics. The Duke of Portland assumed the Treasury. With no clear separation between two parties, the Commons was splintered along divides over the Catholic question, reform and royal prerogative.[95] In the general election of that year, the London radicals and former members of the LCS, led by Francis Place, secured the election of two radicals to Parliament, Sir Francis Burdett and Thomas Cochrane. The radicals themselves also suffered from a divided leadership.[96] Portland was presiding over the most factious political scene in decades.

---

the Continental system had its philosophical advocates in such European thinkers as Fichte, who believed in closed spheres of free trade, possibly more than one in Europe.

92. As quoted in Sloane 1898, p. 223.

93. The orders issued to 'The general-in-chief of the army' on 12 April 1798. Article 2 reads: 'He will drive the English from all their possessions in the east, and above all destroy their entrepôts in the Red Sea'. Article 3 reads: 'He will have the isthmus of Suez cut through, and will take all the necessary measures to insure the free and exclusive possession of the Red Sea for the French republic'. As quoted in Rose 1893, p. 707.

94. 'At a blow', writes Christie (1982, p. 277), 'the slave trade was reduced to a quarter of its former extent'. The complex matter of the relation between slavery and capitalism is regretfully outside the scope of this work, as it deserves special treatment. Slavery did contribute to the development of capitalism as part and partial of British imperialism. Slavery, though paralleling the 'wage slavery' that Marx wrote of when describing capitalism, is inimical to capitalism by virtue of the fact that it involves the application of extra-economic force. Its abolition at this critical point in time, when industrial capitalism is just beginning to make its impact felt internationally, is consistent with political economy's promotion of unregulated markets and 'free labour'. European slavery was in some respects the logical outcome of a non-capitalist imperialism involving the application of extra-economic force to trade taken to the extreme (see below, Chapter Thirteen, pp. 720–1).

95. Christie 1982, pp. 282, 297 and 303.

96. Legislative repression had driven working-class radicalism completely underground in the North. In London, working-class and artisan radicals still worked with middle-class reformers. Both saw little to choose from between Pittites and Foxites. The election of Burdett and Cochrane to Parliament reflected the strength of London radicalism in general, though it 'scarcely belonged to the artisans, however much they

Portland's troubles only grew as the year progressed. In July, Tsar Alexander made peace with Napoleon aboard a raft in the middle of the Nemunas River. Under the resulting Treaty of Tilsit, Russia recognised all of France's acquisitions and joined the Continental system. Once again, Britain was isolated. In Iberia, Wellesley's efforts to drive out the French invaders were marred by Dalrymple's botched negotiations, which repatriated French troops but allowed them to carry their arms with them. France would invade Portugal again, twice.

The Berlin Decree, meanwhile, threatened to bring ruin to domestic manufactures at a time when trade was already greatly curtailed. Feeling 'the stress of necessity for immediate action of some kind' the Portland ministry issued three orders in council on 11 November 1807, responding in kind to the Berlin Decree by declaring that any neutral states trading in French-controlled ports or colonies were subject to seizure, and suspending the Navigation Acts to invite certain countries (such as the United States) to trade exclusively with Britain. Within a month, however, Britain was evading its own decrees, 'raising the blockade of both the Elbe and the Weser and winking at the contraband trade which immediately sprang up in consequence'.[97] Napoleon would respond in kind with fresh decrees on 17 and 26 December, declaring that any ship searched by, paying taxes to or trading in a port of the British would be treated as a British ship, and therefore subject to seizure. Sweden, Denmark and Prussia, followed by Austria and Russia all adhered to the Continental system. The United States, meanwhile, passed Jefferson's Embargo Act, in theory cutting off trade with both powers, which was followed in 1809 by the Non-Intercourse Act. The dilemma for Britain was that the cost of waging war on France was to be deprived of continental markets where goods uniquely manufactured in Britain were in high demand. For France, the self-blockade meant that vital raw materials for French manufacturing ran in short supply. Policing the system effectively was impossible on either side. Smuggling and the evasion of seizures through the use of false documents were rampant.[98]

Whatever the effects of the self-blockade on the Continent, the general effect of Napoleon's strategy of seeking to ruin British trade was having serious effects at home. Regional deceleration had begun in 1802. Shortages of coin and credit,

---

contributed to it' (Thompson 1991, p. 510). But Burdett and Place would soon come under fire from William Cobbett as 'milk-and-water' radicals, whilst the more populist Cobbett and Henry Hunt would be on-again, off-again friends and rivals. The pragmatist and failed factory owner Major John Cartwright later initiated the Hambden Clubs to promote dialogue between middle-class reformers and lower-class radicals. Burdett felt himself shunned in Parliament by other pro-reform MPs who were wary of his supporters, yet he was also seen as a disappointment among radicals. Turner 1999, p. 95; Thompson 1991, pp. 507–14; Briggs 1979, p.150.

97. Sloane 1898, p. 225.
98. Sloane 1898, pp. 221–9.

spiralling inflation and soaring taxes all compounded problems arising from the absence of 15 percent of the male population that had been pressed into service. But the loss of trade was felt the hardest in manufacturing districts where less imports meant less grain and less exports meant less profit and less wages.[99] British manufacturers blamed the Orders in Council rather than the Berlin Decree for the economic depression at home. They were particularly alarmed by America's closing of its harbours to both British and French ships.[100] Industry had shown steady growth to this point, but exports fell by a quarter in the first half of 1808 and grain imports fell even more sharply.[101] The British economy was sliding into a depression. On 1 April 1808, Henry Brougham presented Parliament with a petition from the manufacturers of Liverpool, Manchester and London, arguing that the Orders in Council were ruining British Commerce. He pointed out that of £12.8 million in exports to the United States, less than a third of that sum came back in the form of direct payments, the remainder being covered by U.S. exports to Europe. '"While the orders in council continue"', Brougham explained, '"you must continue to be cut off from receiving remittances, and ... you are consequently, with your own right hand, cutting off, by two-thirds, your vast traffic with America"'.[102] Even before the Orders were modified in April 1809, however, Napoleon's blunder in forcing the abdication of Charles IV of Spain in favour of his brother Joseph Bonaparte sparked a general rebellion against French rule in Spain and subsequently led to the opening of markets in Central and South America to British commerce. This, according to Rose, 'staved off impending bankruptcy' for British merchants and manufacturers.[103] Meanwhile, under pressure from growers in the West of France, Napoleon was forced to lift some restrictions on trade in grain. Thus a limited but substantial commerce between the two nations ensued, and for Britain it was well timed.[104]

Parliament had re-suspended the Tudor statutes regulating the woollen trade in 1806, and the weavers and cloth workers had continued to press Parliament not to proceed with full repeal. The chaotic succession of ministries contributed to the delay in making a final decision but also sapped the energy for protesting.

99. Gregory 1982, pp. 142–3.
100. Briggs 1979, p. 164.
101. Owen 1975, p. 273; Christie 1982, p. 312.
102. Lord Brougham's speech of 1 April, 1808, as quoted by Rose 1893, p. 718.
103. 'The stocks stored up at home for many a weary month were flung on the new Markets, so that British and Irish exports, which had sunk in 1806, 1807, 1808 from 40,874,000*l*., to 37,245,000*l*., and 37,275,000*l*. respectively, reached in 1809 the extraordinary amount of 47,371,000*l*., and in 1810, 48,438,000*l*. But this speculative mania brought a sharp relapse in 1811' (Rose 1893, p. 720). Napoleon's first invasion of Portugal in 1807, forcing the flight of Portugal's Maria I and family to Brazil, had led to the opening of Brazil to British commerce the year before.
104. Christie 1982, p. 313.

Parliament would finally repeal the old statutes on 15 June 1809.[105] The end of two hundred and fifty years of government-enforced regulation of England's staple trade since medieval times sent a clear signal to all the trades still enjoying government enforcement of custom that they were next. Only a small number of prosecutions under the Statute of Apprentices were carried out after 1809. There were even ongoing petitions to apply the statute to trades not previously regulated, most of which observed apprenticeship rules regardless of the fact that their trade never came under the purview of the Tudor legislation.[106] From the woollen workers' point of view, Parliament had now clearly sided with 'the large manufacturers, the men of capital, the factory owners, men who were destroying old customs and community'.[107] In the midst of the war with France on land, at sea and in trade, Parliament had rather quietly done away with these protections. Undoubtedly the economic pressures to do so were greater than whatever resistance the workers could mount. Weavers' wages fell from a high of 39*s*. 9*d*. in 1795 to 25*s*. in 1800 and 15*s*. in 1810. Rose, writing in 1893, proposed that the steady ruining of the weavers (whose numbers, despite the immiseration, continued to grow) 'was the salvation of the country at this crisis. It counteracted the increase of expense in importing our cloth goods into the continent... Probably at no other stage of our industrial development could we have survived the application of Napoleon's continental system'.[108] Rose went on to explain his reasoning as follows:

> The mistake of the French government from 1793 onwards was in imagining that we were *solely* dependent on foreign trade. At that time we had two vast reserves of land power at home – improved agriculture, and the factory system. The improvements in farming brought about by inclosures had doubled the yield of corn and the weight of the fleece; and these inclosures of common wastes and common fields were stimulated by the high prices of the war period, until in ordinarily good years like those of 1802–1807, home-grown corn nearly sufficed for our increasing population... we no longer depended mainly, as of yore, on our carrying trade and on the export of our corn. We now had, thanks to the introduction of machinery, as a chief source of our wealth, the export of cotton, woollen, muslin goods, and hardware, *i.e.* of goods of small bulk, but of high value, which were therefore peculiarly adapted for secret importation into Napoleon's states.[109]

---

105. Gregory 1982, p. 137.
106. Snell 1985, pp. 264–5. The trades mentioned by Snell are: 'coachmaking, trunk making, periwig making, tobacco pipe making, machine making, patent lockmaking, or paper making.'
107. Randall 1991, p. 248.
108. Rose 1893, p. 721.
109. Rose 1893, pp. 721–2.

Here, we see the recognition that Britain enjoyed the advantage of 'improvement' in agriculture and in manufacturing, the effects of which were higher productivity and cheaper, more abundant goods for export. At the same time, the logic of Rose's argument is that it fell upon the weavers and other workers watching their wages shrink even as prices rose – thus pushing them to the brink of famine, if not beyond – to suffer immiseration in order that Britain should be able to win the commercial war by undercutting France with cheap exports of manufactured goods. What an amazing apologetic for capitalist exploitation! The argument is highly overstated. British manufactures could undersell those of France or any other nation without their prices being depressed further.

This raises the question of whether the Revolutionary and Napoleonic Wars may have actually *hastened* the repeal of the Tudor regulatory legislation by creating the right legitimating environment with the repression of radicalism, and by ensnaring Britain in a commercial war that made repeal a political expediency where otherwise it might have been a matter of greater controversy in Parliament, resulting in a more protracted struggle. Either way, just as the Combination Acts signalled an end of the state's role as neutral arbiter in manufacturing disputes, so the repeal of the Tudor regulatory legislation signalled an end to paternalism, as well as the growing influence of the manufacturers, who now took their place in the state power bloc as a rising force to rival the power of the landed interest.

Luddism and the repeal of Queen Betty's law

Wellesley's victory at the Battle of Talavera in July of 1809, once again driving the French from Portugal, was a turning point in the war and a boost to British morale. He was rewarded by being promoted as Lord Wellington. In September, Portland fell gravely ill and resigned, dying at the end of October. The Treasury passed to the energetic and sturdy Pittite, Spencer Perceval. At the same time, the poor harvest of 1809 led to soaring grain prices and acute regional distress. Combined with the depression in trade resulting from Britain's trade war with France, the shortage hit hardest in industrial regions. Businessmen and craftsmen alike organised petitions for peace. Opposition leaders in Parliament, seeking an issue to exploit, led themselves into the false belief that these bubbles of protest were in response to too much taxation rather than the dislocation of trade. In February 1810, when the Commons sent the radical agitator and former LCS member John Gale Jones to Newgate for the publication of a scurrilous handbill, Francis Burdett denounced the move, sought Jones's release and had Jones's speech republished in Cobbett's *Weekly Register*. This move landed Burdett in the Tower, sparking widespread protest and a deluge of petitions not only calling for Burdett's release but also calling for reform of the franchise. In the heated environment, opposition member Thomas Brand put forward a bill for limited reform by way of eliminating rotten and pocket boroughs (with compensation), a return to triennial parliaments and a very minor extension of the franchise among the propertied. With the failure of this bill and another even weaker measure two years later, the cause of reform lost all momentum inside Parliament and was taken up by such populist radicals as William Cobbett, Gravener Henson and Major John Cartwright, who had led the radical takeover of London's Common Council in 1809.[110]

In December 1810, George III fell ill once more. At long last, in the midst of a war and a period of inflation and profound economic stagnation,[111] the Prince of Wales was to assume powers as Regent.[112] He would become one of the most unpopular sovereigns in British history. Unable to risk simply inviting his friends in the opposition to assume power, lest his father recover, the Prince Regent was forced to allow Perceval to retain his position as Prime Minister overseeing a caretaker administration. It was in the midst of this economic and political crisis that Luddism broke out and the Statute of Apprentices was finally repealed.

The first phase of Luddism began on 11 March 1811 in the town of Arnold, Nottinghamshire. Around sixty-three frames and looms in the shops of local hosiers were destroyed. The hosiers had recently cut the wages of local knitters. Several hundred more were smashed in the surrounding villages of Sutton, Mansfield, Bulwell and Kirby over the next three weeks, with two additional but lesser incidents by July. These early attacks involved no written threats or any mythical leaders. But in late November 'Ned Ludd' made his appearance with a threatening letter during the next round of attacks, when several hundred more frames were attacked in night-time raids across Nottinghamshire, Derbyshire and Leicestershire. The first to die in these attacks was a young Luddite named John Westley of Arnold, who was shot during an exchange of fire between a master

110. Brand did propose to Burdett to hold a general conference on reform, but recoiled when threatened with desertion by his colleagues. Christie 1982, pp. 296 and 303–5.

111. The value of the pound had fallen by twenty per cent since 1807. Christie (Christie 1982, p. 296) notes that what had made it possible for the Government to raise the necessary sums to pay for the war was taking the pound off the gold standard in 1797. This, writes Christie, enabled credit to expand, thus allowing industrial expansion to continue, taxation to continue to expand, and the opposition to continue to exploit the issue of taxation.

112. The Prince's mistreatment of his wife Caroline was notorious, as were his covetous desire for the throne and his callous disregard for his father, 'Good King George'. His dissolute lifestyle was even worse. His 'debts from gambling, drinking, and general profligacy that amounted to an astonishing £630,000 in 1795 – just about half the money Britain was then paying to all the countries of Europe to carry on the war against France' (Sale 1996, p. 63; see also Gregory 1982, p. 144). The patrimonial state seemed in some ways to be alive and well, even if its health lay in some doubt.

weaver named Hollingsworth and Westley's Luddite crew attacking his home at Burwell.[113] In all, over a thousand machines were destroyed. The attacks were all motivated by the same underlying grievances among the workers in the hosiery trade. These included not only wage cuts, but also the widespread use of payment in truck, the payment of sub-standard wages to underemployed domestic stockingers by 'bag hosiers', the undercounting of pieces for piecework, the practice of 'colting' or employing un-apprenticed youths in the shops and finally the production of 'cut-ups' or cheap sewn-together imitations of stockings, gloves, and so on, which threatened to lower prices and thus wages, and make 'dishonourable' this 'honourable' trade. These grievances were not about machinery as such – although the 'wide frames' were a particular target of attack because they were 'engines of mischief' – it was more the 'mischief' than the machines that were being attacked. Only employers involved in unscrupulous or 'mischievous' practices – producing 'cut-ups' driving down wages, violating custom and threatening to ruin the trade – saw their equipment attacked. Other employers were spared.[114] What bears particular emphasis is the fact that this outbreak of unlawful coercion proved its usefulness on 30 November when fifty hosiery firms agreed to increase their piece-rates.[115] This was not a case of open class warfare; many employers sympathised with the plight of the stockingers. But this is not to deny that class conflict was involved. Seen in its full context, this first outbreak of Luddism can be taken as a response by semi-proletarian artisans in the hosiery trade to the efforts of employers to reduce costs by lowering wages. The employers themselves were compelled by the increasing pressures of price competition in an increasingly deregulated trade. And all of these pressures were compounded by the slump in trade and the spike in grain prices, which served to bring matters to a boiling point.

Just as had been the case during the Wiltshire outrages, the local magistrates were staggered by their own inability to make legitimate arrests or to find witnesses who would talk. Most of the raids being made under cover of night, in stealth, by men whose faces were blackened or covered with handkerchiefs, there appeared to be some type of cohesive organisation behind the attacks. Moreover, the unwillingness of members of the local community to come forward heightened fears that the region was entering upon '"a state of insurrection"' as the Duke of Newcastle described it in a letter to the Home Office in January.[116] Whole régiments of soldiers were sent to the region, and some skirmishes

113. Sale 1996, pp. 70–4. Authorities attempting to clear the large gathering for Westley's funeral the next week were unable to get the throng to disperse before the casket was lowered into the ground.
114. Thompson 1991, pp. 579–85.
115. Sale 1996, p. 87.
116. Sale 1996, p. 92.

involving exchange of fire between soldiers and Luddites ensued, but no arrests were made. The Luddites shifted their attacks to smaller villages and by February the attacks began to lessen. The Tory magistrate of Southwell and the Duke of Newcastle were among those who expressed sympathy for the plight of the stockingers, 'but the signal from the ministers in charge was that there was no place in laissez-faire for the soft-hearted "paternalism" of 18th-century governments and that London's only response to violence would be violence: "Whatever the cause of the disorders," Prime Minister Perceval [asked] Parliament, "did anyone deny the necessity of putting them down?" '[117]

On 14 February a bill was introduced to deliver the death penalty for machine-breaking. On the first reading of the bill on 27 February, the young poet Lord Byron gave his first address to the Lords, arguing that the war was the real cause of the distress, calling for pity and conciliation: ' "Is there not blood enough upon your penal code?" ' he asked.[118] Despite Byron's pleas, the bill passed both houses on 5 March, 'a true landmark in the annals of industrialism'.[119] In March, the first Luddite trials began. Ten men were tried, their average age being 19, of whom seven were convicted and transported to Australia (their crimes having been committed prior to the new law taking effect). The first phase of Luddism now seemed at an end. This may have been due in large part to the absence of new targets. The worst-offending employers had been hit and more than one in five stocking-frames in the country had been put out of commission.[120] Gravener Henson sought to capitalise on the notoriety of the disturbances with a bill to redress the stockingers' grievances. Months of lobbying and a petition of over ten thousand signatures came to naught when all it took was a few last-minute petitions by some of the larger hosiery concerns in Leicester and Nottingham to persuade Parliament not to pass the bill.[121]

---

117. Sale 1996, p. 95.
118. As quoted in Sale 1996, pp. 96–7.
119. Sale 1996, p. 98. The Watch and Ward Act (52 Geo. 3, c. 17) of the same year made it possible to appoint citizens as special constables, a milestone in the development of policing in Britain (Munger 1981, p. 114, n. 8). It would later be applied in Ireland under Sir Robert Peel's tenure there as Secretary.
120. Thompson puts the figure at about one thousand frames 'at a cost of between £6,000 and £10,000, and numerous articles damaged' (Thompson 1991, p. 584). Sale 1996, pp. 100–2, points out that officials were dismayed to find out that some informers were only seeking the reward to pay for the men's defence, 'their testimony afterwards proving to be of no use whatever... one senses a real operation of community here in which a Judas would fear to be cut off from the web of village life, vilified and ostracized'. The familiar pattern continued.
121. Thompson 1991, pp. 585–90. The bill was first whittled down to 'emaciated clauses relating to lace and to truck', whereupon it passed the Commons but was voted down by the Lords.

By 1812, there were at least two hundred and twenty factories in the West Riding. The distress felt here from the downturn in the woollen trade was perhaps worse than in any other part of the country. One contemporary report suggests the poor were now reduced to living off of boiled oatmeal and occasional potatoes. The croppers here were well aware that they were among the true elite of working men, earning up to 30*s* a week. Cloth finishing was a specialised process requiring considerable training and skill, and they controlled it. Their organisation (or 'combination'), the Brief Institution, could claim all of the three to five thousand croppers in West Yorkshire as its members, along with some weavers. With the repeal of the ban on gig mills and the increasing introduction of shearing frames into woollen factories, croppers faced the ruin of their trade by the direct application of machinery.[122] On 12 January 1812, a gig mill in Leeds was attacked. The second phase of Luddism had commenced even before the first Midlands phase had ended. Authorities arrested a suspect three days later. On 19 January, a finishing mill housing recently installed gig mills was set on fire, with considerable damage done. Then on 9 February a warehouse containing cloths made with power-looms was completely destroyed by fire. Whether Luddism in West Riding and the North-West was a spontaneous re-enactment by imitation of the first phase in Nottingham or whether there were actual organisational links behind these revolts we may never know, though delegates from Nottingham were spotted at secret meetings.[123] But direct organisational involvement was not necessarily required; the excitement in Nottingham would have been read in the newspapers, now common in local pubs and coffeehouses. In March, around the vicinity of Leeds – including at Rawfolds – an attack on shearing frames ensued, with a hundred machines, as well as cloths, shears, windows and furniture destroyed. The attacks grew bolder, striking Leeds itself, and Huddersfield.

Meanwhile, from February to early April, there were attacks in Stockport on large factories employing power-looms. The obvious suspects were weavers, who stood in the same relation to power-looms as cloth dressers to shearing frames and gig mills. But with the wide variety of occupations for the labouring poor, Luddism in Lancashire took on a broader meaning. The Stockport disturbances were followed on 8 April by a protest in Manchester where a crowd ransacked the Exchange Hall. A contingent of Scots Greys swung their sabres at the dispersing crowd in a scene that anticipated Peterloo.

---

122. See Thompson 1991, pp. 570–83.

123. Authorities reported on two Nottingham delegates who attended a meeting of disgruntled weavers in Stockport, Cheshire on 21 December 1811, followed two weeks later by reports of night time meetings in West Yorkshire prior to the outbreak of violence on 12 January 1812. On 11 February, government spies also reported delegates from Nottingham, Carlisle and Glasgow attending nightly meetings and instigating riot (Sale 1996, pp. 103–6).

Three days later, the legendary attack on William Cartwright's Rawfolds Mill in the heart of West Yorkshire, full of water-powered shearing frames, was met with preparedness. Cartwright had armed himself with four workmen and five soldiers, all having slept over at the mill for six weeks in anticipation of another attack. Returning fire, Cartwright and his men shot and killed four Luddites. This was a key turning point in the Luddite 'war' for several reasons. For the Luddites, they could no longer count on finding mills standing empty or undefended: 'For the manufacturers and their allies, it was the first signal that a resolute defense of property might halt the heretofore successful Luddite rebellion and that violence in service to Britain's new industrialism, with the soldiers of the state right alongside the masters of the mills, might well assure the new technology in the long run. Indeed, Cartwright was for a time a hero to magistrate and merchant alike all over Britain . . .'[124]

For the landed classes, this action proved 'how vital such mill owners as William Cartwright were at the local level for establishing control over the numerous laborers', and thus helped to forge an alliance 'between the British government and British industrial enterprise'.[125] Contrasted with Cartwright's heroism was the court martial of one of the soldiers at Rawfolds who refused to fire on the Luddites. Found guilty, he was given three hundred lashes.

The Luddite attacks continued. On 14 April in Sheffield, a food protest turned into a raid on the local armoury, while in Stockport a crowd attacked the home and the factory of the clothier John Goodair. Food protests erupted at markets in and around Manchester on the 18 and 20 April. Also on 20 April, an attack on a factory at Middleton met with gunfire; four or five Luddites were shot dead and eighteen wounded. The crowd then departed for the factory owner's mansion whereupon two daughters of a Luddite weaver set it ablaze. On 24 April, a mill at Westhoughton was burnt down, prompting vicious reprisals by one Colonel Fletcher, a spy who may have unwittingly instigated the attack.

Reprisals called for reprisals, and now Luddism entered its third phase, one involving armed attacks. Cartwright had already been shot at, and more shootings were reported. On 27 April, William Trentham, 63, a Nottingham manufacturer was shot in the chest by two men who were never identified. Trentham survived the attack. The next day, the Huddersfield manufacturer William Horsfall was shot whilst travelling from Marsden and died the day after. Somewhere between fourteen and forty workingmen had been killed in April, one factory had been burnt down and a dozen attacked, and food protests had broken out across the North. Hysteria had set in on the part of the authorities, who were beginning to convince themselves that there was a revolutionary conspiracy behind the

124. Sale 1996, p. 126.
125. Sale 1996, pp. 195–6.

insurrection. Some 14,400 soldiers were dispatched to the Luddite triangle, an area the size of Delaware. Sale has dubbed it 'the invasion of middle Britain'.[126]

On 9 May, a handbill was posted about Nottingham that spoke of making 'foul blood, run clear and fine of Tyrants great and small!' and included the line 'Make Perceval your aim'.[127] On 11 May, Prime Minister Perceval was shot dead in the lobby of Parliament by a merchant named John Bellingham, whom authorities determined to be mentally unstable. No foul play was suspected, though the swiftness of the hanging, which took place on 18 May, should give an initial pause. A crowd in Nottingham openly celebrated and Cobbett wrote of Bellingham as a saviour who had rid the country of the man who had led the assault on English liberties. Threatening letters were sent to the Prince Regent and notices chalked on West Riding Walls offering a hundred guineas for his head.[128] 'Sheer insurrectionary fury', writes Thompson, 'has rarely been more widespread in English history'. 'Almost every historian of the period agrees', writes Sale, 'that if there was ever going to be a revolution in Britain, it would have been at that moment'.[129] What was clearly lacking was a convergence of an uprising in both city and countryside. Paine's parting shot in 1792 was the clearest articulation of a call for insurrection from a recognised leader that we have come across, but it is worth bearing in mind that the memory of the brutal suppression of the 'Liberty Riots' of 1780 was still fresh. The disturbances of 1780 had no political strategy or clear leadership. In neither year – 1780 or 1792 – was there a sympathetic rising waiting to happen outside of London. And now in 1812, it was the countryside in insurrection whilst the City was quiet. Christie points out that 'no dumps of arms, no wide network of organisation, no plan of revolution could be unearthed by the authorities'.[130]

Meanwhile in the North, the celebration of Perceval's death was short-lived, for the authorities there were on the hunt for the murderers of Horsfall. In the presence of armed occupation, tactics shifted from strategic attacks on machines and factories to burglaries, raids on arms caches and secret meetings at night for taking oaths. To the authorities, the collecting of arms appeared as preparation for an armed rising. In May, assize courts were held in Lancaster and Cheshire. Ten suspects, including a boy of 16, were hanged. Nearly forty were transported and a dozen others imprisoned. Not until October would authorities manage

126. Sale 1996, pp. 126–49. 14,400 was a figure greater than the 8,700 men Wellington had taken with him to Portugal in 1808. Sale points out, however, that Wellington had joined a force of over 11,000 troops already stationed in Portugal, correcting Thompson and Dorvall's misperception that he had less than 10,000 men when he went into battle.

127. As quoted in Sale 1996, p. 153.

128. Thompson 1991, pp. 623–4.

129. Sale 1996, p. 156.

130. Christie 1982, p. 179.

to break the silence on William Horsfall's murderers and arrest three suspects: George Mellor, 22; William Thorpe, 23 and Thomas Smith, 22. They would be tried and hanged in York in January. All three plead not guilty.[131] Having made examples, the Government could now think of offering mercy.[132] Sale provides an inventory of the property destruction carried out by the Luddites. Nottingham: perhaps twelve hundred stocking-frames plus dozens of lace, bobbin-net and other machines. West Riding: a minimum of two hundred shearing frames and gig mills plus one factory completely destroyed and others damaged. In Lancashire and Cheshire: two factories totally destroyed and two houses burned down, the Manchester Exchange and many shop stalls badly damaged and much food stolen. Adding in the cost of maintaining an army of over 12,000 soldiers in the region to suppress the revolt, including salaries, food, lodging and equipment, the cost of assize sessions and the costs of maintaining a network of informers plus losses by mill owners from the disruption of production and the defence of their mills, Sale estimates the total cost of Luddism at around £1.5 million.[133]

1812 was a year in which history exposed the futility of war as never before. On 24 June, Napoleon led the *Grande Armée* of six hundred thousand men across the Niemen to begin his doomed advance on Moscow. One day prior, the Orders in Council had been lifted, a move welcomed with the ringing of church bells in Britain's manufacturing districts. It was a major concession to the manufacturing interest, perhaps hastened by Luddism itself.[134] But it came too late to prevent war with America. The Americans had wanted to negotiate an end to British harassment of their merchant fleet under the Orders of Council and an end to the arbitrary impressments of American citizens born in Britain whom the British claimed as citizens and who were thus subject to conscription.[135] But on 18 June, the United States had declared war on the United Kingdom. In July, the Americans invaded Canada from Detroit, but were driven out by combined British and Iroquois forces that seized Detroit in August. That same month, Wellington led forty thousand British and Portuguese troops to capture Madrid. When news of the victory reached Britain, criticism of the war began to subside. While forced to fall back to Portugal, the victory allowed Spanish nationalists to recap-

---

131. Carpenter (ed.) 1972, pp. xiv–xviii and 71.

132. The Treasury solicitor Henry Hobhouse had been sent to Cheshire with special instructions from the Government 'that "perhaps the guilt of the convicted was not of prime importance as long as the violated laws were upheld and sacrificial victims could be found as an example to the rest of society"' (as quoted in Sale 1996, p. 167). The fact that the Government could so openly declare its intent to find 'sacrificial victims' for setting 'an example to the rest of society' bears out Hay's thesis of the levers of terror and mercy (see above, Chapter Ten, p. 528).

133. Sale 1996, p. 192.

134. Thompson 1991, p. 618.

135. See Benn 2002, pp. 32–6.

ture their capital by the end of the year.[136] On 13 September, Napoleon arrived in Moscow only to find it strategically abandoned. The city was burned. With its supply lines in tatters, the *Grande Armée* began its long and terrible retreat in which its numbers would be reduced from over 450,000 to less than 40,000.[137] Returning to Paris on a sled, Napoleon managed to stave off a coup, initially hiding the extent of his disastrous campaign. The Continental system was now in a state of collapse. The effects of this turn toward normalisation of trade, however, would not bring immediate relief to England's textile districts.

Astonishingly, Napoleon was able quickly to raise another impressive army and inflict major losses on Russia and Prussia in his victories at Lützen and Bautzen in May 1813, followed by a brief armistice in Germany from June to August during which Austria joined the Sixth Coalition. Meanwhile, Wellington's victory at Vitoria on 21 June 1813 spelled the collapse of French rule in Spain. When fighting resumed in Germany in August, Napoleon scored his last major victory at Dresden. But his defeat at Leipzig in October signalled the collapse of French rule in Germany.[138] Heavily outnumbered, the French army began a steady retreat to Paris. By 31 March 1814, Paris was occupied. Napoleon subsequently abdicated and the Bourbon dynasty was restored with the accession of Louis XVIII to power.[139] In April, the Treaty of Fontainebleau was signed, calling for the Congress of Vienna at which the victorious powers would begin to address the many issues left outstanding from the war. In America, the war continued, with British blockades and raids on American ports and ships, climaxing with the British occupation of Washington DC and the burning of the White House in August 1814.

The repeal of the Tudor legislation regulating the weaving trade in 1809 had sent a shiver throughout the other crafts where apprenticeship rules were still in force, or still observed. Observance of the seven-year apprenticeship rule was strengthened in some trades. The Woolstaplers, for example, increased the

---

136. Christie 1982, p. 317.

137. Hobsbawm (1994, p. 112) puts the figure of the surviving army at 100,000. Owen (1975, p. 275) writes that by the time Napoleon reached Paris in December 'he had lost half a million men'. But 'lost' should not be understood to mean deaths only, one must also account for desertions and the large numbers of prisoners of war take by the Russians.

138. German nationalism played a strong role in the defeat. Prussia's alliance with Russia had been signed in February, and was followed by Frederick William III's 'Appeal to My People', echoing Fichte's earlier 'Addresses to the German Nation' which called for German unification and a rising against Napoleon. While the nationalist risings that occurred before Leipzig were brutally suppressed and played only a minor role in the subsequent battles, it was an early example of the nationalist spirit that shape subsequent events in Europe between 1815 and 1848. Moreover, Napoleon's German conscripts were unreliable and prone to desertions. See Grab 2003, pp. 108–10.

139. Owen 1975, p. 275; Christie 1982, p. 299.

requisite number of years from five to seven. In London, the courts heard nineteen cases against illegal men between 1809 and 1812, delivering twelve acquittals and only seven prosecutions resulting in penalties amounting to less than £12 at a cost of over £40 in legal expenses. Winning such moral victories was thus proving increasingly futile. A drive for petitioning Parliament was led by the 'mechanics of the metropolis' and regular meetings were held, attended by representatives from many of the City companies. A petition of some 32,000 signatures was sent to Parliament on 28 April 1813 complaining of the inadequacy of the fines exacted on those prosecuted and proposing a bill to amend the Statute of Apprentices and strengthen its provisions. George Rose, Treasurer of the Navy, the same Member who had introduced Pitt's first measure against combinations in 1799 but who supported apprenticeship in principle, was approached once more. Rose warned that such a measure was likely to produce the opposite effect intended by the artisans, but agreed to strike a Select Committee. With little time to prepare, the case put forward by the small masters of the London companies was weak. They asserted that the non-apprenticed workers undercut prices and hampered exports. They pointed out that apprenticeship was assiduously observed at the London dockyards. And while they came out strongly against combinations amongst journeymen, they registered their preference for employees who had served their apprenticeships. The poorly attended Committee issued no report and the measure stalled.[140]

Meanwhile, a counter-measure came forward in the form of a bill to repeal entirely the apprenticeship provisions found in the Statute of Apprentices. The member putting forward the bill was Serjeant Arthur Onslow. Among those assisting in drafting the bill was Sir Robert Peel. London's master manufacturers appointed a committee to support Onslow's measure, chaired by Alexander Galloway, who along with another employer had recently been prosecuted for violating the Statute of Apprentices. The importance of this appointment is that Galloway was in fact a very active London radical. A former member of the LCS, he had spent the years 1798–1801 in prison for working with the United Englishmen. Nevertheless, as an employer Galloway was strongly opposed to combinations and sought to subvert them by signing individual contracts with each of his employees. Galloway's position of leadership in pursuing the repeal of 5 Elizabeth c. iv suggests that popular-radicals could be strong supporters of reform and civil liberties whilst holding in contempt the arguments of artisans and the now illegal trade unions seeking to uphold custom in their trades. Francis Place regarded the opposition to Onslow's measure as a form of 'bigotry'. In November and December 1813, a petition opposing Onslow's measure with

140. Derry 1931, pp. 67–76.

sixty thousand signatures was presented to Parliament. Notices in London newspapers argued that '"it is clearly unjust to take away the whole of the ancient established property and rights of any one class of the community, unless, at the same time, the rights and property of the whole commonwealth should be dissolved, and parceled out anew for the public good"'.[141] In April, Parliament was flooded with appeals from not only artisans, but many 'respectable' figures such as the Leeds magistrates. Another petition with three hundred thousand signatures followed, against a mere two thousand signatures from the counter-petitioners. This enormous effort went virtually ignored. Upon introducing the bill, Onslow made three simple points. First, apprenticeship had since the time of Elizabeth been superseded by the introduction of education and religious instruction as part of the system of outdoor relief. Second, as many trades not covered under 5 Elizabeth still observed apprenticeships, the present measure need not mean the end of the practice. Third, the coming of peace and subsequent decommissioning would result in greater unemployment should workers continue to be prevented from moving to other occupations. Here was a clear indication that employers were coming to see the need for greater labour mobility. On 18 July 1814, statutory enforcement of the customary apprenticeship rules of guilds and trade associations came to an end. Significantly, those provisions of Queen Betty's Law that made it a legal offence to leave one's work unfinished were left intact.[142]

The teachings of political economy do not appear to have played a major role in all of this. The most persuasive argument appears to have been the idea that apprenticeship fostered the existence of combinations among journeymen, and that despite the Combination Acts, combinations could be seen everywhere. A last-minute appeal from the cutler manufacturers of Sheffield complained that the masters were 'at the mercy' of their journeymen.[143] Even the Artisans' General Committee in London was accused of being a kind of combination that had been gathered to promote their amending measure. While Luddism was on the wane and the Northern counties were still under martial law, this did not prevent the stockingers from being so bold as to seek legal redress. It did not prevent the feltmakers in Manchester, the hatters in Glasgow or the wool-combers in Coventry from holding regular meetings. In February 1813, the magistrates in

141. As quoted in Derry 1931, p. 78.

142. Alderman 1986, p. 50.

143. The opposite argument was also made: 'A journeyman speaking to the Artisans and Machinery Committee in 1824 put his finger on the essential point: "The men are more naturally in the power of the master if entry is not limited"' (Leeson 1979, pp. 109–10). In an apparent response to their intervention the masters were rewarded with the Sheffield Cutlers' Act, which specifically did away with apprenticeship restrictions in their trade. The Spitalfields Acts regulating wages and conditions for silk-weavers were repealed in 1823.

Lancashire had sought a measure to make unlawful the meetings of any unregistered societies, including friendly societies. In 1814, the master engineers declared during an open meeting at the Museum Tavern in London that the Combination Acts 'had been "evaded and defeated" '.[144] The repeal of 5 Elizabeth, however, did not strike a blow against combinations. What it did do was snap the organic bond between master and journeyman, a bond that was under enormous strain in the workshops and long ignored by larger firms and of course in factories, where the division of labour anyway rendered the idea of apprenticeship of little value to workers performing only discrete tasks in a complex process of product-assembly.[145]

Conclusion

On 1 March 1815 Napoleon, having escaped from exile on the island of Elba, re-appeared in France and quickly began raising a new army. The news from Vienna was that the Eastern powers were at odds over control of Poland and Saxony. Napoleon hoped to make the most of it. He deposed Louis XVIII and by June marched into Belgium with an army of about 125,000 men. Wellington had relocated from Vienna to the Netherlands and took command of the combined British and Dutch forces. On 18 June, after forcing the Prussians to retreat at Ligny two days earlier, Napoleon moved against Wellington near Waterloo, hoping to defeat and divide the two forces. But the arrival of Prussian forces during the battle spelled the final defeat of Napoleon. He was forced to abdicate once more, and spent the rest of his life in exile on the remote island of St. Helena. In November Britain, Russia, Austria and Prussia would sign the Quadruple Alliance against any resurgence of French imperialism.[146] Over the course of the previous century, France had lost its position as the pre-eminent power in Europe. The long struggle between France and Britain had come to an end. Britain's position as the leading world power was now undisputed. Over the course of the nineteenth century, the European powers would scramble to emulate British industrial capitalism.

At home in Britain, capitalism was triumphant as well. But just as Britain stood out as the only capitalist power in alliance with Europe's reactionary régimes, within the domestic economy capitalist production on farms and factories was still confronted with resistance from customary practices and methods

---

144. One of the spokesmen for the engineers was the famous engineer and inventor Henry Maudslay (Leeson 1979, p. 104).

145. Chase 2000, pp. 95–100; Derry 1931, pp. 77–87.

146. The 20-year agreement bound the parties to reconvene at periodic conferences. It also banned any attempt to restore the Bonaparte dynasty (Christie 1982, pp. 325–6).

of production. Indeed, if Luddism represents the last major revolt of custom against capitalism, the battle may have been lost, but the resistance did not end. Luddism is most commonly viewed as a movement clinging to a traditional way of life whose doom was spelled in the coming of the factory. Luddism certainly involved an attempt to conserve the customary practices that had for so long helped to maintain the bonds that held communities of workers together. The breaking of machinery was not mindless vandalism, but an assertion of ancient rights set out in company by-laws, including search and seizure and such extraordinary measures as were necessary to check the 'illegal' competition of 'forrens' and interlopers. Such rights had been called into question at common law as long ago as 1599.

But in 1812, machine-breaking was made a capital offence. Even if it is to be seen as little more than a historical echo, machine-breaking under Luddism must also be seen as an attempt to prevent interloping by asserting ancient rights designed to protect the trade. In other words, the practice still enjoyed legitimacy in *custom*, even if it was proscribed by law, as the virtually impenetrable silence and support of the local communities where the Luddites were active testifies. Even more reviled were the Combination Acts, which put the legal status of all workers' associations in at best a semi-legal status: 'What had been perhaps even harder to bear than their jealously guarded traditions being denied Parliamentary protection was the way in which they had been abused by a state which, from behind the screen of its Combination Acts, chose to suspect all signs of solidarity among working people, whatever their true motives, as indications of disaffections and invitations to treachery'.[147]

These measures brought on a deep sense of betrayal, and were very much felt as violations of an ancient contract whereby the landed classes and the state enjoyed the allegiance of artisans in return for upholding the ancient rights and privileges of the trades. The fact that by the early nineteenth century the growth of the domestic market and the intrusion of capitalist factories and capitalist entrepreneurs into the sphere of manufacturing had nearly worn through the fabric of custom does not mean that capitalism had won widespread adherence among the working artisans – quite the contrary. As the vision of a future landscape dominated by factories billowing smoke and employing vast pools of unskilled labourers working for starvation wages came into view, it was strongly rejected. Thus when understood in its true context, Luddism also appears as a forward-looking movement, not simply by virtue of its rejection of the capitalist logic of the factory system, but in the desire to project the positive, normative values of artisan communities into the future. Luddism displayed a considerable

147. Gregory 1982, p. 141.

level of organisation in its revolt against state authority across regions and communities. It is in this sense, as Thompson has argued, that Luddism displayed a certain tendency toward democracy. This organising capacity did not come to a halt upon the defeat of Luddism (if defeat is an accurate depiction, for many of its aims were achieved early on), but was immediately channelled into petitioning campaigns for relief.

We can only suspect that the sense of betrayal on the part of artisans was also shared by commoners or smallholders practicing subsistence farming. Indeed, it would be absurd to make a sharp distinction between the two since many if not most of these families earned their subsistence from both farming and weaving or knitting. Thus the final wave of parliamentary enclosures and the closure upon rights of common, which was also met with even more widespread if less dramatic forms of resistance, contributed to the sense of betrayal experienced by commoners and artisans. What both the copyholder and the artisan were resisting was the real subordination of their labour to capital,[148] which is the same thing as saying that they were resisting the transformation of a labour process regulated by custom into abstract labour regulated by the market alone. The major difference between the one and the other, a difference which speaks to the distinction between agrarian capitalism and industrial capitalism, is that one process was nearing its completion, whilst the other process was only gathering steam.

Factories were, in effect, a kind of enclosure of the labour of manufactures. Just as the enclosure movement was a means by which land and agrarian labour could be stripped of the normative regulation of manorial, customary law and subjected to market regulation – in a word, commodified – so the factory was a means by which the labour of artisanal manufacturers would be stripped of the normative regulation of production passed down from the time of the guilds and Queen Betty and subjected to market forces. In identifying these parallel, but not simultaneous large-scale historical processes at work in British history, we hope to point up a major blind spot in much of the literature. For there is a tendency to simply associate the landed classes, along with agrarian commoners and peasants and artisans, with paternalism, tradition and *custom*, all of which capitalism as *industrial* capitalism had to overcome in order to emerge. The specificity of agrarian capitalism and its unique three-class system is thus

148. As Gregory explains, the signs of this coming subordination 'were obvious enough – the new machines making old skills obsolete; the move away from the time-worn rituals of the Cloth Hall; the breakdown of traditional labour discipline and the decay of the apprenticeship system; the scorn of mutuality and the prestige accorded to profit; the erosion of long-established perquisites and familiar customs: the list goes on – it was much harder for most of the clothiers and clothworkers to *read* them' (Gregory 1982, p. 138).

entirely missed. This blind spot fails to come to terms with two crucial facts about agrarian capitalism. First, the struggle between forces promoting agrarian capitalism and forces resisting them has a long history, one that pre-dates the Luddites by centuries. To speak of any 'capitalism' as such existing over the period from 1450 to 1750 may invite confusion if it is understood to suggest that a 'fully-developed' capitalism was ever at work. Rather, there was a long-term struggle between enclosers seeking to convert land and labour to market regulation and those who sought to resist this and preserve extra-economic forms of property and social regulation. Second, by the time we reach the turbulent period beginning in the 1790s, the triumph of capitalism within British agriculture had effectively been achieved. But this was not the case within manufacturing, where not only was most production still carried on by artisans operating under the normative regulations of their company by-laws, but where it was also the case that with population growth, the rising demand for manufactured articles in the growing towns and cities and the growing number of rural dwellers who were losing possession of plots sufficient to maintain their families' subsistence, the absolute number of those engaged in domestic manufacturing grew, and continued to grow even after the Napoleonic wars, despite increasing levels of immiseration. Much of this new growth in domestic production was subject to systems of putting-out where the labour of the workers was subordinated to capital (often merchant capital), a relation Marx defined as the formal subordination of labour. But even under such conditions, the workers enjoyed direct control over the labour process, just as peasants once enjoyed direct control over the land in the form of the strips they farmed. So long as this was true, that is so long as there was no real subordination of labour to capital, the employer was hard-pressed to find ways to increase his profits by either lengthening the working day or intensifying production through a rigorous division of labour or the introduction of machinery. Thus even though the 'defeat' of Luddism may have signalled to contemporaries that there would be no stopping the spread of the factory system, it is nonetheless appropriate to see Luddism as coming not at the end of the long process whereby capital subordinated labour to its economic logic, but near the beginning.

The repeal of the Tudor legislation that made mandatory the observance of the customary rules governing production relations inherited from feudal times dealt a severe blow to the struggle of independent craft workers. But custom and customary resistance to capitalism continued, surviving repeal because it was rooted in *culture*. The Tudor laws had never done more than facilitate the observance of custom; they did not determine it. Well into the nineteenth century, and in some cases on into the twentieth, there were skymington ridings, parades involving rough musick, wife sales, well dressings or rush-bearings. We can name several reasons why. First, as mentioned, the number of domestic artisans did not decline relative to the growth of the factory, and to a large extent because factories continued to need weavers as well as mechanics and builders whose trades were regulated by companies observing such customs as apprenticeship. At Bean Ing, Benjamin Gott subcontracted control over the weavers employed in his factory to supervisors.[149] In 1815, the number of domestic workers would still be greater than the number of those employed in factories. Even within factories, various forms of subcontracting persisted. Mule-workers were widely able to negotiate a system whereby they hired their own hands and operated under subcontract, thus preserving a degree of control over the labour process. So custom continued to enjoy a strong economic basis. At the same time, the observance of custom that is rooted in the culture of local communities was even more resilient. What would be necessary for the continued elaboration of the capitalist system in the long run was for workers themselves to begin to accept *capitalist* norms and ideologies. Such acceptance has always been a difficult prospect, as capitalism's structural inequalities have always meant that lower-income and working populations have far less to gain from capitalism than its wealthy beneficiaries.

149. Randall 1991, p. 209.

Chapter Twelve
Class and the State

> What is Freedom? Ye can tell. That which Slavery is too well. For its very name has grown, to an echo of your own.
>
> Percy Bysshe Shelley[1]

On a cloudless, late-summer day, a large crowd dressed in their 'Sunday best' arrived in Manchester in orderly fashion, gathering at St. Peter's Field to hear from leaders of the reform movement, most notably Henry Hunt, who had been invited by Joseph Johnson, leader of the Manchester Patriotic Union, to address the crowd on the urgent necessity of parliamentary reform. In his letter of invitation, Johnson had described the wretched conditions of the working population in Lancashire: '"Nothing but ruin and starvation stare one in the face, the state of this district is truly dreadful, and I believe nothing but the greatest exertions can prevent an insurrection. Oh, that you in London were prepared for it"'.[2] This letter was intercepted and copied by the authorities and mistakenly taken to mean that an actual insurrection was being planned. The gathering was first set to take place on 2 August 1819, but faced with delays the organisers postponed it seven days whereupon the authorities banned the gathering but subsequently allowed for an event to take place on 16 August. By 1 pm, when Hunt's carriage arrived, there were possibly more than fifty thousand

1. Shelley 1892, p. 20.
2. As quoted in Reid 1989, p. 115.

assembled, an impressive gathering, no doubt aided by the fine weather. The participants were drawn mainly from the towns surrounding Manchester and the level of organisation and discipline also alarmed the authorities. Seeing Hunt's warm reception from the crowd, the local magistrate William Hulton issued a warrant for his arrest, along with Johnson and two other organisers. Sixty members of the Manchester Yeomanry were summoned and ordered to arrest Hunt. They rode their horses along the narrow route toward the hustings and when members of the crowd linked arms to prevent their progress, they began striking at the crowd with their sabres. Although they soon succeeded in arresting Hunt, Johnson and several others, the crowd resorted to pelting them with bricks and stones, whereupon they began cutting at the banners and flags. Hulton then ordered the Fifteenth Hussars to disperse the crowd. They charged St. Peter's Field from the eastern end while the Cheshire Yeomanry charged from the southern end, swinging their sabres as they went. Ten minutes later, the crowd had left the square, leaving behind approximately a dozen dead, over six hundred injured and a river of blood.[3]

'Peterloo', the name immediately given to the massacre, occupies a place of far greater importance in British history than the so-called Gordon Riots of 1780, even though the number of those left dead in 1780 was vastly greater. One obvious reason for this is that the crowd in Manchester had formed an orderly assembly, a fact which evoked immediate indignation and outrage amongst the poor and working classes across Britain. Derry argues that 'panic and incompetence explain what happened, rather than brutal designs upon the common people . . . Had the advice of the home office been followed by the Manchester magistrates, there would have been no Peterloo incident'.[4] Undoubtedly a level of incompetence, as well as the over-readiness on the part of the authorities to suspect a violent plot where there was none, both played a role in precipitating the tragedy. When put in the context of the extensive measures of repression enacted by the Liverpool Government, however, Peterloo can also be seen as a point where the *potential* for the application of brute coercion by the state against unarmed subjects was realised. The hardened class attitudes were reflected in the fact that no aid to the victims and their families was later forthcoming from the government, while the incident was almost immediately met with a further tightening of legislative repression in the form of the Six Acts. Had Peterloo been seen by the Government and the ruling classes as merely a tragic mistake, the response would

3. Thompson 1991, p. 754. By the end of 1819 the Peterloo Relief Committee had authenticated 421 claims (with another 150 cases still awaiting investigation), among which 161 victims had received sabre wounds and over a hundred were women or girls. The Peterloo Relief Committee was not affiliated with the Government.

4. Derry 2001, p. 143.

surely have been aid, sympathy and conciliation. The way in which the lives of the victims were so callously disregarded by the landed classes in power formed the basis for the massacre's enormous psychological impact. Taken together, the Combination Act and Peterloo served to reinforce an understanding that the ruling elite and working people had separate class interests. But Peterloo added a visceral dimension.

We would search in vain for a defining moment at which the paternalistic eighteenth-century order of patrician elites and artisanal plebs was converted into the new order of capitalists and proletarians. In 1819, the great majority of the working population effectively remained artisans. Proletarian factory workers comprised only a minority of the working class, but their numbers were growing as surely as the wealth and political muscle of their factory masters. So while Peterloo was clearly no such watershed, it may come as close as any event in serving as a *sign* of a new order in which working people were compelled to think of themselves as belonging to a 'working class' with a distinct set of interests separate from, and often in opposition to, the interests of a ruling or 'capitalist' class of landowners and manufacturers.

Everywhere in nineteenth-century Britain, the pace of economy and of public life was quickening as the logic of agrarian capitalism and industrial capitalism continued to transform British social relations. It is important to remember this, for the first half of the nineteenth century was a period of transition for Britain, transition of classes and transition of the state. First of all, where in the eighteenth century Parliament had been dominated by the gentry, with a few dozen peers occupying the House of Lords, the simultaneous expansion of peerages alongside an enormous concentration of landholdings was now leading to a near reversal of the situation, whereby it was the aristocracy and not the gentry which dominated Parliament. Of some 658 members in the House of Commons, at least 253 were titled aristocrats.[5] With the final wave of enclosures came the disappearance of commoners as rights of access to the commons were lost. Regions experiencing de-industrialisation also saw the disappearance of independent cottagers engaging in domestic handicraft production. Those who remained were landlords, tenant-farmers, and agrarian wage labourers whose only protection against the threat of famine was the distribution of poor relief. In short, the period after the French Wars saw changes signalling the approaching completion of the agrarian-capitalist project. And, in this sense, the pre-Victorian and early Victorian era was governed by what could rightly be called an agrarian-capitalist state. Such a claim means, of course, that the entire period of the

5. This figure included some 144 for England, 15 for Wales, 30 for Scotland and 64 for Ireland. 'Behind the House of Commons frowned the battlements of the House of Lords' (Kitson Clark 1951, p. 3).

early Industrial Revolution, up to and including the railway age, was governed by a state formed out of the centuries-long evolution of agrarian capitalism. The impact of the Industrial Revolution upon the state was only beginning to be felt. One of two central questions we wish to explore in this chapter is this tension between the ruling landed elite and a rising class of capitalist industrialists.

It bears reminding that the modern European state arose out of the militarist culture of feudalism. In 'the intervals between slaughtering their fellow men', writes Upton, the ruling warrior-class 'filled in much of their time in the hunting and slaughter of animals'.[6] If war had been the natural state of affairs, it was up to the monarch to function as the impartial referee in 'a condition of endless rivalry and competition for relative advantage' between a 'mosaic of self-governing collectives',[7] wielding the tool of patronage. Yet even in the seventeenth century, England was unique economically, legally and in terms of its unprecedented unity. It was also the first state to witness the dismantling of feudal institutions dedicated to extracting extra-economic rents and obligations.[8] At the same time, however, a general theme in much of the literature on the Industrial Revolution is that the British state played the role of passive agent, facilitating perhaps, but not actively promoting industrialisation, and worse: diverting precious resources away from industry to be consumed in its costly wars. If this were truly the case, then we might be left with the general impression that after the first fifty years of industrialisation, Britain had a modern, forward-looking economy presided over by an archaic, backward-looking state.

The reactionary character of the Liverpool Government and the continuation of repression after Waterloo may present the false appearance of a resurgent 'feudal' or 'traditional' landed class in Britain. It is worth asking whether the simultaneity of reaction on the continent and 'Tory' repression in Britain has served to disguise the specificity of British agrarian capitalism or is one reason why so much scholarship has failed to recognise its full importance. It is certainly true that after Waterloo, Britain not only took part in, but even played the leading role in the restoration of the Bourbons, and in general supported the conservative reaction to radicalism across Europe. Revolutionary France had been defeated, but Jacobin ideas and radical societies were still active in Britain. On the continent, popular-radicalism would spill over into the emergence of new movements by ethnic minorities for national independence. In Britain, even

6. Upton 2001, p. 39.
7. Upton 2001, p. 25.
8. See Mooers 1991, p. 154. According to Mooers, the separation between state and civil society in England had begun by the seventeenth century. Civil society is a problematic term, but it is worth posing the question of whether such a relatively autonomous sphere of social relations would be possible in the absence of the conversion to market-dependency under conditions of capitalism.

though the landed oligarchy was still very much in charge of the state through its dominance in Parliament, it would be wrong to equate the repression of radicalism under Liverpool with the restoration of the non-capitalist and neo-feudal régimes rooted in the economics of feudalism and peasant agriculture on the continent. Feudalism in Britain was now truly a dead letter, and the last remnants of the 'peasantry' were being cleared from the open fields and commons. Like the customary manor in the countryside, the customary company in the town and the patrimonial powers of the Crown declined, and the state assumed a new role as neutral arbiter not between self-governing collectives seeking to protect monopoly privileges and other extra-economic forms of property, but between employers and workers engaged in what were assumed to be strictly economic contracts. Yet this presented a dilemma, for how could a state in the hands of a ruling class of capitalist landlords assert its neutrality in the conflict between the interests of an emerging working class and the interests of capitalist farmers and industrialists? The answer of the political economists was to simply assert the neutrality of the market. There was no clear solution to this dilemma at the level of politics. But the stage was set for reform, and a protracted process of gradual, begrudging concessions to be granted by the ruling elite.

What is more, the growing and extraordinary wealth of the rising industrial class was also a unique spectacle, even though European governments were taking notice and were now beginning to seek out British experience, know-how and machinery in an effort to lay the foundations for an industrial revolution on the continent. The fact that this period saw a vast concentration of landed wealth, the proliferation of titles, the rise of the 'Tory' faction led by Lord Liverpool and Britain's participation in the Europe-wide reaction against popular-radicalism does not simply mean that, as in Russia, Prussia and Germany, the 'traditional' landed classes in Britain were restored to power. It is true that landed wealth was now increasingly concentrated in the hands of a growing number of peers at the top of the social pyramid. But this was only a shift in the balance of power between the peerage and the gentry *within* the landed class; the dominance of Britain's ruling agrarian-capitalist elite had not been interrupted by the upheaval of the French Wars. To equate the fact that the power of the landed interest in Britain was at its apex in the early decades of the nineteenth century with a return to 'traditional' rule is to mask entirely the dynamism of not only the growing industrial-capitalist economy in Britain, but more importantly of the agrarian-capitalist base which had played such a fundamental role in creating the conditions that had made industrialisation possible.

This leads us to the second question we wish to explore, here, which concerns the relationship between capital and the state. How had the state been reshaped and how was it continuing to be reshaped by the expansion of capitalist relations of production? In the previous chapter we saw that the passage of the Combination Acts marked a point at which the government began to see its role in industrial relations not as one of regulation but as that of offering arbitration between various individuals engaged in forming contracts of buying and selling. As we shall see, it was hardly the case that the working classes readily conformed to such an outlook of liberal individualism as preached by the economists. The Combination Acts and the repeal of the Tudor statutes were major defeats for the efforts to resist the imposition of a new capitalist order, but the resistance would continue well into the nineteenth century. Where the eighteenth century had been the century which saw the conversion of land to capital, the nineteenth century would be the century in which capital would seek to achieve the broad-scale conversion of labour into abstract labour, into capital itself. As this process advanced, so too did the power of the manufacturing class. In the meantime, however, the British state was dominated by a ruling landed elite with the trappings of a neo-feudal aristocracy, but whose true power resided in their ownership of land as means of production let out for use by tenant-farmers engaged in improving the land, maximising production and specialisation in the pursuit of profits – land as capital.

The post-war crisis

Britain faced a multi-faceted economic crisis upon the peace that followed after Waterloo. The Liverpool administration faced a barrage of demands from pressure groups and lobbyists representing a host of conflicting sectional and regional interests. To a large extent, the contending parties on the major issues of the day fell into two camps, representing a virtual generation gap. On the one hand were those whose livelihoods had been disrupted by the war and who wanted a return to 'normalcy'. On the other hand were those whose fortunes were launched during the war and for whom the loss of government contracts and protection was a serious disruption of what they had come to experience as the norm. The latter camp included landlords and farmers who borrowed money during wartime inflation to undertake improvements on marginal lands, businessmen who had borrowed to expand their trade and Canadian merchants who had benefited from the collapse of the Baltic timber trade. The former camp included agriculturalists on the better lands who had no need for government protection, larger and more established industrialists, and the Baltic merchants who now sought to recapture their lost trade. In general, Lord Liverpool employed defensive tactics in order to keep the most contentious and substantive policy decision-making away from public view as much as possible. To this end, he deliberately filled the Cabinet with politicians who enjoyed the most influence at elections, whilst reserving hard policy decisions for informal meetings with his 'little committee' of insiders or, when the issue was too contentious to be handled in the back room, he would appoint a select committee to investigate the matter.[9]

During the war, farmers and landlords – though not agrarian labourers – had benefited from a boom in prices. To take advantage, many had taken out loans to invest in improvements. The bumper crop of 1813 had precipitated a drastic fall in prices, and was followed by a poor harvest in 1814, leading to renewed imports of grain from Ireland, prompting Irish complaints. Criticism of Irish calls for protection was drowned out by similar calls from English agriculturalists. With the Government itself facing unprecedented levels of debt, pressure was put on farmers to simply adjust and not insist upon government regulation. But Liverpool also needed the support of farmers and landlords. As a result, the Corn Law of 1815 was passed in the face of opposition from the London crowds gathered outside Parliament. The law restricted the imports of grain until wheat reached 80s. a quarter.[10] The measure had been strongly opposed by the factory masters of Manchester, who had flooded Parliament with petitions in opposition. The fact that the landed interest was able to carry the day reflected several things: the continuing dominance of the political power of the landed classes, the Government's willingness to accommodate their fears of a flood of post-war grain imports from the Continent, the degree to which they had yet to fully accept the doctrines of *laissez-faire* and political economy and in general the way in which a majority in the political community continued to associate the national interest with the landed interest. The passage of the Corn Law was thus very much a political decision, and it was seen as such. Radicals saw it as a blatant symbol of greed and selfishness on the part of the ruling landed classes in the midst of the widespread distress being experienced by the poor and working classes.[11]

During the war, high grain prices and low wages had facilitated the decline of servants-in-husbandry: young persons working on one-year contracts and typically aiding middling farmers in dairying, husbandry and ploughing.[12] The

9. Hilton 1988, pp. 153–6.
10. Hilton 1988, p. 159.
11. Turner 1999, pp. 130–2; Briggs 1979, pp. 201–3; Thompson 1991, p. 596; Derry 2001, pp. 137–41. The Corn Law of 1815 was not the first such measure of the period; it had been presaged by those of 1791 and 1804 (Owen 1975, p. 302).
12. Kussmaul 1979, pp. 329–31. Kussmaul frames both 'the early modern popularity of farm service and its selective modern abandonment . . . in ecological terms . . . a process of environmental change drove it to extinction'. Both the presence of commons and wastes and scattered patterns rather than nuclear settlement increased the demand for by-employment, particularly among medium-sized farms. Thus a major force behind the decline of servants-in-husbandry was the enclosure of wastes and commons, and the associated concentration of holdings. The period during the French Wars provided conditions which accelerated both of these developments.

ongoing enclosure of wastes and commons, the concentration of holdings and the shift to more seasonal agriculture also contributed to making the hiring of day-labourers more economical. This development further contributed toward the making of a national labour market.

Upon the onset of a recession, the widened pool of wage labourers in agriculture found themselves caught up in a vicious cycle of falling wages, decreasing employment opportunities and increasing dependence upon parish relief. The demobilisation of as many as three hundred thousand soldiers put an enormous strain on wages in the towns and swamped an already saturated rural labour market, affecting both agrarian and rural handicraft employment. Landowners in the Southern counties seeking to alleviate the burden of the poor rates looked for any means by which they could prevent labourers from settling in their parishes and thereby collect relief. While no cottages were torn down during the agricultural boom of the French Wars, many were torn down now. For the first time, slums appeared in the country towns.[13] The introduction of agricultural machinery, including the threshing-machine, added further strain. The meliorist position in the standard of living debate holds that the pace of the growth of the standard of living slowed during the wars and recovered after 1815,[14] while the deteriorationist position holds that wages fell in both 1793 and 1815,[15] but whereas prices rose during the wars, the cost of living fell after 1815, resulting in a rise of real wages. Since neither side in the debate disputes that the standard of living generally rose after 1840, the years of greatest controversy over the standard of living are 1815–40. Mulhall argued that *per capita* consumption of meat, sugar, tea, beer and eggs increased between 1811 and 1850.[16] Thompson concedes that between 1790 and 1840 the growth of the national product likely outstripped population growth, but countered that the skewed distribution of that product led to a general decline in *per capita* consumption of wheat (in favour of potatoes) and of roast beef.[17]

The end of the war brought a fall in prices, which was felt internationally. This brought hardship to many sectors of the British economy, particularly woollens, which would struggle for recovery into the 1830s.[18] This price fall was felt harder

13. One editor 'doubted whether destroying cottages would check improvident marriages: "Somehow it would seem that the peasantry of Hampshire contrive to multiply in spite of the pains which have been taken to withhold from them the wicked encouragement of comfortable cottages"' (Rule 1986, pp. 76–81, quoting Blackwoods Edinburgh Magazine, 27 April 1830, p. 554).

14. Hartwell 1975, p. 116.

15. Tucker 1975, p. 32.

16. Mulhall 1892, pp. 120, 158, 281, 286, 354 and 544; as cited by Hartwell 1975, p. 108, n. 3. Hartwell mentions that: 'Mulhall also gives statistics for increasing *per capita* consumption of soap, leather, linen, cotton and coal'.

17. Thompson 1975, pp. 144–6.

18. Gregory 1982, p. 97.

on the Continent, where the 'self-blockade' of the Continental system and the loss of trade during the war had led to the virtual collapse of the Atlantic trade, with entrepôts having been reduced back to the status of regional ports. The industries of the Atlantic seaboard in Holland and especially South-West France, as well as Languedoc along the Mediterranean were pushed into a lasting de-industrialisation. Silk and wool needed little protection from British competition, but were it not for protection against British imports, the emerging cotton industry based upon the application of machinery following the British model would have suffered a major setback.[19] As it was, protection afforded the cotton industry to take hold, and thus the seed of an industrial revolution, and industrial capitalism, was planted on the Continent.

Despite the recovery of continental markets, British industry would struggle through serious financial instability. On top of the Corn Law controversy, Prime Minister Liverpool was faced with the greatest currency crisis since 1797 and a debt which now stood at the enormous sum of some £876 million. To put this in perspective, the national debt at the end of the Seven Years' War in 1763 stood at just over £132 million, while at the outset of the French Wars in 1793 it stood at £228 million. In 1815, the annual interest payments alone topped £10 million, eclipsing the amount of the Government's entire budget in 1792.[20] Expenditures on the wars had exceeded £1 billion in total. This 'could scarcely have been achieved without severely limiting the funds that might otherwise have been available for industrial expansion, though the most desperate shortage appears to have been in those areas of social expenditure which were essential for mitigating the harmful effects of over-rapid industrialisation and urbanization'.[21] Thus it was the poor who absorbed the worst shocks of the war. While Pitt had resorted to massive borrowing to subsidise the early years of the wars, nearly half of total government expenditure during the war years was covered through taxation. The land tax continued to decline into insignificance while the income tax, which did not become truly effective until 1806, contributed £172 million between that year and its abolition in 1816. The largest share was thus raised through customs and excise, which fell heaviest upon the poor, though prompting the loudest complaints from the 'middle classes'.[22] The Grand Union Canal

19. Crouzet 1964, pp. 567–88.

20. Briggs 1979, p. 170; Turner 1999, p. 108. Owen (Owen 1975, p. 307) cites a lower figure for the 1815 debt of £744.9 million.

21. Owen 1975, p. 307.

22. 'Such complaints helped to forge middle class consciousness', writes Briggs, as the poor were 'politically paralysed and had fewer opportunities of ventilating their far more serious tax grievances'. Since there was as yet no discernible managerial class within industry, it is necessary to be careful not to give too much weight to the term 'middle-class', although the term did come into usage during this period. There was a small but growing section of urban professionals and shopkeepers in the towns and cities, whose incomes and relative independence would have qualified them to be regarded as 'in the

opened in 1815, for the first time connecting London to the industrial Midlands. The total of private investment in the scheme may have reached £20 million. Thus despite the massive amounts of borrowing by the Government, the war had served to deliver only temporary setbacks to economic growth. Indeed, Patrick Colquhoun expressed wonder at the progress of the Industrial Revolution in Britain by 1814 as follows:

> It is impossible to contemplate the progress of manufactures in Great Britain within the last thirty years without wonder and astonishment. Its rapidity... exceeds all credibility. The improvement of the steam engines, but above all the facilities afforded to the great branches of the woolen and cotton manufactories by ingenious machinery, invigorated by capital and skill, are beyond all calculation...[23]

By contrast, France had endured 'national bankruptcy, revolution, dictatorship and decisive military defeat'.[24] For Britain's ruling classes, extraordinary levels of taxation and borrowing were acceptable burdens, having now achieved the goal of military victory. Yet clearly retrenchment was the order of the day. The 'fiscal-military' state of the eighteenth century was now poised to undergo a 'dramatic scaling back', putting it on course to become what some historians have called the '*laissez-faire* state'.[25]

The 'Malthusian moment'

Let us reflect on these terms. Britain was very much a player in the European game of imperialism, a game which it engaged in on the same non-capitalist terms as the other powers, pursuing extra-economic forms of property. There was no question what the main function of the fiscal-military state had been for well over a century:

> Warfare remained the chief function of the state from the beginning to the end of the eighteenth and indeed well into the nineteenth century. Parliamentary supremacy within the constitutional framework, itself largely a product

middle' between the wealthy and the poor. But it is significant that Briggs points out that association of Protestant nonconformist sentiment with these 'middle-class' grievances, and the fact that the term 'middle class' itself 'was first popularised in dissenting periodicals' (Briggs 1979, p. 170, n. 3). Probably a far larger number of 'middling' sorts were persons whose relative independence was supported by their family connections, being subsidised out of the rent-based incomes of rural estates.

23. As quoted in Mokyr 1999, p. 4.
24. Owen 1975, pp. 324 and 339.
25. Harling 2001, pp. 40 and 70.

> of the chronic warfare of the 1690s and beyond, helped to make the British state the most efficient war machine in Europe. It provided the [necessary] financial support...[26]

Britain's unique advantage in the game of European imperialism was its agrarian-capitalist economy, which allowed for expansion to the point where it could uniquely sustain unprecedented levels of government borrowing, without which Britain could hardly have hoped to have sustained repeated victories over France between 1688 and 1815. The high degree of political consensus with government in the hands of the ruling landed elite underpinned the confidence of the lenders. 'England was not a "bourgeois state"', Hobsbawm has written emphatically, 'It was an oligarchy of landed interests, headed by a tight, self-perpetuating peerage of some two hundred persons, a system of powerful rich cousinages under the aegis of the ducal heads of the great Whig families...'[27] Yet despite recognising this, Hobsbawm has also put forward the thesis of the 'dual revolution', implying that there was a fundamental parallel between the French Revolution of 1789 and Britain's Industrial Revolution. 'The crucial achievement of the two revolutions', he writes, was 'that they opened careers to talent, or at any rate to energy, shrewdness, hard work and greed'.[28] If one must search for parallels between these two 'revolutions', perhaps this is as close as one can get, but this statement is remarkably reductionist. We have mentioned that in 1815, the Continent saw the incipient beginnings of an industrial revolution in the form of the factory spinning of cotton. Yet despite the fact that the revolution had swept away many forms of politically-constituted property as well as feudal bonds of servitude and patronage, traditional modes of production actually saw a revival in the period after 1815. Guilds and journeymen-led organisations such as the *compagnages* in France saw their authority restored as handicraft production underwent a major expansion. Continental societies were still overwhelmingly dominated by the landed interest while manufacturers and would be manufacturers were deeply frustrated by the enforcement all sorts of customary rights and obligations within a legal system which continued to respect politically-constituted property. What is more, economic liberalism was viewed with suspicion by the reactionary governments. Britain itself saw the development of a conservative school of thought which partook in the general reactionary attack on revolutionary principles and on Enlightenment philosophy, which it saw as having inspired the Revolution. But capitalism and the doctrines of political economy had advanced too far in Britain not to be embraced. Conservative

26. Harling 2001, p. 40.
27. Hobsbawm 1986, p. 31.
28. Hobsbawm 1994, p. 232.

landlords focused their economic arguments instead upon resisting pressures from the more advanced class of manufacturers vying for greater representation in Parliament.[29] The challenge to landed hegemony posed by the rising manufacturing class in Britain was real, if not quite yet manifest. But as we have argued, the danger of amalgamating the 'Tory' reaction in Britain with the conservative reaction on the continent is that we may lose sight of the specificity of capitalism as it was developing in Britain.

Even the term 'Tory' is itself misleading, although it had come back into use. The temptation to dub the younger Pitt a Tory proved irresistible to the Whigs, who found this 'a neat and convenient way of giving clarity and consistency to the party differences of the period'.[30] As applied to Liverpool and his following, the designation 'Tory' was meant to distinguish the Pittite tradition from the Foxites, now led by Grey and Grenville. While Liverpool's politics were in fact highly conservative and reactionary, his government nevertheless followed through with the dismantling of the eighteenth-century system of perquisites and patronage that had begun under Pitt. As a result, Liverpool lacked the patronage once wielded by Walpole to enforce party discipline. This points to the irony that the followers of Fox should have appropriated to themselves the term 'Whig' when they had been but a minority opposition faction in what was in reality a Whig government under Pitt. More than any other, it was the issue of Catholic emancipation which divided the Pittite 'Tories' from the Foxite 'Whigs'. Yet here too is irony, for as we have seen, Pitt himself had moved a bill in favour of Catholic emancipation, a measure which cost him his office the first time. Moreover, it would be under Wellington's Tory government that the measure would finally succeed. The reality is that at no point during or after the long rule of Liverpool did ministers operate within a framework of strict party lines or ideologies that would enable historians to discern predictable patterns of political behaviour.[31] Nonetheless, there was a discernible tension between opponents and supporters of the Corn Laws, and more broadly over the issue of free trade. The opponents on either side of this debate were generally associated with the landed and mercantile/industrial interests respectively.

The most influential apologist for the landed class was the Reverend Dr. Thomas Robert Malthus, whose 1798 publication *An Essay on the Principle of Population*[32] was by 1815 coming to be recognised as second only to Smith's *Wealth of Nations* among the standard texts of political economy. Malthus's greatest impact may have been upon the reform of the Old Poor Law in 1834, a

---

29. Breunig 1977, pp. 181–3 and 233.
30. Derry 2001, pp. ix and 43.
31. Derry 2001, pp. 121–8; Turner 1999, pp. 81–2 and 142.
32. Malthus 1960.

topic to be addressed below. Our concern, here, is with both the way in which economic developments since Smith had shaped the discourse of political economy and simultaneously how Malthus and Ricardo, the two principal successors to Smith, shaped the discourse of the period. The debate between Malthus and Ricardo was in effect a debate between the interests of the landed classes and that of the rising manufacturers. In the course of this debate, the tendency to naturalise capitalist economics was taken to new heights.

In his 1798 *Essay*, Malthus advanced the law of diminishing returns, which held that since the quantity of land was finite, the average level of productivity in agriculture would decline as cultivation expanded and farmers were forced to put less productive lands under the plough. It can hardly be a coincidence that such a theory would be advanced at a time when the enclosure movement was running out of arable to enclose and attention was turning to the remaining wastes and commons. What is extraordinary about Malthus is the way in which he interpreted the growing immiseration in the countryside not as resulting from enclosure, but rather as the logical outcome of poor relief, which he viewed as tending to both depress wages and also thereby promote population growth. The central tenet of Malthus's work was his simple dictum that population would tend to outstrip the growth of the food supply, leading to famine where no other 'checks' on population, such as abstinence, had applied. This principle went largely unchallenged outside radical circles, probably because to contemporaries and particularly landowners and tenant-farmers now groaning at the level of the poor rates in the wake of the decommissioning of soldiers and the necessity of large-scale food imports, it seemed self-evident that population-growth was out of control relative to the growth of the food supply.

In his 1817 publication *The Principles of Political Economy and Taxation*,[33] David Ricardo launched what came to be regarded as an attack on the landed classes. Ricardo's highly theoretical model took the law of diminishing returns in a new direction. Rent was for Ricardo differential rent, effectively the result of a monopoly, and did not make up part of either the value of the produce or a part of its price. On superior lands, rents claimed that portion of the produce equivalent to the surplus above what was produced upon the most marginal lands where the rent was zero. Ricardo reached this formula by conceiving of an economy based upon corn as the currency. Adopting this model enabled Ricardo to dispense with issues of quality since the quantity and the value of corn were reduced to the same thing. Ricardo reasoned that as marginal lands were taken under cultivation, the inevitable result for the capitalist tenant-farmer would be diminishing returns and falling profits. Meanwhile, rents would increase on

33. Malthus 1960.

the better lands. Once profits reached a certain minimum, accumulation would cease and so too by implication would population growth. Once all available marginal lands had been put under cultivation, the law of diminishing returns would cease to operate and a 'stationary state' would be reached in which rent, profits and population growth would level off and the working classes would experience poverty, suffering and death. This nightmare scenario could be 'happily checked', however 'by improvements in machinery connected with the production of necessaries, as well as by discoveries in the science of agriculture, which enable the relinquishment of a portion of labour formerly required, and therefore to lower the price of the prime necessary of the labourer'.[34] Improvements in productivity, alongside cheap imports of corn and the discovery of new and fertile lands, however, could only temporarily check the law of diminishing returns. By contrast to the landlords who consumed the bulk of their unproductive income through rents, the manufacturing classes were compelled to re-invest in the economy.

Thus, while Ricardo had appropriated the law of diminishing returns in a critique of rent and the interest of the landed classes, he appropriated Malthus's economic fatalism in the process. But the economic fatalism in Malthus's original 1798 *Essay* ran deeper, for Malthus's primary aim was to discredit radical claims to a fair share in the wealth in an expanding economy. Where Burke had refuted radicalism on the basis that it incited the poor to act on the sinister passions of jealousy, hatred and revenge, 'Malthus maintained that radical dreams of social improvement were incompatible with the fundamental laws of nature. Whereas for Burke radicalism was undesirable', Malthus sought to refute 'that there could be *any* significant improvement in the conditions of the poor'.[35] The more extreme pessimism of Malthus's first *Essay* – in particular his criticism of Smith for believing that all accumulation involved an expansion of wage-goods[36] – were abandoned in subsequent revisions, but the twin themes of an attack on radicalism and on the poor laws remained. Malthus now accepted that individuals had the power to avoid the evil consequences of the principle of population by modifying their behaviour, and in so doing completely undermined the economic fatalism of his original argument by conceding that improvement was in fact possible. In 1820, Malthus completed his about-face by publishing

34. Ricardo 1987, p. 71.
35. McNally 1993, pp. 75–6.
36. The heart of the first essay, writes McNally (McNally 1993, p. 77), is a critique of Smith for not recognising that 'it is possible to have capital accumulation, which draws labour out of agriculture and into manufacturing and thus results in a diminution of the food supply and a decline in real levels of consumption'. This did not mean, however, that preserving a majority share in the economy for the agricultural sector could 'delay the onset of subsistence crises', for 'such crises were nevertheless inevitable'.

his *Principles of Political Economy*, whose main concern lay in refuting Say's Law, which held that overproduction was impossible because expanding production, by generating both commodities for the market and the incomes necessary for buying them, meant that expanding supply created its own demand. Malthus now put forward the argument that workers and capitalists produced more than they could consume, and thus replaced *underproduction*, the basis of his earlier argument, with a theory of *overproduction*.[37] In order to maintain a balance between annual production and consumption, he argued, there must be a class of consumers who *unproductively* consume the surplus. Since he believed wages could never rise to be able to gobble up the surplus, only the rentier class was in a position to play this useful role. Thus, in countering Ricardo, Malthus claimed that rent, which he viewed as being only a partial monopoly, served not one but two grandiose functions. First, it allowed costs of production and profits to reach equilibrium on production of lands of differing fertility. Second, it provided the revenue needed to unproductively consume the surplus produce that was in excess of that needed for productive consumption.[38] Malthus thus confirmed the long-established and still widely-held view that the interests of the landlord were consistent with the interests of society in general.

By refuting Ricardo's attack, Malthus satisfied the need of the landed classes for a champion in the field of political economy. But his real popularity among the upper classes in general lay in his attack on the arguments of Paine, Owen and the Spenceans, and their 'delusive' defence of a right to subsistence. Here we offer but one of the milder samples of Malthus's often odious statements against the right of subsistence:

> Man cannot live in the midst of plenty. All cannot share alike the bounties of nature. Were there no established administration of property, man would be obliged to guard with force his little store. Selfishness would be triumphant. The subjects of contention would be perpetual. Every individual would be under a constant anxiety about corporal support, and not a single intellect would be left free to expatiate in the field of thought.[39]

Since the right to subsistence was implicit in the institution of the poor laws, he advocated their total abolition, and what is more, for him even the workhouse was too generous. It is worth noting that Ricardo fully adopted Malthus's principle of population into his own thinking and equally rejected the poor laws. Thus while one may have promoted the landed interest while the other that of the industrialists, they were united in their rejection of the radical claim of the poor

37. McNally 1993, p. 85.
38. Malthus 1836, p. 41.
39. Malthus 1986, p. 331.

to rights of subsistence, rights that had long been implicit in customary law and craft by-laws. While Ricardo's work demonstrated a level of intellectual rigour to stand alongside that of Smith, the profound inconsistencies and reversals of position in Malthus's work did not diminish his popularity. On the contrary:

> Malthus defined the discourse of poverty which dominated political economy for fifty years. He constructed a pessimistic market economics which jettisoned Smith's hopes for material improvement for the majority. And in so doing, he made classical economics an open enemy of the working class.[40]

McNally describes this period of Malthus's rising popularity as the 'Malthusian Moment'. Malthus's popularity can only be understood as arising from telling the upper classes what – in the midst of a crisis that they neither fully grasped nor wished to confront their role in creating – they wanted to hear: that the rich were not to blame for the suffering of the poor, for this was either the hand of nature at work, or worse, the result of overly generous social policies which even if well-intentioned, exacerbated the tendency for the poor to have too many children and thereby compound their inevitable misery. Social inequality was necessary for a minority to arise out of poverty and achieve a superior measure of virtue and moral status. It was inevitable that these arguments would draw the most vituperative fire from later radical thinkers.

'Bread or blood'

In the chaotic atmosphere of 1815, few politicians had the wherewithal to apply the abstract theories of political economy to practical issues of the day, and 'not until the mid-1820s did the cabinet's command of commercial and financial details become more convincing (and even then there was much disagreement among ministers.)'[41] Behind the reactionary policies of the post-war years lay financial instability, a slump in trade, agricultural depression and a good deal of ongoing hysteria over the fact that radicalism in Britain continued to grow and was attracting a mass following. Radicals did not appear to be cowed in the wake of the defeat of France; instead, they appeared to be more confident than before, with their 'defiant and emotive slogans, and inclusive mobilisation'.[42] Robert Owen observed in 1815 'that "the general diffusion of manufactures throughout a county generates a new character in its inhabitants . . . an essential change in the general character of the mass of the people"'.[43] As Thompson has explained,

40. McNally 1993, p. 91.
41. Turner 1999, p. 128.
42. Turner 1999, p. 149.
43. As quoted in Thompson 1991, p. 208.

reformers may have complained about the apathy of the people, but they nonetheless enjoyed a general level of security that the support of working-class communities afforded them, 'while the authorities were forced to build barracks and take precautions against the "revolutionary crowd". This is one of those facts of history so big that it is easily overlooked…'[44] Reformers, protestors and conservatives alike draped themselves in notions of liberty and the 'Englishman's birthright' that enjoyed widespread acceptance as rights guaranteed by the British constitution. The anti-absolutist 'moral consensus' around the 'liberties of the subject' was perhaps the major factor why the British rejected, down to 1829, having a standing police force in the country, as a policy that was 'too French'.

Radical leaders such as William Cobbett and Joseph Hume sought to build upon this moral consensus in putting forward the claim that the Liverpool administration was pursuing military despotism,[45] and was wasting huge sums of money, especially on war. The call for cheaper government had been sounded. Liverpool's ministers opened the 1816 session of Parliament with unbounded confidence. They were certain that the passage of the Corn Law in the previous year, as well as the victory at Waterloo, meant that the ministry would enjoy the unstinting support of the landed interest. But when the progressive Whig leader Henry Brougham led a successful backbench rebellion against the unpopular income tax, leading to its abolition in April, it was a humiliating defeat. The £172 million yielded by the income tax in the past ten years was no more than a sixth of the budget. With the debt having grown to £902 million by 1816 with interest payments exceeding £30 million, its loss would force the Government into a programme of retrenchment. Between 1816 and 1821, the Tories would make deep cuts in the Civil List and official salaries were reduced by ten percent. The contradiction facing the Tories was that the majority of the body politic demanded such austerity measures but simultaneously cried out in pain at the consequences.[46]

A wet spring in 1816 meant late planting, and this was followed by heavy summer rains. Even before the terrible harvest that followed, the abject poverty among agrarian labourers in East Anglia provoked them to outrages and demonstrations against the high price of bread. The tactics were familiar: nightly meetings and threatening letters leading to demonstrations and violence in April. East Anglia textile workers, now confronted with what would prove to

44. Thompson 1991, p. 85.
45. Derry 2001, p. 138. 'This accusation was spread abroad by the government's opponents when Wellington joined the ministry in 1818'. Although the accusation was unfounded, Wellington would go on to do considerable justice to the charge with his heavy-handed approach to governing.
46. Briggs 1979, pp. 169–70; Turner 1999, p. 109; Hilton 1988, p. 155; Gash 1978, p. 152.

be the terminal crisis of their regional trades, played a leading role.[47] The protestors demanded secure employment and that poor relief be replaced instead by fixed wages from the employing farmers, as well as a fixed 'just' price for flour, consistent with customary expectations. Marching crowds with horns and drums bedecked themselves with garlands and ribbons and recruited passers-by as a way of seeking the full participation of the community. According to Cobbett's *Weekly Register*, the 'breaking of threshing machines, and the destruction of barns, corn-stacks &c. by fire' were outrages which the public in County Sussex 'have been for some time apprised of... the agents in which are presumed to be agricultural labourers, discontented because employment and advance of wages did not immediately follow the recent rise in the price of corn'.[48] In the latter part of May, large disturbances erupted at Brandon, Sussex, where a crowd of 1500, demanding fixed maximum prices for bread and meat and armed with 'brick-bats, stones, clubs, &c'. destroyed several houses and seized flour and bread. Magistrates were cowed into signing statements agreeing to the demands of fixed prices and 'full wages'.[49] At Huntingdon, two hundred protestors armed with 'implements of agriculture' were dispersed by cavalry. In the fen-district of the Isle of Ely in Cambridgeshire, another crowd of vandals armed with sticks studded with spikes carrying a banner with the slogan 'Bread or Blood in Brandon this day!' marched to Ely and threatened to march on London. Despite the implicit threat behind such slogans, the protests were remarkably absent of any violence against persons, but violence against property continued. Several houses, flour mills and a silk manufactory were attacked and a number of threshing-machines were destroyed. Soon the fen-dwellers, who were not wage labourers, joined in the revolt, themselves facing the destruction of their customary habitat in the face of plans to 'improve' and drain the fens. Dragoons were summoned and the matter came to a head at Littleport, where shots were exchanged and two protesters killed. Several more were wounded, as were several soldiers. Over a hundred protestors were captured. Having thus been suppressed, the disorder was 'thrust back into the underground of the poaching war, the anonymous letter, the flaming corn rick'.[50] At the Special Assize at Ely in June, twenty-four capital convictions were handed out and five protestors were actually hung. Nine more were transported and ten were gaoled.[51] What was remarkable about the

47. Wells 1988, p. 116.

48. Cobbett 1816, pp. 707–8. Rule 1986, p. 356 notes that attacks on threshing-machines had begun in 1815 in Suffolk 'where given their limited diffusion protest must be seen as against a potential rather than an actual threat.'

49. Seal 1988, pp. 156–8.

50. Thompson 1991, pp. 249–50. The burning of corn ricks continued into the 1840s, most frequent in the years 1832, 1834–5 and 1842 (Hobsbawm 1968, p. 285).

51. Hammond and Hammond 1974a, pp. 152–4; Cobbett 1816.

'Bread or Blood' protests is that while the tactics employed were similar to those of the Luddites, it was a revolt by and in the interests of agricultural labourers, although 'some of the arms and organization of the protesters seemed to owe something to army training',[52] suggesting the involvement of recently decommissioned soldiers. While the state had swiftly and successfully suppressed the protest, this had only put a lid on a boiling cauldron of discontent.[53] It was an almost symbolic prelude to larger agrarian disturbances to come. It also took place at the same time as Bussa's Rebellion, when a rising by hundreds of slaves led to the destruction of nearly a quarter of a cane crop. A thousand slaves died in the fighting or were executed afterward. The planters blamed the abolitionist MP William Wilberforce for inciting a rebellion which '"well nigh deluged our fields with blood"'.[54]

Likewise, it seemed as if the invasion of Middle Britain had not completely extinguished the flames of Luddism when the lace factory of the inventor John Heathcoat was attacked in Loughborough, Leicestershire. On 28 June, seventeen men broke into the factory, shooting and wounding a guard, and smashing fifty-five of Heathcoat's patented machines with hammers and axes, as well as burning the cloth. The leader, James Towle, 36, was a well-known 'old Ludd' and was therefore easily identified. Towle was hanged in November at the Leicester courthouse, followed in death five months later by six of his accomplices. According to some of the defendants, however, local manufacturers resentful of the low wages Heathcoat paid his workers had paid the attackers more than £100 for their efforts. Whether the Loughborough attack belongs to the tradition of true Luddism remains an open question.[55]

After a miserably wet and cold summer, the grain harvest of 1816 was scant and full of mould. The poor harvest brought home the fact that the anticipated post-war trade boom had not materialised. The loss of wartime contracts was compounded further by the recovery of manufacturing on the continent. The high price and shortage of bread exacerbated the distress of widespread unemployment, and this was further compounded by the now highly resented forms of regressive taxation. Food protests were seen in virtually every county. In the countryside, landlords received many notices from tenant-farmers announcing their intentions to quit and many farms went out of cultivation. Conditions were once again ripe for revolt. In some parishes, more than half the population was receiving poor relief.

---

52. Gash 1978, p. 150.
53. Wells 1988, p. 116; Rule 1986, pp. 356–7.
54. Linebaugh 2000, p. 302.
55. Sale 1996, pp. 188–9.

The use of pauper children in factories now became an issue for poor law commissioners. The Factory Act of 1802, because it was widely disregarded, had done little to improve the condition of pauper children in the factories. An employer in Dublin reportedly locked up his printshop with the children inside each night, taking them out to the countryside on weekends for exercise, before the children were taken away entirely by his apprentices. London was still sending wagon loads of pauper children to work in the cotton mills of Yorkshire and Lancashire. The 'free', effectively slave labour of the children displaced that of grown men and women. Parliament passed legislation in 1816 banning the removal of children over a distance of 40 miles.[56] In 1817, the poor law commissioners of Nottingham were so scandalised by conditions in the hosiery factories that they simply refused to permit the employment of pauper apprentices.[57] Was this simply a moral equation? Or did the displacement of adult workers by children amount to transferring the burden of poor relief from London to Nottingham? If the latter were the case, this was not so much an act of morality as of county revolt.

Toward the end of 1816, Cartwright's Hampden Clubs or Union societies were attracting scores of new members, and 'within weeks of their formation these clubs were pressing outwards for regional and national contacts which were illegal under the Seditious Societies Act'.[58] On 15 November, a gathering of radicals was broken up by the Government, whose paid informants had passed along rumours of a plot to march upon and burn the Tower. A second meeting on 2 December was dispersed only after several fiery speeches had been given. This time, the crowd marched into the City and stormed the shop of a gunsmith, wounding a bystander. Arrests followed. In January 1817, reformers held a meeting in Middleton outside London, where Hunt, Cobbett and Cartwright all quarrelled.[59] Being a radical leader was an expensive business, and there were tensions over money, although vanity may have been the larger factor.[60] At the

---

56. Subsequently in 1819, the Cotton Mills and Factories Act banned cotton-mill owners from employing children less than nine years of age, and limited the working day to twelve hours for children between the ages of nine and sixteen. Both acts were largely ignored. Not until 1823 would the Home Office begin regular inspections (Aspin 1995, p. 94).

57. Berg 1979, pp. 106 and 109.

58. Thompson 1991, p. 678.

59. Turner 1999, p. 114.

60. 'The greatest cause of Radical disagreement', Thompson explains, 'was sheer vanity. And vanity was so common a disorder among the Radical leaders that it appears less as a cause of disagreement than as a symptom of the general lack of coherent organization'. Orators like Hunt 'became addicted to the sight and sound of the throng cheering below the hustings... The demagogue is a bad or ineffectual leader. Hunt voiced, not principle nor even well-formulated Radical strategy, but the emotions of the movement. Striving always to say whatever would provoke the loudest cheer, he was not the leader but the captive of the least stable portion of the crowd' (Thompson 1991, pp. 686–90).

meeting it was resolved that all petitioning bodies in the United Kingdom should 'assist in bringing forth all the strength of the Unions into one point of view'.[61] Deputies were appointed to travel through the manufacturing districts and meetings were to be held in Yorkshire. In Lancashire, the term 'union' was now increasingly used to refer exclusively to working-class organisation, while in the more artisanal Birmingham the term still referred to united actions by employers and workers, such as the agitations against the Orders in Council in 1812. Once a Tory stronghold, Manchester was now the centre of radicalism.

A kind of hysteria gripped the Ministry in 1817. Fears of a genuine insurrection were out of proportion with reality, but were informed by the perception that the ruling landed class now faced agitation from artisans, factory- and agrarian labourers, as well as middle-class radicals still very much inspired by the writings of Tom Paine. A stone thrown through the Prince Regent's coach on its way home from Parliament on 28 January provided the pretext for another wave of repressive legislation. Secret committees in Parliament heard the testimony of paid informants such as Mr. Castle, who told them that the object of the Spencean philanthropists and Union clubs was 'a total overthrow of all existing establishments and a division of the land and extinction of the funded property of the country'.[62] In that moment, the Spenceans were to be taken at their word and vague ideological promises were treated as hard plotting for revolution. Foreign Secretary Castlereagh introduced bills granting emergency powers, including the suspension of *habeas corpus*. Parliament passed a new Seditious Meetings Act, requiring that licenses be obtained for public meetings and lectures, which remained in force until July 1818, as well as enacting Sidmouth's call for the arrest of anyone charged with publishing or writing blasphemous or seditious literature. The bombastic radical journalist William Cobbett had only recently lowered the price of his *Weekly Political Register* from one shilling and a halfpenny to two pence, making a radical progressive journal available to the lower classes for the first time. Now faced with paying stamp duty on his journal, he was prompted to flee to America.

As Parliament passed this legislation in Westminster, petitioners in Manchester gathered for what one authority has described as 'the world's first hunger march', setting out for London on 10 March in the hope of presenting petitions of

---

The power to be gained by flattering the crowd will always remain a vexing problem for the cause of democracy.

61. Thompson 1991, p. 678.

62. Ward, Prothero and Leathes 1911, pp. 577–8. Thompson (1991, p. 543) writes that the authorities suspected Spenceans to be one of the 'hidden hands' behind the disorder. Spence had been arrested on a charge of sedition after the bread protests of 1800 and 1801. And again in 1817 the Commons suspected a conspiracy but Place informed his colleagues that the Spenceans were harmless.

grievance to the Prince Regent.[63] As each petitioner carried a blanket, this 'March of the Blanketeers' got no further than Stockport before the unarmed protestors were turned back by dragoons and yeomanry. Subsequently, on 9 June, a force of some two to three hundred men set out from the White Horse Inn in Pentrich, Derbyshire: 'They set off in the rain to march the fourteen miles to Nottingham, calling at farms and houses and demanding arms and support on the way. At one of these farms the only blood of the rising was shed; [their leader, Jeremiah] Brandreth, demanding imperiously entrance to a house where it was believed there was a gun, fired through the window and killed a farm servant'.[64]

After this tragic and fateful incident, Brandreth led his grim and dwindling party on, promising that they would meet '"a cloud of men" sweeping down from Scotland and Yorkshire on their way to London'.[65] They were instead met by dragoons and forty-six were arrested. A simultaneous rising further North, known as the 'Folley Hall Rising', involved some exchange of gunfire between several hundred clothing workers advancing on Huddersfield and a detachment of soldiers, but no loss of life, and fewer arrests. Because some of those involved in planning these would be rebellions were veteran Luddites, the whole affair has sometimes been viewed as the dying breath of Luddism. Thompson sees the Pentrich affair as a moment of transition between Luddism and the popular-radicalism of 1818 to 1832, writing:

> We may see the Pentridge [*sic*] rising as one of the first attempts in history to mount a wholly proletarian insurrection, without any middle-class support... There is a sense in which Peterloo followed directly, and inevitably, upon Pentridge. It was the outcome of an extra-ordinarily powerful and determined 'constitutionalist' agitation, largely working class in character, within a potentially revolutionary context.[66]

The *Leeds Mercury* subsequently exposed the role of William Oliver, a spy working for Home Secretary Sidmouth, in instigating the whole affair.[67]

Since 1794, the Home Office's use of spies to infiltrate radical organisations had become routine. Despite this, the revelation that a government agent had instigated the whole affair shocked public opinion and remained a matter of controversy for decades. Thompson, however, cautions against accepting the

63. Aspin 1995, p. 59.
64. Thompson 1991, p. 724.
65. Sale 1996, p. 188–90.
66. Thompson 1991, p. 733–6. Thompson's usage of 'Pentridge' throughout is in lieu of the modern spelling for Pentrich, Derbyshire, and is not to be confused with the village of Pentridge, Dorset.
67. Sale 1996, pp. 188–90. Sale gives Oliver the spy's real name as W.O. Jones, while Thompson's index (Thompson 1991, p. 954) identifies him as W.J. Richards.

Whig interpretation that the participants were mere dupes. There are 'overwhelming reasons', he writes, 'for supposing that some kind of "physical force" conspiracy was under preparation in 1817, which was inextricably intertwined with the counter-conspiracy of Government provocateurs'.[68] Thompson cites government reports of pre-planning by secret committees taking place in the Midlands, Birmingham, Lancashire and Yorkshire. The organising was hampered by the fact that many radical leaders were still awaiting trial for their role in the Spa Fields affair. This left Oliver in a position to make empty promises of support from London as he toured the Northern towns and met with radical leaders plotting the uprising. Just as Brandreth and his cohorts were being arrested in Derbyshire, the government was deeply embarrassed when juries acquitted Watson and the other Spa Fields protestors.[69] More embarrassments would come later in the year with the acquittals of the Folley Hall conspirators, and of the publishers Wooler and Hone who had been brought up on charges of seditious libel. The Government's theory that a general conspiracy was at work was discredited. Certainly the threat of Jacobinism was abated with the defeat of revolutionary France and the restoration of the Bourbons. Still, the ministry was determined to set an example by exacting blood and after carefully selecting a compliant jury managed to see that Brandreth and two of his fellow conspirators were hung, with fourteen others being transported and nine imprisoned.[70] Oliver's name was not even mentioned at the trial. Thompson suggests that the defence might have declined to pursue the Government's hand in the affair in order to avoid exposing the full extent of the operation as well as to cut a deal with the prosecution in order to spare the lives of some of the defendants and as well to spare the implication of many more reformers. As with 1780 and with Luddism, the full details of the affair may never be known, due to the imperative of maintaining secrecy and anonymity on the part of the organisers. Regardless, while the Government managed to put a chill on radical agitation with the examples made in Derbyshire, the greater effect may have been to induce public revulsion at the ministry's employment of informants on the model of a 'continental spy system'.[71] Even if the public was unaware of the full extent of the conspiracy in 1817, had the plan been better organised and not co-opted by the government

68. Thompson 1991, p. 713.

69. According to Linebaugh 2000, p. 301, the Spa Fields protesters were 'led by Spenceans and waged by canal diggers, porters, coal and ballast heavers, sailors, dockworkers, and factory workers. Among the leaders was Thomas Preston, a Spencean who had traveled to the West Indies and considered himself an "unregistered slave"'. As Linebaugh documents, increasing linkages between slaves, sailors, the Irish and English working-class radicals were deeply disturbing to authorities.

70. Sale 1996, pp. 188–90. (Turner 1999, p. 114) gives different numbers, claiming that thirty of the Pentrich protesters were transported.

71. Thompson 1991, p. 727; see the full account from pp. 711–34.

in the context of universal 'bread riots' in the midst of agrarian and industrial slump, it might have enjoyed broader support.

The widespread perception that the ministry was indifferent to the suffering was not entirely accurate. Aside from collecting and distributing record levels of poor relief, on 16 June the government passed the Poor Employment Act. The act set up a fund of £1.75 million for the provision of three-year loans to employers who could provide employment by building public works and fisheries. Within two months over a hundred applications had been received for an endless variety of projects, from repairing docks to erecting gasworks. Canal companies claimed the largest share of the loans. While the initial sum was clearly inadequate to the moment of crisis, the powers of the commissioners that had been appointed were subsequently expanded and the amounts extended. The act serves as another milestone that should not be seen as transformative in its own right, but symbolic of a more long-term evolution of public policy. Loans for public works had been issued previously, especially in Scotland. And while the 1817 act was rushed through Parliament as an emergency measure intended to be temporary, it remained active until 1842, when payments out of the Exchequer ceased and the newly formed Public Works Loan Commission was established with its own consolidated fund. Nonetheless, the act amounted to an admission on the part of the Government that it had a responsibility to respond to economic depression by finding ways of providing employment.[72]

Of course, the act was passed in the face of opposition not only from strict adherents of *laissez-faire* principles, but also from radical libertarians who vehemently adhered to the belief that 'those societies in which governments governed less and taxed little were likely to be the most happy and the most free'.[73] The split between libertarian and trade unionist radicalism persisted. As Thompson notes, 'Huntite Radicalism had little to say about factory reform, or social questions in general. The main channel for the energy of the factory workers of 1816–20 was within their own trade union organization'.[74] While the thrust of agitation came from hand-loom weavers, stockingers and other artisans, the

72. Flinn 1961, pp. 82–92 comments: 'Whether one views the act as an extension of the Elizabethan solution of "setting the poor on work", or as another nail in the coffin of *laissez-faire*, or merely as a logical extension of the tentative eighteenth and early nineteenth century excursions into new fields of public finance, it remains a welcome remove from Oliver the Spy and Habeas Corpus suspended'. Since we are seeking to show how capitalist markets advanced by the *gradual* process of deregulation and extinguishing of customary and extra-economic forms of social regulation, it is at least worth asking whether the act should be viewed as a departure from existing policies of *laissez-faire*, or has having some continuity with eighteenth-century policies of direct state intervention.

73. Derry 2001, p. 140.

74. Thompson 1991, p. 707.

cause of reform attracted 'small masters, tradesmen, publicans, booksellers and professional men'[75] who, while willing to condemn the ministry's coercive methods and express sympathy for the plight of workers and peaceful agitations such as the March of the Blanketeers, remained uncomfortable with the use of threatening language and what they saw as irresponsible tactics employed in working-class actions.[76] From 1816 onwards, argues Thompson, the ideas, actions and experiments in organising taken by the trade unionists 'prefigure the developments of the 1830s'.[77] Yet Thompson goes on to stress the 'scale and intensity' of the 'multiform popular agitation' throughout the period from 1811 to 1832 and after, which gave rise to 'the sense of some catastrophic change'.[78] Leeson suggests that 'a kind of revolution, an industrial civil war' was in progress, at the heart of which was a struggle over control of the labour process whereby larger masters and factory owners sought to introduce machinery and techniques of mass-production whilst also seeking to break 'the power of the old style craftsman, master and journeyman alike'.[79] Middle-class reformers could maintain a distance from this great power struggle because it did not touch them directly. Where middle-class radicalism and trade unionism converged was in the call for suffrage, though *universal* male suffrage and annual parliaments were demands that went too far for the former. For the latter, each new round of repressive legislation only underscored the need for working people to secure the right to vote in order that they might prevent such legislative repression from being enacted again in future.

The makings of a working class

E.P. Thompson's writings on the decades between 1790 and 1820 continue to cause controversy. His assertion that this was a critical period for the formation of a working class in England has come under particular scrutiny. Thompson himself was critical of notions of 'class structure', within which he perceives the reification of class. As Thompson explains:

> There is today an ever-present temptation to suppose that class is a thing. This was not Marx's meaning, in his own historical writing, yet the error vitiates much latter-day 'Marxist' writing. 'It', the working class, is assumed to have a real existence, which can be defined almost mathematically – so many men who stand in a certain relation to the means of production. Once this

75. Thompson 1991, p. 664.
76. Turner 1999, p. 116.
77. Thompson 1991, p. 937.
78. Thompson 1991, p. 209.
79. Leeson 1979, p. 102.

> is assumed it becomes possible to deduce the class-consciousness which 'it' ought to have (but seldom does have) if 'it' was properly aware of its own position and real interests.[80]

What is deeply ironic is that the majority of Thompson's critics tend to assume that in his efforts to tell the history of the 'making' of the working class in England, Thompson himself sees the working class as a 'thing' or worse, commits the long-standing Marxist sin of reading 'class consciousness' into a heterodox group of workers where there is no such thing because no class has yet formed, or will ever fully form. For example, Kirkpatrick Sale's work depends upon, and is highly sympathetic to, Thompson's work. Yet Sale sounds dismissive when he writes of the 'making' of the working class which 'Thompson tries so hard to prove', and seeks to supplant the notion of 'class consciousness' with what he calls 'class concept'.[81] One suspects that in engaging in such semantics, Sale is seeking to distance himself from the taint of vulgar Marxist reductions of the concept of class to Platonic structures which precede and infiltrate history, 'determining' class consciousness and the outcomes of class struggle. In his critique of demographic and commercial models of historical change, Robert Brenner argued that the 'structure of class relations, of class power... will determine [how] demographic and commercial changes will affect long-term trends in... economic growth – and not vice-versa'.[82] Brenner too has been (mis)understood to mean by this that he embraces a crude Marxist model, replacing economic determinism with class determinism.[83] While Thompson and Brenner apply the concept

80. Thompson 1991, p. 9.
81. The concept of class, writes Sale (1996, pp. 196–7), 'is a very useful construct for social manipulation and stratification. Once an idea like 'class' can be established to explain how society operates, it becomes a way of seeing the proper, or at least ordained, segmentation of the populace, the division between rich and poor, as an eternal and acceptable given of Britain, like bad weather and abundant coal. As such, then, it is a useful tool for those in power, relegating some populations to labor and poverty as if it were God's will...' There is much to disentangle, here. While political economy does naturalise the market, when we think of ruling elites seeking to indoctrinate the lower orders to accept their inferior position as 'God's will', we typically think back to the Middle Ages and the notion that one's station in life is fixed, a doctrine very much reinforced by the Church. Perhaps not so much in the early nineteenth century, but certainly by the twentieth century, the hegemonic ideologies of capitalism tend to promote quite the opposite notion: that one's station is not fixed and that in a free economy social advancement is both possible and necessary ('equality of opportunity'). Beyond that, Sale's apparent attempt to reduce class to little more than an ideology seems to contradict his earlier claim that Luddism facilitated the forging of 'an identity of interests' between landed gentlemen and millowners: 'a bond between aristocrat and plutocrat that was never really to be sundered', whilst meanwhile bringing about 'a permanent breach between worker and master'. Sale may present these 'bonds' as being strictly ideological, but the real work is to identify their social, legal and economic underpinnings.
82. Brenner 1985a, pp. 10–11.
83. See Bois 1978, pp. 60–9.

of class in quite different ways – Thompson in its social context, Brenner in its broader economic context – both have come under the same kind of criticism with regards to class: there is an assumption that by 'class' they can only be referring to two classes, capital and labour, bound together in the exploitative relationship of capital.

Thompson's disavowal of any such notions can be seen in his rather extreme statement that: 'Class is defined by men as they live their own history, and, in the end, this is the only definition'.[84] This type of comment by Thompson has led critics like Perry Anderson to suggest that Thompson is guilty of collapsing the '"complex manifold of objective-subjective determinations whose totalisation actually generated the English working class into a simple dialectic between suffering and resistance whose whole movement is internal to the subjectivity of class"'.[85] Anderson appears to be suggesting that Thompson is merely telling the story of the subjective 'self-making' of the English working class rather than actually telling the story of its objective 'making'. Thompson's emphasis is certainly on the *experience* of being alive as a worker during the formative era of the English working class, but to reduce experience to subjectivity is also to reduce class to an objective, 'determining' structural category of an analysis that never tells us how the actions of historical agents help bring social classes into being, or for that matter how such objective structures shape the lives of real people. As Ellen Meiksins Wood points out: 'Class as "structure" conceptualises away the very fact that defines the role of class as the driving force of historical movement: the fact that class at the beginning of a historical mode of production is not what it is at the end'.[86] Thompson instead treats class as a historical process. It is certainly one of the methodological goals of the present work to strike a balance between applying class as an objective, descriptive category when discussing broad-scale historical change and seeking to understand how contemporary agents of history applied, understood and recognised themselves as 'class' agents.

Richard Price sees the mass radical actions after 1815 as:

> the first of a series of great social movements that climaxed in Chartism in the 1840s. These movements exposed the social and political tensions that were associated with industrialization. But, of course, they did more than that. Historians have long argued that they revealed the alterations that industrialization forced in class relations and, in particular, that they forged the making of the English working class.[87]

---

84. Thompson 1991, p. 10.
85. Anderson 1980, p. 39, as cited in Wood 1995, p. 84; see Wood's Chapter Three, 'Class as process and relationship', pp. 76–107, for a full discussion of Thompson's alleged bias toward subjectivity.
86. Wood 1995, p. 99.
87. Price 1986, p. 49.

Price seeks to complement the idea of the *making* of the working class with the idea of the *decomposition* of the state of industrial social relations that had first emerged in the late seventeenth century. The specific changes in motion in the early nineteenth century – the vast expansion of artisanal production alongside the dismantling of the customary regulation that had sustained it, and the steady progress of the factory mode of production – coincided with the decline of ruling-class hegemony and the 'boisterous rowdyism of plebeian crowds' that shocked foreign visitors. Price suggests that rather than seeing an embryonic modern working class emerging in this period, a more accurate portrayal of the process might be 'to see them as the vast expansion of themes common to customary consciousness and moral economy into one last, magnificent, bellowing of [the] popular culture and radicalism of the eighteenth century'.[88] For example, Price notes that artisans were less immediately concerned with resisting the real subordination to capital and the loss of direct control over the labour process than they were with the way in which market forces were bringing about the deterioration of their condition. The analysis of working-class theorists of the time focused not on production relations, but on commercial relations, and saw the pursuit of reform as a means by which to confront 'old corruption' and unequal exchange, and restore the traditional mechanisms that had ensured that artisans received a 'just price' for their trade. Political reform would allow a return to political remedies.[89] Price's emphasis on the continuity and even the *expansion* of the customary mode of manufacturing throughout the early period of the Industrial Revolution and deep into the nineteenth century is justifiable. We have already covered much of the terrain in the previous chapter on custom. We will revisit the controversy below.

What we have tried to show to this point is how by 1815 the battles over the legal framework supporting customary modes of manufacture had already been decided against the artisans. This set the stage for the coming decades of struggle in which artisans and other workers reasserted their customary rights, including the control of the labour process, in the face of both the advance of the factory and the deteriorating terms of trade, just as Price suggests. Yet this should not negate the fact that by January 1817 trade unionists were already recognising the need to bring 'all the strength of the Unions into one point of view', or in other words to build class solidarity. The growing tendency to seek solidarity across trades and even a national union movement reflected an increasing understanding that working people *in general* were confronted with a new set of conditions, even if only a minority of workers were as yet subject to *direct* exploitation by capitalists in the factory. No one, and certainly not Thompson, is saying that

88. Price 1986, p. 50.
89. Price 1986, pp. 50–3.

there were two well-defined classes of capital and labour facing each other in the early nineteenth century. But making this point should not negate the fact that *capital*, capital as a social relation, dynamic capital, was advancing in industry.

Let us be clear, lest we leave the impression that capital is here being viewed as some metaphysical force slowly swallowing production just as a black hole eats a star. In order for capital to exist as a social relation, it requires that the owner of the means of production, to whom all profits accrue, must have the capacity to transform production in order to respond to the competitive market pressures, or market imperatives, by applying innovation, specialisation, maximisation in the interests of engaging in price competition and in pursuit of a profit. It is only fitting and proper that the artisans who still formed the backbone of the working classes in 1817 should focus their concern on the issue of unequal or unfair exchange, for it was in the market and not inside the workshop that they increasingly felt the encroaching power of the capitalist. For lack of a better word, we could say that their labour had not yet been 'enclosed' in factories. In the age of the guild, it had been monopoly control *over* markets that spoke to the rights of labour. When that form of control was supplanted, what remained was for artisans to secure themselves *behind* the market, first by vigorously asserting their customary right to control the labour process and then ultimately through the threat of withdrawing their labour entirely. Thus the rights of labour were no longer located *in* the market, but in the control of the labour process. And thus the appeal to custom, which in the past was little noticed, became so prominent in this era.

There were some trades, such as watchmakers, who faced no imminent moment of real subsumption to capital. 'The desire to maintain respectability', writes Chase, was 'the keynote of the watchmakers' ideology'.[90] But in 1817 even the watchmakers lamented the repeal of 5 Elizabeth, c. iv, complaining that this had brought distress to their trade by lifting the limitation on interlopers. A resolution passed by their association reflects precisely the artisanal conception of society in which Price sees the continuity of eighteenth-century conditions: '"That the pretension to the allowance of universal uncontrolled freedom of action to every individual . . . are wholly inapplicable to the insular situation of this kingdom, and if allowed to prevail, will hasten the destruction of the social system so happily arranged in the existing form and substance of the British Constitution, established by law"'.[91] These artisans sought to preserve the old 'social system' with which they were familiar. What else should we expect

90. Chase 2000, p. 106.
91. Rule 1981, p. 213 citing the Select Committee on Petitions of Coventry Watchmakers, P.P. 1817, VI, p. 18.

of them? But it is noteworthy that they were aware that a system of 'universal uncontrolled freedom' was encroaching upon it.

Moreover, the growth of combination continued to gather momentum up until the repeal of the Combination Acts in 1824–5. In 1817, for example, Scottish colliers formed the Glasgow and Clydesdale Association of Operative Colliers, representing some two thousand colliers at 38 mines. In its rules, this national network of colliers openly stated its aim to fix wage rates and to exclude those who had not served apprenticeships. In October 1817 it merged with a similar combination in Ayrshire, which had recently seen some partially successful strikes. The leaders were quickly arrested under Scotland's own Combination Act (which had passed in the same year) and the union was dissolved, but this movement only foreshadowed a more impressive attempt at unionisation in 1824.[92]

The year 1818 brought a general thawing of the crisis: a good harvest meant an easing of food prices, *habeas corpus* was permanently restored on 1 March, and so peaceful was the situation in France that the four occupying powers decided to withdraw from their occupation of French fortresses at the Congress of Aix-la-Chapelle. Lord Liverpool took the opportunity to call for parliamentary elections a year ahead of schedule, only to see the opposition gain seats, riding a wave of indignation at the ministry's inability to stabilise the nation's finances.[93]

Even the protests of that year seemed orderly and tranquil. Observing a march by unemployed cotton spinners in Manchester, a local military commander commented that '"The peaceable demeanour of so many thousand unemployed men is not natural"'.[94] While this remark reflects the fact that Britain's rulers may have feared plebeian *order* more than plebeian *disorder*, coming from a military man it also suggests that what he had in mind was the semi-militarised character of the marchers. The Government was aware that unemployed soldiers had been involved in the Despard affair, the Spa Field Riots, and the risings at Pentrich and Huddersfield.[95]

In 1812, cotton textile workers in Lancashire had elected delegates from each mill to a central committee and launched a series of mass strike actions. In all there were four separate strikes by Manchester mule-spinners, by Stockport mule-spinners, by Stockport jenny spinners and by hand-loom weavers throughout the area. The 'Great Strike' was quickly joined by other artisans: 'hand-loom weavers, dyers, "bricksetters and their labourers", carpenters and joiners, glassworkers and

92. Campbell 1988, pp. 149–50 and Chase 2000, p. 83.

93. Turner 1999, p. 110.

94. Chase 2000, p. 104. Thompson (1991, p. 746) attributes the quote to General Byng. Perhaps these are one and the same person.

95. Gash 1978, p. 151. The use of banners and marching in step to music was also part of the Peterloo spectacle before the massacre.

colliers'.[96] Here was an instance of factory workers (albeit mule-spinners who still enjoyed a measure of control and independence within the factory setting) taking the lead in an industrial action. In 1816, when trade was slack and food prices were low, the mule-spinners had accepted a wage reduction. Now, in 1818, they demanded a restoration of their pre-1816 wages, which they claimed they had been promised. The employers had responded with the argument that as the spinners did not share in the risks of capital, they had no rights to the gains. In August, a 'Union of all Trades' known as the Philanthropic Society was formed. In September a meeting at Todmorden in West Riding received delegates from surrounding, counties who discussed ways to extend the union. In December, the Philanthropic Hercules emerged, representing between thirty and forty trades, in emulation of the Manchester union, led by the shipyard labour leader and Spencean John Gast. Gast's vision was to build the Hercules into a working man's parliament.[97] After seven weeks and the near exhaustion of the strike fund, the Manchester union collapsed, but only after its leaders had been arrested. Here, the full force of the Combination Acts was now felt, with prison sentences of one and two years being handed out to three of the strike's organisers. Mule-spinners returning to work had not only to accept the 1816 rates, but many were forced to sign a document foreswearing any future involvement with trade unions. Hundreds were blacklisted.[98] The Philanthropic Hercules in London survived longer, but the strikes of artisanal London did not compare in intensity with those of factory Manchester.

If Price wishes us to see not only the events of 1816–19, but the whole of the labour struggles into the 1840s as being shaped fundamentally by an artisanal outlook, how then to explain that the Great Strike of 1818 centred around mule-spinners striking for better wages in factories and combining in the action with artisans of all sorts? One spinner addressing the crowds spoke of the masters as 'a class of men unlike all other master tradesmen . . . ignorant, proud and tyrannical'.[99] What this spinner's address does, writes Thompson, 'is to itemize one after another the grievances felt by working people as to changes in the character of capitalist exploitation: the *rise* of a master class without traditional authority or obligations; the *growing* distance between master and man; the transparency of the exploitation at the source of their *new* wealth and power;

96. Chase 2000, p. 104.
97. Chase 2000, p. 137.
98. Rule 1986, pp. 271–2. Rule notes that despite the decline of their condition due to the enormous influx of workers dislocated from other fields of employment, the handloom weavers referred to themselves as 'an immense body of artisans'. The fact that the mule-spinners did not identify themselves as artisans is equally significant.
99. 'Address of a Journeyman Cotton Spinner', *Black Dwarf*, 30 September 1818, as quoted in Thompson 1991, pp. 218–21.

the loss of status and above all of independence for the worker, his *reduction* to total dependence on the master's instruments of production; the partiality of the law; the *disruption* of the traditional family economy; the discipline, monotony, hours and conditions of work; loss of leisure and amenities; the reduction of the man to the status of an "instrument"'.[100]

The emphasis in this quote is added to highlight Thompson's attention to and awareness that this was a *process* of transition; that conditions were *changing* from one state of affairs to another. Price himself cites the above passage and points out that the beneath the instability of the period was a struggle by working people 'to control or escape from the clutches of a dependence upon free market relations'.[101] Price's apparent notion that the modern working class was only made when it (or privileged and leading members of it) ceased in this struggle against the market is highly problematic.

The relative prosperity of 1818 encouraged speculative overproduction, leading to a slow-down in 1819. Calls for a return to the gold standard by landlords and manufacturers who sought a return to pre-war conditions were growing. A return to convertibility would allow the Government to reduce its dependence on high-interest borrowing, better manage debt payments and guarantee the security of government bonds. Secret committees were set up in both houses. On 6 May the reports from the committees, arguing in favour of a gradual restoration of convertibility, were presented to Parliament. In keeping with Liverpool's tactic of busying the Cabinet with ceremonial affairs and as much as possible out of policy matters, the Cabinet's members only received the reports two days *after* Parliament renewed them.[102] Parliament was soon besieged with petitions of protest. Many merchants and industrialists complained that the return to 'sound money' would contract the money-supply, increase the burden of debts and raise the unemployment rate.[103] The measure was also bitterly opposed by agriculturalists who had contracted debts during the boom years of the war and now complained that they would face burdensome interest rates on their loans. As it happened, thousands of tenant-farmers would be forced out of business over the next several years. Factory masters in the cotton industry, however, strongly

100. Thompson 1991, p. 221–2. Emphasis not found in the original.
101. Price 1986, p. 45.
102. Hilton 1988, p. 158.
103. A petition against the measure argued that it would '"tend to a forced, precipitate, and highly injurious contraction of the circulating medium of the country"', the consequences of which would '"be to add to the burthen of the public debt, greatly to increase the pressure of the taxes, to lower the value of all landed and commercial property, seriously to affect both public and private credit, to embarrass and reduce all the operations of agriculture, manufactures and commerce, and to throw out of employment a great proportion of the Industrious and laboring men of the community"': Spofford (ed.) 1879, p. 122.

backed the measure as being beneficial to the credit supply and exports.[104] The government had good reason to listen to the cotton masters; from 1816 to 1850, cotton manufactures accounted for between forty and fifty percent of all British exports. By 1835, Britain's cotton industry, which was concentrated in Lancashire, would account for 62 percent of all cotton spindles in the world. Some 864 innovations were patented for the cotton industry alone between 1750 and 1850.[105] The fortunes of 'King Cotton' had become a bellwether for the economy. 'Only agriculture had a comparable power, and that was visibly declining'.[106] The bill, which received royal assent on 2 July, provided for a gradual return to convertibility over the course of four years. The resumption of specie payments was only part of a larger plan for financial restructuring, which also included debt redemption, a reorganisation of the sinking fund, and measures to curb inflation. There remained the problem of paying for government and paying down the debt, and for this more new taxes and a further expansion of customs and excise meant more regressive taxation.[107] This part of the financial recovery plan was unlikely to garner much favour amongst working people and radical agitators.

While the lessening of economic pressure in 1818 had enabled a focus on industrial action, the failure of the Great Strike seemed to demonstrate that trade union action was by itself incapable of addressing the crisis. With the fall in prices in the 'bad year' of 1819, and a heightening of economic distress, mainly in the form of more widespread unemployment, the political campaign for reform took centre-stage once more. Most towns now had their own radical associations holding regular meetings, and in the Summer months held open-air assemblies in favour of reform. The Government was alarmed by reports of former soldiers leading drill practice in anticipation of parades, seeing in them more plans for an insurrection. A renewed round of harassment of the radical press and mobilising of conservative loyalists to denounce unpatriotic behaviour ensued. Radicals meeting on 12 July in Birmingham appointed a 'legislatory attorney' to represent their city at a national convention, prompting rumours of radical plans to organise an alternative parliament and spurring the Home Office to declare any such proceedings illegal.[108] The revolutionary black tailor and minister Robert Wedderburn, whose abolitionist journal *The Axe Laid Root* was reaching its intended audiences – slaves and slave owners – in the West Indies, held a meeting in London at which the question was put to those present whether the slave had the right to slay his master. The question '"was decided in Favour of the Slave

104. Briggs 1979, pp. 204–5.
105. King and Timmins 2001, p. 49.
106. Hobsbawm 1994, p. 54.
107. Turner 1999, pp. 131 and 171.
108. Turner 1999, pp. 115–17 and Briggs 1979, p. 208. As we shall see below, the Chartists followed through on this effort to organise an alternative parliament.

without a dissenting Voice, by a numerous and enlightened Assembly... Several Gentlemen declared their readiness to assist them"'.[109] For this, Wedderburn would serve the first of several prison terms after being tried for sedition. This increasing momentum of radical organising and this increasing tension between radicals and the Government forms the background of events leading up to the climax of Peterloo. Thompson explains it this way:

> Confronted by this swelling power, Old Corruption faced the alternatives of meeting the reformers with repression or concession. But concession, in 1819, would have meant concession to a largely working-class reform movement; the middle-class reformers were not yet strong enough (as they were in 1832) to offer a more moderate line of advance. This is why Peterloo took place.[110]

Thompson has stated unequivocally that '1819 was a rehearsal for 1832. In both years a revolution was possible (and in the second year it was very close)'.[111] Thompson has taken much criticism for his regular tendency to see the real possibility of revolution at such points of crisis. Since we are dealing with an *if*, the whole matter remains a hypothetical, but the question must also deal with the balance of revolutionary and counter-revolutionary forces. In other words, the more weight one gives to the threat to the Hanoverian state, the more weight one also grants to the virulence of the state's opposition to any attempts to challenge the new economic and political reality of the early nineteenth century. This virulence was most vividly demonstrated at Peterloo. To the authorities, the cost was acceptable. Even though the over-reaction by local authorities had sullied the preferred face of the government as a firm but not blood-thirsty authority, and had served to heightened class tensions to an uncomfortable level, '... the operational men on the spot had made their decision, had run personal risks to uphold order and the status quo, and the code demanded that they be supported'.[112] They were even publicly praised, whilst Earl Fitzwilliam was dismissed from his post as Lord Lieutenant of Yorkshire for speaking out against the massacre, 'an extremely rare event'.[113] No measures of contrition could be afforded. The Government did not even undertake an official inquiry into the events of that day, 'and inquests, trials and other efforts to attach responsibility to government, magistrates and yeomanry were entirely unsuccessful'.[114]

Fitzwilliam was but one of many voices of a more moderate persuasion who made a point of publicly condemning the massacre and calling for redress.

109. Fryer 1993, p. 50.
110. Thompson 1991, p. 749.
111. Thompson 1991, p. 737.
112. Fox 1985, p. 83.
113. Ibid.
114. Turner 1999, p. 118.

Among radicals, the mood was indignant. Meetings were held throughout the country. Extremists called for vengeance and armed revolt. The radical press flourished. The tensions between radical leaders were forgotten in a moment of perceived opportunity for action. Released on bail, Hunt received a hero's welcome in London in September. In November, Cobbett returned from America bearing the exhumed bones of Thomas Paine.[115]

In response to the popular outcry against the brutality of Peterloo, the Government responded only with more legislative repression, passing the Six Acts in November of 1819. The acts targeted the actions and methods of the radicals, banning unauthorised military training or drilling, empowering magistrates to seize weapons, speeding up court procedures by reducing opportunities for bail, banning assemblies of over fifty people, increasing the penalty for seditious libel and increasing the stamp duty on publications in an effort to curb the radical press. The army was also increased by ten thousand men.[116]

Thompson sees the Six Acts as the ministry's way of codifying and extending the repressive measures of 1794–5 and 1817. Derry argues that they were 'little more than gestures, a response to reassure backbench opinion in the House of Commons and conservative opinion in the country, rather than a prelude to a sustained reign of terror. Compared with what Metternich initiated in Austria and Germany they were tame indeed...'[117] Yet Peterloo had been brutal enough for some to question whether Britain was abandoning the rule of law and drifting toward the practices of 'arbitrary rule backed by overt coercion' so common in Europe.[118] It remains an open question whether the cycle of protest and repression would have continued to spiral out of control had the economic distress underlying the whole period of agitation not abated after 1820. As it was, the Six Acts may have helped to divert the energy of popular protest into religion on the one hand, with large Methodist revivals taking place in Lancashire and as far away as Cumberland, and back into trade unionism on the other.[119]

'A land of Roast Beef and Plum Pudding'

In 1780, the population of England and Wales had stood at 7.57 million; corn-output at 16,106,000 quarters and imports at 238,000 quarters. Forty years later the population was nearly twelve million (less than thirty percent of which was engaged in agriculture, forestry or fishing); corn output stood at over twenty-five

115. Turner 1999, pp. 117–18.
116. Breunig 1977, p. 207.
117. Thompson 1991, p. 768 and Derry 2001, p. 141.
118. Fox 1985, p. 83.
119. Briggs 1979, p. 212.

million quarters and imports at over two million quarters. Corn production had actually kept pace with population growth.[120] The disproportionate increase in food imports attests to the fact that with the boom in manufactured exports, Britons could afford to eat more than they had in the past. This, of course, did not mean that all Britons, or even the majority, were eating more or better food each year. But here was another contradiction for the working poor, for why should they earn less and eat less if the well-to-do were enjoying ever better fare? Across Europe, the year 1820 seemed to mark an end to the period of adjustment from war to peace. England's condition in 1820 has been compared with that of an armed camp, with 120,000 troops in uniform who had little by way of a mission other than to be on call to put down popular protests.[121] After five years, high food prices, low wages and widespread unemployment had stimulated the bitterness toward the government that lay beneath much of the agitation of those years – prices began to fall as employment levels rose. While the Liverpool administration could congratulate itself for the wisdom of returning to the gold standard, non-monetary factors such as increasing industrial productivity and a sound harvest contributed to economic recovery.[122] In the context of a return to economic stability and dozens of radical leaders arrested and waiting to stand trial, the radical movement was forced to undergo a reassessment of its methods and ideas.[123]

There were essentially three vectors at work. In this period, working people faced three options. The first option was to continue the struggle to preserve custom and the independence of the small producer. However, between the government's violent suppression of reformist gatherings and the failure of large-scale strikes, it was increasingly clear that something new had to be tried. The second option was to acquiesce, and work within the confines of the new order. Certainly this was what middle-class reformers like Burdett had been pursuing all along. This option presented a deep paradox for artisans because the new, capitalist order presented them with, at best, an insecure future, and already many trades had succumbed to the factory. The third option was to pursue an alternative future, an alternative order to capitalism. This was of course the most difficult option to consider, for it required imagination and a willingness to break with old habits. If only the House of Commons were made to express '"the real voice of the people"', said one Manchester reformer in 1816, speaking to shouts

120. Berg 1985, p. 94 and Rule 1986, p. 8. Rule points out that as early as 1801 the share of the population engaged in agriculture, then standing at 35.9 percent, was less than the combined share of the British population engaged in manufacturing (29.7 percent) and commerce (11.2 per cent).

121. Hay and Rogers 1997, p. 206.

122. Briggs 1979, p. 205.

123. Turner 1999, p. 106; Hay and Rogers 1997, p. 206

of applause, then '"England will again become, what it once was and what it ought to be, A land of Roast Beef and Plum Pudding"'.[124] This succinctly captures the artisan outlook prevalent at the time. But also noteworthy is the way the speaker folds past and future into one utopian vision of an England as it 'once was and ... ought to be'.

Not coincidentally, there were visionaries who came forward to offer an alternative conception of how society ought to be. Probably the most prominent self-styled prophet of the new order was Robert Owen. Owen was a Welshmen who had risen to be a factory manager in Manchester. In 1799, Owen had purchased the Arkwright mill run by his father-in-law David Dale at New Lanark, Scotland. He was subsequently so moved by the plight of pauper children in his factory that he was inspired to humanitarian and 'socialist' ideals, turning his factory into an experiment in collectivism combined with the pursuit of moral improvement. Owen's leadership among Scottish factory owners had helped to bring about the Factory Act of 1819, limiting the hours of work for factory children. Many Owenite societies were formed to disseminate Owen's ideas. In 1820, an Owenite society was founded in London and in 1821 it began publishing the *Economist*, which ran for a year, to be replaced later by the *Universal Philanthropist* (1823) and *The Advocate of the Working Classes* (1827). The 1820s was the decade in which the concept of socialism and the word itself emerged, and in turn it was socialists in France, viewing events in Britain as somehow analogous to the French Revolution, who gave us the term 'Industrial Revolution'.[125] Since the present study is an inquiry into the origins of industrial capitalism, not the origins of socialism, there is no space to consider Owen's philosophies and early experiments in utopian communism. Yet neither can the man be ignored, for as Thompson notes, despite his atheism, Owen's messianic message gained him a following that 'had the force of a secular religion'.[126] Thus one of the outlets of the momentum of radicalism building prior to Peterloo and the Six Acts was was not only into trade unionism, but also into Owen's particular brand of trade unionism and the co-operative movement. Owen's emphasis on personal morality shared much in common with religious reformers. Methodism, for example, was credited by Anglican clergymen for putting an end to such low cultural forms as public wrestling matches in Cornwall. In place of uncontrolled outbursts of public carnival, Methodists organised such events as 'Gipsey parties', funded from weekly contributions from workers' wages, topped off with employer contributions. Rule comments that 'Methodism poses one of the most difficult questions to answer for "social control" theory in which the forces of pressure are

124. As quoted in Collier 1965, p. 10, n. 4.
125. Hobsbawm 1994, pp. 43 and 255.
126. Thompson 1991, pp. 866–7.

seen as a successful external imposition of middle-class values upon the working classes'.[127] In the same way, Owen the reformer was no longer himself a member of the working class. As we shall see below, Owen's idealism and his top-down approach to organising would become deeply problematic for the trade union movement, even if Owen inspired some of its most audacious experiments.

As Richard Price has pointed out, Owenism incorporated a duality, even if it stood on the progressive end of the spectrum against more conservative or artisanal strains of working-class ideology. On the one hand, Owenism appealed to the effectively conservative, artisanal worldview, which identified the problem as unrestrained competition within the commercial sphere threatening to break down the standards of decency and social harmony associated with the independence of small producers. As Owen and Cobbett saw things, having failed to protect these bonds, these 'chains of connection', the nation's rulers had effectively abdicated their position of authority. On the other hand, Owenism provided:

> An alternative framework of organizing social relationships that spoke directly to the collectivist, co-operative themes of lower-class experience such as the local friendly society. It offered an analysis of economic development that integrated notions of justice and morality . . . in its social and recreational aspects, Owenism endeavoured to erect a community that would embody an area of cultural independence within which the fellowship of co-operation and morality could thrive.[128]

What Owenism did not provide, however, was any effective strategy for how such a benevolent community could be won in the midst of a fast-moving industrial capitalism. In retrospect, to point out that the reformers of this era vastly underestimated the dynamism of industrial capitalism is an understatement. But the same has been said of the political economists themselves.

'A ramshackle and cumbersome machinery of government'

On 29 January 1820, King George III, now completely blind and almost deaf, passed away after suffering in a state of complete madness for a decade. Liverpool's ministry was beset with a period of crisis. In the midst of this crisis, a group of extremists led by a veteran radical named Arthur Thistelwood saw their chance to pursue a plot to overthrow the Government. The conspirators had conducted secret meetings in a loft on Cato Street, where a variety of insurrectionary fantasies were entertained. One George Edwards hatched a plot to murder the Prime

127. Rule 1986, p. 220.
128. Price 1986, p. 55.

Minister and his Cabinet members at an official dinner, in hopes of stirring a general uprising. Once again, the whole affair was closely monitored by the Government. A false newspaper advertisement announced the dinner, and the conspirators were rounded up after a skirmish in which Thistlewood ran one of the Bow Street Runners through with his sword. Thistlewood and four others were hanged and five additional men transported.[129] The revelation that Edwards, who had proposed the specific action, had been a government *provocateur*, led to cries of entrapment. The ministry certainly wasted no time in arguing that the Cato Street Conspiracy confirmed the necessity of the Six Acts. The subsequent outbreak of a general strike in Glasgow, an armed rising in Huddersfield and a plot to attack the barracks at Sheffield also suggested to many that the Cato Street plotters were not acting in isolation.[130]

Scottish radicals had responded to Peterloo with a large demonstration of their own on 11 September, 1819. Bearing banners and with bands playing, a crowd of some 16,000 marched in orderly fashion to Meikleriggs Muir near Paisley, where they passed resolutions in favour of political reform. When a banner was seized by an official, the orderly gathering quickly developed from a scuffle into days of violent protest, with sympathetic protests in Glasgow and Bridgetown being put down by cavalry.[131] Later in 1819, Scottish radicals in Glasgow were holding weekly meetings to discuss plans to join a tax revolt in England, but on 15 January 1820 they began talking of instigating an insurrection by way of a general strike, in coordination with fellow radicals in Manchester. Presaging the Chartists, the conspirators talked of setting up a General Convention and a new constitution based on radical principles. Betrayed by an informer, their meeting of 22 February was raided by authorities, who made thirty arrests. Most of those arrested were artisans: weavers and cotton spinners. With these arrests being made on the heels of the Cato conspiracy, authorities in London, Manchester and Glasgow conferred over the possibility of a larger conspiracy. Meanwhile, in spite of the arrests, the Glasgow radicals set 1 April as the date for the commencement of the general strike.[132] On 31 March and 1 April, some 2,000 copies of an address to the people were printed and distributed through a city alehouse to be distributed throughout Glasgow and surrounding counties. The address was issued by a little-known 'Committee of Organisation for Forming a Provisional Government', which proclaimed that 'Liberty or Death is our motto' and called for direct action in demand of manhood suffrage and annual parliaments.[133] Subsequently, on

---

129. Thompson 1991, pp. 769–80.
130. Turner 1999, p. 119.
131. Straka 1972, p. 42; Davidson 2003, p. 145.
132. Thomis and Holt 1977, pp. 71–3.
133. Straka 1972, p. 43.

3 April, through a 'combination of persuasion and intimidation with spontaneous support' the radicals managed to bring 'virtually the whole of Glasgow's workers out on strike', as well as workers in 'a wide range of towns, villages and trades' within the economic region around Glasgow, but not beyond.[134] Pickets shut down mills in Glasgow while in Paisley three hundred men-in-arms shut down all the mills in the town.[135] While 'the overwhelming majority of strikers did not take up arms', writes Thomis: 'it is worth noting that a few did. From various accounts of activity in Glasgow and its suburbs, in Paisley and Kilbarchan in Renfrewshire, Duntocher and Kirkintilloch in Dunbartonshire, and Balfron in Stirlingshire, it is clear that pikes were being made and arms stolen, and that men were drilling'.

Thomis estimates the total number of men bearing arms as around fifteen hundred, with probably less than five hundred actually having paraded their weapons. And only two actual insurrections took place. Echoing Pentrich, a band of perhaps twenty to forty men under the leadership of 63-year-old James Wilson, a stocking-weaver, set out from Strathaven for Glasgow on the night before 6 April, only to be disappointed when they found that Glasgow was not in rebel hands. Another group of a few dozen rebels, led by the young weaver Andrew Hardie, left Glasgow for Stirlingshire in hopes of meeting a large party of fellow rebels at Condorrat, a weaving village, where they did in fact meet with a handful of men led by John Baird, also a weaver, before being found at Bonnymuir by a small contingent of Hussars. The rebels, numbering perhaps twenty-five, chose to stand and fight with pikes and a few pistols, rather than flee or surrender. There were casualties on both sides and when it was over, eighteen of the rebels were taken prisoner.[136] On 4 April, radicals from Glasgow raided the Carron ironworks near Falkirk in an apparent effort to recruit more rebels to the cause.[137] Between 6 and 9 April, most of the workers on strike were compelled to return to work, many accepting lower wages. At Greenhead, however, strikers held out against this pay cut for another six or seven weeks, returning to work only after their employer, Barr and Company, agreed to restore their wages to their original level.[138] Between the Strathaven and Bonnymuir risings, the violent demonstrations in Paisley and Kilsyth and a gaol attack at Greencock, 88 true bills of treason were issued but only 30 persons tried, with

---

134. Thomis and Holt 1977, p. 74.

135. Davidson 2003, p. 133.

136. Thomis and Holt 1977, p. 76; Davidson 2003, p. 134.

137. The raid on Carron ironworks has been widely interpreted as an attempt to seize cannonry (see Donnelly 1976, p. 32) but according to Thomis and Holt (1977, p. 76), this 'was a much later addition to the story of which there is no contemporary mention . . . it was manpower which the rebels sought'.

138. Thomis and Holt 1977, p. 76.

20 being transported and the three leaders: Wilson, Hardie and Baird, being executed.[139] This 'Radical War' of 1820[140] was rather unique in two respects. First, it may be the first attempt at a general strike in the history of capitalism, a distinction typically given to the strike of 1842. But rather than being a work action, that is, a strike for higher wages or better working conditions in the *economic* sphere, it was a strike with specifically *political* motivations. Moreover, as noted by Davidson, since the strike was intended to coincide with similar risings South of the Scottish border, these actions were intended to secure British objectives. Rather than arising out of Scottish nationalist sentiments, they were a response by artisanal workers in Scotland to capitalism's rapid advance in Scotland. As such, concludes Straka, 'they were not a grey mass unaware of their own existence, but an element which was gradually becoming conscious of its position and prepared to assert its collective interest'.[141]

In June, London was the scene of a different sort of mass protests when the spurned Queen Caroline returned from exile to claim her rights as Queen. The subdued voice of radicalism found a relatively safe cause to latch onto, taking the side of the wronged woman bravely 'standing up to a wicked king and corrupt ministers who had violated the people's liberty'.[142] A huge crowd of Londoners greeted her upon her return in June.[143] What ensued was a public debate about the status of women in the midst of Parliament's scrutinising the details of several of her alleged affairs. Throughout 1820, Cobbett wrote in defence of the Queen in his weekly *Register*, and even partook in the handling of her affairs. Parliament's subsequent withdrawal of a bill to strip Caroline of her rights as Queen was announced to the rejoicing of the London crowds. For a time it seemed as if the Caroline affair had revived mass protests. But if it may serve as a barometer of the real state of radicalism, in Manchester only a thousand souls turned out to mark the anniversary of Peterloo in August 1820.[144] When Caroline finally elected to accept a grant and a residence in early 1821, the public became disillusioned with their rebel. When Caroline sought to attend her husband's coronation at Westminster Abbey on 19 July 1821, demanding that she

139. Thomis and Holt 1977, pp. 76–7.
140. A term used by Straka 1970, p. 17.
141. Straka 1970, p. 18.
142. Turner 1999, p. 120.
143. Thompson 1991, p. 778.
144. Counting heads is not necessarily an accurate way of gauging the level of public support for causes. It is entirely likely that many who would have wished to commemorate Peterloo stayed home out of intimidation and fear of more official reprisals. Feiling (Feiling 1938, p. 305), notes that 'hardly an echo of Peterloo was audible in the elections' of March 1820, though this is less surprising. To take a different example, the coronation of George IV was heavily attended. But as Hay and Rogers (1997, p. 207) comment: 'What [royal jubilees] meant to the poor beyond a good meal and a bumper of beer is another matter'.

also be crowned, she was refused admittance. She fell ill the same day, dying on 7 August, certain in her belief that she had been poisoned. The coronation of the overweight and dissolute George IV, whose sole accomplishment aside from addictions and extramarital affairs was to have racked up a debt of 'an astonishing £630,000 in 1795 – just about half the money Britain was then paying to all the countries of Europe to carry on the war against France',[145] fittingly cost the taxpayers approximately £243,000, next to the £10,000 spent on his father's coronation.

Not only was George both unpopular and relatively inept as a politician, but the power and influence of the crown he was inheriting had been in steady decline for some time, thanks in large part to reforms started under the younger Pitt that had resulted in a major decline in the availability of funds for, and the use of, royal patronage.[146] Additionally, Liverpool enjoyed a situation in which, should the King dismiss his First Minister, the entire Cabinet would resign along with him, forcing a change of government. This became accepted convention after 1823. Collective appointment and collective resignation meant collective responsibility, and Liverpool believed this would strengthen the effectiveness of government. It also strengthened his hand in dealing with a sensitive and treacherous King.[147]

The end of the Caroline affair came as a mixed blessing for the ministry. The excitement of so many mass protests began to die down at long last, the Six Acts had successfully stymied the radical reformist movement and there were signs of economic recovery. But in the absence of such major political diversions, Cabinet members and various contending parties began to take a stronger interest in policy matters once more.

Liverpool was able to pull off two more major policy coups. The first matter arose out of the controversy between the merchants operating in the Baltic who petitioned the Government to abandon the preference for Canadian timber that had been established during the war, and merchants operating in Canada who called for government protection against the loss of their trade. Liverpool's strategy was to encourage the London merchants' petition calling for free trade, a policy which he generally supported. But he referred the matter to committees in both houses. In the Commons, he bypassed MP David Ricardo, the famous liberal political economist and champion of free trade recently elected to the Commons representing Portarlington, in favour of a junior Tory minister and political outsider named Thomas Wallace. The result was a declaration in favour

145. Sale 1996, p. 63.
146. Turner 1999, p. 52.
147. Derry 2001, p. 151–2 and Turner 1999, p. 50.

of free trade *in principle*, pleasing to the Baltic traders. In the Lords, he appointed the Marquis of Lansdowne, a doctrinaire free trader, and the committee recommended only that the duty on Baltic timber be reduced, which by falling short of openly advocating free trade, pleased the Canada traders. Grupp argues that this measure amounted to Liverpool's conversion to *laissez-faire*, and with the suspension of the Corn Laws in 1846 and the Navigation Laws in 1849, confirmed Britain's conversion to free trade.[148] Here again we can say that a milestone has been identified, but it is more symbolic than real, and but a small part of a much larger and more protracted process. The second matter, also arising in 1820, began when the backbench squires, who since 1816 had been clamouring for even greater protection than the 1815 Corn Law afforded, demanded their own select committee to consider the seriousness of agrarian distress and strengthen the Corn Laws. The fight lasted three rounds, with the ministry coming out on top each time. In the first committee the terms of the inquiry were restricted to a technicality. In the second committee, Liverpool now appointed the arch-liberal David Ricardo along with William Huskisson, knowing that they would be able to 'bamboozle the bumpkins' and produce a report favouring free trade over protection. When the agricultural protectionists demanded a third committee, Liverpool consented to the passage of the Importation Act of 1822, which amended the old Corn Law by tacking on additional duties to corn imports on a sliding scale, but with an added provision that the new law would not take effect until the 80s. threshold set out in the 1815 law was reached. By issuing orders in council to release bonded wheat from the warehouses in 1825 and 1826, Liverpool made sure that the threshold was never reached during his tenure, rendering the new measure moot.[149]

In 1821 the post-war contradictions, and the defensive tactics Liverpool had employed to deal with them, were catching up with him. The flip-side of his stringent efforts to keep the Cabinet out of policy-making had been his efforts to keep those ministers and officials he felt were competent enough to be involved in policy decisions *out* of the political limelight. But now he saw his own situation as being 'politically desperate, hated by the king, opposed by the Whigs and radicals, and winged by "a crossfire from Canning, Peel and the Grenville connexion". It was to do something about this crossfire that Liverpool set about the work of cabinet reconstruction'.[150] And this meant bringing the policy wonks into the public sphere of popular politics. This shift was partly driven by the

148. Hilton 1988, p. 158.
149. Hilton 1988, pp. 158–9.
150. Ibid., quoting a letter from Liverpool to Charles Bathurst, 29 December 1820, Liverpool Papers, B1., Add., MS 38288, fps. 386–8.

external pressures that were changing the nature of British politics. The post-war crisis inherited by Pitt in 1784 was dealt with mainly by political arrangements made outside the public view. Whichever faction or party governed had relatively little effect on the material lives of ordinary citizens at that time. Forty years later, British citizens were far more invested in and dependent upon market relations, and, therefore, more directly affected by economic policy, as we have attempted to explain. The Government itself was much more deeply entangled in financial markets in 1822, with £36 million out of an annual revenue intake of £55 million being swallowed up by debt charges alone.[151] Liverpool's first move was to strike a deal with the Grenvillites by offering a Cabinet position to Charles Watkin Williams-Wynn. Grenville himself did not join the Tory Government, but he consented to allowing his followers to do so. Few knew that Grenville had actually been counted among the members of Liverpool's informal 'little committee' for some time. Liverpool had now succeeded in reuniting the Pittites once again.[152] The stability of the administration was greatly improved. The Whigs were left with only 150 seats in the Commons under the leadership of Grey, who now moved to the left, more openly identifying with reform and other causes championed by the radicals. Over the next decade, the Tories would move to a more centrist position, seeking the respect of moderate opinion by playing up the virtues of competence and ministerial responsibility whilst continuing Pitt's work of reducing patronage, promoting trade and pursuing retrenchment and further financial reforms.[153] The vacancy of Home Secretary created by Sidmouth's resignation in January 1822 was filled by the appointment of the up-and-coming young High Anglican Sir Robert Peel Jr., the red-headed son of the famous cotton factory master. When Castlereagh (now the Marquess of Londonderry) committed suicide the following August, the vacancy of Foreign Secretary was filled by the appointment of George Canning. As Liverpool was serving in the Lords, Canning's oratory skills made him invaluable as leader of the House of Commons. Other young talent promoted into the cabinet included William Huskisson to head the Board of Trade and John Frederick Robinson to be Chancellor of the Exchequer. While Derry finds that the Cabinet reshuffle amounted to a 'superficial' move toward liberalism, in that any 'difference was one of character and temperament, rather than of policy',[154] Hilton argues that it was the prior ascendance of these 'liberal Tories' that made the shift away from the 'managerial' and behind-the-scenes approach of the 'high Tories' necessary. Their disagreement on this point may reflect two approaches

151. Gash 1978, p. 135–6.
152. Turner 1999, pp. 82 and 133.
153. Turner 1999, p. 147.
154. Derry 2001, pp. 147–8.

to the same problem. Significant as the 1820 reports announcing support for free trade were, they did not translate directly into policy, and politicians remained politicians rather than theorists. Ricardo as economist turned politician serves as the exception to prove the rule; doubly so, since he enjoyed little success as a politician. So Derry is right to stress the overall continuity of the Liverpool administration. But Hilton's emphasis on the differences in administrative style between high and liberal Tories speaks to an entirely different point, which is the overall transition from 'old corruption' and 'a ramshackle and cumbersome machine of government',[155] to a new ethic of professionalism and of 'civil service' and bureaucratic efficiency. What was driving this transition?

The legacy of the younger Pitt was far more influential than any of the teachings of political economy upon the state officials of post-war Britain, both in terms of his personal example of selfless service to the state and the agenda for reform that he had initiated but was forced to abandon when the war with France ensued. Even during the war Pitt had made significant headway in terms of reducing state expenditure on forms of patronage. Sinecures and reversions were cut and officials were offered salaries and superannuities in the place of fees and gratuities. The budget had grown from under £7.5 million per annum in the first quarter of the eighteenth century to nearly £30 million per annum during the French Wars, transforming the British state in terms of both its size and efficiency.[156] The number of public officials grew accordingly, especially during the French Wars when their numbers rose from 16,297 in 1797 to 24,598 in 1815. Since the bulk of the new taxation to pay for the war came from the expansion of regressive taxation, the largest part of this growth was in customs officials, an area where Pitt had made considerable headway in trimming patronage. But in other areas of expansion, such as armed services and transports, centralisation was still lacking and wasteful emoluments continued to expand. Peter Jupp associates the trend toward streamlining the operations of government in the interest of greater efficiency with the rise of officials who ostensibly came from outside the landed elite, 'men of exceptional talent or aptitude', with a 'high level of education coupled with a talent for business' whose qualification for office depended upon 'talent rather than on rank'.[157] To back up this claim, Jupp argues that despite the vast expansion of the peers in this period, their number rising from 195 in 1784 to 372 in 1830, a large share, if not the majority of the new peers, arose out of the military, the bureaucracy or the judiciary. Likewise, Jupp argues, the House of Commons saw an influx of 'self-made men ... merchants, bankers, and industrialists', who claimed 19 percent of all seats by 1820 and 22 percent by

155. Clarkson 1974, p. 18.
156. Harling and Mandler 1993, pp. 44–55.
157. Jupp 1990, pp. 64–5.

1830, and who made up about a quarter of the most active MPs. 'A new kind of politician began to make the running in the Commons', writes Jupp, leading '"a silent revolution", in the composition of the House'.[158] Jupp's method of distinguishing between these 'new men' and landed men has been challenged by Harling and Mandler, who point out that many of these supposedly self-made men actually held estates, and that in any event their being 'made' often depended upon their connections with the landed gentry and aristocracy.[159] Rather than seeing the landed interest as having to adapt to an influx of outsiders, they see a convergence of interests in which the landed class itself was gradually remade, whereby many landowners were simultaneously involved in trade, industry or the bureaucracy. Jupp's modernisation thesis implies that the move toward both larger and more efficient government was driven by a rising entrepreneurial class looking to overthrow the power of the landed oligarchy. Harling and Mandler reject the implication in Jupp's work that Britain experienced a 'virtual bourgeois revolution',[160] pointing out that the growth of the bureaucracy was fundamentally driven by Britain's engagement in a series of ever more expensive wars, with the share of the budget taken up by military spending and debt servicing combined never falling below 85 percent between 1700 and 1815, while spending on civil government *declined* over the same period from around ten to less than seven per cent. As such, the growth of the state was fundamentally driven by the war machine. Rather than seeing the Pittite movement for cheaper and more efficient government as driven by the growth of the bureaucracy or the rise of 'new men', Harling and Mandler argue that it was in fact a *reaction to* what was widely seen as an excessive growth of the budget during the French Wars, that included a considerable expansion of wasteful spending.

> The fiscal-military state was the ultimate casualty of the French wars because the public was no longer willing to pay the price of maintaining it. An assortment of political interests from popular-radicals to country gentlemen felt that the high tax regime necessitated by decades of practically continuous warfare had not only bled them dry but [had also channelled] a good deal of their tax money [into areas] they deemed wasteful and inefficient. The postwar Tory ministries embarked on a program of financial and administrative reform both because they themselves saw minimal government as a fillip to executive authority in an age when almost no one could find any redeeming social value in 'big government'.... Retrenchment, rather than an extension of government responsibilities, accounts for a good deal of the increase in the length

158. Jupp 1990, pp. 67–73, quoting Aspinall 1952, p. xxx.
159. Harling and Mandler 1993, pp. 61–3.
160. Harling and Mandler 1993, p. 46.

> of parliamentary sessions since the opposition began to contest in detail items of government expenditure in the House of Commons.... How did professionalism and efficiency manifest themselves? In the fiscal sphere, they did so through the effort to keep the state credit-worthy and to preserve the tax base while substantially reducing revenue and spending.[161]

For twenty years after 1822, the budget in Britain continued to decline, in sharp contrast with France, whose budget grew by fifty per cent over the same period.[162]

This debate has had little to say about the role of capitalism in the British state's conversion to *laissez-faire* and free trade. The work of Harling and Mandler provides clear and objective pressures, both political and economic, that compelled the programme of retrenchment, which in turn steered state policy in the direction of *laissez-faire*. In rejecting what they call the 'social interpretation', they appear to minimise the role played by ideology, specifically the doctrines of political economy. But ideologies generally operate in concert with objective social and economic pressures and interests, and political economy was no exception. The doctrines of free trade and *laissez-faire* were more salient than ever before in the context of forced retrenchment and a general popular outcry against excessive state expenditure. According to John Davis, economic historians in general tend to share 'the view that the state played little or no useful part in the development of the early European industrial economies'.[163] Harling and Mandler state that they 'see no reason to doubt H.C.G. Matthew's conclusion that "no industrial society can ever have existed in which the state played a smaller role than that of the United Kingdom in the 1860s"'.[164] The 1860s comes only after forty and more years of retrenchment and conversion to *laissez-faire*, but what of the period during the Napoleonic Wars, when state spending reached its apex? According to Jupp:

> In both war and peace, the state was drawn into regulating all aspects of the economy – agricultural, financial, commercial, industrial – to a degree that was unprecedented... there was an undoubted increase in the role of the state in the fields of industrial relations, law and order, factory conditions, poverty, and even madhouses. Our knowledge on these subjects is at the moment slim because research has traditionally been concentrated on developments after 1830... But there is sufficient information to suggest that it was in this period

161. Harling and Mandler 1993, pp. 52–3.
162. Harling and Mandler 1993, p. 59. Sweden and Belgium are cited as following the French pattern, while Austria-Hungary is noted as the only major power that also saw prolonged post-war deflation.
163. Davis 1990, p. 63.
164. Harling and Mandler 1993, p. 60, citing Matthew 1986, p. 169.

> that the state's role as a regulator and supervisor in these fields was firmly established.[165]

Jupp's claim that the state played an *increasing* role in the economy rests on citing parliamentary legislation: the Combination Acts, the Poor Laws, The Thames Police Act of 1800, the Metropolitan Police Act of 1829 and so on. Certainly Jupp is not talking about government expenditure in the economy. Excepting the impact which wartime contracting had in stimulating certain industries, we have already seen that government civil expenditure remained minimal throughout the eighteenth century, and decreased as a percentage of the budget in the early nineteenth century. So we have a contradiction. On the one hand, the British Government made minimal expenditure on the economy. On the other hand, even if government legislation brought about the decline of customary forms of economic regulation in agriculture, industry and trade, Parliament continued to exert its authority over economic affairs through a range of legislative measures that were certainly even more comprehensive and more detailed than those of its Tudor forebears. If we are to solve this apparent riddle, we must ask: what was it that the emerging capitalist economy required of the state?

'A prey to be plundered': the reversal of the combination laws

The Industrial Revolution was not presided over by a strictly passive and non-interventionist state. As we have seen, in abolishing the Tudor legislation which upheld the customary rights of direct producers, the state engaged in the active suppression of resistance to the imposition of capitalist control over production, first in agriculture and then in manufactures. In so doing, the state ensured the successful transition from peasant agriculture to agrarian-capitalist farming and from customary manufacturing to capitalist industry. As Harling and Mandler point out, Tory governments from Pitt to Peel 'thought of the state as the ultimate safeguard of property and, thus, of the social hierarchy that rested on its possession'.[166] In the seventeenth and eighteenth centuries, the British state actively promoted and supported the elaboration of a framework for an agrarian-capitalist economy, especially through parliamentary enclosures, while at the same time engaging in an imperialist project that was driven by the long-standing rules and logic of the 'game' of imperialist geopolitical rivalry. In its origins, this imperialist project had nothing to do with industrial or agrarian capitalism; its rules and logic were very much rooted in the non-capitalist international framework of state relations. Presided over by a landed aristocracy that

165. Jupp 1990, p. 60.
166. Harling and Mandler 1993, p. 68.

was busy consolidating a new form of surplus-appropriation in the form of agrarian capitalism, and preoccupied with consolidating and expanding its revenue-base through customs and excise by seeking to expand international trade along the lines of traditional imperialist and 'mercantilist' practice, the British state initially played the role of neutral arbiter in the struggle over customary versus market regulation of manufacturing. Eventually the state not only abandoned the defence of craftsmen and of custom, but engaged in active suppression of resistance to incipient capitalist industrialisation. In the process, a new type of industrial-capitalist state began to emerge, one that was in many respects a police state with new repressive laws and new methods of policing.

The same British state overseeing the transition to industrial capitalism now belonged to an alliance of reactionary, aristocratic régimes, known as the Quintuple Alliance after France's admission in 1818. But the fact that Britain was effectively the only capitalist power within the alliance, and that it was in general hostile to the extra-economic forms of property still predominant in the reactionary states, made for some sharp policy disagreements. At the Congress of Verona in 1822, Canning stated that Britain would not tolerate the subsequent invasion of Spain by France to crush the liberal revolutionaries in Madrid and restore absolutism under Ferdinand VII, but at the same time had no desire actually to prosecute a war.[167] While Castlereagh voiced disapproval at Austria's moves to put down liberal uprisings in Naples and Piedmont, measured support for the Spanish liberals and, to the delight of the merchant community, open support for the emerging independent states of Latin America – the United Kingdom would recognise Mexico, Buenos Aires, Colombia and the Kingdom of Brazil in 1825 – it was Wellington who represented the United Kingdom in Verona. Wellington made no distinction between revolutionaries, radicals and reformers and saw reaction as the end for which the great wars with France had been fought. Commenting on the situation in Greece, where Greek nationalists were up in arms for independence from Turkey, Wellington commented that Greek independence 'would be founded "on the principles of modern democracy and therefore inimical to this country"'.[168]

Greece, Italy and Spain were not the only places where nationalism was rearing its head. A year after what would be the first in a series of potato blights to hit Ireland, the Catholic Association was founded in Dublin in 1823. The

167. Briggs 1979, pp. 346–7.
168. As quoted in Feiling 1938, pp. 330–1, no citation given. The French intervention in Spain became awkward for Britain when Rafael del Riego y Nuñez, the leader of the Spanish liberals, was shot and then hung 'on a gallows fifty feet high' at La Cebada square in Madrid, his widow subsequently taking refuge in England. The emergence of liberal movements mixed with nationalist aspirations marked the beginning of a new type of struggle on the Continent that would culminate in the revolutionary year of 1848.

Association quickly became the 'legislature of Irish Catholics; it held open session, collected "rent" in every parish, and enjoined national discipline that they might concentrate against the Orangemen. Its programme extended far beyond Emancipation, to destroy the Anglican Church and to repeal the Union'.[169] Its leader, Daniel O'Connell, was arrested for comparing himself to Simón Bolívar. Parliament sought to put a lid on rising tensions with and within Ireland by passing a bill to suppress secret societies.[170] Greek independence might be consistent with liberal notions of liberty, but Irish independence posed a security risk. And besides, the Irish stood to benefit, as the argument ran, under the tutelage of the advanced British state.

While Harling and Mandler are not wrong to argue that the conversion of the state to a project of *laissez-faire* liberalism came about in large part as a reaction to the excessive wartime budgets, their account says nothing about *how* Britain's agrarian-capitalist economy made such an unprecedented expansion of state finances possible, giving Britain a unique edge over its enemies. Nor do they have anything to say about how *capitalism* made such a conversion to a laissez-faire state possible. To assert, as they do, that the propertied classes relied upon the state as the ultimate guarantor of their property actually tells us nothing new. The same could have been said of propertied nobles in ancient Mesopotamia, Egypt or Rome. The critical aspect of the Pittite revolution is that it represented the first active campaign within the British state to begin clearing away extra-economic forms of property, allowing for the conversion of even state officials to reliance upon wages and ultimately upon the market. This programme was only possible because capitalism afforded an alternative to politically-constituted property in the form of a mode of surplus-extraction that was uniquely dependent upon market exchange. Not only were labourers in Britain becoming increasingly dependent upon the market for a living wage with which to secure the necessaries of life, but landlords now drew their rents from the action of tenant-farmers who were themselves dependent upon the market. Tenant-farmers were now engaged in a competition for access to land through a market in land leases, and were also dependent upon the market for their inputs, for labour and for the sale of their produce in order to realise a profit. At the level of bare essentials, the same principles applied to factory masters. Since customary regulations interfered with their access to free wage labour and barred the full conversion of markets, estates and units of manufacturing in production to the control of capital – meaning that these forms of extra-economic property stood in the way of the ability to transform production in response to market

169. Feiling 1938, p. 336.
170. Feiling 1938, pp. 336–7.

imperatives in the interest of increasing profits – landlords, tenant-farmers and industrialists supported their abolition.

As in all state societies, the propertied required a state to guarantee their property. That is really the fundamental role of the state. But what do they specifically require under conditions of capitalism? Specifically, they require the guarantee of economic *contract*, rather than the guarantee of some state-sanctioned or state-regulated privilege or monopoly. The Master and Servant Act of 1823 provides a useful illustration of the gradual process by which the state was transforming into the role of an enforcer of contracts between employer and employee. When most of the trade-regulating provisions of 5 Elizabeth were overturned in 1814, the authors of the repealing legislation were careful to leave unmolested that part of the Tudor code which made it an offence for the labourer to leave work unfinished. Sixteenth-century labour contracts were based upon the completion of discrete tasks, not hourly wages. In 1766, the penalty for leaving work unfinished was increased in some cases to three months' hard labour. In the Master and Servant Act of 1823 (the same year as a minority of silk masters managed – against a petition campaign that had gathered the signatures of eleven thousand silk-weavers – to overturn the Spitalfields Acts of 1773, 1792 and 1811 that had provided extra-economic wage and working conditions protection to silk-weavers),[171] employers managed not only to get Parliament to reaffirm the three-month rule, but to allow the alternative punishments of deducting from wages or sacking the employee. At the individual level, this provided a huge disincentive for partaking in strike actions. What is more, the act recognised the validity of verbal contracts, set out procedures for summary justice and made actions against workers a matter of criminal law requiring magistrates to issue not summonses but warrants.[172] By 1823, 'the concept of "service" no longer related to the fulfilment

---

171. Leeson 1979, p. 110. In 1773 (as noted above, Chapter Ten, pp. 530–1), Parliament had responded to a violent dispute between masters and workmen by yielding to the demands of the journeymen and fixing wages. The journeymen were emboldened by this and actually managed at times thereafter to win *advances* of wages from employers who complied lest their looms be destroyed. The act was amended in 1792 to include weavers working upon mixed fabrics and in 1811 to include female silk-weavers. The argument for overturning these acts in 1823–4 was that profitability had declined, owing to fixed wages scaring off investors. Business 'improved' thereafter, aided in part by the introduction of the Jacquard loom from France, which was initially only popular among Spitalfields workers, allowing them to fetch higher wages and to dispense with the need for a child attendant at the loom (Knight 1851, pp. 394–5 and Berg 1985, p. 247). We note in passing that the Jacquard loom, being one of France's greatest contributions to the industrial machinery of the era, was perfectly suited for domestic production and while producing a superior product to earlier looms, provided little advantage in terms of speeding up production or lowering costs. In other words, it was a piece of machinery that reflected the absence of capitalist relations of production in French manufacturing.

172. Chase 2000, pp. 110–11. Actions against employers, however, still came only under civil law. 'It is hardly exaggerating', writes Chase, 'to say that this was the single most

of an obligation to complete a particular task but had embraced the whole contractual relationship between employer and employee'.[173] The class bias of the act is unmistakeable, given the harshness of the penalties. And the criminalisation of breach of contract could be taken to mean that employers won more than just state enforcement of contract, even a degree of state patronage. But this should serve as a reminder that there has never been, nor will there ever be, a purely economic or purely capitalist economy in which politics plays no role, for the development and expansion of the capitalist market, however much it may be increasingly unregulated, always requires the state's backing for private property to exist in the first place.

Would retrenchment leading to *laissez-faire* have worked in the 1820s in France? In Belgium? In Holland? The answer is doubtful, for even though by this time these countries saw some beginnings of a factory system modelled on that in capitalist Britain, extra-economic forms of property continued to dominate the economy in these societies. Only in Britain had capitalism advanced to the point where policies of economic liberalism could begin to be applied successfully. This is not to say that by this time the social relation of capital was fully entrenched in Britain; there were still all kinds of ways in which the economy was not purely market-driven. With the labour process in most lines of manufacturing still under the control of the labourers, the greater part of the long struggle by capital to achieve the real subsumption of labour and a capitalist labour market still lay ahead. Of course, in retrospect, we know that this goal was largely achieved (although because labour is a fictitious commodity, capital has not achieved the total subsumption of labour even today, nor can it ever). But to contemporaries in early eighteenth-century Britain it was far from clear that the owners of capital would go on to prevail.

The significance of the Pentrich rising and the other various insurrectionary schemes we have covered is that the Government took the rhetoric of these would be Levellers quite seriously. We are less inclined than E.P. Thompson is to see 1792 or 1819 or 1832 as moments when the Hanoverian régime nearly fell to a revolutionary uprising, even if these were the points at which the régime was the most susceptible. In the unlikely scenario that the Hanoverian régime had fallen, the new state-power bloc would most likely have been made up of some kind of alliance between libertarian radicals and liberal-minded landowners, possibly with a seat at the table for trade unionists. Trade unionists most likely remained on the outside looking in, because among their ranks were radicals who had revived the ideas of Winstanley and the Diggers in advocating a

---

serious legal issue that confronted labour in the nineteenth century. Yet few historians notice it and systematic study of the law's application is conspicuously lacking…'

173. Chase 2000, p. 111.

redistribution of property, namely the Spenceans, standing somewhat to the left of those who at least saw the need for political regulation of the economy to protect small, independent producers from the depredations of the market (largely true of Owenism). Radical reformers drawn from independent shopkeepers and urban professionals gravitated toward libertarianism, and at the level of ideology shared a greater affinity to *laissez-faireists* not only in opposing big government but in seeing government's primary role as one of safeguarding personal liberty and personal property. This general divide within radicalism was crucial for Liverpool's administration in the wake of Peterloo. Retrenchment and the programme of rendering government cheap and efficient was not only welcomed but demanded by radical-libertarian reformers as well as wealthy landowners, merchants and manufacturers, all of whom saw state intervention in the economy in defence of private property as both natural and just, and for whom the tendency toward levelling or socialism was therefore anathema. When one considers that by 1822, out of a total government income of £55 million, an entire £36 million was being paid out to cover 'debt-charges, Sinking Fund contributions and the dead-weight of service half-pay and pensions', one gets an idea of just how fortunate it was for the Tories that some of the most influential spokespersons for the radical opposition, like William Cobbett, were rabid advocates of retrenchment, since circumstance offered little choice in the matter.

For the sake of making a simple point, let us suppose that the Spenceans or Owenites had managed to swing public opinion around to their point of view and take power over the British Government at this point in time. How would they have dealt with such a massive fiscal crisis? Assuming they enjoyed sufficient public support to carry it off, they would have undoubtedly cancelled much of the Government's debt to wealthy placemen and treated such debts as odious. They might also have confiscated many of the largest estates either to sell them off or to employ them in production in order to subsidise the Government. It may be argued that the propertied classes would have responded violently to such an attempt at outright appropriation of their property, prompting violence on the part of the revolutionaries as well, and further, that a levelling project such as this would have led to economic and social crisis as the dynamic of capitalism would have been seriously compromised or even terminated. There is plenty of room for debate over such hypotheticals. The point here is that the national debt is all too often taken-for-granted as a 'natural' function of the economy, rather than a political arrangement. But there is nothing inherently natural about enormous fortunes, especially those made by private citizens lending to governments borrowing against the collateral of future taxation.

The effects of retrenchment were felt far and wide. In East Anglia, while many farmers had been employing threshing-machines since they had come into use in the region around 1805, reapers were only just beginning to appear. In spite of critics who pointed out that with the abundance of rural labour the machines offered no direct financial advantage; in the context of a labour surplus, manual and machine threshing were comparable in cost. *The Times* noted another disincentive when the editors wrote in October that '"farmers do not consider thrashing machines of much advantage; seeing that they throw the labourers out of work, and consequently on the parish"'.[174] But the thresher allowed the farmer to get his produce to market faster.[175] The harvest of 1821 was interrupted by heavy rains. Families that relied on harvest-time employment faced a hard winter, and they blamed the threshing-machines. Between 13 February and 21 December 1822, a total of some fifty-two threshing-machines as well as some mole ploughs were destroyed in Norfolk and Suffolk, concentrated along the border region. The East Anglian protestors of 1822 appear to have been single-minded in their intent to destroy threshing-machines. The only two protestors who were executed, Noah Peak and George Fortis, had also set fire to the property of a farmer named John Kent. At trial, they stated that their motive against Kent was that he had been '"so hard hearted as to reduce the allowance of the poor"'.[176] This reflects the contradictory situation faced by poor law commissioners operating in the context of retrenchment, who were under pressure to reduce costs during a period of high unemployment. There was no evidence of a larger conspiracy, although Peak and Fortis were veterans of Waterloo, and this had raised some level of suspicion. The majority of the 123 protesters arrested were given short gaol sentences.[177]

Retrenchment may have factored into the decision to repeal the Combination Acts in 1824 as well, but the fact that they were universally defied by workers along with the Government's general lack of interest in enforcing them, were probably the overriding factors. The way in which the acts were set up, effectively leaving employers to fend for themselves in terms of enforcement, with government interference being relatively rare, speaks not only to a certain level of disinterestedness on the part of the ruling landed elite with regard to industrial labour relations, but more importantly to the way in which the state was moving from regulation to arbitration, as we have discussed above. For the Liverpool ministry, dealing with constant complaints from employers combined with

174. *The Times*, 14 October 1830, as quoted in Hobsbawm and Rudé 1968, p. 100.

175. Wells 1988, p. 105.

176. Muskett (1984, p. 8) notes that the regions where the protests took place had been subject to recent, late enclosure, but follows reports by contemporary authorities, which discounted any role that enclosures may have played in sparking the protests. While it appears clear that the threshing-machine was the focus of the discontent: 1) it is less likely that threshing-machines would have been introduced in the absence of enclosure (that is, on open fields) and 2) Muskett does not appear to consider ongoing disgruntlement at enclosure as possibly playing an indirect role.

177. Rule 1986, p. 357; Wells 1988, pp. 116–17 and Archer 2000, pp. 15–16.

such widespread defiance must have been seen as a nuisance adding unnecessary stress to an existing crisis. The Combination Acts had been intended to strengthen the common-law prohibition against forming a conspiracy in restraint of trade. But in the context of a vast expansion of wage labour under conditions of price competition, with employers seeking to lower the cost of production by keeping wages low, and the abandonment of paying wages according to the rate that was customary for the given trade, it was becoming increasingly obvious that both workers and their employers were compelled to pursue their interests collectively, and that should the laws stay on the books, the state would either be drawn inexorably into an endless series of regional wage battles, where it was expected to break up combinations, or would continue to suffer the embarrassment of having a law on the books which it could not enforce. Or both. In other words, the law against combinations was increasingly coming to be seen as a way in which the state was not deregulating the economy, but increasingly distorting it precisely by attempting to regulate wage negotiations. From the perspective of workers, the Combination Acts appeared to make plain the convergence of the interests of landlords and factory owners, both property owners whose interests now appeared to be clearly opposed to the interests of labour. The traditions of craftsmen stretched back to time immemorial. The Combination Acts had cast the time-honoured associations of the 'honourable' tradesmen into the role of being enemies of the state. Resisting and defying them was a point of honour. The effect which the Combination Acts had upon trade unionism was not to stamp it out but to stimulate 'crucial changes' made during the intense period 'when every power – industrial and legal – was ranged against them'.[178] The observance of 'secrecy and ritual became more deeply ingrained'.[179] While parochial unions organised and recruited locally and in secret, the more difficult work of forming unions between different trades and in different towns was also advancing slowly. The local union might now find itself able to sustain a strike longer with support from the strike fund of another trade or a union in the same trade from another town. Leeson estimates that whereas in 1799 and 1800 some seventeen trades were involved in networks of tramping and interregional contact, by 1824 virtually all of some twenty-eight major trades were now involved in issuing papers to allow members to go tramping in search of work in other towns, a supremely useful tactic for evading prosecution under the acts. By 1824, despite there being perhaps hundreds in gaol for violating the acts, the existence of extended networks of secret trade union activity made simultaneous action against all of them simply impossible.[180] Of course, in many trades,

178. Leeson 1979, p. 104.
179. Chase 2000, p. 85.
180. Leeson 1979, pp. 110–15.

the masters had already acquiesced to the inoperability of the laws, as in the case of the London printers, who after a bitter dispute in 1810 had agreed never again to invoke the law against combinations.[181]

Alexander Galloway, the successful engineering employer and one-time LCS member who had led the employers' charge in repealing the apprenticeship clauses of 5 Elizabeth in 1814, reflected ten years later that this act of repeal had '"broke the neck of all combinations, because then the excluding party were so overwhelmed by new men that we could do without them"'.[182] Yet in many trades, especially those where the transmission of manual skills was still critical to the production process, apprenticeship stayed in the by-laws and its continued observance rested on the strength of the workers' organisations. The London shipwrights, for example, had maintained the practice of apprenticeship and this aided their success in resisting moves by the shipowners to throw the trade open to an unregulated market for labour and products. '"The men are more naturally in the power of the master if entry is not limited"', one journeyman stated before a parliamentary committee in 1824.[183] This is the obverse of the employers' claim that unless combinations were banned, they were at the mercy of their workmen. Apprenticeship survived because artisan craft labour survived, and because as the artisans had argued before Parliament in 1814, the completion of apprenticeship was seen as conferring a special right of property. This sentiment is perfectly reflected in a petition from the silk-weavers calling for the restoration of the Spitalfields Acts:

> All persons whose incomes are derived from landed property, the funds, tythes, law-fees, and from monopolies of every kind, are subject to, and protected by legislative or conventional regulations... as the Artisan's power of labour is his only property, it is irreconcilable with every sense of justice, and of common-right, that the incomes and property of all other classes should be protected, whilst the Artisans and Labourers alone are left a prey to be plundered by needy, rapacious, and unprincipled Employers.[184]

181. Moher 1988, pp. 88–9.

182. Rule 1981, p. 118. Strangely, in a later book Rule (1986, p. 147) references this quote only to 'an engineering employer,' not referring to Galloway directly and replacing 'broke the neck' with 'broke the back'.

183. As quoted in Leeson 1979, p. 109.

184. *The Petition of the Journeymen Broad Silk Weavers of Spitalfields, and its vicinity, for a 'Wages Protection Bill'*, pp. 6–7 as quoted in Chase 2000, p. 106. Chase guesses the date of the petition to be 1828. Rule (1981, p. 106) offers another quote, this time from a cotton weaver speaking during a depression in his trade: '"The weaver's qualifications may be considered as his property and support. It is as real property to him as buildings and land are to others"'. Elsewhere, Rule (1987, p. 106) notes that by 1823 weavers were ready to admit that they no longer belonged to the 'aristocracy of labour' but continued

The use of the phrase 'all other classes' is noteworthy. What possession of the 'mysteries' of the trade by way of serving an apprenticeship conferred in turn was respectability within the trade. This type of respectability of the traditional and honourable trades should not be confused with the sense of respectability that would later come in the Victorian era with the adoption of middle-class values by skilled workers, which we shall discuss below. Artisan respectability was far more a matter of honour. When Parliament overturned the Spitalfields Acts that had fixed the wages of silk-weavers in 1824, some silk-weavers chose starvation over the shame of accepting poor relief. Distaste for charity, says Chase, was second only to the universal desire among artisans 'to avoid the indignity of a pauper's grave, provision against which was the commonest motive for joining a friendly society'.[185] By 1824, there were still more than four times as many hand-loom weavers (two hundred and ten thousand) as power-weavers (forty-five thousand) in Britain.[186] Even if we add the one hundred and twenty-two thousand factory spinners, it is clear that in textiles, artisan labour continued to predominate within the still highly decentralised textile industry. The number of hand-loom weavers would peak at nearly a quarter of a million before the 1820s were over, falling 'to just over 100,000 by the early 1840s, to little more than 50,000 starving wretches by the middle 1850s'.[187] This decline of artisan labour after a period of expansion serves as the essential background to the labour struggles of the second quarter of the nineteenth century.

Francis Place, the tailor and one-time LCS member who had become a firm supporter of the idea of a free labour market, was the force behind the bill to repeal the Combination Acts in 1824, which he quietly guided through Parliament with the support of the Scottish MP Joseph Hume and the Scottish economist J.R. McCulloch (the leading disciple of David Ricardo). In the pages of the *Edinburgh Review* they put forward their case, rooted in the wisdom of political economy. The heart of the argument was that unions were incapable of forcing wages above their 'natural' level, since wages were now determined by competition in the marketplace. Since the market itself would keep wages in check, the combination laws were unnecessary. There were plenty of other laws to prosecute trade unionists who resorted to violent tactics, and thus the combination laws were doubly superfluous. Unions, they argued, would only be able to affect the price of labour when it fell below its natural price. But trade unionists had yet to discover this fact because they were prone to strike more often due to their

to reaffirm that, as in other crafts, apprenticeship conferred '"property rights"... and were properly supported by "internal regulations"'.

185. Chase 2000, pp. 106–7.
186. Berg 1985, p. 259.
187. Hobsbawm 1986, p. 64.

correct perception that the combination laws were biased against them and fundamentally unjust. Repeal would thus *decrease* the frequency of trade actions.[188] Central to Place's thinking was his own experience as the son of an illiterate baker who during his upbringing had excelled mainly in '"drinking, whoring, gaming, fishing and fighting"'.[189] Sitting before the sympathetic Committee on Artisans and Machinery in February 1824, Place put forward the idea that respectability among craftsmen was something that had only come about in the course of his lifetime, citing the decline in drinking. Certainly one of the added motivations behind the desire of employers to check union activity was the all-too common tendency toward drinking and other rough behaviour. But what a sell! According to Place, repeal would not only result in a decline in union activity, but also, by implication, the rough and intemperate behaviours associated with it. While not all the witnesses before the committees concurred with Place's argument, there was sufficient support from exasperated manufacturers to see that the measure passed quickly.[190] What is more, the bill not only repealed the Combination Acts, but it also specifically exempted trade unionists from prosecution for attempting to form a conspiracy in restraint of trade.[191]

One reason why Parliament may have felt sufficiently at ease about labour relations to pass such a generous measure was that it had only recently tightened up labour legislation with the new provisions under the Master and Servant Act. Another reason may have been the trade boom of 1824. The years 1824 to 1825 were the culminating years of an overall improvement in economic conditions. Conditions improved in the industrial districts as the trade recovery meant more jobs, rising prices in key commodities such as iron and cheap and abundant credit leading to a wave of speculative investment in the building or expansion of cotton mills.[192] The Government felt confident enough about economic conditions to repeal laws banning the export of wool, of certain machinery and the emigration of skilled labourers. In March 1825, the law restricting the formation of joint-stock companies (the so-called 'Bubble Act') was also lifted. These measures were all in keeping with Huskisson and Robinson's programme of economic liberalisation through reform of the tariff system, customs and excise and the Navigation Acts. The largest free-trade area in the world was expanded further by removing all remaining tariffs between Britain and Ireland, and in a nod toward Scotland, the English could now buy Scottish whisky. Duties on the London coal supply were lifted. The salt excise was reduced and then abolished.

---

188. Rule 1986, p. 285.
189. Rule 1981, p. 205.
190. Rule 1981, pp. 205–6; Moher 1988, p. 93.
191. Thompson 1991, p. 564; Moher 1988, p. 91.
192. Briggs 1979, p. 211 and Collier 1965, p. 11.

Duties on imported iron and silk were reduced, although a level of 'defensible protection' for industry was preserved. At the height of the boom, investment funds poured out of the country, with £150 million flowing to newly independent states in Latin America.[193] The Corn Law, however, was left untouched, and 'stood out as a glaring offence', marking the widening gap between the ruling landed class and the growing strength of merchants and manufacturers.[194]

Contrary to the predictions Francis Place had made in making the case for repeal, however, what actually ensued in the wake of the repeal of the Combination Laws was a wave of strikes and wage negotiations that often included non-unionists across the sphere of manufactures. Manchester's spinners went on strike and sought a county-wide union. They also sent delegates to support a strike by cotton spinners in Glasgow. The Glasgow strike failed but unionising efforts moved forward.[195] In August, the Thames Shipwrights' Provident Union emerged, with John Gast as its secretary, boasting membership within nearly all mercantile yards and even some naval yards, and launching a 'great strike' that lasted well into the next year. In West Riding, the weaver and comber societies quickly amalgamated into a single union. By August, a strike for higher wages had engulfed the region. Wielding the threat of introducing machinery, the employers refused to recognise the union until November, when the strikers settled for union recognition over wage increases.[196]

From late 1824 to 1826, Scottish colliers launched a wave of strikes aimed at securing higher wages and upholding apprenticeship rules. The practice of legal serfdom in Scottish collieries had continued down to its abolition in 1799. As in the Northeast of England after the bond was discontinued, the result was not a free labour market, but a space for 'new channels of social mediation ... the structure of the industry allowed for a deep implantation of the tradition and practice of control and autonomy in the labour process which reinforced the importance of the dependencies masters wielded above ground'.[197] Mine owners introduced schools and tied housing and tommy shops in this period. In Scotland, the Combination Laws had only taken effect with a legal decision in a case involving a Weavers' Association in 1813, and were used to break the previously mentioned effort by Scottish colliers in 1817 to form a national union. With repeal and boom conditions driving up the price of coal, colliers quickly

193. Feiling 1938, p. 340.
194. Feiling 1938, pp. 318–21.
195. Rule 1986, p. 290.
196. Chase 2000, p. 126–7. The strikers also 'launched an abortive effort to establish a combers' co-operative and "developed an intellectual critique of the political economy of laissez-faire"' (quoting Smith 1981, pp. 74–6). Increasingly, trade unions were producing not just organisers, but social critics and lecturers thinking at the level of economic theory as well.
197. Price 1986, p. 77.

began resurrecting the network of unions aborted in 1817,[198] establishing even more elaborate rules of operation. By December, some eighty collieries were subscribed to what was to become the Associated Colliers of Scotland. By January 1825, Colliers at Renfrewshire had won reduced hours and an eighty per cent pay rise. Other local unions were quick to follow their example. The strikers were blamed for causing an artificial spike in the price of coal now travelling along the recently completed Union Canal to Glasgow and Edinburgh. At Redding, employers brought in 'blacklegs' to replace the colliers over the Winter and in April several of the union's delegates were arrested, leading to the collapse of the local strike and a fall in the price of coal, despite considerable expenditure by the union out of collective strike funds. But the union did not collapse, and a subsequent strike at Dunlop over the summer of 1825 succeeded in winning a pay rise for the colliers.[199]

While the outbreak of strikes may be seen in part as the celebration of a victory by trade unionists, any credit given directly to trade unionists themselves for the repeal measure is dubious. In fact, Place was careful to rush through his bill, introduced by Hume, before Parliament could consider a bill written by Gravenor Henson and George White, which would have repealed 44 statutes. Place considered the Gravenor-White bill 'absurd', as indeed it was if viewed through the lens of political economy. What it represented was 'the last and most comprehensive attempt to legislate in defence of a traditional artisan way of life'.[200] Certainly there is room for a debate as to whether Place actually usurped a measure which might have led to considerable improvements for working people, but it seems far more likely that had such a measure been introduced, there would have been no repeal at all. In either event, Campbell is certainly correct to point out that, contrary to the view that the Combination Acts were repealed in response to worker agitation, 'it would be truer to say that those laws were nearly *re*-imposed in 1825 due to the threatening bearing of the artisanate'.[201]

As the first anniversary of the repeal neared, employers had seen enough. They cited the Scottish colliers' strikes in particular as virtually tantamount to an insurrection. '"No sooner were the laws repealed"', howled the editors of

198. See above, p. 638.

199. Campbell 1988, p. 143–55. It is interesting how machinery appears to have brokered no controversy in any of these strikes.

200. Haynes 1988, p. 243. The Gravenor-Henson bill 'was a comprehensive measure of reform of the master and servant legislation to include provision for written contracts; written recording of tools and materials lent out; of rates and pay and so on. Henson and White saw this aspect as more significant than removing combination legislation which they thought little used...' Chase (2000, pp. 110–11) similarly argues that the importance of the Master and Servant Act has not been adequately addressed by historians.

201. Campbell 1988, p. 93 (emphasis not found in the original). Campbell attributes such a view to Marx, the Webbs and the Hammonds.

Blackwoods Magazine, '"than combinations filled with the worst spirit sprung up in all quarters... they thought it was in their interest to place the masters under the most grinding tyranny. It was now for the servant to command, and the master to obey"'.[202] They cited the handful of violent episodes in their call for a re-imposition of the Combination Laws. The Government joined and supported this counter-attack, appointing a new committee that was expected to find in favour of the employers' call for reversing the repeal. Francis Place now set about a new campaign of seeking to prevent the undoing of his efforts the year before. What resulted was a compromise measure passed in the Summer of 1825. The common law of conspiracy in restraint of trade was made to apply to unions once more, but the right of workers to combine in order to press for higher wages, shorter hours and better working conditions was retained.

Once it was clear that the repeal of the Combination Laws would not itself be repealed, trade unionists could at last formalise what had heretofore appeared to the outside world as only underground tramping networks. They began to turn their attention to improving administrative efficiency by giving uniformity to their rule books, appointing regular officers and, as in the case of the brushmakers in 1826, centralising their accounting methods and bringing them up to date. Accounting was of course crucial to the ability to strike. Thus the ability for unions to formalise their administrative practices surely played an important role in enabling the strikes that followed repeal.

To a degree, what had changed was more apparent than real, meaning that the appearance of legality for unions disguised the continuation of a whole range of legal weaponry that employers could still deploy against striking employees, not least laws against oath-taking,[203] while at the same time the ability of unions successfully to win wage increases or better working conditions still depended, as it had before, on the level of organisation, timing, and economic conditions. Price sees very little change in all of this, arguing that a radical break with eighteenth-century labour law only came about with the statutes of the 1870s.[204] But certainly there was a palpable feeling among trade unionists that the long night of their illegality had ended, and what we should seek to understand is what this meant in terms of what actually was and was not changed by the state's (admittedly circumscribed) recognition of the trade unions' right to exist. One of the signs of a change was the emergence of a newspaper organised by trade unionists. The *Trades' Newspaper* emerged in July 1825, shortly after the passage of the amended Combination Laws Repeal Act.

202. *Blackwoods Magazine*, 18 (1825), pp. 24–5, as quoted in Rule 1986, p. 286.
203. Harling 2001, p. 98.
204. Price 1986, p. 40.

Economic conditions had taken a major turn for the worse in mid-1825 as the boom began to collapse, putting strikers on the defensive and causing a loss of momentum. The crisis worsened as Winter approached, with a string of bank-failures and bankruptcies bringing about not only an economic crisis, but a new round of crisis for the state. William Huskisson, the liberal Tory who had been appointed president of the Board of Trade in 1823, was now widely blamed for imposing his 'theories' of liberalisation of commerce on the nation, despite the fact that these reforms had only proceeded cautiously in the face of merchants, manufacturers and shippers who felt they might lose money under conditions of freer trade.[205] Some economic historians have since treated the boom and collapse of the mid-1820s as 'the first truly modern cyclical boom in British economic history'.[206] In the context of the present study, what is significant about the collapse of 1825–6 is that, unlike the depression of 1816–19, and most prior downturns, this downturn does not appear to have been precipitated by a failed harvest, the harvests of 1824 and 1825 having been good ones. Even if it was more a financial and commercial than industrial crisis (though we cannot discount the degree to which the strike wave itself may contributed to the crisis by causing prices to rise and profits to fall), the downturn may represent a point at which fluctuations of boom and bust, which were certainly not unknown under conditions of agrarian capitalism, are no longer dominated by forces within the agrarian economy.

For contemporaries, the downturn from late 1825, which lasted until the end of the decade, stimulated fresh debate about the factory system. As the conditions of artisanal labour for weavers and even for cloth dressers declined into misery, and as conditions in many factories improved, factory work was beginning to gain appeal. Mule-spinners in Lancashire earned high wages of 40*s*. or more per week. The work that factories offered to factory hands was steadier than that offered to domestic outworkers, who were the first to be let go during downturns. And many factory workers were anxious to show off their earning power by wearing bright clothes, investing in furniture, drinking tea with sugar and eating white bread. These may not have compensated for such occupational hazards as accidents with machinery, trade-related diseases like potter's rot, long hours of work under harsh supervision, payment by truck and other 'deductions'

205. Briggs 1979, p. 221; Turner 1999, p. 143.

206. Briggs 1979, p. 211. Out of nine theorists listed by Lloyd-Jones (1990, p. 83, Table 1), only two (Mendel and De Wolf) cite 1825 as the 'upper turning point' of the first Kondratieff wave, meaning a long-term oscillation between upturns and downturns in the economy. The first wave is associated with the onset of the Industrial Revolution and the cotton boom, the second with the railroad boom. The other seven theorists put the upper point at somewhere between 1808 and 1817. 1824–5 happens to be the year in which Britain saw its first (albeit tiny) railway boom, when the first seventy miles of rails were opened.

from wages, the lax morals and sexual advances toward female employees by male factory owners or the pollution that in the 1820s began to blacken the fascias of the buildings in the factory towns, but for those like the hand-loom weavers suffering under greater poverty and insecurity, it might have seemed better to suffer and enjoy such rewards than to suffer and enjoy none at all.[207] This would have been particularly true in situations like that which prevailed in West Riding in the 1820s, where domestic producers: 'were complaining loudly of decline in their trade and shifts in the organization pattern away from cottage production to proto-factories and factories, from independence to dependence on a few large manufacturers and merchants ... what was really striking here was that the factory was superimposed on a co-existing domestic industry in which people had begun to suffer hardship by the 1820s as industrial involution augured structural unemployment, longer hours for less pay and disinvestment'.[208]

This was precisely the context in which the Bradford wool-combers' strike suffered defeat in the aftermath of the economic downturn of 1825.

The downturn also spelled eventual defeat for the Associated Colliers of Scotland. By late 1825, the strike still held, with colliers in control of the supply at many collieries and thus continuing to drive the price of coal upward. The situation approached a state of syndicalism, with new members being sworn in with 'the grips' and as 'brethren'. The shared experience of the collier's fathers having been collier-serfs probably conditioned the colliers to think of their positions of employment as a form of hereditary birthright, the rewards of which they were now reaping. By April and May of 1826, economic depression meant that employers could draw on a large pool of unemployed workers to replace the unionists with 'blacklegs', and the colliers' 'temporary mastery of the coal trade was soon broken'.[209] However, the Scottish colliers continued to assert their control over the labour process through solidarity and independent action. Apprenticeship rules persisted among the Scottish colliers into the 1880s,[210] surpassing the survival of apprenticeship among the coachmakers, iron founders and London compositors by some thirty years.[211]

---

207. King and Timmins 2001, pp. 53–7.

208. King and Timmins 2001, p. 48. The passage cited is taken out of the specific context of a discussion of how 'proto-industrialisation' could lead to de-industrialisation – in this example, even *as* the factory system was being introduced. This provides yet another example of why the use of the term 'proto-industrialisation' is entirely problematic.

209. Campbell 1988, pp. 155–8.

210. Beyond that, 'resolutions for high entry fees to exclude the unskilled from the mines was still being passed at Scottish Miners' Federation conferences as late as 1911' (Campbell 1988, pp. 158).

211. Apprenticeship finally ending in these trades between 1848 and 1857. See Leeson 1979, p. 111.

In Lancashire, after the defeat of strikes at Hyde, Preston, Stockport and Oldham in early 1825, the economic slump brought a wave of protests and bouts of machine-breaking by distressed hand-loom weavers alongside strikes by cotton-spinners protesting against wage-cuts in 'Manchester, Ashton, Stockport, Bolton and Oldham, all of which were defeated'.[212] By early 1826, most hand-loom weavers were probably out of work, and perhaps half of those who did have work were working only half time. Wages had fallen to a miserable six shillings a week. The Weavers Union Society of Blackburn wrote to the Home Secretary '"in the unadorned language of British mechanics"', noting that seven thousand were unemployed in Blackburn alone, pleading: '"Were a humane man, Sir, to visit the dwellings of four-fifths of the weavers and see the miserable pittance, which sixteen hours of labour can procure, divided between the parents and the starving little ones, he would sicken at the sight and blush for the patience of humanity"'.[213] On 24 April 1826, a crowd of a thousand disgruntled hand-loom weavers demanding living wages and an end to the Corn Laws gathered bearing 'pikes, cudgels and sledgehammers' near Accrington and marched upon a nearby mill where they destroyed 60 power-looms, sparking a wave of machine-breaking reminiscent of high Luddism in which some 21 factories were attacked and 1,139 power-looms destroyed. An army officer wrote to the Home Secretary on 26 April, describing how a crowd of three thousand smashed power-looms in three mills at Haslingden. The protestors responded to the reading of the Riot Act by pelting the militia with stones, prompting return fire, which killed six. It '"is to be feared from that incessant firing"', wrote the officer:

> which was kept up for more than a quarter of an hour, that a considerable number must have been wounded. Between 500 and 600 shots were fired. The populace then dispersed gradually, but with the avowed intention of returning with an overbearing force. They were supplied mostly with bludgeons, clubs, etc., but no arms were observed. The obstinacy and determination of the rioters was most extraordinary and such as I could not have credited had I not witnessed it myself.[214]

The officer's account suggests that this was not Luddism, with its pre-emptive strategies aimed at successfully intimidating masters into submission. This was a whole community on the brink of starvation. In subsequent days, facing the usual pattern of community silence frustrating arrests, the authorities managed to end the disturbance by 'disappearing' many of the leaders from their beds at

---

212. Rule 1986, p. 291.
213. As quoted in Aspin 1995, p. 67; no citation given.
214. As quoted in Aspin 1995, p. 69; no citation given.

night. In general, the rising proved futile. While a number of manufacturers had agreed to return to paying standard wages for out-weaving, this promise did not hold. Moreover, employers were reimbursed by the government and quickly had their power-looms up and running again. The assizes to follow mixed severity and mercy – of the 65 arrested, 12 of them being women, 35 were sentenced to death by hanging but had their sentences commuted, ten finally being transported and the other 25 being sent to gaol.[215] Yet conditions for the hand-loom weavers continued to deteriorate to such a point that the local manufacturers sent an appeal to Huskisson, endorsing the weavers' statement and urging him to act. In his reply, Huskisson called it vain to '"attempt to interpose the authority of the law between the labourer and his employer in regulating the demand for labour and the price to be paid for it"'.[216] Here was the voice of political economy speaking through the government.

Conclusion

It was in the aftermath of the defeated strikes in Lancashire that John Doherty, a local trade union leader, analysed the failure of all the Lancashire strikes since the Great Strike of 1818 and decided that independent strikes by local unions were doomed because the local strike fund was too quickly exhausted. Doherty proposed that the remedy lay in trade federation and building a centralised strike fund to allow support to flow to the locality where it was needed, when it was needed and for a longer duration. This strategy would later be put into practice by the National Association for the Protection of Labour (NAPL). 'Only very gradually did local control give way to centralisation of funds, while rotation of leadership among the branches was only slowly replaced during the 1830s and 1840s'.[217] But by the late 1820s, the trend towards trade federations, or *trades* unions, was clear.

At the same time, new ways of thinking about society were emerging out of the ranks of the working class. From November 1825, the *Trades Newspaper* published the work of the radical economist Thomas Hodgskin. In his book *Labour Defended against the Claims of Capital*, Hodgskin developed the view, pioneered by Cobbett and Thelwall, that labour was the sole source of all wealth, seeing 'parasitic capitalists' as denying labourers the full value of their work, thus putting the wage relation and the labour process at the centre of his thinking. Although continuing to focus upon unequal exchange as the source of economic

215. Johnson 2004, p. 35 and Archer 2000, pp. 54–5.
216. As quoted in Aspin 1995, p. 70; no reference cited.
217. Rule 1988, p. 18.

injustice, Hodgskin was highly influential and his thinking reflected and articulated a general trend toward recognising the need to defend customary worker-control over the labour process as being 'as central and as shared an issue as that of apprenticeship had long been'.[218]

On the other side of the wage relation, more than one author has noted the 'strange absence of management theory' to guide the thinking of capitalist employers in this period.[219] Price finds it curious that 'the first industrial nation failed to develop a distinctive managerial ethos or ethic' and even more curious that political economy, 'the one area where one might expect to find an alternative body of belief – was generally silent' on important issues such as control over the labour process, the breaking down of skills into discrete tasks or how to keep workers in regular attendance at work.[220] Yet this seems to treat early capitalists in an anachronistic fashion, transporting them out of their own time instead of seeing them as products of their time. Employers certainly pushed for the Combination Acts and the repeal of the Tudor statutes, but we must be careful not to simply reduce them to the living embodiment of free markets and capital whilst treating artisans as the living embodiment of custom. The 'field of force' exerted by custom, which E.P. Thompson discusses, was not restricted to relations within and among labourers after 1814, any more than the repeal of 5 Elizabeth simply terminated the force of custom in trade. Social norms are by nature extra-economic; what they affect most is *behaviour*. And even if the behaviour of capitalist employers was increasingly subject to compulsions generated by market competition, this did not make factory owners or tenant-farmers immune to the influence of customary understandings of how the workplace should operate, as we have seen above in any number of cases where employers so easily capitulated to the demands of protesting employees, often under the least duress. King and Timmins offer the example of David Whitehead of Cowpe, Lancashire, who

> was caught up in the riots of 1826, when workers from other local mills, fearful of their future because of mechanization, broke windows and forced his workers out on strike. During the mid- and late 1820s he watched his workers become ever poorer both because of their own imprudence and because market conditions obliged him to pare wages to the bone. In better times he

---

218. Rule 1986, pp. 288–9. Other thinkers of this period mentioned by Rule are Bray, Thompson, Lovett, Gast and the Owenites who broke with Owen's own class-collaborationist proposals. Chase 2000, p. 123.

219. Haynes 1988, p. 251 quoting Pollard 1965, p. 159. The latter notes that although by 1830 there were 'well-defined groups of managers in many industries', it remained the case that there was, as yet, 'hardly a managerial profession as such'.

220. Price 1986, pp. 35–8.

> lamented their tendency to luxury and their seeming mental block on the concept of saving for the future. However, ultimately he was a paternalistic employer, providing a subsidized shop and education for children, and giving away substantial sums in charity on a regular basis.[221]

Workers and their masters did, after all, share the same social setting, and in this instance the same social origins. Whitehead himself began as a pauper, but by the 1840s would be living like a prince. The fact that he shared the same social origins as his workers might seem to explain his relative benevolence, but he was far from being the only benevolent master. The social distance between workers and masters was certainly greater in factories than in the workshop, but not as great as the distance between workers and those landed gentlemen owning huge estates and whose tiny social sphere of elites was isolated from the rest of society. If working-class economists in 1825 were only beginning to appreciate the value of labour and the importance of control over the labour process, perhaps the same was true of 'bourgeois' economists as well. And if that is so, then surely politicians were no further ahead. The Tories were only tendentiously venturing into the uncharted waters of modern free trade. And was it not still a form of paternalism toward employers for the state to rush in a cadre of dragoons every time a factory owner paying starvation wages was threatened by a crowd of angry workers?

The mid-1820s seem to have presented all sides with the lesson that the old methods were no longer working. For employers, relying on the state's coercive powers alone would never inculcate habits of 'general obedience and consent to the rhythm of capitalist production' among their workers. For workers, sporadic, localised protests and strikes had achieved only rare victories, most temporary, and a chain of bitter defeats. And for the landed oligarchy, the cyclical application of repression in response to each social crisis was only serving as a method of postponement. With the pace of economic life under an emerging industrial capitalism accelerating the rate of social change, with the bulk of social relations only recently coming into a state of market dependence, the future for Britons had never been more uncertain. But its outlines were beginning to take shape.

221. King and Timmins 2001, p. 369.

Chapter Thirteen
Reform and the Oligarchy

> I have just been to Scotland and Lancashire. I have made as careful a study as I can and can accurately describe the state of society in these areas. As for the industrial aspect, you can imagine I felt only one thing, admiration – they make machines in this country as we plant cabbages in ours . . . They are afraid of nothing, so plentiful are funds; they raze hills, fill in valleys, to open up communications they dig tunnels under towns and they don't consider such things worthy of mention . . . [However . . .] The physical condition of the working class is very uneven.
>
> Gustave d'Eichthal, French Sociologist writing from Britain in 1828[1]

The unevenness noted by this astonished visitor from France was intensified by an ongoing economic downturn. Poor harvests in 1826 and 1827 compounded the financial crisis. The boom of 1824 had led to a condition of excess capacity in the factories. The fall in profits was so severe that 'no new mills were built in Manchester between 1825 and 1833'.[2] Urban expansion, and the building of row houses for factory workers, however, was at an all-time high. Across Lancashire, the condition of the hand-loom weavers continued to be one of desperation, wages falling as low as 4*s*. per week

1. D'Eichthal 1977, p. 7.
2. Collier 1965, p. 12.

for those who could find work.[3] In West Riding, a strike by the combined union of weavers and wool-combers ('croppers') resulted in collapse, marking for the croppers the end to over a century of trade union activity.[4] In the countryside, the poor rates had doubled, with an estimated eight hundred and fifty thousand receiving poor relief, half of them in the agrarian South East.[5] The rapid increase in population meant that there were more young couples and children in Britain than at almost any other time.[6] This was reflected in the factories, where children under 14 comprised thirteen percent of all factory operatives, children aged between 15 and 18 comprised twelve percent and women formed thirteen percent.[7] Against the background of distress lasting into the 1830s, the Tory Party of Pitt and Liverpool fractured, while radicalism enjoyed a revival.[8]

High politics

Tragedy at the outset of 1827 marked a turning point in politics. On 5 January 1827, Prince Frederick, the presumptive heir to the throne – later immortalised and pilloried for eternity in nursery rhyme as 'the grand old Duke of York' – died of dropsy. Forty-three days later, on 17 February, Lord Liverpool suffered a stroke and was paralysed. He would die the following year. George Canning, whose 'golden tongue' had served to keep the Commons in line with the ministry's agenda, succeeded as Prime Minister. As debate on the issues of corn and Catholics ensued in March, sharp differences amongst the Tories emerged, with a particular animosity between the 'high' Tory Wellington and the 'liberal' Tory Canning, symbolically at least representing a split within the Tory party between the old-school aristocracy and those among the landed classes who read the political economists, supported the liberalisation of commerce and were more inclined to accept the necessity of piecemeal reform. Wellington, Peel and other prominent 'high' Tories resigned rather than serve under Canning, infuriating George IV, who saw this as an act of supreme disloyalty to the Crown. What it reflected was the increasing importance of party feeling and ministerial independence. After taking office on 1 March, Canning reached out to Lansdowne in the hopes of forming a new coalition government with the Whigs. Canning, who had caught a chill at the funeral of Prince Frederick from which he never

3. Aspin 1995, p. 72, citing the *Liverpool Commercial Chronicle*.
4. Chase 2000, p. 127.
5. Feiling 1938, p. 374.
6. Hobsbawm 1994, p. 208.
7. Deane and Cole 1969, p. 294.
8. Turner 1999, pp. 169, 122. The character of radicalism throughout the 1820s had taken on greater airs of 'respectability', with greater involvement by radicals in philanthropic causes such as promoting 'improved' education.

recovered, died on 8 August from the effects of a cold and overwork, passing the ministry to John Frederick Robinson, now Viscount Goderich. He would serve only a short term, during which Britain was drawn into the conflict in Greece, joining France and Russia in helping the Greeks to score a victory over the Turks at the Battle of Navarino in October. Incapable of managing the Lords, Goderich resigned in January. The ministry then passed to a national hero, the vainglorious Wellington. In a letter of congratulations from Austria, Metternich wrote that good had triumphed over evil.[9] Where Canning had sent British troops to Portugal in support of the Liberals in 1826, Wellington withdrew them, thereby allowing Dom Miguel to restore absolutism. He withdrew from engagement with France, thereby allowing the reactionary governments of Charles X and Nicholas I to establish closer ties. The Canningites were appalled.[10]

In May, the Whigs enjoyed a resurgence based on improved popularity with Dissenters when Parliament passed a bill introduced in February by Lord Russell for the repeal of the Test and Corporation Acts.[11] This represented a first step toward a break with the constitution of 1688 and emancipation for Catholics, The measure also exposed the weakness of Wellington's ministry, which lacked the support of the Canningites. It infuriated the 'Ultras', the staunchest supporters of the Anglican Church among the landed elite, who blamed Wellington and Peel for failing to properly manage the Commons, and allowing for the special relationship between the Government and the Anglican Church to be compromised. Wellington declared he would not allow measures for Catholic emancipation to move forward. The Ultras were not mollified by a revision to the Corn Laws in 1828; the decision to amend the laws had already been decided before the 1826 elections. The new law allowed for grain imports to resume by lowering the price threshold to 64*s*., whilst at the same time introducing a new sliding scale in order to maintain high prices for English grain. However, by causing dramatic fluctuations in grain prices during a period of high unemployment, the sliding scale drew a storm of angry protest from workers and industrialists. On 19 May a measure that would have enfranchised Manchester and Birmingham by transferring the seats from two rotten boroughs was defeated in the Commons, having been bitterly opposed by the Ultras and leading to further division in the Cabinet, with the resignation of Huskisson arising out of the matter. Peel

9. Feiling 1938, p. 363.
10. Briggs 1979, p. 350.
11. Turner 1999, pp. 147 and 159–60; Harling 2001, p. 80. The measure repealed the Test Act of 1673 and the Corporation Act of 1661, which respectively had barred anyone not accepting Anglican communion from holding office or being recognised as a member of a chartered town.

would later complain over the Ultras' wearisome '"obstruction over each rotten borough"'.[12]

Refusing enfranchisement for Manchester and insisting upon protection in the midst of a general trend towards free trade only served to widen the rift between popular-radicalism and the aristocracy. Working-class radicals talked increasingly of building independent unions and co-operatives. During a carpet-weavers' strike at Kidderminster, a 'Union of Unions' was proposed, while in London, John Gast led regular meetings of representatives of the London trades, all part of the 'General Association'.[13] Builders, carpenters and bricklayers were also moving toward a national union. Robert Owen, returning from the United States, where his experiment in communitarian living at New Harmony, Indiana had ended in failure, found his following stronger than ever. The increasing frustration over the failure of strikes to achieve their objective, combined with the trend toward trade federation, made for a historical moment in which even some of Owen's sceptics were prepared to listen to his personal doctrine of overcoming the machine and capitalism through worker co-operation.

Ireland was also caught up not only in economic distress but civil and religious strife as well. When Vesey Fitzgerald, the Irish Protestant member from Clare currently serving in Huskisson's former role as President of the Board of Trade, lost his seat to Daniel O'Connell, who was a Catholic and was therefore not allowed to be seated in Parliament, the long-standing grievance of Irish Catholics at being granted what was effectively limited citizenship in the Act of Union of 1801 came to the fore. Against the wishes of the Younger Pitt, George III had refused to agree to full emancipation for Irish Catholics, and this created 'an anomalous situation... in which Catholics had the right to vote – if they possessed the requisite property qualification – but could not sit in parliament itself, could become barristers, but not King's Counsel or judges, and could serve in the army and navy, but not attain the rank of general or admiral'.[14] Several motions to grant Catholic emancipation had passed in the Commons only to be defeated in the Lords, most recently Burdett's bill of 8 May, which had cleared the Commons by just six votes.

With the state of unrest in Ireland approaching something of an insurrection, Home Secretary Peel, who had served as Irish Chief Secretary from 1812–18, concluded that circumstances had made it necessary to grant some form of Catholic relief. Peel was deeply conflicted, as he personally opposed emancipation, and had already lost credibility with the Ultras over the repeal of the Test

12. Feiling 1938, p. 387, no citation given. The two boroughs in question were Penryn and East Retford.
13. Chase 2000, p. 129.
14. Jenkins 1999, p. 10.

and Corporation Acts the year before. He probably also understood that even though the matter cut across party lines, if there was one issue that had served to keep the Tories in office throughout the Liverpool years it was the Catholic question, since majority opinion in England opposed relief. Protestant zeal and anti-Catholic sentiment had gained momentum in the 1820s, bringing with it a 'godliness unknown to Walpolean England... making family prayers a part of country-house custom, or firing politicians like Liverpool or Grant to champion church-building and foreign missions'.[15] What is more, upon his accession, George IV, taking after his father after all, had made up his mind that he was firmly opposed to any lifting of the restrictions on Catholics. Approached by Wellington and Peel on the matter, the King threatened to replace the ministry, but ultimately relented. Debates in Parliament amidst increasing agitation out-of-doors were equally bitter. What eventually passed with large majorities in both houses was a compromise measure which lifted restrictions on Catholics in return for O'Connell's agreement to abolish the Catholic Association, and a rolling back of democracy in Ireland by withdrawing the vote that had been granted to 40*s*. freeholders under Pitt in 1793. Peel and Wellington were never to be forgiven by the Ultras for steering this matter through Parliament. They changed their tactics to supporting reform in the interest of weakening the cabinet. The stage was now set for the ministry to collapse and for the consideration of further reform measures that might not have come forward so soon.[16]

In Summer 1829, conditions in the textile districts were as volatile as they had been in 1826, and there were rumours that the distressed hand-loom weavers would once again launch an attack on power-looms. The power-loom continued to make progress, with 55,000 in operation by 1829, while hand-looms had fallen in number slightly from a around a quarter of a million to two hundred and twenty-five thousand.[17] Hand-loom weavers' wages had fallen to absurd lows: between 1*s*. 1½*d*. and 2*s*. 4½*d*. per week in Burnley, with thousands living on two or three pence a day at Colne. When strikes were called by the mule-spinners, they were accompanied by violence and machine-breaking. One factory master, T. Ashton, was shot in the heart and his assailant was never found. The firm of Horsfall and Garnett, whose Edisford Mill had been attacked in 1826, actually chose to build a moat around the mill in order to protect it from protesters.[18] Before the strikes, which were called in Manchester, Stockport, Ashton and Stalybridge, the mule-spinners were earning thirty to thirty-five shillings per week. After the spinners' strike in Manchester failed, a thousand workers from over

15. Feiling 1938, p. 334; Turner 1999, p. 162.
16. Turner 1999, p. 163; Derry 2001, p. 149.
17. Berg 1985, p. 249; Hobsbawm 1986, p. 64.
18. Aspin 1995, p. 2.

twenty trades met in Manchester on 30 September. This was just one week prior to the opening of the Rainhill trials, held ten miles outside Liverpool, at which Robert Stephenson's *Rocket* would astonish a crowd of over 10,000 as it went '"shooting past the spectators [at 24 m.p.h.] and dropping red hot cinders as it proceeded"'.[19]

The delegates at Manchester identified the source of their systematic exploitation as the unbridled competition between factory masters, which involved falling profits putting downward pressure on piece-rates and wages while fostering further innovation, which in turn drove prices and thus profits down further in a vicious spiral. The most aggrieved workers were the hand-loom weavers, who had been calling upon authorities to intervene and set a fixed standard for piece-rates and equalise working hours across trades. John Doherty put forward his strategy of creating a general fund to be used in an effort to support local strikes so as to check the ability of employers to 'pick off individual towns or districts, factories or sectors of industry; it was also seen as the only effective answer to combinations of employers, and the only realistic form of unionization in a period of depression'.[20] For a fundraising strategy, Doherty also drew lessons from the Catholic Association's use of a 'Catholic Rent' in Ireland. It was out of this meeting that the National Association for the Protection of Labour (NAPL) would formally emerge in late 1830, with John Doherty as its full-time secretary.

By that point, nearly all the strikes in the textiles had ended in failure and the workers were forced to return to their jobs at reduced wages. The total wages lost by the spinners during these strikes ran into the hundreds of thousands of pounds.[21] At its height, Doherty's NAPL had between sixty and seventy thousand members, mostly from Lancashire and Cheshire, but it also enjoyed a loose affiliation with many unions outside Lancashire. Welsh miners joined the NAPL in April, prior to a major strike at Merthyr Tydfil in June that resulted in a lockout, and violent suppression of protests by miners and ironworkers in which more than twenty were killed and seventy wounded. Despite the failure of the strike, Welsh miners continued to organise afterwards, possibly under the influence of the NAPL.[22] As tens of thousands of troops still patrolled the manufacturing

19. Aspin 1995, pp. 15–9. Rainhill was a competition held by the Liverpool and Manchester Railway to decide whether to use locomotives or stationary engines. Stephenson wan a prize of £500, and more importantly the contract to build locomotives for the new line. An example had already been set in the previous year with the opening of the Bolton-Leigh line on 1 August 1828, driven by Stephenson's *Lancashire Witch*.

20. Chase 2000, pp. 140–3. Textile workers noted the irony that to the extent that competition was limited, this was only due to capitalist employers combining amongst themselves in order to collectively depress wages and piece-rates further.

21. Aspin 1995, pp. 2 and 75.

22. Chase 2000, pp. 134 and 140–2. A strike by miners in Northumberland and Durham the following year also resulted in defeat and the 'complete destruction of the union' (see Rule 1986, pp. 313–6).

districts, ostensibly to check violence against property, the state took effectively no action other than the provision of outdoor relief and some employment of the poor in public works programmes to check the downward spiral on piece-rates, described in a recent pamphlet in Manchester as a '"grinding system"', and, '"not something uncertain, accidental, temporary and unavoidable"',[23] directly contradicting the tendency popularised by the economists to view the economy as a natural system, and state intervention in the economy as unwarranted interference. The Hammonds interpret the ruling oligarchy's policy of not intervening to check falling piece-rates and wages, combined with the use of force to suppress working-class resistance, as amounting to a policy of seeking to foster in the working classes a slave-like mentality, writing: 'It seemed to this oligarchy the most natural thing in the world that the economic should resemble the political structure, and that in the mill, as in the State, all this power should be concentrated in the hands of a few men, who were to act and think for the rest. Economic science seemed to add a sanction to the law of inequality, for it showed that the sovereign authority of capital was the condition of success in the world of trade'.[24] This gets to the heart of the matter, which is the way in which a new form of property, capital, retained the singular quality of 'sovereign' authority, which it inherited from pre-capitalist, 'feudal' or politically-constituted forms of property. For even if the exchange, production and price of property were now to be regulated not directly by the state but by the market, the 'economy', *ownership* of property was still firmly backed by the state through the judicial system. 'Property', write the Hammonds, 'was the great civilising force of the world', and quoting Macaulay, '"that great institution for the sake of which chiefly all other institutions exist, that great institution to which we owe all knowledge, all commerce, all industry, all civilization, all that makes us to differ from the tattooed savages of the Pacific Ocean"'.[25] Continuing, they write that for the likes of Sidmouth and Castlereagh, the problem was 'simple enough', namely that:

> A small class was set to defend its own property and that of a larger class against the turbulence of a large unpropertied population. The mass of people was liable to be infected with Jacobin doctrines, and if the State was to be made safe from revolutionary agitation, it was essential that the proletariat should be excluded from all opportunity of discussion, association, education, and remonstrance. The more the ignorant masses seemed tempted by

23. Longson 1827, p. 16, as quoted in Sykes 1988, p. 181.
24. Hammond and Hammond 1995, pp. 324–5.
25. Hammond and Hammond 1995, p. 320. The quote from Macaulay is from a speech on the reform bill. The open display of racism would have been unremarkable in his time period.

> dangerous and seductive principles, the more necessary it was to drive out that temptation by terror.[26]

Certainly the Hammonds have captured an element of the hardened attitudes of the ruling class in this period. Yet such polemics suffer from a large degree of oversimplification. While this passage also brings out the ruling oligarchy's hysteria at the 'levelling' language of Spencean radicals and even Owenism, we have seen little evidence in what has been presented thus far that the ruling landed oligarchy was so interested in *actively* fostering any *new* form of deference to authority. On the contrary, the character of the oligarchy during this period appears to be that of one whose attention is far less fixed on the threat of working-class agitation in the form of strikes and renewed calls for government regulation than it is concerned with the threat posed by the rise of commercial and industrial 'middle' classes calling for a share in state power commensurate with their newfound economic power. To the hand-loom weavers, no doubt, it seemed clear that the once-paternal state now sought their outright reduction to a state worse than slavery. But what events in 1826 and 1829 show are the beginnings of a system in which the market, more so than the soldiers patrolling the industrial towns, was coming to play a predominant role in disciplining the labour force. When the mule-spinners returned to work in 1830, at lower wages than before their strike began, it was their dependence upon the market for subsistence, for the wages necessary to sustain life, and not the bayonets of the soldiers which drove them back.

Could market discipline, by itself, have sufficed to complete the real subsumption of labour to capital, even if over a longer time period? The fact that such a process of subsumption remains incomplete even today, and the fact that the application of police and military force are still relied upon by the state to suppress radical protests and strikes would seem to make the question moot. But there remains the inverse question, which is: what would Britain have looked like if coercive force had not been used to suppress dissent and radical trade unionism verging towards some kind of socialism? As noted, E.P. Thompson's optimism at the prospects for revolution in this period is not widely shared. It seems safe to suggest that the strikers and machine-breakers of the late 1820s were considerably less inclined than their Luddite forebears had been to imagine that their actions might lead to an end that they would find satisfactory. But this is certainly true only because they were looking back at a string of defeats at the hands of the state applying coercive force. The problem with such questions is that they ask us to telescope the long and complex evolution of capitalism down to certain moments of crisis or tipping points. The victory by the

26. Hammond and Hammond 1995, p. 321.

Spitalfields silk-weavers in 1773 might be one example of the historical current flowing against the tide of capitalism, but really turning the tide, or moving the current in an entirely different direction, would have required hundreds more of such historical moments. One of the major objectives of this work is to demonstrate that by the onset of the Industrial Revolution in Britain, a powerful capitalist dynamic rooted in agrarian social relations was already transforming British social and property relations. The point is not to suggest that we should simply stand, mouths agape, and observe the awesome power of the social relation of capital as it proceeds along some teleological course towards dominating all social relations. Quite the contrary, our thesis is that because capitalism was resisted, it was not an inevitable development. And the narrative presented here seeks to identify the social forces and agents which and who ensured capitalism's survival, one of those forces being the state and its interventions in the political economy of Britain by way of applying military force to suppress various revolts and other forms of opposition to the imposition of capitalist social relations.

Yet the fact that by 1830 worker discipline could be conditioned at least as much by the market as by outright coercion appears to indicate that British society was crossing another threshold and entering an era in which, soon enough, factory owners would no longer need to urge the local magistrate to call for military intervention when their factory was threatened by a crowd, an era in which the direct application of force was required less and less and could be replaced by a more routine force protecting private property.

When Home Secretary Peel steered the Metropolitan Police Act through Parliament in 1829, a decade after the first meeting of a committee proposed by James Mackintosh in 1819 to consider penal reform, the stated objective was to improve methods for dealing with the rising tide of crime in the capital, particularly within the emerging slums. But we can hardly ignore the fact that this move came at a time when the industrial towns of the North remained under a form of military occupation. W.R. Cornish writes: 'The authorities were also compelled to find new techniques for controlling public disturbances'.[27] There was also a certain obvious logic to the fact that if the state needed to maintain a continuous presence of armed enforcers in various regions where there were frequent outbreaks of revolt and rebellion, it should consider the establishment of a regular force of armed officers in place of the repeated use of soldiers responding to declarations of emergency. Local magistrates, after all, did not enjoy direct authority over the military and so found it 'impossible to lay down any simple legal prescription as to when and how far the magistrates' commands should be obeyed. Nor was it possible to state precisely what the military should do in

27. Cornish 1969, p. 1484.

the absence of a magistrate to give direction'.[28] Appointed as Chief Secretary of Ireland at the age of 24, Peel had responded to the ongoing state of revolt and disorder there with the Peace Preservation Act of 1814, allowing superintendents and special constables to be appointed to disorderly districts. He also introduced the Insurrection Act of 1817, which allowed for curfews and the confiscation of arms.[29] Upon becoming Home Secretary in 1822, Peel was now equipped to introduce a similar policing principle to the whole of the United Kingdom, and saw the establishment of regular police forces as the only means by which he might make his plans to reform criminal and penal laws effective. The Metropolitan Police Act of 1829 created a new cadre of uniformed police serving directly under the Home Secretary, and no longer under any local magistrates, to patrol the City of London and all areas within a ten-mile radius of it. Peel's stated objectives, in keeping with the programme of the liberal Tories, were to provide the whole system with efficiency and consistency. Between 1825 and 1828, Peel managed to see that some 278 statutes – around two hundred of which carried the death penalty – were consolidated into eight statutes. Such obscure laws as those against cutting down hop vines or impersonating Greenwich pensioners were dropped. It was not actually Peel's objective to reduce the number of executions carried out each year in Britain, but only to remove from the books the myriad of rarely used, self-contradictory or arbitrary laws in order to, in his words, '"add to the solemnity and efficiency of the laws"'.[30] Peel supported the use of the whip and the treadwheel, a device upon which even petty offenders were made to walk for up to ten hours a day. While Peel found the treadwheel 'admirable', one JP saw it as '"the most tiresome, distressing, exemplary punishment that has ever been contrived by human ingenuity"'.[31] Peel's reforms of the prison system involved new laws requiring that most large and medium-sized towns establish their own prisons, with annual inspections to be reported to the Home Office by the JPs.

As a historical figure, Home Secretary and future Prime Minister Peel is of particular interest to this study as the first prominent British statesman to trace his origins to a family of industrialists. The Peels were descended from a long line of yeomen peasants living in the Lancashire hills who since at least the Civil Wars had combined farming with domestic manufacturing. Peel's grandfather,

28. Cornish 1969, p. 1485.
29. Jenkins 1999, pp. 15–6.
30. Peel, as quoted in Jenkins 1999, p. 27. Peel stated in 1827: '"Tory as I am... I have the satisfaction of knowing that there is not a single law connected with my name, which has not had for its object some mitigation of the severity of criminal law, some prevention of abuse in the exercise of it, or some security for its impartial administration"' (as quoted in Briggs 1979, p. 218).
31. As quoted in Harling 2001, p. 95; citing Ignatieff 1978, p. 177.

Robert 'Parsley' Peel (1723–92), was a Lancashire freeholder who inherited land worth between £2,000 and £4,000, which he mortgaged in the 1760s in order to set up a calico-printing factory, which later added spinning, carding and weaving, and went on to set up additional cotton mills in Staffordshire. Parsley Peel's son Robert (1750–1830) continued his father's partnership, and the firm grew to be one of the largest in Lancashire. He then bought his way into the gentry by purchasing Drayton Bassett manor in Staffordshire, and was elected to Parliament for the borough of Tamworth. A staunch Pittite, he subsequently helped to pass the Factory Act of 1802.[32] He would leave behind the vast sum of £1.5 million upon his death in 1830.[33] Robert Peel III (1788–1850), while growing up in the environment of the family firm, never worked in the textile business. He studied at Oxford and was elected to Parliament shortly after graduating.[34] The Peels were exceptional in that factory-owning families tended to be Dissenters and Whigs, while the Peels were high Anglican Tories. The Irish Catholic leader O'Connell once referred to 'Orange' Peel as '"a fop made out of factory slavery"',[35] an insult motivated by more than religious animosity, obviously cutting at the Peels' shallow roots among the landed elite. Peel would go on to become a champion of free-trade policies. At a personal level, he was known for his arrogance, and his career demonstrates a considerable degree of opportunism, perhaps reflecting the mentality of a profit-seeking industrialist. Between his declarations of being a staunch Anglican and his commitment to bureaucratic rationalisation, he stood somewhere between the high and liberal Tories. And as we have seen, whilst professing strong opposition to Catholic emancipation, he played a major role in moving it forward. In his bigotry toward the Irish, Catholics, Africans and Jews, Peel seems like a convert seeking to outdo the aristocracy in its prejudices and condescensions. No doubt this attitude of superiority made him a suitable figure to introduce policing to the United Kingdom.

While Parliament was reluctant to create a continental-style police force, within five years the effect which the new police force in London had on reducing the crime rate would mean that, outside of radical circles, the new force ceased to be seen as a threat. Policing the mass rallies of the coming reform years would now be conducted with batons and staves, not sabres. The Metropolitan Police provided a model, and they were sent to other towns to assist as they developed their own forces. The Municipal Corporations Act of 1835 would see the creation of professional forces in the boroughs and the County Police Act initiated the

---

32. See Chapter Eleven, pp. 581–2.
33. Hobsbawm 1986, p. 62.
34. Jenkins 1999, pp. 3–7. 'Parsley' Peel was so-named because one of his calico prints used a parsley symbol.
35. As quoted in Feiling 1938, p. 336; no citation given.

development of a rural policing force.[36] This came too late for dealing with the labourers' revolt, which followed upon the dreadful harvest and harsh winter of 1829–30.

Upon the dissolution of Parliament in the summer of 1830, George IV reassured his audience that the distress in the countryside lay '"beyond the reach of legislative control"'.[37] On 26 June he would die, unmourned, 'with Maria Fitzherbert's locket on his heart',[38] leaving the crown to his brother William. In July, Charles X of France suspended press freedom and dissolved the just-elected Chamber of Deputies, sparking the July Revolution. On 2 August, Charles was deposed, abdicating the throne to his grandson, Louis-Philippe, who would rule France for the next eighteen years as the popular 'bourgeois King'. The example of a popular overthrow of a monarchy involving minimal violence prompted a renewed outpouring of cries for reform, which confronted candidates even in the most rotten boroughs.[39] As English and Irish volunteers sailed to help spread the revolution in Belgium, Tory authors talked of rallying the Pittite party again around a counter-revolutionary war. But the Tories fared poorly in the election, while pro-reform candidates did well. Breunig credits the 'cumulative effect of the Industrial Revolution upon British society', which 'had created social groups, forces, and problems which the old Tory leaders were incapable of handling'.[40] One of these forces was the emergence of municipal political unions. In London, the London Radical Reform Association brought together 'respectable' reformers, whilst the National Union of the Working Classes (NUWC) assembled trade unionists. Other cities followed suit.[41] In the aftermath of elections, the Tories found themselves politically adrift while the Whigs were busy forming a new alliance with the Canningites. William Huskisson became the first person to die in a train accident while attending the opening of the Liverpool-Manchester Railway on 15 September. Afterward, both parties vied for his followers.[42] On 2 November,

36. Cornish 1969, pp. 1484–6; Breunig 1977, p. 203.
37. As quoted in Feiling 1938, p. 375.
38. Feiling 1938, p. 377.
39. Feiling 1938, p. 379.
40. Breunig 1977, p. 209.
41. Turner 1999, pp. 169–72. The Birmingham Political Union and the Sheffield Political Union both represented employers and workers from the many small workshops dominating manufactures in these two cities. In Manchester, class divisions were evident with the establishment of the Manchester Political Union in November, dominated by shopkeepers and smaller employers, and the Political Union of the Working Classes ten months later to represent the working class. In Leeds, three separate unions emerged. The Metropolitan Political Union was formed in London in March 1830, under the guidance of Henry Hunt and Daniel O'Connell, drawing on the strength of artisan radicalism.
42. Feiling 1938, pp. 379–80. Huskisson was standing on the line with the *Rocket* approaching, looking to shake hands with the Duke of Wellington. When told to stand clear, he became confused and reached for the Duke's carriage, but not in time to prevent being struck and having his left leg crushed. 'As the dying man was placed in the musi-

Wellington declared before the Lords his implacable hostility to reform, asserting that the present system of representation could not be improved upon, and expressing regret for the Belgians' revolt against the Netherlands. The Lords were stunned. Sitting down, Wellington turned to Lord Aberdeen, his Foreign Secretary, and asked what the commotion was about. 'You have announced the fall of your government, that is all', came the reply.[43]

Swing

If there had been doubts on the part of the authorities about expanding policing into the countryside, the events of 1830–1 probably laid those doubts to rest. Poor relief payments had shown a moderate decline in the boom years of the mid-1820s, rising somewhat thereafter. By 1830, the agrarian districts of South and East England were subject to 'the rapid intensification of all the existing factors' precipitating the decline of rural textile manufacturing: high food prices, low wages, massive unemployment, migration and poor rates that had fallen to the barest of subsistence levels.[44] In 1826, William Cobbett had observed that the decline of rural manufacturing in the South had brought about ' "a vast change in the condition of the people, and in the state of property and of manners of morals" '.[45] With the enclosure of more than ninety percent of arable land in Britain now achieved, only pockets of 'peasants' working on open fields remained in villages like Laxton.[46] Reformers seeking to transform the pastimes of the working classes and put an end to such barbarous amusements as bearbaiting and

---

cians' car and taken at full speed by the *Northumbrian* to Eccles, deep gloom replaced the gaiety and shortly afterwards a thunderstorm added to the discomfort' (Aspin 1995, p. 27). Certainly a deep gloom hung over Wellington's ministry during its last days, and over Peel in particular, who expressed a willingness to retire. It is remarkable that such a prominent symbol of progress and modernisation as the *Rocket* would so dramatically come between the symbolic leaders of the high and liberal Tories at the point of their greatest division politically, only shortly before the Tories fell and the oligarchy begrudgingly conceded to the first limited act of reform.

43. Evans 1994, p. 49.
44. Wells 1988, p. 116.
45. As quoted in King and Timmins 2001, p. 48.
46. Laxton in Nottinghamshire remains an open field village to this day. In the 1950s, most of the farms were purchased by the Ministry of Agriculture. The system in Laxton has continued to evolve. The fields are still tilled in common, but the strips have been widened to allow them to be worked with tractors and other modern agricultural machinery. After an outbreak of hoof-and-mouth disease in the 1960s, the sheep were slaughtered and the commons were converted to being sown by grass, which is reaped and auctioned off each year to make winter hay for the animals. Only residents who 'put up smoke' may bid at the meeting of the court leet, which takes place at the local pub. Each purchaser must pay 50 pence upon the fall of the gavel to cover the cost of ale and bitters (village of Laxton and Laxton Museum, visit by author, October 1997).

cock-fighting noted that in the countryside the labourers had lost public spaces left for recreation or for celebrating the harvest and other traditional feasts.[47] The general loss of rights of estover and turbary meant fuel had become not only scarce but expensive, limiting the ability of agricultural labourers to cook their own food or bake their own bread. Many now depended upon purchases of ready-made bread.[48] Decades of agricultural boom and recession had facilitated the proletarianisation and monetisation of the rural economy. In a condition of an absolute surplus of labour, the agricultural worker hovered somewhere between being a proletarian wage worker and a pauper. His or her grandparents might speak of a time when commoners enjoyed a range of rights that had now been taken from them. In 1797, Arthur Young had expressed shock that poor relief which had previously been associated as a form of disgrace was now demanded as a right. What other 'rights' did the agrarian poor have?

The low cost of labour had by now induced most farmers to dismiss their servants-in-husbandry and adopt the practice of paying all their workers in money wages. Yet as Hobsbawm and Rudé point out, a 'fundamental contradiction' in agrarian society was now becoming obvious: 'Its rulers wanted it to be both capitalist and stable, traditionalist and hierarchical. In other words they wanted it to be governed by the universal free market of the liberal economist (which was inevitably a market for land and men as well as for goods), but only to the extent that suited nobles, squires and farmers; they advocated an economy which implied mutually antagonistic classes, but did not want it to disrupt a society of ordered ranks'.[49]

This contradiction lay not only at the heart of agrarian society, but also coloured the tension between the landed oligarchy in control of the state and the expansion of a proletarian workforce in general. 'Thanks to the preponderant political power of the "landed interest" ', Hobsbawm and Rudé continue, 'the

47. Rule 1986, pp. 214–6.

48. Rule 1986, p. 47.

49. Hobsbawm and Rudé 1968, p. 47; see also pp. 15–6 and 42. Hobsbawm and Rudé, writing before Mark Blaug's critique (see above, Chapter Ten, pp. 550–2), take it as axiomatic that the Speenhamland system, and not a labour surplus combined with loss of customary economic rights, was to blame for the low wages and 'universal pauperism' found in the English agrarian countryside in 1830 when they write (p. 51): 'Agrarian capitalism degenerated into a general lunacy, in which farmers were encouraged to pay as little as they could (since wages would be supplemented by the parish) and used the mass of pauper labour as an excuse for not raising their productivity; whilst their most rational calculations would be, how to bet the maximum subsidy for their wage-bill from the rest of the ratepayers'. This appears to be the only usage of the term 'agrarian capitalism' in their treatment of the Swing riots, and is problematic inasmuch as the pauperisation of the agrarian workforce is laid at the door of Speenhamland *and* because agrarian capitalism is associated with the emergence of a 'cash-nexus', rather than a centuries-long restructuring of agrarian class relations.

universal market of capitalism stopped short of land. This was not freely bought and sold, except at the margin of the great and legally buttressed monopoly of the nobility and gentry'.[50] But this is to overlook the essential point. For what made agrarian capitalism capitalist was not the spread of the wage relation, it was the way in which members of the rising 'class' of capitalist tenant-farmers were subject to market imperatives, arising from competition between them for land leases, which made the transformation of production in the direction of greater efficiency a necessity for their economic survival. This competition was further intensified as improvements in efficiency led to higher productivity and falling prices. While most tenant-farmers were not the actual 'owners' of land as the means of production, after deducting the rent they paid to the real owner or the landlord, they retained the remaining profit for themselves. One might draw a parallel between the tenant-farmer leasing the means of production in land and the small master or domestic producer in the workshop or garret also paying a rent on his loom. The problem with such a parallel is that the tenant-farmer enters only after enclosure has abolished customary rights in the manor, giving the leaseholder access to and exclusive control over the means of production in land via the lease and thus the capacity to transform the production process that was essential to his economic survival. In the small workshop, customary modes of regulating production persisted and were specifically intended to protect the master and his journeymen from open market competition. The proper comparison is between the tenant-farmer and the factory owner – even if most factory owners owned (though some of them surely rented) their factories – both of whom were subject to price competition in the marketplace which made their economic survival dependent upon the capacity to assume direct control of production in order to systematically improve efficiency.

The most fundamental proximate cause of the agrarian distress of our period was a surplus of labour, which combined with the decline of rural manufacturing, resulted in soaring levels of unemployment. We have tried to show how it came to this. Agrarian capitalism was now approaching its logical conclusion: a fully-enclosed countryside, the complete extinction of customary rights of access to land and the conversion of the rural workforce to wage and market dependence. The growth of the factory system must be credited with robbing the rural workforce of the agrarian counties of their traditional source of supplemental income in the form of cottage manufacturing through the systematic lowering of price owing to factory innovation. We might entertain a scenario in which the Industrial Revolution never happens and rural labourers continue to subsist happily under conditions of agrarian capitalism by compensating for loss of customary access

50. Hobsbawm and Rudé 1968, p. 48.

to the means of subsistence through rural handicraft production. This is after all what happened throughout much of the countryside into the last decades of the eighteenth century. But we must qualify this picture with two points: 1) even in the form of agrarian capitalism, capitalism is a system that must constantly revolutionise production; and 2) agrarian capitalism in the absence of an Industrial Revolution would have continued to generate falling food prices, falling wages and the associated falling profits, leading to further dislocations and contradictions. For example, had population continued to expand, it is doubtful whether rural manufacturing could have continued to absorb the labour surplus. Second, even if the conversion of manufacturing to a capitalist logic as a process generally followed in the wake of the conversion of British agriculture to capitalism, the two processes were intermixed and inseparable. A fundamental purpose of this work is to demonstrate that the Industrial Revolution grew out of and grew up *within* the expanding social relations of agrarian capitalism.

Having said this, the fact that the largest outbreak of rural machine-breaking came well *after* Luddism might seem contradictory. Here it bears remembering that the Luddites drew their ranks in large part from rural handicraft workers. The question of why the use of machinery and the displacement of labour by machinery spread more slowly in agriculture than industry requires further study, but some of the reasons are obvious. Agricultural innovations like the seed drill and the improved plough were more labour-enhancing than labour-replacing. Rural labour in general, including rural handicrafts, was dispersed and could not be concentrated under one roof allowing for the imposition of the rigorous labour discipline necessary for ensuring the proper functioning of machinery that replaced the tool aspect of manual labour and made the worker an accessory to the machine. Yet it is not as if innovation in agriculture was standing still. The 1780s saw the introduction of Ransome's self-sharpening cast-iron plough, the Scotsman Andrew Meikle's introduction of the first widely-used threshing-machine and the first improvement in Tull's seed drill (which came into general use only in the 1830s). While the first successful reapers came into use in the 1820s, it was the increasing use of the threshing-machine by farmers that sparked the outbreak of agrarian protests in 1830–1.[51] The very bad harvest of 1829 created near famine conditions in the countryside, and many agricultural labours in different counties concluded that the adoption of mechanic threshing had increased their misery.

The first signs of agrarian unrest were seen in the form of fires set in the West of Kent during the summer of 1830. Then, on August 28 and 29, some four hundred labourers destroyed a number of threshing-machines at Lower Hardres, near

51. Beckett 1990, pp. 25–9.

Canterbury.[52] Over the course of the next year, these initial outbreaks of violence against property would spread to 34 counties, with over one thousand four hundred incidents recorded by the authorities, who would arrest some two thousand persons, of whom five hundred would serve prison sentences and nineteen would be executed. More than 425 threshing-machines were destroyed, making this 'the greatest machine-breaking episode in English history – and by far the most successful'.[53] Successful not only because the protesters were able to get many farmers to consent to dismantle their own threshing-machines, but also because a virtual prohibition on the use of the threshing machine in the agrarian South held for more than a decade after the event.[54] As a revolt against authority with any transformative power, however, the revolt was a failure and a disaster.

Machine-breaking was only one of many forms of violence taken by the protests, other forms including sedition, threatening letters from a mythical 'Captain Swing', arson, burglary, cattle-maiming, attacks on poorhouses, attacks on saw- and paper mills, protests against rents and enclosures and even strikes.[55] As with previous customary protests, the attacks were discerning. A report by the poor law commissioners, commenting specifically on the Swing revolt, noted that: 'To a certain extent the burning of ricks is a mode of revenge which has always been practiced among the labourers. They make a wide distinction between burning a rick and burning a house; between destroying property and endangering life'.[56]

Machine-breaking continued in northeast Kent through September until most of the protesters had been arrested. By early October, however, the violence had spread south and east to Dover, and Lyminge, where the leaders and some fifty participants were rounded up by Reverend Price and Sir Edward Knatchbull, leader of the ultra-Tories. When seven machine-breakers plead guilty at the East Kent Quarter Sessions in late October, they were given light sentences and a tongue-lashing from Knatchbull. For his part, the reverend found his ricks fired. As with Luddism and many of the local protests we have explored, the protesters appear to have enjoyed solid support from the community and such acts of retribution were condoned. Offers of large rewards to informants were ignored

52. Hammond and Hammond 1974a, pp. 220–1; Hobsbawm and Rudé 1968, pp. 97–9.
53. Rule 1986, p. 357; Hobsbawm and Rudé 1968, p. 17.
54. Hobsbawm and Rudé 1968, p. 299. The 1822 protests must also have been successful in this regard, since very few machines were destroyed in the regions of Norfolk and Suffolk where some 54 machines had been destroyed eight years earlier (Archer 2000, pp. 15–6).
55. Hobsbawm and Rudé 1968, p. 311, 'Table of Incidents'; Wells 1988, p. 119; Turner 1999, p. 174.
56. R.C. Poor Law XXIX of 1834, p. 200, as cited in Hobsbawm and Rudé 1968, p. 188. They are careful to point out that: 'This was written in the immediate aftermath of the rising, and about it . . . the opposite of their betters', for whom property was more precious to law than life'.

as rick-burning and the issuing of threatening letters from Swing continued. Frustrated, the authorities resorted to gaoling for three months a ten-year-old girl alleged to have valuable information, but excessive interrogation caused the child to clam up. Home Secretary Peel's frustration was also growing: '"I will adopt any measure – will incur any expense at the public charge"' he wrote upon dispatching cavalry – and subsequently artillery – to suppress the outbreak of violence around Maidstone and Sittingbourne in north-west Kent.[57]

The raising of a tricolour at Newington was the first sign of any connection between the Swing revolt and radicalism. Since the 1790s, the influence of radical politics had been felt in the countryside, where sympathy for the cause of reform combined with anger at the high levels of rent, taxation and tithes. How deep these connections ran is a source of contention, but the authorities were certainly aware of them and this prompted a more forceful effort at suppressing the revolt.[58] As the disturbances spread south into Sussex, the demand for a living wage of 2*s*. 6*d*. per day became central to the labourers' agenda, with farmers expressing their willingness to acquiesce to the demand so long as rents and tithes were also reduced, whereupon the labourers began visiting their demands upon the rectory. Declining an invitation to join the yeomanry to suppress the revolt, the farmers of east Kent passed a resolution declaring that landowners and clergy had a duty to lower rents and tithes. Some farmers actually left their machines out to be destroyed. The light sentencing by magistrates and the sympathies shown by farmers caused great alarm among local landlords and moreso at the Home Office, which sent about 'a sharply worded circular in 1830 to point out that "machines are as entitled to the protection of the law as any other description of property"'.[59] A handful of farmers would subsequently stand trial for breaking ranks with the landed classes.[60]

As predicted by Aberdeen, Wellington's speech of 2 November was followed within a fortnight by the collapse of his administration. Under Earl Grey, the Whigs assumed control of the Ministry. While the passage of a reform measure was all but certain, the Whigs differed little from the Tories in their handling of the rural labourers' revolt. The Home Office passed to Lord Melbourne, who would proceed to 'repress the outbreaks ruthlessly and without mercy',[61] demonstrating that there would be 'no lowering of the aristocratic flag' under the Whigs.[62]

57. Hammond and Hammond 1974a, pp. 221–3; Hobsbawm and Rudé 1968, p. 99.
58. Wells 1988, p. 118; Chase 2000, p. 72.
59. Hammond and Hammond 1974a, p. 232 and Hobsbawm 1994, p. 247.
60. Wells 1988, p. 120.
61. Briggs 1979, p. 249; '"Whig", hitherto a political term, became part of the popular vocabulary of abuse' (Chase 2000, p. 134).
62. Feiling 1938, p. 385.

Meanwhile, the revolt that had started in Kent, East Sussex and Surrey had begun to spread westwards into West Sussex, Berkshire, Hampshire and Wiltshire. The explosion lasted little more than a week, and when it was over, there were at least three hundred prisoners awaiting trial in each county. Here the emphasis on machinery was marked, with attacks not only upon threshing-machines, but upon winnowing and chaffing machines, ploughs and industrial machinery at textile factories as well. At Selborne and Headley, there were attacks upon the workhouses. When the estate of the local MP for Wiltshire was attacked on 25 November, the yeomanry were summoned and upon being pelted with stones fired into the crowd, killing one. The juries in the trials concerning both of these events refused to convict. The rioting spread to Gloucestershire, Berkshire and Oxfordshire, then to Buckinghamshire and Dorset. At Kintbury, Berkshire, the town was overtaken by rebels and a crowd armed with hammers and bludgeons led by a wheelwright named William Oakley who addressed the magistrates, demanding a minimum wage and £5 in their pockets before departing. While they got their way, the leaders were arrested the next day, but not before the example had spread. In Buckinghamshire there was destruction of papermaking machinery by the unemployed. At Bensington, Oxfordshire, a thousand rebels gathered at the home of one Mr. Newton, who had been attempting unsuccessfully to receive an act of enclosure, and made him promise to forego his pursuit. Was enclosure a factor in the disturbance? Hobsbawm and Rudé think so. They note that of nine parishes enclosed since 1800 at Eynsford, Kent, four were involved in the revolt, while only nine out of a total 31 parishes saw disturbances. At Erphingham South in Norfolk, the figure was three of five recently enclosed parishes rioting, while only six of the 38 parishes there saw trouble. The obvious potential link between still-smouldering grievances against enclosure and grievances against farm machinery was that enclosure had fostered market dependency, which made manual threshing far more important. The revolt continued to spread, moving west into Somerset and Devon, north into Bedfordshire, Herefordshire, Norfolk, Suffolk and Essex.[63] Geography – the persistence of rights of common on the wastes, heath and woodlands in Surrey and Essex, along with the upward pull of market demand from the metropolis, may explain why there were few incidents in the radius around Middlesex.[64] The incidents tapered off slowly over the month of December, but continued through the winter, and there were several incidents in many counties during the Summer of 1831. Thereafter, occasional

63. Hobsbawm and Rudé 1968, pp. 116–70; Hammond and Hammond 1974a, pp. 234–5.

64. Hobsbawm and Rudé 1968, p. 74.

revivals occurred sporadically down to 1848. Some historians suggest that these later attacks became more vengeful than the attacks of 1830.[65]

Hobsbawm and Rudé estimate the damages to be around £100,000 from arson, and £8,000 in machinery.[66] Despite rumours of French and Irish agents and other 'itinerant radicals' taking part in the violence, and the appearance of radical leader Henry Hunt at Winchester, Hampshire in late November, invited by farmers to arbitrate with the labourers over wages, radicalism seems only to have 'touched' these protests. Often it was local blacksmiths, cobblers and other craftsmen who emerged as leaders, perhaps applying organising skills they had learned as participants in trade organisations, but overall the protests overwhelmingly involved agrarian labourers.[67] This is not to suggest that the protesters saw no stake in reform. Swing had its own politicised leaders, like Robert Mason, who 'speculated in jail while awaiting transportation in February 1831, that "there must be a reformed Parliament or a Revolution before next summer is over..."'[68] The reform movement also extended its reach into the countryside in the years approaching the Great Reform Bill. But much like the Luddites, the aims of the protesters were clearly focused upon economic interests such as obtaining a minimum wage and securing employment in the Winter, not on gaining the right to vote. To the degree that Swing was successful in achieving its immediate aims, it was aided by the considerable level of sympathy shown by farmers, the local community, juries and magistrates. 'Maintaining concessions won during Swing', however, 'necessitated collective action to resist vestries reducing relief, farmers cutting wages, and re-engaging itinerant labour'.[69] This helps explain the sporadic outbreaks of 'Swingism' over the following decades. But there was, of course, a way in which the lasting impact of Swing ran contrary to the aims of the protestors. For Swing helped stimulate a lively debate over the poor laws, leading to the discontinuation of outdoor relief in 1834. The events also had a lasting psychological impact on British society, raising awareness of the degree of poverty, suffering and social dislocation in the countryside.[70] Rule sees Swing 'in part a protest against the decline of paternalism'.[71] Certainly in the statements made by the protestors themselves, there was an awareness and a resentment at the ostentatious wealth of the aristocrat and the healthy profiteering of the farmer in the midst of such distress. Swing operated along the lines of the traditional protest in the context of the rapid decline of customary

65. Rule 1986, p. 361.
66. Hobsbawm and Rudé 1968, pp. 223–5.
67. Hobsbawm and Rudé 1968, p. 207.
68. Wells 1988, p. 120.
69. Wells 1988, p. 121.
70. Chase 2000, p. 134.
71. Rule 1986, p. 357.

rights and observance of paternal obligations. At the same time, however, the protestors operated almost like an informal union engaging in what was in this case a literal example of 'collective bargaining by riot'.[72] The focus on wages and machinery suggests that Swing was less an outcry against the betrayal and non-observance of traditional obligations than a mostly spontaneous strike for better wages and working conditions. In other words, Swing belonged very much to a capitalist social order.

After Swing, there was a renewed push for intensification of cultivation in rural Britain which became known as 'high farming', involving the introduction of the Norfolk four-course rotation, and more capital-intensive processes including a greater emphasis on breeding and dairying. 'In a sense, the operations of the farmer became more like those of the factory', writes Beckett, 'farming changed from being an occupation primarily concerned with extraction from the soil into one involving the purchase of raw materials which were processed to produce a saleable product'.[73] Kirkpatrick Sale speaks of a spirit of resignation taking over whole segments of the working class in the aftermath of Luddism and Swing – 'talents no longer marketable, whole villages no longer needed. Their history, ignored by Whigs and Marxists alike in their enthusiasm for reform, is probably the basic one of the next fifty years'.[74] While overstated, this statement certainly applied to much of the agrarian South and East of England in the mid-nineteenth century, which now provided a huge 'reserve army of labour' not only for high farming and dairying, but for industry as well. Emigration and the flight to the cities in search of work were two release-valves for the ongoing pressures of population and poverty.

'No kings, No lords, No inequalities'

Both political parties were heading for dissolution or transformation in 1830, not just the Tories. Fundamental to understanding why this was the case is that both parties were dominated by landed oligarchs. The new ministry of Lord Grey was made up of eleven Whigs and three Canningites, almost all of whom were 'members of the aristocracy and to a large extent of peers; there were only three commoners in a cabinet of thirteen'.[75] On the matter of reform, both 'Whigs and Tories were agreed during the crucial debates of 1830–2 that democracy was an unpalatable and dangerous form of government, that "a stake in the country" was

72. See Hobsbawm 1952, p. 59.
73. Beckett 1990, pp. 19 and 25.
74. Sale 1996, p. 195.
75. Briggs 1979, pp. 236–9.

an essential title to political power...'[76] Where the two parties differed most was in assessing the likely consequences of reform. For the Tories, reform spelled certain disaster; for the Whigs, *not* granting some measure of reform would certainly spell disaster. The traditional allies of the Whigs were the commercial and industrial interests, particularly those who supported free trade, as well as middle-class reformers such as the Utilitarians or Benthamites. Even so, the representation of the landed classes under the Whigs was out of proportion with the growing size and strength of commerce and industry, for the core of the party itself was deeply committed to the primacy of the landed oligarchy. In fact, oligarchic power was at its zenith in 1832, and the Whig formula for reform was 'Reform on a conservative principle'.[77]

Since the beginning of the century, agriculture and manufacturing had roughly traded places in terms of the percentage of the workforce they employed, with agriculture falling from around a third to around a quarter and manufacturing moving in the opposite direction. During the 1830s, agriculture's share actually rose while manufacturing held steady.[78] Crafts's suggestion that the total factor productivity growth in agriculture outstripped that in industry by a factor of *three* before 1851,[79] even if exaggerated, at least provokes us to rethink the common mental picture of factories blazing the trail whilst agriculture followed behind. To make sense of this, we must keep in mind that the large majority of workers employed in manufactures were domestic weavers and other self-employed artisans in domestic workshops, where there was little or no revolutionising of the means of production going on. Undoubtedly factory production, if taken alone, outstripped agriculture in terms of productivity advances. The slow-down of aggregate productivity advances in the 1830s may be explained in part by the widespread distribution of strikes and shut-downs. The advent of high farming coupled with the more even distribution of agricultural machinery may help explain agriculture's advance in this decade. It also helps to explain how the landed oligarchy remained in power in 1830, and was able to maintain its hegemony even after the reform bill. And it helps explain the willingness of the landed elite, despite the paranoia of the Ultras, to move forward with a broad programme of reform that would surely have been far too threatening for most of the reactionary régimes on the Continent. As progress-minded landlords, Britain's landed oligarchs now had a strong interest in supporting and enforcing the social property relations of capitalism, even if that meant conceding some measure of state power to class and sectoral interests outside the oligarchy.

---

76. Briggs 1979, p. 239.
77. Kriegel 1968, pp. 65–7.
78. Deane and Cole 1969, p. 144.
79. King and Timmins 2001, p. 165.

The Whig programme included retrenchment, an expansion of domestic spending, reform, abolition, and peace. Catholic Emancipation had already been accomplished under Wellington. The necessity of retrenchment meant that the Whigs were faced with the problem of how to meet demands for the expansion of domestic services when the remaining budget after debt servicing was shrinking.[80] The Swing Riots had also put grievances over the high expenditure on the poor rates back into the centre of politics. As for reform, majority opinion now favoured some kind of measure. And with unrest in the countryside, Manchester on strike and discontent across Britain moving toward strikes and even open revolt, the Whigs saw reform as an urgent measure to release some of the pressure for change.

A committee of four, led by the Whigs' acknowledged expert on reform, Lord John Russell, was tasked with drafting the bill in secret. When the bill was introduced on 1 March 1831, the Tories were shocked to discover that Russell was now putting forward the most far-reaching programme yet. It included the elimination of rotten boroughs and the reduction of the representation of small boroughs with under four thousand inhabitants from two representatives to one, the seats to be redistributed to larger towns, including previously unrepresented Manchester, Leeds and Birmingham, as well as seventeen new seats going to London, Scotland, Ireland and Wales. The bill also included the granting of the right to vote to any £10 householder in the boroughs, whilst retaining voting rights for 40s. freeholders in the counties. The Tories laughed aloud as the list of sixty boroughs to be scratched was read out. But their laughter 'turned to a foreboding that what was at stake was nothing less than all the world. "No King, no Lords, no inequalities in the social system", exclaimed Croker – "wickedness and atrocity", echoed faithful Arbuthnot'.[81] The Tories immediately declared that by shifting influence away from the landed oligarchy to the industrial towns, robbing the Crown of much of its powers of patronage and encouraging further such reforms in future, the passage of such a bill would result in nothing short of revolution. Russell and the Whigs countered that the measure was an attempt to save the constitution by removing its most irrational elements, and emphasised that the redistribution of seats was based not upon population so much as wealth and influence, the industrial towns having to this point been sorely underrepresented in this regard. In the Commons on 23 March, the bill passed its second reading by the narrowest of margins, 302 votes for to 301 against, in the largest recorded division in the Commons to date. But a third reading was never held. A motion by the Tory member Gascoyne objecting to the reduction of the total number of

80. Harling and Mandler 1993, p. 59.
81. Feiling 1938, pp. 385–6.

MPs for England and Wales was carried against the Government, leading to William IV's dissolution of Parliament.

The question of reform was now in the hands of the propertied electorate, but this excited disenfranchised radicals to pro-reform action as well. Henry Hunt, now MP for Preston, having won a by-election in 1830, was to be found once again addressing mass rallies, arguing in tones more fiery than ever that the effect of Russell's bill would be to win the middle classes over to their side and to leave the working classes isolated. The NUWC in London published a manifesto reiterating the working-class radical demands: full manhood suffrage without property qualifications, annual parliaments and the ballot. But these were minority positions. More moderate radicals like Cobbett, O'Connell, Hume and others welcomed Russell's bill as a step forward. The political unions, which continued to spread to all the major cities and towns, had also become more favourable to widening the franchise than they had been a year before, and while they welcomed Russell's bill, many also saw the need for agitation out-of-doors, of which there was aplenty. The ensuing election resulted in major gains for the Whigs, widespread defeats for the Tories, and a clear mandate for reform.[82]

Russell submitted a new bill, with only minor modifications, on 24 June. The Tories engaged in delaying tactics, including a measure by the Marquis of Chandos to extend the franchise to tenant-farmers occupying farms renting at £50 or more per year, which carried. Hunt's amendment to extend the vote to all urban householders received only one vote, his own. Despite delaying tactics by the Tories and calls from the King to amend the bill, the measure passed the Commons by 109 votes on 22 September. As the bill headed to the Lords, the Birmingham Political Union threatened a tax revolt should the Lords fail to pass it. But the Tories felt that the public was losing interest, as victories for opponents of reform in several by-elections seemed to show. Wellington, seeing his chance to save the country, gathered his old allies, including the bishops. At five o'clock in the morning on the 8 October, the Lords defeated the bill, 199 to 158.

An immediate uproar of indignant protest swept the country. Newcastle was swamped by a crowd of protesters. Nottingham Castle was sacked. Parts of Derby were burnt down and Worcester and Bath also saw rioting and arson. In the coming months the middle- and working-class elements within radicalism would contend for control over the direction of the movement in each city and town. In London, Francis Place and his old LCS compatriot Thelwall led huge protest meetings and formed the National Political Union. Meanwhile in Birmingham, the BPU, led by Thomas Attwood, proposed to establish a citizens' militia to defend against the outbreak of plebeian violence on the one hand

82. Briggs 1979, pp. 240–51; Turner 1999, pp. 174–84.

and a conservative backlash on the other. Attwood took credit for the absence of violence in Birmingham. The radical trade unionist Bronterre O'Brien noted that class antagonisms in Manchester were markedly less evident in Birmingham, as:

> The Brummagem operatives seemed really to believe that they would be *virtually*, though not actually, represented in the 'reformed' parliament... To this body, more than any other, is confessedly due the triumph (such as it was) of the Reform Bill. Its well-ordered proceedings, extended organization, and immense assemblages of people, at critical periods of its progress, rendered the measure irresistible.[83]

At Bristol, the Government lost control of the city during three days of protesting with the prisons being attacked in a manner reminiscent of London in 1780.[84] The violence in Bristol was not something welcomed by trade unionists. The writings of Edward Gibbon Wakefield reveal his awareness of the danger of unleashing 'the destructive energies of the criminal classes', something he feared that the NUWC might do, especially once a cholera epidemic swept much of the country over winter and added to the hardships of the poor. For the NUWC was able to mobilise some seventy thousand to march in October, and perhaps one hundred thousand the following March. Many of the members, according to O'Brien, were provided with arms. In Manchester and Bolton, the political unions split over the question of manhood suffrage. A protest of some six thousand in Bolton shouted, as if in answer to Croker: '"Down with Bishops!", "No Peers"'.[85] Thompson backs his assertion that 'Britain was within an ace of a revolution' between October 1831 and May 1832 with revealing quotes from middle-class reformers, ministers and even the King. William IV wrote in November that he was '"by no means displeased that the measures contemplated by the [NUWC] are so violent... as he trusts that the manifestation of such intentions and such purposes may afford the opportunity... of checking the progress of the political unions"'.[86] The same month Earl Grey reassured the House that

83. Bronterre O'Brien, *Destructive*, 2 February and 9 March 1833; as quoted in Thompson 1991, p. 897. Emphasis found in the original. Briggs 1979, p. 253.

84. Several conservative historians would later reflect upon the Bristol protests: 'Cities have been sacked and burned by foreign enemies, and the wretched citizens honourably buried in their ruins; but here, did a band of *patriot* ruffians for two days triumph in outrage unchecked; and the ill-disposed citizens looked on in apathy, in sufferance, and too many in approbation. *They thought it was the first step of a revolution*, which a wicked press and a singularly unfortunate coincidence of evil circumstances, under the sanction of an insane Government, had led them in a strong delusion to desire' (Eagles, Brereton and Warrington 1832, p. 162, emphasis found in the original). What is remarkable is how the familiar 'approbation' of the community so enrages these contemporary authors.

85. Brimelow 1882, p. 111, as quoted in Thompson 1991, p. 897.

86. Thompson 1991, p. 891, following Jephson 1892, Chapter 15, p. 11.

'"no one is more decided against annual parliaments, universal suffrage, and the ballot, than I am. My object is not to favour, but to put an end to such hopes and projects"'.[87] He also made the class politics of the reform bill quite explicit when he stated that '"It is of the utmost importance to associate the middle with the higher orders of society in the love and support of institutions and government of the country"'.[88] Voicing the view of a middle-class reformer looking back on the crisis, Francis Place wrote: '"We were within a moment of general rebellion . . . [which] would have been the act of the whole people to a greater extent than any which had ever before been accomplished"'.[89] Edward Baines took a survey to determine '"the numbers and respectability of the £10 householders in Leeds"', and was surprised to discover how few would actually win the right to vote. Here, the discourse and the class arrangements of the Victorian era was already taking shape. Of course it was not all roses between middle-class reformers and the oligarchs. The latter accused the former of fomenting the violence, which was mostly untrue, but they had little mind to stop it before their object was won.

In the aftermath of the October vote, the Cabinet divided over the proposal to approach and suggest to the King the creation of additional peers in order to obtain the votes necessary for passage. Not only would William IV have no part in such a scheme, he continued to press for amendments. In December, Russell presented a modified bill to Parliament. It incorporated the Gascoyne amendment, ensuring that the total number of members for England and Wales was not reduced, and that rather than determine disenfranchisement by population it was now to be determined by dwellings and taxes. The new bill once again passed the Commons and then managed to pass a second reading in the Lords. But when on 7 May Lord Lyndhurst succeeded in a motion to split the vote into two parts so that the disenfranchisement clauses could be voted on separately, Grey refused and once again approached the King, asking for fifty new peerages. The King would not go above twenty, and the impasse led to the resignation of the ministry on 9 May. When Peel refused to reunite with Wellington to form a new ministry, there was escalating excitement out-of-doors. This included a momentary truce between middle class and popular reformers in many cities and a joint meeting of political unions attended by over one hundred thousand at Birmingham. In light of such agitation, William had no choice but to accede to Grey's demands and to recall his ministry. The waverers in the Lords backed down, many choosing simply to avoid attendance at divisions.

87. Thompson 1991, p. 892; no citation given.
88. As quoted in Briggs 1960, p. 56; also partially referenced in Thompson 1991, p. 899.
89. As quoted in Thompson 1991, p. 898.

On 4 June, the Great Reform Act 'was finally passed on its third reading in a poorly attended upper house. In a final show of displeasure, William IV refused to give the royal assent in person, but this made little difference'.[90] Was this merely a phenomenal display of arrogant disinterest in a matter of enormous import to the population, or was it genuine displeasure? One suspects the latter to be the case. William IV had just lost 'most of the electoral patronage that the crown still possessed, and shortly thereafter it became obvious that the choice of prime minister now depended not on the will of the king, but on that of the Commons majority'.[91] The Lords had just lost all of their rotten and pocket boroughs, in which they had since time immemorial enjoyed the power to name their own representatives.[92] There is more than a degree of symmetry between their displeasure and the displeasure of the crafts in 1799 and 1814. Adam Smith may have been applauding from his grave, for surely he would have approved of the clearing away of such extra-economic 'monopoly-' privileges. Yet we can carry the analogy further, for just as artisans retained control of the labour process and apprenticeship continued to be practiced widely after 1814, the hegemonic position of the landed class was far from broken in 1832.

The debate over whether the Reform Bill of 1832 was a 'culminating event' or whether it left the political landscape looking 'much as it had done before' has been extensive and is ongoing, with the familiar pessimists and optimists taking sides. It has been estimated that over the course of the eighteenth century the electorate actually shrank from about 23.9 percent of all adult males in 1715 to 14.4 percent in 1831. By extending the franchise to perhaps one in fifty adult males, the Reform Bill of 1832 only restored the vote to some 4 percent of the adult-male population bringing the voting percentage back up to something like 18.4 percent. Those with little or no property saw no gains at all, and in some poorer towns the number of voters was actually reduced.[93] Part of the case for the optimists is made simply by presenting these figures in a more positive light. So Phillips and Wetherell point out that the bill expanded the electorate to some six hundred and fifty thousand,[94] thereby delivering on a promise to achieve 'an overall increase of perhaps 50 percent in the *already large number of Englishmen who had a right to vote*'.[95] Clever polemics, though we are not told: large in comparison to what? Harling points out that what had a greater impact than

90. Turner 1999, pp. 188–91.
91. Harling 2001, p. 81.
92. Old Sarum was the most notorious rotten borough. It had once been a flourishing medieval town, but by the nineteenth century was officially uninhabited. A pocket borough was one in which the lord exercised so much influence that he could name his own candidates (Breunig 1977, p. 210).
93. Harling 2001, p. 39; Thompson 1991, pp. 900, 904–16; Price 1986, p. 56.
94. Phillips and Wetherell 1995, p. 414.
95. Phillips and Wetherell 1991, p. 622. Emphasis not found in the original.

this limited extension of the franchise was the redistribution of seats; the disenfranchisement of lesser boroughs freed up 144 seats in the Commons. Their redistribution brought voting for the first time to the new industrial cities of Manchester, Birmingham, Sheffield and Leeds.[96] Phillips and Wetherell associate this with 'a wave of political modernisation' that followed after 1832, which: 'the Whig Party eagerly harnessed and the Tory Party grudgingly, but no less effectively embraced. Reform quickly destroyed the political system that had prevailed during the long reign of George III and replaced it with an essentially modern electoral system based on rigid partisanship and clearly articulated political principle'.[97]

Before 1832, voters in Shrewsbury tended to either 'split' their vote between Whig and Tory candidates or 'plumped', meaning that they declined to cast their second vote. But after 1832, these passive voting tendencies decreased in frequency. In other words, Phillips and Wetherell argue, 'the agitation surrounding the Great Reform Bill politicized Shrewsbury's voters'.[98] There is nothing to dispute in this, although when the authors go on to credit the Reform Bill with the 'foundation of a new party system that may have lasted longer than Victoria herself',[99] this is clearly overstated. For what is missing from this discussion is precisely the question of class; in fact most of the working class is entirely missing from view. Another enthusiast, Derry, credits Pitt and Liverpool with laying the foundation for the passage of the bill under the Whigs, who being agreed with the Tories on the essential issue, 'showed a traditional concern for the security of property as the surest foundation for liberty'.[100] Here at least we have the heart of the matter, already revealed in the quote above from Grey about the urgent need to 'associate the middle with the higher orders of society'.

Notice that Grey speaks of the middle *order* and not the middle *class*. Eighteenth-century parlance referred to the 'middling sort' not the middle class. According to Margaret Hunt: 'The composition and outline of the middling sort is, and must remain somewhat vague . . . Most middling people had incomes between £50 and £2,000 [a considerable range], and the bulk of these were concentrated within the range of £80 to £150 . . . The center of gravity of the middling sort . . . was families that were engaged directly in trade or commerce'.[101]

We can see in this a fairly clear definition of what the middling sort were not: they did not belong to the gentry or the aristocracy. Hunt's emphasis on commerce seems an attempt at juxtaposition between commerce and agriculture

96. Harling 2001, p. 79.
97. Phillips and Wetherell 1995, p. 412.
98. Phillips and Wetherell 1991, p. 645.
99. Phillips and Wetherell 1995, p. 435.
100. Derry 2001, pp. 154–5.
101. Hunt 1996, pp. 15 and 19.

and overlooks the large number of second sons, daughters and other extended family members who received stipends paid out of the rents of their family's estates. It is striking that, even in the contemporary debate, the participants are at pains to offer a precise definition of what constituted the 'middle class' in mid-nineteenth century Britain.[102] Middle class or the middling sort are terms that have always been best defined along the lines of those whose incomes fall in the middle range between workers as direct producers and the few who possess large fortunes in property and capital. Lawyers, doctors and other highly-paid professionals have always belonged to this group. The position of skilled craftsmen and other skilled labourers is more ambiguous, as is the position of clerks. What is interesting is that the Reform Bill itself delegated voting rights according to property and income values, and just as artisans were sometimes included in popular definitions of the middle orders, so most skilled artisans in London now possessed the right to vote. In the countryside, meanwhile, one had to be a 40s. freeholder. There were plenty of 40s. cottagers and copyholders, but only freeholders were allowed to vote. The ancient distinction between freemen and bondsmen had retained its grip over power relations in the countryside.

There is no doubt that the Reform Bill was a significant milestone in the development of party politics in Britain, although we must keep in mind that had there been no fragmentation of the Pittite coalition that had formed the second Tory Party, there probably would also have been no Great Reform Act of 1832. The measure also made possible a further expansion of the electorate by some 62 per cent – before the second Reform Bill of 1867 widened it further – under the combined effects of population growth and inflation, which lowered the value of the £10 household franchise requirement. But there is no reason to assume that these were intended outcomes. 'In short', writes Harling: 'the Reform Act was a constitutional innovation that the Tories had never dreamt of making. It evinced a positive conception of the state's duty to promote social fairness, depriving many borough proprietors of much of their glaringly disproportionate influence within the electoral system while acknowledging a much broader range of legitimate interests within that system, notably the interests of middling property owners in hitherto unenfranchised towns'.[103]

102. In two review essays, Julian Hoppit and Jonathan Barry each stress the need for further research. Hoppit 1991, pp. 345–9 concludes: 'Much more work needs to be done, particularly in terms of the regional and local development of the middle class'. Meanwhile, Barry (Barry 1994, pp. 194–208) writes that a 'crucial requirement . . . at least in the British context, is detailed research on how the middle classes at all levels were recruited and trained for their occupations'. Combined, the two authors are commenting on a total of six books written about the emergence of the middle class.

103. Harling 2001, pp. 79–80.

The Reform Act was a concession, made on the part of the parliamentary landed class to stop the exclusion of people who were important and who increasingly did have a say in public opinion. But to see it as a major concession, a blow to those at the top of society, is to misunderstand the composition of the British economy in the early nineteenth century. The peers were living off of rents from their vast and consolidated estates, rents being paid by tenant-farmers now engaging in systematic methods of improving productivity. Britain's peers had never known better times, and there had never been more of them.

The obvious pressure that had been building was the threat of an alliance between working people and the wide variety of middle-order people, from lawyers to merchants to pensioners to industrialists, rising up to *depose* and dispossess the landed oligarchy. Was reform part and parcel of the European reaction then? It emphatically was not. The vast inheritances in question were no longer worked by unfree peasants still under obligation to provide unpaid services to their neo-feudal overlords, as was much of the peasantry of Eastern Europe well into the nineteenth century, or by free peasants, as in France, but by 'free' wage labourers working for capitalist tenant-farmers. What is more, the land they worked was no longer a politically-constituted form but was rather an economically-constituted form of property, increasingly treated as a commodity abstracted from nature, forming but one essential component in an agrarian process of production. Foregoing a large measure of electoral patronage to protect such inheritances may have brought displeasure, but to the lord, who may have felt that the threat of a levelling revolution was actually real, the choice would have been obvious. More importantly, such forms of patronage were coming to stand out as glaring inconsistencies as other forms of patronage and politically-constituted property were being abolished. Wasson argues that historians have overlooked those 'advanced' Whig reformers who were 'imbued with a strong spirit of reform', being 'ready to play with fire and push reform much further than many ministers wished to go',[104] but nonetheless recognised that the current measure would have an impact on public opinion and open the door to further reforms in future. 'Politicians and newspapers', writes Wasson, 'did not shrink from calling it a revolution, and they compared it to 1688'.[105] Combined with the repeal of the Test and Corporation Acts and the emancipation of Catholics, the legislation of this period marks a constitutional revolution, the end of a century and a half of *exclusive* dominance by the Anglican landed oligarchy, and the turn toward secular pluralism under the dominance of a class of property owners marked by the

104. Phillips and Wetherell 1995, p. 166.
105. Wasson 1980, p. 170.

convergence of agrarian, industrial, mercantile and banking interests.[106] Notably, there were no comparisons made between 1832 and 1649. But the comparison with 1688 was apt. To the extent that 1688 was truly a revolution, it was also the culmination of a counter-revolution against such 'advanced' and progressive forces as the Levellers and the Diggers pressing for the universal franchise and greater equality, and marked the rediscovered unity of the landed classes expressing their power through Parliament. Likewise, if we are tempted to see a kind of 'bourgeois revolution' in 1832, it is important to remember that it was precisely to *forestall* the prospect of revolution and protect the vast inheritances of the oligarchs that concessions were made.

John Rule sees it as a 'bitter irony' that following the passage of the bill the newly reformed Parliament set upon a programme to crush trade unions, as a flurry of anti-trade union pamphleteering ensued.[107] Bitter it was, but why should it be seen as ironic? Elsewhere, Rule himself has pointed out that what united the great powers at the Congress of Vienna in 1814 was a shared fear of the revolutionary potential of popular-radicalism, which had demonstrated its awesome potential in France after 1789. Rule has further pointed out that the increasing momentum of middle-class pressure for parliamentary reform had origins in the development of the 'vigorous urban middle-class "club" culture' that had emerged in the eighteenth century.[108] And he cites O'Gorman, who argues that reform was able to come off in 1832 largely thanks to the already existing 'capacity of the unreformed system to make accommodations and compromises with the middling orders'.[109] Roger Wells defines the formula for reform quite succinctly when he writes:

---

106. Chase 2000, p. 134; Harling 2001, p. 80. For Owen (1975, p. 339): 'the era which had opened in 1688 draw to its peaceful close' in 1832, by which he no doubt means to imply at least that Britain had managed to avoid violent domestic revolution. That same century-and-a-half was also marked by almost constant warfare as Britain expanded its empire. If the period of oligarchy ended 'peacefully', there was nevertheless much blood mixed into the formula.

107. Rule 1986, pp. 312–5; Rule, 1988, p. 193.

108. Rule 1992a, pp. 101–4.

109. O'Gorman 1986, p. 52, as cited in Rule 1992a, p. 101. Michael Beaud writes that 'while it would be tempting to present the great reforms of the British nineteenth century as the successive victories of the rising liberal bourgeoisie over the declining conservative aristocracy, this view, without being entirely false – since the landed aristocracy lost in the course of the century its quasi-monopoly over political power and local administration – would be at the least simplistic... In fact, on the one hand the overthrow of royal absolutism in the seventeenth century sealed a sort of unwritten pact between the landed aristocracy and the high families of finance, banking, and international trade. On the other hand, between these two poles there was never an insurmountable barrier: members of the first group invested in commercial and financial businesses, and even in mining and manufacturing, while for the bankers, manufacturers, and traders who had grown wealthy, the purchase of an estate, before becoming a social symbol, was a means of entering parliament. And finally, the aristocracy and the bourgeoisie reacted with a

> The Whigs, by excluding most of the industrial, and the entire rural proletariat from the post-reform electorate, contrived to strengthen the political significance of the industrial middle class, while maintaining the aristocratic and therefore the agricultural interest's domination of the political system, thus preserving the hegemony of agrarian capital.[110]

On the part of those working-class radicals who had previously felt that they were making common cause with middle order reformers there was a widespread sense of betrayal at their exclusion from the franchise. But could there have been much surprise?

What Reform did in 1832 is more sharply circumscribe the interest of the working-class population as separate from the interests of the propertied classes. 'In every manufacturing district,' writes Thompson, 'a hundred experiences confirmed the new consciousness of class which the Bill had, by its own provisions, so carefully defined.'[111] Further, he suggests that Chartism's true point of origin may not have been the drafting of the six points in 1838, but the moment of Royal assent to the Reform Act in 1832.[112] It is important to peer ahead to the era of Chartism at this stage, because the optimists build their case for the Reform Act of 1832 as paving the way for the larger extensions of the franchise that followed much later, crediting enlightened Whigs for their foresight at the expense of giving due credit to the working classes for continuing the struggle for democracy. The continuing expansion of the proletariat, increasingly market-dependent, increasingly pressed into factories and gradually losing direct control of the production process, along with rising wages commanding greater purchasing power, all added up to structural changes in the economy that virtually guaranteed that the working class would exert ever greater pressures for political representation. Had that not been the case, had the precise economic conditions of 1832 been frozen in a stationary state, the landed, industrial and commercial interests united in their command of property might have been quite content to settle for the limited reform that had been achieved in 1832.

---

common reflex of "solidarity" when faced with radical movements and popular-uprisings which threatened property' (Beaud 1983, p. 92). Aside from Beaud's problematic usage of the terms 'aristocracy' (leaving out the gentry) and 'bourgeoisie' (by which Beaud would conflate the commercial and industrial interests in Britain with those in France as all belonging to one big, happy family of capitalists), this statement has it about right.

110. Wells 1988, p. 120.
111. Thompson 1991, p. 908.
112. Thompson 1991, p. 909.

Free labour

The election of December 1832, producing in January the first reformed Parliament, resulted in a Whig landslide. The Whigs now had a mandate to pursue their programme of liberalisation, such as passing the Bank Charter Act of 1833, which suspended the upper limit of 5 percent on the interest rate under the ancient usury laws. Parliament at last took direct control of governing South Asia upon the passage of the Government of India Act. Private merchants were now given full and unrestricted access to the Indian economy, leading to the widespread establishment of opium and cotton plantations in India. The most pressing issue was to deal with a situation of rising violence and crime in Ireland, most of it being organised by O'Connell, who was still agitating for a repeal of the Union.

In 1832, O'Connell had openly called for the impeachment of Lord Stanley, Chief Secretary for Ireland, on grounds of gross misconduct.[113] In Ireland, Catholics tilled and Protestants collected rents. Now Irish Catholics, many having recently lost the right to vote when the 40s. freehold franchise was rescinded in exchange for an end to prohibitions upon Catholics achieving higher rank or serving in higher office, were showing their displeasure by refusing to pay the tithe and the cess (an Easter Tax) by which the Anglican Church in Ireland was funded. Grey's Ministry felt that they had to act quickly, before a rebellion against the tithe became a rebellion against rents in general. A committee was appointed. The Whigs were deeply divided over how to handle the Irish situation. The solution put forward by Stanley was to strike a 'delicate balance of coercion and conciliation'[114] by passing a bill that would suppress agitation, by targeting Irish trade unionists and introducing a conciliation bill to abolish the cess and commute the tithe. There was little trouble in convincing the Lords to pass the Coercion Bill, which suspended *habeas corpus*, trial by jury, the right of petition and freedom of the press in Ireland. Backbenchers among the Whigs in Parliament condemned the measure as befitting a Tory but not a Whig administration, but the bill passed nevertheless. With the measure in place, the government proceeded to prosecute many trade unionists on conspiracy charges over the Winter of 1833–4.[115] The commutation of tithes was another matter, for any measure that threatened to weaken the position of the Protestant Church of Ireland was likely to get a hostile reception in the Lords. On the other hand, advanced Whigs like Anglesey, Russell and Althorp found it obnoxious that Catholics should provide such large subsidies to a Protestant church. Althorp proposed that after a

113. Briggs 1979, p. 269.
114. Kriegel 1971, p. 22.
115. Chase 2000, p. 147.

reduction of sinecures most of the tithe money be dedicated to general service efforts such as the provision of education. But he was only successful in winning some measures for disciplining absentee clergy.

The Church Bill passed the Lords on 30 July 1834. Grey resigned the premiership over attempts to modify the Coercion Bill and retired to a leisurely life on his estates in Northumberland. Lord Melbourne reluctantly took his place.[116] Upon succeeding Melbourne at the Home Office, Lord John Russell announced the pardon of 264 rural machine-breakers.[117] The commutation of tithes in Ireland was followed by the Tithes Commutation Act of 1836 for England, which brought to an end the payment of tithes in kind, commuting them to monetary payments. The Church of England had stepped out of the Middle Ages at last.

It was not only the English and Irish countryside that saw open revolt during the period in which the Reform Act was passed. Under the influence of Methodist, Baptist and Moravian missionaries, there were sporadic incidents of violence and revolt by slaves in the 1820s, leading up to the large-scale revolt by some fifty thousand slaves in Jamaica, led by Samuel Sharp. The militia was called in to crush the rebellion. While the pattern resembles the use of force against protesting agrarian labourers and Luddites, the plantation owners saw no need for a mixture of terror and mercy, only terror. Five hundred slaves were executed, including Sharp, and a hundred were flogged. Charges were brought against the missionaries and later dropped, but not before several Baptist and Methodist chapels were ransacked by white slavers.[118] The brutal response by the slavers and their lack of support for reform at home helped to turn public opinion against them. The West-Indian slave interest lost 16 seats in the election of the first reformed parliament. There were now 104 members who favoured immediate emancipation. The abolitionists and advanced Whigs, warning of a full-scale slave war, now pressed their agenda for a measure to go further than the 1807 act that had merely abolished the trading of slaves within the Empire, but not slavery itself. A committee was appointed with Lord Stanley again taking the lead. While the details of the negotiations between the abolitionists seeking emancipation and the West-Indian slave owners seeking a long-term, gradual emancipation and huge sums from the Government as compensation are not known, one of the proposals put forward by Stanley is revealing:

> Slave children under six were to be entirely set free, if maintained by their parents; otherwise they were to be subject to certain restrictions. All other slaves were to be freed in all spheres, except that of labour, where they were to be apprenticed to their former masters for them under certain conditions for

116. Kriegel 1971, pp. 33–42; Briggs 1979, pp. 269–70.
117. Hobsbawm and Rudé 1968, p. 273.
118. Honeychurch 2000, pp. 66–70.

> several years... Stanley explained that he intended to oblige the apprentices to work for their ex-owners three-quarters of the day, which was understood to be ten working hours. For the remaining quarter of his time the apprentice was free, or, if he preferred, could demand to be employed by his master at such a rate of wages that would enable him to buy his complete freedom in twelve years by working all his spare time.[119]

The stipulation requiring the slave to purchase his own freedom was subsequently removed at the behest of protesting abolitionists, and the apprenticeship period was cut in half, but in a manner reminiscent of the Tudor provisions exacting punishments for work left unfinished that survived the repeal of 1814, the final bill allowed masters to exact extra work from the apprentice for periods of wilful absence 'by making him work overtime or for any period less than seven years after the expiry of his apprenticeship'.[120] What is fascinating about this measure is how slaveowners and statesmen could agree that the slave was to be liberated from servitude in all areas except for labour, that being the critical aspect of true value to the master. Since converting the slave into a full wage labourer would be seen as unfair to the former slaveowner because it would oblige him to incur the cost of wages where he had once enjoyed labour already paid for upon the purchase of the slave, the middle ground was to call the slave an apprentice, thus putting the newly emancipated slave at the same status as apprenticed pauper children working in the factories, both of whom would effectively be required to earn the right to one day be paid actual wages. Such was the method for commuting slavery and converting it to what Marx would later call 'wage slavery'. The system was now all of a piece: slavery would henceforth be merged into the wage labour market via the route of pauper apprenticeship. Sir Robert Peel played an intermediary role in seeking to double the compensation for plantation owners from £15 to £30 million, but the final bill set the compensation at a figure that was not to exceed £20 million. The Abolition of Slavery Act received royal assent on 29 August 1833. It would not take effect until 1 August 1834.

Three years prior, the well-known Yorkshire land agent by the name of Richard Oastler, recently awakened to the truth about the condition of children working in the factories, published a letter in Edward Baines's *Leeds Mercury*, writing: 'The pious and able champions of negro liberty and colonial rights should, if I mistake not, have gone farther than they did; or perhaps, to speak more correctly, before they had travelled so far as the West Indies, should, at least for a few moments, have sojourned in our own immediate neighbourhood, and have

119. Gross 1980, p. 72.
120. Gross 1980, pp. 63–74

directed the attention of the meeting to scenes of misery, acts of oppression, and victims of slavery, even on the threshold of our homes'.[121]

Reflecting on his conversion years later, Oastler wrote:

> I had lived for many years in the very heart of the Factory districts, I had been on terms of intimacy and of friendship with very many Factory masters . . . and I had all the while fancied that Factories were blessings to the poor. Perhaps there was not, in Yorkshire, one man so unlikely as myself to engage in a war against the Factory Monster. But, what could I do? I did not seek the conflict. The secret was revealed to me unasked, and I was horrified! I did not before believe that human nature could have been so cruel – nor that the human frame could have endured such protracted torture! [With God's help], I will war to conquest, against that monster which binds so many Britons in abject slavery.[122]

Oastler was immediately welcomed as the friend of working men, but outside such circles his comments were initially met with denial. Baines continued to publish calls for a shortened working day and regulation of child labour in factories.[123] Baines' agitation was partly responsible for the Althorp's Factory Act of 1833, which passed the Lords on 29 August, precisely the same date as the Abolition of Slavery Act. This measure differed from the Factory Act of 1802 in that routine inspections of factories were established and its provisions were enforced as hundreds of employers were fined or prosecuted in the years that followed. The employment of children under the age of nine was now prohibited. The working day for children aged 9 to 13 was now limited to eight hours and to twelve hours for children aged 14 to 18. Nightwork for all children under the age of 18 was prohibited. The numbers of children working in the textile industry were in fact reduced as a result of the act, the number of children under the age of 14 employed falling from 28,000 in 1835 to 12,300 in 1838.[124] Yet despite that fact that this was 'the first really solid contribution to factory legislation, [it] had the singular result of pleasing nobody'.[125] There was by now a strong movement among workers and trade unionists for the state to limit the working day to ten hours, but when this measure was brought forward as an amendment to the bill, it was soundly defeated by a vote of 238 to 93. 'Manufacturers' – as

121. Oastler 1830.

122. Oastler 1841, p. 104.

123. In April 1831 Baines published his *Manifesto to the Working Classes of the West Riding* (Baines 1831).

124. Anderson, Ekelund and Tollison 1989, p. 78, citing Chapman 1904, p. 92.

125. Cooke-Taylor 1894, pp. 77–85. Anderson, Ekelund and Tollison 1989, p. 80, quoting Senior.

factory owners were now often called[126] – complained meanwhile that whilst mines and domestic manufacturing remained unregulated with regards to the employment of children, their factories were being singled out for such restrictions. They therefore sought every means of evading enforcement. Age certificates were regularly forged to inflate the apparent ages of the apprentices, by factory owners and desperate parents alike. And a relay system was implemented whereby factory children worked in shifts from 5:30 a.m. to 1:30 p.m. and 1:30 to 8:30 p.m. The mandated one-and-a-half hour 'lunch break' was thereby offered only before or after the shift. Getting children to work in 'double sets' was actually condoned by the commissioners as a compromise measure to allow factories to continue to operate at full capacity. An absolute reduction in the hours worked by children would necessitate an absolute reduction in the hours worked by adults, and for the commissioners that was a greater evil than the evil of working children for excessive hours.[127] By now, the self-acting mule was rapidly coming into operation. It was the prime example of a piece of machinery which Andrew Ure touted as a means by which employers could discipline labour and dispense with skilled workers like the mule-spinners, and along with them their relative control over the labour process. The response of the mule-spinners was to try to 'maintain their position in face of the threat from the self-acting mule, by fighting for control over the new machinery, rather than by trying to stop its progress altogether'.[128] In this they enjoyed considerable success.

Nassau Senior, who became the spokesman for the manufacturers' lobby against attempts to regulate factory hours, could thus argue that child labour was becoming less onerous, comparing the work of attending a self-acting mule to the work of a shopkeeper, as it requires '"mere confinement, attention, and attendance"'.[129] In making the case for retaining the long working day, Senior made his famous 'last hour' argument in which he suggested by laying down his spade, the worker '"renders useless, for that period, a capital worth eighteen pence. When one of our people leaves the mill, he renders useless a capital that has cost £100,000"'.[130] Writing decades later, Karl Marx would respond: 'Only

126. Andrew Ure would observe in 1835 that the owners of factories and manufactories (where domestic and machine production were combined) had taken over the term 'manufacturer' by 1835, writing: '"manufacture is a word, which, in the vicissitude of language, has come to signify the reverse of its intrinsic meaning, for now it denotes every extensive product of art which is made by machinery, with little or no aid of the human hand"'. The term 'industrialist' would actually not come into widespread use until the 1860s (Rule 1992a, pp. 81–2, quoting Ure).

127. Cooke-Taylor 1894, pp. 77–85.

128. Berg 1985, p. 43.

129. Anderson, Ekelund and Tollison 1989, p. 15 quoting Senior.

130. Letter from Senior to Thomson, 28 March 1837, in Senior 1966, p. 14, as quoted by Anderson, Ekelund and Tollison 1989, p. 74; Marx 1906, p. 443.

fancy! Making "useless" for a single moment, a capital that has cost £100,000! It is, in truth monstrous, that a single one of our people should ever leave the factory!'[131] Seeking to rehabilitate Senior's 'last hour' argument, which evolved over the coming decade and has been dismissed by Marxists and liberal economists alike, Anderson points out that while Senior severely exaggerated his case when suggesting that elimination of the 'last hour' would wipe out all profits in the industry, his argument was rooted in the concern that a lowering of the ratio of circulating to fixed capital would mean a reduction in the marginal efficiency of capital and in the efficiency of resource allocation, leading to a lower return on capital investment, disinvestment, unemployment and the loss of market share to foreign competitors not subject to such restrictions.[132] While we need not be detained further, here, with the details of the debate, what Senior's intervention shows is the extent to which industrial arguments rooted in the discourse of abstract economic theory were being deployed against demands based on moral arguments for state intervention in the 1830s.

The same group of reformers responsible for all this new legislation responding to the threat of revolt in Ireland and the West Indies, and agitation for a ten-hour workday in the factories were also deeply involved in a royal commission in 1832 to carry out a reform of the poor laws. At the height of the Swing revolt, Nassau Senior emerged as the mouthpiece for the view that outdoor relief was the cause of low wages, high population growth and revolt in the countryside. The instigator of the reform process was Lord Brougham, who was profoundly committed to reducing the amount of public assistance to the poor, but was opposed to its total abolition. For his part, Brougham recognised that a labour surplus existed and his proposed solution was to provide employment through the extension of public works and to put up funds for the emigration of fifty thousand able-bodied persons to the colonies. But Parliament was unwilling to pay for his scheme. In December 1831, Brougham then announced that he would bring forth his own measure for reform to deal with the obvious distress in the countryside, but Grey's ministry was in the thick of the debate on the Reform Bill

131. Marx 1906, p. 443.

132. Anderson, Ekelund and Tollison 1989, pp. 73–4. The authors argue that Marx's ridicule amounts to a misinterpretation of Senior's position. Employing Ricardo's labour theory of value, Marx was concerned to point out 'the economical paradox, that the most powerful instrument for shortening labour-time, becomes the most unfailing means for placing every moment of the labourer's time and that of his family, at the disposal of the capitalist for the purpose of expanding the value of his capital' (Marx 1906, p. 445). Thus there are two sets of concerns at work, here, which are not antagonistic: one regarding the internal dynamic of the factory and the effects of machinery on the working day, and another regarding domestic and foreign competition between capitalists and the disadvantages to employers forced to limit the working day in the face of unrestricted foreign competition.

and he was shunned by his peers. Althorp and others warned that making drastic changes to the system of poor relief might do more harm than good. By the time a royal commission was appointed to explore the matter in 1832, the Swing Revolt was still dragging on in such places as the Romney Marshes and would continue to flare up later on in some of its early strongholds. The commission was seen by most ministers as simply a way of forestalling Brougham's embarrassing adamance that the system of poor relief should be reformed. Privately, however, the ministers conceded that if some way could be found to ameliorate the condition of the poor, it would bring a much-needed benefit to social stability. But they saw no means of doing so. The commissioners came to see it as their task to come up with a solution.[133] In the process, their agenda was shaped by their own class-based assumptions and ideological suppositions. More will be said below about the rationale behind the passage of the New Poor Law in 1834, as well as the Municipal Reform Act of 1835, a product of the work of a royal commission appointed in July 1833 to review the state of municipal government.

More than a hundred such royal commissions would be appointed between 1815 and 1849. By the 1830s, the use of royal commissions became the standard method of determining the course of legislation and helped both to moderate and legitimate reform measures.[134] The commutation of tithes, the emancipation of slavery, the retention of an unlimited working day in the factory and the New Poor Law, all belonging to the Whig reform package of the years 1833–4, shared certain commonalities. Most broadly speaking, all involved actions which undermined normative systems of labour regulation, whether through the Church, the institution of slavery or the paternalism associated with the Old Poor Law. The Factory Act is a special case, since virtually no regulation existed within the factory, the bill being a measure of compromise designed to check the demand by workers for a ten-hour day whilst responding to calls by reformers to further reduce the use of child labour. In all of this new policy, we can see the influence of *laissez-faire* ideology and political economy. While ideologies played important roles in facilitating and shaping these changes, to a large extent the new policies were simply ways that the state was adapting to changed circumstances.[135] By effectively extricating itself from overseeing various extra-economic forms of labour control, the state was positioning itself to play the role of neutral enforcer and

133. Dunkley 1981, pp. 125–34.
134. Briggs 1979, p. 275.
135. As Dunkley (1981, pp. 146–7) points out: 'It is not the case that the Whigs and their advisers saw economic activities simply as a means to traditional ends... Only two or three generations before 1834, any comparable attempt to nurture such a transformation in social attitudes would have encountered widespread opposition from England's rulers... While the seminal contributions of Senior and Chadwick to the rationalization and articulation of this model cannot be ignored, it must also be recognized that their views dovetailed nicely with authority's changing needs'.

arbiter of economic contracts between free and independent parties exchanging commodities, including 'fictitious' commodities like abstract land and labour.

Grand Union

Two outcomes for the working classes in the aftermath of the Reform Bill were to be expected: first, efforts at building trade federations to represent the working class would be redoubled; second, these efforts would be coloured with rising expectations. The effective end of an unsteady alliance with middle-order radicalism may have left labour more isolated and politically shut out, but to a large degree it also enabled organisers to speak more openly about working-class aspirations. The working classes, said Bronterre O'Brien, ' "aspire to be at the top instead of at the bottom of society – or rather that there should be no bottom or top at all" '.[136] The years 1829–34 saw a flurry of trade union organising motivated by this spirit of union and a strong unity of purpose.[137]

At the same time as reformers were organising upwards of 130 metropolitan political unions across Britain, trade unionists were founding metropolitan and regional trade federations. The Sheffield Trades' General Union had formed by March 1930, while the Leicester Union had a Trades Union Secret Committee by September 1833. The Trades Union at Leeds and the Bradford Trades' Union were part of a larger Yorkshire Trades' Union which authorities blamed for the murder of a Farsley woollen weaver in December 1832. In London, the Metropolitan Trades' Union emerged out of Gast's Philanthropic Hercules. Led by the General Union of Carpenters, it became the National Union of the Working Classes (NUWC), which focused its efforts on reform, while the Grand Union of England focused on workplace issues. In Scotland, Alexander Campbell organised the United Trades of Glasgow, who supported a female operatives' union strike at Aberdeen and who would gather thirty thousand signatures for the Tolpuddle Martyrs. There was talk of a Scottish Confederation of Trades. Edinburgh had its own monthly journal for trade unionists. Tramping was now common in Ireland, but unions were under severe pressure with widespread prosecutions against trade unionists on conspiracy charges in 1833 and 1834. Many trades such as the house furnishers, cabinet makers, bricklayers and carpenters simply affiliated with their English counterparts. A Belfast Branch of the General Trades' Union

136. *Poor Man's Guardian*, 19 October 1833; as quoted in Briggs 1979, p. 290.

137. Chase 2000, pp. 137–8; Thompson (1991, pp. 913–14) argues that 'collective self-consciousness was indeed the great spiritual gain of the Industrial Revolution... It was perhaps a unique formation, this British working class of 1832... Enriched by the experiences of the seventeenth century, carrying through the eighteenth century intellectual and libertarian traditions which we have described, forming their own traditions of mutuality in the friendly society and trades club...'

(the future GNCTU) survived until the Summer of 1834 and marched in Belfast protesting against Tolpuddle.[138]

The years 1830–6 witnessed a general recovery. The year 1833 in particular saw rapid economic growth, presenting the opportunity for trade unionists to try and make up for the losses suffered during the depression years of the late 1820s. But the wave of strikes beginning in the Summer of 1833 were also coloured by the anger felt by working people at being excluded from the franchise. In Norfolk, agrarian labourers struck and there were incidents of arson in the fields to support the strike or intimidate the farmers into freezing wages.[139] In Birmingham, a protracted strike by workmen in the heavy steel tool trade successfully pressured employers to stop making deductions from the prices paid for piecework and resulted in the formation of a union.[140] In Lancashire and Cheshire, John Doherty's NAPL began to fall apart between late 1831 and early 1832 due to an inadequate funding mechanism and the effective end to a temporary alliance between factory spinners and domestic textile workers jointly seeking to combat wage reductions. By 1833, the NAPL existed mostly in name only. Leeds employers in the summer of 1833 drew up a 'bond', agreeing not to employ any members of the union, and a series of strikes ensued which would fail by the following year.[141] In the Potteries of Staffordshire, there had been interest in Owenism and co-operatives since the time of the failed strike of 1825–6. In October 1830, delegates from the NAPL had visited during a strike against payment by truck and proposed that low wages were the real source of the potters' distress. An act of 1831 intended to limit the use of truck proved ineffective.[142] Doherty himself subsequently visited and a local NAPL committee was organised, which was involved in supporting local strikes by spinners and miners. The potters were urged to form their own union and affiliate with the NAPL. Between 1831 and 1833, the National Union of Operative Potters (NUOP) emerged and was able to negotiate a wage-increase. By October 1833, it claimed to have six thousand members in the Potteries and two thousand additional members beyond north Staffordshire. Owen paid several visits to the Potteries that Autumn, and by November there were plans for a network of co-operative stores, a labour bank producing its own notes, a campaign against intemperance, elementary schools and a co-operative factory whose wares were to be sold in the co-operative stores. A co-operative factory was in fact established in Burslem, but it proved unprofitable.[143]

---

138. Chase 2000, pp. 134–47; Rule 1986, p. 293.
139. Wells 1988, p. 121.
140. Behagg 1988, p. 164.
141. Rule 1986, p. 293.
142. Rule 1986, p. 64.
143. Fyson 1988, pp. 201–13.

The building trades had remained to this point both untouched by technology and dominated by small craftsmen who observed the 'time-honoured method of contracting' which 'was for one craftsman to make himself responsible for the job'.[144] But they were now facing reorganisation by contractors from outside the trade who called themselves 'builders' and who inserted themselves as middlemen between the craftsmen and the architects. In Lancashire, contractors drafted 'the document', an agreement not to hire unionised workmen. In response, associations of journeymen and small masters among the carpenters, joiners, masons, bricklayers and plumbers organised a strike in August to demand uniform wage rates and an end to piecework in the building trades. In September, a Builders' Parliament was called in Manchester and while addressing the two hundred and seventy assembled delegates representing thirty thousand operatives, Robert Owen called for a Grand National Guild of Builders based on the principle of co-operative production. Meanwhile, one of the largest Birmingham contractors dismissed all union hands. Birmingham was the city where Owenites predominated among the builders and where they sought to establish the Guildhall, which was to be 'the great showpiece of direct contracting'.[145] By the end of 1833, work on the Guildhall halted due to a lack of funds and organisational problems. Owen envisioned a socialist future in which co-operatives of craftsmen would engage in direct contracting and thereby bring about an end to the ruthless competition between large masters and contractors that led to wage deductions and price reductions. To the highly-skilled craftsmen in the building trades who still observed Saint Monday, Owen's vision seemed to offer the prospect of reclaiming for the artisan 'his status, his pride, his well-being and his independence: the just reward of the special property of skilled labour which he possessed.'[146]

The Builders Union, however, did not admit unskilled labourers such as brickmakers and quarrymen, and Owen was put off by the reluctance of the 'exclusives' to participate in combining with unskilled labour to form a general union. The builders' strikes in Lancashire failed at the end of 1833. In London, the beer strike of 1834 marked the end of the union when a boycott of non-union beer was met by William Cubitt (who had taken over the firm from his brother Thomas) with a refusal to allow any *other* beer onto the worksite, followed by a lockout and presentation of 'the document'. Cubitt, who employed over one thousand workers, was one of the exceptional few large builders in a trade where the 'small man was dominant'.[147] The Cubitts provide another example of capitalist

144. Pollard 1965, p. 85.
145. Rule 1986, p. 298.
146. Rule 1986, pp. 294–6.
147. Mathias 1983, pp. 139 and 241.

organisation without technological innovation.[148] In a manner reminiscent of Josiah Wedgwood, Thomas Cubitt had emerged after the wars with an operation that dispensed with subcontractors and revolutionised the trade through a rigorous labour discipline. For contracting firms maintaining a large force of craftsmen like the Cubitts, busting the union in London meant gaining unrestricted control over the labour process. Local builders' unions were meanwhile content to remain 'exclusives' and admit only skilled workmen among their ranks.[149] Disillusioned with the builders, Owen took his vision and his journal, the *Pioneer*, to London.

Our attention is now drawn back to the silk industry in Derby, where thanks to significant trades-union organising, the silk workers now had a strong union, one which had belonged to the NAPL, paying £60 to it during its existence. On 19 November 1833, a bitter strike and lockout ensued when a silk worker in a silk factory just east and a bit north of the Old Silk Mill refused to accept the usual deductions to his wages and was sacked. This in turn led to a walk-out by nearly seven hundred silk workers. On 23 November, the employers – including William Taylor, current owner of the Old Silk Mill – met and passed a resolution agreeing to a lockout. They made a controversy over the fact that union members were apparently required to swear an oath upon joining, an act still prohibited under law. The *Pioneer* now took up the cause and helped make the Derby strike the focal point for the trades-union movement. Doherty's strategy and Owen's millenarian tone are both seen in its cry: '"The Crusade is commenced against us – the enemy has taken the field: – forward to Derby! – One concentrated effort in that quarter will suffice to plant in triumph the Standard of Union. Neglect in this opportunity and we shall have the curse of protracted warfare – weakness and disorganization..."'[150]

By the end of December there were nearly one thousand five hundred silk, lace and smallware-weaving textile workers on strike in a town of twenty-three thousand, including 430 men, 498 women and 454 children. Strikers received 7s. per week out of national union levies. By now the strike had become a national *cause célèbre*, and would be credited as a catalyst in the formation of the Grand National Consolidated Trades Union (GNCTU) in February.[151]

The politicisation of the countryside had informed Swing and during the build-up to the reform bill there was increasing contact developing between the countryside and the political unions. In 1833, sporadic strikes and arson incidents designed to sustain victories won during Swing coincided with strikes in agrarian

148. Rule 1986, p. 294.
149. Rule 1986, pp. 294–8.
150. Butterton 1996, p. 90.
151. Butterton 1996, pp. 85–95; Whitehead 1999.

towns, and employers retaliated with lock-outs against unionists extending into the countryside. Throughout 1833, there was tremendous excitement over proposals to form the GNCTU. The Co-Operative Boot and Shoemakers of Northampton voted to observe the rules and regulations of the National Trades' Union before any such body existed. In October, a rural organiser and former Swing protestor named George Loveless organised a Friendly Society of Agricultural Labourers in the tiny village of Tolpuddle, Dorset. It was intended to serve as the local hub for rural union-building by the GNCTU. Loveless's group was apparently visited by delegates of the GNCTU even though the GNCTU had not actually formed yet. Meanwhile in London that October, the Owenites held a conference in London to form a 'Grand National Moral Union of the Productive Classes of the United Kingdom', which aimed to bring the co-operative and trades-union movements together and wage a general strike to form a co-operative society. The urgency of the Derby strike, however, apparently hastened the bypassing of this project and the formation of the GNCTU in February 1834, by which time the silk workers were growing desperate as the owners had recruited enough strikebreakers to get their silk factories partially operative.[152]

By the spring of 1834, there was a 'real sense of crisis in the relationship between trade unionism, the employers and the State'.[153] The GNCTU had extended its reach into the countryside as agricultural labourers came to events in cities like Brighton and were encouraged to take GNCTU propaganda back to the villages. Fearing a recurrence of Swing, James Frampton, JP for Dorset, took note of the use of oath-taking at Tolpuddle and arrested six poor labourers, subsequently gaining approval from Lord Melbourne in the Home Office to try them under the 1797 statute against the taking of oaths.[154] On 19 March, they were sentenced to seven years' transportation. Judge Williams of the circuit handed out the sentences and was quoted two days later in *The Times* as observing that the '"use of all punishment is not with a view to the particular offenders or for the sake of revenge – that is not the view of those who administer the law, nor the intention of the law itself; it is for the sake of example"'.[155] Within the trade-union movement, this fact was widely recognised and the case of the Tolpuddle martyrs immediately came to be seen, rightly, as an open move by the Home Office to dampen efforts at extending unionisation into the countryside as well as a threat to the trade-union

152. Butterton 1996, pp. 92–3. The only physical violence related to the strike came on 8 February 1834, when a group of union men confronted a group of strikebreakers returning from the Seven Stars pub and an innocent by-standing hawker was stabbed. The hawker survived, but one of the strikebreakers, Henry Ingram, was subsequently tried and sentenced to death before his sentence was commuted to transportation for life.

153. Sykes 1988, p. 193.

154. Wells 1988, pp. 120–3.

155. From *The Times*, 21 March 1834, as quoted in Chase 2000, p. 166.

movement itself.[156] Tolpuddle quickly eclipsed the Derby strike as the focus of efforts to form a grand union and call for a general strike.

There is insufficient data to determine the actual numbers of workers who participated in the GNCTU. While some estimates have put the figure as high as a million, surviving records put the formal paying membership at little more than sixteen thousand.[157] The NAPL had far more *formal* members and lasted considerably longer than the GNCTU, but historians have paid far more attention to the latter, most likely because of the involvement and leadership of Robert Owen. During his absence in America, Owen's proposals for co-operatives and education programmes had gained popularity among trade unionists. With both Cobbett and Hunt suffering ill health and Feargus O'Connor still an unknown quantity, Owen now assumed leadership of the union movement almost by default. One of the advantages of marrying Owenism to trade unionism was the broadening of the appeal, as craftsmen-like printers and engineers who had eschewed trade unionism were open to Owenite principles. The arguments put forward in favour of forming the GNCTU were based on a conception of building a 'moral union' around unity of purpose. In the factories, Owen proposed that masters would be replaced by superintendents elected from the workers. This strategy dovetailed neatly with the aspirations of skilled artisans who sought to restore control of the labour process as one means by which they could forestall being fully proletarianised, or being reduced to the status of sweatshop labourers like the hand-loom weavers. While such practices as apprenticeship and the search were still observed in many trades,[158] the independent status of skilled craft workers – whose numbers in the 1830s were still significant – was clearly in decline. Not only in factories, but as we have seen in the building trades, in the mines and in agriculture, the labour force was increasingly being reorganised by capitalistic employers hiring large workforces on an individual contract basis. The increasing pressure from the threat of full exposure to an emerging labour market made the search for solutions and alternatives more urgent. The appeal of Owenism 'lay in the way it provided a coherent analysis of social trends which

156. There was no question of the Tolpuddle Martyrs being involved in any attempt at inciting sedition, which is what the Naval Mutinies Act against the administering of oaths sought to suppress. It was clearly a wilful misuse of the law in the interests of class suppression. In April, five potters were brought before Judge Williams in Staffordshire on the same charge of administering oaths. But the situation had changed, for not only had Tolpuddle served to make an example, but the GNCTU itself was already showing signs of falling apart, so the threat did not seem so imminent (Fyson 1988, p. 208). Judge Williams's decision to acquit the defendants also serves as an example of the kind of discretionary use of the law that the central government would subsequently attempt to discourage through the reform of the Old Poor Law.

157. Chase 2000, pp. 148–9.

158. Leeson 1979, p. 90.

confirmed the focus on competition as disruptive to decent standards and social peace'.[159] As John Rule comments, skilled labour *did* have something more to lose than just its chains.

Owenism also brought with it the proposal of worker co-operatives and labour exchanges. Truck was universally despised, and co-operatives would not only allow workers to buy food and clothing on credit, but would prevent such abuses as the adulteration of food and the practice of short weight by employers and middlemen.[160] Thus during the very brief period of the GNCTU's formal existence between the publication of its rules on 1 March and its disintegration in July 1834, there were significant experiments in collectivism and co-operation as part of a grandiose and fatally-flawed attempt to combat the advance of industrial capitalism by putting forward an alternative arrangement of social relations simultaneously rooted in the conservative tradition of sturdy, independent craftsmen combined with the Owenite thrust of co-operation as a means to displace the evils of market competition.

To speak of 'Owenism' as a single, coherent body of ideology is misleading. By the time of Owen's return from the United States in 1828, Owenism in practice had taken on many different forms, and in theory had taken on a life independent of Owen's own writings and teachings, in large part because Owenism sought to bring together skilled craftsmen with poor and unskilled labourers, working alongside well-intentioned middle-class philanthropists. The involvement of wealthier elements with little at stake led to lavish overspending on such projects as the London labour exchange. At the same time, the millenarian overtones in Owen's confident prophesies of a future moral society was bound to draw the interest of the growing numbers of followers of such self-proclaimed prophets such as Zion Ward, the crippled shoemaker and former Methodist who believed himself to be Christ and had preached to thousands before being sentenced to two years in prison for blasphemy in 1832. Ward's following was one of many to break away from Methodism, a religion that was particularly popular among craftsmen and miners, and to a lesser degree among unskilled labourers. Aside from the three hundred and twenty thousand 'hearers' affiliated with Methodism by 1830 (a figure that had grown from seventy-two thousand in 1791) another one hundred thousand followers were now faithful to groups that had splintered from Methodism.[161] Despite his atheism, Owen's tendency toward

159. Price 1986, p. 54.

160. Rule 1986, pp. 64–9 and 199. The importance of better access to clothing was not insignificant: 'some historians have followed contemporaries in suggesting that even the demographic revolution owed something to the mortality-decreasing effect of cheap, washable, cotton underclothing!'

161. Hay and Rogers 1997, 168–72. The impact of Methodism upon working-class organisation during this whole period should not be underestimated. It is likely that

prophecy and his open invitation to the very poor to participate in his projects helped to make Owenism a part of this milieu.

Owenism's inclusion of women was also significant as a challenge to the sexism rife in many trades:

> [T]he Cotton Spinners' Union of 1829 specifically excluded women. The handloom weavers consistently refused to admit women to their unions and in 1834 the London tailors struck work to drive women from the trade. The women did come to organize on their own, but combinations that had once been sexually integrated were being replaced by sex-segregated ones. The increasing tension between men and women with the debasement of craft skills revealed to many women workers that 'the men are as bad as their masters'. Not only did workers' organizations become increasingly segmented, but the language of artisans' institutions and the perception of skill itself became increasingly identified with masculinity.[162]

Women who worked in factories gained an undeserved reputation for sexual promiscuity, perhaps due to the fact that many young and single women without families were now earning enough disposable income to engage in flashy dressing. Their relative independence was also exceptional and therefore feared and envied. Outside the factories the rule still held that women's work was supplementary and their wages were correspondingly lower than men's. Worse still, many women were caught in the widening web of urban sweatshop labour, based on piecework and requiring ever-increasing levels of labour-time or labour intensity to offset the effect of falling prices. Such 'sweated workers inverted capitalist development to make the family an economic unit again, but this time in squalid urban tenement rather than rural cottage'.[163] Such women became the subject of middle-class attacks on their inadequacy and lack of 'respectability', seeing working-class women as brutal and indifferent towards their children, a view that has survived with the condescension of posterity but which is unfounded.[164] It also seems unfounded to suggest that such views pervaded the working class itself, as evidenced by the nation-wide support for the Derby strikers, more than a third of whom were women, as well as the support in Scotland for the union of women power-loom weavers by the United Trades of Glasgow and the formation of two London lodges for female workers within the GNCTU.

---

radicals appropriated Methodism's organising methods, such as the division of congregations into discussion 'classes'.

162. Berg 1985, p. 160.

163. Rule 1986, pp. 179–87.

164. Anxieties may have increased, writes Rule, 'but there is no need to accept at face value a generally levelled accusation that indifference, brutality and an exploitative attitude toward children were the norms of working-class life' (Rule 1986, p. 205).

At its core, the GNCTU was fundamentally a trade-union body that had grown out of the various committees set up by trade unions to support the Derby strike and then the Tolpuddle Martyrs; the extent to which Owenism pervaded the whole experiment has been exaggerated. Founded in London, it also was unable to plant strong roots in Lancashire, perhaps owing to the lasting influence of the NAPL. In the wake of the defeated strikes in Lancashire, John Fielden, the radical MP for Oldham, launched a campaign among Lancashire factory workers to call for an eight-hour day. Under the name of the Regeneration Society, the campaign was to begin on 1 March, the same day as the GNCTU published its rules and the same day as the 1833 Factory Act was to take effect. Owen, one of the first factory owners to voluntarily limit the working day (to 11 hours) in New Lanark, happily endorsed the campaign. As nominal leader of the GNCTU, Owen's limited involvement typified his leadership style, which was more about moving from town to town to give speeches than being involved in the details of local organising and tactics. When the experiment began to unravel as one local strike after another ended in disaster over the course of 1834, Owen lost interest and moved away from trades-union organising back to his focus on collectivism and co-operation. At Derby, despite discussion within the GNCTU about purchasing silk machinery and building a syndicalist factory, the strike was broken by late April when many strikers quit the union and returned to work, some six hundred of them being left unemployed and apparently struggling on into May to maintain the strike.[165] The GNCTU subsequently became more London-centred, involving more than twenty London trades but dominated by the tailors and shoemakers. On 21 April, some thirty thousand members marched in support of the Tolpuddle Martyrs.

Only a week earlier, on 14 April, two police officers in Oldham, Lancashire interrupted a union meeting where several single-mill strikes that were crippling the town were being discussed. Two men who had been involved with disputes with their masters over attempts to increase their hours were arrested and some papers were seized. The next morning, not a mill in the town was active. The Regeneration Society was able to make demands for an eight-hour day a part of the strike, but had not initiated it. Apparently afraid that Tolpuddle was being repeated in Oldham, angry residents attacked the officers and freed the prisoners as they were being escorted to see the magistrate. A crowd of some ten thousand then proceeded to the mill of a Mr. Thompson who, in the interest of keeping his machines running, had already employed armed 'knobsticks', who fired upon the stone-throwing crowd, killing one and wounding two others. The mill, its machines and Mr. Thompson's residence were subsequently ransacked.

165. Butterton 1996, pp. 93–5.

By 16 April, the strike had spread to surrounding towns, and in Oldham itself some twelve thousand were now on strike. A public jury acquitted those arrested and effected the eventual dismissal of the arresting officers. 'The effect of all this unabashed justice', writes Weaver, 'was a considerable lessening of tension in Oldham, and on 26 April the workers began returning to the mills on the masters' terms. By May the strike was over'.[166] In Manchester, the tailors also waged a long and bitter strike, but without the 'convulsive effect on the local economy of the textile and mining strikes of 1829–31'.[167] Both the Manchester tailors and the Oldham strikers expressed interest in, but stopped short of joining, the GNCTU.

In London, the Tailors launched a strike at what seemed an optimal time: April was their best month, the economy was in recovery and the GNCTU offered the promise of a large strike fund. But Owen and his followers condemned the strike, Owen himself complaining of ' "little petty proceedings about strikes for wages" ', and Morisson, the Owenite editor of the *Pioneer*, added: ' "We depend for deliverance entirely upon grand and national movements, and not upon the limited struggles of individual trades" '.[168] It was one thing to call upon all members of a grand union to rush to the aid of local strikers or martyrs outside the City, and quite another thing for a core member group to call a strike in *anticipation* of support from the collective. By mid-May, the strike was failing and the GNCTU's executive suddenly recognised the implications of its failure and sprang to action too late, putting out a call on 2 June for all members to contribute one day's wages each week. The call received scant reply. The strike failed and the disappointed tailors seceded, followed by the shoemakers, thus withdrawing the core of support from the GNCTU, which lingered on mostly in name only until the following August.[169]

The motivating idea behind the formation of the GNCTU, that of a grand union with pockets deep enough to support multiple local strikes simultaneously and involving various strata of working men, women and children, had swiftly proved to be unworkable. It was romantic in a way that the NAPL had not been, and the lack of realism may partly account for its rapid fall. But the nation-wide support for the Derby strikers and the Tolpuddle martyrs had been

166. Weaver 1987, pp. 108–12. Foster (Foster 1974) attempts to portray the Oldham strike as being 'fundamentally trade unionist' and led by the workers' 'vanguard'. Sykes (Sykes 1988, p. 190) comments that this is to miss the importance of Oldham's general strike, which because it was a general strike involving the town as a whole, 'illustrated the intensity of working-class communal solidarity in the face of aggressive action by authorities'. The Oldham strike was also the exception to the rule for Lancashire in this year.

167. Sykes 1988, p. 189.

168. As quoted in Rule 1986, p. 302. The executive committee echoed these sentiments.

169. Rule 1986, pp. 302–3; Sykes 1988, p. 186; Briggs 1979, p. 291.

an unprecedented display of solidarity amongst workers of nearly all sorts. As Leeson notes: 'The rules of every single one of those organisations would have barred the men of Dorset who had served no formal apprenticeship, from joining them. Yet those craft-proud journeymen recognized that brotherhood had a wider meaning than the old exclusive one'.[170] Exclusion from the franchise was still a fresh grievance and in this way the Reform Bill coloured these events. A simultaneous factor is the degree to which all of these workers were increasingly coming to share the same condition of being propertyless wage labourers. E.P. Thompson writes that 'From 1830 onwards a more clearly defined class consciousness, in the customary Marxist sense, was maturing, in which working people were aware of continuing both old and new battles on their own'.[171] John Rule adds that while in the eighteenth century social class was merely manifest, in the nineteenth century 'social cleavage' was being replaced with 'horizontal class divisions'.[172] But in the 'making' of the working class, Rule feels that one thing is for certain: 'there can be no presumption of a uniform and wholly homogeneous experience'.[173] There is no question that the emerging working class was heterogeneous. Consider the way in which Irish labourers were migrating within Britain to take over 'whole classes of work', such as portside hauling and heaving. English workers 'either refused the menial, unpleasant tasks or could not keep up with the pace'.[174] The Irish thus took up much of the work of unskilled labourers, just as women and children had done in the early factories. The skilled versus unskilled labour divide was perhaps the most important distinction within the working class. There were also important regional differences, including the disparity between the industrial North and the agrarian South, and regional de-industrialisation in such parts as the West of England, which by the 1830s was in 'terminal decline'.[175] And, of course, there was the divide between traditional craftsmen enjoying control over the labour process and still practicing St. Monday, and fully-proletarian factory workers subject to a labour process characterised by 'regularity, routine and monotony quite unlike pre-industrial rhythms of work'.[176] What was remarkable about the GNCTU was the *attempt* to bring such a diversity of types of labour together under one umbrella in the interest of providing mutual protection and co-operation. There was certainly something very forward-looking in this, but at the same time it was a vision rooted in notions of 'brotherhood' between traditional craftsmen.

---

170. Leeson 1979, p. 120.
171. Thompson 1991, p. 782. If there was one form of class consciousness in the eighteenth century, writes Rule, it was of the consumer class (Rule 1981, p. 212).
172. John Rule 1981, pp. 208–9.
173. Rule 1986, p. 21.
174. Thompson 1991, p. 474.
175. Randall 1991, p. 286.
176. Hobsbawm 1986, p. 85–6.

To paint Owenism as nostalgic does point out what it shared with the traditional artisanal outlook rooted in custom, for Owenism sought to reintroduce a form of normative ('moral') regulation of the market that may have borrowed from traditional forms, but was new in its design. This raises an important question. For if capital is a social relation that demands that no form of extra-economic regulation impede it as it flows through its various circuits, is there no other way to resist the imposition of the social relation of capital than to counter it by imposing or reimposing some form of normative economic regulation? As for class consciousness, what else can this term mean in relation to our period other than an increasing awareness of the shared condition of being (mostly) disenfranchised, and increasingly pressed into the service of factories as proletarian wage labourers whose labour-power was treated as a commodity, as the property and capital of the factory owner or the farmer? What made class relations horizontal was the divide between owners of capital increasingly asserting control over production and the labour process, and direct producers increasingly lacking such control. The fact that the most vociferous opponents of this emerging set of capitalist class relations were the only semi-proletarian craftsmen still holding onto control of the labour process only makes sense, for they stood to lose the most. But the participation of tens of thousands of factory workers, including thousands of children, in large and increasingly well-organised strikes is also very important as a proletarian form of resistance to capitalist production that, while not reclaiming control over the labour process, asserts considerable power over it by the *withdrawal* of labour-power. And does a strike not require solidarity and a shared sense of morality?

The New Poor Law

Another factor in the emergence of an increasingly shared identity among working people in the United Kingdom was the simultaneous decline of institutional practices of paternalism, which along with the removal of the legal underpinnings of custom effectively forced working people to start looking at the world in new ways, and to do more thinking for themselves. By the 1830s, the working classes:

> had become what Pitt and Castlereagh tried so hard to prevent them from becoming, politicians. They talked about the affairs of the State: they discussed the basis of rights and duties, they took an ominous interest in taxes and sinecures, and it was not the phrases of 1789 but the cry of Church and King that awakened their execrations... What came about during this period was the alienation of the working classes, due not to the positive influence of ideas or enthusiasms, but to the effect of experience on ways of thinking and looking

> at life . . . There was no general revolt against the established order in 1790. The normal working man accepted the government and institutions of the country with as little question as the normal aristocrat. But the Industrial Revolution obliged everybody whom it affected to think about the problems it raised, and when they addressed themselves to these problems the rich and the poor started from different standpoints: the rich from the abstractions of poverty, the poor from the facts of their own lives.[177]

One of these 'facts of their own lives' that the poor were made never to forget was that they were not owners of property. In making their case for asserting longstanding privileges and rights rooted in custom, they argued for workplace democracy and the need for state regulation in order to shield workers from the worst effects of market dependency. Trade unionists put forward their case for regulation by arguing that if property was sacrosanct and if the state's role was to protect property, then fairness only dictated that the state should also protect the only property that the labouring poor had: their labour. When this argument was dismissed out of hand, open revolt seemed a legitimate option. And when open revolt was put down, there remained few means by which they might resist the imposition of a capital relation. The choice was increasingly that between resignation or accommodation.

The upper crust of the working class, small masters and skilled labourers whose earnings were sufficient to entitle them to vote for the reformed Parliament as well as to save money, were now faced with the open invitation to abandon resistance and consider themselves part of the so-called 'middle class'. Belonging to the middle class depended first and foremost upon gaining 'respectability', which itself was based upon ability to pay, or in other words on having enough wealth or property to be a trustworthy borrower. An attitude of superiority was also important. Being middle-class meant belonging to the 'civilised' world set apart from the 'barbarians'. The world of the middle class, writes Hobsbawm, was 'freely open to all. Those who failed to enter its gates therefore demonstrated a lack of personal intelligence, moral force or energy which automatically condemned them; or at best a historic or racial heritage which must permanently cripple them, or else they would already have made use of their opportunities'.[178] Middle-order reformers saw it as their duty to inculcate 'improved' morals and behaviours among the working poor, and this underlay the growing consensus on the need for an educational system. Violent revolt seemed to demonstrate that the poor were not ready to be included in the body politic and enjoy the franchise. The trade unionists' movement for

177. Hammond and Hammond 1995, pp. 288–9.
178. Hobsbawm 1994, pp. 241–2.

democracy in the workplace was treated by middle-class reformers as dangerous for a number of reasons. The period saw a tenacious struggle by workers to preserve subcontracting and the gang system and prevent the conversion of direct employment by individual contract. The initiation ceremonies and other secret rituals, violence against knobsticks, trade funerals and internal systems of discipline including fines ran counter to 'liberal' middle-order notions of individual liberty. Their practices of direct democracy set a dangerous precedent and served as a challenge to the system of representative democracy qualified by property ownership that had recently been extended. The Factory Commissioner E.C. Tufnell thought that trade unions practiced '"the worst of democracies – where power is based on outrage, – whose practice is tyranny – and whose end is self destruction"'.[179] Many newly voting 'middle-class' citizens saw it as their contribution to the body politic to demand that the government run a tight ship. Violence and rebellion could not be tolerated. Withdrawing state assistance would break the false sense of entitlement exhibited by many among the poor, and the workhouse would teach the values of thrift, discipline and obedience that were required for imposing what amounted to a new moral order, the moral order of liberalism.

By 1834, the Speenhamland system had been widely abandoned and spending on poor rates had actually reached its lowest point since peaking in 1817,[180] yet the poor law commissioners based their case for reform of the system upon the unsound argument that outdoor relief was the principal culprit in the widespread immiseration of agrarian labourers by allowing wages to fall below their natural rate. In Chapter Ten, it was suggested that the actual cause of low wages was a surplus of labour and high unemployment.[181] But this fact was not acknowledged by the commissioners. Nor could they seriously consider the contribution of enclosures to creating such a vast, market-dependent, agrarian wage labour force, for to explore these avenues would be to call the whole system of agrarian capitalism into question. Embedded within their Malthusian argument that the system of outdoor relief was itself the cause of immiseration were deep-seated notions that agrarian labourers:

> were improvident loafers who deserved to be stigmatized... [a stigma which had been] enshrined in the 1832 reform act, which debarred anyone from voting in a general election who had received parish relief at any time during the previous year... [T]he report recommended a dramatic extension of the centralizing principle as a means of forcing the able-bodied paupers to throw themselves on the mercy of the labour market. It embodied a potent blend

179. Tufnell 1834, p. 125, as quoted In Rule, 1988, pp. 170–2.
180. Harling and Mandler 1993, p. 56.
181. See Chapter Ten, pp. 551–3.

> of evangelical retribution and laissez-faire optimism, which assumed that there was a hard core of feckless labourers who needed to be disciplined into self-reliance, and that the free labour market at all times generated enough employment to permit them to be self-reliant.[182]

Combined with Hannah More's campaign for establishing rudimentary education programmes to inculcate habits of 'obedience, industry and thrift',[183] we have the formula for Victorianism, beneath which was the powerful dynamic of market dependency and the rise of capital. Hobsbawm sees in the poor law reform and the subsequent abolition of the Corn Laws in 1846 the final defeat of efforts to 'safeguard the old rural society against the corrosion of the cash nexus',[184] or in other words to keep agriculture from being fully thrown open to regulation by market forces. While this may be true of the Corn Laws, poor relief is a more complex matter, not only because outdoor relief was never uniformly practiced, but more importantly because when we put the poor laws in historical context we see that they not only provided a way of staving off starvation, but also in the context of low wages and high unemployment they may have increased workers' calorie intake, thereby increasing their productivity.[185] The reform of the poor laws was not in fact so much of a *passive* act of lifting the 'fetters' on the free action of the market, as one of *actively* seeking a solution to the problem of rural poverty in the marketplace itself.

Hobsbawm and Rudé claim that 'the only connection which can be legitimately claimed' between Swing and the Poor Law Amendment Act of 1834 'is one of probability, and nobody would argue that the protesting labourers were more than one factor among several'.[186] This claim deflects attention from the most direct connection between the Swing Revolt and the Amendment Act, namely the degree to which the concessions made by local authorities to the protesters alarmed the central government and became the focal point of the commission's proposals. To Nassau Senior, the most outrageous aspect of Swing was the apparent view of the labourers that ' "wages are not a matter of contract but a matter of right" '.[187] Here was the influence of Arthur Young and Reverend Malthus, who had advocated the abolition of the poor laws on the grounds that

---

182. Harling 2001, pp. 89–91. Hobsbawm 1986, pp. 88–9 concurs: 'The Poor Law was not so much intended to help the unfortunate as to stigmatize the self-confessed failures of society... There have been few more inhuman statutes than the Poor Law Act of 1834'.

183. Owen 1975, p. 321.

184. Hobsbawm 1994, p. 65.

185. Blaug 1964, p. 241; as already mentioned above, see Chapter Ten, pp. 551–2.

186. Hobsbawm and Rudé 1968, p. 297.

187. N.W. Senior to Lord Brougham, 14 September 1832, as quoted in Dunkley 1981, p. 139. Contrast this with Arthur Young's criticism that the labourers had come to see poor relief as a right and not a badge of humiliation; see p. 690 above.

they merely served to maintain the poor without increasing the supply of food, and who saw it as delusive to argue that any individual possesses '"a right to subsistence when his labour will not fairly purchase it"'.[188] Led by Senior and the urban-sanitation reformer Edwin Chadwick, what the commissioners found most disturbing about the Swing protestors were the 'anarchical' attitudes of the rebels, who seemed unrepentant and stood by their convictions that their distress was a result of the fraud and mismanagement of the poor law overseers, and continued to hold on to 'threadbare' customary expectations that the local authority was responsible for providing them with relief in times of distress. The root of the problem, then, lay with the capitulation of local administrators to these customary expectations, and the task of reform was to eliminate the persisting bonds of paternal benevolence that clearly had survived to a considerable degree under conditions of post-enclosure agrarian capitalism. The fact that poor relief remained in the hands of parochial administrators meant that the eighteenth-century principle of administrative justice still applied. The granting or denial of an appeal for relief was still made at the discretion of the local magistrate, who through occasional or even frequent displays of benevolence could enhance his own authority, and simultaneously play the role of the neutral arbiter, passing judgment upon 'the supplicant's value to the community and his right to the means of life', thereby reinforcing 'personal ties and esteem, providing a means for patronage to bridge the great vertical distances in the social order'.[189] To the poor law commissioners, this not only invited maladministration and abuse of the rate-payers but also led to accommodation with protestors in open revolt, which simply would not do. The solution proposed by the commissioners was not only to centralise poor relief administration and thereby take it out of the hands of parochial and discretionary control by substituting the universal, mechanical and impersonal system of workhouse discipline for the contingent, paternal and personal system of local parish relief, thereby breaking the 'link between action and responsibility in administrative decision-making... [which] was absolutely vital to the paternal ideal',[190] but the commissioners also sought to divorce the system of providing poor relief from the operations of the labour market itself. Dunkley provides a breathtaking summary of the commissioners' logic:

> The recommendation to confine able-bodied relief to 'well-regulated' workhouses was intended specifically to extricate labor from the throes of a system

188. Malthus 1986, p. 505 as quoted in McNally 1993, pp. 77–9, who notes that while Malthus's position that no individual had a natural right to subsistence remained constant through the different versions of his essay, the later editions dropped his earlier reservations about placing the poor in workhouses.
189. Dunkley 1981, p. 141.
190. Dunkley 1981, p. 148.

> that destroyed incentive, discouraged efficiency, and extinguished ambition. Severing public aid from private employment, in conjunction with a substantial degree of stringency in the administration of that aid, promised effectively to deter the workers from resorting to the parish for support; this in turn would expose them to the rigors of open competition for employment. Once strictly enforced, a free market in labor would foster the full range of economic virtues in each worker, and individual self-interest would thereby be enlisted in the fight to release the productive energies of a population that had been foolishly insulated from the 'natural' struggle for subsistence. The expected results pointed to a spectacular transformation in the condition of the laboring poor: the greater industry of independent labor would augment employers' profits, which then would create a larger wages fund; at the same time, the increased efficiency of labor would provide sufficient motivation for the hiring of more workers, such demand necessarily resulting in higher wages.
>
> This faith in the absorptive powers of the economy in general, and the elasticity of demand in the agrarian employment market in particular, seemed for the first time to offer an escape from the Malthusian trap of unremitting population pressure on the resources of the poor. As long as poverty was seen as the result of some immutable law of nature, the reduction or abolition of poor relief entailed, at least in the short-term, crisis for the poor and dislocation of the social order. In rejecting this view, the commissioners looked instead to the marketplace as the key factor in determining the state of the poor. It was on the basis of the capacity of the competitive market to raise wages that the commissioners appealed to the propertied classes to work toward sharp reductions in aid to the able-bodied, the workhouses ensuring provision for what was believed to be a small number of involuntary poor. In thus denying the existence of a genuine surplus population in the south, the commissioners cut through the impasse that had hitherto defeated all attempts to devise a comprehensive poor law measure. While the fallacies of the commissioners' propositions may now appear obvious, the Whig ministers clutched at this apparent answer to a problem that continued to arouse their deepest concern. Further incidents of violence in the countryside, despite judicial retaliation against the Swing rioters, persisted in highlighting the ineffectiveness of government policy.[191]

What is simply remarkable about his passage from Dunkley is how fully he has explicated the *active* efforts of the state to create a capitalist labour market. This level of ordering and intervention in structuring the market goes well beyond simply positioning the state to play the role of neutral arbiter between contract-

191. Dunkley 1981, pp. 135–6.

ing parties in an ostensibly free labour market, though that was already assumed. And certainly the process does involve the intentional dismantling of the parochial system of parish relief, which had enabled the survival of a large measure of benevolent paternalism despite the growth of agrarian capitalism and a force of market-dependent agrarian wage labourers. But that is only a clearing away of the old to make room for the new, and what was new and 'unprecedented was the scope and boldness of the theoretical underpinnings of [the commissioners'] palliatives'.[192] The assumptions that went into this landmark legislation, the degree of market idealism or market fundamentalism, are startlingly salient even to twenty-first century conditions. In the place of deference to paternalism, market coercion and the threat of privation by unemployment would become the mechanism to discipline labour, and better still, would help to inculcate the positive virtues of 'obedience, industry and thrift'. Unencumbered by normative social restrictions, capitalist farmers could now pick and choose the most desirable employees in a free labour market, thereby reinforcing a process of selection which would promote the most hard-working and well-behaved. At the other extreme, those prone to idleness and indolence would find themselves forced to earn their bread in a workhouse, where they were to be schooled in the proper moral behaviours.

Life in the workhouse was now *intended* to be so intolerable, and the stigma of dependence was so well enforced, that rural paupers would accept any job offered to them. Inside the workhouse, husbands were separated from their families 'in order to discourage the sentimental and unmalthusian habit of thoughtless procreation'.[193] The conditions within the workhouses varied from county to county. Cases of scandalous neglect were sometimes reported. It was discovered in 1845 that the paupers at a workhouse in Andover, Hampshire who had been put to work crushing bones were so hungry they had taken to sucking the marrow out of the bones.[194]

The most optimistic assumption of the commissioners lay in their conviction that the problem of low wages would be remedied by the improved productivity of labour under the lash of market competition, resulting in higher profits, more investment, more jobs and better wages. What actually happened is that rural immiseration persisted into the 1850s.[195] Not surprisingly, many parishes continued to practice outdoor relief. But the Poor Law Amendment Act, which received royal assent on 14 August 1834, established the new principle that the state was now the guardian of market forces in the countryside. Bread riots would

192. Dunkley 1981, p. 135.
193. Hobsbawm 1977, pp. 188, 203.
194. Harling 2001, p. 92.
195. Hobsbawm 1977, p. 203.

henceforth decline sharply as their effectiveness waned, the local guardians of poor administration now being elected in secret by the rate-payers. Country policing would be converted from the recruitment of volunteer forces to a force of paid professionals – 'the "plague of blue locusts" as it was called in Huddersfield'.[196]

Was there famine as a result of the termination of outdoor relief? Aside from the rare cases where an historical record exists, tracking or measuring the number of isolated incidents of death by famine, or more commonly by disease hastened as a result of malnutrition is very difficult. However, as the new system went into effect, the most vulnerable populations of British society, urban and rural, typically wound up in workhouses. By the late eighteenth century, workhouses and other poor law institutions would become perhaps the most common place for a poor person to die.[197] This is one of the places the rural labourer who could not find employment found him or herself. Other options included relocating to towns and cities in search of work or emigration to the colonies.

The rift over the handling of the Irish question continued to divide the Whigs in 1834. The fear of the more conservative members of the party was that they were losing control to the 'Destructives', meaning the Irish and Radical factions, among whom O'Connell was the most effective leader. 'O'Connell's Tail', as it was known, was tallied by the Tories in 1833 at some 190 '"thick-and-thin Radicals, Repealers from Ireland, members or friends of the political Unions, and so forth"', whose 'most cohesive characteristic seemed to be their estrangement from the aristocracy'.[198] While the 'Tail' rarely voted as a bloc, there was the possibility that it *could* serve to heighten anxieties and deepen the growing rift between moderate and liberal Whigs. William IV was in no doubt as to where his sympathies lay. In November, Althorp resigned, leaving Melbourne without a leader in the Commons. When Melbourne met with the King and proposed to recruit the reformer Lord Russell to the post, William was appalled. He dismissed the Whigs and recalled his favourite arch-Tory, the Duke of Wellington, to form a government. The Duke agreed to serve only until Peel returned from his travels abroad.

Upon his return to assume office in December, Peel as Prime Minister issued the so-called Tamworth Manifesto, a declaration that 'conservatives' under his leadership accepted the Reform Bill as a final settlement of the constitution and

196. Price 1986, p. 56.

197. By 1871, 11.3 per cent of all deaths in London and 5.6 percent of all deaths in England and Wales would take place inside workhouses and other poor law institutions. These figures would rise to 20.9 per cent for London and 9.7 percent for England and Wales by 1906. About twice as many persons died in workhouses and other poor law institutions as died in hospitals over the same period. Crowther 1981, p. 57.

198. Kriegel 1968, p. 69, quoting a letter from Lord Mahon to Sir Robert Peel dated 8 January 1833.

that his government would proceed cautiously with any further reformist measures so as not to infringe upon established rights and privileges. Peel also introduced the Municipal Reform Act or Municipal Corporations Act which despite being the result of the work of a royal commission set up under Grey's government was also a continuation of Peel's efforts at penal reform and the introduction of policing, as it required 178 incorporated boroughs to establish new police forces overseen by local watch committees. By enabling unincorporated towns such as Manchester and Birmingham to at long last petition for incorporation, the act completed the work of the Reform Bill, eventually incorporating 62 additional boroughs.[199] Peel's first ministry enjoyed the smallest of majorities in Parliament. His attempts to court Stanley's faction proved unsuccessful. Stanley and his followers declared a third 'party' independent of the Whigs and Tories, though his following was insubstantial. Meanwhile, O'Connell had been making overtures to the Whigs since September. Peel saw no choice but to dissolve Parliament and call for a general election in December. The new elections produced a House with 290 Tories, 218 Whigs, of which 40 or more were 'doubtful' and 150 Radicals and O'Connellites. While moderate Whigs like Grey and Melbourne found any conciliation with the Radicals distasteful, more reformist members of the party came to an agreement with O'Connell and the Radicals in February 1835 under what became known as the Lichfield House Compact, by which the Radicals would support a Whig government in exchange for O'Connell getting to handpick the appointments to posts in Ireland. It was over a new Irish Church bill to appropriate Irish Church funds for secular purposes, carried by the Whigs by 285 to 258 on 7 April, that Peel would resign, causing Melbourne to suffer 'the embarrassment of victory' and return to the premiership. The compromise that had returned the Whigs to power, however, did not significantly weaken the oligarchic exclusiveness of the Whigs, whose power would steadily decline over the next six years.[200]

In the aftermath of the failure of the GNCTU and the passage of the New Poor Law, trade-union activity presumably became more practical and more limited, although Leeson sees the period as '"not a hiatus, but a richly active one"'.[201] The struggle for workplace control, apprenticeship, universal suffrage and short parliaments continued, as did efforts to amalgamate. There were few trades that did not belong to a larger network. 'In 1834 "union" usually implied an organization with from 20 to 80 member societies and by the 1840s the term "branch" had come into use'.[202] The National Union of Operative Potters (NUOP) now

199. Harling 2001, pp. 94 and 109.
200. Kriegel 1968, pp. 69–91.
201. Leeson 1984, pp. 15–17; Rule (ed.) 1988, p. 216; Rule 1986, p. 320.
202. Rule (ed.) 1988, p. 17.

included not only the Staffordshire potteries but 'branches' in a dozen or more additional towns, including Bristol, Liverpool, Derby and Newcastle-upon-Tyne.

In the countryside, the brief experience of GNCTU rural organising had a lasting effect, and the Poor Law Amendment Act stimulated additional regional efforts at rural union organising. There were protests against the new law in Chertsey, Surrey and meetings and strikes held along the Norfolk-Suffolk border.[203] In the South-East, the United Brothers was formed in anticipation of the act. Recruitment through the summer of 1835 was done in anticipation of a potential strike action at harvest-time. 'The new law's role in defeating the union' was 'of importance in quickly swinging the greater agrarian capitalists solidly behind the Poor Law Amendment Act'.[204] Farmers imposed a lockout from spring to early summer, which quickly sapped the union's strength as the strikefund could not support so many members sufficient to keep them out of the workhouse. The lockout made it easy for farmers to divide the rural proletariat between 'rough' and 'respectable' elements. The United Brothers collapsed after its last recorded strike at Wilmington in July. Strikes by other agricultural unions in Hampshire and Wiltshire were also easily crushed.[205] In 1836, Norfolk saw sporadic violence and rural union organising took place in Essex, and a strike in Kent. The parochial structure of relief after the Poor Law Amendment Act was passed was preserved to a large extent because the Settlement Laws still applied and because contributions were still paid on a *per capita* basis. The new law was evaded for a host of reasons, including a reluctance on the part of authorities to send male breadwinners to the workhouse, resulting in discrimination against single men, who were subject to the workhouse's increasingly punitive character. Finding any means to avoid going to the workhouse became a universal preoccupation among the poor – a kind of rural crimewave ensued, and thousands of petty entrepreneurs suddenly emerged.[206] Some families continued to receive outdoor relief disguised as relief for sick children. The roundsman system was reshaped into a new 'ticket' system. The employment of men on the highways swelled. One Kent farmer remarked that ' "the highways have become the workhouse" '.[207] It soon became evident, however, that the Poor Law Amendment Act did not produce the expected result of rising wages. One farmer remarked: ' "Labour is a marketable article" ', adding that if labourers demanded higher wages, 'He would not have had it . . . we could get them at our own price" '.[208] Where railway construction arrived, young and impoverished rural labourers alongside semi- or

203. Hobsbawm and Rudé 1968, p. 283.
204. Wells 1988, p. 124.
205. Wells 1988, pp. 111 and 124–5.
206. Wells 1988, p. 126.
207. Wells 1988, pp. 109–10.
208. As quoted Wells 1988, p. 110; see n. 65; source attribution unclear.

unemployed craftsmen flocked to find work as navvies.[209] In such regions, action for better wages tended to have greater success.

The Potteries also serve as an insightful example of how the implementation of the Poor Law Amendment Act was met with resistance and evasion. Attendance at vestry meetings by workers had swelled in 1833 when a proposal to incorporate the towns was put forward and ultimately defeated. In 1834, NUOP President William Stacey unsuccessfully objected to the reinstatement of the poor law overseer, citing his harsh treatment of applicants. At Stoke, the union attempted to influence the election of the workhouse governor and the poor rate collectors.[210] Perhaps because the NUOP had not formally affiliated with the GNCTU, it was able to win notable victories on the strength of the strike that lasted from November 1834 – when the pottery masters at Burslem and Tunstall sought to reduce the potters' wages by as much as 35 percent, sparking a fifteen-week strike – until the employers gave in during March 1835.[211] It took time for the employers to organise their counter-attack. In the summer of 1835, employers brought forward charges for breach of contract, neglect of work and intimidation. In November 1835, the poor law overseer at Stoke was dismissed for his leniency in:

> offering parish relief to the families of men imprisoned for striking at a factory owned by one of the select vestry's members. [He was temporarily re-instated] until the arrival of a commissioner from London to supervise the implementation of the 1834 Poor Law Amendment Act in the parish. Tangled parochial finances, allegations of corruption and inefficiency, and the levying of four rates within a year to clear a backlog of debt, meant that working-class ratepayers, as well as middle-class manufacturers, wanted to see a fresh start.[212]

Here we see a clear example of the kind of parochial control and mismanagement which the New Poor Law was intended to root out. In March 1836, the new commissioner arrived and expressed shocked at the influence of the union. A Chamber of Commerce was formed and a new tactic was announced: if one factory struck, a general lockout would ensue. The union called a strike at fourteen factories in September. Control of the distribution of relief was a key issue in the strike. The employers countered with a general lockout, affecting 15,660 men, women and child employees. Troops were called in on the pretext of keeping order. The new commissioner met with union representatives, and in a duplicitous move, promised to lower the property qualification for voting in elections

209. Wells 1988, p. 108.
210. Fyson 1988, p. 210.
211. Wells 1988, p. 121.
212. Fyson 1988, p. 210.

for the Board of Guardians to £6, but subsequently set the level at £20. Only one candidate on the union's list of preferred candidates was elected. On the advice of Edwin Chadwick, the board refused relief to any worker presently receiving strike pay. Unable to sustain the strike, the potters returned to work by January 1837 and the NUOP folded a few months later.[213]

Capital formation and the railway boom

Deane and Cole cite the period after 1830 as the point where a 'radical change in both the level and structure of capital formation took place'.[214] Why do we talk about capital *formation*? Money-wealth and stocks are *accumulated*, but capital is *formed*. In economics, the term 'capital formation' is generally used to refer to the transfer of assets into productive investment. But is it not precisely because capital invested in the production process includes circulating capital, human labour-power, that we speak of capital *formation*? The term would seem to capture the fact that capital is a form of property that encompasses human social relations within its scope. Let us then consider briefly the social factors that may have played a role in the upward turn in capital formation after 1830.

Table 13.1. The decline of hand-loom weaving: 1788–1860[215]

	Hand-loom weavers	Factory weavers	spinners
1788	108,000	0	60,000
1806	184,000	*100s*	90,000
1824	210,000	45,000	122,000
1833	213,000	73,000	133,000
		Factory workers	
1837	160,000	240,000	
1840	123,000	262,000	
1850	43,000	331,000	
1856	25,000	379,000	
1860	10,000	427,000	

213. Fyson 1988, pp. 210–17.
214. Deane and Cole 1969, p. 273.
215. Sources: Berg 1985, p. 259; Rule 1986, p. 37; Burnett 1994, p. 64. Burnett puts the number of hand-loom weavers in 1824 at around two hundred and forty thousand. Figures for factory workers from 1837 to 1860 are drawn from Mitchell and Deane 1971, p. 187, Table 8. See also: Timmins 1993, p. 28.

The United Kingdom's industrial lead over other countries by the 1830s was unquestioned. The pursuit of free-trade policies of tariff reform and reduction were driven by the ability to undersell all competitors as the increasing use of machinery in textiles was causing a constant lowering of cost per unit of production, and thus prices. There were seven cotton factories in Manchester employing more than 1,000 workers, thirty employing more than 500. Manchester's red-brick cotton factories and warehouses awed visitors. But machinofacture of textiles was little known outside of silk, cotton and wool in 1830. It was also not until the 1830s that political economy began to recognise the significance of machinery.[216] The wool market was in fact only just recovering from the effects of the war, and wool spinning had only recently been mechanised.[217] In 1830, virtually all hosiery was still manufactured by hand, and while this was still true of the majority of hosiery by 1850, machinofacture began to advance in this field in the 1830s.[218] If we look at the growth in the numbers of weavers and spinners by 1833 as shown in Table 13.1, it may seem surprising to notice that some 109 years after the Old Silk Mill became fully operational, there were still little more than 200,000 factory hands employed in factory spinning and weaving of cotton, wool and silk in Britain. And yet more surprising that this figure was still fewer than the total number of hand-loom weavers, which had virtually doubled in the past 45 years. This growth came about for the simple reason that power-weaving did not become more cost-effective than outsourcing to hand-loom weavers until the 1840s, which is when their numbers began to decline precipitously. Hand-loom weavers' wages had fallen to around 5*s*. or less per week by the 1830s, a 60 percent fall since their high point in the 1790s.[219] Widespread unemployment and the advance of the power-loom formed the scissors that trimmed away their wages and ultimately their livelihood. There were some two thousand four hundred power-looms in England by 1813. In England and Scotland combined, there were 69,000 by 1829, 100,000 by 1833, 225,000 by around 1845 and nearly a quarter of a million by 1850.[220] While some 30 percent of the adult male workforce was engaged in manufactures by 1851, only a sixth of this, or 5 percent

---

216. As Price (1986, p. 18) notes, McCulloch criticised Smith's focus upon the division of labour at the expense of the considering the role of machinery. This is but a reflection of how far machinery had advanced in the sixty years that lay between these two economists.

217. Gregory 1982, p. 97; Rule 1986, p. 275.

218. King and Timmins 2001, p. 51.

219. Stearns 1998, p. 27; Rule 1986, p. 37; Braudel 1988, p. 567.

220. Burnett 1994, pp. 64–5; Hobsbawm 1986, p. 64. King and Timmins (2001, p. 51) give the numbers for power-looms and power-weavers in woollen textile production as 5,000 and 15,000 respectively in 1835, and 42,000 and 154,000 in 1850.

overall, were employed in factories.[221] This helps explain why the artisanal outlook continued to prevail among trade unionists and later, among the Chartists, who we shall discuss below.

The estimated share of the national capital stock held by machinery in 1830 is 5 per cent, versus 15 per cent for buildings and transport infrastructure.[222] Land had meanwhile fallen from a share of about 64 percent in 1688 (according to Gregory King) to hold steady at around 54 percent from 1798 to 1832. If we add farmers' capital, the figure climbs back to around 64 per cent. Of course, 'steady' can be misleading, here, since the *total* national capital stock grew considerably in this period. Thus total investment in land continued to grow in proportion to the overall level of investment. It is remarkable to consider that even as the share of the population employed in agriculture fell to below a third by 1832, the *majority* of the national capital of Great Britain remained in agriculture.[223] By converting open fields to capitalist farming, parliamentary enclosures effected the final conversion of land into capital, thereby inviting a higher overall level of investment. Improved methods brought productivity advances, expanding output and further expanding the formation of capital in land. We cannot discount the conversion of self-subsistent producers into wage labourers, which also facilitated the widening of the share of *agrarian labour* in the national capital stock.[224] By 1832, fifty years after the major upward turn in British exports, industrial, commercial and finance capital *combined* amounted to less than 20 per cent of the national capital stock, a proportion that would nearly double over the course of the following fifty years.[225] These figures, which demonstrate the continuing dominance of agrarian capital in the first half of the nineteenth century, help to explain why the landed class continued to dominate the state.

---

221. King and Timmins 2001, p. 51.
222. Ibid.
223. Deane and Cole 1969, p. 271, see Table 70.
224. Calculating this share would be a complicated task: on the one hand enclosure was causing large numbers of labourers to be extruded from open field production, compelling many to take up handicraft production, while on the other hand, the area under cultivation was being expanded and investment was increasing enough to enable an increasing absorption of labour in agriculture for these reasons. Population growth also meant that even as the overall share of the population engaged in agriculture fell, the absolute numbers employed could have risen (though this too must be qualified, as a large share of such 'increasing' numbers of agricultural labourers would have been employed only part-time or seasonally). We must add to the picture regional de-industrialisation, particularly in the South, the resulting misery of which we have already considered above. What the numbers provided in the present section should demonstrate is that even after 1830, the expansion of industrial employment was not great enough to absorb a share of the growing population sufficient to prevent widespread immiseration in the countryside. Only after 1850 did this process of absorption begin in earnest.
225. Deane and Cole 1969, p. 271, see Table 70.

While the term 'capitalist' had been used by the physiocrat Turgot as early as 1769 and by William Godwin in 1794, the word 'capitalism' is not to be found in the literature before Thackeray used it in 1853.[226] That the term *agrarian* capitalism did not catch on until much later and was not used at all during the whole period of agrarian capitalism that we have here been discussing should therefore not be surprising. It has been suggested above that one of the reasons that scholars may have failed to recognise the distinctiveness of agrarian capitalism in the early nineteenth century could be due to Britain's participation in the political reaction after Waterloo, causing a kind of conflation of the continuing dominance of landed property in Britain in the form of land as *capital* with the continuing dominance of *extra-economic* forms of landed property on the Continent. The fact that the word *capitalism* arrives only with the major progress of the factory may help explain why capitalism in general has generally been so closely associated with industry at the expense of market-dependent agriculture.

We have already discussed above the respective roles of merchant capital and capital in land as a source of investment for industrialisation. Pat Hudson identifies a third form of 'capital' that was of particular importance in the mechanisation and industrialisation of the production of woollen textiles in Yorkshire, namely artisan capital.[227] The term is problematic and made more so by Hudson's acceptance of the concept of proto-industrialisation, thereby in a sense making the artisan workshop master into a 'proto-capitalist', at least in the woollen industry. But we need not entirely balk at the concept, which is consistent with Marx's 'way I' or the conversion of the petty commodity producer into a capitalist. As we have seen, the structure of Yorkshire's woollen trade was conditioned by late enclosures and the persistence of copyholders and leaseholders who continued to enjoy direct access to the means of subsistence, which in turn made their position as independent domestic producers more secure as they were less exposed to the market or to proletarianisation. Absentee landlordism was also common and this left a space for the emergence of artisans who could accumulate and thus, alongside investing estate-owners, finance early fulling, carding, scribbling and wool-spinning mills. Hudson writes: 'The company mill was a product of the peculiarly artisanal nature of proto-industrial production in the woollen branch and spawned a form of "co-operative capitalism" rather different from the norm. The organization of company mills and their financial and credit dealings

226. William Makepeace Thackeray first used the word capitalism in his novel *The Newcomes* (1853–55). 'A.R.J. Turgot used the word *capitaliste* in his essay "Reflection on the Formation and Distribution of Wealth" (1769–1770), and William Godwin used its English version, "capitalist" in his *Political Justice* (1794)' (Lawson 2007).

227. Hudson 1986, pp. 259–60.

embodied a collective and communitarian spirit whose aim tended toward stability rather than radical change'.[228]

To the extent that such mills continued to exhibit a collective control over the labour process and forms of collective ownership, it is difficult to see them as actually being meaningfully 'capitalist'. At issue would be the degree to which customary regulation of the labour process remained versus the degree to which they were able to make production decisions, including introducing innovations, in response to competitive market pressures. With the advance of machinery in woollen production after 1830, we anticipate that research will show a rich and interesting history, lasting well into the second half of the nineteenth century, as the company factory struggled to survive against increasing pressures to conform to the more 'advanced' capitalist model of factory ownership whereby the owner takes direct control of the labour process.

The sharp, upward trend in capital formation after 1830 could have had numerous proximate causes. Most proximate was the period of economic boom and the good harvests lasting from 1830 to 1837. The railway boom starting in the 1830s is another proximate cause. Certainly the railways were a cause of enormous financial speculation, and thus may have served to accelerate the rate of investment and the overall speed of capital transactions. The railway boom is also typically associated with the second Kondratieff cycle and an overall period of higher economic growth starting in the 1830s. Finally, we might suggest that with the general end of outdoor relief under the Speenhamland system, this termination of state subsidisation of subsistence would have deepened the level of market dependency, and while perhaps actually causing a short-term *drop* in demand for subsistence commodities in poorer agricultural regions, would nevertheless have stimulated overall levels of demand by forcing a significant percentage of labourers out of impoverished regions into towns in search of employment. During periods of prosperity and expanding employment, these labourers would have added to effective demand, whilst the overall effect of a release of labour into the labour market would have been downward pressure on wages, translating into lower costs of production and higher profits, thus facilitating capital formation. While we have addressed the erroneous assumption of the poor law commissioners that outdoor relief and not rampant unemployment was the primary cause of rural distress, the degree to which this view was conditioned by a conscious or unconscious understanding that ending outdoor relief would spell even greater unemployment, as in an oversupply of labour, translating into rock-bottom wages and maximum rates of profit, is a question worthy of further research.

228. Hudson 1986, pp. 260–1.

In 1830, the 35-mile long Manchester to Liverpool line opened. It was the longest line in the world and the first inter-city passenger line with a regular timetable. Once its success was demonstrated, a fury of speculative investment and building followed between 1831 and 1837, with some additional four hundred to five hundred miles of track being built before financial crisis set in. Only extension lines were built between 1839 and 1843, but by 1840 some £50 million had been invested in railways. By now, there were lines being built in France, Germany, Belgium, Russia and the United States. Railways always shared an intimate connection with the coal and iron industries, both because rail hauling was a product of mining and because the railway boom required prodigious sums of iron for the rails, cars and coal to fire them. Thus, spurred on by the railway boom, between 1830 and 1850 British iron output would treble from six hundred and eighty thousand to two million, two hundred and fifty thousand tons per annum, each mile of track requiring 300 tons of iron. Meanwhile, coal output for the United Kingdom more than doubled over the same period from 22.4 million to 49.4 million tons per annum.[229] Like the canals, the railways in Britain were built entirely from private enterprise, with no state subsidies or guarantees. All the risk was borne by private entrepreneurs, and Britain remains the only country where this held true. The railway mania of this period was not entirely rational, since profits were modest. Hobsbawm explains that during 'the first two generations of the Industrial Revolution . . . the comfortable and rich classes accumulated income so fast and in such vast quantities as to exceed all available possibilities of spending and investment'. Railway building provided a useful sponge to absorb the surplus of investment funds, especially after much investing in South America in the 1820s and in North America in the 1830s went sour.[230] While railways provided a comparatively stable site for investment, the railway boom was nevertheless subject to some extremely poor planning. The cost of financing the British lines could exceed five to seven times the cost per mile of lines built in Sweden, Prussia or the United States.[231] The romantic attraction to railway investing, the thought that one was investing in the future, with the railway a symbol of progress, could help explain the mania. The canals had already demonstrated the utility of improved transport, and the certainty

229. Britain already produced some ninety per cent of world coal output in 1800 at around eleven million tons. 'Its nearest competitor, France, produced less than a million' (Hobsbawm 1977, pp. 59–60); Deane and Cole 1969, p. 216, see Table 54; Deane 1997, p. 112. Sweezy (1938, p. 38) notes that London coal markets remained subject to an accumulated plethora of 'regulations and prohibitions until by 1830 it was a veritable Augean stable of fraud and abuse', thus catching the eye of the cabinet reformers . . . 'The Committees of 1829 and 1830, along with the Act of 1831, performed the Herculean labor of clearing it out'.

230. Hobsbawm 1977, pp. 61–4 and 216.

231. Hobsbawm 1986, pp. 113–4.

that the railways would likewise reduce transport costs and speed up transaction times was probably a sufficient compulsion for capitalists to invest in railways, regardless of the rate of return.

The beginnings of the railway mania in the 1830s coincide with an increase in the overall level of investment in Britain, approaching ten percent of GNP by 1840 and thus clearing Rostow's ten to fifteen percent threshold for 'take-off'.[232] Railways were not the only new game in town. Steamships had also made their debut by 1830, and were already numerous enough to prompt complaints about air quality in the *Liverpool Times*.[233] As a share of national capital, however, railways and all transport combined probably still formed something less than five percent of the national capital stock. Railways were more the effect than the cause of the upswing in national capital formation in this period, the beneficiary of a deepening of the market and the progress of capitalist forms of production, in both agriculture and industry. Capitalist production involved the market compulsion to lower production costs in response to price competition by revolutionising the production process. Maximising profits yielded ever larger surpluses (even if average profits were steady or declining in any given trade), creating larger net surpluses for investment. In 1832, financial, commercial and industrial capital formed some 16 percent of the national capital stock, but by 1885 would approach fifty percent (of which railway capital would make up 10 per cent), while agriculture would fall from 64 percent to just over 23 per cent over the same period.[234]

What these figures suggest is that the power of capital in the form of land being leased out to tenant-farmers paying rents based upon capitalist production in agriculture was still predominant and quite secure in the 1830s, but was set to decline in relative importance over the next half-century. Alongside the decline of the landlord in *importance* would come the absolute decline of the independent artisan. The beginning of the decline of these two familiar figures from the eighteenth century and earlier is central to the rest of our narrative.

Conclusion

The reforms undertaken in Britain between the mid-1820s and the mid-1830s were part of a process by which an agrarian-capitalist state adjusted to changing economic conditions that were themselves largely the result of the development

232. Rule 1986, p. 32.
233. '"During the last ten years the nuisance has gone on increasing until it has become almost intolerable"', wrote the editors, '"and if nothing is done to check it, it will increase every year until the atmosphere of Liverpool will become as much defiled as that of Birmingham"'. As quoted in Aspin 1995, p. 43; no citation given.
234. Deane and Cole 1969, p. 271, see Table 70.

of the capitalist system. By establishing a property-based boundary between the middle and working classes upon the inclusion of the former in the voting body politic, the Great Reform Act served to sharpen a sense of identity on the part of the working 'class', or what Marx would soon label the 'proletariat'. But the growing awareness among workers of a common 'working-class' identity, to which the early experiments in trade federations or *trades* unions were a testament, also had a foundation outside the political system. It was based in the shared experience of declining wages driven by open competition between employers seeking to increase or maintain their level of profits by cutting costs. While the early experiments in mass working-class organisation seem, in retrospect, remarkably ambitious, when we situate them in the context of *both* accelerated wage competition between employers in manufacturing and chronic unemployment in the countryside, they can also be seen as logical attempts to respond to a general crisis facing wage labourers.

The final onslaught on the last remaining open fields and commons through parliamentary enclosures that had begun in the 1790s reached its apex in the 1820s. Although the 'last labourers' revolt' came too late to have a hope or even a prayer of halting or slowing the conversion of agrarian labourers to a condition of total market dependency, as the last major revolt against the introduction of machinery into production, Swing did achieve its immediate ends of forestalling the use of the threshing-machine. But this was truly a pyrrhic victory. For the long-term effect of Swing was to draw the attention of central authorities to the way in which local rural authorities continued to practice a large measure of benevolent paternalism and even respect for the customary authority of the crowd in acceding to the demands of the protestors. The 'outrages' against property would set the poor law commissioners on a path of replacing local control over poor relief with centralised administration, one which responded directly to the interests of capitalist tenant-farmer employers seeking greater disciplinary control over labour and which served as a means to differentiate between productive and unproductive workers.

In this way, Swing did inform the Poor Law Reform of 1834. Yet to what extent did Swing inform the Great Reform Act of 1832? Certainly there was awareness in the cities and towns that a general insurrection was spreading across the countryside in 1830–1, and also that it was being almost immediately suppressed wherever it arose. It is unclear how deep this awareness was, however, or what significance urban trade unionists and radicals attached to it. We can point to efforts to make common cause with the labourers of the countryside, but perhaps a more direct link was the way in which a logic of price competition was now taking firm hold of manufacturing, presenting urban artisans in particular with the challenge of how to cope with falling prices for their products even as they continued to maintain control of the labour process and sought to pay themselves 'customary wages'. The experience of agrarian labourers may have provided urban artisans with a picture of the future they were being swept toward by a vortex of free-market forces that was increasingly hostile to the customary modes of craft organisation.

At the level of politics, the previously discussed unresolved tension within radicalism now came to the fore. With some 190 seats in Parliament, the combined force of Irish and English radicalism had reached its highest point of influence. Radicals inside Parliament were content to allow working-class agitation if it meant sufficiently shaking the nerve of the ruling oligarchy into passing a measure that would extend the franchise to the middling sort. But too much should not be made of this. As Grey's speech indicated, for the Whig oligarchs and probably a fair number of Tories as well, reform was a calculated measure designed not only to release the pressure for reform that had been building for the better part of half a century, but more specifically to guarantee that the hegemony of the landed classes would be preserved. This calculated, 'divide-and-conquer' strategy of co-opting the 'middle classes' into a junior partnership in governance would almost immediately prove successful in its primary aim of forestalling revolution.

While the goal of counter-revolution is something which Britain's landed classes shared with the general European reaction, the system which the rulers in Britain sought to preserve was not the social production relations of a kind of neo-feudal order, but of an agrarian and a growing industrial capitalism. This can be seen quite clearly in the nature of the legislation that followed reform, for as we have seen, what was sought was not a restoration of extra-economic forms of extracting surplus from peasant labour, but the quite deliberate and conscious effort at establishing a national labour market by a process of steady elimination of normative modes of labour regulation in favour of a system of wage labour operating according to 'free' contracts between employers and employees, with the state repositioning itself by taking on the role of neutral arbitrator between buyers and sellers of the increasingly popular commodity known as labour. Certainly this general shift away from state paternalism (which as we shall see in the next chapter, would be temporarily revived in a new form) was largely driven by the spread of market dependence and the creation of a mass labour force dependent upon wages for access to the means of subsistence – a proletariat. But the example of how political economy shaped Nassau senior's thinking testifies to the influence of ideology and the way in which the state by-passed other options, such as continuing the Old Poor Law, and *actively* promoted the development of a national market in free wage labour. The termination of outdoor relief and the strict enforcement of the workhouse test was, after all, an extreme policy shift, one which put hundreds of thousands of labouring families at risk of privation or even starvation. Whether the flawed analysis of the poor law commissioners in blaming the Speenhamland system for rural immiseration was based on innocent or wilful ignorance, the fact remains that the policy fitted the desired outcome of employers. Another way of putting this is that even if economic developments (in this case the generalisation of wage labour and market dependency) form the conditions that make major policy shifts necessary, the policy shift in question (the abolition of Speenhamland and outdoor relief) still requires the political will and the guiding ideology for it to be made.

When we combine the political circumscription of working class identity by collective exclusion from the extension of the franchise with the termination of outdoor relief and the harsh imposition of a system of wage labour where the discipline of the market was backed up by the discipline of the workhouse, the almost immediate working-class response in the form of a succession of different efforts at general combination appears somewhat logical and even predictable. But like the General Chamber of Manufacturers, the inherent contradictions between artisan, factory and rural labourers and the growing competition among them made collective action based on class solidarity a largely illusory goal in the short term. And when collective economic action failed, the obvious next step was to turn again to the political system in seeking redress. Yet for the time being, what interest would middle-class 'bourgeois' employers have in extending the right to vote to what would immediately become a working-class majority when the working class was still made up mainly of artisans who sought to preserve and revive normative modes of labour regulation and thereby put an end to the free market in wage labour that was proving so profitable to employers? No longer was the question of labour in manufacturing secondary to that of labour in agriculture, for agrarian labourers no longer made up a majority of the wage labourers in the nation, even if the landed classes still controlled the largest share of the national wealth. This meant that it was now possible to a certain extent for the Industrial Revolution to produce a 'backward flow' and influence the continuing evolution of agrarian capitalism, which had up until now been mainly concerned with the commodification of land but which could begin to concentrate more sharply on the commodification of labour. Perhaps what has often been interpreted as an outright confrontation between the rising 'bourgeoisie' of employers in manufacturing and the landed classes had more to do, as we shall see, with a division within the landed class itself, presenting the somewhat unexpected possibility of a loose alliance between old-school Tory conservatives and radical working-class Chartists in opposition to *laissez-faire* Liberals.

Chapter Fourteen
Chartists and Liberals

> The first generation of pottery workers were taught by their masters the importance of time; the second generation formed their short-time committees in the ten-hour movement; the third generation struck for overtime or time-and-a half. They had accepted the categories of their employers and learned to fight back within them. They had learned their lesson, that time is money, only too well.
>
> E.P. Thompson[1]

> All men have an equal right to the free development of their faculties; they have an equal right to the impartial protection of the state; but... it is against the eternal nature of things, that the indolent man and the laborious man, the spendthrift and the economist, the imprudent and the wise, should obtain and enjoy an equal amount of goods.
>
> Victor Cousin[2]

The period of good harvests and strong economic growth, culminating in the railway mania and boom conditions in the cotton industry in 1835, could not last forever. A failed harvest in 1836 coincided with the inevitable bust that comes after a period of rampant speculation. The winter of 1836–7 saw soaring unemployment. A trade slump ensued, lasting until 1842. For the Radical faction in Parliament, 1836 was a frustrating year.

1. Thompson 1993, p. 390.
2. Pascal 1869, p. 212, n. 1.

A new bill for the reform of Irish Tithes, an Irish Municipal Corporations Bill, a Registration of Voters Bill, a Post Office Bill and a Catholic Marriages Bill had all been successfully steered through the House only to be defeated in the Lords. The only successful radical measures were a bill for Dissenters' marriages and a bill for the civil registration of births, marriages and deaths. Out of doors, however, radicalism was alive and well, as attested by the extraordinary growth of radical newspapers.[3] The cause of the Tolpuddle Martyrs continued to provoke radical outcries for justice. Agitation against the Corn Laws was perhaps the other major cause of the day.

In London on 17 July, the Owenite William Lovett convened the first meeting of the London Working Men's Association (LWMA). The LWMA's aims were far-reaching. They included research and publication, gathering labour statistics, and the establishment of a meeting place with a library. It also aspired to serve as a kind of steering committee for the working class. Yet at the same time, it was decidedly an association for skilled workmen, charging a high membership fee. The founding 33 members grew to only a hundred, with another 35 honorary (non-working-class) members including, among others, Francis Place and Feargus O'Connor. Under its leadership, the '"intelligent and influential portion of the working classes" were to be united to secure equal political and social rights for their class and the removal of "the cruel laws that prevent the free circulation of thought".'[4] In November 1836, the LWMA published a pamphlet entitled *The Rotten House of Commons*, levelling an attack on middle-class reformers for abandoning the working classes after the passage of the Reform Bill and setting out the six demands that would later be incorporated into the People's Charter, along with a seventh demand for a completely free press. Around this time, the London Anti-Corn Law Association was formed. Thus the Chartists and the Anti-Corn Law League had their origins at virtually the same place and time. This simultaneity would continue, suggesting that the two movements were connected at a deeper level.

The People's Charter and the National Petition

In 1837, as recession set in, merchants and manufacturers began petitioning Parliament to take action to relieve the distress. On 28 February at the Crown and Anchor Tavern on the Strand, members of the LWMA drew up the People's Charter, which quickly garnered three thousand signatures. The Charter's six points were demands for: universal suffrage, the ballot, annual parliaments, the

3. Maccoby 2001, pp. 140–4.
4. Maccoby 2001, pp. 159–61.

lifting of the property qualification, payment to members, and equal electoral divisions. These were not new demands, but old ones. The Westminster Reform Committee had set out the same points in its nine-point programme in 1780. The London Corresponding Society and the Benthamites had carried the demands forward since then.[5] This leads Price to argue that Chartism represents the climax of a process of the increasing politicisation of artisan ideology, as opposed to the 'constant mistake of historiography' of treating Chartism as characterised by a tension between progressive, forward-looking and backward-looking elements, a 'Whiggish hare' that Price accuses Engels of starting.[6] In what follows, we hope to show that while Price is right at the level of economic agency, the implication that the artisanal outlook of Chartism was in no way progressive or forward-looking is too strong.

The distress from the recession increased over the Summer of 1837 and in Manchester there were already fifty thousand workers unemployed or on short-time.[7] Meanwhile in Birmingham, the Birmingham Reform Association had formed in 1836, and in response to the slump in trade was reconstituted in 1837, reviving the name of the Birmingham Political Union, under the guidance of the local MP Thomas Attwood, whose chief cause was to reverse the decision made to return to the gold standard in 1919, in the interest of promoting trade and alleviating unemployment. While Attwood himself had not yet come to favour universal suffrage, the BPU formed a committee to draw up the National Petition which happened to embody five of the six points found in the People's Charter (excluding equal divisions). There was immediate excitement, and some fifty thousand would attend a BPU meeting in June. Lord Roebuck, who was assisting Lovett in editing the draft of the Charter, was prepared to introduce a bill for universal suffrage. In May, the LWMA held meetings with O'Connell, Hume and several other Radical MPs, agreeing to set up a joint committee to pursue the aims of the charter. But this effort was cut short on 20 June when William IV died from heart failure.[8]

The King's death cleared the air of a petty dispute between the King and Victoire, widow to William's brother, Edward Duke of Kent. The Duke and Duchess were the parents of Alexandrina Victoria. As William IV left no surviving children upon his death, the crown now passed to Victoria, who was all of eighteen.

5. Bloy 2007. Earlier still, Major Cartwright included the main ideas in his parliamentary reform programme of 1776. Fox (1986, p. 57) writes that the six points of the Charter itself 'were merely restatements of a radical agenda of 80 years' standing'. But he gives no reference to any document from 1758. Of course the demand for universal manhood-suffrage in English history goes back to the Levellers and the Diggers.
6. Price 1986, p. 57.
7. Briggs 1979, p. 295, citing the *Manchester Times*, 17 June 1837; Collier 1965, pp. 12–13.
8. Maccoby 2001, pp. 161–3; Gonner 1889, pp. 630–1.

Disappointing the ambitions of her mother's controller, Sir John Conroy, the young Queen Victoria developed a fondness for Lord Melbourne, the charming old aristocrat out of touch with the sufferings of the poor and working people. The Whigs would enjoy a period of royal favour one last time.[9]

As according to the custom, an election was held upon the event of a new sovereign taking the throne. Peel's 'Conservatives' made considerable gains and the Whig majority was trimmed from 71 to 30 seats. While O'Connell's Irish faction remained as strong as ever, the Radicals in Parliament suffered serious setbacks. When the Radical MPs Wakley and Molesworth sought to amend the 'Address' to include the promise of a more just representation of the people, Lord Russell, now the leader in the Commons, responded on 20 November, by saying: 'having now only five years ago reformed the representation, having placed it on a new basis, it would be a most unwise and unsound experiment now to begin the process again, to form a new suffrage, to make an alteration in the manner of voting, and to look for other and new securities for the representation of the people'.[10] This drew a response from the BPU on 7 December in the form an address to the reformers of Great Britain and Ireland, as well as angry demonstrations in Birmingham where Attwood declared his support for universal suffrage and attacked reluctant reformers in Parliament.

Meanwhile in the North, the Tory activist Richard Oastler and the Reverend J.R. Stephens were busy touring and giving speeches against the implementation of the New Poor Law. Their cause was aided by swirling rumours that the poor-law commissioners intended to commit infanticide against any infant beyond the third child and to spay all pauper girls. It was well understood that to simply end outdoor relief in the North would drive whole masses of domestic workers straight to the poor house. Because of this the commissioners were busy creating alternatives that were weaker variants of public-works programmes, such as establishing labour yards for stone breaking. Feargus O'Connor, the Irish lawyer and former MP for Cork, supported the cause of Oastler and Stephens with his *Northern Star* journal, which was first published in November 1837 and which also became O'Connor's mouthpiece as a virulent advocate for universal suffrage.[11]

After considerable delay and long effort by Lovett, the People's Charter was officially published on 8 May, a month before the festivities of the Queen's coronation. The Chartists' goal of having Parliament make the Charter into a statute was proposed as 'the principal end of all working-class politics'.[12] Mass meetings followed in Glasgow and Birmingham. As the briefer of the two documents, the

9. Clarke and Ridley 2000, pp. 62–9.
10. Russell 2008.
11. Maccoby 2001, pp. 171–9.
12. Maccoby 2001, p. 167.

National Petition was more often read in public and was thus more important than the Charter in terms of winning public support. In August, the BPU proposed a General Convention of the Industrious Classes and the appointment by the localities of 49 delegates, so as to avoid violating the ban on assemblies over fifty persons.[13]

London, Birmingham and the North were of course areas where artisanal production in manufactures continued to predominate, even if on increasingly difficult terms. While all this momentum was building for Chartism in those regions, in Manchester manufacturers were growing increasingly distressed in the face of falling profits. Despite a slight recovery in 1838, the harvest had been quite wet, causing wheat prices to rise, and with them the price of bread. At Manchester in September, after listening to a speech at the York Hotel by Sir John Bowring, one of the Radical MPs to lose his seat in the recent election, a group of manufacturers and merchants met to form the Anti-Corn Law League (ACLL) to agitate for repeal of the Corn Laws, in order to allow the price of bread – and wages – to fall, thus restoring profitability. The argument was as old as political economy itself. In 1826 and 1827 the economist Thomas Peronnet Thompson, a close associate of Bowring, had published two influential pamphlets: *The True Theory of Rent*, analysing Smith and Ricardo's writings on rent, and *A Catechism on the Corn Laws*, laying out the case against the Corn Laws.[14] The *Catechism* quickly became a bestseller. In his lectures during the year of 1838, Thompson had argued for unity between the goal of extending the suffrage and repealing the Corn Laws, two reforms which together 'would solve the central problem which vexed the British people: how to ensure for all responsible citizens a share of legislative power'.[15] The Leaguers, of course, enjoyed a certain obvious advantage in their cause, which is that while working men and women shared in their interest of lowering the price of bread (if not wages), not all employers were inclined toward any further reform, much less radical reform. An inaugural meeting of the ACLL was held on 24 September and the nominal leaders included Richard Cobden, a cotton merchant; the Quaker John Bright, a Rochdale carpet manufacturer and James Wilson, the Scottish journalist who would later found the *Economist*. Like the Chartists, the ACLL's methods included petitions and demonstrations, and if less strident, the ACLL nonetheless 'created a widespread animus against the territorial aristocracy, and against Peel Himself'.[16] At the same time, however, being in the 'middle' of the working and landed classes, the repealers were also

13. Maccoby 2001, pp. 166–9.
14. Thompson 1826; 1827.
15. Turner 1998, pp. 1013–16.
16. Harvie 1986, p. 442.

alarmed at the increasing level of organisation and militancy of their employees.

Chartism surely added to the urgency of the ACLL's mission, for on the very same day as the ACLL's inaugural meeting, Feargus O'Connor spoke to a huge crowd in Manchester, proceeding to Sheffield the following day. At a meeting in West Riding in October, O'Connor spoke of tyrannicide. Stephens spoke of five thousand men ready at arms in his district. He was apprehended for sedition on 27 September before being released on bail. There were 'torchlit meetings' reminiscent of Luddism being held 'in the evenings on the moors outside impoverished industrial towns . . . The Chartists might claim that they held torchlight meetings because their long working hours gave them no opportunity of coming together save at night. But undoubtedly they relished the subtle flavour of revolution and incendiarism which such assemblages conveyed to worried "respectables" '.[17]

Parliament responded with a declaration against torchlight assemblies on 12 December. O'Connor was a student of O'Connell's use of the threat of 'physical force' in Ireland, and he spoke openly of such threats in November, issuing the ultimatum that Parliament had one year to act before trouble might ensue. O'Connor subsequently backed off, reassuring the BPU of his commitment to the use of 'moral force', but even before the first Chartist convention met, the divisions between the North and South over moral versus physical force, which was equally a division between the skilled artisans of London and Birmingham and the distressed artisans in the heartland of Luddism, were evident.

The first Chartist Convention was convened at the British Coffee House with 53 delegates in attendance on 4 February 1839, one day before the opening of Parliament. More than half a million signatures had already been collected and some £967 in 'National Rent' had been raised to support the activities of the delegates. The delegates displayed a certain hubris, perhaps owing to the fact that their 'constituency could justifiably be counted as vastly exceeding that of the House of Commons'.[18] At one moment the delegates were 'demanding a conference with the commons, at another summoning the printer of the *Chronicle* to the bar, while on still another occasion they published grave recommendations "to all and in particular to their constituents" as to the attitude they should adopt towards the anti-corn-law agitation, which was then rising into prominence'. This was the hubris of skilled artisans, 'honourable' tradesmen, imagining themselves to have at long last achieved equal status to that of statesmen, and acting accordingly. Should any other behaviour have been expected? On 13 February Bronterre O'Brien carried a resolution inviting the House of Commons

17. Maccoby 2001, p. 182.
18. Maccoby 2001, pp. 169 and 188.

to meet with the Convention. Six days later a motion in the Commons for the repeal of the Corn Laws moved by Charles Pelham Villiers was defeated 311–172.[19] On 18 March, the Convention delegates violently denounced the measure for rural policing, currently before Parliament. Despite the strenuous efforts of Lovett and other 'moral force' advocates, the majority clearly favoured a rapid presentation of the petition under the threat of violence out-of-doors should it be rejected by Parliament. The delegates were receiving information that much of the country was ready to rise at their word. There was reportedly a brisk trade in pikes in the North, with common halberds going for as little as 9*d.* and those with sharp-edged hooks selling for an additional 2*s.*[20] Nervous magistrates were calling for troops to stand guard over their homes. On 3 May, the Government issued a royal proclamation against drilling, though drilling continued even as arrests commenced. On 6 May, the delegates openly discussed arming, and in the evening retired to another location to meet in secret. On 7 May, the orderly assembly marched two abreast to deliver the National Petition with 1,283,000 signatures to Attwood in Parliament.[21] The organisers had taken elaborate precautions so as to give the authorities no excuse to disrupt the proceedings. Chartism had 'laid down a pattern that virtually all later North American and Western European crowd activism was to follow', namely the public demonstration.[22]

As it happened, the Whigs had lost a division on 6 May and with rebellion in Canada, a looming war with Egypt in the Middle East and rumours of armed insurrection, the Whigs were only too ready to hand over power to Peel. Considering the more serious threat that a Peel government would pose to the Convention, the delegates proposed to remove to Birmingham, where better treatment could be expected from a police force made up of the radical followers of Attwood. Even as Melbourne's government was recalled in the aftermath of a dispute between Peel and the Queen over bedchamber appointments, the Convention reconvened at Birmingham on 13 May. Drilling and arming supporters was again discussed openly. Proposals to put out a call for local agitation for reform and local meetings across the countryside after the next Whitsuntide (Sunday, 19 May) carried prior to the Convention's adjournment on the 17 May.

---

19. Turner 1998, p. 1017.
20. Aspin 1995, p. 153.
21. Maccoby 2001, pp. 188–94; Gonner 1889, pp. 637–8.
22. Plotz 2000, pp. 87–9 credits Bronterre O'Brien with helping to precipitate this new form of public speech when he organised a procession to accompany his petition against the '"tyrannical and inhuman enactment miscalled the Poor Law Amendment Act"' in 1837. According to Plotz, the innovation lay in the demand of an assembly of the people to be 'construed of a desire to be represented'. It is an important development, reflecting the emergence of a national political awareness among the working classes as well as a willingness to submit to representative government, if allowed to participate.

Throughout the week following Whitsuntide there were Chartist meetings in many cities across Britain, the largest at Kersal Moor outside Manchester, with a crowd variously estimated at between thirty thousand and half a million. The fact that the largest turnout among the demonstrations took place just outside Manchester surely reflects the wide participation in Chartism by not only domestic workers but factory workers as well. The speeches given were inflammatory, and participants were encouraged to prepare for a 'Sacred Month' during which they should withdraw all their money from the banks, boycott all excisable articles and be ready for 'physical force' upon Parliament's rejection of the petition. Despite the inflammatory rhetoric, General Sir Charles Napier, in charge of the Northern command, expressed outright disappointment at the lack of violence at the meetings. The petition was introduced by Attwood on 14 June and debate on the measure was set for 12 July. On 1 July the Convention reconvened at Birmingham. On 3 July, Dr. John Taylor moved for a meeting of the Convention on 13 July, at which time the Convention would declare the Sacred Month, on the supposition that Parliament would reject the petition.[23]

The outbreak of violence, however, did not wait until July 13. Ultra-radicals in Birmingham had been meeting regularly in the Bull Ring, and had lately been ignoring a magistrate's notice for them to clear out. With a Birmingham Police Bill still pending before Parliament, the mayor had only street-keepers and a handful of constables at his disposal, and so he resorted to a visit to London, returning with two additional magistrates and sixty metropolitan police officers who were sent at once and without warning to clear the Bull Ring even as a meeting was in progress on the evening of 4 July. Fighting ensued and military reinforcements were called in. Dr. Taylor was arrested on suspicion of having been a 'ringleader' the next day. The Convention responded with placards criticising the police's handling of the matter. For their part in issuing the placards, delegates Lovett and Collins were arrested on charges of sedition.

Thinned by arrests and desertions, only 24 delegates attended the Convention's meeting in London on 10 July, whence a call for replacements was put out. The BPU had temporarily withdrawn its support. As expected, the petition failed in Parliament on July 12 by a vote of 46 in favour and 230 against. The delegates convened on 13 July, and 13 of 24 attending voted in favour of fixing a date for the Sacred Month. That evening, the New Toll House at Swansea, Wales was attacked by 'Rebecca' and her followers. The tradition of protesting led by an imaginary folk hero had resurfaced once more. The so-called 'Rebecca Riots' would last into 1843. On 17 July, the delegates fixed the dates for the Sacred Month, only to reconsider the matter on July 24. Should it be a month or only

---

23. Maccoby 2001, pp. 194–8; Gonner 1889, pp. 639–41.

a few days? Support for the Sacred Month had never enjoyed more than a slim majority and now even former champions of 'physical force' like O'Connor began to draw back as it was becoming clear that they were beginning to lose public support and that the Government was far more powerful and far more prepared to counter any attempt at the use of force than they had previously imagined.[24] In August, there were outbreaks of protests involving the use of troops to suppress them at Nottingham, Sheffield and Bolton as well as London. Given the level of mobilisation under Napier, the failure of any general rising was an effective certainty.

The only actual rising on the appointed date took place in Newport in Monmouthshire, Wales when a body of armed men numbering anywhere from two hundred to twenty thousand, among whom were blast-furnace workers and colliers, marched on the town in November. Their intention was to march in the night, but heavy rains found the men drenched as they approached the town at nine o'clock in the morning. In a scene reminiscent of Brandreth's folly at Pentrich,[25] the men attempted to break into the Westgate Arms Inn only to be fired upon at close range by soldiers lying in wait. Nine were shot dead. The wounded were carried off. Local authorities made arrests the following day. The leader, John Frost, was caught with three pistols on his person. He and 13 others would be charged with high treason, the trials to begin on 31 December. While Birmingham and Bradford also came close to staging risings, Monmouthshire saw the only 'physical force' rising. The Sacred Month was over before it had started.[26]

In his account published in 1889, Gonner portrays the early Chartists as subject to intense folly and recklessness, suggesting that the delegates squandered an extraordinary opportunity by succumbing to the demands for a rising and 'physical force' over the advice of cooler heads. This ignores the fact that local supporters were deeply distrustful of moderate voices, given their recent experience of exclusion in the passage of the Reform Act. The widespread resort to physical force had already been seen in the countryside and there are obvious parallels between early Chartism and Luddism. Strangely, the early Chartists proceeded much further in terms of arming and drilling, but resorted to nowhere near the amount of physical force as the Luddites or the Swing protestors.

One reason is obviously that by 1839 the extension of policing was advancing rapidly. In 1839 alone, Parliament passed the County Policing Act and separate acts to introduce regular policing to Birmingham, Bolton, Dublin and Manchester. The preparedness of the authorities in Monmouthshire reflects the

24. Harrison and Hollis 1967, p. 514.
25. See Chapter Twelve, pp. 630–2.
26. Maccoby 2001, pp. 198–208; Gonner 1889, pp. 641–3.

overall readiness of the authorities to pre-empt the Chartists. It is likely that the use of informants had also developed to a point of routine and advanced professionalism, thus facilitating the pre-emption. The primary object of policing was to enforce property laws, though harassing local plebeian amusements such as cockfighting became another preoccupation. The ancient amusements of the poor: the 'rush bearing, wrestling matches, cock-fighting and bull baiting', along with the folk song as a predominant idiom amongst workers, began to fade away in the 1840s.[27] Policing could give the authorities tighter control over each locality, but this did not necessarily weaken local sympathy for the resistance. Policing did not spread rapidly, but its gradual introduction did effect a change in terms of a general decline in criminality alongside a rise in the number of incarcerated persons from the 1840s, and a general change toward the new moral authoritarianism commonly associated with Victorianism. After 1838, only those guilty of murder or attempted murder were hanged.[28] In the Chartist arrests, the authorities successfully deployed the tactic of making mass arrests to sow doubt in the movement as a whole, whilst taking the sting out of such arrests by commuting sentences and granting the early release of leaders on bail.

Where Chartism clearly differed from Luddism and Swing was in its political focus. Although spurred on by distress, the core grievance was no longer rooted in commercial or production relations but in a demand for inclusion in the body politic, which if won, would presumably enable workers and artisans to *legislate* regulations in the workplace. The general shift toward a political strategy had come about after the collapse of the general strike in 1834. Hopes were high when the Convention met, as the appearance of a unified movement was thereby created. But as with the GNCTU, complex divisions lay beneath this apparent unity, divisions which were effectively destined to break it up. Not only was there enormous mistrust on the part of trade unionists towards those reformers who appeared quite content with the extent of reform reached in 1832, but to the extent to which non-working-class radicals supported the Chartist cause, theirs was generally a libertarian approach which advocated maximum political freedom in the form of (male) suffrage alongside strict enforcement of property rights. Key figures within Chartism, however, continued to pursue socialist aims, including a redistribution of property. Bronterre O'Brien wrote in 1836: '"No working man will ever again expect justice, morals or mercy at the hands of a profit-mongering legislature".... he sought, with considerable genius,

27. Hobsbawm 1986, p. 91.

28. Harling 2001, pp. 94–5, writes: 'There is no greater testament to the moral authoritarianism of the Victorian state than the increasingly centralized prison system over which it presided, which sought simultaneously to discipline and to redeem the convict through an increasingly elaborate set of punishments directed more at the mind than at the body'. Capital punishment for attempted murder ended in 1861.

to twist together the tradition of ultra-Radicalism with that of Owenism, into a revolutionary socialism…: "Property – property – that is the thing we must be at. Without a change in the institution of property, no improvement can take place"'.[29]

This can hardly be seen as the position of the majority. While every county had its own core of radical organisers by the time Chartism arrived,[30] radicalism itself was by no means a unitary phenomenon. The rift between libertarian and socialist radicalism was one layer of tension, to which another must be added. The 'moral force' Chartists were based in the more well-established unions of London and Birmingham, whose primary goal remained one of maintaining the 'honourable' independence of their trade by securing Parliamentary legislation to regulate manufactures. They were 'more likely to settle for the half-loaf than put it at hazard by reaching for what might be seen as dangerously ambitious political solutions',[31] while the younger, more transient unions of the North and the villages tended toward greater militancy. There were also intense ethnic hostilities, such as the fight between Irish railroad navvies working on the Preston to Wigan line and local cotton-mill operatives that broke out in May 1838 and left one dead and forty wounded.[32]

What also separates Chartism from Swing and Luddism is the general absence of appeals to custom. While this reflects the shift from strikes to a political campaign, it also reflects the decline of such appeals in general. This apparent abandonment of the cause of defending customary regulation of labour also represents the beginnings of the so-called 'mid-Victorian compromise'. In this context, it is worth asking whether the 'physical force' advocates of the hinterland were not rebelling as much against what they perceived to be a position of accommodation and compromise on the part of the labour 'aristocracy' as against their exclusion from the franchise. Fox criticises the Webbs for portraying the labour movement of the 1830s and 1840s as being broadly class-conscious

29. Thompson 1991, p. 904. Class analysis was central to Chartist literature, particularly early Chartist literature. The central problem still lay with unregulated competition reducing wages, but the language of class conflict was sharpening. A Chartist journal wrote in 1839 that '"it is the interest of the capitalist to grind as much as he can out of the workman's toil, and the workman vice-versa; and never can the interests of the two become amalgamated until labour and capital be wielded by one and the same class of individuals"' (McNulty 1988, pp. 226–7). McNulty summarises the Chartist economic perspective: 'The present corrupt political system was based on a monopoly of land and capital which had been achieved by usurpation and was now sustained by class legislation secured by a monopoly of representation. It was reinforced by taxation and the national debt. Universal suffrage would eradicate distress and unemployment by eliminating class legislation and restoring to property its proper uses and duties…'

30. Thompson 1991, p. 806.

31. Fox 1985, p. 13.

32. Aspin 1995, p. 38.

and militant up to the middle of the century, after which it 'accepted' capitalism through accommodation, and argues that early nineteenth-century trade unionism showed both militant and accommodating trends, suggesting that accommodation was the dominant tide with various forms of radical militancy acting as an 'undertow'. The thrust toward 'business unionism' and 'prudent accommodation to middle-class values and manners' was:

> increasingly apparent from the 1830s onwards... Food riots, collective bargaining by riot and Luddism were dying out; pre-industrial direct action was giving way to more organized forms... some newer groups within the factories, such as the cotton-spinners – all men – found it possible to establish effective restrictions on entry which elevated them nearer to the higher craft category than to 'factory operatives' as ordinarily understood... In such a context, union restraint, preservation of good order and promotion of respectability were becoming, in a society moving towards an increased outward prosperity, no more or less than possible contributors to effective action... The insistence by strike leaders on restraint and good order was designed, therefore, to ensure that the strike would not be closed down prematurely and that they would be left free to exert such a degree of market strength against the employers as they could muster.[33]

The matter is very much bound up with the question of whether the standard of living was rising, and more specifically *whose* standard of living was rising. Gender becomes a major issue here as well. While it would be dubious to suggest that the 'physical force' advocates within Chartism were well aware of the long-term implications of the development of capitalism as a *system*, they were on the one hand responding directly to the effects and the horrors of proletarianisation and deregulation, and on the other hand, even if they lacked any clear or effective strategy for getting there, they nonetheless looked to the promise of some kind of alternative that would alleviate their suffering in both the short and long term, whether it be through Owenism, trades unionism or extension of the franchise. Only with the advantage of hindsight can Engels be accused of mistakenly seeing in Chartism a progressive element, for we now know that no nineteenth-century alternatives were arrived at. As Price notes, no one in the 1840s knew for certain that capitalist industrialisation was here to stay.[34] Price's criticism of Engels is thus teleological. Here again, we must stress the *active* suppression of resistance to capitalism, without which any number of alternative projects could have been more successfully pursued. The various forms of resistance to capitalism,

33. Fox 1985, p. 115.
34. Price 1986, p. 58. Many of those who took part in the Chartist strike of 1842 could still remember when the first spinning mills were set up.

or resistance to particular aspects of capitalism that we have addressed, were of course 'traditional' or 'backward-looking' inasmuch as they sought to hold on to older 'extra-economic' or customary forms of social regulation. But what else would we expect? How could they have resisted capitalism on capitalist terms?

John Rule describes Chartism as 'the world's first national labour movement' and 'the world's first widely supported movement for universal male suffrage'.[35] At the same time, Rule writes that it was more than a tactical failure; it was the 'end of an epoch'.[36] So here we have Rule pointing out that while Chartism was indeed, as Price puts it, 'the climax to an increasingly politicized artisan ideology', it was also something more: an experiment in organising the working class for a political cause on a national scale. In this sense, it was neither forward- nor backward-looking; it was both.[37] As with Luddism and Swing, underlying Chartism was an intense economic distress. And in this sense Chartism belongs to a decades-long period of British history characterised by 'waves of discontent' and extreme desperation and dissatisfaction on the part of the working class and the poor. 'No period of British history', writes Hobsbawm, 'has been as tense, as politically and socially disturbed, as the 1830s and early 1840s, when both the working class and the middle class, separately or in conjunction, demanded what they regarded as fundamental changes'.[38] These 'waves of discontent' were more than just attempts to emulate the revolutions in America and France; they were also responses to the imposition of the social property relations of capitalism.

The age of petitioning

The depression that had been felt harder in the Northern manufacturing districts now began to hit London.[39] The ongoing depression and widespread unemployment provided the appropriate context for sustaining Chartism. But it was the fact that well over five hundred Chartists were now in gaol that gave Chartists a cause to carry forward. The focal point was the Newport rising, and as the trials approached, hundreds of statements from around the country were issued in support of Frost and his accomplices. Feargus O'Connor raised a defence fund. A semi-formal meeting of convention delegates was held to discuss the trials. Meanwhile, the authorities uncovered several plots of armed insurrection in

35. Rule 1986, pp. 3 and 329.
36. Rule 1987, p. 117.
37. Breunig (1977, p. 187) sees Chartism as the only exception to the general absence of 'organized political activity by the working classes in the first half of the nineteenth century'. This underscores the point that Chartism was both exceptional and experimental.
38. Hobsbawm 1986, pp. 73–7.
39. Gossman 1983, p. 58.

solidarity with Frost. There were disturbances and arrests in Bradford, Sheffield and in several towns in West Riding. On 1 February 1840, a reprieve was announced in the trials to allow for the celebration of the Queen's wedding to Prince Albert. This, and the subsequent commutation of three death sentences, to which Lord Melbourne reluctantly consented, helped diffuse tensions. Chartism now enjoyed nowhere near the public support it had seen in early 1839, and as the second phase of Chartism began, 'physical force' was a term 'only mentioned to be disowned'.[40] Meetings in Glasgow the previous August had sought to set up a Scottish Charter organisation on a 'moral force' basis only, and the language of the Northern Political Union as well as the Metropolitan Charter Union was now more muted.

Meeting in Manchester on 20 July, Chartist delegates put forward an ambitious programme for a National Charter Association (NCA), involving the establishment of wards in each town with dues collectors, with wards to be divided into classes of ten members (a number low enough to evade the still-enforceable Corresponding Societies Act of 1799), each member being expected to pay 1p a week in order to sustain a new National Executive. Falling into step with the growing temperance movement, the Convention advocated sobriety for members. While in theory the local Chartist ward or class was to be kept distinct from any local trade union, in reality it was often the local trade union's membership and executive who comprised the Chartist chapter. The plan was most successfully carried out in London, Manchester and Dundee, Scotland.[41] The NCA fell under O'Connor's sway and was evaded by those who did not support him, notably William Lovett, who had been the object of fierce attacks by O'Connor, along with Bronterre O'Brien, who would break with O'Connor in 1842.[42]

Having lost so much momentum, Chartism was in danger of being overshadowed by the ACLL. The League was by now sponsoring eight hundred lectures and circulating one and a half million handbills annually. By June, the League would collect 1,144,380 signatures on a petition for repeal. For their part, the Chartists would collect 1.3 million signatures on a petition calling of the release of Chartist prisoners. Most Chartists were cynical about the League, seeing in the campaign to abolish the Corn Laws a motive only to increase profits. Chartists like William Cuffay who still looked to 'physical force' solutions took part in disrupting

40. Maccoby 2001, pp. 209–12.

41. Dundee was where the Chartist leader Peter McDouall had formed the Trades Democratic Universal Suffrage Association, which largely served as a model for the NCA (Chase 2000, pp. 190–1). Another source of inspiration was a book written by Lovett and Collins while in prison entitled *Chartism: A New Organisation of the People*, which envisioned an elaborate scheme of collecting 1p per week from all signatories to the Charter in order to fund the establishment of schools, libraries, printing houses and travelling lecturers (Maccoby 2001, pp. 213–14).

42. Briggs 1979, pp. 309–10.

League meetings, whilst 'moral force' advocates like Robert Lowery urged against such actions.[43] When a proposal came forward in August for a meeting in Leeds, just in advance of the opening of Parliament, to discuss an alliance between the two movements to unite all radicals, it was met with widespread suspicion as a scheme leading to a repeat of the betrayal of 1832. Several Chartist delegates attended alongside such notables and O'Connell, Hume, Roebuck, and Marshall, the great flax-spinning master of Leeds. Chartist delegates attended with the object of promoting the Charter and the meeting ended with cheers for the prisoners Frost and O'Connor. This was hardly the outcome the organisers were hoping for, and it gave them no additional leverage with Parliament.[44]

When Parliament met that summer, it was reported that the national debt now stood at £1,842,000 and would surpass £2.4 million by the coming year if no remedial measures were taken. As the Whigs continued occasionally to lose in divisions, Peel moved in June for a vote of no-confidence and elections were called. Peel's Conservatives enjoyed a majority of 92 when Parliament convened on 19 August, making it the first time the opposition party had held the majority. The Conservatives amended the address to express lack of confidence in the Ministers, who subsequently tendered their resignations, to the chagrin of Queen Victoria. Peel was invited to form a new ministry on 30 August. Almost deaf now, old Wellington was retained for his prestige as a minister without portfolio. Knatchbull and Lyndhurst were appointed to appease the ultra-Tories. James Graham became Home Secretary, Lord Aberdeen became Foreign Secretary and Lord Stanley assumed the aptly-named post of Secretary of State for War and the Colonies. Peel's return to power demonstrated that the Reform Bill of 1832 had not precipitated the immediate collapse of the power of the landed classes. Eight of the fourteen Cabinet ministers were peers, and only one was untitled.[45] 'Over 80 per cent of the MPs in the 1841 House had close family ties to broad acres', a trend that was to continue through the century, for 'as late as 1895, 60 per cent of MPs were gentlemen of leisure, most of whom derived a significant portion of their income from the land'.[46]

The economic crisis worsened in 1841 as recession rolled over into depression. Wheat had reached 86*s*. a quarter on 14 August. Thompson suggests that between four and five million souls, more than twenty percent of the population, were living in absolute poverty.[47] The honourable trade of the croppers had come to its end as cloth dressing was now almost exclusively done on the shearing frame

43. Gossman 1983, p. 59; Harrison and Hollis 1967, p. 509.
44. Maccoby 2001, pp. 221–3.
45. Jenkins 1999, pp. 96–7; Briggs 1979, pp. 328–9.
46. Harling 2001, p. 82.
47. Thompson 1991, pp. 256–7 gives the total population of Britain in 1841 as 18.1 million. See also Briggs 1979, p. 295.

and the few remaining croppers were either earning pitiful wages or turning at last to find other means of employment.[48] Roughly a third of the labour force was now engaged in both domestic and factory manufactures combined, a share that would change little until after the First World War.[49] While cotton led the way in terms of proletarianisation, with 53 percent of operatives working in factories,[50] in terms of business organisation it remained highly decentralised.[51] Peel was faced with demands for immediate action to alleviate the widespread level of destitution. The distress only worsened over the course of the Winter.

Out of the Leeds meeting, the Complete Suffrage Union emerged and by the end of March 1842 there were chapters in nearly all the important towns. In April, nine Chartist delegates attended a Complete Suffrage Conference meeting in Birmingham, despite the condemnations of Feargus O'Connor, whose writings from prison were printed in the *Northern Star*. O'Connor's efforts and trade unionism in general probably received some momentum from the rapid expansion of friendly societies and building societies in the 1840s, which were fostering the spirit of self-help and collectivism. There were also the beginnings of genuine, if compromising, feelings for the 'deserving poor' on the part of members of the rising middle orders. Disraeli's novel *Sybil*, depicting the harsh life of the working class, was widely read. Prince Albert became president of the Society for Improving the Condition of the Poor. But those harsh conditions had instilled a deep sense of class hatred amongst a large part of the working classes, especially the increasingly pressured artisans struggling to maintain their independence, for whom class collaboration was unthinkable.

On 21 April, the MP for Rochdale Sharman Crawford moved another measure for reform, resulting in a division of 67 in favour, 226 against and general abstention by the Whigs. Another defeat for suffrage did not deter the Chartists. The second Chartist National Petition was marched to Parliament on 2 May 1842 by an orderly congregation numbering as many as twenty thousand, bearing flags and banners, and including half a dozen musical bands.

> Containing 3,317,702 signatures the second Chartist National Petition was more than six miles in length and weighed more than six hundredweight. For carriage the petition had been tightly encased in a wooden frame bearing the simple inscriptions, 'the Charter', 'justice', as well as the famous six points and the total number of signatures. Such was the weight that it took about 30 Chartists –

48. Thompson 1991, p. 602, citing Dodd 1968, p. 15. 'It was a sad end to an honourable craft', Thompson eulogises.
49. Deane and Cole 1969, p. 144.
50. King and Timmins 2001, p. 51.
51. Hobsbawm 1986, p. 64.

> mainly representatives of the London trades – to lift the petition, and they required regular replacement as the petition was carried.[52]

By the time they reached Palace Yard their numbers swelled to a number *The Times* estimated at fifty thousand. Upon reaching the members' entrance to the House, the Grand Petition got jammed in the doorway, and perhaps symbolically could not be moved either forward or backwards until a part of the door frame was removed. Once inside, the box was opened and petitions flowed out from a table such that to William Lovett, 'the House looked as if it had been snowing paper'.[53] The violent and somewhat vulgar language of the new petition was enough to dismay the Scottish Chartists into several years of estrangement from the movement, but was probably intended as a kind of mockery, given that there was virtually no chance of success. The next day, Duncombe's motion to allow six Chartists to address the bar was defeated. In the debate that followed, Macaulay spoke of universal suffrage leading to the nightmare scenario of the abolition of all private property and the collapse of civilisation itself. Roebuck countered with an argument suggesting that full suffrage was the best guarantee of private property. The vote was 49 Radicals in favour, 287 Tories and Whigs against. With no 'ulterior measures' in place this time, and suffering from internal divisions, the Chartists were not in a position to control the aftermath.

The strike of 1842

1842 was the grimmest year of the nineteenth century. A full 'four years of harvest dearth made England unhappy and afraid, a country of conflict and despair. Bread was dear, and flesh and blood were cheap'.[54] While working-class household expenditure showed an overall increase of one-third between the late eighteenth and mid-nineteenth centuries, they declined in the early 1840s.[55] Trade was stagnant: workhouses were overcrowded. Wages were shrinking in both real and absolute terms, for the price of bread was soaring and employers had been engaging in widespread wage reductions since 1840. According to the Chartist Thomas Cooper, the Plug Plot disturbances 'began in reductions of wages by the Anti-Corn Law manufacturers, who did not conceal their purpose of driving

52. Pickering 2001, pp. 368–9; Chase (2000, p. 174) notes that the figure of 3.3 million contrasts mightily with the number of some eight hundred and thirteen thousand voters who were added to the franchise in 1832.
53. Pickering 2001, p. 369.
54. Briggs 1979, p. 295.
55. King and Timmins 2001, p. 152, citing a sampling of 283 household budgets by Horrell.

the people to desperation, in order to paralyse the Government'.[56] This could as easily be truth as it could be Chartist folklore based on suspicions of League manufacturers. While Hobsbawm sees the general strike of 1842 as a 'point of spontaneous social combustion' that was 'unplanned',[57] this view has been corrected by assessments that suggest the strikes were in fact coordinated by Chartists from an early stage. Malcolm Chase observes:

> The strike wave of 1842 was a unique phenomenon. There was no further occasion in nineteenth-century Britain when strikes were either so extensive or so closely identified with political objectives . . . The Chartist and strike movements of 1842 constituted the last point in British history when a revolution in the nature of government, economy and society seemed not only imperative but actually achievable to many of the population.[58]

As we know, many local chapters of the Chartists were in fact organised trade unions. It thus seems likely that it was local trade unionists who attended summer meetings in Manchester at which resolutions were carried calling for a general work stoppage until the Charter was passed.

The general strike itself began among the colliers of North Staffordshire on 8 July, who engaged in pulling the plugs of the boilers to force a cessation of work. Their grievance was over wages and against payment in truck. By early August the miners were joined by Lancashire cotton operatives, first at Stalybridge and then in Manchester itself, calling for a ten-hour bill and a restoration of 1840 level wages. A meeting of 7 August at Mottram Moor was held and a resolution passed '"that all labour should cease until the *People's Charter* became the law of the land" . . . tens of thousands [holding up] their hands in favour of it'.[59] There was a near complete labour stoppage in dozens of towns in thirty-two counties. There were 'armies of strikers' to be found 'marching from town to town and mine to mine enforcing a turn-out that became general in the manufacturing districts of Lancashire and Cheshire and the West Riding, and reached into Leicestershire and Nottinghamshire'.[60] During this climactic period there were two separate conferences of Chartist delegates meeting in Manchester, the NCA meeting on 16 and 17 August and an alternate group meeting from August 11 to August 20.[61]

---

56. Cooper 1875, p. 190.
57. Hobsbawm 1994, p. 208.
58. Chase 2000, p. 202. Mather likewise saw 'the two months into which the action was squeezed' as 'the most intense threat to order in the early industrial period' (Rule 1986, p. 332).
59. Cooper 1875, p. 191.
60. Rule 1986, pp. 332–3.
61. According to Cooper there were nearly sixty delegates present at the NCA meeting, including McDouall and Feargus O'Connor. When William Hill, the editor of O'Connor's *Northern Star* moved to condemn the strikes as playing right into the strategy of the

Word was sent out from these meetings to link the demand of the Charter to the wage demands of the strikes. The Potteries had already been forced into a slow-down by the absence of coal and rather than giving a hostile response, the potters willingly endured the forced work stoppage, declaring their solidarity with the colliers. Saint Monday was still widely observed among the Potters, so it was a matter of observing Saint Tuesday, Saint Wednesday or Saint Week.[62] The Potters joined the general strike on 13 August. Peel was reluctant, but Wellington prevailed upon him to send armed force to the aid of the industrialists. There were open clashes with the military at the Potteries, as well as at Preston and Blackburn in Lancashire. Conflicts in Halifax left three dead, including a soldier, and thirty-six were arrested and put on trial. From 20 August into September the strike began to fall apart in the face of a combined army of soldiers, yeomanry, police and special constables. The intense hostility in the newspapers was also felt. The cotton workers in Lancashire and the miners in Staffordshire held out for a restoration of wages for another month and the cotton workers in Lanarkshire, Scotland held out until March of 1843.[63]

The usual round of Assize trials and Special Commissions followed, this time with what Maccoby calls 'wholesale bludgeonings of the law'.[64] In all some one thousand five hundred arrests were made, of whom 79 were transported, 54 from Staffordshire alone, for between seven and twenty-one years.[65] O'Connor and Cooper were detained. Upon his release from prison on 30 August O'Connor began touring again. In mid-November, 'Rebecca' struck again in Wales, this

---

ACLL, O'Connor hesitated before voting against the motion (which failed with only six votes), but personally did nothing to assist the strike (Cooper 1875, pp. 209–10). Cooper himself had been wary at the prospect of violence, condemning those he met who had engaged in destruction of property. But his account reveals a kind of conversion to the cause. As a far more notorious figure, O'Connor had more reason to be nervous about the violence, but the whole Plug Plot affair reveals the tension between trade unionists and non-trade unionists within Chartism. If it was indeed the case that employers had driven down wages to deliberately provoke a strike, Hill's amendment, and O'Connor's hesitation, would be arising from a sense of being manipulated, on top of a sense of having lost control.

62. Chase 2000, pp. 193–8. St. Monday would persist into the 1860s in many trades. Joseph Rogers, an employer of grinders at Sheffield, complained of grinders observing St. Monday and taking Tuesday as a '"natty day...when nothing will persuade them to work – not even a barrel of ale, and yet [we] have more control over this class of workmen than any other manufacturers"' (as quoted in Rule 1986, p. 134). The Sheffield cutlery grinders had reason enough to grieve. While grinders' disease was little known half a century earlier, by 1842 fully 50 percent of grinders in their thirties, 79 percent in their forties and all grinders in their fifties 'retched out their lungs with it' (Hobsbawm 1994, p. 252).

63. Rule 1986, pp. 333 and 336; Maccoby 2001, p. 240.

64. Maccoby 2001, p. 241.

65. Maccoby 2001, p. 241; Spartacus Educational 2008.

time destroying several toll gates in the vicinity of St. Clears.[66] While the only connection with the Chartist strike may be the economic distress of the time, it was a signal of the next round of dissenting violence that would occupy the attention of authorities in the following year.

Reform and disorder under Peel

Like Feargus O'Connor, Peel had boundless energy and personally supervised all of his ministers. His technocratic style – not unlike that of a factory master – stood in sharp contrast to the passivity of Melbourne. At the Foreign Office, however, where the almost inept Aberdeen had taken over from Palmerston, the reverse was true. During the previous eleven years Palmerston, in the name of 'free trade', had entered Britain into a Quadruple Alliance with France, Spain and Portugal in 1834 as a counterweight to absolutist régime; had overseen the unification of Upper and Lower Canada through the Canada Act as an effort to resolve the economic and social issues that had led to the rebellions of 1837; had entered Britain into an alliance with Austria and Turkey in 1841 to oust Muhammad Ali Pasha's forces from Syria,[67] subsequently forcing Egypt to lift its high tariffs; and in 1842 had prosecuted the Opium Wars to force China to lift its ban on British imports of opium from India.[68] Under Aberdeen, who did

66. Including the recently built 'Mermaid' gate. Jones 1989, pp. 207–8.

67. The forced reduction of tariffs in the interest of opening up colonial economies was quite successful in facilitating the expansion of British exports, but it had disastrous consequences for the countries in question. In 1838, Muhammad Ali Pasha had invested millions of pounds in industrial establishments, including modern factories employing some thirty thousand workers. The factories were primarily geared toward supplying the military, and enjoyed the protection of a wall of high tariffs. Once the tariffs were lifted, the factories could not compete with imported wares and were sold, leased or liquidated under Ali's successors (Issawi 1980, p. 472). Egypt was not the only country to face de-industrialisation at the hands of Britain. India's domestic hand-loom manufacturing sector, the mighty competitor that had forced Britain to enact bans on Indian cotton imports from the turn of the eighteenth century, was effectively destroyed by 1840. 'Between 1815 and 1832 the value of Indian cotton goods exported from the country fell from £1.3 million to less than £100,000 while the import of British cotton goods increased sixteen times over. By 1840 an observer already warned against the disastrous effects of turning India into "the agricultural farm of England; she is a manufacturing country, her manufactures of various descriptions have existed for ages... To reduce her now to an agricultural country would be an injustice to India"' (Martin 1841, p. 61). Not only was India reduced to an agrarian country, but the policies that were implemented were based on the concept that a rent should be collected from India's peasants just as the landlord collected a rent from his tenant-farmer. In other words, the taxation scheme of the British Raj was based on the fiction that agrarian capitalism existed in India. This policy would contribute to cyclic famine on a massive scale. See Hobsbawm 1994, pp. 196–201.

68. While the rationale behind the Opium Wars – breaking down trade-barriers in China – was quite consistent with the British policy of opening up colonial economies

not share Palmerston's mistrust of France, the Queen consented to *rapprochement* with France.[69] With China subdued and Egyptian aggression in check, Peel sought to bring the mushrooming debt under control and to carry forward Pitt's campaign for bureaucratic efficiency. To address the debt, he proposed a reintroduction of an income tax of 7*d.* on the pound, both to service the debt itself and to allow the reduction of some 750 out of 1,200 existing tariffs in 1842, with another 430 articles to be removed by 1845. The major and most notable exception was the Corn Law. Peel's lowering of the corn tariff upon the introduction of a new sliding scale in 1842 seemed to please neither the Leaguers nor the Anti-Leaguers. There was no question that the poor law would be renewed when it came up for debate early in Peel's term, but in response to petitions Peel agreed to establish a commission of inquiry.

In the meantime, the results from two previously established commissions came in. Lord Ashley's 'blue book' of the Royal Commission on Children's Employment in Mines, the first government report to include pictures, shocked the British public with stories of naked men, women, boys and girls all working together in the mines, wading through knee-deep water in dark tunnels, perhaps more so than the reports of associated lung diseases and the frequent use of brutal methods of discipline.[70] Ashley's report prompted the passage of the 1842 Coal Mines Act, which received royal assent on 10 August and which did for the mines what the Factory Acts had done for the textile industry. The employment of boys under the age of ten and girls of any age was prohibited.[71] The other

---

to trade in British goods, by now the Raj in India was also quite dependent upon the sale of opium to China. Thus without the Opium Wars, British rule in India might have been jeopardised. By August 1842, the British fleet had sacked both Guangdong (Canton) and Shanghai and had seized China's tax ships, bringing the imperial government to its knees. Under the Treaty of Nanjing (Nanking), Hong Kong was ceded to Britain, while Shanghai and four other ports were opened up to British trade (Plumb 1963, p. 177 and Briggs 1979, p. 364).

69. Victoria's visit to Paris and meeting with Louis Philippe was the first direct meeting between an English sovereign and a foreign sovereign since Henry VIII. Clarke and Ridley 2001, pp. 73–5.

70. 'In unemotive language which made its subject matter all the more chilling, [the report] detailed how six-year olds spent twelve hours a day under the earth harnessed to trucks of coal, dragging them along tunnels knee-deep in water, while their mothers heaved coal on their heads up to the top of the mine. That was how Britain was obtaining the coal which made her "the workshop of the world" ' (Fraser 2005, pp. 535–6). Lord Ashley also held the title Lord Shaftesbury, by which he was perhaps more commonly known at this time.

71. Boys of 10 years of age would continue to be sent into the pits until the age restriction was raised to 12 in 1860. Certification and training of managers would only be introduced in 1872. The Royal School of Mines was established in 1843 to train inspectors. The Miners' Association of Great Britain and Ireland was founded after the Act's passage in late 1842. The Association would experience astonishing growth over the next two years, and played a central role in the Great Strike of 1844, which we shall discuss below. Ibid.

report was Edwin Chadwick's *Sanitary Condition of the Labouring Population*,[72] which exposed the dreadful conditions of working-class families crowded into the cheap one and two-room 'court' houses that had begun to spread rapidly in the vicinity of textile mills and coalmines. The conditions involved inadequate ventilation, open doors, communal privies, a shared water standpipe, overcrowding and rampant susceptibility to disease.[73] This report from Chadwick, one of the authors of the Poor Law Report, amounted to an admission *pace* Malthus that the poor could not be blamed for the fact that they were forced to live in unhealthy surroundings and that the state had an obligation to intervene in the economy to protect the most vulnerable from the dislocating effects of a free-market economy. The following year, Ashley would lead a revolt within the Conservative Party by backbenchers that was at least in part a move towards restoring some form of Tory paternalism.

Despite the continuing depression, there were no major strikes or violent disturbances in England in 1843. It was West Wales that became the centre of disturbances in May when followers of 'Rebecca' launched a series of attacks on toll houses. The record suggests these attacks were also in part a rebellion against the implementation of the poor laws in Wales.[74] In England, it was the ACLL that was on the move. In January, a Free Trade Hall capable of holding eight thousand persons at St. Peter's Field in Manchester, the very site of the Peterloo massacre, was built in just six weeks. With the Chartists still divided and disorganised, the ACLL quickly grew to become the most influential public campaign organisation in Britain. Free-trade tea parties and bazaars attracted middle-class housewives, who could buy anti-monopoly teapots and pin cushions.[75] A campaign to get the countryside behind the repeal of the Corn Law was launched. League members

72. Chadwick 1843.

73. The building of 'court' housing was not abolished until 1864, and many were still inhabited in the twentieth century. James Newlands began designing and installing sewer systems in Liverpool in the 1850s. He persuaded the city council to provide wash-houses, street paving and lighting. (Living Life Museum, Liverpool, visit by author, 29 October 1997).

74. Some two thousand Rebecca supporters marched into Carmarthen in broad daylight on 19 June, whence they presented a petition to the magistrates of the Guildhall before marching to the workhouse, which they ransacked after moving the children outside. Whilst preparing to burn the workhouse down, they instead panicked and fled upon hearing that the 4th Light Dragoons sent from Cardiff were approaching. Sixty Rebecca supporters were arrested. The attacks continued through September before nearly fifty additional Rebeccaists were arrested, the ringleaders receiving between seven and twenty years' transportation, with lighter sentences being meted out to the others. 'Rebecca Riots' 2008.

75. Briggs 1979, pp. 317–22. The League now had a central fund of £50,000 which would double in a year, and its own weekly, the *Anti-Corn Law Circular*. It was supported by the new magazine, the *Economist*. Also in 1843, the League moved its headquarters, where it would begin to make headway with the London press.

sought to persuade tenant-farmers that their prosperity depended upon the health of industry, since industrial progress meant more demand for their grain and livestock. Farmers were not an easy sell, however, and there was a short-lived attempt at forming a kind of 'Anti-League'.[76]

Another organisation on the move in England was the Miners' Association, which by August had attracted the support of colliers from Wales, Scotland, the Midlands, Lancashire and Cumberland, and reasonably claimed some 30,000 to 40,000 colliers as members.[77] The initial tactic proffered by the Chartist lawyer W.P. Roberts was to wage a legal war of attrition against the owners, in a battle over the bond.[78] Roberts was also keeping a watchful eye on Parliament, where employers were seeking to smuggle through A Bill for Enlarging the Powers of Justices in Determining Complaints between Masters, Servants and Artificers, and for the More Effectual Recovery of Wages before Justices, introduced by Graham on 22 February. Under the pretence of merely seeking to clarify legal definitions of employment, the bill included such draconian provisions as penalising employees for 'misbehaviour' with up to two months in gaol, with or without hard labour. A campaign to oppose the measure was led by Roberts and the Association, with strong support from the Potters and numerous other unions as local trade associations. Some 213 petitions were delivered to Parliament in opposition to the measure. Chartist leaders joined the campaign and paternalist Tories in Parliament actually booed the measure as it was being read in committee, where it was defeated by a vote of 97–54 on 1 May. The *Northern Star* celebrated this victory as a ' "triumph of labour," ' over an attempt by the government to make the workman ' "a very slave to his employer." '[79]

In part, the renewed push by members of the landed class to ameliorate the harshness of the New Poor Law and to revive paternalism came in response to the growing influence of League spokesmen like Cobden, Villiers and Thompson, who increasingly tended to argue that repeal of the Corn Laws would alleviate the sufferings of the poor. Tory landlords countered by pointing out the scandalous

---

76. Briggs 1979, pp. 317–22. The Quaker Joseph Sturge's Complete Suffrage Union had dissolved after a meeting in December 1842. The meeting was attended by O'Connor and his followers, who effectively took it over, leading Sturge and his followers to leave the hall.

77. Chase 2000, p. 206. Staffordshire had yet to recover from the repression of the previous year's strike.

78. The bond, or annual contract, was still in use but had undergone considerable changes. Traditionally, the bond was read and signed at around the same time of the autumn as hiring fairs were hosted by farmers, thus reflecting its agrarian origins, a time of high demand for labour and thus favouring the men. But in 1812 the owners changed the period of the bond to run from April to April, a time of low demand for labour and thus advantaging the owners (Scott 2004).

79. From the *Northern Star*, 4 May 1844, p. 290, as quoted in Hay and Craven 2004, pp. 413–20; Maccoby 2001, pp. 401–2.

working conditions in the factories. On 6 February 1844, Graham introduced a new factory bill.[80] On 15 March, Lord Ashley, in part out of sincere paternalism, in part out of hostility to the industrialists, moved an amendment to reduce the working day to ten hours. The motion carried 163 to 155. This being unacceptable to the ministry, a second vote later in the week overturned the amendment, but the twelve-hour day was not restored. Unwilling to compromise for an eleven-hour day, the entire bill was temporarily withdrawn.[81]

The Great Strike of 1844, which Chase describes as 'heroic, desperate, tragic'[82] proved a case study in why the hardest time to strike is during a depression in the trade. The conflict over the bond between the Miners' Association and the mine owners reached a breaking point in the Spring. The Association had adopted a policy of opposing local strikes, seeing a general strike as offering the best chance for success. In the meantime, a tactic of job action by voluntarily lowering earnings to 3*s*. per day was adopted. But as the conflict intensified, the Association had little choice but to agree to a strike. The strike began in the Northeast with an orderly walk-out by some thirty-four thousand colliers. The owners retaliated viciously by reducing the bond to a monthly contract and with wholesale evictions of colliers and their families from their tied housing, with no regard for women, infants, the infirm or the aged. Echoing the constant appeals of Chartists for non-violence during the strike of 1842, Roberts advised the colliers ' "Let them *carry* you out" '.[83] The Association put out an appeal for workmen throughout Britain to refuse to accept employment in disregard for the strike, but many blacklegs were recruited. Those from Cornwall were dubbed 'Black Jacks'.[84] The strikers held out on minimal strike pay until mid-August before the strike failed.

---

80. Graham was re-introducing his 1843 Factory Bill for reducing the working day for factory children to six and a half hours, which had been withdrawn under pressure from Nonconformists who protested its provisions that the Anglican Church should be put in charge of factory schools.

81. When re-submitted later in the session, Ashley acquiesced and the twelve hour day was sustained. Peel was faced with another revolt in June, when an amendment to lower the duty on colonial sugar to 20s. per cwt. overrode the ministry's proposal of a 24s. tariff. Again the ministry succeeded in overturning the amendment, but this time only after Peel threatened to resign. Once Peel's ship was back on course, he sought to reassure his Conservative followers by giving a speech restating his steadfast opposition to repeal of the Corn Laws. Jenkins 1999, pp. 112–17; Steward 1969, pp. 35–57.

82. Chase 2000, p. 207. Rule 1986, p. 333, puts the figure for the membership of the Miners' Association of Great Britain and Ireland at 60,000 by the end of 1842, which made the effort 'an national union in an occupation where strong locality orientations made national union in itself a striking achievement,' but Chase's figures may be based on more current research.

83. As quoted in Rule 1986, p. 339. Emphasis found in the original.

84. Scott 2004.

Those who returned were subject to reprisals. Support for unions subsequently dropped among the demoralised colliers of the North-East.[85]

During the economic recovery in 1845, another trades-union was established. At the founding conference of the National Association of United Trades for the Protection of Labour (NAUT), calls for all trades to abandon 'aristocratic pretensions' were heard. The driving force behind this effort was Sam Jacobs, a Chartist from Bristol and a member of the cabinetmakers' society.[86] As heir to the NAPL and the GNCTU, the NAUT differed in several important respects from its predecessors. Aside from building solidarity and providing mutual assistance, the NAUT promoted arbitration boards, which had begun to appear in the 1830s, and the avoidance of strikes. Jacobs also proposed combining trade organisation with a scheme to purchase land for industrial buildings, an idea that resonated with the freeholder movement, a topic to which we shall return.

The repeal of the Corn Laws and the Irish Potato Famine

Ireland had been subject to the introduction of an agrarian capitalism since the late sixteenth century, with the forcible expropriation of the peasantry and their conversion into mostly subsistence-farming tenants on large Protestant estates. By at least the 1830s, rapid population growth in Ireland had led to extensive subdivision of holdings, widespread poverty and chronic levels of unemployment or underemployment. The potato had by now become the staple food for most households in Ireland.

Since 1843, O'Connell's campaign for repeal of the Union had been gaining momentum in Ireland. Staging a series of mass rallies, he now enjoyed the open support of the Catholic bishops and clergy. Like his seventeenth- and eighteenth-century predecessors, Peel saw Ireland as a security threat in terms of a possible alliance between Ireland and France. Hoping to find ways of providing new employment and mollifying the Catholics, Peel set up a commission in early 1844 to look into problems of land tenure in Ireland. The Commission's report in 1845 proposed compensating evicted tenants for any improvements they had made to the land and appointing a Commissioner of Improvements to promote further improvements. But these proposals were voted down in a House dominated

---

85. By contrast, coalfield strikes across Lancashire in early 1844 succeeded in resisting owners' attempts to impose a North-East style bond and to establish what were effectively closed shops. In Yorkshire, a three-month strike beginning on 12 May had been defeated by October through the recruiting of 'blacklegs'. Lanarkshire also saw a strike lasting three months. Rule 1986, pp. 339–40; Chase 2000, p. 207.

86. Disillusioned with the failure of the 1842 strikes, Jacobs was seeking alternatives and in 1844 led the formation of the United Trades Association in Bristol. Fox 1985, p. 131; Chase 2000, p. 208.

by landlords. Peel then put forward measures to establish three colleges where Irish Catholics could attend – in Belfast, Cork and Galway – and endowments for Catholic priests. These met little resistance in the Commons but when Peel proposed tripling the annual grant to the Maynooth Catholic seminary in County Kildare, it set off a firestorm of Protestant protest and prompted petitions with a million and a half signatures. While the bill carried with Whig support, it was significant that the Conservative Party split on the measure by 149 to 148.[87]

In October 1845, news reached London that a blight had ruined half of the Irish potato crop. The blight happened to strike at a time of low grain production and poor harvests in Europe generally, a factor that would contribute to the famine that followed. The more practical aspects of the ministry's response were to spend £750,000 on public works projects and to purchase maize from America to send to Ireland. But Peel also seized the opportunity to call for a full repeal of the Corn Laws. Since the Irish lacked the means to buy grain whether it was cheap or dear, this had the appearance of an act of sheer opportunism on Peel's part. His call for repeal was in part an attempt to pre-empt the League in asserting that the Corn Laws were to blame for the famine in Ireland, but there was a deeper motive at work as well. Lacking Cabinet support for the move, Peel resigned in December to allow the pro-repeal Russell to form a ministry, but the Whigs were as divided on the issue as the Conservatives and, as in 1839, Peel resumed his post.

Peel's reversal of his position on the Corn Laws was seen by many an old Tory squire, who had not forgotten Peel's betrayals on currency reform in 1819 and on Catholic Emancipation in 1829, as yet another act of betrayal against the landed interest. But Peel, who was by now a genuine convert to free trade, was not without his supporters among the landed class. There was an economic basis to the schism that went beyond class and party loyalties. 'The crux of the problem', writes D.C. Moore, 'lay in the dialectical opposition between those customs and policies on the one hand which served to reinforce the hierarchical structure of rural society and the cohesion of the rural interest group, and, on the other hand, the exigencies of agricultural prosperity in an era of high farming'.[88] The problem was not at all unlike that of the so-called agrarian depression of a century before: as the accumulation of capital continued to accelerate, the traditional privileges and perquisites associated with traditional landownership tended increasingly to serve as a drag on agricultural profitability. While Peel and others committed to high farming firmly believed that only through the application of scientific

87. Jenkins 1999, pp. 120–3. An analysis of the transformation of Irish agriculture lies beyond the scope of the present work, though a full study of the introduction of agrarian capitalism into Ireland and Ireland's late enclosures is needed.

88. Moore 1965, p. 551.

methods could the landed class maintain its hegemonic position in society, the dilemma for smaller owners was that investing in improvements posed a very high risk of failure, while simply investing in further acquisitions of land was still a far more profitable route toward wealth creation in the short-term.

The General Inclosure Act of 1845 only served to intensify this schism. With the enclosure of arable lands effectively complete, the main purpose of the Act was to facilitate the final wave of enclosure of the commons, meadows and stinted pastures which obstructed cultivation or the introduction of scientific methods of 'high' farming.[89] High farming did improve yields, but the capital required for investing in drainage schemes, fertiliser, adding livestock, dairying or adding new rotations was simply insurmountable for many farmers and lesser landowners. The use of machinery was now gathering momentum as well. The chill which Swing had successfully put on the use of the threshing-machine across much of South England began to thaw after 1843.[90] Farmers had as yet no legal guarantee that the investments they made were secure and not subject to forfeiture upon the termination of the lease.[91] Since the capitalist entrepreneur was typically not the *owner* of the means of production, agrarian capitalism had a built-in hurdle standing in the way of its own further progression along capitalist lines. It was this hurdle which Peel and his associates were determined to surmount, even if it meant leaving some members of the landed class behind.

Upon introducing the bill for repeal in January 1846, Peel sought to console farmers that they had nothing to fear by repeal, and he sought to induce farmers to undertake improvements by including reductions on duties for grass and clover seeds, maize and buckwheat for fattening cattle, linseed and rape-cake. He also sought to lower the burden of the poor rates by providing more employment on mending and building the highways. A final sop was the drainage loan, more a symbolic programme than real, since it was minimally funded. For Peel, it was intended as a psychological inducement to encourage farmers to change their habits and attitudes toward scientific and high farming. The package as a whole was intended as a free-trade bill. Building on the success of Peel's tariff-reductions of 1842, the bill included tariff reductions on coarse textile and food imports as a benefit to the poor. Finally, to soften the blow, the Corn Laws were to be reduced gradually until full repeal on 1 February 1849. The non-high farmers

89. To this end the act appointed commissioners empowered to enclose any lands outside a 15-mile radius around London and outside specified boundaries of other cities and towns. Adkin 1907, pp. 166–7.

90. Hobsbawm and Rudé 1968, pp. 30 and 299. The lingering threat of Luddism had lasted into the 1840s in some regions as well. According to Sale, 'as late as 1842 one traveler reported that almost no cotton was worked in Westhoughton, where the vast factory had been destroyed in April 1812, because of "the fear of Luddism" ' (Sale 1996, p. 194).

91. Moore 1965, pp. 550–3.

of the Anti-League would have none of this. The protectionists had formed the Central Agricultural Protection Association with Lord Bentinck, 'whose exploits had up to that date been in the field of horse racing',[92] as the chair and Disraeli as a spokesman. This body was driven by the interests of farmers who were digging in their heels against the agenda of the English Agricultural Society (later renamed the Royal Agricultural Society of England), to which Peel belonged. Not only were they appalled that Peel had apparently been resolved against protection for some time, but they also felt that Peel 'was proposing to surrender the fundamental interests of the landowning class' in favour of the narrow interests of a group of industrialists. Assailed by shouting and cries of betrayal from his own party, Peel, with Whig and Radical support, was able to secure passage of the Corn and Customs Bill in May, against 222 Conservative votes and only 106 Conservative votes in favour. On 29 June, Peel tendered his resignation.[93]

The much criticised view of the repeal of the Corn Laws as a triumph of the rising class of urban industrialists, merchants and bankers over the landed aristocracy and gentry is wrong, but not entirely wrong.[94] It is not entirely wrong because the repeal of the Corn Laws is a milestone marking the transition from a condition of agrarian capitalism with an industrial capitalism growing up alongside it to a *capitalism* in which agriculture continued to play perhaps even the dominant role for some time, but now was to be incorporated into a *general* economic system under which land, labour and money were to be commodified and subordinated to market regulation. The view is wrong, however, on two counts. First, seeing Peel's actions as a betrayal of his class in general is a misnomer. Roughly half of the landowners in Parliament voted in favour of repeal, and these 'were not, socially, inconsiderable men. They included the heirs of two dukedoms, a marquisate and eight earldoms, others of noble birth, as well as many eminent representatives of "the gentlemen of England" '.[95] In short, they represented that part of the landed class that was engaged in, and supported, high farming. Second, seeing the repeal of the Corn Laws as a *defeat* for landed-

92. Kitson Clark 1951, p. 3.

93. Jenkins 1999, pp. 124–34; Kitson Clark 1951, p. 10; Moore 1965, p. 548.

94. For example, Thomas 1929, pp. 56–60, examines the voting on the second and third readings of the bill and concludes that there is no question that the crucial support for the bill came from the industrial and commercial classes. He explains away the exception, that of the railway interest, as a faction whose interests were inextricably tied with the fate of the land. What he seems to overlook, however, is that the landholders were almost evenly split: 176–84 on the second reading, 203–197 on the third. It is the case that the landed classes tended to take a dim view of the factory system. During the factory hours agitation and the Corn Law debates in the 1840s 'the wickedness of the system became an article of faith of the agricultural interest' (Fitton and Wadsworth 1958, p. 232).

95. Aydelotte 1967, p. 52. The large Whig vote included many of these gentlemen, the Whig party itself being dominated by many great landowners.

class power, leading to its rapid decline, is also mistaken. Repeal led to virtually no crisis at all for farmers and landlords, in part because the anticipated flood of imports of foreign grain imports did not materialize, due to limited supplies, but also owing to the fact that a run of good harvests meant prices were already low in 1846, yet repeal did not appear to have the much-anticipated effect of lowering grain prices any further. As with 1832, repeal in 1846 amounted to a concession or timely retreat on the part of the ruling landed class, in the interest of preserving its power and hegemonic position, whilst sacrificing very little. In fact, what followed was a kind of golden age for high farming, or what has been called the 'Indian summer of the British aristocracy'.[96]

Peel's resignation led to the return of the Whigs to power under Lord Russell, who retained many of the figures of Melbourne's cabinet, most notably Palmerston at Foreign Secretary and Earl Grey himself (now Lord Howick) as Secretary for War and the Colonies. The situation in Ireland was extremely dire, and the usual instruments at the Government's disposal were relief to deal with the hunger and coercion to deal with a rising tide of violence and murders. O'Connell's 'moral force' position was losing ground to the new Young Ireland movement, led by the young Smith O'Brien. A Coercion Bill was introduced in the face of protest from the Radicals in Parliament and was subsequently dropped. In the Autumn, the situation deteriorated further as the failure of the potato crop was worse than the year before. Russell's government further expanded the public works programme in Ireland to provide employment, the numbers working on the roads rising from four hundred and fifty thousand to seven hundred thousand. On top of this, the Irish Poor Law of 1838 was amended to restore outdoor relief to paupers holding less than a quarter-acre of land, and to appoint medical and relief officers under the Board of Guardians. By June 1847, no less than three million Irish were receiving government relief, a testament to the extraordinary poverty under conditions of the enormous concentration of property in the hands of Protestant landowners seeking to practice a kind of agrarian capitalism. By the autumn of 1847, the worst was over, but in all around one million Irish would perish in the famine, and another one million would emigrate. Of a population of 8,172,124 in 1841, there were only 6,552,385 alive and residing in Ireland in 1851.[97]

96. Kitson Clark 1951, p. 13; Aydelotte 1967, p. 50. Perhaps the greatest beneficiaries of repeal were the colonies, whose grain exports to Britain were stimulated by the lowering of the tariff until the Great Depression struck in 1873 (Hobsbawm 1986, p. 138).

97. Maccoby 2001, p. 271; Marriott 2006, pp. 152–4. There would be no rapid recovery. Ireland's population would drop by a third between 1831 and 1881, whilst over the same period the population of England and Wales would increase by 87 percent. It should be pointed out that while the famine of 1845–6 was certainly the worst in Irish history, it was by no means the first, and some previous famines were quite devastating, as for example the famine of 1740–1, one of four famines in the first half of the eighteenth

'All men are brethren'

Alongside the Irish famine came the peak of the railway boom with £200 million invested between the years 1846 and 1848. The economy as a whole was seeing unprecedented levels of capital investment. The textile phase of the Industrial Revolution was giving way to railways and capital goods. Iron output doubled and the production and export of capital goods in general surged in response to demand for railway building. The surge in exports was in part due to the building of railways on the Continent, which 'were built to a large extent with British capital, British materials and equipment, and often by British contractors'.[98] Britain was not just exporting railroads, it was exporting capitalism. Some thirteen thousand miles of rails were laid in Europe in the 1840s, over six thousand of them in the United Kingdom. Another seven thousand were laid in America. Railway building in the colonies would commence in the 1850s, accelerating the import of primary goods to the 'workshop of the world'. At the peak of building in 1844–7, some two hundred and fifty thousand uniformed railway navvies laid more than two thousand miles of rails, with an expenditure of £52 million in 1847 alone. Expenditure on transportation building had stood at two per cent of GNP in 1800; it now approached ten percent and 'probably accounted for more than half of gross domestic fixed capital formation'.[99]

During this period of accelerated economic activity, Chartists and trade unionists showed signs of renewed activity themselves, organising some 249 petitions bearing one million four hundred thousand signatures calling for the release of Frost, Williams and Jones, the leaders of the 1839 rising in Monmouthshire who still languished in gaol.[100] For his part, Feargus O'Connor had now turned his full attention to the Land Plan, purchasing the first estate for the purpose of breaking it up and settling workers in cottages in March 1846.

Since 1841 O'Connor had been writing about the possibility of extending the franchise to working people by subdividing estates into small plots in freehold, thereby enabling the residents to meet the 40s. (£2) freehold requirement. He estimated that a four-acre smallholder could earn £100 per year or more. Putting

---

century and one which claimed between 250,000 and 400,000 lives or 'roughly 20 per cent of the population, a number proportionally higher than the more famous Famine in the 1840s' (Patriquin 2006, pp. 232–4, following Kelly 1991–2, p. 65). Patriquin also identifies a series of '"minor"' or regional famines in Ireland prior to 1845, these coming in the years: 1822, 1831, 1835–1837, 1839 and 1842.

98. Hobsbawm 1986, pp. 114–5.

99. Deane and Cole 1969, pp. 232, 238 and 295. The trend would peak in the 1870s, when railway building was overcome by the building of steamships, which began to accelerate in the 1840s. Only by 1900 would transportation's share of the GNP fall back to two per cent. Deane 1997, p. 169–70; Hobsbawm 1986, pp. 114–5. Rule 1986, p. 12 puts the total number of railworkers at 182,963 in 1848.

100. Slosson 1916, p. 94.

forward his idea at successive Chartist conventions, O'Connor was able to get it approved in 1845 and he began raising subscriptions with the goal of putting some 24,000 working-class families on the land within five years. By April 1846 the first 35 settlers were chosen to be settled at the subdivided estate at Heronsgate, near Watford, just northwest of London. On 17 August, between twelve thousand and twenty thousand visitors attended an exhibition at the colony, renamed 'O'Connorville', one year before the official opening.[101]

Meanwhile, the NAUT had by October of 1846 recruited fifty thousand members and was still growing. It also had a huge strike fund. At Bristol, a two-week-long strike by the cabinet makers had succeeded in winning a wage increase of 50 per cent. Jacobs was hopeful of opening a factory for striking cabinet makers. His role in the NAUT was terminated when his cabinet makers chose not to affiliate with the NAUT in May. This reflected a trend within the NAUT that had become clear by 1847, whereby the more skilled artisan-based crafts as well as the power-spinners declined affiliation, leaving the NAUT's support base rooted in smaller local unions. The return of relative prosperity generally improved prospects for skilled labour to score higher incomes and better working conditions without threatening to strike. Jacobs had decried the new attitude of workers seeking self-promotion over solidarity as '"ten times more tyrannical than the middle-class themselves... They will have the aristocracy of labour who ape the gentlemen and despise the plain, sensible, honest operative..."'[102] Accommodation lay just on the horizon.

As elections approached in early 1847, the Radicals in Parliament introduced a host of new reform measures, including amendments to the Reform Act of 1832 and a measure to abolish capital punishment, both of which failed. But Fielden's Ten Hours Bill overcame the opposition, led by Peel and Graham, as well as Palmerston's call for an 11-hour bill, and was passed.[103] While the measure applied specifically only to women and children aged 13 to 18 in the cotton mills, it 'had the practical effect of limiting the working day of adult males as well'.[104] It was hailed as a major victory for Ashley and Oastler's Short-Time Committee, and a defeat for the cotton masters.[105] Writing in 1850, Engels would ascribe the victory to a loose alliance between workers and aristocratic reactionaries against the industrial 'bourgeoisie', passed 'at a time marked by neither prosperity nor crisis'.[106] Engels noted that this alliance had 'contaminated the working-class movement with a considerable influx of reactionary elements, which is taking

101. Armytage 1958, pp. 88–90.
102. *Northern Star*, 18 June 1842, as quoted in McNulty 1988, p. 232.
103. Maccoby 2001, p. 272.
104. Breunig 1977, p. 213.
105. Harling 2001, p. 102.
106. Engels 1975b, p. 103.

a long time to disappear'.[107] The attention given to the ten-hours bill probably outweighs the direct impact it had on the state of industry. Factory masters were able within a few years to reintroduce the relay system and effectively amend the act to lengthen the working day to ten and a half hours. The importance attached to the measure probably has to do mainly with the fact that just one year after their apparent triumph over the landed class in securing the passage of the Corn Laws, the factory masters had suffered a defeat of their own, not only at the hands of the landed class but also at the hands of the allied working class. For the first time, wrote Marx, '"in broad daylight the political economy of the middle class succumbed to the political economy of the working class"'.[108] It has been argued both that the Ten Hours Bill marked an end to open *laissez-faire* economics in Britain and alternately, that *laissez-faire* had 'never held undisputed sway'.[109] What is significant is that the measure came at precisely that point when both the state and labour were moderating their strategies in the class struggle over relations in production. What we have seen in the foregoing is effectively a period of cyclic violence, whereby explosions of protests in the form of 'riots' and strikes were met with severe state repression in the form of mobilising military and police units. With the large spending on Ireland and the restriction of the working day, the British state began to earnestly intervene in the free operations of the market to protect working people. A serious push toward the creation of arbitration boards would not come until the 1860s, but the fact that officials were appointed to inspect factories, and that fines were levied against offending factory masters demonstrates that the state was developing institutional responses to deal with labour issues, breaking with the pattern of simply applying repression as needed wherever rights of property appeared to be under threat.

The general election of 1847 returned the Whigs to power with a bare majority. The Conservatives held 325 seats, the Whigs 292. But with 36 Irish Repeal seats, the Whigs could claim a majority of three votes. To this one might add the vote of Feargus O'Connor, elected to represent Nottingham as a Chartist. Meeting in

107. Engels 1975b, p. 99. Engels's optimism that such elements would disappear would not be borne out by later events. Moreover, the support of Chartists and workers in general for the ten-hours bill was only a part of the growing involvement of the working class in the emerging discourse of liberalism, and by no means the central part.

108. Marx and Engels 1945, p. 439 as quoted in Thompson 1991, pp. 603–4. It has been asserted that Marx had opposed the Ten Hours Bill, but this claim has been effectively refuted. See Rappard 1913, pp. 530–5.

109. Breunig 1977, p. 213. While Breunig argues the latter view, Thompson argues that 'During the critical decades of the Industrial revolution, working people suffered total exposure to one of the most humanly degrading dogmas in history – that of irresponsible and unlicensed competition – and generations of outworkers died under this exposure' (Thompson 1991, p. 603). Certainly there is a question of to what *degree* one can say that markets went unrestrained from 1834 to 1847, but it also seems clear that during no other period in British history was labour as unregulated as this.

the autumn, the Chartists began to prepare another petition, which O'Connor himself could now introduce. Upon its rejection, a Convention was to be held, but beyond this the details of the plan were still sketchy.[110]

On 17 August, O'Connorville was officially opened. By now O'Connor had established his own Land and Labour Bank and had renamed his Chartist Land Company as the National Land Company. Accused of seeking to build communism, O'Connor denied the charge, saying he was instead for co-operation and calling himself an 'elevator' rather than a leveller. He was also accused of starting a speculative bubble, having already raised well more than £50,000 and on his way to purchasing his fifth estate for settlement.[111] O'Connor was certainly a pioneer in land settlement, but the idea was also being taken up by middle-class liberals who started the Birmingham Freehold Land Society in 1847.[112]

High prices and a modest harvest made conditions hard for working people in the winter of 1847 and 1848. As a result of the distress, the Chartist cause gained renewed momentum. Despite a modestly better harvest on the British Isles, the harvest in France and Germany was poor, contributing to the high prices as well as to a spate of bank closings. Nonetheless, Britain was also hit by a financial crisis, particularly in the speculative business of railway construction as numerous railway firms declared bankruptcy. In late November, Karl Marx, then living in Brussels, travelled to London to attend a ten-day conference sponsored by the Communist League, at which the old slogan 'All Men Are Brethren' was supplanted by the call to revolution: 'Proletarians of All Countries, Unite!'[113]

The revolutions of 1848 began in Italy on 12 January, when the citizens of Palermo revolted against Ferdinand II, King of Naples and Sicily. The uprising was barely noticed, but it was the spark that ignited nearly fifty revolutions that summer. The situation in France was compounded by a lack of sufficient new markets to absorb the increasing output of industrial and manufactured goods, meaning a crisis of overproduction had arrived, leading to business closures and unemployment. In February 1848, the distress would play a part in the February Revolution in Paris and the fall of Louis Philippe, the last king of the French. With the establishment of the Second Republic, nine million new voters were added to the electorate with the declaration of universal suffrage on 2 March and the 'right to work' was to be guaranteed through the establishment of National

110. Slosson 1916, p. 95.
111. Armytage 1958, pp. 92–3.
112. Chase 1991, p. 320.
113. Returning to Brussels, Marx would complete the Communist Manifesto by the end of January and send it to London, where 500 copies were published in German in an edition with no author cited. An English version did not appear before 1850. As the juggernaut of revolt that followed cannot be attributed to this publication, what can be suggested is that Marx had tapped into the pulse of revolutionary fever that was rising in Europe. Padover 1978, pp. 126–8.

Workshops. The February Revolution provided the inspiration for risings across Europe in March:

> first in the Austrian empire, then in many of the lesser German states, and finally in Prussia. During the same period revolts spread northward in the Italian peninsula from Naples and Sicily into Sardinia, Tuscany, the Papal States, and finally the regions directly under Austrian control. In this initial stage the frightened rulers capitulated with practically no resistance to the revolutionary demands, promising their subjects constitutions and representative assemblies and hastily granting the freedoms which had been denied their peoples. Unlike Louis Philippe, the central European rulers managed to retain their thrones while their more unpopular ministers were dismissed or, like Metternich, forced to flee.[114]

With Paris now in the hands of the 'Red Republicans', and communists in control of establishing state-run workshops to guarantee employment for the poor, it appeared to working-class radicals across Europe as if the revolution had actually arrived.[115]

In Britain, the Chartists were inspired into action. Local associations passed resolutions in solidarity with the Paris revolutionaries and decrying the mass-arrests of the Young Irish in Ireland. Chartist periodicals began calling openly for a republic in Britain. A rally in defiance of the authorities was held on 6 March in Trafalgar Square. On 4 April, the Convention met in London with no 'moral force' advocates present, led by O'Connor, Edward Jones, Bronterre O'Brien and G.W.M. Reynolds. Falling out again with O'Connor, O'Brien resigned on April 9. The contingency plan this time was to set up a National Assembly upon rejection of the petition, to sit until the Charter was passed into law.

On 10 April, the Chartists gathered at Kennington Common. So alarmed were the authorities that a now obscure statute passed during the reign of Charles II banning assemblies of greater than ten persons was revived, and no less than one hundred and seventy thousand special constables were sworn in for the occasion, Louis Napoleon Bonaparte among them. This figure was likely greater than the number of protesters themselves, variously estimated at between some tens of thousands to O'Connor's high figure of three hundred thousand. When the congregation arrived at Parliament, the 'monster petition was greeted with shouts of relieved laughter' for the authorities, who had put Wellington in charge of the safety of the City, 'were surprised to find out how grossly they had magnified the danger'.[116] While O'Connor and Jones had estimated the number of

114. Breunig 1977, p. 253.
115. Maccoby 2001, p. 284.
116. Slosson 1916, pp. 95–100.

signatures to be as high as six million, the committee in charge put the figure at 1,975,496 and reported widespread fraud in the form of signatures such as 'Punch' and 'Queen Victoria'. O'Connor defended these, arguing that many did not know how to write their own name, and refused to believe that such a large number of signatures could be counted in so little time. O'Connor himself spoke against the meeting of the Assembly, which was subsequently convened by Ernest Jones but adjourned on 13 April with no actions taken. Outside of London, arming and drilling recommenced and there were demonstrations and arrests in Lancashire and Yorkshire, with 18 arrested in Bradford in May. June brought bad fortunes for the Chartists, who were short of funds. The authorities arrested Jones and four others on charges of sedition, hoping to forestall plans for mass meetings on 12 June, Whit Monday.[117]

In France, a revolt by disillusioned workers in May had led to suppression and then to counter-revolution in June. As before, the rest of Europe followed France's lead and armies still faithful to the shaken rulers of Europe were ordered to suppress the revolutionaries. By December, the revolutionaries had been defeated in virtually every state and principality where they had rebelled. In France, elections were held, bringing Louis Napoleon Bonaparte to power as the new president (and future emperor) of France.[118]

The devastation in Ireland aside, events in Britain were nowhere near as dramatic, but the authorities remained on high alert, as the wave of protest and violence that had followed the peaceful procession of 10 April had taken them by surprise. All assemblies in London were banned. On 3 July, O'Connor moved a motion in support of the principles of the Charter, which was defeated by a vote of 224 to 15.[119] That same month, Jones and associates were sentenced to two or more years in prison, and McDouall was arrested and later served the same sentence. In August, a revolt in Ashton resulted in the murder of a police officer before it could be suppressed. Reminiscent of the Despard Affair, several Chartists began meeting at such public houses to plan an insurrection in late July that was to take place on 16 August. A government infiltrator going by the name of Johnson alerted the authorities to the plot, which involved the ambitious goal of overthrowing the Government and declaring a republic. The conspirators were arrested while meeting at the Orange Tree on 15 August. Arrests were made

117. Slosson 1916, pp. 95–103; Maccoby 2001, pp. 284–5. Only in the West Riding at Toftshaw Moore between Bradford and Leeds did any sizeable Chartist meeting take place.

118. The elections demonstrated that much like Britain, radicalism was concentrated in the capital, and the countryside was still deeply conservative as a rule. French peasants, 'alarmed by radical statements that implied a threat to property, had united with the bourgeoisie against the radical republicans and the Paris proletariat' (Breunig 1977, pp. 253–4).

119. Slosson 1916, pp. 95–103. On 11 July 1850, he would make the motion again, only to face a loss of quorum.

outside London as well, in Manchester, Liverpool and Bolton. Weapons including guns, pikes and 'ginger bottles filled with gunpowder and pieces of iron' were seized.[120] Some one thousand conspirators were later said to have been involved. Those arrested were imprisoned or transported upon the testimony of the government's spies.[121]

Chartism would survive for another ten years, and in some locations it remained strong, as in Sheffield where Chartists held nearly half of the seats on the city council in 1849.[122] But in general, Chartism after 1848 would never approach the levels of support it had attracted in 1839, 1842 and 1848. In part, personal and ideological divisions at the leadership level were to blame for its failure. With his Land Plan in disarray, O'Connor handed over the leadership to Ernest Jones. William Lovett established a People's League in May of 1848, but it lasted only until September of 1849. O'Brien and G.W.M. Reynolds sought to unite the Chartists and Socialists with the National Reform League, which advocated land nationalisation. Thomas Clark would set up a rival National Chartist Society in 1850. A rival to the NAUT was also established in the autumn of 1848 in the form of the National Association of Organised Trades for the Industrial, Social and Political Emancipation of Labour (NAOT). Leaders of the two associations became embroiled in a bitter public debate in the pages of the radical journals and Feargus O'Connor, his mental health now failing, was unable to mend fences.[123] Chartists in general had never achieved national consensus on the physical- versus moral force issue, or the issue of working with middle-class reformers. A revival of trade that began slowly in 1848 took the urgency out of agitation as employers were more ready to accede to working-class demands. Economic recovery also facilitated the growth of self-help and friendly societies. There 'developed among many radicals a conviction that it was now possible to work within the political system to enforce economy and to promote greater religious liberty'.[124] Accommodation was in the air.

---

120. Gossman 1983, pp. 58–63. The plot has been dubbed 'Cuffay's Conspiracy,' probably because as a black Chartist Cuffay gave the affair added notoriety even though it is unlikely that Cuffay was the ringleader. Cuffay was arrested at his home the next day. A loaded pistol was found among his belongings. Cuffay was not a minor figure in Chartism, however. An organiser with the Metropolitan Tailors Chartist Association, he had been elected to the National Executive in 1842. He later served as an auditor for O'Connor's National Land Company (see below). Arriving in Hobart, Tasmania at the age of 61 in November of 1849, Cuffay lived in Tasmania to the age of 82, and resumed his political work after his free pardon in 1856.

121. Gossman 1983, p. 63.

122. Hobsbawm 1994, p. 258.

123. Chase 2000, p. 215.

124. Harling 2001, p. 87.

'A paddock and a pigsty'

What did in mean to 'work within the system' after 1848? And why did radical convictions increasingly gravitate toward accommodation in the 1840s, especially after the failure of the third Chartist petition? As we have seen, Chartism never regained the level of sympathy and support it had enjoyed up to the meeting of the first Convention. With the unplanned outbreak of violence at the Bull Ring in Birmingham, followed by arrests, and the solitary attempt at a rising in Monmouthshire, followed by more arrests, Chartism's weakness was exposed in the face of a highly organised state response – itself in many ways pre-emptive – in the form of coercion and suppression by military and police. The threat of arrest itself was enough to frighten many otherwise open supporters into quietude. Indeed, it is apparent that Chartism continued to enjoy broad working-class support even in 1848, as the volume of signatures on the second and third petitions suggests, even accounting for the fact that a certain percentage of the signatures were forgeries or duplicates. Yet there is a clear progression of decline, with each effort appearing more desperate than the last. By the time of the second petition, Chartism had lost ground to middle-class League reformers, whose campaign, in contrast with three failed petition initiatives, achieved – or were allowed to achieve – success in 1846. The tension within Chartism between moral- and physical force advocates really represents a tension between those for whom the overarching goal was universal suffrage and those who saw that capitalism offered no secure future to the independent craftsman, and who therefore continued to hold out hope for revolution leading possibly to republicanism and ultimately to a broader programme of property redistribution or the abolition of private property in the name of co-operative syndicalism or what had by now come to be known as socialism.

The backbone of Chartism and virtually all of the struggles to resist capitalism that we have reviewed thus far were made up of associations of independent, domestic artisan producers. Their ability to resist the imposition of capitalist relations of production lay precisely in the fact that they continued to exercise control over the labour process and often over the means of production, for so long as this 'independence' was maintained, a complete subsumption of labour to capital could be prevented. To men like these, writes Fox, 'the campaign for the Charter was a stage in a long and protracted struggle not to win something new but to reclaim ancient and "natural" rights'.[125] But to a large extent it was also the final stage. Price argues that their dependence had already been achieved through 'capitalist market relations for work' – which we equate with Marx's formal subsumption of labour – and that once 'Chartism and Owenism had

125. Fox 1985, p. 120, citing Rudé 1981, p. 179.

failed to find ways of escaping from this dependence, the reliance of even skilled workers upon employers' provision of work was implicit'.[126] Price is adamant in arguing that:

> The progress of industrial capitalism lay in the triumph of capitalist market relations and not in the restructuring of the labour process. The source of capitalist influence over labour at work did not lie in its control over the execution of work. Indeed, as we have seen, large areas of the labour process were quite deliberately evacuated by management.[127]

Presumably, it is the mule-spinners that Price has in mind, here, as one of an increasing number of 'industries where machinery and factories had recomposed the division of labour but where a variety of circumstances combined to allow for craft organisation and control over work execution to persist against the grain of the logic of technical organisation'.[128] This is an important point, for the defeat of Luddism, the GNCTU and Chartism did not lead straight to the formation of a fully-expropriated proletariat. Where skilled workers entered or engaged with factory production, they often became a kind of semi-independent, semi-proletarian workforce. Two other types of 'independent' craft worker are cited by Price, one being the 'mid-Victorian craftsman' such as the cabinet maker or leather worker, characterised by a 'continued reliance upon handicraft skill within a labour process that had not been recomposed either by technical change or by drastic changes in market structure', the other being the 'trades where labour was totally dependent upon the uncontrolled labour market' such as garrets and sweatshops (as in tailoring) which also expanded rapidly starting around mid-century.[129] 'Sweating', for Price, represents a perversion of traditional patterns of dependence. With the cycle of boom and bust, each recession led to a flight on the part of the newly unemployed to independent handicraft-production such as hand-loom weaving. Price notes this 'cruel inversion': what were once considered trades of honourable independence now 'marked a step down the social scale to a deeper entanglement in market forces'.[130] By mid-century, the long artisan-led resistance to the commodification of labour in the name of custom had effectively been defeated. Henceforth, the centre of the struggle would take place wherever workers retained a significant element of control over the labour process, whether inside the factory or in the large mining operation.

126. Price 1986, pp. 71–2.
127. Price 1986, p. 72.
128. Price 1986, p. 73.
129. Price 1986, pp. 73–4.
130. Price 1986, p. 73.

The various forces of nationalism, liberalism and radicalism all played a part in precipitating the continental rebellions of 1848, and while an economic crisis was the most proximate cause, the upheavals of that year can in no way be reduced to economic causes. Whether the limited conversion of manufacturing to capitalist industry and the process of proletarianisation on the Continent played any role in the economic crisis behind the revolutions of 1848 is doubtful. But price competition from the cheaply manufactured articles produced in more advanced British factories certainly would have put downward pressure on wages. While the working class on the Continent was still overwhelmingly made up of independent artisan producers, increasing market dependence and the growing formal subsumption of labour meant that artisanal workers on the Continent were, like Britain's hand-loom weavers, subject to extreme deprivation during periods of economic downturn, providing one source for an explosive social response in the midst of a crisis. We raise these points only by way of making a contrast. For not only was it the case that Britain came nowhere near as close to revolution as some fifty large and small states on the continent, but 1848 was also effectively the last, and one of the weakest, of a long series of 'waves of revolt' in Britain. As we have seen, the British state continued to adapt to resistance to domestic revolts and to improve policing and the management of dissent to such an extent that the Government was both over-prepared for the Chartist march of 10 April and had readily infiltrated the most violent elements plotting an insurrection, whereupon the plotters and Chartist leaders were arrested. It is important to account for the state's active infiltration and readiness to suppress dissent in its various forms, without which alternative projects might have had a greater chance of success. This is a point that both Price and Fox seem to overlook, or at least take for granted in overemphasising the dominance of the traditional, artisanal outlook in these waves of resistance to capitalism.

It is striking that the English version of the *Communist Manifesto* appeared in Britain in 1850, at approximately the same point in time as the 'mid-Victorian compromise' against the backdrop of a general economic recovery.[131] In noting that as Ernest Jones led the rump of Chartism into the 1850s he became influenced by the writings of Marx and Engels, Fox writes that:

> such doctrines never secured the adhesion of the more stable unions, nor of substantial sections of their members. Mediating between working-class experience of conflict in the workplace and much influential working-class political behaviour were social, political and religious values often shared with

131. See p. 781, n. 113 above.

> substantial elements of the middle class. It was a sharing which, though fostered by middle-class indoctrination, had its principal roots in much older and deeper structures of circumstance. These values ensured that a considerable amount of economic conflict was only to a very limited degree translated into political class conflict.[132]

In going well beyond the Charter's call for the male working class to be given a formal role in government via the vote, the secret ballot and the abolition of the property qualification, the call in the *Communist Manifesto* for the abolition of all property in land, of inheritance and the centralisation of property in the hands of a worker-dominated state surely came across to many British workers as far more extreme. And given their failure to win Parliament's acceptance of the Charter, the idea of a complete expropriation of the state by the working class must have seemed sheer fantasy to many British workers. Of course, the idea of abolishing private property was nothing new, it could be traced at least as far back as Gerard Winstanley's writings of the seventeenth century through those of Thomas Spence in the late eighteenth century. As such, the positions of those who now styled themselves as socialists and communists would have been familiar to most working-class organisers of early and mid-nineteenth-century Britain – as well as to the authorities. What was new about Marxism, building upon the progressive aspects of Owenism, was the way it looked for a way out of market dependence and subordination to capital by seeing the fully-expropriated proletariat as the force which would raise the torch and lead the way forward for the working class. This was where, as one might say, there was a disconnect between Marxism and the long tradition of British working-class struggle, which was for the most part led by skilled artisans. The adoption of the proletariat as the truly progressive force within the working class also amounted to a rejection of the increasing influence of 'middle-class indoctrination' upon the 'consciousness' of skilled labourers.

Perhaps no other movement better exemplified the growing influence of middle-class values and the 'spirit of class co-operation' than the freehold land movement, which although part of a widening movement of self-help societies in this period, 'came close to dominating popular politics' in the wake of Parliament's rejection of the April 10 petition.[133] It formed one of the main channels that the energy of the ACLL moved into after 1846. Free traders were as eager as O'Connor and the Chartists to expand Radical influence in Parliament by way of settlement. As the 1832 Reform Act had retained the ancient provision granting the vote to all freeholders owning property valued at 40s. in its successful

132. Fox 1985, p. 121.
133. Chase 1991, pp. 319, 344.

effort at blocking the proposed enfranchisement of £50 tenants-at-will, this left available the opportunity for smallholders to buy their way into enfranchisement simply by purchasing a few acres of land. As has been observed in the case of Country Durham, it '"did not take much more than a paddock and a pigsty to qualify"'.[134] A number of court decisions affirmed the legality of subdivisions for such purposes over the course of the 1840s. Both the ACLL and the Chartists were now encouraging supporters to purchase 40*s*. freehold lands in order to be able to vote in the next election, efforts which would soon lead to two different but related self-help movements. This movement was indirectly aided by the passage of the General Inclosure Act in 1845. The Act 'professed to make ample provision, by means of gardens and public allotments, for the labouring poor'. By 1867 it would become clear that this promise was but an illusion, as only 2,119 acres had been assigned to the poor out of 450,000 acres enclosed since the passing of the Act.[135] For the time being, however, there was still faith in the idea.

Observers of O'Connor's Land Plan suggested that if successful it would instil the middle-class values of thrift and hard work associated with the ownership of property. These were the values which the freehold movement sought to promote, perhaps even more than the right to vote. Certainly O'Connor appeared to be moving from success to success by early 1848, having now purchased some five estates for a Company with some 270 branches and seventy thousand members.[136] When a poor law commissioner by the name of John Revans visited O'Connorville in 1848, he reported that the Chartist settlers were growing inferior crops; that their animals had no hay or straw, and that nine of the original 36 settlers had already left. He also expressed his concern, which later proved largely correct, that the settlers would ultimately wind up as a charge on the local poor rates. A Committee of Enquiry found O'Connor's National Land Company in violation of the Friendly Societies Act and a financial discrepancy of £3,000 in O'Connor's favour. At the Land Conference in October 1848, O'Connor faced serious criticism as his scheme was now beginning to unravel, primarily due to poor management. Early in 1849, settlers began to drift from the colonies and later in the year the courts refused to legalise the Company. Faced with tenants at the newer colonies of Minster Lovell and Snig's End who both refused either to pay or leave, O'Connor was forced to resort to evictions, and eventually to liquidate

134. Nossiter 1975, p. 58, as quoted in Chase 1991, p. 321. The average size of a farm in 1851 was around one hundred and ten acres, and in all there were two hundred and twenty-five thousand farms in Britain (Hobsbawm and Rudé 1968, p. 24).

135. Chamberlain 1885, p. 121. During the debates on the bill, the Earl of Lincoln complained that nineteen of every twenty enclosure bills passed by Parliament had ignored the rights of the poor. Thus the bill's ostensible purpose was to rectify this situation by restoring gardens and certain lost rights of common. When Parliament failed to fulfil this promise, self-help efforts stepped in to pursue the goal on their own initiative.

136. Chase 2000, p. 202.

the company. O'Connorville, the most successful of the ventures, was bought out by the tenants themselves under the name of the National Loan Society. Though his company had failed, some of the settlements continued to operate.[137]

Middle-class tradesmen and higher paid skilled labourers were, of course, better equipped with sufficient disposable income to make a go of it. The freehold land movement served as 'an archetype of the ethic of self-help'.[138] Ownership of freehold property also conferred a significant measure of additional status. To a certain extent the movement was also a reaction to the advent of high farming, which was seen to be throwing off the balance of land ownership in the countryside and engaging in unnatural transformation of the landscape by such practices as drainage. The 1850s was the decade when rural conditions began to improve as the surplus population in the countryside began to move to the cities, to workhouses or to emigrate.[139] The goal of expanding the franchise did achieve a measure of success, as the influence of 'fancy franchises' would be cited as a cause for the defeat of the second Derby ministry in 1859, but the numbers of votes added were never extensive.[140] In general, the self-help movement offered the better-off sections of the working class the chance to fulfil a number of long-sought goals: increased independence through property ownership, enfranchisement in the case of freehold ownership and, above all, respectability.

Conclusion

Liberalism 'was not a conspiracy', writes Price, 'it was the convergence of themes common to both working-class and middle-class culture in the space created by the demise of artisan radicalism'.[141] Part of this convergence came in the form of a relaxation of negative attitudes towards working people on the part of the middle classes. In the aftermath of the terrible defeat of the Miners Association in 1846, the owners reassessed the situation and realised that with the ending of the bond and other normative modes of labour regulation, they needed something to replace such non-coercive methods of control. This is what led them, for the first time, to take a direct interest in social reform, and out of

137. The settlers at Charterville in Oxfordshire, the largest of the five settlements, continued to do well, with a local monopoly on potatoes, until 1887. By 1902, all but two of the settler families had relocated back to the towns. When O'Connorville was auctioned off in 1857, only three of the original settlers remained. O'Connor himself was committed to an asylum in 1852 and died three years later. Some fifty thousand came to pay their respects at his funeral. Armytage 1958, pp. 95–6.

138. Chase 1991, p. 324.

139. Wells 1988, p. 127.

140. Chase 1991, pp. 325–40. The movement continued to expand. By 1854 no less than 58 freeholder-societies operated in London.

141. Price 1986, p. 64.

that came the building of worker housing with schools and libraries, which they now recognised would facilitate a rebuilding of the 'chains of social connection that industrialisation itself threatened to undermine'.[142] What the convergence allowed was a reconstruction of paternalism in a new 'benevolent' form where working-class aspirations for respectability were confirmed within terms set by the middle-class discourse of personal virtue, discipline, obedience, thriftiness and industry. Saint Monday, which had once been the defining practice that stood as the expression of the artisan's independence in the form of the right to set one's own hours, would now undergo a transformation such that by the 1860s those who observed Saint Monday were no longer seen as belonging to the 'respectable' layer of the working class.[143]

The controversial and problematic Marxian concept of 'false consciousness' has been used to portray the 'labour aristocrats' who took an active part in the creation and emergence of late nineteenth-century liberalism in Britain as traitors to their class. Foster, for example, dismisses liberalism as little more than 'a collective ruling-class response to a social system in crisis and integrally related to a preceding period of working-class consciousness'.[144] But what exactly was working-class consciousness in the early nineteenth century? Price has pointed out that Britain's skilled artisans had always held unskilled workers in a certain measure of contempt, while the high value they placed on being 'honourable' tradesmen is a value they carried over into their participation in the making of liberalism.[145] The present study seeks to shed light on this apparent controversy by challenging the undue prominence given to psychology. Both Foster and Price seem to suggest a high degree of voluntarism on the part of those members of the upper strata of the working class in their 'decision' to pursue middle-class self-help as a means to greater personal status and respectability, effectively abandoning Chartism and the much longer struggle to regain the ancient rights of the independent craftsman. Important as it may be to consider such states of mind as 'values' and 'consciousness', it is important not to lose sight of social factors, *both* political and economic, in shaping the so-called mid-Victorian compromise.

The strong economic recovery after 1849 not only improved market opportunities but also strengthened those market imperatives that shaped the decision-making of economic agents, including the labour aristocracy. Add to this the long *political* process we have traced here, by which the governing

142. Price 1986, p. 42.
143. Price 1986, pp. 62–7.
144. Foster 1974, pp. 3 and 6.
145. Price 1986, pp. 6–7. Fox 1985, p. 118 notes: 'Groups of the relatively privileged were doing well, but then they had always done so, and the gulf between them and the rest of manual labour – mostly regarded as unorganisable – was as great as ever'.

classes of Britain essentially ground down any resistance to the emerging capitalist system, thereby narrowing the range of options available to workers, and it becomes worth asking whether convergence and compromise were merely choices and not compulsions and imperatives. We have identified that a shift in the meaning of 'respectability' had taken place by the end of Chartism, from an emphasis on custom and communal values to an emphasis on personal behaviour.[146] But it is as important to contextualise this shift within the overall context of the development of the social relation of capital, which implies the commodification of labour. Coercion alone would never have been enough to ensure the security of capitalism, but it was clearly necessary to contain the cyclical explosions of discontent that had resulted largely as a result of the social dislocations and deprivations that capitalism had heretofore brought about. For now, collectivised resistance to capitalism had effectively been defeated. The Miners Association held its last conference in Lancashire in 1847, and by 1849 was finished by a slow-down in trade. The same year, a Manchester cotton-manufacture would remark that '"unions, trade combinations, and strikes have gone greatly out of fashion"'.[147] In such a context, the pursuit of individual gain by many workers made obvious sense, and with the recovery of trade and economic stability, employers were in a better position to provide inducements and benefits. Accommodation had arrived.

146. See McNulty 1988, pp. 223–4.

147. Rule 1986, p. 341 quoting Razzell and Wainwright (eds.) 1973, pp. 215–16, 229, 240 and 171.

Conclusion

> We pray that the happy influence of this undertaking may be to incite a generous and laudable competition among the sons of science, art, and labour, throughout the world...
>
> Bishop Wainright, prayer at the opening of the Crystal Palace, New York City, 1853[1]

It is a long journey from the age of the medieval guilds to Crystal Palace. This work has not sought to explicate the operations and historical development of the transitional process of agrarian capitalism as such. Its purpose, rather, has been to trace the evolution of British manufactures from their feudal and early modern origins to the Industrial Revolution in the context of the operations of agrarian capitalism. Specifically, we have sought to demonstrate that the world's first industrial revolution did not come about as the result of the operation of natural and immutable economic laws but rather through a series of processes that involved conscious decisions and actions by social agents engaged in a long train of struggles over the preservation of customary modes of economic regulation versus the expansion of market regulation of the economy and the subsumption of social relations to capital.

This series of processes by which pristine capitalism and pristine industrialisation first developed in Britain was protracted and complex. Indeed, it was too protracted and complex a process to be explained away by theories based upon intermediate 'phases',

1. Greeley, 1853, p. 21.

'stages', 'proto-capitalist' forms or by way of a 'bourgeois revolution' that would clear away the 'fetters' of monopoly and custom to make way for the full emergence of capitalism. By offering a narrative of half a millennium of the economic and social history of England and the British Isles, this study challenges readers to rethink long-standing notions about the Industrial Revolution by offering an alternative explanation for its development.

It was deemed necessary to present an analysis that weaves socio-economic *and* political history together in one narrative in order to emphasise the critical role of the state in shaping economic outcomes as capitalism developed. This proved increasingly difficult as the writing progressed, mainly because the literature becomes increasingly divided between economic, social and political histories as one enters the eighteenth century. This would seem to be, at least in part, a reflection of the very process by which the capitalist economy was 'dis-embedded' from social relations, producing an apparent separation of the economy from the polity.[2]

Another challenge was addressing the separate histories of England, Wales, Scotland and Ireland, which was generally not done except by way of discussing the history of England's 'periphery' – Wales, Scotland, Ireland and the colonies – as these societies were annexed and/or converted to agrarian and industrial capitalism, and to the extent that they actually were. While numerous topics for future study of the development of agrarian capitalism and the Industrial Revolution in England, Great Britain or the United Kingdom have been identified at various points throughout this work, separate studies addressing the specific ways in which Wales, Scotland and Ireland were involved in the processes we have discussed are also needed. A counter-study is needed to consider the claims made here that capitalism made little headway in continental Europe before the end of the French and Napoleonic Wars in 1815. And finally, as a rebel colony of Great Britain, the social property relations of the United States were clearly informed by those of agrarian capitalism even if it proved impossible to transplant that system to colonies with no history of feudalism or a feudal aristocracy. Thus there remains much to be explained about the specific development of capitalism and industry in the United States in light of the theory of agrarian capitalism as pioneered by Brenner, Wood and Comninel and the present treatment of the first industrial revolution.

Probably the most surprising aspect of this research was the recognition that even by the mid-nineteenth century, some three-quarters of a century into the Industrial Revolution, the United Kingdom was still very much ruled by a landed oligarchy whose interests were converging with those of the industrial,

2. See Wood 1981 and Polanyi 1957, p. 129.

mercantile and banking 'bourgeoisie'. Tocqueville took note of this convergence during his visit to Britain in 1835:

> He found it extraordinary that his English friends were 'still convinced that extreme inequality of wealth is in the natural order of things'. But Tocqueville found an explanation for the peculiar tenacity of aristocratic power in England. Unlike the French nobility, English aristocracy was not a caste. It soaked up new money and those who acquired it.[3]

Despite the ability of the British oligarchy to absorb other social groups into itself, however, economic rents earned from land ownership continued to be the primary form of wealth which sustained the elite. This fact has probably not been seen as particularly remarkable considering that the rest of Europe also continued to be dominated by landed aristocrats. But once we understand that industrial capitalism grew up out of and alongside agrarian capitalism, this fact takes on particular significance. It helps us address the problem of why the *first* industrial revolution did not come about as the result of an urban 'bourgeoisie' of industrialists, merchants and bankers overthrowing the aristocracy. Britain's aristocracy was really no longer an aristocracy, it was a landed oligarchy which had overseen the development of agrarian capitalism and had actually *ensured* that the same principles of political economy that had been used to abolish feudalism and the peasantry in favour of a system of capitalist tenant-farming were equally applied to manufacturing, by force when necessary.

How then are Hobsbawm's 'three key questions'[4] to be addressed? Britain became the 'workshop of the world' because the superior economic might of its agrarian-capitalist economy provided the financial and military strength necessary to defeat first Holland and then France in a series of wars from the late seventeenth and eighteenth centuries in order to emerge as the pre-eminent commercial power in the world. At the very same time, the manufacturing sector of Britain's economy was transformed along capitalist lines, allowing for unprecedented increases in productivity and output of goods that could be marketed at the most competitive prices in the colonies and world-wide. Secondly, this 'breakthrough' happened in the latter half of the eighteenth century because the same terms of trade that in the first half of the century had enabled agrarian capitalism to respond to falling prices by intensifying production shifted to favour manufacturing in ways that made innovation and the application of machinery to production uniquely profitable. Thirdly, the Industrial Revolution was 'ignited' and did not fizzle out, because just as self-sustaining growth had already been achieved in agriculture, the process of capitalist development in

3. Buruma 1998, pp. 91–2.
4. See the Introduction in this volume, p. 40.

manufacturing also involved self-reinforcing mechanisms based upon the conversion to open market competition. The application of state force was required, however, in order to suppress a long struggle characterised by episodic violence waged by traditional craft artisans seeking to preserve the customary mode of production that was the basis of their livelihood, their independence and their honour.

We now turn to a review and a discussion of our findings and of our argument.

The crisis of feudalism and the origin of agrarian capitalism

In order to understand the origin of capitalism, it is necessary to understand England's distinctive path of development out of feudalism. The feudal system of agriculture in Europe may well have been the most intensively regulated economic system in human history. While this system had its origins in post-Carolingian France, it was introduced into England with the Conquest in 1066. English feudalism differed from French feudalism, however, in that the Norman lords under King William I were never able to appropriate the powers of the ban and thus England never experienced the parcellisation of sovereignty that was the hallmark of French feudalism. England was conquered as a unitary state in which all men, free and unfree, were the subjects of a single sovereign. On the French *seigneurie*, the lord of the land simultaneously enjoyed the public power of the ban: the power to tax and to judge. English lords did have manors on which they extracted surplus from dependent tenants, but this relationship was private and domestic in character. The English lord's legal status was effectively that of a private proprietor of land whose tenure was recognised by the royal courts. Peasant tenures were regulated by the customary law of the lord's manor. But some tenures were held in freehold, meaning that they enjoyed legal protection under the King's law. This distinction was crucial to the mid-twelfth century development of the common law, 'a system of property law based upon the right literally to exclude others from land for which one held greater lawful interest'.[5] In 1166, the Assize of Novel Disseisin provided an expedient legal means for an aggrieved freeholding tenant to regain possession of his land when it had been encroached upon by another party. English lords, however, whose tenure was also effectively held in freehold, found such strong legal protection for the right to private property in land attractive, and in 1235, just twenty years after the signing of the Magna Carta, gained the right to enclose common land on their estates under the Statute of Merton.[6] While enclosures in the thirteenth century

5. Comninel 2000, pp. 17–52.
6. Baker 1990, pp. 262–4; Tate 1967, p. 44.

were relatively few and far between, the fact that English lords had nonetheless attained the right to enclose, and thereby assert absolute private ownership of land as freehold land under common law unencumbered by the customary law of the manor, would have far-reaching consequences.

English towns and guilds received royal charters, and in a sense therefore enjoyed protection under common law much as freeholders did. The charter empowered the guild with a monopoly over the production and sale of a particular craft item, and enabled the establishment of the 'industrial court', a body which could seek to enforce that monopoly by exercising rights of search and seizure and by enforcing apprenticeship and other guild by-laws. While journeymen and small masters were in fact wage labourers producing for the market, making them market-dependent in the sense of being both dependent upon wages and upon the realisation of the sale of their product, and while there certainly was competition between small masters for pre-eminence and between guilds over the setting of boundaries, the general orientation of guilds was to *limit* the harmful effects of their dependence on the market by exercising their monopoly powers. In the typical craft workshop under the supervision of the master, the production process was controlled by the craftsmen themselves, and much in the same way as agrarian production was geared toward subsistence needs, craft production was geared toward fulfilling the immediate use-value needs of the customer. Just as production on the open fields was regulated by the customary laws of the manor, production decisions in the crafts were regulated not in response to market prices and fluctuations but in accordance with normative understandings of what constituted 'fair play', a 'just price' and mutual interest or solidarity.

In the transition debate, Sweezy had equated capitalism with trade and mercantilism and Dobb had rejected this, instead posing the question of how the laws of motion of the feudal mode of production gave rise to a capitalist mode of production. The more specific question guiding the present work is one of how the relations of production in the traditional crafts were 'dis-embedded' from the 'general organisation of society' by normative, customary regulations to enable the development of industrialisation, factories and an industrial-capitalist economy in which the direct producers are free wage labourers who have lost direct control over the production process. These two questions are not one and the same, but the twin processes of transition to capitalism in both agriculture and manufacturing are deeply intertwined.

The crisis of the fourteenth century played an important role in disrupting the customary social relations of European feudalism. By the middle of that century, the arrival of the plague came as an external shock, but it was the internal contradictions of European feudalism that had generated the conditions under which the plague would have such a devastating impact. Feudalism's highly regulated, intensive system of agricultural production had been wildly successful by any contemporary standards in both expanding the area of arable land under cultivation and in promoting population growth. A population that had doubled during the period of high feudalism would fall again by half over the course of a century. In England, the relatively unified landed class reacted almost immediately to the crisis by passing the Statute of Labourers to deal with the shortage of labour, setting up an administration of enforcers charged with going about the country to enforce a limitation on wages. Subsequently, all guilds were compelled to register. The lordly reaction to falling rents also included attempts by the House of Lords to limit intra-lordly competition for labour and to restrict peasant mobility. These efforts were moderately successful down to the Peasants' Revolt of 1381 and perhaps a short time after, but by the early fifteenth century, peasant mobility and peasant resistance managed to break what had been effectively an attempt to re-instate serfdom and rents.[7]

In comparison to their counterparts on the Continent, English lords generally held a much higher percentage of their estates as demesne lands. And now, with many tenancies lying vacant and some villages wholly depopulated, many English lords began to expand their holdings even further through the addition and consolidation of vacant holdings to their demesnes. What is more, they increasingly began to let out such lands under contracts, or what were in effect strictly economic leases, finding this an expedient method of increasing their rent-rolls. This in turn facilitated a more rapid stabilisation of the economy.[8] It also fostered the beginnings of the application of 'improved' agrarian techniques.

While the conversion of a tenancy to an economic leasehold implied the absence of customary law, enclosure was the specific means by which land could be formally removed from the purview of the local manorial court which enforced the customary law of the manor, which governed the production and allocation of furrows on the open fields. This lifting of the customary 'fetters' from the land through enclosure did not mean, however, that a set of production

7. Brenner 1985b, pp. 267–72. Brenner notes that population and rents had already been declining several decades before the plague struck England.

8. Brenner 1985b, pp. 293–6. Other factors facilitated England's recovery relative to the sustained chaos in France, most notably the simple fact that the Hundred Years' War was fought on French and not English soil. Another factor was the unity of England's ruling landed elite relative to the parcellised sovereignty of the lords in France. In the long run, French lords would turn to the office of state and state taxation as an alternative means of increasing their lordly revenues. In the process, they would lay the foundation for the centralisation of the French state and French absolutism. English developments moved in nearly the opposite direction, with English lords engrossing and improving their estates, thereby expanding the *private* source of their wealth and power, and thereby weakening the power of the crown in relative terms.

relations that could be characterised as agrarian capitalism was automatically brought into being. The social relation of capital requires a set of circumstances whereby the means of production are consolidated into the hands of the owner-occupier, who in the case of agrarian capitalism may be represented in both the landlord as owner and the tenant-farmer as the occupier acting in some sense on behalf of the owner. It has been suggested that the social relation of capital may have made its first appearance in East Yorkshire by the late fifteenth century. The lesser-quality land on the high Wolds of East Yorkshire was widely enclosed for pasturing sheep, in direct response to a rise in prices for sheep products.[9] When grain prices recovered relative to animal products, there was widespread conversion of lands to mixed farming, or what became known as 'up-and-down' husbandry, 'sheep-and-corn' farming or simply 'improved' agriculture. In other words, here was a situation in which production decisions by the owner-occupier were being made in accordance with the movement of market prices, quite independently of all considerations of local custom. With the owner-occupier in command of the means of production and enjoying the ability to transform production in accordance with market dictates unencumbered by extra-economic or normative economic regulations, this appears to be an early expression of capital understood as a social property relation.

Over the course of the late fifteenth and sixteenth centuries, as more lands were converted to sheep runs or enclosed and leased to tenant-farmers practicing mixed farming, the production decisions made in these operations were increasingly made in the context of a growing competition between current and would be farmers over leases for access to enclosed farms and a growing price competition between farmers practicing mixed farming and between speculating merchants employing shepherds overseeing profitable sheep runs. As these arrangements spread gradually, a new and competitive logic began to take hold of agrarian production in England, a logic driven by the market compulsion to transform production through innovation and specialisation in pursuit of higher levels of output, which translated into higher profits. In short, a system of agrarian capitalism emerged. There were, as yet, too few 'free' labourers to be identified as an agrarian proletariat, for the new system of capitalist agriculture was not yet predominant and what is more, improved productivity meant that demand for labour on enclosed or agrarian-capitalist farms was reduced in comparison with the intensive use of labour on open fields. On sheep runs, the labour demands were extremely minimal.

As we have shown, the craft guilds were also undergoing a process of transformation during the same period. The lordly reaction of the late fourteenth

---

9. See the Introduction in this volume, pp. 26–7.

century had bolstered the position of wealthier employers, and from the early fifteenth century we have seen that there was a process of stratification within the guilds, one in which the trading element within many or most guilds elevated itself to a position of greater prestige, privilege and wealth, forming an upper strata of those who became exclusively entitled to dress in fine 'livery'. Many craft masters also began employing greater numbers of journeymen and also expanded their operations into the countryside, where apprenticeship regulations were easily evaded, by 'putting-out' unfinished products to rural, domestic producers. In the face of shrinking opportunities for advancement to the level of master, journeymen began forming associations of 'yeomen' within many of the crafts and waged a struggle to limit these developments. These struggles resembled class struggle in many ways, with combined action being met with stricter oversight and control, but we have argued that because the struggles were largely contained within each craft and because the greater rift that had opened lay between traders and craftsmen, rather than among the craftsmen themselves, the process could more properly be identified as one of increasing differentiation between varying strata within the crafts.

The sixteenth century

In examining the Tudor era, we find much evidence of an economy in transition, with all the contradictions that this implies. The conclusion of the Wars of the Roses saw English lords, increasingly dependent upon rents derived from strictly economic leases, become the first ruling class in Europe to demilitarise. Peace brought stability and growing prosperity. Although the Tudors passed laws restricting enclosures, the dissolution of the monasteries under Henry VIII gave a major boost to the enclosure movement by putting large, new estates that were unencumbered by customary laws in the hands of improving lords. The Tudor statutes sought to stabilise the existing social relations of production by balancing the interests of all the various strata, rather than to facilitate change. 'Queen Betty's Law', the Statute of Apprentices, enshrined the customary regulations of the guilds in common law, even though the courts during this time were increasingly loath to hear arguments based upon custom. Paradoxically, despite the fact that the craft guilds were dependent upon the market for the sale of their products and enjoyed no direct access to the means of subsistence, the enshrinement of the customary regulation of labour in the Tudor statutes would mean that custom in manufacturing would generally outlive custom in agriculture.

Accelerated population growth after 1520, as well as a growing level of population dislocation through enclosures and the introduction of less labour-intensive methods of farming, were now beginning to give rise to significant numbers of landless poor. The 'problem of the poor' was met with the poor laws, a state-mandated form of locally-funded social safety net. This institution, a precursor to the modern welfare system, helped to lessen the hardships faced by a growing segment of the rural population that no longer enjoyed direct access to the means of subsistence. It also facilitated the growth of rural handicraft production and aided in the monetisation of the rural economy. The Statute of Apprentices did not apply to rural domestic producers, and so between state subsidisation of rural, market-dependent petty producers and the ease with which rural producers could take up domestic production by purchasing or renting a loom, a stocking-frame or a spinning wheel, the ability of the urban guilds to assert their monopoly powers over the countryside was profoundly undermined. Additionally, while 'Queen Betty's Law' did help to shore up wages amongst the lowest-paid journeymen, it also enforced the powers of the master over those under his employ. This built-in contradiction of the law would shape generations of struggle among craftsmen. As the ability of the guilds to *control* markets through chartered monopolies waned, the workmen would ever more forcefully assert their customary right to maintain their privileged position as skilled labourers passing the secrets of the trade from one generation to the next, most of all by jealously guarding mastery over the production process. By doing so, they were able to shield themselves from being 'hurled' amidst the growing ranks of the fully market-dependent poor.

England was the beneficiary of numerous technical advances brought across the Channel by immigrants from the Continent. New industries such as silk-weaving appeared. And in several lines of industry such as glass-making, ship-building and especially mining, there arose a few large, concentrated operations employing hundreds of workers. The naval yards, employing thousands, were state-run, and other large operations such as iron-making grew in size on the basis of state contracts for such items as cannons. In the mining industries, especially in the coal mines around the Tyneside in the North-East, the scale of operations reached impressive proportions at an early stage. Mining presents a special case, since it is not strictly a handicraft industry, but actually shares with agriculture the fact that it involves land as a means of production. In fact, mining concessions were granted in virtually the same manner as enclosures, enabling the landowners to lease out land to mining companies by asserting absolute property rights under common law, thereby trumping the customary rights of local peasant producers *prior to* the use of enclosure to extinguish local customary tenures altogether, as we saw in the case of seventeenth century Whickham, a region subjected to what might be described as 'coal enclosures'.

If anything, proletarianisation in mining preceded the dispossession of peasants from the means of subsistence in land by enclosures. This has led to the widespread conclusion that the production relations of mining were 'capitalist' across Europe in general as early as the thirteenth century. But dispossession from the means of production and the conversion to wage labour do not necessarily mean that there exists a social relation of capital in which the owner of the means of production enjoys the freedom to transform production according to the competitive pressures of the market. Indeed, large-scale mining concessions in the Middle Ages were typically obtained through monopolistic charters and therefore faced limited competition. The coal mines of North-East England would be largely controlled by a cartel of monopolists well into the eighteenth century. Under monopoly conditions, there was limited pressure to transform production by seizing control of the production process. The question greatly deserves further study, but our research indicates that while a wide variety of different labour arrangements developed in different mining centres, miners were generally able to assert their customary rights to maintain control over the labour process as possessors of both the skill and the courage necessary to the trade. Among the colliers, this could involve extraordinary sacrifice, such as submitting to the yearly labour bond in the North-East, or more strikingly in Scotland, submitting to collier-serfdom, an anachronism which lasted down to the end of the eighteenth century. Subcontracting was also pervasive in mining and other concentrated operations, with the contractor operating much as would the master of a small workshop observing custom.

Many of the large-scale operations of the sixteenth century did not last, but the general robustness of late sixteenth-century manufactures was at least partly a result of the growth of the national market, with demand for manufactured goods increasing at a rate eclipsing population growth, due to the expanding number of market-dependent producers in both the countryside and the growing cities and towns. The expansion of coal mining in particular was largely a function of the growing demand for coal, for both direct consumption in the form of being used to heat homes in the growing towns, and indirect consumption in the form of growing demand for goods produced in workshops and larger manufactories, which used coal to heat buildings, or in some cases applied coal directly to the production process, such as glassblowing or brickmaking. Thus did England pioneer the transition from dependence upon human, animal and vegetable sources of energy – energy derived, that is, from recent, direct sunlight – to dependence upon so-called fossil fuels.

Control of the enormous silver mines in South America vaulted Spain to the status of the most powerful nation in Europe in the sixteenth century. The flood of silver coinage led to a pan-European crisis of inflation. Philip II, as King of the leading Catholic power and widower of Elizabeth's elder sister Mary, chose to devote Spain's vast resources in building one armada after another in a series of unsuccessful attempts at invading Britain to dethrone Elizabeth, the Protestant Queen. The Spanish threat served to strengthen both the depth of adherence to the English Church and the unity of the English landed classes.

The seventeenth century

As the process of differentiation within the crafts continued, with the guild companies increasingly being overtaken by the trading interest, the term 'guild' came to denote less a craft organisation than a company of merchants, often operating out of the town 'guildhall'. Before 'Liberal' arguments calling for their abolition, the Stuarts found the granting of charters useful as an additional source of extra-parliamentary revenue, granting a record number of new charters. In 1620, a crisis in the wool trade, still by far England's primary export, brought on a period of economic crisis complicated by poor harvests and outbreaks of the plague and forming the background against which the Civil Wars of the 1640s would unfold. The crisis fell hardest on the poor, who were caught between rising food prices and falling wages. With an abundant supply of labour, masters increasingly ignored the apprenticeship rules and the numbers of journeymen swelled. Many journeyman companies were able to win charters for their independent companies from the willing Stuarts. But overall, the craft guilds in England were the first in Europe to decline. While the question of what precisely caused this early decline remains a topic for further study, we have seen that the position of merchants and employers was bolstered by the lordly reaction, facilitating the process of stratification. Another probable factor was the spread of improved agriculture, which gradually brought about falling grain prices and thus facilitated regional specialisation in an expanding domestic market. The monopoly of the guild was premised upon a conception of the market as relatively static, but in the face of steadily expanding markets for manufactured articles, the monopolistic logic of the guild would come under increasing strain. The Stuarts equivocated on the issue of customary forms of economic regulation in other areas. In response to protests, laws against forestalling and regrating were issued in the *Book of Orders* in 1627, only to be discontinued in 1631. Laws against enclosure remained on the books, but were poorly enforced and enclosing continued apace.

This was not the only contradiction involving the state. As the landed class was becoming increasingly dependent upon incomes derived from economic rents on enclosed farms, they nonetheless needed a strong state to guarantee their property rights. Yet at the same time, the Stuart tendency toward an absolutist style of governance, expressed during considerable periods of arbitrary rule when James I and then Charles I dismissed Parliament, was widely seen as a threat to the 'liberties of the subject'. A faction of opposition emerged inside of Parliament; the landed classes were divided.

Charles I briefly managed to alienate many of the company merchants before reining them in, but the opposition faction in Parliament found allies in the non-chartered, interloping merchants as well as in the London artisan community, which was instrumental in a popular takeover of London's Common Council in 1641–2. The power struggle between Charles I and a Parliament now dominated by the opposition faction, a struggle over the control of state finances, came to a head over the question of how to raise the necessary funds to supply an army for crushing the rebellion in Ireland. Separate armies were raised and civil war was the result. Parliament's New Model Army under General Cromwell, raised only as a result of the co-operation of London, ultimately routed the Royalist forces. But the growth of democratic radicalism amongst the London artisans and within the army itself gave rise to radical proposals for reorganising society, including the 'levelling' of classes. While the radicals were neither monolithic nor particularly well organised, even the more modest radical calls for democracy were seen as a serious threat to an emerging economy of private estates earning economic rents and the concentration of wealth in the hands of the gentry and aristocracy. After the telling debate at Putney, the democratic radical faction was effectively silenced. Power now fell to a group of moderately radical Independents and Oliver Cromwell became king in all but name.

During the Interregnum, Cromwell pursued a militant and expansionist foreign policy in co-operation with the new merchants, whose cry was for 'free trade', meaning freedom to violate monopoly charters. The abolition of the Court of Wards under Cromwell, confirmed at the Restoration, converted all land in England to the status of freehold tenure. Where the radical artisans pursuing democracy and greater equality were suppressed, their counterparts on the land, the copyholders, sought legal recognition of their possession of land, but were defeated. The landed classes were able to carry off this important legal development which favoured their own rights of property during the Interregnum, but by 1660 they were tired of a régime that represented the narrow range of interests of the Independents and were ready to accept the return of the King rather than continue to subsidise an expensive and over-sized army. In the area of commercial policy, the Interregnum left an enduring legacy as the later Stuarts continued Cromwell's policy of moving away from the direct regulation of commerce. Increasing imports of consumables such as tea, coffee and tobacco supplied an expanding consumerism in the growing towns. The happy accommodation with the Stuarts proved impossible to sustain, however, when James II openly displayed his Catholic leanings, thereby threatening to undermine the direction of a Protestant-oriented foreign policy. William of Orange was invited by Parliament to invade from Holland and claim the English throne. The Stuart tendencies toward absolutism and

Catholicism were thereby removed, and the ruling landed class enjoyed a period of 'glorious' solidarity not known since the armadas.

Henceforth, Parliament would serve as the political vessel through which the landed peerage and gentry would pursue their collective interests, and through which the landed classes would govern in partnership with the Crown. The ruling class in England after 1688 was in no way a 'bourgeoisie' and the Glorious Revolution of 1688 was neither the beginning of capitalism in England nor the end of the transition from feudalism to capitalism. Furthermore, inasmuch as a majority of (land-) lords in the late seventeenth century still collected extra-economic or 'feudal' rents from peasants on unenclosed lands, the ruling class was not entirely or even predominantly a capitalist class. However, by taking charge of the commanding heights of the state, the landed classes were now in a position to more aggressively promote the further development of agrarian capitalism; there would be no more state opposition to enclosures. In the context of this discussion, it is important to reiterate the transitional nature of agrarian capitalism. Unlike capitalist tenant-farmers and later capitalist factory masters, English landlords collecting agrarian-capitalist rents were not themselves directly subject to market pressures and the market compulsion to transform production, but were caught up in a different kind of competition driven by such extra-economic considerations as the quest for status or the contest to see who could build the most magnificent mansions or establish the grandest parks and gardens.

The most outstanding reforms under William came with the founding of a permanent, publicly-funded national debt alongside the founding of the Bank of England. The attempt to establish a National Land Bank by drawing upon land, the primary form of wealth in England at the time, resulted in disaster and demonstrated that English landlords were anxious to borrow but not to lend. After a turbulent beginning, the Bank of England soon proved indispensable. A new type of economic agent arose, the financier, whose capital was money itself, in all its various paper forms. The specific and immediate reasons for the establishment of the national debt and the Bank of England were to provide William with urgently needed funds for prosecuting what would become the first of six major wars with France. The question of what role, if any, agrarian capitalism played in bringing about William's so-called 'financial revolution' is a topic worthy of further study. What is clear, however, is that the financial revolution would prove crucial to the further development of agrarian capitalism in two respects. First, the ability to raise unprecedented sums for war provided England with deep pockets for directly financing its own army and navy and for providing huge subsidies to continental allies in a strategy which, except in the case of the American War, helped England (Britain after 1707) to defeat France and establish itself as the pre-eminent imperial power. The expansion of empire meant new markets for British exports. Thus war indirectly facilitated the further expansion of the domestic market. Second, the expansion of the supply of credit facilitated not only the expanding domestic market and the growth of manufactures, but more importantly perhaps it would also permit a tremendous acceleration in enclosing and improving land over the course of the eighteenth century.

The 1690s saw a legislative revolution meant to secure the Hanoverian succession in the face of Stuart claims that their rights of succession had been improperly abrogated. Additionally, the legislative revolution laid the foundations for a more tolerant society in England. The lifting of restrictions on the press led to the growth of newspapers and public literacy. The trend toward 'liberalisation' was felt not only in the sphere of civil society but also in the economy. As joint-stock charters appeared, the great merchant companies were one by one thrown open to 'free trade'. Rampant speculation on the new stock market would lead to economic crisis in 1697. At the close of the seventeenth century, England was in a state of financial and economic turmoil.

The eighteenth century

Even before the Glorious Revolution, the Whig and Tory parties had emerged on either side of the controversy surrounding James II's Catholicism and absolutist tendencies. The schism grew bitter during the first fifteen years of the eighteenth century as the spectre of a Jacobite invasion backed by France loomed. Security concerns lay behind the move to formally unite the two kingdoms of England and Scotland in 1707. The conclusion of peace at Ryswick in 1713 and the failed rising of 'the '15' exposed the weakness of the Jacobite cause, effectively putting an end to the schism and ushering in decades of peace, political stability as well as extraordinary corruption under the hegemony of Whig rule.

The popularity of Indian calicoes and other printed cotton cloths in the early eighteenth century prompted domestic cotton manufacturers to put pressure on the Government to ban such imports. Thus while the policy of promoting 'free trade' meant opening up monopolies to outside competition, it did not apply to international trade. The establishment of import bans and tariffs to protect home industries such as cotton and silk would have enormous long-term implications. At the same time, as stock-jobbing and speculation in joint-stock and other money-making schemes was left largely unregulated, an enormous bubble of speculation in the South Sea Company ultimately burst in 1720, leading to the banning of joint-stock charters with the passage of the Bubble Act. The man who devised a recovery plan was Robert Walpole. He earned the gratitude of the elite by 'screening' key members of the ruling class from facing losses and accountability. Upon taking office as Britain's first Prime Minister, Walpole pursued a mostly liberal economic policy. Yet this was not the secret to his success. While a supporter of unregulated markets, Walpole was only able to maintain his extended tenure in office by mastering the art of dispensing political patronage, thereby controlling Parliament. Walpole further ingratiated himself with the landed elite by constantly seeking ways to reduce the jealously guarded land tax, which had long exemplified and served as a kind of guarantee of the control of Parliament by the landed elite. This was his primary motive for pursuing peace in international affairs. Within Europe, England was the only country in which the land tax was applied to the ruling landed class. Walpole sought to reduce it not only by pursuing peace but also by shifting the burden of taxation onto the consumer through the expansion of customs and excise. This move toward regressive taxation was only sustainable because of the extraordinary growth of consumer demand, driven by falling prices, which stimulated exports of grain and manufactured articles in return for ever higher levels of imports. At the same time, the Whigs responded to the limitless desire among improving landlords for security of tenure in land by elaborating a 'bloody code' of legislation, adding dozens of new and often trivial crimes to the list of capital offences. Thus where 1688 represented the triumph of the landed class acting through Parliament, the establishment of Whig hegemony paved the way for a full consolidation of the political régime of agrarian capitalism.

The early eighteenth century was a period of unprecedented innovation. The appearance of Newcomen's steam engine and Lombe's silk mill, Britain's first factory, were indications of what lay ahead for manufacturing. Yet the growing body of literature on agricultural improvement and the appearance of a host of new devices aimed at raising agricultural productivity attest to the centrality of agriculture and to the unprecedented dynamism of the British economy in the early eighteenth century. The growing numbers of tenant-farmers were *compelled* to find new ways to increase their productivity as a response to competitive market pressures which made innovation an *imperative*. With more than half the arable land in England now enclosed, the capitalist economic logic that had taken hold of agriculture was evident in the systematic drive to improve yields by adopting new techniques, primarily in the form of convertible husbandry, while other techniques – fen drainage, floating water-meadows, the introduction of clover and turnips for fodder and new mechanisms such as Tull's seed drill – were adopted only gradually. The market imperative stimulated not only intensive but also extensive expansion of production, for this was a period of engrossment and consolidation of holdings and large estates.

A central factor in the new economic logic was the fact that increasing output of grain meant increasing supply, which in turn meant steadily falling prices of grain. Falling grain prices contributed to the apparent agrarian depression of the second quarter of the eighteenth century. But rather than withdrawing land from production in the way the pre-capitalist economies had always responded to a drop-off in grain prices, Britain's emerging agrarian capitalist economy responded with redoubled efforts to intensify production, rising levels of investment and, remarkably, rising rents. And all of this was happening during a demographic pause. Experience now demonstrated what Adam Smith would later argue, that trade did not have to be a zero-sum game and that the wealth of the nation could be expanded indefinitely in an economy premised upon self-sustaining growth driven by unbridled price competition. This process also involved a deepening of the class fissures in society through a process of differentiation in the countryside. A minority of farmers achieved extraordinary success. Meanwhile, peasants and agricultural labourers faced increasing loss of customary rights of access to commons and increasing loss of access to the means of self-subsistence through enclosure, their holdings reduced to a cottage and a small garden. The addition of so many newly market-dependent families to the growing population of Britain now relying upon money wages for their access to subsistence goods further fuelled the growth of consumerism and the domestic market, providing additional demand for domestic manufactures and for grain. At multiple levels, which we explored in Chapter Three as a series of feedback loops,[10] the processes that agrarian capitalism had set in motion were self-reinforcing.

Agrarian prices reached their lowest point in 1743, and grain exports began to drop off a decade later. With the economy even more firmly settled upon an agrarian-capitalist foundation than in 1683–1713, the strength of the economy and of the colonial trade once again provided Britain with the necessary means of providing massive subsidies to its European allies in order to successfully check French expansionism. For the traditional craftsmen, all of this amounted to the conditions for profound crisis. The vast expansion of the supply of wage-labourers enabled employers to circumvent apprenticeship regulations as never before, although the state continued to have an interest in collecting fines levied upon employers hiring 'forrens'. The economy was still very parochial, with wages in many crafts still set by custom, not the law of supply and demand. Yet at the same time, the practice of paying monetary wages to agrarian and craft labourers continued to spread, bringing direct producers into a more intimate connection with consumer markets and laying the foundation for the emergence of a national labour market. With the spread of monetary wages, employers increasingly tended to treat labour as but one of many expenses or inputs in the production processes they controlled, that is as *abstract* labour. Labour was steadily falling under the formal subsumption to capital. In the context of falling

10. See Chapter Three, pp. 193–8.

prices and thus low wages, employers were encouraged to hire more labourers. The scale of operations grew rapidly, particularly in mining, during the period of lowest prices in the 1740s.

Not everyone who was dispossessed of access to land found alternative sources of subsistence in the market. Underemployment was common, and the 'problem of the poor' only intensified. Cries of distress from tenant-farmers and landlords over the rising poor rates reflected a decline in respect for the paternalist notion that the rich had a responsibility to care for the poor. Long before Malthus, the ruling classes and 'middling sort' increasingly developed a pejorative attitude towards those receiving poor relief, viewing their apparent indolence as evidence that they were responsible for their own condition. A number of philanthropic schemes were put forward, but by far the most popular solution was the workhouse, where the able-bodied poor would be required to work in exchange for relief. While workhouses proved impossible to sustain as profitable ventures, they did prove to be useful in deterring the poor from seeking outdoor relief and were therefore expanded. At the same time, the concentration of workers under one roof set to the task of operating textile machinery in the workhouse offered a model for the textile factory. Moreover, the unfeasibility of making workhouses self-sustaining left the door open for private entrepreneurs to find a way to make such operations profitable. The Lombe brothers' silk factory at Derby offered the first successful model of a profitable venture in erecting a large factory employing mostly unskilled women and children operating textile machinery driven by an external power source. By the 1740s, a number of successful silk mills based on the Lombe model would be operating in the Midlands.

The success of Lombe's mill prompted a host of attempts to devise and patent new spinning and weaving machinery. The first operative cotton-spinning mills employed a machine devised by Wyatt and Paul. Although technical difficulties may account for their failure, these mills may also have been the victims of poor timing. For a period of poor harvests from 1751 onward contributed to a reversal in the terms of trade for agricultural and manufactured products. The rise in grain prices contributed to a fairly sharp drop-off in grain exports after 1755, which was further aided thereafter by the resumption of population growth. High grain prices led to stagnation in domestic demand for manufactured goods, freeing up inventories for an export boom. Under such conditions, employers were compelled to find ways to limit rising labour costs or to increase the productivity of existing workers either by extending the working day or by innovating in production. Leaving the production process under the control of the workmen, however, might not allow an employer to achieve a rate of productivity increase necessary to remain competitive. Machinery provided the simplest, but not the only, solution. As larger numbers of cottagers took to hand-loom weaving, the supply of thread from domestic spinning could not keep pace with the demand. In the area of spinning and carding machinery, the race was on to find practical mechanical solutions to these problems.

In both town and country, the response to the increasing levels of dislocation, market dependency and poverty came in the form of growing levels of protest, which accelerated under the pressures of rising food costs, the onset of parliamentary enclosures and renewed population growth in the second half of the eighteenth century. Rising rates of literacy and newspaper circulation contributed to the emergence of an extraordinary show of popular resistance to authority during the Wilkes affairs of the 1760s. Fuelled in part by the Bute legend that the young King George III was a tyrant submitting to 'improper influence', a very loose and tense alliance of sorts arose between the Rockingham party and the mostly artisanal London crowd.

With the conclusion of the Seven Years' War only three years into his reign, George III found himself at the head of a vastly expanded empire. It was a propitious moment to have an export boom, but the very project of empire-building posed a built-in contradiction to the ostensibly liberal project of promoting both free markets and the liberties of the subject at home. Although British imperialism was exceptional to the extent that it was able to export not only high levels of surplus production but also large numbers of surplus population as settlers to its colonies, it was nonetheless subject to the same geopolitical considerations that drove other, non-capitalist nations on to the project of conquering and colonising the globe. Such a project required the application of extra-economic force to subdue and maintain control over native populations, and to make them pay for their occupation by way of exacting or siphoning off large amounts of surplus in the form of tribute or taxation. This spelled disaster for India, as the complete failure of the Directors of the East India Company to grasp the differences between the Indian economy and the British would contribute to the Great Bengal Famine (1769–79), which precipitated a financial melt-down for the Company and would eventually prompt the British state to assume responsibility of governance in India, relieving the East India Company of this charge. In the settler colonies of North America, the continued application of the Navigation Acts and attempts to increase the burden of taxation met with resistance leading to rebellion and eventually to war. In Ireland, the one English colony where the effort to transplant agrarian capitalism met with qualified success, the Catholics followed the American colonists in the direction of open rebellion.

Efforts in Ireland and Canada to recruit Catholics to fight Protestants in New England sparked protests in Scotland in 1779 and in London in 1780. Led by Lord George Gordon, a Scotsman, the so-called Gordon Riots marked a turning point in the relations between the plebeian crowd and the patrician gentry of the eighteenth century. While the protestors themselves kept their violence and vandalism generally within the bounds of acceptable customary behaviours, the state's use of overwhelming military force to suppress them demonstrated that the state was ceasing to observe the normative mores and expectations of the 'moral economy' of the crowd.[11] It was a sobering experience for London's artisan community, but it may have helped to rekindle the flame of radical resistance and the cause of democracy a dozen years later.

In the American war, Britain's commercial rivals – France, Spain and Holland – all saw an opportunity to deal a blow to British dominance of the seas and world-trade. The North American colonies were soon lost, but the Empire survived. Managing to restore trade with France and America not long after the war, Britain quickly resumed its place as the pre-eminent world economic power. This was possible because of the superior dynamism of Britain's agrarian-capitalist economy, the advantages of which France and other rival commercial powers were beginning to take notice.

The periods of warfare in the eighteenth century provided a stimulus to the domestic economy in the form of state demand for metals, foodstuffs, ships and uniforms. But with this came higher taxes, lower profits, the diversion of capital away from private enterprise and weaker consumer power. The end of the American war meant a release of capital back into the domestic economy, prompting a wave of factory-building and a doubling of the pace of enclosure.

In debating the relationship between enclosures and the emergence of a proletariat for the Industrial Revolution, both optimists and pessimists have focused on the question of whether or not large numbers of direct producers actually relocated to find manufacturing work in the towns as a result of being displaced from the countryside as a result of enclosures. In briefly reviewing this 'great debate' in Chapter Five, it was argued that the focus on current enclosures as a proximate cause has come at the expense of considering the impact of prior enclosures on both expanding market dependency and raising the ceiling on the food supply, thereby enabling population growth to rise. Moreover, in stressing the upside of aggregate growth, the optimists understated the level of resistance to enclosures, overstated the value of enclosure to the smallholder whilst understating his or her loss, and unfairly characterised open field agriculture as wasteful, unproductive and backward. Most importantly, the debate generally ignored the significance of agrarian capitalism and the way in which it laid the foundations for the Industrial Revolution by creating an *agrarian* proletariat and deepening the divide between owners of property and propertyless producers rendered increasingly dependent upon wages to earn their livelihoods. In the

11. Thompson 1993, p. 185; Nicholson 1985.

1790s, this agrarian proletariat would face a deep crisis of unemployment resulting from a succession of poor harvests, continued population growth, the acceleration of parliamentary enclosures and the effects of a slow-down in foreign trade during the long war with France, prompting local authorities to increase the level of outdoor relief. However, the economic crisis that arrived simultaneous with France's declaration of war in 1792 was for the state only a secondary crisis to the political crisis that threatened the Hanoverian régime.

Technology and the labour process

Part II of this work turns to the question of technology in the Industrial Revolution. It was necessary at some point to address various currents of thought that amount to a kind of technological determinism, even in the thinking of such lauded writers as Polanyi, Mumford or Landes, since both weak and strong variations of technological determinism, or what we have labelled the technological model, remain pervasive in the way in which attempts to explain the Industrial Revolution are approached. In exploring how twentieth-century debates on technological determinism might influence our view of the role of technology in the Industrial Revolution, we suggested that the unpredictable or unintended consequences of new technological advances amounted to a kind of technological *in*determinism rather than a determinism. Where Brenner has shown that approaches to explaining the transition to capitalism based upon demographic or commercialisation models fail to provide an explanation for England's distinctive development of agrarian capitalism, we have argued that the technological model fails to provide any explanation for why Britain should have been the first nation to experience industrialisation. The main problem with writings that tend to see technology as the prime mover in historical change is that they tend to be devoid of historical specificity. This is perhaps most true of scholars like G.A. Cohen and Heilbroner who have interpreted Marx's base-superstructure metaphor literally to mean that economics determines social change and who narrowly interpret Marx's use of the term 'productive forces' to refer primarily to technology. The result is an economistic Marxism that reproduces the fundamental error of political economy, discussed in the Introduction, which is the tendency to naturalise the economy. The Smithian versus Marxian debate over the role of technology, then, has presented what Wood calls 'false choices' by virtually excluding any examination of how the transformation of social relations, including and specifically the social relations of production, conditions the introduction and the use of technology.

In reviewing the history of technology, we sought to challenge the widespread notion that technological progress in history has been consistently progressive or cumulative. The formation and development of states did result in an increase in the pace of invention, particularly in the area of weaponry. The scholars of classical antiquity were aware of most of the key principles of mechanics, but excelled in other areas of science and technology. The Chinese contributed an astonishing range of fundamental technologies that we still tend to take for granted, such as paper or the compass, but did not revolutionise production. The Arabs excelled in math and astronomy, invented the windmill and for the greater part of a millennium carried forward the scientific and technological knowledge of classical Greece and Rome as Western Europe lapsed into a largely illiterate and rural society during its 'Dark Ages'. In the Americas, the Mayans were extraordinarily advanced in mathematics, astronomy and hydraulic engineering prior to their collapse. If it were actually the case that historical change is driven by technological developments or determined by the level of the productive forces, then how would it be possible that the advance of technology in all of these civilisations collapsed or underwent technological stagnation whilst Britain, long the technological backwater of Europe, became the first society to industrialise? Even the enormous *Manufactures Royales* in sixteenth-century Paris did not bring industrial revolution to France, although French science, basking in royal patronage, made contributions that would be of enormous importance to the British Industrial Revolution. Yet while French science remained dependent upon state patronage, amateur science clubs flourished in Britain and from the eighteenth century onward the field of practical invention geared toward production is dominated by the British.

This underscores the importance of social relations in shaping the uses of technology. Only in Britain had a majority of the population been rendered partially or fully market-dependent through the extinguishing of customary rights of tenure and access to the commons through enclosures. Eighteenth century London was the metropolis of Europe and the centre of world commerce. Urbanisation across England was more advanced than in any other European nation. Mid-eighteenth-century British agriculture was the first in the world to respond to falling grain prices with increased investment in intensifying production.

The same capitalist logic applied to the early Industrial Revolution as large employers responded to the squeeze that rising labour costs put on profits by turning to innovation and machinery; experience had proved that innovation had the potential to pay dividends in the form of profits. In short, the emergence of a new and capitalist economic logic in Britain, where competition uniquely compelled employers to seek ways to cut costs through innovation, provided the economic context in which the systematic application of technology to production made sense in a way that it simply did not and never had in non-capitalist societies.

This is not to suggest that capitalism was already fully-developed in late eighteenth-century Britain. In the early factories, labourers continued to observe traditional rituals and often continued to maintain customary control over the labour process as well. The vast majority of manufacturing continued to be carried on in the home, the garret or the small workshop – that is, in the customary fashion – well into the nineteenth century. And just as customary tenants on open fields were not averse to recognising the advantages of new techniques associated with 'improved' agriculture, so domestic workers in West Yorkshire and Lancashire availed themselves of the advantages of the jenny and – after the initial resistance to it – the shuttle-loom, although in the West of England these machines were fiercely resisted, precisely because under the prevailing social relations of production, their introduction would have put the machines in the hands of the gentleman clothier, the large employer whose ambition leaned toward the construction of factories. Although in the nineteenth century the use of small machinery in the domestic production of woollens in West Riding would develop into 'company' mills that would eventually develop into factories, in the eighteenth century it was the small, domestic clothier who found the jenny a useful machine to incorporate into the domestic workshop, where labour continued to be regulated according to custom. Thus the spread of machinery did not under all circumstances equate with the arrival of capitalist relations of production in industry.

The obverse is also true: capitalist production was not contingent upon the use of machinery. By dividing the labour process into discrete tasks, training unskilled workers in the specific skills that this process required them to perform and instituting a rigorous work discipline to enforce the rules of his assembly-line, Josiah Wedgwood sought, in his own words, to make of his workers 'such Machines of men as cannot err'.[12] It is a telling quote because it betrays a conscious effort on his part to reproduce without the aid of machinery what was to some degree being produced in other lines of industry *by* the application of machinery. What both Wedgwood and machine-driven factory masters like Arkwright required before they were able to transform production was command of the labour process. The compulsion to seize direct control of the labour process, we have argued, was necessitated by the imperatives of market competition, *pace* Marglin's suggestion that capitalist employers wanted control simply in order to establish or maintain hierarchy in the workplace.

There is an obvious parallel between the factory master and the enclosing landlord: both were subject to competitive market pressures that made their

12. McKendrick (1961, p. 34), quoting a letter from Josiah Wedgwood to Thomas Bentley dated 9 October 1769 (see note 93 on p. 586).

economic survival dependent upon making the production process more efficient and both confronted possible resistance from labourers (peasants and traditional craft workers) who claimed customary rights of possession of the means of production as well as the labour process. Enclosing provided the landlord with the means of extinguishing customary law and the village-level organisation of production and distribution of land according to custom. The early factory masters sought first of all to bypass the traditional skilled (and mostly male) craft workers by hiring unskilled women and children. Secondly, they sought to literally supplant the hands of the traditional manual labourer, and thereby also his or her skills, through the introduction of factory machinery which involved a tool aspect, such as the water frame or the mule, whose action could substitute for manual labour. The use of machinery in this manner afforded the owner a means of assuming direct control over the labour process, since the worker was no longer the bearer of the necessary skills required to work the product by hand. Wedgwood achieved relatively the same degree of control by reducing the art of making pots into such minute tasks that his workers were similarly deprived of learning the general skill of how to make pots, and instead learned only such skills as were necessary to carry out discrete tasks performed in endless repetition in much the same manner as would a worker attending a machine.

What made capitalist production in manufacturing capitalist was neither the introduction of technology nor the employment of wage labour, but rather the fact that market-dependent direct producers and their market-dependent employers were increasingly operating according to the compulsions of the market. In order to survive in an increasingly competitive marketplace, it was becoming compulsory for the capitalist owner to assume direct control of the means of production in order to wrest control of the labour process away from the customary labourer by reorganising production in such a way as to vest the critical knowledge and skills necessary for production in the head and hands of the owner and render the knowledge and skills of the traditional worker superfluous. Substituting machinery for handiwork probably offered the most expedient and powerful means of achieving this end but, as the case of Wedgwood demonstrates, was not the only means by which production could be transformed in response to market imperatives.

Introducing machinery into the factory did not come without risks. Through numerous examples, we have seen that most inventions made wealth for someone other than their inventor. Obtaining a patent was not always easy. Enforcing it was harder still, and even success at that did not preclude the emergence of superior inventions. What is more, Arkwright's pioneering of the first broadly successful factory system demonstrated the ease with which factories could be reproduced by simply building more machinery. Wedgwood's system did not offer the same ease of reduplication to his competitors. In both instances, however, it was the ever-increasing pressures of competition between capitalists, not the introduction of machinery itself, which made taking control of and reorganising the production process so as to render production more productive and efficient an imperative. Here we must once again reiterate how common is the misconception that there was some pre-existing capitalism simply awaiting the removal of the customary 'fetters' blocking its inevitable development. In both agriculture and manufactures, it was not the case that once customary regulation of production was cleared away, what remained was a capitalist mode of production. This would imply that the specific intention behind technological and organisational innovation was simply to remove the obstruction of custom. The actual intention was to develop entirely *new* methods of production that were sufficient to enable the owner of the means of production to stay in the game of competition where traditional methods had proved insufficient. In textiles, only specific lines of manufacturing were initially transformed, whilst domestic outsourcing continued for a long time to prove sufficiently productive for continued employment so long as the cost of falling prices and a falling rate of profit could be passed on to the direct producer, as the tragic story of the hand-loom weavers in the early nineteenth century would demonstrate.

This is not the only reason for the persistence of customary modes of labour organisation, however, for the various craft trades did not yield control over the labour processes of their trade without a struggle. Silk, cotton and pottery were unregulated trades. The relative weakness of customary rights in these trades helps to explain why they saw the first or the strongest development of technological and organisational innovation in the form of the factory or manufactory. Woollen production was a regulated trade that had long served as England's staple export. In early enclosed West of England, there was even stronger worker resistance to the introduction of machinery, leading to a technological gap that would ultimately bring about the decline of the woollen trade in this region. The West Riding saw the early adoption of machinery inside the traditional workshop by the small master clothier but slow development of large factories due in part to technical considerations, just as papermaking factories were not built until the introduction of the papermaking machine after 1830 enabled a rapid conversion. But in the case of West Riding's woollen trade, the delay of the factory appears also to have been as a result of the strength of custom. It is in the woollen production districts of West Riding that we find examples of both of Marx's paths by which the capitalist develops: the merchant assuming control over production to ensure the quality of his product ('Way II'), as in the example of Benjamin Gott, and the worker as the small master clothier gradually able to expand the operation by adding machinery for one process after the other until he eventually becomes the master of a factory operating along capitalist lines ('Way I'). Outside of West Yorkshire, however, this study has found little evidence that 'Way I' was the rule in Britain.

The closest approximation to the factory in the metallurgy trades was Matthew Boulton's Soho Manufactory, which struggled with management problems and shared with most large-scale metallurgy and mining operations the character of having incorporated the social production relations of the workshop inside of a larger operation. Boulton and Watt sought to supersede these management issues by later establishing the Soho Foundry for producing separate condenser engines according to a plan that mimicked Wedgwood's methods: rigid division of labour, selective recruiting and a rigorous code of discipline. Even then, Boulton and Watt still had to rely on the skilled labour of experienced engineers, which would have limited the completeness of their control over the production process. Large employers in the metallurgy trade were exceptional in an industry dominated by small workshops producing an endless variety of smallwares. But the number and the scale of large operations in metallurgy and mining did grow. Only a separate and rigorous study can do justice to the complexities of the diverse range of labour arrangements that have been identified in the metallurgy- and mining trades. We can make the general observation, however, that the expansion of output during the early Industrial Revolution in industries outside the factory system was achieved to a greater extent through the expansion of the scale of the operation, including increasing the size of the tools and utensils (as in brewing), and to a lesser extent through innovation in technology and organisation. These operations were informed by innovations in labour organisation in other industries. But where they depended upon highly-skilled labourers, or where the labourers retained a strong collective identity and a distinct culture rooted in the productive skills and knowledge they possessed – thereby providing them with a strong position from which to negotiate – the ability of owners to fully take command of the production process was constrained. In short, the subsumption of labour to capital remained more formal than real. This set the stage for a long-term struggle over control of the production process lasting late into the nineteenth century and beyond.

Capital, custom and the law

If the factory master continued to meet resistance both inside and outside of the factory, the master of the mine or the foundry was bound to encounter his own fair share of resistance as well. The economy during the Industrial Revolution was thus characterised by a tension between the formal versus the real subsumption of labour to capital, but the overall direction of industrial production was moving toward the latter under the influence of competitive market pressures in an increasingly unregulated and expanding domestic market whose expansion continued to be driven by falling prices resulting from constant improvements in agricultural – and now increasingly industrial – output. Much of the scholarship on the Industrial Revolution understands capital according to a strictly economic or what we have also called a static definition, one in which any discussion of labour as a form of circulating capital is conspicuously absent. In a sense, this understanding of capital is little different from what Marx understood as 'merchant-' capital, a definition which understands capital as the merchant's accumulated savings and stock. We have pointed out that the same scholarship that approaches the Industrial Revolution employing an economic or static definition of capital has identified apparently insoluble problems of accounting for the *rate* of capital accumulation in the late eighteenth and into the nineteenth centuries. The distinction between 'merchant-' capital and capital understood as a social property relation is the distinction between capital in the form of the trader's stock being exchanged at domestic fairs or through international trade and a form of capital which *subsumes* social relations in the form of what thereby become 'fictitious' commodities – land, labour and money, as described by Polanyi. By treating land, labour and money as commodities, the owner of capital thereby assumes the power of ownership over: a) the social relations governing the process by which access to the natural environment – *land* – is distributed; b) the social relations governing the process by which the production tasks – *labour* – are allocated; and c) the social relations governing the process by which the medium of exchange – *money* – is regulated or standardised. The story of the origin and development of capitalism is in large part the story of the subsumption of these social relationships to capital by treating land, labour and money as commodities. By *imagining* land, labour and money as interchangeable 'things' independent of the social relations of which they are ultimately inseparable and indistinguishable, and by subsuming them to capital, the very nature of the market was transformed, its scope and powers vastly transformed as the entire population became market-dependent. Stated this way, the conversion to capitalism is probably the most profound transformation in the history of human social relations, one which simply cannot be captured in quantitative terms. Thus in searching for answers to the dilemma of how to account for the dramatic rate of capital accumulation during the first Industrial Revolution, the economists ought to consider adopting a dynamic or social definition of capital.

Whenever and wherever land, labour and money were not yet commodified, when and where the regulation of the social property relationships of land, labour and money were not yet subordinated to market imperatives, those social property relationships were regulated according to widely-accepted, normative social principles, which is to say they were regulated according to custom. Custom was accepted wisdom, the way things had always been done. It was local and contingent. Yet it had the status of law. In the age of custom, there were markets, but goods for sale fetched different prices in different locations. Finding the location where a thing sold dear was in fact a primary objective among merchants. Even the value of the coinage, acting as the medium of exchange, was subject to local variations attributable to social rather than strictly economic standards of value. In a strict sense, Weber is absolutely correct to relate capitalism to the spread of rationality, for once the capitalist market imperative took hold of regional and international markets, such apparently irrational aberrations were quickly dispelled. Yet all too commonly this conception of what was rational and what was irrational has been used to denigrate the customary regulation of the economy as irrational in the sense of being illogical and insane. The decision by peasants to diversify their crops was not irrational or insane, but was rather a rational decision to avoid unnecessary risk given prevailing (pre-capitalist) economic conditions.

One of the major historical landmarks in the process by which customary regulation was de-legitimised was the passage of the Riot Act in 1715, which served to stigmatise the crowd as a 'mob' and the protest as a 'riot'. What followed was an extraordinary series of parliamentary decrees which on the whole served to criminalise acts and behaviours that had once been perfectly acceptable and natural according to local custom. Strolling through the commons became trespass. Collecting firewood off the commons became theft. Taking home the left-over thrums became embezzlement. The elaboration of the 'bloody code' was a logical extension of the process of declaring null and void the local, customary laws of the manor by asserting absolute property rights under common law, which was state law, effected through enclosure. The Code reflects a practical obsession on the part of the ruling landed elite with consolidating their private property. So long as there were still large numbers of rural dwellers who felt they had customary rights to walk upon the fields and enjoy access to the commons, and when, for example there were 'blacks' in Windsor Forest openly violating the new provisions of the Code against hunting deer, fences, hedges and legal title to a plot of land were not enough. That ownership had to be backed up with a kind of legal closure, one which would severely punish the first wave of transgressors, thereby sending a clear signal to any would be future transgressors that the owner's property was inviolable. By the latter half of the eighteenth century, they were in fact using Parliament itself directly as the tool by which they could so declare their absolute property rights in land *one parish at a time* through parliamentary acts of enclosure. Monumental as all this sounds, reciprocal relations between patrician and plebs at the local level nonetheless persisted for a very long time, both because the long arm of the state was not long enough to stamp out each 'riot' in every locality, and because the local JP had a strong interest not only in maintaining order but in preserving the appearance of impartiality, which he did by ensuring that sometimes the crowd seeking to enforce custom emerged victorious.[13]

The observance of custom, both by the state and locally, was already in a serious state of decline, however, by the time the political earthquake that was the French Revolution of 1789 sent a political tidal wave across the English Channel. What 23 years of almost constant warfare with France, beginning in 1792, would mean for artisans and agrarian labourers was an all-out assault by the state on their remaining customary rights. For agrarian labourers, this onslaught came in the form of the final wave of parliamentary enclosures, which targeted wastes and commons, thereby depriving those who had already lost their customary tenures of their customary rights to fish, graze their animals and collect firewood on the commons, or to glean the fields after the harvest. As these ancient rights were transformed into offences under common law, so the role of the local JP shifted from one of upholding the norms and customs regulating the economy, including customary wages, to acting increasingly as the arbiter of contracts between employers and employees.

This onslaught against custom played only a secondary role in the politics of the time, being eclipsed by a resurgent radicalism met with state repression. The French Revolution ignited a rebellious spirit among not only a large segment of the artisan community, but among tradesmen and small masters as well. From the vantage point of the state, dissent in defence of custom and against the imposition of capitalist property relations was tainted with suspicion of being not economic but political protest. With the very real threat of political revolution hanging in the air and endangering the Hanoverian settlement, and with Tom Paine's open call for an overthrow of the régime, the specific grievances motivating the protestors made little difference to King George or the Younger Pitt. To the weavers who pled their case before the parliamentary committee which subsequently voted to suspend the Tudor statutes that regulated their trade, it seemed the state had gone deaf to their suffering in a time of increasing hardship. Of course, individual factory masters and enclosing landlords were only too eager to seize what opportunity fortune had granted and press the speed at

13. As we saw, on a rare occasion, this also happened at the state level. We noted two instances. The first, during the hard times of the 1750s, when the *Book of Orders* and its laws banning forestalling and regrating were revived to the pleasure of the hungry crowds, and in 1773, when extraordinary protests by the Spitalfields silk-weavers won them renewed state support for apprenticeship and other customary rules of their trade.

which the customary rights of tenants and artisans could be abolished. But what preoccupied the minds of most politicians during this period was not the flaming rick but rather actual conspiracies of regicide and revolution, upon which their spies kept a close watch.[14]

It was truly during the French and Napoleonic wars that the writings of Adam Smith and the school of political economy came to the fore, occupying a powerfully influential role in shaping the thinking of high officials, including Pitt, even if the teachings were not readily translated into policy. Smith's concept of 'natural liberty', the idea that direct government regulation in the economy was a form of interference with the rights of the private proprietor to do with his property as he saw fit, offered a definition of freedom that differed radically from its meaning in the French slogan '*Liberté! Fraternité! Égalité!*', where the emphasis was upon freedom from oppression.[15] Yet Smith's conception of a tranquil society in which markets work in equilibrium to promote economic and social harmony did not resonate with a society beset with the burden of war combined with social and economic upheaval. This may explain the popularity of Reverend Malthus, who offered a much darker conception of society than Smith. Malthus's *Principle of Population*, first published in 1798, struck a chord with landowners and tenant-farmers alarmed at the growing crisis of poverty among agrarian labourers. Working within the Smithian universe of a natural economy in which private property is paramount, Malthus blamed rural poverty not on the conversion of rural producers to a state of market dependence through the extinguishing of customary tenures and rights of commons, but on the high rate of population growth which compounded its effects. He instantly became the hero of the landed class and his thesis on population would dominate economic thinking for a generation, contributing to the spread of what the Hammonds would call 'economic fatalism'.

Mark Blaug has argued that the decision of the Berkshire magistrates meeting at Speenhamland in 1795 to adopt a schedule for outdoor relief that became popularised throughout much of Britain was a rational response to chronic

14. The question of to what degree the perceived urgency of repressing revolutionary radicalism was used as a 'cover' for the state's assault on customary rights during the French and Napoleonic wars is, of course, a matter for serious inquiry and debate. The general lack of interest shown by Members of Parliament in the hearings that led to the repeal of the Elizabethan statutes suggests not only that the outcome was already widely considered a *fait accompli*, but that the MPs were preoccupied with what they perceived as weightier matters.

15. This equation of liberty with rights of property persists even to this day. Whether the fact that liberty meant different things to Radicals and economists in Britain made this contested terrain, leading Radicalism to place a greater emphasis on brotherhood and equality, particularly after *la Terreur* of 1793–94, would be a question worth exploring further.

unemployment, one that actually helped sustain agrarian productivity and prevent famine, *pace* Polanyi, who uncritically accepted the oversimplified and ahistorical assumption of Malthus and the poor law commissioners of 1834 that outdoor relief led to wages falling below their 'natural' price. Polanyi was correct, however, in seeing Speenhamland as an attempt to preserve paternalism. Local control over outdoor relief afforded magistrates the ability to maintain a large measure of control and influence over local affairs even though the customary social arrangements of the eighteenth century were increasingly being replaced by a general condition of market dependence and wage labour. During the French and Napoleonic Wars, this control could only have been magnified by the fact that while agrarian labourers were literally faced with the prospect of famine in some regions – particularly as a result of the poor harvests of 1795 and 1800 – high agricultural prices meant good profits for tenant-farmers and healthy rents for landlords. The ability of property owners to increase their rents and profits during a period of economic crisis has remained a defining characteristic of the capitalist mode of production.

The early nineteenth century

If agricultural labourers began the nineteenth century facing dearth and an onslaught upon their traditional rights of access to the commons, for labourers in manufacturing the onslaught came first in the form of the Combination Acts. It seems likely that what served to bring the issue of the 'general disease of combinations' – in the words of Wilberforce, the originator of the acts – directly to the attention of the ruling landowners were strikes by agrarian labourers occurring for the first time outside of the harvest period. The passage of the Combination Act of 1799 was rationalised in terms of strictly enforcing the common law principle of prohibiting conspiracies against trade. While theoretically in keeping with the teachings of political economy against interference with free markets, the act was radical in the way it proscribed centuries of customary labour regulation and self-organisation among craft workers, and in the way it sought to shift the role of the state away from supporting collective and customary regulation of craft work to playing the role of legal arbiter over wage contracts between employers and individual employees.

There is no question that there was a class bias against workers in this legislation, for a major component of the act was to offer employers the option of summary justice in prosecuting strikers and combiners. When labourers protested that employers were still able to combine, the measure was not reversed but merely updated in 1800 to include the placating measure of comparatively light penalties against employers who formed their own combinations. The practical effect of making trade unions illegal was to force them into secrecy, to encourage the growth of the tramping system and to encourage trade unionists and political radicals to make common cause, all of which in turn actually facilitated the growth of combinations. While there were probably more prosecutions under the Combination Acts than we know of, employers were nonetheless reluctant to prosecute for a number of reasons, including financial losses to be incurred when production was brought to a standstill, as well as the fear of retribution. Tramping gave workers threatened with prosecution an effective means of evading trial by relocating to another town. To the extent that these networks facilitated labour mobility and combinations facilitated worker discipline, employers had additional reasons not to prosecute. The greatest effect of the Combination Acts, however, was probably psychological, for by setting the combined interests of the landed and industrial classes against those of worker organisations, the acts served to circumscribe the boundaries of a 'class' of labourers.

Such an open assault on custom was anathema to artisans. For the Combination Acts, when combined with the subsequent repeal of the Tudor statutes enforcing rules of apprenticeship, amounted to an assault on the very heart of the collective power of traditional craft labourers, which was rooted in their ability to transmit their skills to chosen apprentices, thereby preserving the mysteries of the trade and their collective control over the labour process. The ability of craft workers to resist threats to this collective control, despite the Combination Acts, was seen in the Wiltshire Outrages of 1802. Occurring during the trade slump that followed the Peace of Amiens, the machine-breakers were largely successful in pre-emptively checking the introduction of the gig mill. The fact that the Edwardian statute banning use of the gig mill was still in effect aided the machine-breakers' cause. Strikers in West Yorkshire were also successful in checking its introduction at Benjamin Gott's Bean Ing mill. Such successes at checking the introduction of machinery, however, were never permanent. When peace led to the decommissioning of soldiers and weavers responded by forming the Woollen Cloth Weavers' Society in an attempt to limit the influx of newcomers into their trade, employers in turn began to petition Parliament in favour of a repeal of the Tudor legislation limiting the number of looms that could be employed in a workshop. Once war resumed, Napoleon's Berlin Decree and Britain's Orders in Council extended warfare into the commercial sphere, a continent-wide depression in trade ensued. The combined effects of insufficient grain imports and loss of employment due to a fall in exports hit the manufacturing districts the hardest. It was against this background that the Tudor statutes regulating the woollen trade were suspended in 1803 and 1806 and finally repealed in full in 1809, despite the best lobbying efforts of the craftsmen and their lawyers. The fact that their arguments were generally ignored suggests that the association of trade unionism with the threat of radicalism served to delegitimate trade unionists and their arguments in support of keeping the Tudor laws that supported regulation in the trades.

In March 1811, when Luddism first broke out in Nottingham's hosiery trade, it was not machinery but the 'mischief' of employers cutting wages, paying in truck, colting and producing cheap 'cut-ups' that led to the revolt. As in the case of the Wiltshire Outrages, the first wave of Luddism was largely successful in forcing employers to comply with the demands of the machine-breakers, although many of the larger employers were simply put out of commission by having had most of their frames and looms destroyed. Arrests and trials soon followed. When the revolt spread to West Yorkshire, it was led by the croppers, the elite among craft workers. When they sought to destroy the power-shearing frames in the Rawfolds Mill and were caught unawares by a volley of gunfire from awaiting soldiers and armed workmen, all notions of operating according to the traditional and reciprocal 'moral economy' of custom were shattered. Luddism would degenerate from a revolt with a high degree of organisation and a very clear goal of property destruction to disorganised looting and armed attacks in apparent retaliation for the use of deadly force by factory masters. The state's response would come in the form of the 'invasion of middle Britain' by over fourteen thousand soldiers. Meanwhile, Parliament had added to the bloody code a new law under which a man could lose his life for breaking a machine. The customary right to seek out and destroy offending machinery was a dead letter.

Outside the woollen trade, however, the legality of customary apprenticeship was still alive. As Luddism met its end on the scaffold, energy was diverted to a petitioning campaign against the repeal of the Statute of Apprentices. The ease with which 5 Elizabeth was repealed in 1814, in the face of an opposition far better organised than the supporters of the measure, shows how employers in manufacturing could take the support of the ruling landed classes in Parliament for granted. The arguments in favour of repeal actually amounted to an admission that the Combination Acts had failed. Since combinations continued to proliferate despite being outlawed, it was deemed necessary to attack the problem at the root. It would be worth exploring further the degree to which petitioning employers like Alexander Galloway were actually aware of the fact that removing legal support for the practice of apprenticeship would undermine the craftworkers' collective control over the labour process, but employers had anyway been circumventing apprenticeship rules now for well over a century and on an increasing scale, so to employers it must have seemed as though they were merely pushing over a rotted tree. For the artisans, repeal put their organisations in legal limbo.

The French Revolution of 1789 had not given birth to English radicalism, but had only helped to re-ignite it. Thus when Napoleon was defeated once and for all on the fields of Waterloo, clearing the way for the restoration of aristocracy across Europe, the flame of radicalism in Britain was undiminished. The military occupation of middle Britain as well as sporadic outbreaks of Luddism continued after the peace. Britain was not the passive recipient of a wave of radicalism that was born with the French Revolution of 1789 and died on the fields of Waterloo. The war against France itself had intensified existing economic contradictions and pressures in Britain. The repression of radicalism gave the state a free hand in also suppressing resistance to the imposition of near total market dependency in the countryside through enclosures and the abolition of the Tudor laws supporting observance of custom in the crafts. While the exploitation of peasant labour continued in the aristocratic states of reactionary Europe, in Britain the long-term process of subsuming land to capital was nearing completion and the wealth of the ruling class was now very much rooted in ownership of land worked by capitalist tenant-farmers hiring agrarian wage labourers. At the same time, as the number of factories grew from the hundreds into the thousands, the real subsumption of labour to capital had not proceeded nearly as far as the subsumption of land to capital. While the employers' campaign to ban combinations and repeal the Tudor legislation that had for so long served to buttress the role of custom in the workplace had been successful, most manufacturing was still carried out in homes and small workshops where the observance of custom remained strong. This situation in manufacturing could be seen to parallel the situation in English agriculture after 1660, when the legal basis for the customary law of the manor had been undermined but observance of customary rights and tenures had yet to be eliminated in practice. In 1660, the majority of land remained to be enclosed. In 1815, the majority of labour had yet to be subordinated to the rigorous discipline and control of the factory.

Just as Nicholson has sought to rescue the so-called Gordon rioters of 1780 from the condescension of posterity, so Thompson, Sale and others have sought to rescue the Luddites from having become icons of irrational opposition to progress. In both cases, it is not just particular social movements but the observance of custom *in general* that is being afforded a logic of which it has been deprived. The fact that customary forms of protest such as Luddism were generally conservative in their orientation, meaning that they were attempts to preserve or prolong an existing set of social relationships that was under threat, does not mean the participants were irrational or only backward-looking; it merely means that on balance they did not find it in their interests to go along with the development of capitalist industry. What presents itself as a contradiction and a potential source of great confusion about the period between roughly 1814 and 1846 is the fact that those who were mounting the most serious opposition to the advance of capitalism were expressing their resistance through a more codified and emphatic adherence to the observation of custom whilst at the very same time they took part in a radical movement for reform or even revolution that included shopkeepers who had no particular stake in custom, and capitalist employers who had everything to gain from its abolition. Of course radicalism was not a class movement; nor was it even supported by a majority of workers or employers, large or small. Nonetheless, the radical leaders operated as a kind of vanguard leading the opposition to the continuing hegemonic rule of the landed oligarchy. The passage of the Corn Law in 1815 helped to sharpen the lines of conflict by providing a common cause around which both factory masters and workers could rally in opposition to what was perceived as landed-class greed and abuse of privilege.

The multi-faceted post-war crisis spelled harsh conditions for workers and the poor. With the decommissioning of three hundred thousand soldiers, the rural crisis of unemployment persisted and dependence upon poor-relief increased. The tax burden continued to be shifted away from the land tax through the further expansion of customs and excise. This put a heavier strain on the budgets of workers and the poor as the Government sought tax increases in an effort to address the enormous national debt through a policy of retrenchment. The 'bread-or-blood' riots, the Spa Fields affair, the Pentrich and Folley Hall risings and the way in which the Combination Acts were driving worker organisations more stringently to adhere to private rituals and secrecy all contributed to a kind of governmental hysteria and the continuation and intensification of legal repression, which in turn only served to widen the social cleavage between the ruling landed elite and the emerging working class, adding to the sense of betrayal. The more constructive working-class development of the period is the emergence of early attempts at trade federation in the Philanthropic Society and the Philanthropic Hercules led by John Gast, who – in anticipation of Chartism – sought to build a workingman's parliament. The mule-spinners' strike of 1818 demonstrated that resistance to capitalism could also come from inside the factory. Working-class thinkers also began to identify the nature of exploitation under capitalism, questioning the use of state coercion to suppress dissent and enforce a new set of economic and social relationships that the overwhelming majority of the working class and the poor rejected. Whether or not the United Kingdom was anywhere near a revolution in 1819, the oligarchs were clearly worried. While the violence of Peterloo may in fact have resulted from the incompetence of local officials, the fact that there was no state relief forthcoming for the victims and no official inquiry launched into the incident speaks volumes about how the ruling landed elites feared that any concessions made to a radical opposition movement, which at this juncture was predominantly working-class, could fatally undermine their oligarchic rule.

Where outdoor relief on the Speenhamland model had not fallen out of use, the rates were collected locally, provoking widespread resentment toward the poor and the spread in popularity of the teachings of Reverend Malthus. At the state level, the Poor Employment Act initiated a policy of setting up public works programmes to employ the poor. The fact that the act was opposed by libertarian radicals spoke to the ongoing tension between working-class radicals or trade unionists and middle-class radicals and reformers. The state also allocated considerable resources to spy on and infiltrate radical and revolutionary organisations. Even more resented was the continuing presence of some fifteen thousand soldiers in the industrial districts and, after the passage of the Six Acts, the addition of ten thousand soldiers to a peacetime army already over one hundred thousand soldiers strong. In the face of a state determined to put down strikes and 'rioting' with the application of military force, the range of options for radical trade unionists was effectively narrowed to either working within the confines of the new capitalist order or pursuing some kind of alternative. In the decades to follow, both the movement to build *trades* unions and 'utopian socialism' along Owenite lines would emerge.

The necessity of retrenchment factored heavily into efforts to streamline government efficiency, and after 1822 to steadily decrease the size of the budget. While the influx of 'new men' open to careers of talent has given rise to the notion that a kind of silent 'bourgeois revolution' took place during this period, a fuller exploration reveals that most of the 'new men' entering civil service from the military, judiciary or the bureaucracy were themselves estate holders, while landlords were getting more deeply involved in trade and industry, thus making for a *convergence* of interests, one which transformed the ruling class but did not threaten the hegemony of property in land as the predominant source of wealth and power. In a context where there was not only elite consensus but also broad popular support for retrenchment and a move away from the fiscal-military state in favour of *laissez-faire* policies, political economy had never enjoyed greater popularity or perceived relevance. Moreover, the continuation of the reforms that had started under Pitt amounted to a campaign of bringing the operations of the state itself in line with the operations of the capitalist marketplace by clearing away various and sundry sinecures and other extra-economic forms of privilege and patronage and by converting the civil service to a form of waged employment.

No longer was the state an arbiter between various self-governing collectives seeking to extend their extra-economic and monopoly privileges. The new way in which the state maintained the appearance of the 'neutral' arbiter in upholding justice was to enforce contracts between 'free' sellers and buyers of labour. While the appearance of justice depended upon the state assuming the role of 'neutral' arbiter, the application of coercive force against resistance to the introduction of new production methods, including machinery, belied that neutrality. Nonetheless, as the role of the state in relation to production and labour disputes was being redefined in an active manner, it was becoming increasingly clear that the law against combinations had failed and that any attempt to enforce it would only draw the state deeper into direct intervention in disputes over wages and working conditions that would soon amount to another form of state regulation. We are now on the other side of the repression of Luddism. While the use of armed force to intervene in strikes and disturbances continued through the 1820s and 1830s, its application could be seen as a way of applying extra-economic force to discipline labour while the actual legislative and organisational mechanisms for allowing the market itself to discipline labour were still being worked out.

Of course, so long as there were large numbers of independent workmen still observing customary modes of regulating production, including the observance of the apprenticeship rule, the applicability of such mechanisms only extended so far. And artisan labour, even if it was based mostly upon very low-income work, expanded during this period because the Industrial Revolution required it to. The peak of domestic labour was really only reached in the late 1820s, when there were over a quarter of a million hand-loom weavers at work. What remained unfinished was the real subordination of all this artisan labour to capital. The legislation may have been laying a stronger foundation for this process to take place, but this did not mean it would take place without a struggle.

The commodification of social relationships and their subsumption to capital – labour in particular – presupposes the separation of society into a class of property owners on the one hand and a class of 'free' wage labourers on the other. This in turn presupposes the capacity for collective action ('union' or 'combination') on either side of the class divide. But in order for a capitalist marketplace to operate at optimal efficiency, such collective action must abide by the rules of the market itself; that is, combinations must not seek to replace an economy dominated by capital and capitalist social relations of property with something else. Certainly the Combination Acts reflect a consensus among the ruling classes in Britain that worker combinations could not yet be trusted to so abide by the logic of capitalism as it existed in 1799 and 1800. By 1824, however, whether because this lack of trust had diminished or simply because the laws had proved so ineffectual, Parliament was ready (during an economic boom) to follow the advice of Francis Place, Joseph Hume and J.R. McCulloch and repeal the Combination Acts. The argument these gentlemen put forward was couched in the language of political economy: legal combinations, they argued, would only aid the work of the invisible hand because they would only affect the price of labour when it fell below its 'natural' price, at which point combinations could play a positive role by restoring wages to the point of equilibrium. Within a year of repeal, a wave of strikes erupted, provoking employers who felt misled and betrayed to nearly re-impose the Acts before a compromise was arranged. Place and company had not foreseen this outcome, not only because their theory was flawed, but also because as an argument rooted in the thinking of political economy, social and cultural factors were not accounted for in their projections. Even if the ban on combinations had scarcely been enforced while combinations continued to grow, the criminalisation of labour organisation, the suspension of Queen Betty's Law, the legal repression of dissent and the use of coercive force to violently suppress Luddism and other revolts had a profound impact on the psychology and organising tactics of the trade unionists. Legalisation was taken to impart much longed for legitimacy, even 'respectability', and the lifting of the necessity of secrecy meant that organising strikes could now be carried out in the open, allowing for greater effectiveness and efficiency as well as the release of a great deal of pent-up momentum that had not been visible whilst combinations were forced to operate in secrecy, cast in the role of enemies of the state.

Even if from the standpoint of capital the timing of repeal may have been premature, it must be pointed out that *most* of the collective acts of resistance by labourers in Britain after 1825 came not in the form of open revolts or machine-breaking insurrections (though there were some) but in the form of the strike. Moreover, it was for purposes of mounting and sustaining more effective strikes that the organising efforts at building federated trades unions were directed. Such efforts were confounded by the cleavages that continued to divide the working class: the independent artisan and the factory worker, the highly-skilled and well-paid cropper and the impoverished weaver, the trade unionist and the libertarian radical, the Spencean and the Methodist. Given these cleavages, it is perhaps astonishing that the efforts to build mega-combinations to represent working people *in general*, such as the NAPL, the GNCTU, the LWMA, the NUOP or the NUWC, proceeded as far as they did. Yet not only were workers in general being increasingly pulled into an economy of labour based on wages and individual wage contracts, their 'product' was increasingly not a pot or a shoe or a watch so much as labour itself, abstract labour commodified. In other words, the subordination of labour to dominance by money-wealth, to capital, whether formal or real, was a growing general condition that could be felt by labourers of all types.

Critics are likely to object that this statement is going too far by way of imposing theoretical categories upon historical realities. To clarify, the specific reason for making this point is first of all to argue that what gave an objective basis to the common experiences shaping the 'making' of the working class in England and in the United Kingdom was not simply the common experience of becoming wage labourers. Considerable numbers of wage labourers had existed in ancient Greece and Rome, and even under feudalism. What gave the 'making' of the working class under capitalism an objective basis was the subsumption of wage labour to *capital*, which was an entirely new type of social property relation. This is not to suggest that workers during this period had a theoretical understanding of how capital subsumed social relations as commodities. Indeed, the delegates meeting to discuss the 1829 strike at Manchester and working-class theorists like Thomas Hodgskin continued to attribute economic injustice to unequal exchange in the sphere of commerce, where piecework and putting-out operations continued to prevail.[16] What the members of the emerging working class *did* experience quite consciously was the way in which law and policy were being shaped increasingly to accommodate the new social relationships built around the wage contract as the central relationship between labourers and the rest of the economy. Moreover, throughout this work we have tried to show that custom and extra-economic forms of property that are antithetical to the necessity under conditions of capitalism for all forms of property to be freely exchangeable, and, therefore, *not* politically allocated or normatively regulated, continued to exist throughout the whole period of capitalism's development. Even capitalists often bowed to normative expectations based in local custom, in spite of market imperatives. Let us leave this digression by suggesting that it is only through the combination of the application of state coercion to suppress dissent and its legal circumscription of absolute property rights that landlords and industrialists were able to subsume the social relations regulating land, labour and money to their ownership as a form of capital.

An example of the use of the state in 'shaping' economic outcomes in the service of capital is the way in which, after the strikes by Lancashire textile workers had been put down by force of arms in 1826 and 1829, striking mule-spinners in 1830 returned to work and accepted wages lower than they were earning before going on strike, without having faced bayonets. Of course, even when piece-rates for weavers had fallen to starvation levels in 1826, the state held fast to the wisdom of the doctrine of *laissez-faire* and took no action, a decision which may have led to starvation. Abandoning the weavers to their fate actually required the conscious effort of restraint from taking any action to regulate wages, although coercive force was applied in the interest of protecting private property. A decision not to act is itself still an act. In the case of the higher-paid mule-spinners, inaction allowed the now objective fact of their market dependence to drive them back to work. With this mechanism of market discipline in place, the use

16. Hodgskin did, however, identify the process whereby 'parasitic capitalists' denied labourers the full value of their work. This at least anticipated Marx's identification of capital as a form of property-based upon the conversion of social relations into fictitious commodities. This requires an exercise in theory, but it does not follow that because we only arrive at a definition of capital by way of abstract theory that capital does not exist or did not exist as an objective type of social relation of property prior to its discovery.

of coercive military force could be withdrawn and the job of protecting private property turned over to the police, whose main focus was not the enforcement of wage contracts, but dealing with crime, or in other words with the social results of structural unemployment.

With the near completion of the separation of the direct producers from the land through enclosures, the desire of the ruling landed classes to be able to enjoy tradition, stability and hierarchy whilst also converting agrarian production to free-market regulation had proved unworkable when the largest outbreak of machine-breaking in British history broke out across most of southern and central England. The fact that local magistrates in many counties (along with farmers, whole communities as well as juries) capitulated to the demands of the Swing protesters in 1831 and 1832 encouraged the poor law commissioners to adopt a policy of centralising poor relief. Where incentive and ambition languished under the paternal benevolence of the Old Poor Law, the New Poor Law would divorce poor relief from the operations of the labour market, thereby subjecting the poor to open market competition for employment. Rather than be able to appeal to the mercy and decency of the local magistrate, the indolent poor would be driven back to work by the merciless and mechanical discipline of the workhouse, where conditions were *intended* to be worse than any form of employment offered. Since the commissioners blamed overpopulation, not chronic unemployment in a situation of market dependence, for the crisis of rural poverty, they could propose that the discipline of the market itself offered the key to solving the crisis. What actually followed was a wave of rural crime as the anticipated result of rising wages did not materialise and rural families sought any means possible to avoid the workhouse.

This same group of reformers was responsible for the conversion of tithes from payment-in-kind to money payments in Ireland and then in England as well, for freeing Jamaican slaves from all forms of servitude but labour and the conversion of their status into that of apprentices, not unlike pauper children in the factories, and for defeating early efforts to limit the working day for children and women to ten hours on the grounds that this would amount to a form of state interference in the natural liberty of the market. Certainly the reformers' commitment to policies that promoted 'free' labour regulated by the discipline of the market was informed by an understanding arising out of the practical experience that wage labour was the foundation of capitalist profits. But their programme of liberalisation would not likely have been carried out if it had been based on practical experience alone; it was guided by a deep commitment to political economy's doctrine of *laissez-faire*.

The state itself was subjected to a process of reform and liberalisation, and at this level the reformers also faced resistance. A possible explanation why agrarian capitalism has been so little talked about or understood may have to do with the fact that by the early nineteenth century the proliferation of titles and vast concentrations of landed wealth had shifted power in Britain away from the gentry, who had enjoyed greater hegemony in the seventeenth century, back toward the Lords. With a ruling landed elite enjoying all the trappings of a neo-feudal aristocracy, combined with the continuity of repression after the French and Napoleonic Wars, the impression is easily created that the reforms and resistance to those reforms arose out of a classic struggle between a ruling landed aristocracy and a rising industrial 'bourgeoisie' achieving 'victories' in securing the passage of the Reform Act of 1832 and the suspension of the Corn Laws in 1846. The fact that a Tory minister, Robert Peel, was the person most responsible for administrative reform and rationalisation – following through on Huskisson and Robinson's programme of tariff reform, clearing away most of the arcane and obscure laws of the bloody code in order to instil greater efficiency to the process, introducing policing despite long-standing English fears of this 'French' institution and ultimately repealing the Corn Laws – underscores the fact that the oligarchy was not a homogeneous body.

In the case of the Great Reform Act of 1832, we have seen that far from being a capitulation by the landed classes to the rising power of industry and commerce, the whole measure was seen by the Whig oligarchs then in power as an effective means of preserving Whig hegemony by making a timely and strategic concession. In terms of extending the franchise, it was a modest concession at that. A further extension of the franchise would only come in 1867, after the railway boom had made the position of the capitalist ruling class more secure. The Reform Act of 1832 would, in the words of Earl Grey, 'put an end to such hopes and projects' as annual parliaments, universal suffrage and the ballot. In other words, Grey saw reform as necessary to forestall the danger of democratic revolution, which seemed quite real after the Lords' rejection of the first reform-bill in 1831 led to widespread outrage and revolt out-of-doors. Within the ruling class, there was significant and even profound opposition to reform; the 'Ultras' genuinely feared that reform would spell the end of the landed class's oligarchic rule. In fact, reform only spelled the end of *exclusive* rule by a landed oligarchy. What would prove to have a greater impact than the expansion of the electorate by half was the granting of voting rights to the industrial cities of the North as well as the modernisation of the political system in general, changes which over time would bring about the increasing politicisation of urban populations outside of London.[17] Where reform in 1832 actually stung a fair number of oligarchs, however, was in clearing away or diminishing the ability of great landowners to

17. The results of politicising the urban and middle-class populaces would be seen in the growth of municipal political unions (although these had been gathering considerable

essentially hand-pick their politicians. In the same way, the Crown was stung by the loss of electoral patronage under the act. The campaign of governmental reform in the name of efficiency and combating corruption was clearly driven in large part by the imperative of retrenchment, but the difficulty of sorting out which was the greater motor of state reform, retrenchment or the development of capitalism, underscores the complexity of attempting to describe transformations in social relations. If retrenchment was the primary motor, capitalism and its associated doctrines steered the course.

With the interests of the working class now even more sharply circumscribed by the law as separate from the interests of the propertied classes, a series of ambitious strikes ensued in the wake of the Reform Bill, nearly all of which ended in defeat, followed by lock-outs and efforts by employers to break unions through the use of the 'bond' or the 'document'. The extraordinary (and extraordinarily brief) effort at building a Grand National Consolidated Trades Union fell apart after the failure of a strike by the London Tailors, one of the founding groups. Owen and his followers did not see the necessity of supporting the strike before it was too late to save the Union. But underlying this failure was a deeper cause. The facts of having been collectively left out of the extension of the franchise to the 'middle class', on top of a long history of legislative and coercive repression did not mean that conditions for the working class in general were uniform or homogeneous. While there were now over two two hundred thousand factory hands, the majority of textile workers were still independent artisans. Regional differences and disagreements over tactics also undermined the potential for collective working-class action. Once the People's Charter and the National Petition were drawn up, a debate over whether the use of 'physical force' in Luddite fashion or only 'moral force' was appropriate erupted between the more radical workers of the North and those of the South. Preparations for 'physical force' action were extensive, but aside from a single and premature uprising in Monmouthshire, Chartism was notably less violent than previous working-class movements of protest such as Luddism and Swing. To a considerable extent, this can be attributed to the fact that after each successive 'wave of discontent' to break upon the shores of the Industrial Revolution, the state responded with force and with a level of infiltration that became increasingly effective at pre-empting protests and conspiracies of assassination such as the Cato Street or Orange Tree affairs. The Plug Riots of 1842, for example, coming in the wake of Parliament's rejection of the largest of the three Chartist petitions and during the grimmest year for the British economy in the nineteenth century, proved a massive affair, but the decision to pull boiler plugs rather than smash up machinery could be seen

momentum even before 1832), the growth of the Anti-Corn Law League and the vast expansion of petitions as a vehicle for registering political opinion.

to reflect an increasing level of restraint on the part of the participants. Peel also counselled restraint before bowing to Wellington's advice to quell the mayhem by force. After the demoralising defeat of the colliers' 'Great Strike' of 1844, the next effort at building a broad, horizontal trade federation, the National Association of United Trades (NAUT), consciously sought to avoid strikes in favour of promoting arbitration boards.

This shift in the direction of conciliation was matched by and came perhaps in response to entreaties from middle-class reformers and (anti-Corn Law) Leaguers. Poverty was everywhere; it could not be ignored. Gradually, sympathy for the plight of the poor was growing among middle-class reformers, which only increased after Ashley's report on the condition of miners and Chadwick's report on the state of urban sanitation. Yet there was no lack of self-interest, here; the cyclic disruption that working-class strikes and other agitations brought to the social order were costly. In the competition for profits, the advantage went to those employers who could maintain near constant operations. This need for stability can thus explain in part how skilled labourers in particular were able to negotiate wage increases without resorting to strikes. Unskilled labourers were resentful of the privileged position of this 'aristocracy of labour', seen by the more radical trade unionists as betrayers of their class.

Yet there could have been no more famous alleged traitor to his class in this period than Prime Minister Robert Peel. Having voted against the high-Anglican Tories in favour of returning to specie in 1819, and in favour of relief for Catholics in 1829, Peel had already earned the deep mistrust of the Ultras. After Peel's decision to call for the full repeal of the Corn Laws, a move which he justified as necessary in order to address the potato famine in Ireland, he was forced to resign, but not before the repeal measure had passed. It would not have passed without the support of half the landowners in Parliament, and the split vote reflected a schism between proprietors who could and could not afford to lay out the necessary investments to participate in 'high farming'. The intent behind the General Inclosure Act of 1845, as well as a number of provisions in the repeal bill itself, was to encourage landlords and farmers to introduce scientific innovations into their production operations. Just as Grey had argued in 1832 that reform was a necessary concession in order to preserve the hegemony of the landed class, Peel argued in 1846 that repealing the Corn Laws was the only way to further prolong the hegemony of the ruling landed oligarchy. The more obvious part of the argument was that just as the Reform Act of 1832 had taken the momentum out of radical and reformist agitation by extending the right to vote to the middle class, repeal of the Corn Laws would again diffuse the growing Leaguer and Chartist agitation against the landed interest by once again conceding to the primary demand of middle-class Leaguers whilst refusing any concession to working-class Chartists.[18] The more obscure part of the argument was that only high farming, the application of scientific principles to the technological and organisational aspects of agrarian production, would enable agriculture to keep pace with the rapid expansion of industry as a growing rival and thereby extend the dominance of landed capital, which still made up the largest proportion of the national capital, even if a greater number of hands were now employed in manufacturing and industry. Peel also argued that repeal of the Corn Laws would not have the much feared effect of causing grain prices to plummet. On all counts, Peel's prognoses would turn out to be correct. In the wake of the Second World War, observers found it remarkable that while the monarchies and great landowners of the Continent had mostly disappeared, England's 'aristocracy' had survived, and what is more, an aristocratic culture had survived, one which was 'aspired to and imitated by the upper middle class'.[19] Despite seeking to extinguish the role of custom in production, the landed oligarchy retained a deep attachment to ancient titles and rituals.

Understanding all of this, the surface-level impression of 1846 as a victory for the combined middle ('bourgeois') and working classes over the oligarchy is at least insufficiently nuanced if not an actual misnomer. Similarly, the passage of the ten-hours bill would be hailed as a victory for the working class over the industrialists, but this effort and the effort to defeat the draconian bill of 1844 that would have granted despotic powers to employers were actually led by old-school paternalist Tory landowners like Lord Ashley. In a three-class system, two against one was a winning formula.

When nationalists, liberals and popular-radicals rose in revolution against the reactionary regimes of the Continent in 1848, the unique social property relations of Britain conditioned a distinctly different and generally milder course of events. The Chartist agitation of that year was not revolutionary agitation, but began with the presentation of the third and final Chartist petition on 10 April. The state was massively over-prepared for dealing with any possible outbreak of violence. In response to the arming and drilling which followed, the state responded swiftly with repressive legislation. In its inability to overcome the moral- versus physical force schism, Chartism had always been engaged in a flirtation with ('physical force') revolution. But its public face and its core-organising strategy reflected the way in which a series of defeats dealt by the state to working-class agitators and revolutionaries over the course of many genera-

18. Notably, this concession came not in direct response to public agitation for repeal, but on the pretext that it was necessary in dealing with the situation in Ireland. Had it come, as the concession in 1832 had, in response to a revolutionary fervour, it seems likely that the oligarchs might have been more united in their resistance to the measure.

19. Buruma 1998, p. 10.

tions had foreclosed the option of open revolt, thereby channelling the energy of working-class agitation into what amounted to a rather polite exercise: petitioning. Once the 'physical-force' activities such as arming and drilling in the wake of Parliament's rather contemptuous rejection of the third Chartist petition had successfully been suppressed with policing and repression, and with the recovery of trade later that year, as well as the fact that independent producers such as the hand-loom weavers were now rapidly declining in number, the long story of artisan-based mass resistance to capitalism effectively came to a close. Despite itself, Chartism had served as a kind of bridge between open revolt in resistance to capitalism and accommodation in the form of the mid-Victorian compromise.

In the aftermath of the repeal of the Corn Laws, the rising middle class would seek to expand its voter base and counter the effects of the concentration and transformation of the land under high farming by promoting the freehold ownership of land. Feargus O'Connor's ultimately tragic pioneering into this field in the name of working-class self-help may to an extent reflect his own middle-class aspirations and that of his followers. But the campaign to 'return to the land' had something in common with the co-operative movement inspired by Owenism in the way that it was an attempt by working people to manage the effects of their exposure to the market by directly regulating exchange, or in this case production. It also anticipated later experiments with communes under conditions of advanced capitalism in the romantic and ultimately flawed conception that a return to self-subsistence was feasible. Where O'Connor failed, middle-class settlers would succeed on the basis of their allegedly superior virtues of personal discipline. Victorianism would bring a middle-class paternalism that would punish rebellion and idleness with transportation and the workhouse whilst rewarding obedience with advancement and a shot at earning 'respectability', a term whose meaning had now changed from enjoying the 'honourable' status of belonging to a self-governing group of independent, skilled craft workers to inculcating in oneself the personal virtues of obedience, thrift and industry necessary to succeed in the new capitalist labour market. The offer of a path to 'respectability' promised at least partial fulfilment of the long-standing yet frustrated aspirations of skilled labourers for social advancement. It was based upon a growing recognition by employers that coercion alone would never bring about the internalisation of the requisite qualities of discipline and obedience necessary for capitalist production operations to maximise the efficiency of labour. This is where labour leaders and employers met halfway to forge the mid-Victorian compromise and to lay the foundations of liberalism in the United Kingdom. Liberals ever since have emphasised the voluntary aspect of the compromise whilst socialists have emphasised the element of class betrayal. This same struggle really underlies one of the major disputes in the literature on the

Industrial Revolution: the standard of living debate. In that debate over whether real wages and consumption levels were rising in early nineteenth-century Britain, Hobsbawm reflected upon his exchanges with Hartwell by suggesting they were trivial in comparison to the questions E.P. Thompson was bringing to the debate: 'The Hartwell-Hobsbawm debate therefore has little in common with the debate as conducted by Thompson, though as it happens Hobsbawm and Thompson would jointly as well as severally oppose the "optimistic" view. Each debate stands on its own feet, though my personal view is that the question as formulated by Thompson is important, because it raises the whole nature of society and industrialisation under capitalist conditions and the changes produced by one in the other, whereas the problem as formulated in the Hobsbawm-Hartwell exchanges is trivial, because the question whether the working people received marginally greater or smaller real incomes in one period of the nineteenth century is in itself not of great consequence'.[20]

What is of true significance, then, is the 'nature of society and industrialisation under capitalist conditions' and, by implication, understanding the process through which this society came into existence out of a very different type of society, namely feudalism.

Summary

At the centre of the long and protracted process of transition between feudalism and capitalism in England was the class struggle between direct producers and surplus appropriators, both acting as economic agents intending to reproduce themselves as they were, but producing the unintended consequence of general market dependence. Peasants lost their access to the means of subsistence and the new class of direct producers were agrarian wage labourers. They would be employed by a new class of capitalist tenant-farmers competing amongst themselves for access to land through economic leases. The tenant-farmer's economic survival soon came to depend upon finding ways to maximise output by improving productivity through specialisation and innovation. Economic leasehold gave the tenant-farmer command over all production decisions, allowing for the transformation of production in response to market indicators, and thus making possible the emergence of a new type of social property relationship, that of capital. The market imperative was only reinforced by the growth of output, the growth of demand, the steady improvement of agrarian productivity and the decline in the cost of living. With the abolition of customary law

20. Hobsbawm 1975, p. 187. In the preface to this book (Taylor 1975, p. vii), Peter Mathias calls the standard of living debate 'the most sustained single controversy in British economic history'.

and customary tenure and the conversion of all land to freehold tenure under common law, the role of the state was redefined away from upholding social relations rooted in custom in favour of a new role as enforcer of property rights and economic contracts between buyers and sellers. Thus could the coercive powers of the state be invoked to suppress resistance to enclosures and the advance of agrarian capitalism.

Manufacturing in England also went through a considerable degree of transformation in the centuries prior to the first industrial revolution, although in general, production in manufacturing continued to be regulated by customary or extra-economic forms of regulation, based on the labour of independent artisans. Moreover, the numbers of independent craftsmen and craftswomen expanded tremendously as direct producers in agriculture were extruded from agrarian production and looked to domestic handicraft production as an alternative or supplementary means to a livelihood. The growing power of capital and the market imperative were first felt by such domestic craft workers through the loss of direct access to markets as the trading element separated itself out from and eventually subsumed most guild organisations. Merchants engaged in 'putting-out' also gained effective control over the means of production in the crafts. However, the growing power of capital versus the strength of the artisans' associations and the enshrinement of the customary mode of craft labour organisation in Tudor law set the stage for an epochal class struggle between an artisan-led resistance waged in the name of defending custom and employers who, responding to market imperatives, sought to abolish all customary forms of labour regulation and ultimately to realise fully the social relation of capital in manufacturing by assuming direct command over the labour process and all production decisions. The artisan-led resistance to these efforts was only successfully suppressed through the application of the full powers of the state, both legislative and coercive, and only after many generations of class struggle involving successive waves of often violent conflict.

Having managed to gain general control over state power in the seventeenth century, as expressed through Parliament, the ruling landed oligarchy managed to retain this control into the latter half of the nineteenth century. Based on their experience with the success of 'improved' agriculture, the landed oligarchs shared an ideological bias in favour of the efforts of capitalist employers to 'improve' production in manufacturing. In addition to economic reasons, political factors drew the state into taking sides in the class struggle between capital and labour in manufacturing as well. Since much of the leadership and the core of support for the radical movement for popular democracy were drawn from the artisans and trade unionists, these workers came to be perceived as a serious political threat to the Hanoverian régime, thus demanding their suppression. The state's response to the revival of radicalism in Britain during and after the French and Napoleonic Wars thus hastened the advance of capital's subsumption of labour in manufacturing.

Contrary to the view of the state's role as passive, the fact that the artisan-led resistance to the conversion of British manufacturing to capitalism was only overcome through the direct application of state power demonstrates that the state played a very active and central role in the Industrial Revolution. Moreover, the fact that this application of state power was directed not by the rising class of industrialists but by the ruling landed oligarchy testifies to the fact that the Industrial Revolution in Britain grew up out of and continued to be shaped by the social property relations of agrarian capitalism.

While the emergence of capital as a social property relation and its associated market imperatives arose from the unintended consequences of class struggle, being first realised in agrarian capitalism, the fact that the development of both agrarian and industrial capitalism involved class struggle and the application of state force means that it is untenable to view capitalism as an economic system that resulted from the 'natural' evolution of European society and economy out of feudalism, fulfilling the latent potentialities of pre-capitalist commerce and industry. Rather, one must look at the long-term process shaping this moment of transition, one must account for the use of the workhouse, the regulation of poor relief and the application of machinery in structuring social relationships in such a way as to allow the 'invisible hand' of the market 'freely' to regulate wage contracts and discipline labourers. One must account for all the application of force, all of the bloodshed, to understand that the modern capitalist economy did not simply 'evolve naturally', but was only brought into being by suppressing attempts to resist its imposition and to pursue alternatives which, if left unchecked, might have resulted in an entirely different social order.

Epilogue

In 1849, Karl Marx moved to London, as one of the scores of radical exiles faced with the choice of doing time in prison at home in Europe or relocating to England, where they could live freely.[1] Here, Marx would spend the rest of his life, much of it among the impoverished and alienated workers and urban poor, analysing the capitalist system that had transformed Britain and that was now beginning to transform the rest of Europe. This, he would do by applying the theoretical toolkit of political economy. As discussed in Chapter One, it was only later in Marx's life that he began to follow through on his own critique of the tendency of the economists to naturalise the economy and reach an understanding of the importance of how it was the structure of the social relations of property in any given society that shaped the development of its productive forces and not the other way around. This allowed Marx to grasp the fact that it was in

1. Buruma 1998, pp. 105–7, comments: 'It was a peculiar setting for so much revolutionary fervour, this most stable of nations, governed by an aristocracy of landed and commercial wealth, freely elected by an energetic, prosperous bourgeoisie, which was proud of its liberty to own property and conduct its business in peace. The slums were appalling and the gap between rich and poor was immense, but the potential sting of rebellion had been drawn by the promise of prosperity, by civil liberties, and by the officially encouraged notion that however much one suffered at home, to be born in England was still a slice of God-blessed fortune envied by all those unlucky enough to have been born anywhere else. The poor man was as proud of his country as the rich, especially at times of war, which, happily for those who benefited from patriotic deference, were quite frequent... The demand for universal suffrage, or Chartism, had lost its mass appeal now that its most radical leaders had been shipped off to Australia. Industry boomed, and foreign wars beckoned.' While Buruma's own Anglomaniac bias drips from the pages, this observation does reveal the profound disjuncture that Marx and others would face in London, surrounded by poverty but enjoying their civil liberties. 'The paradox of Britain, which all of them recognized', writes Buruma, 'was that it may have been boring and conservative, but it was also the freest society in Europe'.

England alone that the 'classic form' of capitalist development had proceeded through the use of enclosures to divorce the direct producers from the means of production, thereby giving rise to the proletariat. Despite such insights into Britain's unique path to capitalist development, Marx and Engels were less concerned with the question of where capitalism came from, than with the question of where it was going. After 1789, the question of revolution was the dominant topic of intellectual discourse in the Rhine Valley where Marx grew up, and the question of revolution continued to dominate Marx's thought throughout his life. Most of all, long after the publication of the *Communist Manifesto*, Marx and Engels remained committed to the concept of 'bourgeois revolution' as a model for socialist revolution whereby the proletariat could serve as the agent of epochal social transformation just as the bourgeoisie had before it. This commitment to the idea that such a rapid restructuring of social relations was possible may explain why Marx and most of the Marxist scholarship that followed did not explore fully enough the process by which labour was commodified and labourers in England were subjected to the disciplining force of market regulation, a process which developed over centuries. It may also explain why Marx and Engels, as emigrants from Germany, were shocked by the degree to which the development of capitalist social relations had advanced in Britain and saw the prospects for revolution there as good, whilst British thinkers tended to take those social relations for granted and to perceive the mid-Victorian compromise that had been enacted as involving a general abandonment of not only revolutionary, but also reformist agitation, in exchange for greater opportunities for advancement and social stability.

In 1850, Sir Robert Peel died after suffering injury by falling off of his horse. Strangely, the man who during his life had been accused of betraying his class and his party during his tenure as Prime Minister was widely mourned as though he were a national hero. It is as if, in death, all his sins were forgiven by his enemies. Here was the man who had suppressed revolt in Ireland, reformed the legal code without making it more merciful, introduced policing against the general consensus that this would threaten the traditional liberties of the English, reformed the tariff system to the chagrin of the less capitalistically advanced trades, and who had, of course, repealed the Corn Laws. In fact, Peel had done far more than the younger Pitt himself to reform the state and the law in the interest of abolishing extra-economic forms of property whilst promoting markets. With the return of prosperity, those who were now enjoying the benefits of the expansion of wealth could now express gratitude toward a man who had aggressively and perhaps ruthlessly pursued the establishment of a capitalist social order.

In 1851, the 'workshop of the world' was put on display inside the Crystal Palace at Hyde Park. The sixty-foot-wide ornamental gates at the entrance had been cast at Coalbrookdale.[2] Guests and dignitaries from all over the world were invited to come to the Great Exhibition and bear witness to the marvels of British innovation and ingenuity. Nationalism had always had a strong pull in Britain, especially when citizens were urged to rally around the cause of war, but here was an opportunity for ordinary, working-class Britons to take pride in the collective achievements of a nation. Factory masters and workers alike were invited to catch the 'mood, at once buoyant, optimistic and arrogantly confident of limitless progress, which seems almost to have been born in that year'.[3] The boom 'wrecked the hopes of the revolutionaries',[4] but it opened up spaces for considerable numbers of the working class to pursue individual advancement according to the new system of rewards and punishments that defined the logic of an economic system that had yet to be named.[5]

The British labouring class was unique in the world in having a majority of hands employed in manufacturing and industry, but the ruling class of Britain was still dominated by titled nobility and landed gentlemen. The instruments of high farming were on prominent display, a sign that British agriculture was in the process of being reorganised along lines more fully resembling the logic under which production was organised in the factory. Henceforward, agrarian capitalism was to become increasingly drawn into a *general* system under which a common market would supplant virtually all normative systems of regulation governing production.

It was not the beginning of the end of capitalism; it was the end of the beginning.

---

2. Coalbrookdale also contributed a thirty-foot cast-iron dome 'sheltering the figure of an Eagle-Slayer with his bow, and the slain eagle pinned to the roof by the arrow which had transfixed him' (Trinder 1974, p. 61), reflecting the overall theme of triumph.

3. Fox 1985, p. 125.

4. Hobsbawm 1994, p. 45 as quoted in Fox 1985, p. 125.

5. See Chapter Thirteen, p. 741.

References

Addis, John P. 1957, *The Crawshay Dynasty: A Study in Industrial Organisation and Development, 1765–1867*, Cardiff: University of Wales Press.

Adkin, Benaiah Whitley 1907, *Copyhold and other Land Tenures of England*, London: Sweet and Maxwell.

Albritton, Robert 1986, *A Japanese Reconstruction of Marxist Theory*, New York: St. Martin's Press.

—— 1993, 'Did Agrarian Capitalism Really Exist?', *The Journal of Peasant Studies*, 20, 3: 419–41.

—— 2000, 'Agrarian Capitalism: A Response to Michael Zmolek', *The Journal of Peasant Studies*, 28, 1: 147–54.

—— 2002, 'Theory and History in Thinking the Transition to Capitalism: A Reply to Zmolek', *The Journal of Peasant Studies*, 29, 2: 125–34.

—— 2004, 'Clarifying the Root Differences: Considerations on the Debate with Zmolek', *The Journal of Peasant Studies*, 31, 2: 306–12.

Albritton, Robert and Thomas Sekine (eds.) 1991, *A Japanese Approach to Stages of Capitalist Development: Unoist Variations*, New York: St. Martin's Press.

Alderman, Geoffrey 1986, *Modern Britain, 1700–1983: A Domestic History*, London: Routledge.

Amin, Samir 1976, *Unequal Development: An Essay on the Social Formations of Peripheral Capitalism*, New York: Monthly Review Press.

Anderson, Gary M., Robert B. Ekelund, Jr. and Robert D. Tollison 1989, 'Nassau Senior as Economic Consultant: The Factory Acts Reconsidered', *Economica*, n.s., 56, 221: 71–81.

Anderson, Matthew Smith 1995, *The War of the Austrian Succession, 1740–1748*, London: Longman.

Anderson, Perry 1964, 'Origins of the Present Crisis', *New Left Review*, I/23: 27–53.

—— 1980, *Arguments within English Marxism*, London: New Left Books.

—— 1987, 'The Figures of Descent', *New Left Review*, I/161: 20–77.

Anitei, Stefan 2006, 'A 2,100 Years Old Astronomical Computer from Ancient Greece', *Softpedia News*, 30 November, available at: <http://news.softpedia.com/news/A-2-100-Years-Old-Astronomical-Computer-from-Ancient-Greek-41393.shtml>.

Archer, John Edward 2000, *Social Unrest and Popular Protest in England, 1780–1840*, Cambridge University Press.

Arkwright Society 1971, *Arkwright and the Mills at Cromford*, Matlock: Arkwright Society.

Armet, Helen (ed.) 1963, *Records of the Burgh of Edinburgh, 1701–1718*, Edinburgh.

Armytage, William H.G. 1958, 'The Chartist Land Colonies 1846–1848', *Agricultural History*, 32, 2: 87–96.

Ashley, William James 1948 [1914], *The Economic Organization of England: An Outline History*, second edition, London: Longmans.

Ashton, Thomas Southcliffe 1959, *Economic Fluctuations in England 1700–1800*, Oxford: Clarendon Press.

—— 1963, *Iron and Steel in the Industrial Revolution*, New York: Augustus M. Kelley Publishers.

—— 1964 [1955] *An Economic History of England: The Eighteenth Century*, reprint, London: Methuen and Co. Ltd.

—— 1969 [1948], *The Industrial Revolution 1760–1830*, reprint, Oxford: Oxford University Press.

Aspin, Chris 1995, *The First Industrial Society, Lancashire 1750–1850*, Preston: Carnegie Publishing.

Aspinall, Arthur 1952, *Three Early Nineteenth Century Diaries*, London: Williams and Norgate.

Aston, Trevor Henry and Charles Harding English Philpin (eds.) 1985, *The Brenner Debate: Agrarian Class Structure and Economic Development in Pre-Industrial Europe*, Cambridge: Cambridge University Press.

Aydelotte, William Osgood 1967, 'The Country Gentlemen and the Repeal of the Corn Laws', *The English Historical Review*, 82, 322: 47–60.

Baker, John Hamilton 1990, *An Introduction to English Legal History*, third edition, London: Butterworths.

Baines, Edward 1831, *Manifesto to the Working Classes of the West Riding*.

—— 1859, 'On the Woollen Manufacture of England, with Special Reference to the Leeds Cloth District', *Journal of the Statistical Society of London*, 22, 1: 4.

—— 1966, *History of the Cotton Manufacture in Great Britain*, New York: A.M. Kelley.

Barry, Jonathan 1994, 'The Making of the Middle Class?' Review of *The Middle Classes in Europe, 1789–1914: France, Germany, Italy and Russia*, by Pamela M. Pilbeam; *Class Formation and Urban Industrial Society: Bradford, 1750–1850*, by Theodore Koditschek; *Class, Sect and Party: The Making of the British Middle Class: Leeds, 1820–1850*, by Robert John Morris; and *The Emergence of the Middle Class: Social Experience in the American City, 1760–1900*, by Stuart M. Blumin, *Past and Present*, 145: 194–208.

BBC News. 'Bow Street court closes its doors', 14 July 2006, available at: <http://news.bbc.co.uk/2/hi/uk_news/england/london/5179270.stm>.

Beattie, John Maurice 1986, *Crime and the Courts in England, 1660–1800*, Princeton, NJ: Princeton University Press.

Beaud, Michel 1983, *A History of Capitalism 1500–1980*, translated by Tom Dickman and Anny Lefebvre, New York: Monthly Review Press.

Beckett, John Vincent 1990, *The Agricultural Revolution*, Cambridge: Basil Blackwell.

Behagg, Clive 1988, 'The Democracy of Work, 1820–1850', in Rule (ed.) 1988.

Beier, A.L., David Cannadine and James M. Rosenheim (eds.) 1989, *The First Modern Society*, Cambridge: Cambridge University Press.

Bellers, John 1980 [1695], *The First Workers Co-operators, Proposals for Raising a Colledge of Industry*, Nottingham: Institute for Workers Control pamphlet, 68.

Benn, Carl 2002, *The War of 1812*, London: Routledge.

Berg, Maxine 1983, 'Political Economy and the Principles of manufacture 1700–1800', in Berg, Hudson and Sonenscher (eds.) 1983, 33–58.

—— 1985, *The Age of Manufactures: Industry. Innovation and Work in Britain 1700–1820*, Oxford: Basil Blackwell.

—— 1987, 'Women's Work, Mechanization and the Early Phases of Industrialization in England', in Joyce (ed.) 1987, 64–98.

—— 1994, 'Factories, Workshops and Industrial Organisation', in Floud and McCloskey (eds.) 1994.

Berg, Marxin, Pat Hudson and Michael Sonenscher (eds.) 1983, *Manufacture in Town and Country Before the Factory*, Cambridge: Cambridge University Press.

Berman, Marshall 1988 [1982], *All That is Solid Melts into Air*, reprint, London: Penguin.

Bimber, Bruce 1990, 'Karl Marx and the Three Faces of Technological Determinism', *Social Studies of Science*, 20, 2: 333–51.

Black, Jeremy 2001, *Eighteenth Century Britain 1688–1783*, Basingstoke: Palgrave.

Blaug, Mark 1963, 'The Myth of the Old Poor Law and the Making of the New', *The Journal of Economic History*, 23, 2: 151–83.

—— 1964, 'The Poor Law Report Re-examined', *Journal of Economic History*, 24: 229–45.

Bloch, Marc 1961, *Feudal Society*, Chicago: Melanges.

Bloy, Marjory 2007, 'The reasons and arguments behind the Chartist demands', 19 August, available at: <http://www.historyhome.co.uk/peel/chartism/demands.htm>.

Bois, Guy 1978, 'Against the Neo-Malthusian Orthodoxy', *Past and Present*, 79: 60–9.

Bottomore, Tom *et al.* (eds.) 1983, *A Dictionary of Marxist Thought*, Cambridge, MA: Harvard University Press.

Bourne, Henry Richard Fox 1876 *The Life of John Locke*, Volume 2, London.

Bowden, Witt 1919, 'The English Manufacturers and the Commercial Treaty of

1786 with France', *The American Historical Review*, 25, 1: 18–35.
—— 1924, 'The Influence of the Manufacturers on Some of the Early Policies of William Pitt', *The American Historical Review*, 29, 4: 655–74.
—— 1965 [1925] *Industrial Society in England Towards the End of the Eighteenth Century*, London: Cass Publishers.
Braverman, Harry 1974, *Labour and Monopoly Capital – the Degradation of Work in the Twentieth Century*, New York: Monthly Review Press.
Braudel, Fernand 1981 [1979], *Civilization and Capitalism 15th–18th Century*, Vol. 1, *The Structures of Everyday Life*, translated from the French by Siân Reynolds, reprint, London: Collins and Harper and Row.
—— 1988 [1979], *Civilization and Capitalism 15th–18th Century*, Vol. 3, *The Perspective of the World*, translated from the French by Siân Reynolds, reprint, London: Collins and Fontana.
Bray, William 1783, *Sketch of a tour into Derbyshire and Yorkshire*, London: Printed for B. White.
Brenner, Robert 1972, 'The Social Basis of English Commercial Expansion, 1550–1650', *Journal of Economic History*, 32, 1: 361–84.
—— 1973, 'The Civil War Politics of London's Merchant Community', *Past and Present*, 58, 1: 53–107.
—— 1977, 'The Origins of Capitalist Development: a Critique of Neo-Smithian Marxism', *New Left Review*, first series, 104: 25–92.
—— 1978, 'Dobb on the Transition from Feudalism to Capitalism', *Cambridge Journal of Economics*, 2, 2: 121–40.
—— 1985a, 'Agrarian Class Structure and Economic Development in Pre-Industrial Europe', in Aston and Philpin (eds.) 1985.
—— 1985b, 'The Agrarian Roots of European Capitalism', in Aston and Philpin (eds.) 1985.
—— 1986, 'The Social Basis of Economic Development', in Roemer (ed.) 1986.
—— 1987, 'Feudalism', in Eatwell and Millgate (eds.) 1987.
—— 1989a, 'Bourgeois Revolution and Transition to Capitalism', in Beier, Cannadine and Rosenheim (eds.) 1989.
—— 1989b, 'The Economic Backwardness of Eastern Europe in Light of Developments in the West', in Chirot (ed.) 1989.
—— 1993, *Merchants and Revolution*, Princeton: Princeton University Press.
—— 2001, 'The Low Countries in the Transition to Capitalism', *Journal of Agrarian Change*, 1, 2: 169–241.
Brentano, Lujo 1870, *On the History and Development of Gilds, and the Origin of Trade-Unions*, London: Trübner & Co.
Breunig, Charles 1977 [1970], *The Age of Revolution and Reaction, 1789–1850*, second edition, New York: W.W. Norton.
Briggs, Asa 1960, 'The Language of "Class"', in Briggs and Saville (eds.) 1960.
—— 1979 [1959], *The Age of Improvement 1783–1867*, Vol. 9 of Medlicott (ed.) 1979.
Briggs, Asa and John Saville (eds.) 1960, *Essays in Labour History*, London: Macmillan.
Brimelow, William 1882, *Political History of Bolton*, Vol. 1, London: British Library.
British History Online 2006a [1771], *Journal of the House of Lords* 15, 1691–96, available at: <http://www.british-history.ac.uk>.
British History Online 2006b [1803], *Journal of the House of Commons* 11: 1693–97, *British History Online*, available at: <http://www.british-history.ac.uk>.
Brock, William H. 1993, *The Norton History of Chemistry*, New York: Norton.
Broich, Ulrich 2007, *Reactions to Revolutions: the 1790s and Their Aftermath*, Berlin: LIT Verlag.
Bruland, Kristine 1990, 'The Transformation of Work in European Industrialization' in Mathias and Davis (eds.) 1990.
Brundage, Anthony 2002, *The English Poor Laws, 1700–1930*, Basingstoke: Palgrave.
Burke, Edmund 1829 [1795], 'Thoughts and Details on Scarcity', in *The Works of the Right Honourable Edmund Burke*, volume VII, London: F. and C. Rivington.
—— 1973, 'Reflections on the Revolution in France', in *Reflections on the Revolution in France by Edmund Burke and the Rights of Man by Thomas Paine*, Garden City, NY: Anchor Books.
Burnett, John 1994, *Idle Hands: The Experience of Unemployment, 1790–1990*, London: Routledge.
Buruma, Ian 1998, *Anglomania: A European Love Affair*, New York: Random House.

Bushaway, Bob 1982a, *By Rite: Custom, Ceremony and Community in England 1700–1880*, London: Junction Books.

Bushaway, Robert 1982b, 'From Custom to Crime: Wood-Gathering in Eighteenth- and Early Nineteenth-Century England: A Focus for Conflict in Hampshire, Wiltshire and the South', in Rule (ed.) 1982.

Butlin, Robin Alan 1979, 'The Enclosure of Open Fields and Extinction of Common Rights in England, circa 1600–1750: a Review', in Fox and Butlin (eds.) 1979.

Butterton, Harry E. 1996, *The Old Derby Silk Mill and its Rivals*, Matlock, Derbyshire: Greenaway Workshop for the Disabled.

Cameron, Rondo 1982, 'The Industrial Revolution: A Misnomer', *The History Teacher*, 15, 3: 377–84.

Campbell, Alan 1988, 'The Scots Colliers' Strikes of 1842–1926: the Years of Freedom and Independence', in Rule (ed.) 1988.

Campbell, Joseph 1988, *The Power of Myth: An Interview with Bill Moyers*, edited by Betty Sue Flowers, New York: Doubleday.

Carpenter, Kenneth E. (ed.) 1972, *The Luddites: Three Pamphlets, 1812–1839*, *British Labour Struggles: Contemporary Pamphlets 1727–1850*, New York: Arno Press.

Carswell, John 1993, *The South Sea Bubble*, London: Alan Sutton.

Cary, John 1972 [1695], *An Essay on the State of England*, in Thirsk and Cooper (eds.) 1972.

Ceruzzi, Paul E. 2005, 'Moore's Law and Technological Determinism: Reflections on the History of Technology', *Technology and Culture*, 46, 3: 584–93.

Chadwick, Edwin 1843, *Report on the Sanitary Condition of the Labouring Population of Great Britain*, London: W. Clowes and Sons.

Chamberlain, Joseph 1885, *The Radical Programme*, London: Chapman and Hall.

Chambers, Jonathan D. 1967, 'Enclosure and the Labour Supply in the Industrial Revolution', in Jones (ed.) 1967.

Chandler, Daniel 2000, *Technological or Media Determinism*, University of Wales Aberystwyth, available at: <http://www.aber.ac.uk/media/Documents/tecdet/tdet05.html>.

Chapman, Sydney J. 1904, *The Lancashire Cotton Industry*, Manchester: Manchester University Press.

Chapman, Stanley D. 1967, *The Early Factory Masters. The Transition to the Factory System in the Midlands Textile Industry*, Newton Abbot: David and Charles.

—— 1974, 'The Textile Factory before Arkwright: A Typology of Factory Development', *The Business History Review*, 48, 4: 451–78.

—— 1987 [1972], *The Cotton Industry in the Industrial Revolution*, second edition, London: Macmillan.

Chapman, Stanley D. and S. Chassagne 1981, *European Textile Printers in the Eighteenth Century: a Study of Peel and Oberkampf*, London: Heinemann.

Chase, Malcolm 1991, 'The Mid-Victorian Freehold Land Movement', *The English Historical Review*, 106, 419: 319–45.

—— 2000, *Early Trade Unionism: Fraternity, Skill and the Politics of Labour*, *Studies in Labour History*, Aldershot Ashgate.

Chattopadhyay, Paresh 1998, 'Value and Exploitation: Marx's Problem and Skillman's Solution', *Science and Society*, 62, 2: 218–40.

Chirot, Daniel (ed.) 1989, *Origins of Backwardness in Eastern Europe*, Berkeley: University of California Press.

Chitty, Joseph, Esq. 1824, *Treatise on the Laws of Commerce and Manufactures and the Contracts Relating Thereto*, Volume 2, London: Henry Butterworth.

Christie, Ian R. 1982, *Wars and Revolutions: Britain, 1760–1815*, Cambridge, MA: Harvard University Press.

Church, Arthur Herbert, F.R.S. 1903, *Josiah Wedgwood*, New York: MacMillan/London: Seeley and Co.

Cipolla, Carlo M. 1973, *The Industrial Revolution, 1700–1914*, Vol. 3 in Cipolla (ed.) 1973.

—— (ed.) 1973, *The Fontana Economic History of Europe*, London: Fontana Books.

—— 1993, *Before the Industrial Revolution: European Society and Economy, 1000–1700*, third edition, London: Routledge.

Claeys, Gregory 1989, *Thomas Paine and Social Thought*, Cambridge: Cambridge University Press.

Clapham, John Harold, Sir 1926, *An Economic History of Modern Britain: The*

Early Railway Age 1820–1850, Cambridge: The University Press.

Clark, Samuel 1995, *State and Status: The Rise of the State and Aristocratic Power in Western Europe*, Montreal: McGill-Queen's University Press.

Clarke, James Freeman 1871, *Ten Great Religions: An Essay in Comparative Theology*, Boston: J.R. Osgood and Company.

Clarke, John and Jasper Ridley 2000, *The Houses of Hanover and Saxe-Coburg-Gotha*, edited by Antonia Fraser, Berkeley: University of California Press.

Clarkson, Leslie A. 1974 [1971], *The Pre-Industrial Economy of England 1500–1750*, third impression, London: Batsford.

—— 1985, *Proto-industrialization: The First Phase of Industrialization?*, Basingstoke: Macmillan.

Clement, Pierre 1874, *Histoire de Colbert et de son administration*, Paris: Libraire Acadḗmique.

Clow, Archibald and Nan L. Clow 1972, 'Vitriol in the Industrial Revolution', in Musson (ed.) 1972.

Cobbett, William 1816, 'To the People of the United States of America', *Weekly Register*, Letter XV (June 8): 705–24.

—— 1824, 'To Lord John Russell: On the Doctrine of Surplus Population', *Weekly Register*, 52, 3, 16 October: 129–52.

Cohen, Gerald A. 2000 [1978], *Karl Marx's Theory of History: A Defence*, second edition, Princeton, NJ: Princeton University Press.

Cole, George Douglas Howard and Alexander Warnock Filson (eds.) 1965, *British Working Class Movements: Select Documents 1789–1875*, London: Macmillan.

Coleman, Donald Cuthbert 1954, 'Combinations of Capital and of Labour in the English Paper Industry, 1789–1825', *Economica*, n.s., 21, 81: 32–53.

—— 1956a, 'Labour in the English Economy of the Seventeenth Century', *The Economic History Review*, n.s., 8, 3.

—— 1956b, 'Industrial Growth and Industrial Revolutions', *Economica*, n.s., 23, 89: 1–22.

—— 1958, *The British Paper Industry 1495–1860: A Study in Industrial Growth*, Oxford University Press.

—— 1973, 'Textile Growth', in Harte and Ponting (eds.) 1973.

—— 1975, *Industry in Tudor and Stuart England*, London: Macmillan.

—— 1977, *The Economy of England 1450–1750*, Oxford: Oxford University Press.

—— 1983, 'Proto-Industrialization: A Concept Too Many', *The Economic History Review*, 36, 3: 435–48.

Collins, Randall 1980, 'Weber's Last Theory of Capitalism: A Systematization', *American Sociological Review*, 45, 6: 925–42.

Comninel, George C. 1987, *Rethinking the French Revolution: Marxism and the Revisionist Challenge*, London: Verso.

—— 2000, 'English Feudalism and the Origins of Capitalism', *The Journal of Peasant Studies*, 27, 4: 1–53.

—— n.d., 'Capital as a Social Relation', draft essay, York University.

Colley, Linda 1982, *In Defiance of Oligarchy: The Tory Party 1714–1760*, Cambridge: Cambridge University Press.

Collier, Frances 1965, *The Family Economy of the Working Classes in the Cotton Industry, 1784–1833*, edited by Richard S. Fitton for the Chetham Society, Manchester: Manchester University Press.

Cooke-Taylor, Richard Whately 1894, *The Factory System and the Factory Acts*, London: Methuen.

Cooper, Thomas 1875, *The Life of Thomas Cooper: Written by Himself*, London: Hodder and Stoughton.

Cornish, William Robert 1969, 'English Law and Order', a review of *A History of English Criminal Law and its Administration from 1750*, Vol. 4: *Grappling for Control*, by Leon Radzinowicz, *The Yale Law Journal*, 78, 8: 1482–91.

Cowie, Leonard Wallace 1956, *Henry Newman: An American in London, 1703–43*. London: S.P.C.K.

Colli, Edgar Leigh and Major Greenwood 1977 [1921], *The Health of the Industrial Worker*, reprint, Manchester: Ayer Publishing.

Cotton Times 2000, 'Thomas Highs and his Spinning Machines', *Understanding the Industrial Revolution*, available at: <http://www.cottontimes.co.uk/highs.htm>.

Counsell, Christine and Chris Steer 1993, *Industrial Britain the Workshop of the World*, Cambridge: Cambridge University Press.

Crafts, Nicholas F.R. 1985, *British Economic Growth During the Industrial Revolution*, Oxford: Oxford University Press.

—— 1994, 'The Industrial Revolution', in Floud and McCloskey (eds.) 1994.

Crafts, Nicholas F.R. and Charles Knickerbocker Harley 1992, 'Output Growth and the British Industrial Revolution: A Restatement of the Crafts-Harley View', *Economic History Review*, 45, 4: 703–30.

Crouzet, François 1964, 'Wars, Blockade, and Economic Change in Europe, 1792–1815', *The Journal of Economic History*, 24, 4: 567–88.

Crowther, Margaret Anne 1981, *The Workhouse System*, Athens, GA: The University of Georgia Press.

Daintith, John 1994, *Biographical Encyclopedia of Scientists*, London: CRC Press.

Dale, Richard 2004, *The First Crash: Lessons from the South Sea Bubble*, Princeton, NJ: Princeton University Press.

Davidson, Neil 2003, 'Class Consciousness and National Consciousness in the Scottish General Strike of 1820', in Flett and Renton (eds.) 2003.

Davis, John A. 1990, 'Industrialization in Britain and Europe before 1850: New Perspectives and Old Problems', in Mathias and Davis (eds.) 1990

Davison, Lee *et al.* (eds.) 1992, *Stilling the Grumbling Hive: The Response to Social and Economic Problems in England, 1689–1750*, New York: St. Martin's Press.

Deane, Phyllis 1987 [1965], *The First Industrial Revolution*, second edition, Cambridge: Cambridge University Press.

Deane, Phyllis and William Alan Cole 1969, *British Economic Growth, 1688–1959 Trends and Structure*, Cambridge: Cambridge University Press.

DeCastro, John Paul 1926, *The Gordon Riots*, London: H. Milford.

Defoe, Daniel 1971 [1796], *A Tour through the Whole Island of Great Britain*, edited with an introduction and notes by Pat Rogers, Harmondsworth: Penguin Books.

D'Eichtal, Gustave 1977 [1828], *A French Sociologist Looks at Britain: Gustave d'Eichthal and British Society in 1828*, translated and edited by Barrie M. Ratcliffe and W.H. Chaloner, Manchester: Manchester University Press.

Delieb, Eric 1971, *Matthew Boulton: Master Silversmith 1760–1790*; New York: Clarkson N. Potter; also published as *The Great Silver Manufactory. Matthew Boulton and the Birmingham Silversmiths 1760–1790*, London: Studio Vista.

Derry, John Wesley 2001, *Politics in the Age of Fox, Pitt and Liverpool*, London: Palgrave.

Derry, Thomas K. 1931, 'The Repeal of the Apprenticeship Clauses of the Statute of Apprentices', *The Economic History Review*, 3, 1: 67–87.

De Vries, Jan 1994, 'The Industrial Revolution and the Industrious Revolution', papers presented at the Fifty-Third Annual Meeting of the Economic History Association, *The Journal of Economic History*, 54, 2: 249–70.

Dickinson, Henry Winram 1937, *Matthew Boulton*, Cambridge: Cambridge University Press.

Dickson, Peter George Muir 1967, *The Financial Revolution in England: A Study in the Development of Public Credit, 1688–1756*, London: Macmillan.

Dinwiddy, John Rowland 1974, 'The 'Black Lamp' in Yorkshire 1801–1880', *Past and Present*, 64: 113–23.

Dobb, Maurice 1947, *Studies in the Development of Capitalism*, New York: International Publishers.

—— 1978 [1950], 'A Reply', in Sweezy *et al.* (eds.) 1978.

Dobson, C.R. 1980, *Masters and Journeymen: A Pre-History of Industrial Relations, 1771–1800*, London: Rowman and Littlefield.

Dodd, William 1968, *The Factory System Illustrated*, new edition, New York: A.M. Kelley.

Donnelly, F.K. 1976, 'The Scottish Rising of 1820: A Reinterpretation', *Scottish Tradition*, 6: 27–37.

Douglas, David *et al.* (eds.) 1996, *English Historical Documents*, London: Routledge.

Dublin, Thomas 1991, 'Rural Putting-Out Work in Early Nineteenth-Century New England: Women and the Transition to Capitalism in the Countryside', *The New England Quarterly*, 64, 4: 531–73.

Dunkley, Peter 1981, 'Whigs and Paupers: The Reform of the English Poor Laws, 1830–1834', *The Journal of British Studies*, 20, 2: 124–49.

Durie, Alastair John Lindsay 1979, *The Scottish Linen Industry in the Eighteenth Century*, Edinburgh: John Donald Publishers.

Eagles, John, Thomas Brereton and William Henry Warrington 1832, *The Bristol Riots: Their Causes, Progress, and Consequences*, London: Cadell.

Eatwell, John and Murray Millgate (eds.) 1987, *The New Palgrave Marxian Economics*, Vol. 2: *E-J*, London: MacMillan.

Ede, Andrew 2006, *The Chemical Element: A Historical Perspective*, Westport, CT: Greenwood Press.

Eden, Sir Frederick 1996, 'On the State of the Poor in 1797', in Douglas *et al.* (eds.) 1996.

Ehrenberg, Richard 1985, *Capital and Finance in the Age of the Renaissance: A Study of the Fuggers and their Connections*, translated from the German by H.M. Lucas, Fairfield, NJ: August M. Kelley Publishers.

Ellison, Thomas 1886, *The Cotton Trade of Great Britain, Including a History of the Liverpool Cotton Market and of the Liverpool Cotton Brokers' Association*, London: E. Wilson.

Emsley, Clive 1985, 'Repression, "Terror" and the Rule of Law during the Decade of the French Revolution', *The English Historical Review*, 100, 397: 801–25.

Encyclopedia Britannica 1910–11, *The Encyclopedia Britannica: a dictionary of arts, sciences, literature and general information*, Volume 11, New York: The Encyclopedia Britannica Company.

Engdahl, F. William 2004, *Century Of War: Anglo-American Oil Politics and the New World Order*, London: Pluto Press.

Engels, Frederick 1975a, 'The Position of England: The Eighteenth Century', in Marx and Engels 1975.

—— 1975b [1850], 'The English Ten Hours Bill', in Marx and Engels 1975.

—— 1993 [1845] *The Condition of the Working Class in England*, Oxford: Oxford University Press.

Engerman, Stanley L. 1994, 'Mercantilism and Overseas Trade, 1700–1800', in Floud and McCloskey (eds.) 1994.

Epstein, Steven A. 1991, *Wage Labor & Guilds in Medieval Europe*, Chapel Hill: University of North Carolina Press.

Evans, Eric J. 1994, *The Great Reform Act of 1832*, London: Routledge.

Evans, Neil 1989, 'Two Paths to Economic Development', in Huson (ed.) 1989.

Evans, Nesta 1985, *The East Anglian Linen Industry: Rural Industry and Local Economy, 1500–1850*, Brookfield, VT: Gower Publishing.

Everard, William, *et al.* 1973, 'The True Levellers' Standard Advanced: Or, The State of Community Opened and Presented to the Sons of Men', in Hill (ed.) 1973.

Feavearyear, Albert Edgar 1931, *The Pound Sterling: A History of English Money*, Oxford: Clarendon Press.

Feiling, Keith Grahame 1938, *The Second Tory Party, 1714–1832*, London: MacMillan and Co.

Fiennes, Celia 1949, *The Journeys of Celia Fiennes*, revised edition, edited and with an introduction by Christopher Morris, foreword by G.M. Trevelyan, London: Cresset Press.

Fischer, Frederick Jack (ed.) 1961, *Essays in the Economic and Social History of Tudor and Stuart England: in Honour of R.H. Tawney*, Cambridge: Cambridge University Press.

Fitton, Robert Sucksmith 1989, *The Arkwrights Spinners of Fortune*, Manchester: Manchester University Press.

Fitton, Robert Sucksmith and Alfred P. Wadsworth 1958, *The Strutts and the Arkwrights. 1758–1830: a Study of the Early Factory System*, Manchester: Manchester University Press.

Flett, Keith and David Renton (eds.) 2003, *New Approaches to Socialist History*, Cheltenham: New Clarion Press.

Flick, Alexander Clarence 1909, *The Rise of the Mediaeval Church and its Influence on the Civilization of Western Europe from the First to the Thirteenth Century*, London: G.P. Putnam's Sons.

Flinn, Michael Walter 1957, 'Introduction' to *The Law Book of the Crowley Iron Works*, London: Bernard Quaritch.

—— 1961, 'The Poor Employment Act of 1817', *The Economic History Review*, n.s., 14, 1: 82–92.

—— 1966, *The Origins of the Industrial Revolution*, New York: Barnes and Noble.

Floud, Roderick 1997, *The People and the British Economy, 1830–1914*, Oxford: Oxford University Press.

Floud, Roderick and David N. McCloskey (eds.) 1994 [1981], *The Economic History of Britain Since 1700*, Vol. 1: *1700–1860*, second edition, Cambridge: Cambridge University Press.

Flynn, John Thomas 1941, *Men of Wealth: The Story of Twelve Significant Fortunes from the Renaissance to the Present Day*, New York: Simon and Schuster.

Fried, Morton Herbert 1967, *The Evolution of Political Society: An Essay in Political Anthropology*, New York: Random House.

Fryer, Peter 1993, *Aspects of British Black History*, London: Index Books.

Fortier, Rénald 2004, *The Balloon Era*, Ottawa: Canada Aviation Museum.

Foster, John 1974, *Class Struggle and the Industrial Revolution: Early Industrial Capitalism in Three English Towns*, with an introduction by Eric J. Hobsbawm, London: Weidenfeld and Nicholson.

Fox, Alan 1985, *History and Heritage: The Social Origins of the British Industrial Relations System*, London: Allen and Unwin.

Fox, Harold S.A. 1979, 'Local Farmers' Associations and the Circulation of Agricultural Information in Nineteenth-Century England', in Fox and Butlin (eds.) 1979.

Fox, Harold S.A. and Robin Alan Butlin (eds.) 1979, *Change in the Countryside: Essays on Rural England, 1500–1900*, London: Institute of British Geographers.

Fraser, Rebecca 2005, *The Story of Britain: From the Romans to the Present: a Narrative History*, New York: W.W. Norton and Company.

Fyson, Robert 1988, 'Unionism, Class and Community in the 1830s: Aspects of the National Union of Operative Potters', in Rule (ed.) 1988.

Gale, Walter Keith Vernon 1952, *Boulton. Watt & the Soho Undertakings*, with an appendix by W.A. Sealy, Birmingham: City of Birmingham Museum and Art Gallery, Department of Science and Industry.

Gardiner, Leslie 1961, *Stage-Coach to John o'Groats*, London: Hollis & Carter.

Gash, Norman 1978, 'After Waterloo: British Society and the Legacy of the Napoleonic Wars', *Transactions of the Royal Historical Society*, fifth series, 28: 145–57.

George, Mary Dorothy 1936, 'Revisions in Economic History: IV. The Combination Laws', *The Economic History Review*, 6, 2: 172–8.

—— 1965, *London Life in the Eighteenth Century*, New York: Capricorn Books.

Geraghty, Thomas M. 2006, 'Complementarity and the Rise of the Factory System in English Textiles, 1800–1850', Department of Economics, University of North Carolina, Chapel Hill, available at: <http://www.unc.edu/~tgeraght/personal/Textiles.pdf>.

Gibbs, Graham C. 1969, 'The Revolution in Foreign Policy', in Holmes (ed.) 1969.

Gilboy, Elizabeth Waterman 1936, 'The Cost of Living and Real Wages in Eighteenth Century England', *Review of Economic Statistics*, 18, 3: 134–44.

Goodison, Nicholas 1974, *Ormolu: The Work of Matthew Boulton*, London: Phaidon.

Gonner, Edward Carter Kersey 1889, 'The Early History of Chartism', *The English Historical Review*, 4, 16: 625–44.

—— 1966 [1912], *Common Land and Inclosure*, second edition, London: Routledge.

Gossman, Norbert J. 1983, 'William Cuffay: London's Black Chartist', *Phylon*, 44, 1: 56–65.

Grab, Alexander Israel 2003, *Napoleon and the Transformation of Europe*, London: Macmillan.

Gray, Jane 2005, *Spinning the Threads of Uneven Development: Gender and Industrialization in Ireland during the Long Eighteenth Century*, Oxford: Lexington Books.

Greeley, Horace 1853, *Art and Industry: As Represented in the Exhibition at the Crystal Palace, New York—1853–4: Showing the Progress and State of the Various Useful and Esthetic Pursuits*, New York: Redfield, New York Exhibition of the Industry of All Nations.

Greenburg, Arthur 2007, *From Alchemy to Chemistry in Picture and Story*, Hoboken, NJ: John Wiley and Sons.

Gregg, Edward 1980, *Queen Anne*, London: Routledge and Kegan Paul.

Gregory, Derek 1982, *Regional Transformation and Industrial Revolution: A Geography of the Yorkshire Woollen Industry*, Minneapolis: University of Minnesota Press.

Gross, Izhak 1980, 'The Abolition of Negro Slavery and British Parliamentary Politics 1832–3', *The Historical Journal*, 23, 1: 63–85.

Guest, Richard Arkwright 1823, *A Compendious History of the Cotton-Manufacture; with a Disproval of the Claim of Sir Richard Arkwright to the Invention of its Ingenious Machinery*, Manchester: Joseph Pratt.

Gullickson, Gay L. 1983, 'Agriculture and Cottage Industry: Redefining the Causes of Proto-Industrialization', *Journal of Economic History*, 43, 4: 831–50.

Habakkuk, Hrothgar John 1956, 'The Eighteenth Century', *Economic History Review*, second series, 8, 3: 434–8.

Hammond, John Lawrence and Barbara Hammond 1974a [1911], *The Village Labourer, 1760–1832: A Study in the Government of England before the Reform Bill*, London: Longman, Green and Company.

—— 1974b [1925], *The Rise of Modern Industry*, reprint, New York: Haskell House.

—— 1995 [1917], *The Town Labourer, 1760–1832: The New Civilisation*, London: Longmans, Green and Co.

Hardcastle, Peter 2005, *Canals and Waterways: Roots and Routes* (1994–2004), available at: <http://www.canals.btinternet.co.uk/canals/fossdykewithamroot.htm>.

Hardie, David W.F. 1972, 'The Macintoshes and the Origins of the Chemical Industry', in Musson (ed.) 1972, 168–94.

Harling, Philip 2001, *The Modern British State: An Historical Introduction*, Cambridge, UK: Polity; Malden, Massachusetts: Blackwell.

Harling, Philip and Peter Mandler 1993, 'From "Fiscal-Military" State to Laissez-Faire State, 1760–1850', *The Journal of British Studies*, 32, 1: 44–70.

Harrison, Brian and Patricia Hollis 1967, 'Liberalism and the Life of Robert Lowery', *The English Historical Review*, 82, 324: 503–35.

Harte, Negley B. 1973, 'The Rise of Protection and the English Linen Trade, 1690–1790', in Jenkins and Ponting (eds.) 1973.

Harte, Negley B. and Kenneth G. Ponting (eds.) 1973, *Textile History and Economic History: Essays in Honour of Miss Julia de Lacy Mann*, Manchester: Manchester University Press.

Hartmann, Thom 2004 [1998], *The Last Hours of Ancient Sunlight: Revised and Updated: The Fate of the World and What We Can Do Before It's Too Late*, revised edition, New York: Three Rivers Press.

Hartwell, Ronald Maxwell 1975, 'The Rising Standard of Living in England, 1800–50', in Taylor (ed.) 1975.

Harvie, Christopher 1986, 'Revolution and the Rule of Law (1789–1851)', in Morgan (ed.) 1986.

Hatcher, John 1984, *The History of the British Coal Industry*, Volume 1: *Before 1700: Towards the Age of Coal*, Oxford: Clarendon Press.

Hay, Douglas 1975, 'Property, Authority and the Criminal Law', in Hay *et al.* (eds.) 1975.

—— 1982, 'War, Dearth and Theft in the Eighteenth Century: The Record of the English Courts', *Past and Present*, 95, 1: 117–60.

Hay, Douglas and Paul Craven 2004, *Masters, Servants and Magistrates in Britain and the Empire, 1562–1955*, Chapel Hill: University of North Carolina Press.

Hay, Douglas and Nicholas Rogers 1997, *Eighteenth Century English Society*, Oxford: Oxford University Press.

Hay, Douglas *et al.* 1975, *Albion's Fatal Tree: Crime and Society in Eighteenth-Century England*, New York: Pantheon Books.

Haynes, Michael 1988, 'Employers and Trade Unions, 1824–1850', in Rule (ed.) 1988.

Heilbroner, Robert L. 1967, 'Do Machines Make History?', *Technology and Culture*, 8, 3: 335–45.

Henrycort.com 2007, 'Fining before Cort', available at: <http://henrycort.net/fgprehc.htm>.

Herbruck, Wendell 1929, 'Forestalling, Regrating and Engrossing', *Michigan Law Review*, 27, 4: 365–88.

Hertz, Gerald Berkeley 1909 'The English Silk Industry in the Eighteenth Century', *The English Historical Review*, 24, 96: 710–27.

Hibbert, Christopher 1958, *King Mob: The Story of Lord George Gordon and the London Riots of 1780*, first edition, Cleveland: World Publishing Co.

Hibbert, Francis Aidan 1970 [1891], *The Influence and Development of English Guilds: As Illustrated by the History of the Craft Gilds of Shrewsbury*, reprint, New York: A.M. Kelley.

Hidden, Norman 1989, 'Jethro Tull I, II and III', *The Agricultural History Review*, 37, 1: 26–35.

Hill, Christopher 1961, *The Century of Revolution 1603–1714*, London: W.W. Norton.

—— 1967, *Reformation to Industrial Revolution*, volume 2 of *The Pelican Economic History of Britain, 1530–1780*, London: Penguin.

—— 1991 [1972], *The World Turned Upside Down: Radical Ideas During the English Revolution*, reprint, London: Penguin.

—— (ed.) 1973, *Winstanley: The Law of Freedom and Other Writings*, Harmondsworth: Penguin.

Hilton, Boyd 1988, 'The Political Arts of Lord Liverpool', *Transactions of the Royal Historical Society*, fifth series, 38: 147–70.

Hilton, Rodney J. 1978 [1976] 'Introduction', in Sweezy *et al.* 1978.

—— 1985, 'A Crisis of Feudalism', in Aston and Philpin (eds.) 1985.

Hitchcock, Tim 1992, 'Paupers and Preachers: The SPCK and the Parochial Workhouse Movement', in Davison *et al.* (eds.) 1992.

Hobsbawm, Eric John Ernest 1952, 'The Machine Breakers', *Past and Present*, 1: 57–70.

—— 1986 [1968], *Industry and Empire: From 1750 to the Present Day*, reprint, New York: Penguin Books.

—— 1994 [1962], *The Age of Revolution 1789–1848*, reprint, London: Abacus.

Hobsbawm, Eric John Ernest and George Rudé 1968, *Captain Swing*, New York: Random House.

Hodgson, R.I. 1979, 'The Progress of Enclosure in County Durham, 1550–1870' in Fox and Butlin (eds.) 1979, 83–102.

Hoffmann, Walther G. 1955, *British industry, 1700–1950*, translated by W.O. Henderson and W.H. Chaloner, Oxford: Basil Blackwell.

Holcroft, Thomas 1944 [1780], *Thomas Holcroft's 'A Plain and Succinct Narrative of the Gordon Riots'*, reprint, Atlanta: Emory University.

Holkham Hall and Estate 2008, available at: <http://www.holkham.co.uk/>.

Holmes, Geoffrey (ed.) 1969, *Britain After the Glorious Revolution 1689–1714*. London: Macmillan.

—— 1969, 'Harley, St John and the Death of the Tory Party', in Holmes (ed.) 1969.

Honeychurch, Lennox 2000, *The Caribbean People*, Book 3, Cheltenham: Nelson Thornes.

Honeyman, Katrina 1983, *Origins of Enterprise: Business Leadership in the Industrial Revolution*, Manchester: Manchester University Press.

Honigsheim, Paul 1949, 'Max Weber as Historian of Agriculture and Rural Life', *Agricultural History*, 23, 3: 179–213.

Hoppit, Julian 1991, 'A Very Polite and Commercial People', review of *The Making of the English Middle Class: Business, Society and Family Life in London 1660–1730*, by Peter Earle and *The Culture of Capital: Art, Power and the Nineteenth-Century Middle Class*, by Janet Wolff and John Seed, *The Journal of British Studies*, 30, 3: 345–9.

—— 2000, *A Land of Liberty? England 1689–1727*, Oxford: Oxford University Press.

Hopwood, Edwin 1969, *The Lancashire Weavers' Story: A History of the Lancashire cotton Industry and the Amalgamated Weavers' Association*, Manchester: Amalgamated Weavers Association.

Hoskins, William George 1935, *Industry, Trade and People in Exeter, 1688–1800: With Special Reference to the Serge Industry*, Manchester: Manchester University Press.

Hough, Granville W. 2005, 'How Global Conflict Influenced the Outcome of the American War for Independence and Postwar World Development', The National Society of the Sons of the American Revolution, South Coast Chapter CASSAR, available at: <http://www.sar.org/history/global-1.htm>.

Houston, Rab and Keith D.M. Snell 1984, 'Proto-Industrialization? Cottage Industry. Social Change and Industrial Revolution', *The Historical Journal*, 27, 2: 473–92.

Howell, David Luke 1992, 'Proto-Industrial Origins of Japanese Capitalism', *Journal of Asian Studies*, 51, 2: 269–86.

Hudson, Pat 1981, 'Proto-industrialization: the case of the West Riding Wool Textile Industry in the 18th and early 19th

centuries', *History Workshop: A Journal of Socialist Historians*, 12: 34–53.
—— 1983, 'From Manor to Mill: The West Riding in Transition', in Berg (ed.) 1983.
—— 1986, *The Genesis of Industrial Capital: A Study of the West Riding Wool Textile Industry, c. 1750–1850*, Cambridge: Cambridge University Press.
—— 1989, 'Capital and credit in the West Riding Wool Textile Industry c. 1750–1850', in Hudson (ed.) 1989.
—— (ed.) 1989, *Regions and Industries*, Cambridge: Cambridge University Press.
—— 1992, *The Industrial Revolution*, New York: Routledge, Chapman and Hall.
—— 1996, 'Proto-industrialization in England', in Ogilvie and Cerman 1996.
Hunt, Margaret R. 1996, *The Middling Sort: Commerce, Gender, and the Family in England, 1680–1780*, Berkeley: University of California Press.
Hurlstone, Tyrrell and Francis Joseph Coltman (eds.) 1866, *Exchequer Reports: Reports of Cases Argued and Determined in the Courts of Exchequer and Exchequer Chamber*, Vol. 3, Easter Term, 27 Vict., to Trinity Vacation, 29 Vict, London: H. Sweet, W. Maxwell and Stevens and Sons.
Hutchins, John Harold 1940, *Jonas Hanway, 1712–1786*, London, Society for Promoting Christian Knowledge.
Hutton, Ronald 1993, *The Restoration: A Political and Religious History of England and Wales, 1658–1667*, Oxford: Clarendon.
Hutton, William 1817, *The History of Derby*, London: Nichols, Son and Bentley.
Ignatieff, Michael 1978, *A Just Measure of Pain: The Penitentiary in the Industrial Revolution, 1750–1850*, New York: Pantheon.
Innes, Joanna 1987, 'Prisons for the Poor: English Bridewells, 1555–1800', in Snyder and Hay (eds.) 1987.
Inwood, Stephen 1998, *A History of London*, New York: Carroll and Graf.
Issawi, Charles 1980, 'De-Industrialization and Re-Industrialization in the Middle East since 1800', *International Journal of Middle East Studies*, 12, 4: 469–79.
Jackson, Christine (ed.) 2004, *Newbury Kendrick Workhouse Records 1627–1641*, Reading: Berkshire Record Society.
James, Lawrence 1994, *The Rise and Fall of the British Empire*, New York: St. Martin's.
James, Peter and Nick Thorpe 1994, *Ancient Inventions*, New York: Ballantine Books.
Jefferson, Thomas 1774, *A Summary View of the Rights of British America set forth in some Resolutions intended for the Inspection of the present Delegates of the People of Virginia, now in Convention*, London: re-printed for G. Kearsly.
Jenkins, David T. 1973, 'Early Factory Development in the West Riding of Yorkshire, 1770–1800', in Harte and Ponting (eds.) 1973.
Jenkins, David T. and Kenneth G. Ponting 1982, *The British Wool Textile Industry 1770–1914*, London: Heinemann.
Jenkins, Terence Andrew 1999, *Sir Robert Peel*, British History in Perspective Series, edited by Jeremy Black, London: Macmillan.
Jephson, Henry Lorenzo, *The Platform: its rise and progress*, Vol. 2, New York: Macmillan.
John, A.H. 1961, 'Aspects of English Economic Growth in the First Half of the Eighteenth Century', *Economica*, new series 28, 110: 176–90.
—— 1965, 'Agricultural Productivity and Economic Growth in England, 1700–1760', *Journal of Economic History*, 25, 1: 19–34.
Johnson, Matthew 1996, *An Archaeology of Capitalism*, Oxford: Blackwell.
Johnson, Ross 2004, *Sentenced to Cross the Raging Sea: The Story of Sam Johnson Victim of Oldham*, Sydney: Wild and Woolley.
Jones, Dwyryd Wyn 1988, *War and Economy in the Age of William III and Marlborough*, Oxford: Basil Blackwell.
Jones, David John Victor 1989, *Rebecca's Children: A Study of Rural Society, Crime and Protest*, Oxford: Clarendon.
Jones, Eric Lionel (ed.) 1967, *Agriculture and Economic Growth in England 1650–1815*, London: Methuen.
—— 1974 [1968], 'Agricultural Origins of Industry', in Jones (ed.) 1974.
—— (ed.) 1974, *Agriculture and the Industrial Revolution*, New York: Wiley.
—— 1977, 'Environment, Agriculture and Industrialization in Europe', *Agricultural History*, 51, 3: 491–502.

—— 1981, *The European Miracle: Environments, Economies, and Geopolitics in the History of Europe and Asia*, Cambridge: Cambridge University Press.

Jones, Mary Gwladys 1938, *The Charity School Movement: A Study of Eighteenth Century Puritanism in Action*, Cambridge: Cambridge University Press.

Jones, Steven R.H. 1987, 'Technology, Transaction Costs, and the Transition to Factory Production in the British Silk Industry, 1700–1870', *The Journal of Economic History*, 47, 1: 71–96.

Joyce, Patrick (ed.) 1987, *The Historical Meanings of Work*, Cambridge: Cambridge University Press.

Jubb, Michael 1984, 'Economic Policy and Economic Development', in Black (ed.) 1984.

Jupp, Peter T. 1990, 'The Landed Elite and Political Authority in Britain, ca. 1760–1850', *The Journal of British Studies*, 29, 1: 53–79.

Kahrl, Robert C. 2001, *Patent Claim Construction*, New York: Aspen Law and Business.

Kellett, James R. 1958, 'The Breakdown of Gild and Corporation Control over the Handicraft and Retail Trade in London', *The Economic History Review*, 10, 3: 381–94.

Kelly, James 1991–92, 'Harvests and Hardship: Famine and Scarcity in Ireland in the Late 1720s', *Studia Hibernica*, 26.

Kerridge, Eric 1968 [1967], *The Agricultural Revolution*, New York: A.M. Kelley.

Key, Newton and R.O. Bucholz (eds.) 2004, *Sources and Debates in English History, 1485–1714*, Oxford: Blackwell.

Kiernan, Victor Gordon 1983, 'Revolution', in Bottomore *et al.* (eds.) 1983.

King, Steven and Alannah Tomkins (eds.) 2003, *The poor in England 1700–1850: An economy of makeshifts*, Manchester: Manchester University Press.

King, Steven and Geoffrey Timmins 2001, *Making Sense of the Industrial Revolution: English Economy and Society 1700–1850*, Manchester: Manchester University Press.

Kitson Clark, George 1951, 'The Repeal of the Corn Laws and the Politics of the Forties', *The Economic History Review*, 4, 1: 1–13.

Klíma, Arnošt 1987, 'Agrarian Class Structure and Economic Development in Pre-Industrial Bohemia', in Aston and Philpin (eds.) 1987.

Kriedte, Peter, Hans Medick and Jürgen Schlumbohm 1981, *Industrialization Before Industrialization: Rural Industry in the Genesis of Capitalism*, translated by Beate Schempp, Cambridge: Cambridge University Press.

Knight, Charles 1851, *London*, London: H.G. Bohn.

Kriegel, Abraham D. 1968, 'The Politics of the Whigs in Opposition, 1834–1835', *The Journal of British Studies*, 7, 2: 65–91.

—— 1971, 'The Irish Policy of Lord Grey's Government', *The English Historical Review*, 86, 338: 22–45.

Kussmaul, Ann S. 1979, 'Servants in Husbandry in Early Modern England', *The Journal of Economic History*, 39, 1: 329–31.

—— 1994 [1981], 'The Pattern of Work as the Eighteenth Century Began', in Floud and McCloskey (eds.) 1994.

Lacher, Hannes 2006, *Beyond Globalization: Capitalism, territoriality and the international relations of modernity*, London: Routledge.

Landes, David Saul 1986, 'What Do Bosses Really Do?' *The Journal of Economic History*, 46, 3: 585–623.

—— 1991 [1961], *The Unbound Prometheus: Technological Change in Industrial Development in Western Europe from 1750 to the Present*, reprint, Cambridge: Cambridge University Press.

Langford, Paul 1986 [1984], 'The Eighteenth Century (1688–1789)', in Morgan (ed.) 1986.

Langton, John 2000, 'Proletarianization in the Industrial Revolution: Regionalism and Kinship in the Labour Markets of the British Coal Industry from the Seventeenth to the Nineteenth Centuries', *Transactions of the Institute of British Geographers*, new series, 25, 1: 31–49.

Latimer, Jon 2008, 'The Battle of Fishguard: The Last Invasion of Great Britain', available at: <http://www.wargame.ch/wc/nwc/newsletter/21st_edition/Newsletter21/fishguard.html>.

Lavrovsky, Vladimir M. 1933, 'Tithe Commutation as a Factor in the Gradual Decrease of Landownership by the English Peasantry', *Economic History Review*, first series, 4: 273–89.

Lawson, Robert 2007, 'Origin of the Word Capitalism: Thackeray not Marx?', *Adam Smith's Lost Legacy*, available at: <http://adamsmithslostlegacy.com/2007/02/origins-of-word-capitalism-thackeray.html>.

Lazonick, William 1974, 'Karl Marx and Enclosures in England', *Review of Radical Political Economics*, 6, 2: 1–59.

Leadam, Isaac Saunders 1969 [1912], *The Political History of England*, volume 9: *From the Accession of Anne to the Death of George II*, New York: Greenwood Press.

Leeson, Robert Arthur 1979, *Travelling Brothers: The Six Centuries' Road from Craft Fellowship to Trade Unionism*, London: Allen & Unwin.

—— 1984, 'Business as Usual: Craft Union Developments 1834–1851', *Bulletin of the Society for the Study of Labour History*, 49: 15–17.

L'Estrange, Alfred Guy 1874, *History of English Humour: With an Introduction Upon Ancient Humour*, Vol. 2, London: Hurst and Blackett.

Letwin, William L. 1954, 'The English Common Law Concerning Monopolies', *The University of Chicago Law Review*, 21, 3: 355–85.

Levine, David and Keith Wrightson 1991, *The Making of an Industrial Society: Whickham 1560–1765*, Oxford: Clarendon Press.

Libby, Douglas Cole 1991, 'Proto-Industrialisation in a Slave Society: The Case of Minas Gerais', *Journal of Latin American Studies*, 23, 1: 1–35.

Linebaugh, Peter 1975, 'The Tyburn Riot Against the Surgeons', in Hay *et al.* 1975.

—— 2000, *The Many-Headed Hydra: Sailors, Slaves, Commoners, and the Hidden History of the Revolutionary Atlantic*, London: Verso.

Lloyd-Jones, Roger 1990, 'The First Kondratieff: The Long Wave and the British Industrial Revolution', *Journal of Interdisciplinary History*, 20, 4: 581–605.

Locke, John 1876 [1697], 'Report of the Board of Trade, 31 August 1697', in Bourne 1876.

The London Quarterly Review 1860, 'Cotton-Spinning Machines and their Inventors', *The London Quarterly Review*, 107, London: Theodore Foster.

Longson, William 1827, *An Appeal to Masters, Workmen and the Public Showing the Cause of the Distress of the Labouring Classes*, Manchester.

Lord, John 1966, *Capital and Steam Power 1750–1800*, London: Frank Cass.

Love, John 1986, 'Max Weber and the Theory of Ancient Capitalism', *History and Theory*, 25, 2: 152–72.

Lythe, Samuel George Edgar 1958, 'The Union of Crowns in 1603 and the Debate on Economic Integration', *The Scottish Journal of Political Economy*, 5: 219–28.

Macpherson, David 1805, *Annals of Commerce, Manufactures, Fisheries and Navigation*, London: Nichols and Son.

Macaulay, Thomas Babington, Lord 1858 [1830], *Essays Critical and Miscellaneous*, revised edition, Boston: Phillips, Samson and Company.

—— 1886, *The History of England from the Accession of James II*, Vol. 2, London: Longmans, Green and Company.

—— 1886a, *The History of England from the Accession of James II*, Vol. 5, London: Longmans, Green and Company.

Marfany, Julie 2010, 'Is it still helpful to talk about proto-industrialization? Some suggestions from a Catalan case study', *Economic History Review*, 53, 4: 942–73.

Marglin, Stephen A. 1974, 'What Do Bosses Do?: The Origins and Functions of Hierarchy in Capitalist Production', *Review of Radical Political Economics*, 6, 60: 60–112.

—— 1975, 'What Do Bosses Do? Part II', *Review of Radical Political Economics*, 7, 1: 20–37.

Maccoby, Simon 2001 [1938], *English Radicalism*, Vol. 5: *1886–1914*, Routledge Library of British Political History, London: Routledge.

—— 2001a [1935–1961], *Labour and Radical Politics 1762–1837*, Routledge Library of British Political History, Vol. 8, London: Routledge.

Mackie, John Duncan 1952, *The Early Tudors, 1485–1558*, Oxford: Oxford University Press.

Makdisi, Saree 2003, *William Blake and the Impossible History of the 1790s*, Chicago: University of Chicago Press.

Malcolmson, Robert W. 1981, *Life and labour in England, 1700–1780*, New York: St. Martin's Press.

Malet, Hugh 1990, *Coal, Cotton and Canals*, Radcliffe, Manchester: Neil Richardson.

Malthus, Thomas Robert Rev. 1836, *Principles of Political Economy, Considered with a View to their Practical Application*, second edition, London: William Pickering.

—— 1960 [1827], *Three Essays on Population*, New York: New American Library for World Literature.

—— 1960 [1798], *An Essay on the Principle of Population*, New York: Modern Library.

—— 1986, *The Works of Thomas Robert Malthus*, edited by E.A. Wrigley and David Souden, London: W. Pickering.

Mantoux, Paul 1961 [1928], *The Industrial Revolution in the Eighteenth Century: An Outline of the Beginnings of the Factory System in England*, revised edition, with an introduction by Professor T.S. Ashton, Oxford: The Alden Press.

Marriott, John Arthur Ransome 2006 [1913], *England Since Waterloo*, London: Methuen.

Marshall, John D. 1989, 'Stages of Industrialization in Cumbria', in Hudson (ed.) 1989.

Martin, Robert Montgomery 1841, 'Commercial Injustice Towards India', *The Colonial magazine and commercial-maritime journal*, 5, 51–62.

Marx, Karl 1906, *Capital: A Critique of Political Economy*, Vol. I, edited by Friedrich Engels, first American edition, edited by Ernest Untermann, New York: The Modern Library.

—— 1967 [1894], *Capital, A Critique of Political Economy*, Volume III, edited with an Introduction by Frederick Engels, 11th printing, New York: International Publishers.

—— 1973 [1857], *Grundrisse: Foundations of the Critique of Political Economy*, translated with a Foreword by Martin Nicolaus, New York: Penguin Books.

—— 1989, 'Economic Manuscripts of 1861–3', in Marx and Engels 1975–2005, Vol. 31.

Marx, Karl and Frederick Engels 1975, *Articles on Britain*, Moscow: Progress Publishers.

—— 1945 [1942], *Selected Works*, Volume II, edited by Vladimir Adoratsky, Moscow: Marx-Engels-Lenin Institute.

—— 1975–2005, *Collected Works*, translated by Richard Dixon, *et al.*, New York: International Publishers.

Mathias, Peter 1972, 'Who Unbound Prometheus? Science and Technical Change, 1600–1800', in Musson (ed.) 1972.

—— 1979, *The Transformation of England: Essays in the Economic and Social History of England in the Eighteenth Century*, New York: Columbia University Press.

—— 1983 [1969], *The First Industrial Nation: An Economic History of Britain 1700–1914*, second edition, London: Methuen.

Mathias, Peter and John Anthony Davis (eds.) 1990, *The First Industrial Revolutions*, Oxford: Basil Blackwell.

Matthew, Henry Colin Gray 1986, *Gladstone, 1809–1874*, Oxford: Oxford University Press.

McCloskey, Deirdre 1994, '1780–1860: A Survey', in Floud and McCloskey (eds.) 1994.

McKendrick, Neil 1961, 'Josiah Wedgwood and Factory Discipline', *The Historical Journal*, 4, 1: 30–55.

McLynn, Frank 1989, *Crime and Punishment in Eighteenth Century England*, London: Routledge.

McNally, David 1988, *Political Economy and the Rise of Capitalism: A Reinterpretation*, London: University of California Press.

—— 1993, *Against the Market: Political Economy: Market Socialism and the Marxist Critique*, London: Verso.

McNulty, David 1988, 'Bristol Trade Unions in the Chartist Years', in Rule (ed.) 1988.

Medlicott, William Norton (ed.) 1979, *A History of England*, London: Longman

Mendels, Franklin F. 1972, 'Proto-Industrialization: the First Phase of the Industrialization Process', *Journal of Economic History*, 32, 1: 241–61.

Mendle, Michael (ed.) 2001, *The Putney Debates of 1647: The Army, the Levellers, and the English State*, Cambridge: Cambridge University Press.

Merlant, Joachim 1918, *La France et la guerre de l'independence americaine, 1776–1783*, Paris: F. Alcan.

—— 1920, *Soldiers and Sailors of France in the American War for Independence, 1776–1783*, New York: C. Scribner's Sons.
Merriam-Webster 1993, *Merriam Webster's Collegiate Dictionary*, tenth edition, Springfield, MA: Merriam-Webster.
Mickwitz, Gunnar 1936, 'Die Kartellfunktionen der Zünfte und ihne Bedeutung bei der Enstehung des Zünftwesens', *Finska Vetenskaps-Societenen Commentationes Human Litterarum* 8, 3: 1–250.
Miller, John Chester 1959, *Origins of the American Revolution*, Stanford: Stanford University Press.
Miller, Richard 1985, *Analyzing Marx*, Princeton, NJ: Princeton University Press.
Mingay, Gordon Edmund 1956, 'The Agricultural Depression, 1730–1750', *Economic History Review*, 8, 3: 323–38.
—— 1968, *Enclosure and the Small Farmer in the Age of the Industrial Revolution*, Studies in Economic History Series, edited by M.W. Flinn, London: Macmillan.
—— 1997, *Parliamentary Enclosure in England: An Introduction to its Causes, Incidence and Impact 1750–1850*, London: Longman.
Mitchell, Brian Redman and Phyllis Deane 1971, *Abstract of British Historical Statistics*, University of Cambridge Department of Applied Economics Monographs 17, Cambridge: Cambridge University Press.
Moher, James 1988, 'From Suppression to Containment: Roots of Trade Union Law to 1825', in Rule (ed.) 1988.
Mokyr, Joel 1976, 'Growing-Up and the Industrial Revolution in Europe', *Explorations in Economic History*, 13: 371–96.
—— 1990, *The Lever of Riches*, Oxford: Oxford University Press.
—— 1994, 'Technological Change, 1700–1830', in Floud and McCloskey (eds.) 1994.
—— (ed.) 1999, *The British Industrial Revolution: An Economic Perspective*, second edition, Boulder, CO: Westview Press.
Molella, Arthur P. 2005, 'The *Longue Durée* of Abbott Payson Usher', *Technology and Culture*, 46, 4: 779–96.
Mooers, Colin 1991, *The Making of Bourgeois Europe: Absolutism, Revolution, and the Rise of Capitalism in England, France and Germany*, London: Verso.
Moore, D.C. 1965, 'The Corn Laws and High Farming', *The Economic History Review*, new series, 18, 3: 544–61.
Morgan, Kenneth Owen (ed.) 1986 [1984], *The Oxford Illustrated History of Britain*, Oxford: Oxford University Press.
Mori, Jennifer 1997, *William Pitt and the French Revolution, 1785–1795*, Edinburg: Edinburgh University Press.
Morrill, John S. 1984 [1968], 'Mutiny and Discontent in English Provincial Armies 1645–1647', in Slack (ed.) 1984.
Mueller, Gert Heinz 1986, 'Weber and Mommsen: Non-Marxist Materialism', *The British Journal of Sociology*, 37, 1: 1–20.
Mulhall, Michael George 1892, *The Dictionary of Statistics*, London: G. Routledge and Sons.
Mumford, Lewis 1934, *Technics and Civilization*, New York: Harcourt and Brace.
—— 1970, *The Myth of the Machine*, volume 2: *The Pentagon of Power*, London: Secker and Warburg.
Munger, Frank 1981, 'Suppression of Popular Gatherings in England, 1800–1830', *The American Journal of Legal History*, 25, 2: 111–40.
Muskett, Paul 1984, 'The East Anglian Riots of 1822', *Agricultural History Review*, 32: 1–13.
Musson, Albert Edward (ed.) 1972, *Science. Technology and Economic Growth in the Eighteenth Century*, London: Methuen.
Nairn, Tom 1988, *The Enchanted Glass: Britain and its Monarchy*, London: Radius.
Neal, Larry 1994, 'The Finance of Business During the Industrial Revolution', in Floud and McCloskey (eds.) 1994.
Neeson, Jeanette M. 1996 [1993], *Commoners: Common Right, Enclosure and Social Change in England, 1700–1820*, reprint, Cambridge: Cambridge University Press.
Nef, John Ulric 1934, 'The Progress of Technology and the Growth of Large-Scale Industry in Great Britain, 1540–1640', *Economic History Review*, 5, 1: 3–24.
—— 1943, 'The Industrial Revolution Reconsidered', *The Journal of Economic History*, 3, 1: 1–31.
—— 1964, *Industry and Government in France and England, 1540–1640*, Ithaca, NY: Cornell University Press.

—— 1966a [1932], *The Rise of the British Coal Industry*, Vol. 2, London: Routledge & Sons.

—— 1966b [1932], *The Rise of the British Coal Industry*, Vol. 1, London: Routledge & Sons.

Netherton, Robin and Gale R. Owen-Crocker (eds.) 2007, *Medieval Clothing and Textiles*, Vol. 3, Woodbridge: Boydell Press.

Nicholls, Mark 1999, *A History of the Modern British Isles 1529–1603: the Two Kingdoms*, Oxford: Blackwell.

Nicholson, John 1985, *The great liberty riot of 1780: Being an Account of how the People Destroyed the Prisons of London and Set Free the Prisoners, Together with a Thorough Examination of How this Event has been Portrayed in History and Literature*, London: BM Bozo.

Norris, John M. 1958, 'Samuel Garbett and the Early Development of Industrial Lobbying in Great Britain', *The Economic History Review*, new series, 10, 3: 450–60.

Nossiter, Thomas Johnson 1975, *Influence, Opinion and Political Idioms in Reformed England*, Hassocks: Harvester Press.

Oastler, Richard 1830, 'Yorkshire Slavery', *Leeds Mercury*, 29 September.

—— 1841, 'Letter to Thomas Thornhill, Esq., 27 March, 1841', *The Fleet Papers*, 1, 13, London: W.J. Cleaver.

Ogden, Herbert William 1927, *The Geographical Basis of the Lancashire Cotton Industry*, Manchester: Manchester Geographical Society.

Ogilvie, Sheilagh Catheren 1996, 'Social Institutions and Proto-Industrialization', in Ogilvie and Cerman (eds.) 1996.

Ogilvie, Sheilagh Catheren and Markus Cerman 1996, 'Theories of Proto-Industrialization', in Ogilvie and Cerman (eds.) 1996.

Ogilvie, Sheilagh Catheren and Markus Cerman (eds.) 1996, *European Proto-Industrialization*, Cambridge: Cambridge University Press.

O'Gorman, Frank 1986, 'The Unreformed Electorate of Hanoverian England: The Mid-Eighteenth Century to the Reform Act of 1832', *Social History*, 11, 1: 33–52.

Oldland, John 2007, 'The Finishing of English Woollens, 1300–1550', in Netherton and Owen-Crocker (eds.) 2007

Olsen, Kirstin 1999, *Daily Life in 18th Century England*, London: Greenwood Press.

Orth, John Victor 1987, 'English Combination Acts of the Eighteenth Century', *Law and History Review*, 5, 1: 175–211.

Outhwaite, Richard Brian 1991, *Dearth, Public Policy and Social Disturbance in England, 1550–1800*, London: MacMillan.

Owen, John Beresford 1975, *The Eighteenth Century: 1714–1815*, Totowa, NJ: Rowman and Littlefield.

Padover, Saul Kussiel 1978, *Karl Marx: An Intimate Biography*, New York: Mentor New American Library.

Paine, Thomas 1986 [1776] *Common Sense*, edited with an introduction by Isaac Kramnick, Harmondsworth: Penguin.

Parker, Charles Stuart (ed.) 1907, *Life and Letters of Sir James Graham, Second Baronet of Netherby, P. C., G. C. B.* Vol. 1, London, J. Murray.

Parrott, Richard 1752, *Reflections on Various Subjects Relating to Arts and Commerce, Particularly the Consequences of Admitting Foreign Artists on Easier Terms*, London: printed for George Woodfall and C. Corbett.

Pascal, Blaise 1869, *The Thoughts, Letters, and Opuscules of Blaise Pascal*, London: Hurd and Houghton.

Patnaik, Utsa 1972, 'Development of Capitalism in Agriculture: II', *Social Scientist*, 1, 3: 3–19.

Patriquin, Larry 1996, 'English Poor Relief in Capitalist Context', PhD dissertation, York University.

—— 2004, 'The Agrarian Origins of the Industrial Revolution in England', *Review of Radical Political Economics*, 36, 2: 196–216.

—— 2005, 'Agrarian Capitalism and Poor Relief in England, c. 1500–1790: Rethinking the Origins of the Welfare State', *Research in Political Economy*, 22: 3–49.

—— 2006, 'Why Was There No "Old Poor Law" in Scotland and Ireland?', *Journal of Peasant Studies*, 33: 219–47.

Patterson, Judith and Stephen Alsford 2007, 'Glossary', *Medieval English Towns*, available at: <http://www.trytel.com/~tristan/>.

Pelham, Henry 1976 [1963], *A History of British Trade Unionism*, third edition, London: Penguin Books.

Petulla, Joseph M. 1988, *American Environmental History*, second edition, Columbus, OH: Merrill Publishing.

Phillips, John A. and Charles Wetherell 1991, 'The Great Reform Act of 1832 and the Rise of Partisanship', *The Journal of Modern History*, 63, 4: 621–46.

—— 1995, 'The Great Reform Act of 1832 and the Political Modernization of England', *The American Historical Review*, 100, 2: 411–36.

Philpot, Gordon 1975, 'Enclosure and Population Growth in Eighteenth-Century England', *Explorations in Economic History*, 12: 19–46.

Pickering, Paul A. 2001, '"And Your Petitioners &c": Chartist Petitioning in Popular Politics, 1838–1848', *The English Historical Review*, 116, 466: 368–88.

Pirenne, Henry 1969 [1925], *Medieval Cities: The Origins and the Revival of Trade*, reprint, Princeton, NJ: Princeton University Press.

Platt, Richard 1994, *Smithsonian Visual Timeline of Inventions*, London: Dorling Kindersley.

Plotz, John 2000, 'Crowd Power: Chartism, Carlyle, and the Victorian Public Sphere', *Representations*, 70: 87–114.

Plumb, John Harold 1963 [1950], *England in the Eighteenth Century*, Volume 7 of *The Pelican History of England*, Harmondsworth: Penguin Books.

Polanyi, Karl 1957 [1944], *The Great Transformation*, first Beacon edition, Beacon Hill, Boston: Beacon Press.

Pollard, A. Mark and Carl Heron 1996, *Archaeological Chemistry*, London: Royal Society of Chemistry.

Pollard, Sidney 1965, *The Genesis of Modern Management: A Study of the Industrial Revolution in Great Britain*, Cambridge, MA: Harvard University Press.

—— 1981, *Peaceful Conquest: the Industrialization of Europe, 1760–1970*, Oxford: Oxford University Press.

Post, Charles 2002, 'Comments on the Brenner-Wood Exchange on the Low Countries', *Journal of Agrarian Change*, 2, 1: 88–95.

Powell, Martyn J. 2002, 'Ireland: Radicalism, Rebellion and Union', in Dickinson (ed.) 2002.

Price, Derek J. de Solla 1975, *Science Since Babylon*, second edition, New Haven, CT: Yale University Press.

Price, Richard 1986, *Labour in British Society: An Interpretive History*, London; Sydney; Dover, NH: Croom Helm.

Quataert, Donald 1986, 'Machine Breaking and the Changing Carpet Industry of Western Anatolia, 1860–1908', *Journal of Social History*, 19, 3: 473–89.

Quataert, Jean H. 1988, 'A New View of Industrialization: "Protoindustry" or the Role of Small-Scale, Labor-Intensive Manufacture in the Capitalist Environment', *International Labor and Working-Class History*, 33: 3–22.

Radcliffe, William 1974, *Origin of the New System of Manufacture, Commonly Called 'Power Loom Weaving'*, Clifton, NJ: A.M. Kelly.

Ralph, Philip Lee, *et al.* 1997 [1955], *World Civilizations: Their History and their Culture*, two volumes, ninth edition, London: W.W. Norton.

Randall, Adrian 1982, Review of *Masters and Journeymen*, by C.R. Dobson, *Technology and Culture* 23, 2: 252–6.

—— 1986, 'The Philosophy of Luddism: The Case of the West of England Woollen Workers, ca. 1790–1809', *Technology and Culture*, 27, 1: 1–17.

—— 1989, 'Work, Culture and Resistance to Machinery in the West of England Woollen Industry', in Hudson (ed.) 1989.

—— 1991, *Before the Luddites: Custom, Community and Machinery in the English woolen Industry. 1776–1809*, Cambridge: Cambridge University Press.

Raphael, David Daiches 1985, *Adam Smith*, Past Masters Series, edited by Keith Thomas, Oxford: Oxford University Press.

Rappard, William E. 1913, 'Karl Marx and Labour Legislation', *The Quarterly Journal of Economics*, 27, 3: 530–5.

Razzell, Peter E. and Richard W. Wainwright (eds.) 1973, *The Victorian Working Class: Selections from Letters to the Morning Chronicle*, London: Frank Cass.

Rebecca Riots 2008, available at: <http://www.angelfire.com/ga/BobSanders/REBECCA.html>.

Reid, Robert 1989, *The Peterloo Massacre*, London: Heinemann.

Reilly, Robin 1992, *Josiah Wedgwood 1730–1795*, London: Macmillan.

Renard, Georges 1968 [1918], *Guilds in the Middle Ages*, reprint, New York: Kelley Publishers.

Reynolds, Terry S. 2002, *Stronger than a Hundred Men: A History of the Vertical Water Wheel*, Baltimore: The Johns Hopkins University Press.

Ricardo, David 1987 [1817], *Principles of Political Economy and Taxation*, reprint, London: Dent.

Rider, Christine and Michael J. Thompson (eds.) 2000, *The Industrial Revolution in Comparative Perspective*, Malabar: Krieger Publishing.

Roberts, Philip (ed.) 1975, *The Diary of Sir David Hamilton, 1709–1714*, Oxford: Clarendon Press.

Robinson, Austin 1941, Review of *Monopoly and Competition in the English Coal Trade, 1550–1880* by Paul M. Sweezy, *The Economic Journal*, 51, 201: 101–5.

Roebuck, Derek 1990 [1983], *The Background of the Common Law*, second edition, Oxford: Oxford University Press.

Roemer, John E. (ed.) 1986, *Analytical Marxism*, Cambridge: Press Syndicate of the University of Cambridge.

Rogers, Nicholas 1979, 'Money, Land and Lineage: the Big Bourgeoisie of Hanoverian London', *Social History*, 4, 3: 437–54.

Roll, Eric 2013 [1930], An Early Experiment in Industrial Organization: History of the Firm of Boulton and Watt 1775–1805, London: Taylor and Francis.

Rose, J.H. 1983, 'Napoleon and English Commerce', *The English Historical Review*, 8, 32: 704–25.

Rose, R.B. 1961, 'Eighteenth-Century Price Riots and Public Policy in England', *International Review of Social History*, 6: 277–92.

Rosenberg, Justin 1994, *The Empire of Civil Society: A Critique of the Realist Theory of International Relations*, London: Verso.

Rostow, Walt Whitman 1960, *The Stages of Economic Growth, A Non-Communist Manifesto*, Cambridge: Cambridge University Press.

—— 1975, *How it All Began: Origins of the Modern Economy*, New York: McGraw-Hill.

Rowlands, Marie B. 1989, 'Continuity and Change in an Industrialising Society: The Case of the West Midlands', in Hudson (ed.) 1989.

Rudé, George F.E. 1956, 'The Gordon Riots: A Study of the Rioters and Their Victims: The Alexander Prize Essay', *Transcripts of the Royal Historical Society*, fifth series: 93–114.

—— 1959, 'The London Mob of the Eighteenth Century', *Historical Journal*, 2, 1: 1–18.

—— 1981, *The Crowd in History: A Study of Popular Disturbances in France and England, 1730–1848*, London: Lawrence and Wishart.

Rudgeley, Richard 1999, *The Lost Civilizations of the Stone Age*, New York: The Free Press.

Rule, John 1981, *The Experience of Labour in Eighteenth Century English Industry*, New York: St. Martin's Press.

—— (ed.) 1982, *Outside the Law: Studies in Crime and Order, 1650–1850*, Exeter: University of Exeter.

—— 1986, *The Labouring Classes in Early Industrial England, 1750–1850*, Themes in British Social History Series, edited by Dr. J. Stevenson, London: Longman.

—— 1987, 'The Property of Skill in the Period of Manufacture', in Joyce (ed.) 1987.

—— (ed.) 1988, *British Trade Unionism 1750–1850: The Formative Years*, London: Longman.

—— 1992a, *Albion's People: English Society 1714–1815*, London and New York: Longman.

—— 1992b, *The Vital Century: England's Developing Economy, 1714–1815*, London and New York: Longman.

Rupp, Richard A. and Peter R. Townsend 1999, *The Mills at Remington's Run: A Chronological History of the Arkwright Manufacturing Company 1809–1999*, East Greenwich, RI: Meridian Printing.

Russell, Lord John 2008 [1837], 'finality' speech before the Commons, 20 November 1837, available at: <http://www.historyhome.co.uk/polspeech/final.htm>.

Sale, Kirkpatrick 1996 [1995], *Rebels Against the Future: The Luddites and their War on the Industrial Revolution, Lessons for*

the Computer Age, Reading, MA: Addison-Wesley Publishing Company.
Saville, John 1969, 'Primitive Accumulation and Early Industrialisation in Britain', *The Socialist Register*, 6.
Schofield, Robert E. 1972, 'The Industrial Orientation of Science in the Lunar Society of Birmingham', in Musson (ed.) 1972.
Schofield, Roger 1994, 'British Population Change, 1700–1871', in Floud and McCloskey (eds.) 1994.
Scott, Derrik 2004, 'Great Strike of the Northumberland and Durham Coalfield in 1844', available at: <http://www.durham-miner.org.uk/miner/projects.nsf>.
Seal, Graham 1988, 'Tradition and Agrarian Protest in Nineteenth-Century England and Wales', *Folklore*, 99, 2: 146–69.
Sen, Amartya 1981, Poverty and Famines, Oxford: Oxford University Press.
Senior, Nassau 1966, *Selected Writings on Economics*, New York: Augustus M. Kelley.
Shapiro, Seymour 1967, *Capital and the Cotton Industry*, Ithaca, NY: Cornell University Press.
Shady Solís, Ruth 2006, 'Research at Caral: Its Significance for Peru and the World', Proyecto Especial Arqueológico Caral Supe / I.N.C., available at: <http://www.caralperu.gob.pe/trascendencia_ing.htm>.
Shaw, William H. 1979, '"The Handmill Gives You the Feudal Lord", Marx's Technological Determinism', *History and Theory*, 18, 2: 155–76.
Shelley, Percy Bysshe 1892, *The Masque of Anarchy: A Poem*, London: Reeves and Turner, for the Shelley Society.
Shiva, Vandana (ed.) 1994, *Close to Home: Women Reconnect Ecology, Health and Development*, London: Earthscan.
Skillman, Gilbert L. 1995, '*Ne Hic Saltaveris:* The Marxian Theory of Exploitation after Roemer', *Economics and Philosophy*, 11: 309–31.
—— 1996, 'Marxian Value Theory and the Labor-Labor Power Distinction', *Science and Society*, 60, 4: 427–51.
—— 1999, 'Marx's Value-Theoretic Account of Capitalist Exploitation: Non Sequitur or Tautology?', *Science and Society*, 63, 3: 362–72.
Slack, Paul (ed.) 1984 [1968], *Rebellion, popular protest and the social order in early modern England*, Cambridge: Press Syndicate of the University of Cambridge.
—— 1990, *The English Poor Law 1531–1782*, London: Macmillan Education.
—— 1999, *From Reformation to Improvement: Public Welfare in Early Modern England*, the Ford Lectures Delivered in the University of Oxford 1994–1995, Oxford: Clarendon Press.
Sloane, William M. 1898, 'The Continental System of Napoleon', *Political Science Quarterly*, 13, 2: 213–31.
Slosson, Preston William 1916, *The Decline of the Chartist Movement*, New York: Columbia University.
Smail, John 1999, *Merchants, Markets and Manufacture: The English Wool Textile Industry in the Eighteenth Century*, Basingstoke: Palgrave Macmillan.
Smith, Adam 1957 [1776], *An Inquiry into the Nature and Causes of the Wealth of Nations*, edited by Edwin Cannan, New York: The Modern Library.
—— 1979 [1759], *The Theory of Moral Sentiments*, edited by D.D. Raphael and A.L. Macfie, Indianapolis: Liberty Classics.
Smith, John 1969, *Chronicon Rusticum-Commerciale* or *Memoirs of Wool and Being a Collection of History and Argument Concerning the Woolen Manufacture and the Woolen Trade in General*, Vol. 1, New York: A.M. Kelley.
Smith, Jonathan 1981, 'The Strike of 1825', in Wright and Jowitt (eds.) 1981.
Smith, Thomas 1893 [1581], *A Discourse of the Commonweal of this Realm of England*, edited by Elizabeth Lamond, reprint, Cambridge: The Syndics of the Cambridge University Press.
Smout, Thomas Christopher 1969, 'The Road to Union', in Holmes (ed.) 1969.
Snell, Keith D.M. 1985, *Annals of the Labouring Poor: Social Change and Agrarian England 1660–1900*, Cambridge: Cambridge University Press.
Snyder, Francis and Douglas Hay (eds.) 1987, *Labour, Law, and Crime: An Historical Perspective*, London: Tavistock Publications.
Sokoloff, Kenneth Lee and David Dollar 1997, 'Agricultural Seasonality and the Organization of Manufacturing in Early Industrial Economies: The Contrast

Between England and the United States', *The Journal of Economic History*, 57, 2: 288–321.

Soldon, Norbert C. 1998, *John Wilkinson 1728–1808: English Ironmaster and Inventor*, New York: The Edwin Mellen Press.

Spartacus Educational 2008, 'Plug Riots', available at: <http://www.spartacus.schoolnet.co.uk/CHplug.htm>.

Speck, William Arthur 1977, *Stability and Strife England 1714–1760*, Cambridge, MA: Harvard University Press.

Spofford, Ainsworth Rand (ed.) 1879, *American Almanac and Treasure of Facts for the year 1879*, New York: The American News Company.

Staudenmeier, John M. 1985, *Technology's Storytellers: Reweaving the Human Fabric*, Cambridge, MA: Society for the History of Technology and the MIT Press.

Stedman Jones, Gareth 2004, *An End to Poverty?*, New York: Columbia University Press.

Stearns, Peter N. 1998, *The Industrial Revolution in World History*, second edition, Boulder, CO: Westview Press.

Steward, Robert 1969, 'The Ten Hours and Sugar Crises of 1844: Government and the House of Commons in the Age of Reform', *The Historical Journal* 12, 1: 35–9.

Stokes, Randall G. and Andy B. Anderson 1990, 'Disarticulation and Human Welfare in Less Developed Countries', *American Sociological Review*, 55, 1: 63–74.

Stone, Lawrence 1972, *The Causes of the English Revolution*. London: Harper and Row.

—— (ed.) 1965, *Social Change and Revolution in England 1540–1640*, London: Longman.

—— and Jeanne C. Fawtier Stone 1984, *An Open Elite? England, 1540–1880*, Oxford: Clarendon Press.

Strand, Sigvard (ed.) 1979, *Technology and its Impact on Society* (symposium, 1977), Stockholm: Tekniska Museet.

Straka W.W. 1970, 'Reaction of the Scottish Working Class to Economic and Social Changes in Scotland, 1782–1832', *Scottish Tradition*, 1, 1: 17.

—— 1972, 'Reform in Scotland and the Working Class', *Scottish Tradition*, 2, 2: 32–50.

Strieder, Jacob 1966 [1931], *Jacob Fugger the Rich, Merchant and Banker of Augsburg, 1459–1525*, translated by Mildred L. Hartsough, edited by N.S.B. Gras. Hamden, CT: Archon Books.

Stuard, Susan Mosher 1995, 'Ancillary Evidence for the Decline of Medieval Slavery', *Past and Present*, 149: 3–28.

Styles, John 1983, 'Embezzlement, Industry and the Law in England, 1500–1800', in Berg, Hudson and Sonescher (eds.) 1983, 173–205.

Sunniside Local History Society 2006, 'Keelboats on the River Tyne', available at: <http://www.sunnisidelocalhistorysociety.co.uk/keelboats.html>.

Sweezy, Paul Marlor 1938, *Monopoly and Competition in the English Coal Trade 1550–1850*, Cambridge, MA: Harvard University Press.

—— 1978a [1950], 'A Critique', in Sweezy *et al.* 1978, 33–56; first published as 'The Transition from Feudalism to Capitalism', *Science and Society*, 14, 2: 134–57.

—— 1978b [1953], 'A Rejoinder', in Sweezy *et al.* 1978, 102–8; first published, *Science and Society*, 17, 2: 158–64.

Sweezy, Paul Marlor *et al.* 1978 [1976], *The Transition from Feudalism to Capitalism*, reprint, London: Verso.

Sykes, Ella and Sir Percy Sykes 1920, *Through Deserts and Oases of Central Asia*, London: Macmillan.

Sykes, Robert 1988, 'Trade Unionism and Class Consciousness: the "Revolutionary" Period of General Unionism, 1829–1834', in Rule (ed.) 1988.

Takahashi, Kohachiro 1978 [1951], 'A Contribution to the Discussion', in Sweezy *et al.* 1978.

Tate, William Edward 1967, *The English Village Community and the Enclosure Movements*, London: Victor Gollancz.

Tawney, Richard Henry 1912, *The Agrarian Problem in the Sixteenth Century*, London: Longmans, Green and Company.

Tawney, Richard Henry and Eileen Edna Power (eds.) 1924, *Tudor Economic Documents*, Vol. 1, London: Longmans.

—— 1961, *The Acquisitive Society*, London: Collins.

Taylor, Arthur J. 1975, *The Standard of Living in Britain in the Industrial Revolution*, Debates in Economic History,

Peter Mathias, general editor, London: Methuen.
Tennyson, Alfred, Lord 1892, *The Foresters: Robin Hood and Maid Marian*, London: Macmillan and Company.
Thirsk, Joan 1961, 'Industries in the Countryside', in Fischer (ed.) 1961.
—— 1978, *Economic Policy and Projects: the Development of a Consumer Society in Early Modern England*, Oxford: Clarendon Press.
Thirsk, Joan 1984, *The Rural Economy of England: Collected Essays*. London: Hambledon Press.
—— and John Phillips Cooper (eds.) 1972, *Seventeenth-Century Economic Documents*, Oxford, Clarendon Press.
Thomas, J.A. 1929, 'The Repeal of the Corn Laws, 1846', *Economica*, 25: 53–60.
Thomis, Malcolm Ian and Peter Holt 1977, *Threats of Revolution in Britain 1789–1848*, London: Macmillan, 1977.
Thompson, Edward Palmer 1965, 'The Peculiarities of the English', *Socialist Register*.
—— 1968, 'English Trade Unionism and Other Labour Movements Before 1790', *Bulletin of the Society for the Study of Labour History*, 17.
—— 1975, 'Standards and Experiences', in Taylor 1975.
—— 1978, The Poverty of Theory and Other Essays, London: Monthly Review Press.
—— 1990 [1975], *Whigs and Hunters the Origin of the Black Act*, reprint, London: Penguin.
—— 1991 [1963], *The Making of the English Working Class*, revised edition, London: Penguin.
—— 1993, *Customs in Common*, New York: the New Press.
Thompson, Thomas Peronnet 1826, *The True Theory of Rent, in opposition to Mr. Ricardo and Others*, London: Ridgway.
—— 1827, *Catechism on the Corn Laws; with a List of Fallacies and the Answers*, London: Ridgway.
Timmins, Geoffrey 1993, *The Last Shift: the decline of handloom weaving in nineteenth-century Lancashire*, Manchester: Manchester University Press.
Tomkins, Alannah 2006, *The experience of urban poverty, 1723–82: parish, charity and credit*, Manchester: Manchester University Press.
Trinder, Barrie 1974, *The Darbys of Coalbrookdale*, Chichester: Phillimore and Company.
Trow-Smith, Robert 1951, *English Husbandry*, London: Faber and Faber.
Touzeau, James 1910, *The Rise and Progress of Liverpool from 1551–1835*, Liverpool: Liverpool Booksellers Company.
Toynbee, Arnold 1956 [1884], *The Industrial Revolution*, Boston, MA: Beacon Press.
Trenchard, John and Thomas Gordon 1995, *Cato's Letters: or Essays on Liberty, Civil and Religious, and Other Important Subjects*, Vol. 1, edited by R. Hamovy, Indianapolis: Liberty Fund.
Tucker, Rufus Stickney 1975, 'Real Wages of Artisans in London, 1729–1935', in Taylor 1975.
Tufnell, Edward Carleton 1834, *Character, Objects and Effects of Trades Unions: with some remarks on the law*, London: James Ridgway and Sons.
Turner, Michael E. 1968, *Enclosures in Britain 1750–1830*, Studies in Economic History Series, edited by T.C. Smout, London: Macmillan.
Turner, Michael J. 1998, 'The "Bonaparte of Free Trade" and the Anti-Corn Law League', *The Historical Journal*, 41, 4: 1011–34.
—— 1999, *British Politics in an Age of Reform*, Manchester: Manchester University Press.
Uno, Kozo 1980 [1964], *Principles of Political Economy: Theory of a Purely Capitalist Society*, translated from Japanese by Thomas T. Sekine, reprint, Brighton: Harvester Press.
Unwin, George 1922, 'The Transition to the Factory System', *The English Historical Review*, 37, 146: 206–18.
—— 1925 [1908], *The Gilds and Companies of London*, reprint, London: Methuen.
—— 1963 [1904], *Industrial Organization in the Sixteenth and Seventeenth Centuries*, Oxford: Clarendon Press.
—— 1968 [1924], *Samuel Oldknow and the Arkwrights: The Industrial Revolution at Stockport and Marple*, second edition, Manchester: Manchester University Press.

Upton, Anthony F. 2001, *Europe 1600–1789*, London: Arnold.

Usher, Abbott Payson 1982 [1929], *A History of Mechanical Inventions*, revised edition, New York: Dover Publications.

Wade Martins, Susanna 2004, *Farmers, Landlords and Landscapes: Rural Britain, 1720 to 1870*, Macclesfield: Windgather Press.

Wadsworth, Alfred Powell and Julia De Lacy Mann 1965 [1931], *The Cotton Trade and Industrial Lancashire 1600–1780*, Manchester: Manchester University Press.

Wallace, Anthony F.C. and David J. Jeremy 1977, 'William Pollard and the Arkwright Patents', *The William and Mary Quarterly*, third series, 34, 3: 404–5.

Wallerstein, Immanuel 1974, *The Modern World-System*, Vol. 1: *Capitalist Agriculture and the Origins of the European World-Economy in the Sixteenth Century*, San Diego, CA: Academic Press.

Walter, John and Keith Wrightson 1984 [1968], 'Dearth and the Social Order in Early Modern England', in Slack (ed.) 1984.

Walton, John K. 1989, 'Proto-Industrialisation and the first Industrial Revolution: the case of Lancashire', in Hudson (ed.) 1989.

Ward, Adolphys William, George Walter Prothero and Stanley Leathes 1911 [1907], *The Cambridge Modern History*, volume 10: *The Restoration*, Planned by the late Lord Acton, reprint, New York: Macmillan.

Wasson, Ellis Archer 1980, 'The Spirit of Reform, 1832 and 1867', *Albion: A Quarterly Journal Concerned with British Studies*, 12, 2: 164–74.

Weaver, Stewart Angas 1987, *John Fielden and the Politics of Popular Radicalism, 1832–1847*, Oxford: Oxford University Press.

Webb, Keith 1995, *An Introduction to Problems in the Philosophy of Social Sciences*, London: Cassell.

Webb, Sidney and Beatrice Potter Webb 1902, *The History of Trade Unionism*, compiled by Robert Alexander Peddie, new edition, London; New York; Bombay: Longmans, Green and Co., 1902.

Weber, Max 1961, *General Economic History*, New York: Collier Books.

—— 1974, *The Protestant ethic and the spirit of capitalism*, London: Allen and Unwin.

—— 1976, *The Agrarian Sociology of Ancient Civilizations*, translated by R.I. Frank, London: New Left Books.

—— 1978, *Selections in Translation*, Cambridge: Cambridge University Press.

—— 1994, *Political Writings*, Cambridge: Cambridge University Press, 1994.

Weber, Wolfhard 1979, 'Technology in the 18th Century: A Means of Controlling the Emerging Industrial Society', in Strandh (ed.) 1979.

Wedgwood, Josiah 1903, *Letters of Josiah Wedgwood 1762 to 1770*, edited by Katherine Euphemia, Lady Farrer, Manchester: E.J. Morten and Barlaston; The Wedgwood Museum.

—— 1965, *The Selected Letters of Josiah Wedgwood*, edited by Ann Finer and George Savage, London: Cory, Adams and Mackay.

Wells, Roger A.E. 1977, *Dearth and Distress in Yorkshire 1793–1802*, *Borthwick Papers* 52, York: University of York, Borthwick Institute of Historical Research.

Wells, Roger 1988, 'Tolpuddle in the Context of English Agrarian Labour History, 1780–1850', in Rule (ed.) 1988.

Whipp, Richard 1987, 'A Time to Every Purpose: An Essay and Time and Work', in Joyce (ed.) 1987.

White, Leslie A. 1969 [1949], *The Science of Culture: A Study of Man and Civilization*, New York: Farrar, Straus and Giroux.

White, Lynn Jr. 1965 [1962], *Medieval Technology and Social Change*, Oxford: Oxford University Press.

Whitehead, Bill 1999, 'The Derby Lock-Out of 1833–34 and the Origins of the Labour Movement', available at: <http://www.geocities.com/CapitolHill/Congress/1346/potitlepage.htm>.

Whiter, Leonard 1970, *Spode: A History of the Family. Factory and Wares from 1733 to 1833*, London: Barrie and Jenkins.

Whyte, Ian D. 1989, 'Proto-Industrialization in Scotland', in Hudson (ed.) 1989.

Williamson, Oliver Eaton 1980, 'The Organization of Work: A Comparative Institutional Assessment', *Journal of Economic Behavior and Organization*, 1: 5–38.

Wilkes, John 1766, *North Briton*, 1, 45.

Wilson, Charles 1957, 'The Entrepreneur in the Industrial Revolution', *History*, 42, 145: 101–17.

—— 1984 [1965], *England's Apprenticeship 1603–1763*, second edition, London: Longman.

Wilson, Richard G. 1973, 'The Supremacy of the Yorkshire Cloth Industry in the Eighteenth Century', in Harte and Ponting (eds.) 1973

Wimpey, John 1775, *Rural Improvements, or, Essays on the Most Rational Methods of Improving Estates*, London: J. Dodsley.

Winslow, Cal 1975, 'Sussex Smugglers', in Hay *et al.* 1975.

Wollstonecraft, Mary 1997, *The Vindications: The Rights of Men, The Rights of Women*, edited by D.L. Macdonald and Kathleen Scherf, Orchard Park, NY: Broadview Literary Press.

Wood, Andy 1999, *The Politics of Social Conflict: The Peak Country, 1520–1770*, Cambridge: Cambridge University Press.

Wood, Ellen Meiksins 1981, 'The Separation of the Economic and the Political in Capitalism', *New Left Review*, I/127: 66–95.

—— 1991, *The Pristine Culture of Capitalism*, London: Verso.

—— 1994, 'From Opportunity to Imperative: The History of the Market', *Monthly Review*, 46, 3: 14–40.

—— 1995, *Democracy Against Capitalism*, London: Verso.

—— 1996, 'Capitalism, Merchants and Bourgeois Revolution: Reflections on the Brenner Debate and its Sequel', *International Review of Social History*, 41: 209–32.

—— 1997, *A Trumpet of Sedition*, London: Pluto Press.

—— 2002a, *The Origin of Capitalism: A Longer View*, London: Verso.

—— 2002b, 'The Question of Market Dependence', *Journal of Agrarian Change*, 2, 1: 50–87.

—— 2003, *The Empire of Capital*, London: Verso Press.

Wootton, David (ed.) 2003, *Divine Right and Democracy: An Anthology of Political Writings in Stuart England*, Indianapolis: Hackett Publishing.

Workshop of the World 2007, 'Button Shank Machine', *Invention and Innovation in the West Midlands*, available at: <http://www.workshopoftheworld.co.uk/wow.php?id=250>.

Worlidge, John 1669, *Systema Agriculturæ: The Mystery of Husbandry Discovered*, London: T. Johnson for S. Speed.

Wright, David G. and Jowitt, J. Anthony (eds.) 1981, *Victorian Bradford*, Bradford: City of Bradford Metropolitan Council.

Wright, Robert Eric 2003, 'The Transition from Feudalism to Capitalism: The Role of Mercantilism', PhD dissertation, York University.

Wyatt, John 1885, *John Wyatt, Master Carpenter & Inventor, A.D. 1700–1766. Compiled from Original Manuscripts*, Vol. I, London: Hamilton, Adams & Company.

Yelling, James Alfred 1977, *Common Field and Enclosure in England, 1450–1850*, Hamden, CT: Archon Books.

Youings, Joyce A. 1971, *The Dissolution of the Monasteries*, London, Allen and Unwin.

Young, Arthur 1785, *Annals of agriculture, and other useful arts* Volume IV, London: printed for the editor, and sold by H. Goldney.

—— 1984, *Sixteenth Century England*, London: Allen Lane.

Young, Hilary 1999, 'Manufacturing outside the Capital: The British Porcelain Factories, Their Sales Networks and Their Artists, 1745–1795', *Journal of Design History*, 12, 3: 257–69.

Yule, George 1970, 'Presbyterians and Independents: Some Comments', *Past and Present*, 47: 130–3.

Zagorin, Perez 1965, 'The Social Interpretation of the English Revolution in England', in Stone (ed.) 1965.

Zakai, Avihu 1989, 'Religious Toleration and Its Enemies: The Independent Divines and the Issue of Toleration during the English Civil War', *Albion*, 21, 1: 1–33.

Zmolek, Mike 2000, 'The Case for Agrarian Capitalism: A Response to Albritton', *The Journal of Peasant Studies*, 27, 4: 138–59.

—— 2001, 'Further Thoughts on Agrarian Capitalism: A Reply to Albritton', *The Journal of Peasant Studies*, 29, 1: 129–54.

—— 2004, 'Debating Agrarian Capitalism: A Rejoinder to Albritton', *The Journal of Peasant Studies*, 31, 2: 276–305.

Index

Abercromby, Ralph, General (1734–1801), 573
Aberdeen, Earl of *see* Hamilton-Gordon, George
Aberdeen, Scotland, 384, 716
Abolition of Slavery Act (1833), 711–12
Abolition of the Slave Trade Act (1807), 587–88
Abolitionist Society, 544 n. 137
abolitionists, 532, 563, 627, 710–11; *The Axe Laid Root* journal, 641; *see also* Wedderburn; Wilberforce
absolutism, 85, 216, 679, 707 n. 109, 798, 805; in France, 2, 163, 287, 798 n. 8; in Spain, 501, 657, 679; Stuart threat of, 133–34, 144, 149, 163, 804–5
Académie des Sciences, 332 n. 156, 340, 414
Accrington, Lancashire, 672
ACLL *see* Anti-Corn Law League
Act for the Better Regulation of Linen and Hempen Manufactures in Scotland (1727), 468
Act of Settlement: of 1388, 58; of 1559, 67; of 1662, 137, 158; partially lifted, 550; of 1701, 177
Act of Union with Ireland (1801), 562, 573, 680, 709
Act of Union with Scotland (1707), 108, 140, 148 n. 132, 162, 178–9, 210 n. 175, 240 n. 63, 384, 468
Act to restrain the number and ill-practice of Brokers and Stock-jobbers, 155–156
Adams, Daniel, 546
Addington, Henry, 1st Viscount Sidmouth (1757–1844), 629–30, 652, 683
Additional Sea Venture, 124
aeolipile, 306, 323
Africa and Africans, 107, 122, 160–161, 175 n. 34, 259, 384, 687
agrarian capitalism, 2–9, 40–3, 48, 80, 83, 100–2, 112 n. 24, 117, 134, 142–3, 150, 162–4, 215–18, 248–50, 254, 267–8, 272, 274, 279–80, 288, 292, 356, 369–70, 372, 378, 395–400, 419–20, 458–60, 496, 501–2, 512, 514, 520, 523–5, 542, 553, 558–9, 568, 577, 605–6, 611–13, 618–19, 656–80, 670, 691–2, 729, 731, 733, 741, 747, 775–7, 793–800, 805, 807–12, 831–2, 838–9, 843; and absolutism, 216, 501; key to British power, 165–214, 542; and imperialism, 217; in India, 763 n. 67; in Ireland, 216–17, 236, 773–4; and market imperatives, 419, 691; and market dependency, 28–32, 41; mining and, 86–91; political régime of, 182, 618, 807; in Scotland, 211, 240, 250; Smith a theorist of, 416 n. 53; and poor relief, 369, 690 n. 49, 736; specificity of, 23–8, 605, 741; as transitional period, 255, 793; tripartite structure, 172, 199
agriculture, 40–4, 61, 64, 71, 79, 83, 87, 89, 91, 94, 99, 102, 160, 166–71, 192–96, 198–200, 202, 204, 211–12, 214, 253, 258, 268–69, 271 n. 50, 273, 276, 288, 302, 305, 323, 310, 313, 323, 329, 338, 341, 344–6, 357, 369, 377, 395, 398–9, 423 n. 75, 459, 468, 471, 490, 498 n. 165, 502, 505, 516, 523–4, 529–30, 551, 613, 616, 621–2, 626, 640–1, 643–4, 656, 692, 698, 704, 721, 730, 740–1, 744, 747, 776, 795–7, 799–801, 807, 811, 835; British, 192, 279, 606, 692, 813, 843; capitalist, 37, 553, 799; English, 14, 43, 48, 112 n. 24, 152, 168–70, 194 n. 111, 217 n. 5, 288, 459, 825; feudal or medieval, 49, 51, 54, 310, 313, 796; French, 24, 71, 97 n. 186; improved, 26, 42, 64, 112 n. 24, 193, 196, 200 n. 131, 254, 286 n. 7, 591–2, 692, 799, 803, 814, 838; Irish, 216, 774 n. 87; manorial, 49; and manufacturing, 166–71, 368, 797, 816; productivity, 21, 73, 79, 165–6, 171, 173, 193–4, 218, 257, 261, 268, 807; *see also* agrarian capitalism; enclosures

Agrippa, Marcus Vipsanius (c. 63–12 BC), 305
Albritton, Robert, 27 n. 71, 354 n. 34, 501, n. 171
Alexander I, Tsar (1777–1825), 589
Alexandria, Egypt, 304, 306, 323
Algeciras Bay, Battle of (1801) 573
Ali al-Mawsili, Ammar ib, 312
alkali, 415, 489
Al-Khujandi, Abu-Mahmud (c. 940–1000) inventor of the sextant, 312
Al-khwarizmi, Mohammed ibn (c. 780–850), 308
Althorp, John, 3rd Earl Spencer (1782–1845), 709, 712, 715, 734
Althusser, Louis (1918–1990), 294
America *see* Americas, American colonies, Central America, Latin America, South America, Spanish America
Americas, Pre-Colombian Civilisations, 302 n. 52, 304, 308, 311, 313, 495, 813
American Revolution *see* American War of Independence
American War of Independence (1775–1783), 43–4, 165, 210–43, 218; 261, 264, 267–8, 435, 473, 532–3, 535–7, 544, 546 n. 144, 559, 568, 577, 761, 805, 811; conclusion of, 243–6, 250, 401, 43; loyalists, 243
American colonies, 215, 229, 259, 539, 810–11; Boston Tea Party, 236; restrictive acts prompt rebellion, 229–30, 236–9; trade with, 121, 150, 165, 225, 261; transportation to, 189, 242 n. 71
Amiens, Peace of / Treaty of (1802), 573, 580, 585, 823
ancillae, 51
Andalusia, 316
Anderson, Perry, 25, 162 n. 197, 635
Andes Civilisation, 302, 495
Anglican Church, 148, 177 n. 44, 182, 375, 581, 645, 652, 658, 679, 687, 706, 709, 772 n. 80, 834
Anglo-Dutch Alliance (1688), 146, 178
Anglo-Dutch Wars *see* Dutch Wars
Anglo-Saxons, 517
Anne I (1665–1714), 148 n. 132, 177–8, 182, 191, 212, 229 n. 32, 233, 372; death of, 177, 182, 213; Queen Anne's Bounty, 177
annuities, 150, 186; superannuities, 653
anthrax, 257
Anti-Corn Law League (ACLL), 762, 765–7, 770 n. 75, 788–9, 834; formation, methods and mission, 750–4
Antikythera mechanism, 307
Apollodorus of Pergamon (1st century BC), 344
aqueducts, 305
Arab Civilisation, 308, 311–13, 321, 338, 813
arbitration, 566–70, 614, 662, 773, 780, 834
Archimedes (c. 287 BC – c. 212 BC), 315
Argand, François Pierre Ami (1750–1803), inventor of the Argand Lamp, 336
aristocracy, 15, 26, 118, 136, 143, 162, 205, 525, 559, 611, 654, 656, 664 n. 184, 678, 680, 687, 697, 704, 707 n. 109, 734, 753, 776–7, 779
'aristocracy of labour', 474, 759, 791; neo-feudal, 614
Arkwright, Richard (1732–1792), 158 n. 179, 328–9, 338, 380, 384, 387, 389–90, 414 n. 48, 425, 427, 431–44, 452, 455, 457–8, 462 n. 5, 465–6, 477–9, 487 n. 122, 490 n. 141, 493, 502–3, 505, 582–3, 645, 814–15
Arkwright, Richard II (1755–1843), 505, 582–3
Arminian clergy, 120, 122
army, 107, 122–34, 147–148, 154, 156, 165, 179, 211–12, 260, 336, 544, 558, 560–1, 585 n. 82, 588, 599, 643, 680, 697, 767, 804–5, 827; radicals in, 114, 126–7, 137; Scottish, 122–3; Parliamentary, 125; New Model Army, 125–34, 137, 804; in India, 243
articulation of modes of production, 98, 294
artisans, 22, 41–2, 44, 49, 51–2, 55–6, 103, 106, 122, 128, 176, 188, 235, 241, 259, 284, 326, 378, 389, 395, 398, 419, 423 n. 75, 431 n. 113, 445, 447, 454, 456, 463–4, 476, 508, 524, 539, 542–3, 548, 559, 582, 588 n. 96, 594, 601–2, 604–7, 611, 629, 632, 636–9, 644–6, 647, 649, 664–6, 668, 670, 674, 698, 705, 718, 723, 740–1, 744–747, 751, 753–4, 758, 761, 764, 779, 785–8, 791, 796, 804, 810–1, 820–821, 823–824, 828–9, 833, 836, 838–9; artisan capital, 741; conservative outlook, 570, 575, 646, 727; control over the labour process, 637, 703, 721; 'honourable trades', 85, 754, 112, 141, 224, 345–7, 367, 474, 594, 663–5, 754, 759, 763–4, 786, 791, 836; machine-breaking, 572; and radicalism, 162, 249, 688 n. 41, 790; unions, 352, 577, 838
Artisans' General Committee, 602

Ashley, Lord (Anthony Ashley Cooper, 1768–1851), 769–70, 772, 779, 834–35
Ashton, T., factory master , 681
Ashton, Thomas Sutcliffe (1899–1968), xvii, 198, 259, 354, 356, 360–1, 395–6, 427–8, 470, 492
Ashton-under-Lyme, Lancashire, 391, 672, 681, 783
Asia, 28, 175 n. 34, 193, 310, 545, 709; Asia Minor, 310; East Asia, 193; monopoly on cotton growing, 442; South Asia, 709
Asiento, 184, 208, 212, 218
Assize of Novel Disseisin (1166), 796
Associated Colliers of Scotland, 668, 671
Association for the Preservation of Liberty and Property, 542
atlatl, 302
Atterbury plot, 187
Attwood, Thomas (1783–1856), 700–1, 751–2, 755–6
Augustus, Gaius Julius Caesar (63 BCE 14 CE), 305, 315
Australia: discovery of 235; transportation to 242 n. 71, 595, 841
Austria: 146 n. 128, 191, 209–12, 220–22, 536, 541, 557–8, 572–3, 586, 589, 600, 603, 643, 657, 679, 768, ; Austrian Empire 179 n. 51, 336; in Quadruple Alliance, 184, 603; revolution in 1848, 782; subsidies to 191, 210–11, 541; War of Austrian Succession, 209, 212, 218
Austrian Netherlands, 536, 541, 557
Austrian succession, war of (1740–48), 209–12, 218
Aztecs: Tenochtitlan, 308

Babylon, 82, 539
Baghdad, 312–13, 336 n. 174
Bahamas, 245
balloon *see* hot-air balloon
Baltic trade, 111, 113, 160, 174, 183–4 n. 66, 245, 573, 614, 650–651
Bank Charter Act (1833), 709
Bank Restriction Act (Currency Act) (1797), 560
Banking Act of 1844, 187 n. 77
Bank of England, 147, 149, 151–6, 184–7, 211, 241–2, 249, 545, 560, 576, 805; founding of (1694), 147, 151
banks and banking, 82, 129 n. 73, 148–56, 172, 184–7, 204–5, 254 Diagram 5.1, 309, 355, 484, 497; 533 n. 98, 541, 560, 653, 670, 707, 756, 776, 781, 795; country-banks, 182, 186–7, 254, 493–4, 541, 560; customs farmers, 108; in Holland, 133 n. 87; likened to circulation of blood, 527: *see also* placemen; tax farming
bankruptcies, 111, 149, 152, 187 n. 77, 199, 204, 225 n. 22, 230, 245, 385, 393 n. 181, 441–2, 446, 460, 473, 480, 488, 536, 583, 590, 618, 670, 781; Land Bank, 152–4, 172, 184, 805; Land and Labour Bank, 781; labour bank, 717; Sword Blade Company, 184, 186 n. 75; Barbados, 130
Barebones Parliament (1653), 130
Barlow, William, government informant, 565
Barr and Company, 648
Basra, 312
Bastille Day (1789), 537
Batavian Republic, 557, 585
Battle of the Saintes (1782), 245
Bavaria and Bavarian Republic, 107 n. 8, 173 n. 31, 336, 573, 586
Beavermakers' Company, 113
Beckford, William (1709–1770), 233
Bedford, Duke of *see* Russell, William
begging *see* poverty
Belgium, 536, 547, 557, 603, 655 n. 162, 660, 688, 743; Bruges 161; Brussels, 781; Flanders, 146, 173 n. 31; 176 n. 40; Liége, 585; *see also* Austrian Netherlands; Low Countries; Spanish Netherlands
Benson, Thomas, inventor of water grinding, 405
Bentham, Jeremy (1748–1832), 7, 698, 751
Bentham, Samuel (1757–1831), naval architect and engineer, 335
Bentinck, Lord (William) George Frederick Cavenish-Scott (1802–1848), 776
Berg, Maxine, 167–8, 187 n. 77, 267 n. 46, 348 n. 8, 360, 524
Berthollet, Comte Claude-Louis (1748–1822), inventor of bleaching with chlorine, 336, 487
Besson, Jacques (c. 1540–1573) inventor, 321
Bi Sheng (990–1051) inventor of movable type, 309
Bible, 107; Leviticus 514; King James version, 514
Bifocals, 326 n. 131
Bill of Rights (1689), 146–7, 232–3, 537
Bimber, Bruce, 291–4
Binns, John (1722–1860), 562
Birmingham, 139, 196, 262, 264 n. 34, 333 n. 162, 335, 352, 360, 362–3, 376, 388–90,

470, 472 n. 45, 475–6, 478 n. 82, 480, 487–9, 539, 543 n. 131, 629, 631, 641, 679, 699–702, 704, 717–18, 735, 744 n. 233, 751–7, 759, 764, 781, 785
Birmingham Brass Company, 480
Birmingham Freehold Land Society, 781
Birmingham Guildhall, 718
Birmingham Mining and Manufacturing Company, 480
Birmingham Police Bill (1839), 756
Birmingham Political Union (BPU), 688 n. 41, 700, 751–6
Birmingham Reform Association, 751
Black Act *see* Waltham Black Act (1723)
Blackburn, Lancashire, 421 n. 68, 442 n. 177, 767; Weavers Union Society of, 672
'blacking', 189 n. 87, 190 n. 96
blacksmiths, 59, 68, 333, 350, 491, 696; Blacksmith's Company of London, 60
Blackwoods Magazine, 616 n. 13, 669
Blanc, Honoré (1736–1801), 335
blast-furnace, 77, 80, 166, 316, 318, 324–5, 331, 364, 471, 757
Blaug, Mark (1927–2011), 550–2, 555, 690 n. 49, 821
'bloody code', 24, 44, 189–90, 213, 521, 526, 807, 819, 824, 832
Bloxam and Fourdrinier Company, 337
Blunt, Baronet John (1665–1733), 184–5
Board of Agriculture, 544, 553
Board of Health, 554
Board of Trade, 147, 368, 652, 670, 680
Bohemia, 96, 120, 221, 288 n. 10, 318; Bohemian Revolution (1618), 120
Bois, Guy, 6
Bolívar, Simón (1783–1830), 658
Bolivia, 72
Bolton, Lancashire, 33, 329 n. 142, 431 n. 111, 435, 672, 682 n. 19, 701, 757, 784
Bonaparte, Napoleon (1769–1821), 336, 499, 558, 560–1, 572–3, 585–91, 588, 599–600, 823–4
Bonaparte, Louis Napoleon (1778–1846), 782–3
Bonaparte, Joseph (1768–1844), 590
bond, the, 482, 667, 717, 771–3, 790, 802, 833; definition of, 771 n. 78
bondsmen, 705
Bonnie Prince Charlie *see* Stuart, Charles Edward
Booth, Enoch, inventor of double firing in pottery, 326, 405
Boston, Massachusetts, 233–4, 236–7
Boulsover, Thomas, inventor of silver plate (1705–1788), 236
Boulton, John, 475
Boulton, Matthew (1728–1809), 264 n. 34, 333 n. 162, 336 n. 175, 414, 442, 461, 467, 475–9, 489, 503–5, 817, 850, 852, 862; Boulton & Watt, 442, 467, 478, 504–5, 817; *see also* Fothergill; Soho Foundry; Soho Manufactory; Watt
Boulton, Matthew II, 505, 584
Bourbon, House of, 173 n. 29, 536, 538, 544, 556, 600, 612, 631
bourgeoisie and bourgeois revolution, 13, 15, 17 n. 40, 19, 135–6, 144–6, 162, 205 n. 157, 213, 547 n. 149, 654, 707–8, 747, 779, 783 n. 118, 794, 795, 805, 827, 832, 835, 841–2; agrarian, 85 n. 138; 'bourgeois capitalism', 83; economists, 675; in France, 162, 688; petit-bourgeoisie, 235; bourgeois state, 619
Bourn, Daniel, inventor of carding engine, 327, 329, 390, 432
Bourne, Mary, wife of Richard Crawshay, 473
Bowring, Sir John (1792–1892), 753
BPU *see* Birmingham Political Union
Bradford, West Yorkshire, 464, 671, 716, 757, 762, 783
Bradford-on-Avon, Wiltshire, 467
Bramah, Joseph (1748–1814), 336, 491
Brandreth, Jeremiah (1790–1817), 630–1, 757
brass, 75, 160, 193, 260, 358, 363, 393, 480, 487 n. 122, 488, 506
Braudel, Fernand (1902–1985), xviii, xx, 1, 38–9, 53, 76–7, 166–7, 194 n. 113, 196 n. 119, 290, 325 n. 123, 334, 417, 420
Braxfield, Lord Robert McQueen (1722–1799), 545
Braziers, 477 n. 72, 517
Brazil, Kingdom of, 98, 331 n. 155, 590 n. 103, 657
Brenner, Robert, 2–3, 48, 50, 53, 111 n. 20, 145, 166, 213 n. 3, 286–7, 294, 794, 798 n. 7*;* on Catalonia, 100, 216 n. 3*;* on class structure, 28–31, 297, 634–5; on English civil war, 117–29*;* on the Netherlands, 37*;* on property relations, 17–22*;* on the transition debate, 9, 12–17; *see also* commercialisation model; demographic model
Brenner debate, 6, 50
Breunig, Charles (1920–2003), 688, 761 n. 37, 780 n. 109

brewers and breweries, 71 n. 77, 158, 195, 242 n. 68, 332 n. 158, 350, 373, 472, 483–5, 491–2, 550
bricklayers, 356, 680, 716, 718
brickmakers, 718
bricksetters, 638
Bridewell, 370
bridewells, 371, 373–4, 568
Bridgewater, 3rd Duke Francis Egerton (1736–1803), 205 n. 159, 263, 265, 490–1, 494
Briggs, Asa, 533 n. 96, 542, 617 n. 22
Brindley, James (1716–1772), engineer, 263–4, 491, 538
Bristol, 160, 187 n. 76, 325 n. 121, 362, 374, 422, 428 n. 97, 471 n. 41, 480, 488, 506, 560, 736, 773, 779; Bristol Riots (1831), 701
Britain *see* Great Britain
British Brass Company, 480
British Convention of the Delegates of the People in Edinburgh, 545
British Empire, 216, 235–8, 245
British Isles, 486, 781, 794; *see also* Great Britain
British state, 614, 619, 653, 655, 657–8, 810; actively structuring a capitalist labour market, 657, 780; agrarian capitalist, 614, 656; bureaucracy subjected to market regulation, 652–8, 827; and class, 609–676; efficient war machine, 619; fiscal-military to *laissez-faire*, 618, 654, 827; role in governing India, 243, 247, 768 n. 67; national debt, 184–5, 191, 211–12, 235, 245, 533, 588, 617, 661, 759 n. 29, 763, 805, 826; passive versus active, 42, 612, 656, 839; policy informed by political economy, 521, 602, 615, 619, 624; pre-empting dissent, 758, 787, 833; promotes free-trade, 530; shift to neutral arbiter of wage contracts, 183, 567, 592, 613, 657, 731–2, 822, 827
broadcloth, 351, 427
Brougham, Henry Peter (1778–1868), 590, 625, 714, 715
Brownrigg, William (1711–1800) inventor of water carbonation, 326, 473
Bruland, Kristine, 289 n. 12, 408, 411, 418–19, 453, 460
Brunel, Marc Isambard (1769–1849), 335, 337
Brushmakers, 669
Bubble Act (1720), 188 806; repeal, 666; *see also* South Sea Bubble
Builders, 185, 263, 607, 680, 718–19
Builders Union, 718
Bull Ring Riot (1839), 756, 785
Bunker Hill, Battle of, 238
Burgoyne, General John (1722–1792), 238
Burdett, Francis (1770–1844), 588–9, 592–3, 644, 680
Burke, Edmund (1729–1797), 7, 233, 238, 242, 244 n. 78, 247, 519–23, 537–41, 622
Bushnell, David (1740–1824) inventor of the submarine, 332
Bussa's Rebellion (1816), 627
Bute, Earl John Stuart (1744–1814), 226–7, 229 n. 32, 231–2
Bute legend (also Rockingham legend or Rockingham myth), 229 n. 32, 231–2, 238, 242–5, 249–50, 534, 536, 810
button shank machine, 335
butty system, 472, 482, 504
Byng, Captain John (1704–1757), 220
Byng, John of Oldham, 441
Byron, Lord George Gordon (1788–1824), 595
Byzantium, 306, 310, 317 n. 100

Cabinet of ministers, 226, 233, 238, 364, 565, 588, 614, 624, 640, 647, 650–2, 679, 681, 697, 702, 743 n. 229, 763, 774, 777, 779
cabinetmakers, 716, 773, 779, 786
Cahokia, 308
caissons, 326
calamine, 75, 488
Calcutta, Bengal, 221
Calicoes, 161 n. 193, 175–6, 330, 352, 385–6, 432, 442–3, 571, 687, 806
Calvinism, 119–20
cam, 304, 316
Cambodia, 308
Cambridgeshire, 266, 278, 626
Camden, Earl of *see* Pratt, Charles
camera obscura, 309
Campbell, Alan, 668
Campbell, Alexander, 716
Campbell, John (c. 1719–1790) inventor of the sextant, 327
Campo Formio, Treaty of (1797), 558, 573
Canada, 222 n. 19, 223, 235 n. 46, 246, 755, 810; Canada Act (1791), 538, 768; trade with, 246, 650–1; United States invasion of, 599
canals, 254, 262–5, 279, 302, 406, 442, 471, 482, 490, 494–5, 631–2, 743: in France,

133 n. 87, 254; Canal Acts, 263; Foss Dyke, 263; Bridgewater Canal 263, 265; Trent and Mersey Canal, 264, 442; canal mania, 264, 279, 421, 538; Grand Cross, 264; Leeds and Liverpool Canal 265, 465 n. 17; Grand Union Canal 265; canal lock, 309, 316; Forth and Clyde Canal 333; Oxford Canal 538; Grand Union Canal 538, 617; Coventry Canal, 438 n. 114; Birmingham and Fazeley Canal, 538 n. 114; Union Canal, 668
Canning, George (1770–1827) Prime Minister, 651–2, 657, 678–9, 688, 697
cannons, 75, 77–8, 172, 245, 260, 306, 309, 318, 332 n. 157, 333, 585, 648 n. 137, 801
capital: definition of, 462, 495–500; merchant capital, 18, 22; as a social relation of property, 5, 18–19, 39, 41
capitalism, xvii, 1–129, 134–5, 143–5, 150–1, 163, 168, 171, 217, 223, 247–51, 279, 286–303, 313, 315, 318–19, 322, 332, 341–7, 356, 365–6, 369–72, 378, 383, 395–427, 440–462, 470, 472, 501–6, 510–12, 516, 520–6, 548, 553, 574–7, 582, 585–92, 603–7, 611–14, 617–23, 636–7, 639, 644–6, 649, 656–75, 680–5, 690–2, 697–8, 706, 718, 721–3, 727, 729, 732–3, 741–761, 775–8, 785–7, 792–6, 802, 805–22, 825–33, 836–43; the capitalist, 490–5; co-operative, 741; definition of, 2, 38–9, 83–5, 216, 417, 420, 495–500; elusive origins of, 32–40; first usage of the word, 741; fully-developed, 27 n. 71, 145, 403, 814; origins of, 3, 8, 32–40, 95–6, 289 n. 11, 459, 495–500, 796; pristine capitalism, 793; separation of political and economic, 15, 794; specificity of, 2, 8, 23–28, 39, 83, 620; tendency to naturalise and universalise, 8, 27, 300, 420, 523; 'world-system', 38; *see also* agrarian capitalism; industrial capitalism; market dependency; transition from feudalism to capitalism
capstan, 390, 421
carding, 65, 329, 389–91, 440, 687, 741; carding engine, 327, 329, 390–1, 432–6, 465–6, 810; carding factories, 386
Caribbean, 124, 175 n. 34, 215, 217, 245
Carlisle Peace Commission, 238–9
Carolinas, 175 n. 34, 243
Caroline of Brunswick-Wolfenbüttel (1768–1821), 593, n. 112, 649–50
carpenters, 59, 260, 304, 491, 638, 680, 716, 718; yeomen-carpenters, 137; *see also* General Union of Carpenters
Carr, Robert (1590–1645), 110
Carron, Falkirk, 330
Carron Company ironworks, 245, 331, 472–3, 585; carronade 245, 585, 648
Carteret, John (1690–1763) 2nd Earl Granville, 207 n. 165, 208–10
Cartwright, Edmond (1743–1823) inventor of the power-loom, 330, 455–6, 469
Cartwright, Major John (1740–1824), 455–6, 543 n. 131, 588 n. 96, 593, 628, 751
Cartwright, William, 597
Castlereagh, Lord Robert Stewart, 2nd Marquess of Londonderry (1769–1822), 629, 652, 657, 683, 727
Catherine of Braganza (1638–1704), 137
Catholic Association, 657, 681–2, 657–8, 681–2
Catholic Relief Act: (1778) 240; (1780), 241; (1782), 245
Catholicism, 120, 122, 131, 133, 141–2, 146, 171, 189, 210 n. 175, 227 n. 28, 236, 239–41, 435, 562, 687, 773, 802, 804–6, 810; threat of papacy 119, 133; Catholic relief, 236, 532, 535, 538, 562, 573, 587–8, 620, 678–82, 687, 699, 706, 773–4, 834; Catholic relief in Ireland, 680, 709; Catholic Rent 682, 709; Maynooth Catholic seminary, 774; threat of Stuart Papism, 141–2
Catholic Marriages Bill (1836), 750
Cato Street Conspiracy, 646–7, 833
Causeway Arch, 326 n. 129, 363
Cave, Edward (1691–1754), 390
Cavendish-Bentinck, William Henry, 3rd Duke of Portland (1738–1809), 244, 246, 547, 565, 588–9, 592
Cecil, Robert, 1st Earl of Salisbury (c. 1563–1612), 110
Cecil, William (1521–1598) 1st Baron Burghley, 110
Celsius, Anders (1701–1744) astronomer and inventor of Celsius temperature scale, 327
Celts, 307, 332 n. 159
census, 372; Census Act (1800), 554 n. 177
Central Agricultural Protection Association, 776
Central America, 245
Ceylon, 245, 558

Chadwick, Sir Edwin (1800–1890), 715 n. 135, 731, 738, 770, 834
Chamber of Commerce, 737
Chambers, Jonathon D., 272–4, 439, 515
Champion, William (1709–1789) discoverer of zinc distilling, 480, 488, 505
Chandos, Marquess of *see* Grenville, Richard
Chapman, Stanley D. 425, 431 n. 113 and n. 117, 434, 439, 442, 444, 584
charities, 64, 157, 205 n. 159, 372, 378, 531, 554, 665, 675; *see also* schools
Charles Emmanuel III (1701–1773) Duke of Savoy, King of Sardinia, 209
Charles I (1600–1649), 81 n. 120, 113–15, 120–6, 131, 147–8, 156. 225, 324 n. 120, 803–4
Charles II (1630–1685), 130, 132–4, 137–8, 141–2, 147, 149, 190, 210, 782
Charles IV of Spain (1748–1819), 590
Charles VI, Holy Roman Emperor (1685–1740), 180, 209
Charles X of France and Navarre (1757–1863), 679, 688
Charles XII of Sweden (1682–1718), 184
charcoal, 76, 324–325, 334, 359, 474
Charterville, Oxfordshire, 790 n. 790
Chartism, 4–5, 542, 635, 647, 708, 740, 747, 749–92, 826, 833, 835–6, 841 n. 1; General Convention , 647, 753–6, 758, 762, 781–2, 785; moral versus physical force, 631, 754–5, 759–60, 762–3, 777, 783–5, 833, 835; National Assembly, 782; first petition (1839), 754–5; second petition (1842), 764; third petition (1848), 781–3, 785, 787, 833, 835–6; sacred month, 756–7; Scottish Chartists, 765' see National Petition, People's Charter, petitioning
Chartist Land Company, 781
see National Petition, People's Charter, petitioning
Chase, Malcolm, 567, 570, 577, 637, 659 n. 172, 664 n. 184, 665, 668 n. 200, 765 n. 52, 766, 772, 772 n. 82
Chatham, 1st Earl of, *see* Pitt, William the Elder
Chatham, Kent, 362
chemistry, 311–12, 332 n. 156, 336–7, 340, 413–15, 431 n. 111, 483; chemical industry, 336, 470, 473, 486–9
Cheshire Yeomanry, 610
China, 2, 53, 82, 301, 304, 309, 312–13, 316, 338, 380, 384–5, 410, 442, 495; Han Dynasty 338; Kiangsee 410; Ming Dynasty 338; Opium Wars, 768–9
Choiseul, duc de, Étienne-François (1719–1785), 226
Christianity, 51, 305, 357, 372, 374–5, 538; *see also* Catholicism; Protestantism
Christie, Ian R., 588 n. 94, 593, n. 111, 598
Church Bill (1834), 710
Church of England *see* Anglican Church
Cipolla, Carlo M. (1922–2000), 36–40
Clark, Thomas, 784
class, 609–676; relations, xx, 3, 13, 15–16, 22, 30, 35, 44, 48, 86, 96, 287–8, 295, 298, 339, 634–5, 690, 727; struggle, 3, 5, 11, 16, 30, 40–2, 106, 269, 270, 297–8, 420, 513, 634, 780, 788, 800, 832, 837–9; warfare, 8, 594; *see also* landed class; working class
class determinism, 634
Clifton, Francis, inventor of spinning machine, 387
clockmakers, 68, 328 n. 137, 391, 426, 431 n. 113, 503
clocks, 193, 289 n. 11, 314–18, 320, 322, 335, 379 n. 132, 412, 533 n. 98; alarm clock, 318; 'clocking-in', 412, 459; pendulum clock, 314, 322; escapement clocks, 318; tax on, 533; water clock, 304, 306, 312; weight-driven, 316–7
cloth-dressers, *see* shearmen
clothiers, 64–6, 140, 317, 373, 385–6, 393–4, 422, 435 n. 136, 465, 581; gentleman clothiers, 422, 578; merchant clothiers, 580; Clothiers' Community, 581
clothworkers, 114, 159, 605 n. 148
Clydesdale Association of Operative Colliers, 638
Coachmakers, 671
coal, 37, 75–77, 85–91, 94, 116, 123, 152, 159–60, 169 n. 16, 196–7, 200, 205, 235, 260, 263–5, 299, 311, 316, 323–6, 334, 356–65, 367, 403–6, 409, 427, 429, 466–73, 481–3, 486, 489, 504, 533, 666–8, 671, 743, 767–70, 801–802; 'coal enclosures', 482, 801; enabled the growth of London, 71 n. 77, 123; Newcastle the principal region, 470; *see also* colliers; collieries; Company of Hostmen; Grand Lessees; Newcastle
coal-heavers, 235, 356–7, 427, 631 n. 69
coal miners *see* colliers

Coal Mines Act (1842), 769
coal tar, 488
Coalbrookdale, 264, 325, 330–1, 471, 478, 504–5, 584–5, 843
Coalbrookdale Works, 325 n. 121, 471, 504, 584–5
Coalitions Against France, 165; First Coalition (1792–1797), 557–8; Second Coalition (1798–1802), 572; Third Coalition (1803–1806), 586; Sixth Coalition (1812–1814), 600
Cobbett, William (1763–1835), 574, 588 n. 96, 592–3, 598, 625–6, 628–9, 643, 646, 649, 661, 673, 689, 700, 721
Cobden, Richard (1804–1865), 753, 771
cobblers *see* shoemakers
Cochrane, Lord Admiral Thomas (1775–1860), 588
Cockayne *see* Cokayne
coercive force, 13, 41–4, 83–4, 119, 302–3, 413, 547–8, 633, 675, 684, 827, 829–33, 838; non-coercive methods, 790
Coercive or Intolerable Acts, 237
coffee 137, 193, 206, 358, 804
coffeehouses, 137, 147, 188, 404, 596, 754
Coggeshall, Essex, 140
Cohen, G.A. (1941–2009), 35 n. 90, 294–5, 299, 303, 812
coinage, 72, 154, 304–6, 320, 472, 496, 589, 802, 819; clipping, 150–1; minting, 29; recoinage, 154–5; standardisation, 333; *see also* money
Cokayne Project, 111–12
Cokayne, Sir William (1561–1626), 111
coke (coked coal) 166, 264, 324–6, 330–4, 471–2
Coke, Edward (1552–1634), 114, 203
Coke, Thomas (1697–1759) 1st Earl of Leicester, 204
Colbert, Minister Jean-Baptiste (1619–1683), 133 n. 87, 285, 429
Cole, William Alan, 218, 256, 259, 329 n. 139, 261, 355 n. 39, 393, 429, 490 n. 140, 496–500, 738
Coleman, Donald Cuthbert, 47–8, 72–3, 78, 80, 92, 94–5, 97, 155, 199 n. 129, 200 n. 131, 217, 283, 359, 363 n. 66, 386, 430 n. 108
Coliseum of Rome, 305 n. 63
Collier, Elisha (1788–1856) inventor of flintlock revolver, 338
colliers, 71, 409, 481–3, 504, 521, 638–9, 757, 766–7, 771–3, 802, 834; collier ships, 71 n. 77; Great Strike of 1844, 769 n. 71, 772–3; Scottish, 638, 667–71, 771; serfdom, 483, 802; *see also* coal
collieries or coal mines, 87–9, 123, 324, 357, 359, 364, 471–2, 481–3, 489, 769–70, 773, 802; colliery-serfdom, 483, 802; at Griff, 356; in Scotland, 667–8, 671; at Tipton, 478; in West Lancashire, 482; at Worsley, 482; *see also* coal; miners and mining; serfdom: colliery-serfdom; Wylam
colonialism and colonisation, 21, 39, 73, 107, 121–2, 125, 129, 150, 157, 159–60, 165, 175 n. 34, 182, 191, 206, 208, 212, 216–18, 226–7, 229–39, 246–50, 254, 259, 261, 264, 327, 379, 442, 468, 473, 535, 545, 557, 561, 589, 711, 714, 734, 763, 772, 777–8, 789, 794–5, 808, 810–11; in China, 768–9; of Eastern Europe, 11; of France, 227 n. 26, 557; of Ireland, 21; of New England, 107; old colonial system, 129; of Spanish America, 218, 226; *see also* American colonies; imperialism; merchants
Colquhoun, Patrick (1745–1820), 194 n. 111, 438 n. 149; 546 n. 145, 618
colting, 425 n. 85, 594, 824
Coltman, John, inventor who adapted water frame to worsted spinning, 466
combers *see* wool-combers
Combination Acts (1799, 1800) 351, 530, 549, 562–71, 580–1, 579, 592, 602–4, 611, 614, 638–9, 656; repeal of, 653, 662–73, 822–4, 826, 828
combinations or combines, 42, 59–60, 67, 69, 88, 159, 348–51, 379, 398–9, 453, 462, 485, 486, 518, 524, 530, 543, 549, 563–71, 579 n. 60, 587, 596, 601–3, 638, 663–4, 669, 723, 747, 792, 822–5, 828–30; as conspiracies against trade, 570, 669, 822; of employers 524–5, 682; *see also* trade unions
commerce, 1, 22–3, 27, 30, 36, 49–50, 107–8, 117, 143, 161, 163, 167, 215, 236, 246–7, 250, 300, 417, 494, 510, 523, 545, 585, 683, 698, 704, 737, 804, 813, 830, 832, 839; corrosive effect on production, 22; European, 317; international, 11, 25, 108, 161; Irish, 236; laws of, 7; liberalisation of, 670, 678,; of London, 357; pre-capitalist, 42, 839; rational, 339, 417 n. 58; war and capitalism, 585–92; world, 813; *see also* free-trade
commercial treaty with France (1786), 380 n. 134, 506, 533, 535

commercialisation model, 30, 85, 169, 255, 267, 286, 326 n. 130, 417, 812
commissions *see* royal commissions
Commissioners for Trade and Plantations, 147
Committee of Organisation for Forming a Provisional Government, 647
Committee of Secrecy, 546, 564, 576 n. 54
Committee on Artisans and Machinery, 666
Committee on the Woollen Manufacture of England, 448
commodities, 9, 15, 22, 29, 49, 53, 57, 82, 124, 136, 144, 161, 169, 215, 258, 272, 300, 346, 416, 460, 468, 491, 495, 498, 524, 567, 623, 660, 666, 706, 746, 818, 830; fictitious, 216, 300, 346, 660, 716, 818, 830 n. 16; luxury, 137; subsistence, 742
commodification, 57; of labour or labour-power, 15, 24 n. 61, 57, 102, 479, 495, 504, 567, 575, 605, 747, 776, 786, 818, 829, 842; of land, 43, 102, 144, 152, 216, 300, 495, 499, 504, 553, 605, 716, 747, 776, 786, 792, 818, 828–9, 842; of money, 776, 818; petty producers, 741; of elements or factors of production, 17, 57, 417; of social relations, 300, 830, 828
Common Council of London, 65, 106, 122, 348, 349, 364, 593, 804
common law, 25–8, 41, 61, 66–7, 88, 91, 101–2, 106, 119, 130 n. 77, 135, 203, 276–9, 396, 433 n. 124, 518, 520, 531, 555, 559, 564, 568, 570–1, 604, 663, 669, 796–7, 801, 819–20, 822, 838; of conspiracy in restraint of trade, 349, 663, 666, 669
commoners, 66, 115 n. 31, 152, 189, 203, 275–7, 515–516, 528, 532, 541, 547, 559, 561, 568, 605, 611, 690, 697
common rights, 72, 94, 113, 115 n. 31, 266, 270, 275–6, 482, 513, 515, 555, 664
commonwealth or commonweal, 62, 118, 159, 602
Commonwealth of England (1649–1660), 128–9, 141 n. 116, 159, 372–3; *see also* Interregnum
commons *see* common rights, House of Commons, wastes and commons
Commons Secret Committee, 547
Commons Select Committee, 581–2, 601, 615, 637 n. 91, 651
communism, 4, 126 n. 64, 645, 781–2, 788; Communist League, 781; *Communist Manifesto*, 781 n. 113, 787–8, 842
Comninel, George, 2–3, 6, 13 n. 29, 23, 28 n. 73, 48, 50 n. 7, 278–9, 794
companies of artisans; *see also* artisans; guilds
Company of the Indies, 185
complementarity, 445
Complete Suffrage Union, 764, 771 n. 76
Congress of Aix-la-Chapelle (1818), 638
Congress of Verona (1722), 657
Congress of Vienna (1814), 600, 707
Conroy, Sir John (1786–1854), 752
Conservative Party, 752, 763, 770, 772 n. 81, 774, 776, 780
Constitution, English, 127, 130, 188, 537 n. 111; functions of the monarch 229 n. 32; reform 239, 647, 706, 734; rights under 127, 237, 244, 625, 699; and Glorious Revolution 679; Parliamentary supremacy within 618
construction trade, 106 n. 3, 205, 262 n. 27, 334, 365
consumerism, 182, 804, 808
Continental Association, 237
Continental Congress, 237
contraception, 257–8
contracts and contractual market relations, 16, 26, 41, 50–6, 60, 69 n. 68, 82, 86, 106, 137 n. 99, 201 n. 138, 270, 420, 459, 481–3, 515, 525, 532, 566–7, 581, 570, 601, 604, 613–15, 627, 659–60, 716, 718, 721, 729–30, 732, 737, 746, 771 n. 78, 772, 798, 820, 822, 827, 829–31, 838–9; government and military contracts, 260, 364, 366, 473, 614, 656, 801; subcontracting, 365–6, 452–3, 469, 472, 476–7, 482–3, 607, 719, 729, 802; direct contracting, 718
Convention of Pardo (1739), 208
convertible husbandry, 169 n. 16, 180, 198, 807
Cook, Captain James (1728–1779), 235
Cookson, William, Mayor of Leeds, 576, 579–80
Cooper, Thomas, 765, 767
Cope, General Sir John (1690–1760), 210
Copenhagen, Battle of (1801), 573
copper, 76, 78, 81–2, 87, 155, 160, 260, 304, 318 n. 101, 326 n. 131, 330, 336, 363, 393, 443, 473, 480–482, 505; copper oxide, 404; coppersmiths, 477
copperas (green vitriol), 75, 77
coppersmiths, 477 n. 72
copyhold and copyholders, 26, 28, 59 n. 39, 66, 87–9, 118, 135, 202, 277, 348,

404 n. 8, 464, 514, 605, 705, 741, 804; *see also* tenants
cordwainers, 571
corn *see* grain
Corn Laws, 152, 617, 620, 625; (1815), 615, 651, 667, 730, 762, 780, 826; agitation against, 672, 750, 753–5, 762, 770–1, 772 n. 81; repeal of (1846), 651, 730, 773–7, 832, 834–6, 842; revision of (1828), 679
Cornwall, 354, 480–1, 645, 772
Cornwallis, General Charles (1738–1805), 243
Corporation Act (1661), 142, 236, 679, 681, 706
Corresponding Societies Act (1799), 565, 762
Corsica, 233, 557
Cort, Henry (c. 1741–1800) inventor of puddling, 331, 334, 473–4, 584 n. 75
Cortauld, George and Samuel, 452
Cotchett, Thomas, 380
cottage manufacturing, 66, 79, 93–103, 168–71, 196 n. 119, 254, 344, 357, 360, 381, 383, 404, 418 n. 64, 424, 448, 509, 516, 539, 671, 691, 723, 808, 853, 855
cottagers, 3, 194 n. 11, 202, 205 n. 159, 267, 270, 273, 275, 277, 378, 430, 464, 515–16, 520, 611, 809; forty-shilling, cottagers, 705; definition of, 169
Cotton Spinners' Union of 1829, 723
cotton, 33–35, 75, 158, 175–6, 201, 206, 224, 230, 248, 268, 312, 325, 328, 330, 344, 358, 379–80, 384–94, 403, 417, 423–5, 451, 455–6, 462, 465–9, 478–9, 493, 497, 499–500, 502, 505–6, 530, 535–6, 581, 583, 591, 617–19, 628, 638–41, 647, 652, 666–7, 670, 687, 709, 722–3, 739, 749, 753, 759, 764, 766–8, 779, 792, 806, 809, 816; Asian monopoly on growing, 442; boom, 442, 670 n. 206; Indian cottons, 175, 290 n. 14, 385, 436, 768; 'King Cotton', 428–444, 469, 641; cotton gin, 330; cotton-linen fustians, 312; cotton-muslins, 312; tax on, 533 n. 96, 535; cotton prints, 176, 394, 437, 806; cotton revolution, 417; *see also* Arkwright; Paul; Peel; textiles; Wyatt
cotton spinners, 344, 479, 638–9, 647, 672, 760
Cotton Spinners' Union of 1829, 723
couchancy, 514 n. 11
County Policing Act (1839), 687, 757
courts, 55, 142, 147, 183, 253, 279, 328 n. 136, 364, 399, 487, 498, 513, 520, 528, 531, 571, 578, 598, 601, 789, 796, 800; Assize of Novel Disseisin, 796; Chancery, 392; common law, 66, 130 n. 77; Court of Wards, 134, 804; local assizes, 61, 598–9, 626, 673, 767; London, 61; prerogative, 108, 122, 135; Star Chamber, 66 n. 64, 122; *see also* common law; customary law
Cousin, Victor (1792–1867), 749
Coventry, Warwickshire, 352, 538 n. 114, 602, 637 n. 92
craft companies see artisans, guilds, livery, yeomanry
craftswomen see artisans
trade see commerce, merchants, craft companies
trade secrets, 404–7, 425, 450 n. 208, 665, 823; *see also* skills
Cranage brothers, 331
Crawford, William Sharman (1781–1861), 764
Crawshay, Richard (1739–1810) ironmaster, 473–4, 505, 587 n. 89
credit *see* banking
Croker, John Wilson (1780–1857), 699, 701
Crompton, Samuel (1753–1827) inventor of the spinning mule, 329, 433 n. 126, 435, 437 n. 147, 442 n. 176, 456 n. 230
Cromwell, Oliver (1599–1658), 126, 130–1, 151 n. 116, 156–7, 163, 216, 224, 804
Cromwell, Richard (1626–1712), 131–2
croppers *see* shearmen
crossbow, 309
Crowley, John (1687–1727), 364
Crowley, Sir Ambrose (1658–1712) ironmonger, 123 n. 54, 364, 470, 472, 477; Winlaton Iron Works 87, 364; Crowley Iron Works, 159, 365–7; death of, 364
Crowley, Theodosia (c. 1693–1782) 364
Crusades, 11, 51, 313
Crystal Palace, 793, 842
Ctesibius (285–222 BC) Greek inventor, 306
Cubitt, Thomas (1788–1855) master builder, 718–19
Cubitt, William (1785–1861) engineer, 718–19
Cuffay, William (1788–1870), 762
Cugnot, Nicolas-Joseph (1725–1804) inventor of the *fardier*, 331
Culloden, Battle of (1746), 211, 240 n. 63, 250
Cumberland, 201 n. 141, 204, 480, 482, 643, 771

Cumberland, Duke, Prince William Augustus (1721–1765), 210–11, 220 n. 14
Currency Act, 229 n. 33, 560
custom, 509–556; appeals to losing sway in courts, 531; customary regulation of the labour process in workshops, 102, 367, 407, 454, 458, 674, 742, 814; and dis-embedding of social relations, 26 n. 69, 254 Diagram 5.1, 255, 358, 794, 797
customary law or manorial law, 21, 26–8, 56, 61, 64, 67, 71, 89, 224, 514, 539, 559, 569, 624, 796–800; abolition or extinguishing of, 30, 41, 43, 67, 72, 91, 145, 276, 509–10, 513–14, 555, 568, 605, 815, 819, 837–8; in French agriculture, 71; institutional foundations of, 513, 555; jurisdiction of, 279–80; legal basis for undermined, 825; *see also* Statute of Apprentices; open fields; tenancies; workshops
cutlers, 59, 359; Sheffield Cutlers' Act, 602 n. 143
Cyfarthfa, Wales, 473–4

Daguerre, Louis (1787–1851) inventor of photography, 337
dairying, 168, 193, 202, 258, 482 n. 103, 515 n. 16, 615, 697, 775
Darby, Abraham I (1678–1717), 158 n. 180, 166, 264, 324–5, 330–1, 341, 471–2, 493
Darby, Abraham II (1711–1763), 367, 471–2, 493
Darby, Abraham III (1750–1789), 333, 505, 584, 478, 584–5
Darby, Abraham IV (1804–1878), 504–5
Darby, Edmund, 504–5, 584–5
Darby, Francis, 504–5
Darby, Hannah, wife of Abraham Darby II, 367
Darby, Samuel, 504–5
Darwin, Charles (1809–1882), 7
Davidson, Neil, 649
da Vinci, Leonardo (1452–1519), 37–9, 312, 319–21, 325
Davis, John A., 100, 655
Davy, Sir Humphrey (1778–1829) inventor of miner's safety lamp, 337
Deane, Phyllis, 194 n. 111, 218, 256, 259, 261, 329 n. 139, 261, 355 n. 39, 393, 429, 471 n. 41, 490 n. 140, 494, 496–500, 738
debt, 107–8, 110, 132–33, 153, 204, 219, 232, 246, 278, 336 n. 175, 375, 456, 474, 478, 593 n. 112, 640, 737; debtors prison, 231–3, 242, 389; *see also* National Debt
Declaration of Breda (1660), 132, 134, 211
Declatory Act or American Colonies Act (1766) 229, 233
Defoe, Daniel (c. 1660–1731), 148, 158, 365, 454
de-industrialisation, 92, 94, 95, 170 n. 170, 611, 617 n. 208, 470 n. 224, 768 n. 67; *see also* proto-industrialisation
democracy, 42, 84, 103, 114, 163, 270, 542, 628 n. 60, 708, 804, 811, 832, 838; in America, 237; and capitalism's origin, 4; Civil War Levellers call for, 127; a dangerous form of government, 657, 697, 729; in Ireland, 681; and Jacobinism, 577; and Luddism, 605; in workplace and workshops, 114, 135 n. 94, 140, 728–9; representative, 729
demographic model, 30, 169, 255–6, 259, 267, 286–7
Denmark, 107 n. 8, 146 n. 128, 573, 589
dentistry, 304, 336–7
depopulation of rural villages, 274
depression, 110–11, 123, 128, 132, 230–1, 260, 279, 385, 393, 413, 435, 441, 468, 534, 580, 590, 592, 624, 632, 664, 670–1, 682, 717, 761, 763, 770, 823; agrarian, 165, 441, 624, 807; first agrarian (1690–1715), 175, 199, 212; Great Depression (1873), 777 n. 96; second 'so-called' agrarian (1730–1750), 71, 192–206, 213, 255, 279, 355 n. 39, 774
Derby, Derbyshire, 211, 325, 379–83, 406 n. 20, 424, 431–2, 700, 719–21, 723–6
Derby, Earl of *see* Stanley
Derbyshire, 362 Table 7.2, 380, 432, 436 Table 8.1, 438, 439 n. 159, 480, 482, 583, 593, 630–1
Dereham, Sir Richard (1644–1710), 386, 387 n. 155
Derry, John W., 610, 643, 652–3, 704
Despard Affair (1798), 562, 576, 638, 783
Despard, Edward Marcus (1751–1803), 462, 576
determinism *see* class determinism, economic determinism, technological determinism
Dettingen, Battle of (1743), 210
Devon (Devonshire), 140, 159, 220, 323, 349, 362 Table 7.2, 385, 393
Didot, Saint-Léger Didot (1767–1829) papermaker, 337
Diggers, 4, 114, 126 n. 64, 540, 660, 707, 751 n. 5; as 'true Levellers', 4; *see also* Levellers
Dinwiddy, J.R., 576

dioptra, 306
diplomacy, 129, 161, 233
Dircxz van Sonnevelt, Willem, inventor of Dutch ribbon loom, 321
Disarming Act (1747), 211
disenfranchisement, 116, 131, 244 n. 78, 534, 700, 702, 704, 727
Disraeli, Benjamin (1804–1881) Prime Minister, 764, 776
Disseisin, *see* Assize of Novel Disseisen
Dissenters, 120, 126 n. 60, 141, 148, 182 n. 60, 188, 191, 220 n. 14, 475, 531, 537, 581, 679, 687, 750
distilleries, 195, 227 n. 28, 428 n. 97, 470 n. 37
division of labour, 19–2, 31, 74, 85, 169, 201, 206, 297–8, 408–11, 415–16, 420, 426, 440, 446–8, 457, 470, 474–6, 479, 502–3, 524, 603, 606, 739 n. 216; social, 97, 168, 415; technical, 418
Dobb, Maurice (1900–1976), 9–17, 24, 30, 797
Dobson, C.R., 349–50, 393 n. 182, 563–5
dockworkers, 357, 631 n. 69
docks and dockyards, 78, 197, 365 n. 73, 601, 632; *see also* tidal dock
Doherty, John (1798–1854), 673, 682, 717, 719
Domesday Book (1086), 130 n. 77, 144, 306 n. 66
domestic system, 43, 61, 93–4, 159, 289 n. 12, 293, 347, 361, 385 n. 152, 440, 448, 483, 491–2, 580, 582
Dorothée, Claude-François (1751–1832) marquis de Jouffrey d'Abbans, inventor of steamship, 331
Dorset, 113, 115, 360, 362 Table 7.2, 384, 630 n. 66, 695, 720, 726
double forward commitment, 179–80, 212
Downing, Sir George (1623–1684) 1st Baronet, 149
drainage of fens, etc., 115 n. 31, 124, 144, 168, 199, 202, 263 n. 28, 775, 790, 807; of mines, 263 n. 31, 305, 323–4, 481
drapers and draperies, 59, 360, 385–6; new draperies, 111–12, 116, 139; old draperies, 110
Drinkwater, Peter, factory owner, 479
dual revolution, xix, 619
Dudley, Dud (1600–1684), 324
Dundas, Henry 1st Viscount Melville (1742–1811), 247, 547, 586
Dunkley, Peter, 731–2
Dutch Loom, 139, 321, 376, 381, 387, 530–1
Dutch Republic (1581–1785), 37, 71, 111–12, 116, 119–20, 129, 146, 157, 173, 175–6, 215–16, 217 n. 6, 223, 287, 321–22, 384, 404, 429, 603; Anglo-Dutch Alliance, 146, 178, 179 n. 50, 210; Dutch Ceylon, 245, 558; Dutch East India Company, 129 n. 73, 133 n. 87; Dutch East Indies, 558
Dutch Wars: First (1652–4) 130, 133; Second (1665–7), 141; Third (1672–4), 141
dyers and dyeing, 66, 106. 111, 157 n. 171, 158–9, 324 n. 120, 336, 385, 386, 394 n. 187, 410, 431, 433, 442–3, 465, 486, 489, 530, 533, 638

East Anglia, 73, 94, 112, 266, 359, 384, 393, 467–9, 568, 625, 661–2
East India Company, 109, 121, 129, 150 n. 142, 151, 160–1, 185–6, 191, 231, 236–7, 243, 247–8, 362, 385–6, 490 n. 141, 810; New East India Company 161, 175 n. 36; uniting of the two Companies (1709) 161; Dutch East India Company *see* Dutch Republic
East Retford *see* Retford
Easter tax, 709
Eastland Company, 160–1
ecology, 34 n. 89, 498 n. 165, 615 n. 12
economy: Ancient, 275; of crime, 189; disarticualated, 468; domestic, 62, 79, 166, 173–4, 180, 187 n. 77, 250, 260, 559, 571, 603, 811; Dutch, 173; European, 37; European-Mediterranean, 12; family, 640; French, 185; government regulation in the, 821; Indian, 248, 709, 810; market, 56, 83, 167, 770; market regulation of the, 3, 5, 27, 30, 85–6, 288, 313, 415, 553, 605, 657, 776, 793, 819, 831; money or money-wage, 10–11, 358, 369, 526; moral, 54, 532, 636, 811, 824; of scale, 162, 202, 274, 300, 503; separation from the polity, 794; town, 62; village, 169; world, 38, 53
economics, 6–8, 42, 270, 499, 738, 812; agrarian capitalist, 6; capitalist, 420, 523, 621; classical, 307, 624; consumption, 29, 50, 76, 79, 114, 137, 153, 166, 200, 214, 257 Table 5.1, 258, 275, 385, 358, 454, 561, 616, 622 n. 36, 623, 802, 837; distribution, 30, 54, 75, 152, 303, 428, 484, 815; of feudalism, 613; *laissez-faire*, 780; market, 624; modern, 6; naturalised, 6–8; neoclassical, 450, 521; neoliberal, 446' pre-capitalist, 163,

276; redistribution, 126, 128, 144, 540 n. 120, 661, 758, 785; Smithian, 7; *see also* Marxism; political economy
economic determinism, 501, 634
economic fatalism, 521, 622, 821
economic leaseholds *see* tenants
Eden Treaty (1786), 537
Eden, Sir Frederick (1766–1809), 544, 550 n. 161
Edict of Fraternity (1792), 542
Edict of Nantes (1598), 158 n. 179, 380, 472
Edinburgh, Scotland, 178 n. 47, 207 n. 165, 210, 245, 362, 376, 478 n. 80, 545, 616 n. 13, 668, 716
Edinburgh Review, 665
Edward IV (1442–1483), 60, 66
Edward VI (1537–1553), 370, 420, 517, 519, 578, 823
Edward, Prince and Duke of Kent (1767–1820), 751
Eelers, potters, 404
Egerton, Francis *see* Bridgewater, Duke of
Egypt, 302, 304, 307, 309 n. 77, 312, 326 n. 131, 413, 561, 572–3, 585, 588, 658, 755, 768–9
d'Eichthal, Gustave (1804–1886), 677
elections: for Parliament, 132, 146–7, 179–83, 192 n. 102, 209 n. 170, 211 n. 179, 213, 219, 247, 534, 588, 615, 638, 649 n. 144, 679, 688, 700, 709–10, 729, 735, 752–3, 763, 779–80, 789; in City of London, 231–2; secret ballot 232, 539 n. 117, 788; in Preston, 421 n. 68; ballots, 700, 702, 750, 832; by-elections, 700; at Stoke workhouse, 737; in Potteries for Board of Guardians, 737–8; in France, 738
electricity, 326
elements, table of the, 336
Elizabeth I (1533–1603), 66–9, 76, 81 n. 120, 87, 102, 108–9; 112, 119–20, 177, 240 n. 62, 368, 501, 509, 516, 602, 802–3, 821 n. 14; Elizabethan Companies, 140, 344; Poor Laws, 72, 369, 372, 632 n. 72; death, 107; 5 Elizabeth *see* Statute of Apprentices, welfare
Ellul, Jacques (1912–1994), 291
Embargo Act (1807), 589
embezzlement of raw materials by employees, 188 n. 81, 357, 444, 452, 459–60, 517, 819
emigration, 357, 790; of artisans and skilled labourers, 176, 357, 666; to the colonies, 714, 734; from Ireland, 777
employers *see* managers
Emsley, Clive, 546 n. 144, 566
Enamellers, 409
enclosures, 4–5, 26–31, 41–3, 61–9, 71–2, 80, 87–9, 91–95, 102–3, 113–16, 123, 126, 131, 135–6, 144–5, 153, 157, 163, 167, 169–70, 189–92, 197–203, 212–13, 218, 253–7, 262, 265–80, 334, 344, 346–7, 368–9, 378, 395–7, 439, 463–4, 482, 490, 498, 502–3, 509, 514–16, 525, 538–9, 552–3, 568–71, 605–6, 611, 616, 691–5, 729, 731, 775, 789, 795–820, 825, 831, 838, 842; and the capital relation, 26; coal, 482, 801; converting arable to pasture, 26–7, 240; fines for, 115; great debate on, 270–9; in Ireland, 774 n. 87; high parliamentary, 269; late, 464, 662 n. 176, 741, 774 n. 871; legislation against, 69 n. 68, 800, 803; lifting of legislation against, 539; movement, 28, 64, 72, 270–1, 274, 605, 621, 800; parliamentary, 26, 43, 153, 212, 223–5, 253–5, 265–73, 278, 344, 402, 509, 514–15, 520, 538, 540, 554–5, 568, 605, 656, 695, 740, 745, 789 n. 135, 812, 819–20; Philpot's hypothesis, 257; piecemeal, 271 n. 50, 470, 515; protests against, 4, 103, 116, 123, 135, 272, 514, 543, 838; impact on women, 514
Engels, Frederick (1820–1895), 7–8, 33–4, 295–8, 439 n. 158, 751, 760, 779–80, 787, 842
engineers and engineering, 40, 81, 262–3, 287–8, 318–21, 332–40, 340, 381–3, 388–9, 426, 457, 469, 473 n. 51, 489–91, 834, 603, 664, 721, 817; history of, 426; training of skilled, 478–9; master, 603; hydraulic, 813; *see also* social engineering
England *see* English state
English Agricultural Society, 776
English Civil Wars: of fifteenth century (1455–1485), 61; of the seventeenth century (1642–1651), 77, 85, 110, 114, 116–136, 141, 147, 162, 182, 221, 269, 424, 475, 539, 686, 803–4
English Copper Company, 480
English Guinea Company, 122, 129
English Revolution (1640–1660), 105–54, 224; as bourgeois revolution, 135–6, 146;

city revolution in London (1642–1643), 122, 124–5; Puritan revolution, 123, 125
English state, 57, 171–2, 371 n. 97; not bourgeois, 145 n. 126, 619; bureaucracy, 119, 145 n. 126, 149, 203 n. 149; early centralisation and unity of, 58, 61, 70, 80, 372; contradictions of, 116, 803; and crisis of fourteenth century, 57; became Europe's entrepôt, 157, 175, 212; first in Europe to de-militarise, 26, 61, 800; as imperial, 250–1; intra-elite struggles, 221, 249; and national debt, 147–56, 60 n. 182; state-run enterprises, 80, 101, 362, 801; strength of based on agrarian capitalism, 165–214; subsidies to allies, 212, 220 n. 13, 222–3, 226, 544–5, 805, 808; war materiel demand, 260, 560, 656; *see also* British state; Parliament
Engravers, 409
engrossing of foodstuffs, 114, 136, 518, 520 n. 37, 529, 564, 570
engrossment of land *see* land
Enlightenment, 230, 532, 541, 559, 619; rationality, 339
entrepôt trade, 133 n. 87, 157, 175, 212, 384, 588 n. 93, 617
Episcopalians, 131, 210 n. 175
Epstein, Steven A., 19 n. 46, 50, 55, 371 n. 97
escapement mechanism, 309, 317–18
Essex, 371 n. 96, 376, 452, 568, 695, 736
Etruria and Etruscans, 305, 307, 404; *see also* Wedgwood
Europe and European: ancient, 28, 302 n. 52, 316; Central, 107, 782; class society, 84, 216, 322, 339; continental, 93, 558, 585, 794; Eastern, 11, 14, 25, 71, 96, 109, 216, 285, 287, 706 *see* serfdom: 'second serfdom'; feudal or medieval, 12–15, 50, 308, 313, 316, 797, 813; imperialism, 215–17, 619; Northwestern, 97; Northern, 310–11; pan-European industrialisation, 168; post-feudal, 15, 96; population, 71–2, 311, 313; Renaissance, 315; reaction after Waterloo, 706, 746, 825; scientific revolution pan-european, 286; state-led industrialisation, 341, 415; Western, xx, 1, 9–11, 14, 15, 25, 36–9, 52, 59, 96, 98, 213, 287, 310, 536, 755, 813
Evans, Neil, 85
Evans, Oliver (1755–1819) American inventor, 329
Exchequer, 118, 149, 186, 533 n. 98, 560, 632, 652
Exeter, Devon, 374, 384–5, 393
Exploitation, 13, 18, 58 n. 37, 84, 96, 129 n. 71, 156 n. 169, 172, 271 n. 52, 298, 377, 399, 458, 492, 495, 500, 525, 553–5, 592, 636, 639, 682, 825–6
exports, 61, 63, 76, 80, 107, 110–11, 113–14, 123–4, 136–7, 150 n. 142, 151 n. 146, 157, 159–61, 166, 174–6, 187 n. 77, 191, 193–5, 197 n. 123, 198, 212, 214, 230, 250, 255, 257 Table 5.1, 258–60, 279, 312, 317, 326 n. 130, 330, , 363, 381–2, 384–6, 405, 429, 462–3, 467, 475, 484, 498, 515, 518, 548, 590–2, 601, 651, 644, 666, 740, 768 n. 67, 77 n. 96, 778, 803, 806–10, 823; re-exports, 107, 133 n. 87, 150, 157, 159–61, 175, 203; from Scotland, 178, 468; from China and India, 442; from Ireland, 468
extra-economic social relations, 15–19, 26–9, 41, 50, 75 n. 101, 83–7, 109, 117, 136, 163, 215, 248–51, 366–7, 420, 553, 588 n. 94, 606, 612–13, 618, 632, 657–60, 674, 703, 715, 741, 746, 761, 799, 805, 810, 827–30, 838, 842; *see also* coercive force
eyeglasses, 316–17

factor, 360, 463–4
factors of production, 21, 167, 379, 401, 428
factory, 19, 33–5, 43–4, 79–80, 82, 92, 94–5, 100 n. 197, 112 n. 24, 224, 241, 289–93, 318, 330, 335, 337, 339, 343–47, 361, 365–6, 371 n. 95, 367–8, 379–89, 397, 399–461, 464, 466, 476–9, 481, 486, 489, 491–3, 498, 500–4, 510, 512–13, 516, 521, 523, 532, 543, 548, 568, 572, 577, 580–4, 589, 591, 596–9, 603–7, 611, 629, 631 n. 69, 632–3, 636, 639–40, 644–5, 658, 663, 665, 670–2, 674–5, 677–8, 681–2, 685, 687, 691, 695, 697–8, 708, 711, 717, 721, 723–4, 726–7, 737–42, 747, 756, 760, 764, 768 n. 67, 779–80, 776, 786–7, 797, 805, 809, 811, 814–17, 820, 824–6, 829, 831, 833, 843; alkali, 489; calico-printing, 687; carding, 386; children in, 382, 380–90, 628, 645, 711–14, 772 n. 80; commissioners, 453, 729; co-operative, 717; cotton, 224, 329 n. 139, 380, 387–89, 423, 428–44, 500, 618–19, 652; definition of, 379, 451–6; discipline, 427, 441, 447, 451–4, 469; as enclosures of labour, 60; first, 176, 325–6, 335, 347–8, 379–84, 807, 809; hosiery, 628; 'immature' factory, 408; inspectors, 440, 582; Irish, 535; jenny, 421–3, 435; lace, 627;

machinery absent, 264 n. 34, 403–15, 444–55; machinery in, 401–3, 415–61, 815; mode of production, 636; nail, 364; origins of, 343–400; paper, 486, 816; and prisons, 289 n. 11; porcelain, 415; pin-making, 415, 446 n. 194; pre- or proto-, 444, 464, 490, 492; silk, 325–6, 379–84, 397, 584, 626, 719–20, 809; state-run, 285, 287; syndicalist, 724; throstle, 584 n. 74; weavers, 738 Table 13.1; wool, 580–2; and workhouses, 376–9, 396, 400, 510, 512
Factory Acts, 769; of 1802, 581, 628, 687; of 1819, 628 n. 56, 645; of 1833, 712, 715, 724; of 1844, 772
factory masters or capitalist masters, 438–40, 446, 451, 453, 458, 479, 493, 498, 502, 506, 509, 583, 597, 611, 615, 640–1, 652, 658, 681–2, 712, 763, 768, 779–80, 805, 814–15, 817, 820, 824, 826, 843
factory system, 34, 224, 285, 289 n. 12, 343, 347, 361, 373, 401–3, 406, 410, 416 n. 55, 428, 431 n. 115, 440, 443, 445, 448, 451, 460, 466, 470, 493, 504, 523, 539, 549, 575, 604, 606, 660, 670, 691, 776 n. 94, 815, 817
Fahrenheit, Daniel Gabriel (1686–1736) inventor of thermometer, 327
famine, 179, 236, 515, 529 n. 81, 530, 551 n. 165, 554, 592, 611, 621, 692, 734, 768 n. 67, 822; *see also* Ireland; India
Faraday, Michael (1791–1867) inventor of the electric motor, 337
fardier à vapeur (steam dray), 331
farming *see* tenant-farmer
farm-workers *see* agrarian labourers
Fawr, Jemima (1755–1832), 560
Feiling, Keith Graham (1884–1977), 182–3, 321 n. 38, 649 n. 144
feltmakers, 112–13, 159, 602
fens and fen-dwellers, 115, 244, 626
fents and thrums, 517
fertility rates, 257–8
feudalism, 2–3, 6, 8–20, 24–5, 27–30, 36–7, 39, 42, 49–61, 82, 85, 93, 95–100, 109, 117–19, 134–35, 143, 156, 168–9, 171, 202 n. 145, 296, 311, 313–16, 365, 403, 458, 483, 502, 522, 541, 542, 558–9, 568, 606, 612–14, 619, 683, 793–800, 805, 829, 837, 839; neo–feudalism in Eastern Europe, 216, 287–8; neo-feudal régimes after 1815, 706, 746, 832; in Scotland, 211; *see also* parcellisation of sovereignty; transition debate
fictitious commodities, 216, 346, 660, 716, 818, 830 n. 16
Fielden, John (1784–1849), 724, 779
Fielding, Henry (1707–1754), 219, 231 n. 38, 532 n. 91, 546 n. 145
Fielding, Sir John (1721–1780), 231 n. 38, 531, 546 n. 145
financial revolution, 148–56
firebote, 516; *see also* wood
firewood *see* wood
First Coalition, war of the (1791–8), 557–8
First World War, 764
Fitton, R.S., 436
Fitzherbert, Maria (1756–1837), 688
FitzRoy, Augustus Henry, 3rd Duke of Grafton, Prime Minister (1735–1811), 233
Fitzwilliam, Earl see Wentworth-Fitzwilliam, William
flax, 117, 175, 198 n. 126, 328 n. 136, 371, 374, 387, 444, 468–9, 530 n. 82; flax-spinning, 374, 452, 468–9, 503, 763
Fleurus, Battle of (1794), 547
Flinn, Michael W. (1917–1983), xviii, 166–7, 632
flintlock rifle, 321
fluyt, 37
Flynn, John Thomas (1882–1964), 82
flying shuttle *see* shuttle-loom
flywheel, 316
Foley, Thomas (1670–1737), 152
Folley Hall Rising (1818), 630–1, 826
Fontainebleau, Treaty of (1814), 600
forestalling, 114, 518–20, 523, 529, 555, 564, 570, 803, 820 n. 13
Forest of Dean, 363, 482
forests, 11, 113, 115, 135, 189 n. 87, 190 n. 96, 257 n. 12, 266, 334, 359, 475, 513–14, 540, 543; *see also* Windsor Forest
Foss Dyke *see* canals
Fothergill, John (1730–1782), 476, 478 n. 80
Fourdrinier, Henry (1766–1854), 337
Fourdrinier papermaking machine, 337
Fourdrinier, Sealy, 337
Fourneyron, Benoît (1802–1867), inventor of the outward-flow turbine, 337
Fox, Alan (1920–2002), 525, 751 n. 5, 759, 785, 787, 791 n. 145
Fox, Charles James (1749–1806), 244–7, 534–8, 547, 563, 585; death of, 587; Foxite opposition, 536–8, 547–8, 586–8, 620; India Bill, 247; Ministry of all Talents, 586; Whig Club, 534

Fox, Henry (1705 – 1 July 1774) 1st Baron Holland, 219–20
Fox-North Ministry (1783), 246–7
framework knitters, 362 Table 7.2, 425 n. 85, 431 n. 113, 452, 577; Company of, 424 n. 82
Frampton, James, 720
France, 9, 14, 36, 43, 70–1, 77, 80, 107, 110, 118, 120–1, 134, 139, 141–2, 145–6, 148, 152–3, 165, 171–4, 178–80, 182–5, 187, 191, 195, 197, 207 n. 162, 209–12, 215, 218, 220–3, 225–7, 230 n. 35, 233, 238, 241, 244–6, 250, 256, 259–60, 272, 278–9, 340–1, 354, 363–4, 371, 376, 380, 386–9, 391–2, 395, 410 n. 33, 419, 438 n. 152, 472, 486–7, 515, 523, 531, 533, 536–47, 552, 556–62, 572–3, 577, 580, 584–7, 588–593, 600, 603, 611–19, 625, 631, 638, 645, 650, 653–60, 677, 679, 688, 696, 706–8, 743, 761, 768–9, 773, 781, 783, 794–6, 798 n. 8, 805–8, 811–13, 820–5, 832, 839; absolutism in, 2, 163; agrarian capitalism absent, 14, 24, 195; army of, 336, 558, 561, 585, 600, 603; bourgeois revolution in, 162; Carolingian, 796; coal output, 743 n. 229; commercial treaty of 1786, 506, 533–6; guilds of, 74 n. 90; invasion plans, 178, 182, 239, 558–61; inventors, 317, 321–3, 325 n. 123, 327, 331, 333 n. 162, 335–7, 487; Languedoc, 617; Lyons, 337, 380; Marseilles, 70; new constitution, 559; offices of state, 109; peasantry, 17; population of, 11; Paris, 71, 185 n. 71, 228, 238, 333 n. 161, 337, 425 n. 85, 489, 538, 544–5, 559, 585, 587 n. 91, 600, 769 n. 69, 781–3, 813; *pays de Caux*, 97; railways, 743; slavery, 217 n. 6; state patronage of science and technology, 332 n. 156, 340, 414–15; state regulation of manufacturing, 66, 133 n. 87, 285–7, 391; the *taille,* 71; Tours, 380; trade and trade war with, 157, 176 n. 40, 247, 587–92, 599; *see also* Bonaparte; Revolutionary and Napoleonic Wars; property: tax-state office
Franklin, Benjamin (1706–1790), 236 n. 48, 237, 326, 414 n. 48
Frederick, Prince of Wales (1707–1751), 209, 213 n. 182, 678
Frederick II of Prussia (1712–1786), 209 n. 169, 221–6
Frederick William II of Prussia (1744–1797), 536, 541
Frederick William III of Prussia (1770–1840), 600 n. 138
free-trade, 38, 69 n. 71, 110, 138, 140, 156–62, 230, 239, 246, 351, 510, 513, 519, 522, 530, 535, 575, 587 n. 91, 620, 650–5, 675, 680, 687, 698, 739, 768, 770, 774–5, 788, 804, 806; mercantilism and, 129 n. 73, 138, 140, 564 n. 16; Britain largest free-trade area in Europe, 162, 179, 213–14, 666; Free Trade Hall, 770; *see also laissez-faire*
freeholders and freehold tenancy, 4, 26, 41, 59 n. 39, 66, 88 n. 152, 134, 202, 233, 276–7, 406 n. 20, 464, 514, 681, 687, 699, 773, 778, 788–90, 796–7, 804, 836, 838; forty-shilling freeholders, 116, 705, 709, 778, 789; *see also* Birmingham Freehold Land Society; tenants
freemen, 114, 128, 130, 349, 705; *see also* bondsmen
French Revolutions, xix–xx, 260 n. 21, 327, 364, 531; of 1789, 537–40; of (July) 1830, 688; of (February) 1848, 781–2; Directory, 588; *Grande Armée*, 599–600; National Assembly, 538, 542 n. 127; National Convention, 542, 544; *see also* France; Revolutionary and Napoleonic Wars
French Wars *see* Revolutionary and Napoleonic Wars
friendly societies, 43, 140–1, 159, 345, 347–8, 377, 397, 477, 543–4, 570, 581, 603, 646, 665, 716 n. 137, 764, 784; *see also* welfare
Friendly Societies Act (1793), 789
Friendly Society of Agricultural Labourers, 720
Fugger, Jacob (1459–1525), 81–2
Fuller, Robert, shoemaker, 561
fullers, 63, 462–3
fulling and fulling mills, 66, 317, 354, 359, 362, 373, 402, 465, 487, 502, 580, 741
fustians, 111, 175, 312, 386, 467, 530 n. 82

Galloway, Alexander, 601, 664, 824
Galton Jr., Samuel (1753–1832), 414
Gandhi, Mohandas Karamchand (1869–1948), 303
gaols *see* prisons
Garbett, Samuel, 264 n. 34, 475, 487, 489 n. 137, 505–6, 535
gas works, 489, 632
Gascoigne, Charles (1738–1806), 473
Gascoyne, Isaac (c. 1763–1841), 699, 702

Gast, John, 639, 667, 675 n. 218, 680, 716, 826
gears and gearing, 306–7, 316–7, 320, 340, 426, 457 n. 231, 470, 474, 584 n. 74; crown-and-pinion, 316
General Association, the, 680
General Chamber of Manufacturers, 505, 535–6, 747
General Inclosure Act (1845), 775, 789, 834
general strike *see* strike(s) and strikers
General Trades' Union, 716
General Union of Carpenters, 716
gentry, 115, 118, 124, 130, 136, 145 n. 126, 152, 183, 190, 197 n. 122, 204–5, 213, 243, 258, 272, 358, 505, 512, 522, 527, 587 n. 89, 654, 687, 691, 704, 707 n. 109, 776, 804–5, 810; armigerous, 118; growth of, 118; class power of, 142–3, 611, 805; lesser, 201, 206, 249, 475; land tax and, 229; supplied capital for industry, 490; balance of power between peerage and, 613, 832; *see also* oligarchy
George I (1660–1727); 180–3; accession and coronation, 181; death of, 191
George II (1683–1760), 191, 209, 224, 519; death of, 213 n. 182, 221, 223; rides in battle at Dettingen, 210
George III (1738–1820), 213 n. 182, 224–30, 244–9, 432, 434, 547, 563, 586, 704, 810, 820; accession, 224, 236, 357, 519; American War and, 243–4; death of, 646; opposition to Catholic Relief, 236, 680; porphyria and long illness, 536–7, 573, 593, 646; *see also* Bute legend
George IV (1762–1830), 650, 678; accession and coronation, 649 n. 144; death of, 688; as George Augustus, Prince of Wales, 536, 593; opposition to Catholic Relief, 681; Queen Caroline Affair, 593 n. 112, 649–50; as Regent, 593; unpopularity, 650
George, M. Dorothy (1878–1971), 563–6, 570 n. 35
Georgian calendar, 218
Geraghty, Thomas M., 444–5, 451, 460
Germany and German principalities, 7–9, 51 n. 12, 61 n. 45, 75, 77–8, 81, 97, 107, 111, 118, 146, 157 n. 171, 176, 205 n. 154, 216 n. 3, 220–2, 231 n. 38, 241 n. 64, 297, 310, 318, 327, 336, 341 n. 186, 371, 376 n. 114, 386, 431 n. 113, 468, 472, 486, 541, 558, 573, 600, 613, 643, 743, 781–2, 842; Berlin, 221; Berlin Decree, 587–8, 589–90, 823; Leibzig 600; Münster 133; Westphalia, 11, 133; *see also* Prussia
Gibralter, Spain, 172, 245, 573
Gilbert's Act (1782), 550
Gilboy, Elizabeth W., 356
gild *see* guilds
gilders, 412
Gimblett, John, Birmingham Manufacturer, 475, 478 n. 79
Gin Act (1736), 207, 219
Giotto di Bondone (c. 1266–1337), 317
girdlers, 68
Girondists, 545
Glasgow, Scotland, 240, 394, 430, 456, 487–9, 596 n. 123, 602, 638, 647–8, 667–8; University of Glasgow, 478, 752, 762; United Trades of Glasgow, 716, 723
glass and glassmaking, 71 n. 77, 75–9, 87, 137, 153 n. 153, 158 n. 180, 160, 193, 231, 285, 288 n. 10, 302, 304, 307, 311–12, 324, 336, 357, 363, 393, 394 n. 187, 470 n. 37, 486–9, 535, 801–2; stained glass, 432 n. 123; *see also* eyeglasses; magnifying glass
glassworkers, 638
Glauber, Johann, 486
gleaning, 514–16, 820
glider, 312, 339
Glorious Revolution (1688–1689), 136, 142–6, 160, 162–3, 173 n. 31, 394, 402, 537–8, 540, 805–6; post-revolution settlement, 146–9; *see also* financial revolution
Gloucestershire, 111, 113, 159, 360, 384, 398, 422, 424, 467, 480, 482, 578, 581, 695
glovers, 63, 107
GNCTU *see* Grand National Consolidated Trades Union
Goderich, Viscount *see* Robinson, John Frederick
Godwin, William (1756–1836), 575, 741
goldsmiths, 148, 477 n. 72
Gonner, Edward Carter Kersey (1862–1922), 757
Goodair, John, 597
Gordon, Lord George (1751–1793), 240–2, 249, 810
Gordon Riots *see* Great Liberty Riots
Gott, Benjamin (1762–1840), 466, 491, 502–3, 505, 580, 607, 816; Armley Mills, 465 n. 17; Bean Ing Mill, 466, 580, 607, 823
Government of India Act (1833), 709

gradualist school of thought, 32, 269, 322, 500 n. 169
Grafton, Prime Minister *see* FitzRoy, Augustus Henry
Graham, Sir James Robert George, 2nd Baronet (1792–1861), 763, 771–2, 779
grain and grain markets, 64–5, 71, 117, 276, 280, 317, 398, 515, 527, 529 n. 81, 590, 771, 774, 808; engrossing, 114; exports, 114, 133 n. 87, 136–7, 160, 166, 174, 176, 193–5, 214, 255, 279, 515, 548, 807–9; harvest, 627; imports, 398, 515, 548, 560, 572, 590, 615, 622, 651, 679, 777, 823; prices, 26, 28, 43, 61, 71–2, 101, 112 n. 24, 114–15, 136, 176, 192–3, 199, 201, 212–13, 254 Diagram 5.1, 278, 519, 522, 529, 551 n. 165, 556, 572, 592, 594, 615, 626, 679, 799, 803, 807–9, 813, 835; riots, 114; shortages, 114, 519, 549; siphoning, 114; supply and scarcity, 114 n. 28, 254, 807; surpluses, 114; yields and output, 71, 101, 115 n. 32, 193–8, 258, 265, 257 Table 5.1, 274, 591, 643–4, 775, 807; *see also* gleaning; wheat
Grand Alliance, war of the (1688–97), 146, 171, 173
Grand Lessees, 87
Grand National Consolidated Trades Union (GNCTU), 716–7, 719–26, 735–7, 758, 773, 786, 829, 833
Grand National Moral Union of the Productive Classes of the United Kingdom, 720
Grand Remonstrance (1641), 124
Great Britain, 75, 77 n. 108, 181, 209 n. 169, 381, 406, 740, 752, 794; leading coal producer, 367, 473; formation of, 108, 140; largest free-trade area in world, 213–14; leading imperial power, 248; leading industrial power, 260, 618; most powerful state in world, 225; tariff war with Ireland, 535; 'workshop of the world', 40, 243, 769 n. 79, 778, 795, 1842; *see also* Act of Union with Scotland
Great Exhibition (1851), 843
Great Liberty Riots or 'Gordon Riots' (1780), 240, 249, 531, 555, 610, 810, 825
Great Northern War (1700–20), 184
Great Reform Act of 1832, 696, 701, 703–10, 714–16, 726, 734–5, 745, 750, 757, 763, 772, 788, 832–3, 834; of 1867, 705
Greece, 82, 304, 306, 657, 679, 813, 829; Minoans, 326 n. 131
Gregg, Edward, 182
Grenville, Richard Plantagenet, Marquis of Chandos (1797–1861), 220 n. 14, 227
Grenville, William Wyndham, 1st Baron (1759–1834), 220 n. 14, 586, 620, 651–2
Grenville, George, Prime Minister (1712–1770), 227, 229–30, 234
Grey, Edward, 1st Viscount of Fallodon (1862–1933) Prime Minister, 545, 562 n. 11, 620, 652, 694, 697, 701–4, 709–10, 714, 735, 746, 777, 832, 834
Grimshaw Brothers, 456
guilds (gilds), 22, 29, 43–4, 85, 93, 101, 136, 139, 344–5, 348–9, 371 n. 95, 398, 421 n. 67, 472, 492, 516, 525, 532, 619, 637, 793, 797–801; by-laws and monopolistic regulations, 106, 224, 322, 432, 516, 797, 800–1, 803; charities run by, 64; court of assistants, 63; and custom, 57, 67, 70; decline, 74, 101, 139, 406, 462, 803; evolution of, 57–66, 112 n. 24; Great Companies of London, 63; medieval, 49–56, 320, 344; oligarchy' in, 159; Roman guilds, 49; statutes, 55, 602, 605; stratification within, 58 n. 37, 59–63, 344, 397, 800, 803, 838; wage labour and, 49–57; *see also* apprenticeship; Birmingham: Guildhall; Elizabeth I: Queen Betty's Law; livery
Gullickson, Gay, 97
Gütenberg, Johannes (1398–1468) inventor of the printing press, 309 n. 76, 319

Habakkuk, Sir (Hrothgar) John (1915–2002), 166, 183 n. 65, 200
habeas corpus, writ of, 181, 228, 540, 546–7, 574, 629, 632, 638, 709
haberdashers, 112–13
Habsburg dynasty and empire, 180, 209 n. 169
Hadley, John, inventor of the octant, 327
Haines, Richard, inventor of spinning machinery, 387–8
Haiti *see* Saint-Domingue
Halifax, West Yorkshire, 394, 464, 767
Halifax, Earl of *see* Montagu-Dunk, George
Hamilton-Gordon, George, 4th Earl of Aberdeen (1784–1860), 689, 694, 763, 768
hammermen, 365, 409
Hammond, John Lawrence (1872–1949), xvii, 271–2, 277, 326 n. 130, 349, 405–6, 521, 563, 668 n. 201, 683–4, 821

Hammond, Barbara (1873–1961), xvii, 271–2, 277, 326 n. 130, 349, 405–6, 521, 563, 668 n. 201, 683–4, 821
Hampshire, 190 n. 96, 473, 616 n. 13, 695–6, 733, 736
hang glider *see* glider
hand-loom weaving, 290, 436, 466, 493, 572, 638–9, 672, 723, 809, 816, 828; decline of, 738 Table 13.1; in India, 161, 763 n. 67; *see also* weavers
Hanover, 177, 183 n. 66, 209–10, 220 n. 13, 223, 226 n. 25; mercenaries from, 544; Prussian occupation of, 587
Hanoverian dynasty, 180–1, 189, 203, 209–12, 221, 556, 558; threatened by radicalism, 42, 642, 660, 812, 838; succession and settlement, 178, 180–2, 212, 375, 806, 820; *see also* George I; George II; George III; George IV; William IV; Victoria I
Hanway, Jonas, merchant, 378
Hapsburg *see* Habsburg
Hardy, Thomas (1752–1832), 542, 546–7
Hargreaves, James (1720–1778) inventor of the spinning jenny, 328–9, 421–2, 431–2, 437 n. 147, 438 n. 152; *see also* Hockley Mill
Harley, Robert, 1st Earl of Oxford (1661–1724), 152, 172, 180–4
harness, 310
Harrison, John (1693–1776) inventor of the marine chronometer, 327
Harrison, Samuel, inventor of steel-nib pen, 332
Hay, Douglas, 514, 519, 527–8, 599, 649 n. 144
Health and Morals of Apprentices Act ("Factory Act") (1802), 440, 581
Heathcoat, John (1783–1861) improver of the warp-loom, 627
Hedley, William (1779–1843) railway innovator, 338
Heilbroner, Robert L. (1919–2005), 290–1, 294, 339, 812
Helliker, Thomas (1784–1803), 579
Henry VII (1457–1509), 370
Henry VIII (1491–1547), 64–6, 69 n. 68, 146, 286, 769 n. 69, 800
Henson, Gravenor, 593, 595, 668
Hero of Alexandria (10–70), inventor of the aeolipile; treatise on the five simple machines, 304, 306, 321, 323
Hertfordshire, 118, 362 Table 7.2, 486
Hesse: Hessian mercenaries, 173 n. 31, 544
Hibbert, Christopher (1924–2008), 242
hierarchy, 29, 51, 124, 446–50; ecclesiastical, 105, 119, 124, 511–12, 525, 539, 656, 814, 831; in guilds, 128, 344; in hosiery manufacture, 424
Highs, Thomas, inventor (1718–1803), 328–9, 390 n. 171, 422, 431, 437, 584 n. 74
Hilton, Rodney (1916–2002), 9, 652–3
Hipparchus (c. 190–c. 120 BC), 327
Hobsbawm, Eric John (1917–2012), xix, 35, 40, 286, 541, 579 n. 59, 600 n. 137, 619, 690, 695–6, 728, 730, 743, 761, 766, 795, 837
Hockley Mill, 421, 432
Hodgskin, Thomas (1787–1869), 673–4, 830 n. 16
Holkham Hall, 204
Holland *see* Dutch Republic; Low Countries; Netherlands; Fox, Henry (Lord)
Hollander engine, 362, 393, 485
Holmes, Geoffrey, 181–2
Holy Roman Empire, 120 n. 43, 586
Homfray, Samuel (1762–1822), 474
Honduras, British, 576
de Honnecourt, Villard, 37, 317
Hooke, Robert (1635–1703), 139, 155 n. 164, 322
hospitals, 185 n. 70, 336, 370–1, 373, 375, 734 n. 197
Hostmen, Company of, 87, 123
hot-air balloon, 331
House of Commons, 73, 118, 123–4, 134, 225, 232–4, 534–6, 563, 643–4, 652–5, 701, 735, 750, 754, 763, 765, 773, 798; *see also* Parliament
House of Lords, 123–4, 209, 230, 385, 559, 563, 611; *see also* Parliament
housebot, 513
Huddersfield, West Yorkshire, 464, 579, 596–7, 630, 638, 647, 734
Hudson, Pat, 93–4, 170 n. 19, 741
Hudson's Bay Company, 160
Hughes, Admiral Sir Edward (c. 1720–1794), 245
Huguenot, 158 n. 179, 323 n. 118, 379–80, 387
Hungary, 81, 655
Hunt, Henry (1773–1835), 588 n. 96, 609–10, 628, 632, 643, 688 n. 41, 696, 700, 721
Hunt, Margaret, 704
Hunt, Walter, inventor of lock-stitch sewing machine, 337
Huntsman, Benjamin (1704–1776) steel-maker, 326

husbandry, 28, 91, 169, 194, 196, 202, 464, 525, 615; servants-in-husbandry, 615 n. 12, 690; *see also* convertible husbandry; up-and-down husbandry
Huskisson, William (1770–1830), 651–2, 666, 670, 673, 679–80, 688, 832
Hussars, 610, 648
Hutton, William (1723–1815), 382, 396
Huygens, Christian (1629–1695) inventor, 322–4
hydraulics, 305–6, 312, 320, 336, 813; organ, 306; press, 336; jack, 336
hydrochloric acid, 312, 487
hydrogen, 336
hygrometer, 327

Ibn Firnas, Abbas (810–887), 312
Ibn Yunus, inventor of the pendulum, 312
ideology: of *laissez-faire*, free-trade liberalism and political economy, 38, 510, 655, 661, 715, 722, 747; of Rockingham party, 239; custom and, 513, 555; as an instrument of hegemony, 528; and class, 634 n. 81, 646; Owenism not a coherent, 722; and political economy, 746; artisan ideology, 637, 751, 761
immigrants and immigration, 357; contribution to English manufacturing, 38, 75 n. 101, 76, 112, 357, 380, 387, 801; of Huguenots from France, 158 n. 179; from Ireland, 231
imperialism, 84, 174, 215–18, 225, 244, 248–51, 588 n. 94, 618–19, 805, 810; Puritan imperialism, 124; Spanish, 133 n. 87; patriotic, 225 n. 22; as non-capitalist, 588 n. 94, 656–7; French, 603
Importation Act (1822), 651
Improvement(s), 31, 41, 115, 135, 144, 147 n. 129, 152, 173, 186, 192–202, 206, 214, 253, 258–71, 277–80, 284, 297, 303–4, 311, 316, 321, 323, 329–39, 361, 388 n. 161, 392–3, 405, 416, 421, 424, 428–33, 440, 483, 490, 494, 523–4, 538, 582–4, 591–2, 624
inclosures *see* enclosure movement
India, 82, 121, 211, 221, 223, 231, 235–6, 243, 245–8, 304, 530, 558, 586, 709, 810; Bengal, 221, 223, 231, 236, 243 n. 74, 810; Bihar, 231; Cuddalore, 245; Calcutta, 221; cotton production, 709; expansion into East Indies, 38; Great Bengal Famine (1769–79), 530, 810; Green Revolution in, 498 n. 165; India Act (1781), 243; Madras, 223; Maratha, 586; Pondicherry, 223, 226, 245, 558; manufacturing in, 98; Mogul Empire, 231 n. 36; opium production, 709, 768–9; technology, 308–9, 316–17; textiles and textile industry, 161 n. 193, 175, 193, 248, 290 n. 14, 329 n. 143, 380, 385–6, 394, 429, 435–6, 442, 768 n. 67, 806; trade with, 129 n. 73, 150 n. 141, 175, 246, 248, 380, 385–6, 429, 442, 488, 490 n. 141; Trincomalee, 245; *see also* East India Company; Dutch Republic: Dutch East India Company
Indus Valley Civilisation, 302, 304
industrial capitalism: becomes generalised capitalism, 776; emergence specific to England, 9; grew up alongside agrarian capitalism, 795; longer history, 79, 96; machinery cause or effect, 402; new institutions and social relationships required, 408; had to overcome custom, 605; planted on the continent, 617
Industrial Revolution (the First), xvii, 3, 6, 18, 31–48, 79–80, 95, 101–2, 117, 166–7, 187, 196 n. 119, 214 n. 186, 253–4, 259, 262, 268–9, 273, 279, 283–92, 300–1, 305–7, 315–40, 344–5, 369, 378–9, 397, 401–3, 413–29, 455–65, 470, 486, 490–501, 505, 513, 526, 550, 567, 612, 618, 636, 656, 670 n. 206, 685, 688, 691–2, 716 n. 137, 728, 743, 747, 778, 780, 793–5, 811–12, 817–18, 828, 833, 839; agrarian savings fuelled, 494; capitalist dynamic preceded, 2–3; consequences of, xx; pattern of causal relations, 254 Diagram 5.1; conversion of labour to capital at the heart of, 102; 'early Industrial Revolution', 48, 74–81, 89, 327; Enlightenment rationality the deus ex machina of (Weber), 339; role of machinery, 415–20; many key innovations borrowed, 286; origins, causes and antecedents, xx, 36, 79, 101, 291; substitution of competition for custom its essence (Toynbee), 75; technology of the, 332–8; timing the most difficult question, 32; transmuting circulating to fixed capital key (Mokyr), 428; unprecedented growth of integrated domestic market preceded, 288; war and, 259; why it began in England, 3–8
industrialisation, 1–3, 8, 24, 43, 47–48, 74, 79, 91–101, 165–74, 269, 344, 419, 424,

462–5, 510, 612–613, 657, 740–1, 760, 768, 791, 812, 837; agrarian capitalism lays foundations for, 174; begins only in England, 2; creation of proletariat preceded, 24; de-industrialisation, 92, 94, 96, 611, 617, 671 n. 208, 726, 740 n. 224, 768 n. 67; dis-embedding of relations of production enables, 797; elusive origins of, 32–40; incipient capitalist, 657; pristine, 166, 793; state-led versus private-led, 415; *see also* proto-industrialisation theory
inequality, 624, 683, 795
inflation, 69 n. 68, 71–3, 107 n. 8, 154–5, 469, 486, 549, 553, 560–1, 569, 583, 590, 593, 640–1, 705, 802
innovation *see* production
Insurrection Act (1817), 686
interchangeable parts, 335, 340
internal combustion engine, 90, 284
Interregnum (1649–1660), 132, 134–5, 140, 141 n. 116, 153, 156, 163, 204 n. 153, 539, 804
Iran *see* Persia
Iraq, 312
Ireland, 124, 173 n. 31, 175, 189–90, 216–17, 308, 350, 357, 535, 560–2, 568, 576, 585 n. 82, 595 n. 119, 611 n. 5, 615, 631 n. 69, 658, 680–2, 686–8, 699, 709–10, 714, 716, 726, 734–5, 746, 750, 752, 754, 759, 774, 780, 794, 804, 810, 831, 842; agrarian capitalism introduced in, 216–17, 250, 773–4, 810; Belfast, 716–17, 774; blights and famines, 530, 657, 773–4, 777–8; census not taken, 554 n. 177; Cork 376, 560, 752, 774; Irish Municipal Corporations Bill (1836), 750; Dublin 237 n. 50, 443, 535, 542 n. 127, 562, 628, 657, 757; first colonial project, 216; Galway, 239, 774; Irish Volunteers, 535; linen production, 175, 384, 468; Limerick 209 n. 170; manufacturing in, 443, 468; mining, 479–80; Potato Famine (1845–52), 530, 773–4, 777–8, 783, 834–5; rebellion in and the American Revolution 236–46; silk production, 259; trade, 161 n. 193, 175, 258–9, 385–6, 468, 482, 535, 590, 615, 666, 774; subsidies for textiles, 535; treaty with England, 535; Ulster 561; union into United Kingdom (1801), 562; wool production, 175–6, 468; see also Irish Poor Law; United Irishmen; Young Ireland movement
Ireton, General Henry (1611–51), 105, 126–7
Irish Poor Law (1838), 777
iron and ironmongers, 75–8, 87, 159–60, 167, 172, 175, 259–60, 264, 299, 311, 318, 323–6, 330–5, 341, 357, 359, 363–4, 367, 380, 403, 417, 438, 441, 443, 457, 469–79, 482–3, 491, 504–5, 530, 535–6, 584–7, 666–7, 671, 682, 743, 784, 801; barges, 333; bridges, 333 472 n. 42; cast, 316, 326, 331, 358, 363, 504, 584; pig, 193, 318, 331, 333, 587; puddling, 417; plough, 333, 692; rails, 331; ships, 333; Swedish, 364; wrought, 325, 333–4, 364; *see also* Darby; Crawshay; Crowley
Iron Age, 304
Iroquois, 599
Islam, 310–13, 317
Italy, 9, 19, 36, 38, 49 n. 5, 53, 77, 154 n. 158, 173 n. 31, 178, 205 n. 154, 209, 317, 325, 336, 381–4, 404, 536, 557–8, 572–3, 657, 781; Tuscany, 782; Venice, 301, 317; *see also* Coliseum; Rome

Jābir ibn Hayyān 'Geber' (c. 721–c. 815), 312
Jacobins and Jacobinism, 543–7, 552, 556, 558, 563–5, 567, 577, 586, 612, 631, 683; *see also* Revolutionary and Napoleonic Wars
Jacobite cause and Jacobites, 177–184, 187 n. 78, 189, 211–12, 221, 224, 228, 240 n. 62, 269, 350 n. 14, 375, 546 n. 144, 548, 806; army, 211
Jacquard loom, 337, 659 n. 171
Jacquard, Joseph-Marie (1752–1834), 337
Jamaica, 245, 710, 831
James I (1566–1625) also James VI of Scotland, 108–111, 115 n. 31, 120, 131, 134 n. 89, 321, 324 n. 120, 803; accession (1603), 107; dismisses Parliament, 108, 110; King James Bible, 514
James II (1633–1701), 141–2, 147, 173 n. 31, 177, 182 n. 60, 804; accession (1685), 141; as papist, 142, 804, 806; flees into exile and deposed, 142; death of, 177; *see also* Glorious Revolution
James III *see* Stuart, James Francis Edward
James VI of Scotland *see* James I
James VIII *see* Stuart, James Francis Edward
Javel water *see* potassium hypochlorite
Jay Treaty (1794), 246
Jefferson, Thomas (1743–1826), 237
Jenkins, Captain Robert, 208

Jenkins' ear, war of (1739–48), 208
Jenkinson, Robert Banks, 2nd Earl of Liverpool, Prime Minister (1770–1828), 610–17, 620, 625, 638, 640, 644, 646, 650–3, 661–2, 678, 681, 704; stroke, 678
Jenner, Edward (1749–1823) inventor of vaccination, 337
jenny *see* spinning: jenny
Jewish Naturalisation Act (1753), 219
Jews, 321 n. 38, 357, 687
John, A.H., 193, 200, 214
Johnson, Joseph (1738–1809), 609
joiners, 638, 718
joint-stock, 113, 129, 155–6, 159, 188, 367, 666, 806
Jones, E.L., 166; 'virtuous circle', 194
Jones, Edward, 782
Jones, Ernest, 783–4, 787
Johnes, John Gale, 592, 772
journalism and journalists, 148, 185, 227, 385, 629, 641, 716, 719, 752–3, 759 n. 29, 784
journeymen, 43, 54, 59–60, 63, 65, 68–9, 106, 113–14, 130, 137–9, 159, 224, 285, 344–8, 350, 352, 357, 366, 410, 412, 421, 485, 491, 509, 581, 603, 633, 664, 659 n. 171, 691, 713, 726, 797, 800–1; compagnages in France, 619; custom supported, 399; decline of associations, 69; friendly societies, 348; independent associations, 60, 128, 140, 350 Table 7.1, 601–2, 800, 803; numbers restricted, 352, 530 n. 82; proletarianisation of , 140–1; prospects limited, 59, 120; women and, 348; yeomanry a compromise, 59–60; *see also* apprentices; masters: craft; workshops; yeomanry
JPs *see* Justices of the Peace
Julian calendar, 218
justices of the peace (JPs), 68, 114, 137, 159, 182, 225 n. 22, 350, 358, 398, 519, 521, 530, 532, 563–4, 568, 625, 686, 720, 764, 771, 820; corrupt, 189 n. 83; expansion of, 118; and poor laws, 371–2, 357; as neutral arbiters, 519–21, 532, 569; sweeping powers, 527; wage-setting, 68, 116, 566; *see also* Speenhamland
Justinian, laws of, 55

Kaufsystem see domestic system
Kay, John (1704–c. 1779) of Bury, inventor of the flying shuttle, 326, 328, 387, 391–2, 395, 427, 429–31, 433
Kay, John, Warrington clockmaker, 328 n. 137, 329 n. 139, 437 n. 147
Kennedy, John, 441
Kennington Common, 782
Kent, 75 n. 101, 94, 198 n. 126, 361 Table 7.2, 485, 692–5, 736, 751
Kent, John, farmer, 662
Kent, William (1685–1748) inventor of baby carriage, 326
Kenyon, Lord Lloyd (1732–1802), 520 n. 37, 529 n. 80, 570
kerosene lamp, 336
Kerridge, Eric, 272–3, 278–9
de Kersaint, comte Armand (1742–1793), 545, 588
Kersal Moor, 756
Knatchbull, Sir Edward (1781–1849), 693, 763
Knights, 11, 59 n. 39, 118, 130 n. 77, 134, 136, 310 n. 79, 311
Kondratieff cycles or waves, 417, 670 n. 206, 742
Kriedte, Peter, 91–8, 168–71, 345, 347

labour: abstract labour, 57, 102, 504, 567, 605, 614, 808, 829; discipline, 339, 370, 447, 451, 504, 605 n. 148, 692, 719; labour theory of value, 9; organisation, 325, 360, 366–7, 399, 469, 474, 483, 503–4, 817, 829; real versus formal subsumption to capital, 102, 249, 343–6, 359, 366–7, 399, 403, 413, 446, 460, 504–5, 637, 660, 684, 785, 787, 793, 808, 817–18, 825, 828–9, 839; reserve army of, 102, 510; *see also* commodification of land; division of labour; modes of labour organisation; wage labour
labour market, 19, 54, 278, 347, 351, 355–9, 369, 453 n. 216, 460, 729–33, 742, 786, 831; capitalist, 53, 660, 732, 836; free, 366, 549, 577, 665, 667, 730–3; local, 278; national, 346, 355–9, 369, 399, 377, 616, 746, 808, 616; and slavery, 711
labour process, 21, 455; abstract labour and the, 102; control of the, 5, 20–1, 42, 44, 48, 56, 82, 86, 102, 141, 224, 285, 346–7, 379, 383, 399, 412–14, 426, 446, 450 n. 208, 453–5, 457–60, 469, 483, 486, 502, 504, 411, 606–7, 633–75, 703, 713, 719, 721, 726–7, 742, 745, 785, 802, 814–16, 823–4, 838; custom and the, 56, 407, 420, 454, 458; intensification of the, 379, 447, 457; machinery and the, 35; reorganisation of the, 413, 418,

786; roles in the, 20; structure of the, 285, 726; subdivision of the, 408, 814; technology and the, 343 n. 3, 812–17; wages and the, 673
labourers *see* working class
labour-power, 14 n. 30, 18, 24 n. 61, 29, 102, 265, 275, 295, 298, 347, 416, 458, 504, 567, 727, 738
laissez-faire, 396, 461, 522, 533, 581, 595, 615, 618, 632, 651, 655, 658, 660–1, 667 n. 196, 715, 729, 747, 780, 827, 830–1
Lanarkshire, 436 Table 8.1, 767, 773
Lancashire, 33, 73, 79, 175, 181 Table 3.1, 193, 328–330, 356–7, 384, 386–7, 390, 392, 394–5, 398, 422, 429–31, 434, 436–8, 441, 443, 467, 469, 480, 482, 486, 493, 530–1, 565, 570, 581, 596, 599, 603, 609, 628–9, 631, 638, 641, 643, 670, 672–4, 677, 682, 686–7, 717–18, 724–25, 766–7, 771, 773, 783, 792, 814, 830
Lancaster, Lancashire, 264, 376, 584, 598
land: abstract, 57, 716; agents, 237, 711; as capital, 614, 741; commodification of, 43, 102, 144, 152, 216, 300, 499, 553, 605, 747, 776, 818, 828–9; common, 169, 202 n. 145, 796; delinquent, 153; engrossment of holdings, 25, 183 n. 65, 194, 201, 278, 798 n. 8, 807; markets, 5, 64, 135–6, 183, n. 65, 216; as means of subsistence, 40; prices, 152, 425 n. 84; stewards, 153, 183, 205–6, 351; surveyors, 183, 197, 216; vacant, 25; *see also* enclosure movement; means of subsistence; wastes and commons; tenures
Land and Labour Bank, 781
Land Bank, 152–4, 172, 184, 805
Land Conference (1848), 789
Land Plan, 778, 784, 789
land tax, 118, 148, 153, 171–4, 182, 191, 208, 212–13, 229–30, 235, 272, 274, 533, 573, 617, 807, 826
landed class(es), 103, 109, 117–24, 131–5, 141–4, 148, 153, 162–3, 173–4, 182, 191, 213, 217 n. 6, 221, 269, 368, 377, 498, 525, 549, 559, 567–8, 582, 597, 605–5, 611–15, 620–3, 629, 654, 667, 678, 694, 698, 703, 746–7, 754, 763, 771–80, 803–7, 824, 826, 832, 834; hegemony of, 225 n. 22, 40, 746, 834; parliamentary, 121, 706; ruling elite, 212, 249, 269, 397, 525, 612–15, 619, 629, 662, 667, 684, 777, 805, 807, 824, 826, 831–9; traditional, 612–13; unanimity of, 163, 174, 224, 269; unity of, 212, 249, 707, 798, 803; *see also* aristocracy; gentry; landed oligarchy; landlords; property
landed oligarchy, 42–4; 101, 131, 249–50; 399, 526, 613, 619, 654, 675, 677–747, 794–5, 826, 832, 834–5, 838–9; Whig oligarchy, 183 n. 65, 832; as voting oligarchy, 188, 225 n. 22; *see also* landed classes
Landes, David S., 401–2, 447–50, 486–9, 812
landlords, 3–5, 14–17, 28, 41, 58, 65, 78, 85, 87, 118, 134 n. 89, 135–46, 152–3, 158, 171, 192, 197–206, 213, 217, 225 n. 22, 236–7, 264, 270, 275–80, 360, 465, 490, 524, 555, 572, 582, 611, 614–5, 620, 622, 627, 640, 658–9, 663, 691, 694, 698, 768 n. 67, 771, 774, 777, 799, 805, 809, 822, 827, 830, 834; absentee, 205–6, 237, 741; capitalist, 142, 420, 522, 613; decline of, 744; emergence, 25–6; enclosing; 276, 502, 814, 820; improving, 280, 505, 807; progressive, 698; rentier, 217, 632
Lansdowne, Marquess of *see* Petty-Fitzmaurice, Henry
Larrey, Dominique Jean (1766–1842) inventor of the ambulance, 336
Latin America, 657, 667
Laud, William, Archbishop of Canterbury (1573–1645), 115, 123–5
Lavoisier, Anton (1743–1794) chemist, 332 n. 156, 336
Lavrovsky, V.M., 272
law or legal system; *see also* common law; courts; custom; customary law; Roman Law; policing
Law, John (1671–1729), 184–5
Laxton, Nottinghamshire, 490 n. 141, 689
LCS *see* London Corresponding Society
lead and lead mining, 231, 318 n. 101, 326, 363, 393, 404–5, 428 n. 97, 432, 434, 438, 443, 472, 480–2, 487
leaseholder *see* tenants, tenant-farmers
leatherworkers, 112
LeBlanc, Nicolas (1742–1806) inventor of soda, 336, 415, 487
LeBon, Philippe (1767–1804) inventor of gas lamp, 489
Lee, William (1563–1614) inventor of stocking-frame, 213, 424
Leeds, West Yorkshire, 33, 159, 352, 360, 435 n. 134, 452, 464–6, 469, 591, 543, 576, 579–80, 596, 602, 688 n. 41, 699, 702, 704, 716–71, 763–4, 783 n. 117

Leeds Company, 159
Leeds and Liverpool Canal, 265, 465 n. 17
Leeds Mercury, 574, 630, 711
Leeson, R.A., 59, 70, 128, 138, 570–1, 633, 663, 726, 735
Leicester, Leicestershire, 264, 424–5, 466, 549, 595, 627
Leicester Union, 716
Leicestershire, 362 Table 7.2, 380, 593, 627, 766
Lemon, Sir William, 1st Baronet (1748–1824), 481
Levant Company, 161, 239 n. 57
Levellers, 4, 114, 126–8, 130, 221, 540, 542, 575, 660, 707, 751 n. 5; versus 'elevator', 781; *see also* Diggers
Levine, David, 86, 88 n. 152
Lewis, George *see* George I
Lexington, Massachusetts, 238
Liberal Party, 747
liberals and liberalism, 31, 84, 106, 192, 246, 266, 270, 296–8, 300, 315, 378, 240, 510, 522–5, 544, 558, 567, 575, 650–3, 658, 660, 707 n. 109, 729, 749, 780 n. 107, 781, 787, 790–1, 803, 806, 835–6; economic liberalism and liberalisation, 619, 650–1, 658, 660, 666, 670, 678, 690, 709, 714, 747, 807, 810, 831; liberal individualism, 614 ; liberal Tories, 652–3, 670, 678, 686–9; liberal Whiggism, 174, 734; moral order of, 729; Chartists and, 749–792
Libertarianism, 523 n. 51, 575, 632, 660–1, 716 n. 137, 758–9; libertarian radicals, 827
Licensing Acts (1643), 228
Lichfield, Staffordshire, 352, 531
Lichfield House Compact (1835), 735
Lilburne, John (1614–1657), 114, 126, 130
Lincoln, Lincolnshire, 263
Lincoln's Inn, 241
Lithography, 336
Littleton, Wiltshire, 578
Liverpool, Merseyside, 160, 262, 265, 398, 442, 590, 682, 736; Liverpool and Manchester Railway, 628 n. 19, 688, 743, 744 n. 233, 770 n. 73, 784
Liverpool, Prime Minister *see* Jenkinson, Robert Banks
Liverpool Times, 744
livery and liverymen, 43, 60–8, 114, 137, 349, 800
Locke, John (1632–1704), 368
locomotive engine, 332, 338, 684, 682; *see also* railroads
Loeben, Peace (Treaty) of (1797), 558
Lombe, John (1693–1722), 325, 335, 381–2, 404, 438 n. 152, 809
Lombe, Sir Thomas (1685–1739), 287, 335, 381, 383–4, 387–8, 397, 411, 432 n. 119, 438 n. 152, 451, 477, 807, 809
London, 57–63, 70–4, 87, 91, 105, 147, 151, 157, 160, 179, 185, 187, 193 Table 3.1, 196–8, 207, 211, 230–42, 249, 262–5, 308, 322–4, 333–7, 348–90, 404–12, 424, 434–8, 442–3, 461–9, 472–7, 480–9, 497, 519, 523–27, 530–32, 538–9, 549, 554–5, 563, 569, 574–6, 584– 603, 609, 615, 618, 626–31, 639–50, 664, 666, 671, 680, 686–8, 699–705, 716, 718–25, 734, 737, 743, 750–765, 770, 774–5, 779–84, 790, 804, 810–13, 832–3, 841; Blackfriars Bridge, 242; Great Fire of (1666), 138–41; twelve great companies of, 63, 161
London (Quaker) Lead Company, 480
London and Westminster Police Bill (1785), 532
London Anti-Corn Law Association, 750
London Corporation for the Poor, 373–5
London Corresponding Society (LCS), 539, 545–7, 562, 574–6, 588, 592, 601, 664–5, 700, 751; General Committee of, 546
London Proclamation (1383), 57–8
London Radical Reform Association, 688
London Working Men's Association (LWMA), 750–1, 829
Long Parliament (1640–1648), 123
longbow, 318
lotteries, 150, 185, 513
Louis XIV of France (1638–1715), 141, 146, 177–9, 285, 380
Louis XV of France (1710–1774), 285
Louis XVI of France (1754–1793), 415, 544
Louis XVIII of France (1755–1824), 600, 603
Loveless, George, Tolpuddle martyr, 720
Lovett, William (1800–1877), 674 n. 218, 750–2, 755–6, 762, 765, 784
Low Countries, 36, 74 n. 90, 96, 171, 173 n. 31, 536, 557; *see also* Austrian Netherlands; Belgium; Dutch Republic; Netherlands; Spanish Netherlands
Lowery, Robert, 763
loyalist societies, 542–3, 545, 561, 641
Luddism and Luddite disturbances, xix, 330, 335 n. 171, 456, 459, 574, 577; 592–604, 606–627, 630–1, 634 n. 81, 672, 684, 692–3, 696–7, 710, 754, 757–61, 775 n. 90, 786, 824–5, 828–9, 833; 'Ned Ludd', 593

Lunéville, Treaty of (1801), 573
Luttrell, General Henry Lawes Luttrell, 2nd Earl of Carhampton (1743–1821), 232
LWMA *see* London Working Men's Association
Lyndhurst, Lord John Singleton Copley, 1st Baron (1772–1863), 702, 763

Macadam process of road-building, 262 n. 27, 337
Macaulay, Thomas Babington 1st Baron (1880–1859), 499, 683, 765
machine-breaking, 4, 139, 434–5, 459, 543, 572, 577–8, 595, 604, 672, 681, 684, 692–3, 710, 823–4, 829, 831; *see also* Luddism; Swing
machines and machinery: factories and, 401–60; machine tools, 321, 335–6, 457 n. 231; machinofacture, 344, 420–8, 429, 739; specific role of, 415–428; tool element replaces worker's tools, 426–7, 459; *see also* factory; technology
Macintosh, Charles (1766–1843) inventor of the raincoat, 414 n. 50, 487–9
Mackenzie, James Stuart (c. 1719–1800), 226
Mackintosh, James (1765–1832), 685
Magna Carta (1215), 796
Magnetism, 309
magnifying glass, 317
Malta, 573, 585
Malthus, Reverend Thomas (1766–1834), 7, 13–14, 258, 368, 554–5, 618–24, 729–33, 770, 809, 821–2, 827
maltsters, 491
managers and management, 78, 81 n. 119, 158–9, 329 n. 139, 331, 360, 364–5, 378, 382 n. 142, 383, 391, 396, 407, 413, 418–19, 430 n. 109, 451, 453, 471, 473, 477–8, 480, 490, 493, 579, 617 n. 22, 645, 659, 674, 769, 786, 817; estate managers, 136, 152, 204 n. 153, 205–6, 240 n. 63; *see also* working class
Manchester, 33, 139, 196, 230, 233 n. 41, 241, 262–3, 306 n. 66, 330, 332 n. 159, 348, 351–2, 360, 376, 379, 387, 398, 429–30, 434, 436 Table 8.1, 437–8, 442, 456, 475, 479, 485, 506, 539, 541, 543 n. 131, 563, 583, 590, 596–602, 609–10, 615, 629, 638–9, 644–5, 647, 649, 667, 672, 677, 679–683, 688, 699, 701, 704, 718, 725, 735, 739, 743, 751, 753–7, 762, 766, 770, 784, 792, 830
Manchester Exchange, 599
Manchester Mercury, 391, 436
Manchester Smallware Weavers' Society, 351
Manchester Times, 751 n. 7
Manchester Yeomanry, 610
Mandeville, Bernard (1670–1733), 188, 375
mandrel lathe, 321, 335
Mann, Julia De Lacy (1891–1985), 392, 429, 430
manorialism, 4, 11, 13, 26–7, 29, 49, 78, 89, 94, 135, 167, 199, 464, 553; manorial law, 56, 66, 89, 279, 280, 482 n. 103, 514, 568, 605, 798
Mantoux, Paul (1877–1956), xvii, 285, 324 n. 120, 329 n. 139, 428 n. 99, 429–30, 462, 472, 475, 477
Manufactures Royales, 285, 813
manufacturing, 47–104, 348–54, etc.; centralisation of, 78–81, 87, 89, 92, 97–8; handicraft production, 22, 31, 41, 49–50, 63, 67, 73, 93, 96–7, 301, 611, 619, 692, 786, 801, 838; distinction from industrialisation, 47; versus machinofacture, 420–8; *see also* domestic system; industry; proto-industrialisation theory, putting-out system
manufactory, 365 n. 73, 405, 425, 433 n. 125, 470 n. 37, 476–9, 487–8, 503–4, 584, 618, 626, 713 n. 125, 802, 816–17; *see also* manufacturing; Soho Manufactory
March of the Blanketeers (1817), 630, 633
Marglin, Stephen, 401, 445–51, 814
market imperatives (market compulsions), 3, 5, 24, 29, 37, 41–2, 48, 79–80, 83–4, 86, 91, 101–2, 135, 143–4, 152, 341 n. 186, 194, 216, 251, 270, 276, 280, 288, 341, 358, 360, 366, 391, 396–8, 403, 407, 419, 441, 446–8, 457, 458–9, 491, 496, 501–2, 594, 637, 674, 691, 744, 791–2, 799, 805, 807, 809, 813–19, 830, 837–9
market dependence (market dependency), 5, 17, 21, 24, 28–32, 37, 40–3, 48, 101–2, 116, 136, 157, 170, 249, 254 Diagram 5.1, 267–70, 344–6, 356, 369–70, 296, 399, 403, 464, 495–6, 515, 520, 553–6, 569, 575–6, 612 n. 8, 675, 691, 695, 728–30, 733, 741–7, 787-8, 797, 802, 810–25, 830–7
markets: monopoly rights to hold, 519
Marlborough, 1st Duke of, John Churchill (1650–1722), 179 n. 50, 180, 182

Marriage Act (1753), 219
Marshall, John (1765–1845), 452, 469, 493, 503, 505, 763
Martin, Samuel (1714–1788), 228
Marx, Karl, 7–9, 14, 53, 293–304, 313, 315, 633–4; and 'bourgeois revolution', 842; understands capital as a social relation, 347; commerce corrosive on production, 22; critique of political economy, 8, 450; defeat of Corn Laws a victory for labour , 780; on the dissolution of the monasteries, 64; moves to London (1849), 841; on machinery, 304 n. 58, 416, 420, 426; 'mature' Marx's increasing emphasis on social property relations, 17, 297, 841; on merchant capital, 18–19, 818; theory of modes of production, 8, 19, 23–4; on paradox at heart of industrial capitalism, 456–7; primacy of the productive forces, 295; on Senor's 'last hour', 713–14; formal versus real subsumption of labour to capital, 343–4, 606, 785; and technological determinism, 294; on the transition to capitalism, 202 n. 145, 240 n. 63, 842; on wage-slavery, 588 n. 94, 711; ways I and II, 1–154, 503, 741, 816; on Watt's steam engine , 479
Marxism, 6, 9, 35, 58–9, 270–4, 298–300, 315, 633–4, 697, 714, 726, 788, 791, 812, 842; Althusserian, 294; base and superstructure metaphor, 294–5, 812; economistic, 812; 'heresy' of political Marxism, 6; Japanese, 27 n. 71; neo-marxist approach, 91–2; 'neo-Smithian', 31, 95; Soviet, 298; and the proletariat, 788; vulgar or crude, 634; *see also* transition debate
Mary I (1516–1558), 581, 802
Mary II (1662–1694), 142, 147
Masons, 158, 351, 356, 457, 718
Massachusetts, 236 n. 48, 237, 335; Council, 237
Master and Servant Act (1832), 659, 666, 668 n. 200
masters and master craftsmen, 19, 43, 51–69, 101, 106, 112–15, 120, 128, 130, 137–8, 140, 146, 155, 158–9, 224, 326 n. 130, 344–55, 360–1, 365–6, 371, 380, 387, 393, 399, 405–7, 410, 413, 421–5, 433, 435, 462–4, 466 n. 22, 474–7 ck, 502–3, 505, 529 n. 81, 530 n. 82, 563, 569, 579, 580–3, 594, 601–3, 633–4, 639, 659, 664, 667–9, 672, 675, 691, 710–11, 718, 721–5, 728, 737, 741, 749, 797, 800–3, 820; *see also* factory masters; slave masters
master clothier, 422–3, 435 n. 136, 464, 816
master manufacturer, 198, 450, 587 n. 89, 601; *see* putting-out system
master piece, 57
Mathias, Peter, xviii, 32, 340, 414 n. 50, 415, 491–5
Maudslay, Henry (1771–1831) inventor of machine tool technology, 335–6, 491
Mayans, 304, 308, 311, 313, 813
McAdam, John Loudon (1756–1836), road builder, 337
McCloskey, D., 261, 263, 315–16, 499
McConnel, James, 441
McConnel and Kennedy, mule-spinning firm, 441, 452–3
McCormick, Cyrus (1809–1884) inventor of the reaper, 338
McCulloch, John Ramsey (1789–1864), 665, 828
McDouall, Peter, Chartist, 762 n. 41, 766 n. 61, 783
McKendrick, Neil, 411–13, 427 n. 93
McNally, David, 523 n. 52, 622 n. 36, 624
means of production, 3, 17–24, 29–30, 40–4, 48, 86, 92, 102, 129 n. 73, 141, 144, 196, 216, 283, 289 n. 11, 295, 318, 346–7, 361, 372, 397–8, 401, 411, 414, 427, 460, 462, 470, 496, 502, 504, 548, 614, 633, 637, 691, 698, 775, 785, 799–802, 815–16, 838, 842; artisans retain direct possession of, 548; capital accumulates the, 18; capitalist enjoys complete command of, 397; consolidation of by owner-occupier, 799; direct access to in pre-capitalist societies, 20, 29; merchant-employers control, 41; separation of direct producers, 17–19, 30, 216 n. 3, 289 n. 11, 361, 831
means of subsistence, 3–5, 17, 19, 24, 29, 40, 49, 56, 85, 201, 224, 266, 277, 280, 346, 395–99, 426, 463, 502, 515, 520, 532, 569, 692, 741, 801, 837
measurement *see* weights and measurements
Medick, Hans, 91–6, 100
medieval period (Middle Ages), 11, 29, 29, 33, 49–54, 56, 77 n. 108, 81, 105, 134–135, 152, 61, 197, 286, 302, 307–22, 324 n. 120, 334, 344, 352, 371 n. 97, 408, 426, 486, 591, 634 n. 81, 703 n. 92, 710, 793, 802; *see also* feudalism

Mediterranean, 12, 18, 38, 82 n. 126, 133 n. 87, 172, 310, 315, 585, 587, 617
Meikle, Andrew (1719–1811) inventor of the threshing-machine, 323, 692
Meikleriggs Muir, 647
Melbourne, William Lamb, 2nd Viscount (1779–1848), 694, 710, 720, 734–5, 752, 755, 762, 768, 777
Melville, Lord *see* Dundas, Henry
Mendels, Franklin, 91–3, 96, 170–1
Mercantilism and mercantile trade, 12, 129 n. 73, 156, 521, 525, 657, 797
Mercers, 63
merchant(s), 7, 14, 18, 22, 36, 43, 52, 58, 67–9, 72–4, 81–82, 93, 95, 103–12, 118, 136, 146–51, 160–3, 188, 205, 206, 213, 230, 300, 345–61, 377–9, 381, 387, 408, 423–5, 428, 443, 463–6, 473, 476, 490–2, 502–3, 521, 524–5, 543, 560, 573, 579–80, 583, 597–9, 606, 614, 640, 650, 657, 661, 667, 670–1, 706, 701, 750, 753, 776, 795, 799, 803–6, 816, 818, 819, 838; capital, 14, 18, 22, 82, 95, 345–7, 446, 606, 741, 818; capitalist, 14, 82, 419; clothier, 464, 580; companies and company merchants, 69 n. 71, 74, 109, 120–5, 151, 804–6; elite, 109; employers, 41, 58, 101, 346, 345–6, 379, 355, 379, 524; have always existed, 82; interloping, 87, 109, 121–5, 151, 162, 348–9, 392, 481, 519, 564, 581–3, 604, 637, 804; manufacturers, 14, 361, 408, 424–5, 431; mercantile interest, 58 n. 37, 484, 506, 524, 620, 707, 795; 'new merchants', 121–6, 129, 161, 804; putting-out, 347, 377, 445, 450, 517; role in the Civil Wars and the transformation of social relations, 117–29; *see also* East India Company; livery
Merchant Adventurers, Company of, 111, 152, 160–1
Merchant Taylors, 63 n. 50, 68
Mersey to Trent Canal, 264
Merseyside, 489
Merthyr Tydfil, Wales, 334 n. 166, 473, 584, 682
Merton *see* Statute of Merton
Mesopotamia, 302–4, 316, 336 n. 174, 495, 658
Metalworkers and metallurgy, 75–6, 78, 81 n. 120, 139, 193, 260, 302, 318–19, 325 n. 123, 332–5, 341, 358, 363–7, 393, 412, 416 n. 55, 456, 469–71, 474–6, 479–80, 488, 491, 503–5, 811, 817
Methodism, 539, 574, 643, 645, 710, 722, 829; *see also* Wesley
metric system, 327, 364
Metropolitan Charter Union, 762
Metropolitan Police Act (1829), 656, 685
Metropolitan Trades' Union, 716
Metternich, Prince Klemens Wenzel von (1773–1859), 643, 679, 782
Mexico, 72, 657
Mickwitz, Gunnar, 52, 56
Microscope, 317, 321–2
Middle Ages *see* medieval period
middle class, 118, 136, 182–3, 330, 455–6, 475, 564, 575, 617–19, 629–33, 642–46, 665, 684, 689, 700–8, 722–3, 728–9, 737, 746–7, 750, 760–1, 770, 779–91, 827, 833–6
'middling sort', 158, 368, 490, 615, 704–7, 746, 809
mid-Victorian compromise, 759, 786–7, 791, 836, 842
millwrights, 563, 567
Mine Law Court, 482
Mineral and Battery Works, 78
minerals, 39, 76, 89, 117, 155, 197 n. 122, 200, 471, 481
miners and mining, 72, 76–7, 80–91, 102, 123, 139, 155, 216 n. 3, 287, 318, 324, 326, 338 n. 179, 354, 357, 363, 365–7, 393, 416, 432, 438, 443, 469–70, 472–473, 479–483, 494, 503–504, 707, 725, 743, 786, 801–2, 809, 817; butty system, 472, 482, 504; mine-owners, 82, 198, 323, 667, 772
Miners' Association of Great Britain and Ireland, 769 n. 71, 771–2; defeat of, 790–2
Mines Royal, 78
Ministry of all Talents, 586–8
Minorca, 172, 220, 245
Minutemen, 238
missionaries, 710
Mississippi River, 246
mob *see* protestors
modernisation, 654, 688 n. 42, 704, 832
modes of labour organisation, 56, 82, 156, 396, 435, 469, 474, 483, 503–4, 553, 838
mode of marketing, 408, 447
mode of production, 34, 98, 343, 408 n. 24, 502, 511, 635; 'articulation' of, 98, 294; capitalist, 8, 38, 53, 295, 343, 408–10, 470, 797, 816, 822; customary or traditional, 26, 470, 796; definition of, 9, 12; factory, 636; feudal, 6, 12–13, 28

n. 73, 797; petty, 13; pre-capitalist, 301; theory of *see* Marx
Mohammed (c. 570–632)
Mokyr, Joel, 307, 318 n. 101, 319, 402, 428
Molesworth, Sir William, 8th Baronet (1810–1855), 752
monasteries, 50, 315; Cistercian, 64; dissolution of under Henry VIII, 64–65, 118, 286 n. 7, 800
Monck, General, 1st Duke of Albemarle (1608–1670), 132
money: commodification of, 397, 496, 776; as fictitious commodity, 300, 818; standardisation of, 818
monetisation of the rural economy, 369, 568, 690, 801; *see also* coinage
Mongols, 313
Monmouth, Duke of *see* Scott, James
Monmouth Rebellion (1685), 142, 240 n. 61, 531
Monmouthshire, Wales, 757, 778, 785, 833
monopolies, 22, 52–3 61, 69 n. 72, 75 n. 101, 81, 86–7, 101, 107–18, 111–23, 151, 160–2, 173, 191, 215–18, 308, 322–3, 366–7, 432–42, 465, 481–2, 492, 505, 518–19, 523–7, 536, 559, 564, 575, 582, 613, 621–2, 637, 659, 664, 691, 703, 770, 790, 794, 797, 801–6, 827
Montagu, John, 4th Earl of Sandwich (1718–1792), 228
Montagu-Dunk, George, 2nd Earl of Halifax (1716–1771), 228
Montgolfier Brothers, inventors of the hot-air balloon, 331
Mooers, Colin, 143–5, 612 n. 8
Moravia, 336, 586, 710
Moscow, 599–600
Moslems *see* Islam
mouldboard plow, 310, 316
mule *see* spinning: mule
Mumford, Lewis (1895–1990), 80, 216 n. 3, 286–9, 314, 812; eotechnic, neotechnic and paleotechnic phases, 299–300
Municipal Corporations Act (1835), 687, 735
municipal political unions, 399, 629, 636, 665, 680, 734, 847, 854, 859, 865
Municipal Reform Act (1835), 715, 735
Münster, Treaty of, 133
Murdoch, William (1754–1839), 489, 505, 584
muskets, 335, 398
Muslims *see* Islam
muslins, 175, 329 n. 143, 385–6, 435, 442 n. 176, 451, 591; cotton-muslins, 312
mutiny, 126, 154, 558, 561–2, 721 n. 156

nailers, 140
NAOT *see* National Association of Organised Trades for the Industrial, Social and Political Emancipation of Labour
NAPL *see* National Association for the Protection of Labour
Naples, Kingdom of, 544, 572, 585–6, 647, 781–2
Napoleon *see* Bonaparte
Napoleonic Code, 558
Napoleonic Wars *see* Revolutionary and Napoleonic Wars
naptha, 311, 488
National Association for the Protection of Labour (NAPL), 673, 682, 717, 719, 721, 724–5, 773, 829
National Association of Organised Trades for the Industrial, Social and Political Emancipation of Labour (NAOT), 784
National Association of United Trades for the Protection of Labour (NAUT), 773, 779, 784, 834
National Charter Association (NCA), 762, 766
National Chartist Society, 784
national debt, 147, 149–51, 155 n. 163, 156, 171–87, 191, 211–12, 225 n. 22, 235, 245, 533–6, 545, 588, 615, 617, 625, 640–1, 650, 652, 654, 661, 699, 759 n. 29, 763, 769, 805, 826; in France, 536
National Land Bank *see* Land Bank
National Land Company, 781, 784 n. 120, 789
National Petition, the, 750–3, 755, 764, 833; *see also* Chartism; People's Charter
National Reform League, 784
National Union of Operative Potters (NUOP), 717, 735, 829
National Union of the Working Classes (NUWC), 688, 700–1, 716, 829
nationalism, 545, 600 n. 138; Scottish, 210 n. 175, 242, 649, 657, 787, 835; Spanish, 599; German, 600 n. 138
Natural Light and Heat Company, 337
NAUT *see* National Association of United Trades for the Protection of Labour
Naval dockyards *see* docks and dockyards
Naval mutinies (1797), 561; Naval Mutinies Act, 721 n. 156

Navarino, Battle of (1827), 679
Navigation Acts (1650–1651), 129, 157, 160, 175, 535, 588–9, 666, 810
navvies, 737, 759, 778; *see also* railroads
Navy: English Royal, 108, 125, 148, 160–1, 165, 172, 287; British Royal, 179 n. 52, 183–4, 212, 225 n. 22, 229 n. 33, 244, 260, 362, 364, 366, 473, 533–4, 460, 561, 573, 601, 680, 805; French, 573; impressment, 235; impressment of Americans, 599; mercantile marine, 197 n. 123
NCA *see* National Charter Association
Need, Samuel (1718–1781), 424, 431
Neeson, J.M., 274–80, 344 n. 4
Nef, John Ulric (1899–1988), 48, 66 n. 64, 74–81, 89–90, 92, 101, 259–60, 326 n. 130, 327, 345, 366–7
Nelson, Admiral Horatio, 1st Viscount (1758–1805), 561, 573, 576, 586
Neolithic revolution, 36, 296, 302
neo-Marxism, 91–2
Netherlands or Holland, 37, 77, 85, 100 n. 197, 110–11, 133, 137, 141, 146 n. 128, 152, 157, 173 n. 29, 176, 184, 209, 211, 216, 220 n. 13, 238–9, 301, 321, 371, 384–6, 404, 536, 544, 572, 603, 617, 660, 689, 795, 804, 811; Antwerp, 83, 429; entrepôt trade 175, 384; French invasion of, 557, 585; Utrecht, 379 n. 132; *see also* Austrian Netherlands; Batavia; Dutch Republic; Low Countries; Spanish Netherlands
New Harmony, Indiana, 680
New Model Army, 125–8, 131, 134, disbanded, 137
New Orleans, 222
Newbury, Berkshire, 65–6, 78, 373
Newcastle-upon-Tyne, Northumberland, 85–7, 123, 191, 196, 262, 364–7, 470, 574, 736
Newcastle, Dukes of *see* Pelham, Henry and Pelham Holles, Thomas
Newcomen steam engine, 166, 323–4, 331, 393, 478, 481, 584, 807
Newcomen, Thomas (1664–1729) inventor of the atmospheric engine or beam engine, 323–4, 331, 393, 427, 807
Newfoundland, 226–7, 246, 456; Belleisle, 226
Newgate Prison, 592
newspapers, 146–7, 155, 225 n. 22, 229 n. 33, 239, 362, 546, 563, 596, 602, 647, 669, 673, 706, 750, 767, 806, 810
Newton, Sir Isaac (1642–1727), 37, 155 n. 64, 165, 185 n. 70, 307 n. 69
Nicholas, Jemima *see* Fawr, Jemima
Niépce, Nicéphore (1765–1833) inventor of first permanent photograph, 337
Nile, Battle of the (1798), 561
nobility, 272, 324 n. 120, 691, 843; French, 795
Nonconformists, 772 n. 80
Non-Intercourse Act (1809), 589
Norfolk, 385 n. 152, 463, 568, 662, 693 n. 54, 695, 697, 717, 736, 204
Norman Conquest (1066), 25, 130 n. 77, 796
Normandy, 311 n. 80
North, Lord Frederick, 2nd Earl of Guilford, Prime Minister (1732–1792), 234–9, 243–7, 249; 401, 533; Fox-North ministry, 246–7; resignation, 244
North America *see* American Colonies, Canada, Central America, Mexico, United States
Northampton, Northamptonshire, 266, 278, 362 Table 7.2, 390–1, 414, 720
Northamptonshire, 514
Northern Political Union, 762
Northern Star, 752, 764, 766 n. 61, 771, 779 n. 102
Northumberland, 467, 682 n. 22, 710
Norwich, Norfolk, 138 n. 106, 139, 350, 360, 372, 384–6, 438 n. 152, 463–4
Norwich Post, 362
Nottingham, Nottinghamshire, 241, 360–3, 376, 421, 424–5, 431, 433 n. 126, 434 n. 129, 436 Table 8.1, 438, 442 n. 176, 453, 455–6, 583, 757, 780, 824; Nottingham Castle, 700
Nottinghamshire, 273, 321, 380, 482, 490 n. 141, 515, 593, 595–9, 628, 630, 689, 766
NUOP *see* National Union of Operative Potters (NUOP)
NUWC *see* National Union of the Working Classes (NUWC)

O'Brien, James Bronterre (1805–1864), 701, 716, 754–5, 758, 762, 782, 784
O'Brien, William Smith (1803–1864), 777
O'Connell, Daniel (1775–1847), 658, 680–1, 687–8, 700, 709, 734–5, 751–4, 763, 773, 777
O'Connor, Feargus (1794–1855), 562 n. 11, 721, 750–4, 757, 761–4, 766–8, 771 n. 76, 778–84, 788–90, 836
O'Connorville, Hertfordshire, 779, 781, 789–90

Oakley, William, 695
Oastler, Richard (1789–1861), 711–13, 752; Short-Time Committee, 779
Occasional Conformity Acts (1702 and 1704), 148
Ogilvie, Sheila C., 92, 97, 100, 170–1
Old Pretender *see* Stuart, James Francis Edward
Old Sarum, Wiltshire, 233, 541, 703 n. 92
Old Silk Mill in Derby, 166, 379–80, 396, 432, 719, 739; *see also* silk
Oldham, Lancashire, 435, 441, 672, 724–5
Oldknow, Samuel (1756–1828), 442 n. 176, 451–2; Mellor mill 452
oligarchy *see* landed oligarchy
Olive Branch Petition (1775), 238
Oliver, William, spy, 630
Onslow, Serjeant Arthur (1759–1833), 601–2
Onslow, Colonel George (1731–92), 234
open field system, 4 n. 3, 29, 66, 103, 115, 225, 270, 470, 514–5, 530, 797–9, 814; mining on, 87; in France, 195; advantages of and capable of improvement, 201–2, 271, 274–80, 662 n. 176; enclosing and extinguishing of, 225, 253, 266, 271 n. 52, 273, 277–8, 515, 520, 613, 689, 740, 745; unenclosed lands, 87, 135, 202, 406, 463, 498, 515, 805; *see also* enclosures
opium production, 709
Opium Wars (1839–1860), 768–9
Orange Order and Orangemen, 561, 658
Orange Tree conspiracy (1848), 783–4, 833
Orders in Council, 589–90, 599, 629, 651, 823
Ormolu, 476, 479
Orwell, George, Eric Arthur Blair (1903–1950), 291
Ottoman Turkey, 572
overpopulation, 831
overproduction, 111, 193, 441, 640, 781; Malthus' theory of, 623
Owen, Robert (1771–1858), 452, 493, 623–4, 645–6, 680, 717–25, 833
Owenism, 645–6, 661, 674 n. 218, 684, 721–7, 750, 759–60, 785, 788, 827, 836
Owen, John Beresford, 233, 234 n. 42, 707 n. 106
owners of the means of production *see* employers
ownership *see* property
Oxford, Earl of *see* Harley, Robert
Oxford, Oxfordshire, 137, 193 Table 3.1, 227 n. 28, 356, 518, 538
Oxford Canal, 538
Oxford University, 257 n. 12, 455, 687
Oxfordshire, 203 n. 148, 266, 278, 695, 799 n. 137

Paine, Thomas (1737–1809), 238, 540–2, 575, 586, 598, 623, 629, 643, 820
painters, 410, 412
Palmerston, Lord Henry John Temple (1784–1865) Prime Minister, 768–9, 777, 779
Pantheon, 305
Papacy and Papal States, 9, 354, 539, 782 *see* Catholicism
paper, 75, 77, 176, 231, 242, 309, 311, 317–19, 357, 362–3, 393, 436–7, 421, 437, 482–3, 485–6, 503, 543 n. 132, 566, 591 n. 106, 693, 695, 765, 813, 816; money, 182, 186, 452, 805; papermaking machine, 337; sandpaper, 309; *see also* Fourdrinier
Papermakers' Act, 563, 570
papermaking machine; *see also* Fourdrinier
parachute, 312, 332, 339
parcellisation of sovereignty, 55, 58 n. 36, 311, 798 n. 8, 796, 798
Paris *see* France
Parliament, 4, 43–4, 63, 101, 171–95, 208–49, 233–49, 264–9, 278, 317, 323, 329, 333, 344, 351, 371, 376, 380–6, 392, 422, 436–40, 468, 484–5, 510, 515, 526–7, 530, 536–8, 543–55, 560–2, 568, 578, 581, 586, 588–602, 611–15, 620, 628–32, 640, 649, 656–9, 664–8, 679–81, 685, 687–8, 696, 700, 702, 707, 709, 714, 718, 728, 735, 746–57, 763–4, 771, 776–82, 788–9, 803–7, 819–28, 833–8; Civil War and, 116–37, 475; Irish, 239, 535, 562; Revolution and, 105–65; septennial, 183; triennial, 147, 593; *see also* Chartism; Conservative Party; elections; enclosures: parliamentary; House of Commons; House of Lords; landed classes; Liberal Party; petitioning; Tories; Whigs
Parsley Peel *see* Peel
Parys Mine Company, 480
Parys Mountain, Anglesey, 480
Pasha, Muhammad Ali (1769–1849), 768
paternalism, 183, 249, 477 n. 78, 521, 526–32, 534, 548–9, 567, 569, 577, 592, 595, 605, 611, 675, 684, 696, 697, 715, 727, 731, 733, 745–6, 770–2, 791, 809, 822, 831, 835–6

patriarchy, 295–6, 532
patrimony, 103, 116, 119, 133, 163, 558–9, 593 n. 112, 613
patriotism, 418, 225 n. 22, 226 n. 25, 556–7, 586, 641, 841 n. 1
Patriquin, Larry, 66 n. 64, 373, 377, 552–3, 568, 777 n. 97
Paul I (1754–1801) Emperor of Russia, 572–3
Paul, Lewis (c. 1700–1759) inventor of spinning machine, 326–9, 387–91, 425, 430 n. 109, 431–3, 437–8, 809
Peace Preservation Act (1814), 686
Peace of God (989), 51
Peace of Utrecht (1713), 182, 184
Peace Preservation Act (1714)
Peak District, 435, 491
peasants, 3, 9–11, 13–24, 29–31, 40, 49–50, 56, 58, 64, 80, 88–9, 91, 93, 96, 103, 116–19, 123, 169, 171–2, 194, 201–3, 266, 270–2, 274–5, 277, 287–8, 344–5, 361, 378, 404–5, 491, 502, 509, 512, 516, 530, 540, 553, 555, 568, 605–6, 613, 656, 689, 706, 746, 768, 773, 795–6, 801, 805, 808, 815, 819, 825, 837; in France, 14, 17, 783 n. 118; in Holland, 37; in India, 768 n. 67; in Ireland, 236–7; in Normandy, 311 n. 80; revolts and resistance, 30, 58, 71, 272, 798; yeomen, 686; *see also* feudalism
Peel, Robert 'Parsley' (1723–1792), 433 n. 127, 442–4, 451, 687
Peel, Robert, 1st Baronet (1750–1830), 433, 440, 442–4, 451, 490 n. 141, 505, 535, 581–2, 601, 687
Peel, Robert, 2nd Baronet, Prime Minister (1788–1850), 433, 442, 595 n. 119, 651–2, 656, 678–81, 685–8, 694, 702, 711, 734–5, 752–3, 755, 763–4, 767–9, 773–8, 779, 832, 834–5; death of, 842; resignation, 777
peerage, 65, 110, 118, 134, 136, 143, 183, 205, 211 n. 176, 219, 227–8, 230, 512, 527, 558–9, 611, 613, 619, 653, 697, 701–2, 706, 708, 715, 763, 805; *see also* aristocracy; House of Lords; oligarchy
Peerage Bill (1719), 183
Pelham, Henry, 2nd Duke of Newcastle, Prime Minister, 192 n. 102, 210–12, 219
Pelham Holles, Thomas, 1st Duke of Newcastle (1693–1768), 191, 210, 219–222, 225–7, 233 n. 41, 248, 269, 700
Pembroke Yeomanry, 560
pendulum, 312, 322; pendulum clock, 314, 322
Pennines, 265, 359
Pentrich, Derbyshire and Pentrich affair (1817), 630–1, 638, 648, 660, 757, 826
People's Charter, the, 750–2, 766, 833; *see also* Chartism; National Petition
Perceval, Spencer, Prime Minister (1762–1812), 571, 592–3, 595, 598
Perkins, Jacob (1766–1849) inventor of nail-making machine, 335
Persia, 312, 316–17, 384
Peru: Caral, 495; Incas, 302 n. 52; Nazcas, 331 n. 155
Peterborough, Cambridgeshire, 414
Peterloo Massacre (1819), xix, 532, 596, 609–11, 630, 638 n. 95, 642–9, 661, 770, 826
petitioning, 4, 44, 63, 109, 120 n. 43, 138, 154, 195, 208–9, 230–3, 236–9, 277, 348–9, 381 n. 140, 385–6, 391, 422, 514, 528, 530, 535, 564–5, 578, 581, 587, 590–2, 595, 601–2, 605, 615, 629–30, 637 n. 91, 640, 650, 659, 664, 709, 735, 750–65, 769–71, 774, 778, 781–2, 785, 788, 823–4, 833, 835–6; *see also* Chartism; National Petition; People's Charter
Petty, William (1623–1687), 215–16
Petty, William, 2nd Earl of Shelburne and 1st Marquess of Lansdowne (1737–1805), 321 n. 36, 244–6, 475
Petty-FitzMaurice, Henry, 3rd Marquess of Lansdowne (1780–1863), 651, 678
Philadelphia, Pennsylvania, 237, 437 n. 148
Philanthropic Hercules, 639, 716, 826
Philanthropic Society, 639, 826
Philip II of Spain (1527–1598), 802
Philo of Byzantium (c. 280 BC–c. 220 BC), 306
Philpot, G., 257
phlogistan theory, 336
Phoenicia, 304, 307, 316
photography, 337
Physiocrats, 523, 559
piecework, 60, 357, 452, 475–8, 717–18, 723, 830
Pirenne, Henry (1862–1935), 12, 30 n. 77
Pitt, William the Elder, 1st Earl of Chatham, Prime Minister (1708–1778), 209 n. 170, 210 n. 173, 211, 218–223, 226–31, 233–5, 238, 246, 248, 269
Pitt, William the Younger, Prime Minister (1759–1806), 247, 401, 442, 506, 510, 532–48, 550 n. 161, 561–3, 565, 570, 586–8, 592, 601, 617, 620, 650, 652, 656,

678, 680–1, 687–8, 704–5, 727, 820–1; death of, 586; hiatus from office, 573; legacy, 653–4, 658, 769, 827, 842; 'Pittite Repression', 563, 574; posthumously dubbed a Tory, 620
Place Act, 232
placemen, 174, 190, 204, 207 n. 163, 240, 661; *see* tax farming
plague, 25, 57–9, 70, 73, 113, 141, 179 n. 51, 187, 312, 318, 797, 798, 803; silk-worm plague, 317 n. 100
plantations: Caribbean, 157, 215, 217, 710–11; in India, 709; Plantation Act (1764), 229 n. 33
plastic, 308–9
playing-card makers, 113
plebs or plebeians, 113, 249, 512–13, 531, 548, 611, 636, 638, 700, 758, 810, 820
Plug Plot Riots *see* strike(s) and strikers
Poaching, 189 n. 87, 190 n. 96, 477, 626
pocket watch, 322
Poland, 111, 118, 176, 179 n. 51, 230, 541, 603
Polanyi, Karl (1886–1964), 9, 22–23, 27 n. 71, 28 n. 28, 54–6, 72, 144, 300, 346, 417, 460, 549–551, 554, 812, 818, 822; *see also* custom: dis-embedding of social relations; fictitious commodities
Polhem, Christopher Polhammar (1661–1751) inventor, 335, 379 n. 132
policing, 510, 595 n. 119, 219, 519, 532, 565, 625, 656–7, 684–9, 724, 735, 755–8, 780, 783, 785, 787, 831–2, 836, 842; of combinations, 569; of smuggling, 589; industrial, 358; introduced in UK, 686, 735; country, 687–9, 734, 755; *see also* Fielding, Henry
Polish succession, war of (1733–5), 191
political economy, 6–8, 44, 101, 189 n. 83, 446, 450, 499, 510, 515, 519, 521–32, 559, 567, 588 n. 94, 602, 613, 615, 619–24, 634 n. 81, 646, 650, 655, 665, 667–8, 673–4, 678, 685, 715, 739, 746, 753, 780, 795, 812, 821–2, 827–9, 831, 841; *see also* Malthus; Marx; Mill; Ricardo; Smith
Pollard, Sydney, 78, 365, 382, 449, 472, 481, 517
pollution, 291, 361, 671
Poncelet, Jean-Victor (1788–1867) inventor of inward-flow turbine, 337, 426
Poor Act (1782), *see* Gilbert's Act
Poor Employment Act (1817), 632, 827
poor houses, 374, 693, 752
poor laws, 72, 89, 368, 372, 377, 396, 520, 525, 532, 534, 551–3, 622–3, 656, 696, 737, 801; commissioners, 551, 555, 628, 662, 693, 714, 731, 742, 747, 789, 822, 831; New Poor Law (1834), 715, 727–38, 752, 771, 831; Old Poor Law, 550–1, 620, 715, 721 n. 156, 746, 831; in Wales, 770; *see also* Irish Poor Law; workhouses
Poor Law Commissioners' Report (1834), 551, 770
Poor Law Amendment Act (1834), 730, 733, 736–7, 745, 755 n. 22
poor rates, 137, 275–7, 369, 375–7, 469, 516, 520–1, 550–6, 616, 621, 678, 689, 699, 729, 775, 789, 809
porcelain, 193, 301, 336, 340, 405, 410, 415
Porthouse, John, inventor, 469, 503
Portland, Duke of *see* Cavendish-Bentinck, William Henry
Portsmouth, Hampshire, 221 n. 16; naval shipyards at, 362
Portugal, 110, 179 n. 50, 545, 572, 586, 589, 590 n. 103, 592, 598 n. 126, 599, 679, 768; Lagos, 222; Liberal Party in, 679; Lisbon, 331 n. 155
Post Office Bill (1836), 750
potassium hypochlorite, 487
Potteries (the), Staffordshire, 264, 353, 359, 403–7, 413, 438, 475, 717, 736–7, 767
pottery manufacture, 264, 302, 326, 353, 362 Table 7.2, 403–15, 418, 427, 438, 444, 448, 457–8, 470, 475–6, 486, 500, 502, 536, 670, 717, 721 n. 156, 735–9, 749, 767, 771, 816; potter's rot, 404–5, 670; *see also* National Union of Operative Potters; Spode; Wedgwood; Whielden
poverty and vagrancy, 10, 58, 60, 64, 72, 116, 130, 137–8, 188, 190, 236, 330, 361, 370–1, 374, 400, 435, 440, 456, 469, 510, 520, 526–7, 551–5, 622–5, 634, 655, 671, 696–7, 728, 730, 732, 763, 773, 777, 810, 821, 831, 834; 'professional' beggars, 371; 'solutions' for, 368–379; 'sturdy beggars', 370; *see also* Poor Laws; workhouses
Pratt, Charles, 1st Earl of Camden (1714–1794), 228, 233, 561
Presbyterians, 125, 127–8, 132, 178 n. 48; Irish, 236
Pressburg, Treaty of (1805), 586
Preston, Lancashire, 421 n. 68, 431, 434, 672, 700, 759, 767
Prestonpans, East Lothia, Scotland, 211, 487, 489 n. 137
Price, Richard, 635–40, 646, 669, 674, 739 n. 216, 751, 760–1, 785–7, 790–1

Price, Reverand Dr. Richard (1723–91), 537, 635, 693
prime mover, xviii, 9 n. 16, 35, 284, 300–1, 812
Primogeniture, 203
printers, 234, 236 n. 48, 533, 664, 721, 754; calico printers, 352, 386, 571; hand-printers, 330
printing press *see* Gütenberg
prisons and gaols, 85, 121 n. 45, 130, 189 ns. 83 and 86, 190, 207 n. 165, 228, 242, 349–50, 367, 514, 520 n. 37, 542, 546 n. 144, 548, 560–2, 564, 568, 570, 578, 598, 600 n. 137, 601, 631, 626, 639, 642, 648, 662–3, 673, 686, 693–5, 701, 722, 724, 737, 758, 761–4, 767, 771, 778, 783–4, 841; factory compared to, 289 n. 11; Fleet prison, 528; prison-hospitals, 371; *see also* Newgate; debt: debtors prison
private property *see* property
Privy Council, 579
production: innovation, maximisation and specialisation in, xviii, 18, 21, 41, 144, 280, 360, 415, 614, 637, 837; mass production, xviii, 633; re-organisation of the relations of, 169, 448, 451–5, 486; techniques, xviii, 17, 29, 37, 76, 79, 81, 90, 157, 158, 167, 176, 198, 202, 314, 319, 325, 334, 401, 407, 410, 413, 425, 442, 448–51, 459, 491, 501, 553, 633, 798, 807, 814; technological versus organisational innovation, 444–450; *see also* means of production
productive forces, 24, 35, 294–303, 313, 343 n. 3, 812–13, 841; primacy of, 294–5
productivity, 13, 31, 35–36, 48, 320, 322, 346, 592; of agriculture, 21–2, 30, 41, 43, 61, 71, 73, 91, 165–6, 169–171, 173, 192–194, 196 n. 119, 199, 206 n. 159, 213–14, 216–218, 240 n. 63, 253–61, 265–70, 549, 621–2, 690–1, 698, 706, 740, 799, 807, 822, 837; concept of, 313–15; in industry, 401–2, 418, 429, 441, 448, 451–452, 486, 644, 795, 809; of labour, 24, 379, 423, 549, 552, 730, 733; of manufacturing, 274, 301, 387, 423, 795
profit, 3–4, 22, 36–9, 43, 53, 57, 65–7, 82–6, 91, 107, 115 n. 31, 136, 143–4, 150 n. 141, 152–3, 162, 167, 184–99, 217 n. 6, 250, 260, 270, 272, 274, 277–8, 285, 322–3, 341, 345–6, 365, 374–82, 397, 411–12, 415–16, 419, 424–7, 437, 458, 462–3, 472–3, 476–83, 488, 493–500, 521, 524, 533, 553, 572, 590, 606, 614, 621–3, 637, 658–9, 670, 677, 682, 687, 691–2, 714, 732, 742–7, 753, 762, 799, 811, 822, 831, 834; margins, 171; maximisation, 36, 53; rate of, 494, 816
proletariat, 13, 15, 19, 24, 33, 64, 85, 91, 141, 159, 203, 216 n. 3, 224, 271–3, 345, 358, 367, 398, 419, 474, 547 n. 149, 552, 611, 630, 683, 690, 708, 726–7, 736, 745–746, 781, 733 n. 118, 786, 788, 799, 811–12, 842; proletarianisation, 86, 93, 216 n. 3, 273, 318, 415, 423, 454, 464, 469, 515, 549, 552, 690, 721 741, 760, 764, 787, 801; semi-proletarian, 13, 29, 398, 532, 594, 727
Prometheus, 34, 447
propertied classes, 5, 84, 142, 172, 431, 490, 526, 593, 658–9, 661, 700, 708, 732, 833
property, 2–28, 36–44, 50–1, 61–2, 82–5, 88–95, 101–5, 110, 118–39, 144, 163, 171, 184, 189–92, 202–6, 213, 216, 232, 240–50, 271, 276–80, 286, 295–99, 341–50, 361, 372, 396, 413, 421–2, 433, 458, 461, 469, 495–8, 504–6, 512–13, 521, 526–8, 539–40, 545, 554–9, 575–82, 597–606, 613–29, 640, 656–65, 680–708, 718, 727–45, 751, 758–67, 777, 780–804, 811, 818–31, 837–42; abolition of private, 4, 126 n. 64, 163, 575, 785, 788; ancient, 84; feudal, 27; 'great civilizing force', 683; hegemony of landed, 827; landed, 36, 127, 136, 526, 664, 741; middling, 705; politically-constituted, 25, 558, 619, 658, 683, 706; qualification for voting, 539 n. 117, 737, 751, 788; redistribution of, 126, 144, 660–1, 540 n. 120, 661, 758, 785; 'real estate', 28, 279; sacredness of, 540, 575, 819; tax-state office, 25; violent (crimes or offences) against, 4, 190, 241–2, 526–7, 626, 683, 693, 745, 766 n. 61, 824
propertyless classes, 5, 726, 811
protectionism, 38, 107, 380, 651, 776
Protestants and Protestantism, 119–20, 131, 133, 146, 180, 236 n. 49, 239, 240–2, 562, 617 n. 22, 680–1, 709, 773–4, 777, 803–4, 810; Protestant Succession, the, 177 n. 44, 219
proto-industrialisation theory, 47–8, 74 n. 90–101, 145 n. 126, 168–71, 344, 347 n. 7, 418 n. 64, 423, 430 n. 108, 444, 671, 741; *see also* domestic system; putting-out system
Prussia, 145 n. 126, 173 n. 31, 191, 209–10, 220–2, 226–7, 536, 541, 544, 557, 561,

573, 587, 600, 603, 613, 743, 782; army, 221; Bautzen, 600; Lützen, 600; *see also* Germany
Ptolemy, Claudius, (90–c. 168), 308
Public Works Loan Commission, 632
Puckle, James (1667–1724) inventor of machine gun, 325
Puffing Billy, 338
Pulteney, William, 1st Earl of Bath (1684–1764), 207 n. 162, 209
Puritans: 107, 120, 123–5, 372; Puritan Imperialism, 124
Putney Debates, 5, 105, 126, 539–40, 804
putting-out system, 14, 41, 43, 61, 73, 93–4, 96 n. 181, 100–1, 345–7, 355, 360–1, 365, 377, 396, 401, 418 n. 64, 422–3, 430, 445–7, 450, 463–4, 491, 517, 524, 580, 606, 800, 838
Pym, John (1584–1643), 124, 207 n. 162
pyramids, 295, 302, 308, 446

Quakers, 324, 374, 471 n. 41, 480, 542, 585, 753, 771 n. 76
Quebec, 222, 241
Quebec Act (1774), 240
Quesnay, François (1694–1774), 523
Quintuple Alliance (1818), 657

Radical Party, 745–53, 765, 776–9, 785, 788
Radical War (1820), 649
radicalism, 42, 588–93, 601, 622–36, 642–61, 678–688, 694, 696, 700–1, 707–8, 716, 745–6, 750, 756–9, 763, 782–90, 820–7, 835, 839; and the Combination Acts, 562–77; definition of, 548; economists, 673; European reaction to, 612–13; Irish, 535, 734, 746; Jacobin popular, 577; libertarian, 632, 660–1, 827, 829; Malthus on, 622; middle class, 633, 827; 'milk-and-water', 588 n. 96; press, 643, 750, 784; repression under Pitt, 548, 556–7, 592, 820; repression under Liverpool, 613, 641–6, 661, 825; return of in late eighteenth century, 523–48; Scottish, 647–9; seventeenth century, 103–43, 162–3, 221, 224, 229–31, 804; Socialist, 759; Spencean, 684, 829; tension within, 572–7, 661; and Swing, 694; trade unionist, 632; ultra, 756, 759; and Wilkes affair, 233–5, 240–2, 249; *see also* Chartism; London Corresponding Society; London Radical Reform Organisation; Owen; Reform Acts
railroads and railways, 299 n. 44, 326, 332, 338, 442, 482, 490, 493, 497, 505, 584–5, 612, 688, 736, 749, 759, 778, 781, 831; the boom, 497, 504, 670 n. 206, 738–44, 778, 832; mania, 743; railworkers, 778; Rainhill trials, 682; underground, 482; *see also* navvies
Rainsborough, Colonel Thomas (1610–1648), 126
Ramsden, Jesse (1735–1800) inventor of screw-cutting lathe, 335
Randall, Adrian, 94, 422–3, 563, 565–6, 578–9
Ransome, Robert (1753–1830) inventor of the self-sharpening plough, 692
rationality, 27, 297, 417, 819; economic rationality, 2, 17, 36; rational capitalism, 53, 83, 276; rational commerce, 339; rational self-interest, 17, 20–1; rationality model, 339; *see also* Enlightenment
Rawfolds Mill, 596–7, 824
de Réamur, René Antoine Ferchault (1683–1757), 386
reaper (reaping machine), 337–8, 340, 661, 692
Rebecca Riots (1843), 756, 767, 770
Rebuilding Act (1667), 138
reductionism, 294, 339, 501 n. 171, 619
Reeves, John (1752–1829), 542–3
Reform Bill of 1831, 699
Reform Act (Reform Bill) of 1832 *see* Great Reform Act of 1832
Reformation, the, 64
Registration of Voters Bill (1836), 750
regrating, 136 n. 98, 518–20, 529 n. 80, 555, 564, 570, 803, 820 n. 13
Rehe, Samuel, inventor of tool sharpener, 335
Republic of England *see* Commonwealth of England
republicanism, 25, 119, 132, 173, 238, 541–2, 557, 559, 577, 585, 587 n. 91, 588, 782–3, 785
'reserve army of labour', 510, 697
Restoration of Stuart Monarchy (1660), 130–2, 134–6, 147 n. 130, 152, 160, 163, 174, 182, 204 n. 153, 212, 221, 324 n. 120, 343, 374, 424, 475, 480, 559, 804
Retford, Nottinghamshire, 456, 680 n. 12
retrenchment, 618, 625, 652, 654–5, 660–2, 699, 826–7, 833
Revenue Act (1767), 231

reverbatory furnace, 331, 334
'revisionist' history, 272–9; counter-revisionists, 272
Revolution Society, 537
Revolutionary and Napoleonic Wars, 42, 44, 256, 260 n. 21, 272, 278–9, 487, 515, 558, 584, 592, 606, 611–17, 653–4, 794, 821–2, 832, 839
Revolutions of 1848, 657 n. 168, 781–3
revolver, 338
Rhazes (Ali-Rhazi) (c. 850–925) chemist, 312
Rhineland, 557–8
Ricardo, David (1772–1823), 494, 621–4, 650–1, 653, 665, 714 n. 132, 753
Riot Act (1715), 181, 189, 556, 672, 819
Roberts, Richard (1789–1864) inventor of the self-acting mule, 453
Roberts, W.P., 771–2
Robespierre, Maximilien (1758–1794), 548
Robinson, John Frederick, Viscount Goderich, Prime Minister, (1782–1859) 652, 666, 679, 832
Rochdale, Lancashire, 33, 430, 753, 764
Rockingham, Prime Minister *see* Watson-Wentworth, Charles
Roebuck, John (1718–1794) inventor of sulfuric acid, 414 n. 50, 472–3, 478, 486–7, 489 n. 137, 751, 763
Roebuck, John Arthur (1802–1879), 751, 763, 765
Rogers, Nicholas, 514, 519
Roman law, 52; *ager publicus* and *ager privatus*, 83; early modern revival of, 52; private property in land, 84; *see also* common law; property
Rome (ancient), 2, 13, 29, 38, 81–3, 296, 301–17, 338, 363, 480–1; architecture, 305, 326 n. 129; canals, 263; capitalism present or absent, 53, 84, 301; *collegiae*, 49, 51 n. 12, 55; large-scale production, 79; excelled in public works, 305; gearing, 307; hydraulics, 263 n. 28, 305; why no industrial revolution in, 307; roads, 197, 262 n. 27, 305; science , 338; nature of the state, 84; borrowed technologies, 307, 310; waterwheel, 306; weaponry, 306; *see also* Byzantium; feudalism
Romney Marshes of Kent and East Sussex, 715
Rose Copper Company, 480
Rostow, Walt Whitman (1916–2003), 32, 261, 496, 497, 567, 744
rotary motion, 304, 320
rotative engine, 333
Rotherham plough, 198
rotten boroughs, 232, 240, 534, 679–80, 688, 699, 703 n. 92; definition of, 233 n. 41; *see also* Old Sarum
rough musick, 512, 606
roundsman system, 549, 552–3, 568, 736
Rousseau, Jean-Jacques (1712–1778), 559
Royal Africa Company, 160
Royal Agricultural Society of England, 776
Royal Army *see* army
royal commissions, 714–15, 735, 769
Royal Commission on Children's Employment in Mines, 769
Royal Decree of 1360, 57
Royal Lustring Company, 380
Royal Navy *see* Navy
Royal Society, 322, 414, 424
Royalists, English Civil War, 123, 125, 128, 131–3, 141 n. 116, 204, 221; French Royalists, 572
Rudé, George (1910–1993), 690, 695–6, 730
Rule, John G (1944–2011), 205, 215, 369, 398–9, 439, 551–3, 626 n. 48, 639 n. 98, 644–5, 664 n. 184, 696, 707, 722–3, 726, 761
Rump Parliament (1648), 128, 130, 132
Rupert, Prince, 1st Duke of Cumberland (1619–1682), 324 n. 120, 387
Russell, 1st Earl Lord John, Prime Minister (1792–1878), 702, 777; and church reform in Ireland, 709; drafter of reform bill, 699–700; 'finality' speech opposing greater reforms, 752; pardons machine-breakers, 710; promoted to leader in the Commons, 734, 752; repeal of Test and Corporations Acts, 679; second term as prime minister, 774, 777
Russell, William, 1st Duke of Bedford (1613–1700), 124
Russia, 167, 176, 179 n. 51, 220 n. 13, 221, 226, 230 n. 35, 325 n. 123, 473, 536, 541, 572–3, 586–7, 589, 600, 603, 613, 679, 743
Russia Company, 161, 378
Ryswick, Treaty of (1697), 174–5, 177, 806

Sacheverell affair (1710), 180
Saddlers, 509
sailmakers, 260
St. Clears, Wales, 768

Saint-Domingue (Haiti), 585
St. George's Fields, 231 n. 38, 232, 241
St. Giles-in-the-Fields, 373
St. Helena, 603
St. James' Palace, 132
St. John, Henry, 1st Viscount Bolingbroke (1678–1751), 180
St. John, Knights of, 585
'Saint Monday', 354–5, 378, 454
St. Peter's Field, Manchester, 609–10, 770
Sale, Kirkpatrick, 595 n. 120, 598–9, 634, 697, 775 n. 90, 825
Sandwich, Earl of *see* Montagu, John
Sardinia, Kingdom of, 209, 211, 382 n. 141, 544, 558, 782
Sarum *see* Old Sarum
de Saussure, Horace (1740–1799) inventor of hygrometer
Savery, Thomas (1650–1715) inventor of steam engine, 323
Savoy, Kingdom of, 154 n. 158, 173 n. 31, 179 n. 50
Sawyers, 138, 350, 357
Saxony, 173–4, 179 n. 51, 221, 603; *see also* Anglo-Saxons
Say's Law, 623
Scheele, Carl Wilhelm (1742–1786) discoverer of chlorine, 336
schools and schooling, 371, 379, 667, 717, 762 n. 41, 791; charity schools, 372, 375; factory schools, 772 n. 80; of industry, 534; spinning schools, 343; in workhouses, 733
science, 2, 7, 35, 158, 284, 288, 299, 301–8, 314–27, 336–41, 414–15, 484–6, 500, 505, 523, 554, 793, 813, 834–5; of agriculture, 622, 774–5; amateur science in Britain, 340–1, 376, 15, 505, 813, 414; clubs, 505, 813; economic, 683; engineering, 40; state patronage of in France, 414–15, 813; of history, 291; and industrial revolution, 415; natural, 327, 522–3; social, 8, 99, 496; of statistics, 155; *see also Académie des Sciences*; Lunar Society
scientific revolution, 286–7, 320–7
Scotland, 85, 122–4, 128, 132, 142, 155, 158 n. 162, 178–179, 181, 184 n. 67, 210–11, 213, 222, 239–41, 250, 258, 330–1, 333, 362, 384, 386, 394 n. 185, 430, 443, 452, 463, 467–9, 478, 480–1, 483, 486–7, 543 n. 132, 554, 611, 630, 632, 638, 645, 649, 666–71, 677, 699, 716, 723, 739, 762, 767, 771, 794, 802, 806, 810; army of Scottish Covenanters, 123; Combination Laws in, 638, 667; Highlanders, 190, 240 n. 63, 489 n. 137, 211; highlands, 240 n. 63; rapid advance of industrial capitalism in, 649; linen manufacture primary, 469; lowlands, 470–2; population, 554 n. 177; rising of 1820, 647–9; united with England under James I (1603), 107–8, 178 n. 48; union with England and Wales (1707), 148 n. 132, 162, 178–9, 213, 468, 806; wholesale conversion to agrarian capitalism, 211, 250; *see also* serfdom: colliery-serfdom
Scott, James, 1st Duke of Monmouth, also 1st Duke of Buccleuch (1649–1685), 142, 240 n. 61
scribblers and scribbling, 423, 463, 465, 580
scribbling engines, 465–7, 502, 543, 580
scribbling mills, 580, 741
scriveners, 148, 204 n. 153
Second Coalition, war of the (1798–1802), 572
Second World War, 246, 835
Seditious Meetings Act: of 1795, 547, 562, 574; of 1817, 629
Seduction from Duties Act (1797), 561
Segner, Ján Andrej (1704–1777) inventor of reactive turbine, 337
seigneuries, 13, 16, 50, 796
seismometer, 309
Senefelder, Aloys (1771–1834) inventor of lithography, 336
Senior, Nassau William (1790–1864), 583, 713–14, 730–1, 746
Septennial Bill (1716), 183
serfdom, 9–13, 16, 19, 25, 50–1, 71, 798, 802; colliery-serfdom in Scotland, 483, 667, 671, 802; 'second serfdom' in Eastern Europe, 96
servi, 51
Seven Years' War (1756–63), 218, 222 n. 17, 225, 246, 248, 341 n. 186, 587 n. 91, 617, 810
Seville, Treaty of (1729), 191
sewers, 304–305, 307 n. 73, 770 n. 73; Commissioners of Sewers, 115 n. 31
sextant, 312, 327
Sharp, Samuel (1801–1832), 710
Shaw, William, 294, 298, 301, 313, 320
shearmen, 'croppers' or cloth-dressers, 63, 224, 304, 344, 388 n. 161, 462, 543, 572, 577–82, 596, 670, 678, 763–4, 824, 829

shearing frame or engine, 320, 330, 572, 578, 596–7, 599, 763; power shears, 335, 824
sheep farming 26, 89, 144, 240 n. 63, 257, 259, 464, 505, 526, 689 n. 46, 799
Sheer, 598
Sheffield, South Yorkshire, 196, 264, 326, 330, 359, 362 Table 7.2, 486, 563, 565, 597, 602, 647, 704, 754, 757, 762, 784
Sheffield Society for Constitutional Information, 543
Sheffield Trades' General Union, 716
Shelburne, Earl of *see* Petty, WIlliam
Shelley, Percy Bysshe (1792–1822), 609
Sheppard, Jack (1702–1724), 526
Shepton Mallet, Somerset, 422, 467
Sheridan, Richard Brinsley Butler (1751–1816), 536, 538, 562 n. 11
shipbuilders or shipwrights, 205, 287
shipping, 155–6, 160, 172, 197, 239, 245–6, 307, 362, 468; coastal, 197, 262; ships, 75, 78, 125, 129, 141, 172, 185, 208–11, 223, 245 n. 80, 259, 304–305, 312, 362, 484, 560, 573, 587, 590, 600, 768 n. 68, 811; carrack, 316; collier, 71 n. 77; iron, 333; sailing, 322, 335; steamships, 744, 778; tax, 769; tonnage, 121 n. 45, 153 n. 153, 160shipwrights, 517, 664, 667
shivarees, 512
shoemakers, 359, 546, 561, 696, 722, 724–5
shopkeepers, 122, 139, 158, 232, 393, 617 n. 22, 661, 688 n. 41, 713, 826
Shrapnel, Henry (1761–1842) inventor of shrapnel shell, 333
Shropshire, 324 n. 120, 325, 364, 367, 585
shuttle-loom, 290, 320 n. 107, 326, 328, 391–2, 424–5, 427, 429–30, 433 n. 127, 457, 467 n. 25, 503, 543, 549, 814
Sicily, 184, 572, 586, 781–2; *see also* Naples
Sidmouth, Viscount *see* Addington, Henry
Silesia, 209–10
silk, 77, 81, 160, 166, 175–176, 285, 302, 304, 309, 344, 357–62, 379–87, 393, 396, 404, 423–424, 429–32, 438, 445, 530, 617, 626, 659, 664–7, 685, 719–20, 724, 739, 801, 806–9, 816; China, 304, 309, 384–5; France, 337, 380; Irish silk trade collapses, 269; Italy 287, 317, 325–6, 384; India, 385; first factory (the Old Silk Mill), 166, 325–6, 379–84, 396, 432, 719, 739, 807–9; inventors of winding apparatus, 320; organzine thread, 381; protection, 176, 380, 386, 617; silkworms, 317; tram, 384; *see also* Spitalfields
silk-weavers, 230, 235, 337, 348, 398, 531, 602, 659, 664–5, 685, 719, 801, 820; *see also* Spitalfields, Spitalfields Acts
sinecures, 534, 558, 710, 727, 827
Six Acts, 610, 643, 645, 647, 650, 827
skills or 'secrets of the trade' (transmission of), 450, 451–3, 458, 665, 801, 823; de-skilling, 411, 459
skimmington ridings, 115, 512–13
Slack, Paul, 372
slate quarries, 481–2
slavery, 30, 49–51, 98, 175, 184, 207, 217, 299, 384, 447, 544, 585, 587–8, 609, 627–8, 631 n. 69, 641–2, 683–4, 710–712, 715, 831; abolition of, 554, 587–8; Atlantic trade, 122, 160, 175 n. 34, 184, 215, 217; artisanal opposition to, 207 n. 162; Bussa's Rebellion, 627; Committee of reformers, 710–12; decline from the tenth century, 50–5; relation to capitalism, 588 n. 94, 711, 831; Roman, 49; Sharp Rebellion, 710; *see also* Abolition of Slavery Acts; abolitionists
slave labour, 416, 447, 588 n. 94, 609, 628, 683–4, 687, 711, 771
slave masters, 217 n. 6
sledgehammers, 672
slubbing billy, 442, 465, 502
smallpox, 309
smelting, 76, 81, 264, 324–5, 330, 428
Smith, Adam (1723–1790), 6–8, 17–20, 28, 31, 57, 246, 286, 356, 368, 388 n. 161, 420, 446, 521–9, 533–534, 620–622, 624, 667, 703, 753, 808, 812, 821; and agrarian capitalism, 6, 522–3; on corrupting influence of commerce, 7; division of labour key to capitalism, 19, 31, 409, 415–16, 446, 739 n. 216; on forestalling and engrossing, 529; supporter of high wages, 524; on machinery, 415–16, 524; on monopolies, 52–3; on the Poor Laws, 525; property sacrosanct, 527; champion of rural artisans, 524–5; on self-sustaining growth, 7, 17, 28; Smithian socialists, 525; stage theory of history, 8; tendency to naturalise economics and universalise capitalism, 6, 8, 17, 276, 300, 522; tension in his work, 525
Smith, Sir Thomas (1513–1577), 62
Smith, Thomas (Luddite), 599
smuggling and smugglers, 53, 190–1, 207–8, 230, 236, 317 n. 100, 385, 517, 533, 589, 771

social engineering, 372
social property relations, 5, 8, 24, 37, 41–2, 171, 250, 255, 459, 461, 577, 698, 761, 794, 799, 818–19, 828, 830, 835, 837, 839, 841
social relations of production, 8, 23, 170–1, 296, 303, 320, 341, 392, 414, 557, 559, 800, 812, 814; mode of, xx
socialism, 103, 126, 290 n. 15, 296, 525, 539 n. 117, 645, 661, 684, 718, 758–9, 784–5, 788, 836, 842; agrarian, 574; utopian, 827
Society for Commemorating the Revolution, 537; *see also* Revolution Society
Society for Constitutional Information, 543, 546
Society for the Promotion of Christian Knowledge (SPCK), 372, 375
soda (sodium carbonate), 336, 414–15, 487; soda ash, 489
sodium chloride, 336
sodium sulphate, 489
Soho Foundry, 479, 489, 505, 584
Soho Manufactory, 476–9, 817
Soho, Birmingham, 478; Soho House Museum, 33, n. 162
Solvay Process, 487
Somerset, 159, 183, 422, 467, 578, 581, 695
Sophia of Hanover, Electress (1630–1714)
Sorocold, George (c. 1668–c. 1738), 177, 180, 182
South America, 81, 590, 743, 802; *see also* Spain: colonies
South Sea Bubble (1720), 153, 165, 182, 185 n. 70, 188 n. 81, 203 n. 149; *see also* Bubble Act
South Sea Company, 183, 185–8, 208, 364, 806
Southwark, 241 356, 484
sovereignty, 55, 58, 125–8, 133 n. 87; popular, 125, 128, 212; parliamentary, 128, 536; *see also* parcellisation of sovereignty
Soviet Union, 272, 298
Spa Fields affair (1816), 631, 638, 826
Spain, 9, 72, 107 n. 8, 110, 120–3, 131, 133 n. 87, 143, 178–84, 191, 208, 212, 215, 218, 222, 226, 235 n. 46, 238, 245–6, 386, 501, 538, 544–5, 557–8, 587, 590, 599–600, 657, 768, 802–3, 811; absolutist, 215, 501; Armadas, 210, 501, 560, 803; *Asiento*, 184, 208, 212, 218; colonies in the Americas, 72–3, 120, 124, 178 n. 45, 184, 208, 218, 226 ; Conquistadors, 308; liberal revolutionaries, 657; Madrid, 599, 657; 'no peace without Spain', 179; *see also* Spanish Succession, war of
Spanish Netherlands, 178
Spanish Succession, War of (1702–13), 133 n. 87, 171, 176, 178, 191
SPCK see Society for the Promotion of Christian Knowledge
Speenhamland, Berkshire, 549, 821
Speenhamland system, 510, 549–53, 556, 569, 690 n. 49, 729, 742, 747, 822, 826
Spence, Thomas (1750–1814), 562 n. 12, 574–5, 629 n. 62, 788; Spencean followers, 577, 623, 629, 631 n. 69, 639, 661, 684, 829
Spencer, Earl of *see* Althorp, John
spices, 81, 107, 160, 175
spinning and spinners, 61–6, 93, 138, 248, 283, 319, 325–30, 343, 357, 360, 373–4, 381–91, 402, 404, 410, 417, 421–43, 451–69, 478–93, 502–3, 516, 549, 580–1, 583–4, 619, 638–9, 647, 665, 667, 670, 681–4, 687, 713, 717, 723, 738–41, 760, 763, 786, 801, 809–10, 825, 830; distaff, 65, 302; jenny, 328–30, 391, 402, 417, 421–5, 430–7, 441–2, 452, 462, 466, 503, 549, 584 n. 74, 638, 814; mule and mule-spinners, 329–30, 366, 433–7, 441–3, 448, 451–5, 460, 486, 500, 583–4, 607, 638–9, 670, 670, 681, 684, 713, 786, 796, 815, 826, 830; water frame, 384, 417, 430, 328–9, 366, 380, 384, 390 n. 171, 417, 422 n. 70, 429–37, 442–3, 452, 462 n. 5, 466, 468, 486–7, 500, 584 n. 74, 815; roller spinning, 326, 387 n. 155, 389 n. 165, 433 n. 126; spinning wheel, 65, 79, 224, 309, 316–17, 328, 486, 491, 801; spinsters, 423; throstle, 437 n. 147, 442, 584
Spitalfields, London, 230–1, 348 n. 8, 362 Table 7.2, 380–3, 389, 530–1
Spitalfields Acts, 659, 664; of 1773, 530, 659, 684, 820 n. 13; of 1792, 659; of 1811, 659; repeal, 602 n. 143, 659, 665
Spode, Josiah (1733–1797), 406, 409 n. 29
Spode, Josiah II (1755–1827), 409 n. 29, 505
Stacey, William, 737
Staffordshire, 324 n. 120
Stalin, Joseph Vissarionovich (1878–1953), 298
Stalinism, 294
Stamp Act (1765), 229, 233
standardisation of production, 327, 334–5, 479; *see also* coinage; interchangeable

parts; money; weights and measurements
Stanley, Edward, 14th Earl of Derby (1799–1869), 709–11, 735, 763
state(s): and civil liberties, 248–9; capitalism requires state to guarantee property rights, 660; development of, 3, 813; and the drive toward greater productivity, 313–15; as enforcer of property rights, 41, 838; international system of states, 39; Italian city-states, 11, 25, 36, 39, 50; rise of national states after 1648, 11; role in regulating social relations, 12; role in shaping economic outcomes, 794; separation from civil society, 145, 612 n. 8; stationary, 622; stratification and formation of earliest states, 302–3; *see also* British state; coercive force; English state; Rome
stationers, 337, 485
Stationers' Company, 139
Statute of Apprentices, 'Queen Betty's Law' or 5 Elizabeth (1564–1814), 66–72, 105–6, 116, 138, 140–1, 224, 348–52, 371, 406, 485, 509–10, 530, 539, 550, 564, 570, 581, 581–3, 591, 593, 601–3, 637, 659, 664, 674, 800–1, 824, 829; repeal of, 510, 592–603, 824
Statute of Artificers *see Statute of Apprentices*
Statute of Labourers (1349–51), 57–8, 66, 69 n. 68, 798
statute law, 66 n. 64, 67, 232
steam engine, 90, 299, 306, 314–15, 323 n. 118, 329 n. 141, 413, 426, 461, 467, 478–9, 485, 504, 584, 618, 807; Newcomen's atmospheric engine, 166, 324, 807; rotary steam engine, 417; Savery's engine, 323; and steam boats, 333; and steam locomotive, 338, 584; Watt's double-acting engine, 332; Watt's separate condenser engine, 289 n. 12, 332, 334, 442; *see also*: *aeolipile*; *fardier*
steel and steel-making 76, 259, 236, 334, 454, 488, 717; wootz steel, 308; steel-nib pen, 332
Stephenson, George (1781–1848) railway industrialist, 338
Stephenson, Robert (1803–1859) inventor of the *Rocket* locomotive, 682
stewards *see* land
Stewart, Robert *see* Castlereagh
stock exchange or stock market, 151, 155, 188, 265, 806
stockingers, 357, 594–5, 602, 632
stock-jobbing, 151, 155–6, 806
Stone, Lawrence (1919–1999), 117–118, 205, 490 n. 141
Strafford, Earl of *see* Wentworth, Thomas
strike(s) and strikers, 69, 159, 232, 235, 314, 349–51, 367, 398, 412, 483, 534, 543, 563, 568–9, 571, 575, 578, 580, 638–84, 693–9, 709, 716–27, 736 -8, 758–60, 765–769, 770–773, 779–80, 792, 822–34; in France, 337 n. 178; Great Strike of 1820, 647–9; General Strike of 1834, 724–5, 735, 758; General Strike (Plug Plot Riots) of 1842, 765–8; Great Strike of 1844, 769 n. 71, 772–3, 834; Mule-Spinners' Great Strike of 1818, 638–41, 673, 826; Oldham strike of 1834, 724–5; 'Radical War' of 1820, 647, 649; Scottish Colliers' Strike of 1824–5, 667–71, 717; *see also* arbitration
structuralism, 294
Strutt, Jedediah (1726–1797), 328, 424–5, 431–2, 440, 443, 452, 477, 505
Stuart dynasty: *see* James I; Charles I; Charles II; James II; Stuart, James Francis Edward; Stuart, Charles Edward Louis
Stuart, Charles Edward Louis, 'Bonnie Prince Charlie' or the 'Young Pretender' (1720–1788), 210–11, 406 n. 20
Stuart, James Francis Edward, the 'Old Pretender' (1688–1766), 177–81, 213; the '15, 182
Stuart, John *see* Bute, Earl John
subcontracting, 365, 453, 472, 607, 719; *see also* butty system
submarine, 321–2, 332
suffrage: struggle for universal manhood suffrage, 4–5, 126–7, 539, 633, 700–2, 735, 750–3, 758–9, 761–5, 771 n. 76, 781, 785, 832, 841 n. 1; *see also* Complete Suffrage Union
sugar: consumption of increasing in England and Britain, 71 n. 77, 137, 193, 201 n. 140, 217, 358, 616, 670; originated in India, 308; planting, 121, 205; production, 75; refining and processing, 77, 160, 312, 362, 428 n. 97, 489, 535; smuggling, 230; sugar islands of West Indies, 215, 245; trade, 150, 160, 174–5, 772 n. 81
sulphuric acid, 414, 486–7
Suppression of Seditious and Treasonable Societies Act, 562

Suraj-ud-Daulah, Nawáb of Bengal (1729–1757), 221
surgery and surgeons, 302, 308–9, 312, 351
surplus-value, 343 n. 3, 416, 458; absolute surplus, 346
surplus(es), 16–17, 24, 27, 30, 97, 168, 170, 621, 623, 732, 743–4, 810; surplus-appropriation or extraction, 3–6, 16, 19, 21, 25, 29–30, 40, 50, 84–5, 101, 114, 134, 206, 248, 255, 396, 399, 496, 657–8, 746, 796, 837; distribution of the social surplus, 303; surplus labour, 13, 64, 73, 96 n. 181, 168, 377, 500, 662, 690–2, 714, 729; surplus population, 73, 137–8, 217, 250, 254 Diagram 5.1, 273–274, 790, 810
surveyors *see* land
Sussex, 208 n. 167, 362 Table 7.2, 387, 499, 626, 694–5
swape, 304
sweatshops, 721, 723, 786
Sweden, 80, 141, 167, 173 n. 29, 184, 230 n. 35, 325 n. 123, 335–6, 573, 586, 589, 743; iron exports, 364, 473; Stjärnsund, 335
Sweezy, Paul M. (1910–2004), 9–15, 17–18, 24, 98 n. 189, 367 n. 84, 743 n. 229, 797
Swift, Jonathan (1667–1745), 148 n. 132, 188
Swing revolt (1830–1831), xix, 689–97, 699, 714–15, 719–20, 730–2, 745, 757–61, 775, 831, 833
Switzerland, 96, 171, 386, 572, 585
Sword Blade Company, 184, 186 n. 75
Symington, William (1764–1831) inventor of first practical steamboat, 333
syndicalism, 671, 785
Syria, 768

tailors, 55, 140, 349–50, 567, 723–5, 784 n. 120; London Tailors, 833; *see also* Merchant Taylors
Takahashi, Kohachiro, 11, 14
Talavera, Battle of (1809), 592
Tamworth Manifesto (1834), 687, 734
tanners, 359
Tate, Colonel William, 560
Tate, John, 579
Tawney, Richard Henry (1880–1962), 14, 253, 271, 523
tax farming 109, 149, 558; *see also* placemen
taxes and taxation, 49, 60, 93, 107, 115 n. 31, 119–21, 125, 131–2, 146–56, 171, 191–2, 213, 223, 235–40, 248, 260, 369, 376, 485–6, 533–5, 589–93, 617–21, 632, 641, 653–5, 661, 694, 702, 709, 727, 759, 796, 807, 810–11, 826; arbitrary, 121; on clocks, 533–4; on coal, 87, 533; on cotton, 533 n. 96, 535; the excise, 107, 111, 134 n. 89, 148–9, 171, 198, 206–10, 219, 385, 484, 533, 587, 617, 641, 657, 666, 807, 826; decimation, 131; on dwellings, 702; external, 230; on hearths, 134 n. 89; income, 573, 587, 617, 625, 769; in India, 768 n. 67; indirect, 172; on linen, 533 n. 96 on luxuries, 235; on peasants, 118; regressive, 627, 641, 653, 807; tax revolt, 647, 700; on royalists, 125; on shops, 533; on tea, 231; on trade, 109; wartime, 199; unparliamentary, 110, 121; *see also* Easter tax; France: the *taille*; land tax; tax farming; Townshend duties; placemen
Taylor, James, inventor of spinning machinery, 391
Taylor, Dr. John, Chartist, 756
Taylor, John, industrialist, 475–7, 489, 505
Taylor, William, 719
Taylorism, 407
technological determinism, 23, 35, 284, 288–302, 311, 313, 315, 339, 420, 449, 812
technological indeterminism, 291, 812
technological inevitability, 284
technological model, 268, 286–7, 300, 420, 444–5, 812
technology, 1–2, 40, 43, 94, 155 n. 164, 158, 245, 255, 263, 269, 395, 401–403, 413–415, 417, 420, 433, 443, 449–50, 460, 469, 484, 488, 490, 501, 506, 584, 597, 718–19, 812–813, 815, 817, 835; of antiquity, 301–7; backwardness, 284; and history, 283–342; innovation, 284, 444–50, 817; and the labour process, 812–17; machine, 31–5, 288, 299, 413–14, 420–8; medieval and early modern, 307–22; of the industrial revolution, 322–38; and progress, 23, 288, 313, 340, 812; *see also* productive forces
telegraph, 336
teleology, 688
telephone, 284
telescope, 317, 321, 684
Temple, William, 1st Baronet (1628–1699), 368, 454
tenants and tenancies, 27, 64, 89, 371 n. 97, 513, 798; forty-shilling. freeholders, 116, 670, 681, 699, 705, 709, 778; conversion of, 25, 89; copyhold, 26, 59 n. 39, 66, 87–8, 118, 135, 202, 277,

348, 404 n. 8, 464, 514, 605, 705, 741, 804; customary tenants, 91, 101, 134, 267, 270, 279, 513, 814; economic leasehold, 25, 27, 31, 41, 89, 101, 253, 798, 800, 837; freehold, 4, 26, 41, 59 n. 39, 66, 88 n. 152, 134, 202, 233, 276–7, 406 n. 20, 464, 514, 681, 687, 705, 773, 778, 788–90, 796–7, 836, 838; reversion of, 134 n. 89, 135; subidivision of, 73; tenants-at-will, 26, 789; vacant, 798; villein tenants, 17; *see also* enclosure; land; means of subsistence; open field system; tenant-farmers
tenant-farmers, 3–5, 31, 40, 59 n. 39, 64, 71, 89, 137, 163, 199, 216–17, 258, 267, 274, 276, 280, 344, 346, 378, 397, 501, 521–2, 524, 556, 611, 614, 627, 640, 658–9, 674, 691, 700, 744, 768 n. 67, 771, 799, 807, 809, 821–2, 837; capitalist, 7, 40–3, 79, 103, 172, 194, 201, 213, 249, 397, 495, 525, 621, 706, 745, 795, 805, 825, 837; competitive market in leases, 27, 31, 40, 136, 216–17, 235, 280, 501, 658, 691, 799, 836; as leaseholders, 118, 464, 691, 741, 397; subject to market imperative, 27, 143; yeoman, 549; *see also* enclosure; tenants
Tennant, Charles (1768–1838) inventor, 487–8
Test Act (1673), 141–2, 236, 679, 706; *see also* Corporation Act; Workhouse Test Act
textile trades, 68, 73–82, 88, 97, 139, 157, 168, 174–176, 180, 193, 259–60, 268, 289–93, 309, 312, 320, 323, 329–330, 337, 353–5, 359, 373, 379–80, 384, 388, 391–5, 402, 417, 423–4, 432–45, 442, 461–9, 481–92, 499–504, 517, 530, 533–5, 549, 552, 563, 572, 583, 625, 638, 665, 682, 687, 689, 695, 712, 717, 725, 739–41, 769–70, 775, 809, 816, 830, 833; bays, says, camlets and fustians, 111; cottage industry in, 97 n. 186; Damasks, 312; districts, 600, 681; jean, velvet, velveteen, corduroy, 468; new draperies, 111–12, 116, 139; phase of industrial revolution, 778; revolution in, 38, 327, 504; revolution anticipated by da Vinci, 38, 319–20, 325; serges, 140, 350, 384–5; shaloons, 394; workers, 88, 309, 517, 625, 638, 682 n. 20, 717, 719, 830, 833; workshops, 51; *see also* artisans; cotton; fulling; fustian; linen; printing; silk; slubbing; spinning; woollens; worsted
Thackeray, William Makepeace (1811–1863), 741
Thames Police Act (1800), 656
Thames Shipwrights' Provident Union, 667
Thelwall, John (1764–1834), 543 n. 131, 546–7, 673, 700
Theodolite, 306
Thinomnier, Barthélemy (1793–1857), 337
Thirsk, Joan, 168, 524
Thirty Years' War (1618–1648), 107, 112, 120, 133, 179 n. 51, 260 n. 21, 321
Thistelwood, Arthur (1774–1820), 646
Thompson, Edward Palmer (1924–1993), 85 n. 138, 88 n. 149, 144–5, 188 n. 82, 277, 454, 511–12, 523, 527, 529, 531–3, 539, 557, 562–4, 567, 570, 574, 576–7, 586, 595, 598, 605, 616, 624–5, 628 n. 60, 629 n. 62, 630–649, 660, 674, 684, 701, 708, 726, 749, 763, 780 n. 109, 825, 837
Thompson, Thomas Peronnet (1783–1869), economist, 753, 771
Thorpe, William, 599
threshing-machine or thresher, 323, 417, 616, 626, 661–2, 692–3, 745, 775
throstle *see* spinning: throstle
Thurlow, 1st Baron Edward (1730–1806), 536
Thurzo, Johan (1437–1508), 81
tidal dock, 304
tidal mill, 312
Tilsit, Treaty of (1807), 589
timber: supply, 76, 90–1, 189 n. 87, 246, 363; trade, 34, 175, 246, 307, 362, 614, 650–1; *see also* wood
time-measurement *versus* task-orienation, 454–5, 501
time-discipline, 454
tin, 324, 363, 393, 472, 481; tin-plate, 364; tin-glazed wares, 406
tithes, 29, 694, 709–10, 715, 750, 831
Tithes Commutation Act (1836), 710
titled peerage *see* peerage
tobacco, 121, 137, 150, 153 n. 153, 159, 161, 174–5, 193, 206, 215, 217, 358, 362, 470 n. 37, 591 n. 106, 804
de Tocqueville, Alexis (1805–1859), 795
Toffler, Alvin, 291
toilet, 303; toilet paper, 311 n. 84; flushing toilet, 336
Toleration Act (1689), 147
toll roads and turnpikes, 197–8, 242, 254, 261–2, 279, 406, 421, 473, 490, 494, 538, 756, 768, 770

Tolpuddle Martyrs, 716–17, 720–1, 724–5, 750
Tooke, John Horne (1736–1812), 543 n. 131, 546–7
tool-makers, 359
toothbrush, 309
toothpaste, 309 n. 77
Tories and Tory Party, 141–2, 174–92, 204, 211–3, 220–4, 230, 269, 581, 595, 612–13, 620, 625, 629, 650–6, 661, 670, 675, 678, 681, 686–9, 693–700, 704–5, 709, 734–7, 752, 763, 765, 770–4, 806, 832–5; 'Church in Danger', 177; country squires, 183, 191, 204, 222 n. 19, 224, 774; dissolution of the old Party, 183 n. 65; fragmentation of the Pittite coalition, 678, 705; high Anglican, 581, 687, 834; new Pittite Party, 620; reaction after Waterloo, 612, 620; Ultra-Tories, 679–81, 698, 832, 834; *see also* Conservative Party; Peel
Tower of London, 186 n. 75, 333, 484, 476, 592, 628
towns, 9–13, 18–19, 22, 33, 49–57, 61–5, 69, 74, 97, 131, 137, 139, 152, 158, 170, 181, 196, 205, 262, 264, 346, 352–353, 356, 360, 366, 371–3, 377, 393, 404,, 414, 424, 429, 431, 438–9, 464–5, 467, 475, 485, 494, 510, 518–19, 524, 528, 539, 541, 555, 580, 606, 610, 616–17, 631, 641, 648, 663, 671, 677, 682, 684–7, 699–700, 703, 705, 719–20, 734–7, 745, 754, 762, 764, 766, 797, 802–4, 811; coastal or port, 118, 196–7, 262, 362
Townshend duties, 231–3, 236 n. 47
Townshend, Charles (1725–1767), 230–1, 237
Townshend, Charles "Turnip", 2nd Viscount (1674–1738), 187 n. 78, 191, 198
Toynbee, Arnold (1852–1883), 74–75, 289 n. 12, 293, 327, 384, 402
trade: age of trade wars and trade treaties, 157; American boycott, 229–30; balance of, 176, 212; booms in, 176, 214, 422, 441, 442, 538, 627, 640, 666–7, 670, 677, 689, 738–747, 786, 809–10, 828, 832, 843; dissolves feudal relations, 95; and expansion of domestic market, 43, 91, 173, 213, 218, 255, 261, 267, 369, 395, 399, 503, 517, 526, 571, 806; English supremacy in, 157; external to feudalism (Sweezy), 12; free competition in, 121; international or foreign, 37–8, 56, 69 n. 71, 108, 156, 158, 162, 169, 213, 258, 261, 288, 290, 442, 498, 506, 537, 583, 591, 657 n. 109, 806, 812, 818; mercantile, 12, 345; re-export, 160, 175, 206; rise of in early modern Europe, 10–13, 39, 71, 85, 286; slave, 122, 184, 217, 544, 587–8; triangular, 122, 384; *see also* commerce; merchants; smugglers
trade unions, 4, 42, 59, 140, 159, 347–9, 351–2, 398–9, 425 n. 85, 482, 506, 543 n. 132, 565–7, 570, 579, 581, 601, 629, 632–3, 643, 645–6, 638–9, 641, 646, 660, 663, 665–9, 671, 678, 680, 682, 688, 697, 701, 707, 709, 728–9, 735–8, 740, 745, 758–60, 762, 764, 766–7, 778, 771–3, 778–9, 792, 823–4, 827–9, 833–4; agricultural unions, 736; of artisans, 352, 577, 601; 'business unionism', 760; federated trades unions, 140, 159, 506, 639, 673, 680, 716–727, 745, 827, 829; in France, 337 n. 178; in Ireland, 709; of journeymen; radicalism or Jacobinism, links with, 567, 575, 632; and socialism, 684; ten hours movement, 712; unionising, 138, 349, 682; 'worst of democracies', 729; *see also* combinations, Combination Acts, co-operatives, friendly societies
Trafalgar, Battle of (1805), 586
Trafalgar Square, 782
train of mechanism, 304 n. 58, 306, 366, 426
trains *see* railroads
Trajan, Roman Emperor (53–117), 305
tramping, 138, 377, 459, 571, 663, 669, 716, 823
transition debate, 8–17, 24, 797
transition from feudalism to capitalism, 2, 8–9, 15, 18–19, 22–3, 40, 48, 100, 199 n. 130, 296, 657, 797, 805, 812, 837, 839
transition from pre-class to class society, 296, 303; *see also* states
Transportation Act (1718), 189
transportation as a form of punishment, 157, 189, 207, 219, 242, 545, 561, 595, 598, 626, 631, 647, 649, 673, 696, 720, 767, 770 n. 74, 784, 836
transportation system and infrastructure, 61, 71 n. 77, 147 n. 129, 196–8, 254, 262–5, 331, 334, 338, 362–4, 421, 428, 431 n. 117, 463, 470–1, 483, 489, 494, 653, 740, 743–4, 778; as infrastructure of trade, 261, 265; coastal shipping, 197, 262, 362; *see also* canals; rivers; toll roads

Treasonable Practices Act (1795), 547, 574
Treasury and Treasurer, 149, 152, 184, 186, 219–20, 244–5, 247, 547, 563, 573, 586, 588, 592, 599 n. 132, 601; treasury bonds, 442
trepanation, 312
Trevithick, Richard (1771–1833) railway pioneer, 338, 584
Triennial Act (1694), 147
Trimmers, 451
Triple Alliance, 536
Trowbridge, Wiltshire, 139–40, 424, 467, 578
truck system or payment in truck, 350, 366, 452, 472, 594–5, 670, 717, 722, 766, 824
Tudors: *see* Edward VI, Elizabeth I, Henry VII, Henry VIII, Mary I
Tull, Jethro (1674–1741), inventor of seed drill, 198, 692, 807
turbary, rights of, 514, 516, 690
turbines, 337
Turgot, Minister Anne-Robert-Jacques (1727–1781), 741
Turkey, 230 n. 35, 536, 572, 657, 768
Turner, Michael E., 272–4, 278
turners, 409, 433 n. 126
turnpikes *see* toll roads
Turpin, Dick (1705–1739), 526
twist mills and twisting machines, 390, 431, 435
Tyneside, 86, 91, 489, 801
Typewriter, 340
Tyrolia, 81

Ultras *see* Tories
underclass, 241, 369, 396
under-employment, 354, 369, 396
unemployment, 65, 72–3, 97 n. 186, 113, 157, 224, 230–1, 354, 369–78, 389, 393 n. 181, 396, 510, 543, 550 n. 160, 552–6, 580–3, 602, 627, 638, 640–1, 644, 662, 671–2, 679, 689, 681, 695, 714, 724, 729–30, 733, 737–9, 742, 745, 749, 751, 759 n. 29, 761, 776, 781, 786, 812, 822, 826, 831
unions *see* combinations, trade unions, municipal political unions
United Irishmen, 542 n. 127, 559–62, 576
United Kingdom, 562, 599, 629, 655, 657, 686–7, 727, 739, 743, 778, 794, 826, 829, 836; *see also* Act of Union of 1801
United States of America, 173 n. 29, 245–6, 335, 559, 599, 629, 634, 680, 721–2, 743, 774; commercial treaty, 246, 535, 589–90; cotton production, 442; harbours closed during Napoleonic wars, 589–90; inventions, 327–332, 337–8; influence of agrarian capitalism, 217, 250, 794; railways laid, 778; republic, 541; resurgence of trade with (1780s), 259, 279, 442; *see also* American War of Independence; American colonies; War of 1812
Universal Philanthropist, 645
University of Glasgow, 478
underdevelopment, underdeveloped countries, 496, 498 n. 165
Uno, Kozo (1897–1977), 27 n. 71
up-and-down husbandry, 799; *see also* convertible husbandry
urbanisation, 11, 13, 34 n. 89, 69, 74 n. 90, 98, 195, 200, 617, 813; de-urbanisation, 19 n. 46, 49, 310
Usher, Abbott Payson (1883–1964), 290–1, 304 n. 58, 306 n. 66, 317 n. 97, 318–20, 323 n. 118, 340, 426
Usher, Archbishop of Armagh, 308
Utilitarians, 698
utopianism, 447 n. 196, 575, 645; utopian socialism, 827
Utrecht, Treaty of (1713), 182, 184, 384

vacuum pump, 322
vagrancy see poverty
Vagrancy Act (1744), 190
vagrancy laws, 64, 116, 510
Verlagssystem see putting-out system
Versailles, Second Treaty of (1757), 221
Vesey-Fitzgerald, Sir William Robert Seymour (1818–1885), 680
Victoria I (1819–1901), 704, 751–2, 763, 769 n. 69, 783; coronation, 751; death of, 181
Victorian era and Victorianism, 611, 665, 702, 730, 758, 836; *see also* mid-Victorian compromise
victuallers *see* brewers
Vienna, Austria, 558, 573, 586, 600, 603, 707
Villiers, Charles Pelham (1802–1898), 755
violence see coercive force, property
vitriol, *see* sulphuric acid, copperas
Voltaire, François-Marie (1694–1778), 559

Wadsworth, Alfred P., 327 n. 132, 343, 388–90, 402–3
wage dependency, 552

wage labour, 3, 14–15, 18, 21, 33, 80–1, 86, 96, 142–3, 172, 202, 217, 275, 344–5, 354, 369–71, 395, 403, 419, 491, 548, 553, 569, 611, 616, 626, 658, 663, 706, 711, 726–33, 740, 745–7, 797, 802, 815, 822–1, 837; and the guilds, 49–57; in medieval society, 54
Wakefield, Edward Gibbon (1796–1862), 701
Wakefield, Yorkshire, 464
Wakley, Thomas (1795–1862), 752
Wales, 70, 94, 126, 256–7, 306 n. 66, 318, 323, 330–1, 334, 364, 438 n. 149, 463, 467, 470, 472–3, 480–2, 485 Table 9.1, 496, 552, 554 n. 177, 558–60, 611 n. 5, 643, 682, 699–700, 702, 734 n. 197, 756–7, 767, 770–1, 777 n. 97, 794; *see also* Myrthyr Tydfil
Wales, Prince of, *see* Frederick, George IV
Wallerstein, Immanuel Maurice, 38–9, 53
Walpole, Horace (1717–1797), 4th Earl of Orford, 212
Walpole, Robert, 1st Earl of Orford, Prime Minister, (1676–1745), 186–92, 206–9, 219, 221, 248, 620, 681, 806–7; and the Bubble, 182, 186; and the land tax, 191, 206, 807; first Prime Minister, 186, 213; resignation, 209; 'skreenmaster general', 186; *see also* Waltham Black Act
Waltham Black Act (1723), 190, 350, 526–7
War of 1812, 599–600
Ward, Joshua (1684–1761) improver of sulphuric acid, 486
Ward, Zion (1781–1837), 722
warehousemen and warehouses, 360, 364–5, 379, 387 n. 157, 441, 444, 472, 476, 596, 651, 739
warfare, 10, 51, 133 n. 87, 303–4, 311, 321–22, 618–19, 654, 707 n. 106, 719, 811, 820, 823
Warmley, Gloucestershire, 488
Warmley Company, 480
Wars of the Roses (1455–1485), 61, 71, 800
wastes and commons, 4, 89, 115, 135, 137, 201, 203, 257, 266–7, 274–5, 278, 514–15, 520, 526, 553, 591, 611, 616, 621, 695, 813, 819–22; enclosure of and reclaiming, 144, 374, 464
watchmakers, 637
water clock, 304, 306, 312
water frame: see spinning: water frame
Waterloo, Battle of, 558, 612, 614, 625, 662, 741, 825
watermill, 299, 308, 312, 316, 405, 463
waterwheel, 90, 306, 308, 316–17, 324–5, 334 n. 164, 337, 382–3, 390, 426, 443, 461, 476, 481; overshot versus undershot, 427
Watson-Wentworth, Charles, 2nd Marquess of Rockingham, Prime Minister (1730–1782), 229–230, 238, 240–245, 249–250, 534; death of, 245; first ministry, 230; second ministry, 240–5; Rockingham Party, 230, 234, 238–239, 243–5, 247, 534, 810; Rockingham legend or myth *see* Bute legend
Watt, James (1736–1819) inventor of separate condenser steam engine, 289 n. 12, 317, 323 n. 118, 331–334, 336 n. 177, 338 n. 179, 414, 442, 467, 473 n. 51, 478–479, 493, 500, 504, 817; *see also* Soho Foundry
Watt II, James (1769–1848), 505, 584
Watts, Nathaniel, 424
Weald, the, 94, 362–363
weaponry, 302–3, 306, 579, 643, 648, 784, 813
Wear, River, 333, 363
weavers and weaving, 61–6, 93, 111–13, 138–9, 159–60, 211, 230–1, 235, 288, 290, 302, 321, 326, 328–30, 337, 344, 348–51, 357, 360, 362, 380–8, 391–5, 398, 404, 410, 423–30, 443–4, 454–6, 462–3, 466, 469, 491, 493, 502–3, 516, 524, 530–1, 565–6, 572, 577, 580–1, 590–7, 600, 605, 607, 632, 638–9, 647–8, 659, 664–7, 670–87, 698, 716–23, 738–9, 786–7, 816, 809, 820, 823, 828–30, 836; peak of (1790s), 572; slow decline of the trade, 572; tragic plight of, 456
Weavers' Act (1555), 64
Weavers' Association, 667
Weavers Union Society of Blackburn, 672
Webb, Martha Beatrice (1858–1943), 373, 563–4, 759
Webb, Sidney James, 1st Baron Passfield (1859–1947), 373, 563–4, 759
Weber, Max (1864–1920), 52–3, 61 n. 45, 63, 339, 341 n. 186, 379 n. 132, 416–417, 420, 819; equates capitalism with trade, 39, 53, 85; on mining in the 13th century, 81–5, 215 n. 3
Wedderburn, Robert (1762–c. 1835), 641–2
Wedgwood, Gilbert (1588–1678), 404
Wedgwood, Josiah (1730–1795), master potter, 264, 352–3, 403–15, 418, 434–5, 437, 444, 448, 451, 457–8, 476–9, 489

n. 135, 500, 502, 506, 719; capitalism without machinery, 413–14, 427, 458, 814–15; creamware, 406; Etruria works, 264 n. 34, 410 n. 33, 413; leads General Chamber of Manufacturers, 535–6; glazes as technical innovation, 413; jasper ware, 409; marketing, 408–9; organisational innovator, 406–8, 410–413, 427, 457, 817; state assistance in suppressing strikes, 412–13
Wedgwood, Josiah II (1769–1843), 505
Wedgwood, Thomas (c. 1650–?), 404
weights and measurements, 262, 321, 335, 388, 484, 518; France's chaotic system, 327 n. 133; scientific revolution preoccupied with, 327; standardisation of, 133 n. 327, 303; *see also* time-measurement
welfare: Poor Laws as an early form of, 72, 369, 372–3, 553, 801; employer-provided schemes for workers, 480; friendly societies provide social, 159, 543
Wellesley, Field Marshal Arthur, 1st Duke of Wellington (1769–1852), 598–600, 603, 620, 625 n. 45, 657, 678–679, 681, 688–9, 694, 699–700, 702, 734, 763, 767, 782, 834; as Major General Wellesley, 589, 592; made Duke of Wellington, 592
Wellington, Duke of *see* Wellesley
Wentworth, Thomas, 1st Earl of Strafford (1593–1641), 123–4
Wentworth-Fitzwilliam, William, 4th Earl Fitzwilliam (1748–1833), 543, 576, 642
Wesley, John (1703–1791), 235, 539
Western Rising (1628–1631), 113
Westminster, 178 n. 48, 356, 547, 629
Westminster Abbey, 649
Westminster Police Bill, 532
Westminster Reform Committee, 751
Westphalia, Treaty of, 11, 133
wheat, 192, 198 n. 126, 505, 549, 552, 615–16, 651, 753, 763
wheelbarrow, 309, 316
Wheeler, Artemis, inventor of revolver, 338
Whickham, Tyne and Wear, 86–91, 801
Whieldon, Thomas (1719–1795), master potter, 406
Whigs and Whig Party, 141–2, 174, 177 n. 44, 179–92, 211, 213, 219–30, 269, 534, 538, 619–20, 625, 631, 651–2, 678–9, 687–8, 694, 697–710, 715, 732–5, 746, 751–2, 763–5, 774–80, 806–7, 832; 'old corruption', 182–92, 642, 653; Whig Club, 534; 'Whig state of mind', 521–32, 527; *see also* Liberal Party
Whitbread, Samuel Jr. (1758–1815), 543 n. 131, 550
White Horse Inn, 630
White House, 600
White, George, 668
White, John, 486
White, Leslie A. (1900–1975), 293–4, 311
Whiteboy movement, 217
Whitehall, 177
Whitehead, David, 674–5
Whitehurst, John (1713–1788), 414
whitener: flint, 404–5; sour milk, 486
Wilberforce, William (1759–1833), 532, 544 n. 137, 563, 568, 570, 587, 627, 822
Wild, Jonathan (1683–1725), 189 n. 83, 526
Wilkes, John (1725–1797), 223, 227–9, 231–25, 240–241, 249, 350 n. 15, 546–7, 810
Wilkinson, Isaac (1697–1784), 331–2, 472, 493, 505
Wilkinson, John (1728–1808), 331–3, 472, 474, 478, 480, 505, 585
Willey ironworks, 472, 478
William, Duke of Gloucester (1689–1700), 177
William I 'the conqueror (c. 1028–1087), 130 n. 77, 796
William III (1650–1702), 142, 146–9, 152, 154, 158–9, 177, 372; 'conquered' England as William of Orange, 133 n. 87, 14, 142, 173 n. 31, 404, 804; financial reforms under, 148–56, 173–4, 212, 805; death of, 177
William IV (1765–1837), 688, 700–3, 734; death of, 751
Williams, Thomas (1737–1802) copper magnate, 505
Williams-Wynn, Charles Watkin the Elder (1775–1850), 652
Williamson, Oliver, 449–450
Wilson, Charles Henry (1914–1991), 76, 115 n. 31, 117, 129 n. 71, 138, 152, 173, 199 n. 128, 260, 343, 361, 368, 378–9, 394 n. 185, 492
Wilson, James, stocking-weaver, 648–9, 753
Wiltshire, 111, 113, 115, 159, 233 n. 41, 333, 371, 422, 467, 578–579, 581, 695, 736; Wiltshire Outrages (1802), 578, 594, 823–4
Winchcombe, John (Jack of Newbury) (?–1519), 33 n. 87, 65–66, 78, 373

windmills, 299, 312, 316–19, 813
Windsor Forest, 819
Winstanley, Gerard (1609–1676), 114, 126 n. 64, 540, 660, 788
Winzler, Zachäus, inventor of gas stove, 336
Wolfe, Major General James P. (1727–1759), 222
Wolfe, Theobald, 559
Wollstonecraft, Mary (1759–1797), 540
Wolverhampton, Staffordshire, 324, 352, 427 n. 45, 476
women, 20 n. 49, 51, 65, 73, 115–16, 196, 203, 224, 347–8, 352, 356–7, 360, 371, 375, 383, 389, 411, 438–40, 474, 476, 482, 513–15, 527, 531 n. 86, 540, 610 n. 3, 628, 649, 673, 678, 719, 723, 725–726, 737, 753, 769, 772, 779, 809, 815, 831, 838; and contraception, 257–8; craftswomen, 348, 503; and poor relief, 369; and spinning, 357, 423–7; stereotyped as docile, 423
wood or wooden: customary rights to gather or cut, 189 n. 87, 513, 271 n. 52, 482, 514, 516, 527, 695, 819–20; commerce in *see* timber; in eotechnic phase, 299; house construction, 138; lathe, 299; and paper industry, 362–3; pulley blocks, 335; rails, 326; supply of *see* timber; tally-sticks, 533; use in production, 76–77, 90, 158 n. 180, 169 n. 16, 382, 457 n. 231, 474; wheels, 332 n. 159, 363; wood block printing, 309 n. 76, 319; wood-screw, 478 n. 79; *see also firebote*; timber
Wood, Ellen Meiksins, 2, 3, 6, 22–31, 37–48, 84–5, 294, 297, 417, 794; on class as structure, 635; on the market imperatives, 23–4; on market as opportunity versus as imperative, 29; on non-capitalist empire, 248; on the Marxian debate over technology, 812
Wood, James, 186
Wood, Robert, 228
Wood, William (1671–1730) inventor of potting and stamping, 334
wool trade and woollens, 26, 33, 61, 65–66, 75, 77, 80, 77, 94, 113, 115, 117, 138, 140, 144, 160, 168, 172–6, 180, 192, 259–60, 286, 319, 325, 328, 344, 348, 359, 371, 377, 384–9, 393, 422–4, 430, 437, 442, 444, 448, 456, 473, 486, 491, 502–5, 517, 530, 580–4, 578–83, 590–6, 616–18, 666, 716, 739, 741–2, 803, 814, 816, 823–4; survival of customary regulation of, 344; as primary British export, 80, 175; predominance of hand-loom weaving, 290; mechanisation of, 497; manufacture banned in Ireland, 175–6, 468; and 'way I', 503, 816–17; and worsted, 462–7; *see also* worsted
wool-combers, 140, 349–50, 377, 571, 602, 631, 671, 678
Wooler and Hone, publishers, 631
Woolstaplers, 600
Worcestershire, 466 n. 22
working class, 7, 450, 454, 506, 525–6, 539, 574, 588 n. 96, 610–15, 622–5, 629–3, 673–89, 679, 689, 697, 700, 704, 708, 716, 722–8, 737, 745–65, 770, 779– 91, 826–36, 843; consumers, 158; economists among, 675; ideology, 646, 673; imposition of middle class values upon, 646; making(s) of the English, 633–43; Malthus makes economics enemy of, 624; radical movement rooted in artisans, 241, 637; self-organised, 44; *see also* artisans; labourers
Workhouse Test Act (1723), 190, 376, 379, 431 n. 115
workhouse, 43, 89, 137, 343, 352 n. 25, 372–9, 393 n. 181, 396, 400, 422–3, 431 n. 115, 458, 510, 513, 534, 550, 554, 623, 695, 729, 731–7, 746–7, 765, 770 n. 74, 790, 809, 831, 836, 839; at Andover, 733; and bridewell movement, 373; at Bristol, 374; at Clerkenwell, 374; in Cork, 376; corporations for the poor, 375, 431 n. 115; cruelties of, 378; in Edinburgh, 376; emergence of, 801; in Essex, 376; at Exeter, 374; a financial failure, 374, 376; intended to be intolerable, 733; Malthus on, 623; in Manchester, 376; as an instrument for imposing a new moral order, 729; at Newbury, 373; in Nottingham, 376; as remedy for poverty, 368–79, 458; at the Potteries, 737–8; as prototype for the factory, 396; at St. Giles-in-the-Fields, 373; at Shepton Mallet, 422; role of the SPCK, 375; at Swalwell, 89; as part of a welfare system; at Worcester, 374; *see also* bridewells; London Corporation for the Poor; Poor Laws; Workhouse Test Act
workshop, 137, 339, 351, 365–7, 371, 373, 389, 407, 409, 412–13, 416, 421, 423,

425–6, 431–5, 442, 444, 452, 466, 475–7, 491, 502–3, 516–17, 571, 603, 637, 675, 691, 741, 778, 797, 802, 814–17, 823, 825; regulated by custom, 19; expansion in size, 361, 395; in France, 285, 335, 782; state-run, 782; jenny factories, 423, 435; labour discipline in, 416; 'legal' and 'fair' number of apprentices, 68; medieval, 51; retained in large mining operations, 475; traditional arrangement of master, journeymen and apprentices, 54, 366; as Chapman's 'Type I', 444; proto-capitalist small master, 347, 741, 794; *see also* apprentices; butty system; craft companies; domestic system; sub-contracting
Worsley colliery, 263, 482
Worstead, Norfolk, 463
worsteds, 138 n. 106, 290, 351, 353, 384–6, 393–4, 398, 423 n. 73, 444, 456, 462–7, 502–3, 517, 580
Wren, Christopher (1632–1723), 139
Wright Brothers, 312
Wright, Lemuel, inventor of pin-making machine, 338
Wrightson, Keith, 86, 88 n. 152, 217 n. 6
Writ of *Habeas Corpus* see *Habeas Corpus*
Wyatt, John (1700–66) inventor of roller spinning, 326–9, 387–91, 425, 430 n. 109, 431, 478 n. 79, 809
Wylam Colliery Railway, 338
Wyvill, Christopher (1740–1822), 239–40, 244, 541

yeomanry, 59–63, 66–9, 134, 137, 140, 80; etymology, 59 n. 38; yeomen founders, 115; yeomen carpenters, 137; yeoman farmers, 13, 136, 205 n. 159, 522, 549; yeomen peasants, 686; as policing force, 560, 610, 630, 642, 694–5, 767; swelling numbers, 113; yeowoman, 59 n. 38
Yi Xing (683–727) inventor of escapement mechanism, 309
York, Yorkshire, 141, 262, 599
York Courant, 192
York Hotel, Manchester, 753
Yorkshire, 26–7, 186 n. 75, 193, 239, 316, 317, 354, 362 Table 7.2, 363, 384–6, 393–4, 422–3, 455, 462–7, 472, 483, 486, 499, 517, 562 n. 12, 576 n. 54, 579–81, 596–7, 628–31, 642, 711–12, 716, 741, 773 n. 85, 799, 814, 817, 823–4; Yorkshire Wolds, 26
Yorktown, 243
Young Ireland Movement, 777, 782
Young Pretender *see* Stuart, Charles Edward Louis
Young, Arthur (1741–1820) agronomist, 14, 195, 217 n. 5, 368 n. 87, 454, 553–4, 690, 730

Zhang Heng (78–139), 309, 338
ziggurats, 302
zinc, 480, 488
Zonca, Vittorio (1568–1603) inventor of silk winding apparatus, 320, 325

www.ingramcontent.com/pod-product-compliance
Ingram Content Group UK Ltd.
Pitfield, Milton Keynes, MK11 3LW, UK
UKHW021853100926
8556IPUK00020B/1212

9 781608 463756